ENGLISH VERSIONS OF THE BIBLE

BY

VERY REV. HUGH POPE, O.P.

REVISED AND AMPLIFIED BY

REV. SEBASTIAN BULLOUGH, O.P.

B. HERDER BOOK CO.
15 & 17 SOUTH BROADWAY, ST. LOUIS 2, MO.
AND
33 QUEEN SQUARE, LONDON, W. C.
1952

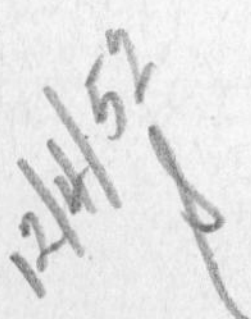

Printed in U.S.A.

IMPRIMATUR

Fr. Hilarius J. Carpenter, O.P.,

Prior Provincialis Provinciae Angliae

LONDONI, die 20a Julii 1950

NIHIL OBSTAT

Fr. Innocentius Swoboda, O.F.M.

Censor Librorum

IMPRIMATUR

✠ *Joseph E. Ritter*

Archiepiscopus

Sancti Ludovici, die 6a mensis Martii 1952

Vail-Ballou Press, Inc., Binghamton and New York

Foreword

FATHER HUGH POPE was a great teacher for many years in various Houses of Study of the Dominican Order, both in Rome and in his own English Province. He died at Edinburgh on November 26, 1946. At that time his manuscript was already with the publishers in America, but it was still in need of considerable adjustment and revision, and this task was first of all undertaken on behalf of the publishers by a Benedictine Father who is one of their literary editors. His notes are signed [Ed.]. He also checked the innumerable bibliographical references. For these labors the English Dominicans owe him a great debt of gratitude. The English Provincial then asked me to go through the text and, where necessary, to adjust, amplify, and bring it up to date. In accordance with this desire I have rewritten several sections, added a few notes, and supplied some entire new chapters. These supplementary sections are indicated, sometimes by [S.B.].

There were certain lacunae in the manuscript: the one on the pre-Wycliffite versions was filled from the chapter in Father Pope's earlier work, *The Catholic Student's "Aids" to the Study of the Bible* (1926), I, 248–52; the lacuna on the "private versions" of the seventeenth, eighteenth, and nineteenth centuries is one that occurs in most histories of the English Bible, and I have supplied these chapters myself. With regard to most of the modern translations, Father Pope's manuscript provided the merest sketch, and of course several translations have appeared since he stopped work. In view, however, of the detail in which the earlier versions were studied in this book, I felt that recent work deserved to be noticed with equal attention. I therefore ventured to recast the last two chapters on Catholic versions and editions, and to supply the last two chapters on recent non-Catholic work.

Finally all this material, both old and new, was rearranged and in part remodeled by the literary editor to form a more coherent whole. It should, however, be stated that it has not been possible to check every statement in the original parts of the book or to trace every bibliographical reference.

We cannot suppose that Father Pope had the opportunity of recording every text of the older versions which has been published, or that I have been able to note all the "private versions" or catalogue without omission every modern version; yet it may be said that a comprehensive account is given in this volume. Of the fortunes of Rheims-Douay and its editions, and of the other Catholic texts of the eighteenth and nineteenth centuries, no such elaborate account has been published since Dr. Cotton's work of 1855, so that much of the material here will not be found elsewhere; nor has there, I believe, been previously presented such a detailed account of the Catholic and non-Catholic versions of the last quarter-century.

I would like to express my gratitude not only to Herder's literary editors for their immense work, but also to the staff of the University Library in Cambridge (England) who have assisted me in my researches, and to Mr. M. T Slater of Burns, Oates and Washbourne, and Mr. C. B. Ogden of Heffer's, who helped me to check recent publications.

When Father Pope was preparing this work, the final fruit of many years' labor conducted amid many other duties of preaching, teaching, administration, and other writing, he was unknowingly preparing his own memorial. It is the hope of those of us who have been concerned that it will be a worthy memorial to one who was a great Dominican, and whose long life was spent in preaching God's truth and in the pursuit of sacred science.

Sebastian Bullough, O.P.

BLACKFRIARS SCHOOL, LAXTON,
England
July, 1950

Preface

ENGLAND has always been a Bible-loving country, and the MSS. produced by Irish and English copyists have always been famous. Many of the Latin MSS. of English origin are highly regarded by biblical scholars, and the *Codex Amiatinus,* which was copied in England and sent to Rome (716) by Abbot Ceolfrid, Benedict Biscop's successor, is regarded as the greatest of all the existing Latin codices. At an early date, too, the Saxon scribes translated parts of the Bible into the vernacular.

Several versions of the Bible translated in England before the art of printing was discovered have been preserved in manuscripts. These fall into two classes: the Anglo-Saxon versions and glosses (about A.D. 1000), and the two Wycliffite versions (between 1380 and 1390). Then, as the art of printing developed, came the long series of translations of the Bible which marked the sixteenth century in England. Indeed it was an age of translation such as St. Augustine envisaged when he complained that, whereas "we can count the translators of the Hebrew Scriptures into Greek, it is impossible to count up those who have translated into Latin. For, in the early days of the faith, any person who found himself in possession of a Greek manuscript and could claim some familiarity with the two tongues [Greek and Latin], promptly embarked on a translation." [1] In England the result, after a century of translations of varying merit, was the appearance in 1611 of the world-famous Authorized Version, which, whatever its defects, has left its stamp on the English language for all time.

In the pages which follow we shall be able to trace the genealogy of this version from its parent, the Latin Vulgate, through the Anglo-Saxon versions and glosses, the versions by Wycliffe, Tyndale, Coverdale, Matthew, Taverner, the Genevan Puritans, Matthew Parker and

[1] *De doctrina Christiana,* II, xi, 16.

the Elizabethan bishops, and finally, though most unexpectedly, through the Rheims-Douay version. It is a history of which any nation might be proud; indeed, no other country has, in its efforts to provide a translation as exact as possible, produced so many versions of the Bible. Not the least remarkable feature in the story is the way in which version succeeded version, and each, as it was displaced, was allowed to fall into oblivion.[2]

[2] Fortunately, at an early date lists were made of the successive versions to perpetuate their memory. Cf. chap. 8.

Contents

PART ONE

Anglo-Saxon and Early English Manuscript Versions

CHAPTER		PAGE
I.	Saxon Versions and Glosses	3
II.	Anglo-Saxon and Norman-Saxon Writers	15
III.	The Anglo-Saxon Versions of the Gospels	31
IV.	The Lindisfarne and Rushworth Gospels	41
V.	Anglo-Saxon Psalters	52
VI.	Pre-Wycliffite Versions	62
VII.	The Wycliffite Versions of the Bible	67

PART TWO

Early Printed Editions

VIII.	Published Lists of Printed Editions of the Scriptures in English	91
IX.	Sixteenth-Century Latin Versions of the Bible	99
X.	Tyndale's Translation of the Bible	130
XI.	Coverdale's Version, 1535	153
XII.	Matthew's Bible, 1537	175
XIII.	The Great Bible, 1539	187
XIV.	Taverner's Version, 1539	205
XV.	The Geneva Bible	216
XVI.	The Bishops' Bible, 1568	234

PART THREE

The Rheims-Douay and Authorized Versions

XVII.	The Rheims Version of the New Testament, 1582	249
XVIII.	The Storm of Controversy	273

CHAPTER PAGE

XIX. The Douay Version of the Old Testament, 1609–10 . 294
XX. The Authorized Version, or King James Bible, 1611 . 308
XXI. Ward's Errata of the Protestant Bible 331

PART FOUR

Catholic Versions since Rheims-Douay

Introductory 337
XXII. Dr. Nary's Version of the New Testament, 1718 . . . 339
XXIII. Dr. Witham's Version of the New Testament, 1730 . . 346
XXIV. Fifth and Sixth Editions of the Rheims New Testament 351
XXV. Dr. Challoner's Revisions, 1749–72 355
XXVI. MacMahon's Editions of the Bible, 1783–1810 372
XXVII. The Biblical Work of Alexander Geddes, 1786–1802 . . 379
XXVIII. The Editions of 1790 and 1792 386
XXIX. Editions at the Beginning of the Nineteenth Century 391
XXX. The Catholic Board Edition, 1815 401
XXXI. Editions from 1816 to 1818 412
XXXII. Editions Immediately before the Catholic Emancipation, 1820–29 425
XXXIII. Editions Immediately after Catholic Emancipation, 1830–39 434
XXXIV. Dr. Lingard's Version of the Gospels, 1836 442
XXXV. Editions Immediately before the Re-establishment of the Hierarchy, 1840–49 448
XXXVI. Dr. Kenrick's Version of the Bible, 1849–60 458
XXXVII. Editions Immediately after the Re-establishment of the Hierarchy, 1851–60 464
XXXVIII. Editions between 1861 and 1896 470
XXXIX. Editions of Rheims-Douay since 1896 479
XL. Independent Catholic Versions of the Twentieth Century 497

PART FIVE

Protestant Versions since the Authorized Version

Introductory 509
XLI. Private Versions of the Seventeenth Century 511

CHAPTER PAGE
XLII. Private Versions of the Eighteenth Century 520
XLIII. Private Versions of the Nineteenth Century 538
XLIV. The Revision of the Authorized Version, 1870–85 . . . 551
XLV. Westcott and Hort 558
XLVI. Criticism of the Revised Version 566
XLVII. The American Standard Version and Its Revision . . . 578
XLVIII. The Modern-Speech Versions 585
Appendix I. Preface to the Rheims New Testament, 1582 . . . 601
Appendix II. Preface to the Douay Old Testament, 1609 651
Appendix III. Catholic Editions of the Bible, 1505–1950 666
Appendix IV. Private Versions between the Authorized and the Revised Versions 683
Bibliography 686
Supplement. American Editions of the Catholic Bible 719
Index 747

PART ONE

Anglo-Saxon and Early English Manuscript Versions

CHAPTER I

Saxon Versions and Glosses

DEVELOPMENT OF SAXON CULTURE AND LITERATURE

THE Saxons invaded England in the year 449. About a hundred and fifty years later St. Augustine arrived in England and converted Kent. The conversion of the North, the Midlands, and the East followed, the Saxons of the South being the last to embrace Christianity, through the labors of St. Wilfrid.[1] It is difficult to realize that a nation, formerly conspicuous for savagery,[2] became Christian in less than a hundred years; still more difficult is it to grasp the fact that the once ignorant and barbaric Saxons almost immediately took rank as a literary nation among the peoples of Europe.[3]

These Saxons who applied themselves to literature manifested the strength of their intellectual powers by a success which could not have been expected and can scarcely be surpassed. That within a hundred years after Christianity and literature came to the Anglo-Saxons two such men as Bede and Boniface should have arisen, the one from the most northerly part of England, the other from the most southerly part, —from Durham and Devonshire—is an adequate proof that the previous absence of literary knowledge arose not from want of intellect, but from want of opportunity for its cultivation.[4]

[1] Bede, *Historia,* II, chap. 9; III, chaps. 5, 21 f.; IV, chap. 13.

[2] A Cotton MS., Caligula XV, fol. 122, verso, speaks of "Sapientia Graecorum, invidia Judaeorum, superbia Romanorum, largitas Longobardorum, sobrietas Gothorum, elevatio Francorum, gula Gallorum, ora Brittonum, stultitia Saxonum, libido Scottorum, crudelitas Pictorum." (Wright, *Biographia Britannica literaria,* I, 43 note.)

[3] "Their superiority," says Lingard, "was, for more than a century, felt and acknowledged by the other nations of Europe. . . . By the end of a century from the death of Adrian (c. 690) the literary reputation of the Anglo-Saxon clergy was established in every part of the Western Church" (*The History and Antiquities of the Anglo-Saxon Church,* II, 142, 150). Even people on the continent were not unfamiliar with the Celtic tongue; cf. Sulpicius Severus, *Dialogue,* I, 20; Lingard, *op. cit.,* I, 9.

[4] J. Bosworth, *The Gothic and Anglo-Saxon Gospels* (1886), p. x; cf. Wright, *op. cit.,*

The most recent historian of the period, Stenton, gives a similar testimony:

Within a hundred years England had become the home of a Christian culture which influenced the whole development of letters and learning in western Europe. The greatest historical work of the early Middle Ages had been written in a northern monastery, and English poets had begun to give a permanent form to heroic traditions. There is nothing in European history closely parallel to this sudden development of a civilisation by one of the most primitive peoples established within the ancient Roman Empire.[5]

The inspiring principle, the sole *raison d'être* of all the literary and artistic work of the Saxons was their love of the Bible.[6] The original impulse in this direction came from the copies of the Bible sent over by St. Gregory to St. Augustine.[7] From these manuscripts were copied such famous Irish Bibles as the books of Armagh, Durrow, Kells, and so forth. For, as Berger truly says, "The history of the Vulgate followed hard upon the progress of the Church of Rome in Ireland and Great Britain. For the history of the Bible in Celtic districts is simply that of the relations subsisting between them and the Continent, more especially with the Church of Rome." [8] A further impulse was given by Benet Biscop, "a man," says St. Bede, "who was well skilled in the knowledge of Holy Scripture, and who for the space of sixteen years, amid

---

pp. 31 f. It is clear that the Saxons had books in plenty; cf. Lingard, *op. cit.*, II, 315 note.

[5] *Anglo-Saxon England,* p. 177.

[6] How eloquent in this respect is Bede's account of his own monastic life: "Spending all the remaining time of my life in that monastery [Wearmouth or Jarrow] I wholly applied myself to the study of Scripture, and amidst the observance of regular discipline, and the daily care of singing in the Church, I always took delight in learning, teaching, and writing" (*Historia,* V, chap. 24).

[7] See John the Deacon, *Vita S. Gregorii,* for an account of the volumes sent by the Pope; St. Bede (*Historia,* I, chap. 29) merely says that Gregory sent "many books." In the library of Trinity Hall, Cambridge, is a MS. catalogue of these same books, drawn up perhaps under Henry V (1413–22); among the books listed is the *Biblia Gregoriana,* a volume which has more than a passing interest for English Catholics, for in the *Petition of the Catholic laity* offered to James I in 1604, they speak of "the very original Bible, the selfsame Numero which St. Gregory sent in with our Apostle St. Augustine, being as yet preserved by God's special Providence." The above catalogue also includes a Psalter sent by St. Gregory to St. Augustine; cf. Wanley, *Librorum veterum septentrionalium qui in Angliae bibliothecis extant catalogus historico-criticus,* p. 151. Of another MS., Corpus L. 15, Wanley says: "This very ancient MS. in 4to, is, I regret to say, damaged at the beginning. It contains the four Gospels in Latin written in large rounded Roman characters. In some important readings it differs from the Vulgate; indeed it differs very much from other exceedingly ancient MSS. which were certainly written in England. For myself I am inclined to believe that this volume is one of those sent eleven hundred years ago by Pope Gregory to the Apostle Augustine, the first Archbishop of Canterbury."

[8] *Histoire de la Vulgate,* p. 29.

innumerable perils in journeyings and in illness, brought back a large number of books which he had either bought at a price or received as gifts from his friends. The large and noble library which he brought from Rome, and which was necessary for the building up of his church, he commanded to be kept entire, and neither to be injured nor dispersed." [9]

The good work was furthered by the arrival, in the year 669, of Archbishop Theodore and his companion, Adrian, abbot of a monastery near Naples. St. Bede says of both these men:

> They were well read both in sacred and in secular literature, so that they gathered a crowd of disciples, and there daily flowed from them rivers of knowledge to water the hearts of their hearers; and together with the Books of Holy Writ, they also taught them the arts of ecclesiastical poetry, astronomy, and arithmetic. A testimony of which is that there are still living at this day some of their scholars who are as well versed in the Greek and Latin tongues as in their own in which they were born.[10]

Nor were the arts neglected: "When the Celts ceased to accept the Scotch date for the celebration of Easter, the monks of Lindisfarne did not therefore lay aside their national art, but offered to God and St. Cuthbert masterpieces such as only the Irish or their disciples could have produced; and these artists bore Saxon names." [11] Of St. Dunstan himself (924–88 A.D.) we are told that, "though fully occupied with literary work, yet, in his anxiety to fit himself for any task, he laboriously cultivated the arts of writing, playing on the harp, and painting; with the result that he soon became known as a keen critic in every department." [12] There still exists a portrait, drawn by himself, of Dunstan kneeling at the foot of a crucifix.[13] "With the sole exception of the Moeso-Gothic," says Skeat, "the Anglo-Saxon MSS. are the oldest and best of all those produced by any Teutonic race." [14]

There are many references to the skill of the Anglo-Saxon monks as

[9] *The Lives of the Holy Abbots of Wearmouth and Jarrow;* cf. Lingard, *op. cit.*, II, 372, who shows how well the Saxons were provided with books. For some account of the libraries at Canterbury, Wearmouth, and York, see *ibid.*, II, 145 f.; for that of the Sion House Monastery, see *The Myroure of oure Ladye,* pp. 339 f.

[10] *Historia,* IV, chap. 2.

[11] Berger, *Histoire de la Vulgate,* p. 39.

[12] Cotton MS. Faustina B.13.

[13] MS. N.E.D. 2.19, in the Bodleian; cf. G. Hickes, *Linguarum veterum septentrionalium thesaurus grammatico-criticus et archaeologicus,* I, 144; also Cotton MS. Faustina B.13.

[14] See G. Miles, *The Bishops of Lindisfarne, Hexham, Chester-le-Street and Durham,* p. 53.

calligraphers. Wanley, for instance, points to the fact that all the names of the benefactors of the church of Durham, kings, bishops, abbots, and so forth, "are written in gold and silver about the time of King Alfred, d. 901—as is evident from the script itself and from the name of Aethelstan, nephew to Alfred." [15] Again, at the end of a *Benedictional* in the possession of the Duke of Devonshire is written:

Atque Patri magno jussit qui scribere librum hunc
Omnes cernentes biblum hunc semper rogitent hoc,
Post metam carnis valeam caelis inhaerere,
Obnixe hoc rogitat scriptor supplex Godemann.[16]

"The history of English sculpture," says Stenton, "shews that Anglo-Saxon artists, once set in the way of invention, came very quickly to complete mastery of form. In the decoration of manuscripts, as in sculpture, achievement may well have come through individual genius rather than the slow elaboration of design." [17]

THE EXTENT OF SAXON VERSIONS

It would be interesting to know how much of the Bible was current in the vernacular in Saxon days. The nuns in convents, of course, had to recite their breviary in Latin,[18] but there was nothing to prevent their having translations, whether in French or English, which presumably had always to be authorized.[19] The monks possessed the Scriptures in

[15] Cotton MS. Domitian A.7; Wanley, *op. cit.*, p. 249.

[16] This Godemann was a monk of Hyde (New Minster) towards the close of the tenth century; the MS. was made for Ethelwold, bishop of Winchester, 963–84; cf. William of Malmesbury, *Historia Novella* (1815), p. 172, who says of St. Wulfstan, bishop of Worcester (1602): "Habebat magistrum Ervenium nomine, inscribendo et quidlibet coloribus effingendo peritum. Ille, preciosiorum apicum captus miraculo, dum pulcritudinem oculis rimatur, scientiam litterarum internis hausit oculis. Verum doctor ad saeculi spectans commodum spe majoris pretii sacramentarium regi, tunc temporis Cnutoni, Psalterium Emmae reginae, contribuit."

[17] *Anglo-Saxon England,* p. 191; see G. Baldwin Brown, *The Arts in Early England,* vol. IV of *The Arts and Crafts of Our Teutonic Forefathers* (1903).

[18] So far as we know, the nuns at Easebourne Priory had only a French Bible; cf. A. C. Paues, *A Fourteenth Century English Biblical Version,* p. xxvii. Archbishop Parker, in his Preface to Asser's *Annales rerum gestarum Alfredi Magni* (ed. Wise, 1722), refers to communities of nuns, especially those at Tavistock, who devoted themselves to the study of the Anglo-Saxon language "lest through its neglect [such] knowledge should wholly disappear."

[19] This was certainly the case after Archbishop Arundel's Constitution of 1408; nor is it anywhere suggested that such authorization was difficult to obtain. The author of *The Myroure of oure Ladye,* writing after 1415, says: "And for as moche as yt is forboden

Latin and could read them. How much of it did they translate for the benefit of the laity? The remains of contemporary literature are all too scanty, and it would be easy to formulate conclusions of too sweeping a character, such as the following: "At the time of the Norman Conquest the Gospels and the Psalms had been translated into English, and the Old Testament narrative was likewise accessible in the language of the people; but there is no reason to suppose that such books had any wide circulation. The language of the Church was still Latin, and such works of theology as were either written or read were for the most part Latin too." [20] But is such a conclusion really justified by the facts? Would not the converse proposition hold equally good: "There is no reason to suppose that such books had not a wide circulation"? Wright may be nearer the mark when he says:

> The writings which are still extant shew that the Anglo-Saxon Church must have had in her own tongue a considerable amount of Scriptural instruction. But these cannot be the full measure of what our forefathers possessed. Much, it cannot be doubted, perished in the troubles and confusions attending the incursions and pillages of the Danes; and much, subsequently, through the disfavour shewn by the Normans to Anglo-Saxon language and literature.[21]

Similarly Moulton:

> We cannot doubt that much of the work accomplished in this field is lost to us. Tradition points to translations of the whole Bible as existing in these early times. Thus Purvey (writing about 1388) appeals to chronicles and books as showing that "Bede translatide the bible, expoundide mych in Saxon, that was English, either comoun langage of this lond, in his tyme"; and similar statements are found in early writers in regard to Aldred, Eadfrith, and others. It were to be wished that the documents which time has spared had received a fuller examination. We are still uncertain what relation exists between the copies of the same book of Scripture, whether they are independent of each other, or merely varieties of one translation. All these relics of antiquity are rich in philological interest; but they are still more valuable as monuments of the love of the Bible among our forefathers. It is of course impossible to determine to what extent these vernacular

---

under payne of cursynge that no man schulde haue ne drewe eny texte of holy scrypture in-to Englysshe wythout lycense of the bysshop dyocesan, . . . therfore I asked and haue lysence of oure bysshop to drawe suche things in-to Englysshe" (Studer, *The Study of Anglo-Norman*, p. 4; Paues, *loc. cit.*).

[20] British Museum, *Guide to the Manuscripts and Printed Books Exhibited in Celebration of the Tercentenary of the Authorized Version*, p. 5.

[21] *Biographia Britannica literaria*, p. 60; cf. Skeat, *The Gospel of St. Mark in Gothic according to the Translation Made by Wulfila in the Fourth Century*, p. iv; *idem*, *The New Testament in English according to the Version of John Wycliffe, . . . reprinted with introduction*, I, p. iii.

translations were known and read. Some were evidently intended for private use: others, if we may judge from the number of copies preserved, seem to have been widely circulated.[22]

Indeed, the very fact that so much has survived suggests that it represents a much larger output of glosses and translations than is generally supposed; and while the number of Anglo-Norman versions of the Apocalypse, for example, shows that the use of English was at least partially checked, the work of Rolle and others shows that a new English was emerging by degrees.

> Gradually and in all likelihood before the great Oxford versions attributed to Wycliffe and his school had spread over the country, the whole of the New Testament had been translated into English of the South or of the North Midlands. . . . The Apocalypse with a Commentary was for a long time attributed to Wycliffe, but I found that in reality it was nothing but a verbal rendering of the famous Norman Apocalypse which dates as far back as the latter half of the twelfth century.[23]

The unknown author of *The Myroure of oure Ladye* tells the nuns for whom he writes that they can get the Psalms in English of "Rycharde Hampoules drawynge [i.e., translation], and out of Englysshe bibles if ye have lysence therto." On this Dr. Blunt comments: "This reference to the English Bibles seems to imply that they were very common in the middle of the fifteenth century. These may have been copies of the Wicliffite version, but it seems unlikely that the sisters would have received 'license' to read these, especially as 'de quibus cavendum est' is written against some works of Wicliffe in the Library Catalogue preserved at Corpus Christi College, Cambridge." [24] As a matter of fact, the sisters at Sion House Monastery had in their library William Wodforde's *Contra Johannem Wyclyffe de sacramento eucharistiae*. Many of the English nobility, notably Duke Humphrey, Sir Thomas Croftys, and William Montagu, possessed precious copies of the Bible in French.[25]

Tradition to the effect that the entire Bible had been translated is certainly more positive than is generally thought. Purvey, writing about 1388, says: "For if worldli clerkis loken wel here croniclis and bokis, thei shulden fynde that Bede translatide the bible, expoundide myche in Saxon, that was English, either comoun language of this land, in his

[22] *The History of the English Bible,* revised edition, p. 11.

[23] A. C. Paues, *A Fourteenth Century English Biblical Version,* pp. xxxvi f.

[24] *The Myroure of oure Ladye,* ed. J. H. Blunt, p. 339.

[25] *Ibid.,* p. 344; Berger, *La Bible française au moyen âge,* p. 299.

tyme; and not onli Bede, but also King Alured, that foundide Oxenford, translatide in his laste daies the begynninge of the Sauter into Saxon."[26] Forshall and Madden, too, who have closely investigated the material before arriving at a judgment, say unhesitatingly:

> Before the year 1200 the Anglo-Normans had translated into their own dialect, in prose, the Psalter and canticles of the church (Cotton, Nero C.4; Trinity College, Cambridge, R.17.1), and towards the middle of the following century appear to have possessed not only a history of the Old Testament in verse, as far as the end of the books of Kings, but also a prose version of the entire Bible.[27] The knowledge of Scripture communicated to the higher classes of society in England by means of these productions, contributed, by satisfying the demand of those who were the more powerful, to delay any attempt to put the sacred volumes within the reach of the great mass of the people.[28] Nevertheless the Anglo-Saxon versions and glosses of the Gospels, and other portions of Scripture, remained partially in use, as is proved by the copies still extant, transcribed in the eleventh and twelfth centuries.[29]

Long before the exhaustive studies of Forshall and Madden, Lewis had written emphatically: "We are sure that the Saxons had the whole Bible in their own characters and language, and that the Four Gospels in the same language were read in their religious assemblies."[30] Whether this statement is fully justified in the case of the earlier Anglo-Saxons may be disputed, but there can be no doubt about the existence of a fourteenth-century prose translation of the Bible.[31] Vising declares: "Thus it appears that the great religious literature, the most valuable translations of biblical books, as well as the great epic literature, belong to the twelfth century; that the smaller pieces, including sermons, are very numerous in the thirteenth century; that didactic and practical literature . . . belongs principally to the thirteenth and fourteenth centuries, . . . and that Anglo-Norman literature comes to an end in the fifteenth century."[32]

[26] Introduction to *The Holy Bible, . . . made from the Latin Vulgate by John Wycliffe and his followers,* ed. by Forshall and Madden, 1850.

[27] In a note (*ibid.,* p. xv) the editors add: "A MS. of the first volume of this translation of the Bible executed in England about the year 1260, was recently in the possession of Edward Aysford Sanford, Esq., of Nynehead, Somersetshire."

[28] Presuming, of course, that "the great mass" could read them if they had copies!

[29] "The Gospels in the MSS. Hatten 65, and British Museum 1.A.14; Psalters in Trinity College, Cambridge, MS. R.17.1, and in Salisbury Cathedral, MS. 141" (*ibid.,* p. iii).

[30] *A Complete History of the Several Translations of the Holy Bible and New Testament, etc., into English,* pp. 3, 7.

[31] See Vising, *Anglo-Norman Language and Literature,* p. 71.

[32] *Ibid.,* p. 39.

At least portions of the Pentateuch were translated into Saxon. A Cotton MS. (Claudius B.4) "contains historical extracts from the *Pentateuch* and *Josue* written in Saxon shortly before the Conquest, the whole is illustrated with historical representations drawn by a rather unskilful hand";[33] this was dedicated to Aethelward by Aelfric. The latter's *Treatise Concerning the Old and the New Testament* was printed by Lisle in 1623, "corrected in innumerable places by Francis Junius, famed for his knowledge of the Saxon tongue."[34] A prose rendering of the four books of Kings is thought to belong to the twelfth century, though based on an earlier version; some scholars think that the translation was made in England.[35] Another Cotton MS. (Vespasian D.6) contains *Parabolae Salomonis Latine vetustis characteribus Saxonicis,* some words being glossed in Saxon.[36] *The Proverbs of Solomon with glosses,* by Samson de Nantuil, for Lady Aalix de Cunde, of Horncastle, Lincs, is referred to the middle of the twelfth century; while a prose commentary on Proverbs is referred to the middle of the twelfth century.[37]

Three translations of the Apocalypse are supposed to date from the first half of the thirteenth century: (a) the prose version at Trinity College, Cambridge, translated about 1240 A.D., probably at St. Alban's, published in part by Montague James in 1909; (b) a metrical version by William Giffard; (c) another version by an anonymous author.[38] The *Miroir,* or *Evangiles des domées* (i.e., *Dimanches*) is an exposition in poetical form of the Sunday Gospels and is referred to the first half of the thirteenth century. Rhymed versions of the *Gospel of Nicodemus* date from about 1330 or even earlier.[39]

33 Wanley, *op. cit.,* p. 253; see also p. 103: *Josue-Judges,* thirteenth century from (?) Christ Church, Canterbury; Warner and Gilson, *Catalogue of the Western Manuscripts in the Old Royal and King's Collections in the British Museum,* I.C. vii f.; pp. 27 b and 154 b.

34 MS. Mareschal 72. Liber impressus per Guil. L'isle. London, 1623: *A Saxon Treatise concerning the Old and New Testament;* "cujus [Lisle's] versionem Anglicam infinitis fere locis emendavit linguae Saxonicae peritissimus F. Junius."

35 *Les Quatre Livres des Reis traduits en français au XIIe siècle,* published by Le Roux de Lincy, 1841; cf. Wright, *Biographia Britannica literaria,* p. xviii; Berger, *Histoire de la Vulgate,* pp. 51–63.

36 Wanley, *op. cit.,* p. 243.

37 Vising, *op. cit.,* p. 51; Skeat, *The Holy Gospels in Anglo-Saxon,* St. Mark, p. iii note; Berger, *La Bible française au moyen âge,* pp. 78, 88, 94, 97.

38 *Apocalypse,* with prologue and commentary in Anglo-Norman; cf. L. Delisle and P. Meyer, *L'Apocalypse en français au XIIIe siècle,* pp. cxviii, cclxxvii; Berger, *La Bible française au moyen âge,* p. 86; Warner and Gilson, *op. cit.,* II, 329 (Royal MS. 19 B.xv).

39 Cf. Vising, *op. cit.,* p. 52.

THE PRACTICE OF GLOSSING

During the Saxon period, "glossing was a very common practice. . . . The process was applied, not only to the Scriptures, but to other books, as Prosper, Prudentius, Sedulius, Dunstan's Rule for English Monks, etc. The gloss was neither a free nor yet a literal translation, but the interlinear insertion of the vernacular, word against word of the original, so that the order of the former was really kept irrespective of the idiom and usage." [40] Nor should the glossing which appears in the Anglo-Saxon MSS. be confused with the brief commentaries enshrined, for instance, in the *Glossa ordinaria* by Walafrid Strabo (d. 849 A.D.),[41] or in the *Glossa interlinearis* of Anselm of Laon (about 1090).[42] The *Postillae* —from the opening formulae of most paragraphs, *"Post illa verba"*—by Nicholas of Lyra, who devoted forty years to their construction (1293–1339), were a development of these brief comments.[43] The practice of glossing, as followed by Anglo-Saxon scribes, is thus described:

> A gloss construes a text word for word, without much regard for the grammatical arrangement of the words of the vernacular tongue thus substituted. Its sole aim is to supply a clue to the meaning of the words of the original separately, that the original itself may be more easily understood. But a *translation* goes a great deal further; it is conformed to the grammatical laws of the vernacular tongue, and is intended to replace the original so completely that the reader may be rendered quite independent of it.[44]

[40] Eadie, *The English Bible: an External and Critical History of the Various English Translations of Scripture,* I, 14 note.

[41] So called because in ordinary use for a long time; cf. B. Smalley, "Gilbertus Porretanus, and the Problem of the Glossa Ordinaria," in *Recherches de théologie ancienne et médiévale,* 1936, pp. 51–60; *idem, The Study of the Bible in the Middle Ages,* pp. 33 ff.

[42] To such glosses, or "Helps for Preachers,"—paraphrases of the text interspersed with anecdotes wherewith the unready sermonizer could eke out his scanty matter—Chaucer presumably refers when he represents the Sompnour as saying:

> I have this day ben at your Chirche at Mess,
> And saied a Sermon after my simple witte,
> Not alle after the Text of Holie writte,
> For it is harde to you as I suppose,
> And therefore I woll teche you all the Glose.
> Glosing is a glorious thing certaine,
> For Lettir slayith, as we Clerkis faine.

(*The Sompnour's Tale,* ed. John Urry [1721], lines, 524–30.)

[43] Cf. Glunz, *The History of the Vulgate in England from Alcuin to Roger Bacon,* pp. 103 ff.

[44] Skeat, *The Holy Gospels in Anglo-Saxon,* St. Mark, p. xvii.

Portions of Scripture of most liturgical importance, as the Gospels and the Psalter, were furnished with an interlineary gloss, in which every word of the Latin text was literally, nay servilely interpreted into the vulgar tongue, serving partly as a translation, partly as a running vocabulary. . . . Where they failed it was from want of Latin, not from lack of painstaking; their anxiety to give every particle in the text its vernacular equivalent is attested by the abundance and variety of compound words in the versions; and whenever they were dissatisfied with the first gloss of a word, a second, third, or even fourth display their zeal.[45]

Idiomatic correctness in the vernacular was sacrificed to an exact representation of each Latin vocable. The result was a Gloss, differing from a formal translation, but calculated to serve the student in lieu of a dictionary, and so offer the teacher a vehicle for orally explaining to his pupils the rules of Latin etymology and syntax. The same procedure was applied to those parts of Holy Scripture most used in the Liturgy of the Anglo-Saxon Church, namely the Psalms and the Gospels. This was done for the benefit of that large body of monks whose acquaintance with Latin was slender, in order that they might understand what it was their daily duty to read or chant.[46]

Yet the magnificent glossed Gospels, those of Lindisfarne and the Rushworth MS., for instance, constitute a real problem. For the gloss there given could not be read without continual reference to the underlying Latin text. Moreover, if made simply for the use of students, it should hardly have been necessary, so it would seem, to gloss all four Gospels. Still less would such volumes for the use of students have been so sumptuously bound and illuminated. These magnificent volumes could not have been intended for public use in the monastic library; they were not made to be handled, but would seem to have been regarded, not so much as tools for craftsmen, but as treasures. Yet such tools, such helps for students, must have been in demand. This would suggest that many similar glossed copies of the Bible, though not of so elaborate a kind, must have existed in every monastery and, owing to their more perishable character, must have disappeared.

There must have been some special reason for this cumbersome glossing of the Latin text. Some have supposed that this was done not for the sake of the laity, "since the full Latin text always stands first, but rather

[45] Waring, *The Lindisfarne and Rushworth Gospels,* IV, p. cii. An example of excessive zeal in this respect occurs in the Lindisfarne gloss which renders the Latin *malum* by "evil" or "apple-tree" (Luke 6:22).

[46] *Ibid.,* III, p. viii. We see the converse process in Aelfric's *Colloquium: Ad pueros Linguae Latinae exercendos.* For here a line in Latin serves as a gloss on the Anglo-Saxon line above; the pupils beg their preceptor: "Ut doceas nos loqui Latialiter recte quia idiotae sumus, et corrupte loquimur" (Thorpe, *Analecta Anglo-Saxonica,* p. 101).

for the less educated class of priests." [47] But is it correct to say that "the Latin text always stands first"? For the gloss is nearly always supralinear, not infralinear; in other words, it stands first. Nor it is easy to imagine these very large glossed Gospels and Psalters as a convenient means for teaching, whether Latin or Anglo-Saxon. Perhaps the real reason for this double presentation of the text is preserved for us by the author of a *Treatise on the Ten Commandments* (c. 1420–34). For in his Preface he says: "And therefore for the blessing and love of God and Our Lady; and of Saint Michael, and of him that made this book, that never man nor woman lette depart the English from the Latin, for divers causes that be good and lawful to my feeling." [48] The same sense of what we might term the sacrosanct character of the Latin text appears in *The Chastising of Goddis Children:* "Nevertheless I would not reprove such translations, nor I reprove not to have them on English, nor to read on them where they more stir you to more devotion and to love of God. But utterly to use them on English and leave the Latin I hold it not commendable." [49]

BIBLIOGRAPHY

Canton, W. *The Bible and the Anglo-Saxon People,* 1914.
Carter, E. H., and R. A. F. Mears. *A History of Great Britain,* 1937, chaps. 2–4.
Chadwick, H. M. *The Origin of the English Nation,* Cambridge, 1907.
———. *Studies in Anglo-Saxon Institutions,* Cambridge, 1905.
Colegrave, Bertram. *Two Lives of St. Cuthbert,* Cambridge, 1840.
Crawford, S. J. *Anglo-Saxon Influence on Western Christendom,* Oxford, 1933.
Gasquet, F. A. *The Life of St. Gregory the Great.*
Hodgkin, R. H. *History of the Anglo-Saxons,* Oxford, 1935, 2 vols.
Lingard, John. *The Antiquities of the Anglo-Saxon Church,* 2nd ed., Newcastle, 1810.
———. *The History and Antiquities of the Anglo-Saxon Church,* 1845, 2 vols.; 2nd ed., 1858.
Michel, F. X. *Bibliothèque Anglo-Saxone,* Paris, 1837.
Palgrave, Francis (Cohen). *A History of the Anglo-Saxons,* London, 1831.
Robinson, J. Armitage. *The Times of St. Dunstan,* Oxford, 1923.
Soames, H. *The Anglo-Saxon Church: its history, revenues, and general character,* London, 1835.

[47] Lechler, *John Wycliffe and His English Precursors,* translated by Lorimer, 1884.

[48] M. J. Powell, *The Pauline Epistles contained in MS. Parker 32,* p. lvii: from MS. 94, fol. 101 f., St. John's College, Oxford, ed. by J. F. Royster.

[49] A fifteenth-century MS., Trin. Coll. Camb. B.14, 19, quoted by Powell, *op. cit.,* p. lviii; by Paues, *op. cit.,* pp. xxv, xxviii.

Stenton, F. M. *Anglo-Saxon England* (vol. 2 of *Oxford History of England*), Oxford, 1943.

Thorpe, Benjamin. *Analecta Anglo-Saxonica,* 1834.

Vinogradoff, Paul. *English Society in the Eleventh Century,* Oxford, 1908.

Wright, Thomas. *Biographia Britannica literaria,* 1842–46, 2 vols.

———. *The Celt, the Roman, and the Saxon,* 1852; 4th ed., 1885.

CHAPTER II

Anglo-Saxon and Norman-Saxon Writers[1]

To grasp the full significance of the Saxon biblical translations which have survived, we must know something of the writers whose works have come down to us. The ten outstanding translators of this period were:

1. Caedmon, c. 670
2. St. Aldhelm, 640–709.
3. St. Bede, the Venerable, 673–735
4. Guthlac, the Abbot, d. c. 714
5. King Alfred, 849–901
6. Aelfric, the Abbot, c. 1000
7. Orm and the Ormulum, c. 1200
8. Rolle of Hampole, d. 1349
9. William of Shoreham, c. 1270–1350
10. Trevisa, d. c. 1408

[1] The terms "Anglo-Saxon," "Anglo-Norman," "Dano-Saxon," and so forth, are used indiscriminately by various writers. But briefly: Anglo-Saxon lasted from about 500 to 1150 A.D.; Middle English, whether Northern, Midland, or Southern, from 1150 to 1500. Anglo-Saxon passed through Dano-Saxon, which would perhaps best describe the language in general use from the beginning of the ninth century to the middle of the tenth century, to Norman-Saxon, which lasted till the reign of Henry II (1154–89), perhaps till 1366. Cf. Vising, *Anglo-Norman Language and Literature,* pp. 1–40; Eadie, *The English Bible,* pp. 24, 60; Lewis, *A Complete History of the Several Translations of the Holy Bible and New Testament, etc., into English,* pp. 12, 50. It has to be borne in mind that until 1350 French was the dominant language, the one spoken at court and in the convents. "Anglo-Norman," says Studer, "would have been the language, not English, before the Tudors, ruling from the Conquest to the time when the two races, with their respective languages and characteristics, blended into *one* homogeneous race" (*The Study of Anglo-Norman,* pp. 11 f.).

CAEDMON

Caedmon the herdsman (c. 670) lived under St. Hilda, abbess of Whitby.[2] St. Bede has preserved the story of the gift, divinely bestowed on this illiterate man, of singing in verse the story of Genesis and Exodus and parts of Daniel.[3] A tenth century MS. of his works has been repeatedly edited.[4] The New Testament narratives sometimes regarded as the work of Caedmon are apparently of later date. Despite efforts to treat these fragments—for they are little else—like the Homeric poems, it is impossible to doubt the substantial accuracy of Bede's story;[5] the title, "the Milton of our forefathers," will always be attached to the name of Caedmon.

The Paraphrase on Genesis opens with an account of the fall of the angels and of the consequent gap in the angelic ranks:

For us it is much right that we the Guardian of the skies
the Glory-King of hosts with our words praise,
in our minds love. He is of power the essence,
the head of all exalted creatures,
the Lord Almighty.

The Fallen Cherub

The All-powerful had angel tribes,
through might of hand, the holy Lord,
ten established, in whom He trusted well
that they His service would follow,
work his will; therefore He gave them wit
and shaped them with His hands, the holy Lord.

[2] See Atkinson, *Memorials of Old Whitby*, pp. 8–34.

[3] *Historia Eccles.*, IV, chap. 24; cf. William of Malmesbury, *Gesta pontificum Anglorum* (3rd ed.), p. 154.

[4] *Codex Junianus*, XI, in the Bodleian Library, edited first of all by Francis Junius, *Caedmonis monachi paraphrasis Geneseos ac praecipuarum sacrae paginae historiarum, abhinc annos MLXX Anglo-Saxonice conscripta, et nunc demum edita a Francisco Junio, F.F.*, Amsterdam, 1655. Wanley (*Catalogus historico-criticus librorum veterum septentrionalium* [1705], p. 77) makes the somewhat startling remark: "Some years ago I heard with great pleasure (*magna cum voluptate*) George Hickes, the most competent restorer of Saxon literature, treating of Caedmon and maintaining that the author of the above Paraphrase was not that divinely inspired Caedmon of whom the Ven. Bede wrote so eloquently in his *History*, but another of the same name who wrote poems in his own Dano-Saxon dialect at a much later date, probably in the tenth century."

[5] Yet Westwood, *Palaeographia sacra pictoria, s. v.* Caedmon, speaks of "the metrical Paraphrase by the pseudo-Caedmon." Wanley (p. 103) mentions *Codex Junianus 113*, an index made by Junius of words used by Caedmon; but this MS., he says, has unfortunately been stolen.

He had placed them so happily, one he had made so powerful,
so mighty in his mind's thought, He let him sway over so much,
highest after Himself in heaven's kingdom. . . .
But he turned it for himself to a worse thing, began to raise war upon Him,
against the highest Ruler of heaven, who sitteth in the holy seat.

The fall of the angels is then described, and after a gap in the MS.,—two leaves have been lost—the formation of Eve and the temptation of our first parents is depicted. The following passage describes Melchisedech's blessing of Abraham.

Melchisedech

Salem's treasures' guardian,
that was the great Melchisedech, the peoples' bishop,
who came with gifts, the chief of martial leaders
Fair to greet, Abram honourably,
And on him set God's blessing.

Then come Abraham's complaint that he has no son (§31), the story of Agar (§32), the story of Lot and his flight from Sodom (§36), the birth of Isaac: "Abraham had a hundred winters when to him his wife a son gratefully bare" (§40), the sacrifice of Isaac (§41), the Exodus (§§42–49), the decline of Israel, the Exile, Babylon, the story of Daniel, and the curse on Nabuchodonosor. Book II consists of three separate poems: the first, again on the fall and punishment of the angels (§§1–7); the second, on the Resurrection, Ascension, and Last Judgment; the third, only a fragment, on the temptation of Christ in the wilderness. Quite true is Wright's assertion that "the collection which goes by the name of Caedmon is rather a series of pieces on scriptural subjects than a continuous poem." [6] How much of what remains to us is the genuine work of Caedmon is difficult to determine.[7]

Of the authenticity of at least one poem attributed to Caedmon there can be no doubt, for it was translated by Bede himself; it also found a place in King Alfred's translation of the *Historia* and in a MS. now in the library of the university at Cambridge. Bede thus introduces his Latin version: "This is the sense, but not the words in order as he sang them in his sleep; for verses, though never so well composed, cannot be literally translated out of one language into another without losing

[6] *Biographia Britannica literaria,* I, 25.
[7] Cf. *The Encyclopedia Britannica,* "Caedmon." [Ed.]

much of their beauty and loftiness." This, then, is given as the song which Caedmon sang:

Now we should praise of heaven the Sovereign,
the Creator's might and His mind's thought,
the works of the Father of glory, how He of each wonder,
eternal Lord! the beginning formed.
He first did shape for children of earth
heaven for roof, holy Creator!
then the middle earth, of mankind the guardian,
eternal Lord! afterwards made
for men the ground, Ruler Almighty! [8]

"Illiterate though Caedmon was," says St. Bede, "he never yet has met with an equal." [9]

ST. ALDHELM

St. Aldhelm (640–709) was abbot of Malmesbury and later bishop of Sherborne. Of his work on the Bible little is known with certainty, though tradition has it that he translated parts of the Scriptures, if not all of it; Ussher says that "a successor of St. Aidan's, Bishop Eadfrid, turned most of the Bible into English about the time that St. Aldhelm was doing the same good work in the south of England." [10] According

[8] Trans. by Dr. Lingard, *History and Antiquities of the Anglo-Saxon Church,* II, 408. Hickes laments the absence of early Saxon writings: "Nulla, proh dolor! istius aevi [Anglo-Saxonici, i.e. of the period previous to the coming of the Danes] literaria monumenta, neque membranis inscripta, neque lignis saxisve incisa extant quae scio praeter veri Caedmonis fragmentum quot in libro IV cap. 24 Eccles. Hist. Bedae regia (scil. Alfredi) versione extat" (*Linguarum veterum septentrionalium thesaurus,* p. 88). Still it may be questioned whether the fragment is Caedmon's original or the King's retranslation from Bede's Latin.

[9] *The Ecclesiastical History of the English Nation,* IV, chap. 24. For a more detailed account of Caedmon and his work, see: J. Blackburn, *Caedmon: Exodus and Daniel,* 1907; H. Bradley, "The Caedmonian Genesis," in *Essays and Studies,* vol. 7 (1920); *idem,* "Caedmon," in *Dictionary of National Biography; idem,* "Caedmon," in *The Encyclopedia Britannica;* Sir H. Ellis, *An Account of Caedmon's Metrical Paraphrases of Scripture History,* 1833; Sir Israel Gollancz, *The Caedmon Manuscript of Anglo-Saxon Biblical Poetry,* Oxford, 1927; C. W. Grein, *Caedmon, Exodus und Daniel,* 1883; C. W. Kennedy, *The Caedmon Poems, Translated into English Prose,* 1916; R. Morris, *The Story of Genesis and Exodus,* 2nd ed. revised, 1895; B. Thorpe, *Caedmon's Metrical Paraphrase of Parts of the Holy Scriptures, in Anglo-Saxon,* 1832; R. S. Watson, *Caedmon, the First English Poet,* 1875.

[10] Foxe, John Caius (*De antiqua academia Cantabrigiensi,* I, p. 150), and Bale (*Centuriae scriptorum Britannicorum,* II, chap. 1) also affirm that Aldhelm translated the whole Bible. See J. H. Blunt, *A Plain Account of the English Bible,* p. 2; *idem, The Reformation of the Church of England,* I, 503; Eadie, *The English Bible,* I, 11; R. Simon, *The Critical History of the Versions of the New Testament,* p. 353.

to his biographer, Faricius, Aldhelm could read Hebrew,[11] and there seems no doubt about his having translated the Psalms from the Latin. "His version of the Psalms," says Kenyon, "was the first direct translation of any book of the Bible into English with the exception of Caedmon's work, but it is now lost." [12] It is doubtful whether the earliest extant Anglo-Saxon gloss on the Psalms,[13] written in a tiny script of perhaps the ninth century over a seventh to eighth century Latin text of St. Jerome's first or "Roman" revision of the Latin Psalter, which was once the property of St. Augustine's and may well be a copy of a Psalter brought over by St. Augustine himself, can be attributed to St. Aldhelm.[14] The scholarly Thorpe declares:

> It must be confessed that the information that can be gleaned from the language is so scant and so uncertain an index to the age of any Anglo-Saxon MS., that reliance on such information alone would not justify us in making any positive assertions. Moreover, though there is in the version a certain inherent majesty and gravity, and the versification is by no means commonplace, yet, as is so often the case with Saxon translations from the Latin, frequent departures from the Latin original make one regret that the translator was not more scrupulous. Hence I consider it highly improbable that this version could have been due to a man so learned as we know Aldhelm to have been.[15]

Thorpe himself thinks that the language is not earlier than the tenth century, in which case we could suppose that what was fundamentally Aldhelm's work has been retouched by a later hand.

Many scholars maintain that a MS. in the Royal Library, Paris, represents Aldhelm's version, but its claims seem no more certain than those of the Cotton MS. mentioned above.[16]

[11] *Opera Sti Aldhelmi quae extant,* ed. Giles, 1844; the same, ed. Ehwald, 1913–19.

[12] *Facsimiles of Biblical Manuscripts in the* [British] *Museum,* Plate XXII.

[13] Cotton MS. Vespasian A.I.

[14] *Libri Psalmorum versio antiqua Latina cum paraphrasi Anglo-Saxonica, partim soluta oratione, partim metrice composita, nunc primum e codice MS. in Bibliotheca Parisiensi adservato, descripsit et edidit* B. Thorpe, Oxford University Press, 1835. Cf. also J. Stevenson, *An Anglo-Saxon and Early English Psalter,* 1843 and 1847; H. Sweet, *The Oldest English Texts* (E.E.T. Soc., Vol. 83), 1885; Kenyon, *op. cit.,* Plate X.

[15] Introduction to his edition, 1835.

[16] Mombert, *English Versions of the Bible,* p. 9. Forshall and Madden declare: "The Anglo-Saxon version discovered in the Royal Library at Paris about the beginning of the present century [the nineteenth] has been supposed to be at least in part St. Aldhelm's production" (*The Holy Bible, . . . made from the Latin Vulgate by John Wycliffe and his followers,* Preface, p. 1). Bale, quoted by Le Long (*Biblia Sacra seu Syllabus omnium ferme S. Scripturae editionum ac versionum . . . ,* ed. Boernerius, II, 299 f.), is very guarded: "Eum transtulisse Psalterium in linguam Anglo-Saxonicam, haec inquam

But whatever the value of the tradition that Aldhelm was the author of an Anglo-Saxon version of the Psalms, there can be no doubt about his reputation as a scholar and a poet. "Nor was his fame confined to the Anglo-Saxons: it quickly spread itself over the neighbouring nations, and foreigners were eager to submit their works to Aldhelm for revision and approbation." [17] He has justly been styled "the Father of Anglo-Latin poetry," [18] while Mr. Hunt says he "was widely known as one of the most learned men of his time. . . . When learning was at its lowest ebb in the rest of Europe it flourished in England. . . . This new spirit of learning extended to nunneries, for Aldhelm addressed his treatise, *De laude virginitatis* to the Abbess of Barking." [19]

BEDE THE VENERABLE

A fellow historian, J. R. Green, speaks of the famous author of the *Ecclesiastical History of the English Nation* as "first among English scholars, first among English theologians, first among English historians —it is in the monk of Jarrow that English learning strikes its roots"; while Pitts says: "Europe scarce ever produced a greater scholar; even while he was living his writings were of so great authority that a council ordered them to be publicly read in churches." Simeon of Durham has left us this testimony:

> Many have thought it incredible that a man living thus in a remote corner of the world, one who never crossed the seas in pursuit of knowledge, who never frequented the philosophical schools, should have become so famed for his learning, and have been known everywhere through the many books he wrote. Yet it is not to be wondered at that a person brought up as he was amid some six hundred monks, remarkable alike for the holiness of their lives and their great learning, should by the illumination of the Holy Spirit, have absorbed something of what each of them had to give him. For he had at his disposal a copious supply of all kinds of books brought by his Abbot Benedict [Biscop] to the monastery owing to the generosity of the Pontiffs Popes Vitalian and Agatho. Moreover he was living

absque ullo veterum testimonio" (*Centuriae scriptorum Britannicorum,* I, chap. 83). Cf. *The West-Saxon Psalms: the first Fifty from the so-called "Paris Psalter,"* anonymous, Boston, 1907.

[17] Lingard, *History and Antiquities of the Anglo-Saxon Church,* II, 186.

[18] Thomas Wright, *Biographia Britannica literaria,* p. 214. See also Montague James, *Two Ancient English Scholars, St. Aldhelm and William of Malmesbury,* 1931. "As a man of letters," says F. M. Stenton, "Aldhelm represents the culture of his age in its most highly developed form, and his writings influenced English and continental scholarship for more than a century" (*Anglo-Saxon England,* p. 182).

[19] *Dictionary of National Biography,* "Aldhelm."

at a time when studies flourished remarkably in England, when the Archbishop Theodore and Abbot Adrian journeyed through the island, and wherever they found Englishmen dwelling, established schools of sacred and secular learning so that all who were desirous to learn could readily find masters who could teach them.[20]

Bede wrote voluminous commentaries on the greater part of the Bible, and these have come down to us. All are familiar, too, with the account given by Cuthbert, one of his disciples, describing how his last sickness overtook him when he had already translated the Gospel of St. John down to 6:9. But Cuthbert, who says sadly, "What are these amongst so many?" goes on to say that the dying saint finished his work "for the benefit of the Church" by dictating the final words of the Gospel with his dying breath. It is generally supposed that no fragment of this precious work has survived, yet in Foxe's edition of the Anglo-Saxon Gospels (1571), republished by Junius and Marshall in 1665, it is suggested that some of the peculiarities noted in that version of the Fourth Gospel may really represent Bede's translation.

We can hardly believe that Bede, devoted as he was to the study of the Bible, would have been content to translate but a single book; indeed there is a tradition that he actually did translate a great deal of the Bible, if not all of it. Archbishop Ussher of Armagh, for instance, quotes "a fragment from the Worcester Cathedral Library" which affirms that "the Venerable Bede translated the Bible, at least the greater part of it, into English, and many copies of his version are still to be found in English monasteries. Moreover, the Bishop of Chester (*Cestrensis*), Lib. V, cap. xxiv, declares that Bede also translated the Gospel of St. John into English, and he adds that the other Gospels in an English dialect, which hardly any Englishman can now read, are still preserved in many places." Perhaps from the same source Ussher cites the instance of "a Bible translated in the dialect of Northern England and belonging to a citizen of London, by name Werung; this," he says, "was seen by many, and it was supposed to be some two hundred years old." [21]

Purver, too, says: "If worldli clerkis loken wel here croniclis and bokis, thei shulden fynde, that Bede translatide the bible." [22] There are not a

[20] *De archiepiscopis Eboraci.* For Bede's knowledge of Hebrew, see E. F. Sutcliffe, S.J., in *Biblica,* 1935, pp. 300 ff.

[21] *Historia dogmatica* (1763), XII, 356.

[22] *A New and Literal Translation of all the Books of the Old and New Testaments, with Notes Critical and Explanatory,* quoted by Lupton in Hastings' *Dictionary of the*

few similar testimonies, and it seems hardly critical to reject them en bloc.

KING ALFRED

Alfred, king of the West Saxons (849–901), was a great translator, turning into Anglo-Saxon the *De consolatione philosophiae* of Boethius, Bede's *Historia,* and that by Orosius. He also translated portions of Exodus and the conciliar letter of the Acts of the Apostles (chap. 15) as an Introduction to his *Code of Saxon Laws,* and for devotional purposes, St. Augustine's *Soliloquia.* In the Preface to his version of St. Gregory's *De cura pastorali,*[23] Alfred expressed his desire that "all the freeborn youth of my people who possess the means, may persevere in learning so long as they have no other affairs to prosecute, until they can perfectly read the English Scriptures." William of Malmesbury says Alfred "died just as he had begun a translation of the Psalms." [24] The "Paris" Psalter, the first fifty psalms in prose, the remainder in verse, has been supposed to be the version made by Alfred,[25] but there is no positive proof of this; many scholars, indeed, regard it as of a later date.[26] How much more of the Bible the King translated is uncertain; [27] for while Polydore Vergil [28] and others mention only his version of the Psalms, others like Boston of Bury affirm that he translated the whole Bible.[29] But perhaps it was in-

---

Bible, "Versions of the Bible," extra vol., p. 236. For further details see A. Hamilton Thompson, *Bede: His Life, Times, and Writings,* 1935, with a discussion (pp. 237–66) by M. L. Laistner on the contents of his library.

[23] *Alfred's Anglo-Saxon Version of Gregory's "Pastoral Care," with an English Translation, Latin Text; Notes and Introduction,* by H. Sweet.

[24] *Chronicle,* II, chap. 4, ed. by J. A. Giles, p. 120.

[25] *Angliae historia,* V, *ad annum 893;* cf. William of Malmesbury, *Gesta regum Anglorum,* chap. 2; also Asser, Bishop of Sherborn (c. 890) and Alfred's biographer, *Annales rerum gestarum Alfredi Magni,* p. 16. All these mention Alfred's translation of the Psalms.

[26] Lupton (*op. cit.,* p. 237) feels that there is no evidence that this version is by the King or that it dates from so early a period.

[27] At the close of Book I of the *Historia Eliensis* we read: "Totum Novum et Vetus Testamentum in eulogiam Angliae gentis transmutaverit"; similarly Boston of Bury (c. 1410): "Totum fere Testamentum in linguam Anglicam transtulit." Cf. Le Long, *Bibliotheca sacra,* II, 201.

[28] Cf. *Angliae historial libri xxvi.*

[29] Bale (*op. cit.,* II, chap. 27) says: "Verti fecit in Anglo-Saxonicum idioma ex purissimis Hebraeorum fontibus per quosdam Hebraeos ad Christianismum, ut credere par est, in suo regno conversos." The Alfred Committee, Oxford and Cambridge, published in 1852–53 *The Whole Works of King Alfred the Great.* See C. Plummer, *The Life and Times of Alfred the Great,* 1902; Asser, *Annales rerum gestarum Alfredi Magni,* ed.

evitable that such claims should be made, as in the case of Bede the Venerable, King Ethelstan, and, most notoriously of all, Wycliffe.

AELFRIC

Aelfric (c. 1000) was a monk at Abingdon, then abbot, first of Cerne in Dorset, then of Eynsham in Oxfordshire; [30] he was the author of a paraphrase on the Pentateuch, Josue, and Judges,[31] and of *A Treatise Concerning the Old and the New Testament,*[32] in which he mentions a translation he had made of part of the Books of Kings, a Homily on Job, and a translation, "briefly, after my manner," [33] of Esther, Judith, and Machabees; of these only the books from Genesis to Josue, the Homily on Job, and a fragment on Esther remain. In the Preface to his *Homilies on the Gospels for Sundays and Feasts,*[34] Aelfric remarks that the English "had not at that time the evangelical doctrines [namely, the Gospels] among their writings, those only excepted who knew Latin, and those books excepted which King Alfred wisely translated from Latin into English, and which are to be had." [35]

F. Wise, 1722; J. C. Wall, *Alfred the Great, His Abbeys of Hyde, Athelney and Shaftesbury,* 1900.

[30] Aelfric must not be confused with the archbishops of Canterbury and York of the same name; cf. William of Malmesbury, *Gesta regum Anglorum,* II, chap. 123; Lingard, *The History and Antiquities of the Anglo-Saxon Church,* II, 312, 318.

[31] *Heptateuchus, liber Job, et evangelium Nicodemi, Anglo-Saxonice, historiae Judith fragmentum, Dano-Saxonice. Edidit nunc primum ex MSS. codicibus Edwardus Thwaites,* Oxford, 1698; reprinted by B. Thorpe in *Analecta Anglo-Saxonica,* 1834. Cf. S. J. Crawford, *Exameron Anglice, or the Old English Hexameron,* 1921; *idem, The Old English Version of the Heptateuch: Aelfric's Treatise on the Old and New Testament, and His Preface to Genesis,* Early English Text Society, no. 160, 1922. Aelfric's text is given in Migne, *P.L.,* CXXXIX. This paraphrase of his is the earliest instance which has come down to us of translations of the Old Testament narrative; there may, of course, have been many others which have perished. See for example: Thwaites, *Versio Heptateuchi Saxonica, praeter alia quaedam Aelfrici Abbatis,* 1688, from Bodleian MS. Laud. E.19; Bodleian MS. Laud. E.33.1 (c. 1066); *Saxon-English Remains of the Pentateuch, Josua, Judges, Ruth, etc., out of Sir Rob. Cotton's MSS. of most reverend antiquity, now first new Englished and set out by W[illiam] L[isle];* Wanley, *op. cit.,* p. 99; K. Sisam, "Aelfric's Catholic Homilies," in *Review of English Studies,* 1931–32; Kenyon, *Facsimiles of Biblical Manuscripts,* Plate XXI.

[32] First edited by Lisle, 1623.

[33] "After my manner" may perhaps refer to omissions of such parts of Scripture as would not appeal to the readers he had in view.

[34] *The Homilies of the Anglo-Saxon Church, . . . with an English Version,* ed. by B. Thorpe for the Aelfric Society, 1843–46.

[35] See Kenyon, *Facsimiles of Biblical Manuscripts,* Plate XXI. Aelfric's statement here is hard to understand in view of the unquestionable existence of Anglo-Saxon versions

Aelfric's remark that he has translated "briefly, after my manner," is best illustrated by his own statement of the principles which should govern a translator of Holy Scripture. "Nothing," he says, "should be written in English but what is found in the Latin, nor should the order of the words be changed, except when the Latin and English modes of expression differ. For he who interprets, or translates from the Latin into English, should carefully preserve the English idiom, or else those who are unacquainted with the idiom of the Latin may be led into many errors." Aelfric would, presumably, have been careful to distinguish between a translation and a paraphrase and would have classed his version of Job and of the Books of Kings as paraphrases rather than as translations strictly so called. He was aware, too, that such translations into the vernacular might not always be opportune: "It thinketh me that that work [he is referring to his version of Genesis] is very dangerous for me or any men to undertake; because I dread lest some foolish man read this book, or hear it read, who should ween that he may live now under the New Law even as the old fathers [the Patriarchs] lived then in that time." [36] He gives as example the case of Jacob and Leah and the handmaids.

What profit he felt was to be derived from reading the written word of God and how intensely the Abbot loved it will appear from his noteworthy words on the subject:

> Whoever would be one with God, must often and often read the Holy Scriptures. For when we pray we speak to God; and when we read the Bible, God speaks to us. The reading of the Scriptures produces a twofold advantage to the reader. It renders him wiser by informing his mind; and also leads him from the vanities of the world to the love of God. The reading of the Scriptures is truly an honorable employment, and greatly conduces to the purity of the soul. For as the body is nourished by natural food, so the sublimer man, that is, the soul, is nour-

of the Gospels (see chap. 3). Mombert declares, without attempting to justify his statement, that Aelfric's "history is shrouded in an obscurity for which he is unquestionably indebted to the *odium theologicum* of the Romish fraternity" (*English Versions of the Bible,* 3rd ed., p. 2).

[36] Mombert, *op. cit.,* p. 13. Ever since the days of Foxe (*Actes and Monumentes,* VIII [v], ed. Townsend, 1846, p. 277), it has been the fashion to represent Aelfric as denying the Real Presence; see his letter to St. Wulstan there printed. But only elementary knowledge of the doctrine is necessary to discover that Aelfric never said anything of the sort. See W. Hunt, *The English Church to the Norman Conquest,* p. 376; Thos. Wright, *Biographia Britannica literaria,* the Anglo-Saxon Period, pp. 484–507; *The Month,* June, 1906; Lingard, *The History and Antiquities of the Anglo-Saxon Church,* II, 314, 456–65; C. L. White, *Aelfric: A New Study of His Life and Work,* 1898.

ished by the divine saying, according to the words of the Psalmist: "How sweet are thy words unto my taste, yea, sweeter than honey to my mouth." Happy is he, then, who reads the Scriptures, if he convert the words into actions. The whole of the Scriptures are written for our salvation, and by them we obtain the knowledge of the truth. The blind man stumbles oftener than he who sees; so he who is ignorant of the precepts of Scripture offends more frequently than he who knows them.[37]

Aelfric of course knew no Hebrew: the Books of Kings, so he says, are called *Malachim* from the name of their author; nor was he familiar with the geography of the East: for instance, he supposes that the whale carried Jonas right up to Nineveh. In the New Testament the order of the books is unusual; St. Paul's epistles follow after the catholic epistles, and that to the Laodiceans is included. Then follow the Acts of the Apostles, and lastly, the Apocalypse.

Apropos of Aelfric and Anglo-Saxon translations of the Bible, Marshall declares in his *Obversationes* in the edition of the Gothic and Anglo-Saxon Gospels published by himself and Francis Junius:

> From this Latin version of Holy Scripture, accessible indeed to literary people, but wholly inaccessible to the unlearned folk, various Anglo-Saxon translations were unquestionably made. . . . If Abbot Aelfric produced a vernacular version of the Old Testament, including even the "Apocrypha," it would seem a certain conclusion that the New Testament must have already been adapted to Anglo-Saxon ears. A glance at the variant readings from four MSS which stand in the margin of the Psalter published by Spelman will convince any investigator that many Saxons translated the Psalter. . . . From what I have written above it will be evident that the English of old time had various and old versions of the Bible.[38]

THE ORMULUM

About the close of the twelfth century there lived an Augustinian Canon called Orm or Ormin, who compiled the *Ormulum*,[39] which is described by Thorpe as a "metrical paraphrase of the Gospels interspersed with moralizations, by an Ecclesiastic named Orm or Ormin, by whom it is addressed to his brother, Walter. It is without rime, in lines of fifteen syllables, which for smoothness of rhythm may vie with

[37] Given by Mombert, *op. cit.*, pp. 17 f.

[38] *Domini Nostri Jesu Christi Evangelia Gothice et Anglo-Saxonice, seu Evangeliorum versiones perantiquae duae, Gothica scilicet et Anglo-Saxonica, quorum illam ex celeberrimo Codice Argenteo, nunc primum deprompsit Franciscus Junius, F. F. Hanc autem ex codicibus MSS. collatis emandatius recudi curavit Thomas Mareschallus, Anglus. Cujus etiam Observationes in utramque Versionem subnectuntur,* 1665, p. 488.

[39] Bodleian MS. Junius I. *Liber Homiliarum Normanno-Saxonice, auctore Orm vel Ormin.*

many modern productions." [40] "Thiss Boc," says the author, "is nemmed Ormulum, forrthi thatt Orrm itt wrochte." This unique MS. in the Bodleian, Junius I, preserves for us only about one eighth of the original, so far as can be calculated.[41] It may possibly have been the author's own copy. Written in Transitional or Middle English, it is of interest if only because Orm tells us that he has devoted himself "to turning into English speech the Gospels of the year so that people might thereby be led to salvation"; moreover, the work is the first piece that has come down to us of Northern English subsequent to the Conquest.

At the close of the Dedication Orm writes:

I have composed this English
For to teach Englishmen.
I was, there where I was christened,
Named Ormin by name.
And I Ormin very sincerely
With mouth and also with heart
Here ask the Christian men
Who hear others read
This book, them I ask that they
For me offer this prayer,
That brother that writ this English writing
First of all writ and made,
That brother in reward for his labour
True bliss may find. Amen.

RICHARD ROLLE

Richard Rolle (d. 1349) was probably an Augustinian, but is best known as the Hermit of Hampole, near Doncaster. He was "a man of sincere piety and deep learning" [42] who by devotional treatises, such as

[40] *Analecta Anglo-Saxonica,* 1834.

[41] Ormin's work seems to have consisted originally of some 240 chapters divided among several "books"; for at one point in the Index of Gospel texts is written: "So far the first volume," but from column 426 on all is wanting (Wanley, *op. cit.,* p. 63). Cf. *The Ormulum, with Notes and Glossary,* ed. R. White, 1852; *ibid.,* re-edited by R. Holt, Clarendon Press, 1878. Many specimens of Orm's work are given by G. P. Marsh, *Origin and History of the English Language;* also by John E. Wells, *A Manual of the Writings in Middle English, 1050–1400,* London, 1916. A brief account of Orm and his work is given in the *Encyclopedia Britannica.*

[42] "Richardus Pampolitanus, Anglo-Saxo, eremita, vir sincerae pietatis et eruditionis" (Sixtus of Siena, *Bibliotheca sancta,* IV, 544).

De incendio amoris and *The Pricke of Conscience,*[43] exercised a profound and lasting influence on English religious life. He seems to have translated or at least paraphrased various portions of the Scriptures: a translation in verse of Job (still in manuscript), paraphrases on Jeremias and Job, and possibly a version of at least portions of the New Testament.[44] But his best-known work is his prose version of the Psalter with an adaptation of Peter Lombard's gloss.[45] Of this universally popular work, various editions appeared, Rolle's Northumbrian dialect being modified locally. A literal English rendering, with a few lines of devotional exposition, follows each verse of the Latin.[46] At the close of his Prologue Rolle says:

> In this work I seek no strange English, but the lightest and commonest, and such that is most like to the Latin, so that they that know not Latin by the English may come to many Latin words. In the translation I follow the letter as much as I may. And where I find no proper English, I follow the wit of the word so that they that shall read it shall read not erring. In expounding I follow holy Doctors, for it may come in some envious man's hand that knows not what he should say, that will say that I wist not what I said, and so do harm to him and to others, if he despise the work that is profitable to him and others.[47]

Rolle's rendering of the opening verses of psalm one shows how literally he translated the Latin text.

> *Beatus vir qui non abiit in consilio impiorum,*
> Blisful man the whilk oway ged noght in the counsaile of wicked
> *Et in via peccatorum non stetit*
> And in the way of synful stode noght

[43] *The Pricke of Conscience, written in English for such as do not understand Latin,* ed. R. Morris, 1863; *English Prose Treatises,* ed. G. G. Parry, Early English Text Society, 1866.

[44] Though Lewis throws doubts on this statement (*A Complete History of the Several Translations of the Holy Bible and New Testament,* p. 12), Rolle's translation of the New Testament included the *Epistle to the Laodiceans;* cf. Dore, *Old Bibles,* p. 6.

[45] British Museum, Royal MSS. 18.D.i; Kenyon, *op. cit.,* Plate XXIII. H. Middendorff holds that Rolle's commentary was founded for the most part on that of Peter Lombard (*Studien über Richard Rolle von Hampole,* Magdeburg, 1888).

[46] *The Psalter or Psalms of David, and Certain Canticles, with a Translation and Exposition in English, by Richard Rolle of Hampole,* ed. by H. R. Bramley, 1884. The "Canticles" are those of Moses (Exod., chap. 15, and Deut., chap. 32), Anna (I Kings, chap. 2), Isaias (chap. 12), Ezechias (Isa., chap. 38), Habacuc (chap. 3), and the Magnificat. Bramley consulted fourteen MSS. See the *Guide* to British Museum Bible Exhibition, 1911, §22.

[47] The author of *The Myroure of oure Ladye* (c. 1470) says: "I have given but a few psalms translated into English, because you have them at hand of the version of Richard Hampole, or that of the English Bible, if you have but leave to read them" (ed. from the Original Black-letter Text by J. H. Blunt, for the Early English Text Society, p. 3).

Et in cathedra pestilencie non sedit
And in the chaire of pestilens he noght sate
Sed in lege Domini voluntatis ejus
Bot in laghe of lord the will of him
Et in lege ejus meditabitur die ac nocte.
And in his laghe he sall thynke day and nyght.

This is pure glossing; there is no attempt at translating or producing a running version which could be read currently. It is clearly meant to help the reader—or shall we say the student?—to spell out the Latin and so be able to profit by the brief commentary which follows.[48]

WILLIAM OF SHOREHAM (c. 1270–1350)

A MS. in the British Museum [49] contains a version of the Psalms in prose and a collection of devotional works in Anglo-Saxon: *The Seven Sacraments; The Hours of the Cross, or Meditations on the Passion; The Ten Commandments; The Seven Deadly Sins; The Five Joys of the Blessed Virgin;* and a dogmatic *Treatise on the Holy Trinity, the Creation, the Existence of Evil, the Devil, and the Fall of Man.* There is no doubt about the authorship, for a colophon at the end of the treatise on the sacraments runs: "Pray for the soul of William of Schorham, formerly Vicar of Chart near Leeds,[50] who made this compilation"; and at the end of the treatise on *The Seven Deadly Sins* we read: "Pray for the soul of Master William of Schorham, formerly Vicar of Chart near Leeds, who compiled this Treatise on the Seven Mortal Sins. And to all who shall say the Lord's Prayer and the Angelic Salutation [the Hail Mary], Simon, Archbishop of Canterbury, grants forty days indulgence." This Simon (of Mepham) was archbishop from 1327 to 1333.

It seems, then, that William wrote in the first quarter of the fourteenth century. In the MS. in the British Museum, the version of the Psalms and William's devotional treatises are written by the same hand, whence

[48] Cf. C. Horstmann, *Richard Rolle of Hampole and His Followers,* 2 vols., 1895; Frances Comper, *A Life of Richard Rolle,* 1928.

[49] Addit. MSS. 17376. *The Poems of William of Shoreham, c. 1320, Vicar of Chart-Sutton,* re-edited by M. Konrath, Early English Text Society, 1902; only Part I has appeared. The former edition, *The Religious Poems of William of Shoreham,* was edited for the Percy Society by Thos. Wright in 1849. Cf. Kenyon, *Facsimiles of Biblical Manuscripts,* Plate XXII.

[50] He was probably instituted as vicar of Chart, near Sevenoaks in Kent, by the Priory of Canons Regular to whom the living belonged; and he himself may have been one of the Canons.

it used to be concluded that William was the author of this Anglo-Saxon version of the Psalter. The difficulty is the dialect. For whereas his unquestioned work is in a West Kent dialect, the Psalms are in a West Midland dialect. Hence the latter work has been attributed to some unknown author.[51]

JOHN OF TREVISA

John of Trevisa (1326-1412) was born at Caradock in Cornwall; he entered at Exeter College, later at Queen's, Oxford; he became canon of Westbury, Wilts, and vicar of Berkeley, Glos. He was a great translator, turning into English Glanville's *De proprietatibus rerum* and a treatise on the passion of Christ. He was the author of *Dialogus militem inter et clericum;* but he is best known for his translation of Higden's *Polychronicon,* at the end of which is the entry: *Versio ista finita est die Jovis die 18 Aprilis, Anno Domini 1357. Anno autem 35 Patroni mei Thomae Domini de Barkeley, qui me versionem istam adornari fecit.*

That Trevisa also translated the Bible into English is positively affirmed by Caxton and Bale, while Anthony à Wood declares: "Conspicuous for learning and eloquence, Trevisa was the first who endeavoured to polish our language and remove barbarous expressions from it. He also, though without any orders to that effect, translated the Bible into the vernacular, a bold and unprofitable undertaking at a time when such a task was fraught with danger." [52] Churchill Babington, the editor of the *Polychronicon,* says in his introduction: "Of his other translations, that of the Bible, *said* by Caxton, Bale, and others to have been made by Trevisa, and *possibly still extant at Rome,* is the most important on all accounts. It is not, however, certain, though by no means improbable, that Trevisa ever translated the Scriptures at all."

In his *Dialogue between a Lord and a Clerk,* Trevisa mentions the fact that "the Apocalipse is wryten on the walles and roof of a chapel in Latyn and Frensshe," a writing which was still on the walls and roof of

[51] See below, chap. 5, note 36.

[52] *History and Antiquities of the University of Oxford,* p. 85. Trevisa himself, following what is known as the longer MSS. of the *Polychronicon,* wherein Higden explains the corrupt state of the English language as being chiefly due to the fact that after the Conquest children were taught French instead of English, tells us that one John Carnwaille, and after him Richard Pencriche, changed all this, with the result that by the year 1385 children "were able to leave French and construe and learn in English" (*Polychronicon,* ed. by Churchill Babington, II, chap. 59, p. 161).

the chapel at Berkeley in 1805. Horne's commentary on this is worth quoting: "John de Trevisa, at the desire of his patron, Lord Berkeley, is said to have translated the Old and New Testament into the English language. But as no part of this work appears ever to have been printed, the translation ascribed to him is supposed to have been confined to a few texts which are scattered in some parts of his works (several copies of which are known to have existed in manuscript) or which were painted on the walls of his patron's chapel at Berkeley Castle." [53] It would be hard to find a more purely gratuitous supposition. Baber may have been Horne's authority for the above suggestion, for he declares:

> Trevisa enjoys the reputation in the estimation of some men of letters of having produced an English translation of the Bible; but his title to this fame had hitherto eluded all attempts I have made to trace it. . . . It may however be considered to rest solely on the authority of Caxton, who in his Preface to the *Polychronicon* says: "It is thought that the translation ascribed to him consisted only of texts painted on the walls of the chapel at Berkeley Castle and the church at Berkeley." [54]

Caxton, Baber, and Horne, then, are responsible for what, after all, is but a vague surmise repeated in various histories of the English versions. There seems no valid reason for disregarding the positive statement of the Preface to the Authorized Version, that "even in our king Richard the second dayes, John Trevisa translated them [the Scriptures] into English, and many English Bibles in written hand are yet to be seen translated, . . . as is very probable, in that age."

[53] Hartwell Horne, *An Introduction to the Critical Study and Knowledge of the Scriptures* (1839), II, ii, p. 66.

[54] *The New Testament Translated by John Wyclif,* ed. H. Baber, 1810. See W. J. Wilkins, *John de Trevisa; His Life and Work,* 1915.

CHAPTER III

The Anglo-Saxon Versions of the Gospels

WE still possess eight manuscripts of the Anglo-Saxon Gospels. These, minutely described by Humphrey Wanley in 1705,[1] and edited in whole or in part by John Foxe, the Martyrologist,[2] Junius and Mareschal (Marshall), Thorpe, and Bosworth,[3] have now been carefully edited by Skeat, who completed a work begun by Kemble and Hardwick.[4] These eight MSS. fall into two classes according as they represent real translations from the Latin without any corresponding Latin text being given (six MSS., namely, Corpus cxl, Cambridge Ii.2.11, Bodley 441, Cotton, Otho C.i, Hatton 38, and Royal I.A.xiv), or a gloss written in Anglo-Saxon between the lines of a Latin text (the Lindisfarne and Rushworth Gospels).

The problem is to discover what relationship, if any, exists between the six Saxon versions of an original Latin text, and between them and the

[1] *Catalogus historico-criticus*, 1705.

[2] *The Gospels of the Fower Evangelistes translated in the olde Saxons tyme out of Latin into the vulgare toung of the Saxons, and now published for testimonie of the same*, 1571. The English text, taken from the Bishops' Bible, 1568, is printed in black letter in parallel columns with the Anglo-Saxon.

[3] *Quatuor Domini Nostri Jesu Christi . . . Evangeliorum versiones perantiquae duae, Gothica scil.* [ed. by F. Junius], *et Anglo-Saxonice* [ed. by T. Marshall], 1665; cf. Wood, *Fasti Oxonienses* (ed. 1691), p. 875.

Da Halgan Godspel on Englisc: The Anglo-Saxon Version of the Holy Gospels, ed. by B. Thorpe, 1842; the text adopted is that of the Cambridge MS. Ii.2.11, collated with the Corpus MS. cxl, Bodley 441, and Otho C.i.

The Gothic and Anglo-Saxon Gospels in Parallel Columns with the Versions of Wycliffe and Tyndale, ed. by Bosworth, 1865; 3rd ed., 1888.

[4] *The Holy Gospels in Anglo-Saxon, Northumbrian, and Old Mercian Versions, synoptically arranged, with collations exhibiting all the readings of all the MSS.; together with the Early Latin Version as contained in the Lindisfarne MS.; collated with the Latin Version in the Rushworth MS.*, Cambridge University Press, 1871–87.

two Latin Gospels with their glosses. Now it is remarkable that not one of the above eight MSS. has Matt. 23:14 ("Woe to you, scribes and Pharisees . . . judgment"). But while such an omission is intelligible in the case of the six versions which, as we shall see, are but slightly varying reproductions of an archetype, it is difficult to understand how two Latin texts differing so considerably as those glossed in the Lindisfarne and Rushworth Gospels should also have omitted the verse. Similarly the words "without a cause" (Matt. 5:22) are absent in the six versions and the two glosses.

On the other hand, whereas the six versions—or rather, six editions of the one version—all have the lengthy addition in Matt. 20:28,[5] yet this passage finds no place in the Lindisfarne and Rushworth texts. It would seem, then, that the versions which present this addition must have been made from a Latin original which, in some respects at least, differed from that glossed by the Lindisfarne and Rushworth scribes.[6]

THE ANGLO-SAXON MANUSCRIPTS

To grasp the literary problems involved, we must have a clear idea of the history and contents of the various manuscripts.

a. Corpus MS. cxl, at Corpus Christi College, Cambridge (Bosworth's I, or B), is "a small folio volume copied, so it would seem, from an older MS. before the Conquest; it contains the Four Gospels in Saxon." [7]

[5] An ultraliteral version of the passage, as found in the Curetonian Syriac, is thus given by Scrivener (*A Plain Introduction* [4th ed., 1894], I, 8): "But you, seek ye that from little things ye may become great, and not from great things may become little. Whenever ye are invited to the house of a supper, be not sitting down in the honoured place, lest should come he that is more honoured than you, and to thee the Lord of the supper should say, Come near below, and be thou ashamed in the eyes of the guests. But if thou sit down in the little place, and he that is less than thee should come, and to thee the Lord of the supper shall say, Come near, and come up and sit down, thou also shall have more glory in the eyes of the guests."

A more polished version is offered by Skeat: "Ye seek to become great in a small matter, and to be minished in the greatest matter. Verily, when ye shall be bidden to a feast, sit ye not in the first seats, lest a more worthy man come after thee, and the householder bid thee rise and make room for the other and thou be put to shame. If thou sittest at a feast, in the outermost seat, and after thee cometh another guest, and the bidder say to thee, Friend, sit nearer; then shalt thou be more honourable than the man put into the outer (seat)."

[6] See Skeat, *op. cit.*, St. Matthew, pp. x f., for the Latin MSS. which have this addition, notably *Codex Bezae* (D) and the *Codex Aureus,* perhaps written in England about the year 850.

[7] Wanley, *Catalogus historico-criticus,* p. 116.

Marshall declares: "Rarely have I noticed any difference between this MS. and that of Oxford [Bodley 441; see *c.*], and I take them both to be very ancient." [8] A note at the end of St. Matthew's Gospel has: "Finit Amen. Sit sic hoc interim. Ego Aelfricus scripsi hunc librum in monasterio Bathonio et dedi Brithwaldo praeposito. Qui scripsit vivat in pace, in hoc mundo et in futuro seculo, et qui legit legator in eternum." This reference to Bath as the original home of the MS. is supported by the forms of manumission prefixed later, several of them mentioning Aelfsige of Bath, who died in 1087. If the *praepositus* Brithwald was the Brithwald who was bishop of Sherborne from 1006 to 1046, we could, with Bosworth, assign the copying of the volume to between 990 and 1030.

One page, Mark 12:26–39, is wanting from the original, though later it was written in by an inferior hand. After St. Luke comes a long list of popes, ending with Alexander II (1061–73), probably added later, as were the forms of manumission. For the relationship between this MS. and the other five, see below. "It is almost certain," says Skeat, "that the Corpus, Bodley, and Cotton MSS. had all a common origin." Bosworth based his edition on this Corpus MS. collated with the other five.[9]

b. The Cambridge MS. Ii.2.11 is in Cambridge University Library (Bosworth II, or C). After the Four Gospels we have an Anglo-Saxon version of the Apocryphal *Gospel of Nicodemus,* or *The Harrowing of Hell,* the embassy of Nathan the Jew to Tiberius, and the story of Veronica. An inscription at the end of St. Matthew's Gospel runs: "Hunc textum Evangeliorum dedit Leofricus Episcopus Ecclesiae Sancti Petri Apostoli in Exonia ad utilitatem successorum suorum." Since Leofric was bishop of Devon and Cornwall from 1046 to 1073, we are able to date the MS. at least some time before the Conquest. The cathedral chapter presented the MS. to Matthew Parker in 1566, and a note adds that he

[8] *Quatuor Domini Nostri Jesu Christi . . . Evangeliorum versiones perantiquae duae, Gothica scil.* [ed. by F. Junius], *et Anglo-Saxonice* [ed. by T. Marshall], p. 490.

[9] *The Gothic and Anglo-Saxon Gospels in Parallel Columns with the Versions of Wycliffe and Tyndale,* 1865; 3rd ed. 1888. For a detailed account of all six MSS., see Skeat, *The Gospel of St. Mark,* pp. v–xii. Bosworth's edition, however, being more readily accessible than Skeat's costly volume, we add the designation of each MS. as given by Bosworth. The names assigned to Cotton MSS., Vespasian, Galba, and so forth, are due to the fact that in Sir Robert Cotton's library the volumes were kept in fourteen presses over which stood busts of the Roman emperors whose names were attached to the respective presses.

"bequeathed it to Sir Nicholas Bacon Knight, etc., who do give the same to the Universitie of Cambridge. Anno 1574."

c. Bodley 441 (Bosworth VI) is "a folio volume written previous to the Conquest and containing the Four Gospels in a Saxon version." [10] It was, at Archbishop Parker's direction, published by Foxe.[11] In this edition the Anglo-Saxon text, in beautiful type, is faced by an English version from the Bishops' Bible of 1568 in black letter. No Saxon text had ever before been printed. Prefixed is an address by Foxe to "the most vertuous and noble Princesse, Queene Elizabeth"; in it he defends the use of vernacular versions.[12] His statement that "by Archbishop Parker's industrious diligence and learned labours, this booke hed bene collected and searched out of the Saxons Monumentes," suggests that the work was in some sort a compilation; and in point of fact, as Skeat shows, Mark 1:1; 4:37; the last three verses of St. Luke; and John 20:9; 21:25, have been supplied from the Corpus MS. (cxl) mentioned above (*a*). The latter is closely related to the Bodley MS., which is also closely related to the Cotton MS. (*d*), of which Skeat considers it a duplicate.[13]

d. Cotton MS. Otho C.i (Bosworth III, or "Cot") is one of the many MSS. damaged by the fire in Sir Robert Cotton's library on October 23, 1731. Complete to Matt. 27:6 in 1704, when Wanley described it, the subsequent fire destroyed twenty-five folio sheets; the remainder was repaired by Sir Frederic Madden, and though St. Matthew's Gospel still remains damaged, those of St. Mark and St. John are nearly complete.

[10] Wanley, *op. cit.*, p. 64.

[11] *The Gospels of the Fower Evangelistes translated in the olde Saxons tyme out of Latin into the vulgare toung of the Saxons, newly collected out of Auncient monumentes of the sayd Saxons, and now published for testimonie of the same. At London. Printed by John Daye dwelling over Aldersgate, 1571. Cum privilegio Regiae Majestatis per decennium.*

[12] Parker himself says: "Foxe also edited the Four Gospels in the Saxon language so as to make it clear that the people of England used to be familiar with the Scriptures in the vernacular" (Preface to Asser's *Annales rerum gestarum Alfredi Magni,* ed. 1722, p. ix).

[13] "It is absolutely certain," says Skeat, "that Bodley, Corpus, and Cotton are copies from a common original" (*The Gospel of St. Mark,* p. vii). MS. Bodley 441 was afterwards edited by Junius and Marshall in 1665, by Benjamin Thorpe in 1824, by Bosworth in 1865; see Lewis, *A Complete History of the Several Translations of the Holy Bible and New Testament,* pp. 4 f.; *Guide to the Manuscripts and Printed Books,* British Museum Bible Exhibition, 1911, §21. Marshall notes that the Bodley and Corpus MSS. rarely disagree and are better and older than the Cambridge and Hatton MSS., which are later in date; of the latter two the Cambridge MS. is older and *longe politissimum,* while the Hatton MS. is *manu plane recentiori ac stylo novitate spirante conscriptum.*

At the end of the Gospel of St. John the copyist has written: "Wulfri me wrat." Between the Gospels of St. Luke and St. John a chapter relating to St. Aldhelm, abbot of Malmesbury and afterwards bishop of Sherborne, suggests some connection with Malmesbury and St. Aldhelm; the relation between this MS. and the Corpus MS. (*a*) may point to the same conclusion.[14] Between the Gospels of St. Luke and St. John is a Saxon version of certain privileges granted by Pope Sergius to Aldhelm, abbot of Meldun, and his successors, with a confirmation of them by Aethelred, king of the Mercians, and Ina, king of the West Saxons.[15]

e. The Hatton MS., in the Bodleian, No. 38 (Bosworth IV, or H), has the Four Gospels in Anglo-Saxon.[16] The translation agrees remarkably with the Corpus MS. (*a*), though the dialect is very different; authorities refer it to the twelfth century. Since the copyist of this MS. wrote into the Royal MS. (*f*) the passage in St. Mark's Gospel omitted in that MS. (16:14–20), and since the text of this MS. and of the Royal MS. is almost verbally the same, it seems to follow that the Hatton MS. was copied from the Royal MS., and that the copyist had at his disposal other MSS. whence to fill the gap.[17] The Hatton MS. originally belonged to St. Augustine's, Canterbury; at the Dissolution it came into the hands of Cranmer, whose signature stands on the first folio. A missing folio containing Luke, chap. 16, was copied in under the direction of John Parker, son of the Archbishop.[18]

f. The Royal MS., British Museum, Bibliotheca Regia, I.A.xiv (Bosworth V, or RL), is an "Anglo-Saxon or Wessex version, produced early in the eleventh century. This is the earliest English version of the Gospels, apart from interlinear word-for-word translations inserted in Latin MSS. (as in the Lindisfarne Gospels or the Bosworth Psalter) . . . written early in the eleventh century." [19] Originally the property of Christ Church, Canterbury, this MS. came into the possession of Cranmer.

[14] Skeat, *op. cit.*, p. ix.

[15] Wanley, *op. cit.*, pp. 211–212.

[16] "Potius Normanno-Saxonice," Wanley, *op. cit.*, p. 76.

[17] Skeat, *op. cit.*, St. John, p. x.

[18] "Cujus labore folium ex Evangelio D. Lucae abscissum, nitide scriptum, restituitur" (Wanley, *op. cit.*, p. 76).

[19] *Guide* to the British Museum Bible Exhibition, 1911, § 21. "A twelfth century copy of a translation made in the tenth or eleventh century in the Wessex dialect. The first version—as distinct from a gloss. Six copies of it remain, viz., the other five Anglo-Saxon MSS" (Kenyon, *op. cit.*, Plate XX).

Wanley (p. 181) would refer it to the time of Henry II (1154–89), Skeat, to that of Stephen (1135–54).[20] The relationship between this MS. and the Hatton MS. is described above.

DATES OF THE MANUSCRIPTS

It is idle to attempt to assign definite dates to these six Anglo-Saxon MSS. of the Gospels.

It is difficult to decide upon the age of a Saxon MS. from any peculiarity of orthography; *place* has an influence, in this respect, as great as *time*. In fact, Saxon MSS. ought to be locally classified before any attempt be made at chronological arrangement; nor will this appear strange when we consider, that in early times the several divisions of the kingdom were, comparatively speaking, almost like foreign countries to each other; that in some parts the Saxon must have continued uninfluenced by foreign idioms much longer than others; that the various provincial dialects must have been much more strongly marked than they are at present, and that they were all equally employed in literary composition.[21]

It is well, too, to bear in mind words written by Wanley to Pepys when the latter had sent him some manuscripts with enquiries as to their probable age. After excusing himself on various grounds, Wanley says:

Nor have I, as I remember, for twelve months lookt into any MS. with intention to observe the handwriting of it. . . . By such long disuse I have lost (I fear) a great deal of that niceness in discerning, which the daily use of so many thousands of MSS. as are in the Bodleian Library, had at length given me: and with that the benefit of many observations, which cost me much time to make. I must needs say too, Sir, that I think it requires a man of great experience to give judgement on the age of an entire book, from the handwriting of it: and much more so when, instead of a whole book, he has only a leaf or a piece of a leaf to judge by.[22]

Without claiming any paramount authority for Wanley, who was, after all, but one of the pioneers in this field, Westwood says: "He had more practice in the examination of Anglo-Saxon MSS. than perhaps any other person who has yet studied them; he could not have mistaken a MS. of the eighth century for one of the eleventh or twelfth; such a consideration is of itself unworthy of a moment's consideration."[23]

[20] *Op. cit.,* St. Mark, p. x.
[21] Thorpe, Preface to *Caedmon's Metrical Paraphrase,* p. xii.
[22] Sir Henry Ellis, *Original Letters of Eminent Literary Men,* Camden Society, p. 203.
[23] *Palaeographia sacra pictoria,* p. 3.

THE RELATIONSHIP OF THE ANGLO-SAXON VERSIONS

Pioneer Anglo-Saxon scholars, presuming that these MSS. represent independent versions, concluded that similar versions must have been common before the Conquest. Marshall, for instance, says: "From the original Latin version, an open book indeed to the educated, but a sealed book to others, there must unquestionably have been made various versions in Anglo-Saxon meant to meet the needs of the prevailing ignorance." He instances the case of King Alfred, who, as we read in the *History of Ely* and in the Preface to Asser's history of that king, "translated both the Old and New Testament for the use of his people." Marshall also points out that the fact that

> Abbot Aelfric was content to translate only certain portions of the Old Testament—and included among them even the Apocrypha (Deuterocanonical books)—would seem to put it beyond doubt that by his time the Gospels already existed in Anglo-Saxon; while anyone who considers the number of variant readings from four different MSS. which are to be found in the margin of the interlinear psalter published by Spelman in 1640, will be convinced that several people translated the Psalms into Anglo-Saxon; there is, further, an admirable MS. in the possession of Francis Junius containing the Psalms beautifully translated and exquisitely written, both the Latin and the Saxon text, which latter differs very much from the foregoing MSS. This makes it clear that our Saxon forefathers had very old as well as widely differing translations of the Bible.[24]

Skeat, however, urges that, while Marshall's arguments may avail for the Bible as a whole, "the actual evidence (so far as the existing MSS. of the Gospels are concerned) is all the other way." His evidence, based on a similarity of the existing MSS., is, briefly, as follows: the last page of St. Mark's Gospel, easily detached from the original, was omitted by the scribe of the Bodley MS. (*c*), but was copied in by a later hand from the Corpus MS. (*a*), probably by the direction of Archbishop Parker. Further, the fact that the Royal MS. (*f*) omitted the same passage suggests that this latter MS. may have been copied from the Bodley MS., a

[24] *Domini Nostri Jesu Christi Evangelia Gothice et Anglo-Saxonice, seu Evangeliorum versiones perantiquae duae, Gothica scilicet et Anglo-Saxonica, quorum illam ex celeberrimo Codice Argenteo, nunc primum depromsit Franciscus Junius F. F. Hanc autem ex codicibus MSS. collatis emandatius recudi curavit Thomas Mareschallus, Anglus. Cujus etiam Observationes in utramque Versionem subnectuntur. Accessit et Glossarium Gothicum: cui praemittitur Alphabetum Gothicum Runicum, etc. opera ejusdem Francisci Junii,* 1665, p. 488.

suggestion corroborated by the failure of the scribe of the Bodley MS. to notice the omission of another page containing Luke 16:14–31, a passage omitted by the copyists of the Hatton MS. (*e*), and of the Royal MS. both of which also omitted Luke 24:51–53. Re-examining the MSS. in the light of these facts, and finding that "the Cotton MS. [*d*] is an absolute *duplicate,* word for word, and letter for letter, of the Bodley MS., whilst both of these, in their turn, agree so closely with the Corpus MS., also word for word and *almost* letter for letter," [25] Skeat drew the conclusion that "all three [the Cotton, Bodley, and Corpus MSS.] must be mere copies of one and the same original not now forthcoming." The same argument holds good for the Cambridge MS. (*b*), "which is exactly the same text, word for word." [26] "We are almost irresistibly led to conclude that perhaps *not* very many of the copies have perished, that they may *never* have been very numerous, and that there is at the present not the faintest trace of any *other* version. I feel the more bound to say this, because the results differ from what I expected to find."

The first conclusion at which Skeat arrives seems irrefutable: "We ought to conclude that there never was but one Anglo-Saxon version"; [27] but his further conclusion seems more hazardous: "the copies of it were never numerous, and there is little to show that many copies have been lost." [28] For, in the first place, the version attributed to Bede will always remain to be accounted for. Moreover, when we consider the wealth and learning of at least some of the Saxons, the sumptuous character of their manuscripts and their binding; [29] when we reflect on King Alfred's statement that he "was incited to translate these books [Orosius, Boethius, Bede, etc.] into English because the churches which had formerly numerous libraries, had, together with their books, been burnt by the Danes"; [30] when, finally, we read of the precious copies of the Latin Bible sent by St. Gregory for use in England [31] and for so long the pride of St. Augustine's, Canterbury, we find it hard not to regard our eight

[25] Introduction to *St. Luke's Gospel in Anglo-Saxon,* p. 21.

[26] *Idem,* Introduction to *St. Mark's Gospel,* p. 132.

[27] *The Holy Gospels in Anglo-Saxon,* St. Mark, p. xiii, and St. Luke, p. xi.

[28] *Ibid.,* St. Luke, p. vi.

[29] See Eadfrith's account of the binding of the Lindisfarne Gospels at the beginning of the following chapter. Cf. Maitland, *The Dark Ages,* pp. 68, 204 ff., 213.

[30] Cf. *ibid.,* p. 228.

[31] For St. Gregory's gift of books see John the Deacon, *Vita Sancti Gregorii,* chap. 37; Bede, *Historia,* I, chap. 39.

remaining MSS. as but a tiny remnant of a very large number of copies.

As we saw above, Foxe published his edition of the Bodley MS. 441 in order to prove that our forefathers had the Scriptures in the vernacular; and Lewis ventures to say: "We are sure they [the Saxons] had the whole Bible in their own country characters and language, and that the four Gospels in the same language were read in their religious assemblies," and he repeats Marshall's argument based on Aelfric's translation of a great part of the Old Testament.[32]

Forshall and Madden, indeed, suggested a *via media* by regarding the Corpus MS., Otho C.i, Bodley 441, Cambridge Ii.2.11, Royal MS. I.A. xiv, and the Hatton MS. as adapted transcriptions of the Anglo-Saxon translations put in the form of glosses;[33] but Skeat's conclusions are endorsed by Scrivener:

> There is but one known version of the four Gospels (the only portion of the New Testament that was translated into Anglo-Saxon); this version was made, probably in the South-West of England at or near Bath, in the last quarter of the tenth century. It is preserved in four MSS.: (Corp.) Corpus Christi College, Cambridge, MS. 140; (B) Bodleian Library MS. 441; (C) Cotton MS. Otho C.I; . . . and (A) Cambridge University Library, MS. Ii.2.11. Of these the first three may be dated, in round number, about the year 1000; the fourth (A) belongs to the following half century. . . . There are in the British Museum two additional copies of this version (Bibl. Regia, MS. I.A.xiv, and Hatton MS. 38). These belong to a period after the Conquest and have no critical value, for the first is copied from B [Bodleian MS. 441], and the second is copied from the first [Bibl. Regia, MS. I.A.xiv].
>
> This version is based upon a type of the Vulgate MSS. that has not yet been definitely determined. Old Latin readings make it certain that the original MS. was of the mixed type.[34]

[32] Lewis, *A Complete History of the Several Translations of the Holy Bible and New Testament, etc., into English,* pp. 3, 7.

[33] *The Holy Bible, . . . made from the Latin Vulgate by John Wycliffe and his followers,* Introduction, p. ii.

[34] *A Plain Introduction to the Criticism of the New Testament* (4th ed., 1894), II, 164.

PRESUMED PEDIGREE OF THE ANGLO-SAXON VERSION OF THE GOSPELS

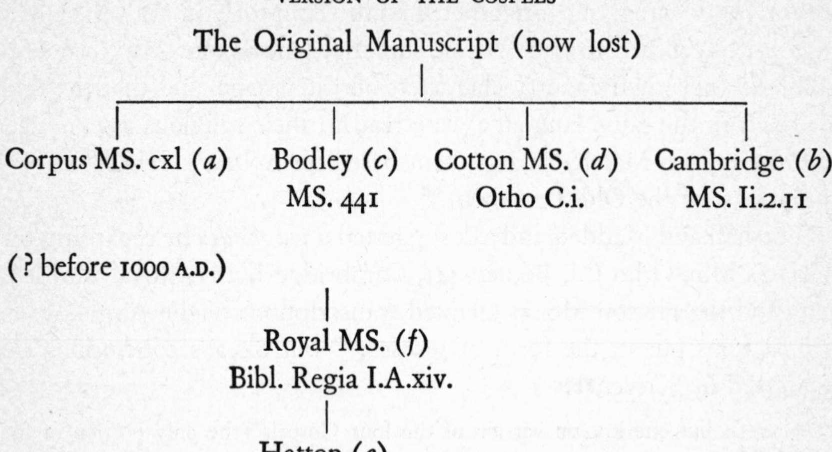

The above six MSS. present Anglo-Saxon versions of a Latin text; two other ancient manuscripts (the Lindisfarne and Rushworth Gospels) present a Latin text of the Gospels with an interlinear Anglo-Saxon gloss, which is, therefore, not strictly a current translation.

CHAPTER IV

The Lindisfarne and Rushworth Gospels

THE LINDISFARNE MANUSCRIPT

THE Lindisfarne Gospels (Cotton MS., Nero D.iv), also called the "Book of St. Cuthbert" or "Durham Book," is a large volume, 13½ inches by 9½ inches, containing the four Gospels: the Vulgate text with an interlinear Anglo-Saxon gloss. It is "one of the most valuable, as it is one of the most splendid volumes which have come down to us, . . . not exceeded in beauty by any known MS. That the Latin text is from one of the Bibles sent by St. Gregory seems proved by the catalogue of the monastery of St. Augustine drawn up in the time of Henry V: *Primitie librorum totius Ecclesiae Anglicanae*."[1]

At the beginning of the MS. is a picture of the cross *magno labore delineata*. There follow St. Jerome's Prefaces, the Eusebian Canons, and other pieces; then a portrait of St. Matthew, followed by another cross: *Imago Crucis incredibili diligentia et venustate delineata*.[2] Before each Gospel the same picture of the cross is repeated, together with a representation of each Evangelist. Before St. Matthew's Gospel is a picture of the Evangelist seated, while on his knee he writes with a metal pen. A saint is dictating to him and an angel holds up a book with his left hand; in his right hand he holds a horn trumpet to his mouth. Over the angel's head is written: *Imago hominis;* and over the Evangelist is the inscription: *O Agios Matthaeus*. Both inscriptions are in square Saxon characters.

The names of those who copied the Latin text, who bound it, who

[1] Westwood, *Palaeographia sacra pictoria;* see note 10 below.

[2] Wanley, *Catalogus historico-criticus,* p. 250.

ornamented it, and who was responsible for the Anglo-Saxon gloss, are preserved in an Anglo-Saxon note at the close:

Eadfrith,[3] bishop of Lindisfarne church, (was) he (who) at the first wrote this book in honor of God and St. Cuthbert, and all the saints in common that are in the island. And Ethilwold, bishop of the people of the Lindisfarne Island, made it firm on the outside and covered it as well as he could. And Bilfrith,[4] the anchorite, he wrought in smith's work the ornaments that are on the outside, and adorned it with gold, and also with gems, overlaid with silver, unalloyed metal.[5] And Aldred,[6] an unworthy and most miserable priest, with the help of God and St. Cuthbert, glossed it above in English, and made himself at home with the three parts: Matthew's part, for the honor of God and St. Cuthbert; Mark's part, for the Bishop; and Luke's part, for the brotherhood, together with eight oras[7] of silver for his admission. And St. John's part for himself, together with four oras of silver, (deposited) with God and St. Cuthbert; to the end that he may gain admittance into heaven through God's mercy, and on earth happiness and peace, promotion, dignity, wisdom, and prudence, through St. Cuthbert's merits. Eadfrith, Ethilwold, Bilfrith, and Aldred made and adorned this Gospel Book in honor of God and St. Cuthbert.

"From the expression of Aldred that he glossed the Gospel of St. John 'for himself,' we conclude that the glosses to this Gospel are in his own handwriting, whilst those to the other Gospels (in a different hand) were merely made under his superintendence, though he claims credit for the whole work. This is shown more clearly by the short entry at the beginning of St. Mark's Gospel: 'Thou, living God, be mindful of Eadfrith, and Ethilwold, and Bilfrith, and Aldred, sinners; these four, with God's help, were employed upon this book.'"[8]

It is clear that Eadfrid copied the whole with his own hand; so beautifully did he perform his task that the Codex is deservedly regarded as an incomparable specimen of Anglo-Saxon calligraphy. It is to be hoped that it will always be preserved. When the copying was completed, St. Athelstan, who succeeded Eadfrid in the See of Lindisfarne, illuminated the volume by painting in with incredible toil the initial letters, and drawing and painting the various figures of

[3] Bede dedicated his *Life of St. Cuthbert* to Eadfrith.

[4] Is he to be identified with a Bridfrith who was a monk of Ramsey Abbey and who commented on Bede's scientific writings? See Lingard, *History and Antiquities of the Anglo-Saxon Church,* II, 311.

[5] The sumptuous binding was, of course, destroyed centuries ago; the present splendid covering is due to Dr. Maltby, bishop of Durham, 1833.

[6] An Aldred was bishop of Durham from 946 to 968.

[7] The ora was a Danish coin, sixteen to the pound, according to one valuation; twenty to the pound according to another. In the gloss *mna* (Luke, chap. 19) is rendered indifferently by ora or by libra.

[8] Skeat, *The Holy Gospels in Anglo-Saxon,* St. Mark, p. ix.

the cross and of the Evangelists. After him Bilfrid the Hermit took the illuminated text and bound it in silver, gold, and precious stones. Finally the Priest Aldred glossed the Latin text with a Dano-(Anglo-)Saxon version in the dialect of the North; he also added a few brief notes of his own in some places, more especially on the Gospel of St. Matthew. I have discovered the names of these men written in gold and silver—presumably on account of the wonderful task thay had performed—in the Register of the Benefactors of the Church of Durham. Of the date at which Aldred worked I have no definite knowledge, but from the dialect and the handwriting I should be inclined to place him in the time of King Alfred, or eight hundred years ago.[9]

Only those who have seen it for themselves can appreciate this wonderful manuscript. "The whole," says Professor Westwood, "is written in a beautifully clear large rounded hand, and most exquisitely ornamented with drawings, illuminated initials and tesselated designs; the entire volume being in an extraordinarily perfect state of preservation, although now nearly twelve centuries old." [10] The stains of sea water are still there. Sir Frederic Madden says: "The stains on the vellum I believe to have been occasioned by sea water when the book was brought from Lindisfarne. It was no doubt secured tightly in a *theca,* or with clasps, and the stains exhibit just the appearance that water would make if oozing by force through a minute aperture." [11] To quote Professor Westwood again:

The wonderful precision and delicacy of touch exhibited in the ornamental patterns composing the large initials have justly attracted the admiration of every writer on the subject. It is difficult to imagine what were the instruments used by the calligrapher, so perfectly regular and free from error is the drawing. . . .

[9] Wanley, *op. cit.,* p. 252. "There did lie on the High Altar an excellent fine book, very richly covered with gold and silver, containing the names of all the benefactors towards St. Cuthbert's Church from the very original foundation thereof"; this was known as the *Liber vitae.* Under the heading *Nomina anchoritarum* stand Bilfrith (p. 6) and Aldred (p. 7). Cf. *Ancient Rites and Monuments of the Monastical and Cathedral Church of Durham,* ed. J. Davies, 1672.

[10] *Palaeographia sacra pictoria: being a series of illustrations of the ancient versions of the Bible, copied from illuminated manuscripts executed between the fourth and sixteenth centuries,* London, 1843–45. It is regrettable that the author numbers neither his pages nor his plates, hence references to his work cannot be more precise. Some faint idea of the marvelous scroll work can be gathered from Sir Frederic Kenyon's *Our Bible and the Ancient Manuscripts* (4th ed., 1939), pp. 184 f., Plate XXVI; see also his *Facsimiles of Biblical Manuscripts,* Plate XI. An even better illustration appears in the British Museum *Guide to the Manuscripts and Printed Books Exhibited in Celebration of the Tercentenary of the Authorized Version,* 1911, Plate opposite p. 24; see E. G. Millar, *The Lindisfarne Gospels,* 1923.

[11] Ellis, *Original Letters of Eminent Literary Men,* p. 267, quoted by Waring, *The Lindisfarne and Rushworth Gospels,* IV, p. xxviii.

It seems clear that a very hard instrument must have been used. In addition to the illuminated title-pages, each of the five divisions of the volume is preceded by a page completely covered with coloured tesselated patterns of the utmost intricacy, generally disposed so as to form a cruciform design in the centre of the page. This elaborately beautiful feature is entirely peculiar to manuscripts executed in Ireland or by Irish scholars; and in its neatness, precision and delicacy, surpasses the productions of contemporary nations on the continent.

With the exception of the Book of Kells, this is the most elaborate and beautiful specimen extant of the style of ornament which distinguished the Celtic school.[12]

And Berger declares:

It is beyond controversy that no district in the West produced such beautiful manuscripts as the Book of Kells and the Book of Lindisfarne. The esteem, then, in which these wonderful monuments of the national art have been held is but natural; natural too, perhaps, that learned people in England have been at pains to disprove their claim to what they regarded as a purely legendary antiquity. We must, however, concede to these manuscripts the place they rightly have in the history of Irish life and culture; in other words, the first place. On this point their testimony is authoritative in proportion to its unanimous character.[13]

HISTORY OF THE MANUSCRIPT

Nothing more romantic than the history of the vicissitudes of this venerable codex could be imagined. On the deaths of Penda and Ceadwalla in 634, St. Aidan became bishop of Lindisfarne, known as Holy Island because of those martyred there by the Danes. When St. Cuthbert, who had succeeded to the See, died in 687, he was succeeded by Egbert, who in turn was followed by Eadfrith, the scribe who, as we have seen, copied the Latin text of these Gospels. When the Northmen again ravaged the country some two hundred years later, the reigning abbot, following St. Cuthbert's dying instructions, removed the saint's body together with the above copy of the Gospels, which at one stage in the ensuing seven years' wanderings, fell into the sea but was miraculously recovered.[14]

[12] Waring, *op. cit.*, p. xl and Plates I f.

[13] *Histoire de la Vulgate pendant les premiers siècles du moyen âge*, p. 29.

[14] Wanley has a note on this remarkable preservation of the codex: "Ego autem codicem diligenter evolvens, haud pauca signa quae eum ab aqua laesum fuisse ostendunt observavi. Quos locos codicis aqua vitiatos, si excipias, in caeteris, videas membranas tam perpolitas, atramentum, etiamnum tam nigrum et nitens, ac si septem solum ab hinc annis scriptus fuisset. Qui quidem splendor et nitor Codicum Anglo-Saxonicorum antiquissimorum bonitati atramenti maxima ex parte meo judicio tribuendus est. Nuspiam enim vidi quempiam codicem antiquis litteris, sive Graecis, sive Romanis, sive Copticis, Syriacisve, sive Hebraicis, aut Arabicis, sive denique Gallicis, Germanicis, aut Longo-

St. Cuthbert's body, with this copy of the Gospels, rested at Chester-le-Street until 998, when another barbarian irruption compelled a further move, this time to Durham, where his body still remains. But the precious codex, presented to the restored Priory of Lindisfarne, remained there until the dissolution under Henry VIII. Up to that date the monks had regularly entered in their annual register of property: *Liber Beati Cuthberti qui demersus erat in mari.* The last such entry was in the lifetime of the last prior, Thomas Sparke, whose register bears the date: "From the Feast of Pentecost 1536 to the same Feast 1537." We hear no more of the precious volume until it was presented to Sir Robert Cotton by Robert Bowyer, Clerk to the House of Commons. Cotton presented it to the British Museum, where it is labelled Cott. MS. Nero D.iv.[15]

CONNECTION WITH NAPLES

A series of discoveries enabled Dom Morin to show that there existed a hitherto unexpected connection between the Lindisfarne Gospels and Naples. For an examination of the list of feast days given in the Lindisfarne MS. showed that they included those of SS. Januarius and Vitus, also that of the dedication of the *Basilica Stephani.*[16] These two saints were, of course, Neapolitan; and the Basilica of St. Stephen was named after its second founder, Stephen I, archbishop of Naples at the beginning of the sixth century. This connection of the MS. with Naples appears in clearer light when we realize that Theodore of Tarsus had for

bardicis, exaratum qui perinde ac scripta Anglo-Saxonica, pristinum adhuc retinent suum nitorem. Neque vero a me solo hoc est observatum: Nam in *Vita S. Cuthberti,* Codd. MSS. Bodl. et Cotton., sic dicit antiquus ejus auctor: Hunc (S. Cuthbertum puerum) beatus Boisilus pro insita illi puritate ac pia intentione, prae ceteris dilexit, et Scripturarum scientia erudivit. Sicut in hac Ecclesia (Dunelmensi) servatur Codex (Evangelia S. Johannis, septem quaternionibus constans) in quo eo (Boisilo) docente, ipse (Cuthbertus) didicerat, per tanta annorum curricula, prisca novitatae decore mirabilis, hodieque demonstrat" (*op. cit.,* p. 253). See Cotton MSS. Domitian A.7 and Faustina A.5.

[15] We owe this brief account to G. Waring, in his Preface to *The Lindisfarne and Rushworth Gospels,* Surtees Society, Part IV. See too the various lives of St. Cuthbert, especially J. Raine, *St. Cuthbert, with an account of the state in which his remains were found upon the opening of his tomb in Durham Cathedral in the year 1827,* Durham, 1828; G. Miles, *The Bishops of Lindisfarne, Hexham, Chester-le-Street, and Durham,* 1898; E. G. Millar, *The Lindisfarne Gospels. An Introduction, with Plates,* 1923; M. Callaway, *Studies in the Syntax of the Lindisfarne Gospels,* 1918; L. M. Harris, *Studies in the Anglo-Saxon Version of the Gospels,* 1901; M. A. Harris, *A Glossary of the West-Saxon Gospels,* 1899.

[16] "La liturgie de Naples au temps de S. Gregoire," in the *Revue Bénédictine,* 1891, p. 481, quoted by Berger, *op. cit.,* pp. 39 f.

his companion when he was sent to stabilize the Church in England a certain Adrian, abbot of a monastery near Naples, and that Theodore, as St. Bede tells us,[17] took Adrian with him when he went to consecrate the church recently built at Lindisfarne. It would seem eminently probable, then, that they brought with them the venerable copy of the Vulgate from which the Latin text of the Lindisfarne Gospels was shortly to be copied and later glossed in Anglo-Saxon.

At the end of the manuscript Eadmer penned the following lines:

Litera me pandat sermonis fida ministra
Omnes alme meos fratres voce saluta:
Trinus et unus Deus evangelium hoc ante saecula constituit
Matthaeus ex ore Christi scripsit
Marcus ex ore Petri scripsit
Lucas de ore Pauli apostoli scripsit
Johannes in prochemio deinde eructavit Deo donante et spiritu sancto scripsit.

THE RUSHWORTH MANUSCRIPT

The Rushworth Gospels, MS. Auct. D.ii.19, was presented to the Bodleian by Rushworth, a barrister of Lincoln's Inn and Deputy Clerk to the Long Parliament. The MS. measures 14 inches by 11 inches, somewhat larger than the Lindisfarne MS. (13½ inches by 9½ inches). There is no preliminary matter, the MS. giving at once the Latin version with an interlinear Anglo-Saxon version, which in the Gospel of St. Matthew is in the old Mercian dialect; in the other Gospels the dialect is that of Northumbria and is a mere verbal gloss: that is, it follows the order of the Latin words irrespective of consecutive sense; whereas in St. Matthew we have what almost amounts to a translation distinctly intelligible by itself.[18]

A note at the end of the Gospel of St. Luke runs: *Macregol dipincxit hoc Evangelium, quicunque legerit et intellexerit istam narrationem orat pro Macreguil scriptori.* Wanley interprets *dipincxit* as implying that Macregol not only transcribed the Latin text but was also responsible for the pictures of the Evangelists and illuminated the initial letters. He adds: "Learned people say that this Codex was once the property of the Ven. Bede, and it certainly has the characteristics of writing of the age of Bede." [19] It is impossible to identify Macregol; the only person known

[17] *Historia,* IV, chap. 2.
[18] Skeat, *op. cit.,* St. John, p. xiii.
[19] *Catalogus historico-criticus,* pp. 81 f. Wanley describes the text as written in large

to us bearing that name died in 820, according to Irish annals.[20] If this Macregol is to be identified with the copyist of the Latin text, his work would date some seventy years later than Bede, who died in 735.

Notes at the end of the Gospels of St. Matthew and of St. Luke give us the names of two glossators: "Faerman the priest thus glossed this book; may the Lord forgive him all his sins, if it can be so with God"; the latter note runs: "Let him that makes use of me [this book] pray for Owun who glossed this book for Faerman the priest at Harewood." [21] There follows a distich:

> "Have now a written book; use it with good will
> Ever with true faith: peace is dearest to every man." [22]

The handwriting shows that Faerman glossed the Gospel of St. Matthew and began that of St. Mark (as far as 2:15), and that Owun glossed the rest of the Gospels with the exception of John 18:1–3, which is in Faerman's hand. In glossing St. Matthew, Faerman presented a wholly independent gloss, which almost amounts to an independent translation; but in St. Mark he followed the Lindisfarne gloss, though he adapted the dialect to the southern forms of speech, as Owun does throughout his work. Yet strangely enough in John 18:1–3 Faerman reverted to the independent rendering he had adopted in his version of St. Matthew.

THE RELATION BETWEEN THE LINDISFARNE AND RUSHWORTH GOSPELS

It used to be supposed that the Lindisfarne and Rushworth glosses were "sister" documents depending on the same original gloss. Waring contended that this was evidenced by the way in which they have the same gloss even when the Latin texts are different. For example, the Lindis-

Saxon characters with an interlinear Dano-Saxon version differing from that in the Lindisfarne Gospels. By "Saxon" writing he means that the Latin is in a Saxon form of script, as in the Gospels of St. Chad.

[20] Waring, *op. cit.*, IV, p. l. *"Mac Riagoil, nepos Magleni, Scriba et Episcopus Abbas Biror,"* viz., Birr (Parsonstown).

[21] Harewood, according to Camden, *Britannia,* lies in the West Riding, on the River Wharfe.

[22] Waring, *op. cit.*, p. li, thus renders the latter note: "Let him who profits by my labour pray for Owun who glossed this book, (and for) Faermen the priest at Harewood (who) has now written this book; use it ever with good will, (and) with true faith; the best peace be with all." But see Skeat, *op. cit.*, St. John, pp. xi and xiv.

farne text had *inopinantur* where the Rushworth text has *operantur,* yet both are glossed by the same *inwoen sint.* Waring gives a number of such instances and concludes: "It will therefore be rightly inferred that beside the current Anglo-Saxon version, made from a comparatively correct Latin text, there was in circulation among the monastic brotherhoods an interpretation made from a less trustworthy source and by men imperfectly versed in Latin, intended to make the text more intelligible to ill-educated monks." But Skeat has proved conclusively that Faerman and Owun, the glossators of the Rushworth Gospels, consulted the Lindisfarne gloss with the result that, though often exercising an independent judgment on its renderings, their work proved in the end little more than a copy of the Lindisfarne gloss.

A careful examination of the work done by these copyists and glossators reveals some interesting phenomena. For example: the number of omissions of small words in the Rushworth MS. is remarkable; in the first chapter of St. Luke's Gospel there are twelve such omissions and fifteen additional words. Some Latin readings are curious: *liberavit nos ab inimicis nostris* (Luke 1:71) instead of *salutem ab inimicis nostris; tulerunt ut adsisterent illum Domino* (2:22) where the Latin of the Lindisfarne MS. has simply *tulerunt illum in Jerusalem.* There are also some more striking omissions: *cui nomen Jairus* (Luke 8:41); *quia Joannes surrexit a mortuis* (9:8); *facite illos discumbere per convivia quinquagenos* (9:14); *At Jesus videns cogitationes eorum* (9:47); *in quancunque domum intraveritis* (10:5); *si autem ego in Beelzebub ejicio daemonia* (11:19); *trahat apud judicem, et judex* (12:58); *in universis quae gloriosae fiebant ab eo* (13:17); *dicebat ergo* (13:18); *et cui simile est* (13:20); *tunc incipietis dicere manducavimus coram te et bibimus, et in plateis nostris docuisti. Et dicet vobis, Nescio vos unde sitis* (13:26 f.); *illam et ipse mortuus est sine filio* (20:30). For *respice in filium meum* (Luke 9:38), the Rushworth MS. has *respice in me, Domine;* and for *Intravit autem cogitatio in eos quis eorum* (Luke 9:46), it has *Interrogavit autem. . . .* For *etiam pulverem qui adhaesit nobis de civitate vestra extergimus in vos, tamen hoc scitote quia appropinquavit regnum Dei* (Luke 10:11), the Rushworth MS. has simply *etiam quia appropinquavit regnum Dei.*

Anyone accustomed to a copyist's work knows how easy it is to omit words, even lines, especially through *homoioteleuta;* but here we are faced with an immense number of lesser omissions as well as the larger ones just given. Moreover the frequent repetitions of words (*mulier, te, et Jesus, timebant, eum* in Luke 13:21; 14:8; 19:8; 22:2; and 24:21) seem to indicate carelessness. The marvel is that the corrector, who has generally made real corrections, failed to see the above blemishes. His changes, however, are not always corrections; for example, when he changed *cilium* (Luke 4:29), "the brow of the hill," to *cilicium*. These Saxon glossators showed a remarkable independence at times; for their renderings are often not in harmony with either the Greek or the Latin texts.[23]

How far these scribes were ignorant or how far some of their strange mistakes are to be attributed to fatigue, monotony, or cold and cramped fingers, it is not easy to decide. Yet only ignorance of what they were reading seems to explain the translation of *Nonne duo passeres asse veneunt?* (Matt 10:29) by "two sparrows coming to him," where *asse* has been read as *ad se* by Faerman; nor does the Lindisfarne scribe mend matters by his: "Do not two sparrows come out of one?" reading *asse* as *a se*. Macregol, the scribe of the Rushworth Latin text, is guilty of some weird errors: we can understand his omission of *Ego non ascendo ad diem festum istum* (John 7:8) or his repetition of John 4:16 and part of 4:17; but when he had written *daemonium hab* (John 8:52), he seems to have been called away, and upon returning to his task forgot to add *es* (*habes*), but continuing with the name of (H)abraham, wrote *daemonium habracham mortuus est,* which would mean: "the devil Abraham is dead." Very often, too, the scribes are weak in their natural history. The Baptist, for instance, is said to have dined on "polypus (or lobster) and wild honey" (Mark 1:6), and he is even said to have been clad in elephant's hair. In Luke 12:7 *passeribus* has been read as *passionibus,* and the gloss, in accordance, thus has: "ye shall be all the better for many troubles."

On the last page of the Rushworth Gospels the following is arranged in six compartments:

Mathaeus instituit virtutum tramite moras bene vivendi justo dedit ordine leges	Marcus amat terras inter caelumque volare et vehymens aquila stricto secat omnia labsu	Lucas uberius de- scripsit proelia christi juresacrato vitulus quia natum moenia fatur

[23] See Westwood, *Palaeographia sacra pictoria,* p. 3, on the Anglo-Saxon Gospels.

Johannis fremit ore leo similisque rudenti intonat (intonat) eterne pandens ministeria	Macregol dipincxit hoc evangelium: Qui- cunque legerit	et intellexerit istam narrationem orat pro Macreguil scriptori

DATE OF THE LINDISFARNE AND RUSHWORTH GOSPELS

The date of the Latin text of the Lindisfarne Gospels seems definitely established. For Eadfrith was bishop of Lindisfarne from 698 to 721, and since we can hardly suppose that he continued to work in the monastic scriptorium after he had become bishop, we can safely assign his Latin transcript to about 690, and the task of binding it to his successor, Ethelwold (721–37).[24] Of Aldred, who glossed it in Anglo-Saxon, a marginal note says: "I am named Aldred, the son of Alfred; I who speak am the eminent son of a good woman," [25] and he has told us that he had glossed "St. John's part for himself," meaning "for his soul," according to Stevenson.[26] But since he had also said that he "made himself at home with the three parts," or on the gloss on Matthew, Mark, and Luke, and since the gloss on St. John is in a different hand and written for the most part in red ink, it would seem that, while content to supervise the glossing of the first three Gospels, he reserved for himself the glossing of the Fourth Gospel. This seems confirmed by an entry after the *capitula secundum Marcum:* "Thou, living God, be mindful of Eadfrith and Ethelwold and Bilfrith and Aldred, sinners; these four, with God's help, were employed upon this book." Moreover, that Aldred actually did supervise the glossing of the other Gospels appears from the additional glosses on St. Luke's Gospel which are in red ink like those in Aldred's work on St. John.[27]

The Latin text, then, of the Lindisfarne and Rushworth Gospels can be assigned to the close of the seventh century, and the two glosses towards the end of the tenth century, that on the Rushworth Gospels being somewhat later than the former, on which it often depends. "The gloss of the Lindisfarne Gospels and also that of the Durham Ritual," says Waring, "were written in the neighbourhood of Durham, and fairly represent the dialect as spoken in that district during the tenth century: the Rushworth gloss takes us as far south as the West-Riding; while

[24] Waring, *op. cit.*, p. xlv.
[25] Skeat, *op. cit.*, St. John, p. ix.
[26] Waring, *loc. cit.*
[27] Cf. Skeat, *loc. cit.*

that of the Cotton Psalter (the oldest of the four) probably exhibits the dialect of the country immediately south of the Humber." [28] Yet we realize how delicate, if not precarious, are these arguments from linguistic peculiarities when Waring himself feels compelled to point out that while it is beyond doubt that Faerman and Owun, the two glossators of the Rushworth Gospels, were contemporaries, "yet the Saxon of Faerman, a man of some cultivation, might at first sight be referred to an earlier period than that of his less educated fellow-worker." [29] Much the same phenomenon appears when we compare the Lord's Prayer as given in MS. Arundel 57, written about 1340 in the Kentish dialect, with the same prayer as it stands in a letter of Gregory VIII to Henry II (1187 A.D.) written in a dialect apparently more modern than that in the Arundel MS.

All that can be said with certainty is that the glossator of the Rushworth Gospels was familiar with the gloss on the Lindisfarne Latin text. Skeat would suggest the close of the tenth century for these Anglo-Saxon glosses.[30]

[28] *Op. cit.*, p. cix note.

[29] *Ibid.*, p. cii note.

[30] *Op. cit.*, St. Mark, p. xii. For a more detailed study see, besides the works already mentioned: J. W. Bright, *The Gospel of St. Luke in Anglo-Saxon,* Oxford, 1893; M. Deanesly, *The Lollard Bible and Other Medieval Biblical Versions,* Cambridge, 1920 (pp. 311 f.); Allison Drake, *The Authorship of the West-Saxon Gospels,* New York, 1894; *Da Halgan Godspel on Englisc. The Anglo-Saxon Version of the Holy Gospels,* ed. from the original manuscripts by Benjamin Thorpe, London, 1842; L. M. Harris, *Studies in the Anglo-Saxon Version of the Gospels,* 1901; L. J. Hopkins-James, *The Celtic Gospels; Their Story and Their Text,* Oxford, 1934 (perhaps the title should rather be, "The Celtic Editions of the Vulgate Gospels"); H. C. Leonard, *A Translation of the Anglo-Saxon Version of St. Mark's Gospel,* 1881; J. H. Lupton, in Hastings' *Dictionary of the Bible,* extra vol., pp. 236–38. Cf. *Journal of Theological Studies,* April, 1935; *Revue Bénédictine,* January, 1935, pp. 119 ff.

CHAPTER V

Anglo-Saxon Psalters

THE large number of manuscripts surviving indicate that there must have been many Anglo-Saxon versions and glosses on the Psalter. Some were based on St. Jerome's first revision, the Roman Psalter; others on his second revision, the Gallican Psalter; [1] others on a mixed text: the revised and unrevised Latin version; others, finally, were based on St. Jerome's translation direct from the Hebrew.

These manuscript Psalters in England deserve more than a passing notice, affording as they do some idea of the amount of delicate and minute work done by our Saxon forefathers in making the Psalms—not to speak of other parts of the Bible—accessible to those ignorant of Latin. Only a study of the plates provided by Kenyon, Warner, and Westwood [2] can give those who cannot see the MSS. for themselves some idea of their beauty.

The Psalms were translated, or rather glossed, at an early date. The earliest specimens that have come down to us are those attributed to St. Guthlac of Croyland Abbey (d. 714) [3] and to St. Aldhelm (see chapter 2).

NINTH CENTURY MSS. OF THE PSALTER

Cotton MS. Vespasian A.I (xv), a Latin Psalter, Roman recension with

[1] Michel (*Bible française,* p. 64) speaks of ninety-nine Norman-French MSS., most of which, if not all, seem based on the Gallican version.

[2] Sir Frederic Kenyon, *Facsimiles of Biblical Manuscripts in the British Museum,* 1900; Sir G. F. Warner, *Illuminated Manuscripts in the British Museum: miniatures, borders, and initials reproduced in gold and colours,* Series I–IV, 1903; J. O. Westwood, *Palaeographia sacra pictoria, being a series of illustrations of ancient versions of the Bible, copied from illuminated manuscripts executed between the fourth and sixteenth centuries,* 1843–45. Unfortunately Westwood does not number either his plates or even his pages, so that it is impossible to make exact references to his work.

[3] *Vita et miracula Sancti Guthlaci Anachoretae, per Felicem Croylandensem Monachum, primum Latine scripta, et deinde ab incerto scriptore Saxonice versa,* Wanley, *Catalogus historico-criticus,* p. 245; Cotton MS. Vespas. D. xxi, assigned by Warner and Gilson to the late tenth century. See also *Memorials of St. Guthlac,* ed. W. de Gray Birch, 1881.

interlinear Anglo-Saxon version, is known as *The Psalter of St. Augustine,* from Christ Church, Canterbury. The MS., "not exceeded in beauty by any known MS.," [4] came into the possession of Sir Robert Cotton in 1599. After psalm 25 is a picture of David playing on the harp, with his chief singers, Asaph, Heman, Than, and Idithun, grouped on either side. A MS. note says: *scriptus videtur anno 700 a Nativitate Christi,* and Westwood holds that since it is written in parts in rustic Roman capitals with the words not divided, it must be "as old or older than the time of St. Augustine." [5] But whether it really is one of the MSS. sent over by St. Gregory is uncertain; Wanley would prefer to regard it as only "a copy of the Gregorian Psalter." [6] The interlinear Saxon gloss is, at any rate, held to be "the earliest extant English translation of any part of the Bible." [7] Stevenson, who edited it for the Surtees Society,[8] thought the Saxon text was "probably of Northumbrian origin since it closely agrees in the general structure of its language with the Lindisfarne and Rushworth Gospels." Sweet, however, maintained that the dialect is Kentish, as "in numerous charters, most of which belong to the first half of the ninth century." [9]

The first printed edition of the Anglo-Saxon Psalter was produced by Spelman: *Psalterium Davidis Latino-Saxonicum vetus, a Joh. Spelmanno, D. Henrici filio editum. E vetustissimo exemplari MS. in Bibliotheca ipsius Henrici et cum tribus aliis non multo minus vetustis collatum,* London, 1640.[10] In marginal notes Spelman refers to four other MSS., without, however, giving any account of them. Forshall and Madden, who think this gloss is "probably of the ninth century," [11] mention six others with similar glosses; but this does not exhaust the number of glosses, which may be simply varying copies or, as Vising suggests, "new

[4] Westwood, *op. cit.;* Kenyon, *op. cit.,* Plate X; Wanley, *op. cit.,* pp. 221 f.; Thompson and Warner, *Ancient MSS. in the British Museum,* Part II (Latin), pp. 8–11.

[5] Westwood, *op. cit.*

[6] *Op. cit.,* p. 173.

[7] Kenyon, *op. cit.,* Plate X.

[8] *An Anglo-Saxon and Early English Psalter, now first printed from MSS. in the British Museum,* ed. by Rev. J. Stevenson, Surtees Society, Nos. xvi and xix, 1843–47, 2 vols.

[9] *The Oldest English Texts,* p. 184. Sweet re-edited the MS., *ibid.,* pp. 184–430. The Latin may be of the eighth century, the gloss of the ninth. Cf. *Transactions of the Phil. Society,* 1877, III, 555, quoted by Skeat, *op. cit.,* St. John, p. xix.

[10] Wanley, *op. cit.,* p. 76.

[11] *The Holy Bible, . . . made from the Latin Vulgate by John Wycliffe and his followers,* Introduction.

versions." [12] Among the MSS. used by Spelman was *Codex Stowensis,*[13] which Astle regards as King Alfred's version, even dating it between 872 and 878.[14] The gloss is said to be almost identical with *Codex Vitellius* E.18.6 and *Codex Arundel,* 60.[15]

TENTH CENTURY MSS.

Bodley MS. Junius 27, known as *Codex Vossius* since it was presented by Isaac Voss to Francis Junius, gives the Psalms in the Roman recension with an interlinear Anglo-Saxon version in minute but carefully formed characters. Wanley would refer it to the time of Aethelstan (c. 900–960).[16] The appended Calendar gives the obits of King Alfred and Gildas.

British Museum, Additional MSS. 37517: the Roman Psalter with an Anglo-Saxon gloss that has contemporary marginal notes in Latin. This MS., which may date from the tenth century, is known as the *Bosworth Psalter* from the fact that it came to the Museum from the library of Francis Fortescue Turville, of Bosworth Hall, Leicestershire, whose bookplate is in the MS.[17]

Lambeth MS. 4.188: portion of St. Jerome's Preface to his Gallican Psalter, the Psalms according to the same version, with Anglo-Saxon gloss; in the Latin text are the asterisks and obeli inserted by Jerome to show where the text varied from the original; certain dots are regarded by Wanley as musical indications, and he would refer the MS. to "the time of King Eadgar or earlier" (957–75).[18]

Tiberius C.6: Gallican recension of the Psalter with interlinear Anglo-Saxon version; "Beautifully written shortly before the Conquest, and, so it would seem, for some nobleman or lady." The MS. is deficient from psalm 107 on.[19]

Cotton MS. E.18.6: Gallican recension with interlinear version and brief introduction in Saxon to each psalm down to psalm 51. The Latin

[12] *Anglo-Norman Language and Literature,* p. 41.

[13] Given in Westwood, *op. cit.*

[14] *The Origin and Progress of Writing,* p. 85.

[15] For these two MSS. see below.

[16] Wanley, *op. cit.,* p. 76.

[17] See *ibid.,* p. 182; *Guide* to the British Museum Bible Exhibition, 1911, §19; *The Bosworth Psalter,* ed. F. A. Gasquet and Edmund Bishop, 1908.

[18] Wanley, *op. cit.,* p. 268. Westwood, *op. cit.,* is skeptical about the musical character of these dots.

[19] Wanley, *op. cit.,* p. 224.

text of psalm 151 is added. Then follow six canticles, *"Hymnus quem S. Ambrosius et S. Augustinus invicem condiderunt,"* four more canticles, the Lord's Prayer (Matt., chap. 6), the Apostles' Creed, the Gloria, *"Fides Catholica Athanasii Episcopi Alexandrini"*—all with an interlinear Saxon version. *"Anno, ut videtur, MXXXI manu scripta."* [20]

ELEVENTH CENTURY MSS.

Bodleian MS. Douce 320: the *Oxford Psalter,* "the prototype of nearly all Norman-French Psalters down to the sixteenth century." [21]

British Museum MS., Arundel 60: Latin Psalter, Gallican recension, with interlinear Anglo-Saxon version; ten canticles, the Magnificat, the *canticum Zachariae,* the Lord's Prayer without the doxology, all with an Anglo-Saxon version. Presented to the Royal Society in 1667 by the Duke of Norfolk, the MS. came to the Museum in 1831. Wanley refers it to the time of Edward the Confessor.[22]

British Museum MS., Arundel 155: Latin Psalter with Anglo-Saxon interlinear version, "written and illuminated in the first half of the eleventh century, most probably for Christ Church, Canterbury," dating from the days of Canute.[23] The canticles are added by a later hand, with a picture of St. Benedict, to whom a monk presents a volume, presumably the MS. in question. The hymns for the ecclesiastical year are appended, also thirty-seven Collects by the same hand that copied the Psalms, several of them with an interlinear Saxon version.

Cambridge University Library, MS. F.f.i.23: the Roman Psalter with interlinear Anglo-Saxon gloss by the same hand.[24] The frontispiece represents David playing on his harp and accompanied by the other psalmists: Eman, Asaph, Idithun, and Ethan.[25] A note says: "This booke was be-

[20] *Ibid.,* p. 223.

[21] *Libri Psalmorum versio antiqua Gallica, e codice manuscripto in Bibliotheca Bodleiana asservato, una cum versione metrica aliisque monumentis pervetustis, nunc primum descripsit et edidit Franciscus Michel,* Oxford, 1860. Michel refers this Psalter to about 1130; Berger to the beginning of the eleventh century (Vising, *Anglo-Norman Language and Literature,* p. 41).

[22] *Op. cit.,* p. 291; Kenyon, *op. cit.,* Plate XI; Warner, *op. cit.,* Series II (1900), Plate I.

[23] Berger regards this as the oldest MS. of the Gallican recension (*La Bible française au moyen âge*). Wanley regards this as a Roman recension; but Warner declares that it has been "corrected in harmony with the Gallican recension" (*op. cit.,* Plate X).

[24] Wanley, *op. cit.,* p. 152. F. Michel edited the MS., *Le Livre des Psaumes,* Paris, 1876. For the illustrations see Westwood and Kenyon.

[25] Westwood, *op. cit.,* has very fine reproductions of these and most of the following

quethed by the Right Reverend Mathewe Parker, Archbishop of Canterburye, to Sir Nicholas Bacon Knight Lord Keeper etc., who do give the same to the Universitie of Cambridge. Anno 1574." Hence the MS. is spoken of as the "Baconian" or as the *Cambridge Psalter.* Wanley regarded it as pre-Conquest in date, but Michel refers it to the early part of the twelfth century.[26] The two texts, Latin and Anglo-Saxon, are contemporaneous.

TWELFTH CENTURY MSS.

The most interesting of these early Psalters is that known as the *Canterbury Psalter,* owing to its origin, or as the *Cambridge Psalter,* for the MS. belongs to Trinity College, Cambridge, where it is known as the *Psalterium Triplex,* owing to the fact that it presents St. Jerome's three editions of the Latin Psalter. A large folio, written in letters of gold and silver, painted and illuminated, it is furnished with historical pictures, patently copies of older illustrations.[27] Commentaries, prefaces, and prayers are prefixed to each psalm. The Gallican version has a Latin gloss, the Roman version an interlinear gloss in Anglo-Saxon, while the version from the Hebrew has a gloss in Norman-French.[28] After the

MSS. of the Psalms. Wanley (p. 152) makes no allusion to the pictures of David and the other psalmists: see above, Cotton MS. Vespasian A.I (xv).

[26] *Le Livre des Psaumes,* Paris, 1876.

[27] An appropriate picture is prefixed to each Psalm. See Berger, *op. cit.,* p. 8, for the relationship between this Psalter and that of Utrecht. The Harleian MS. 606 has the same illustrations and may be the source of those in the Trinity MS.

[28] Wanley, *op. cit.,* p. 169. Elsewhere he writes enthusiastically about his discovery of the MS. "I have by me," he writes to Dr. Charlett, Master of University College, Oxford, "a great folio which I borrowed out of Trinity College. It contains the three Latin versions of the Psalms made by St. Hierome, viz. the Hebrew, Roman, and Gallican. The Hebrew is interlined all along with a French version. The Roman likewise with a Saxon version, and the Gallican with a Latin Gloss, besides other marginal Notes. After the Psalter come the Cantici Sacri, Pater noster, Creeds, etc., in Latin, French, and Saxon. Before every Psalm is a large picture explaining it: which, notwithstanding of the drawing, if they were well considered, may be of good use to an industrious philologer. . . At the end there is a picture of Eadwin, a Monk that wrote the book, and a large Draught of the Monastery that he lived in." Wanley asked Charlett to consult Tanner: "If he has met with any Eadwin about the time of King Stephen (for the book seems to me to be so old) that was famous for writing and painting, as several others have been noted to be, both before and since this Monk's time" (Sir Henry Ellis, *Original Letters of Eminent Literary Men,* p. 289).

A Critical edition of this MS. was published by F. Michel: *Le Livre des Psaumes, ancienne traduction française, publiée, d'après les MSS. de Cambridge et de Paris,* Paris, 1876. An edition was also published by Harsley, who, like Bülbring, was content to publish the text with a promise (never fulfilled) to write a full Introduction later on:

Psalms come six canticles from the Old Testament, the Te Deum, the Lord's Prayer, the Apostles' Creed, the Creed of St. Athanasius, the *Nunc dimittis,* the Gloria, the Benedictus, the Magnificat, and psalm 151: *David cum pugnavit cum Goliath.* These additions, in a Latin text with Anglo-Saxon and Anglo-Norman glosses, are followed by Latin commentaries on the Lord's Prayer and the Apostles' Creed. The *Glossa ordinaria* of Walafrid Strabo is on either side of the Gallican recension; between the lines is the gloss by Anselm of Laon. A note in the manuscript says: *"Hunc Codicem praeclarissimum scripsit et ornavit Eadwinus quidam Monachus, circa tempora Stephani Anglorum Regis* (A.D. *1135–54*)*,"* a date which appears justified by the entry under date *xi. Kal. Maii: "Obiit pie memorie Anselmus Archiepiscopus."* Eadwine the scribe ingenuously says of himself:

Scriptorum princeps ego, nec obitura deinceps
  Laus mea nec fama; quis sim, mea littera, clama.
Te tua scriptura, quem signat picta figura,
  Praedicat Eadwinum fama per saecula vivum,
Ingenium cujus libri decus indicat hujus.
  Quem tibi sequi datum munus, Deus, accipe gratum.

Since the Calendar includes St. Augustine, Theodore, Dunstan, and Lanfranc, Eadwine must have been a monk at Canterbury. In fact, the MS. ends with a bird's-eye view of Christ Church, Canterbury, and a portrait of Eadwine himself. In the Catalogue of the Canterbury library [29] occurs *Liber Eadwini Anglici, Biblia Eadwini,* and this very MS. of the Psalter, *Tripartitum Psalterium Edwini,* referred by Michel to about 1170.[30] A copy of it was in the possession of the nuns at Sion House, for whom *The Myroure of oure Ladye* was written.[31]

Eadwine's Canterbury Psalter, ed. with Introduction and Notes from the MS. in Trinity College, Cambridge, Part II, Text and Notes, Early English Text Society, 1889. No Part I has appeared.

[29] Cotton MS. Galba E.4, drawn up in 1315.

[30] Berger, *La Bible française au moyen âge,* p. 1. Michel maintains that Eadwine's text was derived from an older MS.; another Cotton MS., Caligula A.7, seems to have been written by the same hand, Eadwine's. A copy in the National Library, Paris, has the same arrangement as in Eadwine's text, though without any interlinear gloss; Michel regards the two MSS. as "sisters." In the British Museum, Harleian MS. 603, referred to the time of King Edgar, has the same pictures; from them indeed, those of Eadwine may have been copied.

[31] See the edition by Blunt, Early English Text Society, p. 344. Those who recite the breviary may like to copy the beautiful prayer composed by Eadwine (fol. 255 of the

The *Shaftesbury Psalter,* Cotton MS. Nero C.4: from the convent at Shaftesbury, Dorset. The omission of St. Thomas à Becket from the Calendar (canonized in 1173) and the insertion of St. Hugh of Lincoln (canonized in 1121) determine the years between which the MS. must have been written.[32]

Stevenson adds a metrical version of the time of Edward II (1307–27), with a collation of the *Kirkham Psalter,* Harleian MS. 1170 (fourteenth century), from Kirkham Abbey, York. This has St. Jerome's three Psalters: the Roman, the Gallican, and his version from the Hebrew. The Gallican recension has an interlinear English metrical version.[33] Stevenson also added a collation of another metrical version *in lingua veteri Anglica* between the lines of a Gallican Psalter, C.C.C.C. MS. O.6.[34]

Vising [35] refers to another metrical version with a commentary from St. Augustine at the close of the twelfth century. Forshall and Madden remark that "before the end of the thirteenth century an important step had been taken in scriptural interpretation by turning into verse the whole of the Psalter." Now it is true that the gigantic Bodley MS. 779 (23 inches in height, 15 in breadth, and 5 in depth), a metrical paraphrase of the Old and New Testaments, probably does date from the thirteenth century; but the above-quoted words seem to suggest that the production of such metrical versions constituted a new departure on the part of the Church, a suggestion hard to reconcile with the fact that such versions are of different and widely separated periods.

THIRTEENTH CENTURY MSS.

In the Royal Library, Paris, is a MS. (4.A.xiv) of the Psalms given by the Duke of Berry to the Church at Bourges in 1406. The Latin text has an Anglo-Saxon gloss of the thirteenth (?) century. It was published by Thorpe: *Libri Psalmorum versio antiqua Latina, cum paraphrasi Anglo-Saxonica partim soluta oratione, partim metrice composita, nunc primum*

MS.): "Omnipotens et misericors Deus, clementiam suppliciter deprecor ut me, famulum tuum, Eadwinum, tibi fideliter servire concedas, et perseverantiam bonam et felicem consummationem mihi largire digneris: et hoc psalterium quod in conspectu tuo cantavi, ad salutem et ad remedium animae meae proficiat sempiternum. Amen." Cf. *Catalogue of the Library of Syon Monastery, Isleworth,* M. Bateson, Cambridge, 1898.

[32] Cf. Warner, *op. cit.,* Plate XII.

[33] Cf. Berger, *op. cit.,* p. 17.

[34] Cf. Wanley, *op. cit.,* p. 151.

[35] *Anglo-Norman Language and Literature,* p. 42.

e codice manuscripto in Bibliotheca Regia Parisiensi servato, Oxford, 1835. The Saxon gloss here is not interlinear, as is generally the case, but written in parallel columns with the Latin.

FOURTEENTH CENTURY MSS.

In 1891 Karl D. Bülbring published *The Earliest Complete English Prose Psalter. Together with the Eleven Canticles and a Translation of the Athanasian Creed, edited from the only two MSS. in the libraries of the British Museum and Trinity College, Dublin,* Part I, the Preface and Text, Early English Text Society, London. Part II has, alas, never appeared. The two MSS. used were: British Museum, Additional MSS. 17376 (fourteenth century), containing the Psalms and canticles and also poems by William of Shoreham; [36] and Trinity College, Dublin, MS. A.4.4 (formerly H.32), regarded by Bülbring as a revision of the preceding.

Since only psalms 1 to 50 in the version attributed to King Alfred are in prose,[37] the remainder being in meter, Bülbring claims that the version he publishes is "the oldest complete English Psalter in prose," adding that while many editions had "glossed" the Latin text, this MS. "is the earliest *version* in English prose of any *entire* Book of Scripture." In this MS. the Vulgate text is itself glossed in Latin, and the translator follows that Latin gloss rather than the Vulgate text. For example, Ps. 1:1 reads: "Blessed be the man that sede naught in the counsel of wicked, ne stode in false judgement"; here the Latin ran: *"et in cathedra, i(d est) judicio pestilencie, i(d est) falsitatis non sedit."* It will be seen that the translator has rejected the first gloss and preferred the second.

The character of this version will be still more apparent from the following psalms.

Psalm 83

1. Ha Lord of vertu, ful luuesum ben thyn tabernacles; my soule coveiteth, and failed in the halles of our Lord.

2. Myn herte and my flesshe ioiden in God liveand.

3. For the sparrowe fonde hym an hous, and the turtel nest, ther she liggeth her briddes.

[36] Cf. Kenyon, *op. cit.,* Plate XXII. Since both these MSS. contain Shoreham's poetical works, this version of the Psalter was attributed to him; but the dialect is West Midland, while Shoreham uses the Kentish dialect.

[37] See *The West-Saxon Psalms: the first fifty from the so-called Paris Psalter,* Boston, 1907.

4. Thyn auters, Lord, boeth of vertus, thou art my kyng and my God.

5. And hij ben bliscid that wonen in thyn hous, hij shul herien the in heven.

6. Bliscid be the man of whom the help is of the; he ordeined steizienge in his hert, in the valei of teres, in the stede that he sett.

7. For the berar of the lawe shal geve blisceinge to God; hij shal go fram vertu to vertu, and the God of goddes shal be sen in the heven.

8. Lord, God of vertu, here myn orison, ha God of sones of Jacob, take it wyth thyn ere.

9. Ha God, our defendour, se and loke in-to the face of thy preste anoint wyth creme.

10. For o day is better in thy ioies up a thousand ioies of the wicked.

11. Y ches to be cast out of the hous of my God more than to wonen in the tabernacles of syngers.

12. For God loveth mercy and sothenes, our Lord shal gyf grace and glorie to the gode.

13. He ne shal nought deprive hem of goddes, that gon in innocente; ha Lord of vertu, blisced be the man that hopeth in the.

Psalm 22

Our Lord governeth me, and nothyng shal defailen to me;
In the state of pasture he sett me ther.
He norissed me up water of fyllynge; he turned my soule from the fende;
He lad me up the bistiges of rightfulness; for his name.
For gyf that ich have gone amiddes of the shadowe of deth;
I shall naught douten ivels, for thou art with me.
Thy discipline and thyn amending; comforted me.
Thou madest radi grace in my sight, agens hem that trublen me;
Thou madest fatt myn head with mercy; and my drinke makand drunken ys ful clere
And thy mercy shal folwen me, alle daies of mi lif.
And that ich wonne in the house of our Lord; in length of daies.

Of uncertain date is a MS. in the Bodleian, Laud. D.85.i. The Psalms are in Latin, written in black, the interlinear Anglo-Saxon in red, the titles in green. At the end of the MS. is a noteworthy prayer "before receiving the Sacrament of the Altar: *Concede quaesumus, Omnipotens Deus ut Quem aenigmatice et sub aliena specie cernimus, quo sacramentaliter cibamur in terris, facie ad faciem Eum videamus, Eo sicut est veraciter et realiter frui mereamur in coelis. Per eundem D.N.J.C. Amen.*"[38] Lisle was granted a license to print this Psalter in 1630, but never succeeded in doing so. In his prospectus he describes the MS. as:

The Saxon-English Psalter to preserve the memory of our mother Churche and Language, and to further the studye of our Antiquityes and Lawes out of MSS.

[38] This is "taken out of the Nunes Rules of St. James Order."

most auntient remaining still in the University Library and that of Trinity and Corpus Christi College in Cambridge. Taken and fitted with the Phrase of our time; not as a new English Translation but as the ouldest of all, to th' aforesaid end, received and made known by W(illiam) L(isle), late of Kings College there.[39]

Though it is outside the scope of this volume, which is concerned solely with English versions, we cannot pass over *Queen Mary's Psalter*,[40] containing the Psalms in Latin without any Saxon gloss or translation. It derives its name from the fact that a port official [41] held up some Portuguese sailors who were smuggling out of the country this beautifully bound and illuminated volume. This he impounded just when it was uncertain whether Lady Jane Grey or Mary Tudor would accede to the throne. Waiting on the event, the official in question presented it to Queen Mary. The volume is now in the British Museum, Royal MS. 2.B.vii. In it are no less than 223 tinted drawings illustrating scenes from the Old Testament,[42] all of them seemingly by the same hand. The only English saints depicted are St. Thomas of Canterbury, whose name has been erased, and SS. Dunstan, Grimbald, and Etheldreda. But in the Calendar the name of St. Thomas stands on his feast day, December 29, and also on his translation (1220), July 7. On fol. 84 is written: "This boke was sume tyme the Erle of Rutelands, and it was his wil that it shuld by succession all way go to the lande of Ruteland or to him that linyally succedis by reson of inheritaunce in the seide lande." The first Earl of Rutland was Thomas Manner; Henry, the second Earl, was imprisoned at the accession of Mary Tudor.

39 Cf. Wanley, *op. cit.*, p. 100; he suggests no date for the MS.

40 Warner and Gilson, *op. cit.*, IV, Plates XXIV f.

41 A note on fol. 39 gives his name as Baldwin Smith, and the date, October, 1553.

42 A detailed account of these is given by Warner and Gilson, I, 42–47; they assign this MS. to the fourteenth century. See N. H. Westlake and W. Purdue, *The Illustrations of Old Testament History in Queen Mary's Psalter by an Artist of the Fourteenth Century*, quarto, 1865. These illustrations are extraordinarily naïve: Noe, for instance, is depicted climbing up a ladder to deposit his sons in the Ark, while his wife remains at the foot of the ladder; Samson is shown presenting Delilah to his parents.

CHAPTER VI

Pre-Wycliffite Versions[1]

PROTESTANT writers commonly insist that Wycliffe was the first to translate the Bible into English, and that he did this in opposition to the Church, which desired at all costs to keep the Bible from the people. This only too-popular view is thus set out by Froude with his usual exaggeration: "Of the Gospels and Epistles so much only was known by the laity as was read in the church services, and that intoned as if to be purposely unintelligible to the understanding. Of the rest of the Bible, nothing was known at all, because nothing was supposed to be necessary"[2]

How untrue and how unjust this accusation is may be thus briefly shown:

1. We have already seen that there were translations of the Psalter in the fourteenth century.

2. We have also noticed the Anglo-Saxon versions.

3. It should be remembered that all who could read used French and Latin, which were the official languages of the educated world; the people as a whole could not have read the Bible had it been put before them in any language.

4. The art of printing had not yet come in, and the price of a manuscript Bible was prohibitive; we find £25 paid for a Breviary in 1518 A.D.[3]

[1] Death called Father Hugh Pope before he could rewrite this chapter. The present section, inserted here for the sake of completeness, is taken from his earlier work, *The Catholic Student's "Aids" to the Study of the Bible* (1926), I, 248–52. But we cannot be too certain that Father Pope, after more than twenty years of further study on the problem, would have endorsed in his later years all the conclusions arrived at in his earlier work. Compare the last paragraph of this chapter with his more recent conclusions on pp. 86 f. [Ed.]

[2] See *History of England* (1873), III, 76–84.

[3] Basing his calculations on M. Leber, *Appréciations de la fortune privée au Moyen Age,* Buckingham estimates that the cost of a copy of the Catholic Bible would work

5. Thomas More says in his *Dialogue:* "The whole Bible was long before his [Wycliffe's] days by virtuous and well-learned men translated into the English tongue, and by good and godly people with devotion and soberness, well and reverently read." And again: "As for old traditions before Wyclif's time, they remain lawful and be in some folk's hands. Myself have seen and can show you Bibles, fair and old, in English, which have been known and seen by the Bishop of the diocese, and left in laymen's hands and women's." [4]

6. It is the fashion to say that St. Thomas More was mistaken. But his witness is fully borne out by that of Cranmer, who in his prologue to the second edition of the Great Bible says:

> If the matter should be tried by custom, we might also allege custom for the reading of the Scripture in the vulgar tongue, and prescribe the more ancient custom. For it is not much above one hundred years ago since Scripture hath not been accustomed to be read in the vulgar tongue within this realm, and many hundred years before that it was translated and read in the Saxon's tongue . . . and when this language waxed old and out of common usage, because folk should not lack the fruit of reading, it was again translated into the newer language, whereof yet also many copies remain and be daily found.

7. Even Foxe, the martyrologist, makes the same acknowledgment: "If histories be well examined we shall find both before the Conquest and after, as well before John Wickliffe was born as since, the whole body of the Scriptures was by sundry men translated into our country tongue." [5]

---

out at the present day at £218 (or about $1000), of which £35 ($170) would have gone to pay for the parchment (*The Bible in the Middle Ages,* pp. 2, 38, 63).

[4] Published in 1530, p. 138. "More was a busy and much-practised lawyer in times when printing was very rare indeed. So he would have had constantly in his hands parchments, deeds, reports, and letters—ancient and of his own day. To hold him liable of gross error, or almost sure to make one over documents and handwritings—the accurate treatment of which was habitual and essential to him—would show a dismal want of knowledge about More's education and profession" (John Pollen, S. J., in a letter to the writer, March 1, 1921).

[5] This was in 1571, in the Dedication to Queen Elizabeth, written by Foxe, prefixed to Archbishop Cranmer's *The Gospels of the Fower Evangelistes translated in the olde Saxons tyme out of Latin into the vulgare toung of the Saxons, newly collected out of Auncient Monumentes of the sayd Saxons, and now published for testimonie of the same.* Thus note the Preface to the Rheims version: "In our own countrie, notwithstanding the Latin tonge was ever (to use Venerable Bede's wordes) common to all the provinces of the same for meditation or studie of Scriptures, and no translation commonly used or occupied of the multitude, yet they were extant in English even before the troubles that Wicleffe and his folowers raised in our Church, as appeareth as well by the testimonie of Malmesburie recording that V. Bede translated divers partes

8. In the British Museum catalogue of 1892 we find that the museum possesses eleven German editions of the Bible dating from 1466 to 1518, three Bohemian editions between 1488 and 1506, one Dutch edition of 1477, five French editions from 1510 to 1531, seven Italian editions from 1471 to 1532. All these are, of course, pre-Lutheran; they are Catholic versions in different languages. It must be remembered, too, that these only represent a tithe of the copies which exist; they are merely those which the museum has collected in the course of years.

In 1911 the British Museum authorities held a Bible exhibition, and the official *Guide* tells us that exhibit No. 21 is the *Gospels in English* produced early in the eleventh century; it also says that the Apocalypse appeared in the course of the fourteenth century. The library of Corpus Christi College contains a manuscript giving the Gospels of St. Mark and St. Luke, as well as St. Paul's epistles; this is attributed to the early part of the fourteenth century.[6] Thus Buckingham quotes from Dugdale's *Monasticon* (III, 309–324) the statement that at the visitation of St. Paul's Cathedral in 1295, there were found twelve copies of the Gospels bound in silver, six copies of the epistles, glossed copies of the epistles, the minor prophets, the Gospels with the commentary of St. Thomas Aquinas (presumably the *Catena aurea*—and St. Thomas died only in 1274). He also quotes Martene as saying that at Metz he had seen a Bible seven or eight hundred years old, and a copy of the major and minor prophets in Saxon characters.[7] The same writer instances from the collection of Cotton MSS. in the British Museum "a copy of the Book of Proverbs in Latin with an interlinear Anglo-Saxon translation, a copy of the Book of Genesis in Anglo-Saxon, with extracts from the other Books of Moses and from Joshua, a Book of Precepts extracted from the Proverbs, and a Harmony of the Four Gospels"; and he adds that "among the Harleian MSS. we find the Four Gospels in Anglo-Saxon; and copies

into the vulgar tonge of his time, and by some peeces yet remaining: as by a provincial Constitution of Thomas Arundel, Archbishop of Canturburie." Then there follows an abstract of the Constitution of the Council of Oxford given below. Thus note Luther's own express testimony: "It was an effect of God's power, that in the Papacy should have remained, in the first place, sacred baptism; secondly, the text of the Holy Gospel, which it was the custom to read from the pulpit in the vernacular tongue of every nation; thirdly, the sacred forgiveness and absolution of sin, as well privately in confession as in public; fourthly, the most holy sacrament of the altar" (*De Missa privata,* ed. by Jensen, VI, fol. 92; quoted by Buckingham, *The Bible in the Middle Ages,* p. 58).

[6] *The English Hexapla,* p. 3. For pre-Reformation versions see C. Russell, "The Bible and the Reformation," *Dublin Review,* III, 428 ff.—incorrectly ascribed to Wiseman. [Ed.]

[7] Martene, *Voyage littéraire* (1717), I, 177; Buckingham, *op. cit.,* pp. 9 f.

of the Heptateuch (namely, the Pentateuch, Josue, Judges and Ruth), the Psalter and the Gospels, in the same language abound in various repositories." [8]

9. No proof has ever been brought forward to show that the Church forbade, or even discouraged, the translation of the Bible into the vernacular. This may come as a surprise even to Catholics, for we have been accustomed to hear accusations to the contrary all our lives. But the proof is easy, for in 1408 the Council of Oxford, under Archbishop Arundel, published the following Constitution:

> It is dangerous, as St. Jerome declares, to translate the text of Holy Scripture out of one idiom into another, since it is not easy in translations to preserve exactly the same meaning in all things. . . . We therefore command and ordain that henceforth no one translate any text [it is question of passages, *texta* in the heading of the Constitution] of Holy Scripture into English or any other language in a book, booklet, or tract, and that no one read any book, booklet, or tract of this kind lately made in the time of the said John Wycliffe or since, or that hereafter may be made either in part or wholly, either publicly or privately, under pain of excommunication, until such translation shall have been approved and allowed by the diocesan of the place, or (if need be) by the Provincial Council. He who shall act otherwise let him be punished as an abettor of heresy and error.[9]

Thomas More's comment on this law is striking:

> And this is a law that so many long have spoken of, and so few have in all this while sought to seek (or find out) whether they say the truth or no. For I trow that in this law you see nothing unreasonable. For it neither forbiddeth the translations to be read that were already well done of old before Wyclif's days, nor damneth his because it was new, but because it was naught; nor prohibiteth new to be made, but provideth that they shall not be read, if they be made amiss, till they be by good examination amended.

Thus three times in the course of the *Dialogue* does More repeat the statement that the Bible was translated into English before Wycliffe's days.

10. Cardinal Gasquet has argued with great plausibility that the so-called "Wycliffite" Bibles, of which something like 200 copies exist, are really nothing else than old English orthodox Bibles; that Wycliffe himself has only the most shadowy of claims ever to have translated more

[8] Harleian MS. 3449; Wanley, *Librorum veterum septentrionalium qui in Angliae bibliothecis extant catalogus historico-criticus,* 64, 67, 76, 98, 152, 211.

[9] For the text see Wilkins, *Concilia,* III, 317. As it was a common taunt leveled at the Catholic translators that they had only thrown the Bible open to the people from necessity and because the Reformers had already made it accessible, it is well to point out that this constitution antedates the Reformation by more than a hundred years.

than the Gospels; and that even the famous Bible reposing on its velvet cushion in the King's Library at the British Museum and labelled "The English Bible, Wycliffe's Translation," is but an orthodox Catholic Bible dating from a time anterior to Wycliffe.[10] Here we will give but one of the many arguments which the Cardinal has brought forward in support of his view.

Even St. Thomas More, when combating the often repeated statement that the Ecclesiastical Commissioners burnt every copy of the Bible on which they could lay hands, says: "If this were done so, it were not well done; but . . . I believe that ye mistake it." And in answer to the objection that the Bible of a Lollard named Hun was burnt in the prison of the Bishop of London, he says:

> This I remember well, that . . . there were in the prologue of that Bible such words touching the Blessed Sacrament as good Christian men did abhor to hear, and that gave the readers undoubted occasion to think that the book was written after Wyclif's copy and by him translated into our tongue, and that this Bible was destroyed not because it was in English, but because it contained gross and manifest heresy.

From this it is clear that the Wycliffite Bibles, i.e., those which emanated from him or his followers, were distinctly heretical, as indeed the whole story supposes. Since the existing Bibles bear no trace of any heretical tendency, the conclusion is inevitable: these Bibles are not Wycliffite at all, but pure, orthodox, Catholic, pre-Reformation Bibles.[11] This conclusion is startling, but it is supported by a wealth of learning on the part of Cardinal Gasquet, and if further proof were wanting it would be found in the various attempts at replies.[12]

[10] "The Pre-Reformation English Bible," essays IV f. in *The Old English Bible,* 1897, republished from the *Dublin Review,* CXV (1894), 122–52. See also Gasquet, *The Eve of the Reformation* (1900), chap. 8, "The Printed English Bible."

[11] See above, note 1.

[12] See the *English Historical Review,* January, 1895, an article by Matthew; Sir Frederic Kenyon, *Our Bible and the Ancient Manuscripts* (1939), pp. 206–9; J. H. Lupton, in Hastings' *Dictionary of the Bible,* extra vol., "Versions (English)." A more determined effort to undermine Gasquet's position has recently been made by Miss Margaret Deanesly, M. A., in *The Lollard Bible and Other Medieval Biblical Versions,* Cambridge University Press, 1920. See also: The *Holy Bible, with the Apocryphal Books, in the Earliest English Versions, made from the Latin Vulgate by Wycliffe and his followers,* ed. by Forshall and Madden, Oxford, 1850; also *The New Testament in English, translated by John Wycliffe, circa 1380, now First Printed from a Contemporary Manuscript formerly in the Monastery of Sion, Middlesex,* 1848; *A Fourteenth Century English Biblical Version,* A. C. Paues, Cambridge University Press, 1904.

CHAPTER VII

The Wycliffite Versions of the Bible

FOR a long time it was the general impression, and still is in many quarters, that towards the close of the fourteenth century Wycliffe [1] presented the English people with a complete version of the Bible in their own language, and by so doing brought about a revolution against the Church authorities. That he was in some sort responsible for a translation of the Bible seems beyond question. Knighton, a Canon of St. Mary's, Leicester, and Wycliffe's contemporary, states as an accepted fact:

> This Master John Wiclif translated from Latin into English—the Angle, not the Angel speech—the Scriptures which Christ gave to the clergy and doctors of the Church that they might sweetly minister to the laity and the weaker persons according to the message of the season, the wants of man, and the hunger of their souls. Thence by his means it is become vulgar and more open to laymen and women who can read than it is wont to be to lettered clerks of good intelligence. Thus the pearl of the Gospel is scattered abroad and trodden under foot by swine, the jewel of clerics is turned to the sport of the laity, so that what before had been the heavenly talent for clerks and doctors of the Church is now the *commune aeternum* of the laity.[2]

Huss, too, writing in 1411, says: "The English say that Wycliffe translated the whole Bible from Latin into English." [3] Forshall and Madden, whose authority is paramount on the subject (see below), speak with caution, though they themselves are convinced of the soundness of their views:

[1] It has been calculated that his name is spelled in no less than twenty-five different ways; except when quoting authorities, we adhere to the now more general spelling, Wycliffe.

[2] *Compilatio de eventibus Angliae,* II, 152.

[3] *Monumenta Hussiana,* I, 198. Wycliffe, says Gairdner, only aimed at a new version; there is no proof that he himself made it (*Lollardy and the Reformation in England,* I, 103). Strype simply states it as a well-known fact that Wycliffe "translated the Holy Bible into the mother tongue" (*Ecclesiastical Memorials,* I, 433). See also: R. W. Dixon, *History of the Church of England,* I, 451.

Within less than twenty-five years [after 1360] a prose version of the whole Bible, including as well the apocryphal as the canonical books, had been completed, and was in circulation among the people. For this invaluable gift England is indebted to John Wycliffe. It may be impossible to determine with certainty the exact share which his own pen had in the translation, but there can be no doubt that he took a part in the labour of producing it, and that the accomplishment of the work must be attributed mainly to his zeal, encouragement and direction. . . . The undertaking was not completed until after several preliminary efforts. . . . The evidence indeed which bears upon the point is scanty, and only sufficient, it should be remembered, to afford to the conclusions which it suggests, a presumption of their truth.[4]

ORIGIN OF THE WYCLIFFITE BIBLE

The genesis of the New Testament portion of the Wycliffite Bible was, they suggest, somewhat as follows: Wycliffe had, about 1360, written a commentary on the Apocalypse, the outcome, it may be, of his *Last Age of the Church,* written in 1356,[5] both being markedly critical of existing ecclesiastical authorities. Later came commentaries on Matthew, Luke, and John, largely based on the *Catena aurea* of St. Thomas Aquinas. These commentaries and his *Harmony of the Gospels,* as well as other commentaries on other portions of the New Testament by unknown authors, served, it is presumed, as the basis for a fresh version of the whole New Testament.[6]

It would be hard to overrate the importance of the Wycliffite version. Every subsequent translator made abundant use of it, generally without acknowledgment. But the account given by Forshall and Madden of the effect which these editors imagine the version had is apt to raise a smile: "The effect of this circulation of Scripture among the people in their own tongue was just what might have been expected. Men reading with their own eyes the words of the Saviour and of His apostles, found a marked

[4] *The Holy Bible, . . . made from the Latin Vulgate by John Wycliffe and his followers,* Introduction, §15.

[5] *The Last Age of the Church,* by John Wycliffe, ed. by Todd (Dublin, 1840). Todd declines to affirm its authorship by Wycliffe. "The style, the matter, the writers quoted, all combine to prove that it is not by Wyclif. To print it was to condemn it" (Shirley, *Fasciculi zizaniorum,* p. xiv note). This commentary on the Apocalypse—only doubtfully attributed to Wycliffe—has the ordinary Catholic text, not that of either Wycliffite version (Gasquet, *The Old English Bible,* p. 147).

[6] Forshall and Madden, *op. cit.,* Introduction, §§18, 25. See also: A. C. Paues, *A Fourteenth Century English Biblical Version,* 1904; M. J. Powell, *The Pauline Epistles Contained in MS. Parker 32,* Cambridge, 1916.

contrast between the principles which they inculcated and many parts of the system upheld by the Romish church." [7]

What truth there is in the often repeated statement that England was at any time clamoring for a vernacular version of the Scriptures it is hard to say. Considering that very few could read at all, such a demand seems based merely on wishful thinking.[8] Wycliffe himself undoubtedly wished for a vernacular version; but he could hardly be described as "one of the illiterate people hungering for the Word of God in their own tongue." Still, the English language was making headway.

Early in the fourteenth century Higden complained that children in England were obliged "to construe their lessons in French, to the neglect of their own language"; [9] but by the close of the century Trevisa could say with truth that "this manner is somewhat changed. For John Cornwall, a master of grammar, changed the lore in grammar school and construing of French into English. So that now in all the grammar schools of England, children leaveth French and construeth and learneth in English." Versions of the Bible in languages other than English were in use, at least among the more educated classes, and Wycliffe naturally complained that "as lords have the Bible in French, so it were not against reason that hadden the same in English"; [10] and again: "since it was allowable for the Queen of England (Anne of Bohemia) to have copies of the Gospels in three languages, Bohemian, German, and Latin, and that to dub her a heretic on that account was simply diabolical stupidity, so ought the English to defend the right to read it in their tongue." [11]

[7] *Loc. cit.*, §60, p. xxxiii.

[8] See Chapter X: Tyndale's Version.

[9] *Polychronicon,* I, chap. 59.

[10] *De officio pastorali,* quoted by Hoare, *The Evolution of the English Bible* (1901), p. 96. Cf. Cambridge University Library Ms. Ii.6.26: "Summe ther ben that kunnen rede but litle, or noght understonde, and for hen ben ordent bookis of her moder tongue, to Frensche men bokis of Frensche, to Ytaliens bokis of Latyne corrupte, to Duche men bokis Duche, to Englische men bokis of Englische; in whiche bokis thei mowen rede to konne God and his lawe . . . and that [it] is leful to christeyn peple [to] rede and connen holy Scripture, in destruction of synne and in cresynge of vertu, it is opyne in many placis of Goddis lawe, both old and newe."

[11] *De triplice vinculo amoris,* quoted by John Huss against Stokes; cf. Ussher, *Historia dogmatica,* p. 352. At the funeral of Queen Anne of Bohemia in 1394, Arundel, then archbishop of York and Chancellor, "especially praised her because, though a stranger, she had the Gospels translated into English with commentaries by learned men, and read them assiduously" (Foxe, *Actes and Monumentes,* VI [viii], 674). Cf. Parker, *History of the Archbishops of Canterbury;* Ussher, *Historia dogmatica,* xxi, p. 352.

THE FIRST TRANSLATION OF THE OLD TESTAMENT: NICHOLAS OF HEREFORD

The Bodleian MS. 959 contains an English version from Genesis to Bar. 3:20, where it breaks off in the middle of a sentence. This MS.,[12] said to have been written before 1390, was copied before the original had been corrected; and the copy (MS. Douce 369, also in the Bodleian) was itself corrected in three different hands, also, so it is claimed, before 1390. The latter also breaks off at Bar. 3:20: "And other men in the place of hem risen. The young. . . ."[13] At this point a contemporary hand has written in the Bodley MS., Douce 369: *Explict translacom Nicholay de Herford,*[14] words which can only mean that the translation up to that point was due to the well-known Wycliffite of that name.[15]

Workman suggests that Queen Anne's copy of the Gospels "can scarcely have been other than Purvey's version" (*John Wyclif, a Study of the English Medieval Church,* II, 193). But as he himself assigns Purvey's Prologue to 1395 (*ibid.,* II, 165), his suggestion is difficult to reconcile with her death in 1394. Cf. Lewis, *A Complete History of the Several Translations of the Holy Bible,* p. 198; Deanesly, *The Lollard Bible and Other Medieval Biblical Versions,* pp. 437, 445.

[12] "The original copy of the translator" (Forshall and Madden, *op. cit.,* §27).

[13] The Vulgate has here: *et alii loco eorum surrexerunt. Juvenes. . . ."*

[14] Workman, *op. cit.,* gives a facsimile of Hereford's interrupted copy, "the last folio of the original corrected copy of the translator, MS. Bodl. 959"; also of "a folio transcribed from the preceding before its correction, with a note assigning the translation to Hereford, MS. Douce, 369."

[15] Hereford had a stormy career. Condemned for heresy in 1382, he appealed to Pope Urban VI. Unsuccessful in defending his cause at Rome, he was, at the instance of the Pope, condemned to lifelong imprisonment instead of being executed as a heretic. In 1385 he escaped and returned to England, where he was imprisoned by the Archbishop of Canterbury. He then made his submission, but was shortly after inhibited by the Bishop of Worcester on a charge of preaching Lollard views. Yet in 1394 he was made Chancellor of Hereford, and finally died as a Carthusian at Coventry. "De supradicto Nicholao Herforde," says MS. Bodl. 117, "certum est, quod in senectute sua intravit Ordinem Cartu[sianorum] apud Covent[riam] in domo sancte Anne matris beate Mariae virginis, et in eadem domo catholice vixit et obiit." Of the heretical character of his teachings there can be no question. Netter says succinctly: "Magister Johannes Wyclif in multis excessit; sed ipse [Hereford] superbissimus intolerabilia et nefandissima dixit in sermonibus; et semper commovendo populum ad insurrectionem" (*Fasciculi zizaniorum,* p. 29). For Hereford's false "Conclusiones," cf. *ibid.,* p. 303. See also: Antony à Wood, *History and Antiquities of the University of Oxford,* ed. Gutch, I, 492 f.; Wilkins, *Concilia,* III, 202; Foxe, *Actes and Monumentes,* V (iii), pp. 24–41, 47, 187, 257 f., 807–9.

In the appeal of the four Mendicant Orders against Hereford (February 18, 1381, to John Duke of Lancaster), they speak of him as "Magister Nicholas de Hereford, paginae sacrae professor, et utinam non perversor" (Netter, *Fasciculi zizaniorum,* p. 292). Yet Hereford's recantation must have been sincere, for in 1393 we find him one of the commissioners who tried Walter Brut for Lollardism; cf. Foxe, *op. cit.,* III (v), pp. 187–9.

The portion thus translated is exceedingly literal, often obscure and incorrect; [16] but the remainder, from Bar. 3:20 to the end of the Old Testament, "was completed by a different hand, and not improbably by Wycliffe himself." [17] This last suggestion, though perhaps generally accepted,[18] is, however, no more than a hypothesis. Lupton declares: "Who continued and finished the Old Testament we do not know. It would no doubt be under Wiclif's superintendence; but it was in this year, 1382, that he had his first seizure of illness, and it is difficult to believe that he could, single-handed, have finished his own New Testament work and also what was wanting of Hereford's. It is usual, however, to assign to him the whole of the New Testament translation and the remainder of the Old Testament." [19]

On the supposition that the Old Testament was finished by Wycliffe himself or his disciples, Forshall and Madden suggest that "Probably while the New Testament was in progress, or within a short time of its completion, the Old Testament was taken in hand by one of Wycliffe's coadjutors," and that the translation breaking off at Bar. 3:20 "was completed by a different hand, and not improbably by Wycliffe himself." [20]

But this suggestion has not met with universal acceptance. "The translation," says Pollard, "has been ascribed to Wyclif himself, with more piety than probability"; [21] similarly M. R. James declares: "A dense darkness hangs over the origin and authorship of the translation ascribed to Wycliffe." [22] Blunt puts the case fairly when he says: "There is scarcely any contemporary evidence, except that of his bitterest opponent, that Wyclife was really the author of this translation, but there can be no

[16] Forshall and Madden, *op. cit.*, §32. Hereford's version, says Professor Hales in the *Dictionary of National Biography,* "is in a language hardly to be called English."

[17] Forshall and Madden, *op. cit.*, §27. Various MSS. give Hereford's version in a completed state; e.g., Egerton 617 f.; Corpus, Oxford, No. 94.

[18] "The many resemblances between the New Testament and the latter portion of the Old would seem to prove that Hereford's unfinished work was completed by Wycliffe himself" (Moulton, *The History of the English Bible,* p. 23).

[19] In Hastings, *Dictionary of the Bible,* extra vol., p. 240. Both Baber (*The New Testament Translated from the Latin in 1380 by John Wiclif*) and Lea Wilson (*Catalogue of Bibles, Testaments, etc.,* p. 137) were of the opinion that the translation as a whole was not the work of Wycliffe. But they did not have at their disposal the mass of evidence accumulated by Forshall and Madden. Mombert seems to have proved that Hereford made use of a French version as well as of the Vulgate (*English Versions of the Bible,* p. 53).

[20] *Op. cit.*, §27.

[21] *Records of the English Bible,* p. 1.

[22] *Cambridge Modern History,* i.

doubt that tradition is to be believed when it associates his name with it." [23] "The real difficulty," says another, "lies in the absence of any clear point of contact between this version and Wycliffe's other writings. If a set of sermons on the Sunday Gospels is correctly ascribed to him, and the English is his own, it is noteworthy that the translation of the passages occurring in these is entirely different from that given in the New Testament." [24]

TWO DIFFERENT EDITIONS

So far back as 1690 Wharton had made it clear that there were in reality two distinct versions, both of the Old and of the New Testament, one rough, another more polished.[25] This latter he attributed to John of Trevisa (d. 1412). At the beginning of the eighteenth century, Waterland (1683–1740) at first supposed that both versions of the New Testament were the work of Wycliffe, but later he came to the conclusion that the more polished version, which he mistakenly took to be the earlier, was the work of John Purvey (see below).[26] Waterland's correspondent, John Lewis, accepted this view, and both he [27] and Baber [28] published

[23] *A Plain Account of the English Bible,* pp. 17 f.; cf. Gasquet, *The Old English Bible,* p. 112 note.

[24] Isaacs, in *The Bible in Its Ancient and English Versions,* p. 138; cf. Workman, *op. cit.,* II, 199 note; *Journal of Theological Studies,* April, 1905, p. 456; October, 1912, p. 133; Gasquet, *op. cit.,* p. 147.

[25] *Auctarium,* or Supplement to Ussher's *Historia dogmatica,* p. 424. Henceforth for the sake of brevity these two editions will be referred to as W.I. and W.II.

[26] Writing to Lewis, August 17, 1728, Waterland says: "What I last advanced was that Wycliffe translated the New Testament only [elsewhere Waterland maintained that Knighton (see above) would have said "biblia," not merely "evangelium," had he thought that Wycliffe had translated the whole—unfortunately for this suggestion, Knighton wrote "scripturas," not "evangelium"], and that he was the first *publisher* of such translation. I would rather now say, the first that set out an *entire* and *naked* version: for what was before done was by *parts,* and mingled with notes and comments. Secondly that the translation of the whole Bible came after, and was made by the same person that made the Prologue printed in 1550. Thirdly, that the same person who translated the Bible, and composed that Prologue, translated also the New Testament, which is full of 'forsothes,' by which mark I know that author, and in which the Bible and this author tally exactly. 'Forsothe' occurs no less than eleven times in Matt. 1:1–5. It was a peculiarity of that author to make 'forsothe' generally stand for *autem* or *vero* or *enim*" (*Works,* X, p. 361).

[27] *The New Testament of Our Lord and Saviour Jesus Christ Translated out of the Latin Vulgate by John Wiclif, S.T.P. . . . To which is prefix'd a history of the several translations of the Holy Bible and New Testament, etc., into English, both in manuscript and print, and of the most remarkable editions of them since the invention of printing,* 1731. The frontispiece is a fine portrait of Wycliffe, "a tabula penes Nobilissimum Ducem

the more polished version as being the earlier, a mistake perpetuated in Bagster's *Hexapla* (1841), where the text printed under the heading "Wiclif—1380" is in fact the later, revised text.[29]

The earlier version is given by Bosworth and Waring.[30] It is also found in the reprint of the Sion Monastery MS.,[31] of which Lea Wilson, its owner at one time, says: "The translation of this beautiful volume is not that usually known as Wickliffe's," and he quotes Baber as saying in the Preface to his edition (p. lxix):

Though all these MSS. lay claim to the title of Wiclif's English Version of the Bible, yet there are a few amongst them which differ so materially from the rest, as to warrant the assertion that we enjoy two ancient English translations of the Scriptures. In some places we trace no other similarity betwixt these versions, than that which arises from the circumstance of their being made from one common original, the Latin Vulgate: but in general we discover features of resemblance between them so numerous and so striking, that it is most clear, that the author of the later translation not only saw, but copied very freely from that which had been previously completed.

Dorsettiae." In his later editions, 1738 and 1818, the text of the New Testament was omitted and only the history of the English Versions given.

[28] *The New Testament Translated from the Latin in 1380 by John Wiclif: to which are prefixed memoirs of Dr. Wiclif, and an historical account of the Saxon and English versions of the Scriptures previous to the opening of the fifteenth century,* 1810.

[29] *The English Hexapla, Exhibiting the Six Important English Translations of the New Testament Scriptures: Wiclif, M.CCC.LXXX; Tyndale, M.D.XXXIV; Cranmer, M.D.XXXIX; Genevan, M.D.LVII: Rheims, M.D.LXXXII; Authorized, M.DC.XI. The Original Greek Text after Scholz, preceded by a History of English Translations and Translators.* The first is not Wycliffe's original text, but the revision by Purvey about 1394. The third is really Cromwell's Bible, for Cranmer had nothing to do with the first edition, 1539, but only with the later editions, for which he wrote the Preface. That called the Genevan Bible is Whittingham's version, which was revised when a version of the whole Bible was published in 1560. According to Cotton (*Lists of Editions of the Bible,* p. 130), there have been three editions of this *Hexapla,* 1841, 1845, and 1846; but the one most generally met with bears no date, though often spoken of as of 1841; it has 63 pages of Introduction, whereas the edition dated 1841 has 167 pages. Scrivener, in his Introduction to *The Authorized Edition of the English Bible (1611),* p. 15 note, says the text of the Authorized Version in these editions is sometimes that of 1611, sometimes that of 1612, the divergences being, of course, only of a minute kind.

[30] *The Gothic and Anglo-Saxon Gospels in Parallel Columns with the Versions of Wycliffe and Tyndale,* 1865, 1888, 1907.

[31] *The New Testament in English, translated by John Wycliffe circa Mccclxxx. Now first printed from a contemporary manuscript formerly in the Monastery of Sion, Middlesex, late in the collection of Lea Wilson, F.S.A.,* printed at Chiswick by Charles Whittingham for William Pickering, London, 1858. *Wycliffe's New Testament,* ed. by Lea Wilson, 1848; ed., with a Glossary, by W. Skeat, 1879; and with parts of the Old Testament, 1881.

Wilson concludes "from the greater rudeness of the language" that this copy from Sion Monastery is the earlier. The Catholic epistles follow after the Acts, after which come the Pauline epistles and the Apocalypse. The titles of the books are the briefest imaginable:

> Matheu, Mark, Luke, Joon, ye dedis of ye apostlis, ye pistel of James, ye firste pistel of petre, ye secounde pistel of petre, ye firste pistel of Joon, ye secounde pistel of Joon, ye thridde pistel of Joon, ye pistel to romayne, ye firste pistel to corrintheis, ye secounde pistel to corrintheis, ye pistel to galatheis, ye pistel to ephesies, ye pistel to philipensis, ye pistel to colocenses, ye firste (and secounde) pistel to tessalonicenses, ye firste (and secounde) to tymothe, ye pistel to tyte, ye pistel to ebrues, here bigynns ye apocalips.

At the end of the Apocalypse stands this note: "Here endith ye apocalips. Blesside be ye holy trinite. Amen." And on the last page is written:

> Good Mr. Confessor of Sion with his brethren: Dame Anne Danvers, widow, sometime wife to Sir William Danvers, knight (whose Soul God Assoil) hath given this present Book unto master confessor and his Brethren enclosed in Sion, intending thereby not only the honour, laud and praise to Almighty God, but also that she the more tenderly may be committed unto the mercy of our Lord God by the holy merits of master Confessor and his Brethren aforesaid. [Here follow the names of persons for whom Dame Danvers especially asks prayers.] The Aforesaid Dame Anne Danvers hath delivered this book by the hands of her son, Thomas Danvers, on Mid-Lent Sunday, in the eighth year of the reign of King Henry VIII. In the year of our Lord God, 1517.

While the above-mentioned editions were appearing, the Wycliffite versions had been the subject of minute investigation by Forshall and Madden, who examined 170 MSS., "a considerable portion of their time during nearly twenty-two years having been spent in accomplishing their task." Their scholarly Introduction has done much to clear up obscurities concerning the origin of these versions. Their findings were published in four volumes by the Oxford University Press in 1850.[32]

[32] There exist some 170 MSS. containing the Wycliffite versions in whole or in part. Of these, 140 give the text of W.II (see above, note 25). The most important MSS. of W.I. are:

MS. Bodley 959.

MS. Douce 369 (Forshall and Madden no. 87): the second portion gives, with slight gaps, the text from Isaias to II Maccabees inclusive, the Gospels, Pauline epistles, and Acts 1:1—28:15.

MS. Douce 370 (F. and M. no. 88): Genesis to II Paralipomenon, written before 1400.

MS. Brit. Museum, Royal I.B.vi (F. and M. no. 4): the New Testament, with gaps.

Sir Thomas Phillipps, MS. 9302 (F. and M. no. 168): Matt. 3:4—Tim. 1:15.

Egerton MSS. 617 f. (F. and M. no. 32): Proverbs to II Maccabees inclusive, also the

JOHN PURVEY AND THE REVISED EDITION

Among Wycliffe's intimate friends and supporters was John Purvey. Netter gives a list of his erroneous views, though he speaks of him as a *magnus auctoritate, doctor eximius.*[33] Condemned by Archbishop Arundel in 1401 for his repudiation of traditional Catholic doctrines, Purvey recanted and Arundel gave him a benefice; [34] but his avarice and speedy relapse made the Archbishop regret having done so, as he afterwards declared. Purvey recanted again in 1421.[35]

In a seventeenth century note in MS. A.i.10, Trinity College, Dublin, we have the earliest suggestion that Purvey was the author of W.II: "The author of this translation seems to have beene John Purvey, as Mr. Fox calleth him, both by the verse in the beginning and the character in the end of the Apocalypse [a monogram]: of the care and paines taken therein see the latter end of the Prologue to all the bookes of the Bible which is set in the end of the booke. It should appear thereby that he

---

New Testament, with gaps. These MSS. were once the property of Duke Humphrey and date from about 1420.

British Museum, Additional MSS. 15,580 (F. and M. no. 41). This was written before 1400 and gives, with many gaps, the same portions of the Bible as the Egerton MSS. give.

Oxford, MS. Rawlinson 258 (F. and M. no. 258). Though Rawlinson in a note calls this "Purvey's New Testament," the text—in the order: Gospels, Acts, Catholic epistles, Pauline epistles, Apocalypse—is that of the pre-Purvey or unrevised edition. A contemporary note, written about 1400, says: "Iste liber constat fratri Johanni Lacy, ordinis predicatorum reclus' Novi Castri super Tynam."

Corpus Christi College, Oxford, MS. 4 (F. and M. no. 94): a complete copy of the whole Bible; "perhaps written before 1420."

Of five MSS. referred to a date earlier than 1400, three give the text of W.I, two that of W.II; of nine dated "about 1400 A.D.," three are partly W.I and partly W.II; of ten which give the text of W.I, two contain the whole Bible, save for gaps, and five are of the New Testament only. Of the many MSS. of the second version (W.II), six are of the whole Bible, five of the New Testament, while many contain parts of either Testament.

[33] *Doctrinale antiquitatum fidei Catholicae ecclesiae,* I, 619, 637, a work begun in 1422, edited in Venice, 1757. Richard Lavenham, a Carmelite of Ipswich (d. about 1393) published a list of Purvey's heretical and erroneous tenets, *Contra Johannem Purveium,* drawn from a MS. of Foxe, 1396 (*Actes and Monumentes,* V [iii], 286–92); cf. Netter, *Fasciculi zizaniorum,* pp. 383–407; Gairdner, *Lollardy,* I, 190 f. Waterland, on the authority of à Wood, Bale, and Foxe, styles Purvey *theologus facundus, glossator insignis, legis prudentia clarus, Lollardorum librarius, et Wiclevus glossator;* he also regards him as author of "a famous comment on the Apocalypse."

[34] Wilkins, *Concilia,* III, 262; Foxe, *op. cit.,* pp. 248, 257, 292.

[35] *Ibid.,* Appendix, p. 822.

translated the whole Bible, and made a glose on the hard places, as namely, upon Job and the greater prophets."

The above-mentioned monogram, a capital P with e.r.v.e. in the curve, written in after the Apocalypse, must stand for Purvey, and while it may merely indicate the owner and not necessarily the author of the MS., it is significant that bound up with the MS. of the New Testament is a distinct MS. containing a *General Prologue* or *Introduction to the Old Testament,* which harmonizes with the *Ecclesiae regimen,* a treatise dealing with ecclesiastical corruptions and thought to have been written before 1395.[36] But this treatise agrees so closely with the Articles drawn up for Purvey's recantation in 1401 that it seems a legitimate conclusion that Purvey was author both of the treatise and of the Prologue.[37]

This Prologue, long regarded as Wycliffe's own composition, was printed by John Gowgle in 1536 as *The Dore of Holy Scripture,* and described by Robert Couley as "The true copye of a Prolog wrytten about two C yeres paste by John Wyclyfe." Geoffrey Bliss, bishop of Coventry, 1503–33, was of the same opinion.[38] Lewis dated the Prologue about 1395, and Dr. Workman [39] agrees with him despite Forshall and Madden, who argue strongly for a date nine years earlier, 1386.

Chapters 1–9 of the Prologue give an outline of Old Testament history; chapters 12–14 discuss the rules of interpretation formulated by Tichonius the Donatist and developed by St. Augustine.[40] The author's "Lollardy" betrays itself in his contemptuous words about "the pardouns of

[36] Shirley, editor of the *Fasciculi zizaniorum,* would assign the *Ecclesiae regimen* to 1410 A.D. (p. lxviii).

[37] Forshall and Madden, *op. cit.,* Introduction, pp. xxv–xxviii.

[38] Commenting on chap. 12 of the Prologue, he says: "Nota contra Universitatem Oxonie nequiciam Wyclef, qui ingressus est ut videret. Vana loquebatur, cor ejus congregavit iniquitatem sibi, qui cum cerneret se non posse doctos a fide avertere, voluit et hic suasit omnibus indoctis ad S. Scripturam liberum debere patere ingressum, ut saltem simplices erroris sui veneno corrumperet. Contra cujus errorem et similem arroganciam tota illa laborat epistola pro deinterpretatione omnium librorum sacrae scripturae quae incipit: 'Frater Ambrosius' et communiter praeponitur toti biblie, sed non est mirum si a veritate discedat quae mentita est iniquitas sibi."

[39] *John Wyclif, a Study of the English Medieval Church,* II, 165; cf. Waterland, *Works,* X, 359.

[40] *De doctrina Christiana,* III, chaps. 30–32 (§§42–56); *Epis.,* 40, chap. 2. Cf. F. C. Burkitt, *The Book of Rules of Tichonius* (vol. 9 of *Texts and Studies*), 1894. Purvey, of course, rejects Wisdom and Ecclesiasticus, neither being "books of bileeve," but he quotes both books of Machabees without any such qualification (xi). W.I included III Esdras, but Purvey excluded both III and IV Esdras (Prologue, §1). In W.I the spurious Epistle to the Laodiceans was inserted after Colossians, but Purvey omitted it.

the bisschopis of Rome," and his tirades against worldly prelates, whom he contrasts with the "simple" Lollards: "So now a fewe pore men and idiotis, in camparisoun of clerkis of scole, mown have the treuth of the holy scripture agens many thousande prelatis and religiouse that ben given to worldly pride and conceitise, symonie, ypocrisie and to fleschly synnes."[41] His words on the Holy Eucharist are positively heretical:

All things in holy scripture that seem to unwise men to be full of wickedness against a man himself, or against his neighbor, are figurative speeches, and the privities or ghostly understanding should be sought out by us to the feeding or keeping of charity. Such a rule shall be kept in figurative speeches that so long it be turned in mind by diligent consideration till the expounding or understanding be brought to the room of charity; if any speech of scripture soundeth properly charity it oweth not to be guessed a figurative speech; and forbiddeth wickedness or commendeth profit or good doing, it is no figurative speech; if it seemeth to command cruelty or wickedness or to forbid profit or good doing, it is a figurative speech.

The application of this convenient principle, which will enable a man to reject any doctrine he mislikes, is at once forthcoming: "Christ saith, 'If ye eten not the flesch of mannis sone and drinke not his blood, ye schulen not have lijf in you.' This speech seemeth to command wickedness or cruelty, therefore it is a figurative speech, and commandeth men to commune with Christ's passion and to keep in mind sweetly and profitably that Christ's flesch was wounded and crucified for us."

Chapter 13 is of interest for Purvey's account of the method he followed in translating the Bible: Since it was given

with common charity to save all in our realm, which God would have saved, a simple creature hath translated the Bible out of Latin into English. First this simple creature had much labour, with divers companions and helpers, to gather many old Bibles, and other doctors and common glosses, and to make one Latin Bible somewhat true, and then to study it anew, the text with the gloss, and other doctors, as he might get them, especially Lyranus on the Old Testament,[42] who

[41] Cf. chaps. 10, 12, 15.

[42] Nicholas of Lyra (d. 1340) began his *Postillae super Bibliam* in 1293 and completed the work in 1330; cf. Hody, *De bibliorum textibus originalibus,* pp. 431–43. Whereas in W.I there are no marginal notes in Hereford's portion (Genesis to Bar. 3:20),—though after that point they are frequent—in W.II they are about equally divided between brief comments derived from the *Postillae* of Nicholas of Lyra and statements to the effect that the Hebrew text differs from the Vulgate which he is following. The distribution of these from Genesis to Ruth is interesting. On Deuteronomy there are forty-nine notes from the *Postillae;* on Judges, fifty. Notes on the prophets from the *Postillae* are oddly scattered: a long one on Bar. 6:32, only two on Ezechiel (9:4 and 45:10), none on Jeremias, copious notes on Isaias chaps. 1–8, after which there are very few, many on Daniel, very few on

helped him full much in this work. The third time to counsell with old grammarians and divines of hard words and hard meanings, how they might best be understood and translated; the fourth time, to translate as clearly as he could to the sense, and to have many good fellows and cunning at the correction of the translation. For first we must know that the best translation is out of Latin into English, to translate after the meaning, and not only after the words, so that the meaning be as open, or opener, in English as in Latin, and so not far from the letter. If any one doubts the correctness of his rendering let him look that he examine truly his Latin Bible, and so no doubt he shall find many Bibles in Latin full false, . . . and the common Latin Bibles have more need to be corrected, as many as I have seen in my life, than hath the English Bible lately translated.[43] And no doubt, to a simple [man], with God's grace and great travail, men might expound much more openley and shortly the Bible in English than the old great Doctors have expounded it in Latin. . . .

Furthermore holy Church approveth not only the true translation by mean (ordinary) Christian men, steadfast in Christian faith, but also by open heretics, that did away many mysteries of Jesus Christ by guileful translation, as Jerome witnesseth in one prologue on Job and in the prologue on Daniel. Much more lately the Church of England approved the true and whole translation by simple men that would, for no good on earth, . . . put away the least truth, yea the least letter.[44]

Forshall and Madden argue very strongly in favor of the view that Purvey was the author not only of the Prologue and the revised New Testament (W.II) in the Dublin MS., but also of the revised version of the whole "Wycliffite" Bible contained in whole or in part in some 140 of the still existing 170 MSS. These scholars would not contend that their arguments amount to proof; indeed many find them inconclusive. Kenyon, for instance, points out that "the revision which was almost immediately taken in hand is ascribed to John Purvey, . . . but the attribution, though probable, is not absolutely certain." [45] Sir W. Creighton likewise says: "If the revision was really Purvey's, the fact was either

---

the minor prophets; but copious notes on Proverbs, Wisdom, Ecclesiastes, Ecclesiasticus, and the two books of Maccabees.

In the New Testament portion of W.II, marginal references to the *Postillae* are comparatively rare: the only two on the Gospels being those on Luke 8:30 and 14:26. The notes are more numerous on the epistles, Romans to Galatians, but less frequent afterwards. As Purvey says (Prologue, chap 13), "Lyre cam to me late," it would seem that he began with the revision of the New Testament and perhaps secured a copy of the *Postillae* only after he had revised the Gospels. Among his marginal notes, other than those from Nicholas of Lyra, he quotes the *Glossa ordinaria* of Walafrid Strabo (c. 840) and the *Glossa interlinearis* of Anselm of Laon (c. 1100).

[43] Hereford's version.

[44] Chap. 20. What translation "the Church of England approved" is not clear.

[45] *Facsimiles of Biblical MSS. in the British Museum,* Plate XXV.

generally unknown, or was judiciously ignored in the face of an obvious demand for an English version."[46] It is noteworthy, too, that the English version in Purvey's twelve *Tracts* (1382–95), in which he defends the use of the vernacular, is neither that of W.I or of W.II.

SOME CHARACTERISTICS OF THE TWO EDITIONS

Waterland remarks that Wycliffe's version "of the Gospels read in the Church is more antique in the language [than in his New Testament—he means W.II, which he thought to be the earlier version], and is seldom exactly the same with his translation as now read."[47] "It is," says Scrivener, "much more difficult to a modern ear than Chaucer's *Parson's Discourse*. The obsolete words and phrases are more numerous, and the construction of the sentences is by no means so simple."[48] Purvey himself retains some obsolete terms: mesels (W.I, meselis) for lepers in Luke 4:27; semblaunt (W.I, semelant) in Luke 24:5. The close adherence to the Latin in both versions sometimes makes the sense obscure: W.I, "For why and I am a man ordeyned under power, having under me knightis" (Matt. 8:9), where W.II merely changes the order of the words: "For why I am a man ordeyned undir power, and have undir me knightis"; W.I, "Give to us this day oure breed over other substaunce" (Matt. 6: 11), but W.II italicizes *"ovir other substaunce,"* which is intelligible only in the light of the Latin, *panem nostrum supersubstantialem.*

W.I inserts: (a) alternative renderings: "gendride, *or bigate*" (Matt. 1:2); "just man, *or rightful*" (Matt. 1:19); "kyngis, *or wijs men*" (Matt. 2:1); "unquenchable, *or that never shal be quenched*" (Matt. 3:12); "graves, *or biriels*" (Mark 5:3); "redemptioun, *or again biyng*" (Mark 10:25); "scismes, *or dyvysiouns, dissenciouns, or discords*" (I Cor. 1:10); (b) interpretive additions: "Racha, *that is word of scorn*"; "fool, *that is a word of dispisynge*" (Matt. 5:22); "a libel, *that is a litil boke of forsakyng*" (Matt. 5:31); "Amen, *that is, so be it, so be it*"; "fyndeth his soul, *that is temporal lyf*" (Matt. 10:39); "tetrarcha, *that is prince of the fourthe part*" (Matt. 14:1); "Symon Bariona, *that is the sone of culver*" (Matt. 16:17); "sandalies, *that ben opyn above*" (Mark 6:9); "word,

[46] In *The Bible in Its Ancient and English Versions,* ed. by Robinson, p. 142.

[47] *Works,* X, 357.

[48] *A Supplement to the Authorised English Version,* p. 77. There are no notes on Matthew or Mark; only two on Luke (8:10; 14:26). W.I included III Esdras, but not IV Esdras.

that is Goddis sone" (John 1:1 and 14); "accepciouns of persones, *that is to putt oon before another withoute desert"* (Rom. 2:11).[49]

Some additions seem quite arbitrary: "baptisid, *or cristenyd"* (John 3:22); "Forsothe it was the thridde our, *that men clepen undrun"* (Mark 15:25). Few of the above find place in W.II, though the explanation of "tetrarch" (Matt. 14:1) is retained.

In his Prologue, Purvey dwelt on the various ways of rendering the Latin ablative absolute, and in W.II he avoids participial constructions: for "sothely hym thenkynge" (Matt. 1:20), he writes, "But while he thoughte these thingis"; and for "he rysynge, folowide" (Matt. 9:9), he has, "and he rose and folowide"; "forsothe Jhesus answerynge seide" (Matt. 16:17) becomes "Jhesus answered and said."

W.II is, then, a simplified and polished edition of W.I: "penaunce, *or forthenkynge"* (Matt. 27:3) now becomes "he repented"; "the fame of him" (Mark 1:28) replaces "the tale, or tything" of W.I; and "taris" (tares) replaces "dernils, or cokils" (Matt. 13:26–30). At times, too, W.II presents a better text than W.I. It rightly omits, for instance, "in the blood of the Lamb" (Apoc. 22:14), words which figure in only one MS. of the Vulgate and were omitted by the Rhemists; inserted, however, in the Sixtine and Clementine revisions, they reappear in Challoner's editions. In II Thess. 2:13, both W.I and W.II have "chose us" instead of "chose you," the reading of all the Greek MSS.—the *nos* in the Sixtine and Clementine versions seems otherwise unsupported. In all but two MSS. of W.II, Luke 1:1–4 is omitted; but Bagster's *Hexapla* prints the verses.

One feature of W.I which must strike anyone comparing the two versions, is the really extraordinary use of "forsothe" and "sothli," terms always replaced by others in W.II. For example, in chap. 9 of St. John's Gospel, W.I has "forsothe" fifteen times, "sothli" seven times, the former representing *autem* twelve times, *utique* once, *enim* twice; W.II replaces "forsothe" by "and" nine times, by "but" four times, by "for" once, and once omits any equivalent. Similarly "sothli" is replaced twice by "and," twice by "but," once by "for," and twice is not represented at all. The following passages will exemplify this peculiarity.

[49] Whereas these explanatory notes are frequent in the Old Testament of W.II, they are rare in the New Testament of that revised version. The marginal comments, too, are few on the prophets and Gospels, but there are many on the Sapiential Books and the early portion of Isaias.

W.I	W.II
Luke 5:9. Sothli greet wondir hadde bigon aboute him and alle that weren with him.	For he was on ech side astonyed and all that weren with hym.
Luke 21:1. Forsothe he biholdinge syth tho riche men, whiche senten her giftis in to the tresorie; forsothe he syth also sum litel pore widowe sendynge twei litel moneys.	And he biheeld, and saye tho riche men, that casten her giftis in to the tresorie; but he saye also a litil pore widewe castynge twei ferthingis.

In the Old Testament of W.II, both "forsothe" and "sothli" still find a place, though not to the same extent as in W.I; in Genesis, chaps. 31–35, for instance, W.I rendered *sed, autem, quoque, vero,* by "forsothe," for which W.II four times has "sothli" and once "for whi." Waterland, while pointing out that "forsothe" and "sothli" repeatedly occur in the Wycliffite Old Testament, adds that they do not occur in Wycliffe's New Testament, "which, I doubt not, is really his." He is, of course, speaking of the New Testament as revised by Purvey, which version he took to be the earlier.[50] The following passages will serve to illustrate the differences between W.I and W.II.[51]

Earlier Version (W.I)	Later Version (W.II)
Gen. 49:9–13	
9. The whelp of lyon Juda; to the prey, sone myne, thow steydist up; restynge thow ley down as a lyon, and as a lionesse who shal arere hym?	9. A whelp of lioun is Judas; my sone * [52] thou stiedist to prey; thou restidist, and hast leyn as a lioun, and as a lionesse who schal reise hym?
10. The septre fro Juda shal not be takun awey, and a duke fro the leende of hym, to the tyme that he come that is to be sent, and he shal be the abidynge of folk of kynde,	10. The septre schal not be takun awey fro Juda,* and duyk of his hype, til he come that schal be sent, and he schal be abiding of hethene men;
11. byndynge to a vynyerd his colt, and to a vyn, O my sone, his she asse;	11. and he schal tye his colt at the vyner, and his femal asse at the vyne;

[50] Letter to John Lewis, August 5, 1729, in *Works* (1831), pp. 355 f. In W.I the word "forsothe" occurs twenty-six times in the first six chapters of Genesis, but in W.II it occurs only twelve times; elsewhere it is either omitted or replaced by "sothli" or by "also." Rarely is it used in W.II where it is not found also in W.I; but cf. Judg. 9:1 and Exod. 21:21. Many quotations from Nicholas of Lyra are given in the margin of W.II, mostly in reference to the Hebrew text. Once at least (Exod. 21:21), the marginal note refers to "another translacioun," namely, another Latin text.

[51] For other parallel specimens of W.I and W.II, see Mombert, *op. cit.,* pp. 56 f.; Moulton, *op. cit.,* p. 27.

[52] The inverted phrases of the earlier version are changed in the revision and are here noted with an asterisk (*).

Earlier Version (W.I) (*cont.*)

he shal wasshe in wyne his stoole, and in blood of a grape his mantil;

12. fayrer ben the eyen of hym than wyn, and the teeth of hym whitter than mylk.

13. Zabulon in the brynke of the see shal dwelle, and in the stacioun of shippes, arechynge unto Sidon.

Later Version (W.II) (*cont.*)

A! my sone, he schal waische his stoole in wyn, and his mentil * in the blood of grape;

12. hise iyen ben fairere than wyn, and hise teeth ben whittere than mylk.

13. Zabulon schal dwelle in the brenk of the see, and in the stondyng of schippis; and schal stretche til to Sydon.

Deut. 9:1–3

1. Here, Ysrael; thow shalt to day gon over Jordan, that thow weelde moost naciouns, and strenger than thow; greet cytees, and into heuene wallid;

2. a greet puple, and a hieye; the sones of Enachym, the whiche thi self hast seen, and herd, to the whiche no man may agen withstoond.

3. Thanne to day thow shalt wite, that the Lord thi God he shal go before thee; fier deuowrynge and wastynge, the which brisse hem down, and doo awey, and scatre before thi face swiftly, as he hath spokun to thee.

1. Here thou, Israel; thou schalte passe Jordan to dai,* that thou welde mooste naciouns, and strengere than thou; grete citees, and wallid * til to heuene;

2. a greete puple, and hiy; the sones of Enachym, whiche thi silf siest, and herdist, whiche no man may agenstonde (in the contrarie part).[53]

3. Therfor thou schalt wite to dai,* that thi Lord God hym silf schal passe bifor thee; (he is) a fier deuourynge and wastynge, that schal al to breke hem, and schal do awei, and destrie bifor thi face swiftli, as he spak to thee.

John 2:2 f., 6–9

2. Sothli Jhesus is clepid, and his disciplis to the weddingis. And wyn faylinge, the modir of Jhesu seide to him, Thei han not wyn.

3. And Jhesu seith to hir, What to me and to thee, thou womman? myn our cam not yit. The modir of him seith to the mynystris, What evere thing he schal seie to you, do ye. . . .

6. Forsothe ther weren put sixe stoonen pottis, aftir the clensinge of Jewis, takinge ech tweyne or thre mesuris.

7. Jhesu seith to hem, Fille ye the pottis with watir. And thei filliden hem, til to the highest part.

8. And Jhesu seith to hem, Drawe ye

2. And Jhesus was clepid, and hise disciplis to the weddyngis. And whanne wijn faillide, the modir of Jhesu seide to hym, Thei han not wijn.

3. And Jhesus seith to hir, What to me and to thee, womman? myn our cam not yit. His modir seith to the mynystris, What evere thing he seie to you, do ye. . . .

6. And there weren set sixe stonun cannes, aftir the clensyng of the Jewis, holdynge ech tweyne ether thre metretis.

7. And Jhesus seith to hem, Fille ye the pottis with watir. And thei filliden hem, up to the mouth.

8. And Jhesus seide to hem, Drawe ye

[53] The reviser adds explanatory clauses.

Earlier Version (W.I) (*cont.*)	Later Version (W.II) (*cont.*)
now, and bere ye to architriclyn. And they token.	now, and bere ye to the architriclyn. And thei baren.
9. And as architriclyn tastide the watir maad wyn, and he wiste not wherof it was, sothli the mynystris wisten, that drowen watir, architriclyn clepith the spouse. . . .	9. And whanne the architriclyn hadde tastid the watir maad wijn, and wiste not wherof it was, but the mynystris wisten that drowen the watir, the architriclyn clepith the spouse. . . .

The comparison of a single passage of the New Testament (Matt. 25:1–13) as its stands in W. II with the rendering adopted by the Rhemists in 1582 will show to what extent the latter as well as subsequent translators depended on the Wycliffite Version.

Wycliffe II (c. 1388)	Rheims Version (1582)
1. Thanne the kingdom of hevennes schall be like to ten virgyns, whiche token her lampis and wenten out agen the housbonde and the wiif.	1. Then shall the kingdom of heaven be like to ten virgins, which taking their lampes went forth to meete the bridegrome and the bride.
2. And fyve of hem weren folis, and fyve prudent.	2. And five of them were foolish, and five wise.
3. But the fyve folis token her lampis, and token not oile with hem:	3. But the five foolish, having taken their lampes, did not take oile with them.
4. But the prudent token oile in her vessels with her lampis:	4. But the wise did take oile in their vessels with the lampes.
5. And while the housbonde tariede, alle nappiden and slepten,	5. And the bridegrome tarying long, they slumbered all and slept.
6. But at myd nygt a crie was made, lo the spouse cometh, go ye out to mete with hym.	6. And at midnight there was a clamour made, Behold the bridegrome commeth, goe ye forth to meete him.
7. Thanne all the virgynes risen up: and araiden her lampis,	7. Then arose all those virgins: and they trimmed their lampes.
8. And the folis seiden to the wise yeve ye to us of youre oile? for oure lampis ben quenchid.	8. And the foolish said to the wise, Give us of your oile: because our lamps are going out.
9. The prudent answeriden and seiden, leest peradventure it suffice not to us and to you, go ye rather to men that sellen, and bien to you.	9. The wise answered, saying, lest peradventure there suffise not for us and you, goe rather to them that sell: and bie for yourselves.
10. And while they wenten for to bie: the spouse cam, and tho that weren redi, entrid with hym to the weddingis, and the yate was schit.	10. And whiles they went to bie, the bridegrome was come: and they that were ready, entred with him to the marriage, and the gate was shut.
11. And at last the other virgynes camen and seiden, Lord, Lord: opene to us.	11. But last of al come also the other virgins, saying: Lord, Lord, open to us.

Wycliffe II (c. 1388) (*cont.*)	Rheims Version (1582) (*cont.*)
12. He answeride and seide: truly I seye to you: I knowe you not, therfore wake ye, for ye witen not the day, ne the our.	12. But he answering said to them, Amen I say to you, I know you not.
	13. Watch ye therefore, because you know not the day nor the houre.[54]

In Luke 15:8, both W.I and W.II have preserved the interesting Vulgate reading *evertit* for *everrit,* or "turned up so doun the hous" instead of "swept the house," though all the other English versions have "sweep" in accordance with the Greek. Yet nearly all the Latin MSS. have *evertit,* a reading retained in the Sixtine revision, though the Clementine has *everrit,* reproduced, of course, by Challoner and subsequent English editions. Both W.I and W.II read: "or [not "and"] drink the chalice" (I Cor. 11:27). W.II has a marginal note on Apoc. 22:14 ("in the Blodd of the lamb"): "this that is added in some bookes . . . is not the text, neither is had in elde Bibles. Lire [Lyra] here."

WYCLIFFE'S HERETICAL TENETS

The various propositions extracted from Wycliffe's writings and condemned suffice to show the heretical character of his teachings.[55] "Wicliffe," says Dore, "held views which if carried into practice would have been totally subversive of morality and good order." [56] Blunt, too, declares: "The lawless political principles of Wickliffe, and the still more lawless ones of his followers, created a strong prejudice against vernacular translations of the Scriptures on the part of the rulers of England both in Church and State. The Bible was quoted in support of

[54] Ver. 1. "and the wiif": Vulgate "sponso *et sponsae*" in practically all MSS., but this finds little support in the Greek MSS; Wycliffe and Rheims alone retain it.

5. All have "slumbered and slept": so too Tyndale, Cranmer, Geneva, A.V., and R.V.

6. Tyndale, Cranmer, and Geneva have "even at midnight."

7. All have "trimmed" except Tyndale and Cranmer, who have "prepared."

8. Vulgate, "extinguuntur"; Tyndale and Geneva, "go out"; Cranmer and A.V., "are gone out"; Rheims, followed by R.V.—and surely correct—"are going out."

9. Rheims and R.V. follow Wycliffe, "peradventure"; Tyndale, Cranmer, and A.V., "not so"; Geneva, "we feare."

10. All have "gate" except A.V. and R.V., which have "door."

11. "Last," in Wycliffe and Rheims; but all the rest have "afterwards."

13. The Vulgate, Wycliffe, Rheims, and R.V. omit "when the Son of man will come," which is found in Tyndale, Cranmer, and A.V.

[55] Denzinger, *Enchiridion,* §§581, 651, 657–89; cf. Foxe, *Actes and Monumentes,* V (vii), pp. 46, 809.

[56] *Old Bibles,* p. 6.

rebellion and of the wildest heresy."[57] Similarly Hart: "It cannot be denied that many of the Lollards' opinions were fanatical, while others amounted to positive heresy. That 'God must obey the devil'; that 'everything is God'; that 'dominion is founded upon grace'; and that 'brothers and sisters may lawfully intermarry,' were certainly among their tenets."[58]

Wiclif's attempt to popularise the Scriptures in an English form had been disapproved of by the Church, which considered the clergy as the special custodians and interpreters of Holy Writ, without whose guidance it could too easily be perverted and misconstrued. This was the feeling which inspired the Constitution of Archbishop Arundel in 1408, forbidding the use of any translation which had not been approved by the diocesan of the place or by some provincial council. In days when the sacred writings were only multiplied by copyists, translations of particular books of Scripture, or even of the whole, might be episcopally authorised, if good in themselves, as luxuries for private use, without apparent prejudice to the faith. But Wiclif's version was regarded as a deliberate attempt to vulgarise a literature of peculiar sanctity which required careful exposition by men of learning.

In opposition to the special claims of the Church, the Lollards set up a theory that Scripture was the only true authority for any religious observances and that no special learning was required to interpret it, the true meaning of Holy Writ being always revealed to men of real humility of mind. Men founded their convictions on an infallible book, were confident in their own judgements, and died by hundreds under Mary for beliefs that were only exceptionally held in the beginning of her father's reign.[59]

Hoare declares that Wycliffe was convinced

that the Papal claims were incompatible with what he felt to be the moral truth of things, incompatible with his own conscience, with his instinct of patriotism, and finally with the paramount authority of the inspired Book which was his spiritual Great Charter. Accordingly it was by the standard of the Bible and of the early Fathers that Wycliffe persistently desired that his orthodoxy or his unorthodoxy might be tried. And not his alone, but the orthodoxy even of the Supreme Pontiff himself. . . . From 1378 onwards he no longer limits his hostility to the undue *range* of the Pope's authority, but directs it against the institution of the Papacy itself. . . . He now challenges the very principle of sacerdotalism, and the metaphysical doctrine of transubstantiation.[60]

[57] *The Reformation of the Church of England,* I, 504.

[58] *Ecclesiastical Records,* p. 369. In the *Fasciculi zizaniorum Magistri Johannis Wyclif cum tritico,* ascribed to Thomas Netter of Walden, Provincial of the Carmelite Order in England and confessor to Henry V (ed. by W. W. Shirley, 1858), will be found detailed accounts of the proceedings against the Lollards. The Introduction, pp. ix–lxxxvii, contains a valuable history of the life and times of Wycliffe.

[59] J. Gairdner, *Cambridge Modern History,* II, 464.

[60] *The Evolution of the English Bible* (1901), pp. 64–79.

Many complaints had reached Rome concerning the prevalence of heretical and dangerous teachings in England. Gregory XI, writing in 1377 to Archbishop Sudbury, complained that whereas

the kingdom of England, famous for its power and wealth, more famous owing to its devoted faith, illustrious too by its brilliant expositions of Scripture, has always produced men possessing sound knowledge of the Bible. . . . Yet now we hear with grief that John Wycliffe, professor of Holy Scripture—and would to God he were not a professor of error—has had the audacity insistently to set forth and publicly to preach certain propositions and conclusions of which many are erroneous and false, while others are hardly in conformity with the faith; these propositions amount to an endeavour to overthrow and bring to ruin the whole position of the Church.[61]

The principal tenets of the Wycliffites were formally condemned on May 17, 1382, in the synod held at Blackfriars, when twenty-four propositions were singled out as at least "erroneous," and Nicholas of Hereford and Philip Reppington were excommunicated;[62] likewise Oxford University shortly afterwards.[63]

Yet there is nothing heretical in the Wycliffite versions. Hence, unlike Tyndale's New Testament, the version itself was never condemned either by the English bishops or by the Holy See. The action of the Church was necessitated by the wholly subversive teachings of the Wycliffites.[64] Though the Lollards had long been circulating translations of at least portions of the Bible and had, as some of the condemned propositions show, based their false teachings on them, in none of the many examinations of Lollards given by Foxe is there any reference to vernacular versions as being wrong. It was only in 1408 that the reading of such versions without episcopal license was forbidden; even then Wycliffe's Bible was condemned, not because it was a translation, or a bad one, but because it was an unauthorized one and put in circulation in order to support heretical teachings. As Archbishop Arundel expressed it when writing to John XXIII: Wycliffe, endeavoring in every way possible to assail the faith and the teaching of Holy Church, had, "as a crowning act of wickedness, with a view to this, produced a fresh version

[61] Wilkins, *Concilia,* III, 116 f.

[62] *Ibid.,* 164 f.; cf. *ibid.,* 157 f.: Archbishop Courtney to the Bishop of London. Reppington later became bishop of Lincoln and subsequently cardinal (cf. Gairdner, *Lollardy,* I, 59 f.).

[63] Wilkins, *op. cit.,* III, 166 f.

[64] See, for example, Wycliffe's treatise, *On the Truth of Holy Scripture,* 1379.

of the Bible in the vernacular"; he was "doing the work of Antichrist by the expedient of a new translation of Scripture into the mother tongue." [65]

BIBLIOGRAPHY

A. The Life and Times of Wycliffe.

Chronicle of Adam Murimuth, ed. by E. M. Thompson, Rolls Series, 1889.

Chronicon Angliae, ed. by E. M. Thompson, Rolls Series, 1874.

Deanesly, Margaret. *The Lollard Bible and Other Medieval Biblical Versions,* 1920.

Dene, W. de. *Historia Roffensis,* I, chap. 3 ("anglia sacra").

Gwynn, Aubrey. *The Austin Friars in the Time of Wyclif,* 1940.

Hague, Dyson. *Life and Work of John Wycliffe,* 1935.

Haseltine, G. C. "The Myth of Wycliffe," in *Thought,* 1933, pp. 108–21.

James, Thomas. *An Apologie for John Wickliffe, showing his conformitie with the now Church of England,* Oxford, 1608.

Lechler, G. *Johann von Wiclif und die Vorgeschichte der Reformation,* 1873; English trans. by Lorimer, 1878, 1881, 1884.

Lewis, John. *History of the Life and Sufferings of John Wiclif, together with a collection of papers and records,* 1720, 1820.

Stevenson, Joseph. *The Truth about John Wyclif,* 1885.

Trevelyan, G. M. *England in the Age of Wycliffe,* 1899, 1904, 1909.

Vaughan, R. *The Life and Opinions of Wycliffe, illustrated principally from his unpublished MSS.,* 1828, 1831, 2 vols.

Workman, H. B. *John Wyclif, a Study of the English Medieval Church,* Oxford, 1926.

B. Wycliffe and the Reformation Movement.

Cowell, Herbert. *The Character and Place of Wickliffe as a Reformer,* Oxford, 1857.

Harpsfield, Nicholas. *Historia haeresis Wicleffianae,* in *Historia Anglicana ecclesiastica,* Douay, 1622.

Netter, Thomas (Waldensis). *Fasciculi zizaniorum,* ed. by W. W. Shirley, Rolls Series V, 1858.

Poole, R. L. *Wyclif and Movements for Reform,* 1886.

Rashdall, H. *Universities of Europe in the Middle Ages,* II, ii, pp. 539 ff.

[65] Wilkins, *Concilia,* III, 339–60. "No formal condemnation of Wycliffe's English Bible was ever issued, or, so far as we know, attempted" (F. D. Matthew, *English Historical Review,* X, 95). See *A Compendyous olde tretyse, shewynge howe that we ought to haue the Scripture in Englyshe,* said to be "a tretyse wryten about the yere of our Lorde a thousande fower hundred," given by Foxe in his first edition of *Actes and Monumentes* (1563), but not in his late editions. To this treatise we owe the statement that a bill was brought into the house of Lords for the suppression of the English translation, but thrown out by the exertions of the Duke of Lancaster; also Arundel's sermon on Anne of Bohemia (cf. Forshall and Madden, *op. cit.,* §59, p. xxxiii).

C. Editions of the Works of Wycliffe.

Matthew, F. D. *The English Works of Wyclif,* Early English Text Society, 1880.
Thompson, E. Maunde. *The Wycliffe Exhibition, in the British Museum.*
Winn, H. E. *John Wycliffe: Select English Writings,* 1929.

Separate works and treatises by Wycliffe have been published by Pollard, Harris, Loserth, Lechler, Poole, Buddensieg, and others; also by the Wiclif Society, 1882–90, 14 vols. For his biblical works see the main Bibliography.

PART TWO

Early Printed Editions

CHAPTER VIII

Published Lists of Printed Editions of the Scriptures in English

THE methodical study of printed editions of the English Bible seems to have begun with the work of Rev. John Lewis, of Margate, biographer of Wycliffe, Caxton, and others, who in 1731 brought out an edition of Wycliffe's New Testament in folio. Prefixed to that edition is a lengthy treatise entitled: *A History of the several translations of the Holy Bible into English and of the most remarkable Editions of them since the Invention of Printing.* This important document, now treasured in the University Library at Cambridge (England), was published separately in 1738 and reprinted in 1818. That remarkable bibliographer of the English Bible, Dr. Henry Cotton, in the Preface to his *Lists of Editions of the Bible and Parts Thereof,* looks upon John Lewis as the first who worked in this field.

The next list, quite independent of Lewis' work, was based upon that comprised in a single sheet, MS. 1140 in Lambeth Library, giving the known editions between 1526 and 1776. The editions before 1600 seem to have been copied by Mr. Mark Cephas Tutet, who at the request of Dr. Ducarel, Keeper of the Lambeth MSS. from 1757, continued the list to 1776.[1] Ducarel then brought him another list from Lambeth drawn up by Dr. Gifford, librarian at the British Museum, and containing further editions down to 1757.[2] Gifford himself published the Lambeth

[1] This Lambeth list was first copied by Joseph Ames in his *Typographical Antiquities, or an Historical Account of the Origin and Progress of Printing in Great Britain and Ireland, Containing Memoirs of Our Ancient Printers,* 1749. This was reproduced "considerably augmented" by William Herbert, 3 vols., 1790, and "now greatly enlarged, with copious notes," by the Rev. Thos. Frognall Dibdin, 4 vols., 1810–19.

[2] *A List of Various Editions of the Bible and Parts Thereof in English, 1526–1776. From a MS. in the Archiepiscopal Library at Lambeth (compiled by Joseph Ames) much enlarged and improved by A. C. Ducarel,* 16 pages, published by W. Bower, 1777.

list with additions down to 1778. An enlarged edition was added by the Rev. Clement Cruttwell to his edition of the Authorized Version in three volumes, published at Bath in 1785, and repeated in the Bible published by John Hewlett in 1811. This list, again enlarged, appeared in Archbishop Newcome's *Historical View of the English Biblical Translations* (1792) and, with a few additions, was appended to Lewis' *Complete History of the Several Translations of the Holy Bible and New Testament into English,* edition of 1818.

Anderson's *Annals of the English Bible,* second edition (1862), pages 645–60, has a list comprising editions between 1524 and 1600; but he does not think it incumbent on him even to mention the Rhemist New Testament of 1582, though he does give Fulke's edition of it in parallel columns with the Bishops' Bible of 1589. In 1845 appeared Lea Wilson's sumptuous *Catalogue of Bibles, Testaments, Psalms, and Other Books of the Holy Scripture in English, in the collection of L. W., Esq.* This work, though incomplete, since it lists only the editions in a private collection, serves as a compendious history of the English Bible.

In 1821 Dr. Cotton published *Lists of Editions of the Bible and Parts Thereof in English, from 1505 to 1820.*[3] A second, much enlarged edition giving fuller details was published in 1852, bringing the list down to 1850; it listed no less that 1,155 editions of the Bible or parts thereof. However, all the foregoing lists are eclipsed by the *Historical Catalogue of the Printed Editions of Holy Scripture in the Library of the British and Foreign Bible Society,* in two volumes (1903–11), the first giving the English editions with detailed descriptions of each.

DR. HENRY COTTON

Among the 1,155 editions of the Bible listed by Dr. Cotton, fifty-three were published by the Catholic press. To these latter Cotton now turned his attention, publishing in 1855, *Rhemes and Doway. An attempt to*

[3] Thus appeared the title on the title page. The list of editions of the Bible or parts thereof, of course, opens with Tyndale's New Testament of 1525, and the superscription has "from the year 1525." The section on editions of the Psalms, however, begins in 1505, for in that year appeared John Fisher's translation of the Seven Penitential Psalms. This, with four further editions, was the only biblical text in English recorded by Dr. Cotton as having been printed before Tyndale's New Testament. [S.B.]

Dr. Henry Cotton was educated at Westminster School and Christ Church, Oxford. He became sublibrarian at the Bodleian, then chaplain to Archbishop Laurence, the Ethiopic scholar, and finally archdeacon of Cashel. He died in 1879 at the age of ninety, but he was almost totally blind during his declining years.

shew what has been done by the Roman Catholics for the diffusion of the Holy Scriptures in English (Oxford University Press). Unfortunately the author betrays an extraordinary animus toward Catholics. So marked is his feeling that Dr. Newman (as he then was) felt constrained to pass a very scathing stricture on the volume:

> Painful as it is to say it, in spite of his stating in his preface, that "the design of his book is not controversial but literary," he has made it the vehicle of so much incidental insinuation, sometimes unfair, sometimes ignorant, always ill-natured, to the disadvantage of Catholic ecclesiastics, that we are unable to regard him with that unmixed respect, and to use him with that ready and unfaltering confidence, which would be natural in those who, like ourselves, have long known his claims, both as a gentleman and a scholar, on public estimation. . . . As things stand, while we shall use him in the following pages, we are warned at the same time to verify his various statements, as far as may be, and where this cannot be done, not to adopt them without distinct reference to him as our authority.[4]

This animus appears at every turn, and though it would perhaps be ungenerous to regard the expression, "An attempt to shew what has been done by the Roman Catholics" as a veiled suggestion that such an attempt would prove a failure, yet that is the impression left on the reader's mind. If such was intended by Dr. Cotton, he was most assuredly "hoist with his own petard." For in his lists we find no fewer than forty-six editions or re-impressions of the complete Bible and fifty-three of the New Testament, all published with episcopal approbation. Compared with the prodigious output of Protestant editions, this may seem an insignificant catalogue; yet surely the marvel is that so much should have been done despite the miseries of the penal times. Bishops Murray, Denvir, Crolly, and Troy in Ireland, and bishops Challoner, Wiseman, Gibson, Bramston and others in England deserve our most grateful remembrance in this respect.

Concerning episcopal approbations, Dr. Cotton was particularly in-

[4] In *The Rambler* for July, 1859; reprinted in *Tracts Theological and Ecclesiastical,* Longmans, 1895, pp. 405 f. Cotton seems to have had no idea of the identity of the writer, for on November 21 of that year he wrote to George Offor: "In *The Rambler* for last July there is a paper by a R. C. writer (perhaps a bishop) giving to his Co-Religionists an account of the different English versions of their Bible. The writer owns that it is all taken from me, but he by no means gives a fair account of my descriptions, either of persons or things." Cotton's animus against all things Catholic appears in another letter to Offor (June 2, 1856): "The word of the Lord will yet have its free course in spite of Cardinals and Concordats. . . . Do you ever see a thorough-paced, Popish, priest-ridden, priest-conducted Irish Newspaper? I send you one. I think it will amuse—perhaps instruct you."

trigued by their varying character. He complained, for instance, that the approbation of Challoner's first revision is repeated in various editions, "although not one of them represents the genuine edition of 1749." [5] In particular he complains that Dr. Troy stated that Coyne's edition, 1820, was "particularly conformable" to Cross's edition of 1791, whereas "I am obliged to declare that it differs from Cross's edition in at least five hundred places." [6] Nor can he understand why all approbations are not couched in precisely the same terms, even saying: "I do not believe that those archbishops had the slightest knowledge of what they were doing at the time," a proof, according to his way of thinking, of "the looseness and uncertainty of those fancied safeguards to 'faith and morals,' the positive erroneousness of some of these 'Approbations,' and the utter uselessness of them all." [7]

Dr. Kenrick, archbishop of Baltimore, explained the meaning of such approbations very clearly, though unfortunately too late for Dr. Cotton to profit by it:

> In regard to vernacular versions, the Church is not accustomed to give them a solemn sanction, because it is not easy to ascertain their correctness in the minute details; and the constant changes to which living languages are exposed, may require amendments at no great distance of time. The respective prelates are left free to approve such versions as they deem faithful, and when the approval of the Holy See is added, it is not offered as a guarantee of their exactness so much as an encouragement to the devout study of the Scriptures." [8]

Had Cotton been able to read this, he presumably would not have said: "The professed object [of such approbations] was ever the same, namely to secure what the Court of Rome chose to call soundness of faith and morals," whence he argues that "we might expect not only that the required 'Approbation' should appear in every fresh edition, but likewise that it should always be THE SAME; not indeed in actual terms, but in its tenor and spirit." [9] He then devotes some ten pages to a dissection of the various forms in which these "Approbations" are cast.

No better example of an "Approbation" intended to cover only "faith and morals" could be found than that given by Dr. Walsh and Dr. Wise-

[5] *Rhemes and Doway*, p. 50.

[6] *Ibid.*, p. 120.

[7] *Ibid.*, p. 182.

[8] In the General Introduction to his translation of *The Psalms, Books of Wisdom, and Canticle of Canticles* (Baltimore, 1857), p. ix.

[9] *Op. cit.*, p. 175.

man to the edition of the Bible published in 1847 by Richardson of Derby. The text throughout is that of MacMahon, unfortunately reproduced in every edition of Haydock's Bible. If Dr. Wiseman had studied Richardson's text he must have shuddered when he read (John 2:4): "What is that to me and to thee?"—a reading he had explicitly condemned.[10] Yet there was nothing contrary to faith or morals in the edition of 1847; hence it received his approbation. At the same time it seems clear that publishers sometimes must have drawn up approbations such as they presumed bishops might have framed. Who can believe, for instance, that the archbishop of Armagh and a number of other bishops would in 1794 have signed themselves "R. C. Bishop of" such and such a See?

Despite the anti-Catholic animus displayed in *Rhemes and Doway,* we can be grateful to Dr. Cotton for preserving the information about many editions which would have otherwise passed into oblivion. Moreover, he provides (pages 315–75) a most useful collation of Challoner's first three revisions of the text of the English New Testament, 1749, 1750, and 1752, copies of which are exceedingly rare. At the same time this collation has to be used with caution; for though he describes it as "an exact collation" (page 50), there are many mistakes in it, mistakes for which no one who has attempted such a work of collating will blame him overmuch. Since his volume is by no means rare and of great use to anyone working on our version, we append a list of the errors we have noticed, excluding merely typographical slips.

ERRORS IN DR. COTTON'S COLLATION

Matt. 6:6 (6:7); Mark 13 (13:3); Luke 2:35 (2:3, 5); Rom. 8:19 (10:19); 10:9 (10:2), 10:24 (10:22); II Cor. 8:7 (8:6); I Tim. 4:13 (3:13); Heb. 6:6 (6:5).

Matt. 4:2: the edition of 1750 has "being hungry," thus differing from 1749 and 1752; 5:18: not "of the Laws," but "of the Law" (1749 and 1750); 5:20: not "the Pharisees," but simply "Pharisees" (the article is absent in the editions of 1749 and 1750); 5:29: not "they," but "thy," in all three revisions; 6:9: the *Errata* appended to the edition of 1750 show that the text should have read as in 1749, "thus therefore shall you pray," although as a matter of fact "shalt thou" stood in the text; 8:17: not "Isaias the prophet," but "Isaias the Prophet" (1749); "the Prophet

[10] "Catholic Versions of Scripture," *Dublin Review,* April, 1837.

Isaias" (1750; the name of Isaias was not omitted); 9:9: "arose up," not "rose up," in all three revisions ("rose up" did not appear until the fourth revision, 1764); 10:17: the edition of 1750 had corrected "counsels" to "councils," as in 1752; 13:17: not "many prophets," but "many Prophets" (1750); 16:6: not "Sadducees," but "Saducees" (1749 and 1750); 16:8: not "ye have," but "you have"; 17:26: not "the fish," but "that fish," in all three revisions; 18:34: not "till," but "until"; 19:25: "And when" in all three revisions (the "And" should not be omitted); 21:40: both 1749 and 1750 have "therefore the lord," whereas 1752 has "the lord therefore."

Luke 1:80: "and was strengthened in spirit" was inserted in the revisions of 1750 and 1752; 11:46: not "he saith," but "he said" (1749 and 1750); 13:12: not "unto her," but "to her," in all three revisions; 21:21: not "those that," but "those who." John 6:70: not "we believe and know," but "we believe and have known" (1749). Acts 5:38: should read "counsel" (1749 and 1750) and "council" (1752); 13:31: not "to this present time are," but "to this present are" (1749 and 1750); 19:27: not "reported," but "reputed" (1749 and 1750).

Rom. 2:26: "this uncircumcision" instead of "his uncircumcision" (1750), a misprint which has been perpetuated in many editions; 9:25: a phrase is misplaced in Cotton's collation of 1749, which should read: "I will call that which was not my people, my people; and her, that was not beloved, beloved; and her . . ."; 14:10: not "then, why judgest thou?" but "thou, why judgest thou?" (1749 and 1750). I Cor. 7:15: "servitude" in the edition of 1750 as in that of 1749. Gal. 3:25: "before the faith is come" (1749 and 1750). Eph. 5:8: not "walk thou," but "walk then" (1749 and 1750). Heb. 2:10: not "perfect through suffering," but "perfect by suffering" (1752); 3:6: not "son," but "Son," in all three revisions; 4:1: "the promise being left" (1750), as in 1752; 12:9: not "for instruction," but "for instructors" (1749 and 1750).

James 2:3: "sit thou here well" (1749 and 1750); 3:5: "So the tongue also is indeed" (1749 and 1750). Jude 10: "what things soever," in all of Challoner's revisions.

There are several misprints in Cotton's list (pp. 371–82) of variant readings in the edition of 1791, while one passage noted as varying figures in Challoner's first and second revisions. There are also positive statements which are quite incorrect; for example, Keating and Brown's

New Testament, 1818, is said to be "printed exactly from that of 1749 both in Text and Notes" (p. 237); yet in some twenty passages of St. Matthew the text is that of either 1750 or 1752. Again, the text of Coyne's noteless edition of 1820 is said to be "taken literally from that of Dr. Challoner's second edition, 1750" (p. 120); yet in Matt. 9:9 and Heb. 1:13 the text is that of 1749, while in Matt. 4:2; 7:29; John 21:11; and Heb. 4:1, the text is that of 1752.

VERSIONS OF THE PSALMS

In addition to translations of the whole Bible or of the New Testament, we find an almost incredible number of versions of the Psalms. Cotton enumerates no less than 1,028 versions published between 1550 and 1605, including, of course, versions of single psalms only. The practice of translating the Psalms from the Vulgate continued for a long time. Grafton's translation gives the Latin and English in parallel columns (1540); Whitchurch, another famous printer, published *The Psalter of David in Englysh, truly translated out of Latyn,* 1547.

The Penitential Psalms seem to have made particular appeal to men at the time of the Reformation: Grafton the Printer translated them, perhaps when he was in the Tower (1545; second edition, 1552); St. John Fisher did the same (1555).[11] The titles assigned to these seven psalms at times raise a smile: *Seven Sobs of a Sorrowful Soul,* 1597, 1600, and 1621; *The Dolefull Dove,* 1612; *The Teares or Lamentations of a Sorrowfull Soul,* 1613; *David's Harpe: full of most delectable Armony, newely strynged and set in tune,* 1542.

The Catholics too seem to have turned to these Penitential Psalms during the penal days, often in a *Primer* (St. Omer's, 1617 and 1631); in 1635 with a paraphrase by J(ohn) H(awkins); in a *Manual of Prayers* (1650); in *The Key of Paradise* (St. Omer's, 1675). In 1751 Father Blyth, the Carmelite who, with Bishop Challoner, seems to have been

[11] This edition was published after the accession of Queen Mary. Cotton states (*Lists of Editions of the Bible and Parts Thereof* [1852], p. 133) that John Fisher's version of the Penitential Psalms appeared first in 1505, printed by R. Pynson in London. It was republished by the same printer in 1510. Meanwhile it was published by Wynken de Worde in London in 1508 and 1509, and again in 1525 and 1529. The next edition was that of 1555, published by Thomas Marsche. The only later edition, without place or name, appeared in 1714. The earlier editions are very valuable, and the Cambridge (England) University Library has one of 1508. These editions of John Fisher's Penitential Psalms are the earliest printing of a biblical text in English. [S.B.]

partly responsible for the fifth edition of the Rheims New Testament in 1738, published what Cotton calls "the seventh edition."

Another remarkable aspect of Catholic piety during the penal days was the popularity of the Apocalypse. Nine editions of Dr. Walmesley's *An Exposition of the Apocalypse* appeared between 1771 and 1821, published under the pseudonym Pastorini, while an American edition published in 1851 is labelled, "the fifth American edition."

CATHOLIC VERSIONS OF THE BIBLE

From 1525, when Tyndale's English New Testament appeared, versions by the English Reformers held the field with the exception of St. John Fisher's version of the *Penitential Psalms* and Cardinal Pole's *Prymer*. But with the appearance of the Rheims New Testament, 1582, a new era set in. There could be no greater proof of the determination of our Catholic forefathers to make the Bible accessible to all in an English version than the fact that from 1582 there has issued from the Catholic press, despite all the incredible disabilities of the penal days, at least 102 editions of the whole Bible in English and 131 editions of the New Testament printed separately. If to these we add 34 editions of only portions of the Bible, such as the Psalms and the Apocalypse, and various prymers, the whole total amounts to more than 260 editions.[12] A list of the Catholic English versions of the Bible from the invention of printing to 1950 is given in the Appendix.

[12] These totals do not take into account the fact that sometimes, though rarely, the same edition was published simultaneously by different publishers. This list has been extensively enlarged since Father Pope wrote.

It is interesting to observe that already in 1538 we find a printed edition of *The Pystles and Gospelles for every Sonday and Holy daye in the yere,* printed in Paris, and two others printed at Rouen in the same year. Similar editions were also printed in England in 1539, 1540, 1542, 1546, and 1550, until finally in 1553 it is stated to be "after the Church of England." These editions are listed by Cotton (*op. cit.*) under their respective years. The existence of these printed copies suggests the practice at that time of reading the Epistle and Gospel to the people in the vernacular, and among the cathedral records at Peterborough there is an interesting reference to this custom in the account of a public penance imposed in the parish church of Belton, Rutland, in 1546. For the information about the Peterborough document I am indebted to Father Godfrey Anstruther, O.P. [S.B.]

CHAPTER IX

Sixteenth-Century Latin Versions of the Bible

CERTAIN aspects of the various English versions of the Bible published in the sixteenth century become intelligible only in the light of the Continental craze—for so we must call it—for producing fresh Latin versions. For the Reformers were continually insisting that the Vulgate Latin text was hopelessly corrupt and unreliable; so much so that doctrines based upon its renderings must, at the very least, be regarded as suspect, so it was claimed. This was, in fact, the theme underlying Fulke's *Defense of the Sincere and True Translations of the Holie Scriptures into the English Tong,* and of Whitaker's *De auctoritate scripturae,* 1594.

JACQUES LEFÈVRE (1440–1536)

Jacques Lefèvre d'Étaples, also known as Faber or Stapulensis,[1] was a voluminous but often indiscreet writer who lived to be nearly a hundred years old. He translated into Latin the Epistles and Gospels for the Sundays, and produced also a French version of the Bible. Unfortunately his unbalanced expressions on the need for a vernacular version led to his condemnation by the faculty of the University of Paris. The same faculty also condemned his Commentary on the Gospels, editions of which appeared in 1522, 1526, and 1541. In 1528 he published a "corrected" edition of St. Jerome's Vulgate Bible, which was republished in 1530, 1534, and 1541. He also published a treatise on the three different Marys mentioned in the Gospels and commentaries on the epistles.[2]

[1] Richard Simon, *The Critical History of the Versions of the New Testament,* pp. 175 ff.; Moulton, *The History of the English Bible,* p. 40; Anderson, *Annals of the English Bible,* p. 5; *Cambridge Modern History,* II, 283 ff.; Hurter, *Nomenclator literarius theologiae catholicae,* III, 1301–5; K. H. Graf, *Essai sur la vie et les écrits de J. Lefèvre d'Étaples,* 1842.

[2] *Epistolae divi Pauli apostoli, cum commentariis Jacobi Fabri Stapulensis,* Paris, 1551;

DESIDERIUS ERASMUS (1456–1536)

At first an Augustinian, then ordained as a secular priest in 1592, Erasmus came to England in 1596, where he was warmly befriended by More, Fisher, Colet, Linacre, Tunstall, and Henry VIII, then Prince of Wales.[3] Fisher secured for him the chair of Greek at Cambridge, but he soon returned to the Continent, where a chance perusal of notes on the New Testament by Valla led him from his previous humanistic studies to reading patristic works,[4] and thence to the Greek Testament. By 1505 he had produced a fresh Latin version of the New Testament, and now made up his mind to bring out a critical edition of the Greek Testament. Martin Dorpius alone had the courage to tell him he was ill-equipped for such a task, for Dorpius knew the character of Erasmus and felt that he was far too self-reliant, too impatient of criticism, and too hasty in his judgments to undertake a task calling for minute and patient research.[5]

When Froben the printer and publisher begged him to bring out an edition of the Greek Testament as soon as possible with a view to forestalling the Complutensian edition, Erasmus felt that his chance had come. As Froben's letter is dated April 17, 1515, and Erasmus' edition came out in February, 1516, Dorpius' fears were justified; sound critical work could not have been done in ten months. The work was to have been dedicated to Fisher, but Erasmus aimed higher and dedicated it to Leo X, "preferring," as a contemporary wit put it, "the Fisherman to the Fisher." [6] A second edition appeared in 1518–19, marked by some four

---

included are the Epistle to the Laodiceans, six letters by Seneca, and Linus, *De Passione Petri et Pauli.* He also edited *Biblia Sacra juxta Vulgatam ab aliquot theologis Parisiensibus accurate recognita et emendata; ed. Jacobus Faber cum Scholiis Joan. Benedicti,* Paris, 1573.

[3] To these patrons and friends he pays a grateful tribute: "Quid enim dicam de Britannia, ubi tot sunt mihi Macaenates, inter quos primus Clarissimus Baro, Gulielmus Montejovius: proximus Gulielmus Archiepiscopus Cantuariensis, totius Angliae Primas [Warham]: tertius Thomas Cardinalis Eboracensis [Wolsey], vir acerrimi judicii; summus Rex ipse non minus animi quam fortunae bonis florentissimus . . . Joannem [Fisher] Episcopum Roffensem in hoc catalogo . . . unum pro multis enumerare poteram. Deinde Cuthbertum Tunstallum Episcopum Londinensem."

[4] Of his edition of the *Opera S. Hieronymi,* Scaliger remarks that "it is full of sad blunders."

[5] Letter to Erasmus, October, 1515; see also Erasmus to More, December 15, 1517; *State Papers, Henry VIII,* II, i, no. 1999, note on p. 584; Seebohm, *Oxford Reformers: John Colet, Erasmus, and Thomas More,* p. 313 note.

[6] *State Papers, Henry VIII,* II, i, no. 683; ii, no. 2831.

hundred changes,[7] which Luther used as the basis of his version. A third came out in 1525 with I John 5:7 f. inserted; this was the basis of Tyndale's version, 1525.[8] The fourth edition, 1527,—the basis of nearly all subsequent editions—presented the text in three columns: the Greek, the Vulgate, and Erasmus' own rendering into Latin. The fifth edition omitted the column giving the Vulgate, 1535.[9]

Scholars hailed the production with enthusiasm: Warham, More, Tunstall, Colet, and Fisher all spoke enthusiastically about it.[10] Erasmus' pride in his accomplishment was almost childish; he writes to Wolsey: "The New Testament now stands as it was written by the Apostles"; [11] and he was overwhelmed with joy when More told him how Fox, bishop of Winchester, had "in a great concourse of people declared that Erasmus' translation was more to him than ten commentaries." More added his own congratulations: "it is really wonderful how keenly people are on all sides awaiting its production." [12]

But critics soon awoke to the defects of the version, and Erasmus resented their remarks, though Tunstall told him, to no avail, that he ought to show himself superior to such trifles.[13] A sound criticism was that by Lee, archbishop of York:

> The Greek MSS. of the New Testament are much more corrupt than the Latin; so much so that it seems to me a preposterous notion that we ought to correct the

[7] The bombastic title is typical of the author: *Novum Testamentum omne, multo quam adhuc diligentius ab Erasmo Roterodamo recognitum, emendatum ac translatum, non solum ad Graecam veritatem, verum etiam ad multorum ultriusque codicum, eorumque veterum simul et emendatorum fidem, postremo ad probatissimorum autorum citationem, emendationem et interpretationem, praecipue Origenis, Athanasii, Nazianzeni, Chrysostomi, Cyrilli, Theophylacti, Hieronymi, Cypriani, Ambrosii, Hilarii, Augustini, una cum Annotationibus recognitis, ac magna accessione locupletatis, quae lectorem doceant, quid pro ratione mutatum sit. Quisquis igitur amas veram theologiam, lege, cognosce, ac deinde judica. Neque statim offendere, si quid mutatum offenderis, sed expende, num in melius mutatum sit. Nam morbus est, non judicium, damnare quod non inspexeris. Salvo ubique et illabefacto Ecclesiae judicio.*

[8] An edition of Tyndale's New Testament, 1550, was entitled: *The New Testament in Englishe after the Greeke translation annexed; with the translation of Erasmus in Latin.*

[9] *Novum Testamentum jam quintum accuratissime recognitum a Desiderio Erasmo Roterodamo cum Adnotationibus ejusdem ita locupletatis, ut propemodum opus novum videri possit,* Basle, 1535. Here he made about one hundred changes, chiefly in the Apocalypse, and inserted Acts 8:36 and 9:5 f., which had previously been omitted.

[10] *Epistolae Erasmi,* II, 6 (February 16, 1516); cf. *ibid.,* Appendix, Ep. 221 (December 15, 1517).

[11] *Ibid.,* VIII, 33 (August 30, 1516).

[12] *Ibid.,* Appendix, Ep. 221 (December 15, 1517).

[13] *Ibid.,* III, 2.

Latin text of the Gospels by the much inferior Greek text. . . . If every one who has a smattering of Greek is going to correct the Latin text on his own initiative, the result can only be an ever-increasing number of Latin versions differing from one another. Nothing certain, sacred, stable will remain of the text. Nor is it any good suggesting that we have only to wait till the Supreme Pontiff shall—if he think fit—select and approve the best text. For myself I can only say that I hope I shall not live to see the day when he shall so think fit.[14]

Erasmus replied: "I attach no authority to renderings which are but my private opinion, unless the authority of the Church should approve them"; and again: "I declare, and I would have this declaration published everywhere, that I have no wish whatever to depart by a hair's breadth from the decisions of the Catholic Church." [15] Cambridge University forbade the introduction of the new version, but Erasmus retorted that their own chancellor, John Fisher, had approved it. "You know well," he added, "what kind of man is that great bishop of Rochester." [16]

In his Preface to the first edition, Erasmus explained the lines on which he had proceeded: "I have corrected the New Testament, primarily by having recourse to the 'Greek Truth'; for it is not Jerome and Augustine alone who repeatedly tell us to go to it as the fountain source, decrees issuing from the Roman Pontiff say the same. But while I—in view of its great antiquity and use down the centuries—hesitate to dissent from the original translator, . . . yet whenever it becomes evident that he has either 'nodded' or been mistaken, I do not shrink from pointing that out." Once more in the Preface to the fifth edition, 1535, he says: "It is true that there are places in which our Vulgate is preferable to what appears in the Greek MSS.; yet where all the latter are in agreement we have adapted the Latin text to them." Richard Simon's comment is to the point:

As if our Latin edition were not taken from the Greek Original! Hath he seen all the good MSS. of the New Testament that are extant? He hath indeed cited some of them, and deserves great commendation for the search he has made for them in a time when critical observations were not regarded by the Divines. . . . We shall soon perceive that he hath not read a sufficient number of these MSS. to judge of them exactly and that he hath condemned the ancient Greek readings authorized by our Vulgate because he confided too much in his MSS.[17]

[14] Given in Hody, *De Bibliorum textibus originalibus*, p. 469.

[15] Quoted by Richard Simon, *op. cit.*, p. 184.

[16] *Epis.*, II, 10 (August 31, 1516).

[17] *Op. cit.*, p. 146. Erasmus even maintained "the principle that a manuscript was the

This judgment is of course universally accepted today: Erasmus' edition of the Greek Testament "has no title to be considered as a work of learning or scholarship, yet its influence upon opinion was profound and durable. . . . [But] as an edition of the Greek Testament it has no critical value." [18] Dr. Fairbairn also says: "The inaccuracies of his text, the few and poor authorities he consulted, the haste of the editor, the hurry of the publisher, the carelessness of the printer, and the facility with which he inserted in the third and later editions a text like I John 5:7, which he had omitted in the first and second, are all instances of weakness familiar even to the unlearned." [19] Yet in justice it should not be forgotten that Erasmus was essentially a pioneer, and that while it cannot be pretended that he used his material in a scholarly fashion, he did use the best then accessible.

Erasmus' Latin version was of course made from the "received" Greek text, which he and all others at that time thought unassailable. And who shall blame them? His attitude towards the Vulgate version is difficult to assess. For at one time he praises it, at another condemns it. While maintaining that he never swerved from the Vulgate, yet he straightway gives lists of what he calls "amazing and inexcusable solecisms," [20] and in the Preface to his fifth edition he declares: "I am bound to say that St. Jerome has at times not given us a correct version; he almost seems to have been afraid to do so." Erasmus apparently thought St. Jerome was the translator and not merely the corrector of the current Latin text of the New Testament. Richard Simon's comment is appropriate: "Most judicious persons will prefer the barbarism of the ancient Latin edition before Erasmus' [polished version], because it is not a defect in an interpreter of the Holy Scriptures exactly to follow his Original, and even to represent its hyperbata. If the interpreter of the Church does not use

---

more to be relied on the more it departed from the Vulgate." Cf. Pastor, *History of the Popes*, XXI, p. 199.

[18] Rev. Mark Pattison in the *Encyclopaedia Britannica*, "Erasmus."

[19] *Cambridge Modern History*, II, 699. It is only fair to add that after claiming that the passage "appears in a Greek MS. in England" (the fourteenth-century *Codex Montfortianus*), Erasmus says: "Yet I suspect that that MS. should be corrected in accordance with ours" (the Vulgate). According to Hopfl, *Sirlet*, pp. 22, 36, Erasmus post-dated the Vatican Codex, B, by about five hundred years and his own beloved *Codex Bezae* by nearly a thousand years.

[20] He gave as instances *nubent et nubentur* for *nubunt et nubuntur* (Matt. 22:30); *ad Archisynagogum* for *ab Archisynagogo* (Mark 5:35); *confessus* for *confusus* (Luke 12:8); *suscipiens* for *suspiciens* (Luke 10:30).

very pure Latin expressions, it is because he applies himself faithfully to render the words of the Greek text." [21]

One of the most learned assailants of this new Latin version was the Spaniard, Didacus Lopez of Zuniga, commonly known as Stunica, and one of the chief editors of the Complutensian Polyglot. Simon calls him "one of the most learned men of his time, who knew Greek and Latin at least as well as Erasmus, [and] was, moreover, a good Hebraist," which could not be said of Erasmus.[22] Another severe critic was John Bois, canon of Ely. He collaborated with Sir Henry Savile in editing the works of St. Chrysostom, and was one of the translators for King James's Version. Both Bois and Stunica urged that a new version was not necessary, but "only a correction of the old in those places where it plainly appears not to be conformable to the Greek." [23]

In his Latin version Erasmus sometimes interprets; e.g., *Bethlehem Judaeae* (Matt. 2:1) becomes *Bethlehem civitatem Judaeae.* While repudiating in his footnotes the doxology in Matt. 6:13, he retains it in the text; he changes terms consecrated by long usage, though he is inconsistent, writing *poenitentiam agite* (Matt. 3:8), but with the gratuitous addition of *vitae prioris resipiscite* (4:17), a change which even Melancthon resented: "Let us speak with the Church; why be ashamed of the language of our Mother? For the Church is our Mother, and she so speaks." [24] In John, chap. 1, he replaces *Verbum* by *Sermo,* and verse 41, *Christus* by *Unctus;* verse 42, *quod interpretatur Petrus,* is made to read: *Quod sonat, si interpreteris, lapis."* He could not even keep his hands off the Lord's Prayer, reading *veniat* for *adveniat,* and *quemadmodum in coelo, sic etiam in terra; panem nostrum quotidianum da nobis hodie, et remitte nobis. . . ."* [25]

At times, however, he brings out the force of the Greek better than

[21] Cf. Simon, *The Critical History of the Versions of the New Testament,* pp. 183 ff.

[22] *Annotationes contra Erasmum in defensionem translationis Novi Testamenti,* 1520. Thereupon followed a controversy of pamphlets. On his deathbed Stunica, a man of great holiness, declared that he had assailed Erasmus only in the interests of truth, not out of ill feeling.

[23] Bois, *Veteris interpretis cum Beza aliisque recentioribus collatio in quatuor Evangeliis et Apostolorum Actis. In qua annon saepius absque justa satis causa hi ab illo discesserint disquiritur,* London, 1655.

[24] Cf. Simon, *op. cit.,* p. 190.

[25] Erasmus' Latin version was published with his Greek Testament in 1516 and 1519, and then separately many times between 1510 and 1539. The edition of 1525 (Zurich) is entitled *Novi Testamenti totius aeditio longe optima et accuratissima.*

does the Vulgate: "*that* fatted calf," which, as the whole household well knew, was awaiting the return of the prodigal (Luke 15:23, 27, 30); similarly in the story of Dives and Lazarus: "Son, remember that thou didst receive *thy* good things in thy life" (Luke 16:25).

But the real trouble was Erasmus' lack of theology. Here he was an amateur and laid himself open to criticism. He scoffed at images, relics, pilgrimages, even questioned the immensity of God, and actually pushed his humanistic notions so far as to liken the Good Friday ceremonies to "the mourning for Adonis." He seemed to take pleasure in suggesting doubts about almost every article of Catholic teaching; the Mass, confession, the primacy of the Apostolic See, clerical celibacy, fasting and abstinence, and so forth. Small wonder, then, that he came to be regarded as the man who paved the way for the Reformation by his levity and lack of balance when treating of sacred things, and more especially by his lack of any real theological sense.[26]

THOMAS DE VIO CAJETAN, O.P. (1469–1542) [27]

Thomas de Vio, called *Cajetanus* from his birth-place, Gaeta, is best known for his commentaries on the works of St. Thomas.[28] He is also the author of an exposition of Holy Scripture, his aim being to bring out the literal sense of the Bible. Starting with the Psalter and taking St. Jerome's translation from the Hebrew, he compared it with the Septuagint and later translations. Having no knowledge of Hebrew,[29] he employed a Jewish and a Christian Hebraist to translate the Hebrew word for word "in order to bring St. Jerome's version into exact correspond-

[26] A contemporary cynic has penned these rhyming lines:

Erasmus innuit, Lutherus irruit;
Erasmus parit ova, Lutherus excludit pullos;
Erasmus dubitat, Lutherus asseverat;
Erasmus lutherizat, Lutherus erasmizat.

[27] Cf. Melchior Cano, *Summa apologetica,* VII, iii, 5; Council of Trent, *Diaria,* Soc. Goerresiana, I, 32; II, 379; L. Frigel, *Dissertatio de Cardinale Cajetano;* Hody, *op. cit.,* pp. 478–80; Hurter, *Nomenclator literarius theologiae catholicae* (1903), "Cajetanus"; Mandonnet, "Cajétan (Thomas de Vio)," in *Dictionnaire de théologie catholique,* reprinted separately in 1931; Quétif and Echard, *Scriptores Ordinis Praedicatorum,* II, 14.

[28] Pallavicino remarks that to judge of Cajetan merely by his biblical work is like judging a peacock by his toes rather than by his tail (*History of the Council of Trent,* VI, 17 note).

[29] "Though he had no knowledge of Hebrew, he deals with it much better than many translators endowed with a mediocre knowledge of it" (R. Simon, *Histoire critique des principaux commentateurs du Nouveau Testament,* p. 319).

ence with the original." When these Hebraists insisted on explaining the precise meaning of the words, Cajetan told them "that the meaning was not their concern; their business was to translate, not to expound";[30] for, as he said concerning the Pentateuch, "it is the actual text of Moses we have to expound, not that of his translator." It was the same with the New Testament: when dedicating his Commentary on the Gospels to Clement VII he says: "My sole aim is to bring out the literal meaning."[31]

Cajetan certainly ventilated opinions which were novel, if not hazardous, in those days. He was not afraid to point out, for example, that had St. Matthew written in Hebrew, as was generally held, he would not have gone out of his way to explain such expressions as *Eli, lama sabachtani.* He even ventured to suggest that Matthew might have written his Gospel both in Hebrew and in Greek, or may have himself translated his Greek Gospel into Hebrew. So doubtful did he consider the authenticity of the concluding verses of St. Mark's Gospel that he ventured to say: "These verses are not of such solid authority for establishing the faith as are the unquestionable portions of this Gospel." St. Jerome's words on the authorship of the Epistle to the Hebrews led him to formulate the very doubtful principle that "if not by St. Paul, then it is not canonical, and if not canonical, then not authoritative." On the Apocalypse he declined to comment, but was content to observe: "Apocalypsim enim fateor me nescire exponere juxta sensum litteralem; exponat cui Deus concesserit."

Appearing at a time when men were insisting on the need for a strictly literal interpretation of Scripture, and were ever talking about the corrupt and defective character of the Vulgate, and were continually producing fresh Latin versions purporting to represent the original more

[30] Preface to *Psalmi Davidici ad Hebraicam veritatem castigati et juxta sensum quem literalem dicunt enarrati,* 1530 and 1534; in Cajetan's own words: "Testor ego quod inter hos labores dicebatur mihi ab interpretatoribus: Dictio Hebraica sonat hoc, sed non apparet sensus nisi mutetur in hoc alterum. Respondebam ego, auditis omnibus significationibus: Non sit vobis cura, si sensus non apparet, quia non est vestri officii exponere, sed interpretari: interpretamini sicut jacet, et relinquatis expositoribus curam intelligendi."

[31] *Praefatio in Evangelia cum commentariis Caietani. Reverendissimi Dni. Dni. Thomae de Vio Caietani Cardinalis S. Xisti: in Quatuor Evangelia et Acta Apostolorum ad Graecorum codicum veritatem castigata ad sensum quem vocant literalem Commentarii,* Venice, 1530. Two years later Cajetan published in Paris *Epistolae Pauli et aliorum apostolorum ad Graecam veritatem castigatae et per Reverendissimum Dnm. Dnm. Thomam de Vio, Cardinalis S. Xisti, juxta sensum literalem enarratae. Recens in lucem editae.* As Cajetan's commentaries are not readily accessible, it might be noted that his Commentary on St. Mark is printed in Migne, *Cursus completus S. Scripturae,* vol. 22.

faithfully than the Vulgate; when, too, the prevailing humanistic spirit was, all unconsciously, encouraging such heretical teachers as Luther, Calvin, and the rest, Cajetan's biblical work was of immense value. For he was fighting the Reformers with weapons which they considered peculiarly their own and on a field which they had staked out for themselves.

Authorities, however, were slow to recognize the merits of his work. In fact the Paris faculty condemned his commentaries in 1544 and 1545, though their condemnations were not included in the *Index of Prohibited Books,* 1551 and 1556. His chief opponent was a fellow Dominican, a devoted disciple of Savonarola, Lancelot Politi, better known as Ambrosius Catharinus, who had in his early years written against Luther (1520 and 1521).[32] He persistently attacked Cajetan,[33] but he himself only narrowly escaped condemnation for fifty theses extracted from his works. He became, however, bishop of Minori, near Naples, then archbishop of Conza; he died in 1553 just as he was about to receive the cardinal's hat. Among other complaints, Catharinus inveighed against a passage in Cajetan's commentary on John, chap. 6, where he had suggested that in case of necessity—during a plague, for example—the laity could communicate without the intermediation of a priest. But as Benedict XIV remarked: "It is plain that Catharinus went too far in his criticism; for first of all he did not give Cajetan's words correctly, and secondly his arguments against what Cajetan said can hardly be regarded as solid." [34]

Despite the various attacks on Cajetan, contemporary feeling must have run in favor of the courageous commentator; for his *Jentacula in selecta Novi Testamenti,* 1525, was republished in 1526, and again—long after his death—in 1565 and 1623; his commentaries on the Gospels were published in 1530 and 1536; on the Psalms, 1530 and 1532; on the Pentateuch, 1532 and 1539; on the historical books, 1533 and 1546; on the epistles, 1532, 1537, 1540 and 1544; on Job, 1535; on the poetical books and the prophets down to Isaias, chap. 3, where death overtook him, 1542, 1545, and 1587.

[32] *Apologia pro veritate catholicae fidei ac doctrinae adversus impia Martini Lutheri dogmata,* Florence, 1520.

[33] *Annotationes in excerpta quaedam de commentariis Cardinalis Caietani dogmata,* 1535; *De erroribus annotatis in Caietani commentariis,* 1561.

[34] *De synodo diocesana,* I, xxx, chap. 19, §28.

Cajetan always had the courage of his opinions, in biblical as well as in theological matters. He was not afraid, for instance, to declare that a knowledge of the Latin Bible was insufficient equipment; for the Old Testament, he said, one must know Hebrew, and for the New one must know Greek. He had a feeling, too, that the multitude and variety of versions was not always an advantage: "Would that we now had a version such as the early Fathers had; for then we should have expositions of the Bible based on the text as it stands, not on a text due to the arbitrary views of expositors." [35] In fact, nothing could have been more independent than his whole attitude on biblical questions:

> If we come across some fresh interpretation which, however, squares with the text in question, with the rest of the Bible, and with the Church's teaching, we, as critics, must in fairness be prepared to render to every one his due. Holy Scripture alone is so authoritative that when its authors say a thing is so, we believe them. "When I read other writers," says St. Augustine, "I do not accept what they say merely because they say it, no matter how holy or learned they may be." Let no one, then, reject some fresh interpretation merely on the ground that it does not square with what the early Fathers have held. Let him rather examine the passage in question, bearing in mind, too, its context. If he then finds that the fresh interpretation harmonizes with it, let him give thanks to God, who has not limited interpretation of the Bible to the early Fathers, but has left Scripture to interpret Scripture, yet always under the guidance of the Catholic Church.[36]

Some modern writers, too, have acclaimed Cajetan as a medieval Modernist; one even declares that "Cajetan is far nearer to the Church of England than to the Church of Rome." [37] The same writer dwells with complacency on Cajetan's "remarkable defence of the doctrine of Justification by Faith in his Exposition of the third chapter of the Romans," a passage which he regards as "the source from which our Reformers derived their definition of that doctrine in the *Homily on the Salvation of Mankind*." [38] But two quotations from this critic's writings will suffice to show how little competent he is to deal with matters theo-

[35] This statement distressed Pallavicino, who regretted the way in which so consummate a theologian had, as he thought, allowed himself to be side-tracked into biblical studies. He was driven to assert that whereas Cajetan's theological writings had enhanced his reputation, this was not the case with his biblical work, wherein he had allowed himself to be victimized by a set of Hebrew grammarians (*History of the Council of Trent*, VI, 17).

[36] *Prefatio in Pentateuchum.*

[37] R. C. Jenkins, *Pre-Tridentine Doctrine. A Review of the Commentaries on the Scriptures by Thomas de Vio, Cardinal Cajetan*, p. viii.

[38] *Ibid.*, p. vii.

logical: he speaks of "the Lateran Council, in 1860" [*sic*] as establishing "the doctrine of the Immaculate Conception," and he explains the technical term *res sacramenti* as meaning "the matter or outward part of the sacrament." [39]

When the news of the great Cardinal's death was announced to Clement VII, he mourned over his loss of the *Lumen ecclesiae*. Cajetan lies buried at the door of the Minerva with the simple inscription: Thomas de Vio Cajetanus Card. Si. Sixti. Sacri Ordinis Praedicatorum. A fuller epitaph was penned by a contemporary:

> Felix, O nimium felix, nimiumque beatus
> Mortalem exutus vitam nunc denique vives
> Et fructum vitae innocuae sine fine frueris.

SANTES PAGNINUS, O.P. (c. 1470–1541)

Leo X brought Santes Pagninus of Lucca, a disciple of Savonarola, to Rome as Professor of Oriental languages. From Rome he went to Lyons, where "he was held in great esteem not only for his holy life but also for his profound learning combined with a very real modesty; in addition he was venerated by the Lyonnese for his meritorious work for their city, which, by his earnest sermons, he succeeded in preserving from the errors of the Calvinists. On his death the citizens of Lyons constituted him their patron." [40]

For twenty-five years he was occupied in preparing an edition of the Hebrew Bible with an interlinear Latin translation.[41] For this work, says Sixtus of Siena, "he collated many of the best Hebrew MSS. available and in his Latin version he restored the Hebrew proper names to their original form, unlike the Latin dress in which previous translators had presented them. So carefully was his work done that the most learned of the Hebrew rabbis prefer his version to all others." [42] Pagninus was, says Hurter, "one of the most learned Hebraists of his time, deeply versed, too, in rabbinical literature, truly one of the glories of his Order." [43] His

[39] *Ibid.*, pp. ix, 54.
[40] Hurter, *Nomenclator*, "Pagninus."
[41] *Biblia Sacra Latina, Vetus et Novum Testamentum, nova translatio per S. Pagninum*, 1528. Though published in 1528, the date in the colophon is 1527.
[42] *Bibliotheca sancta* (1626), p. 375. Leusden, the Hebrew grammarian, remarks: "Infinitis fere locis magis congrua est cum textu Hebraeo quam ceterae editiones."
[43] Hurter, *loc. cit.*

edition, first published in 1528, reproduced in 1542, twice in 1564, and twice in 1591, seems to have been the first in which the verses were numbered; accents, too, were provided for establishing the pronunciation. The influence of Pagninus' work on subsequent translations was far-reaching, as we shall see later when dealing with the English versions.

Pagninus certainly took a bold step when he decided to translate direct from the Hebrew original. For at that date the only texts with which his compatriots were familiar were the Vulgate and, in a few cases, the Septuagint version of the Old Testament. But he was warmly encouraged in his arduous undertaking by Adrian VI in 1523 and by Clement VII in 1526.[44] The first edition appeared in 1528; and, as Pico de la Mirandola, in a letter written ten years previously, says that Pagninus had then spent twenty-five years on the translation,[45] the whole must have taken him some thirty-five years. Huetius declared that Pagninus had "furnished an almost perfect example of a translation of Scripture";[46] Genebrard, however, was of the contrary opinion: "Not careful enough, too ambitious, too minute, too much of a grammarian, too much preoccupied with rabbinical subtleties, . . . and sometimes seeming to minimize the mysteries of the Catholic faith."[47]

But the work of Pagninus suffered the usual vicissitudes. Servetus published an edition in 1542 with heretical notes of his own composition, though he endeavored to attribute them to Pagninus.[48] Ecclesiastical authorities had, of course, to intervene; and though Robert Stephens stepped into the breach by publishing an edition with notes derived from Vatablus, he unfortunately replaced Pagninus's version of the New Testament by that of Beza. Later on Arias Montanus re-edited Pagninus' version, adding the Apocrypha, or books not in the Hebrew Bible; he also endeavored to make the version even more literal, and in the New

[44] Preface to the first edition.

[45] Richard Simon, *Histoire critique du Vieux Testament*, p. 314.

[46] Simon (*op. cit.*, p. 316) quotes this from Huetius *De clarissimis interpretibus*, but he rather maliciously adds: "The elogia he passes on the versions by Pagninus and Arias Montanus may be excused seeing that he had never examined either of their versions but was content to quote what other writers had said of them, and even then only from the Prefaces these latter had written."

[47] *Prefatio in Opera Origenis.*

[48] *Biblia Sacra ex Santis Pagnini translatione, sed ad Hebraeam linguam amussim novissime ita recognita*, ed. by M. Servetus, Lyons, 1542. "Habes in hoc libro utriusque instrumenti novam translationem creditam a Santo Pagnino, Epitome."

Testament replaced Pagninus' Latin version by that of the Vulgate.[49] But, as Richard Simon remarks, "Montanus was too much of the grammarian." [50] Simon felt, too, that Pagninus himself was too much impressed by rabbinical learning and that this led him to neglect the work done by previous Christian commentators.[51]

Geddes speaks most unfavorably of Pagninus' work. For, while acknowledging that "the most ancient version, and, in a measure, the model of all the rest, was that of Santes Pagninus, which has been greatly extolled both by Jews and Christians, as the best Latin version that was ever made from the Hebrew, that of Jerome not excepted," he goes on to say: "It is, for all that, a barbarous composition, despicable in almost every point of view, but that of a grammatical glossary. . . . It was made more horribly uncouth by Arias Montanus, who interlined it in his edition of the Hebrew text of the Antwerp polyglott." [52]

Pagninus also published a Hebrew Lexicon which enjoyed a great reputation,[53] also more than one *Isagoge* or Introduction to Holy Scripture.

CONRAD PELLICAN (1478–1556)

Originally a monk, Conrad Pellican threw in his lot with the Lutherans.[54] At Zurich, where he was professor of Hebrew, he exercised an extraordinary influence, as the affectionate letters of his disciples testify. Unquestionably a man of genuine learning, Pellican translated the Talmud into Latin, then the Psalms, and finally undertook a version of the

[49] *Biblia Hebraica, cum interlineari interpretatione Latina Xantis Pagnini Lucensis, quae quidem interpretatio, cum ab Hebraicarum dictionum proprietate discedit, sensum, videlicet, magis quam verba exprimens, in margine libri est collocata; atque alia Ben. Ariae Montani Hispalensis, aliorumque collato studio e verbo reddita, ac diverso characterum genere distincta, in ejus locum est substituta,* 1572, 1584, 1619, 1657. An edition of Pagninus' version of the Old Testament with his notes and those of Vatablus, a translation of the Apocrypha by C. Baduellus, Beza's Latin version of the New Testament (his first edition, 1556), and the Vulgate version of the whole Bible was published by R. Stephens at Geneva in 1557, and again at Zurich in 1564 and 1579—a strange combination of authorities, but indicative of the appreciation in which Pagninus' version was held.

[50] *The Critical History of the Versions of the New Testament,* p. 199.

[51] *Histoire critique du Vieux Testament,* II, 20.

[52] *Prospectus of a New Translation of the Holy Bible,* pp. 74 f.

[53] Republished in an abbreviated form as *Thesauri Hebraicae linguae, olim a Sante Pagnino Lucensi conscripti, Epitome,* Antwerp, 1572.

[54] According to Hody (*op. cit.,* p. 449), his faith was upset by witnessing the routing of a Catholic controversialist by a Jew, and even worse, by a Jewess.

whole Bible, which, however, he did not live to complete. Though often republished, Pellican's edition [55] does not seem to have obtained the popularity accorded to some of the many Latin translations then flooding the market. His death caused consternation; the Earl of Bedford, in a letter to Bullinger, April 26, 1557, declared: "He has most gloriously finished his course in labors, watchings, constant study, and encouragement of learned men; and at length, by dying as he lived, he is translated to a better life in heaven." [56]

LEO JUD (1482–1542)

The Zurich or Tigurine Bible, a new Latin version, was inaugurated by Leo Jud (1482–1542). Despite his name, he was not a converted Jew, his name being derived from Gen. 49:9. A disciple of Zwingli, he translated his works and those of Luther with a view to forwarding the anti-Roman campaign in Switzerland. His unfinished translation of the Bible was completed by Bibliander and Pellican, Cholin adding the Apocrypha and Gualter a revised translation of Erasmus' New Testament.[57]

Geddes speaks highly of the version for the purity of its Latin. But, he adds, the Zurich divines responsible for its production were so convinced of the pre-eminence of the Masoretic Hebrew text "as to enact

[55] See note 57 below. He also produced the *Commentaria biblica et illa brevia quidem ac Catholica Chuonradi Pellicani qui et Vulgatam commentariis inseruit aeditionem, sed ad Hebraicam lectionem accurate emendatam,* Preface by H. Bullinger, Index Bibliorum by C. Pellicano, 1543; the copy in the British Museum formerly belonged to Henry VIII. Another edition added the Apocrypha: *Commentaria Bibliorum, id est canonicorum Veteris Testamenti librorum, opera D. Chuonradi Pellicani elaborata, qui et Vulgatam commentariis aeditionem inseruit, sed ad Hebraicam lectionem accurate emendatam. Accesserunt et commentaria in omnes Veteris Testamenti libros ecclesiasticos* (*seu Apocryphos*), 1536–46.

[56] *Original Letters,* Parker Society, I, 138. See Vigouroux, *Dictionnaire de la Bible,* "Versions latines"; Hody, *op. cit.*, p. 449.

[57] *Biblia sacrosancta Testamenti Veteris et Novi, e sacra Hebraeorum lingua Graecorumque fontibus, consultis simul orthodoxis interpretibus religiosissime translata in sermonem Latinum per theologos Tigurinos* (Leo Jud, Bibliander, and P. Cholin), the New Testament (published separately) revised and corrected from the translation by Erasmus and corrected by R. Gualter, the whole edited by C. Pellican, Zurich, 1543. Both Henry VIII and Edward VI had copies of this edition. Strangely enough, this Tigurine Bible was re-edited by the theologians of Salamanca: *Biblia Sacra cum duplici translatione* (namely, that of the Vulgate and that of Leo Jud with others) *et scholiis Francisci Vatabli nunc denuo a pluribus erroribus repurgatis, doctissimorum theologorum, tam almae Universitatis Salmanticensis, quam Complutensis judicio,* Salamanca, 1584–85. Cf. J. J. Huldricus, professor of theology at Zurich, *Vindiciae pro Bibliorum translatione Tigurina* (that of 1543), 1616.

a canon forbidding any member of their sect to take orders save after a public acknowledgment that the Masoretic text was 'divine and authentic both as to the consonants and the vowels.' "[58] Richard Simon says that a Spanish theologian, Escalente, was so impressed by the very moderate tone of the Preface to the version—the only part he seems to have read—that he described the whole version as "composed by the care and diligence of Leo [Jud] Bishop of Zurich, who being excited by a pious zeal undertook this translation, and this holy man, not being able to finish this version by reason of his extreme old age, and the great labour that he had already sustained, was assisted by some of his brethren who were expert in the knowledge of the languages and of the Holy Scriptures."[59] The good Spaniard evidently thought that Zurich was a Catholic episcopal see and Leo Jud its bishop.

Though fully alive to the defects of the translation, Simon praises the translators for keeping the proper *via media* between

> versions which are too literal wherein the expressions are somewhat rude, and those that are too remote from the letter. They have taken Erasmus for their guide, whom nevertheless they often abandon. . . . They have retained some old expressions which they considered as consecrated to the use of the Church, e.g., "fides," "fidelis," and "benedictus" instead of "fiducia," "fidens"—or "verax" and "laudandus." But while they protest against the current rejection of some terms peculiar to Holy Scripture, they themselves have "resipiscite" instead of "poenitentiam agite"; in John 8:25 for the Vulgate "principium" they read with Erasmus "in primis" and in the margin "omnino," with the note, "id est, omnino hoc ipsum sum quod jam dixi." [At the same time] they blame those who through too much perverseness reject certain forms of speaking that are peculiar to the Sacred Books, . . . [for] there are some phrases in the Holy Scriptures which cannot be elegantly expressed in another language without losing much of their gracefulness, and consequently of that which is mysterious. . . . Their exactness appears in this that they have not presumed to insert anything in their Version but what they firmly believed to be really in the Greek Original.

Simon instances their bracketing the doxology in Matt. 6:13, the omission of the text of "The Three Heavenly Witnesses" (I John 5:7), where, however, they have an excellent note in which, on the authority of the Complutensian Polyglot, they concede that its authenticity is not so impossible of acceptance.

Simon has high praise, too, for the marginal notes on obscure passages; many of these, especially when it is a question of Hebrew turns of ex-

[58] *Op. cit.*, pp. 67, 88.

[59] *The Critical History of the Versions of the New Testament,* p. 200.

pression, "chiefly tend to give light into the knowledge of the style of the Writers of the New Testament; and if they do not always succeed therein; at least they shew evident proofs of their good judgement in a time when people were not as yet very exact in critical enquiries relating to the Sacred Books." [60]

SEBASTIAN MÜNSTER (1489–1552)

Sebastian Münster threw off his religious habit when he became infected with Lutheran ideas. A very good Hebraist, he published more than one Hebrew grammar, and a Hebrew dictionary dedicated to John Fisher, bishop of Rochester.[61] After translating various books of the Bible,[62] he published a Latin version of the whole Bible in 1535, 1539, and 1546.[63] His version exercised a remarkable influence on the English translators; [64] in fact, when the Bishops' Bible was in preparation, Sandys complained that "previous translators followed Münster too much; he swerved from the Hebrew." [65] Yet Huetius on the contrary says: "Münster always adapts his style to the Hebrew, and at the same time is not neglectful of the Latin, though he be not over attentive to the elegancies of it." Richard Simon also praises his work: "No one seems better to have expressed the words and sense of the Hebrew context"; [66] while Geddes says that his version, "though less literal, is more perspicuous than Pagninus'. The rabbins were his chief guides; and his annotations are compiled with no small discernment from their best works." [67] Münster died in 1552, a victim of the plague.

Many of the Reformers were so obsessed by the *Hebraica veritas* that

[60] *Op. cit.*, pp. 198–204. See also the note on Matt. 20:28, "to give His life a ransom for many," with the explanation that "many" is here the equivalent of "all"; also the excellent note on *Logos* (John 1:1–3), rendered *Verbum*, not *Sermo* as in Erasmus.

[61] Cf. Eadie, *The English Bible*, p. 86 note.

[62] His version of the Canticle of Canticles appeared in 1525, of Proverbs in 1548, of Tobias in 1549, of the Pentateuch in 1551, and of Job (posthumously) in 1556.

[63] *Biblia Vetus, opera Sebastiani Münsteri evulgatum*, with a Preface by H. Bullinger, Zurich, 1539; also an edition of his *Evangelium secundum Matthaeum in lingua Hebraea, cum versione Latina et annotationibus Sebastiani Münster; una cum Epistola ad Hebraeos*, Basle, 1557.

[64] In the Latin version of the Book of Common Prayer, 1572 and 1574, the psalms, with the exception of psalm 14 (13), were given in Münster's version.

[65] See Archbishop Parker, Letter 197, p. 257.

[66] See Eadie, *op. cit.*, I, 376 ff.

[67] *Op. cit.*, p. 75; cf. Lewis, *A Complete History of the Several Translations of the Holy Bible and New Testament, etc., into English*, p. 228; *Cambridge Modern History*, II, 355; R. Simon, *The Critical History of the Versions of the New Testament*, pp. 172 ff.

they even preferred the rabbinical commentators to the Christian Fathers This was particularly the case with Münster, who says in his Preface that he followed the Jewish commentators, and that if he has erred in any way, the blame must be laid at their door. But he has the merit of giving the literal signification of the text as interpreted by the Jews of his time, notably the so-called Cabbalists.[68]

ANDREAS OSIANDER (1498–1552)

Andreas Osiander was a Lutheran minister at Geneva and Nuremberg.[69] Of singularly violent temper, even Luther—himself by no means mealymouthed—found his language intemperate, while both Calvin and Melancthon remark that he had very little real religion. Whitaker speaks of him as "a man of the utmost levity and audacity." [70] Like many of those who declaimed against the Vulgate, both Andreas Osiander and his son Luke retained sufficient respect for the familiar version to leave it untouched in their so-called versions, in which, however, they inserted a number of explanatory words as though they were part of the text; for example, in Gen. 1:2 after *ferebatur* they inserted *incubabat.*[71]

ISIDORE CLARIO, O.S.B. (1495–1555)

Thaddeus Cucchi, known as "Clarus" or "Clario" from Chieri, his birthplace, was a thoroughly competent Hebrew and Greek scholar. In 1542 he published an edition of the Vulgate,[72] which, unfortunately, the Church felt bound to condemn, though only because of a passage in the Preface in which, after extolling the merits of the Vulgate version, he went on to say:

[68] *Idem, Histoire critique,* pp. 321–23, 441 f.

[69] Cranmer married a niece of Osiander's wife; cf. Hereford, *Annals,* p. 121.

[70] *The Authority of Scripture,* Parker Society, p. 380.

[71] Andreas Osiander, *Biblia Sacra, quae praeter antiquam Latinae versionis emendationem multas observationes continet,* 1522, 1618; also *Harmoniae Evangelicae, Graece et Latine,* Basle, 1537, 1561; Luke Osiander, *Biblia Sacra. Quae praeter antiquae Latinae versionem necessariam emendationem continent,* 1573, 1586. Le Long (*Bibliotheca sacra*) enumerates no less than eleven editions of these versions, but Vigouroux (in *Dictionnaire de la Bible*) mentions only commentaries on the Pentateuch and on the historical books.

[72] *Vulgata editio Veteris et Novi Testamenti quorum alterum ad Hebraicum, alterum ad Graecam veritatem emendatum ut diligentissime ut nova editio non desyderatur, adjunctis et eruditis scriptoribus scholiis, auctore Isidoro Claro, Brixiano monacho Casinate,* Venice, 1542; another edition in 1557. The copy in the British Museum belonged to Queen Elizabeth.

But two things seem to me to be wanting. For notwithstanding the industry and labour of all these men [previous editors], that edition which the whole Christian world now useth, and as I easily conjecture, will always continue to allow, hath not as yet put off its deformity, neither hath any one taken care to clear it from those innumerable errors with which it abounded.[73] Which matter, in my opinion, deserves so much the more reprehension, by how much the greater number there is in this time of persons who might have remedied this mischief.

The Censors in 1542 excised the entire Preface,[74] but in later editions it was printed except the above passage.

Richard Simon notes that "under pretence of adhering to the originals, Clario very often follows his own caprice," while in the New Testament he accepts Greek readings which not only St. Jerome, but subsequent authorities have discarded, e.g. the "Doxology" (Matt. 6:13).[75] Many of Clario's annotations are based on those of Münster, and Fulke quite unjustifiably quotes him as condemning the veneration of images.[76] At the Council of Trent, Clario—now archbishop of Foligno—maintained in the course of the discussions on the vernacular versions that while none were really equivalent to the original, yet St. Jerome's was entitled to preference, if only by reason of its long use in the Church.[77]

ROBERT STEPHENS (C. 1500–70)

In addition to his various editions of the Greek Testament, Robert Stephens, followed by his son Henry, published several editions of the Latin Bible. The text was, supposedly, that of the Vulgate, but in fact Stephens made large use of the Zurich Bible, as he acknowledged in his Preface to the edition of 1545, though even then he did not name his source, merely saying that he has added to the Vulgate a Latin version which he considered the best. In a later edition, 1577, he preferred the

[73] Clario claims to have discovered 8,000 errors; cf. Copinger, *Incunabula biblica, or the first half century of the Latin Bible, being a bibliographical account of the various editions of the Latin Bible between 1450 and 1500,* p. 224; Fulke, *A Defense of the Sincere and True Translations of the Holie Scriptures into the English Tong,* p. 579.

[74] "Ex Bibliis vero Isidori Clarii Brixiani Prologus et Prolegomena praecidantur: ejus vero textum nemo textum Vulgatae editionis esse praesumat." Hence Le Long remarks: "The editions of Robert Stephens are suspect, that of Benedicti is doubtful, that of Clario quasi-condemned" (*op. cit.,* II, 223). Cotton characteristically remarks: "The authors of that order were ashamed to assign the reason" (*Rhemes and Doway,* p. 14 note). A corrected edition appeared in 1564 with the *caveat, "deputatorum Concilii Tridentini servata censura."*

[75] *The Critical History of the Versions of the New Testament,* pp. 111–13.

[76] *Op. cit.,* p. 372.

[77] Vigouroux, *Dictionnaire de la Bible,* II, 793; III, 124; Hurter, *Nomenclator,* "Clario"; Hody, *op. cit.,* pp. 486–94.

version by Pagninus, but as "emended" by himself. The Paris theological faculty naturally fell foul of him over this and, *perlectis et animadversis erroribus,* condemned his editions published in 1528, 1532, 1534, 1540, 1545, and 1546. Unfortunately these theologians seem to have been too fond of "heresy-hunting," and Stephens indulged in a petty revenge by circulating a canard to the effect that a member of that theological body had acknowledged that it was only when he had reached the age of fifty years that he realized that there was such a thing as the New Testament.[78] The theological faculty at Salamanca, perhaps from a spirit of rivalry, decided that Stephens' editions would be of use to the general reader; they therefore printed an edition in sumptuous style.

JOHN IMMANUEL TREMELLIUS (1510–80)

John Immanuel Tremellius was a Jew who became a Catholic through Cardinal Pole, and then a Protestant through Vermigli, or "Peter Martyr"; he was brought to England by Cranmer and obtained a professorship at Cambridge in 1549, subsequently becoming a prebendary at Carlisle in 1552.[79] When Mary ascended the throne he fled to Heidelberg, where he was imprisoned for Calvinism; finally he was expelled from Heidelberg by the Lutherans.

Tremellius published a Latin translation of the Old Testament and of the Syriac New Testament, dedicating it to Queen Elizabeth.[80] He seems to have thought this Syriac version was due either to the apostles themselves or to some one acquainted with them. He then, with his son-in-law, Junius, produced a Latin version of the Old Testament with long Introductions prefixed to the various books.[81] His Latin text, surrounded by

[78] Richard Simon, *Histoire critique* (1687), pp. 328 f. Stephens defended himself in *Les censures des théologiens de Paris, par lesquelles ils avoyent faulsement condamné les Bibles imprimées par Robert Estienne imprimeur du Roy: avec la réponse d'iceluy Robert Estienne,* 1552; republished at Geneva, 1867. See Le Long's remark, note 74 above.

[79] Strype, *Ecclesiastical Memorials,* II, 335; III, 225; for a fuller account of Tremellius' life and work, see Richard Simon, *Histoire critique du Vieux Testament,* p. 327; also two memoirs: *Immanuel Tremellius. Ein Proselytenleben im Zeitalter der Reformation,* Leipzig, 1890; F. Butters, *Emanuel Tremellius. Erster Rector des Zweibrücker Gymnasiums,* 1859.

[80] *Testamenti Veteris libri canonici, Latini facti ab J. Tremellio et Fr. Junio. Accesserunt libri apocryphi Latine redditi a Fr. Junio, et Novi Testamenti libri ex sermone Syriaco ab eodem Tremellio et ex Graeco a Theod. Beza in Latinum conversi.*

[81] *Biblia Sacra sive libri canonici priscae Judaeorum ecclesiae a Deo traditi, Latini recens ex Hebraeo facta, scholiis illustrata J. Tremellio et F. Junio. Jesu Christi Novum Testamentum Theodoro Beza interprete,* 1575, 1580–81, 1585. Tremellius also published *Grammatica Chaldaea et Syra,* Geneva, 1569, dedicated to Archbishop Parker; cf. Strype, *Memorials of Archbishop Parker,* p. 332.

a very full commentary, sounds strangely in our ears. Genesis, for instance, is headed: "Primus Liber Moschis, sive Genesis. Primus Liber Pentateuchi, Ortum mundi et Ecclesiae Dei describit: doctrinamque hujus, religionem, progressus, et mirificam bis mille trecentorum sexaginta octo annorum gubernationem ad obitum Josephi usque ordine pertexit."

How far Tremellius' new version was removed from the familiar Vulgate will be clear from a few examples: "Terra autem erat res informis et inanis, tenebraeque erant in superficie abyssi, et Spiritus Dei incubabat superficiei aquarum" (Gen. 1:2); "Esto expansum inter aquas ut sit distinguens inter aquas unas et alteras (1:6); "Legislator e medio pedum ejus usquedum venturus erit filius ejus" (49:10). "Ecce virgo concipiet et pariet filium, et vocabis, O virgo, nomen ejus Himmanuelem" (Isa. 7:14). "Reliquae autem res Jechizkija [Ezechiae] et benignitates ejus; ecce sunt scriptae in visione Jeshahjae filii Amotzi, praeter librum Regum Jehudae et Jizraelis" (II Par. 32:32). Tremellius transliterated the Hebrew proper names in the most fantastic fashion; perhaps the readers can divine for whom the following stand: Chavva, Hebelus, Jehoschuha, Schemuel, Kajin, Methuscelschus, Juchannan.

Tremellius had an inordinate love of pronouns, which he inserted lavishly: "Viditque Deus lucem *hanc* esse bonam, et distinctionem fecit Deus inter *hanc* lucem . . ." (Gen. 1:4); "fecit ergo Deus *hoc* expansum, quod distinguit inter *has* aquas quae sunt ab inferiore expansi *illius* et aquas *illas*" (Gen. 1:7). None of the pronouns here in italics appear in the original. Furthermore, Tremellius was not free from the prevailing tendency to adapt the text of the Bible to his own views; for example, II Esd. 8:8 is made to read: "Exponendo sensum, dabant intelligentiam *per Scripturam ipsam,*" the last words having no foundation in the original text. Yet in spite of its stilted phrasing the version proved very popular, twenty editions appearing in the first twenty years, the last in 1764. It exercised a remarkable influence on later English versions. This popularity did not, however, save the version from the attacks of Drusius, the Hebraist; but the revised version which thus became necessary was condemned in its turn by the Emperor Constantine, himself a competent Hebraist.

SEBASTIAN CASTALIO (1515–63)

Sebastian Castalio was that strange anomaly: a Calvinist who rejected the Calvinistic teaching on grace and predestination. In 1551 he published his Latin translation of the Bible,[82] which he endeavored to write in classical Latin, substituting *genius* for *angelus, lotio* for *baptismus,* etc., in the hope that fastidious Latinists might thereby be induced to read it. He even substitutes *Jova Deus* for *Dominus Deus* (Gen. 3:1). The result was an incongruous production, as the following excerpts will testify: "Principio creavit Deus coelum et terram. Cum autem esset terra iners atque rudis tenebrisque offusum profundum, et Divinus Spiritus sese super aquas libraret, jussit Deus ut existeret lux" (Gen. 1:1 f.); "Quin etiam inimicitias inter te et mulierem, interque tuum et ejus semen conciliabo, ut illud tibi caput, tu illius calcem illidas" (3:15); "A Juda sceptrum non recedet, nec de ejus interfemineo rector donec veniat sospitator, cujus erit populorum congregatio" (49:10). "Equidem scio vindicem meum vivere, et postremo in terram surrecturum esse. Et postea hoc ipsum circumdatum iri mea cute, et me ex meo corpore visurum esse Deum, quem quidem ego ipse visurus sum, et meis ipsius, non alterius oculis aspecturus, ego cujus renes in me penitus consummuntur" (Job 19:25–27).

Castalio took equal liberties with the Hebrew text, which he "corrected" freely and on his own arbitrary principles. Yet at the same time he was well aware of the difficulties besetting a translator and acknowledges in his notes that he may have gone astray in many instances.[83]

His renderings in the New Testament are, to say the least, bizarre; for example, "Tu es Petrus, et in hac petra construam meam ecclesiam, quam Orci portae non superabunt" (Matt. 16:18). "Tu vicissim aliquando recreatus confirmato fratres tuos" (Luke 22:32). "Hoc pane vescimini et hoc poculum bibetis" (I Cor. 11:26). I John 5:7 is printed between brackets. On the Apocalypse there are but six notes, all very brief.

Though Westcott speaks of Castalio's version as "a singularly elegant"

[82] Castalio dedicated his Latin version to Edward VI: *Vetus et Novum Testamentum, Latine, interprete Sebastiano Castalione, una cum annotationibus,* 1551 and 1554. An edition in 1573 added an *Historical Supplement from Esdras to the Maccabees.* The last edition was provided with "corrections and an Introduction" by J. Bunemann, and notes by Ludovicus Capellus, 1729–34.

[83] Richard Simon, *Histoire critique du Vieux Testament,* p. 326.

one,[84] Richard Simon very properly points out that "he ought not to make the Evangelists and Apostles speak the language of Catullus and Tibullus," nor should "his chiefest design have been to make the Apostles speak very elegantly. . . . In a word he deserves not the character of a translator of the Holy Scripture." [85] Yet Geddes waxes eloquent on his style. Castalio's version is, he says,

> bold and free, his style clear and concise, his diction pure and perhaps scrupulously elegant. It was reprobated, however, in general by Jews and Christians, by Catholics and Protestants, as a temerarious, insolent and even impious burlesque of Holy Writ. . . . There is an ease and elegance in his translation that are extremely pleasant to the reader, with a conciseness, which one should think hardly compatible with ease and elegance. . . . He had the courage to strike out a path for himself. He translated, indeed, from the present Hebrew text, but he did not Judaically despise the ancient versions; nor did he reject those useful and excellent books (the so-called Apocrypha), which Protestants have, after St. Jerome and his Hebrew preceptors, too rashly thrown out of the canon, and, to connect the Old Testament with the New, he inserted two excellent supplements, abridged from Josephus; the one after the Fourth Book of Esdras, and the other at the end of the Machabees.[86]

Castalio's doctrinal views naturally offended the Calvinistic body, and Beza and the framers of the Genevan version were loud in condemnation. Beza, in particular, insisted that the version was full of errors and complained, somewhat illogically, that Castalio seemed to think he was free to hold whatever form of religion he liked:

> The matter is now come to this point, that the translators of Scripture out of Greek into Latin, or into any other tongue, think that they may lawfully do anything in translating. Whom if men reprehend, he shall be answered by and by, that they do the office of a translator, not that translateth word for word, but that expresseth the sense. So it cometh to pass, that whiles every man will rather freely follow his own judgment, than be a religious interpreter of the Holy Ghost, he doth rather pervert many things than translate them.[87]

Beza quite rightly resented Castalio's changing "baptizing" into

[84] *A General View of the History of the English Bible,* p. 213.

[85] *The Critical History of the Versions of the New Testament,* p. 178. Genebrard indeed bluntly declares: "Castalionis versio est affectata, plus habens pompae et phalerarum quam rei et firmitatis, plus ostentationis quam substantiae, plus fuci quam succi, plus hominis quam flammae, plus humanarum cogitationum quam divinorum sensum, plus folium quam fructum" (*Praefatio in Originem,* quoted by J. W. Whittaker, *An Historical and Critical Enquiry into the Interpretation of the Hebrew Scriptures,* pp. 27 f.).

[86] *Prospectus of a New Translation of the Holy Bible,* pp. 76 f., 86 f.

[87] Quoted by Gregory Martin, *A Discoverie of the Manifold Corruptions of the Holie Scriptures by the Heritikes of our Daies,* p. 155.

"washing"; the old term, he says, "though used of the sacred writers in the mystery or sacrament of the New Testament, and for so many years after, by the secret consent of all churches, consecrated to this one sacrament, so that it is now grown into the vulgar speech almost of all nations, yet they dare presume rashly to change it." [88] Beza omits to comment on Castalio's occasional *respublica* for *Ecclesia*. He might well have complained too of Castalio's expressed doubts about the canonicity of the Canticle of Canticles; his doubts, however, about the descent of Christ into hell Beza would have warmly endorsed.[89]

But whatever the defects of the version, it was very popular. By 1697 there had appeared four editions of the whole Bible and six of the New Testament, three of them with the Greek text as well as Castalio's Latin. His version continued to be published as late as 1780 (in Hannover); editions appeared in London in 1756 and in Glasgow in 1758.

THEODORE BEZA (1519–1605)

Theodore Beza apparently never received sacred orders, yet he held several benefices, which he resigned in 1548 when he joined the Calvinists, whose leader he became on Calvin's death in 1564. At the Poissy debate, 1561, he maintained that the body of Christ was as far removed from the Eucharist as heaven from earth—so far had he strayed from his former Catholic beliefs.[90]

Though destined for law, Beza preferred biblical studies, and by his translations and commentaries profoundly influenced the sixteenth-century English versions of the Bible. His Latin version of the New Testament, often reprinted, first appeared in 1556; [91] the best edition

[88] *Ibid.*, p. 13. Castalio's admirers warmly defended him against Beza: *Biblia Sacra ex Sebastiani Castalionis interpretatione . . . necnon defensio versionis Novi Foederis contra Theodorum Bezam*, Frankfurt, 1797.

[89] Ward, *Errata of the Protestant Bible*, p. 35; cf. *Cambridge Modern History*, II, 375; F. Buisson, *Sébastien Castellion*, Paris, 1892.

[90] There are two contemporary lives of Beza: N. Taillepied, *Vie de Théodore de Bèze*, 1577; Antoine La Faye, *De vita et obitu Theodori Bezae*, 1606. More recently: F. Schlosser, *Leben des Theodore Beza und des Peter Martyr Vermili*, Heidelberg, 1809; J. W. Baum, *Theodor Beza*, Leipzig, 1843, 2 vols.; H. Heppe, *Theodore Beza*, 1861; H. M. Baird, *Theodore Beza*, New York, 1899.

[91] *Novum D.N.J.C. Testamentum Latine jam olim a vetere interprete, nunc denuo a Theodoro Beza versum, cum ejusdem annotationibus in quibus ratio interpretationis redditur*, Rob. Stephani, 1556. The dedication reads: "Serenissimae Reginae, et suis heroicis virtutibus non minus quam R[egalis] M[ajestatis] splendidae, D. Elizabethae Angliae, Franciae, Hiberniae et circumjacentium insularum Reginae, Fidei Christianae

was that of 1642.[92] But Beza's chief work was his *Novum Testamentum: cujus Graeco contextui respondent interpretationes duae, una vetus* [the Vulgate], *altera Theodori Bezae,* 1565.[93] For this he made use of seventeen MSS., but for the second edition, 1582, he added the evidence of *Codex Bezae* for the Gospels and the Acts, and of *Codex Claromontanus* for the epistles. These two famous MSS. constitute Beza's real claim to fame; the former he seems to have secured after the sack of Lyons by the Huguenots in 1562, and later presented it to Cambridge, whence its other title, *Codex Cantabrigiensis;* the *Codex Claromontanus,* found at Claremont, has been preserved at Geneva since 1557.[94]

Seventeen editions of the Latin New Testament were published during Beza's lifetime, and twenty-eight Greek-Latin editions. The numbering of these editions is quite confusing, for Beza regarded his Latin version of 1556 as first, then numbered his second edition of the Greek Testament (1582) as his second, the edition of 1588 as his third, and that of 1598 as the fourth. In addition to the foregoing editions, his *Annotations on the New Testament,* was published in 1556; there appeared most of his unbalanced criticisms. Though best known for his work on the New Testament, Beza did not neglect the Old, translating and commenting on the Psalms and some of the Sapiential Books.[95]

Propugnatrici. Theodorus Beza. Genevensis Ecclesiae Minister." The Vulgate version stands on the inside in small type, while the *nova ex Graeco translatio* is on the outside in larger type. Beza emphasizes the corrupt state of the Vulgate text. The passage on the woman taken in adultery (John 7:53—8:11) is allowed to stand, but doubts of its authenticity are expressed; of I John 5:7 he says: "Hic versiculus omnino mihi retinendus videtur . . . legit Hieronymus, legit Erasmus in codice Britannico et in Complutensi editione. Legimus et nos in nonnullis Roberti nostri veteribus libris."

[92] *Jesu Christi Domini Nostri Novum Testamentum. Ex interpretatione Theodori Bezae,* Cambridge, 1642; reprinted in Berlin, 1909.

[93] *J.C.D.N. Novum Testamentum sive novum foedus, cujus Graeco textui respondent interpretationes duae una, vetus, altera, nova, Theodori Bezae, diligenter ab eo recognita. Ejusdem Th. B. annotationes quas itidem in hac secunda editione recognovit et accessione non parva locupletavit. Indices etiam duo, theologis (praesertim Hebraicae, Graecae et Latinae linguae studiosis) multum profutura adjecti sunt,* Henricus Stephens, Geneva, 1565.

[94] *Codex Claromontanus sive epistulae Pauli omnes, Graece et Latine ex Codice Parisiensi celeberrimo nomine Claromontani plerumque dicto, sexti, ut videtur, post Christum saeculi. Nunc primum edidit Constantius Tischendorf,* 4to, Leipzig, 1852.

[95] *Psalmorum Davidis et aliorum Prophetarum libri V* [the completion of a translation begun by Marot] *et Latina paraphrasi illustrata ac etiam vario carminum genere Latine expressi, Theodoro Beza Vezelio auctore,* London, 1580; *Jobus. Theodori Bezae partim commentariis, partim paraphrasi illustratus, cui etiam additus est Ecclesiastes, Salamonis concio de Summo Bono, ab eodem Theodoro Beza paraphrastice explicata,* London, 1589.

With many English divines, Beza's Latin version found little favor. Andrews, then bishop of Winchester, therefore commissioned John Bois (1561–1644) to expose its deficiencies.[96] Bois prepared his *Veteris interpretis cum Beza aliisque recentioribus collatio in quatuor Evangeliis et Apostolorum Actis. In qua annon saepius absque justa satis causa hi ab illo discesserint disquiritur,* which was published posthumously in 1655, as death overtook the author before he had finished Romans. R. Simon speaks enthusiastically of it: "There has nothing appeared more exact against the later Latin translations of the New Testament, and chiefly against Beza's. . . . It was no caprice [that] induced him to defend the Ancient Interpreter [St. Jerome] of the Church, but his persuasion that the modern Translators had abandoned him upon slight reasons. He gave manifest proofs that he was exactly acquainted with the subject whereof he treated, and understood the Greek and Latin much better than Beza."

Bois particularly objected to the wholly unnecessary changes effected by Beza, his insertions, for example, of *ille,*[97] and his change of *generationes* into *progenies,* of *poenitentiam agite* into *resipiscite,* thereby deserting, says Simon, "an ancient expression of the Western Churches," just as he did when preferring *offendere* to *scandalizare,* "a term long familiar to Christians." Besides the foregoing, there were such changes as *transportatio* for *transmigratio, Nazaritanus* for *Nazaraenus, praescius locutus est* for *providens,* and so forth.

Despite Bois's strictures, Beza had a marked influence on the various English versions. In the Authorized Version, for example, out of one hundred and thirty-one passages examined by Scrivener, Beza's readings are preferred to those of Stephens eighty-one times. This influence of Beza on the English versions was largely due to L. Tomson and his editions of the Geneva New Testament.[98]

The Rhemists justly complained that the Reformers, typified by Beza,

[96] Bois was an exceedingly learned man and so precocious a genius that it was currently reported that he could speak Hebrew before he was six years old. He translated from Chronicles to the Canticle of Canticles, and part of the Apocalypse for the King James's Version, 1611.

[97] "Ex qua natus est Jesus ille"; "David rex ille"; "in principio erat sermo ille, et sermo ille erat apud Deum, eratque ille sermo Deus."

[98] *The New Testament translated out of Greek by Theodore Beza, adjoyned briefe Summaries by T. Beza. Englished by L. Tomson, together with the Annotations of Francis Junius on Revelation,* 1611–12.

mutilated the text for their own purposes "by changing and adding." They instanced, for example, Acts 9:22 ("affirming that this is the Christ"), which appeared in their editions as "proving (by conferring one Scripture with another) that this is the Christ"; and Acts 14:22 ("and when they had ordained to them priests in every church") the Reformers translate: "they ordained to them (by election) Elders in every congregation"—three significant changes. Instead of "He giveth greater grace" (Jas. 4:6), they wrote "the Scripture giveth greater grace," an addition influenced by Beza's translation, which suggested that *Scriptura* of the previous verse was the subject of *offert*. On the Reformers' treatment of I Pet. 2:13 the Rhemists remark: "In king Henries time and king Edwardes they readde 'to the king as chiefe head,' now 'as having pre-eminence,' and 'as to the Superiour,'" renderings no doubt influenced by Beza, who substituted *supereminenti* for the Vulgate *praecellenti;* Rheims retains "to the king as excelling," but A.V. and R.V. read: "to the king as supreme." In addition to the omission of the name of St. Paul in the title of Hebrews, in 11:21 they have "leaning upon his staffe he [Jacob] adored God," thus, say the Rhemists, "adding two wordes 'leaning' and 'God' to the text, against adoration of creatures, called 'dulia.'"

Beza had no respect for the actual text when he disliked it: he omitted "Cainan" from Luke 3:36 as contradictory to Gen. 10:24, where Arphaxad is called the father, not grandfather, of Sale; yet his "received" text and modern critical texts retain "Cainan." As the Rhemists quaintly remark: "Beza was extreme saucie to dash Cainan out of St. Luke's Gospel, and that wittingly and most impudently saying, in his Annotations: 'Non dubitamus expungere (Cainan).' The former English editions, otherwise corrupt in many places, have 'Cainan' in the text of St. Luke's Gospel, but their later translators in this point are pure Bezites."[99] The fact that his beloved *Codex Bezae*—on the critical value of which he was incapable of passing judgment—omitted the name of Cainan, naturally weighed much with Beza.

What most distressed Catholic critics was not so much the changes made by the Reformers as the hatred they so persistently betrayed for traditional doctrinal teaching. Beza, for instance, insisted on reading

[99] "The truth is, Beza was not much of a textual critic. In settling the text, his mind was more influenced by dogmatical than by critical reasons" (W. L. Alexander in Kitto, *Biblical Encyclopaedia*). Cf. Fulke, *op. cit.*, pp. 43, 57.

Hoc est sanguis meus instead of *Hic est* (Luke 22:20), for he called *Hic est* "a dangerous interpretation,"[100] because "he was afraid that if he translated it according to the Vulgar and Erasmus—'Hic est sanguis meus'—the Blood of Christ would be discovered in a place where he would have only wine appear. Thus does Beza adjust his version to the opinions of his party."[101] Again, disliking the article of the Creed, "He descended into hell," Beza changed *non derelinques animam meam in inferno* into *cadaver meum,* boasting that he had thus eliminated limbo and purgatory as well, "foul ideas," he dubs them, though acknowledging that "most of the old Fathers held the same erroneous views." When Castalio insisted that the Greek did not mean *cadaver,* Beza substituted *anima,* agreeing that *cadaver* or "corpse" was not the fitting word;[102] but he did not much improve matters, for he added: "Though I have changed the word, I keep the same meaning still," since he now held that while Christ's body went into the grave, his soul did not go into hell. Bois's only comment is: " 'anima' is correct, and those who render it otherwise than by 'soul' merely betray their audacity."

Matt. 10:2 reads: "The names of the twelve apostles are these: the first, Simon, who is called Peter." On this Beza calmly remarks: "The word 'first' must be due to some one who favoured Peter's Primacy."[103] Again, Wycliffe, Tyndale, and Cranmer had kept to the traditional and correct "Hail, full of grace" (Luke 1:28); but the later reforming translators preferred Beza's *gratis dilecta:* "thou that art freely beloved" (Geneva); "highly favoured" (A.V. and R.V., though a marginal note in R.V. has "endued with grace"). Finally, when the apostles are said to have been "persevering in prayer with the women" (*mulieribus*),

[100] The Rhemists remark that "Beza disregards the Greek, which makes 'which' agree with 'chalice,' and he makes the clause mean 'the chalice of the New Testament in my blood, which blood. . . .'" But editions of Beza's New Testament vary; that of 1642 has: "Hoc poculum est novum illud pactum per sanguinem meum," while an undated edition (Longmans) reads: "Hoc pactum est novum illud foedus per sanguinem meum." Cf. St. Chrysostom: "Hoc quod in calice est, illud ipsum est, quod ex latere fluxit" (*Homilies on First Corinthians,* XXIV, 1).

[101] R. Simon, *op. cit.,* pp. 195 f.

[102] The edition of 1556 had *non derelinques cadaver meum,* but that of 1582 had *animam meam.* Cf. Gregory Martin, *op. cit.,* p. 51; Fulke, *op. cit.,* p. 158.

[103] How differently St. Ambrose: "Andrew followed our Saviour before Peter; yet not he, but Peter, received the primacy" (*Commentary on II Corinthians,* 12:11). Justly did Gregory Martin liken Beza to Marcion, whom Tertullian styled "the mouse of Pontus" for his "nibbling" at the text of the Bible (*Adv. Marcionem,* I, chap. 1); cf. Martin, *op. cit.,* p. 16.

Beza substituted *uxoribus* (wives) on the ground that "it was only fitting that the apostles' wives too should be strengthened." [104]

Beza's Calvinism appears at every turn; his note on Exod., chap. 7, reads: "God so worketh by evil instruments, that he doth not only suffer them to work, not only moderateth the event; but also stirreth them up, driveth them forward, moveth them, ruleth them, (which is most of all) even createth them, that by them he may work that which he appointed." "Beza saith God ordained Adam's fall, but to a good end: and that God justly decreed that which men unjustly have done." [105]

Richard Simon speaks of Beza as a "good Grecian, but a poor Hebraist, . . . more fit to write common Places of Controversie, than to Translate the New Testament. If we believe him, before his time there was no exact version of the Scriptures, either amongst the Greeks or Latins, and all Antiquity lay grovelling in error." [106] Although Westcott gives credit to Beza for correcting the renderings of earlier translators and declares that "on the whole his version is far superior to those which had been made before, and so consequently the Genevan revisions which follow it," the same author adds that "in spite of the great advances which had been made in scholarship, the true principles of Greek criticism were wholly unknown, and the text which served as the basis of the translation [Beza's Latin New Testament] was as faulty as before." [107]

FRANCISCUS JUNIUS (1545–1602)

Franciscus Junius (François Jonghe) started his career as a lawyer, became a Protestant minister at Bourges, and afterwards taught theology at Geneva and Leyden. He was a much married man: *quatuor uxores hactenus duxi,* he complacently remarks, perhaps with emphasis on *hactenus.* When one of his wives, who was the daughter of Tremellius, died in 1580, Junius re-edited, as a seventh edition, the Latin version of

[104] This substitution (Acts 1:14) appeared in the edition of 1556; a similar change was made in I Cor. 7:1 and 9:5 in the edition of 1579.

[105] See the Rhemists' annotations on Exod., chap. 7, and on Ecclus. 15:9.

[106] *The Critical History of the Versions of the New Testament,* pp. 177, 191.

[107] *A General View of the History of the English Bible,* pp. 229, 213. "Non desunt qui auctorem nimis audacem fuisse judicant, dum et recepta lectione saepius sine necessitate recedit; et unius, interdum nullius, codicis auctoritate fretus praetoriam exercet potestatem, conjecturis mutando et interpretando textum Graecum pro libitu" (B. Walton *Prolegomena* to *Biblia sacra polyglotta,* I, 284, 296). Walton instances Luke 3:36; 9:48, 53; I Cor. 15:55, etc.

the Old Testament in the production of which he and his father-in-law had collaborated.[108] In his Dedication to Frederic IV, Count Palatine, he says he has expanded the original notes and corrected the translation in many places. But, remarks Morerius, "though he made it more bulky, it is doubtful whether he made it any better." Later he added the Apocrypha,[109] which included III and IV Esdras as well as III Maccabees, which latter he placed before I and II Maccabees. This addition he dedicated to William, Prince of Orange and Count of Nassau.

Junius also published a new edition of the Latin New Testament, adding Tremellius' version from the Syriac.[110] The proper names in the New Testament are transliterated in the same extravagant fashion as in the Old: Hiraudis, Jaacub, and so forth. He omitted the passage on the woman taken in adultery. The notes are often far from orthodox; thus on Matt. 26:26: "Mark says 'he gave thanks,' therefore 'to bless' (in Matthew) does not mean to consecrate by some sort of magical muttering: the bread and wine are changed, not in their nature but in their quality." Notes signed F are those of Tremellius edited by Junius, those signed B are by Beza; the rest are taken from Beza, Camerarius, and others.

Junius also wrote commentaries on Genesis, the Psalms, and Ezechiel, besides editing a Hebrew Lexicon, controverting with Bellarmine, and attacking Pope Gregory XIII. But Junius has one claim on our gratitude which is almost forgotten: he was one of the earliest collectors of Anglo-Saxon MSS., and his gifts to the Bodleian were numerous. He himself

[108] *Editio septima et germana a permultis mendis et vitiis Genevensis notha et subreptitia scatet, repurgata et emendata. Cum Indice et Nota V.T. triplici: Hebraeo, Graeco et Latino. Accessit seorsum et de novo in eadem Biblia Index locupletissimus, isque geminus: alter rerum et locorum communium: alter nominum propriorum, cum brevi eorundem explicatione et historia. Hanoviae. Anno M.DC. XXIV.* The dedication of this Index reads: "Illustrissimo, Amplissimo Viro, Domino Francisco Walsingham, Equiti aurato, primo Sereniss. Reginae in Anglia Secretario, et Lancastrensis Ducatus Cancellario."

[109] *Accesserunt libri qui vulgo dicuntur Apocryphi, Latine redditi, et Notis quibusdam aucti a Francisco Junio. Multo omnes quam ante emendatius editi et aucti locis innumeris: quibus etiam adjunximus Novi Testamenti libros ex sermone Syro ab eodem Tremellio, et ex Graeco ex Theodoro Beza in Latinum versos, Notisque itidem illustratos.*

[110] *D.N. Jesu Christi Testamentum Novum, sive Fedus Novum, e Graeco Archetypo, Latino sermone redditum, Theodoro Beza interprete, et jam ultimo ab eo recognitum. Cui ex adverso additur ejusdem Novi Testamenti ex vetustissima translatione Syra, Latine translatio Immanuelis Tremeleii conjuncta notis ad linguae et rerum intelligentiam. Franciscus Junius recensuit, auxit, illustravitque. Hanoviae, M.DC.XXIII.*

edited Caedmon's *Poems* (1655) and the *Codex argenteus,* the Moeso-Gothic version by Ulfilas. He is buried in St. George's Chapel, Windsor.

JOANNES BENEDICTI (c. 1540)

While the Reformers were busy producing their own independent Latin versions, Catholic biblical scholars were striving to secure a more correct Vulgate text, with the result that five years before the Tridentine Decree of 1546, Joannes Benedicti brought out his *Biblia Sacra juxta Vulgatam, quam dicunt editionem, a mendis quibus innumeris, partim scribarum incuria, partim sciolorum audacia scatebat, summa curia parique fide repurgata atque ad priscorum probatissimorumque exemplarium normam restituta,* Paris, 1541. But Benedicti gives no variant readings, nor does he tell us on what principles he endeavored to recover St. Jerome's original text, though he says he has compared the Latin text with the Hebrew and the Greek with a view to restoring the Vulgate text to its "pristine integrity." He is careful to add that he has no desire to change in any captious spirit the Latin text adopted throughout the Church and sung in her Offices. Benedicti's edition was republished many times up till at least 1573.

ENGLISH TRANSLATIONS OF THESE LATIN VERSIONS [111]

It should be observed that apart from the influence of these sixteenth-century Latin versions upon the great English translations that are discussed in the following chapters, two of the Latin texts, those of Erasmus and Beza, were translated and published specifically as translations of them. Dr. Cotton lists a *New Testament, translated from the Latin of Erasmus,* published in 1540 by R. Grafton and E. Whitchurch in London; he also mentions a *New Testament in English and Latin, of Erasmus' translation,* published by Powell of London in 1549.[112] In the Cambridge University Library is a two-volume edition of 1548–49 entitled, *The First* [*Second*] *tome or volume of the Paraphrase of Erasmus upon the Newe Testament,* published by E. Whitchurch in London. The catalogue adds the note: "translated by N. Udall, Tho. Key, Princess Mary, M. Coverdale, J. Olde. Continued by Leo Juda, translated by E. Alen."

[111] This section supplied by Rev. Sebastian Bullough, O.P.

[112] *Lists of Editions of the Bible and Parts Thereof in English* (1852), pp. 17, 21.

Beza's Latin text became well known through the English translation of Laurence Tomson, which is often regarded as a mere revision of the Geneva New Testament, with which, of course, Beza was associated. And although Tomson's text follows Geneva closely, yet the edition of 1576 is stated to be *The New Testament, from the Latin of Theodore Beza. . . . Englished by Laurence Tomson.*[113] An edition of 1609 in the Cambridge University Library also claims to be a translation of Beza's text. Tomson's New Testament gained great popularity; there is record of at least eighteen editions up to 1616 of his New Testament alone. In 1603 [114] for the first time we find a Geneva Bible with Tomson's text printed in place of the Geneva New Testament of 1560, and this substitution occurred many times up to 1616, when Tomson's text was last printed, either alone or in a Geneva Bible.

The sixteenth-century work on the Bible, whether the various Latin versions we have been considering or the series of English versions appearing during that period, had two wholly unexpected results: (1) the decision of the Council of Trent to try to recover the text of the Vulgate as it left St. Jerome's hands, and (2) the appearance of the Catholic English version made at Rheims and Douay, 1582–1610. The King James Bible or Authorized Version, published in 1611, marked the culmination of the long series of efforts to produce a satisfactory English Protestant version. But while the Tridentine Vulgate and the Rheims-Douay Version stood for a reassertion of traditional principles regarding the text, its contents, and its interpretation, the Authorized Version, the outcome of a century of independent work, broke away from tradition, if only in its attitude towards the so-called Apocrypha. The eighteenth century was to witness a complete remodeling of the Rheims-Douay Version by Challoner with an approximation in many places to the Authorized Version; the nineteenth century was to witness in the Revised Version the acceptance of many textual readings contended for by the Rhemists but rejected by the Reformers.

[113] *Ibid.*, p. 41. Tomson regularly uses the word "Englished."

[114] *Ibid.*, p. 56. Further details about his work are given in connection with the Geneva Bible, chapter 15.

CHAPTER X

Tyndale's Translation of the Bible

HISTORY OF TYNDALE'S VERSION

William Tyndale (Hotchyn or Hytchins) was born about 1484 at Stinchcombe, Gloucestershire, and was ordained among the Augustinians at Greenwich about 1503. Disappointed in his efforts to secure episcopal support for his projected English version of the Bible,[1] he went to Hamburg, where he translated the New Testament, which was printed at Cologne in 1525 in quarto. Of this edition only thirty-one leaves, containing the Prologue and Matt. 1:1–22:12, are preserved in the British Museum.

Opposition by Cochlaeus[2] drove Tyndale to Worms, where, in 1525, he printed the first complete English translation of the New Testament since Wycliffe's version.[3] In his "Address to the Reader" he

[1] "I had perceaved by experyence how that it was impossible to stablysh the laye people in any truth, excepte the scripture were playnly layde before their eyes in their mother tonge, that they might see the processe, ordre and meaninge of the text" (Preface to Genesis).

[2] Cochlaeus (Johannes Dobneck: 1479–1552), described by Anderson (*Annals of the English Bible,* p. 31) as "the most virulent enemy to the Word of God being translated into any vernacular tongue, who ever breathed," was a canon at Warsaw. A determined opponent of Luther, he published at Mayence, 1549, *Commentaria de actis et scriptis Martini Lutheri;* he also wrote *De canonis Scripturarum auctoritate* and *De novis ex Hebraeo translationibus S. Scripturae disceptatio,* 1544. See Grisar, *Luther* (ed. by Elbe), p. 366; Baronius, *ad annum* 1540, no. 60.

[3] *The First New Testament Printed in the English Language (1525 or 1526), . . . reproduced in facsimile,* published by Francis Fry, 1862; *The First Printed English New Testament, Photolithographed from the Unique Fragment in the B(ritish) M(useum),* ed. by E. Arber, 1871, 1895; *The New Testament . . . by that eminent scholar and martyr William Tyndale, reprinted verbatim with a Memoir of his life and writings,* ed. by George Offor, 1836; *The Beginning of the New Testament Translated by William Tyndale, 1525; facsimiles of the unique fragment of the uncompleted Cologne edition,* Introduction by A. W. Pollard, 1926. The latter contains also Tyndale's text of Matt., chap. 5, as published in 1535, and underneath are given the corresponding texts from the Great Bible of 1539, the Genevan version of 1560, the Bishops' Bible of 1572, the Rheims Version, 1582, and the Authorized Version, 1611.

says: "Consyder howe that I had no man to counterfet, nether was holpe of englysshe of eny that had interpreted the same, or sache lyke thinge in the Scripture before tyme." [4] Only two copies of this octavo edition survive: one, complete except for the first page, at Bristol, the other, mutilated, at St. Paul's, London.[5] Though he himself produced no other edition until 1534, Dutch printers published at least four pirated ones,[6] and as Tyndale still delayed to produce a corrected edition, Joye, the printer, felt himself justified in doing so: [7] "I considred with myself: Englond hath ynow and to many false testaments and is now likely to have many mo." This edition appeared in 1534 with wholly unwarranted changes which provoked Tyndale's wrath.[8] Yet perhaps Joye was not so much to be blamed, for he says:

I had nothing to do with the printing ther of, but correckted their copie only, as where I founde a worde falsely printed, I mended it: and when I came to some derke sentencis that no reason coude be gathered of them whether it was by the ignorance of the translatour or of the prynter, I had the latyn text by me and made yt playn: and where any sentence was unperfite or clene left oute I restored it agene: and gave many wordis their pure and native significacion in their places which thei had not before.[9]

Joye's edition thus "corrected" appeared in 1534,[10] and Tyndale felt compelled to produce a corrected edition: *The newe Testament dylygently corrected and compared with the Greke by Willyam Tindale; and fyneshed in the yere of oure Lorde God* A.M.D. XXXIIII in the

[4] Dore, *Old Bibles*, p. 23.

[5] *Ibid.*, p. 30; Pollard, *op. cit.*, p. 6.

[6] So asserts Joye in his *Apologie*, given in Pollard, *op. cit.*, p. 189.

[7] The only existing copy, in Cambridge University Library, edited by E. Arber.

[8] "I was astonied and wondered not a lytle what furye had dryven him to make soche chaunge and to call it a diligent correction." He especially complained of "lyfe after this lyfe" or "verie lyfe" for "resurrection," for "ye shall understonde that George Joye hath had of a longe tyme marvelouse ymaginacyons aboute this worde resurreccion, that it shuld be taken for the last state of the soules after their departinge from their bodyes." See the whole diatribe given at length in Pollard, *op. cit.*, pp. 178–87.

[9] In his *Apologie*, Joye defended his faith in the doctrine of the resurrection, yet even there he often avoided the term "resurrection," though at times he retained it.

[10] *The New Testament as it was written and caused to be written by them which herde yt. Whom also oure saveoure Christ Jesus commaunded that they shulde preach it unto al creatures.* The colophon at the end runs: "Here endeth the New Testament dylygently oversene and corrected and printed now agayne at Andwarp, by me widow of Christophell of Endhoven. In the yere of oure Lorde A.M.D.XXXIIII in August. Which tytle (reader) I have here put in because by this thou shalt knowe the booke the better. Vale."

moneth of November, printed by Marten Le Emperour (de Keyser).[11] In his "Address to the Reader," Tyndale says: "I have looked [it] over agayne (now at the last) with all dylygence and compared it unto the Greke and have weded oute many fautes which lacke of help at the begyninnge and oversight dyd sowe therein." He defends his renderings, "repentance" for "penance" and "elders" for "priest." There are 232 marginal notes[12] and a Prologue to each book. A copy in the British Museum has "Anna [Boleyn ?] Reginae Angliae" written in red letters on the gilded edges.[13]

In the Preface to the New Testament we read: "Confession, not to the prestes eare, for that is but mannes invencion, but to God." In the "Address to the Reader": "Whether we call them elders or prestes, is to me all one; so that ye onderstonde that they be offycers and servauntes of worde of God, unto the which all men both hie and lowe that will not rebell agaynst Christ must obey as long they preache the rule trylye and no longer."

The edition of 1534 was not Tyndale's final revision; for in 1534–35 he brought out *The newe Testament yet once agayne corrected by Willyam Tindale: Where unto is added a Kalendar and a necessarye Table wherin easely and lightelye maye be founde any storye contayned in the foure Evangelistes and in the Actes of the Apostles. Prynted in the yere of oure Lorde God, MD XXXV*. The monogram "G.H." on the title page probably stands for Godfried van der Hagen, though Fry took it for Guillaume Hytchins.

In this, his final revision, which served as the basis for Matthew's edition, Tyndale made many changes; in 333 places it differs from his previous revision, and in 494 places from Joye's edition.

> Sometimes the changes are made to secure a closer accordance with the Greek; sometimes to gain a more vigorous, or a more idiomatic rendering: sometimes to preserve a just uniformity: sometimes to introduce a new interpretation. The very minuteness of the changes is a singular testimony to the diligence with which

[11] *The New Testament Translated by William Tyndale, 1534. A reprint of the edition of 1534 with the translator's prefaces and notes and the variants of the edition of 1525*, ed. by N. H. Wallis, with Introduction by Isaac Foot, Cambridge University Press, 1938. There is a Prologue to each book, though one serves for the three epistles of St. John.

[12] These notes seem wholly innocuous; e.g., on Rom. 10:10: "Though faith justify, . . . yet is the promise made on the condition that we embrace Christ's doctrine and confess him in word and deed. So that we are justified to do good works, and in them to walk to the salvation promised."

[13] Dore, *op. cit.*, p. 35.

Tyndale still laboured at his appointed task. Nothing seemed trifling to him, we may believe; if only he could better seize or convey to others the meaning of one fragment of Scripture.[14]

A comparison with his first edition (1525) will further show how laboriously Tyndale corrected and refined his renderings. Matt. 5:9: "Blessed are the maynteyners of peace" (1525), "Blessed are the peacemakers" (1534); Matt. 5:15: "see that your light so shine . . ." (1525), "let your light so shine . . ." (1534); Matt. 6:28: "Behold the lilies of the field" (1525), "Consider the lilies of the field" (1534); Matt. 13:23: "some fiftie fold" (1525), a curious slip corrected in 1534 to "sixtie fold"; Matt. 19:14: "For unto such belongeth the kingdom of God" (1525), "For of such is the kingdom of God" (1534); Matt. 26:17 and elsewhere: "unleavened bread" (1525), "swete bred" (1534); Mark 14:5: another slip, "two hundred pence" (1525), corrected in 1534 to "three hundred pence"; Luke 15:17: "then he remembered himself and said . . ." (1525), "then he came to himself and said . . ." (1534); Acts 8:36: "a gelded man" (1525), "a chamberlayne" (1534); Acts 19:24: another slip, "Demetrius a goldsmith" (1525), corrected in 1534 to "silversmith."

Tyndale translated from Erasmus' second edition, 1519, and added I John 5:7 as Erasmus had done in his edition of 1525. In his later editions he departs from the Vulgate and Wycliffe and gives renderings derived from the Latin version by Santes Pagninus, which had appeared in 1528.[15]

In 1530–31 Tyndale brought out in separate volumes *The Five Books of Moses;*[16] the only known copy of which is in the British Museum. He had begun by translating Deuteronomy, but lost it when at sea. At Hamburg, however, he translated the whole Pentateuch between Easter and December, "in the house of one Margaret van Emerson." His version of Jonas came in 1531,[17] with a Prologue in which he called on the king to restrain the prevailing opposition to vernacular versions of the Bible.[18]

[14] Westcott, *A General View of the History of the English Bible* (1905), pp. 144 f.

[15] Cf. *The Quarterly Review,* October, 1911, p. 510.

[16] Reprinted by Mombert in 1884: *William Tyndale's Five Books of Moses Called the Pentateuch, a verbatim reprint of the edition of 1530, compared with Tyndale's Genesis, 1534, the Pentateuch in the Vulgate, etc.* Cf. E. G. Duff, *A Short Account of Tindale's Pentateuch (1530),* 1910.

[17] Reproduced by F. Fry in facsimile, *The Prophete Jonas,* 1863. Cf. Anderson, *op. cit.,* p. 158; Dore, *op. cit.,* p. 78.

[18] "At what time Tyndall had translated the fift book of Moises called Deuteronomium, minding to Printe the same at Hamborough, hee sailed thereward: where by the way

Hall states positively that Tyndale "translated the New Testament into Englishe and fyrst put it in Prynt, and likewise the v. bookes of Moses, Josue, Judicum, Ruth, the bookes of the Kynges and the bookes of Paralipomenon, Nehemias or the fyrst [the second ?] of Esdras, the Prophet Jonas, and no more of holy scripture." [19]

TYNDALE'S LEARNING AND ABILITY AS A TRANSLATOR

Opinions differ regarding Tyndale's learning and the merits of his translation. Blunt declares:

> These works all show the marks of a keen and clear, but extremely self-sufficient man, with enough knowledge of languages to make such a man suppose himself learned, but without any real depth of learning, and with enough facility of expression to lean him to argue, but without any argumentative power. He was also of a very cankered and bitter temper, which led him to fill his pages with abusive language, even when writing of the most sacred subjects. His language respecting the latter was often so shocking, and at the same time so utterly illogical, that it led Sir Thomas More to stigmatize him as a "blasphemous fool." It is certainly a strong evidence of the extent to which party feeling will lead that Tyndale should ever have been respected as a theological writer.[20]

On the other hand Sir Thomas More and Cochlaeus regarded Tyndale as "full prettily learned"; while Herman Bosch even said that he was "so skilled in seven languages, Hebrew, Greek, Latin, Italian, Spanish, English, French, that whichever he spoke you would suppose it was his native tongue." [21] Yet others maintain that he was really ignorant and that his

upon the coast of Holland, he suffred shipwracke, by the which he loste all his bookes, wrytings and copies, and so was compelled to begin all agayne anew" (Foxe, *Actes and Monumentes* [1853], pp. 1076 ff.) Mombert (*op. cit.*, pp. 110 ff.) contends that for Hamburg we should read Wittenburg. See also: E. G. Duff, *op. cit.*; J R. Slater, *The Sources of Tyndale's Version of the Pentateuch*, 1906; E. W. Cleaveland, *A Study of Tindale's Genesis Compared with the Genesis of Coverdale and of the Authorized Version*, Yale Studies in English, XLIII, 1911; a full account will be found in Dore, *op. cit.*, pp. 66 ff.

[19] *Chronicle: The Union of the Two Noble Illustrious Families of Lancastre and Yorke*, p. 818, published by Grafton in 1548; given by Pollard, *op. cit.*, pp. 195 f.

[20] *History of the Reformation of the Church of England* (1882), I, 547 f.

[21] Quoted by Tyndale's friend, John Frith, in a letter to Sir Thomas More. This statement, surely an exaggerated one, seems to be taken over by Dore, who says that Tyndale "had a wonderful faculty for acquiring foreign languages, and was thorough master of English" (*op. cit.*, p. 25). Yet in view of Tyndale's knowledge of Greek it is strange that he should have omitted the definite article in "Art thou (the) Christ?" (Mark 14:61.) The fact that Tyndale made free use of Pagninus' Latin version from the Hebrew,—his version, for instance, of Exod. 15:10 and Num. 22:34 is derived from Pagninus, not from the Vulgate—may perhaps discount efforts made to credit him with a knowledge of Hebrew.

version was simply made from the Vulgate and Luther's German translation.

No one can question, however, that Tyndale was an admirable translator. Geddes, severest of critics, says: "Though Tindall's is far from being a perfect translation, yet few translations will be found preferable to it. It is astonishing how little obsolete the language of it is, even at this day; and in point of perspicuity and noble simplicity, propriety of idiom and purity of style, no English version has yet surpassed it." [22] Froude, too, says: "The peculiar genius—if such a word may be permitted—which breathes through it—the mingled tenderness and majesty—the Saxon simplicity—the preternatural grandeur—unequalled, unapproached in the attempted improvements of modern scholars—all are here, and the impress of the mind of one man—William Tyndale." [23]

Gairdner too pays a handsome tribute to Tyndale's merits as a translator:

> The whole English-speaking world is indebted to him for his vigorous and lucid translation of the Scriptures, which, so far as it extended, became ultimately, with really rather few alterations, the text of the familiar Bible of King James. Tyndale was, for his day, a fair scholar in Greek and Hebrew, and he applied all his learning most conscientiously to the great object he had at heart, of putting the source and fountain of all divinity within the reach even of the least educated readers, that they might form their own views of the Gospel independently of any teaching from professional theologians. That this was a really dangerous design founded on a view of Scripture which was in itself superstitious does not diminish our admiration for the enthusiasm with which he embarked on the great project, and the perseverance with which he carried it through.[24]

Tyndale's version is a mixture of singularly felicitous renderings with some that are decidedly quaint: the young man who fled was "clothed in linnen upon the bare" (Mark 14:51—Vulgate: *vestitus sindone supra nudum*), a rendering surpassed only by the Rhemists: "clothed with sindon on the bare"; the "second-first Sabbath" (Luke 6:1) is the "aftersaboth"; Peter is called a Galilean "because thy speache agreth therto"

[22] *A General Answer to the Queries . . . since the publication of his Proposals,* p. 4. Yet Tyndale is at times almost guilty of colloquialism; e.g., when he represents Pharao as saying to Abraham: "There is thy wife; take her, and be walking."

[23] *History of England,* III, 84, quoted by Ellicott, *Considerations on the Revision of the English Version of the New Testament,* p. 61 note. Ellicott adds: "These words the student will find truly deserved. The more Tyndale's labours are considered, the more will they be valued."

[24] *Lollardy and the Reformation in England,* I, 367 f.

(Mark 14:70, where the Greek text is followed); Pilate is the "leftenaunt of Jewrie" (Luke 3:1); the centurion, "the under captayne" (Mark 15:39); Zachary's "lott was to bren odours" (Luke 1:9); "it came to pass" is given as "it fortuned"; St. Paul calls Ananias "thou paynted wall" (Acts 23:3); "unleavened bread" is "the feast of swete breed which is called ester"; the basket of fragments becomes a basket "of gobbetes."

In Tyndale's version the Baptist was "a burnynge and shyninge light" (John 5:35), where Wycliffe had, correctly, "a lanterne brennynge and schynynge," Rheims, "the lampe burning and shining," and R.V., "the lamp that burneth and shineth"; unfortunately Challoner followed Tyndale, Cranmer, and A.V., substituting "a light" for "the lamp." As a rule "verily" replaces "amen," but in John 6:55: "for my flessche is meate *in dede;* and my bloud is drynke *in dede";* so Cranmer, Geneva, Rheims, A.V., and R.V. (which has a marginal note: "Greek, true meat, true drink"). Among other things, Tyndale seems to have been responsible for the introduction of the word Jehovah into the English. "Where he got it we do not know. Luther knows nothing of the word, which is first heard in the thirteenth century in Raymund Martin, . . . according to Drusius in his *Tetragrammaton* of 1603. 'Ante illum inauditum fuit nomen Jehova.' "[25] Tyndale had, to the dismay of St. Thomas More, read "love" instead of "charity" (I Cor., chap. 13) and "flock" for "fold" (John 10:16), also "except ye turn as little children" (Matt. 18:3). The Authorized Version removed all these blemishes, yet the Revised Version reverted to them.

TYNDALE'S HERETICAL TEACHINGS

Tyndale's emphatic assertion that he "nether was helpe with Englysshe of eny that had interpreted the same"[26] led Pollard to conclude that he had made no use of Wycliffe's version;[27] yet their almost identical renderings of a multitude of passages—e.g., Matt. 12:18; 13:20; Luke 1:38—would argue an intimate relationship between the two versions.[28] Indeed Gairdner, who describes Lollardy as "an influence which arose mainly out

[25] J. Isaacs, in *The Bible in Its Ancient and English Versions,* p. 165.

[26] Epilogue to the quarto edition, 1525.

[27] *Op. cit.,* p. xiii.

[28] A comparison can readily be made in Bosworth's *Gothic and Anglo-Saxon Gospels in Parallel Columns with the Versions of Wycliffe and Tyndale,* 1865.

of Wycliffe's translation of the Bible, and which tended to regard the book more and more as an infallible and all-sufficient guide in faith and morals, capable also of infallible interpretation by private judgement," goes on to say: "this influence was revived by the publication of Tyndale's New Testament and by the power of the printing press in disseminating copies of that and other heretical literature." [29]

It seems idle to deny, as some do,[30] that Tyndale was infected with Lutheranism. Henry himself declared that the new version contained "many corruptions of the holy text, as certain Prefaces and other pestilent glosses in the margents for the advancement and setting forth of his abominable heresies." [31] Sir Thomas More, too, in his *Dialogue* (III, viii) asserts it as an established fact: "For so had Tyndale after Luther's counsayle corrupted and chaunged yt [the New Testament] from the good and holsome doctryne of crist to the devylysh heresyes of their own."

Indeed since Gruber printed Luther's Preface and Tyndale's Prologue in parallel columns, showing that in "the important parts" the latter is "a virtually direct translation from Luther," [32] no doubt on the point can remain. Luther and Tyndale even agree in their Tables of Contents, both inserting the epistles of John before Hebrews and James, both numbering the books I to XXIII, but omitting to number the remaining ones. Again, Tyndale takes over 55 of Luther's 67 notes on Matt. 1:1–22:12, while he adopts 185 of the 208 notes in Luther's third (Wittenberg) edition.

[29] *Op. cit.*, I, 328.

[30] Westcott, *A General View of the History of the English Bible*, p. 36; Anderson, *Annals of the English Bible*, pp. 24 f.; Moulton, *The History of the English Bible*, pp. 76–78. For the opposite view, see Hoare, *The Evolution of the English Bible* (1902), pp. 146 f.; Mombert, *The English Versions of the Bible*, pp. 88–99.

[31] For the king's belief that Tyndale was instigated by Luther, see his answer to the letter addressed to him by Luther, who, writes Henry, "fell in device with one or two lewd pearsons born in this our realm for the translating of the New Testament into English, as well with many corruptions of that holy text, as certain prefaces and other pestilent glosses in the margents for the advancement and setting forth of his abominable heresies." Henry, therefore, with the advice of Wolsey, insisted on copies of Luther's New Testament being burned, 1526–27 (in Pollard, *op. cit.*, pp. 115 f.). See also the Royal Proclamations of May and June, 1530, in which the editions by Tyndale and Joye are condemned (*ibid.*, pp. 161–69). It is also true, of course, that Henry never forgave Tyndale for his opposition to the divorce; see Offor's edition of Tyndale's New Testament, p. 77. The King's repeated efforts to secure his person are well known.

[32] *The Truth of the So-called Luther's Testament in English*, 1917; reprinted from *The Lutheran Church Review*, 1916–17.

"The familiar Prologue to the Romans," writes Workman, "is . . . for the most part a paraphrase or a translation of Luther's Preface," and he goes on to say:

It is in the shorter Prologues to the several books of the New Testament first published in 1534 that the character of the dependence of Tindale on Luther is best seen. Luther has no special Prologues to the Gospels, but Tindale at the close of his Prologue to St. Matthew . . . reproduces in a modified form Luther's famous judgment on the relative worth of the apostolic books in his Preface to the New Testament. . . . [Tindale's Prologue to Galatians] incorporates a large piece of Luther's, but is fuller, . . . that to the Hebrews is a sustained argument against Luther [on the question of the Pauline authenticity of this epistle, which Tyndale upholds].[33]

The conviction that in the contemporary state of affairs vernacular versions of the Scriptures would only lead to the further propagation of the purely subjective ideas on doctrine then in vogue, compelled Tunstall to decline to translate the Acts of the Apostles for Cranmer's proposed version in 1535.[34] It was the same with Stokesley: "Is there none other word of God," he asked, "but that which every sutor and cobbler read in their mother tongue? If ye think that nothing pertaineth to the Christian faith but that only which is written in the Bible, ye err with the Lutherans." And again, apropos of the number of the sacraments: "It is false, and not to be allowed, that all sacraments ought rather to have a manifest ground in Scripture; or show forth some signification of the remission of sins." [35]

As Gardiner pointed out in the course of his controversy with Bucer, the innovators inserted a "but" before "Do this in commemoration of Me" (Luke 22:19) to suggest that the Holy Eucharist was but a reminder

[33] *John Wyclif, a Study of the English Medieval Church,* pp. 147, 150.

[34] Nichols, *Narratives of the Days of the Reformation* (1842), pp. 277 f.; see *Four Supplications of the Commons,* Early English Texts, X–XI, (1871); Dixon, *History of the Church of England,* I, 522 ff.

[35] Constant, *The Reformation in England* (1934), p. 373 note. See Tyndale's *A Briefe Declaration of the Sacraments, expressing the fyrst originall how they came up, and were institute with the true and moost syncere meaning and understandyng of the same very necessarye for all men;* Tyndale there speaks of the sacraments as "bodies of stone only, and there is (in them) none other virtue than to testify and exhibit to the senses and to the understanding the Covenantes and promises of Christ," and again: "The cause of the institution of the Eucharist was to be a memorial, to testify that Christ's body was given and his Blood shed for us." Was it through a determination not to see a divine person in the "Word" that Tyndale, followed by Cranmer and Geneva, rendered John 1:3 f.: "All things were made by it, and without it was made nothing. . . . In it was life"? Wycliffe had written "hym"; so, too, Rheims, A.V., and R.V. adopted this rendering.

of the passion of Christ.[36] But worst of all, in several of his editions of the New Testament, Tyndale omitted I Pet. 2:13 f.: "Be ye subject therefore to every human creature for God's sake: whether it be to the king as excelling, or to governors as sent by him for the punishment of evildoers, and for the praise of the good." "Such an error," says Blunt, "was quite enough justification for the suppression of Tyndale's translation." [37]

Tyndale maintained that so far as the translation was concerned, he was completely honest: "I call God to recorde . . . that I never altered one syllable of Godes worde agaynst my conscyence." [38] And in a protest prefixed to his revised edition of 1534 he emphatically declared that he had not performed his task "either to stir up false doctrine or opinion in the Church, or to be the author of any sect, or to draw disciples after me, or that I would be esteemed above the least child that is born, but only out of pity and compassion which I had, and yet have, on the darkness of my brethren, and to bring them to the knowledge of Christ." [39]

But while accepting this statement unreservedly, agreeing, too, that except for such renderings as "congregation" for "Church," "elder" for "priest," and so forth, there is little to complain about in Tyndale's version, we have to bear in mind that it was not merely the fact that he was presenting an English version, nor even the character of that version, which called for condemnation, so much as the man himself, the rebel against all constituted authority, who stands revealed in chance renderings here and there, and more especially in his notes. Fully to appreciate the situation we have to take into account not only his New Testament, but his translations of other parts of the Bible, his Prologues to various books, and his many anti-clerical publications. As regards Tyndale's actual text, his attitude towards the sacraments appears in Ephes. 5:32: "This is a gret secrete, but I speak bitwene Christ and the congregacion"; so, too, with regard to the royal supremacy: "Submit youre selves . . . unto the kynge as unto the chefe heed" (I Pet. 2:13). Significant also is his rendering of Luke 1:35: "That holy thynge which shall be borne," omitting "of thee."

[36] *A Detection of the Devil's Sophistrie, wherewith he robbeth the unlearned people of the true belief in the Most Blessed Sacrament of the aulter,* 1546.

[37] *History of the Reformation of the Church of England,* p. 514; cf. Gasquet, *The Old English Bible,* p. 131; Dixon, *op. cit.,* I, 451 f.

[38] See the Prologue to his first New Testament, Cologne, 1525; see also the Epilogues to the second edition, Worms, given by Pollard, *op. cit.*, pp. 111–17.

[39] Given by Hoare, *The Evolution of the English Bible* (1902), p. 147.

TYNDALE'S NOTES

But it was the notes to the version which proved especially offensive. Those in his first edition are known to us only from the fragments, and there the note on Matt. 16:16–18 is particularly objectionable. It should not be forgotten that even as a young friar Tyndale cavilled at authority, and that he complained of the way ecclesiastical students were "armed with false principles, with which they are clean shut out of the understanding of the Scripture, . . . which is locked up with false expositions and with false principles of natural philosophy." [40] Purely subjective in outlook, he became a law unto himself. King Henry himself, fully alive to this, the prevailing attitude, condemned subjective interpretations of the Bible, for, he said, "people had forgotten the difference between the teachers and the taught." [41] The same had already been said by Gardiner: "Scripture is a sweet pure flower whereof spiders gather poison and bees honey. . . . Go thither instructed with wholesome doctrine and there thou shalt see it confirmed. Go thither infected with malicious opinions and there thou shalt writhe out matter wherewith to maintain them." [42]

Now this very subjectivism betrays itself at every turn in Tyndale's notes. For example, on "What is this new doctrine?" (Mark 1:27): "That that was then new, after 1536 years, is yet new. When will it be old?" On which Strype comments: "This was to meet the common reproach then given to the religion reformed that it was a new upstart religion." Again, apropos of the prudent virgins who declined to part with their oil, Tyndale notes, against works of supererogation, that "their own good works sufficed not for themselves; and therefore remained none to be distributed to their fellows." Commenting, too, on Matt. 16:19, he claims that the power to bind and loose belonged equally to all the apostles, alleging Matt. 18:18 and John 20:23 in support.

The translation itself provoked criticism, but Tyndale's notes caused such consternation that he felt obliged to omit from his octavo edition in 1525 the distinctively Lutheran marginal notes which had stood in the folio edition of 1525.[43] But in his first revision, November, 1534, he in-

[40] Quoted by R. Demaus, *William Tyndale,* p. 22.

[41] See Lloyd, bishop of Oxford, *Formularies of Faith Under Henry VIII,* p. 215.

[42] Quoted by Constant, *op. cit.,* p. 373.

[43] Dore, *op. cit.,* pp. 20, 25.

serted 232 marginal notes.[44] After his death various notes were inserted by different publishers; Daye and Seres brought out an edition in 1548 with wholly fresh notes attributed by some to Bale, bishop of Ossory.[45] In 1548 Redman's edition introduced notes by Thomas Matthew,[46] though he omitted these as well as chapter headings from another edition he published in the same year, with Erasmus' Latin version side by side with Tyndale's English.[47] Later on, in 1553 and 1554, Jugge set forth an entirely new set of notes, the character of which can be gauged from that on Apoc., chap. 17: "The womannes variable garmentes, betokeneth divers liveries of religious orders, or the rose colour sygnyfye a redines to shed Christen bloude. The cupful of abbominations, etc., the pope's decrees, decretalles, bulles, dispensations, suspentions, and cursynges: the beast she sytteth on, is the papall seate." [48]

On the other hand, nothing could be more orthodox than Tyndale's note on Matt. 1:25 ("he knew her not till she brought forth. . . ."): "Ye shall not," he says, "suppose that he knewe her afterwards, but hit is the maner of the scriptures so to speake as gen. viii c. 'the ravin came. . . .' Evyn so here hit followeth not Joseph knewe oure lady afterwarde." The note on Peter's "confession," too, is quite orthodox (Matt., chap. 16); though on Matt. 26:26, orthodox and unorthodox interpretations of "This is my body" are set down side by side.

In fact, the more we examine Tyndale's writings, the more evident it becomes that the bishops had no alternative but to condemn them. Gairdner says of him:

> His New Testament, like his other works, was intended to produce an ecclesiastical and social revolution, of a highly dangerous character, aided by mistranslations of Holy Writ and sophistical glosses in the margin. . . . There is a perverse and bitter spirit running through the whole design. The marginal glosses have long been dropped, and the most offensive mistranslations have long been corrected, but the spirit of the author was visible in many little turns of expression which look harmless now.[49]

[44] These were omitted in the edition of 1540 as being "offensive" (Strype, *Memorials,* I, 489, 595); nor do they appear in the editions by Offor and Bosworth.

[45] Dore, *op. cit.,* p. 53.

[46] *The New Testament . . . newly set forth after the beste copie of Wyllyam Tindale's translation, whereunto are added the Notes of Thomas Mathewe* (i.e., John Rogers), 1548.

[47] Dore, *op. cit.,* p. 49.

[48] *Ibid.,* p. 64.

[49] Gairdner, *Lollardy,* I, 228; II, 367.

The same must be said even more emphatically of Tyndale's notes on the Pentateuch, which show that "in translating Scripture he wished to hold up Bishops to opprobrium as murderers, though he knew well that heretics were burned only by order of the civil power."[50] "This production," says another, "was provocative in many ways. Tyndale seized the occasion to emphasize the contradiction between the Church practice and the laws of God. His glosses to this end were indeed 'pestilent.'"[51]

Is it to be wondered at, then, that the authorities all over England combined to suppress the new English Testament? Edward Lee, afterwards archbishop of York, saw clearly the inevitable outcome of the ideas then prevailing; for he wrote from Bordeaux to Henry VIII on December 2, 1525, when Tyndale's version was fresh from the press:

> I need not advertis your Grace what infection and danger ensue hereby if it be not withstood. This is the next way to fill your realm with Lutherians, for all Luther's perverse opinions be grounded upon bare words of Scripture not well taken or understood, which your Grace hath opened in sundry places of your Royal Book. All our forefathers, governors of the Church of England, hath with all diligence forbade and excluded publications of English Bibles as appeareth in constitutions provincial of the Church of England.[52]

CONDEMNATION OF TYNDALE'S NEW TESTAMENT

The appearance of this New Testament in English provoked a storm similar to that which arose about fifty years later at the publication of the Rheims New Testament. But rightly to appreciate the attitude of the authorities towards the new version and its accompanying notes, we have to bear in mind the consternation everywhere felt at the flood of heresy let loose on Europe by Luther's teachings. Leo X had denounced him,[53] had conferred on Henry VIII the title of "Defender of the Faith" for his refutation of the heresiarch's attack on the sacraments,[54] and had

[50] *Idem, The English Church in the Sixteenth Century* (1899), p. 190; cf. *idem, Lollardy,* II, 243.

[51] Isaacs, in *The Bible in Its Ancient and English Versions,* ed. by H. W. Robinson, p. 165. Tyndale's *Obedience of a Christian Man* and his *Practice of Prelates* were even more violently anticlerical publications.

[52] An unqualified statement to be understood in the sense in which Archbishop Arundel in his Constitution of 1408 and his commentator Lyndwood understood it.

[53] Foxe, *Actes and Monumentes,* VI (iv), 250; VIII (v), 321, 660–88; Wilkins, *Concilia,* III, 689.

[54] *Ibid.,* III, 695.

bidden him secure the suppression of his works.[55] In pursuance of this aim, Wolsey had drawn up a list of forty-two erroneous propositions therein,[56] and Archbishop Warham, writing in 1526 to Voysey, bishop of Exeter, had said:

> Partisans of the Lutheran faction have cunningly and deceitfully translated into the English tongue, not only the Gospels, but the other parts of the New Testament; instilling pernicious scandals into the minds of simple folk, and profaning the hitherto unsullied majesty of the holy Scriptures by wicked and distorted interpretations whereby they endeavour with subtlety and perverse minds to wrest from the sacred word of God its true meaning. Printed copies of this translation, some, as we hear, with glosses and some without, but presenting the same pestiferous and dangerous teachings in an English dress, are spread throughout your dioceses and the Province of Canterbury, and that promiscuously.[57]

The archbishop concludes: All who within a specified time fail to surrender copies in their possession, incur excommunication. Certain Lutheran works are mentioned by name, *The Supplication of Beggars* and the *Revelation of Antichrist;* likewise "The New Testament of Tindall," his treatises, *The Wicked Mammon* and *The Obedience of a Christian Man,* and his Introduction to Romans.

Perhaps the most damning criticism of Tyndale's version was that by Robert Ridley, brother of Nicholas Ridley, the future bishop of London. When chaplain to Stokesley, bishop of London, Robert Ridley, in a letter to the then chaplain of Archbishop Warham, spoke of Tyndale and Roy as "manifest Lutherans and apostates as doth openly appear not only by their daily and continual company and familiarity with Luther and his disciples, but much more by their commentaries and annotations in Matthew and Mark, their Preface to the second edition and their Prologue to the Romans. . . . The Preface to the first edition is mere phrenzy." Tyndale, he says, makes the Lord's Prayer no part of the Gospel, besides removing other portions. He repudiates the state of virginity, rejects the notion of good works, and "by this translation shall we lose all these Christian words, penance, charity, confession, grace, priest, Church, etc."[58]

[55] *Ibid.,* 690–93.

[56] *Ibid.,* 711.

[57] *Ibid.,* 706.

[58] Given in Pollard, *op. cit.,* pp. 122–24, from a Cotton MS. in the British Museum "dated February 24—almost certainly of the year 1527."

DENUNCIATION BY TUNSTALL

Tunstall was even more emphatic (October 24, 1526):

By the duty of our pastoral office we are bound diligently with all our power to foresee, provide for, root out and put away all those things which seem to tend to the peril and danger of our subjects and specially the destruction of their souls, wherefore we having understanding by the report of divers credible persons, and also by the evident appearance of the matter, that many children of iniquity, maintainers of Luther's sect, blinded through extreme wickedness, wandering from the way of truth and the Catholic faith, craftily have translated the New Testament into our English tongue, entermeddling therewith many heretical articles and erroneous opinions, pernicious and offensive, seducing the simple people, attempting by their wicked and perverse interpretations, to profanate the majesty of the scripture . . . and craftily to abuse the most holy word of God, and the true sense of the same.[59]

Tunstall was not content with verbal denunciations; he bought and burned as many copies as he could. How else could he have acted? But though there is no doubt about the facts, the highly colored account, dwelt upon with such gusto by the prejudiced, rests on the sole authority of Foxe,[60] of whom such an authority as J. S. Brewer says: "Had he been an honest man, his carelessness and credulity would have incapacitated him from being a trustworthy historian. Unfortunately he was not honest; he tampered with the documents that came into his hands, and freely indulged in those very faults of suppression and equivocation for which he condemned his opponents."[61]

How regrettable it is that for so much of the history of the period we have no better authorities than Bale "the foul-mouthed,"[32] and Foxe, a pair of bigots, whom Littledale called "those matchless liars."[63]

Whether ill-advised or not, and however regrettable from the point of view of the biblical student or the bibliophile, so effective were the measures taken by Tunstall that, though no less than six editions appeared between 1525 and 1528, amounting perhaps to as many as 18,000

[59] In Pollard, *op. cit.*, pp. 131 f.

[60] *Actes and Monumentes*, IV, 666, 753; V, 414, 565, 696; cf. Pollard, *op. cit.*, pp. 87 f., 150–53; Strype, *Ecclesiastical Memorials*, I, 537; *Memorials of Archbishop Cranmer*, II, 24; Wilkins, *Concilia*, III, 847. These New Testaments were burned on two occasions, in 1526 and in May, 1530; cf. Hall's *Chronicle*, p. 771; Gairdner, *Lollardy and the Reformation in England*, II, 237; Foxe, *op. cit.*, VI (viii), 696.

[61] *The Reign of Henry VIII*, I, 52.

[62] Gairdner, *op. cit.*, IV, 72.

[63] *Innovations* (1868), p. 42.

copies, only a fragment of the original quarto edition has survived, and only one complete copy of the octavo edition. After all, Tunstall had no monopoly of burning. Tyndale himself had publicly burned the Bull of Leo X and copies of the canon law, while Calvin had burned Servetus' Bible because of the notes, which he disliked.

According to Roy, the heretic, Tunstall declared that there were at least 3,000 mistranslations in Tyndale's New Testament.[64] That is probably a rhetorical statement; the figure is generally given as 2,000.[65] Yet Tunstall was a scholar and familiar with the Greek Testament.

Tyndale naturally was pleased with the profits thus unexpectedly accruing from Tunstall's action. "I am glad, for these two benefits shall come thereof: I shall get money to bring myself out of debt, and the whole world will cry out against the burning of God's word, and the overplus of the money that shall remain to me shall make me more studious to correct the said New Testament, and so newly to imprint the same once again." [66] But, as Dore remarks: "Since he had sold the books to Augustine Packington, well knowing the purpose for which they were being purchased, he was a participator in the crime, and as much to be blamed as the Bishop of London. The fact is the books were full of errors and unsaleable, and Tyndale wanted money to pay the expense of a revised version." [67]

Those who make capital out of Foxe's narrative and picture Tunstall as a simpleton,[68] fail to realize that for him to expend approximately £300 on buying these copies was a disinterested act and regarded by him as a duty.

SIR THOMAS MORE'S "LICENCE" TO READ HERETICAL WORKS

In the following year, 1527, Tunstall took the practical step of inducing Sir Thomas More to take up his pen against the prevailing heretical

[64] Gairdner, *op. cit.*, II, 227.

[65] Gregory Martin, *A Discoverie of the Manifold Corruptions of the Holie Scriptures*, no. 29; Fulke, *Defense of the Sincere and True Translations of the Holie Scriptures*, p. 61; Mombert, *English Versions of the Bible*, p. 102; Burnet, *The Life of William Bedell*, p. 386.

[66] He seems to have used this unexpected windfall to pay for the expenses of his translation of parts of the Old Testament. Cf. Gairdner, *op. cit.*, II, 238.

[67] Dore, *op. cit.*, p. 26.

[68] "Tunstall could scarcely have been such a simpleton as to have no misgivings as to the effect of his policy" (Gairdner, *op. cit.*, II, 234).

tenets. He therefore licensed him to study their works with a view to their refutation. He reminds him that translations replete with the heretical notions of Wycliffe and of Luther, his disciple, are flooding the country, and that unless some competent person will undertake to set out in print these erroneous teachings with the Catholic answer to them, there is grave danger that many may make shipwreck of their faith. He is convinced that Sir Thomas has the requisite qualifications; he has, moreover, an incentive in the good example of the king himself, who by his refutation of Luther's work on the sacraments has earned, not only the title, "Defender of the Faith," but also a deathless reputation. But since effective refutation demands precise knowledge of what these heretics are teaching, Tunstall is sending him copies of some of their recent publications as well as some of the writings of Luther on which they are based; full licence to read and keep such writing is of course accorded him.[69]

The outcome of this "licence" was, of course, the famous *Dialogue,* or rather a series of dialogues, between More and Tyndale. These do not concern us here. Though they have met with discourteous treatment at the hands of certain prejudiced critics,[70] recent students of the period are more open minded.

Tunstall did not stand alone in his condemnation of Tyndale; practically the whole of England followed suit. A synod at Ely, June 19, 1528, forbade the clergy "to use the Bible in the new version in their churches,"[71] while a provincial synod 1529 (?) condemned certain books because "they contain teachings opposed to the Catholic Faith and doctrine of Holy Mother Church." Among these books the bishops specify "the corrupt translation into English of the New Testament made by William Hitchyns, *alias* Tyndall." The bishops assembled at

[69] This licence, granted March 7, 1527, is found in Tunstall's Register, London, fol. 138. Cf. Wilkins, *Concilia,* III, 711-f.; Foxe, *op. cit.,* VI (viii), 679, 697.

[70] Anderson is particularly venomous, showing nothing but contempt for the great Chancellor and his work; the idea of a vernacular version was, he says, "an eyesore" to More (*Annals of the English Bible,* p. 156; cf. pp. 183, 211). See also: Moulton, *History of the English Bible,* pp. 27, 83, 104, 124; Burnet, *History of the Reformation,* I, 263; but on the other hand see: Gairdner, *op. cit.,* I, 100–118; II, 221–303, 426; *idem, The English Church in the Sixteenth Century,* p. 190; J. P. Whitney, in *Cambridge History of English Literature,* pp. 58–63 (ed. of 1907–11, III, 44 ff.).

[71] "Injunctum est quod rectores et curati biblia secundum novam interpretationem in ecclesiis nullo modo utantur, aut per quoscunque alios ecclesias suas accedentes sic uti sinant, nec eadem interpretatione utantur in praedicationibus suis" (Wilkins, *op. cit.,* III, 713).

this synod then proceeded to formulate anew the principles laid down in Archbishop Arundel's famous Constitution of 1408:

Further, still walking in the footsteps of our fathers before us, we forbid any one in future to sell, make presents of, loan, buy, print, write, publish, read, spread abroad or make known, either in whole or in part, whether in public or in private, or to retain possession of, any tractate, works on, programmes of, or any books whatsoever containing Holy Scripture or interpretations of it, translated into the vernacular, unless they have permission in writing from the Bishop of the Diocese, and such books have been shown to him and after diligent examination have been approved by his authority.[72]

JUSTIFICATION OF TUNSTALL AND THE OTHER BISHOPS

It has long been the fashion to speak of Tunstall as a bitter opponent of vernacular versions because he declined to further Tyndale's project for an English version of the Bible after he had an interview with him, and because he burnt copies of the latter's New Testament, which he rightly felt did not faithfully represent the original and was, moreover, replete with notes subversive of the Catholic faith. It is well to realize that Tunstall was a finished Greek scholar, the friend and patron of Erasmus, and perfectly competent to assess Tyndale's version at its true value. St. Thomas More speaks of him as "so excelling in learning, wit and virtue that the whole world hath not at this day any more learned, wiser or better." Strype styles him "a learned and sober prelate," and Burnet "the last and the most eminent of all the Popish clergy." [73] Foxe and Fuller [74] both are loud in his praises; even Cromwell's visitator, the notorious Thomas Legh, wrote in enthusiastic terms of the "gentle and lowly entertainment" he met with at Tunstall's hands.[75] Hereford calls

[72] *Statuta et ordinationes praelatorum in concilio provinciali edita* (almost certainly Canterbury, 1529): Cotton MS. Cleop. F.ii; in Wilkins, *Concilia,* III, 712. Chap. 6, *De haereticis et haereticorum libris,* enumerates, *inter alia,* the following which are condemned: *Parabola Mammonae iniquitatis; Obedientia Christiani hominis; Translatio N. T. in lingua Anglicana a Willielmo Hitchyns, alias Tindall, corrupta; Introductio in epistolam ad Romanos; Practica praelatorum,* et alius qui vocatur *A.B.C. to the Prelacy;* also several works by Luther, Melancthon, Pomeranus, and Brentius; Frith, *The Disputation of Purgatory;* and *Liber compilatus per fratrem Willielmum Roy contra septem Sacramenta ecclesiae* (cf. Wilkins, *op. cit.,* III, 713). Anderson loses all sense of proportion when he comes to the story of Tyndale's version and the opposition it met with at the hands of the bishops (*op. cit.,* pp. 1 ff.). Mombert is more temperate, though very prejudiced against the episcopal authorities (*op. cit.,* pp. 123 ff.).

[73] Strype, *Ecclesiastical Memorials,* III, 88; Burnet, *History of the Reformation,* III, 356.

[74] Fuller, *The Church History of Britain,* IV, 192.

[75] *State Papers, Henry VIII,* Foreign and Domestic, VIII, no. 311.

him "a mild man and of the most sweet conditions, in regard whereof I do not a little wonder that he was so hardly dealt with." [76]

It has been left to modern writers to vilify the fair name of Tunstall. Anderson, for instance, betrays a positively rabid hatred of him, speaking of his "cold barbarity" and "cool malignity," calling him "a worldly-wise man," "an ingenious tormentor," "a leading persecutor of the faith." [77]

> The hostility of Tunstall and his colleagues is not so inexplicable as perhaps it may appear at first sight. In the first place the translation was notoriously opposed to the supremacy of Rome; and this was further made clear by the fact that a large part of the marginal notes were directly translated from Luther's German Bible. But further, an element of novelty, which was naturally regarded as erroneous, if not heretical, was introduced by the fact that Tyndale made his translation direct from the original Greek, and not from the familiar Latin Vulgate; and in so doing he took pains to avoid the old ecclesiastical terms, such as "church" and "priest," and to substitute "congregation," "senior," and the like.[78]

It was not, then, the fact of a translation being made accessible to the people that provoked Tyndale's condemnation, but the unquestioned fact that it was a heretical publication. "It was not as a mere translation of the Bible that Tyndale's work reached England. It came as part of the Lutheran movement, and it bore the Lutheran stamp in its version of ecclesiastical words. . . . We can hardly wonder that More denounced the book as heretical." [79] As Canon Dixon says:

> If the clergy had acted thus, simply because they would have kept the people ignorant of the Word of God, they would have been without excuse. But it was not so. Every one of the little volumes containing portions of the Sacred Text that was issued by Tyndale, contained also a Prologue and notes, written with such a hot fury of vituperation against the prelates and clergy, the monks and friars,

[76] *Annals,* p. 223. In a similar strain Camden says of him: "Omni politiori literatura instructissimus, multis bonorum gradibus domi decursis, et legationibus celebris . . . grandaevus Lambethae in libera custodia obiit" (*Annals of Queen Elizabeth,* p. 37).

[77] *Annals of the English Bible,* pp. 20, 49, 72, and *passim;* cf. *Cuthbert Tunstall,* by Charles Sturge, 1938.

[78] British Museum, *Guide to the Manuscripts and Printed Books Exhibited in Celebration of the Tercentenary of the Authorized Version,* p. 11. "Looking back, we ought to be aware that the great shipwreck of the old system really did produce disastrous and demoralising results; that it set men afloat in tempestuous seas on rafts made of the broken timbers of what had once been Peter's ship; that the attempt to preserve the unity and independence of a national Church only led to cruelty and repression; and that at last we have found peace—if we have found it even now—in what might almost be called the principle of an agnostic State trying to hold the balance between contending denominations" (Gairdner, *Lollardy,* II, 229).

[79] J. R. Green, *History of the English People,* II, 127 f.

the rites and ceremonies of the Church, as . . . was hardly likely to commend it to the favour of those who were attacked.[80]

Dore remarks:

> The only wonder is that Tyndale's animosity to the Church of England, and his strong Lutheran bias, did not produce a still greater crop of errors. The English Bishops carefully examined Tyndale's translation, and instead of making a better one, as they ought to have done, endeavoured to suppress it. They had the greatest reverence for what Tunstall calls "the most holy word of God," and considered Luther's [Tyndale's ?] Testament to be a profanation of it, they therefore felt it their duty to destroy every copy they could obtain.[81]

TYNDALE'S EXECUTION

It is often implied, if not stated in so many words, that Tyndale died for daring to give Englishmen a Testament which they could understand. But there is no proof that churchmen of those days were as a body opposed to having the Bible circulated in English. Nor is there any truth in the widespread notion that Tyndale's version proved an eye opener to the people of England. Yet a modern writer asserts that "the contrast between Christianity as disclosed in the sacred literature, and the version of Christianity which the Medieval Church presented, was so extreme, that not even the simplest reader could fail to see it." [82]

The simple truth is, of course, that Tyndale was put to death for obstinately holding heretical views and that his translation was objected to because it—and, more especially, his marginal notes—was intended to be a means for propagating those views. It is hard to believe that a man of Tyndale's gifts was not perfectly aware of this, though he did say:

> Yet I tell the trouth, yf ye lyst to take hede
> Agaynst theyre frowarde, furious frenesy
> Which recken it for great heresy,
> And unto laye people greuous outrage,
> To haue goddes worde in their natyfe language.

[80] *History of the Church of England,* I, 451 f.

[81] *Old Bibles,* p. 25. Tyndale's *Obedience of a Christian Man* "aimed at nothing less than a complete subversion of the whole system then prevailing; and it was surely not too much for Sir Thomas More to call it Tyndale's 'mad Obedience' " (Gairdner, *op. cit.,* II, 375). How many who sneer at these condemnations have really read these scurrilous productions by Tyndale and his fellows? They can be read in the Parker Society edition of Tyndale's Doctrinal Treatises and his Expositions, especially his *Practice of Prelates* and his *Obedience of a Christian Man.* Anything more crude, illogical, and ignorant would be hard to find; cf. Gairdner, *op. cit.,* I, 366 ff.

[82] H. Hensly Henson, *William Tyndale,* p. 19.

EDITIONS OF TYNDALE'S NEW TESTAMENT

The history of the numerous editions is complicated.[83] The first, in quarto, appeared at Cologne, 1525, and the Prologue to it was reproduced by Tyndale as *A Pathway into the Holy Scriptures,* under which title Thomas More refers to it in his *Dialogue,* though he does not seem to have been aware of its authorship. The second edition, in octavo, was printed at Worms, also in 1525.[84] In 1534 Joye published an edition in 16mo for the widow of Endhover. Again in the same year, 1534, came Tyndale's first personally corrected edition, published by M. Le Emperour.[85]

Many pirated copies, mostly Dutch, appeared. In 1536 no less than seven were published, three in quarto, three in octavo, and one in folio; the latter was entitled, *The newe Testament yet ones agayne corrected by W. Tyndale, and in many places amended where it scaped before by neglygence of the printer. . . . Newly printed in the yere of our Lorde M.D.XXXVI.* Yet even this "corrected" copy was not without mistakes: "the wolf eateth them," for "catcheth them" (John 10:12); "be not afraid of every man," instead of "every shadow" (I Pet. 3:6). The three editions in quarto and octavo all omit "this cup is the new testament in my blood" (I Cor. 11:25).

Publishers took liberties even in those days. Van Meteren of Antwerp was not ashamed to bring out an edition in quarto with the title, *The newe testamente of our savioure Jesu Christ, newly and diligently translated into Englysshe by Thomas Mathew with annotations in ye mergent to helpe the reader to the understandyng of ye Texte. Set forth with the kynges moost gratious lycence. Anno M.D.XXXVIII.* The gratuitous insertion of the name of Thomas Mathew was simply done in the hope that Henry VIII would not notice that the version was really that by

[83] The fullest account of all the editions is that given by F. Fry: *A Bibliographical Description of the Editions of the New Testament: Tyndale's Version in English. With numerous readings, comparisons of texts and historical notices. The Notes in full from the edition of November, 1534.* Fry gives detailed accounts of forty editions of Tyndale's New Testament. But he needs to be supplemented by Dore, *Old Bibles,* p. 26–65; see also Nestle, in *J.T.S.,* October, 1908.

[84] Dore, *op. cit.,* pp. 33–36; Kenyon, *Our Bible and the Ancient Manuscripts* (1939), p. 2. The first copies arrived in England early in 1526.

[85] *The New Testament Translated by William Tyndale, 1534,* ed. by N. Hardy Wallis, Cambridge University Press, 1938; cf. Dore, *op. cit.,* pp. 33–36.

Tyndale, whom he hated. Once more in 1538 Redman of London brought out *The newe Testament in Englyshe and in Latin. Novum Testamentum Anglice et Latine. Anno Dni. 1538.* The colophon runs: "Thus endyth the newe Testament both in Englyshe and in Laten of mayster Erasmus translacio[n], with the Pystles take[n] out of ye Old Testament. Set forthe with the kinges gracious lycence, and Imprinted by Robert Redman dwellyng in Flete Strete at ye signe of the George nexte unto saynte Donstons Churche. The yere of our Lorde, M.CCCCC. XXXVIII. and the thyrty yere of the Kynges most gracious reygne. God save the Kynge." There are no notes or chapter headings.[86]

The long series of editions by Jugge began in 1548, the most important edition being that of 1552: *The Newe Testament of our Saviour Jesu Christe, faythfully translated out of the Greke. Wyth the Notes and Expositions of the darke places therein. . . . The Pearle, which Christ commaunded to be baught Is here to be found, not elles to be sought.* There is a portrait of Edward VI, and the parable of the sower is illustrated by a picture of the devil having a wooden leg.[87] The notes drawn up for this edition continued to appear in the Bishops' Bible until 1619. Between 1547 and 1553 seventeen editions appeared, though it is questionable whether this was due to a popular demand or merely to action by the Government.[88]

The precise date of various editions is difficult to discover, for as Dore points out (p. 56): "No dependence can be put on the titles of many Bibles and Testaments: often printers made inaccurate statements from ignorance; but in other cases the title page was composed in order to sell the book, without any regard to the truth."

BIBLIOGRAPHY

Bullock, C. *Who gave us "The Book"? Or England's Debt to William Tyndale,* 1884.

Clarke, F. L. *The Life of William Tyndale,* 1883.

Cooper, W. B. *The Life and Work of William Tyndale,* 1924.

Demaus, R. *William Tyndale,* 1871; a new ed. (abridged) by W. Watts, 1935.

[86] Dore, *op. cit.,* p. 49. In 1548 and 1550 Daye and Seres issued an edition of *The new Testament in Englishe after the Greeke translation annexed; with the translation of Erasmus in Latin.*

[87] See Fry, *op. cit.,* pp. 118 f., 145–49.

[88] W. P. M. Kennedy, *Studies in Tudor History,* p. 49.

Guppy, H. *William Tindale and the Earlier Translators of the Bible into English, with twelve facsimiles,* The Rylands Library, 1925.

Isaacs, J. "The Sixteenth Century English Versions," in *The Bible in Its Ancient and English Versions,* Oxford, 1940, pp. 149–67.

Kingdon, J. A. *Incidents in the Lives of Thomas Poyntz and Richard Grafton, who suffered loss and incurred danger in common with W. Tyndale in bringing out the Bible in the vulgar tongue,* 1895.

Mozley, J. F. *William Tyndale,* 1937.

——— and J. R. Coates. *Tyndale Commemoration Volume, reproducing parts of the revised Testament of 1534, with some original woodcuts, and an account of the Translator's Life and Influence,* ed. by R. M. Wilson, 1939.

Smith, G. B. *William Tyndale and His Translation of the English Bible,* 1896.

CHAPTER XI

Coverdale's Version, 1535

LIFE AND WORK OF MYLES COVERDALE

MYLES COVERDALE (1488–1569), an Augustinian friar, was ordained priest in 1518. His prior was, at one time, the notorious Dr. Barnes, afterwards burned for heresy. In 1527, or perhaps 1532,—the date is disputed—Coverdale wrote from his convent the following letter to Cromwell,[1] to whose notice he had been brought by a certain Mr. Moore: [2]

Most singular good master, with due humility I beseech unto your mastership all godly comfort, grace and prosperous health. . . . If it like your favour to revocate to your memory the godly communication, which your mastership had with me your orator in master Moores house upon Easter Eve, amongst many and divers fruitful exhortations, especially of your singular favour and by your most comfortable words, I perceive your gracious mind towards me. Wherefore, most honourable master, for the tender love of God, and for the fervent zeal that you have to virtue and godly study, cordis genibus provolutus, I humbly desire and beseech your goodness of your gracious help. Now I begin to taste of holy scriptures: now, honour be to God! I am set to the most sweet smell of holy letters, with the godly savour of holy and ancient doctors, unto whose knowledge I cannot attain without diversity of books, as is not unknown to your most excellent wisdom. Nothing in the world I desire but books, as concerning my learning: they once

[1] *Remains of Bishop Coverdale,* ed. by G. Pearson, Letter I, p. 490. Neither date seems reconcilable with the date of Barnes's trial, 1525; cf. Mombert, *English Versions of the Bible,* p. 150. Gairdner would refer it to "not later than 1527" (*Lollardy and the Reformation in England,* II, 250); cf. *Cambridge Modern History,* II, 465. At any rate it is clear that even if this letter can be referred to the earlier date, only eight years had elapsed since the days when he was a friar and drinking in his love of the Bible in a convent and out of the Vulgate Bible.

[2] "It is quite a mistake to suppose, as some writers have done (e.g., Anderson, *Annals of the English Bible,* p. 557) that the man so named is Sir Thomas More; for the idea that Thomas Cromwell and Coverdale once met in Sir Thomas More's house, and had what they called 'godly communication' there, is absolutely incredible. For what those of Coverdale's school called 'godly communication' would never have been tolerated by Sir Thomas" (Gairdner, *op. cit.,* II, 254). In a footnote Gairdner points out that the spelling "Moorys" and "Moores" in the letters cannot, according to the spelling of the time, stand for "More."

had, I do not doubt but Almighty God shall perform that in me, which he of his most favourable grace hath begun. Moreover as touching my behaviour, (your mastership's mind once known), with all lowliness I offer myself not only to be ordered in all things as shall please your wisdom, but also as concerning the education and instruction of other alonely to ensure your prudent counsel. Nam quidquid est in te consilii, nihil non politicum, nihil non divinum est: [3] quidquid enim agis, nihil inconsulte agis, nusquam te primum philosophum praebes; de rore autem coeli summam, more Jacob, surripuisti benedictionem. De tuo ipso torrente maxime potari exopto, teque coram alloqui non mediocriter cupio. Vale, decus litterarum, consiliorum, omnium denique probitatum.

From the Augustin's, this May-day,

Frere Myles Coverdale

Although the "Mr. Moore" referred to above cannot be identified with St. Thomas More, it may well be that the latter did encourage Coverdale in his self-imposed task of translating the Bible.[4] For Coverdale must have been well aware of More's attack on Tyndale's malicious renderings of certain familiar ecclesiastical terms; it is therefore significant that Coverdale should have restored most of those changed by Tyndale, substituting "charity" for "love" and "priest" for "elder," though he still retained "congregation" instead of "church." Most significant of all, perhaps, are his words on the Greek *metanoia:* "This maner have I used in my translacyon, calling it in some place 'penaunce,' that in another place I call 'repentaunce.' " [5] It is noteworthy, too, that while denouncing Tyndale and Luther by name in his *Dialogue,* More never mentions Coverdale.

When Barnes repudiated Catholicism, Coverdale followed his lead,

[3] Yet no one familiar with Cromwell's record as portrayed in the *State Papers* can refuse to endorse Hoare's words: "Cromwell was an adventurer without a spark of religious principle, and one whose conduct appears to have been consistently regulated by his ambition so to manipulate and manage his master as to secure for himself both fame and fortune by playing Protestantism as the winning political card." The Act of Attainder, §31 (*Henry VIII,* chap. 62), shows his support of every Wycliffite tenet, especially as regards the Blessed Sacrament. Hoare continues: Cromwell was "a man of greater ability and even greater ambition [than Wolsey], trained abroad in the principles of Macchiavelli, but with his fortunes staked on the success of the Reformation, and in that sense therefore a zealous political Protestant" (*Evolution of the English Bible* [1901], pp. 147, 174). Although Collier quotes Foxe as stating that Cromwell knew the Vulgate New Testament by heart, he declares that Cromwell "was neither a Catholic nor a Protestant" (*An Ecclesiastical History of Great Britain,* V, 73).

[4] "Who it was that, against Coverdale's own wish, induced him to undertake the task of translating the Bible is not known; most likely it was the good Sir Thomas More and those of the new learning party with whom he was associated" (Dore, *Old Bibles,* p. 90).

[5] See below, p. 171.

threw off his religious habit, acted as a secular priest, and at length began to preach against the Mass and the practice of confession. Under Edward VI he became a royal chaplain, received a permanent dispensation from the law of abstinence, and had a living conferred on him in London. He even became an active persecutor of priests who failed to remove the name of St. Thomas à Becket from their missals, and actually went to serve as chaplain to the troops sent to suppress the rising in Devon and Cornwall in 1549.[6] When Cromwell fell into disgrace in 1540, Coverdale fled abroad and married, despite his monastic vows. Imprisoned under Mary Tudor but shortly after released at her order, he again went abroad. On the accession of Elizabeth he returned and became the first Protestant bishop of Exeter in place of Voysey; he was one of the assistants at Parker's consecration. Dying at the age of eighty-one, he was buried in St. Bartholomew's, Smithfield, but in 1840 his bones were removed to the church of St. Magnus.[7]

It is strange that one so unassuming, so self-effacing as Coverdale, one, too, who justly enjoys great literary fame, should indulge in the intemperate language of which his controversial writings are full. And while we can understand his condemnation of those whom he calls "the rich and wealthy bellies" and his complaint of "the gorgeous fare and apparel that ye have every day for the proud pomp and appetite of your stinking carcases," [8]—for no doubt the state of the Court called for condemnation —there can be no excuse for the unrestrained language he used about the Church he had left. When dedicating his version of the Bible to Henry VIII, on whom the Pope had conferred the title of "Defender of the Faith," Coverdale was not ashamed to speak of the Supreme Pontiff as comparable only to Caiphas and Balaam, especially to the last named: "Ye blynde bysshoppe of Rome (that blynde Balaam I saye) not understandynge what he dyd, gave unto your grace this tytle: 'Defendour of the faythe,' only because youre hyghness suffred your Bysshoppes to

[6] Strype, *Ecclesiastical Memorials,* III, 46. See Coverdale's letters to Cromwell, February, 1539, on the number of priests at Newbury who, to his thinking, have incurred the penalties of *praemunire* for retaining the name of St. Thomas of Canterbury in their missals and the Office for the Chair of St. Peter in their breviaries, which is "plainly a maintenance of the bishop of Rome's usurped power." He asks, too, that the stained-glass window at Henley commemorating the martyrdom of St. Thomas be broken up. Cf. *State Papers, Henry VIII,* XIV, i, nos. 243, 253, 444.

[7] See Dore, *op. cit.,* pp. 88–90.

[8] Prologue to his Latin and English New Testament.

lurne Gods worde, the root of fayth." Nor does Coverdale leave us in any doubt as to his religious convictions; in the course of his sermon at the funeral of Katherine Parr, he thought it necessary to remind those present that "there shuld none there thinke, say, nor spread abrorde, that the offerynge which was there don, was don anye thinge to proffyht the deade, but for the poore onlye; and also the lights which were caried and stode abowte the cors, were for the honour of the parson, and for none other entente nor purpose." [9]

Bearing in mind, too, that he had for many years been in the habit of saying Mass, what could be in worse taste than Coverdale's sneers at "the whisperings, duckings, and crossings, besides the demure countenance in their turn and half turn"? Not content with this, he goes on to speak of "Romish idolators and diligent students of duncical dregs," while insisting that "those who make it [the Mass] a sacrifice for the redemption of sin receive it to their damnation . . . to hoise it over their heads, to dance it over the cup, to carry it in the streets with great pomp and glory, to bow their knees and to knock their breasts before it, and to lock it up in a pix, to have it ready to serve at all hours all such chapmen as shall call for it, is but a politic cast of the merchants." [10]

EARLY EDITIONS

Coverdale's version of the Bible—perhaps the first complete English translation of the whole Bible—appeared in 1535 with the title: *Biblia: The Bible, that is, the holy Scripture of the Olde and New Testament, faithfully and truly translated out of the Douche and Latyn into English,* M.D.XXXV. It was almost certainly printed at Zurich by Froschover, and the expenses seem to have been borne by Jacob Van Meteren.[11]

[9] Quoted in the *Memorials of Myles Coverdale* (anonymous).

[10] *Treatise on the Lord's Supper;* cf. *A faythful treatyse concernynge the most secret sacrament,* 1549, 1550; *Works of Coverdale,* Parker Society, pp. 422–66. See also Pearson, *Remains of Bishop Coverdale,* p. 490; Mombert, *op. cit.,* 150. "Coverdale was not a figure of marked historical interest. He was somewhat weak and timorous, and all through life he leaned on more powerful natures. Barnes, Cromwell, Cranmer, and Grindal were successively his patrons. In the hour of trouble he was content to remain in obscurity, and left the crown of martyrdom to be earned by men of tougher fibre" (H. Guppy, in *Bulletin of the Rylands Library,* XIX [1935], 327).

[11] There seems to be some controversy about this matter. On Cromwell's fall in 1540, Coverdale seems to have gone to Holland, where, according to an affidavit by Emmanuel Van Meteren, the latter's father "caused the first Bible at his costes to be Englisshed by Mr. Myles Coverdal in Andwerp, the which his father, with Mr. Edward Whytchurch, printed both in Paris and London" (cf. Gairdner, *op. cit.,* II, 273 f.). Yet L. A. Sheppard

Froschover had prefixed certain preliminary pieces, notably a Prologue by Coverdale. But, as it was forbidden to bring into England books already bound, the sheets were sent to Nicolson of Southwark, and he, apparently through fear of adverse comment, omitted the words "out of Douche and Latyn" from the title; he also substituted for Coverdale's original Prologue a Dedication to Henry VIII and a different Prologue, both composed by Coverdale.[12]

After the Dedication to Henry, nine columns long, there follow a long Prologue, "Myles Coverdale to the Reader," [13] and a list of the books of the Bible. The Apocrypha—III and IV Esdras to II Machabees—follow after Malachi. The chapter headings are grouped together at the beginning of each book.[14] In the New Testament the two epistles of St. Peter and the three of St. John come before the Epistle to the Hebrews, which is followed by James, Jude, and Revelation. The colophon at the end reads: "Prynted in the yeare of ore Lorde M.D.XXXV and fynished the fourth daye of October."

This first edition was not "authorized"; in fact, the very year after its publication, Convocation (June, 1536) petitioned the king "that he would graciously indulge unto his subjects of the laity the reading of

seems to have proved that the volume was printed at Zurich by Froschover (cf. "The Printers of the Coverdale Bible, 1535" in *The Library,* 4th series [1935], no. 3, p. 280–89).

[12] This edition is exceedingly rare; Lord Ashburnham's copy, though not quite complete, sold for £820. In 1838 Bagster reprinted the original edition of 1535. Two titles are given: *The Holy Scriptures faithfully and truly translated in to English. M.D.XXXV. S.Paul.ii.Tessa.iii: Praie for us, that the worde of God maie have free passage, and be glorified, etc.; fully and truly translated by Myles Coverdale, Bishop of Exeter, 1535. Reprinted from the copy in the collection of his Royal Highness the Duke of Sussex,* 1838. The second title is in black letter: *Biblia: The Bible, that is, the holy Scriptures of the Olde and New Testament, faithfully and truly translated in to English M.D.XXXV. S.Paul. II.Tessa.iii 'Praie for us, that the worde of God maie have free passage, and be glorified, etc.'*

[13] Given in Pollard, *Records of the English Bible,* pp. 200–206.

[14] In the Prologue, "To the Gentle Reader," prefixed to the first edition but omitted by Nicolson, Coverdale explains this procedure by saying: "I have considered that every man hath not at all times such leisure as to read or to turn the Bible from one chapter to another when they shall have a desire or occasion to seek for any special matter contained herein; this considered, I thought it most needful and necessary to print and set the summaries of all the Books contained in this most sacred Bible together in their order, whereby thou mayest easily find out not only how the Books stand in order and how many chapters every Book containeth, but most especially thou shalt find most speedily how God by the mouth of his most holy Prophets promised the Redemption of the world by our only hope and Saviour Jesus Christ by suffering in that most perfect flesh which it pleased him to take on him in the womb of that most pure virgin Mary" (see Dore, *op. cit.,* pp. 102 f.).

the Bible in the English tongue, and that a new translation of it might be forthwith made for that end and purpose." This looks tantamount to a condemnation, or at least a repudiation, of Coverdale's work. The second edition, published by Nicolson in folio and quarto in 1537, did, however, receive the royal license.[15]

Fifteen years later Froschover reprinted Coverdale's Bible with the title: *The Whole Byble, that is the Olde and Newe Testamente truly and purely translated into Englishe by Mayst Thomas Mathewe. Imprinted at Zurich by Chrysoffer Froschower,* 1550.[16] The strange attribution of the translation to Thomas Matthew (John Rogers) may be due to the hope that, since Matthew's version had received a royal licence, there might be more chance—if the present edition could be taken for the work of Matthew—of securing a sale in England for what was really Coverdale's version.[17] Publishers took amazing liberties even in those days. Meanwhile Hester had bought up Froschover's edition and produced it in the same year, 1550, with a new title.[18] But just as Nicolson had taken liberties with Froschover's original edition, 1535, so did Hester now take liberties with Froschover's reprint, omitting thirty-six pages of preliminary matter, including the Prologue by Coverdale beginning

[15] Dore, *op. cit.,* p. 94; Moulton, *The History of the English Bible,* p. 99.

[16] The words, "translated out of the Douche and Latyn" are again omitted, presumably through fear lest any supposed affinity with the Lutheran body should lead to opposition. Coverdale himself omits them in his Prologue to the Reader, merely speaking of translations in Latin "and in other languages." But in the Introduction to Bagster's reprint, 1838, precisely the opposite interpretation is put on the clause: "The mention of its being translated out of Douche and Latyn was no doubt a bookselling artifice of the time to make the work circulate better, as being intimately connected with the reformed doctrines which were then equally well known by the term of German or Dutch doctrines."

[17] Foxe leaves no doubt about the fictitious character of this attribution to Rogers (Thomas Matthew): "In this translation of this Bible the greatest doer was William Tyndale, . . . but it was thought good to them that had the doing thereof to change the name of William Tyndale, because that name then was odious, and to father it by a strange name of Thomas Matthewe; John Rogers, at the same time, being corrector of the print, who had then translated the residue of the Apocrypha, and added also certain notes thereto in the margin; and therefore came it to be called 'Thomas Matthewe's Bible'" (*Actes and Monumentes,* V [viii], 410). This ruse, adds Foxe, secured the Royal licence for the edition. Foxe wrongly supposed that Tyndale had himself already translated all the Old Testament save the Apocrypha.

[18] *The Whole Byble, that is the holy scripture of the Olde and New Testament faythfully translated into Englyshe by Myles Coverdale and newly oversene and correcte*[*d*]. *M.D.L. Pray for us that the worde of God may have free passage and be glorified, II.Tess.iii. Prynted for Andrewe Hester. dwellynge in Pauls church yard at the synge of the whyte horse and are there to be solde.*

"Gentle Reader." The Dedication to Henry VIII was replaced by one to Edward VI, and a new Prologue to the Reader, also by Coverdale, replaced the one omitted, which is of more interest for the account Coverdale there gives of the origin of his translation.

Considering how excellent knowledge and learning an interpreter of Scripture ought to have in the tongues, and pondering also mine own insufficiency therein, and how weak I am to perform the office of a translator, I was the more loath to meddle with this work. Notwithstanding when I considered how great pity that we should want it so long, and called to my remembrance the adversity of them [Tyndale] which were not only of ripe knowledge, but would also with all their hearts have performed that they began if they had not had impediments: considering, I say, that by reason of their adversity it could not so soon have been brought to an end, as our most prosperous nation would fain have had it: these and other reasonable causes considered I was the more bold to take it in hand, and to help me herein I have had sundry translations, not only in Latin but also in other languages: whom (because of their singular gifts and special diligence in the Bible) I have been glad to follow according as I was required.

But to say the truth before God, it was neither my labour nor desire, to have this work put in my hand, nevertheless it grieved me that other nations should be more plenteously provided with the scripture in their mother tongue, than we in ours; therefore what I was instantly required (though I could not do so well as I would) I thought it yet my duty to do my best, that the scripture might wholly come forth in English. For the which cause (accordynge as I was desyred anno 1.5.34) I toke the more upon me, to set forth this specyall translacyon, not as a cheker, not as a reprover, or despiser of other mens translacyons (for among many as yet I have found none without occasion of great thanksgiving unto God) but lowly and faithfully have I followed mine interpreters, and that under correction. . . . Howbeit, wherein so ever I can perceive myself or by the information of other, that I have failed (as it is no wonder) I shall now by the help of God overlook it and amend it.[19]

In 1553 Jugge reprinted Froschover's edition in quarto, giving it a new title: *The whole Bible, that is the holy scripture of the Olde and New Testament faythfully translated into Englyshe by Myles Coverdale and newly oversene and correcte*[*d*]. *M.D.L.* Like preceding editors, Jugge replaced the former preliminary matter by fresh material.

DEDICATIONS

In dedicating his first edition to Henry VIII, Coverdale employed the nauseating, flattering terms then common:

Unto the most victorious Prince and our most gracious Sovereign Lord King Henry the Eighth, King of England and of France, Lord of Ireland, etc., Defender

[19] "Address to the Christian Reader," prefixed to the first edition, 1535; see Pollard, *op. cit.*, pp. 202–6.

of the Faith, and under God the Chief and Supreme Head of the Church of England. . . .

The right and just administration of the Laws that God gave unto Moses and unto Josua: the testimony of faithfulness that God gave to David: the plenteous abundance of wisdom that God gave unto Solomon: the lucky and prosperous age, with multiplication of seed, which God gave unto Abraham and Sara his wife: be given unto you, most gracious Prince, with your dearest just wife, and most virtuous Princess, queen Anne. Amen.[20]

This was penned in 1535, when Anne Boleyn was already Henry's Queen. But by the time the sheets reached Nicolson, the "virtuous princess" had been executed. Some change had, therefore, to be made, with the result that in the British Museum copy "Anne" has been altered with a pen into "JAne"; one copy at Lambeth has "Anne," another has "Jane"; the Bodleian copy has "Anne," that at Sion College, "Jane"; two other copies have no name at all. Presumably publishers were unable to keep pace with the king's matrimonial ventures.[21]

Coverdale repeated a portion of his Dedication to Henry VIII, including the parallel he drew between "the blind bishop of Rome" and Caiphas and Balaam, when later on the editions by Hester and Jugge had to be dedicated to Henry's son. To Henry he had written in a groveling fashion, but in his Dedication to Edward VI, then hardly thirteen years of age, he surpasses the former production: "Unto the moost victorious Prince, our moost gracious soueruigne lorde, kynge Edward the sixth, kynge of Englonde, Fraunce, and of Irlonde, etc., Defoundor of the Fayth, and under God the chefe and supreme heade of the Church of Englande." The concluding paragraphs of the eight columns which follow, all cast in the same mold, are important:

Considering now (most gracyous prynce) the inestimable treasure, fruit and prosperitie everlasting, that God giveth with his worde, and trusting in his infinite goodnes that he wold bring my simple and rude labour herin to good effect, therefore [what follows is not in the Dedication to Henry VIII] was I boldened in God sixtene yeares agoo, not only to laboure faythfully in the same, but also in most humble wyse to dedicate this my pore translation to your graces moost noble father, as I do now submit this and all other my pore corrections, labours and interprises, to the gracious spirite of trewe knowledge, understanding and judgment, which is in you highnesse, most humbly beseching the same that though this volume be small, and not wholly the texte appoynted for the churches [Matthew's Bible],

[20] Pearson, *op. cit.*, pp. 3–11; Dore, *op. cit.*, p. 94. Hoare is surely guilty of an understatement when he styles this "an elaborate and somewhat obsequious and cringing dedication" (*The Evolution of the English Bible, 1382–1885,* p. 152).

[21] Dore, *loc. cit.;* Mombert, *op. cit.*, p. 153.

it maye yet be exercised in all other places so long as it is used within the compasse of the feare of God, and due obedience unto your moost excellente majestie,[22] whome the same eternal god save and preserve ever more. Amen. Your graces moost humble and faithful subject. Myles Coverdale.[23]

Coverdale's cringing servility did not confine itself to his Dedications.[24] Despite his avowals to the contrary, he actually changed the biblical text in an attempt to justify the repudiation of Queen Catherine. Lev. 18:16 expressly forbade marriage with a man's (living) brother's wife. But Deut. 25:5 excepted the case of a man who died leaving his wife childless, in which case the dead man's brother was bound to "raise up seed" to the dead man, a law which seemed to legalize Henry's marriage with Catherine. Coverdale, by changing "her husband's brother" into "kinsman," put a different complexion on this precept; it was no longer on Henry, brother of Arthur, on whom the duty was now said to devolve, but on some more remote "kinsman." This fact was noted by the ambassador Chapuys in a letter to Granville, February 20, 1536: "A Bible has been printed here in England in which the texts that favour the Queen, especially Deut. xix [a mistake for 25:5] have been translated in the opposite sense." [25]

[22] Compared with this, Arundel's much maligned Constitution, 1408, pales into insignificance. For he had only demanded that people who wanted to read the Bible in the vernacular should procure a licence from their diocesan to do so.

[23] Dore (*op. cit.*, pp. 105–8) is the only author, so far as I am aware, who gives even a portion of this Dedication. Pearson does not seem to realize that it was a Dedication to Edward, not to Henry, although in his footnotes he gives the variant readings (*op. cit.*, p. 2).

[24] The close of Coverdale's Dedication to Henry VIII (1535) well exemplifies this servility: "Agayne, consyderynge youre Imperiall maiestys not onely to be my naturall sueraigne liege Lorde and chefe heade of the church of Englonde, but also the true defender and maynteyner of Gods lawes, I thought it my dutye, and to belonge unto my allegiaunce, whan I had translated this Bible, not onely to dedicate this translacyon unto youre highnesse, but wholy to commytte unto the same, to the intent that yf any thynge therin be translated amysse (for in many thynges we fayle, even whan we thynke to be sure) it may stonde in youre graces handes, to correcte it, to amende it, to improve it, yee and cleane to rejecte it, yf youre godly wysdome shall thynke it necessary. And as I do with all humblenes submitte myne understondynge, and my poore translacyon unto the spirite of trueth in your grace, so make I this protestacyon (having God to recorde in my conscience) that I have nether wrested nor altered so moche as one worde for the mayntenaunce of any maner of secte: but have with a cleare conscience purely and faythfully translated this out of fyve sundry interpreters, havyng onely the manyfest trueth of the scripture before myne eyes" (Pollard, *op. cit.*, p. 201).

[25] *Letters and Papers of Henry VIII*, X, 352, 1696; XIV, i, 186 (v); cf. Constant, *The Reformation in England*, p. 306 note; Gairdner, *Lollardy and the Reformation in England*, II, 276.

ILLUSTRATIONS

The woodcuts surrounding the title of the first edition are worthy of study. At the top the Deity is represented by the name "Jehovah" in Hebrew characters; from it a scroll, directed towards the terror-stricken Adam and Eve, bears the words: "In what day soever thou shalt eat thereof thou shalt die." A similar scroll, directed towards the risen Christ trampling on the serpent, is inscribed: "This is my deare Sonne in whom I delyte," Matth. xvii. The woodcuts on either side of the title represent the giving of the Law on Mt. Sinai (on the left): "These are the laws that thou shalt lay before them," Exod. xxi; and Christ giving his last commission to the apostles, every one of whom is depicted bearing the keys of the kingdom (on the right): "Go your ways into all the worlde and preach the Gospel." Beneath is depicted the day of Pentecost.

Lower on the page Henry VIII is depicted on his throne distributing Bibles to the kneeling bishops, all wearing very tall miters; [26] behind them is David with his harp and a scroll inscribed with the words: "How swete are thy wordes unto my throte, yea more than honey, etc." Ps. cxviii. On the king's left kneel various crowned heads admiring the bestowal of the Bibles on the bishops. Behind stands St. Paul with a sword on which is inscribed: "I am not ashamed of the Gospel of Christ, for it is the power of God," Ro. i.[27]

In accordance with the rendering of Gen. 3:5, "He shall crush," instead of "She shall crush," Christ, not the Blessed Virgin, is shown crushing the head of the serpent. The promise of the keys, made to St. Peter alone (Matt. 16:18), is tacitly denied by picturing all the apostles as bearing the keys. When we come to study Holbein's famous frontispiece to Cromwell's Bible, we shall perceive the source of his inspiration and see how skillfully he adapted his design to the changed attitude of Henry VIII.[28]

[26] In the Introduction to his reprint, 1838, Bagster has misinterpreted this illustration, for he says that "the Bishops are in the act of presenting the Bible to his Majesty, which he graciously receives." Henry's bishops were hardly in a position to do this.

[27] This frontispiece was used more than once, reappearing in Berthelet's edition in 1540, and again in Hyll's edition of Matthew's Bible in 1551.

[28] See below, chap. 13. The *Times* for October 5, 1935, gave reproductions of the title pages both of Coverdale's Bible of 1535 and of Cromwell's Bible of 1539; a very clear reproduction is also given in *The Bulletin of the Rylands Library,* XIX. 8.

COVERDALE'S SOURCES

Coverdale explicitly says: "To help me herein I have had sundry translations, not only in Latin, but also of the Dutch interpreters, whom because of their singular gifts and special diligence in the Bible, I have been the more glad to follow for the most part, according as I was required." [29] Yet some maintain that he translated directly from the original Hebrew and Greek. It is true that, while acknowledging his lack of qualifications for translating from the original,[30] he yet says in a letter written to Cromwell by Grafton and himself while preparing the Great Bible in Paris: "We follow a standing text of the Hebrew, with the interpretation of the Chaldee and the Greek" (June 23, 1538); and a little later (August 9) they refer to the marks they have inserted to show where there is "a diversity of reading among the Hebrews, Chaldees, Greeks, and Latinists." [31]

Internal evidence, however, proves that the version was not made from the originals; [32] and the "fyve [unnamed] sundry interpreters" referred to in the Dedication are now generally held to have been: (1) the Zurich or Swiss Bible published in 1529; (2) Luther's German Version; (3) the Vulgate; (4) the Latin version made from the Hebrew by Santes Pagninus; and (5) Tyndale's translation of Genesis to Chronicles, of Jonas, perhaps also of Job and of the historical books—that is, if it is certain that Tyndale ever did translate those books.

Coverdale seems to have revised the portions taken over from Tyndale by the work of Luther, by the Zurich Bible, by Pagninus, and, in the later editions, by Münster's Latin version. If the translation from Esdras to the end of the Old Testament was not Tyndale's work, then, as with the Apocrypha, it must be due to Coverdale's independent efforts.[33] Follow-

[29] Prologue to the Reader; cf. Pearson, *op. cit.*, p. 12. This declaration is repeated in his Dedication.

[30] Cf. Whittaker, *An Historical and Critical Enquiry into the Interpretation of the Hebrew Scriptures*, pp. 52 ff.; Pearson, *op. cit.*, p. xvii. It is still more astonishing to find that the title of Bagster's *Second Modern Edition of Coverdale's Bible* has "translated from the Hebrewe and Greke by Miles Coverdale." So too the Preface to Bagster's *Hexapla:* "All the remaining part (that is, except the Pentateuch and Job) of the Old Testament and Apocrypha is his own translation. . . . There seems no reason to doubt that he translated from the originals" (p. 23).

[31] Given in Pearson, *op. cit.*, p. 492 (Letter IV); cf. *ibid.*, p. xvii.

[32] Cf. Dore, *op. cit.*, p. 109; Hoare, *op. cit.*, p. 173; Pollard, *op. cit.*, p. 12; Mombert, *op. cit.*, p. 164; Eadie, *The English Bible*, p. 281.

[33] To what extent Coverdale modified Tyndale's version of the Old Testament is

ing the Vulgate as he did, Coverdale retains the headings I, II, III, and IV Kings instead of the later I and II Samuel and I and II Kings. In his Table of Contents, too, he writes Paralipomena and Cantica Canticorum, though his page headings are Chronicles and "Salomons ballettes."[34] The New Testament is Tyndale's version subjected to the same revision.

COVERDALE'S RENDERINGS

Many of Coverdale's renderings sound quaint to modern ears: "The dove had broken of a leaf of an olive tree and bare the olive leaf in her neb" (Gen. 8:11); Cromwell's Bible has: "Lo in hir mouth was an olive leaf that she had pluckt." "The cat of the mountain" (Jer. 5:6) in the edition of 1535 becomes the "leopard" in Cromwell's Bible. The following remain the same in both editions: "He that is a blabbe of his tongue maketh a dyvysion of princes" (Prov. 16:28); "brake his brain panne" (Judg. 9:53); "calamus" (for "cane"), "cockatrices" (for "basilisks"), and "there is no more triacle in Galaad" (Jer. 6:20; 8:17, 33). Other interesting renderings are: "for it soundeth as though it would reyne sore" (III Kings 18:45), a very free paraphrase; "a still soft hyssinge" (III Kings 19:12); "for like as the man of Inde may chaunge his skynne, and the cat of the mountayne his spottes" (Jer. 13:23); "clothed in lynnen upon the bare skynne" (Mark 14:51); the eunuch of Acts, chap. 8, is the "chamberlayne" to Candace.

Aside from strange passages, Coverdale's gift for happy renderings lends a peculiar charm to his version.[35] This is particularly noticeable in the Prayer Book Psalter, his abiding memorial, many phrases of which have become household words. In 1535 he seems to have taken as a basis the Psalms in the Zurich Bible (1524–28); but when preparing the Great Bible (Cromwell's) in 1539, he revised his earlier version by that of Münster; and when the Prayer Book was revised in 1662, this revision

shown by a collation of their respective versions of Gen., chap. 22, and of the New Testament, given by Eadie, *op. cit.*, I, 294 f. Eadie calls Coverdale's Bible a revision of Tyndale's New Testament and a new version of the Old Testament (*ibid.*, I, 277 f.); cf. Lewis, *A Complete History of the Several Translations of the Holy Bible and New Testament*, p. 98.

[34] Gregory Martin protested against this absurd rendering, "The ballad of ballads": "so terming that divine book, Cantica canticorum, containing the high mystery of Christ and his Church, as if it were a ballad of love between Solomon and his concubine, as Castaleo wantonly translateth it."

[35] Scrivener styles him "that consummate master of rhythmical prose" (*A Plain Introduction to the Criticism of the New Testament*, p. 139).

was definitively preferred to that which stood in the Authorized Version of 1611. As examples of felicitous renderings, we may note the following: where Coverdale had originally written (1535) "the yron pearsed his [Joseph's] herte" (Ps. 105:18),[36] in 1539, following Münster's *ferreum (vinculum) intravit usque ad animam ejus,* he changed this to, "the iron entered into his soul." "I have leaned upon thee ever since I was born" (Ps. 71:6) was changed, though not for the better, to, "through thee have I been holden up ever since I was borne." A happier change appears in Ps. 128:2, where "O well is thee, happy art thou," is replaced by "O well is thee, and happy shalt thou be." An unfortunate change, for it is incorrect, occurs in Ps. 119:122, where in 1535 he wrote, "Be thou suretye for thy servant to do him good"; but in 1539, "Make thy servant to delight in that which is good." To Coverdale, too, we owe "the haven where they would be" (Ps. 107:30) and the following happy turns of expression, all found in both editions: "a city that is at unity with itself"; "the thing that good is"; "If thou, O Lord, wilt be extreme to mark what is done amiss."

Yet even in his version of the Psalms there occur expressions which jar: "Fie on thee, fie on thee" (Ps. 35:21), but in 1535, "there, there"; "their forefathers, a froward and overthwarte generation" (78:8), but in 1539 "a faithless and stubborn generation"; "The fool hath said in his heart: Tush, there is no God" (Ps. 14:1; 53:1). Now and again he is somewhat free in his renderings, sometimes indulging in paraphrase: "Or ever your thorns be sharp, the wrath shall take them away quick, like a stormy wind" (Ps. 58:9); in 1539 the same passage reads: "Or ever your pottes be mad whot with thorns so let indignation tear him, even as a thing that is rawe."

To the words "rideth upon the heavens" (Ps. 77:3) Coverdale in 1539 appended "as it were upon a horse," taken over from Münster's *veluti equo insidet;* a similar change appears in verse 26, where, instead of

[36] In the numbering of the psalms some versions follow the Vulgate, others follow the Hebrew. The following table indicates the points at which the divergence occurs.

Vulgate	Hebrew
1–8	1–8
9	9, 10
10	11 etc.
146, 147	147
148	148

"from the fountains of Israel," Coverdale in 1539 wrote, "from the ground of the heart," a rendering apparently due to a misunderstanding of Münster's version. And Coverdale does not hesitate to tone down strong expressions; e.g., the Vulgate *crapulatus a vino* (Ps. 78:65) becomes, "refreshed with wine."

In 1535 Coverdale adhered to the numbering of the Psalms as given in the Latin and Greek Bibles, though notes on psalms 9 and 113 (Vulgate numbering) say: "Here the Hebrues begynne the x. psalme," and "the cxv psalme," respectively; similarly on psalm 147: "This psalme do the Hebrues joyne unto it, that goeth before." In the Prayer Book Version no such notes are inserted, psalm 9 being simply divided at verse 21, and the remaining verses forming psalm 10; the same is the case with psalm 113 (Vulgate), which is divided into two psalms at verse 8, the last part being numbered psalm 115. At the same time psalms 146 and 147 are counted as a single psalm.

In 1535 Coverdale printed psalm 14 (13) with the three verses which have crept in from some marginal note quoting Rom. 3:13–18, but in a note he says: "These verses are not in the Hebrue." In 1539 they are printed in smaller type.

A comparison of four versions of psalm 84 (83)—Coverdale's original translation in his Bible of 1535, his revised version in 1539 for Cromwell's Bible (the Great Bible), the version in the King James Bible, 1611, and Challoner's revision of 1750 of the original Douay Version of 1610—will serve to show the changes made by Coverdale and perpetuated in the Prayer Book Version. The Authorized Version alone inserts the "Selah." This particular psalm also shows to what extent the framers of that version italicised words not exactly represented in the original.[37]

THE APOCRYPHA

Coverdale prefaces his translation of the Apocrypha by an address, "The Translatour to the Reader":

> The bokes (good reader) which be called Apocrypha, are not judged amonge the doctours to be of like reputacion with the other scripture, as thou mayest perceave by S. Jerome in Ep. ad Paulinum. And the chefe cause therof is this: there be many places in them, that seme to be repugnaunt unto the open and manyfest trueth in the other bokes of the byble. Nevertheless I have not gathered them together to the intent that I wolde have them despysed, or little sett by, or that I shulde

[37] See pages 172 ff.

thinke them false, for I am not able to prove it. Yee, I doute not verely, yf they were equally conferred with the other open scripture (tyme, place, and circumstance in all thinges considered) they shulde nether seme contrary, nor be untruly and perversely aledged. Trueth it is, a mans face can not be sene so well in a water, as in a fayre glasse: nether can it be shewed so clearly in a water that is stered or moved, as in a styll water. These and many other darck places of scripture have bene sore stered and myxte with blinde and cuvetous opynions of men, which have cast soche a myst afore the eyes of the symple, that as long as they be not conferred with the other places of scripture, they shall not seme other wyse to be understonde then as cuvetousnes expoundeth them. But who so ever thou be that readeth scripture, let the holy ghoost be thy teacher, and let one text expounde another unto the. As for soche dreames, visions, and darck sentences as be hyd from thy understondynge, commyte them unto God, and make no articles of them: But let the playne text be thy gyde, and the sprete of God (which is the author thereof) shal lede the in all trueth.

As for the prayer of Salomon (which thou findest not herin) the prayer of Azarias, and the swete song that he and his two felowes songe in the fyre: the first (namely the prayer of Salomon) readest thou in the eight chapter of the thirde boke of the kynges, so that it appeareth not to be *Apocryphum:* the other prayer and songe (namely of the thre children) I have not founde amonge eny of the interpreters, but in the olde Latyn text, which reporteth it to be Theodotios translacion. Nevertheless, both because of those that be weake and scrupulous, as for their sakes also that love soche swete songes of thankesgyvynge: I have not left them out: to the intent that the one shulde have no cause to complayne, and that the other also might have the more occasion to geve thankes unto God in adversitie, as the thre children dyd in the fyre. Grace be with the. Amen.

Though Coverdale placed these Apocrypha at the end of the volume, —whence the prevailing practice—his attitude towards them can fairly be described as "non committal." [38] He joins Baruch to Jeremias and Lamentations, though with the *caveat* that Baruch "is not in the Canon of the Hebrue." The famous line in III Esdras 4:41, "magna est veritas et praevalet," is paraphrased,—perhaps not too happily—"As for the trueth, it endureth and is always strong." The name Esdras is correctly spelled in the title, but in the actual text Coverdale writes Eszdras; and while he always writes LORDE in capital letters, he is content to write God in ordinary type.

Coverdale's work seems characterized throughout by the determination not to give such unnecessary offense as Tyndale had done. At that time men, whether Catholics or Protestants, had to reckon with Henry

[38] Quite different is the attitude adopted in Matthew's Bible; see below, pp. 184 f. In the Geneva Bible and in Matthew's Bible the Apocrypha are printed at the end of the Old Testament, not at the end of the volume.

VIII, who, while hating Tyndale for his attitude towards the divorce, yet seemed at times to favor the production of a vernacular version of the Scriptures; hence Coverdale's intentional omission of all controversial matter, even cutting down his notes to a scanty forty-seven in the Old Testament and nineteen in the New. The foregoing may explain, too, the fact that, while dedicating his work in the most fulsome terms to Henry, he never seems to have sought to obtain a royal licence for it; indeed no such licence was granted until 1537.

No one can peruse the foregoing Dedications and Prologues without feeling that Coverdale had found his task no easy one; to use his own expression in the psalm, "the iron had entered into his soul." For not only does he insist more than once on his own "insufficiency" and his lack of the needful qualifications of a translator, but he gives the impression that he had to be almost driven to make his versions: he was "required," and that "instantly"; he was "desyred." It was not his own idea, apparently, and he seems to have submitted his work to "correctors." But who these taskmasters were remains a mystery.

We mentioned at the outset some unpalatable truths about Coverdale, his bitterly antipapal attitude, for instance. Yet—to repeat—no one can read these Prologues and fail to see that unless he was an absolute hypocrite, which is unthinkable, Coverdale was a thoroughly humble-minded man. We shall see further proofs of this when we come to deal with the Great Bible, a revision he made of his previous work, again under some sort of compulsion—a revision, too, with which he himself was far from satisfied, owing, so far as we can judge, to the attitude of those who "oversaw" the work and who seem to have "over-ridden" the author and reviser.

EDITIONS OF THE NEW TESTAMENT

Long before the appearance of the later editions of the whole Bible, Coverdale had brought out a New Testament with the Vulgate Latin and a fresh English version made by himself and distinct from that in his version of the whole Bible. This "diglot edition," as it was called, must have been very popular, as no less than five editions appeared in 1538. The first bore the title: *The New Testament, both Latine and Englyshe, ech correspondent to the other after the vulgar texte, communely called S. Jerome, faythfully translated by Miles Coverdale, printed in Southwarke by James Nicolson. Set forth wyth the kynges most gracious licence.*[39]

In his Dedication to Henry,[40] Coverdale says he prints the Vulgate text which is customarily read in church and has set his own rendering of it, "since some allege that we intend to pervert the Scripture and to condemn the common translation in Latin." This he has no intention of doing, yet feels bound to point out that the existing text of the Vulgate is "so greatly corrupt as I think none other translation is," and he hopes that people ignorant of Latin will be able to realize the extent of this corruption by studying his translation of it. He goes on to explain his rendering of *poenitentiam agite*:

> And though I seem to be all too scrupulous, calling it in one place "penance" that in another I call "repentance," and "gelded" that another calleth "chaste," this methink ought not to offend thee seeing that the Holy Ghost (I trust) is the author of both our doings. If I of mine own head had put into the New Testament these words "Nisi poenitueritis" "poenitemini" "sunt enim eunuchi" "poenitentiam agite," etc., then as I were worthy to be reproved, so should it be right necessary to redress the same. But it is the Holy Ghost that hath put them in, and therefore I heartily require that you think no more harm in me for calling it in one place "penance," that in another I call "repentance," than I think harm in him that calleth it "chaste" which I, by the nature of this word "eunuchus" call "gelded."

As a matter of fact, Coverdale sometimes has "amendment," but far more often "repentance." He also restored the sacrosanct ecclesiastical terminology which Tyndale had rejected, though he retained "congregation" in place of "church." Apart from I Cor. 11:27, "eat this bread *and* dryncke . . . ," there is nothing that can be called heretical in his renderings, passages on the Holy Eucharist (John, chap. 6) and on St. Peter (Matt., chap. 16; Luke, chap. 22) being correctly rendered.

But as Nicolson had once more taken unwarrantable liberties with his text, Coverdale felt bound to bring out another edition: *The New Testament both in Latin and English after the vulgare texte, which is red in the Churche, translated and corrected by Myles Coverdale, and printed in Paris by Frances Regnault, M.CCCCC.XXXVIII, in Novembre, Printed for R. Gratton* [*Grafton*] *and E. Whitchurch.* This was dedicated to "The Right Honourable Lord Cromwell, Lord Privy Seal,

[39] Dore, *Old Bibles*, p. 98.

[40] Pollard, *Records of the English Bible*, pp. 206–10. Bonner bore the cost of printing the first two editions and sent copies to the King; see Foxe, *op. cit.*, V (viii), 161; Dore, *op. cit.*, p. 100; Pollard, *op. cit.*, p. 224.

Vicegerent to the Kings Highness, concerning all his jurisdiction Ecclesiastical within the realme of England." He explains that this fresh edition was necessary owing to the fact that Nicolson's edition, "as it was disagreeable to my former translation in English, so was not the true copy of the Latin text observed." This tampering with his text, he adds, was done entirely unknown to him.[41] In a Prologue to the Reader, Coverdale says that despite the evidence of "the Greek text and the old ancient authors," he has omitted from the Lord's Prayer in Luke, chap. 11, "thy will be done on earth as in heaven" and "but deliver us from evil."

Nicolson, however, was not to be outdone, and promptly produced in the same year: *The Newe Testament both in Latine and Englishe, ech correspondent to the other after the vulgare text, communely called St. Jerome's. Faithfully translated by Johann Hollybushe, ANNo MCCCCCXXXVIII. Prynted in Southwarke by James Nicolson. Set forth wyth the Kynges moost gracious License.* "Whether this name Johann Hollybushe represents a mythical personage or a real person," says Mombert, "belongs to the realm of conjecture." But Duff found in a list of citizens of London in 1535 the name of "John Hollibusche, alias Holybusche of London, Stationer, otherwise bookbinder, born in Ruremond under the obedience of the Emperor." [42] Duff identifies him with Hans von Ruremond, a bookseller in Antwerp, also known as Christopher, imprisoned in 1531 for selling English Testaments in London.[43]

A fourth edition (16mo) has the simple title: *The Newe Testament*

[41] Dore, *op. cit.*, p. 100. On December 1, 1538, Grafton wrote to Cromwell to complain of this: "It chanced since our coming into these parts, that James Nycolson that dwelleth in Southwark put in print the New Testament both in Latin and English, which book was delivered unto us by a stranger. And when Master Coverdale had advised and considered the same he found his name added thereunto as the translator, with the which he never had to do, neither saw he it before it was full printed and ended. And also found the book so foolishly done, yea and so corrupt that it did not only grieve him that the printer had so defamed him and his learning by adding his name to so fond a thing, but also that the common people was deprived of the true and sincere sense of God's true word, and also that such an occasion was ministered to the enemies of God's word that rather seek occasions to rail and slander than to be edified. And therefore, at his most honest and lawful request (although I had enough to do beside) I have printed the same again, translated and corrected by Master Coverdale himself" (*State Papers, Henry VIII,* Foreign and Domestic, II, no. 972.

[42] *Westminster and London Printers,* p. 233.

[43] Pollard, *op. cit.,* pp. 135 f.; Dore, *op. cit.,* p. 101; *State Papers, Henry VIII,* VIII, no. 291, p. 52. Although Nicolson put the name "Hollybush" in the title, he did not remove Coverdale's name from the Dedication.

faythfully and newly corrected by Myles Coverdale. A note in the British Museum copy says: "This small book was once the property of Queen Elizabeth, and actually presented by her to A. Poynts, who was her maid of honour. In it are a few lines of the Queen's own handwriting and signing. Likewise a small drawing of King Edward the 6th when very young (of Windsor Castle) and one of the knight in his robes." [44] The title of the fifth edition is interesting: *The New Testament of oure Savyour Jesu Christ. Faythfully translated and lately correcte*[*d*] *wyth a true concordaunce* [45] *in the margent, and many necessary annotacions declarynge sondry harde places co*[*n*]*teyned in the text. Empreynt in the yeare of our Lorde. M.D.XXXVIII.* Tyndale's Prologues with Coverdale's chapter headings are given. The text is practically that of Coverdale's first edition of the Bible, 1535.[46]

The text in this "diglot" New Testament is not divided into verses, but into paragraphs distinguished by the letters of the alphabet. I John 5:7 is enclosed in brackets; I Cor. 9:5 is rendered, "a sister to wife"; and I Cor. 11:27: "eat this bread, and [not "or"] drink this chalice."

[44] Dore, *op. cit.*, p. 95.

[45] "Concordaunce" means merely the marginal cross references and notes.

[46] See Dore, *op. cit.*, pp. 97 f., for an account of the unexpected discovery of this unique copy. The fullest account of these various editions will be found in the second edition of Dore's *Old Bibles*, 1888.

Psalm 84 (83)

COVERDALE'S VERSION, 1535	COVERDALE'S VERSION, 1539, OR THE PRAYER BOOK VERSION FROM THE GREAT BIBLE
1. O how amiable are thy dwellinges, thou Lorde of hoostes!	1. O how amiable are thy dwellings: thou Lord of hosts!
2. My soule hath a desyre and lonige for the courte of the LORDE, my herte and my flesh rejoyse in the lyvynge God.	2. My soul hath a desire and longing to enter into the courts of the Lord: my heart and my flesh rejoice in the living God.
3. For the sparrow hath founde hir an house, and the swalow a nest, where she maye laye hir yonge; even thy aulters, O LORDE of hoostes, my kynge and my God.	3. Yea, the sparrow hath found her an house, and the swallow a nest where she may lay her young: even thy altars, O Lord of hosts, my King and my God.
4. O how blessed are they that dwell in thy house, they are alwaye praysinge the.	4. Blessed are they that dwell in thy house: they will be always praising thee.
5. Blessed are the men whose strength is in the, in whose herte are thy wayes.	5. Blessed is the man whose strength is in thee; in whose heart are thy ways.
6. Which singe through the vale of misery, use it for a well, and the poles are fylled with water.	6. Who going through the vale of misery use it for a well: and the pools are filled with water.
7. They go from strength to strength, and so the God of Gods apeareth unto them in Sion.	7. They will go from strength to strength; and until the God of Jacob appeareth every one of them in Sion.
8. O LORDE God of hoostes, heare my prayer, herken O God of Jacob.	8. O Lord God of hosts, hear my prayer: hearken O God of Jacob.
9. Behold o God our defence, loke upon the face of thyne anoynted.	9. Behold, O God, our defender: and look upon the face of thine Anointed.
10. For one day in thy courte is better than a thousande.	10. For one day in thy courts: is better than a thousand.
11. I had rather be a dore keper in the house of my God than to dwell in the tentes of the ungodly.	11. I had rather be a door-keeper in the house of my God: than to dwell in the tents of ungodliness.
12. For the LORDE God is a light and defence, the LORDE will give grace and worshipe, and no good thinge shall he witholde from them that lyve a godly life.	12. For the Lord God is a light and defence: the Lord will give grace and worship, and no good thing shall be withheld from them that live a godly life.
13. O LORDE God of hoostes, blessed is the man that putteth his trust in the.	13. O Lord God of hosts: blessed is the man that putteth his trust in thee.

Psalm 84 (83)

THE AUTHORIZED VERSION, 1611

1. How amiable *are* thy tabernacles, O LORD of hosts!

2. My soul longeth, yea, even fainteth for the courts of the LORD: my heart and my flesh crieth out for the living God.

3. Yea, the sparrow hath found an house, and the swallow a nest for herself, where she may lay her young, *even* thine altars, O LORD of hosts, my King, and my God.

4. Blessed *are* they that dwell in thy house: they will be still praising thee. Selah.

5. Blessed *is* the man whose strength *is* in thee; in whose heart *are* the ways *of them.*

6. *Who* passing through the valley of Baca make it a well: the rain also filleth the pools.

7. They go from strength to strength, *every one of them* in Zion appeareth before God.

8. O LORD God of hosts, hear my prayer: give ear, O God of Jacob. Selah.

9. Behold, O God our shield, and look upon the face of thine anointed.

10. For a day in thy courts *is* better than a thousand. I had rather be a doorkeeper in the house of my God, than to dwell in the tents of wickedness.

11. For the LORD God *is* a sun and shield: the LORD will give grace and glory: no good *thing* will he withold from them that walk uprightly.

12. O LORD of hosts, blessed *is* the man that trusteth in thee.

THE DOUAY VERSION, AS REVISED BY CHALLONER, 1750

1. How lovely are thy tabernacles, O Lord of hosts!

2. My soul longeth and fainteth for the courts of the Lord. My heart and my flesh have rejoiced in the living God.

3. For the sparrow hath found herself a house, and the turtle a nest for herself where she may lay her young ones: Thy altars, O Lord of hosts, my king and my God.

4. Blessed are they that dwell in thy house, O Lord: they shall praise thee for ever and ever.

5. Blessed is the man whose help is from thee: in his heart he hath disposed to ascend by steps,

6. In the vale of tears, in the place which he hath set.

7. For the lawgiver shall give a blessing, they shall go from virtue to virtue: the God of gods shall be seen in Sion.

8. O Lord God of hosts, hear my prayer; give ear, O God of Jacob.

9. Behold, O God, our protector: and look on the face of thy Christ.

10. For better is one day in thy courts above thousands. I have chosen to be an abject in the house of my God, rather than to dwell in the tabernacles of sinners.

11. For God loveth mercy and truth: the Lord will give grace and glory.

12. He will not deprive of good things them that walk in innocence: O Lord God of hosts, blessed is the man that trusteth in thee.

BIBLIOGRAPHY

Bagster, Samuel (ed.). *The Holy Scriptures faithfully and truly translated into English . . . by Myles Coverdale, 1535,* 1838.

Cooper and Cooper. "Miles Coverdale," in *Athenae Cantabrigienses,* I, 268–80, Cambridge, 1858.

Fry, Francis. *The Bible by Coverdale, MDXXXV: Remarks on the Titles, the Year of Publication, the Preliminary, the Watermarks, etc.,* London, 1867.

Guppy, Henry. *Miles Coverdale and the English Bible, 1488–1568,* 1935.

Memorials of Myles Coverdale (anonymous), London, 1838.

Pearson, G. (ed.). *Writings and Translatons of M. Coverdale,* Cambridge, 1844, 2 vols.

Sheppard, L. A. "The Printers of the Coverdale Bible, 1535," in *The Library,* December, 1935, pp. 280–89.

Bibliography on Coverdale's Psalter

Carleton, James G. (ed.). *The Psalter of the Church. The Prayer Book Version of the Psalms with Introduction and Notes,* Cambridge, 1909.

Clapton, Ernest (ed.). *Our Prayer Book Psalter, containing Coverdale's version from his 1535 Bible and the Prayer Book version by Coverdale from the Great Bible, 1539–41, printed side by side,* London, 1934.

Earle, J. *The Psalter of 1539, a Landmark in English Literature,* 1894.

King, E. G. (tr.). *The Psalms in Three Collections, translated with notes,* 1898.

Rylands, G. (ed.). *The Psalms of David, Coverdale's Version, edited with Introduction,* London, 1926.

Willoughby, H. R. *The Coverdale Psalter and the Quatrocentenary of the Printed English Bible,* Chicago, 1935.

Wormald, F. *The Book of Psalms from the Version of Miles Coverdale, as published in the "Great Bible" of 1539, with an Introduction,* 1930.

Wright, William Aldis. *The Hexaplar Psalter. The Book of Psalms in Six English Versions,* 1911.

CHAPTER XII

Matthew's Bible, 1537

HISTORY OF THE VERSION

MATTHEW's Bible has a curious history; even the name Matthew is fictitious. Foxe declares that John Rogers is responsible for the version:

> The corrector was John Rogers, a learned divine, and afterwards a canon of St. Paul's, in King Edward's time, and the first martyr in the next reign. The translator was William Tyndale, another learned martyr, with the help of Miles Coverdale, after Bishop of Exeter. But before all this second edition was finished, Tyndale was taken and put to death for his religion, in Flanders, in the year 1536. And his name then growing into ignominy, as one burnt for an heretic, they thought it might prejudice the book if he should be named for the translator thereof; and so they used a feigned name, calling it Thomas Matthew's Bible; though Tyndale, before his death, had translated all but the Apocrypha, which was translated by Rogers, who added also marginal notes.[1]

This John Rogers,[2] born about 1509 in Deritend, Birmingham, was a priest who, influenced by Tyndale, became a Protestant. Implicated in Wyatt's rebellion, Rogers spent some time in Newgate prison. Later in the same year, 1553, he was present at Bourne's sermon at Paul's Cross,[3] and, according to Foxe, helped rescue the Bishop from an infuriated crowd. That Rogers was imprisoned for his share in the uproar appears from an entry in the Acts of the Privy Council for August 18, 1553: "John Rogers, alias Mathewe, a seditious preacher, ordered by the Lords of the Council to keep himself as prisoner in his house at St. Paul's, without conference with any person other than such as be daily with him in household, until such time as he hath contrary commandment." [4] Rogers, Laurence Saunders, Rowland Taylor, and Hooper, *quondam* bishop of

[1] Strype, *Ecclesiastical Memorials,* I, 118. See above, p. 158, note 17.

[2] Cooper, *Athenae Cantabrigienses,* I, 121 ff.

[3] Gairdner, *Lollardy and the Reformation in England,* IV, 13 f.

[4] *Ibid.,* 344–76.

Gloucester, were all condemned at the same time; and Rogers was burnt for contumacy in heresy in 1555.[5] Rogers' writings show that he must have been a strange mixture of genuine piety and amazing fanaticism.[6]

While Rogers' identity with "Matthew" seems beyond doubt, it does not necessarily follow that "Matthew" was a purely mythical person. W. T. Whitley maintains that he was a real person who was fined by Tunstall in 1527 for his connection with a Bible-study circle; he would explain Matthew's absence from Colchester in 1536 as due to the fact that he was then engaged in his translation, which came out in the following year.[7]

In preparing his work for the press, the compiler of Matthew's Bible combined Tyndale's translation of the Old Testament, Genesis to Chronicles, and his corrected edition of the New Testament (1535), with Coverdale's Version of 1535 for the remainder of the Bible.[8] He even took over the latter's version of Jonas, though a translation of that book, with a lengthy Prologue, had been one of Tyndale's earliest ventures in translating. The Prayer of Manasses he translated from a French Bible of 1535, and this is in effect the only portion for which "Thomas Matthew" was responsible. More than half of his Bible, then, was the often anathematized work of Tyndale. Despite Foxe's statement, the preparation of the Bible for the press was the work of Rogers alone, not of Coverdale; for, although he used the text provided by Tyndale and Coverdale, Rogers—or "Matthew"—edited it by adding references to other versions, numbering the Psalms according to the Hebrew enumeration, and prefixing headings to each chapter, instead of putting them all at the beginning as Coverdale had done. Cross references were given in both the Old and the New Testaments, and brief notes at the end of each chapter. The verses were not numbered, but Prov., chap. 31, was arranged correctly, like the alphabetical psalms.

The title, in red and black, runs: *The Byble, which is all the holy Scripture; in which are contayned the Olde and Newe Testament truly and purely translated into Englysh by Thomas Mathew.* A quotation of

[5] *Original Letters,* Thomas Sampson to Calvin, February 23, 1555, Parker Society, I, 171.

[6] Edited by the Parker Society.

[7] "Thomas Matthew of Colchester and Matthew's Bible of 1537," in *The Essex Review,* January, 1934; cf. J. L. Chester, *John Rogers, the Compiler of the First Authorised English Bible, the pioneer of the English Reformation, and its first martyr,* 1861.

[8] A few attempts at revising Coverdale's version were made, e.g., in Esdras, Nehemias, and Esther; the first part of Job, too, was revised, chap. 4, for instance, being practically a fresh version based on Münster's Latin text.

Isa. 1:2 follows, then the important words, "Set forth with the Kinges most Gracyous lyce[n]ce." This title is framed in a series of pictures: Adam and Eve tempted by the serpent; opposite them the Crucifixion; beneath are skeletons and a man rising from the tomb, while a minister points to the cross. This folio volume, printed in black letter, measures 11¼ inches by 6½ inches for the printed matter. On the reverse of the title page is a list of Contents, also an "Exhortation to the Study of the Bible." Beneath are the letters I.R., 2½ inches high. Then follow "The summe and content of the holy Scripture" and a Dedication, "To the moost noble and gracyous Prynce King Henry the eyght," signed by "Youre graces faythful and true subject Thomas Mathew," and followed by the letters H.R. Then comes an "Address to the Chrysten Readers," a "Table of the pryncypal matters conteyned in the Byble," a list of the books, and finally a Chronological Table "sence the begynnynge of the worlde unto this yeare of our Lorde Mccccc.xxxvii."

After the Canticle of Canticles, here called "The Ballet of Ballettes of Salomon," comes a second title; "The Prophetes in Englysh," and on the reverse the initials R.G. above and E.W. below, while after Malachi stand the initials W.T.[9] A third title is prefixed to the Apocrypha.

THE TEXT

In Matthew's Bible psalm 2 is printed practically in dialogue form; the three verses inserted into psalm 14 from Rom., chap. 3, are omitted; psalm 119 has the letters of the Hebrew alphabet inserted before each section. Owing to the rendering in Ps. 91:5, "So that thou shalt not nede to be afrayed for any bugges by night," Matthew's Bible has come to be known as The "Bugge" Bible; but Coverdale had the same rendering in 1535, changing it to "terrour" when preparing the Great Bible. The verses of the psalms are not numbered, but are divided into paragraphs according to the letters of the alphabet. There are interesting notes on liturgical terms in the Psalter, on the titles, and on "Selah."

A comparison of the historical books in Tyndale, Coverdale, and Matthew shows that the latter preferred Tyndale's version; for while both Tyndale and Matthew have "the Ark of the Testament," Coverdale has "the Ark of the Covenant," and whereas the former speak of the "timbrel," the latter has "tabret." Coverdale, Matthew, and the Great

[9] H.R. may stand for Henricus Rex; R.G. and E.W. for Richard Grafton and Edward Whitchurch, the printers; W.T., of course, stands for William Tyndale, while J.R. must stand for John Rogers.

Bible have all the same version of Jonas, which, according to Eadie,[10] is Coverdale's revision of Tyndale's version, a tacit and unexplained repudiation of Tyndale's translation. It is said, too, that Nehemias in Matthew's Bible is not Tyndale's translation.

The text of the New Testament in Matthew's Bible[11] is Tyndale's final correction, 1534–35; prefixed to it is "William Tindale unto the Christen Reader," in eight columns, ending with a defense of his rendering of "elders," for "priests." In the edition of 1549, Tyndale's Prologues to each of the books except the Acts and the Apocalypse (for which he did not compose Prologues), are also given, including the notorious Prologue to Romans in eighteen columns, though varying slightly from the Prologue which Tyndale had himself adapted from that of Luther.

Matthew's Bible, then, was Tyndale's work in a new guise. The only peculiar features were the preliminary matter, including "A Register or a Briefe Rehearsall of the names of the moost famous notable persons mentioned in the Olde and Newe Testamente," and "The Alphabet of Common Places."[12] Despite its origin and the fact that it came into England unheralded, Matthew's Bible was warmly received by Cranmer, who at once obtained for it a royal licence. The second English version to be printed, it served as the basis for the Authorized Version, and it has the questionable honor of securing the perpetuation of Tyndale's version, so often condemned both before and since.

THE ROYAL LICENCE

How a Bible embodying the worst features of Tyndale's often condemned version came to receive a royal licence is interesting, but can be

[10] *The English Bible*, I, 316; Pollard, *Records of the English Bible*, p. 17.

[11] *The New Testament of oure Savyoure Jesu Christ, newly and dylygently translated into Englyshe with Annotacions in the Mergent to helpe the Reader to the Understandynge of the texte. Prynted in the yere of oure Lorde, God. MDXXXVII.* The text itself calls for little notice. Acts 15:34 stops with, "it pleased Sylas to abyde there styll"; John 2:4 reads: "Woman, what have I to do wyth the?" Luke 2:46 reads: "Syttunge in the middes of the doctours, hearyng them and posynge them." I John 5:7 is in small print; Phil. 2:7 reads: "made himself of no reputation"; a colophon after I Tim. reads: "Sent from Laodicia, whiche is the chiefest citye of Phrygia Pacaciana," as in Coverdale's version. There are some remarkable omissions: "Put thy finger into the holes of the nails" (John 20:25); "This cup is the New Testament in my blood" (I Cor. 11:25). For "let us leave the doctrine," the printer has put, "let us love the doctrine" (Heb. 6:1). After the Epistle to Philemon follow the epistles of Peter, the three of St. John, Hebrews, James, and the others.

[12] Other preliminary pieces are mentioned above.

thus explained: In 1537 Grafton sent a copy of it to Cranmer, who at once wrote to Cromwell:

> You shall receive by the bringer a Bible in English, both of a new translation and of a new print, dedicated unto the king's majesty, as farther appeareth by a pistle unto his grace in the beginning of the book, which in mine opinion is very well done, and therefore I pray your lordship to read the same. And as for the translation, so far as I have read thereof, I like it better than any other translation heretofore made; yet not doubting but that there may and will be found some fault therein, as you know no man ever did or can do so well, but it may be from time to time amended. And forasmuch as the book is dedicated unto the king's grace, and also great pains and labour taken in setting forth of the same; I pray you, my lord, that you will exhibit the book unto the king's highness, and to obtain of his grace, if you can, a licence that the same may be sold and read of every person, without danger of any act, proclamation, or ordinance heretofore granted to the contrary, until such time that we the bishops shall set forth a better translation, which I think will not be till a day after doomsday. August 4, 1537.[13]

It will be noted that Cranmer, while well aware of the labor expended on this new version, yet shows no surprise at its sudden appearance, even going out of his way to commend the author's dedicatory letter to the King. Is it possible that Cromwell himself suggested to the author—unnamed by Cranmer, though his name was clearly indicated on the title page—that he should dedicate his work to the King? Why was Cranmer so eager to secure the royal licence and thus override previous ordinances? Why, too, does he say to Cromwell: "If you can"? He is evidently doubtful of even Cromwell's chances of obtaining the King's compliance. Further, though insinuating that he has not read much of the version, yet he warmly commends it. Who, then, can believe that he failed to notice the incriminating signatures, J.R. and W.T.?[14] The whole episode looks like a daring plan to palm off Tyndale's version on an unthinking people. Indeed a daring plan,—if it was one—for the King might have well asked: "Who is this 'Matthew'? And is not this the very version made by Tyndale and so emphatically condemned some years ago?"

[13] Letters 194, 197, and 198, August 4, 13, 28, 1537, in *Miscellaneous Writings and Letters of Thomas Cranmer,* Parker Society (1846), pp. 344–47. When writing to Cromwell on August 28, Grafton, while thanking him for securing the licence, adds significantly: "Yet certain there be which believe not that it pleased the king's grace to licence it to go forth"; he therefore asks that for future security the edition may be licenced under Cromwell's privy seal; cf. *ibid.,* p. 346 note. See also Strype, *Memorials of Archbishop Cranmer* (1853), I, 82–87; Gairdner, *op. cit.,* II, 280–83, 465.

[14] "An impression," says Westcott, "is an intangible argument, but to me Cranmer's letter appears to be that of a man who was not taken by surprise by the new Bible. It is

But whatever the explanation, Cranmer, Cromwell, and Grafton succeeded beyond all expectation. So promptly was the licence accorded that on August 13 Cranmer wrote to Cromwell: "You have shewed me more pleasure herein, than if you had given me a thousand pound"; and a fortnight later: "This deed you shall hear of in the great day, when all things shall be opened and made manifest." On August 28 Grafton wrote to inform Cromwell that printing 1,500 copies had cost him £500, about £6000 at present valuation. Anxious to re-imburse himself, he now urged that every beneficed clergyman, "especially they of the papistical sort," should have to buy a copy, also that every abbey should provide six copies for the use of its members and for visitors.

But Matthew's Bible did not long enjoy royal favor. In 1543, in "An Acte for the advancement of true religion and for the abolishment of the contrary," the King complains that "many seditious people, arrogant and ignorant persons, whereof some pretendinge to be learned and to have the perfite and true knowledge of the sacred and holy scriptures, strive to pervert men. . . . Therefore be it enacted . . . that all manner of bookes of the old and newe testament in englishe, being of the craftie, false, and untrue translacion of Tindall, . . . shall be clerely and utterlie abolished, extinguished, and forbidden to be kept or used in this realme." At the same time the Great Bible was safeguarded: "provided alwayes that the bibles and newe testament in englishe, not being of Tindalles translacions, shall stand in force." [15] Yet the Great Bible was substantially the same as Tyndale's.[16]

---

further to be remarked that Grafton . . . was acquainted with the contents of Cranmer's letter to Crumwell of August 13th, and wrote to Crumwell with a present of six Bibles on the same day that Cranmer wrote the second letter of thanks" (*A General View of the History of the English Bible* [1905], p. 69 note). For Cranmer's letter, see his *Works,* Parker Society, p. 346. Westcott (p. 71) seems to suppose that even Tyndale's Prologues were in this first edition, and marvels that Henry should have failed to detect the work of his old adversary, who in addition to his heretical views had withstood him on the subject of the divorce. But as a matter of fact, the Prologues were added only by Becke in his editions of 1549 and 1551; cf. Dore, *op. cit.,* p. 118.

[15] Dore (pp. 125–36) gives a long extract of this Acte. After his "Injunctions to the Clergy," 1542, Bonner published a list of condemned books, among them "the table, glosses, marginal and preface before the Epistle of St. Paul to the Romans, of Thomas Matthew's doing, and printed beyond the sea without privilege, set in his Bible in English" (in Wilkins, *Concilia,* III, 867). According to Dore (p. 117), the volume was printed by Van Meteren of Antwerp.

[16] Cf. Moulton, *The History of the English Bible,* pp. 144 f. "In the translation of this Bible the greatest doer was in deede William Tyndall" (Foxe, *Actes and Monumentes* [1583], p. 1191).

EDITIONS OF MATTHEW'S BIBLE

Numerous editions of Matthew's Bible appeared, some of them of interest if only for the light they throw on the liberties publishers then felt themselves free to take with books. The second edition, in folio, dates from 1538;[17] a third, in five volumes (16mo), appeared in 1540.[18] In 1549 Raynalde and Hyll produced a faithful reprint of the original edition of 1537; at the end of the volume is the colophon: "To the Honoure and Prayse of God was this Bible prynted and fynisshed in the yeare of oure Lorde God A.M.D.XXXVII. And nowe agayne accordyngly imprented, and finyshed the leaste daye of Octobre. In the yeare of oure Lord God M.D.XLIX. At London By William Hyll and Thomas Reynaldes, Typographers. God save the kynge." This was the first edition to insert Tyndale's Prologues to the Pentateuch and to Jonas; it omitted the Prayer of Manasses. Prefixed to Exodus is a table explaining certain technical terms in the Levitical ritual; e.g. "Brestlappe or brestflap, is soche a flap as thou seest in the brest of a cope"; "Ephod, is a garment somwhat lyke an amyce, save the armes came thorowe and it was gyrd to." This table must have been a useful innovation.[19]

In 1549 Becke published a new edition: *The Bible, that is to say, all the Holy Scripture in which are contayned the Old and the New Testament truley and purely translated into English, imprinted at London by John Day dewling* [dwelling] *at Aldersgate and William Seres dewling in Peter Colledge. Cum privilegio ad imprimendum solum, 17 day of August, M.D.xlix.* The fresh Dedication, drawn up by Becke himself, ran: "To the moost puisant and mighty prince Edwarde the sixt, by the grace of God Kyng of Englande, France and Ireland, defender of the fayth, and of the Churche of Englande and also of Irelande, in earth the supreme head, your graces moost humble and obedient subject Edmunde Becke wysheth all grace and peace from God, with long reygne, honor, healthe and prosperitie." Becke also added an account of the labor involved: "After long travail, great paynes and labours achieved . . .

[17] Lewis, *A Complete History of the Several Translations of the Holy Bible and New Testament,* p. 107; Dore, *loc. cit.;* though Cotton says that "no such edition of this year has yet been ascertained" (*Lists of Editions of the Bible and Parts Thereof in English,* p. 13).

[18] Portions of this edition are known (Dore, *op. cit.,* p. 118), though Cotton (p. 17) questions whether it was ever completed.

[19] See Dore, *op. cit.,* pp. 118–20.

about the edicion and setting forth of an handsome and comodious Byble with prologes, scholyers or briefe Annotations (not hitherto heretofore in our native language published). . . ."

The Frontispiece to "The Thyrd Part" has a cut representing Jonas diving headlong into the mouth of what is intended to be a whale but is really a polar bear with cropped upstanding ears and armed with a formidable set of teeth. The New Testament portion bears the title: *The newe Testament of oure Savyoure Jesu Christe newly and dylygently translated into Englyshe wyth Annotacions in the Mergent to helpe the Reader to the understandynge of the Texte. Prynted in the yeare of oure Lorde God. M.D.XLIX.* Above and below the letterpress are pictured the four evangelists penning their Gospels, St. Mark's lion gazing at him very comically from under the front of the desk. There follow: "William Tindale unto the Christen Reader," in six columns, the list of the books, and a Prologue to the Gospel of St. Matthew. Becke also added very long and offensive notes, which, however, were never reprinted. "The notes to S. Matthew, chapter xix," says Dore, "are indecent, and many others most objectionable, mainly consisting of abuse of the Church, her doctrine, and her clergy." [20] The note on I Pet. 3:7 is startling: "He dwelleth wyth his wyfe according to knowledge, that taketh her as a neccessarye healper, and not as a bonde servante, or a bonde slave. And yf she be not obedient and healpfull unto hym, endeavoureth to beate the feare of God into her heade, that therby she maye be compelled to learne her dutie, and to do it." Becke also added III Maccabees to the Apocrypha.[21]

The last edition was by Hyll in 1551. But no less than eight different publishers' names appear, presumably of booksellers who had subscribed for the edition,[22] for the colophon has:

> Here endeth the whole Byble after the translation of Thomas Mathew, with all hys Prologues, that is to say, upon the V bokes of Moses, the prophet Jonas, and to every of the four Evangelists. And after every Chapter of the boke are there added many playne Annotacions and exposicions of suche places as unto the symple unlearned seame heard to understand. With other dyvers notable matters as ye shall fynde noted nexte unto the Callender. Diligentlye perused and cor-

[20] See Gairdner, *op. cit.*, II, 29 f., for these objectionable notes.

[21] Cotton, *op. cit.*, p. 21; Dore, *op. cit.*, pp. 120–24; Mombert, *English Versions of the Bible*, p. 191; Moulton, *op. cit.*, p. 124.

[22] See Cotton's note on the point, *op. cit.*, p. 33. The names of neither Matthew nor Rogers appear in the editions of 1549 and 1551; in fact, they stood on the title page of the first edition only.

rected. Imprinted at London by Nicolas Hyll, dwelling in Saynt Johns streate, at the coste and charges of certayne honest menne of the occupacyon whose names be upon their bokes."

THE NOTES IN VARIOUS EDITIONS

In the first edition of Matthew's Bible very objectionable notes were inserted. These were omitted in the next few editions, but replaced in later ones. The ordinary marginal notes in, for example, the edition of 1551, are mostly innocuous; e.g., on Matt. 16:18: "I will build (on your confession) my congregation or church"; and on Matt. 26:26, where doubts are expressed as to the precise meaning of the words of consecration. But it was quite otherwise with the "Table of the Pryncypal Matters Conteyned in the Byble." For this, as Foxe says, contained "the commonplaces in the Bible, and texts of Scripture for proving the same; and chiefly the commonplaces of the Lord's Supper, the marriage of priests, and the Mass, of which it was there said that it was not to be found in Scripture. This, giving to the clergy offence, was gotten to be restrained."[23] The word "penance" as well as "works of supererogation" were eliminated, while the Mass was derided and the notion of the Real Presence whittled away. "The word 'Mass,'" says one note, "is not in the Byble translated by St. Jerome, nor in none other that we have seen. . . . The supper of the Lord is a holy memorye and gevyng of thankes for the deth of Christ." The note on Matt. 26:26 ("This is my body") is interesting as an indication of the discussions then prevalent on the precise meaning of the words of institution:

> In these few words lieth all the controversie that had been and is about the belief of the sacrament of Christ's body and blood. Some say . . . he pointed to his own body, as who should say he would speake one thing and poynt another that none might understand his meaning but them that saw him only. Of these men I would axe to what he poynted when he said This is my blood. And another sorte say that by the vertue of these wordes he turned the bread into his very natural body even substantially and really. Of these men I would ask whether his body was then corruptible or not. The third sort . . . that he spake of the bread calling it his body in signification. . . . These men are called heretikes, but are indeed the true Christians.

The note on I Cor. 11:29 explains further the heretical teaching concerning the Eucharist: "The sacramental bread and wine distributed

[23] *Actes and Monumentes,* p. 1191; see Pollard, *op. cit.,* p. 229. For the sources of these notes see Westcott, *op. cit.,* Appendix XI, pp. 336–42.

certify the faithful even (as it were sensybly) of their redemption by Christ." Apropos of the anointing of the sick, the note on Jas. 5:14 has: "We wyth whom such anoyntynge is not in use may under the name of oyle understande the office of charitye in ministering unto the sycke such thynges as he nedeth." The doctrines of purgatory and of prayer for the dead were, of course, repudiated. A note referring to II Mach. 12:44 says:

Judge upon this place whether the opinion hath been to pray for the dead, as to be baptized for them, I Cor. xv., which thing was only done to confirm the hope of the resurrection of the dead, not to deliver them from any pain. St. Paul did not allow the ceremony of Christening for the dead, no more doth any place of the canonical Scripture allow the ceremony of offering for the dead. Furthermore: This whole book of the Maccabees, and especially the second, is not of sufficient authority to make an article of faith.

So too with other traditional teachings. On Matt. 9:6, concerning the power to forgive sins, a note reads: "This remission of sin is the certifying of the conscience of the sinner that his sins be forgiven." And on Matt. 2:6 and the quotation from Mich. 5:2 there is this note: "The Scribes did as some Prelates do when they had rather reherse a pece of Scripture as they fynde it expounded by some of the doctours, then as it lieth in the texte." Other examples are given below, p. 212.

THE APOCRYPHA

In Matthew's Bible there is a lengthy Introduction to the Apocrypha, which is probably taken over from Olivetan and differs from that in Coverdale's Bible of 1535 and in the Great Bible, 1539. In this section, entitled "The volume of the bokes called Apocripha: conteyned in the comen translacion in Latyne, which are not founde in the Hebrue nor in the Chalde," are included III and IV Esdras and The Prayer of Manasses; there are no notes, and the explanation of the term Apocrypha is as novel as it is false. This Introduction embodies the view of the Apocrypha which has since prevailed in the "Reformed" churches.[24]

In consideracion that the bokes before are founde in the Hebrue tonge, receaved of all men, and that the following whych are called Apocripha (because they were wont to be reade, not openly, and in comen, but as it were in secret and aparte) are nether founde in the Hebrue nor in the Chalde, in whyche tonges they have not of long bene wryten (in lesse that it were happyly the boke of Sapience) whereupon it were nowe very harde to repayre and amende them: And that also they are not receaved nor taken as leggytymate and lawful, as wel of the Hebrues as of the

[24] See Mombert, *op. cit.*, p. 181; Eadie, *op. cit.*, I, 316.

whole Churche, as S. Hierome sheweth, we have separated them and set them asyde, that they maye the better be knowen to thyntente that men maye knowe of which bokes wytness oughte to be receaved, and of which not. For the sayd S. Hierome speakinge of the boke of Judith (whyche is Apocripha) sayeth that the autorytie therof is not esteamed worthy and sufficient to confyrme and establysh the thinges that lyght in disputacion. And generally of the bokes called Apocripha he sayethe that men may reade to the edyfyinge of the people but not to confirme and strengthen the doctryne of the church. I leave oute here the Lawe (as they call it) of Can. C. S. Romana xv. *distinct.*[25] where he shewth his judgemente. Lykewyse the Glose of C. Canone xvi. *distinct.* which sayeth that men holdeth them not but in generall; as though he shoulde saye that generally and thorowlye they are not alowed.

And not without cause: for that they have bene corrupted and falsyfyed in many places it appeareth sufficiently in Eusebius his boke called *Historia Ecclesiastica.* Whiche thinge is easy to be knowen even nowe a dayes in certen poyntes, namely in the bokes of Machabees: whose second boke S. Hierome confesseth that he founde not in the Hebrue, by the meanes therof it is become unto us the more suspecte and the lesse receaved. In lyke manner is it of the thyrd and fourth boke of Esdras, which S. Hierome protesteth that he would not have translated them as he took them for dreams, whereas Josephus yet in his boke of his *Antiquities* declareth the summe of the matter after the manner of a storye, as well of the boke of Machabees as of the III of Esdras; although he esteam the bokes compyled from the raigne of king Artaxerxes unto his tyme to be Apocrypha.

Wherefore, then, when thou wylt maynteine any thing for certen, tendrynge a reason of thy fayth, take hede to proceade therin by the lyvynge and pythy Scriptures, folowynge S. Peter when he sayeth, he that speaketh let him speak as though he spake the word of God, as a thinge moost true and certen, opened by the prophetes and Apostles, inspyred with the holy ghoost of whom we have wytnesse moore cleare than the daye. Lawyers havynge greate desyre to confyrme and stablishe their opinions by the lawe of man, say that it is shame to speake without lawe. How much more feare and dreade then oughte he to have that sayeth he is a Christian, the whyche holdeth not hym selfe or readeth not in the lawe of the lyvynge God but in mennes invencyons and phantasyses. Let us: that are bylded on the foundacyon of the holy prophetes and Apostles, and on the heade corner stone (on which they themselves were founded, and whiche they preached, that is Jesus Christ the suer stone) leave the thynges that are uncerten to folowe the certen, holdynge us and reastynge us in them, and fastenynge our ancre there as in a sure place. For oure Christen fayeth consysteth not in doubtful thynges but in a playne and moost certen assurance, and in a moost true persuasion, taken and confirmed by infallyble verytie. In which God graunt us walcke perpetually to thintente that accordinge to it (fulfyllynge his holy wyll in us, and settynge a syde all inventions contrary unto hym) we maye lyve to hys honour and to the edifying of his Churche. So be it.

Although Matthew's Bible had been condemned for its heretical renderings and notes, and was soon to be superseded by Cranmer's Great

[25] That is: Gratian, distinction xv in the chap., *Sancta Romana.*

Bible, it had done its work. For, as Pollard remarks, "its importance was very great, since it formed the starting-point of successive revisions which resulted in the version of 1611, a matter for sincere congratulation as it contained . . . the greatest possible amount of the work of Tyndale, who was a far better scholar than Coverdale." [26] Similarly Westcott declares: "The textual peculiarities of the edition are unimportant. In itself Matthew's has had no original and independent influence upon the authorised text. Its great work was to present the earlier texts in a combined form which might furnish the common basis of later revisions." [27]

[26] *Records of the English Bible*, p. 17.

[27] *Op. cit.*, p. 177. See also C. Roger, *Collation of the Old Testament from the Translations of J. Rogers, the Bishops', the Genevan and the Authorized Version; the New Testament from Wiclif, Rogers, the Rhemes, 1582, the Genevan, the Authorized Version, and G. Wakefield*, 1795; Dundee, 1847.

CHAPTER XIII

The Great Bible, 1539

CROMWELL AND THE GREAT BIBLE

COVERDALE'S Bible proved unsatisfactory, mainly because it had not been translated from the original Greek and Hebrew; therefore Cromwell decided to secure a revision of it. Already in his Injunctions for 1536 he had said: "Ye shall provyde on this side the Feast of . . . next commyng, one boke of the whole Bible of the largest size,[1] in Englyshe, and the same set up in some conveyent place within the said church that ye have cure of."[2] If the date, 1536, is correct,[3] he would seem to be anticipating the production of what came to be known as Cromwell's Bible, owing to his share in its production, or as the Great Bible, owing to

[1] This demand for a Bible "of the largest size" was often repeated: in the Proclamation of 1541, by Elizabeth in 1559, again in 1571, when it was decreed that every archbishop and bishop "must have a copy of the holy Bible of the largest volume as lately printed in London" (Cardwell, *Synodalia,* I, 115); *Thirteen Articles,* 1571, Injunctions for the Laity, no. 4; Grindal, *Works,* Parker Society, p. 133; Strype, *Ecclesiastical Memorials,* II, 78; Wilkins, *Concilia,* IV, 263. The Great Bible, measuring 15 inches by 9 inches outside with a printed page 13 inches by 8½ inches, certainly fulfilled these requirements.

[2] Wilkins, *Concilia,* III, 846–48. Cranmer's Injunctions for Hereford, in the same year, insisted that every parson was to have "a whole Bible in Latin and English, or at least a New Testament, and every day to study one chapter of the said Bible or New Testament, conferring the Latin and English together" (*ibid.,* p. 843).

[3] The date (1536) assigned to these Injunctions constitutes a difficulty. For in 1536 by "a whole Bible of the largest size" Cromwell cannot have meant the Great Bible, which at that date had hardly been contemplated. Nor could the term "largest" have referred to Matthew's Bible, the printed matter in which measured only 11¼ inches by 6½ inches. Foxe avoids the difficulty by saying the Great Bible had been printed "about three years before" (*Actes and Monumentes* [1853], I, 121). Pollard, however, suggests that the date given by Wilkins (*Concilia,* III, 815), 1536, "is probably two years too early"; cf. *ibid.,* III, 262 note; H. Guppy, "The Royal Injunctions of 1536 and 1538 and the Great Bible," in *Bulletin of the Rylands Library,* April, 1938. At any rate the injunctions issued by Henry in 1538 were couched in almost identical terms; cf. *Proclamations,* 1538; Pollard, *op. cit.,* pp. 261–65. Hoare makes the suggestion, an improbable one, that though penned in 1536, these Injunctions were not published till two years later (*The Evolution of the English Bible,* p. 172). See Gairdner, *Lollardy and the Reformation in England,* II, 277–79, for a discussion of the date.

its size, or as Cranmer's Bible, since he wrote the Preface to the second edition.

Meanwhile Matthew's Bible had appeared, 1537, with a royal licence procured by Cromwell; yet it too proved unsatisfactory owing to the character of the notes accompanying it. To prepare, then, for the proposed new version, a proclamation was issued, November, 1538, forbidding the admission into the country of English books printed abroad, compelling printers to submit their work to the Privy Council, and insisting that the words *ad imprimendum solum* should henceforth appear on all title pages.[4] Even notes on biblical subjects had to be submitted for examination, and translators of the Bible or portions of it were obliged to affix their names to their work.

It is difficult to discover how far Cromwell was actuated by any really religious motives in working for this fresh revision and its publication. He was certainly "a very worldly-minded layman," [5] "neither Catholic nor Protestant"; [6] a disciple of Machiavelli, whose doctrines he had assimilated while in Italy, he made "politics . . . chiefly his religion." [7] Probably many regarded him as a conscientious reformer. But whatever may have been his real attitude towards the word of God, Cromwell undoubtedly provided much of the money for the publication of the Great Bible. In fact, he himself told Castillion, the ambassador, that "a ses propres couste et despens luy-mesmes a faict imprimer une bible en vulgaire Angloys," adding that "the said volumes had cost him at least

[4] Printers are "not to put these wordes, *Cum privilegio regali,* without adding *ad imprimendum solum";* in other words, says Pollard, "they are not to make a mere permission to print appear as if any special favour or monopoly were being conferred on the edition" (*Records of the English Bible,* p. 241 note). Grafton, who had already printed on his title page, *Cum gratia et privilegio Regis,* was particularly aggrieved by the insistence on the insertion of *ad imprimendum solum,* "words," he said, "which we never heard before," and which, so he feared, would suggest that "yt is not the kynges acte or mynde to set yt forth, but only lycence the prynters to sell soch as is put forth."

[5] Gairdner, *op. cit.,* I, 315.

[6] Collier, *An Ecclesiastical History of Great Britain,* V, 73; but on p. 71 he says Cromwell was reputed to know the Latin Testament by heart.

[7] Constant, *The Reformation in England,* p. 301. On at least one occasion Cromwell expressed himself openly on the subject of reform; for he said to Chapuys: "Before Christmas I should see all Constitutions made for it [the reform] here, composed by the King, which would be very different from the papistical ones; and he had no doubt it would be a true and singular mirror to all Christendome" (*Papers Foreign and Domestic, Henry VIII,* June 29, 1535). A glazier named Nycolson wrote: "Now help that the holie Bible may come forth. . . . If so, Cromwell will be made more famous than Austen, who, men say, brought the faith first into England" (*ibid.,* IX, 226). Cf. R. B. Merriman, *Life and Letters of Thomas Cromwell,* 1902, 2 vols.

600 marks or 300 *livres tournoys,* et que le tout n'est, sinon pour les donner." [8] Hence Coverdale and Grafton speak of "youre worke of the byble."

ITS REVISION AND PUBLICATION

The new revision commissioned by Cromwell was entrusted to Coverdale, who completed his task by September, 1539, and by the following April the volume was ready for distribution. For his revision of the Old Testament, Coverdale based himself on Matthew's version, 1537, correcting it by Münster's Latin version.[9] For the New Testament he used Tyndale's last corrected edition, 1534–35, Erasmus' Latin version, the Complutensian, and the Vulgate.[10] How far he was an independent reviser is not clear. Who were the unnamed "dyverse excellent learned men, expert in the foresayde tongues" referred to on the title page? And did they work under his direction, or he under theirs?

The Great Bible is no mere reprint of the original versions by Coverdale or Matthew; there are, for instance, no less than forty changes in the fifty-third chapter of Isaias alone. Moreover, wherever Coverdale had in 1535 shown himself indifferent to readings peculiar, for the most part, to the Vulgate, he now inserted from that version, though in smaller

[8] Pollard, *op. cit.,* p. 249. The reference is perhaps to the preparation of Matthew's Bible, the actual printing of which was done by Grafton, who, to reimburse himself, demanded a monopoly of its sale (cf. Strype, *Memorials of Archbishop Cranmer,* Appendix XX; Pollard, *op. cit.,* pp. 219–21). Grafton also printed the Great Bible, though he was succeeded in this by Marler; cf. H. Plomer, "Antony Marler and the Great Bible," in *The Library,* Series III, I, 200 ff. For Marler's petitions for expenses, see Pollard, *op. cit.,* p. 260; Gairdner, *op. cit.,* II, 292; Dore, *Old Bibles,* p. 160; Anderson, *Annals of the English Bible,* 367. These printers naturally looked on the printing and publishing of the Bible as a paying proposition. But Grafton himself fell upon evil days: he had printed Matthew's Bible, only to find it repudiated later on; he had printed the Great Bible, and that too had been repudiated when the religious pendulum swung around and a scape-goat had to be found, with the result that Grafton was fined and had to spend some time in Newgate. Foxe implies that Grafton's imprisonment for printing the Great Bible as well as Matthew's Bible, being at the same time bound over "that he should neither sell, nor imprint or cause to be imprinted, any more Bibles till the king and clergy should agree upon a translation," was contemporaneous with what he styles "the staying of the Bible during the reign of Henry VIII." But Grafton was imprisoned January 5, 1541, and the Convocation which saw the failure of Cranmer's project for a fresh version was not held until thirteen months later, February, 1542. Cf. Gairdner, *op. cit.,* II, 291.

[9] Cromwell commissioned Coverdale "to undertake the charge of a new edition on the basis of Matthew's but with a more complete critical collation of the Hebrew and Latin texts than had hitherto been attempted" (Westcott, *A General View of the History of the English Bible,* pp. 180 f.).

[10] Hoare, *op. cit.,* pp. 187–89; Anderson, *op. cit.,* p. 313.

type and in brackets, clauses not in the current text of the Greek Testament; e.g., "It is I, feare not" (Luke 24:36), "considered not" (Rom. 1:32). So too in the Old Testament, where there are about seventeen additions in Proverbs and several in Job; e.g., "even as it hath pleased the Lord, so is it come to pass" (Job 1:21); "or who may say unto him, why doest thou so?" (Job 11:8.) Similar additions appear in I John 1:4; 2:23; 3:1, 9, and so forth, the whole text differing from that of Tyndale in seventy-one places; I John 5:7 is printed in small black letters. Certain clauses admitted later in the Clementine edition were rightly omitted by Coverdale: "of God" (Mark 15:29); others are bracketed and in small type: "and the bride" (Matt. 25:1), "with whom also I am lodged" (I Cor. 16:19). It is noteworthy that the Great Bible reverts to "one fold" (John 10:16), whereas Coverdale and Matthew both correctly read "one flock." [11]

In his often repeated account of the printing of the Great Bible,[12] Foxe says that when Bonner was ambassador in France, Cromwell "procured of the King of England his gracious letters to the French King to permitte and licence [13] a subject of his to imprint the Bible in English within the Universitie of Paris because paper was there more mete and apt to be had for the doing therof than in the realme of England." Bonner,

[11] Coverdale himself refers to these insertions from the Vulgate (*On Baptism*, xvi). An examination of six of these additional clauses shows that recent textual criticism frequently endorses the readings of the Vulgate; for example, *modo* (Matt. 26:53) appears in the Great Bible as "even now," but in brackets; A.V., "presently"; R.V., "even now"; and without comment in White's *Novum Testamentum Latine. . . . Editio minor. Ego sum, nolite timere* (Luke 24:36) is in brackets in the Great Bible: "It is I, feare not," though omitted in A.V. and R.V.; yet it is endorsed without comment by White. *Non intellexerunt* (Rom. 1:32), retained by White, stands in the Great Bible in small type, "considered not," but is omitted in A.V. and R.V. On the other hand, whereas the Vulgate clauses of Acts 15:33 f. are given in brackets in the Great Bible: "they were let go in peace from the brethren to the Apostles [R.V.: "unto those that had sent them forth"]. Notwithstanding it pleased Silas to abide there still"; the whole of verse 34 is omitted in R.V. and likewise in White's *Editio minor*. The addition in Acts 15:41 (*et praecipiens custodire praecepta Apostolorum et seniorum*) which stands in many MSS., is retained in the Sixtine and Clementine editions but appears neither in A.V. or R.V. or White's edition. Lastly, the addition of *in vobis iram* (Jas. 5:3), which has little MSS. support though retained in the Sixtine and Clementine editions, stands in small type in the Great Bible, though it is absent from the versions by Coverdale and Matthew and is rejected by White.

[12] *Actes and Monumentes* (1583), pp. 1191 ff.; given in Pollard, *op. cit.*, pp. 223–32; see also Strype, *Memorials of Archbishop Cranmer*, I, 119 ff.

[13] For the licence granted by Francis, see Pollard, *op. cit.*, pp. 323–34; Strype, *op. cit.*, II, 303.

he says, was enthusiastic in forwarding the project, even helping in the printing of the amended edition of Coverdale's Latin-English New Testament,[14] and undertaking to "have of your Bibles set up in the Church of Paules, at the least in sundrie places six of them."[15]

But the French king, though he acceded to Henry's request, changed his mind,[16] owing, it is said, to the action of the Inquisitors, who on December 17, 1538, cited the printer, Regnault, for printing the Bible in Paris. These Inquisitors[17] write as follows: "Whereas from the translation of the Holy Scripture alike of the Old and New Testament into the vernacular tongue which has come into the hands of the simple, it has been found lately that some have taken occasion to err in the faith." The Inquisitors therefore summoned Regnault and others engaged in printing the Great Bible in Paris and prohibited them "from proceeding further to the impression of the said Bible in the vernacular tongue and from surrendering and alienating the printed sheets from their possession until, after such Bible has been examined by us, it be otherwise ordained."[18]

[14] "There is no reason to think that Bonner 'caused' it to be printed" (Pollard, *op. cit.*, p. 224 note). How far we are to trust these statements about Bonner's share in the production and forwarding of the Great Bible is a moot question. That he was in Paris and that he was interested in the work on the Bible is clear from his letters to Cromwell announcing that the work had been stopped, October 7, 1538 (cf. *ibid.*, p. 240). But Foxe's account of Bonner's treacherous behavior later on must be taken with many reservations. For, as Collier remarks (*op. cit.*, VI, 125 f.), Foxe defamed Bonner just as much as he did Gardiner for the burning of Cranmer and Ridley. See Burnet, *History of the Reformation,* I, 398, 431 f.; I, ii, 341, 414; iii, 382 f.; Hoare, *op. cit.*, p. 195; Dore, *op. cit.*, pp. 168 f.

[15] That Bonner did set up six copies of the Great Bible in St. Paul's is, of course, true; and it is also true that the resulting brawling and disputing called for energetic suppression; see Gairdner, *The English Church in the Sixteenth Century,* p. 220; *idem, Lollardy and the Reformation in England,* II, 300 f. For the "Admonition" which Bonner found himself compelled to make regarding the disorders, see Wilkins, *Concilia,* III, 863 ff.

[16] In justice the wording of the licence accorded by Francis I should be noted: "Dummodo quod sic imprimetis et excudetis sincere et pure, quantum in vobis erit, citra ullas privatas aut illegitimas opiniones, impressum et excussum fuerit." Cf. Strype, *Memorials of Archbishop Cranmer,* p. 756, Appendix xxx, quoted by Westcott, *op. cit.*, p. 74 note.

[17] "Friar Henry Garvais, Regius Doctor in Sacred Theology, Prior of the Convent of the Preaching Friars at Paris, Vicar-General also of the venerable Father Friar Matthew of the same Order, also Doctor in Sacred Theology, Inquisitor General concerning heretical teachings in the whole kingdom of France, as especially designated by Apostolic and Royal authority, to all priests, vicars—whether with or without the cure of souls—to all public notaries and scriveners wherever so appointed, health in the Lord."

[18] See Pollard, *op. cit.*, pp. 246–49. A note on p. 227 reads: "There is not the slightest reason to attribute the interference of the Inquisition 'to the practice of the Englishe

Coverdale and his assistants had to flee, leaving behind them 2,000 copies. They were able, however, to buy from a haberdasher copies sold him by a venal lieutenant who had been told to see that they were burnt. Coverdale succeeded in getting the printing presses to London, where copies were printed, "yet not without great trouble and loss, for the hatred of the bishops, namely, Steven Gardiner, and his fellowes who mightily did stomacke and maligne the printing therof." [19]

Though no one now gives unqualified credence to Foxe's narrative, there is no reason for questioning its substantial accuracy, discounting, of course, his animus against the bishops. Yet Pollard, while accepting Foxe's account as substantially correct, since it is borne out by the correspondence between Bonner, Grafton, Coverdale, and Cromwell, does not hesitate to say of the foregoing account: "Almost every statement in it which can be tested can be shewn to be inexact." J. S. Brewer says quite simply: "Had Foxe, the Martyrologist, been an honest man, his carelessness and credulity would have incapacitated him from being a trustworthy historian. Unfortunately he was not honest; he tampered with the documents that came into his hands, and freely indulged in those very faults of suppression and equivocation for which he condemned his opponents." [20]

ITS RECEPTION

Strype has also preserved from one of Foxe's MSS. the often quoted description of the enthusiasm with which the Great Bible was received in England.

> It was wonderful to see with what great joy this book of God was received, not only among the learneder sort, and those that were noted for love of the Reformation, but generally all England over, among all the vulgar and common people;

Bishops.' It was a political move, suggested by the French ambassador in London"; see the letter of the imperial ambassador to Charles V, January 9, 1539: "The ambassador informs me that all that was done in France was merely an artifice" (*ibid.*, p. 252).

[19] See too J. A. Kingdon, *Incidents in the Lives of Thomas Poyntz and Richard Grafton*, 1895. In his *Abridgement of the Chronicles of England*, by Hall, Grafton gives his own brief account: "In this yere the Great Bible in English in the Great volume was printed in Paris in as privy a manner as might bee, but when it was knowne, not only the same beeing XXC [2,000, not 2,500, as Foxe has it] in nomber was seased and made confiscat, but also both the printer, marchants, and correctors in great jeapardy of their lyves escaped" (given by Pollard, *op. cit.*, p. 227 note).

[20] *The Reign of Henry VIII*, I, 52. J. F. Mozley, in *John Foxe and His Book*, made a gallant but unavailing attempt to whitewash his hero.

and with what greediness God's word was read, and what resort to places where the reading of it was. Everybody that could bought the book, or busily read it, or got others to read it to them, if they could not themselves. And even little boys flocked among the rest to hear portions of the holy Scripture read.[21]

But this is only one of Foxe's many "terminological inexactitudes" which a gullible people always has accepted, and perhaps always will accept, as "Gospel truth." Dore dryly remarks on it:

This statement is not more true than are many other statements in the *Acts and Monuments*. If the people all England over were so anxious to possess the new translation, what need was there of so many penal enactments to force it into circulation, and of Royal proclamations theatening with the King's displeasure those who neglected to purchase copies? . . . It is strange that this statement of Foxe should have been so often quoted by writers who must have known it to be exaggerated. . . . This great anxiety on the part of the majority of the people of England to possess a vernacular Bible existed only in the imaginations of Foxe and other party writers; for in spite of all the arbitrary proceedings taken to force the Bible into circulation, we find the printers often complaining of the large stocks remaining on their hands, and begging that persons might be compelled to purchase, and that no fresh editions might be issued. . . . The Cornishmen objected to have the new translation of the Bible forced upon them, as the Latin Bible was far more intelligible to them than the English.[22]

When the time came for the distribution of the Bibles, difficulties at once arose over the price to be charged. Cranmer urged 13/4, but Cromwell held out for 10/–, or at least £5 of our money; the printers agreed to the latter.[23] As many churches found it difficult to provide these obligatory Bibles, the printers began to fear lest they should find large stocks of unsold Bibles on their hands. For instance, Marler, though he had obtained leave to charge 2/– more for copies "trymmed with bullions," [24] only six days later urged: "Onles I have by the means of proclamacion some charge or commission that every church not redy provided of one bible . . . shall provide them of a bible of the largest volume, . . . being charged as I am with an importune somme of the said bookes now lying on my hande, I am undone for ever." [25]

[21] *Memorials of Archbishop Cranmer,* I, 91.

[22] *Old Bibles,* pp. 15–17, 155, 169 f., 225 f. See Westcott, *op. cit.,* p. 81; Gairdner, *Lollardy,* I, 159, 333–65; Daiches, *The King James Version of the English Bible* (1936), p. 39.

[23] Cf. Pollard, *op. cit.,* pp. 257 f.

[24] April 25, 1541; cf. *ibid.,* p. 260; Wilkins, *Concilia,* III, 843. See above, note 8.

[25] Pollard, *op. cit.,* pp. 260–62.

THE GREAT BIBLE IN THE CHURCHES

Marler's plea produced the Royal Proclamation of November 14, 1539: "For the Byble of the largest and greatest volume to be had in every church." Addressing "all and singular prynters and sellers of Bookes," the King says he is convinced that his zeal for the spiritual advancement of his people "cannot by any meane take so good effect, as by the graunting to them the free and lyberal use of the Bible, in oure owne maternall English tonge." But, he continues, since such determination necessitates having one standard edition,

> we have therefore appoynted our right truly and welbeloved counsellor the lorde Crumwell, keepor of our pryvye seale, to take for us, and in our name special care and charge, that no manner of persone or persones within this oure realme shall enterprise, attempt, or sett in hand to print any Bible in the English tonge of any manner of volume, duryng the space of fyve yeares next ensuying after the date herof, but only all suche as shall be deputid, assignid, and admitted by the said lord Crumwell.[26]

There was nothing intrinsically wrong in setting up Bibles in church for people to read. The Reformers might in fact have appealed in justification for so doing to the practice of that "primitive Church" to which they so frequently made reference when it harmonized with their own ideas. St. Paulinus of Nola, for instance, had inscribed on the wall of the *secretarium* of his church:

> Si quem sancta tenet meditandi in lege voluntas
> His possit residens sacris intendere libris.[27]

The fact, too, that Christians in Africa who had surrendered their copies of the Scriptures to the persecutors were therefore called *traditores* shows that it was usual for them to have copies in their houses. Had this not been the case, St. Chrysostom could not have said: "We often acquaint you many days beforehand with the subject of our discourse, so that taking the Bible in the meantime into your hands and running over the

[26] *Ibid.*, pp. 258 f. See Strype, *op. cit.*, II, 735 f. Pollard draws attention to the fact that on the receipt of the printers' complaint and their demand for royal protection for their interests, Cromwell wrote on the same day to the King and, characteristically, secured the patent for himself. This proclamation was repeated in even more emphatic form in May, 1541; cf. Rymer, *Foedera,* XIV, 649; Wilkins, *Concilia,* III, 846 f.; Dore, *op. cit.*, p. 161.

[27] *Epis.*, 12, *ad Severum.*

whole passage, you may have your minds better prepared to hear what is to be spoken." [28]

The motive for putting Bibles in the church is all-important. If the idea was that the laity could thus discover for themselves whether the services then being conducted in the sacred building were "in accord with the Word of God," then the action was, like the motive behind it, unjustifiable. When Bonner set up his six copies in St. Paul's, his sole object was to encourage people to become familiar with the Bible, not to use it as a stick wherewith to assail the Church to which they owed those same Scriptures.

But in those turbulent times such a concession was only too liable to be abused. "The Reformation spirit was too strong for men who had no mental balance. They were drunk with the new wine, and liberty degenerated with them into disreputable and offensive licence. The preacher in the pulpit often found his exhortations completely drowned in a tumult of voices shouting verses of the Bible out loud in various parts of the church, and occasionally adding improvised expositions." [29]

If interruptions during the sermon were trying to the preacher, picture the distress of a priest who, while saying Mass, had to hear a man like John Porter bawling out "with a loud and commanding voice" such choice extracts from the violently antipapal notes to be found in Matthew's Bible as "abominations before the Lord are idols and images before whom the people do bow themselves," or "the abuses that be in the Churche ought to be corrected by the Pryncees," or, even worse, "the worde Masse is not in the Byble translated by Jerom, nor in none other that we have," and "God doth curse the blessynges of the preastes and blesseth their curssynge." [30]

Henry himself took alarm at these ebullitions and had to intervene with a Proclamation:

> The Kynges Royal Majestie intended that his lovynge subjectes shulde have and use the commoditie of the readyng of the sayd Bybles, for the purposes above rehersed [namely, to learn how to fear God and honor the King], humbly, reverently and obediently; and not that any of them shulde reade the sayd Bybles, wyth loude and hyghe voyces, in tyme of the celebracyon of the holye Masse, and other dyvyne servyces in the churche, nor that any hys lay subjectes redynge the

[28] *Homilia*, III, *in Lazarum*.

[29] Hoare, *Evolution of the English Bible*, pp. 195 f.; cf. Wilkins, *Concilia*, III, 813–15, 846, 863.

[30] Cf. Gairdner, *Lollardy*, II, 300 f.

same, shulde presume to take upon them, any common dysputacyon, argumente or exposicyon of the mysteries therein conteyned.

Bonner, too, as bishop of London deprecated the unruly way in which people were acting; he demanded "reverence, discretion and quiet behaviour; no exposition of the text to be made save what was declared in the Bible itself which is to be read with all devocyon, humilitie and quyetnesse; the reader levyng behynde hym vayne glorye and hypocrisie, and all other carnal and corrupte affection, bryng with hym discretion, honeste intent, charytie, reverence and quyet behaviour, he is not to expound, nor to reade with a lowde voyce, and without disputacyon." [31]

Bonner even felt obliged to threaten to remove his six copies from St. Paul's. "But that," he added, "I should be right loth to do, considering that I have been always, and still am, right glad that the Scripture, the Word of God, should be well known." [32] These last words are noteworthy; in conformity with them he obliged all his clergy to read daily a chapter of the Bible with some gloss or commentary by approved writers.

THE TITLE PAGE AND FRONTISPIECE

The title page and frontispiece are generally said to be the work of Holbein,[33] and will repay careful study, not only as a work of art or as illustrative of the costumes of the period, but also for the "king worship" there portrayed. No description could portray better than does this picture the complete subordination of both Church and State to a sovereign who had constituted himself his own pope. At the top is depicted the eternal Father addressing the assembly on His right with the words: "Verbum quod egredietur de ore meo, non revertetur ad me vacuum, sed faciet quaecunque volui" (Isa. 55:11). To those on His left He says: "Inveni virum juxta cor meum qui faciet omnes voluntates meas" (Acts 13:22) and "Lucerna pedibus meis verbum tuum" (Ps. 118:105). Be-

[31] Pollard, *op. cit.*, pp. 266 ff.

[32] Wilkins, *Concilia,* III, 864–67; Burnet, *History of the Reformation,* I, ii, 507–10.

[33] This identification is now much disputed. H. R. Willoughby maintains that the frontispiece to Coverdale's Bible, 1535, is the work of Holbein, but not that prefixed to the Great Bible (*The First Authorized English Bible,* pp. ix, 49); see also *The British Museum Catalogue of Printed Books,* XV (1936). Very good reproductions of this frontispiece are given in H. Guppy's *Brief Sketch of the History of the Transmission of the Bible,* 1936; *idem, Miles Coverdale and the English Bible,* 1935; British Museum, *Guide to the Manuscripts and Printed Books Exhibited in Celebration of the Tercentenary of the Authorized Version,* 1911 and 1927; A. W. Pollard, *Last Words on the History of the Title-page,* 1891.

neath we see Henry seated on his throne with Cranmer and the other bishops on his right, and Cromwell with the laity on his left. To Cranmer he hands the *Verbum Dei:* "Haec praecipe et doce" (I Tim. 4:11); while to Cromwell he says: "Quod justum est judicate . . . (nec) ita parvum audietis ut magnum" (Deut. 1:16 f.). Over the king's left shoulder extends a large scroll with the words of Nabuchodonosor: "A me constitutum est decretum ut in universo imperio et regno meo tremiscant et paveant Deum viventem (Danielis)" (Dan. 6:26). Neither Cranmer nor the other bishops are wearing their miters, which lie on the ground at their feet; Cromwell, too, and the laity are hatless. All are smiling—almost smirking—as they receive the royal gifts.

The middle scenes depict Cranmer on the reader's left, now wearing his miter while distributing the *Verbum Dei* to the clergy, to whom he says: "Pascite qui in vobis est gregem Christi" (I Pet. 5:2). Cromwell, no longer hatless, does the same to the laity, whom he addresses with the words: "Diverte a malo et fac bonum, inquire pacem et persequere eam" (Ps. 33:15). At the bottom a preacher, from a pulpit inscribed with the words, "Vivat Rex!" exhorts the populace: "Obsecro igitur primum omnium fieri obsecrationes, orationes, postulationes, gratiarum actiones pro omnibus hominibus, pro regibis, etc." (I Tim. 2:1 f.) The orator is greeted with shouts of "Vivat Rex!" and "God save the King." It is no exaggeration to say with Hoare:

> If this frontispiece means anything it means that, in the eyes of those around him, Henry was himself the English Reformation. For he is the centre and soul of the picture. Not Parliament, not Convocation, not the Council, neither Cromwell himself nor Cranmer, but the King's Grace it is, that, under the guidance of Providence, presents the Bible to Cranmer and Cromwell, as representing respectively the clergy and the laity of his realm.[34]

The picture also has its tragic aspect. For though the arms of Cromwell, the originator of the projected version, figure on the title page of the first three editions, they were removed after his fall in 1540, and though his shield still appeared in the four following editions, it remained blank.

The first edition was entitled: *The Byble in Englyshe, that is to saye the content of all the holy Scripture, bothe of the olde and newe Testament, truly translated after the veryte of the Hebrue and Greke textes,*

[34] *Op. cit.* (1902), pp. 201 f. "It is the most vivid and comprehensive pictorial record we have of the religio-political organisation of Tudor society in England under Henry VIII" (H. R. Willoughby, *The First Authorized English Bible,* p. 11).

by ye dylygent studye of dyverse excellent learned men, expert in the forsayde tonges. Prynted by Rychard Grafton and Edward Whitchurch. Cum privilegio ad imprimendum solum, 1539. There follow lists of the books of the Bible, a "Kalendar,"—the name of St. Thomas à Becket is omitted—an "Almanack" for six years, an "Exhortacyon to the studye of the Scriptures, gathered out of the Byble," the "Summe and Contents of the Byble," a Prologue "expressynge what is meant by certayne signes and tokens that we have set in the Byble" and ending with "Amen, God save the Kynge!" Then comes "A Descripcyon and Successe of the Kinges of Juda and Jerusalem, declarynge whan and what prophets lyved. And what notable thynges happened in their tymes, translated from the Hebrue." Finally we have a section showing "Wyth what judgement the Books of the Old Testament are to be read."

This same frontispiece led to a curious incident. For when during the procession for the coronation of Edward VI someone carried a picture of Henry VIII bearing a book whereon was inscribed *Verbum Dei,* Bishop Gardiner sent for the painter and "demanded to know by whom and why he had been ordered so to depict the late King." The unfortunate man escaped imprisonment in the Fleet only by painting him "shortly after, in the sted of the booke of 'Verbum Dei,' to have in his handes a newe payre of gloves." [35]

No Dedication to the King was prefixed to the Great Bible. Perhaps the scroll indited "Inveni virum juxta cor meum qui facit omnes voluntates meas" was thought sufficient by way of adulation. Holbein, or whoever the artist was, must have had his tongue in his cheek when he penned those lying words. The many cuts in the body of the text constitute a strange gallery of portraits: Abraham and his three visitors, the sacrifice of Isaac, Susanna, Esther, Mardochai, and others. An excellent picture of St. Paul is prefixed to the Epistle to the Romans.

Red print is copiously used on the title page and in the preliminary pieces. Among the feasts figure "The Purifycacion of our Lady, All Soulen day, and Chyldermas day or the Feast of the Holy Innocents." The page headings give the title of each book and, from Genesis to Esther, the subject matter of each page.[36] There are neither Prologues nor notes; nor are the verses numbered. The First and Second Books of

[35] *Chronicle of Queen Jane and Two years of Queen Mary,* p. 79.

[36] Except in the Apocrypha, Matthew's Bible gives the titles of each book as well as the subject matter at the head of each page.

Kings are so entitled at the head of the right hand page, but on the left they are called I or II Samuel. The psalms are numbered according to the Hebrew enumeration, psalm 9 being divided at *Ut quid Domine, recessisti longe?* [37] The opening words of each psalm are given according to the Vulgate; e.g., psalm 54 (53): *Deus, in nomine tuo salvum me fac,* and its title is translated: "To the chaunter in melodies, an instruction of David when the Zephytes came and sayd unto Saul: hath not David hyd himselfe amongest us?" The Hebrew letters, Aleph, etc., are omitted in psalm 119. Malachi, chapter 3, remains undivided, as in the Hebrew text and in the versions by Coverdale and Matthew; the Authorized Version and Revised Version follow the Vulgate in dividing it into two chapters.

COVERDALE'S INTENDED NOTES

Both in the text and in the margins of the first three editions, April, 1539, April, 1540, and July, 1540, appear outline figures of hands (indexes) intended to indicate the annotations which—since the Lutheran notes in Matthew's Bible were not to be reproduced—Coverdale says he had written "in a private table, the dyversities of all textes, with such annotacions, in another table, as shall douteles delucidate and clear the same, as well without any singularyte of opinions, as all checkinges and reprofes." He had prepared these, he adds, "without any pryvate opinion, onlye after the best interpreters of the hebrues for the more clearnesse of the texte." [38] But evidently there was opposition to these proposed notes, for he writes on December 13, 1538:

> I humbly beseche . . . that I maye knowe youre pleasure concernynge the Annotacyons of this Byble, whether I shall proceade therin or no. Pitie it were that the darck places of the text (upon the which I have allwaye set a hande—pointing), shulde so passe undeclared. As for anye pryvate opynion or contencious

[37] Coverdale's revision for the Great Bible of his 1535 version of the Psalms was adopted in the first Prayer Book of Edward VI and was subsequently known as the Prayer Book Psalter; its retention was further insisted on in 1662 and 1669. The version of the Psalms in the Authorized Version may be more correct than that in the Great Bible, but certainly does not so readily lend itself to singing.

[38] Letters to Cromwell, August 9 and December 13, 1538; cf. Pollard, *op. cit.*, pp. 237, 245; Westcott, *op. cit.*, p. 75 note. Foxe (*op. cit.*, VIII [v], 410) says that the continued presence of these pointing "hands" with no corresponding notes gave offense to the clergy; cf. Dore, *op. cit.*, pp. 157–59, 175 f. An edition in 1550 added notes wherein "suche thynges as are darke and hydd from the naturall understandynge [are] briefelye touched." These "pointing hands" are not reproduced in Bagster's reprint, 1838.

wordes, as I wyll utterly avoyde suche, so wyll I offre the annotacions first to my sayde lord of Herdforde; to the intent that he shall so examen the same, afore they be put in prynte, yf it be your lordshippes good pleasure that I shall do so.

These notes, however, were never incorporated in the printed text, a fact which Coverdale tried to explain when giving an account of the "signs" used in his edition.

Forsomuch as there hath not yet bene soffycient tyme minystred to the kynges moost honourable councell, for the oversight and correccyon of the sayde annotacyons, we wyll therfore omyt them, tyll their more convenient leysour, doynge now no more but beseke the, most gentle reader, that when thou commest at soch a place where a hand doth stand . . . then do not rashly presume to make any private interpretacyon therof, but submyt thy selfe to the judgement of those that are godly learned in Christ Jesu.[39]

THE APOCRYPHA AND THE NEW TESTAMENT

Holbein's frontispiece is reproduced before the Apocrypha, the Prologue to which runs:

Of the volume of the Bokes called "Hagiographa": III–IV. Esdras, Tobiah, Judith, reast of the boke of Esther, Wysdome, Ecclesiasticus, Baruch, Song of the Three Children, the Story of Susanna, Bel and the Dragon, the Prayer of Manasses, I–II. Machabees: they are wont to be reade, not openly and as comen, but as it were in secret and aparte. . . . Wherfore, then, when thou wylt maynteyne any thynge for certen, rendrynge a reason of thy fayth, take heade to the lyvynge and pyththye Scriptures.

Oddly enough, though in his original version, 1535, and in the Address to the Reader, Coverdale calls these books Apocrypha, yet here he calls them "Hagiographa," a term normally used to signify "the Sacred Writings," or Job, Psalms, the Canticle of Canticles, Ecclesiastes, Wisdom, and Ecclesiasticus; I and II Machabees coming under the heading "Historical Books."

The New Testament portion of the Great Bible has this title page: *The New testament in englyshe translated after the Greke, contayning these bookes* (the usual list follows). Around the title are devotional pictures of the Annunciation, the Nativity, the shepherds and the angels, the circumcision of Jesus, the magi, the crucifixion, the Tree of Jesse, showing our Blessed Lady and the child, and lastly, the resurrection of Christ. But in the edition of 1541, these were replaced by the pictures figuring on the title page of the whole bible—a change in accordance with the growing change in the religious outlook.

[39] Pollard, *op. cit.,* p. 245.

St. Paul's Epistle to Philemon ends with "sent from Rome by Onesimus a servant"; Hebrews is entitled, "The Epistle of Sainct Paul the Apostle to the Hebrues"; the Apocalypse is "The Revelacyon of Saynct John the divine"; I John 5:7 is in smaller type. The colophon to the whole New Testament runs: "The ende of the new Testament and of the whole Byble, fynisshed in Aprill Anno M.CCCCCXXXIX. A Domino factum est istud."

To what extent was the Great Bible "unorthodox"? Fulke says that he heard Coverdale say in a sermon that when Henry VIII asked his bishops for their opinion of the Great Bible and they expressed dissatisfaction with it, the King then asked: "But are there any heresies maintained therein?" When the bishops replied in the negative, Henry exclaimed: "Then in God's name let it go abroad among our people."[40] But though it would not be easy to single out anything strictly heretical in the version, there are many passages distinctly erroneous and others which are *male sonantes.* For, as we have seen, Cromwell's Bible is to all intents and purposes a reproduction of Tyndale's version of the New Testament with all the renderings that the Henrician bishops and St. Thomas More so much resented. For example, in Acts 14:23 the words "by election" appear, as in Tyndale and the Geneva Bible; "charity" is changed to "love" in the thirteenth chapter of First Corinthians; "temple" is substituted for "altar" in I Cor. 9:13; while the insertion *"the image* of Baal" (Rom. 11:4) here appears for the first time, to be repeated in the Geneva Bible and in A.V. Tyndale's *"the image* which came down from heaven" (Acts 19:35) is reproduced here and also in the Geneva Bible. "Mystery" replaces "sacrament" (Ephes. 5:32); "knowledge" replaces "confess" (Rom. 10:10); while "communion" is now "partaking" (I Cor. 10:16).[41]

VARIOUS EDITIONS

The second edition, April, 1540, appeared with Cranmer's famous Preface; hence Cromwell's Bible came to be known as Cranmer's Bible.[42] The title reads: *The Byble in Englyshe, that is to saye the content of al*

[40] *A Defense of the Sincere and True Translations of the Holie Scriptures,* p. 98; cf. Moulton, *op. cit.,* p. 141.

[41] These examples suffice to show the heretical tendencies of the Great Bible.

[42] See *Works of Cranmer,* Parker Society, pp. 118 ff. The Preface continued to appear even in the Bishops' Bible, 1568. In Bagster's *Hexapla* the column labelled "Cranmer, 1539," should read either "Great Bible" or "Cromwell's Bible, 1539."

the holy scrypture, both of the olde, and newe testament, with a prologe therinto, made by the reverende father in God, Thomas, archbysshop of Canterbury. Printed by Richard Grafton. Cum privilegio ad imprimendum solum, M.D.XL. This is the Byble apoynted to the use of the churches.[43] The colophon has: "The ende of the newe Testament, and of the whole Byble, fynisshed in Apryll, anno M.CCCCC.XL. A Domino factum est istud." [44]

Two more editions appeared in July and November of that same year, 1540. The title of the former, in which the preliminary matter is considerably shortened, is: *The Byble in Englyshe of the largest and greatest volume auctorysed* [45] *and apoynted by the commaundement of oure most redoubted Prynce and soveryngе Lord Kynge Henrye VIII, supreme heade* [46] *of this his church and realme of Englande; to be frequented and used in every churche* [47] *within this his sayd realme, accordynge to the tenour of his former Iniunctions geven in that behalfe.* The November edition adds: *Ouersene and perused at the commaundement of the kynges highness by Cuthbert bysshop of Duresme, and Nicolas, bysshop of Rochester. E. Whitchurch, fynyshed in November, 1540.*[48] Three more editions followed in May, November, and December, 1541. The May edition, the fifth of the series, repeats the statement about the two bishops commissioned to revise the publication. But, as Moulton declares, "It is probable that the association of Tunstall and Heath with this edition was little more than nominal." [49] "Diligent investigation," says Pollard, "has not yet discovered in what the episcopal revision consisted." [50] Mombert, too, thinks that these two bishops "were

[43] These last words constitute an important addition, appearing here for the first time.

[44] Reprinted in 1562, this second edition is the one continually referred to by Gregory Martin in his *Discoverie of the Manifold Corruptions of the Holie Scriptures* and in the annotations in the Rheims Version, 1582. Cf. Fulke, *op. cit.*, p. 68. For a collation of the first two editions, see Eadie, *The English Bible,* I, 379 f.

[45] The expression "authorised" here occurs for the first time.

[46] Another significant addition; the whole series summarizes the King's progress towards totalitarianism.

[47] These words were probably inserted at the insistance of the printers, who maintained that they could cover expenses only if every church was compelled to have a copy.

[48] This edition was marked by the erasure of Cromwell's arms from his shield, which remains blank; Coverdale's "pointing hands" were also removed. Cf. Westcott, *op. cit.*, p. 77; Eadie, *op. cit.*, I, 396 f., 426; Lewis, *A Complete History of the Several Translations of the Holy Bible and New Testament,* pp. 143 f.; Mombert, *op. cit.*, p. 238; Hoare, *op. cit.*, p. 197; Moulton, *op. cit.*, p. 142.

[49] *Op. cit.* (1911), p. 142.

[50] *Op. cit.*, p. 22; cf. Strype, *op. cit.*, I, i, 612; Anderson, *op. cit.*, p. 363.

compelled to give their names to the work, and that the title-page of those editions of the Bible is simply an imposture, for there is no evidence whatever that they had revised the version." [51]

As successive editions came out, Coverdale continued his task of revising.

> In the Prophets the revision was less complete in the first edition, 1539, and Coverdale appears to have gone again carefully through this part of his work at least before the publication of the second edition, April, 1540. (Hence) the text of Cranmer's Bible presents a second revision of the original Coverdale (Matthew), and that again by a more thorough use of Münster. . . . The variations from the first edition, 1539, in the second edition, April, 1540, are far greater in the Hagiographa and the Prophets—the part of Matthew's Bible which was Coverdale's own work—than those in the earlier books: and the variations in the text of 1539 from that of Matthew, 1537, are more important throughout than the changes introduced afterwards. [52]

But strangely enough, "In part the edition of Nov. 1540 goes back from the text of April 1540 to that of 1539." [53]

The revision, says Westcott, was based upon a careful use of the Vulgate and of Erasmus' Latin version; a good instance is the rendering of Jas. 1:13, for whereas in the first edition, 1539, this read, "For God cannot tempt unto evyll, because he tempteth no man," this was changed in 1540 to read, in accordance with Erasmus' version: "For as God cannot be tempted with evill, so nether he hymselfe tempteth not eny man" (p. 194).

Edition followed edition,—twenty-seven appearing before 1568—for printers found it hard to produce sufficient copies for "every church," though it is said that 21,000 copies of the Great Bible were already in circulation between 1540 and 1544. In 1540 Berthelet the printer brought out what seems to have been an independent edition, 12mo, the Old Testament being a reprint of the first edition, the New Testament being an English version of Erasmus. Though Coverdale had to omit all notes,

[51] *Op. cit.*, p. 228; cf. *Cambridge Modern History*, II, 466. Strype says: "Your Majesty appointed two of them (Tunstall and Heath) to overlook the translation of the Bible, they said they had done your Highness' command therein: yea, they set their name thereunto: but when they saw the world somewhat like to wring on the other side, they denied it, and said they never meddled therewith, causing the printer to take out their names." *Ecclesiastical Memorials*, I, 595 f., quoting from Fish, *The Supplication of the Poor Commons*.

[52] Westcott, *op. cit.*, pp. 185, 192; cf. Fulke, *op. cit.*, pp. 68, 98.

[53] Westcott, *op. cit.*, p. 193.

some were added in later editions. This was particularly the case with the "Worcester Bible," 1549, the New Testament portion of which was furnished "with notes and expositions of the darke places therein."[54] One edition, that of 1550, has a curious woodcut prefixed to the epistles of Peter: a schoolmaster birching a boy; "very singular," remarks Lea Wilson, "and far exceeds the bounds of decorum." Several editions came out in 1553; one has I John 5:7 printed in small Roman type as distinct from the black letter of the rest.

These repeated editions seem to have been occasioned by the complaint of the printer, Marler, who said that there was no demand for copies and that unless the parishes were obliged to buy them, he would be ruined. The King thereupon complained, May 6, 1541, that Cromwell's injunctions on this point had not been observed, and proceeded to fix the price: "To thentent they maye have the sayd Bybles of the greatest volume at equall and reasonable pryces, His hyghness by the advyse of his counsayle hath ordeyned and taxed: that the sellers therof, shall not take for any of the sayde Bybles unbounde, above the pryce of ten shyllynges. And for every of the sayde Bybles well and sufficientlye, bounde, trymmed and clasped, not above twelve shyllynges."[55]

The renewed condemnations of Tyndale's version in 1543 and 1546 secured for the Great Bible a predominance which remained unchallenged until the appearance of the Bishops' Bible in 1568. No edition of the Great Bible appeared after 1569.

[54] These notes conclude with an exhortation to the reader: "Geve no credence lyghtelye unto every enterpretation, but fyrste prove the spirites. And if they confesse not Christe to be comen into the fleshe, that is, that there is no maner salvation besyde hym, beleve them not, for they are the spirite of Antichriste."

[55] See Francis Fry, *A Description of the Great Bible, 1539;* Anderson, *op. cit.*, pp. 262 f.; Dore, *op. cit.*, pp. 160–67.

CHAPTER XIV

Taverner's Version, 1539

TAVERNER'S LIFE AND WORK

OF Richard Taverner, 1505–75, we know little save the account given of him by his relative, Antony à Wood. His version, mainly a revision of Matthew's Bible (1537), came suddenly and unexpectedly on the scene in the very year, 1539, in which Cromwell was insisting on the paramount position to be assigned to the version which bears his name, otherwise known as the Great Bible or Cranmer's Bible.

Educated first at Cambridge, then, owing to Wolsey, at Cardinal's College, Oxford, Taverner became a barrister, though whether he ever practiced at the bar seems uncertain.[1] Exceedingly proficient in Greek, he used to annoy his fellow law students by quoting legal items to them in Greek. Attracted by Tyndale's version from the Greek, he was thrown into prison for reading that heretic's New Testament.[2] On being released he seems to have gone abroad in pursuit of his studies, and it was presumably then that he fell under the influence of the German reformers and translated in 1536 a work embodying the tenets of the Augsburg Confession of 1530. Though Anderson calls him a "canon,"[3] he never received any orders but remained a layman all his life. Yet Edward VI licensed him to preach, a function he exercised under Elizabeth in a court dress—he had become a favorite at the court—and wearing a sword.[4] On the fall of Cromwell, July, 1540, Taverner was sent to the Tower, according to some because of rumors he had circulated about Anne of Cleves,[5] according to others for having dared to translate the Bible.[6] But

[1] Cooper, *Athenae Cantabrigienses,* I, 182; cf. *ibid.,* p. 338 f. Foxe speaks of him as a musician and therefore patronized by Wolsey (*Actes and Monumentes,* VI [viii], p. 617).

[2] Mombert, *English Versions of the Bible,* p. 194.

[3] *Annals of the English Bible,* p. 342.

[4] *History,* II, 459.

[5] *State Papers, Henry VIII,* Foreign and Domestic, XVI (1540–41), no. 1414.

[6] Mombert, *op. cit.,* p. 194; Moulton, *op. cit.,* p. 133.

he was soon set free and must in time have become a wealthy man, for through the dissolution of the monasteries he came into possession of the Priory of Alvingham, land at Wood Eaton, Oxford, the Franciscan friary at Northampton, part of Stamford Priory, and other lands in Norfolk, his native country.[7] In 1545 he sat in Parliament for Liverpool. He married twice, and by his second wife he became, through his daughter Penelope, the great grandfather of Antony à Wood.

Though a lawyer by profession, Taverner seems always to have had a predilection for biblical studies. This led him to bring out in 1539, the year marked by the appearance of Cromwell's Bible, his own version,[8] which he dedicated

Unto the most noble, most myghtie, and most redouted prynce Kynge Henry the VIII, Kynge of England and of France, defensour of the fayth, lorde of Ireland, and in erth supreme heed immediately under Chryst of the Churche of England, his humble servaunt Richard Taverner, desireth all joye, felycitie, and longe life. How hyghly all England is bounden to youre incomparable majestie for the infinite and manifolde benefites receyved at your most gracious handes, from tyme to tyme without ceasing . . . truly no mortal tonge is hable with wordes sufficiently to expresse or with secret thoughtes worthely to conceyve. . . . This one thinge I dare ful wel affirm, that amongst al your Majesties deservings, your highnesse never did any thinge more acceptable to God, more profitable to the advancement of true Christianity, more unpleasant to the enemies of the same, and also to your graces enemies, then when your Majestie lycenced and wyled, the moost sacred Bible,[9] contayning the unspotted and lively word of God, to be in the Englyshe tonge set forthe to your highnesse subjects. . . .

Wherefore the premises well considered, forasmuch as the prynters herof were very desirous to have the Byble come forth as faultlesse and emendatly as the shortnes of tyme for the recognysing of the same wold require, they desyred me, your moost humble servaunt, for the default of a better learned, diligently to overloke and peruse the hole copy, and in case I shold fynd any notable default that neded correction, to amende the same according to the true exemplars, which thing

[7] *State Papers, Henry VIII,* Foreign and Domestic, XIV (1539), p. 607.

[8] *The Most Sacred Bible Whiche is the holy scripture, conteyning the old and new testament, translated into English, and newly recognised with great diligence after most faythful exemplars, by Richard Taverner. "Harken thou heven, and thou erth gyve eare: for the Lorde speaketh," Isa.i.2. Prynted at London in Flete strete at the sygne of the sonne by John Byddell, for Thomas Barthlet. Cum privilegio ad imprimendum solum. M.D.xxxix.* This last expression denotes, says Pollard, that "they were not to make a mere permission to print appear as if any special favour or monopoly were being conferred on the edition" (*Records of the English Bible,* p. 241); cf. Wilkins, *Concilia,* III, 847.

[9] The reference is to the licence Henry had so unexpectedly granted to Matthew's Bible; see *supra,* pp. 178 ff. The dignified, even manly, tone of this Dedication stands in marked contrast to the servile effusions of Coverdale.

according to my talent I have gladly done. . . . It is a worke of so great difficultie so absolutely to translate the hole Bible that it be faultlesse that I feared it could scarce be done of one or two persons, but rather requyred both a deeper conferryng of many learned wittes together, and also a juster tyme and longer leysure. . . . These therefore my simple lucubrations and labours to whom might I better dedicate than unto your Majestie?

The "Exhortacion to the Study of the Scriptures," which follows the Dedication, consists of familiar passages from the Bible inculcating the need of attention to the word of God. Next comes "The Summe and Contents of the Scriptures," or a summary of doctrine on God, the creation, the promise of the coming of Christ, the Mosaic Law, the Saviour, the sacrifice of the lamb, peace, the Holy Ghost, love, justice, good works, the Last Judgment, and life everlasting. This is followed by "A briefe rehersall declarynge how longe the world hath endured from the creation of Adam unto this present yere of our Lord. M.D.XXXIX: both after the maner of the reckenyng of the Hebrues, and after the reckenynge of Eusebius, and other Chronyclers." Finally, and most important of all, "A Table for to fynde manye of the cheyfe and principall maters conteyned in the Bible." This occupies fifty-three columns, and though the work of the bigoted Matthew, it is, as edited by Taverner, excellent on the whole.

TAVERNER'S VERSION OF THE OLD TESTAMENT

Though his love of Greek well fitted Taverner for the task of translating the New Testament, he does not seem to have been so well equipped for the translation of the Old Testament, for he seems to have known no Hebrew nor even to have consulted the Septuagint in the course of his work. In fact, whereas we might have expected him to make considerable use of the latter, the only discoverable trace of familiarity with that version is in the note on Gen., chap. 11, where he points out that "the Septuagint interpreters omit the name 'Caynan' "; but that was a universally recognized fact calling for no personal acquaintance with the version. The only piece of textual criticism, so far as I have noticed, occurs in the margin of Gen. 8:11, where Taverner remarks that after the words "till the waters were dried up upon the earth," "some rede 'and never came agayne.' " Becke omits this note, presumably because it did not appear in Matthew's Bible.

In truth, Taverner's Old Testament is mainly a polished revision of

Matthew's version,[10] except the Psalter and Deut. 31 to Jos. 13, where the latter version has been left untouched. However, Taverner, since he was a good Greek scholar, was in a position to translate the Apocrypha for himself; his version, especially of III and IV Esdras, Tobias, and Judith differs greatly from the versions by Coverdale and by Matthew, and that in the Bishops' Bible.[11] Taverner shows a remarkable familiarity with the Vulgate text, often adhering to its renderings. The psalms are numbered as in the Vulgate, and Taverner has four books of Kings, not two of Samuel and two of Kings. The influence of the Vulgate also appears in the strange "incluse" (III Kings 21:21), where the Vulgate has *et clausum.*

Taverner's meticulous polishing of Matthew's version, involving as it did the elimination of Latinisms, resulted in some strange renderings; e.g., "spokesman," for "advocate," and "mercystock," for "propitiation for our sins" (I John 1:1 f.) It is surprising that he should have retained Coverdale's "triacle" (Jer. 8:22), and "bugs" (Ps. 91:5) from the second edition of Matthew's Bible.

[10] The extent to which Taverner changed Matthew's version may be gauged by the following examples from Genesis: Matthew, "and so it was done" throughout Gen., chap. 1, following the Vulgate, *et factum est ita;* but Taverner, "and it was so," "and it came to pass," "and so it was." Where Taverner has "with all theyr furniture" (3:1), Matthew has "apparel"; Taverner, "ye shall be as Goddes" (3:5), Matthew, "as God"; Taverner, "I will put enmities betwene the and the woman, betwene thy sede and his sede. And that sede shall tread on the head, and thou shalt tread it on the hele" (3:15); Great Bible, "The same shall tread downe thy head, and thou shal tread upon his hele." In 41:43, "proclamation was made that every person should bow his knee before hym," Taverner has translated the Egyptian word *Abrek,* which Matthew had retained, although he added in a note, "As much to say 'as tender father' or as some wyl, 'bowe the knee.' " Taverner has, "Into their secretes come not my soule, and into their congregacion be my honour not coupled; for in their wrathe they slewe a manne, and in their luste they threwe downe the walles of the cytye" (49:5); but Matthew and Coverdale thus render the last clause: "In theyr self wyll they houghed an oxe." Taverner, "Tyll he come that is to be sent" (49:10); Matthew, "until Sylo come," "Sylo" being interpreted as "he that maketh hoppe"; Coverdale, "Tyll the Worthie come."

[11] Here is his translation in 1539 of II Mach. 12:43–46; in Becke's edition of 1551 there are only a few orthographical changes. "So he gathered of every one a certen, in so much that he brought together two M drachmas of silver which he sent unto Jerusalem that there might a sacrifice be offered for the mysdede. In the which place he dyd well and right, for he had some consideration and pondering of the life that is after this time. For if he had not thought they which were slain did yet live, it had been superstitious and vain to make any vow or sacrifice for them that were dead. But for so much as he saw that they which die in the favour and belief of God are in good rest and joye he thought it to be good and honourable for a reconciling to do the same for those which were slain, that the offence might be forgiven."

The variations in the versions of such a passage as Deut. 32:28 show how successive translators worked over the text. Matthew, "A nation that hath an unhappy forecast"; Taverner, "that hath no forecast"; Coverdale, "wherein is no council," though he himself changed this to "without forecast" when preparing the Great Bible.

TAVERNER'S VERSION OF THE NEW TESTAMENT

The order of books in Taverner's version of the New Testament [12] is the same as that in Matthew's Bible: after the Epistle to Philemon follow those of Peter and John, the Epistle to the Hebrews, those of James and Jude, and the Apocalypse. At the end: "This is the Table wherein ye shal fynde the Epistles and Gospels after the use of Salsburye." A colophon reads: "The ende of the newe Testament and of the hole Byble. To the honour and prayse of God was this Byble prynted: and fynysshed in the yere of our Lorde God. a.M.D.XXXIX.

In revising the New Testament, Taverner made the translation more exact and polished the English of Matthew's version. Moulton speaks of forty variations in Taverner's text from that of Matthew in Matt., chaps. 21 f. Not all of these, of course, were due to Taverner; many of them had already appeared in earlier versions. But he gave them a wider currency, and some of them have persisted to this day.

Wycliffe, Taverner, and Rheims, "espoused"; Tyndale and Geneva, "betrothed" (Matt. 1:18); Wycliffe and Rheims, "he was dumb"; Tyndale, Cranmer, and Geneva, "he was speechless"; Taverner, "but he said never a word" (Matt. 22:12); another example: Wycliffe, "tormented"; Tyndale, "ungodly"; Cranmer, "shamefully"; Taverner, "foully"; Geneva, "sharply"; Rheims and A.V., "spitefully"; while Challoner, despairingly, "contumeliously" (22:6—the Latin *contumeliose*). "Stopped the Sadducees' mouth" (Matt. 22:34) is peculiarly Taverner's own, all other versions having, "put the Sadducees to silence." The generally accepted substitution of "garment" for "vesture" (in Tyndale, Cranmer, and Geneva) was due to Taverner, followed by Rheims, A.V., and R.V. He was responsible, too, for the "dogs" instead of "whelps" in Matt. 15:27, but strangely enough Challoner reverted to "whelps." Heb.

[12] *The New Testament of our saviour Jesu Christ, translated in to English: and newly recognised with great diligence after moost faythful exemplars, by Richarde Taverner. "Pray for us that the worde of God may run and may be gloried"* 2. *Thess.iii. Prynted in the yeare of our Lorde MD XXXIX.*

11:1–3 provides an instance of the meticulous character of the changes Taverner thought fit to make in Matthew's text; he eliminated three words which he judged to be superfluous and inserted "and." "Fayth is a sine, (a) confydence of (the) thinges which are hoped for, *and* a certayntie of thinges which are not sene. By it the elders were wel reported (of)."

It is in his precision—despite occasional lapses—in rendering the Greek article that Taverner's Greek scholarship is most evident. Tyndale, Cranmer, Matthew, and A.V., "set him on a pynacle"; but Wycliffe, Taverner, Rheims, and R.V. have "the pinnacle" (Matt. 4:5); all, including Taverner, have "on a candlestick," except R.V., "put it on the stand" (Matt. 5:15); Wycliffe, "a verri light"; Geneva, "that light"; but Cranmer, Taverner, Rheims, A.V., and R.V., "the true light" (John 1:9). Wycliffe, Tyndale, Cranmer, Geneva, Rheims, A.V., all read, "Art thou a teacher (master) in Israel?" (John 3:10); Taverner, alone of the older translators, did justice to the definite article, "Art thou the master?" and R.V. follows his lead. Wycliffe and Tyndale, "a prophet"; Matthew, Cranmer, Geneva, and A.V., "that prophet"; Taverner, Rheims, and R.V., "the prophet" (John 1:21); yet in the previous verse Taverner, Tyndale, Cranmer, and Rheims have "I am not Christ," where Geneva, A.V. and R.V. rightly have "the Christ" (cf. John 1:25; 7:40). Conversely Wycliffe and Taverner alone have "a voice" (John 1:23) where other versions wrongly have "the voice."

The same instinctive feeling for the force of the Greek appears in I John 5:1 f., where Taverner changes Matthew's "is begotten" into "was begotten," and "by this we know" into "in this we know"; yet he omits, without warrant, the word "for" in "For this is the love of God." That Matthew had an independent knowledge of Greek also appears in I Cor. 15:29, where, though his text reads "baptized over the dead," the note says: "In my opinion the translation would be better if it were 'for the dead' "—a note taken over by Taverner. Matthew quotes, too, Macrobius' quip apropos of Herod's slaughter of the Innocents: "I should sooner be Herod's sow (ὗς) than his son (υἱός)."

Taverner also has felicitous turns of expression which, though not always originated by himself, betray careful discrimination and a determination to secure the best rendering. Tyndale, followed by Geneva, has "for their unbelief's sake" (Matt. 13:58), but this is inferior to Taverner's rendering, "because of their unbelief," taken over by A.V. and R.V. "The charity of many shall wax cold" (Matt. 24:12), adopted by Taverner from Wycliffe and followed by Rheims, A.V., and R.V., is far preferable to "the love of many shall abate," in Tyndale, Matthew, Cranmer, and Geneva. Again Taverner, with Wycliffe, followed by Rheims and A.V., reads "charity" throughout I Cor., chap. 13, against Tyndale, who notoriously replaced the time-honored "charity" by "love"; so too Cranmer and Geneva. How strange that the Revisers should have reverted to Tyndale's unwarranted change! "Gelded," with Wycliffe and Rheims (Matt. 19:12), and "shall be Easter," with Tyndale, Cranmer, and Geneva, are not so felicitous. Wycliffe and Rheims wrote "Pascha"; A.V. and R.V., "Passover."

Taverner follows Tyndale and Cranmer in omitting "of thee" in the clause "shall be borne of thee" (Luke 1:35), also, in accordance with the best accredited MSS., he omitted "of God" (Mark 15:29), "and the bride" (Matt. 25:1), "with whom I also lodge" (I Cor. 16:19). According to Mombert, Taverner wrote "Tyll at last she brought forth her fyrst borne sonne," but this does not appear in the first edition, 1539, nor in those by Becke, 1549 and 1551. In Luke 12:29 we have the strange rendering, "be not carried in the clouds," where Tyndale and Cranmer have "neither climb ye up on high," Wycliffe, "nyle ye be reisid an hy," Geneva, "neither let your minds wander about these speculations," A.V. and R.V., "neither be ye of doubtful mind."

I John 5:7 is, as so often, printed in smaller type and in brackets. Pointing hands are drawn in the margins throughout the New Testament, those on the inside column being upside down.

THE NOTES IN TAVERNER'S VERSION

Moulton says that the principal difference between Taverner's version and Matthew's Bible is "the absence of so large a proportion of Rogers' notes from the Old Testament." [13] But the same holds good to an even greater extent in the New Testament. For, while not completely omitting Matthew's notes, he rigorously excised all that were in any way offensive; e.g., against clerical celibacy, or what Matthew calls "the wiveless doctrine" (Matt. 19:11; Luke, chap. 20), on the absurdity of fasting on specified days (Matt. 17:20), on the pope as being anti-Christ (Matt. 23:9),

[13] *English Versions of the Bible* (1906), p. 199.

on purgatory (Luke 12:48). The "Table of Principall Matters" drawn up by Matthew was considerably "edited" by Taverner, who omits: "He then that purgeth out hys sinnes through fyer or by any other meanes than by the passyon of Christ, denyeth hys sayd passyon." He omits, too, all unpleasant notes on the Mass, on sacrifice, and on the worship of idols; while apropos of the priesthood he is content to refer to the putting aside of the Levitical priesthood in favor of that of the New Covenant. Matthew's notoriously antipapal notes on the Apocalypse are also omitted, likewise the savage note on I Pet. 3:7, wherein the husband is counselled, "If she [his wife] be not obedient and healpfull unto hym, endeavoureth to beate the feare of God into her heade, that thereby she maye be compelled to learne her dutie and to do it."

Sometimes, however, Taverner omits notes which are not only inoffensive but useful; for example, he might profitably have retained the note on Luke 16:22: "Some by 'the bosom of Abraham' do understand the fayth of Abraham. Other some also understand it of the place where the elect and chose[n] that folow the fayth of Abraham do rest after their death. But where that place is (because the Scripture doth not expressly determine it) can we not tell. And therefore no man may be so bold as to defyne it."

Throughout, indeed, Taverner has toned down even the notes he admitted; how moderate his words on "Elders" (I Pet. 5:3): "Presbyter, that is to say a priest, in Greke signyfieth an elder because commonly they were elderly men that were chosen to teach the people." He omits, too, the note on Matt. 16:18, where it is said that Peter spoke "in the name of all." Again, nothing could be more orthodox than the note on Matt. 1:25 ("He knew her not till she brought forth her first-born son"), in which Taverner succinctly remarks: "Not because she had any after, but by cause she had none before"; even Rogers had written: "The minde of the Evangeliste . . . was to prove that he was the sonne of a virgin, . . . not to declare that Mary had more children after him, as some phantasye."

Taverner's critical attitude towards the distinctively anti-Catholic comments then in vogue does not, of course, mean that Taverner had Catholic leanings. His attitude was rather that of the scholarly minded man revolted as much by prejudice and bigotry as by slovenliness in translating.

EDITIONS OF TAVERNER'S VERSION

The printers who, for reasons unknown to us, were in a hurry, as Taverner tells us, seem to have felt assured of a good sale. Not even the fact that Cromwell's Bible with all its authoritative backing had appeared in April of that same year, 1539, deterred them from publishing in that year two editions of Taverner's Bible, one in folio and another in quarto, as well as two editions of his New Testament, also in folio and quarto. The title of the latter is *The New Testament in Englysshe after the Greke Exemplar: Dilygently translated and corrected by Richard Taverner, M.D.XXXIX. Cum privilegio ad imprimendum solum.* Another edition appeared in 1540, "Imprinted at London by Thomas Raynalde and William Hyll, dwelling in Paules Churcheyeard"; this, like an edition in five volumes 16mo published by Redman in the same year, is very rare.[14]

In 1551 Becke brought out another edition: *The Byble, that is to say, all the holy Scripture conteined in the olde and newe Testament, faythfully set forth according to the Coppy of Thomas Mathewes translatio[n], whereunto are added certaine learned Prologes, and Annotacio[n]s, for the better understanding of many hard places thorowout the whole Bible. Imprinted at London by Jhon Daye dwellyng over Aldersgate. Cum gracia et privilegio ad imprimendum solum. Anno a M.D.LI.* This title is certainly curious. For though the New Testament is (with reservations) taken from Matthew's Bible, the Old is Taverner's version, except from Deuteronomy, chapter 31, to Josue, with some alterations by Becke. The New Testament is thus in substance Tyndale's edition of 1535. A title page such as the above, remarks Dore, "shows us how careful we ought to be in accepting for facts the statements we find on title-pages. It appears as if in many early printed books the publisher and not the author drew up the title-page, and put on them not a true description

[14] A copy, said to be unique, is the property of the dean and chapter of St. Paul's; see the *Times,* February 9, 1938. Dore mentions an edition in five volumes 12mo by Daye and Seres, 1549, in which III Maccabees appeared for the first time as a part of the Bible; see Cotton, *Lists of Editions of the Bible and Parts Thereof in English,* p. 27; Eadie, *The English Bible,* p. 346; Dore, *Old Bibles,* pp. 142, 150 f., where he gives a summary of III Machabees. Abrahams (*Jewish Quarterly,* March, 1896) regards it as historical; cf. *Legacy of Israel,* p. 37 note. The Council of Trent refused to treat it as a portion of Scripture; cf. *Diaria,* V, 33; H. Cotton, *The Five Books of Maccabees,* Oxford, 1832. III Maccabees was also published in 1785 under the superintendance of Dr. Wilson, bishop of Sodor and Man.

of the book, but what he thought most likely to cause the volume to be purchased. The various titles to Coverdale's folio of 1535 are instances of this." [15]

In this edition the title of the New Testament portion is even more misleading than that prefixed to the whole Bible: *The New Testament of oure Saviour Jesu Christe, diligently translated, accordynge to the Greke, with certayne Notes folowynge the chapters. Wherin the hardest doutes are declared for the better understandyng of the unlearned reader.* Next comes Tyndale's Prologue, "Unto the Christen Reader," four pages. A colophon at the end of the whole volume runs: "The ende of the old and newe Testament. To the honour and prayse of God was thys Byble prynted and fynyshed in the yeare of our Lord and Saviour Jesus Christ. M.D.LI. The xxiii daye of Maye. Imprinted at London by Jhon Daye, dwellyng over Aldergate beneth Saynt Martyns. Cum privilegio ad imprimendum solum."

Becke's alterations in this edition of the New Testament are deplorable. For by reverting in nearly every instance to Tyndale's version, he has done an injustice to Taverner by perpetuating mistakes which the latter had corrected. For example: Taverner's rendering of Matt. 22:6, "he intreated them foully" now reads, "ungodly." In Matt. 1:18 Tyndale had "betrothed," Taverner, "espoused," Becke, "married." Worst of all, Taverner was, as we have seen, nearly always correct in attaching due force to the Greek definite article and had written: "that was the true light" (John 1:9), "I am a voice of one crying" (1:23), "art thou the Prophet?" (1:21); but Becke reverted to Tyndale's mistaken renderings in each case.

The only reliable edition of Taverner's Bible, then, is the first, 1539. Copies are, however, exceedingly rare, and are hardly ever complete, the title page and much of the preliminary matter having disappeared. The same is true of Becke's edition of 1551.[16]

Opinions differ as to the real worth of Taverner's version. Pollard surely dismisses it too summarily "as attaining little success at the time, and having no influence on the version of 1611." [17] Moulton, who seems

[15] *Op. cit.*, p. 143.

[16] See H. H. Hutton, "The Ignored Taverner Bible of 1539," in *The Crozier,* July, 1939, pp. 161–76. Taverner's *Postils on the Epistles and Gospels,* 1540, were edited by Cardwell in 1841.

[17] *Op. cit.*, p. 24.

really to have studied the version, speaks of it as "of very unequal merit —the work of a scholar, able and energetic, but somewhat capricious and uncertain." [18] Westcott, however, feels that Taverner's version demands more study than it has hitherto received and is not to be too lightly set aside:

> The work of Taverner is different from that of any of the revisers noticed before, and stamped with a very distinct individuality. . . . Throughout he appears to aim at vigorous and idiomatic language, and his New Testament deserves more attention than has yet been paid to it. . . . It would be tempting to dwell longer on this version, but it appears to have exercised no influence whatever on the later versions. It remains simply as a monument of one man's critical power, and in the very sharp personality of its characteristics is alien from the general history of the English Bible.[19]

[18] *Op. cit.*, p. 135.
[19] *Op. cit.*, p. 207; cf. H. H. Hutton, *op. cit.*

CHAPTER XV

The Geneva Bible

When Henry VIII died, the conflict between Catholic and reforming ideals was at its height. But under the Protectorate, Protestantism triumphed, and Cranmer brought over Bucer, Fagius, and Vermigli (Peter Martyr), all imbued with the teachings of Luther, Calvin, and Beza. But the grasping and irreligious character of the rulers of the Protectorate exasperated the more genuine advocates of reform, who saw that the future of the movement was at the mercy of men whose one aim was to get rich quickly at the expense of the Church. On the accession of Mary Tudor, these extremists fled to Strasburg and Frankfort. But while they all repudiated the First Prayer Book, they could not agree about the Second.[1] The more radical members therefore migrated to Geneva under Knox, and there Calvin, who had taken up his residence with them, so stamped them with his views that Geneva and Calvinism came to be identified just as Wittenberg and Lutheranism. Hence the English version they produced at Geneva was really a Calvinistic manifesto.[2]

THE FRAMERS OF THE VERSION

Since the framers of the Geneva Bible even to this day are spoken of in some quarters with bated breath, some account of them must be given.

[1] See Whittingham's *Brieff Discours off the Troubles begonne at Franckford,* p. 185, where we are told that the English congregation passing by Frankfort and "perceiving the contention among them to be so boiling hot, that it ran over on both sides, and yet no fire quenched, many had small pleasure to tarry there, but went to Basle and other places."

[2] How completely the new version was dominated by the influence of Calvin and Beza is seen in the request made by the authorities at Geneva that these two should "eftsonnes peruse the same (the Geneva Bible of 1560) notwithstandinge their former travells" (quoted by Isaacs, "The Sixteenth Century English Versions," in *The Bible in Its Ancient and English Versions,* p. 182).

William Whittingham (1524 [?]–79) was, according to Wood, "of an opposite and restles humour." [3] As a student at Christ Church, Oxford, he traveled for three years, with leave of the university, for the sake of his studies. He returned in 1553; but fearing the changes introduced by Mary Tudor, he fled to Frankfort, where he joined with Knox in his dispute with Cox and Whitehead over the Edwardine Prayer Book.[4] Succeeding Knox as minister, he received some sort of ordination, many think it was merely a show of hands. Despite his Nonconformist attitude on various points, the Earl of Leicester secured for him the post of Dean of Durham, where he earned the title of "Durham's unworthy Dean" for having desecrated the tombs of former priors of Durham and breaking up the statue of St. Cuthbert, "to the end," says Wood, "that no memory or token of that holy man St. Cuthbert should be left, who was sent, and brought thither by the power and will of Almighty God." [5] Whittingham married a relative of John Calvin and was the author of *A Brieff Discours off the Troubles begonne at Franckford, 1554–1559,* published in 1575.

Christopher Goodman was another turbulent spirit: "A furious hot spirit, and guilty in conscience of wicked attempts, but especially, as was thought, of the conspiracy that would have killed Queen Mary. . . . He ran to Geneva and there joined with John Knox (as quiet a spirit as himself) that was the firebrand of his country. The truth is Goodman was a most violent Nonconformist, and for rigidness in opinion he went beyond his friend Calvin." [6] Bishop Parkhurst's epitaph for him must have been meant ironically:

> Nemo bonus, Servator ait, sed solus Olympum
> Qui regit, is bonus est; Gudman, nemo bonus.

Goodman's attack on Mary Tudor was entitled: *How superior powers ought to be obeyd of their subjects: and wherin they may lawfully by God's Worde be disobeyed and resisted. Wherin also is declared the*

[3] *Athenae Oxonienses,* I, 153.

[4] See *Original Letters,* nos. 357–61.

[5] *Op. cit.,* I, 154; *Dictionary of National Biography;* Dore, *Old Bibles,* pp. 190 f. See *The Life and Death of Mr. William Whittingham, Dean of Durham, who departed this life, A.D. 1579,* edited from a MS. in the Bodleian by Mary A. Everett Green, for the Camden Society, 1871. For the charges against him see the Appendix I, pp. 41–48.

[6] *Athenae Oxonienses,* I, 272.

cause of all the present miserie in England, and the onely way to remedy the same.[7] Whittingham's Preface to this effusion identifies him with its views. Regicides though they were, in intent if not in deed, these men did not scruple to accept preferment from Elizabeth.

Thomas Sampson (1517 [?]–89) was a Calvinist who accepted Anglican orders from Ridley and subsequently became dean of Chichester. Found collecting money in Mary's reign for poor students opposed to Catholicism, he and his wife, a niece of Latimer, fled to Strasburg, where he became intimate with Emmanuel Tremellius. Though under Elizabeth he refused the bishopric of Norwich, owing to his dislike of the principles of Episcopalianism, he yet accepted the deanship of Christ Church, Oxford, a post from which Parker had to remove him owing to his "Nonconformist conscience." He died at Wigston near Leicester, where he had been given charge of a hospital. His epitaph fittingly describes his character: "Hierarchiae Romanae, papaliumque rituum hostis acerrimus; sinceritatis evangelicae assertor constantissimus." [8]

Richard Cox (1500–89) was appointed headmaster of Eton, though he was a Lutheran. In 1542 he was a member of the abortive commission for the production of an "authorized" version of the Bible,[9] and in 1543 one of the commission which produced *The King's Book*, or *A Necessary Doctrine and Erudition for Any Christian Man.* Siding with the Duke of Northumberland, he had to flee to Frankfort, where he upheld the Second Prayer Book against Knox and Calvin, whence arose still deeper divisions among the exiles there. In 1559 he became bishop of Ely, dying in 1580.[10]

Hoare's strong expressions about the morals of the Edwardine councilors apply with equal force to the fanatics of Geneva:

> With the solitary exception of the invertebrate but amiable Cranmer, it would be difficult to name a single disinterested, or unselfish, or even ordinarily honest man among all that clique of greedy nobles who formed the Council of the Regency. No Jesuit could wish the Protestant cause a worse fate than its exploita-

[7] See Maitland, *Essays on Subjects Connected with the Reformation in England,* pp. 103–96. Strype says Goodman recanted (*Ecclesiastical Memorials,* II, i, 140). See Parsons, *A Treatise of Three Conversions of England,* II, 220; Heylyn, *Ecclesia vindicata,* pp. 204 f.

[8] *Athenae,* I, 192 f.

[9] Wilkins, *Concilia,* III, 860; Parsons, *op. cit.,* II, 220.

[10] Cf. *Dictionary of National Biography;* Fuller, *The Church History of Britain from the Birth of Jesus Christ untill the Year 1648,* II, 414.

tion by this band of sordid adventurers, who, under the mask of piety, made such frenzied haste to fill their pockets at the expense of the Church.[11]

HISTORY OF THE REVISION

Four distinct stages in the history of the Geneva Bible have to be borne in mind: (1) Whittingham's original and individual work, the New Testament of 1557; (2) the revision of the same by several hands in 1560, simultaneous with the publication of their version of the Old Testament; (3) later editions of the whole, mostly printed by Robert Barker; (4) the variations introduced into the text and notes by L. Tomson.

The title of Whittingham's edition of the New Testament runs: *The newe Testament of our Lord Jesus Christ. Conferred diligently with the Greke, and best approved translations with the arguments as wel before the Chapters as for every boke and Epistle, also diversities of readings and the most profitable annotations of all harde places, whereunto is added a copious Table. At Geneva. Printed by Conrad Badius M.D. LVII.* Beneath the title Time is depicted bearing a scythe while he drags Truth out of a pit. An inscription reads: "God by Time restoreth Truth, and maketh her victorious." This 12mo volume, 5¼ inches by 3½ inches, is exceedingly rare.[12] Legend has it that on her way to her coronation, Elizabeth was presented with an English Bible, while an old man standing by represented Time and a little child represented Truth.[13] The title page of Whittingham's New Testament suggests that this was the Bible presented to the Queen.

After the title page come a list of the books, "The Epistle declaring that Christ is the ende of the Law, by John Calvin," [14] and "The Translator to the Reader":

> As touching the perusing of the text, it was diligently revised by the most approved Greek examples, and conference of translations in other tongues as the

[11] *Evolution of the English Bible* (1901), p. 186. As the translation of the Old Testament was still unfinished at the date of Elizabeth's accession (1558), at least two of the collaborators, Gilby and Sampson, remained in Geneva to complete it. Cf. Wood, *Athenae Oxonienses,* s.v. "Whittingham."

[12] Dore, *op. cit.,* p. 190. In 1842 Bagster published in quarto a facsimile of the first edition of 1557, with the original notes; the text is also given in Bagster's *Hexapla,* 1841.

[13] Hoare, *op. cit.,* p. 219; Eadie, *The English Bible,* pp. 62 f.; Strype, *Annals of the Reformation in England,* I, i, 43.

[14] This "Epistle" is not given in the revised version, although it appears again in the edition of 1575; many editions omit it.

learned may easily judge, both by the faithful rendering of the sentence, and also by the propriety of the words, and perspicuity of the phrase. Furthermore, that the Reader might be by all means profited, I have divided the text into verses and sections,[15] according to the best editions in other languages, and also, as to this day the ancient Greek copies mention, it was wont to be read. And because the Hebrew and Greek phrases, which are strange to render in other tongues, and also short, should not be so hard, I have sometime interpreted them without any whit diminishing the grace of the sense.[16]

The list of the canonical books following the title page is the traditional one, though the "Catholic Epistles" are now styled the "Generall Epistles." But the name of St. Paul does not appear in the title of the Epistle to the Hebrews, where an explanatory note says: "Forasmuch as divers, both of the Greeke writers and Latines witnes, that the writer of this Epistle for just causes would not have his name knowen, it were curiositie of our part to labour much therein. For seeing the spirit of God is the author thereof, it diminishes nothing the authoritie, although we know not with what pen he wrote it. Whether it were Paul (as it is not the like), or Luke, or Barnabas, or Clement, or some other, his chief purpose is. . . ." The colophon reads: "Written to the Hebrewes from Italy and sent by Timotheus."

This new version, wholly the work of Whittingham alone, was really a revised edition of Tyndale's New Testament rather than a fresh version. The rendering "congregation," which Tyndale had substituted for "Church," was first displaced in this Genevan version, which reverted to "Church." In this version the Gospels are entitled, "The Gospel writ by S. Matthew"—or "S. Luke." Before the Acts and each epistle is an "argument" summarising its contents; there is only one such "argument" for the three epistles of St. John. I John 5:7 is not put in brackets as doubtful, as in Tyndale's editions.

THE OLD TESTAMENT, 1560

Three years after Whittingham's edition of the New Testament appeared, the Old Testament with a revised version of Whittingham's

[15] This division into verses Whittingham derived from Stephens' Greek Testament, 1551, which in turn had been anticipated by Santes Pagninus in his Hebrew-Latin Bible, 1528. Long before that the Masoretes could hardly have counted up the number of verses in every book of the Bible without numbering them in some way. Our present division into chapters is owing to Hugo à S. Charo as seen in his *Concordance*, 1248. Cf. Moulton, *The History of the English Bible*, p. 37; Kenyon, *Our Bible and the Ancient Manuscripts* (1939), p. 225; "Verse-division" in *The Jewish Encyclopaedia*.

[16] Given in Pollard, *op. cit.*, pp. 275–79.

New Testament was published; *The Bible and Holy Scriptures. Conteyned in the Olde and Newe Testament. Translated according to the Ebrue and Greke, and conferred with the best translations in divers languages. With most profitable annotations upon all the hard places, and other things of great importance as may appeare in the Epistle to the Reader. "Feare not, stand stil, and beholde the salvacion of the Lord, which he wil shewe to you this day," Exod. xiv. 13. At Geneva. Printed by Rowland Hall. M.D.LX.* A woodcut depicts the passage of the Red Sea.

The expenses of production were largely borne by Bodley, father of Sir Thomas Bodley, founder of the Bodleian Library; he therefore received from Elizabeth in 1560 a licence constituting him for seven years sole printer of the Geneva Bible. In 1564 Archbishop Parker, though himself engaged in preparing the version known as the Bishops' Bible, secured for Bodley a renewal of his licence for another twelve years, though only four years of the previous licence had expired. Bodley appears to have toned down some of the excessively Puritan features of the version so as to make sure of the archbishop's assistance.[17]

After a "List of the Books of both Testaments" comes an address "To the moste vertuous and noble Quene Elisabeth, Quene of England, France, and Ireland, etc. Your humble subjects of the English Churche at Geneva." In the fulsome manner of the time they compare her work in building up true religion to that of Zerubbabel. Enemies withstood him, and the queen too meets with opponents, "whereof some are Papistes, . . . who traitorously seke to erect idolatrie." Faith in God and trust in His appointed ministers—"for it is their office chefely to understand the Scriptures and teache them"—will be her safeguard, as the whole history of the Jewish people shows; "from Geneva. 10. April. 1560." This is followed by a further address:

> To our Beloved in the Lord, the Brethren of England, Scotland, Ireland, etc., Grace, mercie, and peace, through Christ Jesus. . . . God knoweth with what

[17] His words are worth noting. Writing to Cecil he says that both he and Grindal "thought so well of the first impression and the review of those who had since travailed therein, that they wished it would please him to be a means that twelve years' longer term might be by a special privilege granted him, in consideration of the charges by him and his associates in the first impression, and the review since sustained; and that though one other special Bible for the Churches were meant by them to be set forth, as convenient time and leisure hereafter should permit, yet should it nothing hinder but rather do much good to have diversity of translation and readings" (Strype, *The Life and Acts of Matthew Parker*, I, 412).

feare and trembling we have bene now, for the space of two yeres and more day and night occupied herein, but being earnestly desired and by divers, whose learning and godynes we reverence, exhorted, and also incouraged by the ready willes of suche . . . not to spare any charges for the furtherance of such a benefite and favour of God toward his Churche, . . . we submitted ourselves at length to their godly judgementes, and seeing the great opportunitie and occasions which God presented to us in this Churche by reason of so many godly and learned men; and suche diversities of translations in divers tongues, we undertook this great and wonderful work with all reverence as in the presence of God. . . . And this we may with good conscience protest, that we have in every point and worde . . . faithfully rendered the text, and in all hard places moste syncerely expounded the same. For God is our witnes that we have by all meanes endevored to set forthe the puritie of the worde and the right sense of the holy Gost for the edifying of the brethren in faith and charitie. . . .

Now as we have chiefly observed the sense, and laboured always to restore it to all integritie: so have we most reverently kept the proprietie of the woordes, considering that the Apostles who spake and wrote to the Gentiles in the Greeke tongue, rather constrained them to the lively phrase of the Ebrewe, then enterprised farre by mollifying their language to speake as the Gentiles did. And for this and other causes we have in many places reserved the Ebrew phrases, notwithstanding that they may seem somewhat hard in their eares that are not well practised and also delight in the sweete sounding phrases of the holy Scriptures.[18]

They add that "albeit that many of the Ebrewe names be altered from the olde text, and restored to the true writing and first original, . . . yet in the usual names litle is changed for feare of troubling the simple readers." [19]

Both the text which follows and the notes are in clear Roman type, a great improvement on the older black letter.[20] The rendering, "They sewed figge leaves together, and made themselves breeches" (Gen. 3:7), led to the name of "Breeches Bible," by which the version has since been known.[21] Gen. 3:15 reads: "Hee shall breake thine head, and thou shalt bruise his heele"; Gen. 49:10, "until Shiloh came." On II Chron. 15:16 occurs the note which so displeased James I, who said that he had found in the Geneva Bible "some notes very partiall, untrue, seditious, and savouring too much of dangerous and trayterous conceipts: As for ex-

[18] Pollard, *op. cit.*, pp. 279–83.

[19] But few names appear in the new form; e.g., "Jaakon" and "Ishak" in Genesis.

[20] The black letter type persisted in some editions; e.g. in those of 1589, 1592, and 1608, though the marginal notes remained in Roman type.

[21] This rendering remains unchanged in all editions I have seen. But it already stood in Wycliffe's Bible, and the English version of the Golden Legend has: "took figgelevis and sewed them togyder in maner of brechis."

ample, 2 Chron. xv the note taxeth Asa for deposing, onely, and not killing her," namely, the queen mother.[22]

The psalms are given in the usual place, after Job; but the version is a new one, made from the Hebrew. Psalm 89 (88) opens with, "I will sing the mercies of the Lord for ever," in place of, "My song shall be always of the loving kindnesse of the Lord," as in the Great Bible and Prayer Book Version. The note on Isa. 7:15, "Christ is not only God, but man also," is but one of many proofs of the rigid orthodoxy of these Puritans touching the divinity of Christ; note, too, the emphatic capital letters in Jer. 31:22: "A WOMAN shall compass a man." The Canticle of Canticles is entitled: "An Excellent Song Which is Salomon's." After Chronicles comes "The Prayer of Manasses," but with the *caveat:* "This Prayer is not in the Ebrue, but is translated out of the Greke."

The Apocrypha, placed after Malachias, are prefaced by the statement that they are so called because they comprise "bookes which were not received by a common consent to bee read and expounded publikely in the Church, neither yet served to prove any point of Christian religion save in so much as they had the consent of the other Scriptures called Canonical to confirme the same, or rather whereon they were grounded: but as bookes proceding from godly men, were received to be read for the advancement and furtherance of knowledge of the history and for the instruction of godly maners." The Synod of Dort, 1618, directed that the Apocrypha should be omitted; they therefore do not appear in the edition published in 1633.

The heroic deed of Eleazar, who sacrificed his life in killing an elephant, is condemned: "This example is not to be followed, because it is contrary to the commandment" (I Mach. 6:43–46). Similarly the suicidal act of Razias is likewise condemned (II Mach. 14:41–43): "As this private example ought not to be followed of the godly, because it is contrary to the worde of God, although the author seeme heere to approve it: so that place as touching prayer [for the dead], chap. xii.44, thogh Judas had appointed it, yet were it not sufficient to proove a doctrine, because it is onely a particular example"—a strange argument indeed![23]

[22] William Barlow, *The Summe and Substance . . . of the Conference . . . at Hampton Court, January 14, 1604* (1604), p. 47.

[23] The famous passage referred to, II Mach. 12:44 f., is rendered: "He sent to Jerusalem . . . to offer a sineoffring, doing very well and honestly that he thoght of the

THE REVISED NEW TESTAMENT, 1560

The title of the New Testament portion of the Bible published in 1560 is: *The Newe Testament of Our Lord Jesus Christ, Diligently conferred with the Greke, and best approved translacions in divers languages. Exod.xiv.13: "Feare ye not, Stand stil, and beholde the salvacion of the Lord, which he will shew to you this day." At Geneva. Printed by Rouland Hall. M.D.LX.* The picture of the passage of the Red Sea is repeated. A brief "Description of the Holy Land" precedes a delightfully quaint map depicting immense ships sailing on the sea, in which weird fish disport themselves, among them an octopus and another having a man perched on his back.[24] After the Apocalypse, here called "Revelation of John the Divine," comes "A Briefe Table of all the Propre Names which are chiefly founde in the Olde Testament," comprising fourteen and a half columns. From it readers are exhorted to choose names for their children.[25]

In subsequent editions the title is framed in twenty-eight pictures. Surrounding it the Evangelists are depicted engaged in penning their Gospels. Above the title is the Holy Spirit in the form of a dove; beneath is the Lamb bearing a banner. On the outer side of the six abovementioned pictures are depicted on the left the tribes of Israel, eleven in number,[26] Ephraim and Manasses being represented by Joseph; on the

resurrection. For if he had not hoped that thei which were slaine, shold rise againe, it had been superfluous and vaine to pray for the dead. And therefor he perceived that there was great favour layed up for those that died godly. (It was an holy and good thought.) So he made a reconciliation for the dead that they might be delivered from sinne." The note on this passage says: "From this verse to the end of the chapter the Greeke text is corrupt, so that no good sense, much less certeine doctrine can be gathered therby. Also, it is evident that this place was not written by the holie Ghost, both because it dissenteth from the rest of the holie Scriptures, and also the authour of this booke acknowledging his own infirmitie, desireth pardon if he have not attained to that he should. . . . It is contrary to the custome of the Jewes, even to this day, to pray for the dead. And though Judas had so done yet this particular is not sufficient to establish a doctrine."

[24] On this map Sidon and Joppe are assigned huge basilicas; a river flows into the Dead Sea parallel to the Jordan; Sodom and Gomorrha are placed on the east side of the Dead Sea, Jericho on the west, while southeast of the Sea of Galilee, called Lake Genezar, is depicted a mythical Lake Gadara.

[25] It is doubtful whether children would be grateful to their parents for burdening them with names such as Ahasuerus, Artahshaste, Beraiah, Caseluhim, Dositheus, Eleadah, Elichoeni, Gazabar, Hanameel, Jephunneh, Kerenhappuch, Lysimachus, Mahazioth, Noadiah, Orthosias, Pedahel, Retrabeam Sabteca, Tanhumeth, and Vopsi.

[26] Not twelve, as Dore says, p. 232, but eleven of each.

right side are eleven of the apostles, Judas and St. Paul being omitted. Then follow "The Summe of the Whole Scripture of the Bookes of the Old and New Testament" and "Certaine questions and answeres touching the doctrine of predestination, the use of God's worde and Sacraments."[27] This "catechism" has been justly described as "the most clear and naked exposition of Calvinistic doctrine that can be compressed into a small space." One sample will suffice: "Question. Are all ordained unto eternal life? Answere. Some are vessels of wrath ordained unto destruction, as others are vessels of mercie prepared to glory." As Dore remarks:

> The changes adopted in the Genevan Bible and New Testament synchronise with the gradual spread of the Calvinistic heresy and the contemporaneous development of hatred of the whole Papal system of doctrine. The notes attacked the Sacramental teaching of the Church, substituting for it the Calvinistic doctrines of election and reprobation. They taught that Sacraments are nothing more than signs and seals of grace previously given to the elect. All passages about Sacraments are explained away.

In some editions, e.g., that of 1608, after the title page follows a "Hymn, drawn from the Bible, and dealing with the Incomparable Treasures of the holy Scriptures, with a Prayer before reading." After the Text of the New Testament the above-mentioned tables are reproduced, but now with a very full title:

> Two right profitable and fruitful Concordances, or large and ample Tables Aphabeticall. The first containing the interpreteation of the Hebrew, Caldean, Greek, and Latine words, and names scatteringly dispersed throughout the whole Bible, with their common places following every of them. And the second comprehending all such other principall words and matters, as concerne the sense and meaning of the Scriptures, or direct unto any necessary and good instruction.
>
> The further Contents and use of both the which Tables (for brevitie sake) is expressed more at large in the Preface to the Reader: And will serve as well for the Translation called Geneva, as for the other authorized to be read in Churches. Collected by D.F.H.

These initials are partly explained by the signature attached to the above-mentioned Preface: "This xxii of December, Anno Domini, 1578. Thine in the Lord, Robert F. Herry."[28] Herry (or Fitzhenry) certainly made his Tables ample, for he expanded the previous fourteen and a half columns into one hundred and twenty-seven, and the previous fifty-two

[27] These "questions and answeres" were omitted in Tomson's editions.

[28] Herry's real name was Robert Harrison; turning this into Harri-son, he further translated it into Fitzhenry.

columns into two hundred and eighty-five. His "directions" are distinctly controversial, for example those on images, preachers, and preaching; and while there is much about the need of confessing our sins, there is not a word about auricular confession.

The revisers of Whittingham's version made some changes in 1560; for example: "Then Joseph her houseband, beynge a just man, and loth ("unwilling," 1560) to make her a publike example of infamie" (Matt. 1:19); "chosen by election of the churches"; 1560, "chosen of the churches" (II Cor. 8:19); "free benevolence"; 1560, "good pleasure" (Ephes. 1:9). Similar changes occur throughout; there are, for instance, seven in Luke 15:1–8, eight in Rom. 7:1–4.[29] All editions have "Hail, thou that art freely beloved," and in the margin, "received in favour" (Luke 1:28); "this cup *is* the New Testament in my blood" (Luke 22:20); "made himself of no reputation" (Phil. 2:7); "the whole Scripture *is* given by inspiration of God" (II Tim. 3:16). Some changes involve unjustifiable interpretations; e.g., Wycliffe, A.V., and R.V. may be right in their reading of Jas. 4:6, "but *he* giveth greater grace," though the Greek is ambiguous and Tyndale, Cranmer and Rheims omit the pronoun; but the revisers of the Geneva Bible, in accord with their insistence on the principle that the Bible and the Bible only is the rule of faith, write, "but the Scripture offereth more grace." Another erroneous

[29] For a list of these see Dore, *op. cit.*, pp. 193–97. The following examples will show how the Geneva Bible influenced subsequent versions. The text as given is that of 1557; words in italics were either omitted or changed in the revision of 1560.

Matt. 12:45. "Then he goeth *hys way* and taketh unto him seven other spirits worse than himselfe and *so* they enter in and dwell there, and the ende of that man is worse than the beginning. Even so shall it be with this *evil nation* (wicked generation)."

Matt. 23:27. "*Wo* (Woe) be to you Scribes and Pharisees hypocrites, for you are like unto *paynted* (whited) tombes which appear beautiful outward but are within full of dead mens bones and of all filthiness."

Mark 9:49. "For every *one* (man) shall be salted with fire and every *victime* (sacrifice) shall be salted with salt."

Mark 12:17 underwent even greater revision: 1557, "Then Jesus answered and said unto them: Then give to Caesar that which belongs to Caesar and to God that which belongeth to God"; 1560, "Then Jesus answered and said to him: Give to Caesar the things that are Caesar's and unto God the things that are God's."

In the above examples, the Rhemists adopted "wicked generation" from the revised Genevan version, 1560, and also "whited," though they wrote "sepulchres" in preference to "tombes"; but they adopted "victime" from the unrevised edition, 1557. They realized, too, the superiority of the revised version of Mark 12:17, though here, as throughout, they prefer to use inverted expressions: "the things that are Caesar's to Caesar, and that are God's to God"; but A.V. boldly adopted the rendering of 1560, and Challoner followed suit.

rendering, which stands in all editions, is: "As often as ye shal eat this bread *and* drinke this cup" (I Cor. 11:26).

The marginal notes are remarkable for the absence of controversial bitterness. Some of them are distinctly weak; e.g., the one on Matt. 1:25 ("til she had broght foorth her first borne sonne"): "Christ is here called the first-borne because she had never none before: and not in respect of any she had after"; but the last clause is immediately qualified by: "Neither yet doth this worde [til] import alwais a time following wherin the contrarie may be affirmed." Nothing could be more orthodox than the note on John 6:62: "He meaneth not that his humanitie descended from heaven; but he speaketh touching the union of bothe natures: attributing to thone that which apperteineth to the other."

HERETICAL TENDENCIES OF THE REVISERS

Though the editors of the revised version of the New Testament make no ostentatious parade of their seditious opinions, the true spirit of Puritanism appears both in the notes and in the chapter headings. For example, on Rom. 13:5: "No private man can contemne that government which God hath appointed, without the breach of his conscience; and here he speaketh of civil magistrates: so that Antichrist and his [the pope of Rome, of course] cannot wrest this place to establish their tyrannie over the conscience," a comment which sounds strange, coming from would-be regicides. The note on Rom. 2:12: "As the onely will and purpose of God is the chief cause of election and reprobation; so his free mercy is an inferior cause of salvation, and the hardening of the heart an inferior cause of damnation." Again, through divine intervention the Magi eluded Herod; therefore, they declare, "promises ought not to be kept when God's honour and the preaching of his truth is hindered."

The sacraments, too, are deprived of their real significance; this is particularly the case when there is question of the Holy Eucharist. The note on "This is my body" (Matt. 26:26) reads: "That is, a true signe and testimonie that my body is made yours, and by me your souls are nourished . . . with the blood of Christ spiritually received." On Luke 22:19: "The bread is a true sign and an assured testimony that the body of Jesus Christ is given for the nourishment of our souls, likewise the wine signifieth that his blood is our drink to refresh and quicken us everlastingly." On John 6:54: "To eat the flesh of Christ and drink his blood, is to dwell in Christ and have Christ dwelling in us."

In the note on Matt. 19:11, clerical celibacy is denounced, at least by implication: "Continence is a gift of God, therefore men may not rashly abstain from marriage." The words, "Upon this rock I will build my Church," are interpreted to mean: "Upon that faith whereby thou hast confessed and acknowledged me; for it is grounded upon an infallible trueth"; and on the power of the keys (Matt. 16:19): "the preachers of the Gospel open the gates of heaven with the worde of God, which is the right key, so that where this worde is not purely taught, there is neither key nor authoritie." Again, on Mark 6:34 ("they were like sheep which had no shepherd") the note says: "This declareth that there is an horrible disorder among that people where the true preaching of God's word wanteth."

The pure subjectivism of all that is apparent; all doctrines are to be tested by "the word of God" at every man's discretion according as he chooses to interpret it. This principle is explicitly formulated in the note on Matt. 16:6, "Beware of the leaven of the Pharisees": "We may boldly by Christ's admonition reject and contemne all erroneous doctrines and man's inventions, and ought onely to cleave to the word of God." It is significant that while the notes on the Gospels, Acts, and the epistles are nowhere definitely anti-Roman, this feature is very marked in the notes on the Apocalypse. For example, the locusts of Apoc. 9:3 are "false teachers, heretikes, and worldlie suttill prelates, with Monkes, Friars, Cardinals, Patriarkes, Archbishops, Bishops, Doctors, Baschelers, and Masters which forsake Christ to mainteyne false doctrine." "The beast that cometh out of the bottomless pit" (11:7) is explained as "the Pope which hathe his power out of hel and cometh thence"; and Sodom (11:8) is interpreted of "the whole jurisdiction of the Pope." The note on 13:8 declares that "the Pope's kingdom is of the earth, and leadeth to perdition, and is begun, and established by ambition, covetousness, beastlines, craft, treason, tyranie," etc.[30]

[30] Despite all this, Hoare can complacently remark that the version "stands creditably free from ecclesiastical bias" (*op. cit.*, p. 196). Even in the original edition, 1557, some of the notes on the Apocalypse are very antipapal: "The beast signifieth the ancient Rome: the woman that sitteth thereon the new Rome which is the Papistrie, whose cruelty and bloodshed is declared by scarlet. This woman is the Antichrist, that is, the Pope with the whole bodie of his filthy creatures, whose beauty onely standeth in outward pompe and impudencie, and craft like strumpet" (on 17:3).

Not without reason does Scrivener say of these notes that

in general they comprise a sort of running commentary on the sacred writers, strongly impregnated with the peculiar views of Calvin and Beza, which are set forth in a tone as positive and uncompromising as can well be imagined. When we reflect that the Geneva version was the Family Bible of the middle classes for two full generations after its first appearance, we may conceive how powerful an engine these notes became in the hands of that party, which in the next century laid the throne and altar in the dust.[31]

THE POPULARITY OF THE VERSION

Many factors conduced to the success of the new version: its convenient quarto size indeed sounded the death-knell of the unwieldy Great Bible;[32] its clear type compared favorably with the old black letter; the division into verses made reference easy; and the maps, plans, and tables were helpful. The version appeared, too, just when returning exiles had reason to hope for support from a Protestant queen, though Elizabeth may not have enthusiastically welcomed a Bible in which Knox, who had but recently published his *Monstrous Regiment of Women,* had so large a part. The fact that the version had been made directly from the original enhanced its value. Convocation had in 1534 demanded a vernacular version, and Coverdale's appeared in the following year. But it was unsatisfactory since it was a translation of the Vulgate Latin. His improved version, the Great Bible of 1539, was condemned by Convocation in 1542 for the same reason.

Despite the assertion by the pseudoerudite King James that the Genevan version was, to his thinking, the worst that had so far appeared,[33] there can be no two opinions about the excellence of the translation. Archbishop Trench says of it: "It is evident that there must have been some very good scholarship brought to bear on this version, or revision rather. I have observed on several occasions that it is the first to seize the exact meaning of a passage, which all the preceding versions had missed."[34] He instances: "The tyme of the Fast was now passed" (Acts 27:9), followed by Rheims, A.V., and R.V., instead of Tyndale's

[31] *A Supplement to the Authorized Engish Version of the New Testament,* p. 93.

[32] Not all editions of the Geneva Bible were of this small handy size; Wilson describes the edition published by Barker in 1583 as "magnificently printed in royal folio, with a margin of three inches, on a paper nearly equal to vellum" (*Catalogue of Bibles . . . in the Collection of Lea Wilson*).

[33] At the Hampton Court Conference; cf. below, chap. 20.

[34] *On the Authorized Version of the New Testament* (1859), p. 113 note.

"overlong fasting." Whereas the earlier translators of Jas. 1:13 regarded ἀπείραστος as active and rendered it, "God is not a tempter of evils," the Genevans realized that the word was passive and therefore wrote, "God cannot be tempted with evil," a rendering accepted by A.V. and R.V. The Geneva Bible has "and a house divided against itself falleth" in preference to "and house upon house shall fall" (Luke 11:17); Wycliffe, Tyndale, Cranmer, Rheims, A.V. margin, following the Vulgate *et coepit flere,* have "and he began to weep" (Mark 14:72), but Geneva, taking into account the Greek ἐπιβαλῶν, has "and weighing that with himself, he wept"; A.V. text, "and when he thought thereon, he wept." As a matter of fact, as Westcott points out, the instances given by Trench are really due to Beza.[35] Still it is to the credit of the Genevan translators that they realized how correct Beza was. At the same time theirs was not a wholly new version so much as a revision. Its framers, says Westcott,

> took in the Old Testament the Great Bible as their basis, and corrected its text, without ever substituting for it a new translation. Even where the changes are greatest the original foundation can still be traced, and the new work fairly harmonises with the old. One chief aim of the revisers seems to have been to make the translation as nearly verbal as possible, and consequently in a number of passages they replace the renderings of the Zurich scholars (Coverdale) or Münster by those of Pagninus. At the same time there is abundant evidence to shew that they were perfectly competent to deal independently with points of Hebrew scholarship.[36]

TOMSON'S EDITIONS OF THE GENEVAN NEW TESTAMENT

In 1576 Laurence Tomson (1539–1608) brought out an edition which, while not making many changes in the actual text, yet materially altered the Bible owing to the notes which he added. Tomson, a great traveler, was a good linguist, for he was said to have known twelve languages and was at one time lecturer in Hebrew at Geneva. He made few changes in the text of the New Testament, the most characteristic being his pedantic rendering of the Greek definite article by "that"; e.g., "Thou art that Christ" (Matt. 16:16); "Who is a liar but he that denieth that Jesus is that Christ; the same is that Antichrist that denieth . . ." (I

[35] *A General View of the History of the English Bible,* p. 227. In these instances Beza has: Deus tentari a malis non potest (Jas. 1:13); domus adversus se partita cadit (Luke 11:17); animum adjiciens flevit (Mark 14:72).

[36] *Ibid.,* p. 322. Yet Eason, who also quotes the above, speaks of this Bible as "a new translation" (*The Geneva Bible, Notes on Its Production and Distribution,* 1937). J. H. Blunt, *Encyclopedia Britannica,* VIII, 387, would agree with Westcott.

John 2:22); "He that hath that son hath that life: and he that hath not that Son hath not that life" (I John 5:12). In I Cor. 16:22, for "Let him be in execration, yea excommunicate to death" (1560), he has substituted "Let him be in excommunication, maranatha."

By 1587 no less than twelve editions of this revision had appeared, and by that date Tomson's text and notes had practically supplanted the editions of 1557 and 1560. The revision was often republished, the last edition coming in 1616; it was thereafter replaced in popular esteem by the King James's Version, 1611.

Unfortunately it was the notes added by Tomson which contributed most to the popularity of his edition. These notes were violently anti-Catholic, and while even in the edition of 1560 the notes on the Apocalypse were certainly antipapal, they were mild compared to those in Tomson's first edition, 1576; and even these latter were surpassed in virulence by those he added later from Francis Junius.[37] These, as Pocock remarks, "added to nearly all Tomson Bibles after 1598, must have done much to spread hostility to Rome among the people." [38] Indeed what else could be expected when God-fearing people read such passages in their annotated Bibles:

> The popes arrogated unto themselves a licence to kill whom they would, whiles others were unawares; and without feare established a butchery out of many of the wicked Canons of the Decretals. . . . Gregory, the seventh, a most notorious Necromancer, who before was called Hildebrandus Senensis; for this man being made altogether of impiety and wickedness, as a slave of the devil whom he served, was the most wicked firebrand of the world: he excommunicated the Emperour Henry the Fourth" (on Apoc. 9:6).

Of Boniface VIII it is said that "he entered like a foxe, reigned like a lion, died like a dogge" (on Apoc., chap. 11). In the 1560 edition the note on "the mark of the beast" (Apoc. 13:16) read: "A man must subscribe to the Pope's doctrines; moreover their Chrismatories, greasings,

[37] *The New Testament of our Lord Jesus Christ translated out of the Greeke by Theod. Beza whereunto are adjoined briefe summaries of doctrine upon the Evangelists and Acts of the Apostles, by the said Theod. Beza. And also short Expositions on the phrases and hard places, taken out of the Annotations of the foresaid Author, and Joachim Camerarius, by J. Ls. Villerius. Englished by L. Tomson. Together with the Annotations of Francis Junius upon the Revelation of St. John. Edinburgh. Printed by Andro Hart, and are to be sold at his Buith, on the Northside of the gate, a little beneath the Crosse. Anno Dom. 1610. Cum Privilegio Regiae Majestatis.* See also pp. 123, 129.

[38] Quoted by Eason, *op. cit.*, p. 16, from Pocock, *Saturday Review*, September and November, 1880; also in *The Bibliographer*, 1882–84.

vows, othes, and shavings, are signs of this mark"; to this Tomson added: "to exercise over all their goods and actions, a pederlike abuse of indulgences and dispensations."

The notes on the Gospels, not so abusive as the foregoing, are definitely opposed to the agelong teaching of the Church, a point emphasized by Tomson; for to the note on Matt. 16:18, which in 1560 ran: "Upon that faith whereby thou hast confessed and acknowledged me: for it is grounded upon an infallible truth," he added: "Christ spoke in the Syrian tongue and therefore used not this discanting between Petros which signifieth Peter and Petra which signifieth a rock but in both places used this word Cepha. . . . His mind was that wrote in Greek by the divers terminations to make a difference between Peter who is a man and Christ who is the Rock."

LATER EDITIONS

The Genevan New Testament was translated into Italian in 1562, into French in 1610 and 1616, with a *Nouvel Indice* full of bitterly anti-Roman notes. In England the last edition appeared in 1616; but even after that date no less than 150,000 copies are said to have been imported from Holland. It has been reckoned that some 200 editions, whether of the whole Bible or of the New Testament alone, were printed between 1560 and 1630; the *Catalogue of the British and Foreign Bible Society* lists 149 editions between 1560 and 1644. But it is questionable whether these many "editions" indicate a corresponding demand, for publishers, even publishers of Bibles, are human and must find a market for their goods. Moreover, many "editions" of the Geneva Bible are printed from the same blocks, for they reproduce the same misprints, the only change being a fresh title page asserting that this is a new edition.[39] In fact, the Protestant Synod at Saumur pointed out to the Calvinistic authorities at Geneva that their booksellers were practising fraud by thus prefixing such title pages and passing off the volumes as though they were new editions.[40] The publishers of Coverdale's editions of 1535 and 1550 resorted to the same expedient in order to sell their books.

Many of Barker's editions open with *The Booke of Common Prayer, with the Psalter or Psalmes of David, of that Translation which is ap-*

[39] See Dore, *op. cit.*, p. 207.

[40] See *ibid.*, p. 234. Dore points out, too, that publishers introduced extensive variations, not only into the notes, but into the text as well (*ibid.*, pp. 218 ff.).

pointed to be used in Churches. Then follows the "Address to the Christian Reader" as in the edition of 1560; but there is added a page on "How to take Profit in Reading of the holy Scriptures," also thirty-one pages giving "The Genealogies Recorded in the Sacred Scriptures, According to every Family and Tribe. With the Line of our Saviour Jesus Christ observed from Adam to the blessed Virgin Mary," by J. S. Finally, "A Description of Canaan, and the bordering Countries," with a map which, though quaint to our eyes, is more correct than the previous one of 1560.[41] The text in the Old Testament is, so far as I have observed, unchanged from that of 1560,[42] but the clear type which makes the first edition so convenient to use is replaced by the old black letter. The psalms are given in the new version, and after the Tables which follow the New Testament we have "The Whole Booke of Psalmes. Collected into English Meeter, by Thomas Sternehold, John Hopkins, and others, conferred with the Hebrew, with apt Notes to sing them withal, 1616."

[41] See above, footnote 24.

[42] The only difference I have been able to detect in later editions is the omission of italics, so marked a feature of the Old Testament of 1560; cf. Job, 19:7, 16, 24, 26, 27.

CHAPTER XVI

The Bishops' Bible, 1568

NONE of the translations so far produced had met with general satisfaction. Tyndale's had been condemned repeatedly, though it had, it is true, surreptitiously gained an entrance into the country disguised under the name of Matthew's Bible; Coverdale's version had not been based on the original texts, and Cranmer's Bible had been condemned by the bishops in 1542. The Geneva Bible, too, was far from acceptable to the authorities of the Church of England because of its Calvinistic notes. A new version, then, was urgently needed.

In 1561 Archbishop Parker [1] circulated among the bishops a proposal for a new version, assigning to each of them a portion for revision. On September 22, 1568, he wrote to Cecil that the work was done, and sent copies to the Queen and to Cecil in October, with a list of the revisers and the portions they had done: "The lettres of their names be partlie affixed in the ende of their bookes, which I thought a policie to shewe them, to make them more diligent, as Answerable for their doinges." [2] Strype says:

[1] A letter of Cox of Ely to Parker, January 19, 1561, seems to show that Cox was really the originator of the proposal: "Another thing ther is worthy to be consydered, the translation of the bible to be committed to mete men and to be vewed over and amended. . Ye have men hable to do it thoroughly." On May 3, 1566, he wrote again: "I trust your Grace is well forward with the Bible by this time. I perceive the greatest burden will lie upon your neck touching care and translation. I would wish that such usual words as we English be acquainted with might still remain in their form and sound, so far forth as the Hebrew will well bear. Inkhorn terms to be avoided. The translation of the verbs in the Psalms to be used uniformly in one tense, etc. And if ye translate *bonitas* or *misericordia,* to use it likewise in all places of the Psalms, etc." (see Pollard, *Records of the English Bible,* p. 291; *Epis.* 286, Parker Society Edition).

[2] "After much toil of the printer, and some labour taken of some parties for the setting out and recognising of the English Bible, we be now come to a conclusion for the substance of the book" (*Epis.* 257, Parker Society, 334). Parker at one time had asked Cecil himself to peruse at least one of the epistles: "I have distributed the Bible to divers men, and I am desirous if you could spare so much leasure either in morning or evening,

The Archbishop took upon him the labour to contrive and set the whole work a going in a proper method, by sorting out the whole Bible into parcels . . . and distributing those parcels to able bishops and other learned men, to peruse and collate each the book or books allotted them; sending withal his instructions for the method they should observe; and they to add some short marginal notes for the illustration or correction of the text. And all these portions of the Bible being finished and sent back to the archbishop, he was to add the last hand to them, and so to take care for printing and publishing the whole.[3]

THE RULES FOR REVISION

The rules laid down for the guidance of the revisers are very simple and straightforward:

Firste to followe the Commune Englishe Translacion used in the Churches and not to recede from yt but wher yt varieth manifestlye from the Hebrue or Greke originall.

Item to use such sections and devisions in the Textes as Pagnine[4] in his Translacion useth, and for the veritie of the Hebrue to followe the said Pagnine and Münster specially, and generally others learned in the tonges.

Item to make no bitter notis upon any text, or yet to set downe any determinacion in places of controversie.

Item to note such Chapters and places as conteineth matter of Genealogy or other such places not edefieng, with some strike or note that the Reader may eschue them in his publike readinge.

Item that all such wordes as soundeth in the Olde Translacion to any offence of Lightnes or obscenitie be expressed with more convenient termes and phrases.

The printer hath bestowed his thickest Paper in the newe Testament bicause yt shall be most occupied.[5]

When sending a copy to the Queen, Parker explained that his purpose was "not to make yt varye much from that translacion which was commonlie used by Publike order [the Great Bible], except wher eyther the verytie of the hebrue and greke moved alteracion or wher the text was by sum negligence mutilated from the original." He wished his edition to serve as a counteraction to "sum translacions which have not byn labored in your realme having inspersed diverse prejudicall notis which might have byn also well spared."[6]

---

we had one Epistle of SS. Paul, Peter, or James, perused by you, that ye may be one of the builders of this good work in Christes Churche," a politic suggestion which Cecil took at its face value and declined.

[3] *Parker,* I, 414.

[4] For the influence exercised by Pagninus' version, see Strype, *The Life and Acts of Matthew Parker,* p. 336 note. The revisers depended also on Castalio and Leo Jud; but their real basis was the Great Bible.

[5] Given in Pollard, *op. cit.,* pp. 297 f.

[6] Pollard, *op. cit.,* p. 294.

In his Preface, after pointing out how assiduously the Jews studied the Bible, Parker says: "How much more unadvisedly do such as boast themselfe to be either Christ's vicars, or be of his garde to loth christen men from reading by their covert slanderous reproaches of the Scriptures, or in their authoritie by law or statute to contract this liberty of studying the word of eternal salvation." This was a veiled allusion to Arundel's Constitution of 1408. But a little further on Parker explicitly condemns it. "They can in their constitutions provincial, under pain of excommunication, inhibite al other men to translate them without the ordinaries of the provincial councils agree thereunto, but they will be wel ware never to give counsail to set them out." In support of vernacular versions he even quotes "John, once Bishop of Rochester" as one "who had rightly insisted that knowledge of the Bible must increase as the ages went by." [7]

Parker was fully alive to the defects of the new version, and he exhorts the readers "charitably to examine this translation . . . and not to be offended with diversitie of interpretation, tho' he find it not to agree with his wont text, or yet to disagree from the common translation; . . . not to be offended at seeing the holy scriptures in his own language as a matter newly seene." In support of the vernacular he refers to the fact that the Venerable Bede finished his translation of the Gospel of St. John on his deathbed.[8]

It was the object of the bishops, says Westcott, "to remove from the Great Bible all errors which seemed to impair the sense; and at the same time to produce a popular, and not a literary version. . . . The execution of the work is indeed extremely unequal; and the Greek scholarship of the revisers superior to their Hebrew scholarship." [9]

Since all the revisers were bishops, or afterwards became bishops, the

[7] John Fisher's words are so striking that they may be given in full: "There be yet in the Gospells many darke places, whiche without all doubt to the posteritie shal be made muche more open. For why should we dispayre herein, seeing the Gospel was delivered to this intent, that it might be utterly understanded of us, yea to the very inche. Wherfore, forasmuch as Christe sheweth no lesse love to his Churche now, then hitherto he hath done, the auctoritie wherof is as yet no whit diminished, and forasmuch as that holy spirite (is) the perpetuall keper and gardian of the same Church, whose gyftes and graces do flowe as continually and as abundantly as from the beginning: who can doubt but that such thinges as remayne yet unknowen in the gospells, shal be hereafter made open to the latter wittes of our posteritie, to their cleare understanding?" (Strype, *op. cit.*, I, 412.)

[8] Lewis gives this Preface almost in its entirety (*A Complete History of the Several Translations of the Holy Bible and New Testament*, pp. 242–46).

[9] *A General View of the History of the English Bible*, p. 230.

edition came to be known as the Bishops' Bible. Parker did the greatest share of the work, being responsible for three Prefaces: those to the whole work, to the Psalms, and to the New Testament; he also revised Genesis and Exodus, the Gospels of Matthew and Mark, and the epistles from II Corinthians to Hebrews inclusive. The Psalms were assigned to Guest of Rochester, but Parker disliked his turning "the preterperfect tense into the present," and his retention of the same renderings of the Psalms as appeared in quotations from them in the New Testament. He therefore assigned Romans to Guest; [10] yet even Romans was actually done by Cox of Ely, while the Psalms ultimately fell to Thomas Bickley,[11] afterwards bishop of Chichester. Sandys revised Kings and Chronicles, but complained that previous translators had been too much influenced by the Latin version of Münster. Josue, Judges, and Ruth fell to Davies of St. David's; [12] the Apocrypha were divided between Parkhurst of Norwich and Barlow, then bishop of Chichester. Cox ultimately took over the Gospels of Luke and John as well as the Acts. Esther finds no place in the lists. In the folio editions the signatures of the contributors are appended to the books they revised, but these do not always agree with the list furnished by Parker.[13]

AUTHORIZATION OF THE BISHOPS' BIBLE

The Bishops' Bible, then, was due to the personal initiative of Parker, supported, indeed urged on, by such bishops as Cox and Sandys. The latter writes to Parker: "Your Grace should much benefit the church in hastening forward the Bible which you have in hand. Those that we have be not only falsely printed, but also give great offence to many by reason of the diversity of reading." [14] The edition was not the result of any royal decree, nor had Convocation anything to do with the work of

[10] Strype, *op. cit.* (1821), I, 415–17; also *Correspondence of Parker, Epis.* 191, Parker Society, 1853, p. 250.

[11] Strype supposed the initials T. B. stood for Thomas Becon, Prebendary of Canterbury, but Aldis Wright is almost certainly correct in referring them to Thomas Bickley; see his revised edition of Westcott, *op. cit.*

[12] *Correspondence of Parker, Epis.* 197, February 6, 1565. On April 24, 1566, Davies wrote: "I am well forward in the recognising of that part of the Bible that your Grace hath committed to me" (*ibid., Epis.* 214).

[13] See *ibid., Epis.* 257; Pollard, *op. cit.*, pp. 30–32; Mombert, *English Versions of the Bible*, pp. 268–79; Dore, *Old Bibles*, p. 237; Burnet, *History of the Reformation*, II, 643 f.; V, 559; Lewis, *op. cit.*, pp. 236–38.

[14] *Correspondence of Archbishop Parker, Epis.* 198, p. 257 note.

revision, though in 1571 Convocation enacted that it was to be "read in churches," and in this sense it was, until the appearance of King James's Version, regarded as the official version of the Church of England. Yet this edition does not seem to have been much "read in churches," for in 1587 Whitgift complained that many churches were still without Bibles, or at best had only torn and defaced copies, not "of the translation authorized by the synods of Bishops." He therefore had a larger as well as a smaller edition prepared.

Though superseded in its turn by the King James's Version, just as it had itself superseded the Great Bible, the Bishops' Bible was, in the edition of 1602, to provide the real basis for the King James's Version. "Parker's edition," says Dore, "took the place of the Great Bible in the public services of the Church, but for private use it never displaced the Genevan; and we find that the Puritans, who held many livings in the Church of England, often in defiance of all authority took their text from the 'Breeches' Bible."

THE OLD TESTAMENT

The title of the first edition of the Bishops' Bible was simple: *The holie Bible, conteyning the Olde Testament and the new.* Beneath was an engraving of Elizabeth with emblematic figures of charity and religion.[15] Tables and "Almanachs," Parker's Preface, and Cranmer's Prologue follow.[16] A portrait of the Earl of Leicester is prefixed to Josue, one of Burleigh to the Psalms. There are no less than 143 cuts as well as several maps.[17]

In later editions, such as that by Barker, 1585, the title was amplified: *The Holy Byble conteining the Olde and the New Testament, Authorised and appointed to be read in Churches. Imprinted at London by Christopher Barker, Printer to the Queenes most excellent Majestie. Anno 1585. Cum gratia et privilegio.* At the top are Hebrew letters meant to represent Jehovah, but they are all wrong. On either side are heraldic

[15] An undated edition simply entitled *The Holie Bible* has a pleasing portrait of Elizabeth surrounded by heraldic figures; beneath is inscribed: *Non me pudet . . . omni credenti,* Rom. i. The lessons and psalms for Sundays are indicated, but a note says, "marked parts may be leased [left] unread in the public reading."

[16] Cranmer's Preface originally opened with the words, "Of two sundry sorts. . . ." Besides several other minor changes, this was altered to "Concerning two sundry sorts." The closing, "God save the King," became "Praise be to God."

[17] For details see Lewis, *op. cit.,* pp. 235 ff.; Mombert, *op. cit.,* pp. 272 f.

angels and the letters E.R. (Elizabeth Regina), one on each side of the title. Since this edition is more commonly met with than the first edition, 1568, it will be convenient to base on it the following account of the version.

The text has marginal summaries of the contents of the chapters, the verses are numbered, and the chapter headings are divided by references to the said verses. The first chapter of Genesis reads throughout, "and it was so"; other readings: "It shall tread down thy head, and thou shalt tread upon his heele" (Gen. 3:15); "until Silo come" (Gen. 49:10); the marginal note on Gen. 49:13: "There are many commodious havens about this tribe." After Chronicles we read:

> A verie profitable declaration for the understanding of the histories of Esdras, Nehemias, Esther, Daniel, and divers other places of Scripture, very darke by reason of the discord that is among the Historiographers, and among the expositours of the holy Scriptures, touching the successive order of the kings and Monarchies of Babylon and of Persia: of the yeeres that the said Monarchies lasted from the transmigration of the Jewes under Nabuchodonosor untill the Monarchie of the Greekes, and of the confusion that is in the names of the kings of Persia.

The next title page, with the same framework as the former, embraces "The Psalter or Psalms of David, the Proverbs, Ecclesiastes, and the songs of Solomon, the great prophets Esai, Jeremie, Ezechiel, Daniel; the smal or lesse prophets, Osee to Malachi.[18] Prefixed to the Psalms is "A Prologue of Saint Basil the Great upon the Psalmes," also a passage from St. Augustine's *Confessions* (X, chap. 33). These are followed by Archbishop Parker's admonition to the reader not to be distressed at the unfamiliar renderings in the fresh version of the Psalter.

Each psalm is prefixed by "The argument of the Psalme"; the three verses frequently added to psalm 14 are omitted; psalm 16 is entitled "The golden psalme of David." Some idea of the changes in the new version of the Psalms can be gained from psalm 23: "He will cause me to repose myself in pasture full of grasse, and he will lead me into calm waters. . . . Truely felicitie and mercie shall follow me all the dayes of my life, and I will dwell in the house of God for a long time." In psalm 91 "Thou shalt not be afraid of any terrour of the night," replaces the "bugges" of previous versions; Jer. 8:22 reads: "Is there no tryacle at Gilead?" Chapter 31 of Proverbs is not arranged metrically, but nearly every verse begins with "shee" or "she." Ecclesiastes is "The

[18] The proper names are spelled as in the Vulgate.

Book of the Preacher, otherwise called Ecclesiastes, which is Solomon the king"; The Canticle of Canticles is here called, as in previous versions, "The Ballet of Ballettes of Solomon."

There is a third title page for "The Bookes called Apocrypha," comprising I and II (III and IV) Esdras, I and II Machabees, as well as the others generally known as Apocrypha. At the foot of the title page is the figure of the lion and the unicorn, the whole presentation being distinctly pagan. After "Bel and the Dragon" we have "The Prayer of Manasses king of Juda." After the title page comes "A necessary Table for the knowledge of the state of Juda, from the beginning of the Monarchie of the Greekes (where the Table that we have set forth upon Esdras endeth) untill the death and Passion of Jesus Christ." This Table furnishes lists of the Seleucidan kings and the Machabean rulers. II Mach. 12:43–45 is rendered:

> That there might a sacrifice be offered for the misdeede. In the which he did wel and right, for he had some consideration and pondering of the life that is after this time. For if he had not thought that they which were slaine should rise againe it had been superfluous and vaine to make any vow or sacrifice for them that were dead. But for so much as he saw that they which die in the favour and beliefe of God, are in good rest and joy, he thought it to be good and honorable for a reconciling to do the same for those which were slayne, that the offence might be forgiven. [There it stops.]

The Psalter in the Bishops' Bible was a new version made from the Hebrew and certainly inferior to the Prayer Book Version. This version, which appeared in the first edition, appeared also in the quarto edition of 1569; but in 1572 the version of the Great Bible was published alongside of it, and in 1577 it was entirely replaced by the version of the Great Bible; it appeared for the last time in the edition of 1585. In his Preface, Parker says:

> Let the gentle reader have this Christian consideration within hym selfe that though he findeth the psalmes of this translation following, not so to sounde agreeably to his ears in his wonted wordes and phrases, as he is accustomed with, yet let hym not be to muche offended with the worke, which was wrought for his owne commoditie and comfort. And if he be learned, let hym correct the worde or sentence (which may dislike hym) with the better, and whether his note ryseth eyther of good wyll and charitie, eyther of envie and contention not purely, yet his reprehension, if it may turne to the finding out of the trueth, shall not be repelled with greefe, but applauded to in gladnesse.

In this version of the Psalms there are many bracketed words; e.g., "[as for] the ungodly [it is] not so [with them]" (1:4). Before each psalm appears the opening words of each as they appear in the Vulgate: *Beatus vir,* etc.; while in psalm 119 each set of eight verses has for its heading, *Legem pone, Mirabilia,* etc. In the third edition, 1572, the Psalms were printed twice: in black letter according to the version in the Great Bible (the Prayer Book Version), and in Roman type according to the new version from the Hebrew. Later editions gave only the Prayer Book Version, though the metrical version by Sternhold and Hopkins was often printed at the end of the volume.

In psalms 14 and 53 the rendering of Coverdale and Matthew is retained: "The foolish bodies say in heart: Tush, there is no God"; whereas the Great Bible has, "The foole hath sayd in his hert, there is no God." The Prayer Book Version had in Ps. 37:28 the unfortunate misprint, "the righteous shall be punished"; all editions of the Bishops' Bible which retained this Psalter perpetuated the mistake, which was corrected only in 1661.

THE NEW TESTAMENT

The New Testament portion bears the title: *The Newe Testament of our Saviour Jesus Christ. Imprinted at London by Christopher Barker, printer to the Queenes most excellent Majestie. 1585. Cum gratia et privilegio Regiae Majestatis.* The Preface, by Parker, ends with the words: "God graunt that all readers may take so much profite thereby, as the good translatours meant unto them. Amen." Opposite is a rough map of Palestine and a list of the places mentioned in the Bible. Prefixed to the Gospel of St. Matthew is "A Table to make playne the difficultie that is founde in Saint Matthewe, and Saint Luke touching the generation of Jesus Christ the sonne of David." After St. Matthew's Gospel is another "Table for the better understanding of the xxvi ch. of St. Matthew, the xiiii of St. Marke, the xxii of St. Luke, and the xix of St. John"; this gives the reckoning of the days according to "the Jews, the Romans and ours," the names of the days, and "certaine dayes of the Moneth of March in the yeere that Jesus Christ suffered." After the Acts is "A Chart Cosmographie, of the peregrination or journey of St. Paul," with the distance in miles and a map.

Some of the renderings are noteworthy: "and drink" in place of "or drink" (I Cor. 11:27); "*God* was shewn" (I Tim. 3:16); "All Scripture *is* given by inspiration of God, and *is* profitable" (II Tim. 3:16); I John 5:7 is printed in the same black letter as the rest of the text without being bracketed; "Priests" is replaced by "Elders" throughout. The epistles, patently based on the Genevan version, are the best feature in the Bishops' Bible. At the end of the volume two pages are devoted to an arrangement of the books of the Bible according as they are "Legall, Historicall, Sapientiall, or Propheticall." [19]

MERELY A REVISION

Examination of a few passages in the versions by Coverdale and Matthew, in the Great Bible, and in Parker's revision will show how slight, indeed how unsatisfactory, was the work of revision done by the bishops responsible for their version. For example, Coverdale, Matthew, and the Great Bible had thus rendered Job 19:25 f.: "For I am sure that my Redeemer liveth, and that I shall rise out of the earth in the latter day; that I shall be clothed again with this skin, and see God in my flesh." But the editions of the Bishops' Bible, 1568 and 1575, have: "For I am sure that my Redeemer liveth, that he shall raise up at the latter day them that lie in the dust; and though after my skin the worms destroy this body, yet shall I see God in my flesh"; however, two other editions, those of 1569 and 1595, in the essential wording reverted to the rendering given by Coverdale, Matthew, and the Great Bible.

Again, Coverdale, Matthew, and the Great Bible correctly rendered II Tim. 3:16: "All Scripture given by inspiration of God is profitable," a rendering which Parker retained in his Preface; yet the rendering actually adopted in the text is: "All Scripture is given by inspiration of God and is profitable." The rendering of the Authorized Version, "took up our carriages" (Acts 21:15) has often provoked merriment; yet the rendering differed little from that of the Great Bible and the Bishops' Bible "took up our burdens"; Geneva, "trussed up our fardeles"; R.V., "took up our baggage," with "made ready" in the margin, as in the Vulgate *praeparati ascendebamus;* Matthew and Coverdale, "made ourselves ready."

Some quaint but effective renderings are retained from former versions: the devil is described as showing Christ all the kingdoms of the world "even in the twynkelynge of an eye" (Luke 4:5); standing in the

[19] As copies of the Bishops' Bible are not readily accessible, it is worth noting that in Fulke's *New Testament translated out of the Vulgar Latin by the Papists at Rhemes, whereunto is added the translation out of the Original Greeke,* 1589, the latter is the New Testament according to the version in the Bishops' Bible.

midst of the doctors, He is said to be "hearing them and posing them" (Luke 2:46); so too the Great Bible; but Coverdale has, "opposing them."

Apart from the Psalter, the Bishops' Bible was merely a superficial revision of the Great Bible, from which, especially in the historical books and the Apocrypha, it differed little. The New Testament is, save for some minor changes, Tyndale's version. Had he not been so prejudiced against the Genevan version, Parker could have improved his edition by adopting more of the renderings given in the latter.[20]

The work of many men, who do not seem to have worked in collaboration, this Bible was necessarily of unequal merit.[21] Some bishops liked the Genevan version; others intensely disliked it. Moreover the revisers sometimes "interpreted" by adding explanatory clauses; e.g., "and from beyond the Jordan" (Matt. 4:25) becomes "and from [the regions that laye] beyond Jordane." Such additions are in marked contrast to the usually literal character of the translation. "James the just," for instance, is now "James the little" (Mark 15:40). At times, too, the phrasing is ponderous: "prepare your pre-promised benefice, that it might be ready as a benefice and not as an extortion" (I Cor. 9:5).

Criticism of the revision has always been severe. Hugh Broughton, a great scholar but perhaps too captious a critic, remarked that "the cockles of the Sea shores and the leaves of the Forest, and the granes of the Popy, may as well be numbered as the grosse errours of this Table, disgracing the ground of our own hope." [22] Mombert, too, summing up the investigations made by Westcott, Eadie, and Moulton, says that the conclusion is "one that does not redound to the praise of those revisors who had in hand the Old Testament and the Apocrypha." [23] "There is little to recommend the original renderings of the Bishops' Bible in the Old Testament. As a general rule they appear to be arbitrary and at variance

[20] When Eadie says (*op. cit.*, II, 93) that only seven out of more than fifty notes on First Corinthians are not taken from the Genevan version, while Mombert quotes Moulton as saying that "a few, perhaps a dozen, of the Genevan annotations are retained," they are probably referring to different editions of the Bishops' Bible.

[21] "It is a work of unequal merit from first to last" (Mombert, *op. cit.*, p. 275).

[22] *A Concent of Scripture*, p. 591; see Strype, *The Life and Acts of John Whitgift*, pp. 433, 587. See below, chap. 20.

[23] *Op. cit.*, p. 277. The Apocrypha were not revised at all, but taken over from the Great Bible, where the translation had been made from the Latin rather than from the Greek.

with the exact sense of the Hebrew text. The revision of the New Testament, however, will repay careful study." [24]

VARIOUS EDITIONS

Many editions of the Bishops' Bible were published. Cotton [25] enumerates eleven in folio, six in quarto, and two in octavo between 1568 and 1606, the date of the last edition of the complete Bible. The New Testament portion was published separately in eleven editions, the last appearing in 1619, though editions of Fulke's Rhemish New Testament with the Bishops' version in parallel columns came out in 1589, 1601, twice in 1617, and once in 1633.[26] In the second edition, 1569, a division into verses was attempted by inserting the letters of the alphabet into the text, though in the Psalms the verses were numbered.[27] This edition had received extensive revision: "hundreds of passages having been altered" and all the cuts having been removed.[28]

The third edition, 1572, while ignoring the changes made in the previous one,[29] was based on a careful revision by Laurence, whom Strype calls "a man in those times of great fame for his knowledge in the Greek." [30] Laurence drew up lists of words wrongly translated, of words or sentences omitted or superfluous, of "sentences changed and error in doctrine," and finally, of "modes and tenses changed, and places not well considered by Theodore Beza and Erasmus, as I thynke." But Laurence

[24] Westcott, *op. cit.*, p. 237. "The version can hardly be regarded as much more than a makeshift" (Pollard, *op. cit.*, p. 32).

[25] *Lists of Editions of the Bible and Parts Thereof in English* (1852), pp. 34–68. See also Dore, *op. cit.*, pp. 239, 275–90; Mombert, *English Versions of the Bible*, pp. 271 f.

[26] The last edition, 1633, claims to give the Rhemish New Testament with the Authorized Version, a misprint for the Bishops' Bible.

[27] In the edition of 1576 these letters were replaced by numbers.

[28] Dore, *op. cit.*, p. 247. Parker conceded, however, that the Prayer Book Psalter "might remayne in the Queres (choirs) as they be much multiplied, but wher of their owne accord they wold use this translacion."

[29] On this fact Dore remarks: "It is remarkable that the great improvements made . . . in 1569 should have been so completely ignored in the issue of 1572; and that errors in the first edition of 1568 should be re-introduced, although they had been corrected in the preceding quarto" (*op. cit.*, p. 253). But Mombert speaks of this edition of 1572 as "a very important one, even at this day, for it is the immediate basis of the Authorized Version" (*op. cit.*, p. 275); but see below, note 32.

[30] Strype, *The Life and Acts of Matthew Parker*, II, 223, Appendix lxxxv: "Notes of Errors in the Translation of the New Testament," by Giles Laurence, Professor of Greek at Oxford, not to be confounded with Thomas Laurence, Headmaster of Shrewsbury; see Aldis Wright, note on p. 237 of his edition of Westcott's *A General View of the History of the English Bible*, 1905; Hoare, *Evolution of the English Bible*, p. 203.

had a scholar's temperament, and unlike Hugh Broughton, who thought that "our Bishops' Bible might well give place to the Alkoran, pestred with lyes," Laurence closes his series of criticisms with a candid avowal: "It is more lyke that I should be deceived than either Erasmus or Beza. I wold gladlie they were defended that I might see myne own error. I take them to be deceyved, because I see reason and authoritie for me, and as yet none for them, but because they saye so, and yet bring no proofe for them." [31]

The edition of 1573 has a certain notoriety from its substitution of "love" for "charity" in chap. 13 of First Corinthians, following the example of Tyndale. The fifth edition, 1574, was the first in which the words "Set foorth by auchthoritee" figured on the title page. The ninth edition is of interest since it was, along with the 1562 edition of the Great Bible and the editions of the Genevan version, 1579 and 1580, incriminated by Gregory Martin. The edition of 1602 served as the basis for the King James's Version of 1611.[32]

Many editions of the New Testament continued to appear. Those of 1613 and 1619—the last—had the bad taste to replace Parker's innocuous notes by the pestilential antipapal notes from Jugge's 1552 edition of Tyndale's New Testament,[33] a few examples of which are here given: on I Tim 5:18, of widows who prove wanton: "S. Paul doth not here speake of the everlasting damnation, but by this word damnation, doeth rather understand the shame that those wanton widows shall have in the world for breaking their promise. If this place be well understood, it is able to overthrow all the monkish vowes"; [34] concerning the Magi, who did not return to Herod (Matt. 2:12), the note says: "Promise

[31] Lewis, *op. cit.*, pp. 229–33; Mombert, *op. cit.*, pp. 277–79. But as Moulton points out, "The renderings on which Laurence comments belong, without exception, to the first edition of the Bishops' Bible; some indeed are not found in any other version [edition?] at all" (*op. cit.*, p. 172).

[32] That the 1602 edition of the Bishops' Bible served as the basis of the King James's Version in 1611 is maintained by Fry in *Notes and Queries,* July 28, 1871; cf. Westcott, *op. cit.*, p. 241 note; Dore, *op. cit.*, p. 272. See also note 29 above.

[33] The title of the 1619 edition, differing from any of the preceding titles, is similar to that of Jugge's 1552 edition: *The New Testament of our Saviour Jesus Christ, faithfully translated out of the Greeke, with the Notes and Expositions of the darke places therein.* Then follows the distich (Matt. 13:46):

"The pearle which Christ commaunded to be bought,
"Is here to be founde, not els to be sought."

[34] Cox wrote to Parker: "The Holy Ghost gave a general rule to deacons, priests and bishops that they *should* be the husband of one wife" (*Epis.* 109, Parker Society, p. 151).

ought not to be kept, where God's honour and the preaching of the trueth is hindered, the wise men, notwithstanding their promise made unto Herode, returned home into their owne countrey, by another way." It is needless to say that the Gospel nowhere suggests that the Magi made any such promise. "The very people," remarks Dore, "who complained of the dictum that 'faith should not be kept with heretics' were ready to insert in the New Testament itself that faith was not to be kept with anyone if 'the preaching of the word' was hindered thereby."[35]

[35] *Op. cit.*, p. 284.

PART THREE

The Rheims-Douay and Authorized Versions

CHAPTER XVII

The Rheims Version of the New Testament, 1582

ORIGIN OF THE VERSION

THE title, "Douay Bible," is generally used to denote the complete Catholic version of the Bible as produced by the professors at the English College established on the Continent; but as a matter of fact, the New Testament was translated at Rheims and published there in 1582,[1] while the Old Testament, though translated before the New and also at Rheims, was published at Douay only in 1609. Most interesting is the story of the making of the Rheims New Testament and the Douay Old Testament, and of the lives and labors of the men who produced them.

Surius gives a vivid picture of the position prevailing in religious matters at the time of the Diet of Worms, 1540, or shortly before the Rheims-Douay Version was taken in hand.

> The heretics want the Bible to be the authority, but only on condition that it shall be for them to interpret it. But was there ever a heresy which would not gladly welcome the Bible as the sole arbiter on such conditions? . . . We have no controversy with the heretics about the Bible, but about the meaning of the Bible. They want to unearth its meaning by aid of their own none too erudite brains; we say that that meaning is to be discovered in the perpetual agreement of the Catholic Church. But this idea they wholly repudiate; for they know that their teachings, their false private opinions, diverge entirely from that public agreement of the entire Christian world. They continue to spread the Bible abroad among the illiterate; but learned men readily perceive that the genuine sense of the Bible can no more make for their views than a lie can lead us to the truth. In fact how can they really be appealing in good faith to the Bible when they have more than once changed not only their profession of faith but several of their dogmas? Can the unchanging truth of the Divine Scriptures have any truck with such inconstancy? [2]

[1] To speak, then, of the "Douay New Testament" is misleading.

[2] Quoted by Baronius, *anno* 1540.

If this state of affairs was to be met, a vernacular Catholic version was a necessity. This was realized by Allen, who, writing to the professor of canon law at Douay in 1578, or four years before the Rheims New Testament made its appearance, pointed out the disabilities under which the clergy labored when preaching, owing to the fact that they had no vernacular version:

> Catholics educated in the academies and schools have hardly any knowledge of the Scriptures except in Latin. When they are preaching to the unlearned and are obliged on the spur of the moment to translate some passage into the vernacular, they often do it inaccurately and with unpleasant hesitation because either there is no vernacular version of the words, or it does not occur to them at the moment. Our adversaries, however, have at their finger tips from some heretical version all those passages of Scripture which seem to make for them, and by a certain deceptive adaptation and alteration of the sacred words produce the effect of appearing to say nothing but what comes from the Bible. This evil might be remedied if we too had some Catholic version of the Bible, for all the English versions are most corrupt. . . . If his Holiness shall judge it expedient, we ourselves will endeavor to have the Bible faithfully, purely, and genuinely translated according to the edition approved by the Church, for we already have men most fitted for the work.[3]

Other factors which made necessary the preparation of a new and orthodox English version were the various Latin versions produced on the Continent by men who sneered at the Latin Vulgate and attached undue importance to the Hebrew and Greek text then current[4] and to the existing English versions by Tyndale and Coverdale, Matthew's Bible, the Great Bible, the Geneva Bible, and the Bishops' Bible. The history of the new Catholic version covers four distinct periods: (a) that of the first five editions of the New Testament, 1582–1738, including the two editions of the Old Testament, 1609–10, 1635; (b) the period of Challoner's revisions, 1749–77; (c) what for lack of a better term we may call the "post-Challoner" period, 1778–1825; (d) 1825 to our own day. At present we are concerned only with the first period and with those who were responsible for the Catholic version: Cardinal Allen, who sponsored it, and Gregory Martin, Richard Bristow, and others, who produced the translation and notes. Of these pioneers some account must be given.

William Allen (1532–94) went to Oxford in 1546. In 1550 he was unanimously elected Fellow of Oriel; six years later he became principal

[3] *Letters and Memorials of Cardinal Allen,* pp. 64 f.

[4] See chapter 9 above.

of St. Mary's Hall and a canon of York. Refusing, however, to "conform," he fled to Louvain in 1561. Threatened with consumption, he returned to England; but his Catholic activities were resented; therefore he returned to Flanders and in 1568 opened the English College at Douay, which in 1578 was removed to Rheims. Allen was called to Rome, where he founded another English College.[5] Created cardinal by Sixtus V, he and Cardinal Colonna became members of the commission for the revision of the Sixtine Vulgate, a work finally completed at Zagorola, where Allen's name still stands in the commemorative inscription.

Allen's sojourn in Flanders had familiarized him with the work of Hentenius and Luke of Bruges in preparing a corrected edition of the Vulgate, and he would thus have had a clear idea of the problems presented by the varying Latin texts and so be in a position to secure a new English version resting on the best edition of the Vulgate then to be had. Allen had also collaborated in the preparation of the Sixtine edition of the Septuagint. Thus he was well equipped to produce an English translation that was reliable in every respect.[6]

Gregory Martin (d. 1582), scholar of St. John's, Oxford, and friend of Campion, won for himself an extraordinary reputation at the University. This was made evident when the Duke of Norfolk visited there with Martin, then tutor to his sons; for the students shouted: "Thou hast, O illustrious Duke, our Hebraist, our Grecian, our poet, our honour and glory." Refusing to "conform," Martin fled to Douay in 1570; there he taught until the removal to Rheims in 1578, where he translated the Bible. The *Douay Diaries* contain only tantalizingly brief entries: "October 12, 1578: We began to read the Life of Calvin in the refectory"; then in the margin:

[5] *An Apologie and True Declaration of the Institution and Endeavours of the Two English Colleges, the one in Rome, the other now resident in Rhemes: against certaine sinister information given up against the same,* by William Cardinal Allen, printed at Mounts in Henault, 1581. See also Dodd, *The Church History of England from 1500 to 1688,* II, 156–81; *idem, The History of the English College at Douay, . . . by a Roman Catholic, Chaplain to an English Regiment,* London, 1713; Gasquet, *A History of the Venerable English College, Rome,* 1920.

[6] Gregory XIII held him in such high esteem that he is reported to have said to his cardinals: *Venite, fratres mei, ostendam vobis Alanum* (Pits, *De illustribus Angliae scriptoribus,* p. 793); cf. Fuller, *The Church History of Britain from the Birth of Jesus Christ untill the year 1648,* IX, 139. For further details see Gillow, *Bibliographical Dictionary of the English Catholics; Dictionary of National Biography;* the *Douay Diaries;* Dodd, *op. cit.,* II, 44–52, 60, 219–45; III, 525; Lingard, *History of England* (5th ed.), pp. 331, 498 f., 508, 706; *Letters and Memorials of Cardinal Allen,* pp. 16, 332 f.

On October 16 or thereabouts Mr. Martin started translating the Bible into English in the hope of thus providing an antidote to the corrupt heretical versions which have been for so long a misery to nearly everybody in our own land. With a view to the speedy production of what will, we trust, prove an exceedingly useful work, he will translate two chapters a day; while, to secure its exactitude, Drs. Allen and Bristowe will read these carefully and, if need be, make any corrections which prudence may demand.

Four years later this entry was made: "This month [March, 1582] the final touches were given to the English version of the New Testament." [7]

The next entry in the Diary is ominous: "On the last day of April [1582] Mr. Gregory Martin went to Paris to recuperate, for he has long been suffering in his lungs." On October 28 "Mr. Gregory Martin passed from this life." Allen had to mourn the loss of both his chief supporters, for Bristow had died in the previous year; on July 17, 1582, he wrote: "The death of Bristowe and Martin's illness have rendered me fit for little." In addition to his work on the Bible, Martin, despite his delicate health, found time to write many controversial works.[8]

Richard Bristow (1538–81), a student and Fellow of Exeter College, Oxford, on becoming a Catholic joined Allen at Douay, where he taught until 1578, when Allen put him in charge of the college then removed to Rheims. Always delicate, Bristow died at Harrow on October 14, 1581. He was one of the revisers of Martin's translation of the Bible and has left manuscript annotations on the New Testament. It is sometimes stated that he was responsible for part of the translation, but Dodd says that "the work may be entirely ascribed to Dr. Martin; the others being only revisers. He translated the whole Bible, though it was not published all at one time. The New Testament was first put out at Rheims and Antwerp, with Dr. Bristow's Notes. The Old Testament was not pub-

[7] *Douay Diaries,* I–II, pp. 145, 186. Dodd says that "the work may be entirely ascribed to Mr. Martin; the others [he includes Dr. Reynolds, a Fellow of New College] being only revisers" (*op. cit.,* II, 121). Yet Gillow declares that Bristowe "wrote many of the Commentaries in the New Testament" translated by Martin (*op. cit.,* I, 304).

[8] *A Discoverie of the Manifold Corruptions of the Holie Scriptures by the Heretikes of our Daies, Specially the English Sectaries,* 1582; *A Treatise of Schisme, shewing that al Catholikes ought in any wise to abstaine altogether from heretical Conventicles,* 1578; *Roma Sancta* (posthumous), 1838; *A Treatise of Christian Peregrination* (posthumous), 1583; *Of the Love of the Soule, with Questions to the Protestants* (posthumous), 1603; *Pro veteri et vera Graecarum literarum pronunciatione* (posthumous), Oxford, 1712; and the following which yet remain in manuscript: *St. Chrysostom, contra Gentiles de vita S. Babilae; De consolatione agonizantium; Tragoediam Cyri, regis Persarum; Of the Excommunication of the Emperor Theodosius.* For further details concerning the controversy aroused by his *Discoverie,* see the following chapter.

lished till several years after, when Dr. Worthington put it to the press with his own notes and historical tables." At the time Dodd wrote, then, it was commonly understood that Bristow, not Martin, was the author of the notes on the New Testament.[9] Bristow's best known controversial work was *Motives inducing to the Catholicke Faith.*[10] Even Fuller acknowledged Bristow's powers as a controversialist: "He wrote very solidly, for proof of which, let his books against Dr. Fulke be perused." [11]

William Reynolds (1544–94), of Winchester and New College, became a Catholic through studying the controversy between Jewel and Harding, 1575. At Rheims he lectured on the epistles of St. Paul.[12] Gillow says he "assisted in the translation of the New Testament," Le Long even suggesting that he was the real author of the version.[13] However that may be, Reynolds certainly defended the Rheims version against Whitaker. He also translated some of Allen's works and wrote *A Treatise of the Holy Sacrifice and Sacrament,* 1593, and *A Refutation of sundry Repre-*

[9] *Op. cit.,* p. 121; cf. Charles Butler, *Memoirs of the English, Irish, and Scottish Catholics,* IV, 414; *Dictionary of National Biography,* "Martin," p. 1265. Bristow's *Life* was written by Worthington.

[10] In 1574 Bristow published *A briefe Treatise of diverse plaine and sure wayes to finde out the truthe in this doubtful and dangerous time of Heresie, conteyning sundry worthy motives unto the Catholike faith, or Considerations to move a man to beleve the Catholikes, and not the Heretikes;* the running title of the work is, "Motives to the Catholike Faith." Two years later an epitome of the *Motives* appeared: *Demaundes to bee proposed of Catholickes to the Heretickes, by Richard Bristow, Priest and Doctor of Divinitie. Taken partely out of his late Englishe booke of Motives to the Catholicke faith, parteley out of his intended Latin book of the same matter,* several times printed without place or date; but according to the *Douay Diaries* (p. 102) it seems to have issued from the press in 1576. Bristow enlarged and translated into Latin his original *Briefe Treatise,* and this work was edited by Worthington in 1608 with the title, *Motiva omnibus Catholicae doctrinae orthodoxis cultoribus pernecessaria.* This work was again translated into English by Worthington under the title, *Motives inducing to the Catholicke Faith,* 1641, a much larger work than the original English *Motives.* Cf. *Dictionary of National Biography,* "Bristow," and Gillow, *op. cit.,* "Bristow."

Bristow also wrote: *A Reply to William Fulke in Defence of M. D. Allen's Scrole of Articles and Booke of Purgatorie,* 1580; *Tabula in Summam Theologicam S. Thomae Aquinatis,* 1579; *Veritates aureae S. R. ecclesiae auctoritatibus veterum patrum* (posthumous), 1616.

[11] *Op. cit.,* IX, v–vii, p. 34.

[12] *Douay Diaries,* April, 1581, p. 178.

[13] *Biblia Sacra, seu Syllabus omnium ferme S. Scripturae editionum ac versionum, cum additamentis et notisque auxit C. F. Bornoerus,* 1709, 1723; re-edited by A. G. Masche, 1778–90, 5 vols., p. 418. Archbishop W. Newcome says that "some ascribe the version of the New Testament chiefly to William Raynold" (*An Historical View of the English Biblical Translations,* p. 89), and he refers to Le Long (*loc. cit.*); but the contemporary statement in the *Douay Diary* must outweigh such suppositions. See "Martin" and "Bristowe" in the *Dictionary of National Biography* and in Gillow, *op. cit.*

hensions, Cavils, and false Sleights, by which M. Whitaker laboureth to deface the late English translation and Catholic Annotations of the New Testament, and the Book of Discovery of heretical corruptions, 1583.

To these four men, then, we owe the Douay Bible. Martin appears to have been responsible for the whole translation, though there are reasons for thinking that the other professors also contributed their share. To Allen fell the onerous task of providing the funds for the undertaking and of correcting his companions' work.

To appreciate rightly the translation these men produced, we must bear in mind the following points: These exiles were the pick of the University which had driven them out; they were most learned men. Further, they were apostles in the truest sense of the term, for their whole lives were devoted to the cause of the Catholic faith. Both Martin and Bristow died at a very early date as the result of their strenuous labours, and we can call them "martyrs." Again, they all lived in an atmosphere of controversy such as even in these days we can hardly understand. The heretics had their translations and, in Allen's own words, "have at their finger-tips every text of Scripture which seems to make for them, and that, too, in some heretical version." . . . Consequently there was a feeling of unrest abroad among Catholics; men began to fear lest perhaps the true Scriptures were really being withheld from them. These considerations compelled the Douay professors to present a translation direct from the original, as literal as possible, and replete with notes to illustrate the controverted points.[14]

THE TITLE AND PREFACE

The first fruits of their labors appeared in 1582, when the New Testament was published; the title page reads as follows:

The New Testament of Jesus Christ, translated faithfully into English, out of the authentical Latin, according to the best corrected copies of the same, diligently conferred with the Greeke and other editions in divers languages. With the Arguments of bookes and chapters, Annotations, and other necessarie Helpes, for the better understanding of the text, and specially for the discoverie of the corruptions of divers late translations, and for cleering the Controversies in Religion, of these daies. In the English College of Rhemes.

Give me understanding, and I wil search thy Law: and wil keepe it with my whole hart. Psalm 118.

S. Augustin, tract. 2 in Epist. Joan: Al things that are readde in holie Scriptures, we must heare with great attention, to our instruction and salvation: but those things specially must be commended to memorie, which make most against Heretikes: whose deceites cease not to circumvent and beguile al the weaker sort, and the more negligent persons.

PRINTED AT RHEMES, by Iohn Fogny, 1582. *Cum privilegio.*

[14] Supplemented from Pope's *Catholic Student's "Aids" to the Study of the Bible,* I, 254 f. [Ed.]

On the reverse is the *Censura* and *Approbatio* by four doctors of Rheims:

Whereas the sound faith and learning of the authors of this version and edition are fully known to us, and whereas others well versed in sacred theology and the English language have testified that in this work nothing appears which is out of harmony with Catholic teaching and piety, that is repugnant to civil power or tranquility, but that on the contrary everything in it tends to promote true faith, the good of the state, and uprightness of life and morals; we therefore, relying on their testimony, consider that the work can with profit be printed and published.

Peter Remigius, senior archdeacon of the famous metropolitan Church of Rheims, Doctor of Canon Law, and vicar general of the archbishopric of Rheims.

Hubert More, dean and preacher of the Church of Rheims and doctor in the theological faculty.

John Le Besgue, canon of Rheims, Doctor in Theology, and chancellor of the Academy of Rheims.

William Balbus, professor of theology, and rector of the College at Rheims.

"We come to the understanding of Scriptures through povertie of the spirit: where a man must shew himself meeke-minded, lest by stubborne contentions, he become incapable and unapt to be taught," St. Augustine, *De Sermone Domini in monte,* i.3.

The Preface [15] has always commanded at least unwilling admiration, its most adverse critics speaking of it as "ingenious": "A document of consummate skill and ingenious special pleading," says one; [16] "an elaborate and ingenious document," says another; [17] and a third, "a very interesting and ingenious defence of their method." [18] But this "ingenious" document has defied every critic; in fact its main positions are now more or less accepted, even though but tacitly.

After pointing out that "the Protestants . . . by their false translations have in steede of Gods Law and Testament, and for Christes written will and word, given them their owne wicked writing and phantasies, . . . corrupting both the letter and sense by false translation, adding, detracting, altering, transposing, pointing, and all other guileful meanes: specially where it serveth for the advantage of their private opinions"; the authors say that these facts have led to the production of this new version, to which have been appended such notes as seemed necessary; for just as the Jews "cannot find Christ in the Scriptures," so neither can the misguided readers of the heretical versions discover there the Church

[15] The Preface is printed in full in Appendix I, pp. 601 ff.

[16] Mombert, *English Versions of the Bible,* p. 295.

[17] Moulton, *The History of the English Bible* (1876), p. 183.

[18] Westcott, *A General View of the History of the English Bible,* p. 243.

and her doctrines.[19] They even declare that because of the indiscriminate translating and interpretation of the Scriptures, the country has "fallen to this miserable state in religion." [20]

The authors then give the ten reasons why they translate from the Latin rather than from the Greek; [21] they also explain why they retain certain Latin terms: "In this our translation, because we wish it to be most sincere, as becometh a Catholike translation, and have endeavour'd so to make it: we are very precise & religious in folowing our copie, the old vulgar approv'd Latin, not onely in sense, which we hope we alwaies do, but sometime in the very wordes also and phrases." [22] In concluding they again declare their purpose: "Thus we have endeavoured by al meanes, to satisfie the indifferent reader, and to helpe his understanding every way, both in the text, and by Annotations: and withal to deale most sincerely before God and man, in translating and expounding the most sacred text of the holy Testament." [23]

After the long Preface follow "The Signification or Meaning of the Numbers and Markes used," a list of the books of the New Testament, "The Summe of the New Testament," "The Summe of the 4 Gospels," "The argument of S. Matthewes Gospel," then the text of the New Testament, pp. 3–745. At the end of the volume is "A Table of the Epistles and Gospels" for Sundays and feast days "after the Romane use," "An Ample and Particular Table directing the reader to al Catholike truthes, deduced out of the holy Scriptures, and impugned by the adversaries," "The Explication of certaine wordes in this translation, not familiar to the vulgar reader, which might not conveniently be uttered otherwise," and finally the *Errata,* introduced by the words, "The faultes correct thus"; these supplementary pieces occupy 27 pages. A summary of the contents precedes each chapter of the Testament; the text is printed in paragraphs with the verse numbers in the margin.[24] Cross references are given on the inside margin, the marginal notes on the outside margin, and the copious Annotations at the close of each chapter. There is a

[19] Preface, see Appendix I, pp. 615, 619.

[20] *Ibid.,* p. 613.

[21] Cf. *ibid.,* pp. 621–24.

[22] *Ibid.,* p. 639.

[23] *Ibid.,* p. 650.

[24] Bishop Milner had not averted to this fact when he condemned the edition of the New Testament published by the Catholic Board in 1815 for this, its presentation of the text in paragraphs, one of the features which he deemed objectionable.

marginal line on the inside border only. The whole makes a handsome quarto volume of 778 pages.

SOME DEFECTS OF THE VERSION

No one could be so foolish as to deny that the antiquated English of the new version has always proved a stumbling block. There was justification for Sir Tobie Matthew's exclamation when he read on the title page, "faithfully translated into English": "It is a lie, for it is not English." [25] This same feature of the version led Dr. Nary to complain with feeling:

> We have no Catholick Translation of the Scriptures in the English Tongue but the Doway Bible, and the Rhemish Testament, which have been done now more an hundred years since, the Language whereof is so old, the Words in many Places so obsolete, the Orthography so bad, and the Translation so very literal, that in a number of Places it is unintelligible, and all over so grating to the Ears of such as are accustomed to speak, in a manner, another language, that most People will not be at the Pains of reading them. Besides they are so bulky that they cannot conveniently be carried about for publick Devotion, and so scarce and so dear, that the Generality of the People neither have, nor can procure them for their private use.[26]

Yet it is remarkable that, apart from the Latinized forms retained, the un-English character of the translation does not seem to have aroused contemporary comment. Thomas Ward, however, was conscious of it when, writing a hundred years later, he said:

> As for the English of the said Rhemish translation, which is old, and therefore must needs differ much from the more refined English spoken at this day, the reader ought to consider, not only the place where it was written, but also the time since which the translation was made, and then he will find less fault with it. For my part, because I have referred my reader to the said translation, I have not altered one syllable of the English, though indeed I might in some places have made the word more agreeable to the language of our times.[27]

In judging of the style adopted by the Rhemists, we have to bear in mind that the immediate concern of these pioneer translators was to show that the various Latin translations then appearing and purporting to represent the originals more faithfully than the Vulgate were really not preferable to the latter. The same criticism applied to the various

[25] Quoted by Gillow, *op. cit.*, IV, 489, from the *Crosby Records.*

[26] Preface to his *New Testament, newly translated out of the Latin Vulgat,* 1718 and 1719.

[27] *Errata of the Protestant Bible,* p. 20.

English translations then current. The Rhemists aimed, then, at presenting the traditional Vulgate text in an English dress which should represent it as accurately as possible. If any proof were wanted that these scholarly men could write as good, nervous English as the framers of King James's Version, it can be found in their Preface, the English of which no one has ever quarreled with.

The number of Latinisms in the Rheims Version is much exaggerated; nor are they wholly indefensible. Defending the retention of "Amen," "Alleluia," "Corbona," "Parasceve," "Pascha," "Azymes," "bread of proposition," and so forth, in their original Hebrew or Greek or Latin forms, the translators reasonably argue that if "proselyte" and "phylacteries" and similar words are allowable in the current English versions, then why not "neophyte," "prepuce," "Paraclete," and so forth. Though most of the above terms have by now passed into general usage, no one would now defend the retention of "commessation," "condigne," "Dominical Day," "donaries," "hostes," "repropitiate," and "sages." Some exceedingly quaint renderings raise a smile: "a young man clothed with sindon on the bare" (Mark 14:51); and "he that sate was like in sight . . . to the sardine" (Apoc. 4:3). Likewise, the slavish adherence to purely Latin constructions like "with desire I have desired" (Luke 22:15) and "the voice of thy thunder in a wheel" (Ps. 76:19), is disconcerting, to say the least.

SOME EXCELLENT QUALITIES OF THE VERSION

But the above renderings are the exceptions, the extravagances. Taking the version as a whole, the insistence on *deficiencies* in style is often exaggerated; those loudest in condemnation seem either to have never read the version or to have come to it with their minds made up. Let any one read aloud the parable of the prodigal son in the version and deny, if he can, that "save for some extreme instances the version is in vigorous and noble English." Nor, again, has the Rheims Version a monopoly of quaint phrases and turns of expression. The Geneva Bible writes "haberous" for "hospitable" (Tit. 1:8), and even Coverdale's version abounds in such odd terms as "an overbody coat" for "ephod" (Judg. 17:5). Who can refrain from smiling when reading in Tyndale's version that "Joseph was a lucky fellow" (Gen. 39:2), or in Coverdale's version that Amnon asks Thamar to "make me a syppynge or two" (II Sam. 13:6)? Are the names of the unclean animals in the Douay Version any more weird than Tyndale's "origen and cameleon" (Deut. 14:5)? The Douay Version of Judg. 5:28, "his mother looked out at a window and howled; and she spoke from the dining room," has often been quoted with derision; but are such renderings as the following any better: "looked out the wyndowe and cryed thorow the lattesse" (Great Bible), "looked out at the wyndowe and cried piteously through the trallace" (Coverdale), "thorow a windowe loked Sisera's mother and howled thorow a lattesse" (Matthew's Bible)?

Some renderings are delightful and their loss one is inclined to regret: "For the morrow day shall be careful for itself" (Matt. 6:34); to the tempter Christ said: "avaunt, Satan" (Matt. 4:10); Herod was "deluded" by the Magi (Matt. 2:16); the centurion's son was "sore tormented" (Matt. 8:6). As Pollard remarks with justice:

> The translation is much simpler than popular accounts of it make out. It is quite true [that the translators kept to their principle of] word for word, and point for point, and it is possible to quote verses, especially from the Epistles, which remain utterly unintelligible until we know the original. . . . But it is easy to find long passages in the Gospels without a difficult word in them, and which a good reader would make all the more dramatic because of the abruptness of some of the constructions and transitions.[28]

Some readers may be tempted to smile when an enthusiastic Catholic writes:

> Martin's Translation is terse, close, vigorous, grand old English of the very best era of English literature, coeval with Shakespeare, Bacon, Ben Jonson, Spenser. . . . It came on the Protestant zealots like a thunder-clap. It was learned—for they could not gainsay the capacity of Gregory Martin—it was, in point of language, equal to the best they could shew, and, what galled them most, it was honest, rigidly, thoroughly honest. . . . It stands, and will ever stand, as the first really honest English translation that issued from the press. . . . Bible of our fathers, wrought in the day of Martyrs, read and prized by heroic confessors: it should be a pride in every one of our Catholic institutions, and in the family libraries of Catholic gentlemen, to shew a copy of this venerable and holy book.[29]

Yet Professor J. S. Phillimore endorses those enthusiastic words:

> The Authorized Version . . . is more archaic than the Rhemish, more unfamiliar in diction, more often misleading, even where there is no intention to mislead. . . . On its merits as a piece of English, to be read by those whose taste

[28] *Records of the English Bible,* p. 36.

[29] "English Translations of the Bible," in *The Catholic World,* XII (1870), 164, 157.

and training fit them to add the literary to the spiritual enjoyment, I plead for the Rhemish; and I wish that far from depriving it of recognition, we may see it much more widely known and studied.

There is so little ambition for eloquence or fine language, such a severe resolve to eschew those processes of heightening, . . . which translators of profane originals have always tacitly and avowedly employed, that such occasional unsought for happinesses [as "Marie therefore took a pound of ointment of right spikenard, precious, and anointed the feet of Jesus"] deserve to be given prominence.[30]

THE ACCURACY OF THE VERSION

The title page of the Rheims Testament affirms that the text is "out of the authentical Latin, according to the best corrected copies of the same,[31] diligently conferred with the Greeke and other editions in divers languages." [32] That this was no idle boast and that the attention of the translators to the Greek text was in no sense perfunctory appears in many instances, but most notably in their attention to the presence or absence of the Greek definite article, where, of course, the Latin could give them no enlightenment. It is noteworthy that in all the following instances the Rhemists alone inserted the article, and their renderings have been en-

[30] "Scripture Versions and Variants," in the *Dublin Review,* CLXX (1922), 45, 41. Bacon speaks of "the discretion and tenderness of the Rhemish translation which ever distinguished the Christian grace 'Charity' (ἀγάπη) from 'love' (ἔρως)" (*Concerning the Liturgy;* given in Westcott, *op. cit.,* p. 106, where this reference is attributed to Mr. Plumtre). Eadie speaks of its "stately theological vocabulary" (*op. cit.,* II, 226).

[31] Mombert says (*op. cit.,* p. 305): "It is impossible to tell what edition [of the Vulgate] they used, but it must have been one of the very worst, for quite a number of copies read, 'Beati qui lavant stolas suas in sanguine agni' (Apoc. 22:14)." This is an unfortunate statement, for the Rhemists have simply, "wash their stoles"; the addition *in sanguine agni* is in only the *Codex Bezae* and the Sixtine and Clementine editions. The Greek MSS. are divided, some reading "who keep his commandments," others, "who wash their stoles," which latter reading was adopted by R.V. Challoner, following the Clementine, has "wash their stoles in the blood of the lamb"; so too Wycliffe.

[32] Though the Rhemists translated quite independently from the Latin, they were fully alive to what Westcott calls "the niceties of the Greek"; they made full use, too, of the existing English versions, perhaps especially of the Genevan version. According to Isaacs, Coverdale's *Diglott New Testament,* 1538, was "a deliberate attempt to bring his English version closer to the Vulgate text," and he suggests that from this edition the Rhemists adopted such renderings as "the Son of man hath not where to lay [Luke 9:58, "repose"] his head" (Matt. 8:20), and "I see men as it were trees, walking" (Mark 8:24). According to the same authority, from the Genevan version the Rhemists derived "this wicked generation" (Matt. 12:45); "whited tombs" (Matt. 23:27); "salted with salt" (Mark 9:49); "the things that are Caesars" (Mark 12:17); "sold in the shambles" (I Cor. 10:25). All these renderings were taken over by A.V. except Mark 8:24, where "it were" was omitted and R.V. now reads, "for I behold them as trees, walking." Isaacs is here referring to the second Genevan version, 1560, for that of 1557 differs very much in all the above instances. (In *The Bible in Its Ancient and English Versions,* p. 193.)

dorsed by the Revised Version: "the pinnacle" (Matt. 4:5); "the meat . . . the raiment" (Matt. 6:25); "the outer darkness" (Matt. 25:30); "the mount" (Matt. 28:16); "the light (lamp)" (John 5:35); "the robes" (Apoc. 7:13).

In the following instances the versions vary in their treatment of the article. Rheims has "the five talents, . . . the two, . . . the one" (Matt. 25:16–25); Tyndale, Cranmer, and A.V. are not so consistent; R.V. follows Rheims. No other version has "be merciful to me the sinner" (Luke 18:13), though R.V. suggests it in the margin. But in John 4:27, "They marvelled that he was speaking with the woman. . . . Why talkest thou with her?" only the Rhemists rightly omitted the definite article and wrote "a woman"; R.V. follows the Rhemists. At times, of course, the Rhemists failed in this respect. In John 1:20, Wycliffe, Tyndale, Cranmer, and the Rhemists have "I am not Christ," omitting the definite article; but A.V. and R.V., "I am not the Christ," as in the Greek. In John 1:23, where there is no definite article, Wycliffe and Taverner stand alone in writing simply "a voice." Nicodemus was no chance teacher in Israel; Christ asked him, "Art thou the teacher . . . ?" (John 3:10), not "a teacher," as the Rhemists have. St. Paul did not write "a letter" to the Corinthians (I Cor. 5:9), but "the letter"; R.V. has here "my epistle." Likewise it was a very definite messenger whom the Apostle sent to Corinth, not "a brother" (II Cor. 12:18), as the Rhemists again have. John 1:21 should read, "Art thou the prophet?" but Wycliffe and Tyndale have "a prophet," Cranmer, Geneva, and A.V. have "that prophet," and Rheims and R.V., "the prophet."

Even Westcott commends the Rhemists for their general accuracy in treating the definite article:

> When the Latin was capable of guiding them, they seem to have followed out their principles honestly: but wherever it was inadequate or ambiguous they had the niceties of the Greek at their command. Their treatment of the article offers a good illustration of the care and skill with which they performed this part of their task. The Greek article cannot, as a general rule, be expressed in Latin. Here then the translators were free to follow the Greek text, and the result is that this critical point of scholarship is dealt with more satisfactorily by them than by any earlier translators. And it must be said also that in this respect the revisers of King James were less accurate than the Rhemists, though they had their work before them.[33]

[33] *Op. cit.*, p. 254; cf. Carleton, *The Part of Rheims in the Making of the English Bible*, p. 19; Moulton, *op. cit.*, p. 188; Pollard, *op. cit.*, p. 36. "In addition to the Vulgate," says Isaacs, "the Greek text was closely consulted and produced improved renderings of

Scrivener, too, acknowledges that the Rheims Version "is highly commendable for its scrupulous accuracy and fidelity. In justice it must be observed that no case of wilful perversion of Scripture has ever been brought home to the Rhemish translators." [34] So, too, Dore: "In some places the Douai Bible more accurately hands down the very words of the inspired writers than any English translation then existing. This is owing to the Latin having been taken from earlier MSS. than were accessible to later translators." [35]

The Vulgate text used by the Rhemists, with the Greek text underlying it, has, in the light of modern textual criticism, often proved correct. In Acts 16:7 the Rhemists stood alone in reading, "the Spirit of Jesus suffered them not," the words "of Jesus" being omitted in all other versions, but now inserted in R.V.; the same is the case with the long insertion, "bless them that curse you, do good to them that hate you and which despitefully use you" (Matt. 5:44), omitted by Wycliffe and the Rhemists and now by R.V. The Rhemists stood alone, too, in reading "sanctify the Lord Christ" (I Pet. 3:15), the others having "the Lord God," a reading now rejected by R.V. Again, Wycliffe and the Rhemists rendered Ephes. 4:24, "holiness of truth," to be followed by R.V., whereas the other versions have "true holiness"; likewise in Rom. 8:21, Wycliffe, Rheims, and R.V. have "the liberty of the glory of the sons of God," in place of "the glorious liberty" in Tyndale and his followers: Cranmer, Geneva, and A.V. In Matt. 25:8 the Rhemists correctly render the imperfect tense, "our lamps are going out" (so too R.V.); but they have failed to do so in Luke 5:6, where R.V. alone is correct, "their nets were breaking."

Not without justice, then, G. C. Macaulay describes the Rheims Version as

> a most accurate and scholarly version . . . by thoroughly competent Greek scholars, who carefully compared the Latin with the Greek. . . . In the representation of a simple Greek word occurring in various places by the same English word, in careful discrimination of the senses of the definite article, and in regard of the

---

the article, not without effect on the Authorized and Revised Versions" (in *The Bible in Its Ancient English Versions,* p. 193). Much the same testimony is borne by Mill, *Prolegomena,* p. 142, and by Walton, *Prolegomena* to his *Biblia sacra Polyglotta,* chap. 10.

[34] *A Supplement to the Authorised English Version of the New Testament.*

[35] *Op. cit.,* pp. 316 f. Hugo Grotius shrewdly remarks that "no version is freer from prejudice than the Vulgate owing to its antiquity and the fact that it antedates the Western schisms."

original form, expression, and order of words, this version is far superior to any previously existing. As to the English style of it, a very false impression is created by the usual descriptions. It does no doubt contain a certain number of unfamiliar words which it was thought could not be rendered into common English without losing their theological or ecclesiastical associations; but in the Gospels and the simpler portions of the Epistles we may read for a long time without finding anything unusual in the diction; and such words as "evangelise" and "Paraclete" need not seriously offend us. By far the most shocking instance is "supersubstantial bread" in the Lord's Prayer; but the translators were dealing with a difficulty which had been rather evaded than solved by their predecessors. . . . It is needless here to do more than mention the considerable debt owed by our Authorized Version to the Rhemist translation.[36]

This fidelity to the original was not confined to such details as the due rendering of the article; again quoting Westcott:

> Scrupulous or even servile adherence to the text of the Vulgate was not always without advantage. They frequently reproduced with force the original order of the Greek which is preserved in the Latin; and even while many unpleasant roughnesses occur, there can be little doubt that their version gained on the whole by the faithfulness with which they endeavoured to keep the original form of the sacred writings. . . . The same spirit of fidelity to the letter of their text often led them to keep the phrase of the original where other translators had unnecessarily abandoned it.

THE DEBT OF KING JAMES'S VERSION TO THAT OF RHEIMS

Complaints used to be made, as we have seen, against the Latin forms the Rhemists retained; but time has had its revenge. For, as Westcott remarks, the version "is of considerable importance in the internal history of the authorised text, for it furnished a large proportion of the Latin words which King James' revisers adopted; and it is to this rather than to Coverdale's translations that we owe the final and most powerful action of the Vulgate upon our present version"; and though, as Westcott adds, "the style, so far as it has a style, is unnatural and the phrasing (as a rule) most unrhythmical, yet the language is enriched by the bold reduction of innumerable Latin words to English service. . . . There are also rarer cases in which the Rhemists furnish a true English phrase which has been adopted since." He instances "felow-servant," "kingdom against kingdom," "faile," "darkened," "fore-knew."[37]

[36] "The English Bible," in the *Quarterly Review,* October, 1911.

[37] *Op. cit.,* pp. 245, 249, 255; Matt. 18:29; 24:7; Luke 16:9; Rom. 1:21; 11:2.

A single Epistle (that to the Romans) furnishes the following list of Latin words which King James' translators have taken from the Rhemish Testament: "separated," "consent," "impenitent," "approvest," "propitiation," "remission," "grace," "glory (in tribulations)," "commendeth," "concupiscence," "revealed," "expectation," "conformable," "confession is made (to salvation)," "emulation," "concluded," "conformed," "instant," "contribution." [38]

Elsewhere they stand alone in bold or idiomatic turns of expression: "throttled," "workeman," "stagger not," "overgoe." [39]

Pollard makes the very probable suggestion that the Rheims New Testament influenced the framers of the Authorized Version through the medium of Fulke's republication of the Rhemish text, which had passed through two editions by 1601 and which "was regarded as a standard work on the Protestant side, and probably every reviser of the New Testament for the edition of 1611 possessed it." [40] From the Rhemists, King James's revisers took over such expressions as "this wicked generation" (Matt. 12:45); "salted with salt" (Mark 9:49); "the things that are Caesar's" (Mark 12:17); "in the shambles" (I Cor. 10:25), all of which, however, had already appeared in the Geneva Bible.

The Preface to the version of 1611 makes no reference to the Douay Version of the Old Testament, which in fact appeared only in 1609–10, when King James's Version was practically completed.[41] Their only allusion to the Rheims Testament, of which two editions had already appeared, in 1582 and 1600, is to the Rhemish Preface:

Now the Church of Rome would seem at the length to bear a motherly affection towards her children, and allow them the Scriptures in the mother tongue: but indeed it is a gift not deserving to be called a gift, an unprofitable gift; they must get a licence before they may use them, and to get that, they must approve themselves to their Confessor, that is, to such as are, if not frozen in the dregs, yet

[38] *Ibid.*, p. 253; Rom. 1:1, 32; 2:5, 18; 3:25; 4:4; 5:3, 8; 7:8; 8:18, 19, 29; 10:10; 11:14, 32; 12:2, 12; 15:26.

[39] *Ibid.*, p. 255; Matt. 18:28; 20:1; 21:21; 23:33; 25:7; I Thess. 4:6.

[40] *Records of the English Bible*, p. 37.

[41] What acquaintance King James's revisers had with the Douay Version of the Old Testament is not clear. They say in "The Translators to the Reader": "We affirm and avow that the very meanest translation of the Bible in English by men of our profession [presumably they mean members of the Reformed churches], for we have seen none of theirs of the whole Bible as yet [referring to the Catholic version]." Macaulay (*op. cit.*) indeed tries to show that they used it and that the A.V. shows evident signs of the fact; but though three of the passages he refers to in support of his theory hardly differ in the two versions (Exod. 15:1 f.; II Sam. 1:27; III Kings 8:27), the same can hardly be said of the remaining four (Job 3:17; 4:13; 38:7; Isa. 53:3). See C. H. Collette, *The Authorized Version of the Bible as Compared with the Douay and Rhemish Versions*, 1891; J. S. Phillimore, *op. cit.*

sowr'd with the leaven of superstition. . . . So much are they (the Roman authorities) afraid of the light of the Scripture that they will not trust the people with it, no not as it is set forth by their own sworn men, no, not with the licence of their own Bishops and Inquisitors. Yea, so unwilling they are to communicate the Scriptures to the peoples understanding in any sort, that they are not ashamed to confesse, that wee forced them to translate it into English against their wills. This seemeth to argue a bad cause, or a bad conscience, or both.

Yet these revisers in King James's day owed an immense debt to the Rheims Testament, which "has left its mark on every page of their work."[42] "The revisers," says Pollard (p. 60), "were concerned also, although pride prevented any reference to the fact, to meet the objections which had been urged in the preface and notes to the Rheims New Testament, and it is to their credit that they not only did this, but took from that version much that was good, though with no other acknowledgement than a gibe." What they did to "meet the objections" of the Rhemists would be hard to discover. The Preface to the Revised Version, 1881, makes atonement, though somewhat tardily, for the remissness—or rather, cowardice—of the former revisers: "Their work shows evident traces of the influence of a Version not specified in the rules, the Rhemish, made from the Latin Vulgate, but by scholars conversant with the Greek Original."

THE VALUE OF THE ANNOTATIONS

It is noteworthy that most of the attacks leveled against the Rheims Testament were directed, not against the new Catholic translation, but against the Preface and Annotations in which the framers of the version used very plain and outspoken language. But their strong expressions of feeling become readily understandable when we reflect that the Church they represented and for whose teachings they fought had been in unquestioned possession for fifteen hundred years, whereas now opposing views of the most heterodox and varied type were being openly taught by men who insisted that such ideas were the true teaching of the Bible, the text of which they mutilated in support of such views. Men of weaker mold were, in consequence, falling away from "the faith once (and for all) delivered to the Saints"; great numbers, including the Rhemish translators themselves, were in exile for their faith; even greater numbers were being brutally put to death for their adherence to

[42] Moulton, *op. cit.* (1887), p. 207; cf. J. G. Carleton, *op. cit.*

that same faith. Is it to be wondered at that the annotators defended their Catholic faith openly and in the plain, unvarnished language of the day?

Many of the notes are illustrative of those times of persecution and so-called "reformation"; e.g., those on heretics who preach liberty yet refuse it to those who do not agree with them (II Pet. 2:2); on jailers who treat their Catholic prisoners kindly (Acts 16:32); on the evil fruits of heretical teachings (Matt. 7:16); on attending heretical sermons (Mark 3:12); on Catholics who unhappily conform to the state religion: "All men, but especially nations, must take heed that whiles to save their temporal state, they forsake God, they lose not both" (marginal note on John 11:49). "This is the case of many principal men in such countries where heresie hath the upper hand who know and believe the Catholic faith, but making choise rather to keep man's favour than God's, they dare not confess the same. Such may pray that God and the world agree together, for else it is seen whose part they will take" (marginal note on John 12:42).[43]

What might be called catechetical notes are as valuable today as the day they were penned; e.g., on the value of prayers which are not fully understood (Matt. 21:16); on the conflicting jurisdictions of Church and State (Matt. 22:21; Mark 10:4); on the difficulty involved in the fact of unworthy popes (Matt. 23:2); on God's permitting evil (Mark 10:4); on the prayers used at the ordination of priests (Luke 6:12); on limbo (Luke 16:2); on purgatory (Luke 16:26); on the significance of the rood (John 19:26); on confession (John 20:20).[44]

Many notes were necessarily highly controversial, and it was these which provoked the Reformers: on heretics (Matt. 7:16); on the way the Mass was abolished (Matt. 24:15); on the Holy Eucharist (Matt. 26:26; John, chap. 6; I Cor. 11:20); on the changeable character of Protestantism (II Cor. 1:18); on the heretical corruption of Scripture (II Cor. 2:17; 4:3, 8; II Pet. 3:16; Mark 12:24; Matt. 6:1; John 20:19); on the Reformers' inconsistency in their rendering of Scripture (John 8:34; 6:32; Apoc. 19:4); on the growing diversity of sects (Acts 11:26); on St. Peter's pres-

[43] See also the notes on "New Gospellers" (Gal. 1:8); on the temporal prosperity of non-Catholic countries (Matt. 5:48; John 11:29); on the reward for those who harbour recusants (Matt. 10:42); on the absurdity of saying, "I go straight to Christ" (Matt. 15:36); on the meaning and value of processions (Matt. 21:8).

[44] On Matt. 2:2 the note reads: "Christ's nativity depended not upon this star, as the Priscillianists falsely surmised: but the star upon his nativity, for the service whereof it was created"; cf. St. Gregory, *Homilies on the Gospels,* X.

ence in Rome (Rom., chap. 16; Gal. 2:7; Luke 5:1); on the enormity of schism (Luke 9:5; 13:26; 17:33; John 4:20); on the principle, "Outside the Church there is no salvation" (Mark 4:12; Luke 15:4); on clerical celibacy (Matt. 8:15; 19:5; I Tim. 1:3–20; 3:2; 5:9; Tit. 1:6; 3:10 f.); on the use of Latin in Church services (I Cor., chap. 14); on holy orders (Acts 13:3); on divorce (Matt., chap. 19); on the vows of religious (*ibid.*).

The last annotation, based on the words "Come, Lord Jesus" (Apoc. 22:20), is couched in the form of a prayer:

> And now, O Lord Jesus Christ, most just and merciful, we thy poore creatures that are so afflicted for confession and defense of the holy Catholike and Apostolike truth, conteined in this thy sacred booke, and in the infallible doctrine of thy deerest spouse our mother the Church, wee crie also unto thy Majestie with tenderness of our hartes unspeakable: COME LORD JESUS QUICKLY, and judge betwixt us and our Adversaries, and in the meane time give patience, comfort, and constancie to all that suffer for thy name, and trust in thee. O Lord God, our onely helper and protector, tarie not long. Amen.

PREJUDICED CONDEMNATIONS

In the many histories of the English Bible, but little space is, as a rule, devoted to the Catholic version. It seems to be referred to rather as a curiosity and for the sake of completeness than as a work calling for serious consideration. Indeed, if not wholly ignored, it is treated with contempt.[45] It would, for instance, be hard to find a more prejudiced and unfair account of the version than the following:

> The translators sent forth the Scriptures as explained by tradition, treating them as dubious oracles, whose utterances were not to be properly understood without the aid of an interpreting priesthood. . . . It would be unfair to charge the Rhemish translators with a dishonest perversion of Scripture: it is sufficient condemnation, and one which they deserve—indeed, one which, in their preface, they seem almost to court—to affirm, that they produced a version in many parts quite unintelligible. To leave words untranslated, and then give the explanation of them in the annotations, was to veil the Scriptures, that the Church might come forward and disclose her mysteries,—to silence the voice of inspiration that she might speak

[45] Anderson makes no mention of it, nor of such historic characters as Allen, Martin, and Bristow, in his *Annals of the English Bible,* new edition, 1862; it is the same with Archbishop Newcome, *An Historical View of the English Biblical Translations,* 1792. As late as 1939 Kenyon wrote: "The Romanist Bible had no general success" (*Our Bible and the Ancient Manuscripts,* p. 229). Yet the first two editions must have been very large, since copies are by no means scarce even now.

herself. In short the motto of the Rhemists was not, "Search the Scriptures," but "Hear the Church," and they had honesty enough to avow it.[46]

There can be no excuse for maintaining, as many have done, that the stilted and difficult English style was deliberately adopted with a view to making a version which was—so it is maintained—produced only unwillingly and under a quasi compulsion, so unintelligible that none would care to read it. Says Horne:

> The Romanists in 1582, finding it impossible to withhold the Scriptures any longer from the common people, printed an English Testament at Rheims: which was translated not from the original Greek, but from the Latin Vulgate. The editors, whose names are not known, retained the words Azymes, tunike, holocaust, and a multitude of other Greek words untranslated, under the pretext of wanting proper and adequate English terms by which to render them: and thus contrived to render it unintelligible to common readers.[47]

It is indeed surprising to find a critic of Scrivener's established reputation daring to say: "The Rhemish translators produced a version which is neither English nor Latin, but composed in an obscure and perplexing dialect of their own; such as always must have been (as perhaps it was designed to be), in a great measure unintelligible to all who were unable to read the Vulgate for themselves. On no other supposition can I account for their perpetual employment of barbarous words, which no one ever did or would wish to meet with elsewhere." [48] Fuller's comment is often quoted with gusto: "A translation which needeth to be translated, neither good Greek, Latin, nor English, as everywhere bespeckled with hard words." [49] And a writer in the *Quarterly Review* for January, 1872, boldly declares:

> The Roman Catholic translation of the Scriptures, although it had little influence upon the formation of our English Bible, demands a brief notice in a historical and critical point of view. It was only under strong pressure from without that the version was undertaken and issued. Some leading Roman Catholic divines had charged the various Protestant versions with grievous error and gross misrepresentations, . . . they felt themselves, therefore, bound to establish their charges by producing a translation of their own under the influence and guidance of the

[46] From the Preface to *The Vulgate New Testament, with the Douay Version of 1582 in parallel columns,* London: Samuel Bagster and Sons, 1872.

[47] *Introduction to the Critical Study and Knowledge of the Bible.* Another very prejudiced account of the version is given by Edgar, *The Bibles of England,* pp. 234 ff.

[48] *Supplement to the Authorised Version,* p. 98.

[49] *Op. cit.* (1837), IX, xv–xx, pp. 68 f. Bingham actually states that the Roman Church holds "ignorance to be the mother of devotion" (*Antiquities of the Christian Church,* II, 600).

Church. . . . It is enough to say that it contains all the corruption, errors and interpolations of the Vulgate. . . . It is only too evident that the version was made rather to cloak than to reveal the meaning of Scripture.

Of late, however, scholars have learned to appreciate some of the merits of the version, have even begun to grasp the fact that the Church knew well what she was doing when feeling obliged at times to discountenance, though never entirely to prohibit, vernacular versions. Notable work in this respect has been done by Bishop Westcott and by Carleton.[50]

SUBSEQUENT EDITIONS

The second edition of the Rheims New Testament appeared in 1600, a more compact octavo with the same title page as before, except for minor changes.[51] The Approbation by Remigius and others was undated in the edition of 1582; in the second edition it is repeated and dated 1599 and called "The Censure and Approbation of the Former edition." The "Table of Heretical Corruptions" mentioned on the title page is reproduced as "A Table of Certaine Places of the New Testament corruptly translated in favour of Heresies of these dayes in the English Editions, especially of the yeares 1562.77.79. & 80. by order of the Bookes, Chapters & Verses of the same. Wherein we do not charge our Adversaries for disagreeing from the authentical Latin text (whereof much is saide in the Preface) but for corrupting the Greeke itselfe, which they

[50] Westcott, *A General View of the History of the English Bible,* 3rd ed. by W. A. Wright, 1905; Carleton, *The Part of Rheims in the Making of the English Bible,* 1902.

[51] *The New Testament of Jesus Christ faithfully translated into English, out of the authentical Latin* (*according to the best corrected copies of the same*), *diligently conferred with the Greeke, & other Editions in divers languages: With Arguments of bookes & chapters: Annotations & other helpes, for the better understanding of the text, & specially for the discoverie of Corruptions in divers late translations; & for cleering Controversies in Religion of these daies:* (*By the English College then Resident in Rhemes. Set forth for the second time, by the same College now returned to Doway. With addition of one new Table of Heretical Corruptions, the other Tables and Annotations somewhat augmented*).

Search the Scriptures, Joan. 5.

Give me understanding, & I wil search thy Law: & I wil kepe it with my whole hart, Psalm 118. v. 34.

S. Augustin *Tract. 2 in Epist. Joan.* Al things that are readde in holie Scriptures, we must heare with great attention, to our instruction & salvation: but those things specially must be commended to memorie, which make most against Heretikes: Whose deceites cease not to circumvent or beguile al the weaker sort, & the more negligent persons.

Printed at Antwerp by Daniel Vervliet. 1600. With Privilege.

pretend to translate." It summarises the "Corruptions" discussed in the Preface and in Martin's *Discoverie* and closes with the statement that "The blessed Confessour, Bishop Tonstall, noted no lesse than two thousand corruptions in Tindals translation, in the New Testament only. Wherby, as by these few here cited for examples, the indifferent reader may see how untruly the English Bibles are commended to the people for the pure Word of God." [52] This edition has a curious inside margin with the cross references; there is no outside marginal line. The clause "in the Lord" (Acts 7:60) is still omitted as in 1582.

The third edition of the New Testament, 1621, marked a great change, the cumbersome 4to edition being replaced by one in 16mo with consequently extremely small print. The title, slightly abbreviated from the 1582 edition, runs: *The New Testament of Jesus Christ, translated faithfully into English, out of the authentical Latin, diligently conferred with the Greeke, and other Editions in divers languages. With Annotations, and Other Helpes for the better understanding of the text, specially for the discoverie of Corruptions in divers late translations, and for cleering Controversies in Religion of these dayes. In the English College of Rhemes: Printed at Antwerp, by James Seldenslach. 1621.* The previous Approbations are repeated, with a new one for the present edition.[53] The original Preface is repeated and is followed by a list of twenty-one *Errata* in the text, while at the end of the volume is a list of thirty *Errata* in the Annotations, which have been removed from the end of the chapters to the end of the volume. The "Table of Controversies" is reduced to two pages; the chapter headings disappear, and the text is no longer set out in paragraphs but in verses. In the Table of Epistles and Gospels "after the Romane use" the chapters alone, not the verses, are given, though a note says: "At what verse the Epistles and Gospels begin is set downe in the marginal notes"; in the edition of 1600 the only reference is to the pages of the volume. There follows an "Ample and Particular Table directing the reader to the Catholike truthes deduced out of the

[52] As Dr. Reynolds died only in 1607, he or perhaps Dr. Worthington may have drawn up this "Table." Cf. Martin, *A Discoverie of the Manifold Corruptions of the Holie Scriptures by the Heretikes of our Daies,* no. 29; Fulke, *A Defense of the Sincere and True Translations of the Holie Scriptures into the English Tong* (1843), p. 61.

[53] "Infrascriptus attenta approbatione Eximiorum Dominorum suprascriptorum, et confisus de sinceritate versionis et editionis praesentis, quantum in me est assentior ut ex fide recudatur, et Catholicorum manibus versetur. Act. Antverp. die 10 Aprilis, 1620. Laur.Beyerlink Archipresbyter Eccl. Cathedr. Antverp. Librorumque Censor."

holy Scriptures, and impugned by the Adversaries, especially of our time"; finally, a half page of "The faultes escaped in printing, (which) we trust the gentle reader wil of his courtesie easily amend and pardon." Yet a few slips have passed unnoticed; on p. 195 the heading should be Chap. XV, not XVI; on p. 155 it should be "of the Apostles," not "of S. John." The words "in the Lord" (Acts 7:60) are still omitted.

A fourth edition of the New Testament appeared in 1630. For though the edition of 1633 is entitled "the fourth," and that of 1738 "the fifth," yet Seldenslach reproduced in 1630 the 16mo edition he had published in 1621. But there are some new features, for while the title is the same as in 1621, the Approbations are now omitted and the pagination is a mystery: the text in 1621 occupied 285 pages, but now in 1630, 485 pages, while in both editions the Annotations cover 349 pages. In both editions appears the same inconsistency in the use of the prefix "Saint": "S. Matthew" stands in the title and page headings of his Gospel, whereas the other three Gospels have in their title simply Mark, Luke, and John, although the page headings have S. Mark, S. Luke, and S. John; the titles and page headings of Romans and Second Corinthians have simply "The Epistle of Paul to . . . ," but elsewhere we find "The Epistle of S. Paul to. . . ." This edition has no table of the Epistles and Gospels for the Sundays and feast days.[54]

The fifth edition of the New Testament, 1633, reverted to the quarto form. To the original title is added: *Set forth with Tables of the Epistles & Gospels through the yeare, Controversies, & Heretical Corruptions. The Fourth Edition, enriched with pictures. John Cousturier, 1633,* Rouen (?). The pictures represent the four Evangelists,—St. John engaged in writing the Apocalypse—St. Paul, and the descent of the Holy Ghost. The marginal notes vary somewhat from those in the first edition, following in this respect that of 1600. The original Preface and the patristic statements on the unique position of the Scriptures are repeated. At the end of the volume come "An Explication of certaine wordes . . . ," and a "Table of certaine Places of the New Testament corruptly translated in favour of the Heresies of these dayes in the Eng-

[54] The only copy of this edition (1630) I have ever seen is in the library of the Benedictine Abbey at Fort Augustus, Scotland; there is none in the British Museum. It is not given in Cotton, *Rhemes and Doway,* but he mentions it in his *Lists of Editions of the Bible and Parts Thereof in English, from the Year MDV to MDCCCL,* p. 66, referring to Lewis, *A Complete History of the Several Translations of the Bible* (1818), p. 299.

lish editions, especially of the yeares 1562, 77, 79 & 80, by order of the Bookes, Chapters, and Verses of the same." The latter occupies fourteen columns and is introduced by a *caveat:* "Wherein we do not charge our Adversaries from disagreeing from the authentical Latin text (wherof much is said in the Preface) but for corrupting the Greeke itselfe which they pretende to translate." At the end of this Table: "The Blessed Confessour, Bishop Tonstal noted no less than two thousand corruptions in Tindal's translation, in the New Testament only. Whereby, as by those few here cited for examples, the indifferent reader may see how untruly the English Bibles are commended to the people, for the pure word of God." The order of the above "Explication" and Table is inverted from the edition of 1600, and both are placed immediately after the Preface. The text is in paragraphs, with verse numbers in the margin. The only Approbation is that to the first edition. Misprints are few; the Gospel for the twenty-first Sunday is given as from Matt., chap. 8, instead of chap. 18; the words "in the Lord" (Acts 7:60) are still missing. This edition seems to be less often met with than the first three.

CHAPTER XVIII

The Storm of Controversy

MARTIN'S *DISCOVERIE*

ALMOST immediately after the publication of the Rheims New Testament, appeared *A Discoverie of the Manifold Corruptions of the Holie Scriptures by the Heretikes of our daies, specially the English Sectaries, and of their foule dealing herein, by partial and false translations, to the advantage of their heresies, in their English Bibles used and authorised since the time of the Schisme, by Gregorie Martin, one of the Readers of Divinitie in the English College of Rhemes. "We are not as many, adulterating the Word of God, but of sinceritie and as of God, before God, in Christ we speak," 2.Cor.ii.17.* Printed at Rhemes by John Fogny, 1582.[1]

Martin intended his *Discoverie* to be "as it were a handmaid to his New Testament." He must have felt that the inevitable bulk and expense of the latter would prohibit the circulation he wished to secure for it. "In this Discoverie," he wrote, "I will deal principally with the English Translations, which are in every mans handes within our countrie, the corruptions whereof, as they are partly touched here and there in the Annotations upon the late new English Testament Catholikely translated and printed at Rhemes."

The tiny volume—344 pages, large 12mo, the whole measuring six inches by four inches—roused the English Reformers to fury. For among other things, Martin naturally emphasized the divergences between the various translators who differed from one another. "Every man expoundeth according to his error and heresy. . . . Are not their expositions of one and the same Scripture as diverse and contrary as their

[1] "Sub fine hujus mensis (Junii), typis non ita multo ante mandatus, divulgari coeptus est liber quidam anglice conscriptus de corruptelis et erroribus translationum et editionum sacrorum bibliorum ab haereticis modernis, praecipue vero Anglis nostris, emissarum" (*Douay Diaries*).

opinions differ from one another?"[2] He quotes Zwingli as saying of Luther's version: "Thou corruptest the Word of God, O Luther; thou art seen to be a manifest corrupter of the Holy Scripture; how much are we ashamed of thee, who have hitherto esteemed of thee beyond all measure, and prove thee to be such a man!"[3] To which Luther politely retorted: "the Zwinglians are fools, asses, and deceivers."[4] Since the Elector of Saxony disliked the Genevan version, he replaced it by that of Luther;[5] Beza condemned Castalio's version; Molinoeus complained that Calvin "uses violence to the letter of the Gospel, and besides this, adds to the text," and of Beza said: "I will not note all his errors, for that would require too large a volume."[6]

THE STORM OF ABUSE

The appearance of the new version and of the *Discoverie* provoked a storm among the Reformers. "They inveigh with incredible fury against the Testament so recently translated and published here," wrote Allen in 1583. Against Martin himself the grossest calumnies were circulated; Bale even dared to say, apropos of Martin's treatise on clerical celibacy, that he was "a vicious man himself, and notoriously guilty of uncleanness; and so the more unfit to handle that subject. Nor was he able to write such a book himself, being altogether ignorant in divinity, as his opponent [Fulke], that answered his treatise, asserted."[7] Camden says that "suspicion lighted upon Gregory Martin" as author of a supposed plot to murder Queen Elizabeth.[8] "The better to procure Queen Elizabeth's ruin," says Foulis, "there was a little book composed, and called *A Treatise of Schism,* which among many other things exhorted the women at Court to act the same part against the Queen as Judith had done, with a commendation against Holofernes. The author of this pernicious pamphlet was one Gregory Martin."[9] Lewis, too, apropos of

[2] *Discoverie,* no. 13; cf. nos. 24 f., 28, 33.

[3] *Ad Lutherum, liber de S. Scriptura,* quoted by Ward, *Errata of the Protestant Bible,* p. 10.

[4] Ward, *loc. cit.*

[5] Hospinianus, *Concordia discors,* quoted by Ward, p. 10.

[6] *Translatio Novi Testamenti.*

[7] Given by Strype, *Ecclesiastical Memorials* (1816), IV, 276.

[8] *Annales rerum Anglicarum et Hibernicarum, regnante Elizabetha,* anno 1584.

[9] *History of the Popish Treasons and Usurpations,* p. 437. Carter, "now chief printer for the *Romanists,* keeping two Presses at their devotion, . . . prints above a thousand copies; for which he is tryed, confesseth his printing it, vindicates all contain'd in it, is

Martin's statement that the reforming translators wilfully forsook the Vulgate in order to support their own heresies, says: "After such an introduction, so false and uncharitable, one need not wonder at anything that follows in this book," which, he adds, "had a substantial answer made to it by Dr. William Fulke." [10]

So great was the opposition that priests found with copies of the New Testament were imprisoned; and though Cecil denied that torture was ever used unmercifully (*Execution of Justice,* 1583), his words leave "no doubt that torture was applied to those who circulated this translation of the Testament, and inflicted by those who most zealously advocated the unlimited right of private judgement." [11] When Mary, Queen of Scotts, offered to pledge on the Rheims New Testament her word that she had not conspired against Elizabeth, the Earl of Kent exclaimed: "The book is a popish Testament, and of course an oath on it is of no value." But Mary rejoined; "It is a Catholic Testament, and on that account I prize it the more, and therefore according to your own reasoning you ought to judge my oath the more satisfactory." [12]

The bitter invectives heaped on the translators would lead one to suppose that they were the first to throw a bomb into the placid waters of English religious thought. Yet the translations by Tyndale, Matthew, and the Genevan divines ran counter to the traditional teaching on many doctrinal issues and were filled with bitterly anti-Catholic notes. It had been quite otherwise with the Bishops' Bible, 1568 and onwards, for one of the rules laid down by Archbishop Parker was that "they should make no bitter Notes upon any text, or yet set down any determination in places of controversy." [13]

---

condemn'd and executed, and hath the honour to be Registered amongst their Martyrs."

[10] *A Complete History of the Several Translations of the Holy Bible and New Testament into English,* p. 293. Mombert, while granting that "there is much ability displayed by both [Fulke and Martin]," thinks that "in most instances Fulke gets the better of his adversary" (*English Versions of the Bible,* p. 292).

[11] Dore, *Old Bibles,* p. 292.

[12] *Ibid.,* p. 306; cf. Mombert, *op. cit.,* p. 317; Eadie, *The English Bible,* II, 136. When Shakespeare makes Coriolanus speak of "the cockle of rebellion" (*Coriolanus,* Act III, scene 1), he must be using the Rheims Version of Matt. 13:25–30, for all the other versions have "tares"; so also when he puts in the mouth of Berowne the phrase recalling the parable: "Sow'd cockle, reap'd no corn" (*Love's Labour's Lost,* Act IV, scene 5 at the end). See *The Tablet,* April 17, 1937, p. 545.

[13] The sixth rule for King James's revisers was: "No marginal Notes at all to be affixed, but only for the explanation of the Hebrew or Greek words, which cannot without some circumlocution so briefly and fitly be expressed in the text."

Striking as they did at the very roots of the various sects, the Rhemists' Preface and Annotations could not be allowed to pass without challenge. Indeed the very existence of a Catholic version in English was an offense in the eyes of the Reformers. Worse than all: these audacious "runagate Papists" had actually dared to challenge the scholarship of the day by presenting the world with a version made from the despised Latin Vulgate, which since the days of Erasmus had been regarded contemptuously by many; this, too, in face of the prevailing canonization and supposedly sacrosanct character of the current Greek text. Moreover, the new version was furnished with a Preface, notes, and Annotations which so forcibly insisted on the pre-eminence of that same Latin text and of the Greek text underlying it, that genuine scholars should have felt bound to face the inevitable conclusion that what they were in the habit of styling "the old vulgar Latin" could not be ignored if they really wished to arrive at a text doing justice to the original inspired words.

CARTWRIGHT'S *CONFUTATION*

Many years were to elapse before justice could be done to the contentions of the Rhemists. Prejudices were then too strong and passions too violent to allow of sober judgment. So strong indeed was the feeling—nay, the dread—aroused, that Elizabeth asked Beza to undertake a refutation. Beza, however, referred her to Cartwright the Puritan, who, financed by Leicester and £100 from Walsingham,[14] got as far as Apoc., chap. 15, when Whitgift, resenting his attacks on the Church of England, stopped publication.[15] Still a small portion did appear in

[14] In an "Address by the Publisher to the Reader" we learn that "the chiefe Instrument" was "S. Francis Walsingham . . . who was accounted the mouth and hand of the late Queen and state, by whom M. Cartwright was not only to begin this business (but, it is added, that to this purpose) he sent him a hundred pounds [at least £1000 or $4500 according to present values] towards the charges, which buying of books and procuring of writers was like to bring upon him. This was about the year 1583."

[15] Whitgift's action ceases to be surprising in the light of *Certaine Propositions avouched by William Cartwright and other Puritanes; in their Admonition to the Parliament. About the year 1574.*

1. The present pretended Ecclesiastical Regiment in England by Bishops, Chancelers, Deanes, Archdeacons, etc. is Antichristian.

2. The people must choose their ministers; and so they nede no other ordination.

3. All ministers are of equal auctoritie.

4. The Presbyteri by most voices, is the supreme Judge in spiritual causes: in every province or shire.

5. The Article, of Christs descending into hel is foysted into the Crede.

1602,[16] and the entire work came out belatedly in 1618: *A Confutation of the Rhemists Translation, Glosses and Annotations on the New Testament so farre as they containe manifeste Impieties, Heresies, Idolatries, Superstitions, Prophanesse, Treasons, Slanders, Falsehoods, and other Evills. By occasion whereof the True Sence, Scope, and Doctrine of the Scriptures, and humane Authors by them abused, is now given. Written in England, as the ensuing*[17] *Epistles shew, by that learned, Reverend and Judicious Divine, Thomas Cartwright, sometime Divinitie Reader of Cambridge. Printed in the yeare 1618.*

Cartwright reprinted the Rheims version of St. Matthew with the notes and Annotations, with a "confutation." But finding this method too laborious, he merely summarized the rest of the Annotations. But his work can be described only as a series of studied insults. For example: "The only resort of the Papists lies in the defacing and dis-authorizing of the Scriptures . . . by a false surmise of corruption in them, in the languages wherein they were first written. Which abominable practice

---

6. No holie day is to be kept but the Sabbath day only. *Which is Saturday.*
7. Baptism is not necessary for anie person, Nor to be ministered to infants.
8. The signe of the Crosse is in nowise to be made.
9. No surplice is to be used; nor cope; nor square cappe, etc.
10. It is not lawful to knele when they receive the communion.

Dr. Worthington, who gives these Propositions (*An Anker of Christian Doctrine,* 1618), adds: "Al which, with the like, were impugned by Dr. Whitegift: and others. And are condemned in the Protestants Synode, holden at Hampton court, 1604."

[16] *The Answere to the Preface of the Rhemish Testament. At Edinburgh. Printed by Robert Walde-grave, printer to the Kings Majestie. 1602. Cum privilegio Regis.* This book of 213 pages, 16mo, is now very rare. Cartwright of course attributes the version to the Jesuits, whom he styles "three halfpenny ushers" (p. 46). The English Colleges of Rheims and Douay were not Jesuit foundations, nor had the Society anything to do with the translation, though Father Parsons is said to have been instrumental in securing funds for its publication (cf. *Catholic Record Society,* XXXIX, pp. xl, 174). Though we can understand Cartwright's attributing the work to the Jesuits, for the people of that period connected everything Romish with the Jesuits, yet Pollard in our own century speaks of "the Jesuit New Testament" and "the Jesuit version" (*Records of the English Bible,* p. 36; Introduction to *The Beginning of the New Testament Translated by William Tyndale,* p. xxi). The same mistake occurs in the British Museum *Guide to the Manuscripts and Printed Books Exhibited in Celebration of the Tercentenary of the Authorized Version,* nos. 68 and 70, where the version of 1582 is said to have been necessitated by the needs of "the Jesuit controversialists," and the college at Douay is called a "Jesuit" foundation. Grier, too, in his *Reply to the End of Religious Controversy,* p. 277, speaks of "the Rhemish Jesuits"; see Milner, *Letters to a Prebendary,* Letter VI.

[17] The "ensuing letters" were from ten Cambridge divines: Goade, Whitaker, Fulke, and others.

being attempted in the Old Testament by Lindanus (whom some term Blind-asinus) is now assayed in the New by the Jesuites." [18]

FULKE'S *DEFENSE*

When all these attempts at a refutation, whether of the New Testament or of the *Discoverie,* proved abortive, the task devolved on William Fulke (1538–89), a disciple of Cartwright. Deprived of his Fellowship at Cambridge owing to the "vestiarian" controversy, he was reinstated through Puritan influences, but had to resign it in 1568 owing to grave charges against him.[19] Always a bitter controversialist, "his language was unmeasured, and even in that age he was conspicuous for the virulence of his invectives against his opponents," becoming known, in fact, as *acerrimus Papamastix,* or the "bitter scourge of Papistrie." [20] He held disputations with Bishop Watson and Abbot Feckenham in 1580, and in 1581 three disputations with Edmund Campion.[21] For Gregory Martin he had a positive hatred, speaking of his "malicious and unlearned quarrels" and calling him "a shameless slanderer," for "a devilish madness

[18] Quoted by Cotton, *Rhemes and Doway,* p. 21, from T. Cartwright, *The Answere to the Preface of the Rhemish Testament,* 1602. "To Cartwright's work, now lying neglected and mouse-eaten in parts, the Rhemists durst never return the least answer" (Fuller, *op. cit.,* IX, 70). Fuller forgets that by 1618 all the Rhemish protagonists were dead.

[19] *Dictionary of National Biography,* "Fulke," p. 741; Cooper, *Athenae Cantabrigienses,* II, 57–71.

[20] *Dictionary of National Biography,* VII, 746 f. The epitaph on Fulke's tomb at Dennington runs as follows:

If deepest learning, with zealous love
To Heaven and Truth, could Priviledges prove
To keep back Death, no Hand had written here
Lies Reverend Fulke, 'till Christ in clouds appear;
His Works will shew him free from all Error,
Rome's foe, Truth's Champion, and Rhemishes Terror.

[21] *A Disputation or Conference had within the Tower of London, on Monday, being the 18th. of September, A.D. 1581. Wherein were assembled the Lorde of Glanrikerd, Sir Owen Hopton, Sir William George, Sir Thomas Hinnage, Sir Nicholas Poynes, besides others: Doctour Foulkes and Doctour Goade, Disputants, being sitting at a table, having certaine bookes about them. Mr. Clarke and Mr. Field being as Notaries at the said table, and for the Conference appointed; before whom and right opposite upon a stoole was sette Mr. Campion, Jesuite, having only his Bible. A third Disputation between the said Doctors Fulke and Goade opponents, and Campion the Jesuite respondent, is entitled, The three last days of conferences had in the Tower with Edmund Campion, Jesuite, the 18, 23 and 27 of September, 1581. Collected and faithfully set down by Mr. John Fielde, student in Divinitie. Nowe perused by the learned men themselves, and thought meete to be published.*

possesses your malicious mind." [22] He never forgave Martin for dubbing him "a malapert theologian"; [23] "I am called," he complains, "a malapert Scholler of Bezaes impudent Schools for placing the mysteries of Antichrist, as working in the See of Rome even in St. Peter's times." [24] When Martin spoke of Campion as "reverent, godly, and learned," Fulke sneeringly retorted: "Campion's levity, treason, and ignorance in divinity hath lately been tried among us," adding that in his *Decem rationes,* "besides a little rank rhetoric, more meet for a boy that learneth to practise his figures, than for a grave divine to use in so serious a matter, there is nothing that any learned man may think of any answer." [25] Perhaps Fulke had never forgotten that Campion had defeated him when they competed for a prize at St. Paul's school.

Nothing comparable to this ribaldry appears in Martin's pages, though he does express himself strongly at times. But who would not have done so under the provocation he and the other Rhemists had received? Maitland's words on this subject are noteworthy:

> I do not want to defend the Romish writers, and I hope I have no partiality for them, or for the errors, heresies, and superstitions which they were concerned to maintain; but it really appears to me only simple truth to say that, whether from good or bad motives, they did in fact abstain from that fierce, truculent, and abusive language, and that loathsome ribaldry, which characterised the style of too many of the puritan writers. . . . For senseless cavilling, scurrillous railing and ribaldry, for the most offensive personalities, for the reckless imputation of the worst motives and most odious vices; in short, for all that was calculated to render an opponent hateful in the eyes of those who were no judges of the matter in dispute, some of the puritan party went far beyond their adversaries.[26]

[22] *A Defense of the Sincere and True Translations of the Holie Scriptures,* pp. 75 f., 224.

[23] The Rhemists' note on II Thess. 2:3.

[24] *A Confutation of a Popishe and Sclanderous Libelle,* p. 15.

[25] *A Defense . . . of the Holie Scriptures,* pp. 440, 442. The titles of his controversial writings show the character of a man who was not ashamed to say: "As for our hatred of the malignant antichristian church of Rome, we never dissembled the matter." *A briefe Confutation of a Popish Discourse, by John Howlet,* London, 1581; *A Confutation of a Popishe and Sclanderous Libelle,* London, 1571, 1573, 1574; *D. Heskins, D. Sanders, and M. Rastel, accounted (among their faction) three pillers, and Archpatriarches of the Popish Synagogue (utter enemies to the truth of Christes Gospel and all that syncerely profess the same), overthrowne and detected of their severell blasphemous heresies,* London, 1579; *A Rejoynder to Bristow's Replie in defence of Allens scroll,* London, 1581; *A Retentive to stay good Christians in true faith and religion, against the Motives of R[ichard] B[ristowe],* London, 1580; *A Sermon preached at Hampton Court, Nov. 12, 1570, wherein is plainly prooved Babilon to be Rome, both by Scriptures and Doctours,* London, 1572, 1579.

[26] *Essays on Subjects Connected with the Reformation in England,* pp. 47 f.

But as a plain matter of fact, the Rhemists were transparently honest, stating their beliefs fully and unreservedly, and defending them with a wealth of learning and sound reasoning which finds no parallel in the vituperative "Confutations," "Answers," "Antidotes," etc., of their opponents. There were then no reviewers to pour contempt with a few deft phrases culled from encyclopedias. Book and pamphlet had to be answered by book and pamphlet. Men wrote what they thought, and the thoughts and ideas of the Rhemists on religion were not nebular theories. They knew what they believed, and why they believed it. Moreover, they were witnessing the spectacle of men not half so well equipped as themselves, light-heartedly flooding the world with ideas subversive of the old order and supporting newfangled notions by biblical versions which were not always honest. Whitaker, the opponent of Bellarmine, admits with shame: "Forgery—I blush for the honour of Protestantism, while I write it—seems to have been peculiar to the Reformed. I look in vain for one of these accursed outrages of imposition amongst the disciples of Popery."

Fulke attempted to answer the *Discoverie* by *A Defense of the Sincere and True Translations of the Holie Scriptures into the English Tong, against the manifold cavils, frivolous quarrels, and impudent slaunders of Gregorie Martin,* 1583.[27] But he fails throughout to grasp the point at issue. When, for instance, Martin complained of the substitution of "congregation" for "Church," Fulke called this "a stinking cavil" because "Church" at least stood in the marginal notes, and the translators adopted "congregation" or "assembly" for fear lest people might by "church" understand the building; so, too, they preferred "overseer" to "bishop" lest people might take a bishop "either for such an idol as the Papists used to make of their St. Nicholas, or else for a great lord only that rideth about in a white rochet"; the people are therefore "to be told that the name of a bishop describeth his office, that is, to be an overseer of the flock of Christ." Similarly, "if the word 'deacon' be taken for such an one, as at a popish mass standeth in a disguised tunicle, holding a patten, or some other idolatrous bauble used by them, the people must be taught

[27] This was reprinted, separately paged, in Fulke's edition of the Rhemish New Testament, edited for the Parker Society by C. H. Hartshorne, 1843. As Fulke copies the now very rare *Discoverie* almost in its entirety, for this contribution to posterity we are grateful even to this most acrimonious enemy of the Catholic faith.

that this name signifieth a minister, which was ordained not to serve the popish alter, but the poor man's tables."

Martin's *Discoverie,* against which the *Defense* was directed, was a tiny 12mo volume, but Fulke's *Defense* occupies 591 8vo pages, in which no single argument of any force is urged against Martin. One cannot help wondering whether they had ever really read and weighed the arguments who say, like Mombert, that "in most instances Fulke gets the better of his adversary" and that "his *Defense* is very noble," [28] or who, like Lewis, claim that the *Discoverie* "had a substantial answer made to it by Dr. William Fulke." [29] Even more emphatic is J. Brown in the Preface to his attack on Ward's *Errata:* "Fulke completely refuted Martin's charges . . . and inflicted merited chastisement on the annotators of those detestable notes prefixed [*sic*] to the Rhemish translation of the Bible, which would disgrace a musselmen conclave." [30]

MARTIN VERSUS FULKE

Martin's *Discoverie* embraces four main points which he urges against the Reformers' translations: (a) the changes they have felt compelled to make in successive translations; (b) some deliberate mistranslations; (c) additions to the text for the purpose of supporting their false teachings; (d) their recourse to a new version when one fails.

a. Martin declares that successive translators were compelled "for shame" to correct previous false renderings, for which statement he gives illustrations: the "temple" of the Great Bible becomes "altar" in later editions; [31] "congregation" is changed to "Church"; "the king as chief head," later "as having pre-eminence"; while Beza changed "carcase" into "soul." When Fulke replied that "in Thomas Matthew's translation, the first that was printed in English with authority," "altar" stood in I Cor., chaps. 9 and 10, Martin naturally felt that this was an unworthy

[28] *Op. cit.,* p. 291.

[29] *A Complete History of the Several Translations of the Holy Bible and New Testament into English,* p. 293.

[30] *Ten Lectures on Ward's "Errata of the Protestant Bible,"* 1859.

[31] Fulke insists that this must have been a printer's error, as though he were not perfectly well aware that the text thus stood in Cranmer's Bible, 1539 and 1562, in the Bishops' Bible, edition of 1577, and the Geneva Bible, 1579, though not in the editions of 1557 or 1608 (*Defense,* pp. 112, 516). In Dan. 14:12, 17, 20, they have, conversely, "the altar of Bel" where there is question of the idolatrous "table" of Bel.

evasion of the point at issue; namely, that the various editions did acknowledge, at least tacitly, that there had been mistranslations. He exclaims:

> Where shall we have these good fellows, and how shall we be sure that they will stand by any of their translations? From the first read in their churches they flee to that that is now read, and from this again to the later Genevan English Bibles, neither read in their churches (as we suppose), nor of greatest authority among them; and we doubt not that they will as fast flee from this to the former again, when this shall be proved in some places more false and absurd than the other. If they will not stand to all their translations, but fly to that namely which now is read in their churches: and if that which is now read in their churches, differ in the points aforesaid from that that was read in their churches in king Edward's time; and if from both these they fly to the Geneva Bible, and from that again to the other aforesaid: what shall we judge of the one or the other, but that all is voluntary and as they list? [32]

b. The reforming translators, says Martin, were guilty, like the heretics of old, of rejecting books of the Bible in whole or in part, and of deliberately mistranslating passages when the text as it stood ran counter to their preconceived notions. As for the mutilation of the canon, Luther repudiated the Epistle of St. James, and though Whitaker says this is an ill-founded accusation, Fulke allows its truth. Whitaker himself was even more guilty in this respect, rejecting Tobias, Ecclesiasticus, and Machabees: "We pass not for that Raphael of Tobie, neither do we acknowledge those seven Angels which he speaketh of. Al this is far from Canonical Scriptures, that the same Raphael recordeth, and favoureth I wot not what superstition." And again, "I little care for the place of Ecclesiasticus (31:10), neither wil I beleeve free wil, though he affirms it an hundred times." In like manner he repudiates prayers for the dead and the intercession of saints: "As for the book of Machabees, I do care lesse for it than for the other. Judas dreame concerning Onias (II Mach. 15:12–16) I let passe as a dreame." [33]

The accusation of falsifying the text when it suited their convenience is abundantly supported; Martin instances in particular the Reformers' renderings of such sacrosanct terms as "tradition," "idols," "Church," "priesthood," and their efforts to eliminate traditional teachings on

[32] *Discoverie,* no. 15; Fulke's *Defense,* p. 113. The Bible "now read" was the Bishops' Bible, and, according to Cotton, was the edition published in 1577, or the fourteenth of the twenty-four enumerated (*Lists of Editions of the Bible,* p. 41).

[33] *Ad decem rationes Edmundi Campion,* p. 11.

purgatory, limbo, the descent of Christ into hell, justification, merits, free will, and penance; "faith," he says, they have brought to signify little more than "security."[34] Complaining of the rendering "images" for "idols," Martin says: "Surely the Bible that we most accuse, not only in this point, but for sundry other most gross faults and heretical translations is the Bible which was authorised by Cranmer and read all King Edward's time in their churches, and (as it seemeth by the late printing thereof again, anno 1562) a great part of this queen's reign." The result of this rendering is that people have learned to despise pictures of the crucifixion, even the use of the sign of the cross.[35]

Martin also criticized the Great Bible for want of scholarship in representing the five foolish virgins as saying, "our lamps are gone out," instead of, "are going out" (Matt. 25:8). It was hardly scholarly to say, as does Lewis, "It was either pure ignorance or perfect cavilling that let Martin find fault with its being translated 'their lamps were gone out.' "[36] The Authorized Version follows Cranmer, but the Revisers wrote correctly, "are going out," as had the Rhemists three hundred years before them.

The edition of the Bible published in 1562 had rendered I Pet. 2:12, "to the king as the chief head" (Bishops' Bible, "as pre-eminent"); Martin therefore pointed out that St. Ignatius "exhorted them to honour God, next the Bishop, and then the king"; the words of St. Peter, he added, "maketh not for any spirituall claime of earthly kings, because it giveth no more to any Prince, than may and ought to be done to a heathen magistrate. Neither is there anything in all the New Testament, that proveth the Prince to be head or chiefe governour of the Church in spirituall or ecclesiasticall causes, more than it proveth any heathen Emperour of Rome to have beene."[37] Fulke's retort is characteristic:

> The name of "supreme head," in that sense which Calvin and others abroad did mislike it, it was never allowed, nor by authority granted to the kings, Henry and Edward, but in the same sense it is now granted to queen Elizabeth; whom we acknowledge to have the same authority in causes ecclesiastical, which her father and brother, kings before her, had, and exercised to God's glory. But as Stephen Gardiner understood that title in conference with Bucer at Ratisbon, we do utterly

[34] *Discoverie,* no. 9. See also D'Astros, *La Bible mutilée par les Protestants, ou démonstration de la divinité des Écritures rejetées par la Réforme,* 1817, 1847.

[35] *Discoverie,* no. 11; in Fulke's *Defense,* p. 190.

[36] *Op. cit.,* p. 229.

[37] *Op. cit.,* no. 23.

abhor it, and so did all godly men always, that a king should have absolute power to do in religion what he will.[38]

Concerning St. Ignatius, Fulke is content to say: "These words shew of what shop this *Epistle* of Ignatius came, who was a man of greater religion than that he would have corrected the Scripture in Salomon, or in Peter, both commanding the King to be honoured next unto God." [39] Fulke, as indeed most of the Reformers, was very apt in quoting the Fathers; but only when they seemed to favor their views, as Martin repeatedly complains. The Fathers were repudiated when their statements were inconvenient; Whitaker, for instance, declared that "all the Fathers were wrong in that they regarded exterior penances as satisfactions to God." [40]

c. Not content with mistranslations which seem at times to have been deliberate, the reforming translators even added clauses supporting their own doctrinal vagaries. I Pet. 1:25 is made to read, "This is the word which by the Gospel was preached unto you." The gratuitous addition of "by the Gospel," owing in the first place to Tyndale, was adopted by Cranmer, the Genevans, and A.V., also in the editions of 1562 and 1577; needless to say, it has no MS. authority, either Greek or Latin, and was unknown to Wycliffe and the Rhemists, and was repudiated by the revisers in 1881.[41] Perhaps even worse is the rendering of Acts 14:23, "When they had ordained elders by election in every congregation." The gratuitous insertion of "by election" in favor of a Presbyterian doctrine is enforced by the renderings "elders" and "congregation" for "priests" and "church"; all three disfigurements appear in Tyndale, Cranmer, and the Genevan version, but neither in A.V. nor R.V.[42]

The revision in 1562 of Cranmer's Bible [43] seems to have been prolific in this respect. For example, in II Par. 36:8, where Rheims rightly has "But the rest of the acts of Joakim, and his abominations, which he wrought, and the things that were found in him" (Vulgate, *et quae in-*

[38] *Op. cit.,* p. 488.

[39] Of course neither Martin nor Fulke could at that date have known that the Ignatian epistles existed in more than one recension and had been freely interpolated. The text in the accepted text of the *Epistle to the Smyrneans* (chap. 9) runs: "It is good to honour God and the Bishop"; there is no reference to the king.

[40] Cf. Martin, *op. cit.,* nos. 3, 14 f.; Fulke, *Defense,* pp. 36, 38, 99.

[41] *Discoverie,* no. 3; in Fulke's *Defense,* pp. 548 f.

[42] *Discoverie,* no. 7; in Fulke's *Defense,* pp. 245 f., 466.

[43] According to Hartshorne, editor of the *Defense,* this edition was due to a revision made by Archbishop Parker (p. 67 note).

venta sunt in eo), the last clause is made to read, "and carved images that were laid to his charge." Fulke is compelled to acknowledge that "our first translators added that which is the common interpretation of them that write upon this place; but because that had been better in the note, than in the text, it is corrected in two later translations." [44] Another tendentious addition appears in Acts 9:22, "Saul confounded the Jews, proving (by conferring one scripture with another) that this is the very Christ." The editor of Fulke's *Defense* says in a note on p. 547 that "the bracketed clause is only found in one edition, the Bishops' Bible of 1584"; but Martin says it stood in an edition of 1577; [45] it finds no place in the other English versions, not even in the first Genevan version, 1557.

d. The innumerable versions and revised editions that appeared between 1525 and 1582 are evidence enough that the translations made by the Reformers were defective. The continual changing of the text in subsequent editions makes an account of the development of the English Bible extremely complicated and difficult. In one year the same publisher would sometimes publish several editions of different versions.[46]

[44] *Defense,* pp. 202, 547; cf. Martin's *Discoverie,* no. 1. The passage is omitted in the Bishops' Bible of 1584, the Genevan edition of 1560, and A.V.

[45] The edition referred to must have been one of the Bishops' Bible (see above, note 32), for Martin speaks of this edition as "a Bible read daily in their churches as most authentical," a statement which he could not have made of the Geneva Bible. Fulke, indeed, maintained that the clause in question did not appear in any of the four editions of the Bishops' Bible in his possession, yet as a matter of fact it does appear in the edition of 1584 (cf. *ibid.,* nos. 2, 33; Fulke, *Defense,* pp. 68, 547 f.). The edition of 1577 was also guilty of inserting "by election" in the clause, "when thay had ordained them elders by election in every church" (Acts 14:23). In his *Defense* Fulke makes no comment on this unwarranted addition (cf. p. 582).

On the other hand, Martin is clearly referring to an edition of the Geneva Bible in 1577 when he comments on the omission of Alleluia "nine times in the sixe last Psalms," for that omission is confined to the Genevan version (on Apoc. 14:4; *Discoverie,* no. 13; in Fulke's *Defense,* p. 582). The edition of 1579, incriminated by Martin for its rendering of Gen. 14:19 and for transposing words in Heb. 2:9, seems also to have hailed from Geneva, for the latter transposition certainly occurs in the first Genevan Testament, 1557. Martin notes that in Acts 1:14, instead of "with the women," "heretikes, some in the text, other in the margent, translate 'wives,' see Beza and the English Bible, 1579."

Concerning these various editions Fulke writes: "I guess that the Bible 1562 is that which was of Coverdale's translation, most used in the church service in king Edward's time. The Bible 1577, I take to be that which, being revised by divers Bishops, was first printed in the large volume, and authorised for the churches, about ten or twelve years ago. That of 1579, I know not what translation it be, except it be the same that was first printed at Geneva in the beginning of the queen's Majesty's reign."

[46] For example, an edition both of the Bishops' Bible and of the Geneva Bible was printed by Robert Barker in 1602, and in the following year the same publisher produced two editions of the Geneva Bible; cf. Cotton, *op. cit.,* pp. 26, 56 f.

The multiplicity of revised editions is a condemnation of their authenticity. Martin's words quoted above (p. 282), condemning the fickleness of the Reformers in biblical matters, are noteworthy.

All the English corruptions here noted and refuted are either in all or some of their English Bibles printed in these years, 1562, 1577, 1579. And if the corruption be in one Bible, and not in another, commonly the said Bible or Bibles are noted in the margin [that is, of his *Discoverie*]: if not, yet sure it is that it is in one of them, and so the reader shall find it. And in this case the reader must be very wise and circumspect. . . . For it is their common and known fashion, not only in their translations of the Bible . . . to alter and change, add and put out, in their later editions according as either themselves of the former, or their scholars, that print them again, dissent and disagree from their master.[47]

FULKE'S ATTACK ON THE NEW TESTAMENT OF 1582

Fulke's *Defense* against Martin's *Discoverie* was, however, but a preliminary encounter. For six years later Fulke produced a prodigious volume, *The Text of the New Testament of Jesus Christ, translated out of the vulgar Latine by the Papists of the traiterous Seminarie at Rhemes. With Arguments of Bookes, Chapters, and Annotations, pretending to discover the corruptions of divers Translations, and to cleare the controversies of these dayes. Whereunto is Added the Translation out of the Original Greeke, commonly used in the Church of England* [the Bishops' Bible], London, 1589.

To his double text of the New Testament Fulke added *A Table of Controversies* "gathered according to the Table drawne by the Rhemists," with a reprint of his *Defense* and a list of Martin's "cavils." After this comes "A Briefe Confutation of all such quarrels and cavils as have been of late uttered by divers Papists in their English Pamphlets, against the Writings of the said William Fulke." In this "Confutation"—not to be confused with that by Cartwright, mentioned above—Fulke's language passes all bounds; Bristow is "a shameless beast," "an impudent ass," "ignorant," "blundering"; Cardinal Allen, "brazen-faced and an iron forehead," "an impudent liar"; Stapleton is "a Popish swine," "a cankred stomacked Papist," and a "blockhead"; Lozell is "lewd" and "an unlearned dog-bolt"; while addressing Allen he says: "Shew me, Allen, if thou canst, for thy guts." [48]

[47] *Discoverie,* no. 33; in Fulke's *Defense,* p. 67. For the editions here referred to, see above, note 45.

[48] *A Discoverie of the daungerous Rocke of the Popish Churche,* Parker Society, p. 219.

It seems impossible to believe in Fulke's honesty. When Sander pointed out that Protestants had excluded certain books from the canon, Fulke replies: "The Protestants do admit as many as the Catholic Church ever did or doth to this day"; then concerning Second Machabees he quotes St. Augustine as saying that the book "is received of the Church if it be heard or read soberly." [49] But what Augustine really said was: *recepta est ab Ecclesia non inutiliter, si sobrie legatur aut audiatur,* where the qualifying *non inutiliter,* omitted by Fulke, refers not to the reception of Second Machabees by the Church, but to the profit readers may thence derive. Fulke even denies that there existed any Catholic version of the Bible: "I never saw any; neither is there any translation to be shewed of any Papist into any vulgar tongue" [50]—this from a man who had violently attacked Martin's *Discoverie* as well as the Preface and notes to the Rheims version! When Martin showed up an unjustifiable rendering by Beza, Fulke repudiated Beza's authority; when Sander, on the strength of Luther's assertion that the Epistle of James was "an epistle of straw," maintained that Protestants reject that epistle, Fulke simply repudiated Luther. Finally, he speaks of St. Jerome as "an imperfect Grecian and a very barbarous Latinist." [51]

Fulke dedicated his work to "the Most High and Mighty Princess Elizabeth," and descanting on the glory of England in having now a vernacular version of the Bible, he jeers at the Rhemists for following "the crooked streame of their barbarous vulgar Latine Translation, which (beside all other manifest corruptions) is found defective in more than an hundred places, as your Majestie, according to the excellent knowledge in both tongues [Hebrew and Greek], wherewith God hath blessed you, is very well able to judge." The Preface, forty-two folio pages, is full of virulent abuse of "the Popish Church, the Babylonical harlot, the Spouse of Antichrist, and her one object—the suppression of the truth."

Fulke's attempted refutation of the Annotations can be described only as ludicrous. For example, the Rhemists, commenting on "This is my body" (Luke 22:19), had written: "Though sense tell thee it is bread,

[49] *Ibid.,* p. 221. Fulke refers to *Contra Gaudentium,* II, viii; it should be I, xxxi, 38. For Augustine's real mind on the point he might have looked at *Epis.,* 111, § 5; 204, §§ 6–8; *Ennar.* II.22 on Ps. 33:18; *De Civ. Dei,* XVIII, chap. 36; *Doctrina Christiana,* II, chap. 5; *De cura pro mortuis gerenda,* chap. 1.

[50] *Op. cit.,* p. 223.

[51] *Defense,* pp. 417, 435.

yet it is the body, according to his words," and they quote St. Cyril: "Let faith confirm thee; judge not by sense, after the words of our Lord let no doubt arise in thy mind." The note continues:

> As the former words make and prove his body present, so these words plainly signify that it is present, as given, offered, or sacrificed for us; and being uttered in the present tense it signifieth not only that it should afterward be given or offered on the Cross, but that it was then also in the Sacrament given or offered for us. Whereby it is invincibly proved that his body is present as an host or sacrifice; and that the making or consecrating thereof must needs be sacrificing. And therefore the holy Fathers in this sense call it a sacrifice. [They then refer to some thirty passages from the Fathers and councils.]

Fulke was simply content to deny the doctrine, maintaining, against all evidence, that the Fathers never called the Lord's Supper "a propitiatory sacrifice," "but only a sacrifice of praise and thanksgiving, prayers and memoriall of Christs one sacrifice offered on the Crosse." It is the same throughout his 912 quarto pages; no reasoned argument, but flat contradiction accompanied by abuse. His volume is a veritable arsenal of statements contravening Catholic doctrine; in its pages we have the germ of those accusations against the Church and her doctrines which have for so long passed muster with some people.

A second and a third edition appeared in 1601 and 1617; a fourth, in 1633, by Hester Ogden, Fulke's daughter, adds to the title: *With a Confutation of all such arguments, Glosses, and Annotations as conteine manifest impietie, of Heresie, Treason, and Slander against the Catholike Church of God, and the True Teachers thereof, or the Translations used in the Church of England. The Whole Work Perused and enlarged in divers places by the Authors own hand, before his death, with sundrie Quotations and Authorities out of Holy Scriptures, Counsels, Fathers and Historie. By W. Fulke, D. in Divinitie, Sometimes Mr. of Pembroock Hall in Cambridge. The 4th Edition, wherein are many grosse absurdities corrected. London. Printed by Augustine Mathewes, on[e] of the assignes of Hester Ogden. Cum privilegio Regis,* 1633.

Hester Ogden dedicated this edition "to the Most High and Mighty Monarch, our Deare and dread Soveraigne Lord, CHARLES, by the good providence of God, King of Great Britain, France, and Ireland, Defender of the Faith and most Gracious Patron of the Church." She presents the volume to the King by reason of his "zeale against Poperie . . . as one among others of those prime Forts and strongest Bulwarks your Majesties Kingdome hath to withstand the common in-rode and invasion of a Troupe of Romish and Rhemish Jesuites."

On the left of the title page the figure of a priest with biretta and rosary is labelled, *"Hinc zizania"*; on the right stands a bearded Puritan divine labelled, *"Hinc semen bonum."* In the corners the four Evangelists are depicted, while at the foot SS. Peter and Paul hold up an immense *Novum Testamentum*. At the top, between St. Matthew and St. John, the birth and resurrection of Christ are depicted.

OTHER ASSAILANTS

George Wither dedicated to "The Most Reverend Father in God, John, Archbishop of Canterbury, Primate and Metropolitan of England," *A View of the Marginal Notes of the Popish New Testament translated into English by the English fugitive Papists resiant at Rhemes in France*, London, 1588. His Preface, like that of Fulke, witnesses to the consternation caused by the appearance of the Rheims Version: "The censure, view, and examination thereof hath ever since [1582] been heartily looked [for], or rather longed for, of all both rich and poor, high and low, that feare God and love his truth. But by what occasion I cannot tell, it hath been hitherto delaied. Therefore . . . I tooke in hand to discover the loose, corrupt, unjust, and untrue dealings of our Rhemists in their marginall notes." This task, he adds, is only the preliminary to a much fuller work which was to follow. The Rhemists' version is, he says, "fraudulently framed to make poore men thinke the Scriptures to be more obscure and darke a great deale, than they are, and so to fray them from taking pains to read them." Although Wither undertook to refute the Annotations, all that he really does is to treat them with contempt; for example, apropos of the note on St. Peter's presence in Rome (Rom. 16:15), he is content to remark: "We know that it is not materiall whether Peter were at Rome or not, or whether he were a Bishop there or no."

Edward Bulkeley, the next assailant, directed his attack against the Rhemists' "ten reasons" for translating from the Latin rather than from the Greek: *An Answere to ten frivolous and foolish reasons set doun by the Rhemish Jesuits and Papists in their Preface before the New Testament by them lately translated into English, which have mooved them to forsake the originall fountaine of the Greek, wherein the Spirit of God* *did indite the Gospell, and the holy Apostles did write it, to follow the streame of the Latin translation translated we know not when nor by whom. With a Discoverie of many great Corruptions and Faultes in the said English Translation set out at Rhemes,* London, 1588.

It would be hard to discover anything more "frivolous"—to use Bulkeley's own expression—than his attempt to demolish the "ten reasons": "the Vulgate is not so old as they think: indeed it will be hard for al the Rhemish rout of Jesuits to prove its antiquity"; nor, even if it is ancient, will it follow that it is not corrupt, a fact never disputed by the Rhemists. Bulkeley boldly declared that the Vulgate was not the work of St. Jerome, nor was it the work referred to by St. Augustine, meaning, of course, that the Old Latin version preceded St. Jerome's work. But Bulkeley failed to perceive that this concession went far to prove that very antiquity of the Latin version as a whole, a point on which alone the Rhemists had insisted. Again, to the Rhemists' claim that the Latin Fathers used the Vulgate, Bulkeley was guilty of the schoolboy retort: "Yes, but the Greek fathers did not." And when they urged that the Council of Trent venerated the Vulgate, Bulkeley could find no better answer than, "Quite so; but this cursed conventicle we no more esteeme than the godly fathers esteemed the Councils of Ariminum, Tyre, Ephesus II, and such others." When the Rhemists acclaim the Vulgate as the best of versions, Bulkeley pronounces those by Erasmus [52] and Beza to be better; if they insist on the correctness of the Vulgate, he triumphantly retorts that even their version of the Lord's Prayer is incomplete—he is actually referring to the version in Luke, chap. 11. When they point out that even Beza had spoken highly of the Vulgate, Bulkeley, again in schoolboy fashion, retorts: "Yes, and how disgracefully you Romish folk have treated him ever since!" Finally, when compelled to acknowledge that the various translations in use among the Reformers vary, he makes the feeble rejoinder that "a little variety may better serve to bring out the truth."

Bulkeley undoubtedly had a very real familiarity with the Greek text, but his efforts to show that the Rhemists had departed from it without warrant were hardly felicitous; he contended, for instance, for the reading: Christ "delivered himself to him (Pilate) that judged him *justly*"

[52] Erasmus was Bulkeley's "god," and Bulkeley constituted himself Erasmus' "prophet": "in his daies after the long winter of ignorance, began both the clouds of darknesse to be dispersed, and the sunne of Gods word cleerely to shine forth."

(I Pet. 2:23), and when unable to refute the arguments in favor of the Vulgate, he resorts to abuse, calling the Rhemists "runagates" and a "Jesuit rout." He was particularly angry with Pighius, who, when urging the stupidity of leaving everybody to interpret the Bible for themselves, remarked that "the Bible is like a nose fashioned of wax, which you can easily turn up or down, this way or that way, into any shape you please." Among other things, Bulkeley presents from the Rheims version a list of words which he finds strange in it; e.g., adore, desert, scandalize, impose hands, monument, victim, infirm, erected, congratulate, illuminate, calumniate, deceased, designed, contaminated, impious; yet every one of these has now passed into common usage. Nor was he more fortunate in his list of forty-four omissions in the Rhemists' text, for modern textual criticism has shown that the Rhemists were right in all but seven of these instances.

William Whitaker (1548–95) was another assailant, who, when Master of St. John's, Cambridge, was known as "the pride and ornament of the city." But his Puritanism, Calvinism, and hatred of episcopacy led him to spend his brief life in controversy with both Anglicans and Catholics, assailing among the latter Sander, Reynolds, Stapleton, and especially Bellarmine, who, however, held him in great esteem. Lupton states:

> I have heard it confessed of English Papists themselves, which have been in Italy with Bellarmine himself, that he procured the true portraiture and effigies of this Whitaker to be brought to him, which he kept in his study. For he privately admired this man for his singular learning and ingenuity; and being asked of some of his friends, Jesuits, why he would have the picture of that heretic in his presence? he would answer, "Quod quamvis haereticus erat et adversarius, erat tamen doctus adversarius." [53]

Yet Bellarmine was not ignorant of the fact that Whitaker had accused him of bad faith in controversy.[54]

Though much more learned than Fulke, Martin's "malapert theologian," Whitaker's judgment was warped by his inability to grasp the nature and function of the Church. For example, when faced with patristic declarations on the canonicity of the so-called Apocrypha, he simply repudiated the authority of the Fathers and councils; while

[53] *History of the Moderne Protestant Divines,* quoted in the Preface (p. x) to the edition of Whitaker's Works by the Parker Society, 1849.

[54] *Epistle Dedicatory* on his *Disputatio de sacra Scriptura contra hujus temporis papistas, imprimis Robertum Bellarminum Iesuitam,* 1588, 1590, 1610, quoted in the Parker Society ed. of his works, p. 9.

apropos of the Council of Trent, which had in its fourth session dealt with this question, he could only say: "The legates, cardinals, archbishops, and bishops, who were present, and who published this decree concerning the number of the canonical books, made in all about fifty; and these, almost to a man, Italians and Spaniards." He even went so far as to say that "even after Christ's ascension, and the Holy Ghost's descending upon the Apostles, the whole Church, not only the common sort of Christians, but also even the Apostles themselved, erred in the vocation of the Gentiles, etc.; yea, Peter also erred. He furthermore erred in manners, etc. And these were great errors; and yet we see these to have been in the Apostles, even after the Holy Ghost descended upon them."[55]

Thomas Bilson (1546–1616) was another opponent. He wrote *True Difference between Christian Subjection and Unchristian Rebellion, where the Princes lawful power to command and bear the sword are defended against the Pope's censure and Jesuits' sophisms in their Apology and Defence of English Catholics, also a Demonstration that the Things reformed in the Church of England by the Laws of the Realm are truly Catholic against the Catholic Rhemish Testament,* Oxford, 1585. Antony à Wood says he was

> as reverend and learned a prelate as England ever afforded, a deep and profound scholar, exactly read in ecclesiastical authors and . . . a principal maintainer of the Church of England. . . . He became so complete in [ecclesiastical divinity], so well skill'd in languages, so read in the fathers and schoolmen, so judicious in making use of his readings, that at length he was found to be no longer a soldier but a commander-in-chief of the spiritual warfare, especially when he became a bishop and carried prelature in his very aspect.

But Wood's eulogy hardly agrees with the verdict of Dr. Grosart, who remarks that Bilson's writings "show want of judgement, . . . are superfluously learned, . . . halting in logic and commonplace in proofs."[56]

When an anonymous writer published *The Gagg of the New Gospell . . . for the establishing of the Romane doctrine,* he was answered at once by *Rhimes against Rome: or the Removing of the Gagg of the New Gospell, and rightly placing in the mouthes of the Romanists by the Rhemists; in their English Translation of the Scriptures which Counte-*

[55] *Praelectiones . . . de ecclesia . . . contra Bellarminum,* II, q.4, p. 223.

[56] *Dictionary of National Biography,* "Bilson," II, 505 f. He was bishop, first of Worcester, then of Winchester.

Gagg is heere filled by the industrious hand of Richard Bernard, Rector of Batcomb, in the County of Sommerset. At London, Imprinted by Felix Kingston, for E. Blackmore, and are to be sold at his shop at the great South doore of Pauls, London, 1626. Bernard speaks of his volume as "varyeed, furbished in divers editions," and "I humbly submit my poore labours to our Reverend and blessed Mother the Church of England." The whole argument of his work is that the Bible is the sole rule of faith. Bernard takes all the biblical and patristic citations from the Rheims Version, 1582, and tries to make them prove his point.

EFFECTS OF THE LONG CONTROVERSY

This long-continued campaign of vilification of the Rheims Testament and Catholic teaching had its inevitable results. As Ward wrote a hundred years later:

> How many innocent and well-meaning people are there in England, who have scarce in all their life-time, ever heard any mention of a Catholic, or Catholic Religion, unless under these monstrous and frightful terms of Idolatry, Superstition, Antichristianism, etc.? How many have ever heard a better character of Catholics, than bloody-minded people, Thirsters after Blood, Worshippers of wooden Gods, Prayers to Stocks and Stones, Idolators, Antichrists, the Beast in the Revelations, and what not, that may render them more odious than Hell, and more frightful than the Devil himself, and that from the mouths and pens of their teachers, and ministerial guides? [57]

[57] *Errata of the Protestant Bible,* p. 15. So deep-seated is this prejudice, that so late as 1884 Scrivener could write: "It were endless to enumerate every violation of common sense, or common decency with which the Rhemist notes on the New Testament overflow" (Introduction to *The Cambridge Paragraph Bible,* p. 100).

CHAPTER XIX

The Douay Version of the Old Testament, 1609-10

TITLE PAGE AND PREFACE

ALTHOUGH the Catholic version of the Old Testament was translated before the New, lack of funds prevented its publication until 1609–10, when it appeared in two volumes with the title page: *The Holie Bible, faithfully translated into English out of the authentical Latin. Diligently conferred with the Hebrew, Greeke and other editions in divers languages. With Arguments of the Bookes and Chapters: Annotations: Tables: and other helpes for better understanding of the text: for discoverie of Corruptions in some late translations: and for clearing Controversies in Religion, by the English College of Doway. "Haurietis aquas in gaudio de fontibus Salvatoris," Isaiae 12. "You shal draw waters in joy out of the Saviours fountaines." Printed at Doway by Laurence Kellam at the sign of the holie Lambe, M.DC.IX.* The approbation reads:

We, the undersigned Doctors and Professors of Theology in the University of Douay, certify that this English version of the Old Testament, the work of three learned English theologians,[1] is extremely useful, not only for the faithful (who may read it), but, by reason of the various Annotations attached to it, a very valuable help in propagating and safeguarding the Catholic Faith. Testimonies to this fact, signed by the respective Censors, have been seen by us. Moreover the sound faith and solid learning of the authors of the translation and Annotations are well known to us. We therefore, declare that this work can be published and will be productive of much fruit. Douay, Nov. 8. 1609.

Gulielmus Estius, Sacrae Theologiae Doctor, et in Academia Duacensi Professor.

Bartholomaeus Petrus, Sacrae Theologiae Doctor, et in Universitate Duacensi Professor.

Georgius Colvenerius, S. Theologiae Doctor, et ejusdem in Academia Duacena Professor.

[1] These "three learned English theologians" are probably Allen, Martin, and Bristow, although they had died over twenty years before.

The same Approbation is printed again at the opening of the second volume. It is curious to note that the official *censura* upon which the Approbation is based is printed only at the end of the second volume, which did not appear until 1610. This *censura,* which is repeated in the second edition, 1635, reads:

> Censura trium Theologorum Anglorum, extra Collegium commorantium.
>
> We the undersigned, having carefully read this version of the Old Testament, with the Arguments of the books and chapters, the Annotations and Recapitulations inserted in their respective places, discover nothing contrary to Catholic faith or sound morals. On the contrary, we find that the translation is faithfully made, and the rest learned and useful. For they give the precise series of the ages, of the Church, and her pastors, from the beginning of the world; also a correct statement of Catholic doctrine; they throw light on the more obscure passages of the sacred text, and, while refuting by means of quotations from the same text the heresies now prevalent, they solidly establish practically every point in Catholic dogma. We are therefore of the opinion that the publication of this work will be of great advantage to all its readers if, that is, the official censors of books think fit to give their approval.
>
> Joannes Wrightus, Ecclesiae Collegiatae Gloriosiss. Virginis Cortracensis Decanus.
>
> Matthaeus Kellison, S. Theologiae Doctor ac Professor in Universitate Remensi.
>
> Gulielmus Harisonus, S. Theologiae Doctor. Omnes aliquando Sacrarum Literarum in hoc Collegio Professores.

The Preface [2] is addressed

> To the right well beloved English Reader, Grace and Glorie in Jesus Christ Everlasting:
>
> At last through God's goodnes (most dearly beloved) we send you here the greater part of the Old Testament: as long since you received the New; faithfully translated into English. The residue is in hand to be finished. . . . As for the impediments, which hitherto have hindered this worke, they al proceded (as manie do know) of one general cause, our poore estate in banishment. . . . But you, our dearest, for whom we have dedicated our lives, wil pardon the long delay.

An additional reason for delay was that during the interval between the translation of the Old Testament and its final publication, 1582–1609, there had appeared the Sixtine Vulgate, 1590, and at least three editions of the Clementine Vulgate, 1592, 1593, and 1598. The translation of the Old Testament had been based on the unofficial Louvain Bible, and therefore had now (1609) to be brought into conformity with the official

[2] The complete text is given below in Appendix II, pp. 651 ff. The whole Preface should be read, for it is a touching document illustrative of the spirit and devotion of these exiles.

Clementine text:[3] "We have therefore again conferred this English translation, and conformed it to the most perfect Latin edition."[4] They point out, however, that "few or none of the former varieties [variant readings] touched Controversies of this time." They also explain how it is that a vernacular version is now permitted and what the mind of the Church on this point has always been.

After the Preface comes "The Summe and Partition of the Holie Bible, with a briefe note of the Canonical and Apocryphal Books." Marginal notes, as distinct from the more formal Annotations, indicate the contents of the sections; for instance a note in the above "Summe" runs:

> The old and new Testament differ in time, in manner of uttering, Varietie of Precepts, Means. The old Testament conteyneth figures of the new. A continual visible Church from the beginning of the world to Christ. The same Mystical bodie, but different in state. Divided into six ages. the first age continued 1656 yeares. The second 368 or 398. the third about 430. the fourth 480. The fifth 430. The sixth nere 640. Al the time from the creation to Christ above 4000 yeares.

The text is set out in paragraphs, but the verse numbers are inserted. Exod. 35:23 should read: "If any man had hyacinth and purple and scarlet twice dyed red (fine linen and goats' hair, rams' skins dyed red), and violet-coloured skins"; but the words in parenthesis are omitted. This slip was presumably due to the words "dyed red" occurring twice in

[3] The immense amount of work that had been devoted to the examination of the Vulgate text since the Tridentine demand for its revision, 1546, had resulted in the publication of the Sixtine and Clementine editions. These had to be taken into account by the editors of the Douay Old Testament. What changes they made in the original draft we cannot tell, since it has of course perished; but probably such changes were few. For the Louvain Bible (1547), upon which the original translation was based, was published by John de Hentine immediately after the Tridentine decree for the correction of the existing Vulgate text, and his Bible served as as the basis for the work done by several Roman commissions preparing the revised Vulgate text. Moreover, Allen must have been familiar with the work being done at Louvain during his residence there previous to his founding of the college at Rheims. Later, when the Sixtine edition had to be corrected, Allen was a member of the commission which finally produced the Clementine editions in 1592, 1593, and 1598—the last giving lists of *Errata* in all three editions. The Rhemish translators, then, must have been fully cognizant of the textual problems that faced them, and they must have translated from a Latin text closely similar to the Clementine. Yet modern writers are slow to appreciate the scholarly ability of the Rhemists; Pollard, for instance, suggests that "Gregory Martin, or whoever wrote the preface to the New Testament of 1582, was probably very insufficiently conscious that if the available Greek texts were corrupt, the available Latin texts were very corrupt also, and far from representing what St. Jerome really wrote" (*Records of the English Bible,* p. 36).

[4] Traces of this revision appear in the references to Protestant versions; e.g., to that of 1602 (on Gen. 37:35, p. 118) and that of 1603 (in the Preface to the Old Testament).

the translator's rough draft, for the Latin words *tinctum* and *rubricatas* would not, since they differ, have misled him. The omission was perpetuated in Challoner, as also was the following, where in I Kings 17:49 the translator failed to notice the clause *et infixus est lapis in fronte ejus,* because the word *fronte* occurs twice—*percussit Philistaeum in fronte; et infixus est lapis in fronte ejus*—and his eye passed from the first *fronte* to the second, omitting the intervening clause. Neither of these omissions was corrected in the second edition, 1635.

LITERAL CHARACTER OF THE TRANSLATION

Owing to the excessively close adherence to the Latin, many of the renderings are quaint and may raise a smile: "The ramme he shal immolate for a pacifique hoste to the Lord, offering withal the baskette of azymes, and the libamentes that by custom are dew" (Num. 6:17); "the champion countries of Moab" (Num. 36:13); "And he saw his principalitie, that in his part the doctor was reposed" (Deut. 33:21); "Noemi came from the land of her peregrinations" (Ruth 1:21); Achab "sayd to his cochere" (III Kings 22:34); the harlot is not "able to consist in the house on her feete" (Prov. 7:11); "the Dominatour, the Lord" (Isa. 3:1); "it is day of slaughter and conculcation, . . . the God of hostes . . . magnifical upon the mountain" (Isa. 22:5); "hearing I heard Ephraim going into transmigration" (Jer. 31:18).[5] Challoner succeeded in eliminating most of these disfigurements, but too many remain: "the voice of thy thunder in a wheel" (Ps. 76:19), where R.V. has "in a whirlwind"; in Cant. 8:11 for "the peacemaker" Challoner has "the peaceable," while R.V. has "Solomon."

The work of three men, the version is necessarily uneven, the prophets being perhaps the best, the Psalms the worst: "the most unsatisfactory part of the whole book." [6] As Moulton declares, "the weakest part of the Vulgate, and of all translations made from it, is the Book of Psalms." [7] But it must be remembered that the version of the Psalms was deliberately made from St. Jerome's second or Gallican [8] revision precisely be-

[5] At times the version has preserved a rendering due to St. Jerome alone; e.g., II Kings 17:17, *Non enim poterant videri aut introire civitatem;* Douay, "For they could not be seen nor enter into the citie"; whereas the Hebrew and Greek, followed by A.V. and R.V. have, "they might not be seen to come in the city."

[6] Westcott, *A General View of the History of the English Bible,* p. 251.

[7] *The History of the English Bible,* p. 29.

[8] So called owing to its predominant use by the churches of Gaul.

cause that was, and still is, the version adhered to in the breviary and in the Divine Office of the Church, the version which the Reformers scoffed at and which St. Jerome himself well knew to be defective.[9] Hence, as one writer crudely expresses it, the Douay version of the Psalms "is a positively unintelligible English version of the unintelligible Latin version of a very uncertain Greek translation." [10] The following examples will suffice: "Wash me more amply (50:5); "Deliver me from Bloudes" (50:16); "God they have not invocated" (52:6); "sinners are alienated from the matrice" (57:4); "The king of hoastes the beloved of the beloved; and to the beauty of the house, to divide the spoils" (67:13); "A mountaine crudded as cheese" (67:17); "The Queene stood on thy right hand in golden rayment: compassed with varietie" (44:10), which Challoner hardly improved when he changed it to, "in gilded clothing; surrounded with variety."

But while it is easy enough to criticize the excessively literal character of this version of the Psalms, we have to bear in mind that the translators had no intention of producing a rhythmical version any more than had St. Jerome in making his version from the Hebrew. Unfortunately, in addition to the slavishly literal character of their version, the translators adopted an awkward arrangement of the text. For their marginal notes on nearly every verse are continued from the margin in between the verses, so that at first sight one is tempted to regard them almost as an interlinear version extending at times to eleven lines of interlinear matter (on Ps. 36:25 and 37:2). Added to this, the verses are numbered on the inner margin of each page. These awkward features combine to make the reading of the Psalms exceedingly difficult. But as a strictly accurate rendering of the Latin text used in the Church, the version is, as it was intended to be, most useful. Indeed, such a word for word adherence to the Vulgate, described as "startling" by one critic,[11] and as

[9] See *Epis.*, 106, *ad Sunniam et Fretelam.*

[10] Mombert, *English Versions of the Bible,* p. 313. Here and in the following chapters the Vulgate enumeration of the Psalms will be followed.

[11] Isaacs in *The Bible in Its Ancient and English Versions,* ed. by Robinson, p. 194. But as Dore points out, "The version is, as it professes to be, a literal translation of the Vulgate, and in some places more accurately hands down the very words of the inspired writers, than any English translation then existing. This is owing to the Latin having been taken from earlier manuscripts than were accessible to later translators" (*Old Bibles,* p. 317).

owing to "their Balaamitish resolution" by another,[12] has, despite its inevitable drawbacks, certain compensations.

It is only fair to point out, too, that much the same complaint has been urged against the version of the Psalms in the Authorized Version; its "prosaic tone, however exact and elaborate, is so spiritless as to be willingly used by but few that are familiar with the version in the Book of Common Prayer."[13]

The verses added in Ps. 13:3 are noted, also the additional verse in Ps. 144:14, "The Lord is faithful in al his wordes, and holie in al his workes." An account of the Sapiential Books is given. Prov., chaps. 10–29, are set out in verse form with an explanation of the antithetical form in which they are couched; they are "of great elegancie, especially in the original tong, which could not be expressed in Greeke, nor Latin, much lesse in vulgar language." Chaps. 30 f. are in prose form, though it is pointed out that the section on "the Valiant Woman" is "in an exquisite kind of stile; in Tetramical verse, with perfect order and number of the Alphabet letters."

The canticles of Debbora (Judg., chap. 5), of Anna (I Kings 2:1–10), of Judith (chap. 16), those in Eccles. 3:3–8, Isa., chap. 26 and 38:9–20, and Hab., chap. 3, are all set out in verse form; so too psalm 104 as it is repeated in II Par. 16:8–36 is set out in verse form in the second edition, 1635, this being the only substantial difference between the two editions. Coverdale's Bible has sometimes been called the Treacle Bible, for he translated Jer. 8:22 to read, "Is there no triacle (treacle) in Gilead?" Since the Douay Version here read "rosen" for "triacle," it was at one time known as the "Rosen Bible."

The Prayer of Manasses and III and IV Esdras,[14] "extant in most Latin and Vulgate Bibles, are here placed after al the Canonical Books of the old Testament: because they are not in the Canon of the Divine Scriptures by the Catholique Church." No notes or Annotations are appended.

[12] Edgar, *The Bibles of England;* the expression "Balaamitish" is presumably derived from Coverdale's Dedication of his version to Henry VIII.

[13] Scrivener, *A Plain Introduction to the Criticism of the New Testament,* p. 139.

[14] The text has "the Second and Third," a misprint, as subsequent headings show. Misprints are, apart from those pointed out in the *Errata,* very rare; in fact we have noticed only one, "are" for "art" in Ecclus. 48:10.

THE ANNOTATIONS AND MARGINAL NOTES

The Annotations, or lengthy notes at the end of chapters, are few but important; for example, those on the "locusts" (Joel, chap. 1), on Christ's birth at Bethlehem (Mich., chap. 5), on the Sacrifice of the Mass (Mal., chap. 1), on the kingdom of the Messias (Isa., chap. 32), on the intercession of the saints (Isa., chap. 37, and Jer., chap. 15), on the state of virginity, fasting, and the nature of the beatific vision (Isa., chaps. 56, 58, 63), on the sign "Tau" or the sign of the cross, and on the conditional will of God (Ezech., chaps. 9 and 18), on the mysterious character of the last chapters of Ezechiel, and on Nabuchodonosor's "change" and his repentance (Dan., chap. 4). Strangely enough, there is no note on the prophecy of Emmanuel (Isa. 7:14).

In the Old Testament these Annotations are rarely controversial, that on Ps. 15:10, "Thou wilt not leave my soul in hel," being somewhat of an exception:

> How Calvin and Beza sometimes corrupt this text, always pervert the sense, and most absurdly oppose themselves against al ancient holie Fathers, concerning the Article of Christs descending in soule into that part of hel called *Limbus Patrum,* is largely noted Gen. 37.35, Acts 2.24 and 2.Pet.3.10. Only here we may not omit to advertise the reader, that some Protestant Bibles permitting the word *hel* to remaine in the text, a latter edition for *hel,* putteth *grave,* with this only note in the former place, that *this is chiefly meant of Christ, by whose Resurrection al his members have immortality.* And Acts 2.24 they repeate their new text by this paraphrase: *Thou shalt not leave me in the grave.* Wresting that which perteineth to the bodie rising from the grave, to the soule, which was not at al in the grave, altime the bodie lay there.

These Annotations and marginal notes are almost certainly from the pen of Dr. Thomas Worthington, who went to Douay in 1572 and, after returning to the English mission, suffered for more than two months the torture known as "the Pit." [15] Later he became president of the college and died in 1626. That he was the author of the Annotations is affirmed by Dodd, and a note on II Mach. 15:39 in the earlier editions of Haydock's Bible refers to "the remarks of Dr. Worthington on the six ages in the Douay Bible." Milner says that "Dr. Worthington added the long Annotations with which the Douay Bible is enriched," [16] and Ribadeneira gives in his list of Worthington's writings *Annotationes ad Vetus Testa-*

[15] *Church History,* ed. by Tierney, III, p. 156.

[16] *A Brief Account of the Life of the Late R. R. Richard Challoner,* prefixed to Challoner's *Grounds of the Old Religion,* 5th ed.

mentum, Duaci, 1609.[17] Worthington also wrote *An Anker of Christian Doctrine,* Doway, 1618.

These marginal notes and Annotations constitute, as we have remarked concerning the New Testament, a veritable catechism of Christian doctrine such as must have proved invaluable at a time when the Catholic body was for the most part deprived of pastors, and which to this day is most useful for those seeking a detailed knowledge of their religion. We need only instance the admirably concise, though abundantly documented notes on predestination, the Holy Eucharist, the sacrifice of Melchisedech and of the Mass, and the note on transubstantiation, where a striking passage is quoted from Rabbi David Kimchi on Osee 14:8: "They shal live with wheate, and spring as a vine: Manie of our Doctours (sayth he) expound this, that there shal be mutations of nature in wheat in the time of our Redeemer Christ." There are also excellent notes on schism, tradition, the judge of controversies, on divorce, vows, the intercession of the saints, purgatory, and so forth.

But the annotator seems to have begun his task on too ambitious a scale. For while there are notes on 43 out of the 150 pages devoted to Genesis, there are but 17 on the 115 pages of Exodus; indeed their number decreases steadily book by book. There are, for instance, but few on Daniel, not even on chapter 9, confessedly "one of the more obscure portions of the Sacred Text." In a "Brief Recapitulation of this strange and sacred historie" (the book of Job), the annotators explain why they have felt compelled to "contract our Annotations into the margen (this volume growing great)" (I, p. 1110).

Occasionally a note affords us a glimpse of the troubles of the times and of the difficulties with which Catholics had to contend. There was, for instance, the obvious danger of "conforming" to the "established" religion. Hence the notes on Ps. 90:5 and 118:164 (pp. 169, 232), and on Dan. 3:6: "Now in England personal presence at heretical service or sermon is a distinctive signe of conformitie to the Protestants pretended religion, because such presence is there exacted for this purpose" (p. 777).

[17] *Bibliotheca scriptorum Soc. Jesu;* cf. Gillow, *Bibliographical Dictionary of the English Catholics,* "Martin," IV, 490; Cotton, *Rhemes and Doway,* pp. 25, 88; Lewis, *A Complete History of the Several Translations of the Holy Bible and New Testament into English,* p. 291. There is a tendency, which seems baseless, to attribute the notes on the New Testament also to Worthington; a note in a copy of the Rheims New Testament of 1582 in the British Museum makes this claim; so too in the *Catalogue* of the Rylands Library, Manchester.

The spirit which animated the sixteenth-century Catholic martyrs shines forth in the notes on Job, chaps. 1 and 42: "Job stood immovable in the service of God for example to us that we fall not for anie worldlie damage, losse of dearest friendes or corporal afflictions. And blessed be God, by whose blessing we may now say: O happy English Catholiques, that patiently suffer the very same kind of tribulation. . . . God condemned the errors of Job's friends; it is, then, folly to disregard the Church's condemnations of such men as Luther, Calvin, and Beza." The note on Eccles. 10:16, "Woe to thee, O land, whose king is a child," refers of course to the miseries suffered under the Protectorate; so too that on II Mach., chap. 3, dealing with the three requisites for a good commonwealth.

The Douay theologians could never have approved the methods of government in vogue under Henry, Edward, and Elizabeth. But it is an injustice to suppose, as many have done, that they therefore advocated tyrannicide.[18] There is no trace of anything of the sort in their notes; for such fanatical notions we have to go to the framers of the Geneva Bible.

[18] So insistently were these and similar accusations repeated that even Catholics themselves at times supposed that they were well founded. Daniel O'Connell, for example, went so far as to say that he "would not remain a Catholic one hour longer, if he thought it essential to the Catholic faith to believe that it was lawful to murder Protestants, or that faith might be innocently broken with heretics. Yet such were the doctrines to be deduced from the Rhemish Testament." That O'Connell, however, had little or no personal knowledge of the subject appears in the account he proceeded to give of the origin of the Rheims-Douay Version and its notes: "An English version of the New Testament containing *some* of the notes in question was published at Rheims in the year 1582, through the agency, chiefly of Dr. Allen, Bristow, Sanders, Reynolds, all distinguished for animosity to Elizabeth. . . . Several notes in the Douay version (1609–10) were inserted, breathing the same spirit of hatred to the religion and government then established in England. . . . The notes of the New Testament were undoubtedly intended to prepare the public for the invasion meditated by Philip II. . . . They were in unison with the celebrated sentence and declaration of Pope Sixtus Quintus . . . which designated Elizabeth as an usurper and unjust ruler, who ought to be deposed; and as an heretic and schismatic; whom it was not only lawful but commendable to destroy. This document was circulated in England, accompanied by an admonition of Cardinal Allen to the same effect. . . . It is perfectly clear, therefore, that the notes had their origin in the political hatreds of those unhappy times, of which religion was made the degraded instrument on both sides. If we are to blush for the frenzy of priests who contaminated the word of God by their atrocious interpretations, must not the Protestants blush for tortures. . . . Terrible crimes were perpetrated, unChristian doctrines were promulgated, by both the contending parties. This is a fact which admits of no dispute" (*Dublin Evening Post,* December 1 and 7, quoted by McGhee, *Complete Notes of the Douay Bible and the Rhemish New Testament,* p. xxvi). Cf. Jean Petit, *Question du tyrannicide au commencement du XVe siècle,* ed. by A. Covelle, 1932.

The *locus classicus* in the Bible on this subject is I Sam., chap. 8, where the people demand a king and thereby incurred the divine displeasure; on this the words of our annotators call for careful consideration. They point out that:

> a) Kinges do oftentimes abuse their power by reason of their high dignitie and little fear of controlment, but unjustly and unlawfully. [SS. Cyprian, Jerome, and Gregory are quoted to this effect.] (b) Kinges have great prerogatives, besides and above, but never contrary to the law; (c) albeit they cannot take their subjectes landes or goodes, neither for themselves nor to geve to their servantes at their pleasure; yet in divers cases subjects are bound to contribute of their private goodes to supplie the necessitie of the King, or of the commonwealth, as by nature every part must suffer damage in defence of the principal member, or whole bodie. And if anie refuse to do so they may justly be compelled. (d) Furthermore in case Kinges or other Princes commit excesses, and oppresse their subjectes, yet are they not by and by to be deposed by the people nor commonwealth, but must be tolerated with patience, peace, and meeknes, til God by his sovereign authoritie, left in his Church, dispose of them, which his divine wisdom and goodnes often deferreth to do . . . because he wil punish the sinnes of the people by suffering evil princes to reigne, cf. ver. 18, Job xxxiv.30, and St. Thomas, *Summa Theol.* 2-2.xii.art.2 and other schole Doctors.

God, they point out, Himself deposed Saul for transgressing His law (I Kings 13:13 f.) and disobeying his commandment (chap. 15), and Himself appointed another king "by the ministrie of Samuel" (chap. 16). There is no doubt, however, that had Elizabeth still been on the throne, she would have warmly resented the statement that Debbora, though a prophetess, yet "exercised no jurisdiction in anie causes, for that belonged to the councel of priestes where the High Priest was the Chief Judge."

The annotators must have smiled when they wrote: "Those that kepe innes or ailehouses are always talking, as willing to please al, but in much talking wanteth not sinne" (on Ecclus. 26:28); while concerning Jacob's kissing Rachel at the well we read that "St. Augustin commendeth familiar kissing of kinsfolk and frendes as a laudable custome in some countries. It is nowhere more civil and modest then in England" (on Gen. 29:11).

The more we reflect on the terrible nature of the times through which they were passing, the exile they had to endure, the insults to which they had to submit, and the blasphemous things said about the age-old faith of the Church, the more we are impressed by the self-restraint exercised by these annotators. The religious and political controversies of the time of course find an echo; but how faint an echo it is! The divorce of Henry VIII was, it is true, then a matter of past history; but how few commentators would have resisted the temptation "to point the moral and adorn the tale" apropos of Deut. 24:1? It is the same with the note on Deut. 25:5, of marrying the deceased brother's wife, also on Jos. 2:3, where the note deals with the relation between Church and State as regards spiritual matters. "Men," they say, "may jeer at Catholics for their beliefs and dub them Papists, yet the Psalmist said, 'I spake of thy testimonies in the sight of kings'" (Ps. 118:46); it is then no "base or contemptible thing to be a Christian, to be Catholiques, to be Papistes. No, al these and the like are honorable and glorious titles; importing the true service of Christ; in unitie of the Catholique Church; and spiritual participation with the visible head therof, Christs Vicar in earth."

But alas! "The Douay Bible is a forgotten book," as a recent writer has said.[19] And while nothing would be gained by reprinting the now obsolete translation, yet anyone devoting his leisure to republishing these undeservedly maligned notes and Annotations would be doing a signal service to the Catholic body.

SUPPLEMENTARY PIECES

One very useful feature of these volumes is the series of summaries of the various states through which God's created world, His Church, and His revelation have passed:

a) A Briefe Remonstrance of the State of the Church, and the Face of Religion in the First Age of the world. From the Creation to Noes floud: the space of 1656 yeares, pp. 29–35; (b) The Continuance of the Church and religion in the Second Age of the world. From Noes floud to Abrahams going forth of his countrie. The space of 368 yeares, pp. 47–50; (c) in the Third Age, from Abrahams going forth of Chaldea to the passing of Israel out of Egypt. The space of 430 yeares, pp. 196–206; (d) in the Fourth Age, from the parting of Israel out of Egypt to the fundation of the Temple. The space of 480 yeares, pp. 701–17; (e) in the Fifth Age, from the fundation of the Temple to the Captivitie in Babylon. The space of 530 yeares, pp. 934–43; (f) in the Sixth Age, from the Captivitie in Babylon to the coming of our Saviour, nere the space of 640 yeares, Vol. II, pp. 988–1004.[20]

Apropos of the second age we are given a vivid account of the state of religion on the Continent and in England as a result of the so-called Reformation:

19 Isaacs, in *The Bible in Its Ancient and English Versions.*

20 These are summarized in "An Historical Table of the Times, Special Persons, most Notable Things, and Canonical Bookes of the Old Testament," in Vol. II, pp. 1073–96.

Name we like countries, cities, and townes in these parts of Europe where Luther's scholers have set their feet, consider the forme of Religion and opinions which they hold, and we shal see as unorderlie beginnings and as horrible dissenseions in heresies (which S. Hierom calleth the Idols of the New Testament) as the ancient Fathers have descryed in Paganisme. For Lutherans or Protestants having no lawful generation, but proceeding of bastards race, upstarts of unknown progenie, are no lesse at discord among themselves, only agreeing against Catholikes, like syncretisantes against their common enemies, or Herod, Pilate, and the Jewes against Christ. And in England alone are divers Sects without possible meanes to agree in one. For albeit the civil state endeavoureth prudently and seriously to bring al to uniformitie, at least in publike shew, yet they are but like manie faces under one hood, everie sort keeping their owne opinions; yea almost everie Preacher and meane scholer (to say nothing of artificers and common Ministers) arrogating to be his owne Judge, contemneth to stand to Luther or Calvin, to Geneva or Parliament, to Convocation or Synod of their owne, but to his owne understanding and interpretation of holie Scripture. Nor yet to that alwayes; for when he is pressed with that he once said, he wil forget it, or eat his owne worde, if he have not written it, or that you have readie witness against him, so hard it is to make a deceived Protestant or Puritan confesse that he is convinced, except by very pregnant meanes you can first cast out of him, or bind fast the spirit of presumption, dissention, and contention; whereas the simplest Catholike in the world hath the selfe-same faith in al points with the whole Church, in which he remaineth, and upon whose judgement he dependeth.

After the account of the sixth age is a prayer: "Jesus, Redeemer, correct us in errors, gather the dispersed, conserve them that are and shal be gathered, make al one flock in one fold under one Pastour, thy selfe JESUS Christ. To whom with the Father, and the Holie Ghost be al thanks, praise, honour, and glorie, now and for ever and ever. Amen."

The volume closes with a "Table of the Epistles taken forth of the Old Testament upon certayne Festival days," "An Historical Table of the Times, Special Persons, most Notable Things, and Canonical Books of the Old Testament," and "A Table of the chiefe Contents of the Text and Annotations of the Old Testament." On the last page of all: "You may please (curteous reader) to amend the more especial errors happened in this Edition, by reading thus:" and there follow twelve slight corrections to be made in Vol. I and three in Vol. II. "We have also found some other faultes of lesse importance; and feare there may be more. But we trust the reader may easely correct them, as they occurre."

Though it is the fashion to speak of this edition as cumbersome, yet nothing can be further from the truth. The two small, compact quarto volumes are exceedingly neat and handy; they compare most favorably in the printing and general appearance with any of the volumes then appearing. No edition we have ever handled, whether of Cranmer's Bible, or Matthew's, or Taverner's, or the Bishops', or even of the much-vaunted Geneva Bibles, can vie with them.[21]

THE SECOND EDITION

A second edition of the Douay Old Testament appeared in 1635, published by John Cousturier, Rouen. The spelling differs slightly, but text, marginal notes, and Annotations are the same. The pages are now in double black lines at the top and sides; the numbering of the pages differs since the first edition has 41 lines, the second 45 lines, to the page. In this edition the "Historical Table" and "The Particular Table" are not in such good type as in the first edition, nor are the pages after 1018 numbered. The *Censura* of the three former professors in the college at Rheims, given at the end of the second volume of the first edition, is here repeated. It is followed by a fairly long list of *Errata,* ending with: "We have also found some other faults of lesse importance, and feare there may be more. But we trust the Reader may easily correct them as they occurre, and beseech those that shal set out the next Edition carefully to compare the text with the Latine." But there was no later edition of the Douay Old Testament until Challoner's revision appeared in 1750, nor has the text of the original Douay Version ever since been reprinted.

BIBLIOGRAPHY

A Brief History of the Versions of the Bible of the English and Roman Churches, Dublin, 1830.

Eason, Charles. *The Circulation of the Douay Bible in Ireland,* London, 1931.

Gratet-Duplessis, P. A. *Notice sur une traduction de l'Écriture sainte designée ordinairement sous le titre de Bible de Douai et Nouveau Testament de Rheims,* 1841.

The Douay Bible. Being remarks on what is said by authority in regard to it, 1931.

Shea, J. G. *A Bibliographical Account of the Catholic Bibles, Testaments . . . translated from the Latin Vulgate and printed in the United States,* 1859.

Sheahan, J. F. *The English in English Bibles,* Poughkeepsie, N.Y.

[21] Many will, perhaps, object to this statement, but probably they are acquainted only with old, shabby, and worn-out second-hand editions. If they could get a glimpse of a clean, well-bound copy, they will marvel at the fineness of the paper (2,240 pages) and the beauty of the type.

In Periodical Literature

Hügel, F. von. "The Church and the Bible," in the *Dublin Review*, CXV (1894), 313–41; CXVI (1895), 306–37; CXVII (1895), 275–304.

Pope, Hugh. "The Origin of the Douay Bible," in the *Dublin Review*, CXLVII (1910), 97–118.

———. "The Rheims Version of the New Testament," in the *Dublin Review*, CLII (1913), 276–300; in *The Library*, March to June, 1940; and in the *Downside Review*, October, 1944.

———. "The Rheims Version of the New Testament: the hostile reception accorded to it," in the *Clergy Review*, XVII (1939), 311–25.

———. "Some Omissions in the Rheims-Douay Version," in the *Clergy Review*, XIX (1940), 112–21.

Russell, C. "The Bible and the Reformation," in the *Dublin Review*, III (1837), 428–52.

Wiseman, Nicholas. "Catholic Versions of Scripture," in the *Dublin Review*, II (1837), 475–92; and in *Essays on Various Subjects*, vol. 1.

CHAPTER XX

The Authorized Version, or King James Bible, 1611

ORIGIN OF THE VERSION

ALREADY during the reign of Queen Elizabeth the necessity of a new translation of the Bible was felt, as appears from a document attributed to Whitgift: "An Act for the reducings of the diversities of Bibles now extant in the Englishe tongue to one seteld vulgar translated from the originall." This, say the petitioners, is necessary

> for the avoydinge of the multiplicitie of errors, that are rashly conceaved by the inferior and vulgar sort by the varietie of the translacions of the Bible to the most daungerous increase of papistrie and atheisme. . . . But while everybody has long desired such a fresh version, the absence of any machinery whereby the Universities could be compelled to help in the necessary work has hitherto proved an insuperable difficulty, neither has it been found possible to provide for the charges involved. The Bishops are therefore to be empowered to compel the Universities to assist in the task of its production.[1]

Though nothing came of this petition at the time, when during the Hampton Court Conference, January, 1604, Rainolds the Puritan urged the need of a fresh translation owing to the defective character of the Bishops' Bible then in use,[2] James welcomed the project: [3] "I profess,"

[1] Pollard, *Records of the English Bible,* pp. 329–34; Fuller, *The Church History of Britain from the Birth of Jesus Christ untill the year 1648,* IV, 171 ff.; Eadie, *The English Bible,* II, 180; Anderson, *Annals of the English Bible,* p. 477.

[2] John Rainolds (1549–1607) was a Puritan, Calvinistic controversialist. At one time he held a lectureship at Oxford for the "Confutation of Romish tenets," and wrote *A Defence of the Judgment of the Reformed Churches* (in favor of divorce), 1609; *The Summe of the Conference betwene John Rainoldes and John Hart,* London, 1584; *De Romanae ecclesiae idololatria in cultu sanctorum,* Oxford, 1596. Rainolds formed one of the company of revisers and he seems to have secured the correction of the three instances he had adduced at Hampton Court of renderings "corrupt and not answering to the truth of the originals": "bordereth" (Gal. 4:25) was, he maintained, a mistranslation;

he said, "I could never yet see a Bible wel translated in English; but I think, that of all, that of Geneva is the worst. I wish some special pains were taken for an uniform translation; which should be done by the best-learned men in both Universities, then reviewed by the Bishops, presented to the Privy Council, lastly ratified by Royal authority, to be read in the whole church, and none other." When Bancroft suggested the omission of all notes, James agreed, "for in the Geneva translation, some notes are partial, untrue, seditious, and savouring of traitorous conceits," and he naively instanced those on Exod. 1:19 and II Chron. 15:16, which seemed to teach that disobedience to kings was lawful. He further maintained that translators under Henry VIII were under the influence of Erasmus and Münster, the Genevans under that of Beza, while the Bishops' Bible was full of errors through neglect of the Hebrew original and undue adherence to the Greek version.[4] Later the King presented a

Ps. 105:28 should read, "were *not* disobedient"; while the Vulgate *placavit* of Ps. 106:30 should be rendered, "exercised judgment." These were trifling instances on which to base an accusation of general corruption in the Bishops' Bible, which was then used in churches, indeed "authorized." James laughingly assured Rainolds that these mistakes had been set right long since, though he failed to say when or in which editions; while Bancroft sneeringly remarked that "if every man's humour should be followed, there would be no end of translating." These mistranslations adduced by Rainolds were all corrected in the resulting version.

[3] James had some claim to a hearing in matters theological, for according to Richard Montagu, bishop of Winchester, who published the King's *Collected Works,* 1616, his *Paraphrase on the Book of Revelation* was written "before hee was twenty yeeres of age." He had also translated the Psalter in whole or in part: *The Psalmes of King David,* translated by King James, London, 1647. Charles I authorized the printer to publish "this translation of the Psalmes (whereof our late deare Father was the Author)." The engraved title page depicts David and James receiving the Psalms from on high. There exists also *A Metrical Version of the Psalms* signed in places "J.R.D.S.," or "Jacobus Rex Dominus Scotorum"; but the psalms in this version "have scarcely any resemblance to *The Psalmes of King David,* translated by James I, published in 1631, and which are (?) by William Alexander of Menslie, Earl of Stirling" (see *Letters and Journals of R. Baillie,* ed. by S. Laing, III, 530). See also Warner and Gilson, *Catalogue of the Western Manuscripts in the Old Royal and King's Collections in the British Museum,* II, 293.

[4] *The Summe and Substance . . . of the Conference . . . at Hampton Court,* contracted by William Barlow, 1604. Barlow, then dean of Chester, was one of the translators for the King James's Version, receiving in reward the bishopric of Lincoln. According to Cardwell (*A History of the Conferences . . . 1558–1690,* pp. 213 f.), it was James himself who proposed "that a translation be made of the whole Bible, as consonant as can be to the original Hebrew and Greek; and this to be set out and printed without any marginal notes, and [it] only to be read in all Churches of England in time of Divine Service." The same is emphatically stated by the translators in their Address to the Reader: "For the very historical truth is, that upon the importunate petitions of the Puritans at his Majesty's coming to this crown, the conference at Hampton Court having been appointed for hearing their complaints, when by force of reason they were put

list, presumably suggested to him, of fifty-four men qualified for the work; but various causes reduced their number to forty-seven.

THE RULES FOR REVISION

The fourteen rules drawn up, apparently by James himself,[5] for the guidance of the revisers may thus be briefly summarized:

1. The Bishops' Bible to be followed "and as little altered as the original will permit."

2. The proper names "to be retained as near as may be . . . as vulgarly used."

3. Old ecclesiastical words not to be changed, "as the word 'Church' not to be translated 'congregation.'"[6]

4. Words of varying interpretations to be rendered in accordance with patristic tradition and the analogy of faith.

5. No change to be made in the chapter divisions.

6. No notes except to explain Hebrew or Greek words.

7. Cross references to be inserted.

8. As each reviser completes the portion assigned to him, all his company should compare results and decide on the rendering to be chosen.

9. The completed work of each company to be sent to the other companies "to be considered of seriously and judiciously; for, his Majesty is very careful in this point."

10. Doubts thence arising to be settled "at the general meeting of the chief persons of each company, at the end of the work."

11. In really obscure passages the help of other learned people is to be sought.

12. The bishops are to look for men capable of assisting in the work.

13. The directors to be the deans of Westminster and Chester and the regius professors of Hebrew and Greek.

14. "These translations to be used when they agree better with the

from all other grounds, they had recourse at the last to this shift, that they could not with good conscience subscribe to the Communion book, since it contained the Bible as it was there translated, which was, as they said, a most corrupt translation. And although this was judged to be but a very poor and empty shift, yet did his Majesty begin to bethink himself of the good that might ensue by a new translation, and presently after gave order for this translation which is now presented unto thee."

[5] See Fuller, *op. cit.,* IV, 229; Lewis, *A Complete History of the Several Translations of the Holy Bible and New Testament, etc., into English,* p. 310; Eadie, *op. cit.,* II, 190–92.

[6] "Church" instead of "congregation" is consistently retained in A.V. and R.V., though the latter has "congregation" in the margin in Matt. 18:17.

text than the Bishops' Bible: namely, Tindal's, Matthew's, Coverdale's, Whitchurch's,[7] the Geneva."

Rule 2, that the proper names "be retained as near as may be . . . as vulgarly used," was observed in the case of the Old Testament, the extravagances of some previous translators being avoided. But in the New Testament these proper names stand in the familiar form derived from the Vulgate through the Greek; e.g., "Elias" instead of "Elijah" (Matt. 11:14 and 17:3–12); and "Jesus" instead of "Joshua" (Heb. 4:8), though Tyndale, Cranmer, Geneva, and R.V. have "Joshua."

Though rule 8 provided for a certain amount of collaboration, yet, as Scrivener says, "Our very meagre information respecting the progress of the translators gives us no great reason to believe that this wholesome desire was carried out in practice, while internal evidence points decidedly to the contrary conclusion"; the version of the Psalms is, he adds, a case in point, for it is "prosaic, and however exact and elaborate, spiritless."

THE MODE OF PROCEDURE ADOPTED BY THE REVISERS [8]

In his Address to the Reader,[9] Dr. Smith says that, unlike the Septuagint version, which, so legend has it, was the work of but seventy days,

> the present version hath not bene hudled up in 72 dayes, but hath cost the workemen, as light as it seemeth, the paines of twise seven times seventie two dayes and more. . . . Neither did we thinke much [10] to consult the Translators or Commentators, *Chaldee, Hebrewe, Syrian, Greeke, or Latin,* no nor the *Spanish, French, Italian or Dutch;* neither did we disdaine to revise that which we had done, and to bring back to the anvil that which we had hammered: but having and using as great helpes as were needfull, and fearing no reproch for slownesse, nor coveting praise for expedition, we have at the length, through the good hand of the Lord upon us, brought the worke to that passe that you see.[11]

[7] "Whitchurch" stands for the Great Bible, of which he published the fifth edition in 1541, the second quarto edition in 1550, and others.

[8] For further details on the mode of procedure adopted, see Mombert, *English Versions of the Bible,* pp. 356 f.

[9] Given in full by Scrivener, *A Plain Introduction to the Criticism of the New Testament,* pp. 267–304.

[10] If "much" qualifies "consult" and not "think," we should gather that they did consult them, but not very much.

[11] The pedantic and turgid style of this composition is in startling contrast with that of the version itself as well as with the much maligned Rhemish Preface. And while it is true that the Rheims Version has many quaint phases, yet Dr. Smith himself writes of "a Panary of wholesome food against fenowed traditions," even calling the Holy Spirit "the Enditer of the Bible." For obsolete words, see below.

The revisers were divided into three groups of two companies each, sitting at Westminster, Oxford, and Cambridge. At the head of one group comprising ten members, responsible for the revision of Genesis to I Chronicles (exclusively), was Lancelot Andrews; Barlow, subsequently bishop of Lincoln and historian of the Hampton Court Conference, presided over the second Westminster group of seven, who dealt with the epistles in the New Testament. At Cambridge, Dr. Liveley presided over a company of eight members, who translated from I Chronicles to Ecclesiastes; the other company, one of whose seven members was Dr. Bois, was occupied with the Apocrypha. At Oxford the revision of the prophets was entrusted to a company of seven under the presidency of Harding, who had among his assistants Rainolds the Puritan, who first urged the idea of a fresh version, and Miles Smith, one of the final revisers and author of the Preface; Sir Henry Savile, editor of the Works of St. Chrysostom, was the most prominent of the eight members of the second company at Oxford, which dealt with the Gospels, Acts, and Apocalypse.[12]

Unfortunately we know very little about the methods actually adopted by the revisers. As Scrivener says: "Never was an enterprise like the production of our Authorized Version carried out with less knowledge handed down to posterity of the labourers, their method and order of working." [13] Their work did not begin before 1607 and was completed in less than three years. It was, of course, uneven in character; it is generally agreed that the Pentateuch, historical books, and the prophets were well done, Job and the Psalms not so well done, the epistles poorly done, and the Apocrypha worst of all.[14] The members were remunerated at the rate of thirty shillings a week, about £15 at present values.[15]

[12] The list is given, with variations, in all the authorities: Burnet, *History of the Reformation,* V, 559 ff.; Wilkins, *Concilia,* IV, 407 f.; Fuller, *op. cit.,* IV, 227; Pollard, *op. cit.,* 37–64; Thomas Smith, *Memoirs of the Translators of the Authorized Version,* 1827. The list is appended at the end of this chapter. Westcott (*A General View of the History of the English Bible,* pp. 342–50) gives "Notes about the Translators, July 22, 1604," from a MS. in Lambeth Library.

[13] *Op. cit.,* p. 9.

[14] Cf. Mombert, *op. cit.,* pp. 375, 379. "The company of Translators to whom these books were assigned took no sort of pains to assimilate their portion of the work to that executed by the others" (Scrivener, Introduction to the *Paragraph Bible,* p. xxxvii).

[15] Cf. Mombert, *op. cit.,* p. 359. In 1651 Matthew Barker claimed that his father, Robert Barker, "paid for the amended or corrected translation of the Bible £3500," at least £35,000 at present values. For the efforts made by King James and Bishop Bancroft to raise the requisite funds, see Pollard, *op. cit.,* pp. 331–34.

THE TITLE PAGE AND PREFACE

The result of the extensive labors of the revisers appeared in 1611. The title page of the new version reads as follows: *The Holy Bible, Conteyning the Old Testament and the New: Newly Translated out of the Originall tongues, with the former Translations diligently compared and revised, by his Majesties speciall commandement. Appointed to be read in Churches. Imprinted at London by Robert Barker, Printer to the Kings most Excellent Majestie. Anno Dom. 1611.* On either side stand Moses and Aaron; in the four corners are the Evangelists; at the top the name of God is in Hebrew letters, with the sun and moon on either side. Above is the Paschal Lamb with the apostles; below is a pelican. The New Testament is entitled: *The Newe Testament of our Lord and Savior Jesus Christ, Newly translated out of the Originall Greeke; and with the former Translations diligently compared and revised, by His Majesties speciall Commandement. Imprinted at London by Robert Barker, Printer to the Kings most Excellent Majestie. Anno Dom. 1611. cum Privilegio.*

The expression "newly translated" shows that we are in the presence of a fresh version, in spite of rule 1, which demanded merely a revision of the Bishops' Bible. The version is not said to be "authorized"; yet "appointed to be read in Churches" (not on the title page of the New Testament) could be interpreted to mean that as successor to the Bishops' Bible, which was thus appointed, it might be regarded as "authorized"; moreover the Bishops' Bible was the legitimate successor of the expressly "authorized" Great Bible.[16]

The lengthy Preface, not an inspiring document and omitted in most editions,[17] was the work of Miles Smith. In it, after complaining of the hostile attitude of certain people towards the scheme, he dwells on the

[16] Cf. L. Gruber, *The Version of 1611. Propriety of calling it "Authorized Version,"* 1914; H. R. Willoughby, *The First Authorized English Bible and the Cranmer Preface,* 1942.

[17] Yet Scrivener speaks of "this noble Preface," adding that in "spite of the quaintness of its style and the old fashion of its learning, it deserves no meaner epithet" (*A Plain Introduction to the Criticism of the New Testament* [1884], p. 39). The lengthy Preface has been reproduced by Pollard, *op. cit.,* pp. 340–77; and Dore, *Old Bibles,* Appendix, pp. 355–78. An exact reprint of the original edition was published in 1870, and another by the S.P.C.K. in 1870 and 1880, and another by Simpkins, Marshall and Co., 1911. See E. J. Goodspeed, *The Translators to the Reader: Preface to King James's Version,* 1935; Scrivener, *op. cit.,* pp. 267–304.

need for vernacular versions, instancing their use by the early Church, "even in the Church of Rome, then a true Church," which even now has at length awakened to the same need and produced a version the framers of which "are not ashamed to confesse that wee forced them to translate it into English, against their wills"—a wholly unjustifiable statement many times repeated. The Rhemists' Preface of course comes in for criticism, so too the attitude of the Puritans at the Hampton Court Conference. These latter, he says, have no right to complain of the version now presented,

since they were the principall motives of it, and therefore ought least to quarrell it: for the very Historicall trueth is, that upon the importunate petitions of the Puritanes, at his Majesties coming to this Crowne, the Conference at Hampton having bene appointed for hearing their complaints: when by force of reason they were put from all other grounds, they had recourse at the last, to this shift, that they could not with good conscience subscribe to the Communion booke, since it maintained the Bible as it was there translated, which was, as they said, a most corrupt translation.

Then reverting to the Rhemists' Preface, their translation, and the much-vaunted "vulgar Latin," Miles Smith insists that Thomas James's *Bellum papale* has abundantly shown the extent of the corruption of the latter. While defending the revisers' decision not always to use the same English equivalent for the same word in the original, Dr. Smith takes occasion to comment on the Puritan change of "Church" into "congregation," and others, and the Rhemists' retention of Latin words "whereof their late translation is full, and that of purpose to darken the sence, so that since they must needs translate the Bible, yet by the language thereof it may bee kept from being understood"—another unjustifiable statement.

The Address to King James, which follows and which is retained in modern editions, is couched in the then customary language of fulsome praise: "Upon the setting of that bright Occidental Star, Queen Elizabeth," men feared lest religious chaos should darken the land, but "the appearance of Your Majesty, as of the *Sun* in his strength," dissipated their fears. At the close they pray that the King will support them in the work they have completed "so that if, on the one side, we shall be traduced by Popish persons at home or abroad" who "desire still to keep the people in ignorance and darkness; or if, on the other side, we be maligned by selfconceited brethren, . . . we may rest secure."

SOURCES USED BY THE REVISERS

The statement in the Preface that the revisers "consulted the Translators or Commentators" (see note 10) as well as the originals is borne out by "an analysis of passages of the translation and of the alternative renderings offered in the margin [which show] that the authorities most frequently followed were Beza in the New Testament (both for text and for interpretation), and in the Old Testament the Latin versions of Junius and Tremellius, Münster, Leo Jud, and Pagninus. The influence of the Vulgate was exercised mainly through the Rhemish version."[18] The revisers depended much on Pagninus; Westcott concludes from an examination of Isaias, chapter 53, that seven-eighths of the changes made from the Bishops' Bible in that chapter are derived from the Genevan version, in conjunction or not with Pagninus or Tremellius.[19] Tremellius' version (1575–79) is particularly evident in the Hagiographa, especially in the Psalms; that of Junius in the Apocrypha, with the difficult renderings in II Para. 20:1 and Job 34:33 being traceable to Tremellius, as also the marginal readings in Mark 1:34, Luke 4:41, and Acts 1:8. We must add to the above sources the Complutensian Polyglot and the version of Arias Montanus, 1569–72.

Though rule 1 had laid down that the Bishop's Bible was to be followed as nearly as possible, the revisers seem to have preferred the Genevan and Rhemish versions;[20] to this latter version, as Ellicott says, "though it was not in the list of their authorities, they were certainly more than occasionally indebted. And commonly with advantage, —as the Rhemish, with all its faults and asperities, was a translation of a really good Version, and, at any rate, is very affluent in its vocabulary,

[18] Mombert, *op. cit.,* 377 f. Cf. Eadie, *op. cit.,* II, 208–14; Westcott, *History of the English Bible,* 2nd ed., pp. 268–89; *idem, A General View of the History of the English Bible,* 3rd ed. (1905), pp. 261 ff.

[19] The following are renderings almost wholly derived from Pagninus: "hath believed" and "revealed" (Isa. 53:1); "no form of comeliness" (verse 2); "rejected of men . . . a man of sorrows, and acquainted with grief: and we hid as it were *our* faces from him; he was despised and we esteemed him not" (verse 3).

[20] A collation by Moulton (*History of the English Bible* [1887], pp. 202–206) shows that every verse in Isa. 54:11–17 resembles far more closely the Rhemish version than the Genevan version; in Rom. 12:6–15, verses 7 f. are akin to the Genevan, verses 11 f. combine the Genevan and Rhemish versions, and the influence of the latter is clear both here and in verse 6; verse 13 follows the Bishops' Bible, verse 15 the Genevan. Yet Scrivener maintains that "particular attention was paid to the Bishops' Bible, which was the basis of the Authorised Version" (*op. cit.,* p. 57).

and very useful in converting Latin words into English service."[21] Of this relationship between the Rheims Version and the Authorized Version, Westcott says that "it is most worthy of notice that the Genevan and Rhemish versions, representing as they do the opposite extremes of opinion, contributed most largely of all to the changes which the revisers produced. . . . The use of the Rhemish version is so remarkable that it may be well to add more unequivocal proofs of its reality."[22] He continues: "The changes of words from the Bishops' Bible are far more frequent, and of those numbers introduce phrases identical with those used in the Rhemish version."[23]

In fact it must be acknowledged that the Authorized Version is at times distinctly inferior to Rheims, as Carleton has shown in detail: e.g., "communication" (A.V.) for "talk" (Matt. 5:37); "despitefully use you" for "persecute you" ((5:44); "vain repetition" (6:7) is an interpretation, not a translation. In Matt. 6:12, 14, A.V. is inconsistent, having

[21] Ellicott, *Considerations on the Revision of the English Version of the New Testament,* p. 91. The relationship between the Authorized Version and Rheims Version of the New Testament has been worked out in detail by J. G. Carleton, *The Part of Rheims in the Making of the English Bible,* Oxford, 1902.

[22] *A General View of the History of the English Bible,* pp. 270 ff. He instances thirteen renderings taken over from the Rheims Version in the first thirteen chapters of Romans: "if by any means" (1:10); "not have you ignorant" (1:13); "changed (the glory)" (1:23); "revelation" (2:5); "glory, honour and peace to every (man) that worketh good" (2:10); "for not the hearers of the law are just" (2:13); "the work (of the law)" (2:15); "why (yet) am I also judged as a sinner?" (3:7); "and not only so" (5:3); "but not as the offence, so also . . ." (5:15); "provoke to emulation" (11:14); "(wise) in your own conceits" (12:16); "(owe) no man anything" (13:8). To these we must add the following: Bishops' Bible, "betrothed"; Rheims, "spoused"; A.V., "espoused" (Matt. 1:18); Bishops' Bible, "a citie of Jurie"; Rheims, "of Juda"; A.V., "of Judaea" (2:1); Bishops' Bible, "babblings"; Rheims and A.V., "much speaking."

[23] Alternative renderings suggested in the A.V. margin give the same results, though mainly in the New Testament, the revision of which was based on a careful study of the Bishops' Bible, 1572, the Greek text, Beza's text and his version, and also the versions of Geneva and Rheims, with the result that of thirty-seven marginal alterations in the first nine chapters of Mark, nearly half are due to Geneva, seven to Rheims (1:4; 3:5; 6:20; 7:2, 4, 9, 26; 9:18).

Westcott (*op. cit.,* pp. 373 f.) points out eleven changes in I John made by the revisers of the Authorized Version through the influence of the Rheims Version: "acknowledge" now becomes "confess" (1:9); "he that obtaineth grace for us" is changed to "a propitiation" (2:2 and 4:10); "fulfilleth" becomes "he that doeth" (2:17); "deceive" is now "seduce" (2:26); "be bold" becomes "have confidence" (2:28; 3:21; 5:14); "manslayer" is changed to "murderer" (3:15); and "have a mind to" becomes "understanding" (5:20). See also Bosworth, *The Gothic and Anglo-Saxon Gospels in Parallel Columns with the Versions of Wycliffe and Tyndale,* pp. xxviii f.

"our debts" in verse 12, but "trespasses" in verse 14; but neither is Rheims consistent here, having "debts" in verse 12, but "offences" in verse 14. "Low estate . . . low degree" (Luke 1:48, 52) seem like a deliberate avoidance of the word humble; in verse 72 of the same, "to perform the mercy promised," "the" and "promised" should not have been inserted. "Abiding in the field" (Luke 2:8) is inadequate. "When the day of Pentecost was *fully* come" (Acts 2:1) is an unnecessary amplification.[24] Even the Latinisms of Rheims exercised an influence on the Authorized Version, so much so that the displeasing participial constructions reappear: Matt. 1:10; Mark 7:15; 13:36; 16:3; etc.;[25] yet A.V. has at times profited by the excessive literalism of Rheims: Luke 8:14; Acts 19:32; Rom. 1:5; etc.[26]

BEZA'S INFLUENCE ON THE VERSION.

Apart, however, from these more or less subsidiary sources, it remains true that "our present English Version was based upon the Bishops' Bible of 1568, and that upon Cranmer's of 1539, which was a new edition of Matthew's Bible of 1537, partly from Coverdale, but chiefly from Tyndale; in other words, that our present authorised translation is mainly that of Tyndale." Yet Beza's influence was paramount, as in the case of the ultimate formation of the Genevan version. His version, Scrivener continues, was "the latest and the most excellent of the several Latin Translations executed in the sixteenth century and must have lain open before the Translators throughout the whole course of their labours; it has led them into some of the most conspicuous errors that occur in their text"; he instances II Chron. 20:1; Job 34:33; Mark 1:34; Luke 4:41; Acts 1:8; Rom. 11:17; I Cor. 4:9.[27] The same influence

is just as perceptible in the case of their choice between various readings; the variation approved by Beza is set in the text, that of the others is mostly banished to the margin. On certain occasions, it may be, the Translators yielded too much to Beza's somewhat arbitrary decisions; but they lived at a time when his name was the very highest among Reformed theologians, when means for arriving at an

[24] Cf. Carleton, *op. cit.*, pp. 44 ff.

[25] *Ibid.*, pp. 32 ff.; cf. Mark 4:12, "be converted" instead of "turn," though R.V. reverts to "turn"; see also Matt. 17:16 f.; Luke 6:49; 19:23.

[26] *Ibid.*, pp. 58–83.

[27] Scrivener, *A Plain Introduction to the Criticism of the New Testament* (1884), pp. 37, 44, 57.

independent judgement were few and scattered, and when the first principles of textual criticism had yet to be gathered from a long process of painful induction. His [Beza's] most obvious and glaring errors their good sense easily enabled them to avoid.[28]

The revisers depended on Beza's fourth edition of his Greek Testament (1598), "more esteemed than the fifth, the product of his extreme old age." [29] In 81 out of 131 passages he has examined, Scrivener found that they preferred Beza to Stephens; on 21 occasions they chose to follow Stephens, and 29 times both these authorities are set aside in favor of readings adopted by either the Complutensian, or Erasmus, or the Vulgate.[30]

THE GREEK TEXT USED FOR THE NEW TESTAMENT

The value of any translation must, of course, depend on the value of the original text on which it is based. The Old Testament was translated directly from the Hebrew with the assistance of the translations mentioned above. But the New Testament presented a very different problem. For it seems certain that the translators relied on the Greek text as furnished by the fourth editions of Beza and Stephens, 1598 and 1557 respectively; these being really the same as Beza's third edition, 1588, and Stephens' Greek Testament of 1550. But neither Beza nor Stephens had paid any real attention to MSS. evidence; and since Stephens' Greek text was based on Erasmus' fourth edition, this latter may be justly regarded as the parent of the Greek text used by King James's revisers of

[28] *Idem, Supplement to the Authorised Version,* p. 72. While acknowledging that he "cannot rebut what Campbell (*Preliminary Discussions,* X, parts 4 and 5) has advanced to prove the gross partiality of Beza," Scrivener adds: "It is but equitable for us to bear in mind that the principles of sacred criticism were so little settled in his age that a strong theological bias might very possibly be allowed to influence his translations of Scripture without any serious imputation on his moral honesty" (*Ibid.,* p. 60). There is no need to insist on Beza's blatant Calvinism; commenting on Jas. 1:13 he says: "The Lord leadeth into temptation those whom he permitteth to Satan's arbitrament, or into whom rather he leadeth or bringeth Satan himself to fill their heart" (*Annotations* [1556], on Matt. 6:33). He insisted, too, that circumcision was as much a sacrament as baptism; quoting Rom. 4:11 he asks: "What could be more magnifical of any Sacrament? They, then, that put a real difference between the Sacraments of the Old Testament and ours, never seem to have known how far Christ's office extendeth" (quoted by Gregory Martin, *A Discoverie of the Manifold Corruptions of the Holie Scriptures,* p. 2). For Beza's denial of free will, see *ibid.,* pp. 2, 15.

[29] Cf. Scrivener, *op. cit.,* Preface, p. vi.

[30] Cf. *idem,* Introduction to *The Cambridge Paragraph Bible,* p. xxxii. He also says that "the Complutensian Polyglott, together with the several editions of Erasmus, and Stephens of 1550, were constantly resorted to" (*A Plain Introduction,* p. 60).

the New Testament. Both the Genevans and King James's revisers had, then, says Sir Frederic Kenyon,

> the "received text" of 1550. All alike were in fact accepting as the authentic Greek text the form which it had assumed after 1,400 years of transmission by manuscript, and with the deterioration, small in each detail but cumulatively great, due to the errors of scribes and the well-meant efforts of editors. . . . Beza (1556) made some use of the various readings of Greek Manuscripts which had been collected in a convenient form by Stephens in his Greek Testament of 1550 (ed. Regia), but as yet, in spite of the great advances which had been made in scholarship, the true principles of Greek criticism were wholly unknown, and the text which served as the basis of translation was as faulty as before.[31]

Mombert declares "that in a considerable number of cases—not of great importance—the reading of the Authorized Version is supported *by no known Greek manuscript whatever,* but rests on an error of Erasmus or Beza [he adds instances], and it is safe to say that in more than a *thousand* instances the text used by the translators requires to be corrected." [32]

Some thirty years earlier, in 1582, the Rhemists had already contended in their Preface and Annotations that the Latin Vulgate preserved a Greek text much older than that current in the sixteenth century and regarded as sacrosanct by the Reformers.[33] Nearly a hundred years later, 1690, Ward put the matter bluntly in his *Errata of the Protestant Bible* (pp. 8 f.):

> In vain do Protestants tell us, that their translations are taken immediately from the fountains of the Greek and Hebrew; so is also our Latin Vulgate; only with this difference, that ours was taken when the fountains were clear, and by holy and learned men, who knew which were the crystal waters, and true copies; but theirs is taken from fountains troubled by broachers of Heresies, self-interested and time-serving persons; and after that the Arians, and other Heretics had, I say, corrupted and poisoned them with their false and abominable doctrines.[34]

[31] *The Story of the Bible,* p. 45.

[32] *Op. cit.,* p. 389. "The critical sources at the command of our Translators were very scanty," says Scrivener, who points out, too, that even the *Codex Bezae* was very little used (Introduction to *The Cambridge Paragraph Bible,* p. xxxii).

[33] See above, p. 256, and Appendix I, pp. 621–24.

[34] A good example is furnished by John 8:59, where the Vulgate has, "But Jesus hid himself, and went out of the temple," to which the "received" Greek adds: "But he, passing through the midst of them, went his way," a marginal note from Luke 4:30, as Erasmus and Beza were aware. The editions of 1561, 1562, 1577, and 1579 therefore omitted the insertion; yet it was restored in 1611 and to this day stands in the margin of the Revised Version. Westcott concedes that "this clause must be omitted in accordance with a combination of the best authorities" (*Commentary on St. John's Gospel,* chap. 8).

Indeed, Wordsworth and White do not hesitate to say: "The conviction has been gradually forced upon us, especially in regard to the Gospels according to St. Luke and St. John, that Jerome's Greek MSS exhibited a type of text which is not represented by any one Greek MS or class of MSS, and sometimes not by any existing Greek MS." [35] Among the instances they give, the following are noteworthy: Luke 9:44, where the Vulgate, *ponite in cordibus vestris,* is followed by Wycliffe and Rheims, but all others have "in your ears"; John 9:38, where Wycliffe and Rheims again follow the Vulgate, *et procidens adoravit eum,* but all others omit *procidens;* John 10:16, *ex hoc ovili . . . unum ovile,* where Tyndale and R.V. have "fold . . . flock," in agreement with the Greek while all others read "fold . . . fold," following the Vulgate.

OTHER DEFECTS OF THE VERSION

At times the revisers interpret rather than translate, as the following examples show. Acts 12:19: A.V. has "commanded that they should be put to death," and R.V. margin, "led away to death," though neither the Greek nor the Vulgate justify the addition "to death"; Wycliffe, though hardly correct, was more careful when he wrote, "to be brought to him"; Tyndale, "to departe," is incorrect; Cranmer, "to be caryed away," and Rheims, "to be led away," are correct; "to be led to be punished" in the Geneva Bible is a gratuitous addition. This tendency to interpret led to the introduction of explanatory words: *"the nature of* Angels" (Heb. 2:16); "marriage *is* honourable in all" (Heb. 13:4), perhaps a deliberate perversion, though Wycliffe has the same; here Tyndale, Cranmer, and Geneva have "wedlock is to be in honour," and R.V., "let marriage be in honour." A.V. has *"this is* not to eat the Lord's supper" (I Cor. 11:20); the Rhemists make this a question, "is it not now to eate the Lordes supper," but neither they nor the Greek or Latin texts have a note of in-

[35] *On the Question of What Greek Manuscripts or Class of Greek Manuscripts St. Jerome Used in Revising the Latin Gospels.* Jerome's words to Helvidius on this subject are well known; this heretic had contended that the words "and his father and mother were wondering at those things which were spoken concerning him" were to be found only in incorrect Greek MSS. To which *mira impudentia* St. Jerome replied that "practically all the Greek commentators on the passage retained those words, and even some of the Latins read the passage precisely as it stands in the Greek. Nor is it necessary here to dwell on the variations in copies, since the entire Testament, both the Old and the New, has been translated into Latin from the Greek; and we must needs suppose the water of the fountain-source to be more pure than that of the outflowing streams" (*Adv. Helvidium,* 6, in Migne, *P.L.,* XXIII, 191).

terrogation; A.V. margin, "ye cannot eat"; Tyndale, Cranmer, Geneva, and R.V., "it is not possible to eat"—an interpretation rather than a translation. In the same chapter A.V. has "after the same manner *hee tooke* the cup" (I Cor. 11:25); the italics were omitted in R.V., where, too, it is gratifying to note that the utterly unjustifiable "eat this bread and drink this cup" has at last been corrected to "or drink." Other interpretations: "whether *wee bee* Jewes or Gentiles, whether *wee bee* bond or free" (I Cor. 12:13); "a dispensation (of the Gospel) is committed to me" (I Cor. 9:17); "I pray to God that it may not be" (II Tim. 4:16).

The tenses in the Authorized Version are not always clearly defined. Luke 5:6 should read, "for their net was breaking," as the imperfect tense in both Greek and Latin shows; had it really "brake," as Tyndale, Cranmer, Geneva, and A.V. have, the fish would have already got away. Similarly Matt. 25:8, "our lamps are going out," as Rheims and R.V. have; not "gone out," Cranmer and A.V.; Tyndale and Geneva rightly have "go out."

Justice is not always done to the definite article. In I Cor. 5:9 the Apostle clearly refers to a letter familiar to his readers; R.V. has "in my letter." Nicodemus was not "a teacher in Israel," but "the teacher" (John 3:10). In Matt. 13:2 a particular boat—surely Peter's (cf. Luke 5:3)—is referred to, yet all the English versions, including R.V., have "a boat", except Rheims, which is more precise, "into one boat which was . . ."; again, though the definite article in Acts 17:1 suggests a well-known Jewish synagogue, no version has "the synagogue." [36]

THE STYLE AND CHARACTER OF THE VERSION

Despite its many inaccuracies of translation, the English style of the Authorized Version has always received its due meed of praise. Profiting by the labors as well as by the mistakes of their predecessors, the translators produced a version so remarkable for the majesty and rhythm of

[36] For further examples see Mombert, *op. cit.*, pp. 407 f. The classical treatment of the subject is *The Doctrine of the Greek Article Applied to the Criticism and Illustration of the New Testament,* by T. F. Middleton, 1841. Scrivener maintains that had due attention been paid to the definite article,—e.g., Rom. 15:6; I Cor. 15:24; II Cor. 1:3; Gal. 1:4; Ephes. 1:3; 5:5; Col. 1:3; 2:2; 3:17; Jas. 3:9; I Pet. 1:3—the divinity of Christ would have been brought out more clearly. See also J. Taylor, *What Is the Power of the Greek Article, and how it may be expressed in the English Version of the New Testament?* 1842.

its language that "the music of the English Bible" [37] has become proverbial.

The uncommon beauty and marvellous English of the Protestant Bible . . . lives on in the ear like a music that never can be forgotten, like the sound of church bells which the convert hardly knows how he can forego. Its felicities seem often to be almost things rather than mere words. It is part of the national mind, and the anchor of national seriousness. . . . The memory of the dead passes into it. The potent traditions of childhood are stereotyped in its verses. The power of all the griefs and trials of a man is hidden beneath its words. It is the representative of his best moments, and all that there has been about him of soft, and gentle, and pure, and penitent, and good, speaks to him for ever out of his English Bible. It is this sacred thing which doubt never dimmed and controversy never soiled.[38]

The great merit of the version, says Lightfoot, "is its truly English character"; and he remarks on the phenomenon—for such it is—that "the language is not the language of the age in which the translators lived, but in its grand simplicity stands out in contrast to the ornate and often affected diction of the literature of the time." [39] Scrivener, too, speaks of "the perfect and easy command over the English language exhibited by its authors on every page." [40] Nor is it any disparagement of this beautiful English to say, as a critic remarked some years ago: "That beauty is of course indisputable; but at the same time one must always remember that by reason of its sacred character the English Bible has come to be itself the standard of excellence by which other writings are tried, and it is necessarily unsurpassed in coming up to itself." In the same vein Dean Swift wrote:

If it were not for the Bible and Common Prayer Book in the vulgar tongue, we should hardly be able to understand anything that was written among us a hundred years ago, . . . for those books, being perpetually read in churches, have proved a kind of standard for language. . . . No translation our country ever yet produced has come up to that of the Old and New Testament. . . . I am persuaded that the translators of the Bible were masters of an English style much fitter for that work than any we see in our present writings; which I take to be owing to the simplicity that runs through the whole.[41]

[37] Cf. John Henry Newman, *Grammar of Assent,* chap. 4, § 2, p. 56.

[38] F. W. Faber, *St. Francis of Assisi,* Oratorian Lives of the Saints, pp. 116 f. This passage used to be attributed to Newman, who pointed out that it appeared in an Essay prefixed to the above *Life of St. Francis* and signed "F.W.F." (*Church Opinion,* July 24 and 31, 1869).

[39] *On a Fresh Revision of the English New Testament,* pp. 212, 299.

[40] *The Authorized Edition of the English Bible,* p. 181.

[41] *A Proposal for correcting, improving and ascertaining the English Tongue; a Letter to Robert, Earl of Oxford, and Mortimer, Lord High Treasurer of Great Britain,* 1712, ed. by John Nichols, VI, 55.

Selden, too, in an oft-quoted passage, says: "The English Translation of the Bible is the best Translation in the world, and renders the Sense of the Original best, taking in for the English Translation, the Bishops' Bible as well as King James's." [42]

Still critics have not been wanting. Purver, for instance, maintains that "the language is obsolete, uncouth, clownish." But the examples he gives—"joyous," "solace," "damsel," etc.—hardly support such extravagant language.[43] Geddes, too, always a stern critic says: "I venture to affirm (and I affirm with full conviction) that James' translators have less merit than any of the predecessors; and that the version of Tindall, revised by Coverdale, is a juster representation of the original (such as he had it) than our present Vulgar Version. The truth is that James' translators did little more than copy the Genevan Version; which was little more than a transcript from the revised French; which was chiefly borrowed from Pagninus." [44] Hallam's criticism is more balanced:

> The style of this translation is in general so enthusiastically praised, that no one is permitted either to qualify or even explain the grounds of his approbation. It is held to be the perfection of our English language. I shall not dispute this proposition; but one remark as to a matter of fact cannot reasonably be censured, that in consequence of the principle of adherence to the original versions which had been kept up ever since the reign of Henry VIII, it is not the language of the reign of James I. It may, in the eyes of many, be a better English, but it is not the English of Daniel, Raleigh, or Bacon, as any one may easily perceive. It abounds, in fact, especially in the Old Testament, with obsolete phraseology, and with single words long since abandoned, or retained only in provincial use.[45]

These critics, however, were "stylists," not too much concerned with the really vital question: the merits of the Authorized Version as a faithful witness to the original text. This of course became the subject of minute investigation when the question of a fresh revision (the Revised Version) was mooted. The preparatory work for this was done by

[42] *Table-Talk*, p. 20.

[43] *A New and Literal Translation of all the Books of the Old and New Testaments.* In his introductory remarks, Axiom II (p. v) runs: "The obsolete Words, and uncouth ungrammatical Expressions in the Sacred Text." His accusations would have been better founded had he instanced such words as "advisement" (I Chron. 12:19); "aliant" (Job 19:15), now "alien"; "ambassage" (Luke 14:32); "amerce" (Deut. 22:19); "artillery" (I Sam. 20:40); "daysman" (Job 9:33); "neesing," for "sneezing" (Job 41:18); "ouches" (Exod. 28:13); "purtenance," for "entrails" (Exod. 12:9).

[44] *A General Answer to Queries, Counsels, and Criticisms*, p. 4.

[45] *The Introduction to the Literature of Europe in the Fifteenth, Sixteenth, and Seventeenth Centuries*, II, 464.

Scrivener [46] and, after the heat of controversy had cooled down, by Westcott, who says:

> As a whole their work was done most carefully and honestly; . . . even in the minutest details the translation is that of a Church and not of a party. . . . No kind of emendation appears to have been neglected, and almost every change was an improvement. . . . Throughout the most delicate care is given to the choice of words, and there is scarcely a verse which does not bear witness to the wisdom and instinctive sense of fitness by which it was guided. . . . The scrupulous and watchful care with which the revisers worked is nowhere seen more remarkably than in their use of italics to mark the introduction of words not directly represented in the original, . . . (thus) marking distinctly that the work is a translation; and yet more the use distinguishes in many cases an interpretation from a rendering, e.g. Heb. x.38.[47]

"Nor can we fail to marvel," to quote Scrivener again, "at the perfect and easy command over the English language exhibited by its authors on every page. The fulness and variety of their diction, the raciness of their idiomatic resources, seem almost to defy imitation, while they claim our just and cheerful admiration." [48]

PECULIARITIES OF THE VERSION

Measuring 16 inches by 10½ inches, the King James Bible was even larger than the Great Bible or "Bible of the largest size." It was printed in black letter, and words not standing in the original were printed in small italicised Roman type. The use of italics to indicate words not in the original was inaugurated by Münster in his Latin version, 1534, the Geneva Bible being the first English version to employ them. These were so multiplied in later editions that a formal protest was made against them as "deteriorating the vernacular version, discovering great want of critical taste, unnecessarily exposing the sacred text to the scoffs of infidels, and throwing such stumbling blocks in the way of the unlearned, as are greatly calculated to perplex their minds, and unsettle their confidence in the text of Scripture." [49] These italicized words have been

[46] *The Cambridge Paragraph Bible of the Authorized English Version, with the text revised by a collation of its early and other principal editions, the use of the italic type made uniform, the marginal references remodelled, and a critical Introduction prefixed,* 1870–73, 3 vols. 4to.

[47] *A General View of the History of the English Bible,* pp. 256 ff. In some editions even now the words "any man" in Heb. 10:38 are italicised.

[48] *A Plain Introduction to the Criticism of the New Testament,* p. 141.

[49] In the *Variorum Bible,* edited by Cheyne, Driver, and others, 1876, twenty-six words are italicized in I Cor., chap. 11, against six in the original edition of 1611. None

severely criticized as the "Jacobeans' trick . . . inspired at best by a penny-wise pound-foolish minuteness, . . . or by a hypocritical pretence in detail, . . . [whereby] the simple were assured that nothing was interpolated, but what was printed in italic. To a modern eye the effect of this supposed guarantee offered by the translator to the reader is a humorous exhibition of false emphasis. . . . Whereas in the Rhemish we find a reasonable, civilized, and convenient use of the italic to indicate quotation." [50]

The revisers interpreted in a wide sense rule 6, which precluded notes. In defense of their notes they say: "Though in those things that are plainely set down in the Scriptures all such matters are found that concern faith, hope and charitie, yet . . . it hath pleased God in his divine providence to scatter wordes and sentences of that difficultie and doubtfulnesse, not in doctrinal points that concerne salvation, (for in such it hath been vouched that the Scriptures are plaine) but in matters of lesse moment." [51]

The dates A(nno) M(undi), first inserted by Bishop Lloyd in 1701 [52] and derived from Ussher's conjectural calculations,[53] have been adopted in practically every edition of the English Bible. The fresh chapter headings introduced by the revisers have remained unchanged.

Some misprints in the original edition persisted down to 1881: the first folio of 1611 omitted three lines, Exod. 14:10, while the heading of II Sam., chap. 24, had "eleven thousand" instead of "thirteen hundred thousand" (cf. verse 9). The words "of God" were until 1638 omitted from "he that hath not the Son of God" (I John 5:12).[54] The second

---

of these are in the Rheims version of 1582 nor in Challoner's revisions. For a detailed discussion of this point, see Scrivener, *A Plain Introduction,* pp. 62–81.

[50] J. S. Phillimore, "Scripture Versions and Variants," in the *Dublin Review,* CLXX (1922), 26 f. Cf. Dore, *op. cit.,* pp. 340, 348; Eadie, *op. cit.,* pp. 285 ff.; Mombert, *op. cit.,* pp. 367 f. However the use of italics was upheld by Archbishop Newcome, *An Historical View of the English Biblical Translations,* p. 276; and Scrivener, *A Supplement to the Authorised English Version of the New Testament,* p. 60; cf. Turton, *The Text of the English Bible Considered,* 2nd ed., 1883.

[51] These, dealing mainly with variant readings or the more literal meaning of the original, numbered 6,637 in the Old Testament and 765 in the New. Many were added later, and cross-references have multiplied from about 9,000 to 60,000 in some editions.

[52] Perhaps in 1690 (Lewis, *op. cit.,* p. 347). For details, see Mombert, *op. cit.,* pp. 372 f.

[53] *Annales Veteris et Novi Testamenti,* 1650–54.

[54] But the text is uncertain. Some pre-Clementine editions of the Vulgate omitted the word, others retained it. Rheims and R.V. retain the words; but the *Codex Amiatinus,* followed by the Clementine, A.V., and Challoner, omits them.

folio of 1611 had "then Judas [for "Jesus"] came to Gethsemane" (Matt. 26:36). Both folios of that year printed: "Blind guides, who strain at a gnat" (Matt. 23:34), whereas the Genevan and the Bishops' Bibles correctly had "strain out," and Rheims had "strain a gnat"; yet the error held its place in all editions except that of 1764.

NOTABLE EDITIONS

Editions have, of course, been innumerable; [55] we need mention but a few. Three distinct editions appeared in 1611; one is known as "The great HE edition," [56] the other two as "The great SHE editions," the nomenclature being due to the fact that whereas Ruth 3:15 should read, "He [Boaz] measured six measures of barley, and laid it on her [Ruth]; and she went," the first folio substituted "he" for "she"; subsequent editions based on either the "he" or the "she" folios reproduce their respective readings. Editions of the whole Bible in 4to and 8vo, and of the New Testament in 4to, appeared in 1612.[57]

Some editions are notable for their misprints. The edition of 1631, Cambridge, is known as "The Wicked Bible" for printing the commandment, "Thou shalt commit adultery." According to tradition the publishers were fined £3000, but actually only £300, and even for this, compensation was made by the presentation of a font of Greek type to the University.[58] Another Cambridge edition was guilty of at least four gems in the way of misprints: "sons of Belial," for "sons of Bilhah (Bala)" (Gen. 37:2); "slew two lions like men," for "two lion-like men" (II Sam.

[55] Loftie (*A Century of Bibles, or the Authorised Version from 1611 to 1711*, 1872) enumerates 229 editions (duplicates excluded) of the whole Bible and 38 of the New Testament. Robert Barker, the Royal Printer, had brought out fifty editions by the year 1640.

[56] A copy recently was offered for sale at £500.

[57] Details of various editions are given by Dore, *op. cit.*, Appendix I, pp. 355–78; Cotton, *Lists of Editions of the Bible . . . in English, from the year MDV to MDCCCL;* Newcome, *op. cit.; idem, A List of Various Editions of the English Versions of the Bible*, 1818. "The Great HE edition" was reprinted at Oxford, 1833; ed. by David Nutt, 1903, 6 vols.; ed. by W. A. Wright, 1909, 5 vols., with a fine reproduction of the original frontispiece. A reprint, but in modern spelling, by Cambridge University, has neither date nor Introductory matter, but gives the generally omitted "Address of the Translators to the Reader." See W. E. Smith, *A Study of the Great "SHE" Bible*, 1890; J. Lenox, *Early Editions of King James' Bible in Folio*, 1861.

[58] This fine is said to have been inflicted by Archbishop Laud. Kilburne says: "The printers had to pay £2000 or £3000, as I have heard." Only a single copy of this unfortunate edition is said to survive, at Wolfenbüttel; cf. Scrivener, Introduction to *The Cambridge Paragraph Bible*, p. xviii. For an account of these misprints, see Loftie, *A Century of Bibles*, 1872.

23:20); the Midianites "vex you with their wives," instead of "wiles" (Num. 25:18; here the Douay has, "acted like enemies against you"). Another unfortunate edition was that of 1653, which omitted "or who hath opened his eyes" from John 9:21, and in Rom. 6:13 wrote: "your members as instruments of righteousness," for "unrighteousness"; conversely, in I Cor. 6:9 it has, "know you not that the righteous [for "unrighteous"] shall not possess the kingdom of God?"

One misprint was heart warming, at least to the Puritans. The apostles arranged for the selection by the faithful of seven deacons "whom we may appoint" (Acts 6:3); but the Puritans, finding that "ye" had been printed instead of "we," seized on this misprint as confirmation of their peculiar views on appointment to the ministry. The statement that "the dogs liked ["licked"] Achab's blood" (III Kings 22:38) may raise a smile; but "I will never forgive ["forget"] thy precepts" (Ps. 119:93) is distinctly disedifying.

Several other editions have received nicknames owing to their misprints. One printed at Oxford, 1717, is called the "Vinegar Bible" from the title affixed to Luke, chap. 20, which reads, "The Parable of the Vinegar," for "vineyard"; another, 1795, is dubbed the "Murderers Bible," for Mark 7:27 reads, "Let the children first be killed," instead of "filled." On the other hand, an edition printed by Sir David Hunter Blair and J. Bruce in 1811 is styled the "Immaculate Bible," since the printers claimed that it more nearly reached perfection than any hitherto printed.[59]

BIBLIOGRAPHY

Butterworth, C. C. *The Literary Lineage of the King James Bible,* Philadelphia, 1941.

Cook, A. S. *The Authorized Version of the Bible and Its Influence,* 1910.

Daiches, D. *The King James Version of the English Bible,* Chicago, 1941.

Malan, S. C. *A Plea for the Received Greek Text and for the Authorized Version of the New Testament,* 1869.

———. *A Vindication of the Authorized Version,* 1856.

Scrivener, F. H. *The Authorised Edition of the English Bible* (1611); *its subsequent reprints and modern representatives,* 1884; reprinted from the Introduction to *The Cambridge Paragraph Bible,* 1873.

———. *A Supplement to the Authorised English Version of the New Testament,* 1845.

Todd, H. J. *An Authentic Account of Our Authorised Translation of the Holy Bible,* 1834, 1842.

[59] For a curious account of the vicissitudes of the version, see Isaac Disraeli, *Curiosities of Literature,* II, iii, p. 322.

Todd, H. J. *Vindication of Our Authorized Translation and Translators of the Bible,* 1819.

Trench, R. C. *On the Authorized Version of the New Testament,* 1858, 1859.

Turton, R. *The Text of the English Bible Considered,* 2nd ed., 1833.

Westcott, B. F. *A General View of the History of the English Bible,* 3rd ed. by W. A. Wright, 1905, pp. 255–78.

Whitley, N. T. *The English Bible under Tudor Sovereigns,* London, 1937.

Valuable articles are to be found in the encyclopedias:

Blunt, J. H. *Encyclopedia Britannica,* "English Versions."

Lupton, J. H. "Versions (English)," in Hastings' *Dictionary of the Bible,* extra volume.

Milligan, G. "Versions" in Hastings' *Dictionary of the Bible,* vol. 4.

Plumptre, E. H. "Version, Authorized," in Smith's *Dictionary of the Bible,* vol. 3.

List of Revisers

Genesis—Kings, Westminster

Dr. Lancelot Andrewes
Dr. John Overall
Dr. Hadrian de Saravia
Dr. Richard Clark
Dr. John Layfield
Dr. Robert Teigh
Mr. Francis Burleigh
Mr. Goeffrey King
Mr. Thompson
Mr. William Bedwell

Isaias—Malachy, Oxford

Dr. John Harding
Dr. John Rainolds
Dr. Thomas Holland
Mr. Richard Kilbye
Dr. Miles Smith
Dr. Richard Brett
Mr. Richard Fairclough

The Gospels, Acts, Apocalypse; Oxford

Dr. Thomas Ravis
Dr. George Abbot
Dr. Richard Eedes
Dr. Giles Thompson
Mr. (Sir Henry) Saville
Dr. John Perin
Dr. Ravens
Dr. John Harmer

I Chron.—Eccles., Cambridge

Mr. Edward Lively
Mr. John Richardson
Mr. Laurence Chatterton
Mr. Francis Dillingham
Mr. Thomas Harrison
Mr. Roger Andrewes
Mr. Robert Spalding
Mr. Andrew Byng

The Apocrypha, Cambridge

Dr. John Duport
Dr. William Branthwait
Dr. Jeremiah Radcliffe
Dr. Samuel Ward
Mr. Andrew Downes
Mr. John Bois [60]
Mr. Robert Ward

The Epistles; Westminster

Dr. William Barlow
Dr. William Hutchinson
Dr. John Spencer
Dr. Roger Fenton
Mr. Michael Rabbett
Mr. Thomas Sanderson
Mr. William Dakins

[60] For John Bois, see above, chap. 9, *s.v.* Erasmas.

NOTE

Hugh Broughton (1549–1612), one of the most prominent scholars of his time, does not figure among the revisers. He had long contemplated a revision of the English versions and had in 1588 published *The Concent of Scripture,* in which he defended the Hebrew chronology, the Masoretic text, the vowel points, even the "Keri" and "Kethibh." In Germany he used to dispute with Jewish rabbis and preened himself on his attainments as a Hebraist. "The Jewes," he says, "desired to have me sent to all the synagogues in Constantinople, if it were but *to see* my Angelical countenance"; he speaks of himself as "a man approved over the world," and says "only the Queene is fit to be my Patrone," while he gloats over a remark made by Rainolds the Puritan that "there was as much in Broughton as could bee in a man."

Some few years before the Hampton Court Conference, Broughton published *An Epistle to the learned Nobilitie of England, Touching Translating the Bible from the original, with ancient warrant for evrie worde, unto the full satisfaction of any that have hart,* Middlesburgh, by Richard Schilders. An anonymous riposte to this described the author—justly, I fear—as "a vainglorious Thraso, a fugitive schismatike at home, a tormentor of soules with mysticall riddles, a clamorous trumpetor of his owne praises." Even Scaliger called him *furiosus et maledicus,* and one of his own friends, Morton, afterwards bishop of Durham, said before sitting down to table with him: "I pray you, whatsoever dolts and dullards I may be called, call me so before we begin, that your discourse and mine attention be not interrupted thereby."

This unruly tongue of his as well as the vehemence of his denunciations of any who failed to agree with him, made everyone shy of suggesting him as a member of the revision committees. When Broughton found his name omitted, he wrote to the King asking for "a pension fitt for his age, study and travells past," also for the See of Tuam, a modest request, he says, since the income would amount to only £200 per annum. On the appearance of the new version, Broughton at once denounced it in *A Censure of the late translation for our churches: sent unto a Right Worshipfull Knight, Attendant upon the King,* 1612:

The late Bible . . . was sent to me to censure: which bred in me a sadness that will greeve me while I breath. It is so ill done. Tell his Majest. that I had rather be rent in peces with wild horses, than any such translation by my consent should bee urged upon poore Churches. . . . Bancroft raved. I gave the Anathema. Christ judged his owne cause. The new edition crosseth me. I require it to be burnt. . . . I blame not this that they keepe the usual style of former translations in the Church that the people should not be emazed. For the learned, the Geneva might be made exact: for which paynes whole 30 yeres I have been called upon, and spent much time to my great losse by wicked hinderance.

The rendering, "for an hundred pieces of money," margin, "lambes," as in the Vulgate and its derivatives (Gen. 33:19), especially provoked Broughton's indignation: "The margent note for sheepe burneth the hart of the translatours: who bade them put this errour in the text, and right in the margent? . . . I will suffer no scholer in the world to crosse me in Ebrew and Greek, when I am sure I have the trueth."

John Lightfoot, himself a famous scholar, published Broughton's Works in thirteen volumes under the weird title: *The Works of the Great Albionean Divine, renowned in many Nations for Rare Skill in Salems and Athens Tongues and Familiar Acquaintance with all Rabbinical Learning. Mr. Hugh Broughton,* 1662. This was reprinted in 1825.

CHAPTER XXI

Ward's Errata of the Protestant Bible

THOMAS WARD, 1652–1709, a member of an anti-Catholic family, became a Catholic through studying the religious question for himself. Though disinherited as a "pervert," he ultimately converted his family to the Catholic faith. After a sojourn in Rome, where he became a member of the Papal Guard and saw service against the Turks, he returned to England. Feeling that he could do good by entering into controversy, he published *Cantos on the Reformation*. These were widely read and resulted in many conversions. A comparison he made between Catholic and Protestant translations of the Bible in English led him to publish in 1688 *Errata of the Protestant Bible: or the Truth of the English Translations examined in a Treatise shewing some of the Errors that are to be found in the English Translations of the Sacred Scriptures, used by Protestants, against such Points of Religious Doctrine as are the Subject of Controversy between them and the Members of the Catholic Church. In which also, from their Mistranslating the Twenty-third Verse of the Fourteenth Chapter of the Acts of the Apostles, the Consecration of Dr. Matthew Parker, the first Protestant Archbishop of Canterbury, is occasionally considered.*[1]

Ward's work attracted little attention until the publication of a third edition, 1797, and a fourth, 1810. The attempted answers by Ryan [2] and

[1] Subsequent editions: 1737, 1797, 1810, 1824, and 1844; in America, 1841 and 1899. The title page of some editions reads: *Errata to the Protestant Bible;* but *Errata of* is here uniformly adopted.

[2] *An Analysis of Ward's "Errata of the English Bible,"* 1808.

Grier,[3] and later by Browne,[4] completely missed the points at issue.[5] Subsequent critics have been content with abuse. Lewis styles him "the late Popish merry-Andrew";[6] and Mombert speaks of "the almost savage fanaticism of this bigoted book."[7] Cotton is, of course, equally bitter, speaking of the *Errata* as "a strenuous effort to disparage and discountenance the version of our Church," while he describes Ward's *Cantos on the Reformation* as "a work of coarse humour, filled with gross misrepresentations, and disgraced by a most malignant spirit." Cotton even tries to take the sting out of the *Errata* by suggesting—though he gives no instances—that "a considerable number of the renderings which Ward in his malice against us stigmatises as *heretical corruptions,* have been adopted, and are actually to be found at this day, in the Roman Catholic Bibles sanctioned by the late Archbishop Murray."[8] As a matter of fact the reverse is the case, for the readings advocated by the Rhemists in their Annotations and by Gregory Martin in the *Discoverie,* and condemned by Bulkeley, are now generally accepted.

Gregory Martin's *Discoverie,* 1582, had dealt with the English versions then current, namely, Cranmer's Bible, the Geneva Bible, and the Bishops' Bible of 1568 "appointed to be read in churches." Ward's purpose, then, was to discover how far the framers of the version made in 1611, that is, thirty years after Martin's incriminations of the earlier versions, had corrected the many errors the latter had pointed out. For this purpose he examined various editions of the Authorized Version down to 1683.[9]

[3] Grier speaks of the edition of 1810 with a Preface by Lingard as "in the highest degree illiberal, unfounded and absurd; . . . a performance *sui generis* replete with coarse invective and vulgar abuse, the natural effusions of bigoted malice"; but he gives no examples in support of these wholly unfounded charges. Grier himself was fully answered by Milner in a new edition of Ward's *Errata of the Protestant Bible. . . . To which are added the celebrated Preface of the Rev. Doctor L[ingard] in answer to Ryan's "Analysis"; and a Vindication by the Rt. Rev. Doctor Milner in answer to Grier's "Reply."*

[4] *Ten Lectures on Ward's "Errata of the Protestant Bible,"* 1859.

[5] Yet Mombert says that the *Errata* was "refuted times without number" (*English Versions of the Bible,* p. 330).

[6] *A Complete History of the Several Translations of the Holy Bible and New Testament into English,* p. 157.

[7] *Op. cit.,* p. 227; cf. Eadie, *The English Bible,* II, 267.

[8] *Rhemes and Doway,* pp. 27–30.

[9] Apropos of the "gift of tongues" (I Cor., chap. 14), the edition of the Authorized Version published in 1683 with the notes of the Geneva Bible, always inserts the word "unknown" before "tongue," verses 4, 13, 14, 19, and 27, insinuating that the Latin used by the Church was "an unknown tongue."

This examination enabled him to draw up a list of certain changes for the better in that version; for instance, "Church" replaced "congregation"; "giving thanks" yielded to "blessing"; "contain" was changed to "receive" (Acts 3:21), "temple" to "altar" (I Cor. 9:13; 10:18), "feed" to "rule" (Matt. 2:6), "chaste" to "eunuchs" (Matt. 19:12); "images" yielded to "idols," "grave" to "hell," "ordinances" to "traditions," and so forth.

But there remained some passages still calling for correction: the retention, for example, of "and," instead of "or," in I Cor. 11:27: "Wherefore whosoever shall eat this bread and drink this cup." "Bishops" were still called "overseers" (Acts 20:28), although in the Pastoral Epistles the title "bishop" was retained. Similarly Matt. 19:11 still read: "All men cannot receive this saying" instead of "take not," the implication being that continency is not possible.

Feeling that by such misrepresentations he and many thousands like him had been robbed of his inheritance in "the faith once (and for all) delivered to the saints," Ward was justified in saying: "The nature of the Holy Scripture is such, that whosoever do voluntarily corrupt and pervert it, to maintain their own erroneous doctrines, cannot rightly be characterized by any less infamous title than that of heretics; and their false versions, by the title of heretical Translations. . . . Notwithstanding, I would have the Protestant Reader to take notice, that I neither name nor judge all to be heretics, who hold errors contrary to God's Church, but such as pertinaciously persist in their errors." [10]

Great resentment was felt at the epithet "heretic" which the Rhemists and Ward himself applied so freely to the reformers and their teachings. But we have to bear in mind that in their translations these would-be reformers deliberately and of set purpose assailed the age-old teaching of the Church on the Holy Eucharist, the Mass and the Real Presence, the priesthood and the episcopate, the sacraments, the intercession of the saints, purgatory, limbo, the veneration of images, the doctrine of merits and rewards, free will and good works, and so forth.

That protests such as Ward and Gregory Martin made were not without effect appears in a note prefixed to the *Table of Corruptions* in the fifth edition of the Rheims New Testament, 1738: "The following Table has had so good an Effect, that since the First edition of it (in the second

[10] *Errata*, p. 22.

edition of the Rheims Testament, 1600) the Protestants have had the Grace to correct, by it, their Edition of the New Testament of 1660 in many Places. But as Falsehood is inseparable from Heresy, and None can be fit to translate faithfully the Word of God, who have not first the Spirit of God in them: they have left many other Passages here taken notice of, either totally unalter'd, or not alter'd for the better; sometimes even for the worse."

The Revised Version, 1881–1885, has made further improvements, notably the change from "and" to "or" (I Cor. 11:27), removing the suggestion that St. Paul endorsed the idea that it was necessary to receive Communion under both species. But it is regrettable that the rendering "to lead about a *wife* that is a believer" (I Cor. 9:5) has been allowed to remain. Further changes, too, would have been welcome on the subjects of "grace," "tradition," "hell," and "images." Why, for instance, should "overseers" (Acts 20:28) be now correctly replaced by "bishops" in the text, yet remain in the margin?

PART FOUR

Catholic Versions since Rheims-Douay

Introductory

From its appearance in 1611, the Authorized Version, which marked the culmination of nearly one hundred years of unremitting toil by a series of translators (1525–1611), remained stationary for almost three hundred years, until the Revised Version was finished in 1885, though in the intervening years innumerable editions continued to appear.

The story of the Rheims-Douay Version is quite different. For the penal times, with all the resulting disabilities, precluded the production of new editions after the publication of the fourth edition of the New Testament, 1633, and of the second and last edition of the Old Testament, 1635. But the opening of the eighteenth century marked a great change. It soon became evident that considerable dissatisfaction with the Catholic version was felt, a feeling which manifested itself in a series of attempted revisions due to the labors of Doctors Nary, Witham, and Challoner, of an anonymous editor of the New Testament towards the close of the century (1792), and of the ill-starred Dr. Geddes. Mr. MacMahon, too, had by 1810 revised Challoner's version of the whole Bible twice and the New Testament separately three times.

CHAPTER XXII

Dr. Nary's Version of the New Testament, 1718

EARLY in the century there appeared from a wholly unexpected quarter *The New Testament of our Lord and Saviour Jesus Christ. Newly translated out of the Latin Vulgat, and with the Original Greek, and divers Translations in Vulgar Languages diligently compared and revised. Together with Annotations upon the most remarkable Passages in the Gospels, and Marginal Notes upon other difficult Texts of the same, and upon the rest of the books of the New Testament, for the better understanding of the literal Sense. By C. N. C. F. P. D.* (Cornelius Nary Consultissimae Facultatis Parisiensis Doctor), 1718 and 1719.[1]

Dr. Walsh, archbishop of Dublin, had written to Dr. Nary [2] on November 19, 1715, saying: "It was with a great deal of satisfaction that I read your Manuscript Version of the New Testament from the Latin Vulgate. You have now by your indefatigable labour furnished us with what we so long wished for, and so much wanted. Your happy genius has furnished you with the means of reconciling a literal Translation with the Purity of the English Tongue. And your Annotations . . . show manifestly the Profoundness of your Erudition, and the Brightness of your Wit." As this letter was written four years before the appearance of the volume, and the Approbations by John Farely, *sacrae facultatis*

[1] The second edition was necessitated by the accidental omission of half of Apoc. 18:22, and the ascription of the Epistle of St. Jude to St. Paul; cf. Cotton, *Lists of Editions of the Bible* (1852), p. 84. Cotton adds that Harris, in his edition of Ware's *Writers of Ireland,* mentions an edition of Dr. Nary's New Testament printed in 1705. Cf. *Rhemes and Doway,* pp. 225 f.

[2] Dr. Nary died in 1737. An obituary notice in a Dublin journal ran: "Dublin, March 7, 1737. Last Friday morning died, aged 79, Dr. Nary, a Romish Priest of this Parish of St. Mican's. He was a gentleman of great Charity, Piety and Learning, and very much esteemed by Protestants, as well as by those of his Religion."

Parisiensis Doctor Theologus and President of the Irish College in Paris, and by M. Fogarty, Doctor of the Paris Faculty, are dated so far back as April and July, 1714, the translator must have kept the completed work for some time before publishing it, after the many years he must have consecrated to his task.

In his Preface Dr. Nary explains why he translates from the Latin rather than from the Greek.

Since the *Latin Vulgat* has been declared Authentick by the Council of Trent, and that the same has been by order of Sixtus V and Clement VIII corrected and amended of the Faults and Imperfections crept into it in process of Time, thro' the neglect of Transcribers, it is not to be expected I should translate the New Testament, which is designed for the use of the People, from the *Greek*, or from any other *Latin* copy than that of the said *Vulgat;* because it is fit the People should understand the Scripture as it is read in the Catholick Church, and as they hear it in the publick Service, and at their private Devotion.

He also gives his reasons for venturing on a new translation:

We have no Catholick Translation of the Scriptures in the English Tongue but the *Doway Bible,* and the *Rhemish Testament,* which have been done now more than an Hundred Years since, the Language whereof is so old, the Words in many Places so obsolete, the Orthography so bad, and the Translation so very literal, that in a number of Places it is unintelligible, and all over so grating to the Ears of such as are accustomed to speak, in a manner, another Language, that most People will not be at the Pains of reading them. Besides, they are so bulky, that they cannot conveniently be carried about for publick Devotion; and so scarce and so dear, that the Generality of the People neither have, nor can procure them for their private use.

But Nary had no illusions as to the immensity of the task he had undertaken:

I am not insensible of my Insufficiency for so great an Undertaking, nor of the many Censures and Reprehensions to which my weakness shall render my Work obnoxious. I have always before my eyes the Answer which the learned *Génébrard* made to *Henry* III of France, who being desirous to have a good *French* Translation of the Bible, asked Génébrard how much time would the finishing of such a Work take up, and what would be the Expence thereof. This great man . . . answered "That it would take up Thirty Years, that there should be Thirty Divines well read in the Oriental languages employed in the Work, that no less than two hundred thousand crowns would defray the Charges, and that after all he would not promise his Majesty that the Work should be free from all Manner of Imperfections."

I was always of opinion, that it was morally impossible to succeed in translating the New Testament into any vulgar language out of the *Latin,* without being read in the *Hebrew* and in the *Greek*, by reason of an infinite (as I may say) Number of Phrases that are ambiguous, and may be construed in a double Sense in the *Latin,* which yet are limited and only determined to one Sense in the *Greek,* and according to the *Hebrew* idiom, can have no other: But I am now convinced by Experience that it is not enough to understand the *Greek* of prophane Authors, but that one must withal be thoroughly acquainted with the *Helenist,* or the *Greek* of the Synagogue: For this is the Language into which the Law of Moses and the Prophets were translated (as is commonly believed) by the *Septuagint:* And these Doctors being Jews, gave the *Greek* the very Turn and Genius of the *Hebrew* Phrases and Particles; so as to make them signify very often quite another thing than what they generally do in prophane Authors. Now the Apostles, being Jews also, and being acquainted only with the Turn and Genius of the *Hebrew,* and this *Greek* of the Synagogue; wrote in the Stile of the Septuagint, and gave the same turn to the *Greek* in the New Testament, as the *Septuagint* had given to it in the Old. Hence proceed a great many Ambiguities and Obscurities in the Phrases and Particles of the *Latin Vulgat,* which cannot be understood or determined, but by having recourse to the *Greek* of the Synagogue; so that it is absolutely necessary for a Translator to be well read therein.

Besides, there are several Particles in the *Greek* that are expletive, and serve only for Ornament and Sound, but signify nothing in any vulgar language, on the contrary, would be a great Defect in them should they be expressed: Now the *Latin Vulgat* has retained a great many of these, which if literally translated, would rather spoil than mend the Sense. And that the *Hebrew* being written in a very concise laconick Stile, expressing things by Halfs, and being very barren in Particles and Prepositions, the *Septuagint,* following the same method, wrote in a like Concise, and consequently Obscure Stile; especially as to the rendering of the *Hebrew* Particles and Prepositions, where they were forced very often to render one and the same *Hebrew* Particle by several Particles which have different significations in the *Greek,* as they conceived the *Hebrew* Particle ought to signify in such a Place: so that when there is any Obscurity (as it often happens), or Absurdity, or Ambiguity, or receding from the Analogy of the Faith, arising from the translation of such Sentences, or of such Particles according to their usual Signification; one must have recourse to the *Hebrew* to see what the meaning of such Sentences and Particles and Prepositions must be, in that or in the like place, and render them accordingly in vulgar language, tho' they should happen to signify otherwise upon another Occasion in the *Greek* or *Latin:* And yet I maintain that this is not receding from a literal Translation. For a literal Translation of the Scripture does not consist is giving the Sense or Meaning of the Words in general, but as they are in the Text in Scripture Phrase: Now the *Latin* being taken from the *Greek,* and the *Greek* from the *Hebrew,* it is certain the *Latin* Sentences, and Particles, and Prepositions, can have no other literal Sense in the Text, than that which the *Hebrew* has in the same, or in the like Texts.[8]

[8] Yet he does not rigidly adhere to his principle of giving a strictly literal rendering in the text and relegating explanations to the margin. For example: "even so death passed upon men *by this one man in whom* all have sinned" (Rom. 5:12); "but will with the temptation produce *in you* an increase *of strength*" (I Cor. 10:13); "hath broken down by his flesh, the middle-wall of partition, that is, the enmities *which divided us*" (Ephes. 2:14). The italics are Dr. Nary's.

The principles which he demands of a translator show that in his insistence on the need for study of the common epistolary Greek of the New Testament times if one would rightly appreciate the Greek of the Evangelists, Nary anticipated the work of Deissmann. But he adduces only a few instances of the application of these principles: Matt. 1:20, *quod enim in ea natus est;* Rhemists, "that which is borne in her"; but Nary points out that the child was not yet born, and the Greek demands "begotten" or "conceived"; Challoner has "conceived," which the Rhemists indicated, however, in their use of "in." Luke 11:41, *Quod superest date eleemosynam,* which rightly suggests that alms need be given only out of superfluities. The Greek δέ means "but"; yet to render it by "but" in all the forty places where it occurs in the first chapter of St. Matthew would be intolerable. Hence Nary renders it by "and," "now," "but," "then," "whereupon," "as I judged to be most agreeable to the genius of the *English* tongue, and most proper for connecting Sentences and Periods together." So too with the prepositions: *optabam enim ego ipse anathema esse a Christo,* said the Apostle; can he have meant "an anathema from Christ," as Challoner and R.V. have it? That, says Nary, would do no good either to St. Paul or to his brethren. He points out that the Hebrew *min,* though generally meaning "from," can equally well mean "for." Why not, then, translate "an anathema for the sake of Christ"?

A comparison of Nary's rendering of Rom. 8:18–23 and Luke 5:1–11 with Challoner's first revision, 1749, will afford some idea of the former's independence of judgment. The italicized words indicate the differences between Challoner and Nary. There can be little doubt as to which is the better translation.

Rom. 8:18–23

Nary, 1719	Challoner, 1749
18. For I reckon that the sufferings of this *present* time, are not worthy to be compared *to* the *future* glory, *which* shall be revealed in us.	18. For I reckon that the sufferings of this time are not worthy to be compared *with* the glory *to come, that* shall be revealed in us.
19. For the expectatioı of the creature waiteth for the *manifestation* of the *kingdom* of God.	19. For the expectation of the creature waited for the *revelation* of the *sons* of God.
20. For the creature *is* made subject to vanity, not willingly, but by reason	20. For the creature *was* made subject to vanity, not willingly, but by

Nary, 1719 (*continued*)	Challoner, 1749 (*continued*)
of him, *who hath subjected the same* in hope.	reason of him *that* made *it* subject, in hope:
21. Because the creature it self also shall be delivered from the *bondage* of corruption, into the *glorious* liberty of the children of God.	21. Because the creature itself also shall be delivered from the *servitude* of corruption into the liberty *of the glory* of the children of God.
22. For we know that every creature groneth, and travaileth in pain *until* now.	22. For we know that every creature groaneth, and travaileth in pain *even till* now.
23. And not only *they,* but our selves also, who have the first fruits of the ſpirit, even we our selves grone within our selves, waiting for the adoption of the *children* of God, *to wit,* the redemption of our body.	23. And not only *it,* but ourselves also, who have the first-fruits of the Spirit, even we ourselves groan within ourselves, waiting for the adoption of the *sons* of God, the redemption of our body.[4]

Luke 5:1–11

Nary, 1719	Challoner, 1749
1. And it came to pass that *as* the multitudes pressed upon him to hear the word of God, he stood by the Lake of Genesareth.	1. And it came to pass that *when* the multitude pressed upon him to hear the word of God, he stood by the lake of Genesareth.
2. And saw two ships standing by the Lake; but the fishermen were gone *down,* and were washing their nets.	2. And saw two ships standing by the lake: but the fishermen were gone *out of them* and were washing their nets.
3. And *having gone aboard* one of *them, which* was Simon's, he *prayed* him to *put* back a little from the land, and *he sat down and* taught the *people from aboard* the ship.	3. And *going up into* one of *the ships that* was Simon's, he *desired* him to *draw* back a little from the land. And *sitting he* taught the *multitudes out of* the ship.
4. And when he had *done* speaking, he said *unto* Simon: Launch out into	4. Now when he had *ceased to* speak, he said *to* Simon: Launch out

[4] Ver. 18. There is perhaps little choice between "future glory" and Challoner's rendering.

19. "Kingdom of God," for "sons of God," a paraphrase which should have been relegated to the margin.

20. Nary has a full stop after "hope"; Challoner has a colon, but deprives it of its force by beginning verse 21 with "because" instead of "that"; the passage should read, "in hope that the creature (creation) may be. . . ." "Bondage" is preferrable to "servitude," but Nary's "glorious liberty" hardly does justice to the Hebrew idiom.

22. Adhering to the Latin, neither translator does justice to the compound verbs; R.V., "groaneth and travaileth in pain together" (margin, "or with us") is hardly an improvement.

23. Challoner has "Spirit" with a capital "S" as referring to the Holy Spirit; Nary is surely right. "Not only *they*" is preferable, referring to "every creature."

Nary, 1719 (*continued*)

the deep, and let *loose* your nets for a draught.

5. And Simon answer*ed, and* said *unto* him: Master, we have *toiled* all night, and have taken nothing: But at thy word I will let *loose* the net.

6. And when they had done *so,* they enclosed *so* great a multitude of fish, *that* their net broke.

7. And they beckoned to their *companions, who* were in the other ship, that they should come and help them. And they came, and filled both the ships, so that they almost sank.

8. Which when Simon Peter *perceived,* he fell down at Jesus' knees, saying: Depart from me O Lord, for I am a sinful man.

9. For he was astonished, and all that were with him at the draught of fish, which they had taken.

10. And so were James and John, the sons of Zebedee, who were Simon's *companions.* And Jesus *said unto* Simon: Fear not: From henceforth thou shalt catch men.

11. And having brought their ships to land, they *forsook* all, *and* followed him.

Challoner, 1749 (*continued*)

into the deep, and let *down* your nets for a draught.

5. And Simon answer*ing,* said *to* him: Master, we have *laboured* all *the* night, and have taken nothing; but at thy word I will let *down* the net.

6. And when they had done *this,* they enclosed *a very* great multitude of fish*es, and* their net broke.

7. And they beckoned to their *partners that* were in the other ship, that they should come and help them. And they came, and filled both the ships, so that they *were* almost sink*ing.*

8. Which when Simon Peter *saw,* he fell down at Jesus' knees, saying: Depart from me, for I am a sinful man (O Lord).

9. For he was *wholly* astonished, and all that were with him, at the draught of *the* fish*es* which they had taken.

10. And so were *also* James and John the sons of Zebedee, who were Simon's *partners.* And Jesus *saith to* Simon: Fear not; from henceforth thou shalt catch men.

11. And having brought their ships to land, *leaving* all *things, they* followed him.[5]

[5] Ver. 1. "As" is more correct than "when"; the Greek and Latin mean "he was standing" rather than "he stood." In his third revision, 1752, Challoner has "and *he* saw."

2. It is hard to choose between "gone down" and "gone out of," but the former is more literally exact.

3. For "draw back a little," the edition of 1752 has "thrust out"; Challoner has an unfortunate predilection for "that" in place of "which" (see verse 7 and Rom. 8:18, 20). Nor does Challoner avoid the participial construction which is so marked a feature of the Rheims version; e.g., "sitting he taught," though in 1752 he has, "sitting down"; see verse 5. This whole verse reads better in Nary's version.

4. Nary's "let loose" here and in the following verse is literally correct, but neglects the idiom. The rendering "Master" is perhaps inevitable; no one would like to read "Teacher," though it is St. Luke's characteristic term.

5. Nary's rendering of this whole verse is more rhythmical than Challoner's. Nary has a keen sense of rhythm, for instance, "unto him" (verses 5 and 10), and "until" instead of "till" (Rom. 8:22).

6. Neither version does justice to the imperfect tense of both the Greek and the Latin *rumpebatur,* "was breaking" or "threatening to break." Challoner is slavishly literal by giving "fishes" in the plural in verses 6 and 9.

The notes in Nary's version are comparatively few.[6] Their purpose he thus explains:

My design is to reconcile some apparent Contradictions in the Gospels, and to illustrate the literal Sense of the Text: And for as much as the *Greek* in some Places makes a clearer Sense than the *Latin,* I have now and then put the rendering from the *Greek* Text in the Margin. . . . As to Moral or mystical Reflections, I have industriously omitted to make any. . . . My chief aim is to encourage my Countrymen to read, and to meditate upon the Will and Testament of their Lord and Master; by giving it to them in a Stile and Dress les obscure and somewhat more engaging than it has been many years past.

As one of the official censors of Dr. Witham's version, which frequently refers to Dr. Nary's version, Challoner must have been familiar with the latter, though apparently he never refers to it.

---

8. Nary's rhythm is again seen in the end of this verse, "Depart from me O Lord, for I am a sinful man," though Challoner's order is that of the Greek and the Latin.

11. Here again Nary's order excels; his avoidance of the participial construction secures a compactness which is distinctly pleasing.

[6] There are fifty-three notes on Matthew; those on "Raca" (5:22), the "Corban" (15:5), the Passover (26:2), the Agony in the Garden (26:39), and "In the end of the Sabbath . . ." (28:1) being of considerable length. On Mark there are only six notes, four of them on chap. 9, and a lengthy one on the "shew bread." On Luke we have fourteen notes; those on our Lady's vow (1:34), the genealogy of Christ (2:3), and the "Second first Sabbath" (6:1) being given in detail. There are no notes at all on St. John or the rest of the New Testament. Dr. Nary defends "Passover" for "Pasch," "verily" instead of "Amen," "righteousness" instead of "justice," and the term "shew bread" (Matt. 12:4; Mark 2:26; Luke 6:4; Heb. 9:2).

CHAPTER XXIII

Dr. Witham's Version of the New Testament, 1730

THE task of remodeling the original Rheims version was continued by Dr. Robert Witham,[1] president of the college at Douay when Dr. Challoner was vice-president. With their experience of the English mission and its needs, they must have often discussed the want of a readable English version of the Bible, which they proceeded to produce. In 1730 [2] appeared:

Annotations on the New Testament of Jesus Christ, in which
I. The literal sense is explained according to the Expositions of the Ancient Fathers.

[1] Robert Witham came from a Yorkshire family famous in Catholic annals. After teaching philosophy at Douay, he went on the English mission and was Vicar General of the Northern District until 1714, when he became president of Douay, a post he held until his death on May 29, 1738. Dr. Witham, say the Editors of the *Seventh Douay Diary,* "was a president to whom the college of Douay owed much, but especially in the regularity of its discipline, the care with which its accounts were kept, his strict adherence to authority, and the spirit of almost isolation to which, in the end, he reduced the college. He appears to have been a man of strong but narrow views, with a deep sense of duty and piety, an unswerving loyalty to the House of Stuart, a rooted objection to the subordination of the College to the University of Paris, which—with good reason—he suspected of Jansenism in its theology." Dr. Burton quotes a recent French writer, Msgr. Haudecœur, who thus sums up the character of Dr. Witham: "An exceptional administrator, a solid theologian, a distinguished orator, a man of deep and enlightened piety, and one who exhibited a singular beauty of soul, he has left in the College and in the minds of all the English clergy an undying memory and a stainless reputation" (*Life and Times of Bishop Challoner,* I, 109 note; on p. 39 is a portrait of Dr. Witham as a young man). The *Seventh Douay Diary, 1715–1778,* in *The Catholic Record Society,* vol. 28 (1928): "Dr. Witham himself started this Diary and continued it almost to the day of his death; it alone would be a sufficient memorial to his name."

[2] The second edition, which appeared in 1733, is not merely a reprint of the first, which comprises 536 pages, one page of *Errata,* and two pages of Approbations; the edition of 1733 has 541 pages, one page of Approbations, six pages of Indexes, and no *Errata.* A third edition appeared in 1740.

II. The false Interpretations, both of the ancient and modern writers, which are contrary to the received Doctrine of the Catholic Church, are briefly examined and disproved.

III. With an account of the chief differences betwixt the text of the ancient Latin Version and the Greek in the printed Editions and MSS. By R. W. DD.

The title is misleading, for the English version here given differs from that of Rheims in almost every verse.

Dr. Challoner himself acted as censor of the volume. I have, he says, examined "the English translation of the whole of the New Testament and have found it faithful in every respect and in conformity with the Vulgate. Nor have I discovered anything in the Notes contrary to sound faith or morals; the author's learning and piety appear at every turn" (Sept. 24, 1730, London). The Dominican, Dr. Ambrose Burgis, and the Franciscan, Dr. Antony Codrington, gave their approbations on the Gospels and Acts, but the former was too busy to do more, and the latter was dead before the second volume was completed.

In his Preface,[3] Witham defends the practice of translating from the Vulgate rather than from the Greek, arguing that while it is true that the originals were written in Greek, we always have to ask "where we may find this Greek fountain pure and unmixed, as it was in the beginning," for "out of about 120 MSS. he [Mills] publish'd an. 1707, [there are] thirty thousand different readings," a variety which brought about the publication of those innumerable versions which led Luther himself to exclaim: "Owing to the number of versions, readers were left in a greater state of uncertainty than ever before." Beza likewise said that the number of translators who "perverted rather than converted" was so great that unless something was done to counteract their audacity, we should find ourselves within a very few years stripped of our property.

Dealing with the Rheims Version of 1582, Witham points out that it was made

> before the amendments and corrections made under Sixtus V. and Clement VIII. to reduce the Latin-Vulgat to its former purity. Yet the differences betwixt that Douay-Translation, and the present Latin-Vulgat, are so few, and inconsiderable, that they must have follow'd a very correct Latin-Edition. . . . They perhaps follow'd too scrupulously the Latin, even as to the placing of the words; but what chiefly makes that edition seem so obscure at present, and scarce intelligible, is the difference of the English tongue, as it was spoken at that time.

[3] This Preface, well worth reading in its entirety, is given by Cotton, *Rhemes and Doway,* Appendix IV, pp. 305–14.

Since he entitled his work *Annotations,* Dr. Witham presumably did not at first contemplate making a fresh translation of the text, but merely intended to provide his fellow countrymen with a compendium of Catholic doctrine more suited to their needs than that given by the sixteenth-century Rheims Version. Hence he omitted their Annotations as dealing with controversies long dead, and purposely avoided "any harsh language or reflections on those who have fal'n into the greatest errors and mistakes." [4]

The instructive character of his Annotations is seen in those on the sin against the Holy Ghost (Matt., chap. 20), on St. Peter's faith continuing unshaken in his successors (Matt., chap. 16), on "no one knoweth of the Day of Judgment" (Matt., chap. 24). The eight pages of Annotations on John, chap. 1, deal mainly with the divinity of Christ; he discusses at length the authenticity of the passage on the stirring of the waters (John, chap. 5), but only briefly discusses that of the woman taken in adultery (John, chap. 8). Apropos of Christ's discourse at the Last Supper, he quotes Luther as having said: "Who but the Devil hath granted such a Licence of wresting the words of the Holy Scripture? Who ever read in the Scriptures, that *my Body,* is the same as *the sign of my Body?* or that *is,* is the same as, *it signifies?* . . . Not *one* of the Fathers, though so numerous, ever said: *It is only bread, and wine:* or, *the* Body, and Blood of Christ is not there present" (Luther, *Opera* [Wittenberg], VII, 391).

On Christ's rebuke to St. Peter (Matt. 16:23), Witham notes: "His words may signify 'begone from me,' but out of respect for the ancient Fathers, who would have these words to signify *come after me* or *follow me,* I have put with the Rheims translation, *Go after me."* On Matt. 18:6 he has this note: " 'Scandalize,' being sufficiently understood, and authoriz'd by use, both in English and in French, might, I thought, be retain'd. The words 'offend' and 'offence' in the Prot. Translation do not express sufficiently the sense." And on Heb. 5:7: "Even the last Protestant translation (1611), though much more exact than any of the former, put, 'And was heard in that he feared.' If the Rhem. translation,

[4] The notes are not meant to be controversial. But at times Witham does not hesitate to point out the aberrations of contemporary commentators. The prevalent insistence that the Pope was the Antichrist particularly annoyed him. His lengthy note on Apoc., chap. 18 (pp. 513–20), would have been much longer, he declares, had not a friend (Challoner?) urged him to omit his proposed Appendix on the subject.

which I have not changed ('was heard for his reverence'), be Obscure, I much doubt whether theirs can be better understood."

Witham was familiar with Dr. Nary's version,[5] but not wholly in sympathy with it, thinking him too ready to follow the lead of the Protestant translations. On I Thess. 2:3, for instance, he says he would "prefer the rendering 'and that no man go beyond or circumvent his brother in *the* matter,' to that of the Protestants—and Mr. N.—who even in their translations (as distinct from Notes) add 'in any matter,' because some expound it of frauds and circumventions in any kind of business. But this addition of *any* should be left out, seeing that the best Interpreters expound it of a prohibition of adultery."[6] He complains, too, that "a late English translation from the Latin an. 1719, by C.N." is not consistent in its renderings of the Vulgate *seniores* and *presbyteri*, "the Translators of the Rhem. Testament were more exact." Again, apropos of II Thess. 2:3 he insists on the sound principle—against Dr. Nary—that "when the Expositions are so different, as in this place, whosoever pretends to give a literal Translation, ought never to add words to the text, which determine the sense to such a particular Exposition, and especially in the same print, as Mr. N— on the 7. verse, where he translates, 'only let him that now holdeth the Faith, keep it until he be taken out of the way.'"

Some renderings can hardly be called felicitous; at times we have paraphrases rather than translations: "A Ruler of a Synagogue," instead of, "a certain ruler" (Matt. 9:18); "and he coming forth," with the addition, "out of the boat" (Matt. 14:14); "a hundred Roman pence," where the word "Roman" should rather have been in the margin (Matt. 18:28); "and when he had said these words, his adversaries all blush'd for shame" (Luke 13:17); "pursue peace with all men, *and purity of life,*" for "holiness" (Heb. 12:14); "a mountain palpable" (Heb. 12:18); "that God would open to us a door of utterance" (Col. 4:3); "the long-bearing of our Lord" (II Pet. 3:15); "and a man's enemies *shall be* his own Domesticks" (Matt. 10:36), an unfortunate Latinism, all the more strange since the original Rheims version has, "they of his own household." The use of italics to indicate words not in the original is disput-

[5] Cornelius Nary was a Doctor of Paris University, and perhaps it is not ungenerous to suppose that Dr. Witham's well-known distrust of that university with its Jansenistic tendencies may have unconsciously influenced his judgment when dealing with Nary.

[6] The Revisers in 1881 adopt the same view in their translation.

able; Witham, who seems to have been the first to introduce them into the Catholic versions, defends their use: "If the reader find in this Edition sometimes a word or two in a different character [italics] it is meerly because, tho' they are not express'd in the very *letter* of the text, yet they seem'd necessary, to represent to the reader the true and literal sense." [7]

On the other hand, some renderings might well be preserved: "Judas, is it with a kiss thou betrayest the Son of man?" (Luke 22:48); "cancelling the handwriting of the decree" (Col. 2:14); "dwelling in tents," instead of the unfortunate "cottages" of Rheims and Challoner (Heb. 11:9). Witham is, so far as we have noticed, the only translator who had the courage to differentiate the genders in Luke 15:9: the woman who had recovered her lost groat "calleth together her female friends," though "woman friends" might have been better. "Eternal mansions" (Luke 16:9) is a decided improvement on "eternal tabernacles" (Rheims and R.V.), or "everlasting habitations" (A.V.), or "everlasting dwellings" (Challoner).

Concerning Witham's version Cotton remarks:

> Some severe but seasonable animadversions were made on it a few years after its publication, in an important treatise, which unfortunately has become extremely scarce, entitled, "Popery an Enemy to Scripture: or, an account of the several methods pursued by the Church of Rome, to sink the authority of the *Holy Scriptures;* and of the various falsifications introduced in some versions of the *New Testament,* publish'd by Divines of that communion in French and English; particularly the last in English, by Dr. W. Professor of Divinity at Douay. By *James Serces,* Vicar of Appleby in Lincolnshire." London, 1736. . . . This pamphlet richly deserves to be reprinted at the present day.[8]

[7] This use of the italic first appeared in the Genevan version of 1560. Such a practice may be misleading and is apt to result in undue emphasis by the unwary reader.

[8] *Rhemes and Doway,* pp. 44 f.

CHAPTER XXIV

Fifth and Sixth Editions of the Rheims New Testament

THE FIFTH EDITION, 1738

IN 1738 was published in folio what is known as the Fifth Edition of the Rheims New Testament. The long gap between this edition and that of 1633 grieved the soul of Dr. Cotton, who says: "During the remainder of this century [1635–1700] I find nothing done by the Roman Catholics towards keeping up a supply of the Vernacular Scriptures for the people. . . . No fewer than a hundred and five years had passed since an edition of the Rhemish Testament had been printed." [1] Yet the marvel is that what Cotton himself describes as "a new and imposing edition, . . . in a large handsome folio volume, 'adorned with cuts,' . . . handsomely printed, on a large fine paper, with good type," [2] should have been produced at all in those penal days. The title is substantially the same as in the four previous editions, though there is a slight change in the order of the clauses:

The New Testament of Jesus Christ; with Arguments of Books and Chapters, with Annotations and other Helps, for the better understanding of the Text, and especially for the Discovery of Corruptions in divers late Translations: and for clearing up Religious Controversies of the present Times. To which are added Tables of the Epistles and Gospels, Controversies and Heretical Corruptions. The Text is faithfully translated into English, out of the Authentical Latin, diligently conferred with the Greek, and other Editions in divers Languages, and the Annotations, etc., are affix'd to it by the English College then resident in Rhemes. The Fifth Edition (the First in Folio) adorned with Cuts. Permissu Superiorum. Printed in the year MDCCXXXVIII.

Misled apparently by the name of the engraver of the quaint illustrations, booksellers' catalogues sometimes add, "printed by Van der

[1] *Rhemes and Doway*, pp. 27, 46.
[2] *Ibid.*, pp. 46, 228.

Gucht"; but it was almost certainly produced in London. The frontispiece depicts the Blessed Virgin, standing for the Church, on the right side of the crucifix; on the left stands Aaron, representing the Synagogue. Before each Gospel is a picture of the Evangelist: St. Mark with a truly amazing lion, St. Luke painting a portrait of Our Lady, St. John penning the opening words of his Gospel. The notes are now at the foot of each page instead of at the end of the chapter as in 1582 and 1600, or at the end of the volume as in 1621 and 1630. The Approbations of the first and second editions as well as the Preface are reprinted.

This edition marks a further stage in the revision and modernization of the Rheims Version. For while Cotton speaks only of "some few changes of the antiquated phrases in the Text,"[3] there are in reality many changes; e.g., "there was a cry [for "clamour"] made" (Matt. 25:6); "well done, good and faithful servant," for "wel fare thee" (Matt. 25:21, 23); "swept with a broom," for "besom" (Luke 11:25). Changes were made in the excessive literalism of the previous editions, which had found its worst expression in Mark 14:51, where the Rhemists had rendered *vestitus sindone supra nudum* as "clothed with sindon upon the bare," which is now changed to "cloathed with linnen cloath over his naked body." These few instances—they might be multiplied—show the definite attempts at revision. Yet the editor, like St. Jerome, *temperavit calamo;* for he allowed some of the worst features of the old version to stand: "the domesticall church" (I Cor. 16:19); "containing," for "holding forth" (Phil. 2:16); "celestials, terrestrials and infernals" (Phil. 2:10); "Dominator" (Jude 4); "the countenance of his nativitie" (Jas. 1:23).[4]

Who was this reviser? In some booksellers' catalogues it is categorically stated that this edition was "edited by Bishop Challoner and Father Francis Blyth, O.D.C.,"[5] though no such suggestion appears on the

[3] *Ibid.*, p. 49. "There are some few *verbal* alterations in the text; and the same in the Annotations: but (with exception of *the spelling*) I think the substance of both is unchanged from the editions of 1600 and 1633" (*ibid.*, p. 47). But the Rev. R. Hudleston, in the Preface to his reprint of the version of 1582, in which the notes are omitted (Burns, Oates & Washbourne, 1926), points out that in the edition of 1738 there are "a number of departures from the text of the original."

[4] The variations in subsequent editions are interesting: "his own countenance" (1818, 1820, 1825, etc.); "his natural countenance" (1749, etc.).

[5] Father Blyth (1705–72) was a convert who became Vicar-Provincial of the English Carmelites, 1742–55. For many years he was attached to the Portuguese Embassy, and he published various devotional and controversial works. He was buried in St. Pancras

title page of any copy seen by this author. But the Rev. T. Barnard says: "In the year 1768 [clearly a misprint for 1738, for no edition dates from 1768], he, in conjunction with the Rev. Mr. F. Blyth, published a new and fine edition in folio of the *Rhemes Testament.*" [6] There is no antecedent improbability in this deduction, for in 1730 Challoner had given his Approbation to the version revised by Dr. Witham when the latter was president of the college at Douay and himself vice-president. Moreover, the changes introduced in 1738 are, with few exceptions, precisely those adopted by Challoner in 1749.[7]

THE SIXTH EDITION, 1788, 1789

Seven years after the death of Challoner in 1781, Wogan the printer took the bold step of publishing, with all the original notes of the first edition (1582):

The New Testament of Jesus Christ with Arguments of Books and Chapters: Annotations and Other Helps, for the better understanding of the Text, and especially for the Discovery of Corruptions in divers Translations: and for clearing up the Religious Controversies of these times. To which are added Tables of the Epistles and Gospels. The Text is faithfully translated into English, out of the Authentical Latin, diligently conferred with the Greek, and other editions in divers languages: And the Annotations, etc. are affixed to it: by the English College resident in Rhemes, 1582. The Sixth Edition (the second in folio) adorned with cuts.[8]

Search the Scriptures. John. v

Cemetery. See Gillow, *Bibliographical Dictionary of the English Catholics,* I, 252 f.; Zimmermann, *Carmel in England,* pp. 373–78.

[6] *The Life of the Venerable and Right Rev. Richard Challoner,* p. 128; see Cotton, *op. cit.,* p. 47.

[7] Of sixty-four changes noted in this edition as compared with the four previous editions, and taken quite at random, no less than forty-nine were perpetuated by Challoner in 1749. For example: "invoking," for "invocating" (Acts 7:58), while the words "fell asleep in the Lord" (Acts 7:59), omitted in the previous editions, were inserted in 1738 and in subsequent editions; "towards the south-west and north-west," for "towards Afrike and the Chore" (Acts 27:12); "barbarians," for "barbarous" (Acts 28:3); "captivating," for "captiving" (Rom. 7:23); "uncircumcision," for "prepuce" (I Cor. 7:18 f.); "as long as," for "so long time as" (I Cor. 7:39); "do not keep company with him," for "do not company with him" (II Thess. 3:9); "before the times of the world," instead of "before the secular times" (Tit. 1:2); "hateful," for "odible" (Tit. 3:3). These instances could be multiplied.

[8] The title varies slightly from that of the first edition. This edition is spoken of as the "Sixth," the "Fifth" being the first folio edition of 1738; Challoner's five revisions are totally disregarded. Copies of this edition, which anticipated the ill-fated editions of 1816 and 1818, are exceedingly rare.

Give me understanding, and I wil search Thy Law: and wil keep it with my whole hart. Psalm 118.

[The passage from St. Augustine, as in the first edition (p. 254).]

Liverpool. Printed and sold by P. Wogan, 1789.[9]

The frontispiece is a picture of the crucifixion with the *Ecclesia* looking upwards and the *Synagoga* looking down. The Preface [10] and preliminary pieces of 1582 with the original Annotations are reproduced; but the marginal notes are omitted, though some are incorporated in the Annotations. The text adopted seems to be that of the fifth edition of the Rheims New Testament, 1738, which was a slight revision, by Challoner himself, of the previous editions. There are, however, some variations adopted from his subsequent revisions of 1749 and 1750; e.g., "their [for "the"] Scribes" (Matt. 7:29); the inversion, "I also will" (Mark 11:29). Following the third revision, 1752, the clause omitted from Mark 8:6 in 1749 and 1750 is inserted. In Luke 2:18 we have a wholly independent rendering, "all who heard"; the words, "of God," are not inserted in Mark 15:29, nor are the omissions in Acts 18:10 and Heb. 9:9 made good. The Gospel for the twenty-first Sunday after Pentecost is, as usual, given incorrectly: Matt. 18:23–25 for 18:23–35.

[9] Cotton maintains that this edition was printed in 1788 with the last line of the original title page reading as follows: "Liverpool: printed in the year MDCCLXXXVIII and sold by R. Ferguson, bookseller in Dale Street"; and he declares that in 1789 copies were sold in Dublin with a new title page bearing the name of P. Wogan and a list of Irish subscribers on the reverse (*op. cit.*, p. 233; cf. *ibid.*, p. 56). [Ed.]

[10] Some of the opening and closing clauses of the Preface are omitted.

CHAPTER XXV

Dr. Challoner's Revisions, 1749-72

THE work of Doctors Nary and Witham and the slight revision apparent in the fifth edition of the Rheims New Testament, prepared the way for that text of the English New Testament in use until the present day. This text is the result of the indefatigable work of Bishop Challoner,[1] who, besides being almost certainly responsible for the fifth edition of the Rheims New Testament, 1738, revised the version of the Old Testament twice, in 1750 and 1763, while doing the same for the New Testament no less than five times, in 1749, 1750, 1752, 1763, and 1772. Hence English-speaking Catholics the world over owe Dr. Challoner an immense debt of gratitude, for he provided them for the first time with a portable, cheap, and readable version which in spite of a few inevitable defects has stood the test of two hundred years of use.

The saintly bishop, it is true, did not possess the profound scholarship of Gregory Martin or Richard Bristow, but he did perceive what was needed by his flock. There are, of course, inaccuracies in his renderings; but they are surprisingly few. The Gospels are perhaps the best part of his work, the epistles the least satisfactory. It must be conceded, too, that the necessary simplification he aimed at and secured has resulted in the loss of that dignity, rhythm, and majesty which is so noticeable at times in the original version of 1582, the nervous force of which will be apparent to anyone who will read aloud from it such passages as the parables of the ten virgins and of the ten talents (Matt., chap. 25). Cardinal Wiseman complained of one change made by Challoner, the

[1] Born in 1691, Richard Challoner was vice-president of Douay under Dr. Witham; consecrated as Titular Bishop of Debra and coadjutor to Bishop Petre in 1741, he succeeded the latter as Vicar Apostolic of the London District; he died in 1781, in his ninetieth year. Milner preached his funeral oration and also wrote *A Brief Account of the Life of the Late R. Rev. Richard Challoner, D.D.*, 1798. His life was written as early as 1784 by the Rev. Father Barnard, reprinted in 1793; see Burton, *Life and Times of Bishop Challoner*, 1909, 2 vols.; M. Trappes-Lomax, *Bishop Challoner*, 1936.

substitution of "the Lord" for "Our Lord," though probably few would agree now with the Cardinal.[2]

FIRST REVISION OF THE NEW TESTAMENT, 1749

In 1749 Challoner's first revision of the Rheims New Testament appeared with the title: *The New Testament of our Lord and Saviour Jesus Christ. Translated out of the Latin Vulgat: diligently compared with the original Greek; and first published by the English College at Rhemes, Anno 1582. Newly revised and corrected according to the Clementin edition of the Scriptures. With Annotations for clearing up modern Controversies in Religion, and other Difficulties of Holy Writ. Printed in the year MDCCXLIX.*[3] There is no indication of authorship or of the place of publication. The Approbations to the editions of 1582 and 1600 are repeated, and a further Approbation of the present revision is added:

> Vulgatam Novi Testamenti editionem, olim a Theologis Rhemensibus Anglice redditam, ac demum ab N. N. recognitam et emendatam, attente perlegi: eamque in omnibus fidelem, ac Vulgatae Editionis sensui ubique inhaerentem judico. Breves quoque ejusdem in Novum Testamentum Annotationes, Catholicae veritati consentaneas, et ad difficiliora sacri textus loca illustranda perutiles censeo.
>
> Septimo Calend. Octobris Anno 1748.
>
> GULIELMUS GREEN, S.T.D.
>
> Idem Censeo, 15 Calend. Novembris Anno 1748.
>
> GULIELMUS WALTON, S.T. Professor.

A list of the books of the New Testament precedes the text, which is very well printed in two columns. After the Apocalypse appears this note: "N.B. In the following table, the titles of the books, and the order

[2] In the *Dublin Review,* II (1837), 475–92. This very point was discussed in Convocation two hundred years earlier, March 19, 1541: When it was asked "whether one Christian speaking to another should say, '*The* Lord save thee,' or '*Our* Lord save thee'? The bishops all (Ely and St. Davids excepted) are for '*Our* Lord save thee'; but the archbishop more for 'the' than 'our'; for '*the* Lord' containeth 'immensitatem majestatis Dei, et universalem dominationem et amplitudinem dignitatis'" (Wilkins, *Concilia Magnae Britanniae et Hiberniae,* III, 862).

[3] The copy in the British Museum (two volumes bound into one, but the pagination running throughout) has pencilled on the fly sheet: "This copy contains specimens from the three rare first editions of Dr. Challoner's revision of the Rhemes Testament, namely a complete copy of the first and rarest [of 1749]; part of page 218 of the second edition [1750] at the end of this volume; and the title-page of the third edition [1752] at the beginning of the second volume." The "part of page 218" referred to contains John 21:21–23, corresponding to p. 231 of the second revision. Both the first and second revisions are exceedingly rare; I am acquainted with only three copies of the latter; copies of the third revision, 1752, seem to be more numerous.

of the psalms are quoted as they are set down in the Protestant bible." A Table of Controversies, a Table of the Epistles and Gospels, and a Chronological Table follow. The notes are very few; there are no chapter headings. A comparison of but one passage as it stood in 1582 and as modernized by Challoner in 1749 will give some idea of the changes he made (the italics indicate Challoner's most significant changes).

I Cor., chap. 13

Rheims, 1582	Challoner, 1749
1. If I speake with the tonges of men, and of Angels, and have not charitie: I am become as sounding brasse, or a tinkling cymbal.	1. If I speak with the tongues of men, and of angels, and have not charity, I am become as sounding brass or a tinkling cymbal.
2. And if I should have prophecie, and knew al mysteries, and al knowledge, and if I should have al faith so that I could remove mountaines, and have not charitie, I am nothing.	2. And if I should have prophecy, and *should* know all mysteries, and all knowledge, and if I should have all faith, so that I could remove mountains, and have not charity, I am nothing.
3. And if I should distribute al my goods to be meate for the poore, and if I should deliver my body so that I burne, and have not charitie, it doth profit me nothing.	3. And if I should distribute all my goods to *feed* the poor, and if I should deliver my body *to be burned,* and have not charity, it profiteth me nothing.
4. Charitie is patient, is benigne: Charity envieth not, dealeth not perversely: is not puffed up:	4. Charity is patient, is *kind,* charity envieth not, dealeth not perversely: is not puffed up.
5. Is not ambitious, seeketh not her owne, is not provoked to anger, thinketh no evil:	5. Is not ambitious, seeketh not her own, is not provoked to anger, thinketh no evil.
6. Rejoyceth not upon iniquities, but rejoyceth with the truth:	6. Rejoiceth not *in* iniquity, but rejoiceth with the truth.
7. Suffereth al things, believeth al things, hopeth al things, beareth al things.	7. *Beareth* all things, believeth all things, hopeth all things, *endureth* all things.
8. Charitie never falleth away: whether prophecies shal be made voide, or tonges shal cease, or knowledge shal be destroied.	8. Charity never falleth away: whether prophecies shall be made void, or tongues shall cease, or knowledge shall be destroyed.
9. For in part we know, and in part we prophecie.	9. For we know in part, and prophesy in part. [Inverted.]
10. But when that shal come which is perfect, that shal be made voide that is in part.	10. But when that which is perfect *is* come, that which is in part shall be done away. [Inverted.]
11. When I was a little one, I spake as a little one, I understood as a little	11. When I was a *child* I spoke as a *child,* I understood as a *child,* I thought

Rheims, 1582 (*continued*)	Challoner, 1749 (*continued*)
one. But when I was made a man, I did away the things that belonged to a little one.	as a *child*. But when I *became* a man, I *put* away the things *of a child*.
12. We see now by a glasse in a darke sort: but then face to face. Now I know in part: but then I shall know as also I am knowen.	12. We see now *through* a glass in a dark *manner:* but then face to face. Now I know in part; but then I shall know *even* as I am known.
13. And now there remaine, faith, hope, charitie, these three, but the greater of these is charitie.	13. And now there remain faith, hope, charity, these three: but the great*est* of these is charity.

This, Challoner's first formal revision, as distinct from that initiated in the "Fifth Edition" of the Rheims Version, 1738, has been in the main the standard followed by all printers and publishers since 1825, when Dr. Murray's edition appeared, except for the edition by Walsh and Wiseman in 1847.[4] Yet no really stereotyped form of text, which all should be bound to adhere to, has ever yet been determined, although the Catholic Board in 1815 reproduced the text of 1749 with very few variants and gave an account of its reproduction by subsequent editors. In some passages practically all editions follow the text of 1749 as distinct from that of 1750 and 1752; e.g., "Thus shall you pray" (Matt. 6:9);[5] "arose up" (Matt. 9:9); "when therefore the Lord" (Matt. 21:40). Yet, as we shall repeatedly point out, it is hard to find editions which have not perpetuated the eighteen renderings peculiar to the revision of 1750, as well as some peculiar to those of 1752 and 1764. There are also some renderings quite alien to Challoner's text.

FIRST REVISION OF THE OLD TESTAMENT, 1750

In 1750 Challoner published his revision of the Douay Version of the Old Testament: *The Holy Bible Translated from the Latin Vulgat: Diligently compared with the Hebrew, Greek, and other Editions in divers languages. And first published in the English College at Doway, Anno 1609. Newly revised and corrected, according to the Clementin Edition of the Scriptures. With Annotations for clearing up the principal*

[4] The text of the 1847 edition "appears to agree with that of the Bible, 4to. Dublin 1791, the Testament of 1803, and Haydock's Bible [1811–14]" (Cotton, *Rhemes and Doway,* p. 149); these latter were further revisions of Challoner's version. See below.

[5] So also the *Errata* of 1750; the text has "thus shalt thou pray." For the omissions and misprints, see below, pp. 368–70.

Difficulties of Holy Writ. Printed in the Year 1750; 4 vols., 12mo. The Approbations of 1609 and those of "Other Eminent Divines" are repeated. The Annotations are brief but numerous—250 on the Pentateuch alone. Volume 2 ends with "A Chronological Table" (the Creation to Nehemias); volume 3 ends with "The Order and Distribution of the Psalms for Tenebrae, the Office of the Dead, and for Various Festivals, also the Penitential and Gradual Psalms." At the end of volume 4 is this note: "N.B. The third and fourth book of Machabees; as also the third and fourth books of Esdras (which some call the first and second of Esdras) and the Prayer of Manasses, are here omitted: because they have never been received by the Church."

The original translators of the Old Testament, 1609–10, unfortunately omitted two clauses. In his revisions Challoner omitted these and nine more through oversight, which is hardly to be wondered at in view of his many other labors and the immensity of the task he had undertaken singlehanded. The clauses omitted are here given in parentheses:

Gen. 4:14. "Behold thou dost cast me out this day from the face of the earth (and I shall be hidden from thy face, and I shall be a vagabond and a fugitive on the earth)." The copyist's eye passed from the first "earth" to the second. Challoner's edition of 1750 was responsible for this mistake, which was corrected in all editions subsequent to 1816.

Gen. 36:2. "Esau took wives . . . Oolibama (the daughter of Ana)," an omission due to Challoner, 1750, but corrected in all editions later than 1816 except in that by Duffy, 1847.

Exod. 18:10. "The Lord who hath delivered (you out of the hand of Pharao and out of the hand of the Egyptians, who hath delivered) his people out of the hand of Egypt"; the same kind of mistake as in Gen. 4:14; corrected in all editions later than 1816.

Exod. 35:23. "If any man had violet and purple and scarlet twice dyed, (fine linen and goats' hair, rams' skins dyed) red, and violet-coloured skin"; a mistake like the above, but not owing to Challoner, who only failed to notice the omission in the previous editions of the Douay Old Testament, 1609 and 1635. The text is corrected in editions later than 1816.

Jos. 7:17. "Which being brought by its families, it was found to be the family of Zare. Bringing that also by its houses, he found it to be (Zabdi)," a strange mistake occurring in the 1750 edition.

Judg. 7:18. "When the trumpet shall sound in my hand, do you also blow the trumpets on every side of the camp, and shout together (to the Lord, and Gedeon)." The omission of the last words, corrected by Haydock, was not noticed by Murray in 1825; hence the same gap appears in present-day editions.

Judg. 11:18. Moses "camped on the other side of the Arnon, and he would not enter the bounds of Moab (for the Arnon is the border of the lands of Moab)." Challoner omitted the last clause, and though corrected in Haydock's second edition, the correction passed unnoticed and almost every other edition of the Douay Bible is here defective.

I Kings 1:11. "If thou wilt look down (on the affliction of thy servant) and wilt be mindful of me"; the words in parentheses, first omitted in 1750, appear in all editions since 1816.

I Kings 17:49. David's stone "struck the Philistine in the forehead (and the stone was fixed in his forehead)." The last clause was omitted by the printers of the original Douay Version. Haydock seems to have been the first to rectify the mistake in his second edition, 1813, and though Troy's edition, 1816, again omitted the clause, all later editions give the verse in full.

II Par. 32:32. "The rest of the acts of Ezechias, and of his mercies, are written in (the vision of Isaias the son of Amos, the prophet, and in) the book of the kings of Juda and Israel." Challoner's unfortunate omission of this interesting historical statement was first rectified in the edition brought out by Burns and Oates in 1914.[6]

Agg. 2:2. The verse should read: "In the seventh month (the twenty-first day of the month)"; but the last clause does not stand in any edition of the Douay Bible, so far as I am aware.[7]

Some of the misprints in this edition of 1750 have also been perpetuated: "guard" for "garden" (Neh. 3:15); "Jacob" for "heaven" (Ps. 90:1). Other editions appeared in 1763, 1796, 1805, and 1811. That of 1763, edited by Challoner himself, is to all intents and purposes a verbal reproduction of that of 1750, none of the omissions being corrected. For the other editions, see below. The edition of 1750 is frequently met with, not so that of 1763.

[6] The 1941 edition by Benziger Brothers and The Douay Bible House, New York, has the correction; but current Douay Bible House texts, now printed in Belgium, do not have the correction, nor do the latest Kenedy Bibles (1950). Yet the Bibles published in 1950 by Benziger Brothers and the Catholic Book Publishing Co. complete the text. [Ed.]

[7] Note that this is 2:1 in the Hebrew and A.V.

SECOND REVISION OF THE NEW TESTAMENT, 1750

To the four volumes containing the revised Old Testament, Challoner added a fifth, a cursory revision of his previous revision of the New Testament. The title page is the same as in the first revision, but now it is in red and black lettering; chapter headings are still wanting. The Approbation of 1749 is repeated. The omission of "tempting him" (Matt. 22:35), "strengthened in spirit" (Luke 1:80), and "to hurt thee" (Acts 18:10) is corrected; but not the omission of "and he commanded the people to sit down upon the ground" (Mark 8:6) and "of promise, as in a strange country" (Heb. 11:9). The words, "of God" (Mark 15:29), are now inserted on the authority of the Clementine revision. Capital letters are used lavishly; e.g., "Disciples." The Gospel for the twenty-first Sunday after Pentecost is given as Matt. 18:23–25 instead of 23–35, a misprint perpetuated in the majority of editions to this day. Six notes were added to those in the 1749 edition: on Acts 7:48; Rom. 7:1; I John 3:9; 5:1; 5:18; and II Cor. 9:11. The *Errata* at the end are important.[8]

[8] The *Errata* at the end of Challoner's second revision, 1750:

Matt.	6:9	for	"shalt thou"	read	"shall you"
	8:17	...	"by the prophet"	....	"by Isaias the prophet"
	10:17	...	"counsels"	....	"councils"
	13:25	...	"where"	....	"were"
	15:6	...	"and mother"	....	"or his mother"
Mark	1:45	...	"but be was"	....	"but he was"
	4:19	...	"lust"	....	"lusts"
	8:27	...	"in his way"	....	"in the way"
	15:3	...	"priest"	....	"priests"
Luke	3:16	...	"latchets"	....	"latchet"
	3:31	...	"Melca"	....	"Melea"
	9:33	...	"is it good"	....	"it is good"
	10:35	...	"two pieces"	....	"two pence"
	12:1	...	"yea"	....	"ye"
	13:9	...	"then after"	....	"then after that"
	17:16	...	"given"	....	"giving"
	18:26	...	"who can"	....	"who then can"
	21:21	...	"mountain"	....	"mountains"
	23:29	...	"paps"	....	"paps that"
Acts	4:16	...	"had been"	....	"hath been"
	4:29	...	"which"	....	"with"
	7:31	...	"he drew"	....	"as he drew"
Heb.	4:1	...	"having been"	....	"being"
	10:29	...	"esteemeth"	....	"esteemed"
	11:18	...	"they"	....	"thy"
Jas.	5:20	...	"caused"	....	"causeth"
I Pet.	2:13	...	"to the kings"	....	"to the king"
II John	4	...	"thy children"	....	"of thy children"

One hundred and twenty-four of the changes made from the previous revision were incorporated in the next revision, and nearly all are for the better; they show how meticulously Challoner worked at his self-imposed task amid his many other occupations. But there remain eighteen changes from the previous revision which, though not repeated in the third revision, have had a peculiar influence, for most of them are reproduced in nearly every subsequent edition. The following passages are peculiar to the revision of 1750.[9]

		1749	1750	1752
Matt.	1:17	to the transmigration of Babylon fourteen generations, . . . unto Christ fourteen	to the transmigration of Babylon are fourteen generations, . . . to Christ are fourteen	until the carrying away to Babylon are fourteen generations, . . . to Christ are fourteen
	4:2	afterwards he was hungry	being hungry	he was afterwards hungry
	23:29	because you build	that build	who build
Mark	6:5	miracle	miracles	mighty works
	9:11	who answering saith	who answering said	And he answered & said
	11:29	I also will . . . one word	I will also ask . . .	I will also ask of you one question
Luke	2:18	All that heard wondered at those things	All that heard wondered: and at . . .	All they that heard wondered: and at . . .
John	5:1	After these things there was	After these things was	After this was . . .
Acts	24:4	not further	no further	no farther
	28:7	in those places	in these places	in these quarters
Rom.	2:26	his uncircumcision	this[10] uncircumcision	his uncircumcision
	5:14	who had not	who have not	that had not

The first two *errata* were not noted by Cotton in his collation of the first three revisions by Challoner, hence the former enumerates the uncorrected text as being peculiar to this second revision (*op. cit.*, pp. 317 f.). It should be noted that in the *Errata* itself there are three misprints: Mark 4:19 is given as 4:9; Luke 3:31 is given as 5:31; Acts 7:31 is given as 8:31.

[9] This list differs somewhat from that given by Dr. Cotton, *Rhemes and Doway*, pp. 315–70. Overlooking the *Errata* at the end of the revision of 1750, he failed to notice that Matt. 6:9 should read, "thus therefore shall you pray" both in 1749 and in 1750, not "shalt thou" as in the text of 1750; Matt. 8:17 should read, "the Prophet Isaias," as in 1752. Cotton perhaps should have added Rom. 2:26, but see the following note. He also failed to notice the rendering of Matt. 4:2. On page 370 he speaks of eighteen renderings peculiar to 1750, but his collation includes Matt. 6:9 and 8:17, and omits Matt. 4:2 and Rom. 2:26.

[10] Presumably only a misprint, but it has persisted in many editions, even as late as 1896.

I Cor.	2:14	those things	these things	the things
	16:12	And as touching	And touching	As touching
Gal.	2:2	conferred with them that gospel	. . . the gospel	communicated to them the gospel
Ephes.	2:12	testaments	testament	covenants
I Pet.	1:13	that grace . . . in the	the grace . . .	the grace . . . at the
	5:9	befalls	befals	befalleth

These renderings peculiar to the second revision do not figure in editions by Coyne (1811), Haydock (1811–14), Troy (1816), or MacNamara (1818). They first appear in Syers' Bible, 1813, some too in the edition by Horrabin, 1818, and all of them in that by Keating and Brown, 1818, reprinted in 1832. But these same renderings will be found in practically every edition published since 1818;[11] yet this second revision has never been reproduced in its entirety, although an edition by Coyne in 1820 without any notes deserts it on only seven occasions: "he arose up" (Matt. 9:9), and "thine enemies" (Heb. 1:13), renderings peculiar to 1749; "he was afterwards hungry" (Matt. 4:2), "the Scribes" in place of "their Scribes" (Matt. 7:29), "one hundred and fifty-three fishes" (John 21:11), "the promise being left of entering" (Heb. 4:1), four renderings found only in the third revision; and "What is it to me?" (John 2:4), a rendering foreign to Challoner.

It is impossible to discover at this date how these eighteen variants came to be persistently adopted by nearly every editor after 1818; nor is it easy to understand how so many renderings peculiar to the first revision have persisted even in editions taking the third revision as their basis. Perhaps some explanation is to be found in the Approbation by the three Vicars Apostolic for the New Testament published by Keating and Brown in 1818, in which they expressly state that it is "conformable to that published by Bishop Challoner in 1750." This explicit preference for the second revision seems tantamount to a rejection of the former, 1749, which was reproduced by the Catholic Board in 1815, under the direction of Dr. Poynter. Milner, too, by his emphatic condemnation

[11] Taking quite at random four of the many editions bearing the Approbation of Dr. Denvir, 1847, 1851, 1858, and 1885, also those by Duffy, 1866, Burns and Oates, 1896, and by Archbishop Hayes, 1912, the seventeen passages referred to appear in them all, two exceptions being Gal. 2:2, where the latter edition has "communicated to them the Gospel," as in the third revision; and I Pet. 5:9, where the editions of 1858, 1885, 1896, and 1912 follow the first revision, "befalls"; those of 1820, 1847, 1851, and 1866 keep to the spelling of the second revision, "befals"; none have "befalleth," as in the third revision.

of the edition of 1815, tacitly condemned that of 1749, which he called "the most incorrect edition of the Testament that perhaps ever was published." Yet between these first and second revisions there are only one hundred and twenty-four differences, all of which, except two, are trifling: the omission of "that" before quotations, the substitution of "thy" and "my" for "thine" and "mine," etc.; the only changes of any importance are "footstool" for "footstool of thy feet" (Matt. 22:44), and "merchant" for "merchant man" (Matt. 13:45).

THIRD REVISION OF THE NEW TESTAMENT, 1752

Challoner published his third revision of the New Testament in 1752. It is in the same format as before, with the title in red and black, as in 1750.[12] Chapter headings, the same as those now in use, are inserted for the first time, and there are 119 additional notes—70 on St. Matthew as compared with 38 in 1749 and 41 in 1750. The chapter heading on Mark, chap. 6, has "4000" instead of "5000," but this mistake is corrected in the *Errata*. The "Table of Controversies" opens with the *caveat:* "N.B. the titles of the Books and the order of the Psalms are quoted as they are set down in the protestant bible." The text of this third revision was that in general use until 1815, when the edition produced by the Catholic Board reverted to the text of the first revision, 1749, which differs from that of 1752 in no less that 443 passages of St. Matthew's Gospel alone.

Challoner now made over 2,000 changes in the text of the two former revisions, and these he retained in the later editions of 1764 and 1772.[13]

[12] Prefixed to the title page was this quaint advertisement:

J. P. COGHLAN
Printer, Bookseller, Bookbinder & Stationer, etc.
In Duke-Street, Grosvenor Square,
London

Procures & Sells Books, in all Arts & Sciences, Bibles, Common-Prayers, . . . & School Books. Serves GENTLEMEN with Subscription Books, Magazines, Pamphlets, Plays, & all other occasional Books or Pamphlets. Takes Catalogues of *Gentlemen's* Libraries, gives most Money for any quantity or parcel of old Books, & Binds Books in the best & most elegant Manner.

LIKEWISE

Sells all sorts of fine Writing Papers, Plain, Gilt, Black, etc. Fine Wax, Wafers, black shining Sand, best Black or Red Lead Pencils, Japan Ink, or Ink Powder, Alphabets, Account Books, Copy Books, Cyphering Books, Receipt or Measuring Books, Pocket Books, Memorandum Books, Pounce, Slates, Slate Pencils, Quills, Pens, & the best sorts of red or black Inks.

[13] Challoner made no substantial changes in his subsequent editions.

A distinct effort at greater modernization of the language is noticeable throughout: the "boat" becomes a "ship," "miracles" are now "mighty works," "testament" is replaced by "covenant," "adored" by "worshipped," "cured" by "healed," "illuminated" by "enlightened," "reprobate" by "rejected," etc. Hitherto Challoner had translated *quia* and *quoniam,* though these merely represented the Greek recitative introducing statements: "I say to you that they have received their reward"; but he now omits the redundant "that." The tenses, too, are often corrected: "time should be no longer" is changed to "shall be" (Apoc. 10:6 f.); "thus therefore shall you pray" is changed—not too happily—to "you therefore shall pray in this manner" (Matt. 6:9); "transmigration" is now "carrying away"; "conferred with them" becomes "communicated to them" (Gal. 2:2); "mine" and "thine" become "my" and "thy." But some changes can hardly be called improvements: "who diversely and in many ways" will not bear comparison with "who at sundry times and in divers manners," though it is certainly preferable to the rendering of R.V., "by divers portions and in divers manners" (Heb. 1:1).

In this third revision Challoner avoided the inverted sentences so conspicuous in the original version, 1582, and in his own previous revisions: "diligently enquire" becomes "search diligently" *;[14] "afterwards he was" is replaced by "he was afterwards" *; "if in Sodom had been wrought the miracles that have been wrought in thee, perhaps it had remained" now is made to read: "if the mighty works had been done in Sodom that have been done in thee, perhaps it would have remained" *; "standing in the market place idle" becomes "standing idle in the market place"; "there came to him the blind and the lame" becomes "the blind and the lame came to him" *; "his generation who shall declare?" now reads, "who shall declare his generation?" But, as Wiseman urged,[15] these inverted forms of speech have a beauty of their own, and their removal seems to detract somewhat from the dignity and grace peculiar to the Scriptures. Who would endorse such changes as, "if any man will go to law with thee" ** instead of, "contend with thee in judgement" (Matt. 5:40); or "when he would have put him to

[14] An asterisk (*) indicates renderings which Challoner adopted from the reading of the Authorized Version; two asterisks (**) signify that the rendering was also retained in the Revised Version. These are a few of the renderings adopted from A.V.: Matt. 2:8; 4:2; 11:23; 20:3; 21:14; Acts 8:33, and so forth.

[15] In the *Dublin Review,* II (1837), 475–92.

death" ** instead of, "having a mind to put him to death" (Matt. 14:5)? "Now if God so clothe the grass of the field which to-day is and to-morrow is cast into the oven" ** is hardly preferable to, "if the grass of the field which is to-day and to-morrow is cast into the oven God doth so clothe" (Matt. 6:30). "Babbler" ** instead of "wordsower" (Acts 17:18) is assuredly not an improvement; nor is "the marriage was furnished with guests" * instead of "filled with guests" (Matt. 22:10); here R.V. returns to "filled."

It is true, as the above passages show, that Challoner did not hesitate to adopt renderings from the Authorized Version when he deemed them preferable; but it is puerile to suggest, as Cotton does (p. 51), that "the little differences seem to have been kept up on purpose to escape the odium of appearing to approach too closely to a Protestant translation." Some of the adaptations are certainly for the better, as when he changed the unfortunate "depositum" of the Rhemists (I Tim. 6:20) to "that which is committed to thy trust," in accordance with A.V. and followed by R.V. But in John 5:35, where the Baptist is spoken of as *lucerna et lucens,* and Wycliffe and Rheims correctly had "the [Wycliffe, "a"] lamp burning and shining," Challoner unfortunately changed "lamp" to "light," as had Tyndale, Cranmer, Geneva, and A.V.; but R.V. reverted to the Rhemists' "lamp." Indeed the Revisers frequently paid the Rhemists this compliment; e.g. II Thess. 2:3: Tyndale, Cranmer, and Geneva had changed Wycliffe's "the man of synne" to "that synful man"; A.V., "that man of sin"; but Rheims, correctly, "the man of sin," a rendering followed by R.V.; II Cor. 12:3: Wycliffe, "I woot not"; but Tyndale, Cranmer, Geneva, and A.V., "I cannot tell," followed by Challoner in all his revisions; yet Rheims, "I know not," is followed by R.V. and some modern Catholic texts.[16] II Cor. 5:14 is an example of an unfortunate change made by Challoner: "If one die for all, then all were dead," where the Rhemists correctly have, "if one died for all," though the next phrase, "then all were dead," had been rendered better by Tyndale, "then all died."

The following comparison of Matt. 13:1–9 as it appeared in 1582 and in Challoner's third revision will prove instructive; words in italics indicate the most significant changes.

[16] For further examples see pp. 129, 261 f., 571 f.

Matt. 13:1–9

Rheims Version, 1582	Challoner's Third Revision, 1752
1. The same day Jesus going out of the house, sate by the sea side.	1. The same day Jesus going out of the house, sat by the sea side,
2. And great multitudes were gathered together unto him, in so much that he went up into a *boate* and sate: and al the multitude stood *in* the shore,	2. And great multitudes were gathered together unto him, so that he went into a *ship* and sat: and all the multitude stood *on* the shore;
3. and he spake to them, many things in parables, saying,	3. And he spoke to them many things in parables, saying: Behold the sower went forth to sow.
4. Behold the sower went forth to sow. And whiles he soweth, some fell by the way side, and the *foules* of the aire did come and eate it.	4. And whil*st* he soweth some fell by the way side, and the *birds* of the air came and ate them up.
5. Othersome also fell upon *rockie places,* where they had not much earth: and they *shot up incontinent,* because they had not deepenes of earth,	5. And other some fell upon *stony ground,* where they had not much earth: and they *sprung up immediately,* because they had no deepness of earth,
6. And *after* the sun was up, they *parched:* and because they had not roote, they withered.	6. And *when* the sun was up, they *were scorched:* and because they had not root, they withered away.
7. And other fell among thornes: and the thornes grewe and choked them.	7. And others fell among thorns: and the thorns grew up and choked them.
8. And othersome fell upon good ground: and they *yelded* fruit, *the one* an hundred-fold, *the other* threescore, and *another* thirtie.	8. And others fell upon good ground: and they *brought forth* fruit, *some* a hundred-fold, *some* sixty-fold, and *some* thirty-fold.
9. He that hath eares to heare, let him heare.	9. He that hath ears to hear, let him hear.

The use of italics to indicate words not in the original first appeared in the Rheims Version of the New Testament in its fifth edition, 1738. In his first revision, 1749, Challoner used them sparingly, but they are multiplied to a great extent in his third revision; e.g., the mistake in Acts 2:37 f., "men *and* brethren." One curious feature of this revision is the substitution of "that" for "who" or "which," a reversal of his procedure in 1749, when he had replaced "that" of the original Rheims Version by "who" or "which." The first three revisions exhibit a strange vacillation on the point: "because you build," "that build," "who build" (Matt. 23:29). In 1749 and 1750 he wrote, "foreseeing *this"* (Acts 2:31), but *"this"* is superfluous and misleading, since St. Peter is simply saying that

David, being a prophet, foresaw; Challoner omitted the word in 1752, yet A.V. and R.V. retain it.

One of the most distressing features of the Rheims version is the awkward participial construction: "and he answering said," or worse, "who answering said." Though fully aware of this disfigurement, Challoner did not eliminate it from his first two revisions, but he now attempted a wholesale change: "and when we had heard this" replaces "which when we had heard" (Acts 21:12); "and when we had saluted them" replaces "whom when we had saluted" (Acts 21:19); "so he took him and brought him" replaces "he taking him brought him" (Acts 23:18).

The omission of "and he commanded the people to sit down on the ground" from Mark 8:6 in the two previous editions is corrected; [17] yet this third edition has two omissions peculiar to itself: the words "and he shall abound" being left out in Matt. 13:12, and "thou hast a little strength" from Apoc. 3:8; it also has one addition, a very minor one: Heb. 7:2 reads, "first by interpretation *of his name,* is king." The following eight clauses were omitted in one or the other of Challoner's revisions, some even by the Rhemists.

OMISSIONS IN CHALLONER'S REVISIONS

Matt. 13:12. "He that hath, to him shall be given (and he shall abound)." Challoner overlooked this clause in this third revision, 1752, and again in 1764 and 1772. Hence editions based upon the third revision also omit it, notably those by Haydock, even the last edition of that Bible by Oakley and Law, 1874–78. Most modern editions, based as they are on Challoner's first revision (1749 and 1750), have the clause.

Matt. 22:35. "One of them, a doctor of the Law, asked him (tempting him)." Challoner omitted "tempting him" in 1749, but inserted it in later revisions. It stands in all subsequent editions.

[17] Dr. Cotton points out that the last line on p. 181 of volume 2 is omitted, so that I John 1:5 reads, "And this is the declara- . . . from him"; the line which should read, "-tion which we have heard" having escaped the printer's eye. But in the three copies which I have seen, whereas two are complete, another has the missing line on p. 181 but repeats it on the top of the next page, "-tion which we have heard." In the Catalogue of the British and Foreign Bible Society a note says: "neither of the two copies below contains the error in I John 1:5 which Cotton, p. 230, mentions"; presumably, then, the first copy in their list has the error. I do not know if any one can explain how a book which was printed only once can appear with such divergencies, nor how—seeing that correct copies of the edition of 1752 existed—the next edition, 1764, came out without the correction being made, for at the foot of page 477 it has, "And this is the declaration" (catchword), and at the top of page 478 has "-tion from him, and believe," a whole line being omitted. The verse is correctly printed in the edition of 1772.

Mark 8:6. "(And he commanded the people to sit down on the ground.) And taking seven loaves. . . ." Here the position is the converse of that in Matt. 13:12. Challoner inserted the clause in 1752, and editions based on that revision retain it; but editions based on 1749 and 1750—that is, the vast majority of subsequent editions—omit it, though editions of Haydock's Bible retain it. The New York edition published by Benziger Brothers and The Douay Bible House is about the only recent edition of Challoner that retains the passage. [Ed.]

Mark 15:29. "Thou that destroyest the temple (of God)." The words "of God" were rightly omitted in all the early editions of the Rheims New Testament. Challoner inserted them in his second and subsequent revisions because they appeared in the Sixtine and Clementine editions of the Vulgate, though on what manuscript evidence it is hard to discover. They appear in all our modern editions, but seem to have little or no support from either Greek or Latin MSS.

Luke 1:80. "And the child grew (and was strengthened in spirit)." Challoner omitted the last words in 1749, but added them in later revisions. The Catholic Board edition, 1815, "stereotyped from that of 1749," failed to note the omission, though Bagster's reprint of the Catholic Board edition in 1823 inserted the clause.

Acts 18:10. "No man shall set upon thee (to hurt thee)," an accidental slip by Challoner in 1749 and therefore reproduced in 1815 and in Bagster's reprint in 1823 (see above, on Luke 1:80). All other editions retain the words "to hurt thee."

Heb. 11:9. "By faith he abode in the land (of promise, as in a strange land) dwelling in cottages." Challoner's eye passed from the first "land" to the second in his first two revisions, but he corrected the oversight in 1752. Hence the same result as before: all editions based on the 1749 and 1750 editions omit the clause, and few copies contain it. Even such recent editions as those of 1914 and 1936 omit the words (but not that of 1941 [Ed.]).

Apoc. 3:8. "A door opened which no man can shut (because thou hast a little strength)"; the last clause was omitted by Challoner in 1752, but re-inserted in 1764 and 1772. I know of no subsequent edition which omits them; even Haydock's edition has them, although it was based on the 1752 revision.

Many phrases are omitted in some American editions; e.g., those by Carey (undated), by Cummiskey, 1825, Doyle, 1836, Sadlier, 1851, and

Dunigan's edition of Haydock's Bible, 1852—although not all are equally defective. These American editions are listed on pages 719 ff.

On the other hand, Challoner emended two omissions of the Rhemists:

Acts 7:59. The first four (five?) editions of the Rheims New Testament omitted the words "he [Stephen] fell asleep in the Lord," but they were inserted in the edition of 1738 and in all subsequent editions.

I Cor. 16:19. "With whom also I lodge." As with the words "of God" (see above, Mark 15:29), this clause found no place in the original editions by the Rhemists. Challoner inserted it in all his revisions on the authority of the Sixtine and Clementine editions; but, as in the case of Mark 15:29, manuscript evidence in its favor is wanting. Yet Wycliffe, *c.* 1380, or two hundred years before the Clementine revision, wrote, "at the whiche also I am herborid." Tyndale, Geneva, Rheims, A.V., and R.V. omitted the clause; Cranmer's version gives it in italics as doubtful.

SECOND REVISION OF THE OLD TESTAMENT, 1763–64

Challoner's second revision of the Old Testament appeared in 1763; the title, omissions, and mistakes are the same as in 1750. Lavish use is made of italics for words not in the original. Misprints are few, though "drink a little [of] the wine" (I Kings 1:14) is perpetuated in many editions. The same ten clauses are omitted as in 1750; also the same misprints, "guard," for "garden" (Neh. 3:15), "Jacob," for "heaven" (Ps. 90:1), and the substitution of "artful hand" for "obstetric hand" (Job 26:13). There is no list of *Errata,* nor is the name of printer or publisher given. The first volume was printed in 1763; the following three bear the date 1764.

The fifth volume, 1764, constitutes Challoner's fourth revision, a very slight one, of the New Testament, the only changes noted being "rose up" for "arose up" in the three previous revisions (Matt. 9:9); "you" for "ye" (Col. 3:8); "the Son" (Heb. 3:6), a reversion to the first two revisions, for in the third revision Challoner changed this to "a Son," a reading to which he again reverted in the fifth revision, 1772.[18] The two volumes—their pagination is distinct—are bound up as one. The only

[18] Cotton is incorrect when he says: "This edition is copied, page for page, from that of 1752" (*op. cit.,* p. 202).

clause omitted in the New Testament is, "and he shall abound" (Matt. 13:12).

FIFTH REVISION OF THE NEW TESTAMENT, 1772

Challoner's fifth revision, 1772, reproduces with few variants the text of 1752 and 1764, though "domination" (Ephes. 1:21) is a reversion to 1749; "rose up" (1764) is adopted rather than "arose up" (1749–52). "Known," for "know" (Acts 2:16), occurs here for the first time, to reappear in 1797, 1810, 1812, and such recent editions as that of 1896; "know" of the previous editions is reproduced in editions based on the 1749 revision: 1820, 1823, 1832, etc. There are far more misprints than are pointed out in the *Errata;* e.g., p. 329, Chap. III for Chap. VIII; Matt. 18:53 for 18:35; p. 203, the headline has St. Luke for St. John. Some copies have engravings; some are on poorer paper than others. The only note omitted is that on the "stars" (Matt. 24:29).

Did Challoner make a sixth revision of the New Testament? Charles Butler speaks of an edition published in 1777 as being "the last printed during the Author's lifetime." Milner too says: "I myself, in 1777, received a copy of the last edition of both Testaments from the very hands of the venerable commentator." [19] Yet it is certain that Challoner revised the Old Testament only twice, in 1750 and 1763, and if Milner is referring to the edition of both Testaments in 1763–64, then he is incorrect in terming the edition of the New Testament in 1764 "the last," for that was followed by the edition of 1772.

[19] Cf. Cotton, *op. cit.*, pp. 50, 118.

CHAPTER XXVI

MacMahon's Editions of the Bible, 1783-1810

DR. CHALLONER died in 1781. Since he had begun the work of revision with the fifth edition of the Rheims New Testament in 1738, he had held undisputed possession of his field. During the intervening forty-three years he had published five editions of the New Testament, and since the last two were to all practical purposes reproductions of his third revision, 1752, the latter had held the field for thirty years. But great changes were pending, and a series of attempts at a fresh revision began to appear. The first was by the Rev. Bernard MacMahon,[1] who at the suggestion of Dr. Carpenter, archbishop of Dublin, published in 1783 an edition of the New Testament destined to exercise a most unfortunate influence on our English version: *The New Testament. . . . With Annotations. The Fourth Edition, newly revised and corrected according to the Clementin Edition of the Scripture,* Dublin: Printed by Daniel Graisberry, for R. Cross, MDCCLXXXIII.[2] To the Approbation given to Challoner's first revision in 1749, Dr. Carpenter added: "Hanc quartam Novi Testamenti editionem nunc denuo recognitam et emendatiorem

[1] Bernard MacMahon was born about 1736 in County Louth. He completed his studies at Antwerp, and on returning to Dublin served the Hardwicke Street Chapel till his death in his eightieth year, September 20, 1816. Besides his editing of the Bible, his literary labors seem to have been confined to re-editing Butler's *Lives of the Saints* and other devotional works, as well as producing the annual *Ordo* and *Directory.* He does not seem to have had any special qualifications for revising the English version of the Bible. —The late Mr. Seamus O'Cassaide of Clontarf is the source of this information; see also his article in the *Journal of the County Louth Archeological Society,* "Bernard MacMahon: Priest and Scientist," IX (1940), no. 4.

[2] An exceedingly rare volume; there is no copy in the British Museum, and even Dr. Cotton had seen only two copies; cf. *Rhemes and Doway,* p. 56.

redditam a R^{do} B. M^{c} M. Approbamus. Dublinii, 8 Septembris, 1783. J.C.A.D.H.P.[3]

After the title comes an episcopal Admonition on the right spirit in which the Bible should be read. This Admonition, here printed for the first time, sometimes appears together with the letter of Pope Pius VI commending in 1778 the Italian version by Martini, archbishop of Florence, though more often the Admonition is omitted; in recent editions both the Admonition and the Pope's letter are omitted.

MacMahon apparently began the work of revision about 1778, and by the time Challoner died, he had revised the text of the Gospels, making only about fifty changes in Challoner's text. But after the latter's death, feeling perhaps that he now had a free hand, he made about five hundred changes in the Acts, Epistles, and the Apocalypse.

FIRST EDITION OF THE WHOLE BIBLE, 1791

In 1791 MacMahon produced a revised edition of the whole Bible. In his Approbation, Dr. Troy, who had succeeded Dr. Carpenter, says:

> Novam hanc BIBLIAE SACRAE Anglicam Editionem, typis Ricardi Cross Licentia nostra impressam, et cum Vulgata Clementina, necnon Duacena Veteris Testamenti anni 1609, Novi Testamenti Rhemensi Anni 1582; et Londinensi Veteris et Novi Testamenti Rmi Dni Challenor [sic], Episcopi Deborensis, anni 1752; Anglicis jam approbatis versionibus, a Rdo Dno Bernardo Macmahon diligenter jussu nostro collatam, auctoritate nostra approbamus: eamdemque, debitis servatis conditionibus, a Fidelibus cum fructu legi posse declaramus. Datum Dublinii, die 21 Septembris, 1791. F. Joh. Thomas Troy. A.D.H.P.[4]

MacMahon is here said to have "collated" the Clementine Vulgate, the Rheims New Testament of 1582 and the Douay Old Testament of

[3] Jacobus Carpenter, Archiepiscopus Dublinensis, Hiberniae Praeses. In Carpenter's Approbation as well as in the title, this edition is styled "the fourth"; yet the folio edition of 1738 was "the fifth," and since that date Challoner had published five revisions, if not six. It is possible that MacMahon was not taking into account the editions between 1582 and 1738, and that, starting with Challoner, he may have regarded the latter's fourth and fifth revisions as to all intents identical with his third, and therefore labeled his own edition of 1783 "the fourth" and his subsequent revisions in 1791, 1794, 1803, and 1810 the "fifth," "sixth," "seventh," and "eighth," respectively. Dr. Crolly's edition of 1857 is called "the ninth," though it is hard to understand why the many editions appearing between MacMahon's last, 1810, and 1857 should have been thus disregarded.

[4] Cotton characteristically remarks that "this Approbation cannot be said to be very *warm* or *earnest* in recommending the general study of the Scriptures by the people; when it merely declares that it is *possible* that the faithful may read them with profit, provided they observe certain unnamed conditions" (*op. cit.*, pp. 57 f.). Yet Dr. Troy's *posse* only means that since it is a faithful reproduction it can be read safely.

1609–10, and Challoner's third revision, 1752. This wording is not too clear, for Challoner's revision in 1752 covered the New Testament only. Moreover, since MacMahon's Old Testament text is, save for a few minor changes, that of Challoner's two revisions of it, 1750 and 1763, he must have used that text as his basis.[5] Since, too, Dr. Carpenter had spoken of the edition of 1783 as "freshly revised and made more correct," he must have been fully aware that MacMahon was making many changes in Challoner's text of the New Testament. Now, in 1791, he added another two hundred and fifty changes to the previous five hundred and fifty, or about eight hundred in all.[6] The deplorable character of at least some of these changes will be evident from the following examples.

"If therefore the light that is in thee be darkness, how great will the darkness itself be?" (Matt. 6:23); "and they laughed at him, . . . and when the crowd was turned out" (Matt. 9:24); "go after me, satan, for thou dost not relish the things that are of God" (Mark 8:33); "they began to desire what he always done to them" (Mark 15:8); "all the people were held in suspense to hear him" (Luke 19:48); "but I, and he that sent me, the Father" (John 8:16); "but Peter to them, do penance, said he" (Acts 2:38); "a certain man named Simon, who before had been a magician in the city, seducing the people of Samaria, giving out that he was some great one" (Acts 8:9)—neither here nor in the following verse is there any finite verb; "Barnabas had a mind to take along with him" (Acts 15:37; "after have whipped us" (16:37); "to whom when Paul went down and laid himself upon him; and embracing him said" (Acts 20:10)—faulty grammar; "hath enlightened life and incorruption" (II Tim. 1:10).

Some changes are for the better: "rejoice and be exceeding glad" (Matt. 5:12); "he [John] was a burning and a shining lamp" (John 5:35); "he vigorously convinced the Jews in public" (Acts 18:28).

In the Old Testament the same omissions remain as in Challoner's editions of 1750 and 1763, except that Jos. 7:18 is completed; the only omis-

[5] Though his revision of the New Testament is based on the edition of 1752, some of the renderings of 1749 and 1750 are retained: "if falling down, thou wilt adore me" (Matt. 4:9). Some, too, are peculiar to 1749: "Testaments" (Ephes. 2:12), where 1750 had "testament," and 1752, "covenants."

[6] These variations are tabulated by Cotton, *op. cit.*, pp. 371–83. MacMahon also omitted thirty of Challoner's notes on the Old Testament and sixteen from the New; while adding ninety notes on the Old Testament, altering twenty-six, and altering another twenty on the New; cf. *ibid.*, p. 59.

sion in the New Testament is, "and he shall abound" (Matt. 13:12). But the same misprints are perpetuated: "guard," for "garden" (Neh. 3:15); "Jacob," for "heaven" (Ps. 90:1); "same," for "fame" (II Par. 9:6); "inhabitants"—the plural for the singular (Amos 1:5). The Gospel for the twenty-first Sunday is, as usual, Matt. 18:23–25 instead of 18: 23–35.

SECOND EDITION OF THE WHOLE BIBLE, 1794

MacMahon's 1791 edition of the Bible was republished in folio by Reilly, Dublin, in 1794: *The Holy Bible. . . . With Annotations, references, and an historical and chronological Index. The Sixth Edition,*[7] *newly revised and corrected* (as in 1791). The Approbation at the end of the New Testament reads: "We the undersigned, having carefully examined this New Edition of the Holy Bible printed by Mr. James Reilly, highly approve of the Manner in which the Whole is executed, and do recommend it as well deserving the Encouragement and Support of the Faithful. Most Rev. Richard O'Reilly, R.C. Archbishop of Armagh, Primate and Metropolitan of all Ireland." The seven other bishops whose names follow all sign themselves "R.C. Bishop," a formula which could have emanated only from the publishers. Cotton's statement that "this edition follows the quarto Bible of 1791 exactly, both in *Text* and *Notes,*" needs qualification: 1791 has "*he* called" (Matt. 1:25), but "he" is omitted in 1794, which also omits some notes; e.g., those on IV Kings 24:2 and II Par. 13:9. But the preliminary pieces, omissions, novel renderings, and misprints of 1791 all reappear.

The plates differ in different copies; in one the frontispiece depicts death: "O Mors, ubi est stimulus tuus?" Frequently they are inserted without any regard to the subject matter of the chapters. A picture of St. Lawrence the Deacon is opposite psalm 26; then comes the adoration of the child Jesus by the shepherds, followed by the administration of confirmation, apparently by an Anglican bishop. Facing John, chap. 14, is a picture of the visitation of the sick. In some copies there is only one plate, depicting the visitation of the sick, opposite III Kings, chap. 3.

The Admonition, the rescript of Pope Pius VI, and a prayer before reading the Scriptures occupy one page, on the reverse of which we have the declaration of the Council of Trent on the canon of the Bible. Op-

[7] For this numbering of the edition, see above, note 3.

posite is the list of the books of the Bible. The notes throughout are practically the same as those in later editions; e.g., in that published by Burns and Oates, 1914. But there are some changes that are worth noting: the note on Gen. 9:23 (1914) does not appear; while a note on Gen. 28:18 reads (1794): "A title, that is a pillar or monument"; and on Gen. 44:5: "To divine; this was spoken by Joseph to his steward in jest; alluding to the notion of the people who took him to be a diviner"—a somewhat gratuitous statement. The edition of 1794 has a long note on the manna, (Exod. 16:31); the edition of 1914 omits it, as well as notes on Lev. 13:2, 14; 16:8, 13 f.; 19:27; 21:17; 22:19; but it inserts notes on the fat of the sacrifices and on ignorance (Lev. 3:17; 4:2). The edition of 1914 also has a note on Judith 10:12, where Judith seems to lie: "In this and the following chapter some things are related to have been said by Judith, which seem hard to reconcile with truth. But all that is related in scripture of the servants of God is not approved of by the scripture: and even the saints in their good enterprises may sometimes slip into venial sins." There are other variations between the notes of the editions of 1794 and 1914. It is noticeable, too, that 1794 sometimes adopts the Protestant spelling of proper names; e.g., Nehemiah.

THE FOURTH AND FIFTH EDITIONS OF THE NEW TESTAMENT, 1803 AND 1810

MacMahon's fourth edition (the second of the New Testament published separately) came out in 1803.[8] Dr. Troy's Approbation runs as follows: "Septimam hanc NOVI TESTAMENTI editionem Anglicanam cum prioribus Rhemensi, Londinensi, et Dubliniensi jam approbatis exemplaribus diligenter collatam, nunc denuo recognitam atque in nonnullis a Rdo D. Bernardo MacMahon emendatiorem redditam approbamus; erratis typographicis exceptis, quorum plura ad calcem ejusdem notantur. Datum Dublinii, Idibus Martii 1803. F. Joh. Thomas Troy A.D.H.P." The text differs from that in New Testament portion of the Bible in 1791 in about 115 places, most of them being reversions to the text of 1783. But the last edition, 1810, reverts to the text of 1791 and 1794.

MacMahon's fifth edition appeared in 1810: *The New Testament of*

[8] For information on this edition, as on that of 1783, we have to depend wholly on Dr. Cotton, *op. cit.*, pp. 78, 234, as no copies of either edition are now known to exist.

our Lord and Saviour Jesus Christ, translated from the Latin Vulgat; diligently compared with the Original Greek; and first published by the English College at Rhemes, Anno 1582. With Annotations. The Eighth Edition, newly revised and corrected according to the Clementine Edition of the Scriptures, Dublin, Printed by P. Wogan, 1810. Some copies have on the title page, "Printed by H. Fitzpatrick, . . . Printer and Bookseller to the R. C. College, Maynooth, 1810." Dr. Troy repeats the Approbation given to the former edition, merely changing *septimam* to *octavam* (*editionem*).

The renderings in this, MacMahon's last revision, are even more bizarre than before; for MacMahon made changes in every revision, taking his renderings indiscriminately from Challoner's various revisions and making others of his own. Matt. 2:8–11 follows the text of 1752, but verse 14, "who rising up," differs from any revision by Challoner; verses 15 and 22 are taken from Challoner, 1749–50, but verse 23 is a medley of all three revisions: "and he came and dwelt in a city called Nazareth that it might be fulfilled what [1749–50, "which"] was said by the prophets: That [omitted in 1752] he shall be called a Nazarene [1752]." There is a similar medley of the three revisions in verse 20. The version of 1810 differs from that of 1791 in more than a hundred places.[9]

Dr. Troy regarded the edition of 1791 as the standard definitely approved by himself,[10] but MacMahon changed some of the renderings he had there adopted, generally for the better; for example: "obscured with darkness and alienated" (1791) becomes, "darkened, being alienated" (Ephes. 4:18); the awkward "I the light am come," now reads, "I am come a light" (John 12:46); "destined to death" is replaced by "appointed" (I Cor. 4:9); "natural body," as in 1582, is now "animal body" (I Cor. 15:44); "contumeliously" becomes "shamefully" (I Thess. 2:2); the paraphrastic rendering, "that which appeareth foolish of God . . . that which appeareth weakness" (I Cor. 1:25) now disappears, as does the exceedingly awkward, "But Peter to them, do penance, said he" (Acts 2:38). But MacMahon still omits "there was" from, "Now there was a certain man" (Acts 8:9), with the resulting impossible grammar.

The notes are the usual ones except that the one on St. Peter's rebuke

[9] Cotton says that "in this year [1810], Mr. MacMahon published another edition of his Testament, exactly copied from that of 1803. . . . Both in *Text* and *Notes* it appears to be an exact copy of the edition of 1803." [Ed.]

[10] See his Disclaimer, apropos of Coyne's edition of 1816, *infra,* p. 418.

to Christ is abbreviated; there are slight changes in those on Rom. 8:16 and 10:9, while that on Rom. 4:8 is omitted. The note on Matt. 19:11 reads: "Protestants have altered the text by rendering it, 'All men cannot receive this saying'; to excuse the sacrilegious marriages of their first reformers"; this note is omitted in later editions. Gal. 4:9 has "work" for "weak"; Jas. 2:3 has "your" for "you"; otherwise misprints are few.

If MacMahon's aim was to produce a more polished and readable version than Challoner's, it can hardly be said that he succeeded. Nor did his version effect any substantial change in Challoner's version as a whole. Yet his repeated changes in the text had as a result that the version which was in general circulation became further removed from the text as Challoner had left it. Moreover, since the production of editions of the Bible was at this period almost exclusively in the hands of the Irish bishops,—for the state of affairs in England precluded the Vicars Apostolic from taking a hand in their production—MacMahon's editions, approved as they were by two successive archbishops of Dublin, were sure of an extensive circulation. But the influence of this corrupt text—for so we must call it—was not confined to Irish editions. For all the editions of Haydock's Bible, from 1811 onwards, have the text of 1791, as does the Bible and the New Testament published by Richardson of Derby in 1847 with the Approbation of Doctors Walsh and Wiseman.[11]

[11] Ten years previously, in the *Dublin Review* for April, 1837, Wiseman had reprobated many renderings which nevertheless find a place in this edition of 1847, which he approved.

CHAPTER XXVII

The Biblical Work of Alexander Geddes, 1786-1802

WHILE Challoner and others were thus laboring to provide English Catholics with a more acceptable version of the Bible, another worker was proceeding along entirely different lines. This was Alexander Geddes, 1737–1802, a genuine, though eccentric and unbalanced, biblical scholar. His indiscrete friendship with certain ministers of the Presbyterian body, whose sermons he sometimes attended, thereby giving scandal to his flock, led to difficulties with Bishop Hay. He therefore went to London, where he served the Imperial Embassy Chapel and that in Sardinia Street. In London he became on intimate terms with Dr. Lowth, whose *Lectures on Hebrew Poetry* appeared in 1780, and with Dr. Kennicott, author of *Vetus Testamentum Hebraicum variis lectionibus,* 1776–80. Encouraged by them, Geddes brought out in 1786 a *Prospectus of a New Translation of the Holy Bible, from corrected Texts of the Originals, compared with ancient versions, with various readings, explanatory notes, and critical observations,* necessitated, so he maintained, by "the imperfection and incorrectness of the originals." This was followed in 1787 by *A Letter to the Right Rev. the Lord Bishop of London: containing Queries, Doubts and Difficulties, Relative to a vernacular version of the Holy Scriptures,* which was an Appendix to his *Prospectus of a New Translation of the Holy Bible,* and was followed in 1788 by *Proposals for printing, by subscription, a New Translation of the Holy Bible from corrected Texts of the Original; with various readings, expository Notes, and Critical Observations (with specimens of the work).* This he proposed to publish, with the generous help of Lord Petre, in six volumes. But before any portion appeared, Geddes issued in 1790 *A General Answer to the Queries, Counsels, and Criticisms that have been com-*

municated to him since the publication of His Proposals for printing a New Translation of the Bible.

At length the much-advertised first volume of his translation was published. It bore the somewhat bombastic title: *The Holy Bible, or the Books accounted Sacred by Jews and Christians; otherwise called the Books of the Old and New Covenants: faithfully translated from Corrected Texts of the Originals. With various Readings, Explanatory Notes and Critical Remarks. By the Rev. Alexander Geddes, LL.D.,* London: MDCCXCII. But the author had shown himself so cantankerous,—no milder word will suffice—and his notes were so wholly uncatholic in tone, that the four Vicars Apostolic had no recourse but to forbid its use by the faithful. Bishop Milner's words, though written before he had examined the version, show that Geddes' general attitude on biblical questions had already made the ecclesiastical authorities uneasy:

I shall enter upon the Doctor's translation without any prepossessions, if he can but satisfy my mind as to one point, which, I think, is of essential consequence in a translation of the Sacred Text, namely, that he holds this text to be inspired, and that he considers *Paul of Tarsus* to be something more than *a very extraordinary man.* For I own that the very free manner in which the Doctor is known frequently to express himself on this subject, his representing the history of the Creation as the mythology of the Hebrew people, and his profession to treat the Sacred Text with as little ceremony as he would the text of Homer, Virgil, Milton, or Shakespeare, naturally breeds in my mind a jealousy which will not permit me to trust the translator any farther than I can see him.[1]

Geddes gave offense, too, by his scant respect for St. Jerome's Latin version, the Vulgate; he thought it barbarous and uncritical. He had still less respect for the Douay Version:

It is a literal and barbarous translation from the Vulgate, before its last revision; and accompanied with acrimonious and injurious annotations. The residence in a foreign country, and, what they deemed, exile from their own, corrupted the translators' language; and soured their tempers; and it was, unhappily, the common custom of those lamentable times, to season every religious controversy with gall and vinegar. We do not find that Fulke, Fuller and Cartwright, who drew their quills against the Douay annotators, were a bit more courteous than they.[2]

[1] In *The Gentleman's Magazine,* October, 1779, p. 888. Isaac Disraeli remarks that "Dr. Geddes' version is aridly literal, and often ludicrous by its vulgarity; as when he translates the Passover by the Skipover" (*Curiosities of Literature,* II, 21). But Geddes himself says: "My translation is neither literal nor verbal; but, if I may use the term, strictly sentential; that is, every sentence of the English corresponds as exactly to the Hebrew as the difference of the two idioms will permit."

[2] *Prospectus of a New Translation of the Holy Bible,* p. 110.

By his autocratic handling of the text, Geddes, unlike the Reformers of the sixteenth century who canonized the Hebrew text, was asking the Catholics of his day to accept his own personal views as to what really constituted the original text of the Bible. Yet it should not be thought that Geddes indulged in hasty emendations of the text; his principles, at least, are perfectly sound, even though his practice may not always have accorded with them. Such emendations, he insists, are to be justified only when (a) the grounds for them are convincing; (b) when all other resources have been exhausted; and (c) then only on condition they prove in harmony with the context.[3]

The second volume, Judges to Chronicles, appeared in 1797; and in 1800 he published *Critical Remarks on the Hebrew Scriptures corresponding with a New Translation of the Bible.* In this, says his biographer: "our author considered himself at liberty to throw off every restriction whatever." Indeed it is undeniable that his treatment of inspired Scripture was wholly rationalistic and independent. For example, in his *Critical Remarks* he regards as a "groundless assumption" the notion that Gen. 49:10 contains any prophecy of the future Messias; he takes the word "Shiloh," Vulgate *qui mittendus est,* to mean "peaceful prosperity," referring it to quite another Hebrew root (p. 144). Concerning the passage of the Red Sea he boldly says: "I believe there was nothing miraculous in the event; I am positively for the pass at Suez . . . where at this day there are shallows fordable at low water" (p. 225). Apropos of the words, "My name Adonai (Jehova) I did not show them [the Patriarchs]" (Exod. 6:3), he insists that the occurrence of the name Jehovah in the prayers, etc., of the patriarchs is simply due to the fact that "they are corrupt passages, and that 'Jehova' has slipped into them for 'Elohim' or 'Adonai' " (p. 176). Again, he particularly objects to the rendering of Gen. 3:15 by the singular, maintaining that the rendering should rather be, *"they* shall seek to bruise thee on thy head, and thou to bite *them* in the heel"; and he adds: "So I render the Hebrew: contrary,

[3] *Ibid.*, p. 60. Geddes' translation and his Preface were severely criticized by Father John Earle, *Remarks on the Prefaces prefixed to the First and Second Volumes of a work entitled "The Holy Bible," translated by the Rev. Alexander Geddes,* 1799. On his title page Father Earle aptly quoted:

> "Your learning, like the lunar beam, affords
> Light but no heat: it leaves us undevout,
> Frozen at heart while speculation shines."
> Young, *Night Thoughts,* Night V.

in one respect, to almost all modern translators" (p. 46). Of the poetical fragment in Num. 21: 27–30 he says, "This I believe to be . . . a beautiful fragment of an old ballad, quoted by the writer of the Pentateuch: but such a quotation could not be made by Moses: although Moses may have composed the ballad" (p. 390).

Geddes finds no room for the devil in the story of the fall of our first parents: the whole "is a mythological moral figment." Nor does the story of the deluge fare any better: "A traditional tale is easily exaggerated and improved upon by a credulous posterity, and the first *writer* gives it with all the accumulated circumstances. What reason have we to think that the Hebrew historian was exempt from the common lot? All we can say is, that he has better told his tale. . . . I think the inference to be drawn is: That a good deal of the fabulous is mixed with the history of Noah's flood" (p. 72). He pours contempt, too, on the association between the sacrifice of Melchisedech and that of the Mass: "There is hardly one who would seriously defend it" (p. 93).

The doctrine of the inspiration of the biblical writers does not find any favor with him. After devoting three pages to a discussion on the site of the Garden of Eden, he concludes with the trite remark: "After all, it may well be, that we are labouring to find out a spot that never existed but in the creative imagination of the mythologist. It was necessary for him to place his Paradise somewhere. . . . I believe the narrative of Genesis to be a most beautiful mythos, or philosophical fiction, contrived with great wisdom, dressed up in the garb of real history" (p. 37).[4] The following, too, is unpardonable: "I cannot conceive how Moses could have governed so rude, so stubborn, so turbulent a nation, and made them submit to such a code of laws as he devised for them, without feigning an immediate intercourse with the Deity, and ascribing to Him every injunction laid upon them" (p. 41).

Quite in keeping with Geddes' general attitude on biblical questions is the fact that, while insisting that he is translating from the "original," yet he is convinced that "the present Hebrew text" is very corrupt.[5] What he translates is that text as he thinks it ought to be. For example, every

[4] In effect Geddes denies the existence of anything approaching "inspiration" in the authors of the historical books of the Old Testament, ranking them, as he does, "somewhat lower as historians" than Herodotus, Thucydides, Livy, Sallust, or Caesar; he does, however, contend for "a doctrine of partial and putative inspiration."

[5] *Prospectus of a New Translation of the Holy Bible.*

biblical student is aware that the story of David's visit to the camp of his brothers and the sudden appearance of Goliath, with the narrative that follows, I Kings 17:11–58, contains, as it now stands, certain apparent contradictions. But that did not justify Geddes in pronouncing the story "an incongruous and inconsistent interpolation" and in relegating the whole episode to a footnote, though he acknowledges that "it is in all the copies of the present Hebrew text, and in all the ancient versions, . . . [and] has even stolen into most copies of the Septuagint." [6]

At the same time it is remarkable that despite his very rationalistic attitude on these and similar points, Geddes had no use for the findings of the "dissectionists," whose views were then coming into fashion: "The second chapter of Genesis is at present pretty generally supposed to be another cosmogonical fragment, written by a different person, and inserted by Moses in his commentaries as a curious piece of antiquity. I confess I have never been able to view it in that light: after all the pains that Astruc, Eichhorn and others have taken to prove diversity, I can find nothing in it but a natural resumption of the subject, by the same pen which wrote the first chapter." [7]

While reading his learned pages, one gets the impression that Geddes had had little or no training in defensive or apologetic theology. He would seem never really to have studied any formal treatise on the Church, for instance. Only on this supposition can we explain his confident assertion that

> the Romanists always reasoned in what is termed a vicious circle; and proved the infallibility of the Church from the authority of Scripture, and the authority of Scripture from the Church's infallibility. I know what shifts have been made by Bellarmine, Becan, and many others, to get out of this coil; but I have never met with any one who had succeeded. . . . The bulk of Christians, whether Papists or Protestants, cannot be said to have a rational faith: because their motives of credibility are not rational motives; but the positive assertions of an assumed authority, which they have never discussed, or durst not question: their religion is the fruit of an unenlightened credulity. . . . The vulgar Papist rests his [faith] on the supposed infallibility of his Church; although he knows not where that infallibility is lodged, nor in what it properly consists. . . . From that moment reason is set aside; authority usurps its place. The case of the vulgar Protestant is even worse. For he rests it [his faith] on a book, called the Holy Bible, which he believes to be the infallible word of God. . . . His belief is as implicit as that of the vulgar Papist; and his motives of believing less specious. . . . On the whole, then, I think

[6] *Ibid.*, p. 92.

[7] *Critical Remarks on the Hebrew Scriptures*, p. 29.

that the bulk of Christians, whether Papists or Protestants, cannot be said to have a rational faith; . . . their religion is the fruit of unenlightened credulity.[8]

Geddes himself leaves us in no doubt about his religious views:

The Gospel of Jesus is my religious code: His doctrines are my dearest delight; His yoke to me is easy, and His burden is light. But this yoke I would not put on: —these doctrines I could not admire; that Gospel I would not make my law;— if Reason, pure Reason, were not my prompter and preceptress. I willingly profess myself a sincere though unworthy disciple of Christ. *Christian* is my name, and *Catholic* my surname. Rather than renounce these glorious titles, I would shed my blood: but I would not shed a drop of it for what is neither Catholic nor Christian.

He did not hesitate to say: "I am a Catholic *absolute,* Roman Catholic *secundum quid.*" [9] And again: "I continue to be what I ever professed— *Qualis ab incepto,* that is, neither Papist nor Protestant: but both between, like good Erasmus, in an honest mean, a genuine Catholic." [10] Over his tomb in the churchyard at Paddington is this self-revealing epitaph, which he drafted himself:

Reverend Alexander Geddes, LL.D.
Translator of the Historical Books
Of the Old Testament,
Died Feb. 26th. 1802
Aged 65.

Christian is my name, and Catholic my surname.
I grant, that you are a Christian, as well as I,
And embrace you as my fellow disciple in Jesus:
And, if you are not a disciple of Jesus,
Still I would embrace you as my fellow Man.
(Extracted from his Works.)
Requiescat in Pace.[11]

When Bishop Douglass heard of Geddes' death, he wrote in his diary: "1802. February 26. This morning also died at his lodgings Dr. Alexander Geddes, . . . author of an unfinished translation of the Bible, replete with irreligious and heterodox reflections. He died under ecclesiastical censure." The Bishop then goes on to say that the Rev. William Fryer

[8] *Ibid.,* Preface, pp. v f.

[9] In *The Gentleman's Magazine,* LXVII, 323.

[10] *Ibid.,* LIX (1789), 417. He even went so far as to declare that should his studies "hurt the interests of religion, . . . if it do, I care not."

[11] Given by Charles Butler, *Historical Memoirs of the English, Irish, and Scottish Catholics,* IV, 418 f.

tried repeatedly to see him, but in vain. Bishop Douglass felt bound to refuse the request for a Dirge and a Mass for the deceased.[12]

No one can peruse Geddes' learned pages, betraying as they do the most profound knowledge of the Hebrew text, of every version, and apparently of every commentator, without feeling bitter regret that such splendid talents and such painstaking work should have been thrown away. For thrown away it has been, by the ill-fated author himself, who so persistently defied all authority and went his own way, convinced that he, and he alone, was right. For side by side with the undoubted learning there is always present the ever-recurring *ipse dixi Ego* Geddes, often justified, it is true, yet none the less exasperating, and in the end calculated only to raise doubts as to his reliability.[13]

[12] Cf. Ward, *The Dawn of the Catholic Revival,* II, 246 f.

[13] Dr. Cotton (*op. cit.*) hails Geddes' version as "a remarkable book, by a very remarkable man, . . . [who] met with nothing but opposition, contumely, and injurious treatment" (pp. 62, 66). He declares that "Geddes had a spirit too independent to bow down before usurped authority, and too much learning to yield to the clamour of bigotted ignorance" (p. 66). Cotton even suggests that "there is ground for thinking that some foul play was used respecting his *papers,* immediately upon his death" (p. 70). Geddes' last published work was a translation of psalms 1–117, which appeared in 1807, after his death.

CHAPTER XXVIII

The Editions of 1790 and 1792

BIBLE PUBLISHED IN PHILADELPHIA, 1790

In 1790 Carey, Stewart & Co., Philadelphia, published in large quarto *The Holy Bible translated from the Latin Vulgate, diligently compared with the Hebrew, Greek and other Editions, in divers languages; and first published by the English College at Doway, Anno 1609.* There is no mention of the version of the New Testament made at Rheims, though the text of the New Testament is included together with the Approbations given to the first and second editions of the Rheims New Testament in 1582 and 1600. Then comes an Approbation of "the corrected edition of the New Testament first published in 1750"; but as a matter of fact, it is the Approbation given in 1748 to Challoner's first revision.

The New Testament portion has no title page. At the end of the volume is a Table of References, a Chronological Table, a Table of the Psalms as Arranged for the Breviary, Tables of the Epistles and Gospels, where the usual mistake is perpetuated: the Gospel for the twenty-first Sunday is given as Matt. 18:23–25 instead of 18:23–35. In the Old Testament are the same omissions as in Challoner, 1750, except that Jos. 7:18 is completed. In the New Testament the text generally is that of Challoner's third revision, 1752. But the text of 1749 is followed in Acts 28:7; Rom. 5:14; Ephes. 1:21; that of 1750 in Ephes. 2:12; and that of 1764 in Matt. 9:9. The influence of MacMahon appears in John 2:4: "What is *that* to me?" In I Pet. 1:13 we have a combination of the renderings of 1749 and 1752: "In *that* grace which is offered at *the* revelation." The missing clauses in Mark 8:6 and Heb. 11:9 are inserted as in 1752.

THE EDITION OF 1792

A strange and anonymous edition of the New Testament appeared in 1792: *The New Testament of our Lord and Saviour Jesus Christ; translated from the Latin Vulgate. Compared with the original Greek. With Annotations. Permissu Superiorum. Printed in the year MDCCXCII,* 12mo. This exceedingly rare edition is of great interest. In the *Dublin Review,* April, 1837, Wiseman complained of the rendering, "Woman, what is *it* to me and to thee?" (John 2:4) in an edition published in Edinburgh, 1792. Dr. Cotton, unable to trace any such edition, thought 1792 a misprint for 1797; but later he discovered a mutilated copy dated 1792 and bearing the device of a pelican with a scroll inscribed, *Impendere et superimpendi,* with *McIntyre sculpsit* written beneath.[1]

The text is mainly that of Challoner's third revision, but with many remarkable changes: "When Jesus . . . saw the minstrels and multitude making a noise, he said: Withdraw, for the girl is not dead, but sleepeth" (Matt. 9:23 f.); "laid hold of him by the throat" (Matt. 18:28); "they should ask Barabbas, and make Jesus perish" (Matt. 27:20); the sin against the Holy Spirit "shall not have forgiveness for ever, but shall be liable for an everlasting offence" (Mark 3:29); the shepherds are described as "guarding in the fields" (Luke 2:8); Christ asks Mary and Joseph, "Did you not know that I must be about the concerns of my Father?" (Luke 2:49); the Pharisees "began vehemently to urge him, and to perplex him in discoursing about many things" (Luke 11:53); the salt without savor is said to be "neither of use to profitable land, nor the dunghill" (Luke 14:35); when asked whether He was the Son of God, Christ answers, "You say it, for I am" (Luke 22:70); John 5:39 is given as a statement of fact, not as an exhortation: "You search the Scriptures"; "having therefore intended this, did I act with levity" (II Cor. 1:17); "you look to what is according to outward appearance" (II Cor. 10:7); "which things, along with superstition, have indeed a show of wisdom and humility" (Col. 2:23); "shew-bread" replaces "loaves of proposition."

[1] The only copy of this edition known to the present author is in the British Museum, 3051.aaa.3. See "An Unusual Edition of the Rheims New Testament," by Pope, in *The Irish Ecclesiastical Record,* LV (1940), 468–84; see also below, Newcastle New Testament, 1812.

This unknown editor is fond of intensive expressions: the disciples "being very sorrowful, began every one to say" (Matt. 26:22), and Christ "began to grow sorrowful and to be very sad" (Matt. 26:37); now and again he shirks a difficulty: the "garden" of Gethsemane, for instance, becomes "a certain place" (Matt. 26:36). Against Challoner and A.V., he correctly represents the foolish virgins as saying that their lamps "were going out" (Matt. 25:8) and the fishermen as saying that their net "was breaking" (Luke 5:6).

While basing himself on the text of 1752, the editor at times prefers that of 1749–50; e.g., Matt. 2:22; 10:4; 26:33; Ephes. 1:21. He stands almost alone, however, in retaining "if thou wilt fall down and adore me" (Matt. 4:9) and "you therefore shall pray in this manner" (Matt. 6:9)—both readings of 1752. Following the same revision, he omits the clause in Matt. 13:12, though he completes all the other defective passages: Mark 15:29; Luke 1:80; Acts 18:10; Heb. 11:9. He uses both parentheses and brackets, the latter as a substitute for italics where some explanatory word is required not in the original text: "it is near, [even] at the door," "as your fathers [did] so [do] you." Sometimes both devices appear in the same verse: "Corban (that is a gift), [whatsoever is from me]." These brackets are often explanatory insertions and partake of the nature of a commentary; e.g., "from him shall be taken even that which he hath [seemingly]." The "it" in, "What is it to me and to thee?" (John 2:4) should have been put in brackets, but was not.

When Dr. Cotton says that the author of this edition translates Matt. 3:8, "Bring forth therefore fruit worthy of repentance," uses "passover" instead of "pasch," "cup" for "chalice," and frequently "elders" instead of "ancients," [2] the unwary reader would naturally suppose that such were the usual renderings in this edition. But as a matter of fact, he writes "penance" thirty-three times, "penitence" or "repentance" only eleven times; thirty-six times he writes "ancients," only fourteen times "elders," both being the equivalent of the Greek *πρεσβύτεροι*. Nowhere does he substitute "cup" for "chalice" while speaking of the Holy Eucharist, but only when referring to Christ's prayer in the garden (Matt. 26:39; Luke 22:42), and even in this connection he writes "chalice" once

[2] This statement was made concerning the edition of 1812, which both in text and notes follows exactly the edition of 1792 in the Gospels and the Acts, but after Rom. 2:18 follows Challoner's text of 1752.

(Mark 14:36). But it is true that in the Gospels and Acts he always writes "passover" for "pasch."

There is a quaint misprint in Rom. 3:1: "What is the *prophet* of circumcision?" In Matt. 26:69 there is an unusual archaism: "Peter sat without in the Cove," an old Saxon word for "chamber" used by Caedmon in his Genesis.[3] Some of the nearly four hundred changes in the Gospels and Acts are distinct improvements: "His mother Mary having been betrothed to Joseph" (Matt. 1:18); "which of you by anxious thought can add" (Matt. 6:27); "a piece of undrest cloth" instead of "raw cloth" (Mark 2:21). Chapter headings and cross references are omitted, as in Challoner's first two revisions.

THE NOTES IN 1792

The notes in the edition of 1792 are interesting. As Dr. Cotton points out, "The *Notes* of this edition exhibit the enlightened hand of the translator: they differ from those in Dr. Challoner's edition, in about eighty-five places. Several new ones are inserted; several of Challoner's are left out: and, in all those of his which are retained, the more offensive expressions are omitted." [4] Yet the notes retained are every bit as "offensive" as the omitted ones.[5] In general those on St. Matthew are the same as those given in Challoner's third revision, 1752; but sixteen of these are omitted,[6] while sixteen new ones are added. The omission of the note on Matt. 19:11 is significant,[7] as also is the omission of the last line of

[3] "Cove and key" is, according to the *Oxford Dictionary,* "an ancient legal phrase used by Bracton in reference to the functions and rights of the mistress of a house," signifying her rights and duties with regard to the store chamber.

[4] *Rhemes and Doway,* p. 398.

[5] See the ones on Acts 10:35; Rom. 10:15; I Cor. 7:9; 9:5, 27; Phil. 2:12; 4:3; Heb. 11:21, all of which stand in our present editions save those on I Cor. 9:27 and Phil. 4:3.

[6] Those omitted: on hell fire (5:22); on "justice" (6:1); on the friends of the bridegroom (9:15); on the sign (12:38); on St. Peter's "rebuke" to our Lord (16:22); on faith (17:1); on "talents" (18:24); on "pence" (18:28); on celibacy (19:11); on eunuchs (19:12) "wheresoever the body is there shall the eagles be" (24:28); on the "Blood of the New Testament" (26:28); on the stars (28:29). Only the last three are omitted in current editions.

[7] "*All men take not this word.* Protestants have corrupted the text by rendering it, *all men cannot receive this saying:* to exclude the sacrilegious marriages of their first Reformers." Wycliffe and Rheims have, "take not this word"; Tyndale, "cannot away with that saying"; Cranmer, "cannot comprehend this"; Geneva, A.V., and R.V., "receive not this saying." The note, from Challoner's revisions, though omitted in 1792 and 1812, was reprinted in 1815, 1823, and 1832. In most editions since that by Dr. Murray in 1825 the note appears in a modified form.

the one on Luke 1:48: "Let Protestants examine whether they are in any way concerned with this Prophecy." [8] But the omission of notes is not so interesting as the presence of a series of notes which are unique. There are sixteen of these on St. Matthew alone.[9]

This edition is clearly the work of an independent scholar who, while using the edition of 1752 as his basis, yet introduced many changes into the text and notes. Though presumably familiar with the work of MacMahon, 1783, he struck out on a line of his own and, if his work had a wider reception, it might have originated yet another stream of tradition, thus increasing the confusion in editions of the Bible which was to prevail for so many years.

[8] This note was omitted in the editions of 1792, 1812, 1815, and 1823, but stands in our present editions.

[9] On public prayers (6:6); on "much speaking" (6:7); on following divine calls (8:22); on leather bottles (9:17); on preaching "on the housetops" (10:27); on the obstinacy of the incredulous Jews (13:13) on being "scandalized through weakness and fear" (13:21); 16:28 is explained as a reference to the Transfiguration; on the camel and the eye of the needle (19:24); on the value of the denarius (20:2); "fill ye up the measure of your fathers" is explained as a prophecy, not a command (23:32); on Christ's will (26:39): "As in Christ there were two natures, so there were consequently, two wills, the divine and the human. For the love of us and for our example and encouragement in affliction, he was pleased to suffer a most heavy sadness and a reluctance to pain in his human will; which was nevertheless always most perfectly conformed to the divine will."

CHAPTER XXIX

Editions at the Beginning of the Nineteenth Century

THE CONFUSION IN THE NINETEENTH CENTURY

BEFORE giving a more detailed account of the editions appearing during the first fifty years of the nineteenth century, it will be well to realize the state of confusion, not to say chaos, into which our English version had fallen. Beginning during Challoner's later years, it grew steadily worse during the next half century owing to a variety of causes, as we shall see; nor can it be truly said that we have yet escaped from that confusion. It will come as a shock to many to learn that never yet has a complete Catholic Bible or Testament issued from our press. Quite apart from egregious misprints, there are at least ten omissions of clauses in the Old Testament, and as many again in the New. And while these are not all found in any single edition, no edition is free from some of these blemishes.

To understand how this confusion arose, we have to bear in mind that Challoner's first three revisions gave rise to three distinct types of text: (a) that which followed the first revision, 1749, now adhered to in our current editions: (b) that following the second revision, 1750, the eighteen renderings peculiar to it having been retained in the vast majority of subsequent editions; (c) that following the third revision, 1752, differing from its predecessors in over 2,000 places and exercising a dominant influence since it was reproduced almost word for word in Challoner's fourth and fifth revisions, 1764 and 1772.

Then came MacMahon's editions, 1783–1810, pre-eminent in Ireland till about 1825; then in 1792 an anonymous edition, which fortunately exercised no lasting influence. In 1796–97, and again in 1804–1805,[1] Moir

[1] "In 1796 a printer of Edinburgh put forth a new edition of Challoner's Bible and

of Edinburgh reproduced in five volumes Challoner's second revision of the Old Testament, 1763, and his fourth revision of the New, 1764. Previous Approbations, the Episcopal Admonition, and the letter of Pius VI are repeated. In 1811 Keating and Brown, London, reprinted Moir's edition,[2] which they then sold to Coyne of Dublin, who published it in the same year, 1811; Wogan of Dublin did the same in 1814. In addition to his five volume edition of the whole Bible, Coyne also published in 1811 the New Testament separately; in both editions of the New Testament he follows Challoner's third revision, 1752, with but slight deviations.

Haydock's first edition began to appear in 1811 and gave a new lease of life to MacMahon's renderings. Two years later Syers' Bible, 1813, introduced the renderings peculiar to Challoner's second revision, 1750; while in 1815 the Catholic Board reverted to his first revision, 1749, in an edition often reprinted. In 1816 Coyne republished the text as in the Liverpool edition of 1788–89, which varied but slightly from that of 1582. In the same year Beegan of Manchester followed almost exclu-

---

Testament, in five volumes duodecimo. The Text and Notes of the *Old* Testament exactly follow the edition of 1763–64: and the Text of the *New* Testament in general does the same: but occasionally it deserts that edition for the first, of 1749: as at Matthew i. 25, iii. 13, iv. 9, v. 37, vi. 16, viii. 17, x. 22, xxi. 40; Acts v. 38; Ephes. i. 21; and some other places. In a few passages it agrees with Dr. Troy's Bible of 1791: as at Matthew ii. 23, iv. 9, vi. 7; Galatians vi. 9, etc. This edition was published under the inspection of Dr. Hey, one of the Vicars Apostolic in Scotland.

"In 1804–5 the same printer issued a re-impression, almost page for page and line for line. He stated, in 1830, that he had struck off about 3000 and 2000 copies of these two editions; and that the greater part of them was not sold in Scotland, but in England and Ireland.

"In fact, the unsold copies of the latter were disposed of by Keating and Browne of London to Mr. Richard Coyne of Dublin; who published them, with new titlepages, some engravings, and a long list of subscribers, with the imprint of 'Dublin 1811.' He announced its appearance, as a new book 'Now in the press,' in a long Advertisement filled with unnecessary abuse of Protestants and their version. . . .

"In the same year [1811], Coyne likewise published an *actual reprint,* of the New Testament only: it is, page for page and line for line, the same as in the Edinburgh book; but on smaller and worse paper. . . .

"Although in general appearance and contents, and even in the number of pages, this volume closely resembles the Testament printed in Edinburgh in 1804, copies of which were afterwards issued in Dublin by Coyne with a reprinted title bearing the date of 1811; it is really a distinct impression, as may easily be seen [from several minor faults which are] corrected in the Dublin reprint" (Cotton, *Rhemes and Doway,* pp. 77 f., 83). This and some following notes are supplemented by the editor from Cotton's work, but they are clearly indicated. [Ed.]

[2] Generally called Dr. Hay's Bible, presumably because he authorized its publication. But I have never come across a copy bearing his authorization.

sively the text of 1752. The text preferred by MacNamara of Cork, 1818, was that of 1788, while that printed by Keating and Brown, 1818, is explicitly stated to be that of 1750.

This growing predilection for the text of Challoner's second edition seems to have impressed Coyne; for whereas up to 1811 he had preferred the text of the third revision, in the edition he so unaccountably published for the "Catholic Fund" in 1820 (reprinted in 1825, but now with the notes previously omitted), he adopted, almost in its entirety, the text of the second revision. When in 1825 Dr. Murray gave his Approbation to what was termed the "stereotyped edition," which for the most part followed the first revision, he at the same time admitted most of the renderings peculiar to the second revision; and these have since found a permanent place in all editions except those of Haydock and those based on his work.

We can easily understand, then, the confusion experienced by attentive church goers at the beginning of the nineteenth century. For at least five different types of text were then in use. Listening to the Epistle and Gospel on Sundays, one might in one church hear them read according to Challoner's first revision, 1749, in another from his second revision, 1750, hardly differing from the former except for about one hundred and twenty-four quite trifling variations. In a third church—probably in most—his third revision, 1752, would be heard, differing from the foregoing in more than 2,000 places. After being the predominant text for about sixty years, the third revision yielded place to the first revision, made popular since its reproduction by the Catholic Board edition in 1815. In other churches, especially in Ireland, MacMahon's editions, 1783–1810, would be followed; the same, too, in England, where Haydock's Bible perpetuated that text. In some churches, especially on the Tyne, the faithful might have to listen to the anonymous and anomalous Edinburgh edition of 1792, reproduced, at least in part, in Worswick's edition, Newcastle, 1812.

In Manchester the Epistle and Gospel might be read from Syers' Bible, adhering mostly to Challoner's earlier revisions, unless that huge folio proved too unwieldy in the pulpit. In Liverpool, Dr. Gibson's magnificent folio editions, 1817 and 1822, following Challoner's later revisions, might have been used, if any pulpit could accommodate them. Owing to their condemnation by Dr. Troy, Ireland probably never heard Coyne's edition, 1816, nor MacNamara's, 1818, though if they ever were used in the pulpit, people would have had the privilege of listening to the Epistle and Gospel as originally translated in 1582. Nor is it likely that the Dublin clergy would have tolerated Coyne's New Testament, 1820, in their pulpits, despite the prefixed Approbation by Dr. Troy; for it was published by the Protestants' Fund for the "conversion" of the presumed ignorant Irish Catholics.

Meanwhile, however, the Catholic Board edition, 1815, giving the text of Challoner's first revision, 1749, and his notes in a somewhat mutilated form, was steadily making its way, being reproduced, with variations from the second revision (1750), by Horrabin in 1818, also by Keating and Brown in the same year, and almost precisely as in 1815 by Bagster in 1823 and by Dr. Poynter in 1825. Newman thus summed up the situation as it appeared in 1859:

> The text of the Old Testament as we now have it is practically as it left Challoner's hands, coming down to us through Dr. Troy's editions perpetuated by Drs. Murray and Denvir, who followed Haydock's text, which again was taken over in Cardinal Wiseman's edition of 1847. In the New Testament the editions of Drs. Murray and Denvir may be said to give the text presented in Challoner's earlier editions, while Haydock and Wiseman follow Challoner's later editions and those of Dr. Troy.[3]

COYNE'S EDITIONS, 1811

By 1811 Coyne was coming into deserved prominence as a printer and publisher, and his edition of the Bible, in five volumes 12mo, had a long list of subscribers and an Advertisement which Cotton describes as "filled with unnecessary abuse of Protestants and their version." [4] Each volume of the Old Testament has a frontispiece, often out of keeping with the books contained: vol. 1, Adam and Eve listening to the promise of the redemption; above, Christ holds a cross, to which angels point; vol. 2 (Judges to Nehemias), the meeting of Melchisedech and Abraham, the latter clad in armor and mounted on a very large horse; vol. 3 (Job to Isaias), Job and his friends, one of whom is weeping while another looks on sternly; the third has an evil countenance, and behind him

[3] "History of the Text of the Rheims and Douay Version of the Holy Scripture," in the *Rambler,* July 1859; reprinted in *Tracts Theological and Ecclesiastical,* p. 405; cf. Burton, *Life and Times of Bishop Challoner,* I, 288 f. Newman's words must be read in the light of what is said below of the various editions he mentions.

[4] *Op. cit.,* p. 78; see above, note 1. This Advertisement does not appear in any edition I have seen.

stands the devil; vol. 4 (Jeremias to the end), the slaughter of the first-born in Egypt; above are depicted the Hebrews plodding through the desert, the paschal meal, and the slaughter of the Innocents. The passages omitted in Challoner's two revisions, 1750 and 1763, are not made good, nor are the misprints corrected. In the New Testament volume [5] the text is, in the main, that of 1752; the only rendering peculiar to the fourth revision, so far as I have noticed, is "rose up" (Matt. 9:9) is place of "arose up" (1749) or "arose" (1750–52). This and the frequent reversion to the text of 1749 show that extensive efforts were made in editing the text. In the New Testament volume of his edition of the complete Bible, Coyne omitted the clause in Heb. 11:9.

In the same year Coyne published the New Testament separately. Nowhere in either New Testament does he show any predilection for Challoner's second revision, 1750, but bases himself on the third revision, 1752, with occasional reversions to the first, 1749; e.g., Matt. 1:25; 3:13; 21:10; Ephes. 1:21. In Matt. 9:9 ("rose up") he again follows Challoner's fourth revision and Moir's editions of 1797 and 1805. He corrects the omission of Heb. 11:9 from his edition of the whole Bible,[6] but three lines are omitted from Matt. 24:29. Both editions have, "What is *it* to me?" (John 2:4), thus deviating from Challoner's five revisions; this reading first appeared in the anonymous edition of 1792, while MacMahon's editions, 1791 and 1810, have "What is *that* to me?" The avoidance of renderings peculiar to 1750 is noteworthy, since two years later, 1813, Syers retained practically all those peculiar renderings.

HAYDOCK'S BIBLE, 1811–14

Thomas Haydock, printer and schoolmaster in Manchester, suggested to his brother, the Rev. George Leo Haydock of Ushaw College, the preparation of an edition of the Bible with very ample notes. This work, involving an immense amount of labor, appeared in parts, at first fortnightly and then weekly, being begun on July 11, 1811, and completed on September 11, 1814. Even while this edition was coming out, a re-

[5] *The New Testament. . . . Translated from the Latin Vulgate, with Annotations, etc., newly revised and corrected,* 1811, R. Coyne.

[6] Cotton, then, is not correct in saying that "it is, page for page and line for line, the same as the Edinburgh book [1804]" (*op. cit.,* p. 83).—But Cotton later acknowledges that this "is really a distinct impression, as may easily be seen [from several minor] faults . . . corrected in the Dublin reprint." See above, note 1. [Ed.]

print was called for, which was begun in 1812. The dates on the title pages of the parts are sometimes earlier than the actual dates of appearance, a fact which causes some confusion. The dedication was as follows:

To that Loyal, Religious, and Enlightened Body of men, the Catholics of the United Kingdoms of England, Ireland and Scotland in admiration of the steady zeal with which they have kept the Deposit of Faith bequeathed to them by their forefathers, and handed it down, without interruption or alteration, to their grateful posterity, this Edition of the Douay Bible and Rhemes Testament is with gratitude for past favours and hopes of future encouragement, most respectfully dedicated by their ever devoted and humble servant, Thomas Haydock.[7]

The learned Preface embodied much of the Preface to the Clementine Vulgate, 1592, which in its turn summarises the Preface by Sixtus V to the Sixtine Vulgate, 1590. In the Old Testament, the text is substantially that of Challoner's first revision, 1750, and in the New Testament that of the third revision, 1752. The Notes, based in part on those of the original Rheims-Douay versions, are also taken from Calmet, Estius, Tirinus, and others.[8] At the end of each Testament comes an Historical and Chronological Index; at the end of the New Testament, a Harmony of the Gospels, lists of the miracles and parables, and Tables of Epistles and Gospels. Some of St. Jerome's letters and Prologues are given in the *Addenda.* How such a gigantic work could have been brought to a successful conclusion, especially when we consider the straitened circumstances of the editor and his brother, the printer and publisher, must always be a subject of wonder.

While reproducing in the main Challoner's third revision of the New

[7] This Dedication was repeated in the edition of 1848; also in Husenbeth's abridged edition, 1853.

[8] The plan of its publication is set forth in an Advertisement, quoted by Cotton (*op. cit.,* pp. 86 f.): "In this edition of the Holy Scriptures, we shall adhere to the Text of the Venerable and Right Rev. Dr. Richard Challoner: and we shall insert all his notes either *verbatim,* or at least shall give their full sense, placing his signature, *Ch.* at the end. In like manner, when any additional observation is made, the author from whom it is taken will be specified, either at length or by an abbreviation; which will easily be understood, by attending to the following remarks. The most ancient Greek version, by the Septuagint, or 72 Interpreters, . . . will be designated *Sept.* or 70. The authentic Latin translation of S. Jerom will be written *Vulg.* . . . The other commentators most frequently consulted, will be thus marked—B. Bristow, C. Calmet, Ch. Challoner, D. Du Hamel, E. Estius, M. Monachius, P. Pastorini or Walmesley, T. Tirinus, W. Worthington, Wi. Witham. We shall also sometimes insert a few original observations, or such at least as we cannot easily trace to their real authors. These will be marked with the letter H." [Ed.]

Testament, he unfortunately followed MacMahon's editions of 1783, 1791, 1794, 1803, and 1810, where these differ from that of 1752; in other words; he retained MacMahon's seven to eight hundred "improvements" on Challoner.[9] Yet Haydock has some independent renderings: "if thou shalt remember," for "and there thou remember" (Matt. 5:23); "and they going out," for "but they going out" (Matt. 8:32). In fact Haydock's was essentially an eclectic text: "that it might be fulfilled" (Matt. 2:15) instead of, "that the word might be fulfilled" (1752); "and seeing many" (Matt. 3:7), for "and when he saw many" (1752); "if falling down thou wilt adore me" (Matt. 4:9), as in 1749, for "If thou wilt fall down and adore me" (1752). Some of the renderings are distinctly awkward: "held in suspense to hear him" (Luke 19:48); "dash him to pieces" (Luke 20:18); "I and he that sent me, the Father" (John 8:16); "affiance and access" for "boldness and access" (Ephes. 3:12); "obscured with darkness and alienated" (Ephes. 4:18). Most of these instances, which could be multiplied almost indefinitely, are derived from MacMahon's editions.

No subsequent editors of Haydock's Bible seem to have noticed these aberrations until the Rev. T. G. Law, in his Introduction to the edition published by himself and Canon Oakeley, 1874–78, pointed out that the text of the New Testament, while mainly that of Challoner's third revision, 1752, yet had "apparently some admixture of renderings derived from a Bible known as Dr. Troy's (1794). This text," he adds, "has been intentionally reproduced" (p. xxiii). One rendering, however, proved too much for Oakeley and Law, who replaced the dreadful rendering, "they began to desire what he always done to them," by, "they began to desire that he would do as he had always done to them" (Mark 15:8).

Haydock's Bible achieved an immediate success. The first edition, 1811–14, was followed by a second, 1813, by a third, abridged and full of errors, Dublin, 1822–24,[10] by a fourth, published at London, Edinburgh, Glasgow, 1845–48, and in New York, 1852, a fifth, with notes abridged by Husenbeth, 1853, and a sixth, with a very valuable Introduction, by Oakeley and Law, 1874–78, though no date is given. Editions

[9] This was done at the express wish of Dr. Troy, who, in authorizing the publication of the edition with abbreviated notes in 1822 and 1824, insisted that the edition should be made "conformably to that printed by the late Mr. Richard Cross [1791], some inaccuracies of which are to be corrected by the Rev. Dr. Hamil, V.G.," July 6, 1822 (quoted by Cotton, *op. cit.*, p. 399).

[10] See below, Editions of 1822–24. I have seen one volume of what seems to be an independent edition dated 1875, but can learn nothing more about it.

show remarkable variations in their omission or retention of the clauses; for example: all except 1813 complete Gen. 36:2; Jos. 7:18; Judg. 7:18 (except also 1811); I Kings 1:11. Still all except 1813 are incomplete at Gen. 4:14; Exod. 18:10; 35:23; Judg. 11:18; I Kings 17:49; II Par. 32:32. But all these defects, with the exception of the last, are made good in the edition by Oakeley and Law, 1874–78. In the New Testament all omit Matt. 13:12; but strangely enough, Heb. 11:9, omitted in most editions from 1749 onwards, is given in every edition of Haydock's Bible.

NEWCASTLE NEW TESTAMENT, 1812

In 1812 appeared an unpretentious little volume entitled on a fly sheet, *The New Testament of Our Lord and Saviour Jesus Christ,* and on the title page, *The New Testament of Our Lord and Saviour Jesus Christ, translated out of the Latin Vulgat: diligently compared with the Original Greek: and first published by the English College of Rhemes, Anno 1582. Newly revised and corrected according to the Clementin Edition of the Scriptures. With Annotations for clearing up modern Controversies in Religion, and other Difficulties of Holy Writ. Lex Domini immaculata convertens animas: Testimonium Domini fidele sapientiam praestans parvulis. Ps. xviii. 8.* Beneath is a vignette of the crucifixion. Newcastle upon Tyne: Printed by Preston and Heaton, 1812; 12mo, 412 pages. The Admonition, letter of Pius VI, the Approbations of 1582, 1599, and that to "another edition" (Challoner's of 1749) follow. Though no name appears on the title page, Father Peter Gandolphy told Bishop Marsh that Father Worswick of Newcastle, anxious to provide his flock with a cheap edition, was responsible for it. A member of a well-known Lancashire family of Leighton Hall, Father Worswick was a familiar figure in Newcastle, where he worked from 1795 until his death in 1843.[11]

Certain unusual features in this edition were for a long time a mystery. For the text up to Romans, chap. 2, was an independent one; though based on Challoner's third revision, it differed from it in about four hundred places. There were also a series of fresh notes and a curious system of brackets. But after Rom. 1:13, "I have often proposed to come to you" (instead of Challoner's "purposed"), and Rom. 2:18, "approvest the

[11] Cf. Gillow, *Bibliographical Dictionary of English Catholics,* "Worswick"; Cotton, *op. cit.,* p. 92. Worswick Street in the city is named after him.

things that are more profitable" (Challoner, "more profitable things"), we have no more independent renderings, but simply the text as in 1752; the novel notes, too, as well as the brackets, disappear. Cotton saw in this sudden change "some outward pressure of authority"; [12] but why, in that case, was the independent text of the Gospels and Acts allowed to stand? Probably the expense involved in resetting the type precluded any change.

Previous to the discovery of the edition of 1792,[13] it was difficult to understand how a hard-working parish priest laboring for a poor Tyneside congregation could have equipped himself for the task of producing what seemed to be a wholly independent edition of the New Testament. Now, of course, we realize that the independent work had been done by the anonymous editor of that earlier edition. The edition of 1792 omitted all chapter headings, but Father Worswick inserted them, though he did not add cross references.

SYERS' BIBLE, 1813

When Thomas Haydock, who was engaged in printing his brother's edition of the Bible, left Manchester for Liverpool, Oswald Syers, another Manchester printer, apparently presuming that the publication of Haydock's Bible was suspended, decided to bring out an edition of his own: *The Holy Bible . . . with Annotations, references, an historical and chronological Index,* Manchester, MDCCCXIII, folio. The usual preliminary pieces are reproduced: the decree of the Council of Trent on the canon, the Admonition, letter of Pius VI, and so forth. Dr. Cotton says: "This edition has no 'Approbation' by any living authority. At first, Bishop Gibson, the Vicar Apostolic of the Northern District, patronized the work, and it was publicly advertised by the printer as 'dedicated by permission' to him. But circumstances afterwards arose to change Dr. Gibson's sentiments on this matter; and the book, as published, does not contain any mention of his name." [14] But while it is true that no formal episcopal Approbation appears in the volume, Dr. Gibson, in giving his approbation to the undertaking, stipulated that "the correction of the press must be most carefully attended to: if this point be secured, I

[12] *Op. cit.,* p. 92.
[13] For further details of the peculiarities of this edition, see above, chap. 28.
[14] *Op. cit.,* p. 208.

sincerely wish good success to you and your undertaking"; accordingly he appointed Father Thomas Sadler and Father Edward Kenyon as supervisers.[15]

In the Old Testament the text and notes are those of Challoner, 1750, with four additional notes on Genesis. In the New Testament, too, the text is that of 1750, with only occasional reversions to the text of 1749; [16] but Challoner's notes are replaced by those in Dr. Witham's edition, 1730.[17] Uncommon even when Cotton wrote in 1855, this edition is now rarely to be met with.

WOGAN'S EDITION, 1814

In 1814 Wogan, Dublin, republished Challoner's New Testament; he followed the edition by Moir of Edinburgh, 1797 and 1805, though correcting a misprint in Acts 25:18. The text is that of 1752 with occasional reversions to that of 1749; e.g., in Matt. 3:13; 1:25; 4:9; 5:37, etc. There is no trace of the second revision, 1750. The only clause omitted is that in Matt. 13:12, those in Mark 8:6; 11:29; 15:29 all being made good.

[15] Cf. *ibid.,* p. 90.

[16] E.g., Matt. 2:1; 6:9; 9:9; 21:40; I Cor. 15:12, etc.

[17] See above, chap. 23.

CHAPTER XXX

The Catholic Board Edition, 1815

THE ROMAN CATHOLIC BIBLE SOCIETY

WE come now to a little-known and very curious piece of history which was to have an unexpected influence on the Catholic version of the New Testament. When, at the opening of the nineteenth century, Bible societies came into being, Catholics, who felt that they could not cooperate with them, came to be regarded as "enemies of the word of God." This feeling reached its climax with the formation of "The Catholic Fund, established for the sole purpose of printing the Rhemish version of the New Testament, and dispersing it gratuitously, or at a low price, among the Roman Catholics in the United Kingdom, . . . [reprinting] most faithfully and correctly, their own Rhemish translation, without note, comment, or addition, excepting that the Letter of Pope Pius VI. to the Archbishop of Florence, and the Approbation of the English Colleges of Rheims and Douay, always prefixed to this version, will also be reprinted." [1] This was to be done in order "to reflect some rays of light among their brethren, who are still sitting in darkness and the shadow of death."

The Catholic Board, feeling that if such an edition was to be thus broadcast, it should be undertaken by the Catholics themselves, inaugurated in March, 1813, "The Roman Catholic Bible Society," the object of which was to facilitate "the distribution of the Holy Scriptures, and particularly the New Testament, among the poor of the Catholic Communion." [2] Dr. Milner stormed against this novel "society," denouncing

[1] Quoted by Cotton, *op. cit.*, p. 94, from a Prospectus issued January 12, 1812, by The Catholic Fund, which was predominantly a Protestant organization having some Catholics among its members. [Ed.]

[2] *Correspondence on the formation, objects, and plan, of the Roman Catholic Bible Society; including Letters from the Earl of Shrewsbury, Lord Clifford, Right Rev. Bishop*

it in more than one pastoral letter,[3] but Dr. Poynter thought it wise to accept the post of president and thus ensure that the Society should proceed on sound lines.

THE PROBLEM OF THE NOTES

The Board entered on its task light-heartedly enough. But they were speedily faced with delicate problems: What English text was to be used? And what about the notes? This latter question caused much dissension in the Committee. The lay members seem to have been quite unaware that the Church insisted on the insertion of notes. They had vague and uneasy recollections of the Annotations in the original Rheims version, the polemical character of which had been grossly exaggerated by anti-Catholic writers. The Board was influenced, too, by the fact that the "Catholic Fund" had decided "to reprint the Rhemish Version of the New Testament, without notes." Consequently some members, headed by Charles Butler,[4] proposed to omit all notes in their contemplated edition. This suggestion, however, was successfully opposed by Dr. Poynter, the president, and on May 11 it was finally agreed "that the Board decidedly disapproves of every publication, either illiberal in language or uncharitable in substance, injurious to the character or offensive to the just feelings of any of our Christian brethren, with all whom the Roman Catholics of England sincerely wish to preserve harmony and mutual good will, in the spirit of Christian charity."

Charles Butler, now agreeing that notes were necessary, compromised: Challoner's notes were to be retained in a modified form, and "such notes as are offensive to the just feelings of our Christian Brethren to be omitted." As a matter of fact, Butler himself, in a letter to Blair, April 19, 1813, had said: "I believe no harsh expression, in respect to our

Poynter, Rev. Peter Gandolphy, Anty. Richd. Blake, and Charles Butler, Esqrs. With Notes and Observations, exhibiting the genuine principles of Roman Catholics, London, 1813. A full account of the above proceedings will be found in Ward, *The Eve of Catholic Emancipation,* II, pp. 189–204; a very different account, biassed and prejudiced, is given by Cotton, *op. cit.,* pp. 94–110.

[3] Husenbeth, *The Life of R. R. John Milner,* pp. 228, 248, 323, 380; Milner in *The Orthodox Journal,* I, 126, 179; III, 313, VII, 9–11; *idem, Supplementary Memoirs of English Catholics,* pp. 239–43. Milner described the Catholic Bible Society as being "in its very title a departure from the Catholic Rule of Faith."

[4] Nephew of Alban Butler, whose *Lives of the Saints* he brought down to his own time. He also wrote *Horae biblicae,* 1797, 1799, 1817, and four volumes of *Memoirs,* 3rd ed., 1822.

Protestant Brethren, is to be found among them." This statement is perfectly true; there is not a single note in any edition of Challoner's revision to which anybody could take the slightest exception. Indeed it is difficult to understand on what grounds any of them were omitted in this edition by the Catholic Board. The only note to which exception might have been taken is that on Matt. 19:11, apropos of the sacrilegious character of the marriages of those Reformers who had been ordained priests, and that note was retained, though it does not now stand in modern editions.[5]

But Milner proved implacable: "It is plain," he says, "that the cancelled part of our former Catholic Notes is precisely the part that is wanted at the present day, to render an English translation of the sacred text *safe* and profitable in the hands of the laity, . . . and that the Notes which were left were for form's sake and to avoid the censure of the rules of the Index; to the Congregation of which the stereotype ought to have been denounced, as its progeny ought to be at the present day."[6] As for the edition brought out in 1818 in six-penny parts by Sidney and Horrabin, he could only say that it was "the revival of a work avowedly made to disguise the true religion, and to favour a false one, connected also, as it evidently is, with the modern plan of educating Catholic children in Methodist schools." Cotton maliciously remarks that Milner's attitude was only what was to be expected of a "Bishop who wished to keep his own laity in ignorance of the Word of Inspiration." Just as malicious and quite without foundation is his declaration that "the omission of even a part of them [Challoner's notes] by later editors was violently denounced [by Milner] as no less than treason against the supremacy of Rome."[7]

Milner, who had not a good word to say for the venture, also complained that the text ought not to have been printed in paragraph form

[5] This note originally ran: "*All men receive not this word:* Protestants have corrupted the text, by rendering it, *all men cannot receive this saying;* to excuse the sacrilegious marriages of their first reformers." In the current editions this is replaced by: "That is, all receive not the gift of living singly and chastely, unless they pray for the grace of God to enable them to live so, and for some it may be necessary to that end to fast as well as pray: and to those it is given from above." Yet Cotton says: "From many Notes the controversial parts and the abusive expressions are honourably withdrawn" (*op. cit.,* p. 103); he would have a difficult time trying to find a single "abusive" expression in Challoner's notes.

[6] Husenbeth, *op. cit.,* p. 381.

[7] *Op. cit.,* pp. 109, 52.

and with the omission of the verse numbers; yet the verses are numbered in the margin, and the paragraph form had been employed in the original edition of 1582. There is likewise no justification for his further complaint that "almost every note of Bishop Challoner's edition, which was necessary for rendering the Testament safe in the hands of the ignorant, was left out." For although the forty on St. Matthew are reduced to thirty,[8] the seven on St. Mark are retained, and thirteen of the sixteen on St. Luke,[9] and twenty-one of the twenty-two on St. John are retained.[10] All the notes on Acts, Second Corinthians, Galatians, and Colossians are retained. Only one of the forty-four excellent dogmatical notes on Romans is omitted: on "how shall they preach unless they be sent out" (10:15); similarly, of the twenty-seven on First Corinthians, only that on 11:28 is omitted, as also is the note on "the man of sin" (II Thess. 2:3). The remaining fifty-eight notes on the rest of the New Testament remain as they were. In all, then, Challoner's 240 notes (in 1749) were reduced to 226.

THE PROBLEM OF THE TEXT

Although the choice of the English text to be reproduced was a far more complicated question than that of the notes, yet it does not seem to have troubled the members of the committee very much; in fact it involved problems with which they were incompetent to deal. They began by circulating a specimen page taken from the edition of 1805, a

[8] The notes removed were: those on "guilty of judgement," on "Raca," and "thou fool" (5:21 f.); "simple as doves" (10:16); on forgiveness of sin and the doctrine of purgatory (12:32); on idle words (12:36); "who are my brethren?" (13:55); "whatsoever thou shalt loose on earth" (16:19); on indulgences (*ibid.*); on Christ's addressing Peter as "Satan" (16:23); on continency (19:11); on the words Azymes and Pasch (26:17). The notes on 5:39; 6:11; 12:4, 48, were much abbreviated; those on 15:9 and 11 were cut down to half, and that on blasphemy against the Holy Spirit shortened and couched in very different words. The editors based their text, and presumably their notes too, on the first revision, 1749. If, however, Milner had in mind the notes in the third revision, 1752, an edition familiar to the editors, his strictures would have had more justification, for on St. Matthew alone that revision had thirty-five more notes than in the two previous revisions.

[9] The only ones omitted were those on "that seeing they may not see" (8:10); "Wo to you lawyers" (11:52); and that on almsdeeds (16:9). Perhaps Charles Butler, the lawyer, felt that the explanation in the second note was hardly sufficient to clear the character of the legal fraternity. The concluding line of the note on 1:48 is omitted, though the words still appear in current editions: "Let Protestants examine whether they are in any way concerned in this prophecy."

[10] The sole omission, one hard to justify, is that of the note on "except my Father draw him" (John 6:44).

reprint of the Bible of 1796–97 by Moir of Edinburgh and based in the main on Challoner's fourth revision, 1764, though reverting at times to his first revision, 1749, and even adopting at times renderings from MacMahon's Bible of 1791. The Board, however, changed its mind, and though we have no record of what led them to do so, it printed instead Challoner's first revision, 1749, with the result that it replaced the third revision, 1752, which, with its more than 2,000 variations from the 1749 revision, had been predominant until that time.

The fruit of the labors of the Board appeared in 1815: *The New Testament of Our Lord and Saviour Jesus Christ translated from the Latin Vulgate, and diligently compared with the original Greek. Stereotyped from the edition published by authority in 1749.* London, A. Wilson, Camden Town, 1815. Two editions were issued, one in 8vo, the other in 12mo.

The Approbation of Challoner's first revision is repeated, and there follows an Address by Dr. Poynter, who insists on the pre-eminence of the Vulgate Latin version and emphasizes the fact that "the Greek edition of the New Testament, printed at Oxford, 1675, gives, out of divers manuscripts, about 12,000 different readings. Hence the editions of the Scriptures in Hebrew or Greek, from which the Protestant translations are made, cannot be shewn to be exactly conformable to the originals." He then gives a brief history of the Vulgate and of the labors of St. Jerome, Cassiodorus, Alcuin, Lanfranc, and St. Stephen Harding, scholars who strove to purify St. Jerome's text from the errors which had inevitably crept in. "Surely," concludes Dr. Poynter, "the Sacred Scriptures have not been neglected in the Roman Catholic Church, nor withheld from the Catholic Public. Surely Scriptural truth has been faithfully preserved, and freely disseminated, by this most ancient and widely established Society." [11]

After Dr. Poynter's Address comes a Historical Index, "in which the Life of Christ is shown in the Concordance of the Four Gospels"; this, actually a harmony of the Gospels, is not mentioned on the title page. The text, admirably printed, is in paragraphs, with the verse numbers in the margin. The Table of Epistles and Gospels at the end contrasts favorably with the miserable ones now generally produced; the Gospel

[11] Quoted by Cotton, *op. cit.*, pp. 100, 102. The whole Address is given at the end of this chapter. [Ed.]

for the twenty-first Sunday is correctly given: Matt. 18:23–35. Cross references seem to have been first introduced in this edition. None appear in any revision by Challoner himself, but from 1815 they are given in every edition except that by Richardson, Derby, in 1847.

Though Cotton says, "The *Text* differs from that of 1749 in a single word, at Philippians 2. 7, viz. *debased* [1752], instead of *emptied* [1749–50]," [12] it is clear that some editing of Challoner's first revision was done, that whoever [13] prepared this edition for the Catholic Board, was familiar with Challoner's second and third revisions, while ignoring MacMahon's strange renderings. For, apart from his omissions of the redundant "that" in introducing quotations (Matt. 14:26; 16:8, etc.), the change from "thine" and "mine" to "thy" and "my" (Mark 12:23, etc.), and the substitution of "said" for "saith" (Mark 9:11, etc.), the text of the second revision, 1750, is deliberately preferred in Luke 2:18: "and all that heard wondered: and at . . . ," instead of, "all that heard wondered at . . ." (1749), or, "all they that heard wondered; and at . . ." (1752). This third revision is adopted at Phil. 2:7, as Cotton has pointed out, and also at Matt. 5:29, the insertion of "that." Frequently, too, the text adopted is that found in both the second and third revisions; e.g., "he called" (Matt. 1:25); "the Jordan" (Matt. 3:13); "merchant" for "merchant-man" (Matt. 13:45); "there," for "thither" (Matt. 24:28), etc.

Despite his evident familiarity with the second and third revisions, the editor of this edition of 1815 did not make good the clauses which, though omitted in 1749, were filled in either in 1750 or 1752: Matt. 23:35; Mark 8:6; 15:29; Luke 1:80; [14] Acts 18:10; Heb. 11:9. In a list containing twenty-four *Errata,* prefixed to the book, these clauses omitted in 1749 still remain incomplete, though strangely enough, "and he shall abound" (Matt. 13:12), omitted in the editions of 1749 and 1750, is now inserted as in the third revision, 1752; and the unfortunate misprint is corrected, whereby the unjust steward was represented as saying, "I know not what I shall do" (Luke 16:4).

It is remarkable that the efforts of the Board should have resulted in perpetuating the text of Challoner's very rare first revision of 1749, which, according to Charles Butler, "is the most correct; alterations were made

[12] *Op. cit.,* p. 103.
[13] Dr. Rigby; see below, note 16.
[14] This omission was made good in Bagster's reprint, 1823; see below, note 19.

in every one, to Dr. Challoner's dissatisfaction." Probably no one familiar with the third revision, with its more than 2,000 variations from that of 1749, will regret its disappearance, though, with the exception of MacMahon's editions, it seems to have been the generally accepted text till the Catholic Board edition was published.

JUSTIFICATION OF THE CATHOLIC BOARD

The Catholic Board deserves every commendation for its action in bringing out an edition of the New Testament with abridged notes.[15] It should not be supposed that these members of the Catholic laity arrogated to themselves the right to choose the text to be followed or the notes to be inserted. Dr. Poynter is explicit on the point: "The text is that of Bishop Challoner in 1749. As to the notes, a few only have been omitted, under the revision of the late Dr. Rigby,[16] who judged those he omitted as of very little use. . . . The Board had nothing to do with the text or notes."

Further difficulties arose when, a year after the appearance of the edition, the Holy See condemned a Bible Society in Poland. This led many to suppose that the condemnation also affected the Catholic Society in England. But the Polish society was condemned, not for circulating the Bible, but for circulating a non-Catholic edition of it, a thing the British society had purposely avoided; in fact, that society had come into existence owing to the necessity of preventing the work from being done by a Protestant society that proposed to publish an edition which, though Catholic, was to have no notes at all.[17]

This edition by the Catholic Board was reproduced almost exactly by Sidney and Horrabin in 1818 and in the same year by Keating and Brown,

[15] See the admirable letter of Lord Clifford to Dr. Poynter, given by Ward, *op. cit.*, II, 197–99.

[16] Dr. Thomas Rigby was senior chaplain at the Sardinia Street Embassy for twenty years, and Grand Vicar of the London District, not "Vicar Apostolic," as Dr. Cotton styles him (*op. cit.*, p. 103). He died in January, 1815. The changes in the text and the gradual diminution noticed above in the omission or revision of the notes would suggest that the editor began by making a considerable number of changes, but grew tired of his attempt by the time he had come to the end of St. Luke's Gospel.

[17] Maziere Brady misrepresents the matter when he says that Dr. Poynter "suffered himself to be persuaded into becoming president of the 'Catholic Bible Society,' an institution founded in 1813 and in 1816 condemned by the holy see as 'a crafty device for weakening the foundations of religion'" (*Episcopal Succession in England, Scotland, and Ireland,* III, 181).

though in this latter edition nearly all the peculiarities of Challoner's second revision, 1750, were retained.[18] In 1823 the text of 1815, as well as the notes, was republished by Bagster: *Translation of the New Testament of our Lord and Saviour Jesus Christ, from the Latin Vulgate. Published by authority and diligently compared with the original Greek,* MDCCCXXIII. The clause, "stereotyped from the edition published by authority in 1749" was omitted. The text, says Cotton, "exactly resembles in appearance the London edition of 1815; and I judge it to be struck off from the same stereotyped plates: but all the Errata (except three) mentioned in the edition of 1815 are here corrected." [19] Dr. Poynter's valuable Address, however, is sadly mutilated, its five pages being reduced to one.

In 1825 Dr. Poynter republished the edition, though seven times he prefers the renderings of the second revision. This tendency became more marked in the edition by Keating and Brown in 1832, which prefers the second revision some fifteen times. The text of 1815 was reprinted twice in 1826, again in 1834, 1835, 1837, 1840, 1843, and 1850.

ADDRESS [20]

THE ROMAN CATHOLIC CHURCH has at all times been attentive to preserve the precious deposit of the Holy Scriptures, and to impart the true word of GOD to the People.

The autographs, or original manuscripts, of the Scriptures are not known to exist. The manuscript copies now extant, in Hebrew and Greek, differ in their readings one from another,[21] and also from the text of various editions printed in those languages. The Greek edition of the New Testament, printed at Oxford, 1675, gives, out of divers manuscripts, about 12,000 different readings. Hence the editions of the Scriptures in Hebrew or Greek, from which the Protestant translations are made, cannot be shewn to be exactly conformable to the originals.

Amongst the several translations of the Bible into Latin, which were made, some perhaps in the time of the Apostles, and others soon after, one version, called

[18] See below, pp. 422 ff. We have already referred to these reversions to the text of 1750; the matter may seem of small importance, but, as we shall see, it exercised a peculiar influence on all subsequent editions.

[19] *Op. cit.*, p. 239. This edition incorporates the *Errata* printed in 1815 with the exception of I Cor. 6:10, which still reads "liars" instead of "liers"; II Cor. 5:13, "it is to you," for "it is for you"; II Cor. 6:13, where "also" is omitted in "be you also enlarged." It is remarkable that Bagster's reprint fails to make these corrections, for they are said to have been "made in the plates, but not in time for the present edition" (1815). For other differences between these two editions, see the account of Bagster's reprint below, chap. 32.

[20] Dr. Poynter's Address prefixed to the Catholic Board edition, 1815, as given by Cotton, *op. cit.*, pp. 99–103. The footnotes (21–30) are also from Cotton. [Ed.]

[21] Kennicott, *Present printed Hebrew Text considered.*

the *Italic,* was held in particular estimation, and was preferred to all the others. As many various readings were observed in the copies of this version, St. JEROM was commissioned by Pope DAMASUS, in the 4th age, to correct the translation of the Gospels by the original Greek. St. JEROM accordingly corrected, first, the translation of the Gospels,—afterwards, that of the rest of the New Testament, from the best Greek manuscripts that could then be found. This Latin Vulgate of the New Testament, with St. JEROM's amendments, was much esteemed by learned men, and was gradually brought into use in the Western Church: as was also the Latin Vulgate of the Old Testament, which consists partly of St. JEROM's translation, and partly of the old Vulgate or Italic, corrected by St. JEROM. This Latin Vulgate of the Old and New Testament has been constantly used in the service of the Roman Catholic Church, has been cited in Councils, explained by Commentators, and from time to time diligently revised.

The learned CASSIODORUS,[22] in the 6th age, spared no labour to have the faults corrected, which had crept into the copies of the Vulgate, through the ignorance or negligence of transcribers.

In the 9th age, the Emperor CHARLEMAGNE [23] engaged ALCUIN, and other learned men, to correct the *Errata,* which were then observed in a number of written copies of the Latin version, both of the Old and New Testament.

LANFRANC,[24] in the 11th age, employed much time in correcting the copies of the Vulgate.

St. STEPHEN of Citeaux,[25] in the 12th age, with the assistance of his Religious, prepared and transcribed a very correct copy of the Vulgate, after having collated it with innumerable manuscripts, and consulted many learned Jews on the Hebrew Text.

The Council of Trent,[26] without deciding anything concerning the Hebrew and Greek editions of the Scriptures, declared, that, amongst the Latin versions, the Vulgate should be held to be authentic. The Council ordered that a most correct edition of the same should be published.

Learned men in most of the Universities, and in all parts of the Western Church, were employed by Pope SIXTUS V. and CLEMENT VIII. to revise the Latin Vulgate, and to collate it with the best copies of the Hebrew and Greek manuscripts and editions of the Holy Scriptures. From the result of the remarks and discoveries of these learned men, a corrected edition of the Latin Vulgate was published at Rome, by SIXTUS V. in 1590: another, more correct, by CLEMENT VIII. in 1592: and again, with some further amendments, in 1593.

The most learned Protestants in biblical criticism, such as MILL,[27] WALTON,[28] and others, have professed the greatest esteem for the Latin Vulgate. It has been justly observed, that the Vulgate of St. JEROM is very ancient, and that it was made long before the divisions in religion that have taken place in the West: on which

[22] Cassiodorus, *De instit.,* cap. 12, 13.
[23] Capitul. Caroli Magni, p. 203.
[24] Mabillon. Tom. IX. Actorum, p. 639.
[25] Ad calcem Tom. IV. Operum S. Bernardi.
[26] Concil. Trident. Sess. 4.
[27] Mill, *Prolegom.,* p. 142.
[28] Walton, *Prolegom. in Polyglott.,* chap. 10.

account, it must be acknowledged to be further removed from the suspicion of prejudice and partiality than any other version.[29]

It is reasonable to suppose, that those Hebrew and Greek manuscripts, from which the Latin Vulgate was translated and corrected by St. JEROM in the 4th age, were more exact and conformable to the originals than any at present extant.

From the above-mentioned corrected Vulgate, Catholic translations of the Old and New Testament have been published in almost all the modern languages of Europe.

A translation of the New Testament into English was published by the English College at *Rheims,* in 1582. The *Douay* Bible, translated from the Vulgate, diligently compared with the Hebrew, Greek, and other editions in divers languages, was printed at Douay, in 1609. New editions of the same, revised and corrected by Dr. Challoner, have been printed in England, Ireland, and Scotland: two are now in the press.[30] Besides these, a translation of the New Testament, with very useful notes, was published at Douay, by Dr. WITHAM, in 1730.

In the course of theological studies, in Catholic Universities, and Colleges of ecclesiastical education, the Sacred Scriptures are well read, and deeply explored. The Scriptures, together with the perpetual tradition of the Church, are the pure source from which the Minister of CHRIST derives the knowledge of Salvation, which he is commissioned to impart to the people.

In our Catholic Chapels, the Epistle and Gospel appointed for the day are read to the faithful, by their Pastors every Sunday. The instructions delivered at the same time are frequently an explanation of the sacred text that has been read; and may in general be regarded as an exposition of the principles and articles of faith, and of the rules of morality, contained in the Bible.

In order to direct the reader to a right understanding of many obscure and difficult passages of the Scriptures, the English Catholic translation is accompanied with explanatory notes, which are extracted chiefly from the Commentaries of the Holy Fathers, and shew the sense in which these passages have been always understood in the Church.

Surely the Sacred Scriptures have not been neglected in the Roman Catholic

[29] "Il n'y a pas de version, au jugement de Grotius, qui soit plus éloignée de toutes sortes de préjugés que la Vulgate, parce qu'elle est très ancienne et antérieure à tous les schismes d'occident." *Diction. Hist. de Feller*. art. *Jérôme*.

Grotius in annotationes suas in Vetere Testamento. Vulgatum interpretem semper plurimi feci, non modo quod nulla dogmata insalubria continet, sed etiam quod multum habet in se eruditionis.

[30] I am not certain *what* are the two editions of the Bible here alluded to, as being *then* in the press. Most probably, *one* of them was the 4° Bible published at Dublin in 1816, with the supposed sanction of Dr. Troy, the appearance of which led to a very curious correspondence, etc. (which may be seen in Rev. R. M'Ghee's "Notes of the Douay Bible, etc." 8°. 1837). Possibly the other was Haydock's: or, it may be, that which was published at Manchester by Oswald Syers.—But I think that both these latter were *completely finished* before 1815. Perhaps it was the folio edition executed at Liverpool in 1816 and 1817. Mr. Charles Butler, in a letter to Mr. Blair, dated 29th April, 1813, mentions that two editions "on large paper are now in the press [probably the folio editions of Haydock and Syers], and a third, on a small type has been lately printed." Quaere, does he mean by this last, the Newcastle edition, issued by Mr. Worswick, in 12°?

Church, nor withheld from the Catholic Public. Surely Scriptural truth has been faithfully preserved, and freely disseminated, by this most ancient and wisely established Society.

With a view of facilitating the means of religious instruction among the Roman Catholics of Great Britain, the English Catholic Board proposes to raise a fund, for the purpose of printing and circulating, at a very cheap rate, an approved edition of the Catholic version of the Sacred Scriptures in *English,* especially of the New Testament, with notes. It is moreover the intention of the Catholic Board, if the fund to be collected shall be found sufficient for the purpose, to extend its plan, and to provide means of supplying, for the benefit of the poorer Catholics, cheap editions of the most approved and useful books of piety and religious instruction.

CHAPTER XXXI

Editions from 1816 to 1818

BEEGAN'S EDITION, 1816

IN 1816 M. Beegan & Co. published *The New Testament of Our Lord and Saviour Jesus Christ. . . . With Annotations comprising those of Drs. Witham and Challoner and a selection from other approved Commentators. Enriched with Four Superb Engravings,* Manchester. The Dedication in Haydock's edition, 1811–14, is reproduced in a modified form: "In gratitude to the Catholics of the British Empire, for the steady zeal which they have at all times manifested for the Catholick and Apostolick Faith, in opposition to the intolerance and calumnies of their enemies, this Edition of the Rhemes Testament is inscribed by their obedient, and very humble servants, the Publishers." [1] The text is that of Challoner's third revision, 1752; that of 1749 is followed in Matt. 1:17 and Ephes. 1:21; there is no trace of renderings peculiar to 1750.

The editor of the *Orthodox Journal,* W. E. Andrews, announced in 1816 that he was publishing in weekly numbers an edition of the New Testament in quarto, but no portion of it seems to have survived.[2]

GIBSON'S EDITIONS, 1816–17, 1822–24, 1829

The Holy Bible translated from the Latin Vulgate; diligently compared with the Hebrew, Greek, and other editions in divers languages. The Old Testament, first published by the English College at Douay, A.D. 1609. And the New Testament, first published by the English College at Rheims, A.D. 1582. Newly revised and corrected, according to the Clementin edition of the Scriptures, with Annotations for clearing up the principal difficulties of Holy Writ. Published with the Approbation of the Right Reverend Dr. Gibson, Vicar Apostolic of the Northern District. Liverpool, Printed at the Caxton Press, by Henry Fisher [no date].

[1] Quoted by Cotton, *Rhemes and Doway,* p. 399. [Ed.]

[2] Cf. *ibid.,* p. 171.

The New Testament portion of this Bible which appeared in 1816–17 has a separate title page:

The New Testament of our Lord and Saviour Jesus Christ, translated from the Latin Vulgate: diligently compared with the original Greek; and first published by the English College at Rheims, A.D. 1582. Newly revised and corrected, according to the Clementin edition of the Scriptures. With Annotations, for clearing up modern controversies in religion, and other difficulties of Holy Writ. London, Printed at the Caxton Press by Henry Fisher.

Previous Approbations of the original Douay-Rheims versions and of Challoner's first revision, 1749, are repeated; also, somewhat strangely, Dr. Troy's Approbation of MacMahon's fifth revision of the New Testament, 1810, "from which the present edition is correctly copied." But this Approbation is not confined to that edition of the New Testament, for it repeats that given to MacMahon's revision of the whole Bible in 1791, a fact which raises some interesting problems. Unfortunately I have never been able to discover a copy of this first edition of Dr. Gibson's Bible, but only of the second edition, undated, but referred by Dr. Cotton to 1822–24, owing to the fact that some of the plates are dated 1823. Now this second edition adds to the title page, "Revised and Corrected by the Rev. T. Robinson and the Rev. V. Glover, of Liverpool." These revisers must have done their work very thoroughly; for if the text in the first edition, 1816–17, was "correctly copied" from MacMahon's edition, as stated above, this statement certainly was not true of the second edition, 1822–24. For in it one of the nine clauses in the Old Testament omitted by MacMahon has been inserted: Jos. 7:18; moreover, every vestige of MacMahon's aberrations—for so we must style them—has disappeared. Whether this was also the case with the first edition, I am unable to say; certainly its title page as given by Cotton makes no reference to the two revisers.

The text of the Old Testament seems to be based on Challoner's second revision, 1764, a few misprints being corrected: "a little of the wine" (I Kings 1:14), "of the" being inserted; "had raised" for "hath raised" (Esd. 1:5); "basis" for "bases" (Esd. 3:3). Of the usual ten omissions of clauses, only two are corrected. Job. 26:13 now reads, "artful hand" instead of "obstetric hand"; Neh. 3:15, "guard" for "garden." The notes are practically unchanged, though that on IV Kings 4:31 is differently expressed, and that on gourds, verse 39, is omitted. In the New Testament

Challoner's third revision is followed, though "name sake" (Matt. 10:22) and "domination" (Ephes. 1:21) are peculiar to the first revision. "What is *it* to me?" (John 2:4) is a departure from all of Challoner's revisions. All omissions are made good except Matt. 13:12.

McGhee says: "Although the Rhemish notes are not contained in it, the celebrated note on Deut. xvii. 8–12, by which the Church of Rome assumes for her priests the right of putting heretics to death for disobedience to their commands, is verbatim the same as the Bibles of 1816 and 1818." [3] Needless to say that not a syllable in this note suggests any such conclusion; it runs: "Here we see what authority God was pleased to give to the Church-guides of the Old Testament in deciding, in that appeal, all controversies relating to the Law, promising that they should not err therein; and punishing with death such as proudly refused to obey their decisions; and surely he has not done less for the Church-guides of the New Testament." [4] It is remarkable that there is no note on Isa. 7:14.

In 1829 a "third" edition came out in folio, but this time with the Approbation of Dr. Bramston: [5]

Novam hanc Sacrorum Bibliorum in linguam Anglicanam versorum editionem typis Henrici Fisher et Sociorum, licentia nostra impressam, cum Duacena Veteris Testamenti anni 1609, Rhemensi Testamenti Novi anni 1582, aliisque jam approbatis Anglicis versionibus diligentissime, jussu nostro collatum, auctoritate nostra approbamus, eandemque, debitis servatis conditionibus, a Fidelibus cum fructu legi posse declaramus. . . . Datum apud Collegium Sti. Edmundi die 27 Martii, An. 1829.

Printed by Henry Fisher and P. Jackson, 38 Newgate Str. London.

The declaration that "the present edition [of the New Testament] is correctly copied from Challoner's first revision," is incorrect; for both in this edition and in that of Dr. Gibson, 1822, and presumably in the first edition, 1817, of thirty-four passages examined, the text peculiar to 1749 is followed four times, that of the third revision, 1752, twenty-seven times, and that first appearing in the fourth revision, 1764, once: "rose up" for "arose up" (Matt. 9:9).

These three editions are magnificently printed on good paper. But seeing that Challoner had in his five revisions put into the hands of

[3] *Romanism as It Rules in Ireland,* I, p. xxxii.

[4] This note is repeated in the "ninth edition," with Dr. Crolly's Approbation, 1857.

[5] After graduating from Trinity College, Cambridge, Dr. Bramston became a solicitor; received into the Church at the age of forty, he was consecrated as coadjutor to Dr. Poynter in 1823. See the note at the end of chap. 32.

Catholics handy 12mo volumes, it is hard to understand how Gibson and Bramston could think it necessary to produce these enormous and exceedingly cumbersome folios,[6] which must have been very expensive.

MACNAMARA'S EDITION, 1813–14

In 1813 MacNamara, a publisher in Cork, announced with a great flourish the coming of a new edition of the New Testament he had in preparation:

The Holy Catholic New Testament. Patronised by the Most Reverend Dr. O'Reilly, . . . [eleven other bishops] and nearly three hundred Roman Catholic Clergymen. . . . Now publishing in Numbers and Parts, by J. A. McNamara, late of Cork (now 86 High Str. Dublin). A new, superior, and elegant edition of the Catholic Bible, containing the whole of the Books in the Sacred Scriptures, explained or illustrated with valuable Notes or Annotations, according to the interpretation of the Catholic Church which is our Infallible and unerring Guide in reading the Holy Scriptures, and leading us unto Salvation. Translated from the Latin Vulgate and diligently compared with the Hebrew, Greek, and other Editions in divers languages. These genuine Translations of the Holy Scriptures into the English Language were first finished and published by the English College at Rhemes, A.D. 1582, and the English Catholic College at Doway, A.D. 1609.

The Catholic Bible will be comprised in one large Quarto Volume now Publishing in Numbers and Parts. These Numbers will be published every Fortnight, and sold to Subscribers only at 1/s. and 8d. each; and one part containing ten numbers will be published quarterly; printed with a new type and very fine paper; and to render it the more complete, the elegant, copious, and instructive Notes or Annotations of the Rhemist Translators will be inserted. These great Notes of the New Testament were never before published in this Kingdom. These will be embellished with beautiful Frontispieces both in the Old and New Testament, and ornamented with a very useful and entertaining Map in which will be clearly pointed out the different Situations of the most remarkable Places mentioned in Sacred History. By Permission of Dr. Thomas Troy,[7] Catholic Lord Primate of Ireland, this work is carefully revising by the Rev. P. A. Walsh, Denmark Street, Dublin. Printed for the Proprietor by James Cumming, Dublin, 1813.

This comprehensive title and advertisement stands on the outside of the cover; there is no title on the inside. The usual preliminary pieces are given: Tables of weights and measures, etc., the decree of the Council of Trent on the canon, the prayer before reading, the Approbations given to the first and second editions, 1582 and 1600, the famous and much

[6] A copy of Dr. Gibson's edition weighs 16½ pounds.

[7] These words, "By permission of Dr. Thos. Troy," should be noted in view of the controversies which followed. No Approbation later than those to the edition of the New Testament in 1582 and 1600 are given, not even that accorded to Challoner in 1748.

controverted Preface, the statement on the infallible authority of Scripture, and the letter of Pius VI. Though this advertisement refers to an edition of the New Testament only, it will be evident from what follows that MacNamara had in preparation an edition of the whole Bible. For in some copies there is added to the Prospectus: "Every number of the Douay Bible of this work will contain thirty-two pages of letter-press, and every number in the Rhemish Testament will contain twenty-four pages."

A new Prospectus provided further information, telling of

> the Historical, geographical, theological and chronological Indices; also of all sects with their rise and fall, and doctrines; of all Popes and more Eminent Saints; also, an historical and geographical description of the ancient and modern cities of Rome and Jerusalem, and other remarkable places mentioned in Holy Writ, in which will be inserted a most beautiful description of St. Peter's Church in Rome and the Temple of Solomon at Jerusalem, they being the most stupendous, admirable, and costly edifices ever erected by the hand of man—one being the metropolitan sanctuary of the faithful in the Old Law, the law of Moses, and the other the metropolitan sanctuary of the faithful in the new Law, or law of Christ; with a particular account of the siege of Jerusalem by the Roman army under Titus. There will be included a list of all the empires, states, principalities, etc. in the world that are united to the Church of Rome at this day; with other useful sketches and observations, deduced from the most eminent Catholic writers.
>
> The first number of every fortnight's publication will be inspected and undergo a critical examination by the Catholic Clergy, one of whose names and place of residence will be inserted in print on the outside cover of each number, to show that the whole work, from Genesis to Revelations, will be in the greatest order and regularity, according to the Clementine edition of the Scriptures.

Then follows a Dedication to the Catholics of Ireland, modeled on that in Haydock's editions:

> To that Orthodox, Loyal, and Enlightened Body of Men, the Catholics of Ireland, in Admiration of their steady zeal in having kept the Deposit of Faith, bequeathed to their Forefathers by that Illustrious Saint and Glorious Luminary of the Church of Christ, PATRICK, and in having handed it down, without interruption, genuine and pure, to their grateful posterity, This Edition of the Catholic Bible is, with gratitude, most respectfully inscribed, by their ever devoted and humble Servant.
>
> James Augustin McNamara.

The second part, ten numbers, came out in 1813, with the names of Dr. Coppinger of Cloyne and Ross being inserted, and Dr. Ryan now "Bishop of Ferns." But by the time the text as far as Romans had been printed, MacNamara went bankrupt. Though his printer, Cumming, hoped that the five hundred copies still in his possession might reimburse him, yet he felt that he, a Protestant, could not well publish this "remainder" of a Catholic Bible. He therefore asked Coyne to undertake it, and the latter agreed on condition that the Rev. P. A. Walsh would continue to act as reviser. The whole was promptly printed afresh and was published in 1816.

COYNE'S REPRINT, 1816, AND SUBSEQUENT DIFFICULTIES

The Holy Bible, translated from the Latin Vulgat: diligently compared with the Hebrew, Greek, and other editions in divers languages; the Old Testament, first published by the English College at Doway, A.D. 1609. And the New Testament, first published by the English College at Rhemes, A.D. 1582. With Annotations, and an Historical and Chronological Index. Revised and corrected according to the Clementin Edition of the Scriptures, and approved of by the Most Reverend Doctor Troy, R.C.A.D. Dublin: printed and published by Richard Coyne, Parliament Street, and sold by Keating, Brown & Keating, Duke Street, Grosvenor Square, London. 1816.

The title of Coyne's edition, it will be noticed, states that it was published with the approval of Dr. Troy; [8] but as the latter had disapproved of MacNamara's edition started in 1813 on the ground that it reproduced the text and notes of 1582, he was naturally dismayed at finding that Coyne had reproduced the same text and notes, thinking that the Archbishop had given his approval to the undertaking. How such a misapprehension came into Coyne's head must remain a mystery.

The republication of these sixteenth century notes, familiar to few in England and to none in Ireland, provoked a storm. The wildest notions on their character prevailed, and the most outrageous interpretations were put upon them. A reviewer in the *British Critic,* September, 1817 (pp. 297–99), interpreted the note on John 15:7 as meaning that "the Prayer of a Protestant cannot be heard in heaven." He also maintained that the Rhemists' Preface taught that "a Christian is bound to burn and deface all heretical books, such as Bibles and Books of Common Prayer." He was convinced, too, that a note on Hebrews, chap. 5, implied that "the translators [of the Protestant versions] ought to be abhorred to the depths of Hell"; while another note (unspecified) was calculated to establish the notion "that the zeal of a Catholic ought to be so great to-

[8] This edition is generally spoken of as "Dr. Troy's Bible," despite his disclaimer (see below); he himself regarded MacMahon's edition of 1791, published by Richard Cross, as the sole edition authorized by himself.

wards all heretics and their doctrines, that he should give them the curse, —the execration—the anathema—though they were never so dear to him, though they were his parents." [9] But a man who can calmly assert, as though it were an established fact, that "with every good Catholic the Rhemish Notes are of the same authority with the Text, as they speak the language of the one infallible Church," betrays his incompetence to pass judgment.

In view of these criticisms, Dr. Troy immediately published a disclaimer:

> Having seen a new edition of the Rhemish Testament, with Annotations, published by Coyne, Dublin, and by Keating, etc., London, 1816, said to be revised, corrected and approved by me, I think it necessary to declare, that I never approved,[10] nor meant to approve, of any edition of the Old or New Testament, which was not entirely conformable, as well in the Notes as in the text, to that which was edited by R. Cross, Dublin, 1791, containing the usual and prescribed formula of my approbation, and which has served as an exemplar to the several editions that have since been published with my sanction.
>
> As in the said new edition, the notes vary essentially from those of the last mentioned editions which exclusively I have sanctioned for publication, I should think that that circumstance alone is fully sufficient to induce me to withhold every kind of approbation from it; but having read, and now, for the first time, considered these notes, I not only do not sanction them, but solemnly declare that I utterly reject them generally, as harsh and irritating in expression, some of them as false and absurd in reasoning, and many of them as uncharitable in sentiment. They further appear to countenance opinions and doctrines, which, in common with the other Roman Catholics of the Empire, I have solemnly disclaimed upon oath.

The Archbishop then adjures clergy and laity alike to beware of "the notes and comments of the said new edition of the Testament. Dublin, October 24, 1817." [11]

Dr. Troy's animadversions on the Rhemist notes show that these had

[9] Grier, *A Reply to the End of Religious Controversy,* p. xvi, gives as examples of the Annotations in the Rheims New Testament of 1582 those on Mark 13:29; John 15:7; Acts 10:9; 28:32; I Tim. 3:12; Heb. 10:7.

[10] Pope Damasus, says Erasmus, *legebat, non "approbavit"* St. Jereome's correction of the Latin New Testament.

[11] In *The Dublin Correspondent,* October 27, 1817. This disclaimer, as well as Coyne's correspondence with Dr. Troy and with Cumming, has been pasted on the inside cover of a copy of the edition of 1816 now in Trinity College Library, Dublin. Copies vary extraordinarily: the title page in one really belongs to the New Testament only; even the Approbation prefixed to the Old Testament speaks "of this Edition of the New Testament." Some copies have twelve plates; another has fourteen, most of them differing from those in the first. Copies of either edition, 1816 or 1818, are now very rare.

evidently been a revelation and a shock to him. For to him, as to all Ireland, the original Rheims-Douay Bible was an unknown book. MacNamara himself had said in his Prospectus: "These great Notes of the New Testament were never before published in this Kingdom." As a matter of fact, ever since 1749 Ireland had depended on Challoner's revisions and MacMahon's editions for English versions of the Bible.

Troy's critics contended that he had given a formal Approbation to MacNamara's contemplated edition, and that now he "became alarmed for the *political* consequences of this untoward event [the fulminations of the *British Critic* and the *Courier*] and in a published letter, dated 24th of October, 1817, stated his surprise at the appearance of such an edition. . . . He withdrew his Approbation from the edition of 1816; and directed his Clergy to discourage and prevent, by every means in their power, its circulation among their parishoners." [12] Dr. Cotton, not content with repeating this calumny, calls attention to what he calls "the startling fact" that at the very time when these transactions were taking place in *Dublin,* . . . this very same Bible, with the same notes, was actually in course of republication, professedly under the same patronage, of the Roman Catholic Bishops and Clergy." [13]

In his Prospectus of 1813, MacNamara had said that his edition was "patronised" by Archbishop O'Reilly and eleven other bishops; similarly of his edition in 1818, that it was "sanctioned and patronised by the Roman Catholic Prelates and Clergy of Ireland." But unfortunately Coyne, when bringing out in 1816 MacNamara's uncompleted edition of 1813, had stated on the title page that it was "approved by Dr. Troy." Presumably Coyne merely meant that the publisher's request for permission to bring out a fresh edition had been acceded to, though he should certainly have been more cautious in expressing it. For formal episcopal approbation is a very different thing from a simple permission to print, and is given only after the printing is completed and is generally based upon an official *censura* by supervisers appointed by the bishop of the diocese.

Dr. Troy had been directly responsible for the edition published by Richard Cross in 1791, and had always regarded that as his official edition. When, then, MacNamara and Coyne asked for permission to pub-

[12] In Cotton, *op. cit.,* p. 112.

[13] *Ibid.,* p. 113. The reference is, of course, to MacNamara's edition in 1818.

lish an edition of the Bible, he took for granted that they would reproduce that text with its notes. Moreover, whereas he had affixed his formal Approbation to MacMahon's editions even so late as 1810, no such Approbation appears in either of the editions in question, those of 1816 and 1818.

MACNAMARA'S REPRINT, 1818

With Dr. Troy's disclaimer the matter might have dropped. But MacNamara, returning from America financially rehabilitated and ignorant of recent controversies, reproduced and completed in 1818 his original edition of 1813, with the new title:

The Holy Catholic Bible, containing the whole of the books in the Sacred Scriptures, translated from the Latin Vulgate, the Old Testament, first published at the English College, at Doway, A.D. 1609. The New Testament, first published at the English College, at Rheims, A.D. 1582. Explained and Illustrated with Valuable and copious notes. To which are added, useful tables of the weights, measures and coins mentioned in Scripture, with an evangelical history and a Controversial Index. Also, The Errata of the Protestant, or Sectarian Bible, with explanations and references, together with the principles of Roman Catholics, and Vindication, shewing their abhorrence of certain tenets commonly alledged against them. Likewise, an epitome of ecclesiastical history, from the Apostles' days to the present time, compiled from the best Authorities, expressly intended for this Edition of the Holy Scriptures. . . . By James A. M'Namara. This Edition of the Catholic Bible, containing the Old and New Testament, is Sanctioned and Patronized by the Roman Catholic Prelates and Clergy of Ireland, and Embellished with appropriate Maps and other Superb Engravings. Cork: printed for the proprietor, A.D. 1818.

The wording of the title page varies; in some copies the following is inserted after the words "copious notes":

To which is added, Explanations and references, according to the interpretation of the Holy Catholic Apostolic Roman Church, Which is our Infalliable and Unerring Guide in reading the Holy Scriptures, and leading us unto Salvation. By James A. M'Namara. This Edition of the Holy Catholic Bible is sanctioned and patronised by the Roman Catholic prelates and clergy of Ireland. "Give me Understanding, and I will search the Law; and will keep it with my whole Heart."—Psalm cxviii, v. 34. Cork, printed for the Proprietor, A.D. 1818.

In both editions, 1816 and 1818, the text of the Old Testament is that of Challoner. Cotton declares that the text in the New Testament is based on that of 1788–89; thus almost identical with that of 1582.[14] But

[14] *Op. cit.*, p. 115.

it seems more likely that, while Challoner's first revision was the basis of this edition, some attempt at revision by Challoner's second and third revisions was made, Mark 8:6 being completed as in the third revision, and Luke 1:80 as in the second and third; yet Mark 15:29, Acts 18:10, and Heb. 11:9 are left incomplete, though completed in 1750 and 1752. Independent renderings appear in Matt. 10:22, "for my name"; Luke 2:18, "and all who heard wondered at those things"; and Rom. 5:14, "them also who had not." The edition of 1818 has at least two egregious misprints: "the wickedness [for "weakness"] of God" (I Cor. 1:25), and "he cannot sin because he is born of sin [for "of God"]" (I John 3:9); another interesting error: "Denomination," for "Domination" (Ephes. 1:21). Both editions agree in John 2:4, "What is it to me?" and in I Tim. 6:20, "depositum." Instances of renderings peculiar to 1750 are rare: "said," for "saith" (Mark 9:11); "from thence" (Acts 28:13).

In the Old Testament the omissions and misprints of earlier editions are perpetuated, only Jos. 7:18 being completed.[15] The notes in the Old Testament are in the main those of Challoner with a few additions and omissions;[16] in the New Testament the original Rhemist notes of 1582 are reproduced.[17]

BELFAST EDITIONS, 1817 AND ONWARDS

In 1817 Belfast firms such as Simms and McIntyre, Baird, Mairs, and Read, began a long series of editions, both of the whole Bible and of the New Testament separately. From 1836 onwards these editions were sponsored by Dr. Denvir of Down and Connor. It is not easy to discover for how many editions Dr. Denvir was responsible; we know of at least nine editions of the complete Bible and as many separate editions of the New Testament.[18]

[15] The headline to the first two chapters of Josue reads "Deuteronomy," chapter 3 of Daniel is labeled "Ezechiel," and Ezech. xlviii is numbered lxviii.

[16] The note on Ps. 20:13, from St. Jerome, is not in the original edition, 1610, while most of those on psalm 48 differ very much from those in the original edition.

[17] Some notes of 1582 are omitted: on Mark 14:71; 15:46; John 5:14; Acts 15:20; Rom. 6:23; Apoc. 22:11; and II Cor. 7:9. The last mentioned is the only note that can be called controversial; it read: "The Catholic teaching on contrition is farre distant from Luthers and Calvins and such wicked Libertines that teach contrition to be altogether a meanes to make sinners either hypocrites or to put them in despair." All the above notes were also omitted in the edition of 1788.

[18] See below, chap. 33.

EDITIONS BY KEATING AND BROWN, 1818

In 1818 Keating and Brown [19] brought out two editions of the New Testament with the usual title. The Approbations are of interest; in one edition the "Approbations to the Present Edition" are by Doctors Poynter, Gibson, and Milner, Vicars Apostolic:

We, the undersigned Vicar Apostolic of the London District, attest that this Stereotype Edition of the translation of the New Testament has been carefully compared with the Edition published by Bishop Challoner in 1750, and that it has been found to be conformable to the same.

London William, Bishop of Halia and
Oct. 13, 1818 Vic. Ap. in the London District.

Having seen a copy of an attestation of the Right Rev. Vicar Apostolic of the London District, that the Stereotype edition of the New Testament, by Messrs. Keating, Brown & Co., has been carefully compared with the Edition published by Bishop Challenor and that it has been found to be conformable to the same, we hereby give our approbation to its publication.

Will. Gibson, Vic. Ap.
of the Northern District.

I, the undersigned, do hereby certify, that having collated the present Edition of the Rheims Testament with that published by the Venerable DR. Challenor, Bishop of Debra, in the year 1750, I have found the former to be conformable to the latter, with respect to the Texts, the Notes, the Table of Controversies, that of the Epistles and Gospels, and the Chronological Table.

John Milner, Bishop of
Castabala, Vic. Ap.

Here it is explicitly stated that the text is that of Challoner's second edition, 1750. This is remarkable in view of the fact that Dr. Poynter had just as explicitly sanctioned the reproduction of the first revision, 1749, in the edition brought out by the Catholic Board three years earlier. And it is surprising too to find Milner endorsing this edition, which varies from that of 1749 (1815) in only 124 places of minor importance, for he condemned in unmeasured terms the reproduction in 1815 of that first revision. Perhaps the fact that the mutilated notes of 1815 were not reproduced mollified him.[20]

[19] The Catholic publishing firm of Keating—sometimes Keating and Brown—was a long established one. Patrick Keating, who took over the business of Coghlan, publisher of Challoner's third revision, when Coghlan died in 1800, had The Catholic Shop in Warwick Str., later in Duke Str., Grosvenor Square; his son George edited *The Laity's Directory* from 1801 until 1839.

[20] Thirty-eight of the forty notes on Matthew in 1749 are retained; in current editions the notes now number seventy-five.

As for the text, the renderings peculiar to the third revision are studiously avoided, though it differed from its predecessors in over 2,000 places; fourteen times the rendering is that peculiar to the second revision, 1750. In spite of these facts, Cotton maintained that Coyne's edition without notes, 1820, was "the first, if not the only representative of that particular text," 1750. He also asserted that this edition "is printed *exactly* from that of 1749, both in Text and Notes. Even the pages agree. The only difference which I have perceived is, that the Table of Controversies contains one addition, from the edition of 1750, and the omission in Luke 1:80 is corrected." [21] How utterly incorrect are his assertions is apparent from the foregoing account, especially from the express statements of the three Vicars Apostolic.

The other edition by Keating and Brown in 1818 has the Approbations of the University of Rhemes (1582), the University of Doway (1599), and that of Gulielmus Green and Gulielmus Walton accorded Challoner's first edition (1749). This edition (British Museum press mark 3050.bb.7) was subsequently republished by Keating and Brown in 1832.

HORRABIN'S EDITION, 1818

In 1818 appeared another edition now rarely met with: *The New Testament of Our Lord and Saviour Jesus Christ translated out of the Latin Vulgate, diligently compared with the original Greek, edited by M. Sidney and carefully revised by the Rev. M. Horrabin.*[22] *The Text is conformable to that of the edition published by authority in 1749.* London, printed by P. and F. Hack, Cullum Str. Fenchurch Str., and sold by P. Fagan, 22 Virginia Str. Wellclose Square, 1818. The letter of Pius VI is printed with this prefatory statement:

> By way of Preface to this edition we insert the following Letter of His Holiness Pius the Sixth, to the late Archbishop of Florence, on his translation of the holy Bible into Italian—*a letter* deserving of particular attention, because it unequivocally shows the benefit which the faithful may reap from their having the Holy

[21] *Op. cit.*, pp. 120, 237. In Matt. 6:9 the text of 1750 is followed, "thus shalt thou pray," though in the *Errata* of 1750 this was changed to "thus shall you pray." In their reprint of 1832, Keating and Brown noted this mistake in their edition of 1818 and corrected it.

[22] Marlow Sidney, a convert and a friend of Bishop Poynter, acted as treasurer of the catholic school in St. Giles; he died in 1839. Richard Horrabin came of a family of recusants; he was chaplain of the Virginia Street Chapel till his death in 1859.

Scriptures in their vulgar tongue, provided they read them with the same spirit of submission as the Eunuch of Queen Candace. (Acts viii.) *See* 2 *Peter* iii. 16 *and* i. 20.[23]

The text, in good black type, reproduced that of 1749 even more faithfully than the Catholic Board edition of 1815, even retaining "footstooll of thy feet" (Matt. 22:44), a redundancy excised in 1750 and 1752. On three occasions the text peculiar to 1750 is followed: Mark 1:29, Luke 2:18, and I Pet. 5:9. This revival of the edition of 1815, which Milner had hoped was defunct, roused his wrath: "I was alarmed with a notice contained in a late printed Report of the Education Committee, which announced that a Catholic Testament, with Dr. Poynter's Notes, was printed and upon sale at the East end of the town in sixpenny numbers. I immediately procured a copy, and found them to be a reprint, as far as regards the Notes, of the ill-fated stereotype." [24] As a matter of fact, some of the notes are taken over from Challoner's third revision; e.g., on "scandalize," "not to swear at all," and on resistance to evil (Matt. 5:29, 34, 39).

[23] In Cotton, *op. cit.*, p. 238.

[24] *Orthodox Journal,* December 29, 1818; in Cotton, *op. cit.*, p. 117. Cotton declares that Horrabin's edition of 1818 itself "was stereotyped in Dublin, in 1826; and with title-pages of various dates according as copies were required, continues in circulation to this day" (*ibid.*, p. 119). [Ed.]

CHAPTER XXXII

Editions Immediately before the Catholic Emancipation, 1820-29

COYNE'S NOTELESS EDITION, 1820

THOUGH the Catholic Board, in view of the efforts of the so-called Catholic Fund to broadcast an edition of the Rheims Testament without any notes, had published in 1815 an edition with comparatively few notes, the Protestants were not satisfied. A new society, therefore, mainly Protestant though with a sprinkling of Catholic members, was formed in Dublin in 1820, and later in London, with the professed object of circulating "the Roman Catholic Version of the New Testament, without Note or Comment." How the famous Catholic publisher, Richard Coyne, could have produced the desired edition must always remain a mystery; [1] but in 1820 appeared:

The New Testament of our Lord and Saviour Jesus Christ, Translated out of the Latin Vulgate: Diligently compared with the Original Greek and first published by the English College of Rhemes: Anno 1582: newly revised and corrected according to the Clementin Edition of the Scriptures. Stereotype Edition. Lex Domini . . . , Ps. xviii. 8. Dublin, Printed by Richard Coyne, 4. Capel Str. Printer and Bookseller to the Royal College of Saint Patrick, Maynooth; and Publisher to the Roman Catholic Bishops of Ireland.

There is no date on the title page, but the Recommendation on the reverse reads: "I certify, that the Sacred Text of the New Testament, in *this edition* of it, as conformable to that of former approved editions; and particularly to that of the Douay English Version sanctioned by me, and published by R. Cross, in the year 1791. + J. T. Troy, D.D, etc.,

[1] Dr. Cotton, in his *Lists of Editions of the Bible and Parts Thereof,* states that a small tract of 36 pages, containing the usual notes, was circulated with this edition (p. 118 note). [S.B.]

Dublin, 9th Feb. 1820." Then comes the translation of an "Extract of a Rescript addressed by His Holiness Pius VII to the Vicars Apostolic of Great Britain."

Vicars Apostolic labouring in the Vineyard of our Lord, direct all your zeal and attention to this, that all the faithfull whom we have committed to your pastoral care, love one another in Charity, Sincerity and Truth: that in the present general agitation, they shew themselves an example of good works: that they obey the king, and be so dutiful and faithful to him, that our adversaries may fear (not having it in their power) to speak ill of us: that they abstain from reading vicious books, by which in these most calamitous times, our religion is in all directions assailed; that by reading pious books, *and above all the* HOLY SCRIPTURES *in the editions approved by the Church,* they conform in faith and good works to you, as their pattern in precept and practice. While we trust from your fidelity and proved veneration for us, that this duty shall be duly performed, we impart to you the Apostolic benediction.

Given at Rome at the College of St. Mary the Greater, on the 18th of April, Year of Grace, 1820, of our Pontificate, 21.

Dr. Troy's assertion that this edition is particularly conformable to the edition of 1791 constitutes a problem. For in it there is no trace of the seven to eight hundred variants from Challoner's editions which disfigured MacMahon's edition of 1791. Likewise incorrect is Cotton's statement that "the text is taken literally from that of Dr. Challoner's second edition, 1750; and is, I believe, the first, if not the only modern representative of that particular text"; [2] for the text is that of 1749 in Heb. 1:13, "thine" for "thy"; while the text of 1752 is preferred in Matt. 4:2; 7:29; John 21:11; Heb. 4:1; and in the omission of the clause in Heb. 11:9, as in 1752 only. Moreover Challoner never wrote "what is *it* to me?" (John 2:4.) At the same time it is clear that Coyne did in other respects follow the second revision, 1750, for in Matt. 6:9 he wrote, "Thus shalt thou," as in the text of that edition, though the list of *Errata,* had he noticed it, would have told him to read, "Thus shall you." The rendering "his own countenance," as against "his natural countenance" (Jas. 1:23) is peculiar to Coyne's edition. The chapter headings are much abbreviated; e.g., the first three chapters of Acts: The Ascension of Christ, The disciples receive the Holy Ghost, The miracle upon the lame man.

This New Testament is still distributed in Ireland, nominally *gratis,* but the Protestant depot in Kildare Street charges sixpence. Opposite the

[2] *Rhemes and Doway,* p. 120; see above, pp. 363, 423.

title page is a slip pasted in: "Douay Version of the New Testament. It is a reprint of the Original Stereotype Edition which was printed and published in Dublin in the year 1820, by the late Mr. Richard Coyne, Printed in Ireland by Sealy, Bryers and Walker, Crow Str. Dublin, 1938." The title, Douay Testament, is of course a misnomer; it should be Rheims Testament. The same misnomer is found on the title page of Dr. Arendzen's edition, 1947.

SMITH'S NEW TESTAMENT, 1821

The New Testament of Our Lord and Saviour Jesus Christ translated from the Latin Vulgat, diligently compared with the original Greek, and first published by the English College at Rhemes, Anno 1582, with Annotations. Liverpool. Printed by E. Smith and Co., 18 Pool Lane, 1821, 16mo. The Admonition, the letter of Pius VI, and the Approbation accorded in 1599 to the second edition are given. Challoner's first revision, 1749, is simply referred to as "another edition." The text is printed in paragraphs, but the verses are numbered. The text is that of 1752, except Rom. 5:14, "who had not," as in 1749, against "who have not" (1750) and "that had not" (1752); and Ephes. 1:21, "domination," instead of "dominion." There is no trace of renderings peculiar to 1750, in which respect this edition stands alone.[3]

HAMIL'S EDITIONS OF HAYDOCK'S BIBLE, 1822–24

In 1822 an edition of Haydock's Bible with abridged notes was published with the authorization of Dr. Troy: *The Holy Bible. . . .* [with the usual title down to Chronological Index, after which is added] *The whole revised and compared with the Latin Vulgate by the Rev. George Leo Haydock, the Compiler of the Notes to the folio Bible. With eight appropriate engravings. The inaccuracies of former editions are corrected in the present copy, by the Very Rev. Dr. Hamil, Vicar General,* Dublin, by Thomas Haydock, 2 volumes, 8vo. In 1824 it was reissued with new titles, calling itself the "second edition" and bearing the imprint "by William Pickering and Son, for Thomas Haydock, David Wogan, and John Coyne"; no date of publication is given. There follow

[3] This is a very rare edition. The only copy I have seen is at St. Edmund's College, Ware. It is not in the British Museum, nor is it mentioned by Cotton, *op. cit.*, or by Lewis or any of the other authorities.

the Admonition, letter of Pius VI, and the prayer before reading. Dr. Troy's authorization reads: "I hereby authorize Mr. Thomas Haydock to publish an edition of the Bible, conformably to that printed by the late Mr. Richard Cross [MacMahon's edition, 1791], some inaccuracies of which are to be corrected by the Rev. Dr. Hamil, V.G. July 6, 1822." But Dr. Hamil failed to notice II Cor. 10:4, where the text has "unto the pulling down of fornications" instead of "fortifications." Christie (see the following page) gives a list of ninety-six errors in the Pentateuch alone.

BAGSTER'S REPRINT OF THE CATHOLIC BOARD EDITION, 1823

Translation of the New Testament of our Lord and Saviour Jesus Christ, from the Latin Vulgate. Published by authority, and diligently compared with the original Greek. London: printed by Samuel Bagster, Paternoster Row, MDCCCXXIII.[4] Dr. Cotton says: "This edition exactly resembles in appearance the London of 1815: and I judge it to be struck off from the same stereotype plates: but all the Errata (except three) mentioned in the edition of 1815 are here corrected. The preliminary pieces and Tables are the same, except that the Address of 1815 is greatly shortened here." [5] But this is a very incomplete account of the edition. The text is on the whole that of 1749, but in several places renderings common to 1750–52 are to be found; e.g., "he called" (Matt. 1:25); "the Jordan" (Matt. 3:13). At least twice the text peculiar to 1750 is given: "who answering said" (Mark 9:11); "all that heard wondered: and at . . ." (Luke 2:18). Renderings peculiar to the third revision, 1752, are: "were astonished" (Mark 9:14); "debased himself," as in 1815, for "emptied himself" (Phil. 2:7). The archaic spelling, "burthened" (Matt. 11:28), the omission of capital letters, so marked a feature in the edition of 1815, as well as the insertion of some clauses omitted in 1815, —"and he shall abound" (Matt. 13:12), "tempting him" (Matt. 22:35), "strengthened in spirit" (Luke 1:80)—though minor details, all serve to show that some editing was attempted. Yet the omissions in Mark 8:6; 15:29, Acts 18:10, and Heb. 11:9 were not corrected.

[4] Compare this title with that of the 1815 edition, above, chap. 30. How Bagster came to publish this peculiarly Catholic edition is a mystery. In fact the firm refused to believe that it had ever done so, and only after two years of correspondence was a copy discovered in the original Samuel Bagster's library and kindly supplied to me.

[5] *Ibid.*, p. 239.

CHRISTIE'S EDITION, 1823–24

James Christie intended to publish in 1823 a reprint of MacMahon's 1791 edition, but in the course of preparation Christie was so impressed by the faulty character of the translation, especially by the omission of clauses, that he laboriously collected as many previous editions as he could. Comparing them with the Vulgate, he drew up a list of forty passages, Genesis to Samuel, which he then corrected by the Latin text. Only thirty weekly numbers appeared, ending with Isa. 13:2. Though no official Approbation is prefixed, since the work was never finished, Christie claims that it was "sanctioned by the late most Rev. Dr. Troy, with the Approbation and under the patronage of the Most Rev. Dr. Murray." [6]

DR. MURRAY'S BIBLE, 1825

The year 1825, remarkable for the appearance of no less than two editions of the Bible and four editions of the New Testament separately, is an important one in the annals of the English Catholic Bible. For in that year, probably as the result of the troubles arising out of MacMahon's ill-fated revisions and the later editions by MacNamara, Dr. Murray, archbishop of Dublin, sanctioned the publication of *The Holy Bible . . . with Annotations, etc. The whole revised and diligently compared with the Latin Vulgate. The Stereotype Edition. With an Historical and Chronological Index to both Testaments; Tables of References and of the Epistles and Gospels for Sundays and Holy Days,* Dublin, printed by Richard Coyne, bookseller, printer, and publisher, to the Royal College of St. Patrick, Maynooth, 1825.[7] There are no preliminary pieces, and the only Approbation reads:

> Novam hanc Sacrorum Bibliorum in linguam Anglicam versorum editionem typis Richardi Coyne licentia nostra impressam, cum Vulgata Clementina, necnon Duacena Veteris Testamenti anni 1609, Rhemensi Novi Testamenti anni 1582, aliisque jam approbatis Anglicis versionibus diligentissime jussu nostro collatam Authoritate nostra approbamus, eamdemque, debitis servatis conditionibus, a Fidelibus cum fructu legi posse declaramus.
>
> Datum Dublinii, die 7 Martii, An. 1825.
>
> ✠ Daniel Murray, A.D.H.P.

[6] Cf. *ibid.,* pp. 171, 399 f.

[7] Presumably the edition of the Bible published in 1825 by Keating and Brown, London, is simply the London edition of the above (British Museum press mark, 1003.g.1).

This edition was often reprinted; e.g. 1829, 1833, 1840, 1844, 1847. In the first reprint, 1829,[8] Dr. Murray's Approbation is given in English and dated September 2, 1829, and twenty-four bishops append their signatures under the words: "We concur with the above Approbation." The so-called "ninth edition" is that published with the Approbation of Dr. Crolly, 1857.

The text adopted in the Old Testament is that of Challoner's revisions of 1750 and 1763; in the New Testament is it in the main that of his first revision, 1749, the renderings of the third revision, 1752, appearing, so far as I have noticed, only in Matt. 8:32, "ran" for "run," and in I Pet. 1:13, "in the grace which is offered you at. . ." The notes in the Old Testament are those of Challoner's revision, 1750 and 1763, though thirty-seven are omitted, fifty altered, and ninety-seven added. Those on the New Testament are, with few exceptions, those of his third revision, 1752, though here again five are omitted, fourty-four altered, and fifty added. The abbreviated notes of the Catholic Board edition, 1815, though frequently republished, were thus eliminated from this stereotyped edition.[9]

Dr. Murray seems to have wished to eliminate the renderings peculiar to Challoner's second revision, 1750, first appearing in Syers' Bible, 1813, and more pronouncedly in the edition by Keating and Brown, 1818, and in Coyne's edition, 1820. For he adhered to the text of 1749 in Matt. 7:29, "their Scribes" in place of "the Scribes" (1752), in Matt. 23:29, "because you build" (1749) rather than "that build" (1750) or "who build" (1752), and in Mark 6:5, "miracle" instead of "miracles" (1750). But in his next edition, 1829, the position is reversed; Matt. 23:29, for instance, reverts to the text of 1750, "that build." In fact nearly every subsequent editor betrays the same penchant for the text of 1750, sometimes adopting all of the seventeen or eighteen renderings peculiar to it, at other times making a purely arbitrary selection from them.

DR. POYNTER'S NEW TESTAMENT, 1825

The New Testament of our Lord and Saviour Jesus Christ, translated from the Latin Vulgate and diligently compared with the Original Greek; with Notes for

[8] See below, note 11.

[9] Dr. Murray's edition met with much criticism by Protestants in Ireland: *Archbishop Murray's Douay and Rhemish Bible and the Bordeaux New Testament Examined in Four Letters, by "Phoenix,"* 1850; *Observations on the present state of the Roman Catholic Bibles,* by G. Hamilton, 1825.

determining the original and genuine meaning of certain Passages in Holy Writ, and wherein is marked the Concordance of particular Parts with other Passages of the Old and New Testament. To which are added Tables of Controversial References and of certain Corruptions in other versions of the Sacred Text; a Table of the Epistles and Gospels for all the Sundays and Holydays throughout the year. Also an Historical Index wherein the Divine Precepts, Miracles, and whole Life, Passion, Death, and Resurrection of Christ are shewn in the Concordance of the Four Gospels. Permissu Superiorum. London. Printed for Ambrose Cudden, 62 Paternoster Ros. MDCCCXXV.

The Approbation of Challoner's revision, 1749, is followed by the Letter of Pius VI and "A Table Pointing Out Some of the Errors, Mistranslations and Corruptions of the Sacred Text, in Versions of the New Testament, made by those who have separated themselves from the Unity of the Holy Catholic Church." Though supposed to be a reprint of the Catholic Board edition, 1815, even to the rendering "debased," for "emptied" (Phil. 2:7), yet it differs from that edition in reading "no further" (Acts 24:4) and "and touching" (I Cor. 16:12) with 1750 rather than with 1749; cf. Mark 9:11; 11:29; Luke 2:18; Acts 24:4; I Cor. 2:14. The notes are those of 1815, there being only twenty-seven on St. Matthew instead of seventy-one as in the current editions.

COYNE'S NEW TESTAMENT WITH NOTES AT THE END, 1825

Mention is made of an edition of the New Testament in 1825 with the usual title, after which is added: "Approved and Recommended by the Four R.C. Archbishops of Ireland. Stereotype Edition. Lex Domini. . . . Ps. xviii. 8. Dublin, Printed by Richard Coyne, and Sold by Joseph Booker, Catholic Bookseller and Publisher, 61 New Bond Street, London, 1825." On the Reverse: "*Approbation.* We approve of this Edition of the Sacred Text of the NEW TESTAMENT according to the Doway English Version; also of the Notes subjoined thereto, 27th. of June. 1820. Patrick Curtis, D.D., etc., Patrick Everard, D.D., etc., J. T. Troy, D.D., etc., Oliver Kelley, D.D., etc." The order in which the bishops' names stand, with the Archbishop of Dublin coming almost last, is strange. Nor is it easy to believe that they would have signed themselves "D.D. etc." Dr. Cotton suggests that the bookseller "faked" the signatures; indeed he is convinced that there never was such an edition, and adds that "this title is sometimes found prefixed to the Dublin edition of 1820, which is entirely *without Annotations.* It is believed that this was done by Booker, the London publisher, in order to assist the sale of copies then lying on his hands. I have likewise seen a *third* titlepage attached to the Testament of 1820; differently worded and without any date." [10]

The text is the same as in the noteless edition of 1820. Challoner's notes, placed at the end of the volume, are greatly reduced; there being only thirty-seven on Matthew,—thirty-nine being omitted—six on St. Mark, fifteen on St. Luke, twenty-two on St. John, twelve on Acts, forty-eight on Romans, thirty-one on First Corinthians, six on Second Corinthians, five on Galatians, six on Ephesians, four on Philippians, four on Colossians, none on First Thessalonians, five on Second Thessalonians, seven on First Timothy, none on Second Timothy, two on Titus, twenty-two on Hebrews, five on St. James, two on First Peter, none on Second Peter, ten on First John, one on Third John, twenty-four on the Apocalypse. The strange Approbation by Dr. Troy prefixed to the noteless edition of 1820, published by the so-called "Catholic Fund," is omitted in this edition. It appears as though the somewhat notorious noteless edition had rightly met with episcopal disapproval and Coyne had been told that he must supply the notes. These he inserted at the end in a mutilated form, as we have seen. One note is new and seems never to have been repeated; on Matt. 1:11: "In the transmigration. That is about the time they were carried away to Babylon."

SMITH'S NEW TESTAMENT, 1825

In 1825 Joseph Smith published the New Testament in Belfast, 12mo. The title is the usual one; the Admonition and also the letter of Pius VI are given. The text is an eclectic one: of twenty-six passages, four follow the text of 1749 (Matt. 1:25; 3:13; I Cor. 16:12, Ephes. 1:21), eighteen follow that of 1752, one, the text of 1750 (Acts 28:7), and one, the text of 1764 (Matt. 9:9). Cotton thinks the edition is a reproduction of a stereotype edition in 1817, of which nothing seems to be known; he also declares that it must have been copied from Wogan's edition, 1814, on the ground that a misprint in Acts 25:18, previously occurring only in Wogan's edition, is here reproduced. But though both editions are based on that of 1752, on at least four occasions they differ from one another: Matt. 2:1; 9:9; 21:40; Acts 28:7.

[10] *Op. cit.*, p. 240. Why Cotton should be so positive that "there never was an edition" like this, I cannot imagine; a copy lies before me as I write, though I must acknowledge that it is the only one I have ever seen.

COYNE'S REPRINT OF THE CATHOLIC BOARD EDITION, 1826

In 1826 Coyne published a reprint of the Catholic Board edition of 1815 at the instance of the Commissioners of Irish Education. They insisted that the edition of 1815 should be adhered to, and even purchased 3,000 copies for distribution. In addition to the Approbation accorded to Challoner's first revision, 1749, the Archbishops of Ireland, Doctors Curtis, Laffan, Murray, and Kelley, add their own Approbation: "We approve of this Stereotyped Edition of the New Testament . . . being according to the Douay [sic] Version, and We authorize Richard Coyne . . . to Print and Publish it. Dublin, Dec. 16, 1825." All the notes of the 1815 edition are given, but Dr. Poynter's Introductory Address is omitted. This stereotyped edition was reprinted in 1834, 1835, 1837, 1840, 1843, and 1847.[11]

11 1829—DR. MURRAY'S BIBLE

"The year, in which the Act of Roman Catholic Emancipation was passed, produced a re-issue of the Bible which Dr. Murray had sanctioned in 1825: and the copies now taken off from the stereotype plates bore an 'Approbation' signed not only by him, but likewise by twenty-four other Roman Catholic Bishops" (Cotton, p. 126). See above, the edition of 1825. [Ed.]

1829—DR. BRAMSTON'S BIBLE

"Messrs. Fisher and Co. of Liverpool and London, who printed a folio Bible at the former town in 1816 and 1817, and a 'second edition' of it in London in 1822, both professing to be approved by the Vicar Apostolic of the Northern District, Dr. Gibson, now issued what they chose to call a 'third edition,' published with the Approbation of Dr. Bramston, Vicar Apostolic of the London District. . . .

"The *Text* appears to agree with that of Dr. Challoner, in 1763–4; and the *Notes,* with very few exceptions, are taken from that edition" (*ibid.,* p. 127). See above, Dr. Gibson's Editions, 1816–17. [Ed.]

CHAPTER XXXIII

Editions Immediately after Catholic Emancipation, 1830-39

THE BALTIMORE EDITION, 1832

An edition of *The Holy Bible* was published in Baltimore in 1832 by F. Lucas. The anonymous episcopal Approbation says: "We hereby recommend it as a genuine copy of the excellent translation long since sanctioned by the Prelates of America and Europe." The Approbations of the original Douay version, 1609, and of the Rheims New Testament, 1582, are prefixed both to the Old Testament and to the New. The decrees of the Council of Trent, session IV, the letter of Pius VI, the Admonition, and the prayer before reading are also given.

The text is strangely eclectic, many renderings peculiar to the first revision (e.g., Matt. 1:17; 7:25) and as many peculiar to 1750 being retained; perhaps, however, the third revision is more consistently followed; e.g., Matt. 8:17; 23:29; Mark 8:6; 9:11. But "What is that to Me?" (John 2:4), and "design" (Acts 5:38) are derived from MacMahon.

NEW TESTAMENT BY KEATING AND BROWN, 1832

In 1832 Keating and Brown reprinted their New Testament of 1818 with the same Approbations by three of the Vicars Apostolic.[1] Though a reprint of the Catholic Board edition, 1815, some slight verbal changes show that a certain amount of editing was done. For example, the *Errata* at the end of Challoner's second edition were examined. The text of that edition had in Matt. 6:9, "thus shalt thou pray," and thus it was printed in 1818; but now in accordance with the *Errata,* it appears as, "thus shall you pray"; "you" replaces "ye" (Luke 12:29, etc.); "that" introducing

[1] See above, Editions by Keating and Brown, 1818.

quotations is generally omitted (Luke 2:15, 23; 9:22, 46); "and" is omitted in Luke 17:7, but inserted in 9:60. These are minor details, but show that editors were alive to variations in the text. This edition escaped the notice of Dr. Cotton.

COYNE'S RE-ISSUE OF DR. MURRAY'S BIBLE, 1833[2]

In 1833 *The Holy Bible, stereotype edition* (Dr. Murray's edition, 1825), was republished by Coyne in three volumes. The clauses in Exod. 18:10; Judg. 7:18; 11:18; II Par. 32:32 are still omitted. We still read "obstetric hand" (Job 26:13), "Jacob" for "heaven" (Ps. 90:1), and "guard" for "garden" (Neh. 3:15).

REPRINT OF THE RHEIMS NEW TESTAMENT, 1834

The New Testament of our Lord and Saviour Jesus Christ; translated out of the Latin Vulgate, diligently compared with the original Greek, and first published by the English College of Rheims, anno 1582. With the original Preface, arguments, and tables, marginal notes, and Annotations. To which are now added, an introductory Essay; and a complete and topical and textual Index. New York: published by Jonathan Leavitt, . . . 1834.

Published for controversial purposes, six Protestant clergymen certify that this is an exact and faithful copy of the Romish Testament and Annotations of the New Testament published at Rheims, 1582. Two hundred and forty-five years previously Fulke had published his enormous volume with the Rheims Version and the New Testament portion of the Bishops' Bible in parallel columns and an attempted refutation of the Rhemists' Annotations. But the introductory pages of the present volume are even more venomous in tone that Fulke's diatribes. We can give only selections, but the interested reader will find the whole Introduction printed, with a sort of gloating satisfaction, by Cotton, *Rhemes and Doway,* pp. 127–34.

One hundred and forty ministers of the Gospel combine to assure their fellow Americans that through the medium of this exact copy of the Rheims New Testament of 1582 they can now see "what Roman Catholics were at that time willing to avow, and what they have been ever since willing to avow, as containing their views of Christian doctrine and worship." Their main contention is that as soon as translations of the

[2] For Coyne's quarto edition of the New Testament, see below, Editions of the New Testament, 1840.

Vulgate New Testament "are appealed to as an authority, the Roman Priests deny both the value of the book, and the obligation of the Papists to believe its contents." In support of this contention they refer to the disputes over Dr. Troy's edition, 1816, referred to above, and the investigation held at Westminster, 1824–25, when—so they say—"the Irish Roman Prelates, . . . upon oath, with all official solemnity, peremptorily disclaimed the volumes published by their own instigation, and under their own supervision and auspices, as books of no authority: because they had not been ratified by the Pope, and received by the whole Papal church."

Since that period only *expurgated* editions are permitted to appear before Protestants. There are several editions printed at Dublin; . . . in all of them the most exceptionable notes are omitted, and nevertheless the volume is presented to Protestants as genuine. The original and the suppressed [?] editions contain lengthened annotations on all the dogmas of Romanism: but Protestant money cannot *now* buy a copy of those editions in the United States. They are reserved for the initiated "faithful" only, who can obtain an order for that purpose from the Vicars General of the different Romish dioceses. . . . If Protestants exhibit the errors in doctrine which they promulge, the palpable incorrectness of the translations, and the corruption which is inculcated in the notes: they are instantly told that the book is of no obligation, that the notes are the private opinions of individuals only; and consequently, that the Papists as a community are not responsible for the unauthorized act or sentiments of any one person. Notwithstanding, it is undeniable, that the Romanists in the United States receive these doctrines as infallible; and practise them whenever their Priests enjoin their obedience. . . .

The repulsive theories and pernicious results of the Popish system are bluntly denied: thereby to conceal the abominations of the apocalyptic Babylon, and to mask "the mystery of iniquity." All the grosser idolatry, pollutions, and malignity, which are continually taught in their Catechisms, and enforced in their Confessionals, are not yet appended to *their* text of the Scriptures, as an infallible exposition, in the editions published in the United States: although the European copies are constantly imported, and *privately* sold to those Papists who can read, or who can purchase, or by any other means obtain, the priestly dispensation to peruse them: and therefore, when the Roman Priests are charged with thus implanting in the minds and hearts of their disciples all antichristian heresy and perverseness and revenge; they deny the fact, and appeal to the ordinary mutilated Romish comments upon the Scriptures as their justification.

To justify their publication of the Rheims Version complete with Annotations, but "without the Christian antidote," the editors declare:

The American people, and particularly the Churches of Christ in the United States, until recently have displayed a morbid incredulity in reference to the Papal system, and an almost settled determination not to be convinced of the "damnable heresies" and soul-killing abominations of Popery. To extirpate this deadly distemper, it is indispensable to administer a strong and plenteous surfeit; which shall excite an irresistible necessity for both the counteracting antidote, and the healthful restorative.

This volume is a genuine, minute, and strikingly exact portraiture of the Papacy delineated by their own Master Artists. The Roman Priests and the Jesuits know, that this, their Babylonian image, will not be worshipped by Americans. The external drapery, however gorgeous and imposing, is too thin to conceal the interior deformity: and therefore they have craftily withheld their dominant goddess from Protestant scrutiny: we only perform that duty, which, in the present state of Romanism in the United States, they are not sufficiently daring to execute.

By way of antidote they propose to republish the replies of Cartwright and Fulke to the edition of 1582. So far they have not done so. The Address concludes with a "fervid prayer to Immanuel, the Prince and Saviour of his Church, that with its associated successor [?] it may constitute a 'standard against the enemy who cometh in like a flood' effectually lifted by the Spirit of the Lord." Some copies are without this introductory address.

GLASGOW EDITION OF THE BIBLE, 1830–36

Kennedy, of Glasgow, published *The Holy Bible,* with the Approbation of eight bishops of Scotland: "This edition has received the special sanction of the following venerable prelates," whose names follow. No date is given, but judging by the dates of their respective consecrations and deaths, we can place the date of publication between 1830 and 1836; the British Museum Catalogue assigns it to 1835.

After the Approbation come the Admonition, the letter of Pius VI, and a "Prayer before Reading." The only previous Approbation is that accorded to Challoner's first revision. In the Old Testament the only omissions seem to be clauses in Exod. 35:23; Judg. 7:18; 11:18; and II Par. 32:32; in this respect the edition compares favorably with most others. In the New Testament Mark 8:6 and Heb. 11:9 are incomplete. The text peculiar to 1749 appears in Matt. 1:25 and I Pet. 5:9; that peculiar to 1752 in Matt. 7:29; at least fourteen of the renderings peculiar to 1750 are retained. John 2:4 reads, with Challoner, "What is to me?"

COYNE'S EDITIONS, 1835

In 1835 Coyne reprinted Dr. Murray's edition of the Bible, 1825. He also reprinted his 1826 edition of the Catholic Board edition of the New Testament, but without any episcopal Approbations, the list of books being the only preliminary piece.

NEW TESTAMENT BY SIMMS AND REEVES, 1835

In 1835 Simms and Reeves, Belfast, published a New Testament in which nearly every rendering peculiar to 1750 is retained; but "the Scribes" (Matt. 7:29) comes from 1752; "counsel" (Acts 5:38) from 1749. Matt. 13:12 is complete; Mark 8:6 is left incomplete.

MAIRS' EDITION OF THE BIBLE, 1836

In 1836 appeared *The Holy Bible,* "with the Approbation of the Most Rev. Dr. Crolly," Belfast; stereotyped and printed by Thomas Mairs, 8vo. There are no preliminary pieces; the text is that of Challoner's second revision of the Old Testament, 1763, and his fourth revision of the New Testament, 1764.[3]

DR. DENVIR'S NEW TESTAMENT, 1836

In his Approbation to an edition of the New Testament published in 1836, Dr. Denvir says:

> This new and portable stereotype edition of the *Douay Testament,* printed by the firm of Messers Simms and Reeves, Donegal Str. Belfast, has been diligently and carefully collated with the most approved Catholic Versions in the English language, by the Rev. John Lynch, P.P., Ahogill, previously to its publication. I hereby approve of its circulation among the faithful; being convinced, that if read with becoming reverence, humility, and pious dispositions, its perusal will be attended with great spiritual advantage.[4]

In all of Dr. Denvir's editions of the New Testament, the basis may be said to be Challoner's first revision, 1749, though wherever a rendering is supported by the second and third revisions, it is adopted. But the curious predilection, so often referred to, for renderings peculiar to the second revision is very marked, nearly all of the eighteen having become part of the traditional current text. Most of the omissions have been made good, yet "he commanded the people to sit down upon the ground" (Mark 8:6), and "in the land of promise, as in a strange country" (Heb. 11:9) are omitted in all of Dr. Denvir's editions; but "and he shall abound" (Matt. 13:12), omitted in Denvir's edition of 1839, is inserted in later editions.

[3] Cotton remarks (p. 216) that "both the *text* and the *notes* appear to agree entirely with Dr. Murray's Bible of 1825." [Ed.]

[4] Quoted by Cotton, *op. cit.,* p. 135.

NEWRY NEW TESTAMENT, 1838

In 1838 Dr. Blake, bishop of Dromore, made arrangements with Greer of Newry for the publication of an edition of the New Testament which should meet the needs of the poorer members of his flock. In his Preface to the book he says:

> Among the duties annexed to out pastoral office, we have always regarded that of nourishing those whom God has committed to our care with the *pure* word of Divine revelation as pre-eminently and incomparably the most important; and accordingly, we have availed ourselves of every facility which the zeal of others afforded to communicate this inestimable food as much as possible to our beloved flock. We now endeavour to add to these facilities. Knowing that there are many who cannot purchase the sacred volume, if it be not very cheap; and others who cannot read it if the type be small: it has been our duty to provide an edition of the *most precious* portion of the sacred writings, suited to the scanty means of the poorer classes of society, and easily legible to readers of every age. Such in our estimation is the New Testament now published by Mr. Robert Greer. To ensure the correctness of this Edition, to the utmost of our ability, we have imposed on ourselves the task of revising every page of it, and of collating it not only with the most approved Catholic versions in the English language, but also with the Clementine Latin Vulgate, and occasionally with the Original Greek.[5]

The text and notes follow Dr. Murray's edition of 1825: the text is that of 1749–50 where they agree; at other times it is eclectic: that peculiar to 1750 being followed in Matt. 23:29 and Gal. 2:2; that peculiar to 1749 in Ephes. 2:12; that of 1752 in Jas. 3:5.

EDITIONS OF THE BIBLE, 1839

Simms and McIntyre, Belfast, published an edition of the Bible in 1839.[6] The text in the Old Testament is that of Challoner's second revision, 1763; the text of the New Testament is that of Challoner's earlier revisions, for in Matt. 23:29, Mark 11:29, Acts 24:4 and 28:7, the text is that peculiar to 1750; while in Matt. 7:29 we have that of 1752. Mark

[5] This Preface was reproduced in an edition of the New Testament published by Simms and McIntyre in 1846.

[6] To this Bible published in Belfast, Bishop Denvir gave his Approbation in the following form: "This new and portable edition of the Douay Bible, printed by the firm of Simms & M'Intyre, Belfast, has been diligently and carefully collated with the most approved versions in the English language, previously to its publication. I hereby sanction its circulation among the faithful, feeling convinced that if read with becoming reverence, humility, and pious dispositions, its perusal will be attended with great spiritual advantage" (in Cotton, *op. cit.,* p. 146). [Ed.]

8:6 is, as usual, incomplete; John 2:4, "What is it to me and to thee?"

In the same year Dolman, London, published an edition of the Bible in 12mo.

NEW TESTAMENT WITH PREFACE BY CUROE, 1839

In his Approbation to a New Testament published in Belfast in 1839, Dr. Denvir says: "The present edition of the Douay Testament, published by the firm of Archer and Sons, Castle Place, Belfast, has been carefully revised and diligently compared with the Latin Vulgate. To promote the spiritual interests of the faithful, I hereby impart to it my Approbation, and earnestly recommend its pious perusal." Prefixed is a remarkable Preface by the Rev. Daniel Curoe, parish priest of Randalstown. He energetically refutes the "antiquated calumny" that the Church discourages the reading of the Bible: "In compliance with the request of two distinguished Prelates, under whose sanction extremely cheap editions have been executed in Belfast, publishers of the first respectability have furnished an authorized statement, recording the sale of three hundred thousand copies of the Douay version." Father Curoe then declares that "of all the false, malevolent charges preferred against our holy religion, there is none more opposed to truth, to facts, and to general practice, than that of our attempting, in the remotest manner, to depreciate the Divine Word, or to debar our people from its invaluable possession." He then quotes Luther, who "acknowledges his obligations to the Mother Church on this head. 'We are,' says he, 'obliged to yield many things to the Papists. . . . With them is the Word of God, which *we receive from them;* otherwise we should have known nothing at all about it.' *Comment on John,* ch. xvi."

Discussing the various English Protestant versions, Father Curoe points out many of the inconsistencies of which the Reformers and their followers are guilty, quoting in particular the words of the Westminster Confession, with the Synod of Ulster the standard of orthodoxy: "There is no ordinary possibility of salvation out of the visible Church: some churches have so far degenerated as to become no churches of Christ, but synagogues of Satan: the Pope is Antichrist, the Man of sin, and Son of perdition." [7]

[7] Cotton reproduces this lengthy Preface in full (pp. 141–45), but dismisses it with the contemptuous remark that it is a "piece of frothy declamation . . . against Protestants" (p. 146).

The basis of the text is that of 1749–50 when in agreement, though every rendering peculiar to 1750 is preserved; there is no vestige of the text of the third revision, 1752.

CHAPTER XXXIV

Dr. Lingard's Version of the Gospels, 1836

A New Version of the Four Gospels, with Notes Critical and Explanatory, by a Catholic, London, 1836, was published anonymously, but it soon became common knowledge that the author was Dr. Lingard,[1] though not until after Dr. Wiseman had reviewed it in the *Dublin Review* without much enthusiasm.[2] He seems to have been puzzled by the appearance of such a scholarly work emanating from any English Catholic, perhaps even a layman; for only seven years had elapsed since the passing of the Catholic Emancipation Act, and the difficulties of penal

[1] A second edition appeared in 1851 with the author's name on the title page.

[2] II (1837), 475–92, "Catholic Versions of the Scriptures." This is an invaluable paper, though hardly a review of Lingard's volume. Dr. Cotton, who never misses an occasion of criticizing the Catholic authorities, says: "Although a revision of the Douay and Rhemish version had long been called for by pious Roman Catholics; and though Dr. Lingard's character as a scholar stood very high among all those of his communion: yet it is beyond question that this New Version of the four Gospels was an undesired and unwelcome book to the high Ecclesiastical party among them. It was coldly received, tamely reviewed, and faintly commended. . . . It is quite evident that this translation, which the learned author was bold enough to publish 'unannounced,' i.e. without waiting for any Clerical 'Approbation,'—which he furnished with critical notes, and openly submitted—'not to the Church (that is the bishops),' but—to 'the consideration of his readers,' was by no means acceptable to some of his brethren" (*op. cit.,* pp. 137 f.). Truly prejudice can blind men. Dr. Cotton does not seem to have understood that Wiseman did not know who the author was. Elsewhere Cotton speaks of this review as the work "of some less liberal modern writer in the *Dublin Review* (Vol. II, p. 475 etc.): who writing under the recent infliction of an independent version of the Gospels, executed by an eminent scholar, Dr. Lingard, and sent forth into the world without leave or 'Approbation' of the high authorities of his church, . . . thus vents his spleen upon the former labours of Dr. Challoner" (*ibid.,* p. 51). This condemnation was occasioned by Wiseman's remark that "the changes made in it [the Douay Version] by Dr. Challoner were in general *for the worse*"; but he was referring to some of the passages we have given above and was not condemning Challoner's work as a whole.

days had excluded Catholics from most educational advantages. Yet readers of the Introduction must surely have seen through the veil of anonymity. For none could fail to recognize the work of a historian, of one accustomed to weigh historical evidence. The same applies to the notes; the freshness and independence of judgment they exhibit is quite characteristic of the fearless historian, Lingard.

Lingard translated from the Greek, though the Vulgate renderings were adhered to so far as possible. Mark 15:29 is a case in point. The Sixtine and Clementine editions had: *Vah, qui destruis templum Dei;* but the Greek and Latin MSS. omitted *Dei,* and Lingard followed them, writing: "Ah, thou destroyer of the sanctuary!" Similarly John 21:22, where Lingard has, "If it is my will that he tarry till I come," a reading followed by only one Latin MS., *Si eum volo,* whereas the majority have *Sic eum volo,* and some combine both readings, *Si sic eum volo,* a reading retained in the Oxford Vulgate.

Wiseman admits that "with several of its verbal changes we are certainly pleased," and most readers will regard "acceptable fruits of repentance" as an improvement on "fruit worthy of penance" (Matt. 3:8); [3] "gabble," however, for "speak not much" (Matt. 6:7), is questionable. In Matt. 25:8, "our lamps are going out," and Luke 5:6, "the net was like to break," full justice is done to the imperfect tenses; it is gratifying, too, to find "one fold" replaced by "one flock" (John 10:16).

But some changes are hardly so acceptable: "Hail, thou favoured of God" (Luke 1:28), though the accompanying note has: "These words are explained by the angel himself, ver. 30, 'thou hast found grace with God' "; "And do thou, when thou hast returned (to thy duty) strengthen thy brethren" (Luke 22:32). Other questionable renderings (in Matthew) are: "a virgin will prove with child" (Matt. 1:23); Joseph "took home his wife" (1:24); Herod was "duped by the Magians" (2:16); "toll-office" (9:9); "the heart of this people is bloated" (13:15); "zizan" for "cockle" or "tares" (13:25); "double drachm" (17:24); "denarius" (20:9); the Pharisees "talk but do not practise" (23:3). In Luke we find "table-book" (1:63) and "tuft of his cloak" (8:44); similar instances might be multiplied.

Lingard, moreover, is fond of paraphrasing: "the children of this

[3] "Do penance" is always replaced by "repent"; the note on Matt. 3:2 rejects the proposed rendering, "reform."

world are more provident in their pursuits than the children of light" (Luke 16:8). Again, the fact that in John 1:11, "He came unto his own, and his own received him not," "his own" is first neuter, then masculine, does not justify, "He came to his own (house), but his own (household) received him not." Nor is he always consistent: "I will it, be thou made clean" (Matt. 8:3), but "I will, be thou made clean" (Luke 5:13); he writes "Noah" (Matt. 24:38) and "Messiah" throughout, yet "Elias," not "Elijah" (Luke 9:8). Then again, though "do penance" is often quite fittingly changed to "repent," it is possible to be too exacting on this point; Christ's rebuke to Corozain would seem to demand "do penance," for insistence seems to be laid precisely on external works as expressive of internal repentance: "They had long ago done penance in sackcloth and ashes" (Matt. 11:21; Luke 10:13).

Only once, so far as I have noticed, does Lingard keep the distressing participial construction with the relative pronoun, which is so characteristic of the Rheims Version and which Challoner himself corrected in his third revision, 1752, but which persists in the current editions, reverting as they do to Challoner's first revision, 1749. "Verily" for "Amen" marks a change long called for, despite the protestations of the Rhemists on the point. A comparison of Lingard's version with the current edition of Challoner's version will afford some idea of the changes he thought expedient.

Matt. 13:1–9

Challoner's Version, ed. of 1898	Dr. Lingard's Version
1. The same day Jesus going out of the house, sat by the seaside.	1. On that day Jesus having gone out of the house, sate down by the sea.
2. And great multitudes were gathered together unto him, so that he went up into a boat and sat: and all the multitude stood on the shore.	2. And a concourse of people gathered about him, so that going into a bark, he sate down, whilst all the people stood on the shore.
3. And he spoke to them many things in parables, saying: Behold the sower went forth to sow.	3. And he spake many things to them in parables, saying: "Behold the sower went out for the purpose of sowing:
4. And whilst he soweth some fell by the wayside, and the birds of the air came and ate them up.	4. And as he sowed, some seed fell by the wayside, and the birds came and eat it up.
5. And other some fell upon stony ground, where they had not much earth: and they sprung up immediately, because they had no deepness of earth.	5. And some fell on rocky ground, where there was little earth. And this sprouted quickly, because it had no depth of soil;

Challoner's Version (*continued*)	Dr. Lingard's Version (*continued*)
6. And when the sun was up they were scorched: and because they had not root they withered away.	6. But, after sunrise, it was scorched, and through want of root, it withered away.
7. And others fell among thorns: and the thorns grew up and choked them.	7. And other some fell upon the thorns: and the thorns grew up and choked it.
8. And others fell upon good ground: and they brought forth fruit, some an hundred fold, some sixty fold, and some thirty fold.	8. But the rest fell upon the good soil, and bare fruit, some a hundred, some sixty, and some thirty fold.
9. He that hath ears to hear let him hear.	9. He that hath ears to hear let him hear."

Opinions will differ as the merits of the translation, but there can be no two opinions about the value of the notes and the Introduction. The opening paragraph of the latter strikes a tone which pervades the notes throughout.

The man who, for the purpose of instruction or edification, peruses the four books of the gospels—the only authentic sources of information respecting the words and actions of our blessed Lord—should be aware that he is reading works composed about eighteen centuries ago, and descriptive of events which happened among a people of different language from his own, of different manners, of different habits of thought, of different institutions—social, political, and religious. He must therefore expect to meet in them with colloquial idioms to which he is a stranger, with allusions to matters of which he is ignorant, and with figures, metaphors and similitudes—the usual vehicles of oriental instruction—the exact import of which, though easily understood by those to whom they were addressed, can now in many instances, be discovered only, if it can be discovered at all, with the aid of long and patient investigation.

It may be proper to inform the reader that the notes, which are appended to the text in the following pages, are not of a controversial character. Their object is the elucidation of obscure passages, of the explication of allusions to national customs, or the statement of the reasons which have induced the translator to differ occasionally from previous interpreters. . . . I shall occasionally quote from the Greek text, as it has been made up by critics from different manuscripts; and at the same time from the Latin, as representing a Greek manuscript of greater antiquity than any now in existence.

He then points out

(a) that the key to the Gospels lies in the expectation of a Redeemer; (b) that Christ's discourses are here presented neither in the language nor in the form in which He gave them; (c) that the writers had not the same meticulous care for accuracy in quoting as is now demanded; (d) that they paid little attention to the niceties of literary form; (e) that Our Lord's teaching, though meant for all time, was couched in a form suitable to His first hearers, uncultured fishermen; (f) that their narratives are imperfect, and are not meant to provide us with a complete biography of Our Saviour, His words and deeds; (g) that, finally, the Evangelists had no intention of providing generations to come with a religious code which should be independent of oral and traditional teaching.

This Preface, as well as the notes, profoundly impressed Wiseman, though, as we have seen, he was unaware of the identity of the learned writer.

Throughout the notes and preface there is a drift which cannot be overlooked, and which has our cordial approbation; it is to place the Gospels in their proper light, as narratives not intended to form a complete digest of our Saviour's life, but as "occasional pieces," so to speak, suggested by particular circumstances, and primarily directed to readers possessing different qualifications from ours, who could understand much that to us must be obscure. The impression on the reader's mind, after having perused this edition, must be, that Christianity never depended, for its code or evidences, upon the compilation of these documents, and that they never could have been intended for a rule of faith. Considering the work in this light, we have an additional pleasure in bearing witness to the learning, diligence and acuteness of its author.

The following excerpts from the notes will prove enlightening and interesting. On the genealogy of Christ (Matt. 1:27):

This is the genealogy of Joseph, not of Jesus; for Joseph was not the father of Jesus. Why then did the evangelist begin his narrative with it? Had he been aware that he was writing for *our* information, he would probably have told us. To the Christian converts of the day such information was unnecessary.

[On Matt. 2:23] A Nazarite. This is a difficult passage for us, though probably very intelligible to the contemporaries of the sacred writer. The obvious meaning is, that from his residence at Nazareth he should be, or should be called, a Nazarite. Now nothing of this tendency is to be found in the prophets; nor did the Jews expect that the Messiah would ever dwell in the town of Nazareth. It is not, however, improbable that the Jewish doctors, when they explained the meaning of the word Nazarite in the Old Testament, particularly in Numbers vi and Judges xiii, 5, were accustomed to teach that the Saviour to come would prove the real Nazarite, of whom the others were but the figure.

[On Matt. 5:23] Thou fool. Moreh. It is generally translated *thou fool,* from the Greek μωρέ. But it is difficult to conceive that such can be the meaning, and more satisfactory to maintain that ῥακά is a copy, in Greek letters, of the Hebrew word *raḳa,* so μωρέ is a copy, in Greek letters, of some other contumelious word in use among the Jews.

[On turning the left cheek (Matt. 5:39)] Is there an individual who believes himself bound to obey this precept to its fullest extent? I imagine not. Yet the evangelist, from his language, must have considered those for whom he wrote to be so bound, or else he must have been aware that his readers would derive, from some additional source, the knowledge how far, and in what circumstances, they would be obliged by it.

On the enigmatic words, "Many shall be first that are last, and last that are first," we have the bold statement:

> The national prepossessions of the apostles might have led them to suppose that the magnificent promise (of the hundredfold in this life and of an everlasting life to come) in the last verse regarded the Jews only. Wherefore, to prevent or to do away with such a delusion, Our Lord proceeds to inform them that many of the Gentiles, though called *last,* should be first; in other words that with regard to the rewards in His Kingdom, both Jews and Gentiles would be placed on an equal footing.

Similarly on Matt. 15:5: "But ye say, whosoever shall say to his father or mother, *of every corban from me the benefit be thine*"; on this the lengthy and admirable note runs: "To those whom our Blessed Lord addressed, and to those for whom the evangelist wrote, this passage would be perfectly intelligible; to us, from our imperfect acquaintance with the peculiar customs and traditions of the Jews, it presents almost insuperable difficulties." Then follows an examination of these difficulties, one which could hardly be improved upon even with the aid of the fuller knowledge of such customs as we are now privileged to possess.

On John 20:30 Lingard notes: "This looks very like the conclusion of the gospel: and it is not improbable that when the evangelist wrote it, he intended it as such, but that he afterwards thought proper to add the following chapter, which bears internal proof of having been also written by him." Similarly on chapter 21:

> The comparison of the conclusion of this chapter with the conclusion of the last suggests the notion that this history of the third appearance of Jesus to his disciples was added by St. John at the request of his hearers, and that he makes the remark in the last verse as an excuse to relieve himself from their farther importunities; as if he had said, you ask what I cannot undertake: to relate all that I remember would be an endless task.

These few notes which we have selected for quotation suffice to show that, while they are hardly to be called "critical" in the modern sense of the term,—there is, for instance, little or no discussion of the text—yet they are truly "critical" in that they help the reader to realize some of the difficulties inherent in the story, and also indicate the spirit in which we should approach these deathless narratives which by reason of their very simplicity are sometimes apt to repel even those most conscious of their appeal.

CHAPTER XXXV

Editions Immediately before the Re-establishment of the Hierarchy, 1840-49

COYNE'S EDITION OF THE BIBLE, 1840

IN 1840 Coyne published an edition of the Bible with several of the clauses usually omitted now inserted; only Judg. 7:18; 11:18; and II Par. 32:32 are left incomplete in the Old Testament, and Mark 8:6 and Heb. 11:9 incomplete in the New. Most of the renderings peculiar to 1750 are retained.

EDITIONS OF THE NEW TESTAMENT, 1840

Coyne is supposed to have published a quarto edition of the New Testament in 1840, but a pencilled note in the only copy I have seen gives the date as 1833. It seems to be a reprint of his 12mo edition in 1826, for out of twenty-nine passages the text is that of 1749 eighteen times; of 1749–50, five times; of 1750–52, twice; of 1750, three times; of 1752 only in Phil. 2:7, "debased," as in 1815 and 1826.

In 1840 Coyne did republish his "stereotype" edition, 12mo. But the text differs substantially from that in his quarto edition, 1833 or 1840 (above). For of twenty-four passages, the text is that of 1750 on fourteen occasions; of 1749–50 seven times; of 1750–52 three times; of 1749 once, "counsel" (Acts 5:38). Nowhere is the text peculiar to 1752 represented; but Coyne supplied "strengthened in spirit" (Luke 1:80), omitted in 1749 and by Dr. Murray, and "of God" (Mark 15:29). Both Dr. Murray and Coyne omit the clauses in Mark 8:6 and Heb. 11:9.

In the same year Cummiskey in Philadelphia published the New Testament "from the last London and Dublin edition . . . with the Approbation of the Right Rev. Francis Patrick Kenrick, and the Right Rev. J. Hughes."[1] This edition seems to be copied from Dr. Murray's edition of 1825.

In this same year Dr. Blake's edition of 1838 was reprinted.

EDITIONS OF 1841

In 1841 Dr. Murray's edition of the Bible, 1825, was reproduced by Coyne.

In this same year Simms and Co. published an exact reimpression of Dr. Denvir's edition of 1839, 16mo.[2] It seems clear that this edition, 1839 and 1841, was copied directly from a copy of Challoner's second revision, for every peculiarity of that revision is retained, even the spelling of "counsel" (Acts 5:38), which is the reading of the text in 1750. There is no trace of Challoner's third revision, 1752.

EDITIONS OF THE NEW TESTAMENT, 1843–44

In 1843 F. A. Little, Catholic Bookseller, London, published a reprint of Bagster's reproduction in 1823 of the Catholic Board edition, 1815, stereotyped from Challoner's first revision, 1749, except for the rendering "debased," instead of "emptied himself" (Phil. 2:7). The same year Coyne reprinted again his edition of 1826, which also was copied from the Catholic Board edition.

[1] Cotton declares that this New Testament "published at Philadelphia, professing to be taken 'from the last London and Dublin edition,' . . . was issued under the sanction of Bishops Kenrick and Hughes; whose 'Approbations' are attached as follows:

"We hereby approve of the edition of the New Testament now published by Eugene Cummiskey, being conformable to the edition previously approved of by various prelates. Given under our hand at Philadelphia, this 1st day of October, 1839.

+ Francis Patrick Kenrick, Bishop, etc.

"We approve of this stereotype edition of the New Testament of our Lord and Saviour Jesus Christ, being according to the Douay version.

+ J. Hughes, Bishop, N.Y."

Cotton was "not able to say *what* was 'the last London and Dublin edition,' or the edition 'previously approved of by various prelates' " (Cotton, pp. 146 f.). [Ed.]

[2] The only change I have noted is the insertion of the clause in Matt. 13:12, omitted in 1839; both editions omit the clauses from Mark 8:6 and Heb. 11:9. According to Cotton, the size of this edition is 24mo (p. 244), but his figures for the sizes of Bibles are hardly reliable; the British Museum Catalogue gives 12mo (3051.aa.8).

In 1844 a New Testament was published in New York which retains the peculiarities of 1750, though following the first revision in Matt. 1:25, "called," in place of "he called."

EDITION OF HAYDOCK'S BIBLE, 1845–48

A new edition of Haydock's Bible was published in Glasgow, Edinburgh, and Dublin by Fullarton, with detailed Approbations by the bishops of Ireland and Scotland and a letter by Father Theobald Mathew, the apostle of temperance. Dr. Kyle, Vicar Apostolic, and Bishop Scott, Vicar Apostolic of the Western District, had insisted that the edition was to be revised by the Rev. W. Gordon of Glasgow, "in whose accuracy I have every confidence," wrote Dr. Kyle. Dr. Gordon was to certify that the edition was "*verbum verbo* the same as the Bible already approved and circulated as Haydock's Catholic Bible." In accordance with this directive, Dr. Gordon's attestation was printed on the original covers of this edition, which came out in parts: "I find the whole printed exactly from the original folio edition of 1811, used by you as your copy." But though Haydock in his second impression, 1812, corrected a misprint in the note on Gen. 1:16, where light is said to be "nearly three thousand years in coming to us from the remotest star in our stratum" (1811), the error was faithfully reproduced in this edition, 1845–48. Yet various corrections were made; e.g., four of the nine omissions in the Old Testament of 1811 were made good: Gen. 36:2; Jos. 7:18; Judg. 11:18, I Kings 1:11. The only omission in the New Testament is the clause, "and he shall abound" (Matt. 13:12), omitted as in 1811.

EDITIONS OF THE BIBLE, 1845–46

The Bible published in Belfast by Simms in 1845 was the first published with the Approbation of Dr. Crolly alone; it is practically identical with Coyne's edition in 1840.

In 1846 Coyne published a reprint of Dr. Murray's edition, 1825, with the letter of Father Mathew prefixed. In the list of the books of the Old Testament, that of Ruth has been omitted.

In the same year Read published the Bible in 24mo [3] with the Approbation of Dr. Denvir: "To this edition of the Douay Bible, published by

[3] As noted before, authorities differ in their estimates of the size of various editions of the Bible. Cotton describes a Bible published in 1846 by Simms and McIntyre, Belfast, and bearing the Approbation of Dr. Denvir and Dr. Crolly (*op. cit.*, p. 216).

Messers Robert and Daniel Read, after being carefully collated with the most approved versions in the English language,[4] I feel happy in giving my sanction and approbation. C. Denvir. This 18th. day of November, 1846." In the Old Testament there are the usual omissions in Judg. 7:18; 11:18; II Par. 32:32; in the New Testament Mark 8:6 is incomplete. The text followed is that of 1749–50; nowhere have we noticed a rendering peculiar to 1752.

DR. MACHALE'S NEW TESTAMENT, 1846

In giving his Approbation to an edition of the New Testament printed by Brennan of Tuam in 1846, Dr. MacHale, the archbishop, says:

> Aware of the manifest dangers to faith and morals, that are found in corrupt versions of the Bible as well as in the Scriptural fragments that are insidiously issued amongst the people, exhibiting strange and inaccurate novelties of language, in which you look in vain for the sound forms of Catholic doctrine; We have not ceased to deplore this great evil, and to labour for its correction. It occurred to us that the publication of genuine versions of the Vulgate, under competent authority, with explanatory notes, would be found among the most efficient means to neutralize the poison of those counterfeit productions.
>
> Accordingly, We approve of this edition of the DOUAY TESTAMENT, with notes and comments, published by Thomas Brennan of this city, and recommend it to the faithful, in the confidence that, for the true sense of the different parts of the Scriptures, they will submissively trust to the authority of the Catholic Church, on which alone all Christians must rely for their authenticity and inspiration.
>
> John, Archbishop of Tuam.[5]

Though the Archbishop of Tuam was presumably referring primarily to current English versions, he probably had in mind, too, the Irish versions of the New Testament by John Kearney assisted by King, a Gaelic scholar,[6] and of the Old Testament by Bedell, bishop of Kilmore, also

[4] It would be interesting to know what the Bishop meant by these "most approved versions in the English language." He would hardly have "approved" of any of the non-Catholic versions.

[5] Given by Cotton, *op. cit.*, p. 148. These outspoken words provoked Cotton's wrath: "The language of this 'Approbation' is gratuitously violent against Protestant versions; and he distinctly avows, that his chief inducement to permit the use of the edition was, that it might 'neutralize the poison of those counterfeit productions' " (*ibid.*, p. 147).

[6] Cooper (*Athenae Cantabrigienses,* I, 515) says that the work was begun by Nicholas Walsh in 1573 with the help of Kearney and O'Donellan, but it was published only in 1602. Le Long attributes the translation of the New Testament from the Greek to William Dornwillium, who presented his version to James I; it was re-edited in 1681 by Robert Boyle, and the Old Testament, without the Apocrypha, was republished in London in 1689–90 (*Biblia Sacra,* II, 371, 426–28). For John Kearney see a letter by A. F. Pollard in the *Times,* October 22, 1935.

assisted by King. Though completed in 1640, Bedell's work was not published until 1685;[7] a second edition appeared in 1690. King, who seems to have been mainly responsible for the version, knew no Hebrew, and apparently contented himself with translating King James's Version of 1611 into Gaelic, while Bishop Bedell revised the work by the Hebrew and the Septuagint with the help of the Italian version by Diodati. The Irish Catholics naturally pointed out that a version made in this fashion would hardly redound to the credit of the Irish Protestant Church.[8] The circulation of this Protestant version induced Dr. MacHale, himself an Irish scholar, to begin a translation of the whole Bible into Irish for the sake of his flock.[9]

For the text of his English New Testament, MacHale follows that of the combined witness of 1749 and 1750, though showing a preference for the renderings peculiar to 1750. Only in I Pet. 5:9 does he retain a rendering peculiar to 1749, and he avoids all renderings characteristic of 1752.[10]

DR. DENVIR'S NEW TESTAMENT, 1846

In 1846 Simms and Reeves, Belfast, published a New Testament with the Approbation of Dr. Denvir and with Dr. Blake's Preface to his edition in 1838 prefixed. Though this might be regarded as the "stereotyped" edition among the many resulting from the energy of Dr. Denvir, yet copies vary.[11] For some prefer the text of 1749 to that of 1750; e.g., in Acts 5:38 and I Pet. 1:13; some copies even read "debased" for "emptied himself" (Phil. 2:7), as in Challoner's third revision and in that brought out

[7] *Leabhuir na Seintiomna, or The Books of the Old Testament translated into Irish by the care and diligence of Dr. William Bedel, late Bishop of Kilmore,* 4to, 1685, 1690, 1852.

[8] Burnet, *more suo,* attributes another motive to the Catholics: "The priests of the communion of the Church of Rome, had reason to oppose the printing of a Book, which hath always prov'd fatal to them" (*The Life of William Bedell, D.D., Bishop of Kilmore in Ireland,* 2nd ed., p. 94).

[9] *An Irish Translation of the Holy Bible, from the Latin Vulgate. With a corresponding English version, chiefly from the Douay,* vol. 1, Genesis to Josue, 1861. This is all that was ever published, and despite the title, the translation of Josue was not included. Dr. MacHale also translated much of the Iliad into Irish.

[10] Cotton declares: "It does not appear, that Dr. MacHale bestowed any special care in preparing this edition, or added any thing by way of improvement; for both the Text and Notes seem to agree exactly with Dr. Murray's Bible published in 1825" (*op. cit.,* p. 148). [Ed.]

[11] For some variations in Dr. Denvir's editions, see below, p. 455.

by the Catholic Board in 1815. These facts show that editors were fully conscious of the variations in the text.[12]

EDITIONS OF THE BIBLE, 1847

The year 1847 was remarkable for the publication of at least five editions of the whole Bible and two separate editions of the New Testament. Coyne published in 8vo a reprint of the stereotyped edition of Dr. Murray, 1825, to which is prefixed, by way of Preface, a letter from Father Mathew, "the Apostle of Temperance," addressed "To the members of the various Total Abstinence Societies of Ireland, England, and Scotland," urging them to read the Bible and thus learn "to join Wisdom to Temperance" (cf. II Pet. 1:5–7). In the list of the books of the Old Testament, that of Ruth is accidentally omitted.

This same year Duffy also published a reprint of Dr. Murray's Bible. This edition and those published by Burns and Lambert, 1853, by Washbourne in 1914, and by the Douay Bible house in 1941, are, so far as I know, the only ones avoiding the misprint "Jacob," for "heaven," in Ps. 90:1, which dates from Challoner's revision, 1750.

The Bible published in 1847 with the Approbation of Archbishop Hughes of New York opens with a brief sketch of the principal epochs of biblical history. In addition to the usual preliminary pieces, others from the original Douay Version are given: the decree of the Council of Trent on the canon, the "Sum of the New Testament," the "Sum of the Gospels." The text of the Old Testament is that of 1750 with trifling exceptions, and the omissions of that revision are not made good; the text of the New Testament is complete with the exception of Mark 8:6, "and he commanded the people to sit down on the ground."

Richardson of Derby also published in 1847 an edition of the Bible "with the Approbation of Bishop Walsh, Vicar Apostolic of the Midland District, and Dr. Wiseman, his Coadjutor," which was of a very different type from the foregoing. How such a text came to be made up is a mystery, for out of some fifty-five passages taken at random, thirty follow Challoner's third revision, nine follow the first, and eight the second. At least six renderings are independent of any previous revision; e.g., Acts. 18:14; I Cor. 15:13; I Pet. 1:13. As Dr. Burton explains, it is a very

[12] This edition was reproduced by Gill and Sons in 1885 and in 1912.

composite text;[13] and the influence of MacMahon's revisions, 1791, 1803, and 1810—unfortunately perpetuated in Haydock's Bible, which was reissued this year in parts—is manifest throughout: "laughed at him . . . when the crowd was turned out" (Matt. 9:24 f.); "and when it was evening" (Matt. 14:15); "Go after me" (Matt. 16:23); "What is that to me and to thee?" (John 2:4); "Grecians," for "Greeks" (Acts 6:1); "these they placed in the presence of the Apostles" (Acts 6:6). In the Old Testament none of the usual omissions are rectified except Judg. 7:18.

EDITIONS OF THE NEW TESTAMENT, 1847

Besides their editions of the whole Bible, both Coyne and Richardson in 1847 published editions of the New Testament separately, and in both instances the text of the separate New Testament differs greatly from the text of the New Testament in the complete Bible. Coyne's edition bears the title: *The New Testament of Our Lord and Saviour Jesus Christ translated out of the Latin Vulgate and diligently compared with the original Greek, with Notes and an Historical Index by which the Life of Christ is shewn in the Concordance of the Four Gospels, and an enlarged Table of the Epistles and Gospels throughout the year.*[14] *Stereotyped Edition,* Dublin, 1847.[15] The Approbation accorded to Challoner's first revision, 1749, is repeated, and a further Approbation by Doctors Curtis, Murray, Laffan, and Kelley is added. Though it is stated on the title page that this New Testament is printed "from the last London and Dublin edition," it is not possible to discover what edition is referred to. The whole is in a good black print.

Richardson's separate edition of the New Testament follows Challoner's first revision far more closely than does the New Testament portion of the whole Bible: Matt. 9:9, "arose up," as in 1749, but the Bible, "rose up," as in 1764; I Pet. 5:9, "befals," as in 1750, but the Bible, "befalleth," as in 1752. One copy has, "is of evil," the other, "cometh of evil" (Matt. 5:37); one reads, "of the Law," the other, "from the Law" (Matt. 5:18).

[13] Cf. *Life and Times of Bishop Challoner,* I, 288.

[14] This table is correct; indeed it is one of the few instances where the Gospel for the twenty-first Sunday is correctly given.

[15] Cotton does not seem to have been aware of this separate edition of the New Testament (British Museum press mark, 3053.bb.14).

In this same year Simms and McIntyre issued a reprint of Dr. Blake's edition of 1838, 12mo.[16]

EDITION OF THE BIBLE, 1849

In 1849 an edition of the Bible was published in 16mo by Simms and Co. with the Approbation of Dr. Denvir. As usual the clauses in Judg. 7:18; 11:18, and II Par. 32:32 are omitted from the Old Testament; Mark 8:6 and Heb. 11:9 from the New Testament. Renderings peculiar to the third revision, 1752, nowhere occur, but practically all those peculiar to the second revision, 1750, are incorporated. John 2:4, "what is to me?" is in accord with all Challoner's revisions.

DIVERGENCES IN THE TEXT

Today we are astonished at the liberties which publishers thought themselves free to take with the word of God. We wonder that Bibles approved by the same bishop should exhibit such a wide variety of readings. The comparison of various editions appearing with Dr. Denvir's Approbation would show interesting results; confining ourselves, however, to two different editions of the Bible published in 1846, to another in 1852, and to a New Testament published separately in 1846, we find: (a) In the Old Testament all omit clauses from Judg. 7:18; 11:18; and II Par. 32:32; one copy of the Bible (1846) also omits a clause from Exod. 18:10. (b) In the New Testament all have the frequently omitted clause, "and he shall abound" (Matt. 13:12); and all omit clauses from Mark 8:6 and Heb. 11:9. (c) Practically every rendering peculiar to Challoner's second revision, 1750, is retained in all. (d) One 1846 edition of the Bible has "counsel" (Acts 5:38), another has "council" with Challoner's third revision (1752), followed by the reimpression published by Gill in 1912; one 1846 edition of the Bible reads "befals" (I Pet. 5:9) with 1750 and is followed by Gill's edition, 1912, another 1846 Bible has "befalls," with 1749; one 1846 edition of the Bible has "their scribes" (Matt. 7:29) with the first and second revisions; the New Testament of 1846 reads "the scribes," with 1752, and is followed by the edition of the same Bible published in 1846 with the original Approbation of Dr. Denvir. These divergences may seem trifling, but they show the liberties which the publishers took with the text.

[16] In his text, p. 245, Cotton describes this edition as 12mo, but in the list of Catholic editions at the beginning of his work, it is described as 24mo. [Ed.]

A comparison of two editions of Dr. Murray's Bible, both published in 1847 by Coyne and Duffy respectively, gives some startling results.

		Coyne's Edition, 1847	Duffy's Edition, 1847
Matt.	23:29	"that build," 1750	"because you build," 1749
Mark	15:29	clause omitted, 1749	clause inserted, 1750–52
John	2:4	"what is to me?" 1749–52	"what is *that* to me," MacMahon, 1791
	5:1	"after these things was," 1750	"after these things there was," 1749
Acts	5:38	"counsel," 1749	"design," MacMahon, 1791
	24:4	"no further," 1750	"no farther," 1752
	28:7	"these places," 1750	"those places," 1749
Rom.	5:14	"who have not," 1750	"that had not," 1752
I Cor.	2:14	"these things," 1750	"the things," 1752
	16:12	"and touching," 1750	"as to our," MacMahon
I Pet.	1:13	"in . . . in," 1750	"that . . . at," MacMahon

An even more striking example of inconsistency is furnished by a comparison of the New Testament portion of the Bible published by Coyne in 1847 with a separate edition of the New Testament which he brought out in the same year:

		The New Testament in Coyne's Edition of Murray's Bible, 1847	The New Testament Published by Coyne Separately in 1847
Matt.	1:17	Three "are," 1750–52	One "are," 1749
	7:25	"on a rock," 1750–52	"upon a rock," 1749
Mark	6:5	"miracles," 1750	"miracle," 1749
John	5:1	"After these things was," 1750	"After these things there was," 1749
	6:70	"have believed and have known," 1750–52	"believed and have known," 1749
Acts	18:10	"to hurt you" (inserted), 1750–52	clause omitted, 1749
	24:4	"no further," 1750	"not farther," 1749
	28:7	"these places," 1750	"those places," 1749
Phil.	2:7	"emptied himself," 1749–50	"debased himself," 1752

To these nine differences it would be easy to add at least a dozen more where in his edition of the Bible Coyne has adopted for the most part the text of 1750, but in his separate edition of the New Testament he reverted over and over again to the text of 1749, and on one occasion took a rendering from the revision of 1752.[17]

[17] Presumably this separate edition of the New Testament is a reprint of his 1826 edition (Catholic Board edition). [Ed.]

Dr. Murray's attempt to establish a stereotyped form of text was thus ruined, and though he did succeed in eliminating almost completely the aberrations of MacMahon's revisions, some of these still appear in various editions, and practically all of them in the various editions of Haydock's Bible and in that sponsored by Walsh and Wiseman in 1847.

CHAPTER XXXVI

Dr. Kenrick's Version of the Bible, 1849-60

SINCE complaints had repeatedly been made about the corrupt state of current editions of the Douay-Rheims version, the Provincial Council of Baltimore in 1829 decided that immediate steps should be taken to secure as correct an edition as possible, with suitable notes. Dr. Kenrick, who during the synod had been nominated Coadjutor Bishop of Philadelphia, set to work, and the results of his labors appeared in 1849: *The Four Gospels. Translated from the Latin Vulgate, and diligently compared with the Original Greek Text, being a revision of the Rhemish translation, with Notes Critical and Explanatory. By Francis Patrick Kenrick, Bishop of Philadelphia.* In dedicating his work "To the Hierarchy of the United States assembled in the Seventh Provincial Council of Baltimore," Dr. Kenrick says:

> I venture to offer to the public a revised translation of the Four Gospels, with notes directed to remove the chief difficulties that may occur in their perusal. My object is not to substitute it in public use for the received version [that of Dr. Challoner], but to submit it to your mature judgement and correction, and in the meantime to facilitate the study of the life of our Divine Redeemer in its only authentic records. The annotations which I have added, are for the most part selected from the holy Fathers, although occasionally I have availed myself of the researches of modern writers, unhappily estranged from Catholic communion. I cannot hope that a work which demands so much erudition and such exercise of judgement, is in every respect faultless, but I offer it as earnest of my zeal for the correct understanding and devout study of the Sacred Scriptures.

The following passage from his Preface to *The Four Gospels* will show the spirit in which the Bishop worked:

> In order to understand the precepts and doctrines which were delivered by Our Lord, we must bear in mind the circumstances in which He spoke, whether in

private to His disciples or in public to the multitude; and compare the various statements of the Evangelists, who manifestly did not undertake to record His very words, so much as the substance of His instructions.

[The Gospels] are the history of a God-man, who disclosed to His chosen disciples the secrets of His Eternal Father. They belonged to the supernatural order: and where divine mysteries are in question, human reason must bow to authority. . . . Wherever a revealed mystery is in question—wherever the sense of a scriptural passage regarding a divine doctrine or institution has been solemnly declared by the Church of God, which is the pillar and the ground of truth—it becomes enlightened reason to embrace the decision. The Scripture otherwise becomes a labyrinth, from which there is no issue.

In 1851 the second volume appeared: *The Acts of the Apostles, the Epistles of St. Paul, the Catholic Epistles, and the Apocalypse. Translated from the Latin Vulgate, and diligently compared with the Greek Text, being a revision of the Rhemish translation, with Notes, critical and explanatory. By Francis Patrick Kenrick, Bishop of Philadelphia,* New York, Edward Dunigan and Brother.

At the next Provincial Synod held in Baltimore, 1858, the bishops suggested that Dr. Kenrick's version of the whole Bible, then nearing completion, should form the basis of the uniform version so repeatedly demanded. They added, however, that "since it was matter of general knowledge that the English Bishops had already arranged for the preparation of a corrected version to be made by the Very Rev. Dr. John Henry Newman,[1] they would suggest that these two men should combine their forces and preparatory work, and thus produce a single version which would suffice for the United States as well as for England."

But Dr. Kenrick continued the good work unaided. Job and the prophets came out in 1859, and the historical books and the Pentateuch in 1860 (two separate volumes), thus completing the Bible, for in 1857 had appeared *The Psalms, Books of Wisdom, and Canticle of Canticles.*

[1] In 1855 the Synod of Westminster had decreed: "With a view to the speedy production of an accurate version of the Bible translated into English from the Vulgate Latin Version, the Fathers decided that the Cardinal Archbishop should entrust the preparation of such an edition to competent persons to be chosen by himself. The Rules laid down by the Congregation of the Index on the point as regards revision of the work and the Notes drawn from the Fathers of the Church and from Catholic commentators, as well as the requisite Approbations and permissions to read it, must of course be observed." Newman undertook in 1857 to forward the decision of the Synod by producing an English version; but nothing came of it. See Ward, *Life of Cardinal Newman,* I, 418 ff.; see also Newman's article in the *Rambler,* July, 1859, "History of the Text of the Rheims and Douay Version of the Holy Scripture," reprinted in *Tracts Theological and Ecclesiastical* (1891), pp. 405–45.

Translated from the Latin Vulgate, diligently compared with the Hebrew and Greek. Being a revised and corrected edition of the Douay Version, Baltimore. This latter he dedicated to Cardinal Wiseman. A second, revised edition of the whole New Testament was published in 1862 by Kelly, Hedian and Piet, Baltimore.[2]

In his Preface to *The Four Gospels* (1849), the Bishop justifies his presentation of a new version. "In France, Spain, Germany and Italy they have been made freely, and new versions substituted for others which had become antiquated in style, or otherwise unsuited to the actual state of the national literature. No restraint has ever been put on efforts of this kind, when made with due regard to the local authorities, and without prejudice to that sanction which the Church has given to the Vulgate." But he was keenly alive to the defects of the various editions passing for reproductions of Challoner's revisions, and he felt, with Charles Butler, that "a more correct version is perhaps the greatest spiritual want of the English Catholics." [3] Later on he wrote: "From the many changes made in the various editions [of the Douay version], it has been found impracticable to point to a standard that might be in all things followed; so that although since the Council, which was held in 1829, not less perhaps than ten very large editions have been issued with permission and approval, it has not been possible to secure their entire accuracy.[4] . . . I present my work as a literary essay, rather than as a substitute for the Douay translation." [5]

TEXT AND NOTES

Kenrick was familiar with Challoner's three main revisions, 1749, 1750, and 1752, taking his renderings from all three indiscriminately,

[2] *The New Testament. Translated from the Latin Vulgate, and diligently compared with the original Greek Text, with Notes, Critical and Explanatory. "How shall we escape, if we neglect so great salvation?" Heb. 2:3.*

[3] Butler, *Historical Memoirs of the English, Irish, and Scottish Catholics,* p. 417.

[4] In particular he condemned the editions of 1791, 1794, 1810, and 1816 (in his Preface to *The Four Gospels*). He refers to three of MacMahon's editions and to that published under Dr. Troy's Approbation in 1816. But Kenrick is not always accurate in his dates, assigning Nary's version to 1709 and 1717 instead of 1718 and 1719, and referring Witham's version to 1736, whereas it first came out in 1730 and was republished in 1733 and 1740. See Pope, "History of the English Version first published at Rheims, 1582," in *The Library,* 1940.

[5] General Introduction to *The Psalms,* 1861.

though in the main he bases himself on the third revision.[6] But Kenrick was a pioneer, and not all his renderings would now meet with universal acceptance; for example: "through Him" (John 1:3, 10), though grammatically correct; "became flesh," for "was made flesh" (John 1:14); "the impression of His substance" (Heb. 1:2); "they seek their country" (Heb. 11:14). "Wary as serpents, guileless as doves" (Matt. 10:16) is good, but better perhaps is "guileful as serpents, guileless as doves." Throughout he renders "Amen" by "verily."

The independence of his judgment appears repeatedly. He says:

> "Repent," does not fully express the force of the original term. "Agite poenitentiam" of the Vulgate is an elegant and precise version: but "do penance," which literally corresponds to the Latin, is by usage determined to signify the practice of penitential works, rather than the exercise of the virtue itself. "Reform" does not express the compunction of the mind, which is the precise force of the Greek term. I have retained the Rhemish translation in other places, where reference is made to external humiliation.[7]

On Apoc. 2:21 he says: "I have alternately translated the Greek term 'repent' and 'do penance,' holding both expressions to be equivalent, although modern usage refers the latter to external acts especially."

He defends at great length his rendering of John 2:4, "What hast thou to do with me?" On phrases peculiar to the Vulgate version of Proverbs he says:

> This, however, does not imply that those verses, or parts of sentences, which are not in the Hebrew, but are borrowed from the Septuagint, must necessarily be regarded as appertaining to the sacred text. . . . It may be conjectured that some of them are a second translation of words already rendered, whilst others contain the glosses of some ancient commentator, transferred accidentally from the margin to the text. The Vulgate generally distinguishes them by leaving them unnumbered, or putting them by themselves, thus intimating that they are wanting in the Hebrew. It should be observed that the translation of St. Jerome from the Hebrew is given in the Vulgate, but with some additions and variations, occasioned by recourse to the Septuagint, or by the retention of some words and phrases from the very ancient Latin version, which was in use before the time of that illustrious interpreter.[8]

[6] Of forty-two passages in the first four chapters of Luke, six are independent renderings, twenty-two follow the reading of 1749–50, five follow the reading of 1750–52, and only in Luke 2:18 does he prefer a rendering peculiar to 1750. In his Introduction he makes no reference to the revision of 1752.

[7] Note on Matt. 3:2 and Mark 1:15. On the whole subject see A. H. Dirksen, *The New Testament Concept of Metanoia,* 1932.—However, both the text and the notes in the edition of 1862 differ from those quoted in this chapter. [Ed.]

[8] Introduction to Proverbs, pp. 265 f.

In the Preface to his version of the Gospels, Kenrick pays a generous tribute to Lingard's version:

A few years ago, a new version of the four gospels, made directly from the Greek, with notes critical and explanatory, was published in England by a "Catholic," who is generally believed to be Dr. Lingard, the justly celebrated historian. I have freely availed myself of his labours, sometimes with special acknowledgement, in the present work, which differs from his in its plan and character. It does not depart so widely as his from the Rhemish version, and it contains a fair number of notes designed to remove, as far as in my power, every difficulty that might present itself to the reader. I offer it only as a literary essay, to aid students of theology, and the faithful generally in the study of the gospels.

Again, when republishing his version of the New Testament in 1862, Kenrick refers to this version by Lingard as "a new and elegant version of the Four Gospels with few but luminous notes. Taking him for my guide, I gave in 1849 a revision of the Rhemish version of the Gospels, the text of which I followed more closely."

Kenrick's notes, though betraying a remarkable familiarity with the work done on the Greek text by Scholz, Griesbach, Bloomfield, and others, are very simple and practical. For example, on "This is the chalice, the new covenant in My Blood, which shall be shed for you" (Luke 22:20), he says: "The present participle is used in the Greek. The Latin interpreter had regard to the latitude in which the Hebrews use the tenses, and rendered it by the future, as referring to the effusion of the Blood of Christ on the cross." In John 10:8, where Challoner reads, "All *others,* as many as have come," Kenrick would like to read, "as many as have come *before Me,"* though he feels that the textual evidence is against him. The whole note should be read, if only to show his minute study of the textual evidence so far as it was then available to him. Another model note is that on the prophecy of Isaias, "Behold a virgin shall conceive," as quoted by Matt. 1:23. Other valuable notes are those on the Baptist's supposed doubts (Matt. 11:3), on "Satan" (Matt. 16:23), on Cyrinus (Luke 2:2), and on "they [Mary and Joseph] understood not the word that He spoke to them" (Luke 2:50).

OTHER AMERICAN EDITIONS, 1850

In 1850 Sadlier, New York, published the New Testament in 12mo. The text is that of 1749–50 where they are in agreement; nearly all the renderings peculiar to 1750 appear, and that so exactly that Matt. 6:9

reads: "thus shalt thou pray," as in the text of that edition, though corrected in the *Errata* to, "thus shall you pray," as in 1749. In Matt. 2:1; 7:29, the text is that of 1752; in I Pet. 5:9, that of 1749; Heb. 11:9 is incomplete. The Gospel for the twenty-first Sunday is given as Matt. 18:23–25 instead of 18:23–35.

In the same year *The Pictorial Catholic New Testament,* in 8vo, was also published in New York. After the usual title is added: "Newly revised and Corrected with Annotations explanatory of the most difficult passages. Illuminated after original drawings by W. H. Hewett, Esqr." The Approbations accorded by seven bishops read as though referring to the illustrations rather than to the whole edition; the illustrations are numerous and, on the whole, pleasing. The text differs from that in the foregoing edition in that the revision of 1749–50 is preferred to that of 1752 in the instances given above.

CHAPTER XXXVII

Editions Immediately after the Re-establishment of the Hierarchy, 1851-60

JUST as Catholic Emancipation had been marked by the publication of many Catholic editions of the Bible, so too the restoration of the English Catholic hierarchy, which had been destroyed by Elizabeth, was marked by numerous editions of the Bible and New Testament, though as a matter of fact the number of editions published during the preceding decade had been remarkable.

EDITIONS OF 1851

In 1851 Dolman, London, published an edition of the Bible with the Approbation of Drs. Denvir and Crolly. In the Old Testament clauses in Judg. 7:18; 11:18; II Par. 32:32; Agg. 2:2, are still omitted, and in the New Testament those in Mark 8:6 and Heb. 11:9. There seems to be no trace of Challoner's third revision, that of 1750 being adhered to throughout. This edition is identical with Coyne's edition, 1835.

This same year marked the publication of six editions of the New Testament. Duffy published a reprint of Dr. Murray's edition of 1825 with the Approbation of Dr. Crolly. The text is that of 1749–50 when they are in agreement; renderings peculiar to 1750 are retained; there seems to be none peculiar to 1752. Two other editions followed, in 1852 and 1853.

Richardson, Derby, published two editions of the New Testament in 1851: one was a reprint of his edition of 1847, with the same Approbations by Doctors Walsh and Wiseman; the other, with an entirely different text (that of Dr. Murray's edition, 1825), bore the Approbation given by Dr. Denvir in 1836.

In the same year J. Brown ("late Keating and Brown") published a New Testament, 8vo, in excellent black type. No Approbations later than 1748 are given. The text is that of Coyne's 1835 edition of Dr. Murray's Bible; the renderings peculiar to 1750 are retained.[1]

Simms and McIntyre published a New Testament in 12mo with the Approbation of Dr. Denvir;[2] and another edition, likewise with the Approbation of Dr. Denvir, following the text of Coyne's 1835 edition, also appeared in 1851 in 16mo (8vo ?).

EDITIONS OF THE BIBLE, 1852

The year 1852 is remarkable for the publication of seven editions of the whole Bible and two of the New Testament separately. Read and Co., Belfast, alone published three editions of the Bible: one in 8vo with the Approbation by Dr. Crolly, one in 12mo with the Approbation of Dr. Denvir, and another in 8vo with the Approbation of Dr. Denvir. In the latter Judg. 7:18, 11:18; II Par. 32:32 are, as usual, left incomplete; so too are Mark 8:6 and Heb. 11:9. The text of 1749 is adhered to in the spelling, "befalls" (I Pet. 5:9), and in Matt. 13:2, "and he shall abound," which was omitted in 1750 and 1752; the text of 1752 in Matt. 8:17, "the prophet Isaias."[3] Elsewhere the text is that of 1749–50, all the peculiarities of 1750 being retained.

A fourth Belfast edition was published by Simms and Co. in 24mo, with the Approbation by Dr. Denvir.

[1] Cotton calls this edition 12mo and says that "the *Text* appears to be that of the edition of 1749: and *Notes* also agree; except that three notes are added from that of 1750, viz., at 1 John iii. 9, v. 1, and 18.—The paging also agrees with the edition of 1750" (*Rhemes and Doway,* p. 248). [Ed.]

[2] Of this edition Cotton says (p. 247): "In this edition the title-page alone is new: the rest of the book is struck off from the stereotype plates used by these publishers in their edition of 1829, described at p. 243," where he says: "The text appears to differ, in a few slight points, from that of the Bible of 1825, and the New Testament of 1838." [Ed.]

[3] The variations here are strange: the Rhemists wrote (1582), "Esay the Prophet," and likewise did Challoner in 1749, "Isaias the Prophet" (not "prophet" as Cotton prints it, *op. cit.,* p. 318). But subsequent editors fluctuated between "the prophet Isaias" (1797, 1829, 1835, 1841, 1851, 1853, 1885, 1914) and "the Prophet Isaias" (1857), and "Isaias the prophet" (Dr. Gibson, 1816–1822). The text of 1750 omitted the word Isaias alto-

This year saw also the publication of two editions of Haydock's Bible: Fullarton issued in 4to a reprint of the edition of 1845–48, and Dunigan, of New York, published a folio edition of the same.[4]

Sadlier, New York, published a Bible with the Approbation of Archbishop Hughes of New York, 2 vols., 4to. The text is that of MacMahon's revision, 1791. Of the nine clauses omitted from the Old Testament in that edition, two are here corrected (Gen. 36:2 and Judg. 7:18). Ward's *Errata of the Protestant Bible* (1841 edition) is added.

EDITIONS OF THE BIBLE, 1853

The year 1853 also saw a number of editions of the Bible and New Testament. Among them was a quarto edition of Haydock's Bible with abridged notes edited by Dr. Husenbeth.[5] In his note on Gen. 1:16, an absurd misprint, "the remotest star in our *stratum"* (for "system"), vexed Haydock, who discovered it too late. Husenbeth tried to solve the difficulty by omitting "in our stratum" and writing, "the remotest star, beyond which are others"—not very helpful.

This same year Dolman, London, published an edition of the Bible in 12mo. Most of the omissions in the Old Testament are corrected, but Judg. 7:18; 11:18; and II Par. 32:32 remain incomplete; also Mark 8:6 and Heb. 11:9 in the New Testament. The text is that of 1749–50, with most of the variants peculiar to 1750 retained. I Pet. 5:9 has "befalls" as in 1749; but Acts 5:38 has "council," as in 1752. The reading of the third revision is also followed in Mark 6:2, 5; Gal. 2:2; Phil. 2:7; the reading of 1764 is followed in Matt. 9:9. "What is to me" (John 2:4) follows all of Challoner's revisions. Other editions of the Bible with the

---

gether, simply reading, "the Prophet"; but this omission was corrected in the *Errata,* a fact which Cotton did not notice.

[4] "A new edition of Haydock's large Bible, with all his collected Notes, was commenced in this year [1852] at *New York*. . . . The book is handsomely printed; and is embellished with some good engravings. It appears to have been copied from Haydock's *first* impression, that of 1811; as it repeats the mistake in the wording of the Note at Genesis i. 16, to which I have already adverted" (Cotton, *op. cit.,* pp. 165 f.). The Approbation was given by Archbishop Hughes. [Ed.]

[5] Shortly before the publication of Haydock's Bible in New York, "it was determined in *England,* that a new edition should be prepared *there,* but with his copious Notes greatly reduced from their original extent. This task of abridgment was committed by the bishops to the Rev. Dr. Husenbeth, a Vicar General and 'Canon of the English chapter': and the book has appeared, handsomely printed in two volumes quarto." (Cotton, *op. cit.,* p. 166). [Ed.]

Approbations of Dr. Hughes and Dr. Cullen respectively were published in the same year.

Sadlier, New York, also published an edition of the Bible with the Approbation of Archbishop Hughes. In the Old Testament the only omission corrected is that in Jos. 7:18; the New Testament portion is that published by Sadlier in 1850 and presents the same eclectic text as appears in Dolman's edition of the Bible, 1853.

About this same time a Bible was published in New York with Approbations by Archbishop Hughes and Doctors Kenrick, Purcell, McCloskey, and Timon. The frontispiece depicts the Baptist in the desert with what an irreverent person might call a "permanent wave." In the Old Testament the only omissions corrected are those in Jos. 7:18 and I Kings 1:11. There are the same misprints, "guard," for "garden" (Neh. 3:15); "Jacob," for "heaven" (Ps. 90:1). In the New Testament the text is that of 1752; sometimes that of 1749–50 when in agreement; none of the readings peculiar to 1750 appear; those peculiar to 1749 are preferred in Matt. 1:17; 7:25; Ephes. 2:12. The influence of MacMahon's editions is seen in Matt. 9:24 f. and Mark 15:8; "rose up" for "arose up" (Matt. 9:9) comes from Challoner's fourth revision, 1764. The Gospel for the twenty-first Sunday is given as Matt. 18:23–25 instead of 18:23–35.

In 1853 there also appeared a reprint of Dr. Murray's edition of 1825, and Burns and Lambert published a Bible with the Approbation by Dr. Denvir.

EDITION OF THE NEW TESTAMENT, 1853

In 1853 Duffy published the New Testament in 16mo with Dr. Murray's Approbation. In writing to the Rev. Patrick Meahan, December 8, 1850, Dr Murray says: "I approve of Mr. James Duffy's wish to publish a portable edition of the New Testament, and I hereby authorize you to revise the proof-sheets of the work previous to its publication, in order that it may be found in all things conformable to the Authorized Edition he published in 1847 with my Approbation." On August 17, 1851 the Archbishop wrote to Father Meahan: "This new Edition . . . carefully collated, by our direction, with the Clementine Vulgate, also with the Rhemish Version of the New Testament of 1582, and with other approved English Versions, we, by our authority, approve." It is hard to imagine what the "other approved English Versions" might have been. Father Meahan's task of collating this English edition with the Vulgate and the Rhemist version was not an easy one. The text here is that of 1749–50, every variant of the latter being adhered to. There is no trace of the third revision, 1752. In fact, the whole text is that of the edition by Brown in 1851. The Gospel for the twenty-first Sunday is given as Matt. 18:23–25 instead of 18:23–35. The British Museum Catalogue describes this edition as 12mo.

EDITIONS OF 1857

The Holy Bible translated from the Latin Vulgate; diligently compared with the Hebrew, Greek, and other Editions in divers languages. The Old Testament, first published by the English College at Douay, A.D. 1609; and the New Testament, first published by the English College at Rheims, A.D. 1582. With Annotations, References, and an Historical and Chronological Index. The whole revised and diligently compared with the Latin Vulgate. First published by the Approbation of the Most Rev. Dr. Crolly, Archbishop of Armagh, and Primate of All Ireland. Ninth Edition. Belfast; Printed and published by Robert and Daniel Read. 1857.

Most of the usual omissions are corrected, though Judg. 7:18; 11:18; II Par. 32:32 are still incomplete. The long-standing misprint, "Jacob," for "heaven" (Ps. 90:1), still persists. In the New Testament the text is eclectic as usual; though based on the readings of 1749 and 1750 where they agree, where they differ the reading is sometimes that of 1749 (e.g., Matt. 2:1; 21:40), sometimes that of 1750 (e.g., Matt. 1:17; 23:29). We have noticed only one rendering peculiar to the third revision, "a promise being left of entering" (Heb. 4:1).

The same "ninth edition" was brought out by Duffy with the Approbation of Dr. Cullen in the same year, 1857, but with some remarkable differences; e.g., Read, "When Jesus therefore"; Duffy, "Now when Jesus" (Matt. 2:1); Read, "on a rock"; Duffy, "upon a rock" (Matt. 7:25); Read, "When the lord therefore"; Duffy, "therefore the lord" (Matt. 21:40). And so throughout the publisher takes at his discretion renderings now from one revision, now from another; yet both editions are called the "ninth." This same edition was brought out again by Burns and Oates with the Approbation of Cardinal Bourne, but no date is indicated.

Duffy also published this year an edition of the New Testament with the Approbation of Cardinal Cullen. The text is extraordinarily eclectic; for whereas that of 1752 is followed in the main, that peculiar to 1749 appears in Matt. 1:17; 7:25; John 5:1; Acts 28:7; Ephes. 2:12; and that common to 1749 and 1750 in Matt. 7:29; 21:40; while the influence of MacMahon's revisions appears in Matt. 1:17 and Acts 5:38.

EDITIONS OF THE NEW TESTAMENT, 1858

In 1858 Burns and Lambert published the New Testament in 12mo with the Approbation by Cardinal Wiseman. The basis of the text seems to be that of 1749 and 1750 when they are in agreement, though every rendering peculiar to 1750 is preserved. The influence of the third revision, 1752, appears in Mark 8:6, where the clause, "he commanded the people to sit down upon the ground," is inserted from that edition, though omitted in 1749 and 1750; yet Heb. 11:9 is still left incomplete. Gal. 2:2 is given according to 1752, "communicated the Gospel." Unlike the Bible and the New Testament published by Richardson in 1847, also with the Approbation of Dr. Wiseman, all the variations introduced by MacMahon are now omitted.

In 1858 Duffy published a New Testament without any Approbations or preliminary pieces, but several plates. The text is that of 1749, though that of 1750 appears in Mark 9:11 and 11:29.

THE CATHOLIC FAMILY BIBLE

Sadlier, New York, published the Bible "with Annotations by the Rev. Dr. Challoner." In his Approbation, Archbishop Hughes terms it "The Catholic Family Bible." No date is given, but it appeared probably in 1860.

CHAPTER XXXVIII

Editions between 1861 and 1896

THE CONFUSION IN 1860

We have already referred to the confusion prevailing at the opening of the nineteenth century owing to the existence of five distinct revisions of the New Testament by Dr. Challoner, five revisions by MacMahon, and one or two independent versions. By the middle of the century the confusion, though confined to minor details, was in a sense even greater. For while the influence of MacMahon, except for a few instances, was confined to Haydock's Bible and the Bible and Testament issued by Richardson of Derby in 1847, editors seem to have felt free to adopt any one of Challoner's main revisions. Nor were they consistent in doing so; for they passed freely from one revision to another, picking and choosing here and there according to their fancy, with the result that in some editions we find renderings taken from the revisions in 1749, 1750, 1752, and 1764, with an occasional reversion to MacMahon's text of 1791.

More astonishing still, we find Bibles and Testaments issuing from the same publishing firm and approved by the same bishop, yet presenting widely different texts. This inconsistency is particularly noticeable in editions approved by Dr. Cullen: in that of 1866 we read, "What is that to me?" (John 2:4); in that of 1857, "What is it to me?" Again, in that of 1866 the text of 1749 is followed in John 5:1; Rom. 5:14; Ephes. 2:12, where the edition of 1857 prefers the text of 1750. But the edition of 1866 keeps the text of 1752 in Gal. 2:2 and I Cor. 2:14, while that of 1857 prefers the renderings of 1750. Such vagaries are indeed hard to explain.

Between the years 1856 and 1867 a series of editions appeared, some with the Approbation of Dr. Cullen, others with that of Dr. Crolly, and published either by Duffy, Dublin, or by Read, Belfast. Generally speaking the Bible published in New York in 1856 (Approbation by Dr. Cullen), that published by Read in 1857 (Approbation by Dr. Crolly) and called the "ninth edition," and an edition of Dr. Murray's New Testament published by Duffy in 1859, all agree: the text in the New Testament portion being that of 1749 and 1750 when they are in agreement, but with many renderings peculiar to 1750; while those peculiar to the third revision, 1752, are notably absent.

But an undated edition of the New Testament printed by Duffy (probably 1857) with the Approbation by Dr. Cullen, an undated edition of the Bible issued with the Approbation of Dr. Crolly and twenty-five Irish bishops, and a pictorial edition of the New Testament in quarto printed by Duffy in 1865 with the Approbation by Dr. Crolly, present a very different type of text, that of the third revision, 1752, being predominant, with occasional preference for that of 1749, though all three prefer the rendering of the fourth and fifth revisions (1764 and 1772) in Matt. 9:9, "rose up," for "arose up." In several places, too, the dateless edition (1857?) of the New Testament retains renderings from the third revision where the other two prefer those of the former revisions. The influence of MacMahon's revisions also appears: "What is that to me?" (John 2:4); "design," for "counsel" or "council" (Acts 5:38); "as to our brother" (I Cor. 16:12); "that . . . at" (I Pet. 1:13), against all Challoner's revisions.

The same lack of agreement appears from a comparison between the pictorial edition of the Bible issued by Duffy in 1865 with the Approbation given by Dr. Cullen in 1857, the New Testament portion (Dr. Murray's edition) of the Bible published in 1866, again with the Approbation given by Dr. Cullen in 1857, the same issued once more in 1867, and the Bible published with Dr. Denvir's approval (1846) prefixed. In fifteen passages examined, the edition of 1865 has nearly always the text of 1752, thrice that of MacMahon, twice that of 1749, and sometimes that of 1750. The edition of 1866 prefers the renderings of 1750, but thrice adopts those of 1752, once a rendering of 1749, and once a rendering of MacMahon. The edition of 1867 also prefers the renderings of 1750, five times those of 1752, twice those of 1749, thrice those of MacMahon. The edition of 1869 also follows 1750, but thrice those of 1749, thrice those of 1752, without any rendering of MacMahon being noted. Two of these editions follow MacMahon in reading, "What is that to me?" (John 2:4);

one has, "What is it to me?" another, following Challoner, "What is to me?" Only the edition of 1865 boldly leaves Challoner's first three revisions in Matt. 9:9 and follows the revisions of 1764 and 1772: "he rose up" for "arose up." In fine, out of the fifteen passages selected, in only two do they all agree: Acts 5:38, "counsel," instead of "council" (1752) or "design" (MacMahon), and Mark 6:5, where all prefer "mighty works" (1752), to "miracle" (1749) or "miracles" (1750).

Well might one ask: Who decided that such and such a verse should read according to Challoner's first revision, 1749, while the next was to follow his second revision, 1750, the next that of 1752, perhaps even that of 1764? Who, again, decided to take over MacMahon's renderings either en bloc or in isolated instances? Lastly, who decided that these should be wholly eliminated?

Bishops could hardly be expected, when giving their approbation, to look closely into such niceties of translation, the very existence of which they were probably unaware of. Nor can we suppose that the revisers sometimes commissioned by their diocesan superior to supervise the text as it issued from the press had any intimate knowledge of the problems involved. In fine, there would seem to have been only one body of people possessed of such knowledge, namely the publishers and printers. Scholarly and painstaking men like Coyne, Wogan, Cross, Christie, Keating, and Brown may have been well acquainted with the various revisions and editions then current,—certainly Coyne was—and it seems that they exercised their own judgment, not only on the general type of text,—whether this or that particular revision was to be reproduced—but upon the rendering of individual passages, taking their text now from one, now from another of the various editions with which they were familiar.

Such tamperings with the English text of the Bible were not confined to the first half of the nineteenth century; indeed they became more pronounced with each successive decade, as we shall see below.

HOLY BIBLE, 1861

The *Holy Bible* printed by Duffy in 1861 omitted Judg. 7:18; 11:18; II Par. 32:32; and Agg. 2:2 in the Old Testament; and Mark 8:6 and Heb. 11:9 in the New. Every peculiarity of 1750 is preserved, but there is no trace of the third revision, 1752.

HOLY BIBLE, 1864–67

In 1864–67 Duffy published a pictorial edition of the Bible in quarto with the same title as in Syers' edition, 1813. In his Approbation, Dr. Cullen says:

> This new Edition of the English Version of the Bible, printed with our permission, by James Duffy, 15 Wellington Quay, Dublin, carefully collated, by our direction, with the Clementine Vulgate, likewise with the Douay Version of the Old Testament of 1609, and with the Rhemish Version of the New Testament of 1582, and with other approved English Versions—WE, by our authority, approve. And we also declare, that the same may be used by the faithful, with great spiritual profit, provided it be read with due reverence, and with the proper dispositions.
>
> Given at Dublin, this 16th day of June, 1864.
>
> Paul Cullen.

Of the many omissions in the Old Testament, only two are corrected, those in Judg. 7:18 and I Kings 17:49; the usual misprints are not corrected. On the other hand, this edition, considering the omissions in the New Testament, is the best we have, for all are made good. On the whole the text is that of 1752, though that of 1749 is preferred in Matt. 1:17; 7:25; John 5:1; Acts 5:38; and Ephes. 2:12; that peculiar to 1750 occurs, so far as I have noticed, only in Mark 9:11 and I Pet. 5:9; that of 1764 in Matt. 9:9; and that of 1791 in I Pet. 1:13 and I Cor. 16:12. The Admonition and the letter of Pius VI are omitted.

NEW TESTAMENT, 1866

The New Testament published in 1866 repeats the Approbation by Dr. Murray (1825) and adds that of Dr. Cullen. The text is very eclectic; but the peculiarities of 1750 are nearly always preserved, though deserted in Mark 6:5; 11:29; and Luke 2:18 in favor of the text of 1752. Mark 8:6 and Heb. 11:9 are incomplete. Despite the prefixed Approbation by Dr. Murray, the text is not that of his stereotyped edition, which adheres to the text of 1750 in Mark 6:5; 11:29; and Luke 2:18.

EDITIONS OF 1867

In 1867 Duffy published an edition of the Bible with Dr. Cullen's Approbation given in 1857. In the Old Testament only Judg. 7:18 and II Par. 32:32 are incomplete. In the New Testament the text of 1752 is followed in Mark 6:5; 11:29; and Luke 2:18; that common to 1749 and 1750 in Matt. 2:1, 23; 6:9; 7:21; 21:40; and Phil. 2:7; that peculiar to

1750 in Matt. 23:29; John 5:1; Acts 24:4; 28:7; Rom. 5:14; I Cor. 2:14; 16:12; Gal. 2:2; Ephes. 2:12; I Pet. 1:13; and 5:9. John 2:4 reads, "What is it to me?" Finally, in spite of the editor's familiarity with the third revision, Mark 8:6 and Heb. 11:9 are left incomplete as in 1749–50, though completed in 1752.

But in a separate edition of the New Testament published the same year with the same Approbation prefixed, John 2:4 reads, "What is that to me?" The text of 1749 is retained in John 5:1; Acts 5:38; Rom. 5:14; while the text of 1752 is retained in Phil. 2:7 and I Pet. 5:9. MacMahon's renderings appear in I Cor. 16:12; I Pet. 1:13; and John 2:4.

HOLY BIBLE, 1869

The Catholic Booksellers' and Publishers' Co. published an edition of the Bible in 1869 with the Approbation of Dr. Denvir. The only omissions in the Old Testament are clauses in Judg. 7:18; 11:18; and II Par. 32:32. In the New Testament all renderings peculiar to 1750 are retained, but the text of 1749 is preferred in Acts 5:38 and Ephes. 2:12; that of 1752 in Mark 6:5; Gal. 2:2; and Phil. 2:7. The fourth revision appears in Matt. 9:9, "rose up," for "arose up."

NEW TESTAMENT, 1872

In 1872 Bagster published *The Vulgate New Testament with the Douay* [*sic*] *version in parallel columns*. But the Vulgate text here is not that translated in 1582: Luke 10:30 reads, *suspiciens autem Jesus,* where the Rhemists clearly translated *suscipiens:* "taking it."

HOLY BIBLE, 1873

In the Bible published in 1873 with Dr. Cullen's Approbation, very few of the clauses usually omitted in the Old Testament are completed; Mark 8:6 is incomplete in the New Testament, in which all the variants peculiar to 1750 are preserved. Renderings peculiar to 1749 appear in Acts 5:38 ("counsel"); Mark 6:5 ("miracle"); and Ephes. 2:12 ("testament"). The text of 1752 is followed in Gal. 2:2 and Matt. 8:17; and "rose up" (Matt. 9:9) comes from Challoner's fourth revision, 1764. "What is it to me?" (John 2:4) departs from all of Challoner's revisions, as also does Jude 10, "whatever," where Challoner always wrote, "what things soever."

NEW TESTAMENTS, 1874

In 1874 Duffy published a New Testament in 12mo (16mo ?) with the Approbation by the Irish episcopate. The text is a mixture. For though it marks a reversion to that of 1752 throughout, yet renderings peculiar to 1749 crop up: "are" (Matt. 1:17) is not thrice repeated as in the other revisions; "upon" (Matt. 7:25); "those places" (Acts 28:7), where 1750 has "these places," and 1752, "those quarters." In Matt. 9:9 we have "rose up" from the 1764 revision, a rendering now becoming common instead of the awkward "arose up" of the first three revisions. MacMahon's influence appears in "design" (Acts 5:38), "that grace . . . at the coming" (I Pet. 1:13), and "as to our brother" (I Cor. 16:12). This edition is remarkable for the fact that all renderings peculiar to 1750 have been removed.

In 1874 and again the following year a New Testament was published with Dr. Cullen's Approbation, in which the text is based on the revision of 1752; but with many of the renderings peculiar to 1750 reproduced; some from 1749 are also reproduced; e.g., "those places" (Acts 28:7), "testaments" (Ephes. 2:12). As usual at this date, the editors preferred "rose up" (Matt. 9:9) to "arose up" of Challoner's first three revisions. John 2:4 reads, "What is it to me?"

PHILADELPHIA EDITION OF THE BIBLE, 1875

The Holy Bible: containing the Entire Canonical Scriptures, according to the Decree of the Council of Trent; translated from the Latin Vulgate: diligently compared with the Hebrew, Greek, and other editions in divers languages. . . . With Annotations by the Rev. Dr. Challoner; together with References, a Historical and Chronological Index, a Table of the Epistles and Gospels for all the Sundays and Holy Days throughout the year, and of the Most Notable Feasts in the Roman Calendar, and other Instructive and Devotional Matter. Philadelphia, John E. Potter and Co. [no date].[1]

On the reverse is a "Certificate of Genuineness": "This Edition of the Holy Scriptures, from the Versions of Douay and Rheims, with Annotations by the Rev. Dr. Challoner, printed in Philadelphia by Messrs.

[1] Although Father Pope assigned the publication of this edition to 1840, it could not have appeared at that early date, for Rev. James Wood did not become bishop of Philadelphia until 1860. This handsome, large quarto Bible was published probably in 1875, for a mutilated copy at hand has on the reverse of a secondary title page: "Entered, according to Act of Congress, in the year one thousand eight hundred and seventy-five. By John E. Potter and Company, in the office of the Librarian of Congress, at Washington." Shortly thereafter Wood became archbishop of Philadelphia. [Ed.]

John E. Potter and Company, from the Stereotype Plates of Fielding Lucas, Jr., Baltimore, is a Genuine and Reliable Edition, and may be used Without Fear or Scruple by the Faithful. James F. Wood, Bishop of Philadelphia." To this is added: "This edition of the Holy Catholic Bible, having been duly examined, is hereby approved of"; the signatures of seven archbishops and forty-four bishops follow.

There are the usual omissions in the Old Testament, except Jos. 7:18 and I Kings 1:11, which are complete. The New Testament text is eclectic: some five renderings peculiar to 1749 being retained, while at least thirteen are those of 1752. Only once is the text that peculiar to 1750 (Ephes. 2:12), and only once is MacMahon's text followed (Matt. 9:24 f.); in Matt. 9:9 "rose" is from Challoner's fourth revision, 1764. Matt. 13:12 is left incomplete, but Heb. 11:9 is complete.

HOLY BIBLE, 1876

In 1876 Burns and Oates published a new edition of Dr. Crolly's Bible (1857) with the Approbation now by Cardinal Manning. This is one of the most complete editions so far published, the only clauses omitted in the Old Testament being those in II Par. 32:32 and Agg. 2:2, and in the New Testament that in Heb. 11:9; the clause in Mark 8:6, omitted in nearly every other edition, is here inserted. The text of the New Testament is consistently that of 1750. There is no trace of renderings peculiar to Challoner's third revision.

NEW TESTAMENTS, 1876

In 1876 McGlashen and Gill published a pictorial edition of the New Testament in quarto with the Approbation by Dr. Cullen in 1857 repeated by him for this edition. The text is eclectic: all the variants of 1750 are retained, while renderings peculiar to 1749 occur; e.g., Matt. 2:1; 6:9; 7:25; 21:40. The text of 1752 appears in Matt. 8:17, and that of 1764 in Matt. 9:9; John 2:4 reads, "What is it to me?" The clause in Mark 8:6 is omitted as usual.

In the same year Gill published a 12mo edition of the New Testament, which differs from the quarto edition only in Matt. 7:25, "on a rock" (1750–52), instead of, "upon a rock" (1749).

The text of these editions published between 1872 and 1876 with the Approbation of either Dr. Crolly or Dr. Cullen, is generally that of Challoner's first or second revision; but at least one edition has in many places preferred the different readings peculiar to the third revision. All these editions are eclectic, following now one, now another of the first two revisions, sometimes deserting them for the fourth or fifth revisions (1764 and 1772). The influence of MacMahon's editions appears in "What is that to me and to thee?" (John 2:4), and "design," for "counsel" (Acts 5:38). These divergences in the text are clearly seen in the following table.

VARIANT READINGS [2]

		1873 Bible Cullen 8vo	1874 N.T. Cullen 12mo Duffy	1875 N.T. Cullen 8vo	1876 N.T. Crolly 4to McGlashen & Gill	1876 N.T. 12mo Gill	1876 Bible Crolly 8vo Burns & Oates
Matt.	1:17	1750–2	1749	1750–2	1750–2	1750–2	1750–2
	2:1		1752	1749–50	1749–50	1749–50	1749–50
	6:9	1749–50	1752	1749–50	1749–50	1749–50	1749–50
	7:25	1750–2	1749	1750–2	1749	1750–2	1750–2
	9:9	1764	1764	1764	1764	1764	1749–1752
Mark	6:5	1749	1752	1750	1750	1750	1750
	8:6	omitted	complete	omitted	omitted	omitted	complete
John	2:4	"is it"	"is that"	"is it"	"is it"	"is it"	"is"
Acts	5:38	1749	1791	1749	1749	1749	1749
	24:4	1750	1752	1752	1750	1750	1750
	28:7	1750	1749	1750	1750	1750	1750
Rom.	5:14	1750	1752	1752	1750	1750	1750
I Cor.	2:14	1750	1752	1750	1750	1750	1750
	16:12	1750	1791	1750	1750	1750	1750
Gal.	2:2	1752	1752	1752	1752	1752	1750
Ephes.	2:12	1749	1749	1749	1749	1749	1750
I Pet.	1:13	1750	1791	1750	1750	1750	1750
	5:9	1750	1752	1750	1750	1750	1750

GILL'S EDITIONS, 1881–85

In 1882 Gill, Dublin, published an edition of the Bible in which the text of the Old Testament is that of the revision of 1763–64. In the New Testament, which was published separately in 1881, all the renderings peculiar to 1750 are retained, but none of those peculiar to 1749. "Put you

[2] 1749, Challoner's first revision; 1750, his second revision; 1752, his third; 1764, his fourth; 1791, MacMahon's edition of the Bible.

also all away" (Col. 3:8) seems to be the sole rendering due to the fourth revision, 1764.

In 1885 Gill published a reprint of Dr. Denvir's edition of the Bible, 1846. "This Edition of the Douay Bible is considered the most accurate in its typography of all the small Catholic Bibles hitherto published. As this issue is printed from the original stereotype plates, it is impossible that any errors can have crept into it since its original publication." But unfortunately that "original publication" continued the omission of clauses in Judg. 7:18; 11:18; II Par. 32:32; "Jacob," instead of "heaven" (Ps. 90:1), and other minor misprints. The renderings peculiar to 1750 are retained; the spelling of "befalls" (I Pet. 5:9), and "the Scribes," instead of "their Scribes" (Matt. 7:29) seem to be the only renderings peculiar to the first and third revisions; "put you also all away" (Col. 3:8) is the only trace of the fourth revision. Mark 8:6 and Heb. 11:9 are left incomplete; John 2:4 keeps Challoner's rendering, "What is to me and to thee?"

HOLY BIBLE, 1886

In 1886 Mairs, Belfast, published a Bible with Dr. Crolly's Approbation reprinted. There are none of the usual preliminary pieces; some omissions remain uncorrected, and there are also some misprints; e.g., "hecause" for "because" (I Mach. 14:35); "inhabitants," plural for singular (Amos 1:5), a mistake which seems to have originated with MacMahon in 1791 and was repeated in the editions of 1811 and 1814.

HOLY BIBLE, 1888

In 1888 Duffy published an edition of the Bible with the Approbation by Dr. Walsh and the rest of the Irish episcopate. Gen. 36:2; Judg. 7:18; and II Par. 32:32 are incomplete; we find the usual misprints: "guard," for "garden" (Neh. 3:15), and "Jacob," for "heaven" (Ps. 90:1). Heb. 11:9 is incomplete, but Matt. 13:12 and Mark 8:6 are correct. No rendering peculiar to 1752 is retained, but those peculiar to 1750 are kept. John 2:4 reads, "What is it to me?"

CHAPTER XXXIX

Editions of Rheims-Douay since 1896[1]

THE editions of Rheims and Douay now current in England and America owe their origin principally to certain texts which were issued about the turn of the century. Certain peculiarities of the text frequently enable us to trace their parentage, though it must be admitted that there are considerable vagaries on the part of the various editors in the choice of a text.

In England the firms of Burns and Oates, and of R. & T. Washbourne united in 1922 to form the great publishing house of Burns, Oates and Washbourne. Yet in the editions previous to this date each firm represents a different tradition: Burns and Oates deriving their text probably from the Irish editions of Dr. Murray, while Washbourne's text is principally based on an American source.

The pocket New Testaments (16mo) of Burns and Oates (1896 and later) and of Washbourne (1909) remained in print until 1937 and 1939 respectively, and an old Burns and Oates text has been reprinted in 1950. These pocket editions are in everyone's hands, and it is therefore not unimportant to make some observations upon the texts they incorporate. The well-known Bible of Burns, Oates and Washbourne, either in the large format which goes back to 1914, or in the smaller edition of 1931, is traceable to the Washbourne text of 1900, which in turn is derived from the Baltimore edition of 1899.

The situation in America is somewhat simpler, for until the advent of Fr. Carey's edition of 1935 and the Douay Bible House texts of 1941, together, of course, with the revised text of the Confraternity Edition in the same year, American texts look back almost unanimously to Cardinal Gibbons' text of 1899.

[1] The beginning of this chapter and certain sections have been rewritten or entirely supplied by Rev. Sebastian Bullough, O.P.

CARDINAL VAUGHAN'S NEW TESTAMENTS

In 1896 Burns and Oates published a New Testament of 448 pages in 16mo with the *Imprimatur* of Cardinal Vaughan dated August 10, 1896. The title page reads: *The New Testament of Our Lord and Saviour Jesus Christ, according to the Rheims Version, revised by Bishop Challoner.* The text is mainly that of 1749, including "counsel" (Acts 5:38), "Nazarite" (Matt. 2:23), and "conferred with" (Gal. 2:2); but it also includes the mistake, "this uncircumcision" (Rom. 2:26), which is proper to 1750. As in all modern editions (except one), it abandons Challoner by reading "What is it?" in John 2:4, a reading which comes from the anonymous edition of 1792. The usual missing passages are still omitted, and Dr. Murray's misprint of "brought" for "bought" in Mark 16:1 is perpetuated. Besides these faults, this edition has some peculiar aberrations of its own, some of which remained in many English editions which followed it. One is to be found in I Tim. 2:1 f.: "intercessions and thanksgivings be made by men, for kings, and for all that are in high stations." This mistake was corrected in the reprint (to be noticed presently) to the usual form: "for all men, for kings, and for all that are in high station," though some later editions retain the plural "stations." Another peculiar reading is that in Acts 11:29: "The disciples proposed to send relief," which is probably a misprint, for no other text has this reading except those editions dependent upon this one; Challoner here wrote "purposed" in 1749–50, and "resolved" in 1752. A plausible misprint, which reappeared in several editions, is the reading in Acts 14:16: "filling our hearts with good [instead of "food"] and gladness."

After the consolidation of the firms in 1922, this edition was reprinted by Burns, Oates and Washbourne, and certain alterations were made, apart from that in the publishers' name on the title page. The edition of 1896 was apparently printed from plates, and corrections therefore involved the excision of part of the plate and the substitution of some letters of moveable type. The effect is clumsy, and the new type appears notably blacker and out of alignment, so that the emendations are instantly recognizable. Notable among the changes, "Nazarite" was changed to "Nazarene" (1752), a reading which is of course more correct. The correction of I Tim. 2:1 f. was made at the same time, and the date of the

Imprimatur was erased. In this form the edition remained in print until 1937.

In 1898 a handsome crown octavo New Testament was published by Burns and Oates with Cardinal Vaughan's *Imprimatur* of November 1, 1897. This edition, known as the "Pulpit Edition," was reprinted in 1914 and again as recently as 1934. It numbers 495 pages.[2] The text is identical with that of the original edition of 1896 with the exception of the correction of I Tim. 2:1 f. and of the misprint "good" for "food" in Acts 14:16 (which, however, was not corrected in the later reprint of the 448-page edition). An unusual feature is the phrase on the title page: "with lawful authority."

An edition almost identical with the above, also having 495 pages, was issued in 1898 in America, with the *Imprimatur* given at New York by Michael Augustine [Corrigan, Archbishop], and dated November 10, 1897—within ten days of Cardinal Vaughan's *Imprimatur*. This text was reprinted by Benziger Brothers of New York with an additional *Imprimatur* of Cardinal Hayes, dated November 16, 1931, and is still on sale. The text is that of Cardinal Vaughan's edition of 1896, and represents the English tradition in America before the Baltimore text of 1899. But this type of text is not common in America.

Another pocket New Testament (16mo) with the *Imprimatur* of Cardinal Vaughan was published about this time by Burns and Oates. Unfortunately it is not now possible to date exactly the first edition of this text, since many of the firm's earlier records were destroyed in an air raid on London, and the later reprints, as in the other edition, have the date of the *Imprimatur* erased. This edition numbers 574 pages, and the title page runs: *The New Testament of Our Lord Jesus Christ, translated from the Latin Vulgate, diligently compared with the original Greek and first published by the English College at Rheims, A.D. 1582. With Annotations and References by Dr. Challoner and an Historical and Chronological Index.* The text mainly corresponds to that of 1896, even including the reading "proposed" in Acts 11:29 and the misprint "good" for "food" in Acts 14:16, which were peculiarities of that edition. But the reading of that edition is abandoned for the 1752 rendering "Nazarene" (Matt. 2:23) and "put you" (Col. 3:8), as well as for the

[2] The number of pages in these editions is frequently the most convenient manner of identifying the exact text.

inferior reading of 1752, "council," in Acts 5:38. Yet this 574-page edition has some peculiarities of its own: an error in Gal. 4:13, "therefore" for "heretofore," which confuses the whole issue of St. Paul's visits to Galatia, appears in no other text; and in II Tim. 1:9 all previous editions have: "[God] called us by His holy calling, not according to our works, but according to his own purpose and grace," prefixing a cross reference to Tit. 3:5 ("Not by the works of justice"). But this edition, by the omission of a line of print, reads grotesquely: "[God] called us by his holy calling, not according to his own purpose and grace." It is strange that Burns, Oates and Washbourne's Bible of 1931 (reprinted in 1946) has perpetuated this error; even the cross reference to Titus remains. It is interesting to observe that the omitted clause appears in the 1914 Bible with a variation, "not according to our own works," which is also followed by Dr. Arendzen's edition of 1947.

The 574-page edition was the one among the pocket New Testaments selected for reprinting by Burns, Oates and Washbourne in 1950. No alterations or corrections (not even in II Tim. 1:9) have been made in the text, but the title page and the headings to the books have been reset in modern type, and a pleasing modern binding has been used. It is a much more legible text than the fine print of the 448-page edition.

EDITIONS OF 1899

An edition of the Bible was published in Baltimore in 1899. In his Preface, Cardinal Gibbons explains the true character of the Bible, the divine inspiration of which can be known only through the Church. Most of the omissions previously noted are made good, except Judg. 7:18; 11:18; II Par. 32:32; Mark 8:6; and Heb. 11:9, which remain incomplete. The basis of the text is that of 1749, but twelve of the renderings peculiar to 1750 are retained, and those of 1752 appear in Matt. 2:23; 7:29; Gal. 2:2, and Acts 5:38 ("council"). John 2:4 reads as in MacMahon's revision: "What is that to me?"

This very eclectic text was the result of minute revision. For example, in Mark 1:2, "thy way" (1752) is rejected in favor of "the way" (1749–50), though the Greek, Latin, and all other English versions have "thy way." Conversely, "the voice" (1752 and all the other versions) is preferred to "a voice" (1749–50). Again, "he taught them" (Mark 1:22) follows 1752 and most other versions, though the Rhemists' rendering, "he was teaching them," followed by the editions of 1749 and 1750, seems more correct.[3] Explanatory clauses are introduced and are not put in brackets as they should have been: "very early (in the morning)" (Mark 1:35); "so that (now) he could not openly go" (Mark 1:45). An unfortunate misprint, "brought" for "bought" (Mark 16:1), first appearing in the 1847 edition of Dr. Murray's Bible and repeated in the New Testament of 1896 published by Burns and Oates, is corrected here and in the Bible of 1900 and of 1914 published by Washbourne.

In this same year, Gill published an edition of the New Testament with Dr. Cullen's Approbation of 1857. The text is that of 1749, though the renderings peculiar to 1750 are retained, except Gal. 2:2, where 1752 is followed: "communicated to them the Gospel." Matt. 9:9 reads as in 1764, "rose up."

WASHBOURNE'S BIBLE, 1900, AND NEW TESTAMENT, 1909

In 1900 Washbourne published a reprint of Cardinal Gibbons' edition of 1899, and for a long time this was the standard Douay Bible in England. There seems to be only one change from the American text, "on a rock" (Matt. 7:25) instead of "upon a rock" (1749 and 1899). This Bible represents the American tradition followed by Washbourne and is the direct parent of the firm's 1914 Bible (with the Preface by Cardinal Bourne), which still remains the standard text in England. In general the text follows Challoner's revision of 1749, but none of the confused passages which occur in Cardinal Vaughan's New Testaments appear here.

In 1909 Washbourne produced a pocket edition (16mo) of the New Testament numbering 707 pages. The title page reads exactly as in the 574-page edition of Burns and Oates noted above, but the text follows that of the 1900 Bible exactly. The *Imprimatur,* dated May 21, 1909, is that of the Vicar General of Westminster, Canon Surmont. This edition remained in print until 1939.

C.T.S. GOSPELS, 1900, 1920

The Catholic Truth Society of London in 1900 published the four Gospels as separate pamphlets, with notes by Canon M'Intyre (later archbishop of Birmingham). These were attractively produced in paper

[3] The Vulgate has, *erat enim docens,* as in the Greek.

covers bearing the symbol of each evangelist. In 1900 the text is identical with the original Burns and Oates edition of 1896, including even "Nazarite" (Matt. 2:23); but in the 1920 reprint of St. John's Gospel there is an alteration which makes this edition almost unique among the texts of the last 160 years, for in John 2:4 the C.T.S. text presents Challoner's own reading: "What is to me and to thee?" when every other text has followed either MacMahon's reading of 1791, "What is that to me and to thee?" or that of the anonymous text of 1792, "What is it to me and to thee?" It is curious that Challoner's consistent reading of this passage in all his revisions was so universally abandoned until this edition. Another merit of this text is that Mark 8:6 is complete.

HOLY BIBLE, PRINTED IN BELGIUM, 1912

In 1912 Etabl. Brepols, Belgium, published an edition of the Bible which appeared with the imprint of various publishers. To the usual title is added: "This edition contains Annotations, References, an Historical and Chronological Index, many maps and illustrations." The Preface is by the Rt. Rev. H. A. Brann. Though described as due to Dr. Challoner and Dr. Ganss, the Annotations and References in the New Testament seem to be simply those in the current editions, except that "pounds" gives place to "dollars" in the note on Luke 19:13. There is an Introducion to the New Testament as a whole as well as to each book. The headings to the books of the Old Testament are the traditional ones, and after Second Machabees is a Historical and Chronological Index to the Old Testament.

Judg. 7:18; 11:18; II Par. 32:32; Agg. 2:2 remain incomplete; "Jacob," for "heaven" (Ps. 90:1), "guard" for "garden" (Neh. 3:15), and "inhabitants" (Amos 1:5) are misprints long calling for correction. The text in the New Testament is eclectic: that peculiar to 1749 appears in the spelling of "befalls" (I Pet. 5:9); every rendering peculiar to the second revision, is preserved; the only renderings peculiar to the third revision, 1752, seem to be "Nazarene," for "Nazarite" (Matt. 2:23), "the Scribes," for "their Scribes" (Matt. 7:29), and "communicated to them the Gospel" (Gal. 2:2). "What is that to me and to thee?" (John 2:4) is due to MacMahon's revision, 1791. Mark 8:6 and Heb. 11:9 are left incomplete. The Gospel for the twenty-first Sunday is given as Matt. 18:23–25 instead of 18:23–35.

This edition was reprinted many times with the imprints of various publishers. Some reimpressions bore no imprint whatever, thus permitting the individual bookseller to stamp on his imprint. It is therefore almost impossible to determine how many publishers and booksellers have attached their name to this edition, which bore no date. The *Imprimaturs* likewise vary. The title page states that this edition was "published with the Imprimatur and Approbation of His Eminence Cardinal Farley, Archbishop of New York"; but besides his *Imprimatur* (dated December 4, 1911), most copies bear also the *Imprimatur* of Dr. Prendergast, archbishop of Philadelphia (September 27, 1911), and of the archbishop of Montreal (December 3, 1912). A fourth *Imprimatur,* that of Dr. Chatard, bishop of Indianapolis (September 5, 1906), was also added to some impressions, either before the Old Testament alone or before both Testaments.

Some copies contain many illustrations, which are photographs of sites in the Holy Land. All copies have maps and diagrams at the end of the book; but whereas some have seventeen maps, others have only four pages of maps (nos. 3, 4, 14, and 15). It is interesting to note that the names on these maps all follow the spelling of the Authorized Version. The sepia illustrations and colored maps are the same in all the copies that have them, but the shade of coloring differs. These differences are interesting, but since none of the impressions were dated, more precise information cannot be given. The illustrated edition is frequently found in England, but without the Preface by Rt. Rev. H. A. Brann.

HOLY BIBLE, 1914

In 1914 Washbourne published *The Holy Bible Translated from the Latin Vulgate and diligently compared with other Editions in divers languages*[4] (*Douay, A.D. 1609; Rheims, A.D. 1582*). *Published as revised and annotated by Authority. With a Preface by the Cardinal Archbishop of Westminster* (Francis Bourne). This edition contains Bishop Challoner's notes, newly compiled indexes, tables, and verified references; also Pope Leo XIII's encyclical on the study of the Holy Scriptures and a new series of maps. After the encyclical comes an "Index to Names of Persons and Places mentioned in Holy Scripture"; there follow a "Table of References" dealing with points of Catholic doctrine, and a

[4] It is hard to imagine what is meant by "other Editions in divers languages."

well arranged "Table of the Epistles and Gospels"; [5] finally a list of the books of the Old and New Testaments. Prefixed to the New Testament is the letter of Pope Benedict XV on the work of the Society of St. Jerome, which distributes gratis copies of the Gospels; at the end we have ten maps and plans.

This deservedly popular edition is more complete than any of its predecessors, though clauses in Judg. 7:18; 11:18; and Agg. 2:2 are still omitted; the same misprints also recur: "guard," for "garden" (Neh. 3:15) and "inhabitants" (Amos 1:5). In the New Testament the peculiarities of 1750 are preserved throughout, but the text of 1752 is adhered to in "Nazarene" (Matt. 2:23), "the scribes" (7:29), and "communicated," for "conferred" (Gal. 2:2). The only vestige of the text of 1749 that we have noted is the spelling of "befalls" (I Pet. 5:9).

DIVERGENCES IN THE TEXT

The following Table will serve to show how these versions published between 1896 and 1914 differed from one another. It is hard to discover by whose authority publishers and printers elected to follow now one type of text, now another. For no single edition adheres throughout to one definite type of any existing text.

		New Test. B. & O. 1896 448 pp. red cross [6]	New Test. B.O.W. reprint 448 pp.	New Test. B. & O. 1898? 574 pp.	Bible Washbourne 1900	Bible Brepols 1912	Bible Washbourne 1914
Matt.		Nazarite	Nazarene	Nazarene	Nazarene	Nazarene	Nazarene
	7:29	their	their	their	the	the	the
Luke	19:48	were	were	were	were	were	were
John	2:4	is it?	is it?	is it?	is that?	is that?	is that?
Acts		counsel	counsel	council	council	council	council
	7:10	king	king	the king	the king	the king	the king
	7:17	and was multiplied	and multiplied	and multiplied	and were multiplied	and were multiplied	and were multiplied
Rom.	6:18	free	free	free	freed	freed	freed
Gal.	2:2	conferred with	conferred with	conferred with	communicated to	communicated to	communicated to
Col.		lay you	lay you	put you	put you	put you	put you

[5] This table is correct. Hitherto publishers had been content to copy slavishly existing tables, sometimes with unfortunate results. For example, the Gospel for the twenty-first Sunday after Pentecost is Matt. 18:23–35; but ever since Challoner drew up the table for his third revision, 1752, the verses have been given as 23–25.

[6] This edition sometimes has a red cross on the cover.

All these editions omit clauses from Mark 8:6 and Heb. 11:9; all are complete in Matt. 13:12. All are independent of Challoner in Luke 19:48, where he wrote "was attentive," instead of "were attentive," and in Acts 3:19, where he always wrote "repent ye therefore," instead of "be penitent," and in Acts 3:16, where Challoner always had "seen and know," instead of "seen and known." By writing "of the law" (Matt. 5:18), they disguise the reference to the Mosaic law, whereas Challoner wrote "of the Laws" in 1749–50, and "from the Law" in 1752; again, in "seek not what you shall eat" (Luke 12:29), the first pronoun—"seek not ye" (1749), "you" (1750–52)—is omitted despite its presence in the Greek text. But in the use of a capital S, "the Son," instead of "the son" (1749–50) or "a son" (1752), these modern editions rightly emphasize the reference to Christ's eternal sonship in Heb. 3:6.

NEW TESTAMENT, 1919

The text of the New Testament published in 1919 with the Approbation of Dr. Hayes, New York, is markedly eclectic; renderings peculiar to 1750 are retained, while those peculiar to 1752 are frequent; the text of 1749 appears in I Pet. 5:9, "befalls." John 2:4 follows MacMahon's edition: "What is that to me?" Mark 8:6 and Heb. 11:9 are left incomplete.

NEW TESTAMENT, 1926

In 1926 Burns, Oates and Washbourne published *The New Testament of Jesus Christ as translated into English out of the authentical Latin in the English College at Rheims and printed at Rheims by John Fogny, 1582. With certain of the Annotations and an Introduction.* This excellent reproduction of our original version should be better known. Father Hudleston, the editor, provides an admirable Introduction and a selection of the very voluminous Annotations by the Rhemists. The spelling in this edition has been modernized.

THE LAYMAN'S NEW TESTAMENT, 1928, 1934

The Layman's New Testament, published by Sheed and Ward in 1928 and edited by Father Hugh Pope, O.P., was never intended to be a critical edition. It was intended for the members of the Catholic Evidence Guild, and therefore provided Challoner's text on the left hand and a running commentary from the apologetical and controversial standpoint on the right.

A second edition of *The Layman's New Testament,* with amplified notes, was published in 1934. But both editions were completely destroyed in the bombing of England. A third edition appeared in 1940.

HOLY BIBLE, 1931–46

In 1931 Burns, Oates and Washbourne published a new edition of the Bible. It was a smaller edition of their standard Bible of 1914, and was printed in Belgium. It bore the same *Imprimatur,* dated 1914, as well as Cardinal Bourne's Preface. The preliminary features are all reproduced exactly, but the feast of Christ the King is inserted into the Table of Epistles and Gospels. The text seems to adhere faithfully to that of the 1914 Bible, down to the misprint in Nah. 2:10, "The heart melteth and the knees fail and all the lions [for "loins"] lose strength," which seems to be proper to the 1914 edition. The old misprint "guard" for "garden" in Neh. 3:15 reappears, as it has done in every edition since 1609, when the word stood at the end of a line with a stroke over the e to represent the n ("gardē"), and was taken to be a misspelling of "guard" instead of "garden." In view of the faithful representation of 1914, it is all the more remarkable that the preposterous misprint in Cardinal Vaughan's 574-page New Testament in II Tim. 1:9 should occur again here: "[God] called us . . . not according to his own purpose and grace," though no other peculiarities of that edition are found here. The format is small and the type rather fine, and the text is printed in verses, as in all these editions.

The subsequent history of this edition is interesting. It was reprinted several times until 1939, when another reprint was made; but owing to the outbreak of the war, the sheets could not be shipped across from Belgium. After the end of hostilities, however, the sheets were found untouched in Belgium, and in 1946 they were brought to England, bound, and placed on sale. This reprint was thus the first postwar Bible that was available in England, having been actually printed in 1939. It was subsequently reprinted again in 1947 and is at present (1950) the only English edition of the Douay Bible that is available.[7]

[7] For these facts I am indebted to Mr. M. T. Slater of Burns, Oates and Washbourne, London. [S.B.]

CAREY'S EDITION OF THE NEW TESTAMENT, 1935

The New Testament of Our Lord and Saviour Jesus Christ, Translated from the Latin Vulgate. Diligently compared with the original Greek, and first published by the English College at Rheims, A.D. 1582. As revised by Dr. Challoner, London, A.D. 1752. With Annotations and References by Dr. Challoner, Canon Haydock, and Dr. H. J. Ganss, and an Historical and Chronological Index. With a Preface of Rev. James A. Carey, M.A., Prof. of Sacred Scripture at St. Joseph's Seminary, Dunwoodie, New York. With the Imprimatur of His Eminence, Patrick Cardinal Hayes, Archbishop of New York. A Wildermann-Brepols Publication.

This edition of the New Testament, which appeared in America in 1935, is of notable importance; for it is an "endeavor . . . to give to American Catholics, who anxiously await publication of a definitive Catholic Version in English, the Reims-Challoner text free from the many literary defects and blemishes which mar its style and otherwise detract from its majesty as the written expression of the Word of God. But in no sense is the present edition a new version. The corrections made have been introduced only where the existing English seems obviously wrong or meaningless" (from the Preface, dated Easter, 1935).[8] Father Carey then proceeds to explain his method of correcting:

> The corrections made fall into three categories:
> (1) changes in punctuation. The traditional punctuation has been revised only (a) where it destroys the sense intended, or (b) where it varies from the general system followed;
> (2) minor errors (for example, Luke, xiv, 1; xxiii, 8; etc.) which are obvious to any careful reader even without reference to the Vulgate or the Greek text;
> (3) more serious defects, naturally fewer in number, where the current text seems hopelessly inaccurate or obscure.

There then follow nearly ten pages of examples, with the usual text in one column and Carey's emendations alongside. Many of these are purely grammatical points, such as "Art thou he that is [for "art"] to come?" (Luke 7:20); others are deliberate substitutions for a supposedly old-fashioned phrase, such as "Far from it," for "God forbid" (Rom. 3:6); while still others involve a change of the sense which seems not

[8] The first fourteen pages of Father Carey's Preface present a well-written history of the Rheims-Challoner version.

entirely warrantable according to the Latin, for example: "For the charity of Christ holdeth us," for "presseth us" (II Cor. 5:14), where the Vulgate has *urget nos,* though the Greek means "constraineth" or "restraineth." In II Cor. 7:8 the punctuation of the Greek is followed rather than that of the Latin and Challoner, and an explanatory phrase is inserted.

In spite of the title page, the only change from the ordinary notes seems to be the substitution of American currency for English currency in the explanations of didrachma, talent, pence, and so forth. The important feature of this edition is that it is a deliberate attempt to carry out the recommendation of the Second Plenary Council of Baltimore in 1866, endorsed by an instruction of the Sacred Congregation for the Propagation of the Faith in 1868, which urged the bishops of America to see that future editions of both the Old and the New Testaments "should be most carefully emended according to the most reliable exemplar." Here for once we have an editor of Rheims-Challoner who candidly announces the fact that he has made alterations in the text and indicates some of the places. The title page states that the text followed is that of 1752, but it corresponds with the text of 1899, which was based on that of 1749, and contains at least fourteen renderings peculiar to 1750. Moreover, in his third revision, 1752, Challoner filled in the missing clauses in Mark 8:6 and Heb. 11:9, but these remain here uncorrected. John 2:4 follows MacMahon (1791): "What is that to me and to thee?"

This edition was printed in Belgium at Brepols' Press, Turnhout, and issued as a "Wildermann-Brepols publication" by the C. Wildermann Co. Inc., New York. It was republished by A. Bassi of Dublin in 1936, and again by Wildermann with an *Imprimatur* of 1937, and again with an *Imprimatur* of 1938.

In 1938 a Bible containing Carey's New Testament was published by Wildermann-Brepols, printed in Belgium, with the *Imprimatur* of Cardinal Hayes dated January 7, 1938.[9] The encyclical *Providentissimus*

[9] *The Holy Bible, translated from the Latin Vulgate, diligently compared with the Hebrew, Greek, and other editions in divers languages. The Old Testament was first published by the English College at Douay, A.D. 1609, and the New Testament was first published by the English College at Rheims, A.D. 1582. The re-edited edition by Rev. James A. Carey, M.A., was first published A.D. 1935. This edition contains annotations, references, an historical and chronological index, maps and a family record. Published with the Imprimatur and Approbation of His Eminence, Patrick Cardinal Hayes, Archbishop of New York,* C. Wildermann Co. Inc., New York. Like the Brepols Bible

Deus is given, with an Introduction by Father Lattey, S.J. Before the New Testament stands Father Carey's Preface giving the history of the Rheims-Douay text and an account of his own emendations, as it was given in the edition of the New Testament alone. In this Bible the text of the Old Testament is that of the edition previously approved by Cardinal Farley in 1911. Judg. 7:18; 11:18; II Par. 32:32; and Agg. 2:2 are incomplete; and the same misprints also occur; for example, "Jacob" for "heaven" (Ps. 90:1).

Father Carey's text represents the last revision of Challoner before the complete remodeling of the Confraternity Edition, 1941.

THE CONFRATERNITY EDITION, 1941

The New Testament of Our Lord and Savior [10] *Jesus Christ, translated from the Latin Vulgate. A Revision of the Challoner-Rheims Version, edited by Catholic Scholars under the Patronage of the Episcopal Committee of the Confraternity of Christian Doctrine,* St. Anthony Guild Press, Paterson, New Jersey, 1941; small cr. 8vo, 768 pages. Admirably set out in paragraph form, this edition of the New Testament has chapter and verse numbers at the head of each page and cross references at the foot; insets show the subject of the text, and quotations from the Old Testament are in verse form. At the end of the volume is a glossary of religious, geographical, and personal terms, a map not overburdened with names, and a handy Table of Epistles and Gospels. The notes might have been more numerous: there are none on John 21:22, 24; some are weak, e.g., on Rom. 5:12; 15:12; I John 5:7; and we cannot agree with the one on John 8:6, 8; but the note on John 7:53–8:11 is excellent. Special attention has been paid in the notes to passages where the Latin Vulgate differs from the Greek text. Recent studies on the Vulgate text have been taken into account, as is explained in the Preface (p. vii): "The readings of the Clementine [Vulgate], however, have been im-

of 1912, this edition with Carey's text of the New Testament has also appeared with the imprint of various publishers; e.g., The E. M. Lohmann Co. and the Herder Book Co. When the recent war cut off their supply from Belgium, the C. Wildermann Co. distributed under the name "Douay Bible House" a Bible printed by Benziger Brothers (see below, p. 493). But when the Brepols Bibles again became available, these latter were sold with the Douay Bible House imprint. The latest re-issue of this text (1950) has a new series of maps at the end. [Ed.]

[10] The correct American spelling is used; previous American editions usually printed the spelling current in England, "Saviour."

proved in not a few instances by recourse to the witnesses for a more ancient text of the Vulgate. This tends to bring the text basic to the present version very close to the modern critical editions of the original Greek. Where the Latin text differs from the Greek in such a way as to affect the meaning, attention is called to the fact in the footnotes." The situation is very different from that in the sixteenth century, when no critical text of either the Greek or the Latin was available, and when the Latin text was at the time more stable.

The text of this edition is rather a remodeling of Challoner's work than a fresh translation. In their Preface the revisers maintain (p. vii):

> To produce the type of version required in our day, it was necessary to eliminate many of the characteristics of the older version, and even to change many of its familiar passages; but there was no reason for setting it aside entirely. In fact, this revised text can claim the advantage of preserving in an improved form the version to which English-speaking Catholics have become accustomed.
>
> The English text now being presented retains as much as possible of the version it seeks to replace. And yet, in striving for expression that is modern, much of the general style of Challoner's work has been improved upon. . . . Only such alterations in the Challoner text have been made in the revised edition as were necessary to give a simple and clear modern version.

It must be admitted that the general impression of the version is that it does not depart greatly from Challoner's style: a certain archaism remains. "Thou" is retained throughout; but verb forms such as "doth" or "committeth" are modernized. Certain phrases are altered, such as "Fear not" (Matt. 1:20), now "Do not be afraid," and "knew her not" (Matt. 1:25), now "did not know her." Participial constructions, such as, "Who having heard the king" (Matt. 2:9), are altered: "Now they, having heard the king." The word "generation" in the first verse of the New Testament is altered to "origin," and the conjunction "now" sometimes replaces "and." "That you may abound the more" in I Thess. 4:1 appears as "make even greater progress." It may therefore be said that, although this revision preserves a distinct flavor of the old version, the translation is greatly eased for the modern reader.[11] An outstanding example may be cited here together with the usual text (in this case that of 1896), where the latter is by no means easy to follow, and the new version is truly a work of beauty.

[11] It should be noted that two of the contributors to the Confraternity Edition, Father C. Lattey and Father Wendell Reilly, had previously worked on the Westminster Version (see the following chapter), and therefore it is not surprising that certain renderings in the Confraternity Edition should be based on that version.

II Cor. 6:11–13

1896	1941
Our mouth is open to you, O ye Corinthians, our heart is enlarged. You are not straitened in us: but in your own bowels you are straitened. But having the same recompense (I speak as to my children) be you also enlarged.	We are frank with you, O Corinthians; our heart is wide open to you. In us there is no lack of room for you, but in your heart there is no room for us. Now as having a recompense in like kind—I speak as to my children—be you also wide open to us.

Yet some renderings are less satisfactory: Herod was "tricked by the Magi" (Matt. 2:16); "fruit befitting repentance" (Matt. 3:8) does not quite express the thought; "except for immorality" (Matt. 19:19) is not correct. "They could not take hold of what he said" (Luke 20:26) is inadequate—why not "contradict"? "Has effected man's purgation from sin and taken his seat" (Heb. 1:3) is hardly a felicitous attempt at expressing the aorist. There is a tendency at times to paraphrase rather than to translate; e.g., Matt. 20:18; Acts 18:10; Phil. 2:6 f. John 2:4 reads thus: "What wouldst thou have me do?" a completely new rendering; but the footnote gives as the literal translation the authentic Challoner reading, which has disappeared from all modern editions: "What is to me and to thee?"

The Confraternity Edition has for practical purposes replaced Challoner's original text for the New Testament in America, and it became widely known all over the English-speaking world through excerpts in *My Sunday Missal* and *Daily Readings from the New Testament,* both edited by Father Joseph Stedman (d. 1946) and distributed by the thousands to the men of the American armed forces during the recent war (1939–45).[12]

BENZIGER AND DOUAY BIBLE HOUSE EDITIONS

The Douay Bible House of New York published a Challoner Bible in 1941 and a New Testament in 1942 which bears on the title page: "As revised by Dr. Challoner, London, A.D. 1752. With Annotations and References by Dr. Challoner, Canon Haydock and Dr. H. J. Ganss." The text is, of course, independent both of Carey's editions and of the Confraternity Edition. In spite of the title page the text follows that of

[12] It was stated at the time of Msgr. Stedman's death that 15,000,000 copies of *My Sunday Missal* had been distributed between 1938 and 1946. (See the *Universe,* April 6, 1946.)

1899, which was based on the text of 1749. MacMahon is followed in John 2:4: "What is that to me and to thee?" The error in the 1750 text, "this uncircumcision" (Rom. 2:26), is followed, although 1752 was correct with "his." A most commendable feature of this 1942 New Testament is that alone among modern editions (apart from the Confraternity Edition) it follows Challoner's 1752 revision in completing the text of Mark 8:6 and Heb. 11:9, inserting the usually omitted clauses: "And he commanded the people to sit down on the ground"; and *"he abode in the land* of promise, as in a strange country, *dwelling in cottages."* It may be said that this edition is the best text in the American tradition. The notes, once more in spite of the title page, do not appear to differ from the usual ones; they even preserve the English currencies. The above Bible appeared also with the Benziger Brothers imprint.

BENZIGER'S RED LETTER EDITION, 1944

With the *Imprimatur* of Cardinal Spellman, dated November 3, 1943, Benziger Brothers of New York published a Challoner Bible, the special feature of which is the use of red type in the New Testament for the words of Christ. The title page runs: *Red Letter Edition. The Holy Bible. The Catholic Bible, Douay-Rheims Version. Translated from the Latin Vulgate and diligently compared with the Hebrew, Greek and other editions in divers languages. With notes by Bishop Challoner and the Encyclical letter "on the study of the Holy Scriptures" by Pope Leo XIII. Also a presentation of the essence of the Encyclical letter "on biblical studies"* (*Divino afflante Spiritu*) *by Pope Pius XII, and an Introduction by Vy. Rev. Charles J. Callan.* Father Callan's Preface contains a vigorous apologia for the old text of Dr. Challoner, which has especial interest in being written at a time when certain revisions were gaining great popularity in the United States. Father Callan's remarks are important since they are the most recent public defense of the unrevised text of the "old version." He wrote:

> It is a great mistake to think that this hallowed Challoner Version which has so long endeared itself to countless millions of Catholics . . . should be changed and modernized as to be something quite new and different. . . . Catholics and other Christians do not want the Bible expressed in the language of newspapers and popular books, which are mostly dead and forgotten as soon as they are read. No, they want the medium in which God's heavenly messages are expressed to exhibit . . . something of the elevated, changeless, heavenly and eternal character of the truths contained in those messages. . . . No changes except the correction of

some obvious errors that had crept into the text through repeated copying and reprinting. . . .

An outstanding example of such a correction is to be found in II Esd. 3:15, where for the first time since the original Douay Version of 1609 we find the correct reading, "garden," instead of the usual misprint, "guard." For this correction alone the edition deserves special mention. In the New Testament the text is the usual American type, based on the edition of 1899; and Mark 8:6 is complete. The book is pleasingly produced; but it should be observed that the names on the maps follow the Protestant spelling. This edition appeared also with the imprint of The Douay Bible House.

DR. ARENDZEN'S NEW TESTAMENT, 1947

This well-produced edition was published by Sheed and Ward in London and is the most easily available Rheims-Challoner New Testament to be found in England today. It bears the title: *The New Testament of Our Lord and Saviour Jesus Christ according to the Douay Version, with an introduction and notes by J. P. Arendzen, D.D., Ph.D., M.A.* Dr. Arendzen in his Introduction defends the misnomer, "Douay Version," on the grounds of popular usage, though it began only with the notorious "Catholic Fund" edition of 1820, and was continued in Dr. Denvir's editions from 1836; but it has not been printed on a Rheims-Challoner New Testament for nearly a hundred years. Douay Version is, of course, the title for the Old Testament, or for the complete Bible; but Rheims is correct for the New Testament. In the same Introduction the author speaks of Dr. Challoner's revision of "1746," presumably indicating that of 1749 as his source, though in fact a number of readings of the 1750 revision are included in his text. But the above details are small blemishes.

This edition appeared at a time when the new translation of Msgr. Knox (1945) had just achieved an enormous popularity in England, and was being read from most of the pulpits in the land. It was felt that some would wish to have "this venerable rendering of the Word of God," either because they were accustomed to it and liked the literal translation, or for purposes of comparison with the new version. In one matter, at least, Dr. Arendzen was able to profit from the example of Msgr. Knox: the layout in paragraphs, with verse numbers in the outside margin, and the pleasing general format of the book are not unlike

Burns, Oates and Washbourne's edition of Knox. The print is even more pleasing.

With regard to the text, it may be said that it represents in general the most satisfactory edition of Challoner that has so far appeared. The basis is the text of 1749, including "counsel" (Acts 5:38), "his uncircumcision" (Rom. 2:26), and "befalls" (I Pet. 5:9). The 1750 revision is followed when it is actually more correct than 1749, as in Matt. 23:29 and Acts 28:7, though "miracle" (Mark 6:5) in 1749 is more correct than the plural form in 1750 and in this edition. One or two other readings of 1750 are followed for the sake of the English. Challoner's many alterations in 1752, often approximating the Authorized Version, are followed only in Matt. 2:23, "Nazarene," which is more correct than "Nazarite" (1749–50); in Gal. 2:2, "communicated to them the gospel" (for *contuli cum illis*); and, rather inexplicably, in Acts 11:29, "purposed" for "resolved" (1749–50). Challoner's text is abandoned altogether in John 2:4, where "What is it to me and to thee?" comes from the anonymous edition of 1792. Mark 8:6 and Heb. 11:9, which Challoner completed in 1752, remain incomplete here. Lastly, the misprint in Mark 16:1, inherited through the Burns and Oates New Testaments (though not the 1914 Bible) from Dr. Murray's edition of 1847, is still here: "brought" for "bought"—the Latin reads, *emerunt aromata.*

It is interesting to observe that the tendency of the recent English editions of Challoner is to follow the text of 1749–50, while the American editors include a few more readings of the 1752 text. Of these two lines we have the most satisfactory fruits in this 1947 edition in England and the Douay Bible House edition in America (1942).

NEW CATHOLIC EDITION OF THE HOLY BIBLE, 1949

The edition of the Bible published in 1949 by the Catholic Book Publishing Co., New York, is eclectic in its sources. The Old Testament is Challoner's revision, except for the Book of Psalms, which is a translation of the New Latin Psalter of 1945. The New Testament is according to the Confraternity Edition.[13]

[13] In 1950 Benziger Brothers, New York, published a similar edition taken from the same eclectic sources. In the same year Kenedy and Sons published a Bible, the Old Testament of which is from their 1944 edition of the Bible; the New Testament is according to the Confraternity Edition. Both of these editions have the *Imprimatur* of Cardinal Spellman. [Ed.]

CHAPTER XL

Independent Catholic Versions of the Twentieth Century[1]

WE have already noticed the work of Dr. Nary in the eighteenth century, who produced a version of the New Testament translated from the Latin and independent of the Rheims tradition. A chapter has been devoted to the somewhat unorthodox labors of Alexander Geddes at the end of that century. In the nineteenth century we find Dr. Lingard translating the Gospels from the Greek, and Archbishop Kenrick translating the whole Bible from the Latin. Not until the eve of the twentieth century do we find another independent work: Father Aloysius Spencer's translation of the Gospels from the Latin, published in America in 1898.

Yet so long ago as 1810–11 the English bishops commissioned Father White of Winchester to prepare a revised version of the English New Testament,[2] but nothing came of the project. The commission by the Westminster Synod of 1855 entrusting Dr. Newman with the task of retranslating the Bible likewise bore no fruit.[3] Not until 1945 did these efforts bear fruit, when Msgr. Knox published his definitive version at the request of the hierarchy of England. But meanwhile there had been two further efforts, both undertaken with the active support of the hierarchy: one being the work of Father Spencer, O.P., in America, be-

[1] This whole chapter is supplied by Rev. Sebastian Bullough, O.P. Father Pope's manuscript included only two pages on Msgr. Knox's version and only a few lines on Father Spencer's version and the Westminster Version. His observations are here incorporated. [S.B.]

[2] This statement is given on the authority of Dr. Cotton, who says that he was so "informed through the Rev. G. L. Haydock" (*Rhemes and Doway,* p. 170).

[3] *Decretum IX Concilii Provincialis Westmonasteriensis Secundi,* MDCCCLV; see *The Month,* May and June, 1908; January, 1911.

gun in 1901 and not completed until 1937; and the other the great undertaking in England of the Westminster Version, begun in 1913 and still in production as regards the Old Testament; the New Testament was completed in 1935. Both Father Spencer's work and the Westminster Version are translations from the original tongues.

THE WORK OF FATHER SPENCER

Father Francis Aloysius Spencer was the son of a distinguished Episcopalian minister, and became a Catholic at the age of 21. He at once joined the Paulist Fathers, but after his ordination he exchanged the Paulist habit for that of the Dominicans at the age of 26. He had a distinguished career in the Order, and in 1898 he published a new translation of the Gospels from the Latin. It was this work that moved him to attempt a new translation from the Greek, as he was an accomplished Greek scholar and skilled also in Hebrew and Syriac. Thus it came about that in 1901 he published *The Four Gospels, a new translation from the Greek text direct, with reference to the Vulgate and Ancient Syriac Version.* Cardinal Gibbons wrote the Preface, and the book was published by Wm. H. Young & Co., New York; four editions appeared in as many years. Father Spencer then set about translating the whole New Testament from the Greek. The final touches were put to the translation and notes only a month or two before he died in 1913.

Not until the annual meeting of the American hierarchy in 1935 was the matter again raised of the need for a new translation of the New Testament, and it was then suggested that the as yet unpublished parts of Father Spencer's work should at last be printed. Two learned fellow Dominicans were thereupon entrusted with the task of preparing the manuscript for the press. These were the distinguished theologians, Charles J. Callan and John A. McHugh, who wrote the Introductions to the different books and provided many additional notes.[4] The fruit of their labor was published in 1937: *The New Testament of Our Lord and Saviour Jesus Christ, translated into English from the Original Greek,* Macmillan Company, New York. It has had a wide appeal in America and has been reprinted five times: in 1940, 1941, 1943, 1945, and 1946.

[4] These facts concerning the history of the version are taken from the editors' Introduction.

The text is printed in paragraphs, each with a subject heading in capitals, under which is the reference of the present passage and also the parallel passages. This device enables the reader to have at a glance all the passages dealing with a particular subject. The verses are numbered on the outer margin. A typographical peculiarity is that the words of Christ are always printed in italics, and quotations from the Old Testament are printed in small capitals. The principal divisions of the text are not the chapter headings, but Parts; such as, "Part II, The Public Life of Christ."

The medium of translation is biblical English; but archaic forms, except "thou," are avoided. Contrary to usual custom in the Bible, quotation marks are used for direct discourse; this practice and the use of italics compel the translator to commit himself in a passage like John 3:16–21: *"For God so loved the world . . . ,"* which is printed as part of our Lord's speech to Nicodemus, though a note states that it may be a comment of the Evangelist. The practice in modern prose of placing "he said" after the beginning of a speech is frequently followed; e.g., John 3:9–11:

> "How can this be?" said Nicodemus in reply. *"Thou art the teacher of Israel,"* said Jesus to him in return, *"and art not aware of these things? Indeed, indeed, I say to thee, that what We know, that We speak, and what We have seen, that We bear witness to. . . ."*

This example also serves to show the care about details such as the article before "teacher," which has been so often disregarded. It also shows the literal but easy style, and the treatment of "Amen, amen." In St. Paul's closely reasoned theology Father Spencer's clear and literal manner is often helpful, as the following example shows: "But if our iniquity evinces the justice of God, what must we say? that God is unjust in inflicting punishment?—I speak humanly. Never! for then how should God judge the world?" (Rom. 3:5 f.) This is almost the only version that does not hesitate to use the theologian's technical term "justification" in the difficult theology of Romans; for instance, Rom. 3:22: "Justification from God by means of the faith of Jesus Christ, for all and upon all who believe—for there is no distinction."

The book is well produced. At the end is a short chronology of New Testament times, an index of subjects for meditation (an unusual feature), an index of names and subjects, and two simple maps.

THE WESTMINSTER VERSION

The Westminster Version is a translation of the Bible from the original tongues into biblical English, which was selected as being the most suitable medium for a literal, yet graceful, rendering. The text is presented in paragraphs, with subject headings in bold type and insets for each main paragraph. The general editor from the beginning has been the English Jesuit, Cuthbert Lattey, who was assisted, particularly on the publication side of the venture, by Father Joseph Keating, editor of *The Month,* until the latter's death in 1939. The New Testament appeared in fascicles, beginning with Father Lattey's own contribution of First and Second Thessalonians in 1913. By 1935 the fascicles of the New Testament were complete. But meanwhile the handsome four-volume edition of the New Testament was begun: Volume III, St. Paul's epistles to the churches appeared in 1921 (2nd ed., 1927); Volume I, the synoptic Gospels, in 1928 (2nd ed., 1938); Volume IV, Hebrews, the pastoral epistles, the catholic epistles, and the Apocalypse, in 1931; and finally, Volume II, St. John and the Acts, in 1936. A special feature of this version is that each book is assigned to a particular contributor, who is totally responsible for the translation, introductions, and notes, working merely under the guidance and supervision of the general editor. In this respect the Westminster Version differs from almost every other version, which is usually either the work of a syndicate, or series of committees, or else principally the work of a single man.[5]

The Westminster Version appears in a long and in a short recension: the long recension is in large 8vo volumes, as indicated above, finely printed and lavishly produced, with elaborate introductions and appendices and fairly full notes all the way through. The short recension of the New Testament appeared in 1948; it is a 16mo volume containing the translation of the earlier volumes, with greatly abbreviated introductions and notes which are the work of Father Lattey, though based on the notes in the full edition.

It seems that the Confraternity Edition of 1941 made use of the West-

[5] The contributors to the New Testament are: Msgr. Joseph Dean (the Synoptics), Dr. W. S. Reilly, of Baltimore (John), Father Lattey, S.J. (Acts, Thess., I Cor., Rom.), Archbishop Goodier, S.J. (Phil., Philem.), Father Keating, S.J. (II Cor., with Father Lattey), Father A. Keogh, S.J. (Gal.), Father J. Rickaby, S.J. (Eph., Col.), Canon P. Boylan, of Dublin (Heb.), Dr. Francis Gigot, of New York (the pastoral epistles, John's epistles, Apoc.), Father W. H. Kent, O.S.C. (Pet., Jas., Jude).

minster Version in so far as a translation made from the Latin would allow, but altered the archaic forms used by the Westminster revisers.[6] The following passage is given for comparison of the texts (John 4:6–9):

Challoner, 1749 (Arendzen, 1947)	Westminster, 1936	Confraternity, 1941
Jesus therefore being wearied with his journey, sat thus on the well. It was about the sixth hour. There cometh a woman of Samaria to draw water. Jesus saith to her: Give me to drink. For his disciples were gone into the city to buy meats.	Jesus therefore, wearied with the journey, sat just as he was by the spring. It was about the sixth hour. There cometh a woman of Samaria to draw water. Jesus saith to her, "Give me to drink." For his disciples were gone away into the town to buy food.	Jesus, therefore, wearied as he was from the journey, was sitting at the well. It was about the sixth hour. There came a Samaritan woman to draw water. Jesus said to her, "Give me to drink"; for his disciples had gone away into the town to buy food.
Then that Samaritan woman saith to him: How dost thou, being a Jew, ask of me to drink, who am a Samaritan woman? For the Jews do not communicate with the Samaritans.	The Samaritan woman therefore saith to him, "How dost thou, being a Jew, ask to drink of me, who am a Samaritan?" For the Jews do not associate with the Samaritans.	The Samaritan woman therefore said to him, "How is it that thou, although thou art a Jew, dost ask drink of me, who am a Samaritan woman?" For Jews do not associate with Samaritans.

The New Testament is now complete in both the long and the short recensions. Work on the Old Testament, translated from the Hebrew or the Greek, began with the publication of Father Lattey's translation of the Book of Malachy in 1934. Between 1934 and 1939 three other of the Minor Prophets, Ruth, and the First Book of Psalms appeared in the long recension; in 1949 Daniel was published. In 1945 the small edition of all the psalms was published.[7]

An unusual feature of the New Testament in both editions is the chronological order of St. Paul's epistles: I and II Thess., I and II Cor., Rom., Eph., Col., Philem., Phil., Heb., followed by the pastoral epistles. The other books stand in their usual order.

[6] See footnote 11 of the preceding chapter.

[7] Contributors to the Old Testament are: Father Lattey (Malachy, Ruth, Psalms, Daniel), Father T. E. Bird (Jona), and Dom Hugh Bévenot (d. 1936—Nahum and Habakkuk). Other contributions are in preparation during 1950. It will be noticed that the Vulgate names in the Old Testament have been abandoned, the forms found in the Authorized Version being for the most part adopted.

THE WORK OF MONSIGNOR KNOX, 1944–49

Again in 1939, as in 1810–11 and in 1855,[8] a request came from the English hierarchy to a single man that he should undertake the translation of the New Testament. By 1944 Msgr. Ronald Knox had his draft ready, and it was printed by subscription. The title page runs: *The New Testament of Our Lord and Saviour Jesus Christ, newly translated from the Vulgate Latin, at the request of their Lordships the Archbishops and Bishops of England and Wales. Printed for private circulation only.* Burns, Oates and Washbourne, 28 Ashley Place, London, 1944. In his Preface Msgr. Knox invited "the readers of this trial edition . . . to express in general their approval or disapproval of the lines he has followed, and to point out any passage which, in their opinion, specially calls for correction."

Msgr. Knox's version is too well known on both sides of the Atlantic to need illustration. But the translator wrote a number of articles in the course of his work, and in 1949 they were collected and published in a book entitled *On Englishing the Bible*. In one of these essays he speaks of his aim in translating the New Testament into "a sort of timeless English that would reproduce the idiom of our own day without its neologisms, and perhaps have something of an old-fashioned flavour about it." [9] He declares that "any translation is a good one in proportion as you can forget, while reading it, that it is a translation at all"; and again: "Your examination of conscience, when you are doing any translating work, is obviously grouped under three heads: Is it accurate? Is it intelligible? Is it readable?" [10] In another of these essays [11] Msgr. Knox defends certain circumlocutions in his version which most readers will have noticed, such as "have sight of" for "see," "it is within your knowledge that " for "you know," and "found faith" or "learned to believe" for "believed." He claims that the so-called literal translation is in fact inaccurate when it does not produce in modern English the effect that the original produces in Latin, Greek, or Hebrew.[12] He exemplifies this view in his translation of Acts 20:18 and 22:19:

[8] Cf. above at footnotes 2 and 3.

[9] "Farewell to Machabees," in *On Englishing the Bible,* p. 97.

[10] *Ibid.,* pp. 92, 84.

[11] "Some Reasons Why," *op. cit.,* pp. 53 ff.

[12] Dr. J. W. C. Wand, Anglican bishop of London, reviewing Msgr. Knox's New Testament in the *Sunday Times* (February 17, 1946), wrote: "The main object of a good trans-

The Latin for "you know" is *scitis,* and the Latin for "they know" is *sciunt.* But it isn't *scitis,* it's *vos scitis;* and it isn't *sciunt,* it's *ipsi sciunt.* St. Luke, here, is not using Aramaic sources, and he must be credited with the intention of emphasizing his pronouns. In English there is no way of emphasizing a pronoun without the use of italics; and I am not going to use italics in my version. Therefore periphrasis is a necessity; you cannot translate your original without it; "you know" is an *inaccurate* translation.[13]

From Msgr. Knox's own statements we are able to understand the principles on which he worked, and it is fortunate that he made them public, since any judgment on his translation must take them into account.

Msgr. Knox worked with a committee (which included Father Pope) which passed the draft edition after some discussion. In 1945 the final edition appeared, which differs from the draft edition in only a few instances.[14] The title page of the final edition reads: *The New Testament of Our Lord and Saviour Jesus Christ, newly translated from the Vulgate Latin, and authorized by the Archbishops and Bishops of England and Wales,* Burnes, Oates and Washbourne Ltd., Publishers to the Holy See, 1945. Msgr. Knox's name appears only in the course of the Preface by Cardinal Griffin, archbishop of Westminster. In that Preface the Cardinal also says: "The official recognition now given by the Hierarchy to this translation does not mean that the Rheims Version of the New Testament is to be displaced. On the contrary, we now have two official versions in the Church in this country."

In 1948 a much larger "Library Edition" was published to form the third volume of the set of which the Old Testament volumes were to be the first two. The text in both editions is presented in paragraphs, as in nearly all the modern versions. There are no other headings than the indication of the chapters, though running heads giving the contents of each page are provided.

In this version Msgr. Knox[15] breaks entirely new ground; he translates the Vulgate into excellent English of a most readable type, of set purpose ignoring all previous versions, even more so than his prede-

lation is to produce in the mind of its readers the same effect as that which was produced by the original in the mind of those to whom the writing was first addressed."

[13] *Op. cit.,* p. 56.

[14] E.g., "Lads" in John 21:5 gave way to "friends"; and "It is within your knowledge" in Acts 20:18 to "You yourselves can testify."

[15] This paragraph represents verbatim Father Pope's criticism, written before the appearance of Msgr. Knox's own apologia.

cessors, Nary, Witham, Lingard, and Kenrick had done. Whether he has succeeded, time alone will show. Most readers will feel that he has made the epistles far more intelligible. His notes, too, though comparatively few, are really helpful. Perhaps critics will complain that intelligibility has been gained at times by paraphrasing rather than strictly translating; this appears borne out when we examine a single chapter taken at random from the Gospels: John, chap. 8, in the original Rheims version, 1582, runs to 1,324 words, reduced by Challoner to 1,281, but increased by Msgr. Knox to 1,515.

The Old Testament appeared in two volumes in 1949. The Douay Version of 1609–10 was divided after Job; Msgr. Knox starts his second volume with Job. The title page to each volume reads: *The Old Testament, newly translated from the Latin Vulgate by Mgr. Ronald A. Knox at the request of the Cardinal Archbishop of Westminster. For private use only.* Thus the Old Testament, though bearing Cardinal Griffin's *Imprimatur,* does not have the same authorization that was accorded to the New Testament, and Msgr. Knox explains the matter in his Preface, adding: "The book gives my idea of how the Old Testament ought to be translated, and does not claim to do anything more." It may be said that the translation is freer in the Old Testament than in the New, and the style is more personal. In fact, in the course of 1,604 pages the translator has evolved a style that is highly characteristic and peculiar to this particular work. The same principles underlie the translation, but of necessity their practical application in the Old Testament proceeds along somewhat different lines.

An "alternative version of the psalms," translated from the Latin text of the Pontifical Biblical Institute, is printed as an Appendix to the second volume. This text of the Psalms, with a few minor differences, had already appeared as a small volume in 1947.[16]

[16] The American edition of the New Testament was first published in 1944 by Sheed & Ward, New York, with the same title as the British edition; *Imprimatur* by Cardinal Spellman. But the title of the third and subsequent impressions reads simply: *The New Testament of Our Lord and Saviour Jesus Christ. A New Translation.* The popularity of this edition, which follows the "trial edition" rather than the final edition, is attested to by the fact that it went through the eleventh printing in 1950. In 1946 a handsome illustrated edition was published, also with the *Imprimatur* of Cardinal Spellman; but this has "friends" instead of "lads" in John 21:5, although Acts 20:18 still reads, "It is within your knowledge." The Old Testament volumes, though printed in America (1948 and 1950), have the same *Imprimaturs* as the British editions and almost the same title page.

HOLY BIBLE, CONFRATERNITY EDITION, BEGUN IN 1948

Up to the time of this writing (1950) only Genesis has appeared in the great undertaking of the Confraternity of Christian Doctrine to publish a new translation of the Old Testament from the original tongues. In approaching the Old Testament the editors have used a different method from that used in the Confraternity Edition of the New Testament in four very important respects. In the first place, the translation is being made from the Hebrew (or Greek), not from the Latin Vulgate.[17] Secondly, it is in no sense a revision of Challoner's work, but is an entirely new translation. Thirdly, the medium used is an entirely modern idiom, all archaisms of biblical English, even including "thou," being abandoned. Lastly, each book has been entrusted to a single translator, although he must work with an editorial board. The title page reads: *The Holy Bible, translated from the original languages, with the critical use of all the ancient sources, by members of the Catholic Biblical Association of America. Sponsored by the Episcopal Committee of the Confraternity of Christian Doctrine. The Book of Genesis.* St. Anthony Guild Press, Paterson, New Jersey, 1948. The format and printing are similar to those of the Confraternity New Testament.

Every translator of the Hebrew Old Testament must perforce at times have recourse to emendation of a corrupt text. At the back of this book there are five pages of "Textual Notes," intended to show where the translator has departed from the Hebrew text as it now stands. There are 106 passages thus indicated, in 66 of which the Septuagint or other ancient version has been followed; on seven other occasions the meaning has been arrived at through the versions; fifteen times the translation is conjectural, and on eighteen occasions a hypothetical emendation of the text has been made. Of these last it must be said that the greater number are generally accepted among exegetes today.

A pure twentieth-century idiom has not been used before by biblical translators among English-speaking Catholics, so this work is something of a departure. A brief example of its style must suffice (Gen. 43:26–30):

The *Imprimatur* to vol. 1 was given by Cardinal Griffin, July 3, 1948; that to vol. 2, by E. Morrogh Bernard, Vicar General, May 2, 1949. [Ed.]

[17] The fact that the translation is made from the Hebrew is undoubtedly due to the encouragement given to such work in Pope Pius XII's encyclical of 1943, *Divino afflante Spiritu.*

When Joseph came home, they presented him with the gift they had with them in the house, and prostrated themselves before him. He inquired about their health, and said, "Is your father, the old man of whom you spoke, in good health? Is he still living?" "Your servant, our father, is well; he is still living," they said, bowing low to him. Then Joseph looked up and saw his brother Benjamin, the son of his own mother, and said, "So this is your youngest brother of whom you spoke to me? God be gracious to you, my son," he continued. Thereupon Joseph broke off and was on the verge of tears, for his heart yearned for his brother. He retired to his room and wept.

Occasionally, however, the modernity of the idiom obtrudes itself in phrases such as those in Gen. 27:19: "Sit up, please! Eat again of my game"; or in Gen. 24:21, 40: "Whether or not the LORD [18] had made his trip successful."

The volume bears the *Imprimatur* of Bishop Edwin V. O'Hara, who, as chairman of the Episcopal Committee, also provides an introductory letter. This is followed by a Preface by the editorial board. The brief notes are for the most part concerned with textual matters.

[18] "The LORD" is thus printed when it translates the Tetragrammaton, as in the Revised Version.

PART FIVE

Protestant Versions since the Authorized Version

Introductory

It is frequently supposed that when the story of the English Protestant Bible reaches its culminating point in the Authorized Version of 1611, it remains at a standstill until work began on the Revised Version in 1870. That the Catholic Bible had a long and complicated history through the eighteenth and nineteenth centuries is better known. In contrast to the vicissitudes of the Catholic Bible, we find the Authorized Version holding a predominant position among English Protestants during this period—so much so, in fact, that of the many biblical translations that appeared in the eighteenth and nineteenth centuries, hardly a single one is ever used nowadays, excepting, of course, the Revised Version. Indeed, as Professor Goodspeed recently remarked: "These private versions, as they may be called, are usually passed over in complete silence by historians of the English Bible, and form a forgotten chapter in its history."[1]

In view of the silence of the historians, one frequently finds a sole authority to be Dr. Henry Cotton's *Lists of Editions of the Bible and Parts Thereof in English, from MDV to MDCCCL.*[2] Apart from Cotton, I have depended on the British Museum Catalogue and on the perusal of the books themselves, a number of which Cotton had not seen, in the University Library at Cambridge.[3] The authors of these translations are frequently persons of notable importance, and in these instances the *Dictionary of National Biography* has often supplied many useful facts.[4] Sometimes the title page of the book has helped to identify the author,

[1] *How to read the Bible* (1948), p. 221.

[2] When Cotton is the sole authority for an edition, I have appended (C) to its title in the following chapters.

[3] In these cases I have appended, where necessary, (BM) or (UL).

[4] When this work has been the sole authority for an edition, I have added (DNB) to the notice.

and in particular to determine whether he was a clergyman of the Established Church or a Dissenter. Such a detail will often be given.

The following chapters will not catalogue the translation of a single book of the Bible, but only editions comprising a substantial part of the Holy Scriptures. Therefore we shall not include publications such as that of 1645 (anonymous), *A bottle of holy tears: or, Jeremie's Threnes and Lamentations, metrically and metaphrastically laid out in verse,* and many other translations of single books recorded by Dr. Cotton. A chronological list of the sixty-seven texts recorded in this part is given in Appendix IV.

CHAPTER XLI

Private Versions of the Seventeenth Century[1]

SEVENTEENTH CENTURY DISSENTERS: HENRY AINSWORTH'S TEXTS, 1616–27

THE first biblical translations made after the Authorized Version and recorded by Dr. Cotton were those of Henry Ainsworth. He was a scholar of Caius College, Cambridge, who went to Amsterdam in 1593 when he became a Brownist, the separatist sect which later became the Independents of the Civil War period, the ancestors of the present-day Congregationalists. A characteristic of the sect that has remained is the autonomous nature of each church, and Ainsworth eventually became the leader of the refugee English congregation of Brownists in Amsterdam, which he founded together with Francis Johnson. He was the sole or part author of the *Confession of Faith of the People called Brownists,* 1596. Of special interest to the Catholic reader is the fact that in 1615 he published a correspondence of courteous controversy between himself and John Ainsworth "and twenty-one other priests in Newgate," which took place in 1614. There is no evidence for or against the supposition that the correspondents were brothers.

In 1616 he published his translation of Genesis, which was followed during the years to 1623 by the rest of the Pentateuch and Solomon's Song. These, together with a version of the Psalms, were published posthumously in 1627, all at Amsterdam. The text is "literally translated" with "Annotations"; and the latter sometimes include renderings in verse. W. E. A. Axon, however, in the *Dictionary of National Biography,*

[1] This entire Part Five, excepting the three chapters on the Revised Version, has been supplied by Rev. Sebastian Bullough, O.P. [Ed.]

says that "his versification is of the baldest"; but it is interesting that the rendering of Exodus, chap. 15, includes the music to which it was sung by Ainsworth's congregation at Amsterdam. The same author further states that Ainsworth left in manuscript works on Hosea, Matthew, and Hebrews, which were never published, and that his annotations proved useful to the scholars engaged on the Revised Version of the Old Testament.

JOHN CANNE'S BIBLE, 1647

At the death of Henry Ainsworth, which occurred probably in 1623, he was succeeded as pastor of the Independent congregation at Amsterdam by a newly arrived refugee scholar named John Canne, who occupied the pulpit for the next seventeen years, until he returned to England for a short visit in 1640. Within a year he had come back to Amsterdam, and in 1647 he published his Reference Bible. The text is that of the Authorized Version, but it is noted here because of the importance of its elaborate system of cross-references. In a prefatory note the editor explains that the best interpreter of Scripture is Scripture itself, and he consequently devised a system of cross-references which was fuller than anything that had so far appeared. His Bible was republished many times, principally at Amsterdam. At Cambridge there are copies of 1682 and 1698.

John Canne was the author of many books in defense of Independency and Presbyterian government, the most important being *A Necessitie of Separation from the Church of England, proved by the Non-conformists' Principles,* 1634. He died probably in 1667 at Amsterdam.

RICHARD BAXTER'S NEW TESTAMENT, 1685

Richard Baxter was one of the most prominent Nonconformist divines of the second half of the seventeenth century. He was born in 1615 and was largely self-educated, but being of a studious and thoughtful nature, before he was twenty he had already read widely in theological literature, including especially St. Thomas Aquinas and Scotus. In 1638 he was ordained in the Church of England, but he had begun to have doubts about the propriety of certain liturgical customs in that Church. It was John Ball's answer to John Canne's treatises mentioned above that first made Baxter realize "what presbytery or independency were." [2] This

[2] Cf. "Canne" and "Baxter" in the *Dictionary of National Biography*.

"conversion" occurred about 1642, when he was at Kidderminster, where his preaching became famous. His sympathies in ecclesiastical affairs were on the Puritan side, and he acted as a chaplain to the parliamentary forces during the Civil War; yet he remained devoted to the ideal of monarchy. Thus at the Restoration in 1660 he was in London to welcome the King, and became one of Charles II's chaplains. He was even offered a bishopric, but this his Puritan conscience forbade him to accept. He then took a prominent part in the Savoy Conference, for which he himself prepared the "Reformed Liturgy" which the Puritan party submitted to the conference. By this time Baxter had become the leading theologian on the Puritan side and was greatly disappointed by the result of the Savoy Conference and the Act of Uniformity which followed it in 1662, according to which the ceremonies of the Church of England were imposed on all. He was one of the first of over two thousand clergymen to refuse the Act and so to become Dissenters, or Nonconformists, and be deprived of their livings. The Conventicle Act and the Five-mile Act of 1664 and 1665 respectively (the first, forbidding any services but those of the Church of England, and the second, forbidding any Nonconformist minister to come within five miles of any town) served to make the division between the Established Church and the Dissenters deeper than ever. With many other Nonconformists, Baxter suffered much during this time.

Early in 1685 Baxter published his *New Testament with a paraphrase and notes.* Just at this time James II was succeeding Charles II, and Baxter was immediately arrested and charged with libeling the Church of England in his "Paraphrase." At the trial he was grossly insulted by the famous Judge Jeffreys, and he lay in prison a year and a half. He was released in November, 1686, and resumed his preaching, always to large audiences. He died in 1691. The British Museum has a copy of the second edition of his paraphrase of the New Testament, 1695. He was a very prolific writer, especially after 1662, and his collected works on religious subjects alone fill twenty-three volumes. Baxter's influence on subsequent dissenting thought was considerable.

SEVENTEENTH CENTURY OXFORD DIVINES

Two volumes of biblical translation of notable importance were published by a group of Oxford divines in the latter half of the seventeenth century. These were: Dr. Henry Hammond's *New Testament with a Paraphrase and Annotations,* 1653, a work which, according to W. P. Courtney's article in the *Dictionary of National Biography,* "gives Hammond a claim to the title of father of English biblical criticism"; and *A Paraphrase and Annotations upon all the Epistles of St. Paul,* first published in 1675, which was the joint work of Abraham Woodhead, Richard Allestry, and Obadiah Walker, the later editions of which were revised by Dr. John Fell. These men, all of notable interest, were contemporaries and friends, or at least acquaintances, and both Woodhead and Walker were secretly Catholics; Walker even publicly professed his faith in the time of James II. All of them were staunch supporters of the Stuart kings, and Hammond, Allestry, and Fell were among the most important members of what might be termed the "high church" party in the Church of England at that time.

HAMMOND'S *PARAPHRASE,* 1653

Henry Hammond (1605–60) was at Oxford from 1619 to 1633, principally engaged in theological studies. He had been ordained in 1629, and in 1633 received the living of Penshurst, Kent. During the Civil War, Hammond was on intimate terms with King Charles I, and joined him at Oxford in 1643. He was public orator of the university in 1645, and, being a chaplain to the King, he was frequently with him at this time and later, including the period at Carisbrooke. Hammond was finally removed and kept under surveillance at Clapham, and the news of the King's death in 1649 distressed him greatly. After the King's death and until his own death he lived in retirement at Westwood in Worcestershire, devoting himself to study and writing.

His *Paraphrase* was first published in folio in London in 1653, with subsequent editions in 1659 and 1702, and finally in four volumes octavo in 1845.[3] In the *Paraphrase* by Woodhead, Allestry, and Walker there is a reference to Hammond's work in connection with I Cor. 9:5, where the Authorized Version, with an allusion to married clergy, translated: "to lead about a sister, a wife." The note in the *Paraphrase* of Woodhead, Allestry, and Walker reads: "To carry about a Sister woman, as Dr. Hammond renders it according to the most literal and proper signification of the Greek, as *viri fratres,*" and calls attention to the women who

[3] Cf. *Dictionary of National Biography,* VIII, 1129. The British Museum Catalogue lists the 1702 edition as the seventeenth edition.

ministered to Christ and the apostles. Hammond's version was recommended by Dr. Johnson as the best commentary on the New Testament.[4]

WOODHEAD, ALLESTRY, AND WALKER

The *Paraphrase on the Epistles of St. Paul,* by Woodhead, Allestry, and Walker, first appeared anonymously in 1675. The edition of 1708 includes "Some Account of the Authors' Lives," and although this does not mention that Woodhead was ever a Catholic, it seems to have been a well known fact after 1660 that he was.[5] With regard to Obadiah Walker, this Preface says: "What should induce so great a Man to change his Religion for that of Rome, (for so he declar'd himself upon the Coming of King James II. to the Throne) is not to be accounted for." The two men were the closest of friends, Walker having come under Woodhead's influence when he came up to Oxford in 1633, when Woodhead was a young tutor there. Woodhead visited Rome some time after 1641, and Walker in his turn after 1648. In 1654 or 1655 Woodhead bought a house at Hogsden, or Hoxton (North London), where he lived with friends, having a common fund and devoted to prayer, meditation, and study. This establishment was sometimes referred to as a "popish seminary," and it seems fairly clear that there was a strong Catholic influence there. Walker must have been interested in it, for Woodhead bequeathed the property to him at his death in 1678. It is more than likely that some of the work on the *Paraphrase* was done there.

Abraham Woodhead (1609–78) came up to University College, Oxford, in 1624, and after being ordained in the Church of England, held various university offices, including that of proctor in 1641. In 1648 he was ejected with all the royalist dons by the Parliamentarian visitors, and, like many others, he found a temporary position as a private tutor. After this incident he first retired to Hoxton, where he remained in seclusion for the rest of his life, except for a brief period in 1660, after his reinstatement as a fellow of his college. He was most probably the author of the *Whole Duty of Man.*

Obadiah Walker (1616–99) lived most of his life at Oxford. He also was ejected in 1648 and reinstated in 1660. He was elected master of University College in 1676, and it appears that his inheritance of the

[4] Cf. Boswell, *Life of Samuel Johnson* (1822), III, 52 (anno 1776).
[5] Cf. *Dictionary of National Biography,* XXI, 870.

Hoxton property in 1678 led people to suspect him of being a Papist. An inquiry was held in 1679, but the master denied that there were any Papists in his college. The next year, however, there were further complaints, this time about his printing popish books—perhaps the *Paraphrase* was among them. In 1685 James II came to the throne, and in the following year he exercised his royal prerogative of dispensing particular subjects from the nation's laws; accordingly Obadiah Walker and three others were granted royal licence "to absent themselves from church, common prayer, and from taking oaths of supremacy and allegiance." [6] At the same time Obadiah Walker received a licence to print for twenty-one years a list of thirty-seven Roman Catholic works, the only restriction being that the sale was not to exceed 20,000 volumes in any one year—in other words, no restriction at all. During that same year Walker had Mass in the Master's Lodging, and a resident Catholic priest named Wakeman was maintained on the foundation. A private printing press was also set up in the college. In 1688 some persons who objected to these happenings had a "poor natural" sing in the college quad the jingle:

Oh, old Obadiah,
Sing Ave Maria.

But the time was short. From 1686 to 1688 Walker had openly professed his Catholicism; and when James II fled the country in 1688, Walker attempted to join him; but he was arrested, deprived of his mastership, and imprisoned until 1690. After his release he lived in retirement until his death in 1699. He was buried next to Woodhead in St. Pancras' churchyard.

The other writers concerned in the *Paraphrase* were Richard Allestry [7] (1619–81) and John Fell (1625–86). In his youth Allestry had for a time attended the same school at Wroxeter as the great Dissenter, Richard Baxter. He was at Christchurch, Oxford, at the same time as John Fell, and together with many students carried arms for the King during the Civil War. He took orders and became a tutor in his college, and in 1648 was ejected with the other supporters of the King. Although he made several visits abroad to King Charles II, both he and Fell continued to reside at Oxford during the Commonwealth, and together with a few

[6] Cf. "Walker" in the *Dictionary of National Biography*.

[7] Thus spelled on the title page. The "Account of the Authors' Lives" adds, "or Allestree," the spelling adopted in the *Dictionary of National Biography*.

other clergymen managed to conduct the services of the Church of England throughout the period, albeit in humble and reduced circumstances. Both Allestry and Fell, at their reinstatement as fellows of Christchurch in 1660, were made canons. In the same year Allestry went to Westwood to visit his friend, Dr. Hammond, in his retirement, but on his arrival he found the funeral procession of his friend leaving the house. He later learned that Hammond had bequeathed him his library. In these facts we find another link between the work of Dr. Hammond and the other three divines. In 1663 Allestry became professor of divinity, and in 1665 provost of Eton.

John Fell was vice-chancellor from 1666 to 1669, and finally bishop of Oxford in 1675. Dr. Fell died in July, 1686, only a few months after Obadiah Walker had obtained his licences from King James II, and he must have known of his friend's Roman Catholic activities.

THE *PARAPHRASE*, 1675

In view of the above history, the work of these three men, Woodhead, Allestry, and Walker, takes on special interest. It first appeared anonymously in 1675, and this edition was reprinted "At the Theater in Oxford" in 1684.[8] The original edition was published while Woodhead was still living at Hoxton; the reprint appeared after the death of both Woodhead and Allestry, just before Obadiah Walker made known his Catholicism. Dr. Fell was then bishop of Oxford.

In 1702 there was another edition, including on the title page: "Done by several Eminent Men at Oxford, Corrected and Improv'd by the late Bishop Fell." [9] In 1708 "The Third Edition" appeared with the names of the three scholars on the title page, and "Corrected and Improv'd by the Late Right Reverend and Learned Dr. John Fell, Bishop of Oxford. To which is prefix'd Some Account of the Authors Lives. London, printed: and Sold by C. Smith at the Buck between the Two Temple-Gates, E. Curll at the Peacock without Temple-Bar, and E. Sanger, at the Post-house at the Middle Temple-Gate." [10] In the account of Walker's life in this edition, the following startling statement is made: "The . . . Paraphrase went wholly under his [Walker's] Name for two Impressions which were Printed at *Oxford,* but at his Death, the Book being very

[8] Cambridge University Library class-mark 7.17.65.

[9] *Ibid.,* 7100.c.38.

[10] *Ibid.,* 7.14.46.

scarce and dear, Mr. *Boyse,* his Executor put a Copy of it into the Hands of Bishop *Fell* to Revise, who in some places where he thought the Text was a little too much wrested to the Sentiments of the Church of *Rome,* took the Liberty to expunge or otherwise alter, and superadded some of his own." Now, this account may be partly true, but in the first place the scene depicted cannot have taken place after Walker's death, for this occurred in 1699, and Dr. Fell died in 1686. If Dr. Fell carried out any revision, it must have been during the last two years of his life, after the edition of 1684, which has no mention of his revision. Furthermore, the first two impressions do not bear Walker's name, although it may have been well known that he had a hand in the work. Lastly, a comparison of the editions of 1684 and of 1708 shows scarcely any difference whatever in the text. The only two alterations I have been able to detect are the merest details: an additional note about Hagar on Gal. 4:26 (p. 192 in 1708), and an unimportant abbreviation of the note on II Tim. 4:8 (p. 333 in 1684; p. 349 in 1708).

Turning to certain passages in both editions, one finds them identical in every respect. A few examples will illustrate the nature of the paraphrase—the insertion of phrases in italics and parentheses into the text of the Authorized Version—and will indicate how far the exegesis is a Catholic one. "I Cor. 10:16. (*At the Table of our Lord in the Christian Feast and Sacrifice,*) the (*sacred*) cup of Blessing, which we (*solemnly, after the example of our Lord,*) bless (*and consecrate,*) is it not the Communion, (*to you that drink of it,*) of the blood of Christ? the bread which we break (*to you,*) is it not the Communion of the body of Christ?" The annotations on this verse and the next include the following:

(*"Bless"*) This seems to be said to make the solemnity of the Eucharist run parallel with the religious ceremonies of sacrifices; called spiritual meat and drink. Vers. 3.

(*"Consecrate"*) The solemn blessing and breaking was performed by the Apostles afterward, according to the pattern, as our Savior did it first, . . . who, besides the blessings of meat, (usual,) before the meal, . . . after supper made another consecration of this bread, and cup, continued ever since by the Holy Clergy.

[On verse 17] For whosoever eat of the Eucharistical sacrifice have Communion with the Deity (See Psal. 106.28) whose bread it is. Lev. 21.6.

The annotation on Heb. 5:10, Christ's "Melchisedechial, or eternal Priesthood," is worthy of note, as well as the annotation on "laying on of hands" in Heb. 6:2, which contains plain allusions to the sacraments of penance and extreme unction.

> . . . As also he hath instituted the same Oblation of his Holy Body and Blood; and Commemoration of his Passion, to be made in the Holy Eucharist to God the Father by his Ministers here on Earth, for the same ends, viz. The application of all the Benefits of his sole meritorious Death and sacrifice on the Cross, till his second return out of the Heavenly Sanctuary.

> The laying on of hands, in Baptism. . . . In Confirmation after Baptism: In Absolution of Penitents for greater Sins committed after Baptism: [11] In Ordination of Clergy: Lastly in curing of the sick, Mark 16.18.

If, therefore, Dr. Fell intended to "expunge or otherwise alter" any passages, he certainly held his hand and allowed the text to stand almost intact. After the two editions bearing his name, the text was once more edited in 1852, without any names on the title page, by Bishop Jacobson, who doubted whether Dr. Fell had any share in the work at all; yet it seems that the work has sometimes gone by the name of "Fell's Paraphrase." [12]

The work of this group of Oxford divines, so rarely mentioned by historians of the Bible, becomes of particular interest in view of the fact that two of them were secretly Roman Catholics in the Restoration period.

[11] This inclusion of the raising of the hand in absolution as an *impositio manuum* is not usual.

[12] Cf. "Fell" in the *Dictionary of National Biography*.

CHAPTER XLII

Private Versions of the Eighteenth Century

THIS chapter sets out to cover a very wide field, and sometimes the notices must be very brief. Occasionally this brevity is due simply to lack of evidence; but in many cases it is due to what must be admitted to be the very ephemeral nature of many of these versions, which, having had but small influence on the course of the history of the English Bible, must in a work like this be merely recorded for the sake of completeness.

As in the preceding chapter, it sometimes happens that the translator is a person of greater importance in the general history of English religious development than in the strictly biblical field, and that his biblical works were no more than sparks, as it were, from his anvil. In such cases it is but fair to give some indication of his historical importance, and thus set the version in its historical background.[1]

VERSIONS BY ANGLICANS EARLY IN THE CENTURY

In 1703 appeared the massive tomes of the *Paraphrase and Commentary on the New Testament,* by Dr. Daniel Whitby (1638–1726) (DNB).[2] It was the most elaborate work of its kind that had so far appeared, and had a second edition in 1706, a third in 1709–10, and a fourth in 1759–60 (UL); these repeated editions are some indication of its popularity. Dr. Whitby was chaplain to the bishop of Salisbury, and precentor of the Cathedral; he was widely known as a controversialist, having published many anti-Roman writings between 1664 and 1688. But

[1] The following account is chronological for the most part; but sometimes writers who were in some way associated have been grouped together out of chronological order.

[2] See footnotes 2–4 on p. 509.

his commentary and somewhat ponderous Preface are chiefly concerned with the defense of the supernatural in Scripture against unbelievers, and contain very little anti-Catholic matter. The paraphrase is a type that was becoming common: the insertion of bracketed explanatory phrases into the text of the Authorized Version. In Whitby's case most of the phrases are explanations of a somewhat obvious nature. In his later years Dr. Whitby was greatly concerned with the refutation of the Arian views that were appearing in the Church of England.

Rev. Edward Wells (1667–1727) achieved distinction as a mathematician and geographer as well as a divine. While he was rector of Bletchley (from 1716 until his death), he turned to the task of publishing a complete correction of the Authorized Version. This was the first time such a task was attempted for the complete Bible. The New Testament appeared in 1718: *The Common Translation corrected, with a paraphrase and notes;* the Old Testament followed in 1724 (C).

In 1726 appeared *The New Testament, a new Version, from the French of Messieurs De Beausobre and Lenfant, done into English* (BM). St. Matthew also appeared separately in 1727 (C). The original was the work of the French Protestants, Isaac de Beausobre (1659–1738) and Jacques Lenfant (1661–1728), and was published at Amsterdam in 1718. Lenfant had visited England in 1707 and preached before Queen Anne.[3]

WILLIAM MACE'S NEW TESTAMENT, 1729

William Mace was a Presbyterian minister, who in 1729 published *The New Testament in Greek and English . . . corrected from the Authority of the most Authentic Manuscripts.* Dean Luther Weigle says that "his corrections of the Greek text were in the direction of sound scholarship; but his English version was too obvious an attempt to copy 'the humour of the age'—the pert colloquial style which was then fashionable. Here are some examples: 'When ye fast, don't put on a dismal air as the Hypocrites do' (Matt. 6:16); ' 'tis the overflowing of the heart that the mouth dischargeth' (Matt. 12:34)."[4]

This text is important because it is one of the first to be based on a critical Greek text, which is printed alongside; also because it deliber-

[3] See "Beausobre" and "Lenfant" in the *Encyclopaedia Britannica.*

[4] *The English New Testament* (1950), p. 82. Dr. Cotton's entry for 1729 suggests that Mace's New Testament was published anonymously.

ately attempts to adjust its style to the language of the time; and lastly, because it is the first of several occasions when a Presbyterian minister prepared his own independent translation.

THE PRESBYTERIAN TEXT OF DODDRIDGE, CAMPBELL, AND MACKNIGHT

In 1818 a New Testament was published combining three earlier translations made by Presbyterians during the eighteenth century. The Gospels were according to the text of Campbell, published in 1789, while the Acts and Revelation were taken from the New Testament published by Doddridge in 1739, and the epistles followed the text of Macknight, published in 1795. The work of these three men should be considered separately.

Philip Doddridge (1702–1751) was probably the most important Nonconformist writer and preacher of the mid-eighteenth century. The son of a clergyman ejected by the Act of Uniformity, he intended from the beginning to enter the dissenting ministry. In 1719 he entered the academy of John Jennings, an Independent, at Kibworth in Leicestershire; and after the removal of the academy to Hinckley in the same county in 1722, he preached his first sermon there in the same year. For two years he was minister at Kibworth; but in 1725 he moved to Market Harborough. Meanwhile Jennings had died (1723), and there was no academy for the training of dissenting ministers in the district to replace it. Therefore in 1729 Doddridge opened his own academy at Market Harborough, but later in the year he moved it to Northampton, whither he had been invited by the Independent congregation there. The next year (1730) he was ordained "presbyter,"—as an Independent or Congregationalist he had refused ordination—and this action did much to bring together the Presbyterian and Congregational elements among the Dissenters. Doddridge remained at Northampton until his death in 1751, and his most important work belongs to this period, during which he was writing, preaching, and directing his academy. His influence on dissenting thought at the time is comparable only to that of Baxter in the preceding century, and great was the spiritual effect of his book, *On the Rise and Progress of Religion in the Soul* (1745). During his residence at Northampton he produced his *Family Expositor, or, a Paraphrase and Version of the New Testament,* including also a commentary. It began to appear in 1739 (C), and was republished at least in 1761 (UL).[5]

George Campbell (1719–96) was a distinguished Presbyterian minister who from 1759 to 1792 was principal of Marischal College, Aberdeen, and professor of divinity there after 1771. While he was at the college he published his large volumes of a *Translation of the Gospels* with preliminary dissertations and notes. His interest in miracles, which had shown itself in his well-known *Dissertation on Miracles* (1762), appears again here among the preliminary essays. The *Translation of the Gospels,* the work of a minister of the Established Church of Scotland (Presbyterian), is dedicated to a bishop of the Established Church of England, the Lord Bishop of Carlisle. It was republished several times: Cotton mentions editions of 1812 and 1813, and the *Dictionary of National Biography* lists a seventh edition in 1834. But Cotton further mentions one of 1838 based on an American printing, which brings interesting evidence of one of these "private versions" being published in America.

James Macknight (1721–1800) was a Presbyterian minister in Ayrshire until he was called to Jedburgh in 1769 and to Edinburgh in 1771. His first publication that has been noticed was *A Harmony of the Four Gospels* (1756); but his great work was *A new Literal Translation of all the Apostolical Epistles . . . the Greek Text, and the old Translation . . . with a Commentary and Notes. . . . To which is added . . . the Life of the Apostle Paul,* four volumes quarto, published at Edinburgh in 1795. This work is said to have been the fruit of thirty years of labor at the rate of ten hours a day. There were several later editions: 1806 (in six volumes), 1816 (C), and 1834 (DNB). The long list of subscribers at the beginning includes the names of the archbishops of the Church of England and many of its bishops. Macknight had published his work on the two Thessalonian Epistles in 1787 as a specimen of the larger work that was to follow.

JOHN GUYSE'S PARAPHRASE, 1739–52

John Guyse (1680–1761) was an Independent minister for twenty-seven years at his home town of Hertford. In 1727 he was invited to be-

[5] See the article in the *Dictionary of National Biography,* V, 1063 ff.; also *The Cambridge History of English Literature,* X, 381–83.

come the minister of the newly formed congregation in London, and there he remained until his death. He was a vigorous opponent of the Arianism that was showing itself in England at the time, and his two lectures published in 1729 under the title, *Christ the Son of God,* raised considerable controversy. Between 1739 and 1752 he published the three volumes of his *Exposition of the New Testament in the form of a Paraphrase* (DNB), a work which went through several editions, a sixth being published at Edinburgh in 1818 (UL), long after his death, with the fuller title: *The Practical Expositor: or, an Exposition. . . .*[6] Dr. Guyse became blind in his old age, "but his blindness was thought to have improved his sermons by compelling him to preach without notes, so that it was said that one of his congregation told him she wished he had become blind twenty years earlier." [7]

THE ARIAN MOVEMENT: WHISTON, CLARKE, AND PYLE

This is not the place to trace the history of the Arian controversy in the Church of England; but since several of the versions that appeared up to the middle of the nineteenth century were made under the influence of its latter phases, especially the Unitarian movement, some reference to it must be made.[8] The first phase, the so-called Socinian controversy, became prominent during the last decade of the seventeenth century, although anti-Trinitarian views had been circulating covertly for some time, among Anglicans and Dissenters alike. The Act of 1698, for the more effectual suppression of blasphemy and profaneness, which remained on the statute book until 1813 and was directed against the anti-Trinitarian views of the Socinians, marks the end of this part of the controversy. None of our translators were numbered among those concerned with this first phase.

The second phase, however, the properly so-called Arian controversy, was not long in developing. Its beginning can best be traced to William Whiston's dismissal from his professorship at Cambridge in 1710 because of his Arian notions. In 1686 Whiston (1667–1752) went to Clare Hall, Cambridge, where he took his degree and became a fellow. His principal interest at the time was mathematics, and he heard Newton's lectures. In 1693 he was ordained a deacon and became chaplain to the

[6] In what edition the fuller title first appeared is not clear.
[7] Edwin Cannan in the *Dictionary of National Biography,* VIII, 837.
[8] Cf. *The Cambridge History of English Literature,* X, 377 ff.

bishop of Norwich. At this time he wrote his first book, *New Theory of the Earth,* which had Newton's approval. In 1698 the Bishop presented him with a living near Norwich; but in 1701 he returned to Cambridge to act as deputy to Newton in the Lucasian professorship, to which he succeeded in the following year. About this time he began his theological speculations, the eccentric nature of which eventually brought him into much trouble. He came to the conclusion that the *Apostolic Constitutions* was "the most sacred of the canonical books of the New Testament," [9] and in 1708 he wrote an essay on this subject, in which he expounded many Arian doctrines. He maintained that he was not an Arian, but only a Eusebian (that is, "semi-Arian"), but nevertheless he was banished from Cambridge for his views. Subsequently he led a somewhat restless life: he wrote, lectured, and sometimes even begged from friends. In 1711 he published his chief work, *Primitive Christianity Revived,* on which Convocation voted an address for his prosecution; the latter, however, was never carried out. In 1715 he started his "Society for Promoting Primitive Christianity," especially by the sale of Arian literature. One queer notion after another, both on mathematical and theological topics, were expounded in print during the remainder of his life. He had a striking wit and had many friends, even when they did not agree with his theories.[10]

In 1745, when Whiston was seventy-eight years old, he published his edition of the New Testament. The title page reads: *Mr. Whiston's Primitive New Testament. Stamford and London, printed for the Author and sold by the Booksellers of London and Westminster.* M.DCC.XLV.[11] The basis of this version is the idea that the *Codex Bezae* (D) of the Gospels and Acts is the "most primitive of all," "being now probably above 1600 years old," and "written within thirty years of the death of John the Apostle." The epistles of St. Paul represent the text of *Codex Claromontanus,* which Whiston places about the year 300; [12] and for the other epistles and the Apocalypse he follows *Codex*

[9] This work as it stands is now generally attributed to the end of the fourth century, and it contains diction that is at least Subordinationist if not extreme Arian. Small wonder, then, that Whiston's conclusion should lead him into heresy.

[10] In 1737 he published his translation of Josephus, which is the one of his works that has lived down to the present day; it is still the usual English text. Cf. the *Dictionary of National Biography,* XXI, 10 ff.

[11] Cambridge University Library class-mark 1.12.47.

[12] Actually, however, the *Codex Bezae* dates from the fifth or sixth century, and the *Codex Claromontanus* from the sixth century.

Alexandrinus. It is surprising to find Whiston's text following the Authorized Version word for word for the most part, except where his codices bid him depart from it, as in the peculiar gloss which is found only in Codex D in Luke 6:5: "On the same day seeing one working on the sabbath, he said unto him, Man, if thou knowest what thou doest, thou art blessed: But if thou dost not know thou art cursed, and art a transgressor of the law." Whiston's old reverence for the *Apostolic Constitutions* was still with him, for we find he places the Gospels in the unusual order: Matthew, John, Luke, Mark, explaining in one of the notes at the back of the book that this order is "according to the original Order in the Apostles first Directions for reading them in publick: Constitution II.57." And shortly after he quotes the same authority for the statement that "Mark was the Son of Peter, and abridged Matthew's Gospel."

One of Whiston's outstanding qualities was his complete honesty. One might have expected his Arianism to appear occasionally in the translation, but not once has he altered the text of the Authorized Version except in order to follow the codex of his choice. Only in 1747, after the publication of his *Primitive New Testament,* did Whiston, then eighty years old, abandon communion with the Church of England and join the Baptists.

The other great Arian leader was Dr. Samuel Clarke (1675–1729), who was born in Norwich and went up to Caius College, Cambridge, in 1691, where he studied brilliantly under Newton. In 1697 he was back at Norwich and chanced to meet Whiston in a coffeehouse there. Whiston was then chaplain to the bishop of Norwich, and Clarke succeeded Whiston in the chaplaincy when the latter was given the living near Norwich during the following year. Clarke's *Paraphrases of the Gospels* was the fruit of his youthful studies at this time, being published in 1701–1702 (DNB). At this time there was no evidence of his future Arianism. He began to achieve fame by his Boyle lectures of 1704 and 1705, during the time of Whiston's professorship. He had now come to be "generally regarded as the first of English metaphysicians." [13]

In 1712 Clarke published his *Scripture Doctrine of the Trinity,* which was the most important book of this phase of the Arian movement and raised a great storm of controversy, including Daniel Waterland's fam-

[13] Leslie Stephen in the *Dictionary of National Biography,* IV, 443.

ous *A Vindication of Christ's Divinity,* 1719. In 1714 the matter was taken up by Convocation, and Clarke submitted in quite orthodox terms. Clarke remained within the Church of England, where he had many friends. Voltaire said that he would have become archbishop of Canterbury had not someone told the queen that "Clarke was the most learned and honest man in her dominions, but had one defect—he was not a Christian." [14]

Thomas Pyle (1674–1756) was a contemporary of Clarke at Caius, and was ordained by Bishop Moore of Norwich in 1697 while Whiston was his chaplain. He held various livings in the Lynn district, and later, through his friendship with Hoadly, became a canon of Sarum. His views became increasingly heterodox, and in later years he scarcely disguised his Unitarianism. That he was a great admirer of Clarke is shown in the title of his work: *Paraphrase of the Acts and Epistles, in the manner of Dr. Clarke,* published in 1725 (DNB). This work went through several editions, the fifth appearing in 1765 (UL); the latter is a small volume for the time, and the title is slightly different from that given above: . . . *Supplement to Dr. Clarke's Paraphrase of the Gospels.* The author is described as "Canon of Sarum, Minister of Lynn Regis, Norfolk." The style of paraphrase is that current in the eighteenth century: italicized explanatory phrases in parentheses inserted into the text of the Authorized Version. Pyle also published a *Paraphrase on the historical books of the Old Testament,* 1717–25 (DNB), and a *Paraphrase on the Revelation of St. John,* 1735 (DNB), which also bears the title, *The Scripture Preservative against Popery.*

Thus from Clarke and Pyle we have a complete paraphrase of the New Testament, and although Clarke's work was published before the Arian controversy had reached its second phase, Pyle's contributions were made when it was at its height. Although Whiston was an older man, his text was not published until much later.

JOHN WESLEY'S TEXT, 1755, 1790

There is no need to emphasize the influence of Wesley on English religious thought. The new movement of Methodism, which is dated either from the group of Charles and John Wesley and George Whitefield at Oxford in 1729, or from the "conversion" of John Wesley in

[14] *Ibid.,* p. 446.

1738, had a profound effect at first in the Church of England itself, and after 1784, when John Wesley ordained Methodist ministers himself, among the Nonconformists. The new movement in great measure overshadowed the previous Arian difficulties within the Church, apart from the growth of the Unitarians from the Arian group.

Our only immediate concern with Wesley is to notice his edition of the New Testament "with Explanatory Notes" in 1755 (BM), the text being that of the Authorized Version slightly altered. Another edition appeared in 1790 (C), in the Preface to which he says: "In this edition the translation is brought as near as possible to the original. The alterations are exceedingly small; but they may be of considerable importance."

ANGLICAN EDITIONS OF HEYLYN (1761) AND WYNNE (1764)

John Heylyn (1685?–1759), known as "the Mystic Doctor," was the first rector of the new St. Mary-le-Strand in London. He published in 1749 a volume entitled, *Theological Lectures at Westminster Abbey, with an Interpretation of the Four Gospels.* This work was continued in a second volume entitled, *An Interpretation of New Testament . . . containing the Acts of the Apostles and the several Epistles,* which was not published until 1761, after his death (C, DNB).

Rev. Richard Wynne, rector of St. Alphege's Church in London, in 1764 published *The New Testament, carefully collated with the Greek, corrected, divided and printed according to the subjects treated of.* The author does not set out so much to make merely a correction of the Authorized Version, as Wells had done in 1724, but more liberally to adapt it. He explains in the Preface that his intention is "to steer a just medium between a servile literal translation and a paraphrastic loose version," and this is probably the first time among these versions that the translator has so plainly enunciated his principle. The statement has a particular force in view of the many paraphrases we have just noticed. Another important feature of this work is the fact that the text is printed in paragraphs and not in verses, as most of the texts derived from the Authorized Version had been.

THE QUAKERS' BIBLE, 1764

Anthony Purver (1702–77) joined the Society of Friends (called the Quakers) before he was thirty, and shortly afterwards began his lifework of translating the whole Bible. The task took him thirty years, and he claimed to be executing it under divine instruction. It is said that when he arrived at a difficult passage, he would shut himself up for two or three days and wait for inspiration. The great folio volumes were published by John Fothergill, a doctor and himself a member of the Society of Friends.

HARWOOD'S *LIBERAL TRANSLATION OF THE NEW TESTAMENT*, 1768

Harwood's *Liberal Translation of the New Testament* (1768) is one of the better known versions of the period, though it is chiefly known as an example of eighteenth-century verbosity at its worst. Yet Harwood was no mean classical scholar, linguist,—he also made translations from the French and German—and textual critic of the New Testament. In 1776 he published a text of the Greek Testament on the basis of *Codex Bezae, Claromontanus,* and *Alexandrinus,* the very codices that Whiston had used for his version. His theology, however, seems to have made him unpopular in some quarters. His first training for the dissenting ministry was acquired in London with David Jennings, brother of John Jennings, whose academy at Kibworth had been attended by Doddridge. Later he came in contact with the Independent academy at Warrington, which was under the Arian influence of Dr. John Taylor. Harwood was ordained a presbyter in 1765, though his Arian views were not generally welcomed among the Presbyterians. He ministered at Bristol until 1772, when he came to London.

The description of his New Testament on the title page is in the style of the version itself, but it explains a method of treatment that at the time was new and is a definite landmark in the history of biblical translation: *A Liberal Translation of the New Testament: being an Attempt to translate the Sacred Writings with the same Freedom, Spirit, and Elegance, with which the other English Translations from the Greek Classics have lately been executed: The Design and Scope of each Author being strictly and impartially explored, the True Significance and Force of the Original critically observed, and, as much as possible, transfused into our Language, and the Whole elucidated and explained upon a new and rational Plan: With Select Notes, Critical and Explanatory. By E. Harwood.* London, M.DCC.LXVIII. The text is printed in verses, as in the Authorized Version. A typographical peculiarity is the use of a dash to introduce a speech. The notes are very few. Titles of the books are remodeled; e.g., "The History of Jesus by Matthew." A few examples, compared with the Authorized Version, will suffice to show Harwood's treatment of the text.

Authorized Version	Harwood's Version
Matt. 13:51 f. Jesus saith unto them, Have ye understood all these things? They say unto him, Yea Lord.	After speaking these parables, Jesus said to his disciples—Do you perfectly understand my meaning and intention? —they answered in the affirmative.
Then said he unto them, Therefore every scribe which is instructed unto the kingdom of heaven is like unto a man that is an householder, which bringeth forth out of his treasure things new and old.	He then said to them—every publick teacher of Christianity ought to study the precepts and doctrines of it with such sedulous application and industry, that he, like a careful and provident master of a large family, may lay up a rich and inexhaustible fund of useful knowledge, and may upon every occasion be always able from a mind replete with wisdom to administer an ample and salutary repast for the consolation and benefit of mankind in every various state and condition.
Matt. 10:28. But rather fear him which is able to destroy both soul and body in hell.	But let that great Being be the object of your fear, who can involve both soul and body in total and everlasting destruction. Let that great Being, I repeat it, be the object of your constant fear.
Matt. 26:26. Take, eat; this is my body.	Take and eat this bread—which I design should represent my own body.

In 1765 Harwood had issued some proposals for a free translation, and in 1771 he published a companion volume to his actual translation. His *Introduction to New Testament Studies* (1767) had earned him a D.D. at Edinburgh University.[15]

WORSLEY'S NEW TESTAMENT, 1770

Worsley's version of the New Testament, published in 1770, deserves special notice in that it is the first deliberate attempt among Protestants since the Authorized Version to produce a modern-speech version. Among Catholics in the eighteenth century, Dr. Nary in 1718 and Dr. Witham in 1730 had already made the attempt; but among Protestants, where the Authorized Version was so universally used for public read-

[15] Cf. the *Dictionary of National Biography,* IX, 102 f.

ing, Worsley's proposal to provide a readable version for private use is certainly interesting. The book was published after the translator's death, and the editors (M. Bradshaw and S. Worsley) write in a prefatory note: "We hope this Book will be found . . . a very improving and therefore welcome Closet-Companion; and in that Persuasion we chearfully leave it to the Candor of those into whose Hands it may fall." The title page runs: *The New Testament or New Covenant of Our Lord and Saviour Jesus Christ. Translated from the Greek according to the Present Idiom of the English Tongue by the late Mr. John Worsley, of Hertford.* 1770.

Worsley himself emphasized that his version is for private use, and in his "author's advertisement" he advocates the retranslation of the "sacred oracles" into the current idiom at least once a century. He thus begins his "advertisement": "The English Translation of the Bible in the Reign of King James I. is, no doubt, a very good one, . . . but it is not to be wondered at if some words and phrases, then in use and well understood, should be by this time become obsolete and almost unintelligible to common readers." He tells us that he deliberately tried not only "to make the form of expression more suitable to our present language," but also to bring it "nearer to the original." For instance:

Authorized Version	Worsley's Version
Matt. 2:16. Then Herod, when he saw that he was mocked of the wise men, was exceeding wroth, and sent forth, and slew all the children that were in Bethlehem, and in all the coasts thereof, from two years old and under, according to the time which he had diligently enquired of the wise men.	Then, Herod, when he saw that he was baffled by the wise-men, was very much enraged; and he sent and slew all the male-children in Bethlehem, and in all its borders, from two years old and under, according to the time which he had exactly inquired of the wise-men.
Phil. 2:7 f. But he made himself of no reputation, and took upon him the form of a servant, and was made in the likeness of men. And being found in fashion as a man, he humbled himself, and became obedient.	Yet he emptied himself, assuming the form of a servant, when made in the likeness of men: and being in the human state, he humbled himself, and was obedient.

GILBERT WAKEFIELD'S NEW TESTAMENT, 1791

Gilbert Wakefield (1756–1801) graduated at Jesus College, Cambridge, in 1776, and shortly afterwards was ordained deacon, an act which he deeply regretted before long, for he soon found himself unable to subscribe to the articles of the Anglican Church. He did not, however, attach himself to any dissenting body, although in 1779 he went as classical tutor to the academy at Warrington, which was strongly Arian or even Unitarian. While he was there he published new translations of First Thessalonians and Matthew, which were eventually to form part of his New Testament. From 1783 to 1790 he was engaged in private teaching, study, and writing, chiefly on classical subjects. From 1790 he lived at Hackney. For a year he taught at a dissenting academy there, but resigned, partly owing to his aversion to any form of public worship. During this time he completed his translation of the New Testament. Wakefield also had strong political views, which he did not hesitate to put into print: he condemned all war as immoral, and considered the prevailing system of government, both civil and ecclesiastical, to be a "bond of iniquity." Under these circumstances it was not surprising that he was prosecuted for libel in 1798. Although he conducted his own defense with much ability, he was committed to prison in 1799. He was released in 1801, but died within a few months. His imprisonment was presumably the "unfortunate event" discreetly referred to by the projectors of the Unitarian Version (1808), who had endeavored just at that time to negotiate with him in order to make use of his text.

Wakefield's *Translation of the New Testament* appeared probably in 1791.[16] In the Preface he enunciates several of his principles, stating that his chief rule is "to adopt the received version upon all possible occasions, and never to supersede it unless some low, obsolete or obscure word, some vulgar idiom, some coarse or uncouth phrase . . . demanded an alteration," further adding that he intended to make his text "as completely vernacular without vulgarity" as possible. When we consider the periphrastic style of Harwood and others, we can understand Wakefield's statement: "What are called liberal translations of the scriptures I could never approve." In fact, his text follows very closely that of the Authorized Version, and in many respects is not dissimilar from that of Archbishop Newcome in 1796, even though the latter text sets out to be no more than a revision of the Authorized Version. In a footnote to the Preface of the 1795 edition Wakefield pays tribute to *An Historical View*

[16] 1791 is the date given by Cotton (*Lists of Editions of the Bible and Parts Thereof*); it is also the date of the Preface in the later edition of 1795 and the date referred to in the Unitarian Version; but the *Dictionary of National Biography* (XX, 453) gives the date of publication as 1792.

of the English Biblical Translations by "that liberal and enlightened scholar, Dr. William Newcome." Wakefield's text had a second edition in 1795 (UL) and a third in 1820 (DNB).

ANGLICAN EDITIONS OF ROBERTS (1794) AND HAWEIS (1795)

Corrections of various passages in the English Version of the Old Testament, the work of Dr. W. H. Roberts, who died in 1791 while provost of Eton, was published posthumously in 1794. The main object was apparently "to reduce the number of italicised supplementary words which occur in the authorised version." [17]

In 1795 Rev. Thomas Haweis published *A Translation of the New Testament from the original Greek*. Haweis is a person of particular interest because of his connection with the Methodist movement. He had been ordained in 1757 and appointed to a curacy in Oxford, from which he was removed because of his Methodist sympathies. He then went to London; but from 1764 until his death in 1820 he was rector of Aldwinkle in Northamptonshire. In 1768 he became chaplain to Selina Hastings, countess of Huntingdon, who was a member of the first Methodist society in 1739 and became prominent through her support of the Calvinistic Methodist group which looked to George Whitefield as their leader and finally seceded from the Wesleyan group in 1764. When Lady Huntingdon died in 1791, Thomas Haweis was made her trustee and executor, and given the management of her chapels, which were registered as dissenting chapels; yet he retained the living of Aldwinkle. During this latter part of his life he made his translation.

ARCHBISHOP NEWCOME'S NEW TESTAMENT, 1796

William Newcome (1729–1800) was a distinguished scholar and eminent tutor of Oxford who became an exemplary bishop and finally, in 1795, primate of the Established Church in Ireland. Most of his extensive biblical work was done during his years as a bishop (from 1766) and was published in Dublin. His first important publication was a harmony of the Greek Gospels in 1776, which was issued in English in 1802, after Dr. Newcome's death. Other books on New Testament subjects followed this work, and in 1785 there appeared *An Attempt towards an Improved Version . . . of the Twelve Minor Prophets,* and in 1788 a similar work

[17] Cf. the *Dictionary of National Biography,* XVI, 1283.

on Ezekiel. He was working on a revision of the whole Bible, and in 1792 published *An Historical View of the English Biblical Translations* (referred to by Wakefield), in which he advocated that the Authorized Version be revised by authority. His was the first plea made by a prelate of the Established Church for an action which was realized almost a century later in the production of the Revised Version. Although various private attempts were afterwards made, as the next chapter will show, no action was taken by authority until 1870. Yet the work of William Newcome undoubtedly prepared the way.

Dr. Newcome's work on the New Testament was printed at Dublin in 1796. He continued the humble form of the title he had used before: *An Attempt towards revising our English Translation of the Greek Scriptures, or the New Covenant of Jesus Christ: and towards illustrating the sense by philological and explanatory notes.* However "the work was withheld from publication until (1800) after Newcome's death; as the impression was damaged in crossing from Dublin, the number of copies for sale was small." [18] The two volumes are handsomely printed with the text in paragraphs and with verse numbers down the margin. Quotation marks are used for direct quotations probably for the first time in biblical translation. This was also the first English translation to make use of the new critical edition of the Greek text published in 1774–75 by J. J. Griesbach in Germany; but the alterations from the Authorized Version are few and in small matters, and there is no attempt to alter the style. The most notable difference is in the typographical presentation. Occasionally a more archaic word seems to be preferred, as "murther" for "murder" in Matt. 19:18. There are frequent notes, for the most part soundly critical and theologically orthodox; for instance, the note on Matt. 1:25 supports the perpetual virginity of Mary: "The suffrage of antiquity is against the natural import of the words, that Joseph, after the birth of Jesus, lived with Mary in the holy state of marriage."

Archbishop Newcome's own interleaved folio Bible, containing his own handwritten proposals for the revision of the Old Testament, is preserved at Lambeth. It is sad that the scholarly labors of this learned man have not received greater recognition.

[18] Alexander Gordon in the *Dictionary of National Biography,* XIV, 323. The rare copy in the University Library at Cambridge has the class-mark, 1.11.32.

SCARLETT'S NEW TESTAMENT, 1798

Though published so late in the century, Scarlett's New Testament is in many respects a typical conceit of the eighteenth century. The book measures no more than 7½ inches by 4½ inches, and was a "pocket volume" at the time. The title page is elaborately engraved with a variety of flourished lettering; it reads: *A Translation of the New Testament from the Original Greek Humbly attempted by Nathaniel Scarlett, Assisted By Men of Piety & Literature: with Notes. London: Printed by T. Gillet; and Sold by Nathaniel Scarlett No. 349 (near Exeter 'Change) Strand, also F. & C. Rivington, St. Paul's Church Yard.* 1798. There follows another elaborately engraved page giving a table of the books of the New Testament, where to find them in this volume (they are in the usual order), their dates (most orthodox), "The Time in which each Book may be read distinctly" (for instance, Matt. requires 1 hour and forty-eight minutes, Mark, one hour and nine minutes, II John, two minutes; and at the foot of the column, the whole, fourteen hours), and the number of chapters and verses in each book. Below is inscribed: "N.B. It will require about 48 hours to read the Old Testament, it bearing a proportion to the New nearly as 17 to 5."

The translation is a notably original work, and though it does not profess to be a work of full scholarship, some of the principles of translation enunciated in the Preface are of interest, one of them being the modernizing of the language.

> The common English Translation of the Bible is generally allowed to be, on the whole, a good one. Yet, it must be granted, that a very material change has taken place in our language, even within the last two centuries: and it will, no doubt, like other living languages, differ much in a century hence from what it is now. . . .
>
> [The Authorized Version] often followed exactly the order of the words as they stand in the original: whereas the genius of the English language requires, frequently, the very reverse. [Some examples are given.] From these few instances, and a thousand others which might be produced, the unlearned reader (for whose use the following Translation is chiefly intended) will perceive that a very considerable improvement may be made, by transposition, even though the very same words are used. . . .
>
> Whilst an attempt is made to bring this sacred Book somewhat nearer to the English idiom at this day, still care is taken to steer between the two extremes, of being too servile and literal on the one hand, or too periphrastic on the other.[19]

[19] The similarity of Scarlett's views and those of Wynne and Worsley (above, pp. 528 and 531) lead one to wonder how much he depended on the work of the two earlier translators.

. . . The learned reader (if such should notice this publication) will readily acknowledge [that Greek idiom differs considerably from English, but that if the Greek idiom can be followed in English] consistently with perspicuity, the meaning of the inspired penmen is better represented, than it can be in a free Translation.

A remarkable modern feature, adopted by so many recent versions, is found here: chapter and verse numbers are retained, but the editor has divided the work into sections, "placing a title over each section expressive of what he conceived to be the leading feature of that section"; and he adds: "If the learned reader should object to this mode, let him remember that this publication was intended chiefly for those, whose temporal concerns afford them but little leisure to read." It would appear that Nathaniel Scarlett was the first editor deliberately to cater to what is now called the casual reader. A peculiarity of this edition is "the personifying, or putting the name of the speaker," as in the text of a play, with the narrative portions marked "Historian." A single example from Mark 14:17–21 will suffice to show Scarlett's treatment of the text.

§72. JESUS AT SUPPER POINTS OUT THE TRAITOR

Hist.—And in the evening he cometh with the twelve. And while they were sitting and eating, Jesus said,

JESUS.—Verily I tell you, One of you who is eating with me, will betray me.

Hist.—And they were grieved, and said to him, one by one,

Disciples.—Is it I?

Hist.—And another said,

Disciple.—Is it I?

Hist.—And he replied,

JESUS.—It is one of the twelve, who is dipping *his hand* with me in the dish. The Son of man, indeed, is going. . . .

Nathaniel [20] Scarlett himself is an interesting character (1753–1802), having been successively shipwright, accountant, and bookseller. Originally he was a Methodist, but then became a Universalist, and finally a Baptist under the influence of William Vidler, a Baptist preacher who held Universalist views and after Scarlett's death became a Unitarian. Scarlett's Baptist belief accounts for his rendering "immerse" for "baptize" whenever it occurs. The *Dictionary of National Biography* tells us who were the "Men of Piety and Literature" who assisted in the work. The basis of the work was a manuscript translation made by James Creighton, an Anglican clergyman, and once a week he and Vidler and

[20] Not Nathan, as Cotton gives it (*op. cit.*).

John Cue, a Sandemanian,[21] met at Scarlett's house to work on the translation. The final arrangement of the text, however, was entirely the work of Scarlett.

THE BIBLE OF J. M. RAY, 1799

The Holy Bible, translated and interpreted after the Eastern manner, from concurrent authorities . . . with philosophical and medical commentary, by J. M. Ray, is a large tome. Although published at the end of the eighteenth century, it belongs more in spirit to the nineteenth century. Its avowed object is to show that there is no conflict between religion and the scientific theories that were then emerging from the recent progress in the physical sciences, from the acquaintance with the East made by recent travelers, from the new evidence of manuscripts, and from the advances made in philology.

The author professes himself to belong to no party or church, and according to Cotton spelled his name variously as D. McRae or McRay, or J. M. Ray. In the copy of the edition of 1815 at Cambridge the name is spelled J. M. Ray. Cotton gives the date for the first edition as 1799.

[21] A follower of Robert Sandeman, who joined the "Glassites," a group of independent Presbyterians started by John Glas in Scotland in 1730. Sandeman spread the movement in England, where it went by his name.

CHAPTER XLIII

Private Versions of the Nineteenth Century

THE study of English Protestant versions of the Bible during the nineteenth century is much easier than the record of the efforts of the Protestant churches during the preceding century. The Protestant bodies had, for the most part, settled down to a regular existence, and the Church of England itself was not torn by doctrinal controversy as it had been in the eighteenth century. These controversies had been reflected in the versions made of the Bible, and the dissenting groups had in many instances produced translations of their own. It is difficult to estimate how many of the versions mentioned in the last chapter were still in use in the nineteenth century, but the very fact that they were so rarely spoken of suggests that they fell into disuse as quickly as they had come into existence. It is more than probable that the Authorized Version continued to hold the same predominant position; but the leaders of religious thought, especially among the Nonconformists, who had produced versions in the seventeenth and eighteenth centuries, had undoubtedly contributed to the fairly stable position which emerged in the earlier nineteenth century. It is an interesting fact that the important effects of the Oxford Movement in the Church of England are in no way reflected in the sphere of biblical translation; a great commentator like Pusey, for instance, was quite content to use the text of the Authorized Version in his *Minor Prophets*.

According to the nature of the history, there is no need in this chapter to present the versions on a historical background, as in the last chapter, except for the first section on the Unitarian versions; but they will be grouped according to the nature of the translation, concluding with the attempts to revise the Authorized Version, which culminated in the Revised Version itself.

THE UNITARIAN VERSIONS

The title Unitarian in the course of the eighteenth century began to be applied to those who held the more extreme Arian or Subordinationist views, either in the Church of England or among the dissenting churches. According to these views, Christ is to be called divine only in a way quite subordinate to the divinity of the Father, and consequently to be regarded as a great human religious leader, albeit in some way divinely endowed. No Unitarian group effected a permanent separation from the church to which it belonged until Theophilus Lindsey seceded from the Church of England in 1773 and set up his independent Unitarian chapel in 1774, devising a liturgy consonant with the doctrines accepted by Unitarians and based on the Arian teaching of Dr. Clarke.[1]

Towards the end of the eighteenth century the Unitarians were becoming a more powerful group, and they had notable influence in the academy at Warrington, where the word "rational" was used of their theology, and they used a "rational" liturgy.[2] Gilbert Wakefield taught here for a time, and though he never attached himself officially to any Unitarian congregation, it appears that they regarded him as a prominent supporter of their views.

The most important Unitarian at the turn of the century was Thomas Belsham (1750–1829), an Independent minister who had received his first training at Kibworth, and then at Daventry, where he was teaching when he resigned in 1789, feeling that he could no longer teach Trinitarianism. He went to the academy at Hackney, where Unitarianism was already strong and where Wakefield was teaching. In 1794 he became an official Unitarian minister, and in 1805 occupied Lindsey's pulpit at the Essex Street Chapel. Belsham wrote the *Memoirs of Theophilus Lindsey,* originally published in 1812 and republished in 1873.[3]

Our immediate concern with Belsham is his connection with the production of an official Unitarian Version. It appears that Belsham was the principal editor, although the work itself is anonymous. The Preface

[1] See above, pp. 526 ff.

[2] Cf. *Cambridge History of English Literature,* X, 385.

[3] The latter was called a "centenary edition"—the centenary of Lindsey's secession in 1773.

of the fifth edition, 1819, gives some account of the history of the version and a plain statement of Unitarian views. The Society for Promoting Christian Knowledge and the Practice of Virtue had been formed by Unitarians to publish Unitarian literature and to spread "pure and practical" Christianity. This society intended to produce a text of the New Testament "divesting the sacred volume of the technical phrases of a systematic theology which has no foundation in the Scriptures themselves." In 1791 the society approached Dr. Wakefield with a view to securing his permission to print his text (issued in that year) as their own. Dr. Wakefield, who had much sympathy for the Unitarians, agreed most readily, but some obstacle connected with the publishing rights prevented the realization of this plan. When the matter was taken up again a few years later, an "unfortunate event"—presumably Dr. Wakefield's imprisonment from 1799 to 1801—and his subsequent death in 1801 compelled the society to abandon the idea of having Wakefield's text. In 1806 they finally decided to adopt Newcome's text as the basis of their version, which appeared in 1808 as *The New Testament in an Improved Version, upon the basis of Archbishop Newcome's New Translation; with a corrected text.* It was decided to place at the foot of the page the reading of the Authorized Version where it differs, but this practice was abandoned in the fourth and fifth editions. In fact the text is not notably altered. It was apparently known at the time that the edition was Belsham's work, for Dr. Stock, bishop of Killala and Achonry, a relative of Dr. Newcome (who had died in 1800), addressed an indignant expostulation to him in 1809 for having without any warrant adapted Dr. Newcome's text for his own sectarian purposes. But the "Improved Version" had several further editions, the fifth being in 1819, a copy of which has "Unitarian Version" on the back.[4]

In 1822 Thomas Belsham published under his own name an edition of *The Epistles of Paul the Apostle, translated with exposition and notes.*

Ten years later another version of the Epistles by a Unitarian appeared in two volumes: *St. Paul's Epistles illustrated; including a new translation,* by Charles Eyre, Clerk. Ipswich, 1832. Charles Eyre (1784–1864) was a somewhat eccentric person. A graduate of Trinity College, Cam-

[4] This title did not appear on the first editions, since until its repeal in 1813, the Act of 1698, forbidding anti-Trinitarian teaching as blasphemous, prevented the overt dissemination of Unitarian doctrines. For further details of this version see "Belsham" and "Newcome" in the *Dictionary of National Biography*.

bridge, he took orders, but later became a Unitarian. He then took to journalism and became the proprietor of three newspapers at Colchester. He was interested in the movement that led to the Reform Bill of 1832. He later took to farming near Dedham in Essex, but when his family pressed him to give up farming, he committed suicide. His translation is mentioned by Cotton and the *Dictionary of National Biography*.[5]

The next Unitarian biblical work appeared in the next decade with the important work of Samuel Sharpe (1799–1881), who was a banker until his retirement in 1861. He became a Unitarian in 1821 and remained a keen member of that group all his life. He had a passionate interest in Egyptology, and published his first work on this subject in 1836, the first of twenty works on Egypt and its history and literature, including an important *Vocabulary of Egyptian Hieroglyphics*. His studies also included other oriental subjects. Shortly after his first work on Egyptology had been published, he turned his attention to the translation of the Bible. In 1840 he published his *New Testament, translated from the Greek of J. J. Griesbach,* which was the second text to be based on that edition of the Greek. It is, in fact, a revision of the Authorized Version according to the critical text of the Greek; he expressly states that he will alter the Authorized Version as little as possible. In 1865 he brought out in three volumes his *Hebrew Scriptures translated,* which was a revision of the Authorized Version of the Old Testament. His New Testament had eight editions, and his Old Testament four editions, the last published in 1881. He continually worked over his text, and the various editions show small alterations and improvements. "As a translator he was distinguished less by originality of scholarship than by excellence of judgment; he is successful beyond others in the difficult experiment of removing the archaisms without impairing the venerable dignity of the English Bible." [6] He held that Hebrew should be read and studied without points, and wrote a grammar on this system in 1877.

Sharpe is of special interest to us for his connection with the Revised Version. The New Testament Company for the production of the Revised Version was to include one Unitarian, as it also included three Presbyterians, one Congregationalist, one Baptist, and one Methodist. Convocation in 1870 invited four Unitarian scholars to select a member

[5] *Ibid.*, VI, 962.
[6] Alexander Gordon in *ibid.*, XVII, 1364.

of their denomination to take part in the work, and Sharpe was one of the four scholars thus invited.[7]

ORIGINAL VERSIONS LISTED BY DR. COTTON

For the following versions I have been unable to find any other evidence than the notice in Cotton's *List of Editions of the Bible and Parts Thereof in English* (1852). It is interesting to note that the first and the last of these versions are translations of the Septuagint Old Testament. Cotton points out that the edition of 1808 appears to be the first such translation into English.

The Old Testament translated from the LXX Version, the New Testament from the original Greek, by Charles Thomson, Philadelphia, 1808.

The New Testament, a modern, correct and close Translation, arranged in order of time, with notes, London, 1812. The translation is anonymous, but is attributed by Cotton to W. Williams. It would seem that this was the first occasion when a strictly chronological order of the books was presented, a method frequently followed in twentieth-century editions. The epithets "modern, correct and close" are also noteworthy.

The New Testament, translated from the Greek, and the four Gospels arranged in harmony, by William Thomson, Kilmarnock, 1816. Dr. Cotton observes that in the Preface it is noted that the translation is made "as literal as possible."

The Holy Bible, an improved version, with notes and reflections, by Benjamin Boothroyd, 1817. Boothroyd (1768–1836) was an Independent minister who lived at Pontefract, where he also opened a bookshop. He was a Hebrew scholar and printed a Hebrew Bible during the years 1810–13 at his own printing press. His English version he also printed at his own press at Pontefract.[8] A second edition was printed in 1824.

The Holy Bible, Hebrew and English, the English a new translation, with notes, by A. Alexander, 1822. Cotton notes the publication of volume one of *The Holy Bible, a revision of the Authorized Version, with notes,* by William Alexander, at York, and questions whether this is to be identified with a Pentateuch issued by William Alexander about 1835;

[7] Cf. *ibid.* and the following chapter.

[8] Cf. the *Dictionary of National Biography,* II, 854.

Cotton also believes that William Alexander was a Quaker. The relationship between these texts is not clear.

In 1828 appeared an anonymous edition, *The Gospel of God's Anointed, the Glory of Israel; being a recent version of the Greek Scriptures (commonly called the New Testament).*

In 1832 appeared *The Revelation of Jesus Christ; newly translated from the original Greek; with a plain reading, divesting it of all its metaphors,* Part I, by George Pilkington.

The Old Testament in the LXX Version according to Codex Vaticanus, translated by Sir Lancelot Brenton, Bt., appeared in 1844.

OTHER ORIGINAL VERSIONS OF THE NINETEENTH CENTURY

The first three of the following editions are listed by Cotton, but the remainder appeared after his time. All these editions are in the University Library at Cambridge. This section does not include those versions which set out to be merely revisions of the Authorized Version; these are listed separately. Most of these translations are characterized by their literalness, except Barlee's, which is professedly free, and Turnbull's, which approaches modern prose in its style.

In 1833 Rodolphus Dickinson published at Boston, U.S.A., *A New and Corrected Version of the New Testament.* The work is a deliberate revolt against the "quaint monotony and affected solemnity" of the Authorized Version, with its "frequent rude and occasionally barbarous attire"; and the translator sets out to adorn the Scriptures with "a splendid and sweetly flowing diction" suited to the use of "accomplished and refined persons." Dean Luther A. Weigle, in quoting the above passages from Dickinson's Preface, refers to that document as "an astonishing exhibition of conceit." [9] The style belongs more to the eighteenth century and is reminiscent of Harwood's version, though by no means so periphrastic. An interesting feature is the use of "you" for the second person singular. Dickinson's is among the first "private versions" to be produced in America.

A free and explanatory version of the Epistles, by Edward Barlee, rector of Worlingworth in Suffolk, was published in 1837. The general style is that of the Authorized Version, and brackets are used for the periphrastic inserts and explanatory phrases, as in the eighteenth-century

[9] *The English New Testament from Tyndale to the Revised Standard Version,* p. 84.

paraphrases. It seems that Barlee's version is the last in which this type of translation was used.

In 1839 *A literal translation of the Apostolical Epistles and Revelation, with a concurrent commentary,* by W. H., was published in London. Cotton evidently did not know the identity of the author, but the *Dictionary of National Biography* and the Cambridge University Library catalogue identify him with William Heberden (1767–1845), a well-known London doctor who in 1809 became physician in ordinary to George III. In 1812, after the death of his wife, he abandoned his medical practice, except his attendance on the king at Windsor, and retired to Datchet, near Windsor, where he began to occupy himself with the education of his nine children and with classical and biblical studies, producing this translation and other works.

The Epistles of St. Paul, an original translation, with critical notes and introduction, by Joseph Turnbull, was published in London in 1854 for the Anglo-Biblical Association. Another edition appeared in 1858, including Revelation, with the words "from the Greek" inserted into the title. This version uses the style of a more modern prose, although the diction is still biblical English.

The year 1854 also saw the first publication, in London, of Herman Heinfetter: *A literal translation of the last eight books of the New Testament* (i.e., the catholic epistles and Revelation). He also brought out *An English Version of the New Testament from the text of the Vatican Manuscript,* a sixth edition of which appeared in 1864. In 1865 he began his great project of translating the Bible; but the work did not get beyond Genesis. The name appears to be a pseudonym, for the Cambridge University Library catalogue, on the entry for the 1865 edition of Genesis, adds to the name Herman Heinfetter: "[= F. Parker]"; but the identity of F. Parker cannot be traced either. The translation is very literal in character.

What is probably the most literal translation ever made is the Bible of Robert Young (1822–88), first published in 1862. The title page reads: *The Holy Bible . . . translated according to the letter and idiom of the original languages;* on the back of the 1929 edition is written: "Young's Literal Translation of the Bible." It is significant that Young's claim to fame is his magnificent *Analytical Concordance to the Bible* (A.V.), first published in 1879, in which every word is traced to its Hebrew and

Greek equivalent. Young's supreme interest in every word was undoubtedly with him when he produced his translation. He was by profession a bookseller, but he had carefully studied Hebrew and Oriental languages. Yet his notions about the Hebrew tongue were vitiated by an eccentric idea of the use of tenses in that language.[10] This defect, combined with his extremely literal approach, produced a queer effect, and two examples may be given to show what is probably the limit of literal translation:

> And it cometh to pass, after these things—the butler of the king of Egypt and the baker have sinned against their lord, the king of Egypt; and Pharaoh is wroth against his two eunuchs, against the chief of the butlers, and against the chief of the bakers, and giveth them in charge in the house of the chief of the executioners, the place where Joseph is a prisoner, and the chief of the executioners chargeth Joseph with them, and he serveth them; and they are days in charge. (Gen. 40:1–4.)
>
> Then shall the reign of the heavens be likened to ten virgins, who, having taken their lamps, went forth to meet the bridegroom; and five of them were prudent, and five foolish; they who were foolish, having taken their lamps, did not take with themselves oil. (Matt. 25:1–4.)

During the nineteenth century there was an increasing interest in the Greek text itself, and we have already noticed two translators (Newcome, 1796, and Sharpe, 1840) who based their work on Griesbach's critical text of 1774–75. Several new critical editions of the Greek Testament appeared during the middle of the nineteenth century, and those used by our translators were those of Lachmann (Berlin, 1831), Tischendorf (Leipzig, 1841; but the most important edition was that of 1864–72), Alford (London, 1844–57; but the edition of 1871 is important), and Tregelles (London, 1857–74).

In 1863 Rev. G. W. Brameld, vicar of East Markham, produced an edition of *The Gospels, translated from the original Greek,* in which, as he tells us, "the spurious passages are expunged; the doubtful bracketed; and the whole revised after the texts of Griesbach, Lachmann, Tischendorf, Alford and Tregelles."

In 1870 *The New Testament, translated from the purest Greek,* by J. Bowes, appeared at Dundee. John Bowes (1804–74) was a Primitive Methodist minister who in 1830 renounced all party affiliations and started a completely independent mission at Dundee.

[10] According to Young, the construction with waw consecutive is a fiction, and all imperfects, even with waw consecutive, are to be translated by the present tense in English.

Dr. Samuel Davidson (1806–99), who was a distinguished Presbyterian scholar, published in 1875 *The New Testament, translated from the critical text of Von Tischendorf.* In 1857 he had been forced to resign from Lancashire Independent College, Manchester, on account of his unorthodox views on the text of the Old Testament.

J. B. Rotherham produced his *New Testament, translated from the text of Tregelles* for the purpose of making what he termed an "emphatic text," in which an elaborate system of underlining (including double and triple underlining), pointing, and pausing was used to indicate suitable inflections of the voice in reading. This edition was published first in 1872, and again in 1878; *The Emphatic Bible* came out in four volumes during the years 1897–1902. Rotherham's interest was rather that of an elocutionist than that of a translator.

The Greek Testament englished, by William Burton Crickmer, curate at Beverley Minster, published in 1881, also served a particular purpose: that of using certain printing devices whereby an exact transference of the Greek words and phrases might be seen in the English text.

TWO MODERN-SPEECH VERSIONS

In the middle of the nineteenth century we find two private versions made in America which were the immediate precursors of the modern-speech versions so common in the twentieth century, the first of which,—that of Ferrar Fenton—though begun in 1883, was not completed until 1903, and is consequently considered in a later chapter.

In 1855 *The Gospels, a new translation,* by Andrew Norton, was published in Boston, employing a contemporary idiom, including "you" in place of "thou," apparently for the first time in biblical translation. All archaisms are excluded, and the style is that of sober nineteenth-century prose.

The other modern-speech text is a version of the entire New Testament: *The New Testament, translated from the original Greek with chronological arrangement of books,* by Leicester Ambrose Sawyer, Boston, 1858. This text also adopts a modern style except in the language of prayer, when "thou" and the familiar archaisms are used. This device was followed by *The Twentieth Century New Testament,* Moffatt, and others.

These two versions, 1855 and 1858, are little known; yet they mark the beginning of the long line of present versions which use current English as the medium of expression.

REVISIONS OF THE AUTHORIZED VERSION

Up to the time of the appearance of the official Revised Version, 1881–85, a number of private attempts were made to revise the text of the Authorized Version. The present section lists these revisions and leads directly to the important work of the Revised Version.

The first is the work of the famous lexicographer, Noah Webster, the original author of Webster's *American Dictionary* (1806), which in its modern form still goes by his name. In 1833 he published *The Holy Bible, containing the Old and New Testaments, in the Common Version, with Amendments of the language.* Weigle writes: "As was to be expected of a dictionary maker, Webster began with an Introduction in which he carefully listed and explained the alterations he had made in the English text of the Authorised Version. There were some one hundred and fifty words and phrases which he found to be erroneous or misleading, and which he corrected in the various passages where they appeared. Practically all of these have been changed by later revisers also, who found his judgment sound as to the need of change, and in most cases accepted the corrections he proposed" (p. 88). It is therefore perhaps legitimate to conjecture that the scholars who produced the Revised Version, or at least its American equivalent, made use of Webster's work.

The Four Gospels: specimens of a proposed translation of the received Greek text, on the basis of the Authorized Version, London, 1834, is attributed by Cotton to Rev. J. G. Tolley; but apart from Cotton's entry, I have found no further information about it.

In 1836–37 Granville Penn, of Oxford, published *The Book of the New Covenant, being a critical revision of the text and translation of English version of the New Testament, with annotations.* Penn was the author of many translations from the Greek classics.

Samuel Sharpe's translation of 1840 we have already noticed. It was, in fact, a revision of the Authorized Version according to Griesbach's text.

For the same year, 1840, Cotton lists *The New Testament, revised from the Authorized Version with the aid of other translations, and made conformable to the Greek text of J. J. Griesbach, by a layman.* Cotton identifies this layman as Edgar Taylor (1793–1839), a Dissenter, the son of John Taylor, who had taught at Warrington. What translations Mr. Taylor used cannot be ascertained. This work appeared posthumously.

Another curious entry of Dr. Cotton is that for the year 1841: an edition of the Authorized Version with nearly 20,000 emendations. This work is attributed to a certain Dr. Conquest, who might have been the famous medical doctor of that name.

In 1844–45 appeared *The Holy Bible . . . with a brief hermeneutic and exegetical commentary and Revised Version,* by Rev. T. J. Hussey, rector of Hayes in Kent. This edition prints the Authorized Version in parallel columns with the revision, which, in fact, is not very extensive.

A Revised Translation of the New Testament, by the Rev. H. Highton, fellow of Queen's College, Oxford, and principal of Cheltenham College, is in fact no more than a revised text of the Authorized Version, retaining even many characteristic details of printing in the latter version. It was published in 1862.

Rev. Robert Ainslie, of Brighton, in 1869 published a pocket edition of *The New Testament, translated from the Greek text of Tischendorf.* This text follows the Authorized Version except when Tischendorf's text departs from it.

In 1869, a year before Convocation started the negotiations which resulted in the Revised Version, one of the staunch advocates of revision and later a member of the New Testament Company, Henry Alford, published his own work: *The New Testament, newly compared with the original Greek, and revised*, London. Alford had completed his own critical edition of the Greek text, and he had contributed to the symposium, *Revision of the Authorized Version, by Five Clergymen,* and to the translation that they made of St. John's Gospel and some of the epistles between 1856 and 1863.[11] Dean Alford's work is thus a direct preparation for the Revised Version itself.

While the Revised Version was in the course of production (1870–85), the ten volumes of *The Speaker's Commentary* appeared under the editorship of Canon F. C. Cook, during the years 1871–81. Thus the work was concluded the very year that the New Testament in the Revised Version appeared. The work contained a commentary and a revision of

[11] See the following chapter.

the text of the Authorized Version. Canon Cook (1810–89) was a distinguished scholar from Cambridge, and since 1864 a canon of Exeter. It is well known that he was strongly opposed to certain principles adopted by the revisers who produced the Revised Version, the production and merits or demerits of which are discussed in the following three chapters. *The Speaker's Commentary,* therefore, represents another approach to the problem of revision, and as such merits a special place in the history of the English Bible.

The last revision of the Authorized Version that preceded the appearance of the Revised Version is *The New Testament, a new translation on the basis of the Authorized Version,* by John Brown McClellan, vicar of Bottisham, near Cambridge. This work appeared in 1875.

PRIVATE VERSIONS AT THE END OF THE CENTURY

Contemporary with and after the publication of the Revised Version, other editions continued to appear. Some of these are deliberate attempts to improve upon the Revised Version, while others are independent of that version. Among the latter is an original translation of the Old Testament by Mrs. Helen Spurrell, which was published in London the very year that the complete Revised Version appeared (1885). Mrs. Spurrell was a remarkable old lady. Already talented in music, painting, and sculpture, she applied herself to the study of Hebrew when she was past fifty years old. She translated from the unpointed Hebrew text, as Samuel Sharpe had done in 1865, and she made free use of the Samaritan Pentateuch and the Septuagint version, substituting their readings for that of the Hebrew text in a number of passages. In her Preface she acknowledges her debt to Benjamin Boothroyd's work on the Hebrew text, whose Hebrew Bible, printed at his own press in 1810–13, she had used. She printed her text in paragraphs, not in verses, with the poetical passages laid out as poetry—devices that had just been adopted in the Revised Version. She was among the first to use "Jehovah" for the name of God in the Old Testament.

Ferrar Fenton's modern-speech version of the Bible, which began to appear in 1883, and *The Twentieth Century New Testament,* another modern-speech version, which came out in three parts beginning in 1898, were not completed until 1903 and 1901 respectively, and are therefore studied in greater detail in the last chapter of this book. Ernest Bilton's modern-speech version of the Gospels, 1888, is also described with the other modern-speech versions.

Mention should here be made of the new translation into biblical English of those books of the Old Testament which appeared in the Polychrome Bible of Paul Haupt in 1898–99.[12]

Dr. Moffatt's *Historical New Testament* of 1901 is an independent translation using biblical English, but it is noticed together with his other work in chapter 48.

[12] The Polychrome Bible, in which Leviticus, Josue, Judges, Isaias, and Ezechiel appeared in English, shows by means of tinting the paper how, according to a documentary hypothesis, the various parts of the book are to be ascribed to various authors or documents. It has sometimes been nicknamed the "Rainbow Bible." Several books of the Old Testament had already been published with the Hebrew text thus printed on variously colored backgrounds.

CHAPTER XLIV

The Revision of the Authorized Version, 1870-85

EARLY INTEREST IN EXISTING TRANSLATIONS

A PETITION addressed to Parliament in 1393 demanding "the annulling of the Bible that time translated into English, and also other books of the Gospel translated into English" (the Wycliffite versions) [1] shows the anxiety the English have always shown concerning the accuracy of vernacular versions of the Bible. The same feeling betrayed itself some two hundred years later, for among the Additional MSS. in the British Museum is a draft of the time of Elizabeth entitled: "An Act for the reducinge of diversities of Bibles now extant in the Englishe tongue to one settled vulgar translation: to compel students of both Universities to assist in the work for avoydinge of the multiplicitie of errors, that are rashly conceaved by the inferiour and vulgar sorte by the varietie of the translacions of Bibles, to the most dangerous increase of Papistrie and Atheisme." [2]

Nearly one hundred years later, a petition was presented to the Long Parliament asking for "a new English translation of the Bible out of the original tongues" (January, 1663). This petition was referred to a committee, which had among its members Brian Walton, editor of the *London Polyglot*. But as the terms of their commission allowed the committee only "to consider the translations and impressions of the Bible," there could be no question of their producing a fresh version.[3]

[1] Deanesly, *The Lollard Bible and Other Medieval Biblical Versions*, p. 282 note.

[2] Pollard, *Records of the English Bible*, pp. 329–31; British Museum, *Guide* to the Biblical Exhibition, 1911.

[3] Hoare, *The Evolution of the English Bible*, p. 247. Fuller (*The Church History of Britain*, II, 868, 878) says that at the Savoy Conference in 1661, the Nonconformists com-

DEMAND FOR THE REVISION OF THE AUTHORIZED VERSION

There matters stood until the opening of the nineteenth century, when there began a definite movement in favor of a revision of the Authorized Version. Yet even then protesting voices were heard, for the idea of tampering with a version already about two hundred years old and endeared to many generations naturally proved repugnant.[4]

One of the earliest publications in support of revision was *Revision of the Authorized Version, by Five Clergymen:* Dr. Barrow, principal of St. Edmund Hall, Oxford; Henry Alford, afterwards dean of Westminster; W. G. Humphry, rector of St. Martin's in the Fields; C. J. Ellicott, afterwards bishop of Gloucester; and Dr. Moberly. Between 1856 and 1863 these five scholars translated the Gospel of St. John and some of the Pauline epistles.[5]

On the other side, S. C. Malan argued energetically,[6] while Archbishop Trench pleaded against any undue haste.[7] But an investigation of the state of the text by E. H. Plumptre in Smith's *Dictionary of the Bible,*[8] came at an opportune moment, for he showed that revision had become an urgent necessity. The matter was then enthusiastically taken up by such scholars as Lightfoot, Hort, Newth, Ellicott, and others,[9] some of them afterwards members of the Revision Companies.

THE COMPANIES FOR REVISION

The Convocation of Canterbury in February, 1870, approved the formation of a Commission for Revision, and the report of this com-

plained of bad translations in the liturgical services; e.g., in that for the first Sunday after Epiphany, "Are ye changed in your shape?" (Rom. 12:2), and in that for the first Sunday after Easter, "found in his appeal [for "apparel"] as a man" (Phil. 2:8).

[4] *A Vindication of our Authorised Translation and Translators of the Bible* (against Bellamy on Genesis and Burges' arguments for a fresh translation), 2nd ed., 1819.

[5] See the *Times,* May 18, 1935, for an interesting account of the minute-book they kept.

[6] *A Vindication of the Authorised Version, from charges brought against it by recent writers,* 1856. Malan returned to the charge in 1869 with *A Plea for the Received Greek Text and for the Authorised Version of the New Testament.*

[7] *On the Authorized Version of the New Testament, in connection with some recent proposals for its revision,* 1858, 1859. Cf. W. Selwyn, *Notes on the Proposed Amendment of the Authorized Version,* 1856.

[8] III, xiii, 1680–83.

[9] Lightfoot, *On a Fresh Revision of the English New Testament,* 3rd ed., 1891; Hort, *Final Suggestions on the Revised Version of Acts to Revelation,* 1879; Newth, *Lectures on Bible Revision,* 1881; Ellicott, *Considerations on the Revision of the English Version of the New Testament,* 1870; Scrivener, *Six Lectures on the Text of the New Testament,* 1875.

mittee, presented in May, was adopted. Shortly afterwards two companies were formed, one for the revision of the Authorized Version of the Old Testament, the other for the revision of the New Testament. In the Old Testament Company were five bishops,—among them Wordsworth of Lincoln—F. Field, J. S. Perowne, W. Aldis Wright, A. B. Davidson with two other Presbyterians, two Baptists, and one Congregationalist. In 1881 were added: R. L. Bensley, J. R. Lumby, and W. Wright (Cambridge), T K. Cheyne, S. R. Driver, and A. H. Sayce (Oxford), one Wesleyan, and four representatives of the Scottish churches, among them W Robertson Smith from Aberdeen. The New Testament Company of seventeen was predominantly Anglican, including Bishop Ellicott, Deans Alford and Stanley, A. J. Hort, B. H. Kennedy, J. B. Lightfoot, F. H. Scrivener, R. C. Trench, C. J. Vaughan, and B. F. Westcott. But there were also three Presbyterians, one Baptist, one Congregationalist, one Methodist, and one Unitarian, whose inclusion—especially his admission to the Sacrament—met with angry but unavailing protest and appeal.[10]

The rules laid down (a) that there should be marginal readings and emendations; (b) that there should be no question of a fresh translation; (c) that necessary alterations from the text of the Authorized Version should be couched in the style of that version; (d) that competent scholars, "to whatever nation or religious body they may belong," should be invited to cooperate.[11] As for the procedure to be adopted: (a) each

[10] *Protest against the Communion of an Unitarian in Westminster Abbey on June 22nd. 1870,* signed by thousands of clergymen; Burgon, *The Revision Revised,* p. 507; *idem, An Unitarian Reviser of Our Authorized Version, Intolerable,* 1872.

[11] Among those thus invited were Dr Newman and Dr. Pusey. On May 28, 1870, Dr. Ellicott wrote to the former, enclosing the resolutions and rules adopted at the first meeting of the Committee: "My dear Sir: I am requested by the Chairman and Committee to forward to you the enclosed and to express to you the very sincere hope that you may feel able to join us. Very faithfully yours, C. J. Ellicott, Glouc. and Bristol."

The draft of Newman's reply runs: "My dear Lord: I feel the high compliment which the Chairman and Committee appointed for the revision of the Authorized Version of the Holy Scripture have done me in asking my cooperation in their work, but while I thank them for it, I must beg them to allow me to decline it. I might assign many serious reasons for my so doing; however, they will perhaps consider it sufficient if I say I have never employed myself on a critical study of the sacred text and in consequence feel myself unfitted to take part in labours to which such study is a necessary preliminary."

To this Dr. Ellicott replied on June 2: "My dear Sir, I cannot leave your most kind reply to my note unanswered. We all feel the friendly kindness of your reply, and regret all the more that we shall not have you with us. I venture to think that you will not feel sorry to hear that the undertaking thus far seems prospered. We have sustained two great losses,—yourself and Dr. Pusey (who wishes to have more time to finish his own

company was to revise its work twice; (b) only changes supported by decidedly preponderating evidence were to be adopted, and, if based on a Greek text differing from that underlying the Authorized Version, the alteration was to be indicated in the margin; (c) changes proposed during the second revision were not to be accepted unless supported by a two-thirds majority; (d) to secure uniformity, the completed work of each company was to be communicated to the other.

The average attendance of the members of the New Testament Company was sixteen,[12] and Dr. Newth thus describes the procedure: "When it was question of textual changes [in the Greek text underlying the A.V.], the duty of stating this evidence by tacit consent devolved on two members of the Company who, from their previous studies are especially entitled to speak with authority—Dr. Scrivener and Dr. Hort. The former gives his judgment, Dr. Hort following and adding any additional matters, stating, if necessary, why he dissents from Dr. Scrivener. After discussion, the vote is taken and the Text is thus settled."[13]

THE GREEK TEXT UNDERLYING THE NEW TESTAMENT

The task of the Revisers was to produce a more accurate version than the Authorized: (a) by correcting misrenderings of the Greek, if any; (b) by basing their revision on what they felt to be a better Greek text than that used in 1611. This did not of course involve the construction of a revised Greek text. Indeed, apropos of the instructions received regarding the Greek text,—instructions which spoke of "the removal of plain and clear errors, whether in the Greek Text originally adopted by the Translators, or in the Translation (A.V.) made from the same"—Dr. Ellicott, the chairman, had said at an early stage in the proceedings: "We

great works). Nearly the whole of the rest have joined: some with very hearty expressions. Permit me to conclude with renewed thanks to you for your friendly words, and with every hearty good wish to remain

Very faithfully yours,
C. J. Ellicott, Glouc. and Bristol."

(These letters were kindly communicated to me by Father Henry Tristram, the Oratory, Edgbaston, Birmingham.)

[12] Ellicott and Palmer, *The Revisers and the Greek Text of the New Testament,* pp. 29 f.

[13] *Op. cit.,* pp. 119 f. Some account of the preliminary arrangements and of the formation of the Revision Companies is given by Westcott, *A General View of the History of the English Bible,* Appendix IX, pp. 320–32.

may be satisfied with the attempt to correct plain and clear errors: but there it is our duty to stop."[14]

Yet the Revisers naturally felt that it was their duty to enable readers to see what changes they had felt justified in making in the current Greek text. Hence the rule that "when the text adopted differs from that from which the Authorized Version was made, the alteration be indicated in the margin." But finding that to do so would encumber the margin, the Revisers drew up a list of readings adopted by them but which were at variance with the Greek "presumed to underlie the Authorized Version." The Cambridge University Press therefore published, under the editorship of Dr. Scrivener, an edition of the Greek Testament[15] in which they "judged it best to set the reading actually adopted by the Revisers at the foot of the page, and to keep the continuous text consistent throughout by making it so far as was possible uniformly representative of the Authorized Version."

The first step was to make sure what Greek text the revisers in 1611 had at their disposal. All agreed "that Beza's fifth and last text of 1598 was more likely than any other to have been in the hands of King James's revisers, and to be accepted by them as the best standard within their reach." By printing Beza's text, then, Dr. Scrivener enables the reader to see at once what was, presumably, the Greek text at the back of the Authorized Version; by giving in footnotes the improvements on that text which the Revisers felt to be justified by textual criticism, he enables the reader to see to what extent the Revised Version presupposed a Greek text varying from the text used in 1611.[16]

[14] *Chronicle of Convocation,* February, 1870, p. 83; cf. Burgon, *The Revision Revised,* pp. 399 f. "Would it be well for the Revisers to agree on a Critical Greek Text? To this question we venture to answer unhesitatingly in the negative. . . . Though we have much critical material, and a very fair amount of critical knowledge, we have certainly not yet acquired sufficient critical judgement for any body of revisers hopefully to undertake such a work as this. . . . No revision in the present day could hope to meet with an hour's acceptance if it failed to preserve the tone, rhythm, and diction of the present Authorized Version" (Ellicott, *op. cit.,* pp. 44, 99); cf. Burgon, *op. cit.,* pp. 369, 509.

[15] *The New Testament in the Original Greek, according to the text followed in the Authorized Version, together with the variations adopted in the Revised Version,* 1881. Dr. Westcott (Preface to *A General View of the History of the English Bible,* p. ix), Dr. Trench (*On the Authorized Version of the New Testament,* p. 3), and Dr. Ellicott himself (Preface to the *Pastoral Epistles* [1861], p. xiv), had all declared that any attempt to revise the Greek text was inopportune.

[16] Among the countless editions of the Greek Testament, the following will prove useful in this respect:

THE GREEK TEXT BY WESTCOTT AND HORT

Since the expressed purpose of the Revisers was to correct the Authorized Version, some agreement was necessary as to the most correct text of the Greek Testament. This was at once provided by Westcott and Hort, who had for twenty-five years been working on the question. Although previous to the discussions over the Greek text to be followed, Dr. Ellicott, the chairman, had stoutly maintained that it was no part of the duty of the New Testament Company to frame a new critical edition of the Greek Testament, that is precisely what was done, and their revision of the Authorized Version was almost wholly based on the fresh edition of the Greek Testament prepared by Westcott and Hort. Their elaborate theory, by which they reconstructed their text, may be thus summarized:

a) They maintained that the works of Origen showed the existence in the third century of three types of text which they labeled *Western, Alexandrian,* and *Neutral.*

b) The wide and early variants—additions, omissions, transpositions, and paraphrasings—in *Codex Bezae,* and in some Old Latin and Old Syriac versions, must be regarded as due to a *Western* type of text prevalent in ante-Nicene times.[17]

The Greek Testament, with the readings adopted by the Revisers of the Authorized Version, ed. by E. Palmer, Oxford, 1881. In addition to the marginal renderings of the Revisers, the variations of the *textus receptus,* the basis of the Authorized Version, are given.

The Parallel New Testament, Greek and English, being the Authorised Version set forth in 1611 arranged in parallel columns with the Revised Version of 1881 and with the Greek Text followed in the Revised Version, to which are added the readings followed in the Authorised Version and the readings noted in the margin of the Revised Version, ed. by Scrivener (?), Oxford, 1882.

The Resultant Greek Testament, ed. by R. Weymouth, 1886; 3rd ed., 1905; this is the basis of his *New Testament in Modern Speech,* 1903; 7th ed., 1938.

The Revisers' Greek Testament. A critical examination of certain readings, textual and marginal, in the original Greek of the New Testament adopted by the late Anglo-American revisers, ed. by S. W. Whitney, 1892, 2 vols.

Novum Testamentum Graece. Textui a retractoribus Anglis adhibito brevem adnotationem criticam subjecit Alexander Souter, 1910.

A very convenient edition is *The Holy Bible: Two Version Edition; being the Authorized Version with the differences of the Revised Version printed in the margins,* Oxford, 1900.

The New Testament in the Original Greek, according to the text followed in the Authorized Version, together with the variations adopted in the Revised Version, ed. by Scrivener, 1881.

[17] Hort in his Introduction (vol. 2) to *The New Testament in the Original Greek,* pp. 120–23.

c) The many MSS. free from such features they group together as a *pre-Syrian* type of text, which, so they maintain, was twice drastically revised at Antioch between 250 and 350 A.D.; the Old Syriac text was revised at the same time, whence we have the Peshitta Syriac version.[18]

d) Readings due to this revised text, called *Syrian* or *Antiochian,* are to be disregarded.

e) A type of text witnessed to by Origen, St. Chrysostom, the Egyptian version, in *Codex Alexandrinus* of the Acts and Epistles, and in codices L, C, T, is termed *Alexandrian,* and though unaffected by the presumed Syrian revision, is yet not free from *Western* readings.[19]

f) A type of text free from pre-Syrian, Syrian, and Alexandrian readings they call *Neutral.* This is represented by codices א and B, and their witness is to be accepted owing to the antiquity of the archetype from which these MSS. were copied.[20]

It will be evident that this seductive theory rests in the final resort upon the supposed Antiochian revision, resulting, it is presumed, in the hitherto universally accepted Greek text commonly known as the *textus receptus.* But is such a revision a historical fact? "Of this twofold authoritative revision of the Greek text," says Scrivener, "of this formal transmutation of the Curetonian Syriac into the Peshitto, . . . although they must have been of necessity public acts of great Churches in ages abounding in Councils General or Provincial, not one trace remains in the history of Christian antiquity; no one writer seems conscious that any modification either of the Greek Scriptures or of the vernacular translation was made in or before his time." [21]

Now, if this supposed Antiochian revision resulting in the *textus receptus,* which retains all those great passages enumerated above, but which are absent in whole or in part from most if not all of the five great codices to which appeal is made, is a historical fact, that can only mean that by insisting on the retention of those passages, the great and learned Fathers from the patriarchates of Alexandria, Antioch, Constantinople, and Jerusalem officially condemned those very MSS. to which Westcott and Hort would have us pin our faith.[22]

18 *Ibid.,* pp. 84 f., 137.
19 *Ibid.,* p. 131.
20 *Ibid.,* pp. 223–25, 246.
21 *A Plain Introduction to the Criticism of the New Testament,* II, 287; cf. Burgon, *op. cit.,* pp. 284–96, 343, 392, 517.
22 *Ibid.,* pp. 277–81.

CHAPTER XLV

Westcott and Hort

Westcott and Hort claim a unique position for their so-called *Neutral* text. Speaking of its two principal representatives, ℵ and B, they say of the latter: "It is found to hold a unique position. Its text throughout is Pre-Syrian, perhaps purely Pre-Syrian"; they make the same claim for ℵ.

Every group containing both ℵ and B, is found, where internal evidence is tolerably unambiguous, to have an apparently more original text than every opposed group containing neither . . . ; the combination ℵ B is the constant element of those variable groups that are found to have habitually the best readings . . . ; the respective ancestries of ℵ and B must have diverged from a common parent extremely near the apostolic autographs; or, if their concordant readings were really derived from a single not remote MS., that MS. must itself have been of the very highest antiquity. . . .

[Every group of two MSS.] containing B is found to offer a large proportion of readings which on the closest scrutiny have the ring of genuineness. . . . The readings of B in ternary variations . . . are habitually those of the original text. . . . With certain limited exceptions the concordance of B and ℵ marks that residual portion of the text of their primitive archetype in which neither of the two ancestries had at any point adopted or originated a wrong reading. . . . This general immunity from substantive errors that can without room for doubt be recognized as errors in the common original of ℵ-B, in conjunction with its very high antiquity, provides in a multitude of places a safe criterion of genuineness, not to be distrusted except on very clear internal evidence. . . .

B must be regarded as having preserved not only a very ancient text, but a very pure line of a very ancient text, and that with comparatively small depravation. . . . On the other hand to take it as the sole authority except where it contains self-betraying errors . . . is an unwarrantable abandonment of criticism, and in our opinion inevitably leads to erroneous results.[1]

Now views such as these unquestionably involve in effect a repudiation of the Greek text current through the centuries. For they ask us to accept

[1] Hort, *op. cit.,* pp. 150 f., 210, 212, 220, 227, 241, 248, 225, 250 f. The last paragraph is quoted by Scrivener, *op. cit.,* Vol. II.

en bloc the evidence of but two MSS., ℵ and B, with occasionally that of a few others which sometimes agree with them, no matter how overwhelming the evidence against them from other sources. Even were it a matter of proved fact that the so-called *Neutral* text is the oldest witness we have,—and we must keep reminding ourselves that ℵ and B date only from the fourth century—their evidence could not outweigh that of the Traditional Text [2] unless the latter could be proved corrupt. It seems like "poisoning the wells" to claim without proof that this Traditional Text is the result of a revision, even a twofold revision, somewhere between 250 and 350 A.D.—a revision which can be called only a "dream." [3]

"No one," as Reich had said many years before, "has ever yet dreamed, nor, I hope, will ever dream of reducing the mighty volume of witnesses to the text to some three or four on whom the rest are presumed to depend; nor will any one, I trust, ever select from these innumerable witnesses some particular guides whose testimony is to be regarded as of such convincing value that the evidence of the rest can forthwith be discounted." [4] Yet this is precisely what has unluckily come to pass; as Canon Cook has declared: "By far the greater number of the innovations in R.V. are adopted on the authority of two MSS, or even of one MS, against the distinct testimony of all other MSS." [5]

THE CHARACTER OF MSS. ℵ AND B

Though Westcott and Hort are of course well aware of the many defects in ℵ and B, they hardly seem conscious of the exceedingly corrupt character of these two manuscripts. Dr. Westcott's own words, written, it is true, in a different context, seem peculiarly applicable to Dr. Hort's Introduction: "He who has long pondered over a train of Reasoning, becomes unable to detect its weak points." [6] We have to adopt some standard of comparison, and no other is available except the "received

[2] We cannot too often insist that by the "Traditional Text" is not meant the present *textus receptus,* which represents the Traditional Text defaced by the corruptions which have inevitably crept into it during the course of time, but that type of text witnessed to by "consentient Antiquity"; and that the sole test for the genuineness of a reading is its universal acceptance. Cf. Burgon, *op. cit.,* pp. 339, 342, 376 f., 387.

[3] *Ibid.,* pp. 121, 284–96, 517.

[4] Observations prefixed to his collations of MSS. in the Paris Library, 1847; cf. Burgon, *op. cit.,* p. 381 note.

[5] *The Revised Version of the First Three Gospels, considered in its bearing upon the record of Our Lord's words and of incidents in His life,* p. 227.

[6] *The Gospel of the Resurrection,* p. viii, quoted by Burgon, *op. cit.,* p. xiv.

text" (*textus receptus*), which, despite the corruptions which have crept in during the course of centuries, represents that Traditional Text which can be traced back to the earliest ages of the Church, and which is to be found in the vast mass of evidence at our disposal: manuscripts, versions, and the Fathers. Here are some tabulated results of such a comparison.

The *textus receptus* of St. Luke's Gospel contains 19,941 words; of these B omits 757, ℵ, 876, and D, 1,662. Of the 11,646 words in the *textus receptus* of St. Mark, B omits 762, ℵ, 870, and D, 900. Again, in the Gospels, B has 589 readings peculiar to itself, or 858 words in all; ℵ has 1,460 such readings, or 2,640 words. Once more, in the Gospels, B differs from the *textus receptus* in 2,370 places, ℵ in 3,392, D in 4,697, and has, moreover, 1,829 words not to be found in the *textus receptus*. In the Gospels, B omits 2,877 words, adds 536, substitutes 935; in other words, B differs from the *textus receptus* in 8,972 different places. Similarly D omits 3,704 words, adds 2,213, and substitutes 2,121; in fine, differs from the *textus receptus* in 13,281 places. How extensive are these variations in D may be gauged from the fact that in eight verses in St. Lukes Gospel (8:35–43) it has 93 readings peculiar to itself, 40 omissions, 4 additions, and 25 substitutions.[7]

Putting it in another way: B omits 330 phrases from St. Matthew's Gospel, or 648 words; 365 phrases, or 762 words, from Mark; 439 phrases, or 757 words, from Luke; 710 words from John. Similarly ℵ omits 808 words from Matthew, 870 from Mark, 876 from Luke, 961 from John. Even Tischendorf speaks of the *magna Scripturae vitiositas* of this MS. and adds that the corrector of B was especially careless. Nor is this all. For not only are these MSS. themselves corrupt, but they do not even agree among themselves. The five oldest manuscripts are, says Scrivener, "scarcely ever in unison; perpetually divided two against three, or perhaps four against one. All the readings these venerable monuments contain must of course be *ancient,* for they would not be found where they are; but they cannot all be true." [8] "These perpetual inconsistencies between

[7] These figures are by Burgon, in the *Quarterly Review,* October, 1881; see his *Revision Revised,* pp. 249, 319, 325; *idem, The Last Twelve Verses of the Gospel according to St. Mark,* p. 77 f. See also, Burgon and Miller, *The Traditional Text of the Holy Gospels Vindicated,* pp. 32, 78, 159; *idem, The Causes of the Corruption of the Traditional Text,* pp. 91, 97, 131. Even *Codex Alexandrinus* (A) and *Codex Ephraemi rescriptus* (C) are far from perfect (Burgon, *The Revision Revised,* p. 249); while the corrupt state of *Codex Bezae* (D) is notorious (*ibid.,* pp. 78, 249); cf. *idem, The Traditional Text of the Holy Gospels Vindicated,* pp. 172–95; Scrivener, *op. cit.,* I, 118.

[8] *Op. cit.,* II, 277. The five manuscripts referred to are codices ℵ, A, B, C, and D.

Codd. B and ℵ," says Burgon, "grave inconsistencies, and occasionally even gross ones, altogether destroy my confidence in them." [9]

As to the origin of codices ℵ and B we can only speculate. Yet certain historical facts have to be taken into account. We know, for instance, that Constantine wrote to Eusebius of Caesarea:

"I have thought it expedient to instruct your Prudence to order fifty copies of the sacred Scriptures . . . to be written on prepared parchment in a legible manner and in a convenient portable form, by professional transcribers thoroughly practised in their art. . . . Take special care that they be completed with as little delay as possible."

The Emperor's commands were followed by the immediate execution of the work itself, which we sent him in magnificently bound volumes of a threefold and fourfold form.[10]

It is highly probable that ℵ and B were among these fifty copies ordered by the Emperor. Now Eusebius was undoubtedly at least tainted with Arianism, a fact which renders his judgment suspicious where passages concerning the doctrine of the Holy Trinity are in question.[11] While there is not "the least cause to believe," as Scrivener says, "that Eusebius had either the power or the will to suppress or tamper with the great doctrinal texts, . . . yet we cannot deny that his prepossessions may have tempted him to arbitrary alterations in other passages, which had no direct bearing on the controversies of his age." [12] In a footnote he quotes Canon Cook: "I will not dwell upon indications of Arian tendencies. They are not such as we should be entitled to rely upon. . . . Eusebius was far more likely to adopt an explanation which coincided with his own system than to incur the risk of exposure and disgrace by obliterating or modifying them in manuscripts which would be always open to public inspection." [13]

But there are passages in ℵ and B which are a source of uneasiness; for example: "The only-begotten God" (John 1:18) stands in the text of Westcott and Hort, the traditional reading, "only begotten Son," being relegated to the margin; R.V. reverses the procedure. In John 1:34, where

[9] *The Last Twelve Verses of the Gospel according to St. Mark*, pp. 177 f.; cf. *idem, The Revision Revised*, p. 330; *idem, The Traditional text of the Holy Gospels Vindicated*, pp. 32 ff.

[10] *Vita Constantini*, IV, xxxvi–xxxviii.

[11] See Theodoret, *Hist. Eccles.*, I, 6; Sozomen, *Hist. Eccles.*, I, 5. For further details see the discussion by McGiffert, *Prolegomena* to his edition of Eusebius's *Church History* in the *Nicene and Post-Nicene Fathers*, Schaff and Wace, 1905, p. 11.

[12] *Op. cit.*, II, 267.

[13] *The Revised Version of the First Three Gospels*, p. 176.

their text has "the Son of God," but "the chosen one of God" in the margin, R.V. has "Son." "Who is in heaven" (John 3:13) is omitted from the text of Westcott and Hort, but stands in the margin; R.V. reverses the procedure. In Matt. 19:17 their text has, "Why askest thou me about good? One is good"; but A.V., "Why callest thou me good? There is none good but one, that is, God"; the Vulgate, *Quid me interrogas de bono? Unus est bonus, Deus* (cf. Mark 10:18; Luke 18:19). The reading accepted by Westcott and Hort would throw doubts on the consubstantiality of the Father and the Son, and R.V. accepts the text as in Westcott and Hort, consigning the traditional reading to the margin.[14] In short, in two of these four crucial passages, R.V. accepts a reading which is at least susceptible of an Arian construction.

For many centuries one of the greatest testimonies to the divinity of Christ has been Rom. 9:5: "Christ as concerning the flesh, who is over all things, God blessed for ever"; and so it stands in the text of R.V. But the margin, by suggesting different punctuation (due to commentators, not to the evidence of manuscripts, the Fathers, or other versions) contrives to minimize the force of this great dogmatic pronouncement.[15]

What has been said above is sufficient to show that the Revised Version is based almost wholly on the Greek text as edited by Westcott and Hort, which edition is in its turn based on the evidence of the five great uncial manuscripts, the so-called *Neutral* type of text, which, so it is claimed, was deliberately set aside by a supposititious revision made at two different times between 250 and 350 A.D. But apart from the purely conjectural character of that revision, it is beyond question that those five manuscripts are exceedingly corrupt and are probably of an Arian origin, and are in conflict with one another and with the immense mass of evidence from other sources.

THE ADOPTION OF WESCOTT AND HORT'S TEXT AND PRINCIPLES

The influence of the Greek text reconstructed by Westcott and Hort in the production of the Revised Version was undoubtedly very great,

[14] Cf. Scrivener, *op. cit.*, pp. 327–29. See also W. Morris, *The Revised and Arianized Versions of the English New Testament*, 1881; G. V. Smith, *Texts and Margins of the Revised New Testament Affecting Theological Doctrine*, in which (p. 47) he rejoices in the R.V. rendering, "in the Name," instead of "at the Name" (Phil. 2:10). Smith also opposes the reading "God" in I Tim. 3:16; cf. his *Bible and Popular Theology*, p. 39.

[15] Cf. Burgon, *The Revision Revised*, pp. 210–14; Routh terms this a *celebre effugium, quod ex falsa verborum constructione Critici quidam haereticis pararunt* (*Reliquiae Sacrae*, III, 322).

as we shall see; but, as Scrivener himself points out, it was "by no means a preponderating one, . . . as a comparison of their text with that adopted by the Revisionists might easily have shown." [16] Though the revisers of the Authorized Version cannot be accused of blind acceptance of the conclusions arrived at by the above highly qualified textual critics, yet we have only to look at the margin of the Revised Version to see that its framers rarely dissent from their masters.

Had this new version—for the title "revision" is really a misnomer—been intended solely for scholars, for people competent to estimate the evidence on which the Greek text presumed to be underlying it is based, no one could have complained. But unfortunately that evidence does not appear in the Revised Version, though Westcott and Hort do provide in their introductory volume detailed evidence for the type of Greek text they themselves preferred. How, then, did it come to pass that the Revisers came to acquiesce to the principles laid down by Westcott and Hort with the result that their Revised Version was in effect based almost wholly on the Greek text as reconstructed by these two great textual critics?

The average attendance of members at meetings of the New Testament Company was sixteen, and of these only four could be described as having first-hand knowledge of the textual problems involved, Bishop Wordsworth and Doctors Westcott, Hort, and Scrivener.[17] Westcott and Hort had for twenty-five years been engaged on the Greek text and had written an Introduction to their Greek text, the advance sheets of which they distributed to the members.[18] This Introduction, by Hort, is a master-

[16] *A Plain Introduction to the Criticism of the New Testament,* II, 285 note.

[17] *The Revisers and the Greek Text of the New Testament,* "by Two Members of the New Testament Company" (Ellicott and Palmer), pp. 29 f.

[18] *The New Testament in the Original Greek. The Text revised by B. F. Westcott and F. J. Hort.* Though this work appeared only in 1881, yet "a confidential copy had been entrusted to every member of the New Testament Company to guide them in their labours, under pledge that they should neither shew nor communicate its contents to any one else" (Burgon, *op. cit.,* p. 24; Hort in his Introduction to *The New Testament in the Original Greek,* p. 18). Dr. Ellicott emphatically denies that Hort's introductory volume was ever "privately communicated to the Revisers. . . . The 'New Greek text' is not based on the text of Westcott and Hort" (*op. cit.,* p. 29), though he adds that they "did indeed place instalments of their Greek text in the hands of each member, . . . to help, not to direct" (*ibid.,* p. 31). But at the same time he naively confesses that "the genealogical method [the pivot on which the whole of Hort's argument in his Introduction turns] was never formally adopted by the Revisers as a Company. But the facts on which that method rests were continually before the Company and had a great effect on its decisions" (*ibid.,* p. 34); in other words, the principles maintained in Hort's Introduction guided the Revisers.

piece of close reasoning and is bound to carry conviction, once certain premises are granted.[19] It led Dr. Ellicott, the chairman, to change his mind on the matter.[20] Even Dr. Scrivener, who was as experienced in matters of textual criticism as any of the other members,—perhaps even more so—was persistently overridden at all the meetings. "It is well known," says Burgon, "that Dr. Scrivener found himself perpetually outvoted by two thirds of those present." [21]

SUBSEQUENT INFLUENCE OF WESTCOTT AND HORT

The effect produced on some minds by Hort's *Introduction* is well illustrated in the *Saturday Review,* August 20, 1881, where the reviewer actually says: "Seeing that the Vatican manuscript does not contain one single passage that can be demonstrated to be spurious, or that by the evidence of other manuscripts and of the context, admits of just doubt as to its authenticity, a position that no other manuscript enjoys, a man is bound to accept the testimony of that manuscript alone, as his present text of the sacred record, wherever he possesses its teaching." [22] But to quote Dr. Scrivener once more: "There is little hope for the stability of their imposing structure, if its foundations have been laid on the sandy ground of ingenious conjecture: and since barely the smallest vestige of historical evidence has ever been alleged in support of the views of these accomplished editors, their teaching must either be received as intuitively true, or dismissed from our consideration as precarious, and even visionary." [23]

The Greek text reconstructed by Westcott and Hort, with the resulting English Revised Version, has so far come to be regarded in many quarters as the last word on the subject that many will regard adverse views as

[19] Namely, that the texts on which it is based are unassailable, and that the Antiochian revision which they postulate is a historical fact.

[20] Compare his words (quoted above) addressed to the committee before it began its work, with his attempted answer to Burgon's articles in the *Quarterly Review.* His change of attitude is not so remarkable when we reflect that though he had read much on the subject, he now came for the first time to the underlying problems involved and was carried away by the arguments of men who had made a life-long—though one-sided—study of the question. See Burgon's answer in *The Revision Revised,* pp. 368–520.

[21] *Ibid.,* pp. 231, 364, 414, 502; cf. also Canon Cook, *Revision of the New Testament.* On the other hand, Dr. Humphry says: "Each of us, times without number, has been outvoted by a 'tyrant majority'" (*A Word on the Revised Version,* p. 21).

[22] Quoted by Scrivener, *op. cit.,* II, 284.

[23] *Ibid.,* II, 285.

hopelessly out of date. But then, how many have actually read and analyzed Hort's Introduction, and then have done the same with Burgon's dissection of it? The latter seems to me unanswerable; Hort's familiarity with the textual evidence, great though it is, cannot compare with Burgon's comprehensive knowledge.[24]

Though I personally can pretend to no competence as a textual critic, I have studied, so far as I have been able, everything written on either side, and have, year by year, become more and more convinced that the position adopted by Westcott and Hort is unsound. Yet having written to an illustrious textual critic some years ago and saying that I was a convinced disciple of Burgon, Scrivener, Cook, and Miller, I received this reply: "I never dreamed that such a fossil existed! You really must grow out of it!" But in vain have I tried to defossilize myself.[25]

[24] Burgon, it should be remembered, had spent five and a half years collating the great uncial manuscripts of the Gospels only, and eight years in all in such work of collating (Burgon, *op. cit.,* pp. 337, 376). No one has attempted to refute his *Last Twelve Verses of the Gospel according to St. Mark* (cf. *Quarterly Review,* October, 1881), nor has his third article in that review ever been answered, while the answer to his first two articles by "Two Members of the New Testament Company" (Dr. Ellicott and E. Palmer) can hardly be called an answer at all.

[25] Surely Father Pope would have welcomed the critical Greek Testament which has been published by Herders at Freiburg im Breisgau (Germany), in two volumes, 1949–50. The text has been edited by the Catholic scholar, H. J. Vogels, of Bonn, and is a re-edition of the text he published in 1920. Dr. Vogels insists on the value of the evidence of the ancient versions, especially the Vulgate, and of patristic sources in determining the text, and turns to this "consentient antiquity" rather than to isolated codices in order to arrive at the genuine reading (see above at footnote 2). The widely used text of Nestle is built upon the findings of Westcott and Hort, Tischendorf (who placed his faith almost exclusively in the codices), and Weiss, so that it is definitely in the Westcott and Hort tradition. Dr. Vogels, however, belongs more to the school of thought represented by Father Pope in this chapter. [S.B.]

CHAPTER XLVI

Criticism of the Revised Version

THE COMPLETION OF THE REVISION

THE New Testament Company, working four days a week, completed its task between June 23, 1870, and November 11, 1880; their revised version was published May 17, 1881. The revision of the Old Testament occupied fourteen years, June 30, 1870, to June 20, 1884; though the fixed character of the Masoretic Hebrew text made the revision of the Old Testament an easier task than that of the New Testament, the amount of work called for was naturally far greater. Both Testaments were published together, May 19, 1885; the Preface by Aldis Wright provides the best introduction to the whole work. The two companies then divided the books of the Apocrypha between them; here the task of revision was rendered difficult by the fact that the revisers in 1611 had done their work somewhat hastily; hence the fresh revision now undertaken lasted from 1882 to 1892.

In the Revised Version the text was set out in paragraphs, as in the Rheims Version of 1582. The copious use of italicized words, so marked a feature of the Authorized Version, was much restricted. Though rule seven had laid down that they were "to revise the headings of chapters and pages, paragraphs, italics, and punctuation," the Revisers felt that "the revision of the headings of chapters and pages would have involved so much of indirect, and indeed frequently of direct interpretation, that we judged it best to omit them altogether."

DISREGARD FOR THE TEXT OF THE AUTHORIZED VERSION

As soon as the Revised Version appeared, severe criticism was heaped upon it, and there followed a war of pamphlets and articles in the *Quarterly Review,* the *Edinburgh Review,* the *Expository Times,* and other periodicals.[1] On all sides the general feeling arose that scant regard had been paid to the rule of not departing unnecessarily from the Authorized Version. Dr. Wordsworth declared: "We meet in every page with small changes which are vexatious, teasing, and irritating; even more so because they are so small (as small insects sting sharply), which seem almost to be made merely for the sake of change." [2] What a shock it must have been for those accustomed to the swing and rhythm of: "God, who at sundry times and in divers manners spake in time past unto the fathers by the prophets, hath in these last days spoken unto us by *his* Son" (Heb. 1:1), to find instead: "God, having of old time spoken unto the fathers in the prophets by divers portions and in divers manners, hath at the end of these days spoken unto us in *his* Son." Could pedanticism go further?

King James's revisers had decided not to attempt always to render the same Greek word by the same English equivalent. But now uniformity in this respect was aimed at, though not always with success; [3] e.g., the Revisers fluctuate between "fastened his eyes upon," and "looked steadfastly" for ἀτενίζω; each of these occurred three times in the 1611 revision, but elsewhere, we read, "earnestly look," "set his eyes," "earnestly behold," "look on," an elasticity perhaps preferable to the comparative stiffness of the Revised Version.

[1] Some of these were afterwards republished; notably: Lightfoot, *On a Fresh Revision of the English New Testament,* 3rd ed., 1891; Westcott, *Some Lessons of the Revised Version of the New Testament,* 1897. Burgon's trenchant attacks in the *Quarterly Review,* October, 1881, to April, 1882, were republished as *The Revision Revised,* 1883; Burgon also left in manuscript *The Traditional Text of the Holy Gospels Vindicated,* and *The Causes of the Corruption of the Traditional Text,* both edited and published by his *fidus Achates,* E. Miller, 1896. Burgon wrote in the same "joyous tone" as in his earlier *The Last Twelve Verses of the Gospel according to St. Mark,* 1871; but his *saeva indignatio* undoubtedly betrayed him at times into intemperate language: the Revisers, he said, "deserved nothing short of stern and well-merited rebuke"; he even dubbed an article by Dean Farrar in the *Contemporary Review* "a vulgar effusion." An attempt to answer the first two articles in the *Quarterly Review* was made by "Two members of the New Testament Company" (Dr. Ellicott and E. Palmer): *The Revisers and the Greek Text of the New Testament. Chiefly in answer to the criticisms by J. W. Burgon in the Quarterly Review of the Greek Testament as revised by B. F. Westcott and F J. A. Hort,* 1882. This was published before the appearance of Burgon's third article, "Westcott and Hort's New Textual Theory," to which no answer has ever been attempted. Burgon answered Dr. Ellicott in *The Revision Revised,* pp. 369–520.

[2] *Address on the Revised Version,* 1881.

[3] Every translator knows how difficult it is to differentiate in English between κατεργάζομαι, ποιέω, and πράσσω.

It would be idle to multiply examples such as "withstand," for "resist," and "sufferings," for "affliction" (I Pet. 5:9), and *"even the sword"* (Apoc. 19:21)—why in italics? Why, too, should the Revisers, following Tyndale, Cranmer, and the Genevans, have reverted to "love" instead of the sacrosanct "charity" of the Vulgate, Wycliffe, Rheims, and A.V in the thirteenth chapter of First Corinthians? Once more, in John 3:25 the Vulgate, the *textus receptus,* and all previous English versions read: "there arose a question between some of John's desciples and the Jews about purifying"; was it necessary for the Revisers to adopt with Scholz the singular form and read, "with a Jew"?

It has been calculated that in Judges, Psalms, Job, Osee, Jeremias, and Ezechiel alone there are about 15,476 changes; Canon Cook indeed reckoned 35,000. He reckons more than 600 changes in St. Mark and more than 800 in St. Luke. Burgon points out that thirty of the thirty-one words in II Pet. 1:5–7 are changed. Bishop Wordsworth reckoned that "36,000 changes have been made; not a fiftieth of which can be shown to be needed, or even desirable." [4]

THE MARGINAL NOTES

The marginal notes proved a stumbling block to many. To say of any particular rendering adopted, "some ancient authorities read . . . ," is futile unless some clue is furnished to identify these; surely the familiar signs א, B, D, would have sufficed. The interpretive notes, too, are of doubtful value: why "or *through* instead of "by the prophet" (Matt. 2:5, 17; 8:17, etc.)? Why replace "hell" by "Gehenna" in the margin (Matt. 5:22; 10:28, etc.)? The statement that "Peter" is "Petros" and that "rock" is "petra" suggests that the margin was intended to serve as a commentary. Though these marginal notes represent the views of a majority as expressed in the course of the second revision, they do not represent the views of that two-thirds majority requisite before a rendering suggested at that stage could be adopted.[5] Furthermore, almost every shade of religious opinion was to be found among the Revisers, and their divergent views appear in the margin. For example: though the evidence in favor of the doxology after the Lord's Prayer (Matt. 6:13) is very slight and it is omitted from the text, yet the margin has: "Many authorities,

[4] Burgon, *op. cit.,* p. 400; Wordsworth, *Address to the Lincoln Diocesan Conference,* p. 27.

[5] See Stanley Cook, *The Old Testament. A Reinterpretation,* p. 13.

some ancient, but with variations, add 'For thine. . . .' " The result is that the unquestionably erroneous "received" Greek text, followed by Tyndale, Cranmer, Genevа, and A.V., is conceded a new lease of life.[6]

The often repeated statement that "many ancient authorities omit" a certain passage,—e.g., the agony and the sweat of blood (Luke 22:43 f.) —would lead the unwary reader to suppose that such passages had little or no textual support, whereas such is not the case at all. Similarly Christ's prayer for his enemies (Luke 23:34) is accompanied by the statement that "some ancient authorities omit" it, which almost suggests that the Revisers retained the passage under protest. Then, what gain could there be in noting on Apoc. 13:18 that in place of 666 being the "number of the beast," "some ancient authorities read 616"?

Another regrettable feature is the absence, if not suppression, of the "miraculous." Three words expressive of the amazing character of Christ's works repeatedly recur: δυνάμεις, σημεῖα, τέρατα; these are rendered by "miracles" in A.V., though more precise renderings would be "mighty works," "works of power," "signs," "wonders," or "marvels." These were *mira* intended to make witnesses admire or wonder, and then, by reflecting on their character, arrive at the truth they were meant to teach.[7] When, for instance, the centurion heard Christ "crying out with a loud voice" at the moment of death, "seeing that crying out in this manner he had given up the Ghost, [he] said, Indeed this man was the Son of God" (Mark 15:36–39). But the Revisers, by omitting "crying out," practically eliminated that very proof of his divinity which so overwhelmed the centurion. The Revised Version, it is true, does sometimes retain the word "miracle"; but when it does so (Luke 23:8; Acts 4:16, 22; 19:11), the margin suggests "signs" or "powers," though "works of power" or "mighty works" would have been preferable.

GRAVE CHANGES IN THE TEXT

The Vulgate and all English versions before R.V. read, "Deliver us from evil" (Matt. 6:13). But all manuscripts of the Greek Testament

[6] See Weymouth, *The Resultant Greek Testament;* Driver and Wright, *On the Marginal Notes of the Revised Version,* 1912.

[7] "Miracula quae fecit Dominus noster Jesus Christus sunt quidem divina opera et ad intelligendum Deum de visibilibus admonent humanam mentem, . . . ut invisibilem Deum per visibilia opera miraremur, et erecti ad fidem et purgati per fidem, etiam ipsum invisibiliter videre cuperemus. . . . [Miracula] habent enim, si intelligantur, linguam suam" (St. Augustine, *Homilies on the Gospel of St. John,* XXIV, 1 f.).

have the definite article, ἀπὸ τοῦ πονηροῦ, both here and in I John 5:18 f.: "and that wicked one toucheth him not. . . . The whole world lieth in wickedness" (A.V). The Revisers, however, forcing the presence of the definite article, relegate the traditional "deliver us from evil" to the margin, and in their text read, "Deliver us from the evil *one*," so that we ought to change our Latin version and say, *Libera nos a diabolo*. Insisting still on the force of the definite article, they render the passage from I John 5:18 f.: "the evil one toucheth him not, . . . the whole world lieth in the evil one"—an appalling statement. All scholars are aware of the difficulty of doing justice to the Greek definite article; but were the Revisers justified in writing "the evil one"? Is it certain that πονηροῦ is masculine? It might perfectly well be simply neuter.[8]

The reading, "good will toward men" (A.V.), instead of "to men of good will" (Luke 2:14), has much to be said in its favor; even Scrivener admits: "If there be one case more prominent than another in the criticism of the New Testament, wherein solid reason and pure taste revolt against the iron yoke of ancient authorities, it is that of the Angelic Hymn sung at the Nativity"; [9] and he insists on the claims of the reading εὐδοκία instead of εὐδοκίας, and the consequent rendering, "good will amongst men," in place of "to men of good will," the rendering of the Latin MSS. and Latin Fathers. But there are notable exceptions in the MSS., for ℵ, B, and D, in which Westcott and Hort have so much faith, here read as the Church has always read, *hominibus bonae voluntatis*. R.V. reads: "Peace among men in whom he is well pleased."

St. Paul's words on the inspired Scriptures (II Tim. 3:16) have proved a difficulty owing to the absence of any finite verb. The sentence, taken as it stands, should read as in R.V.: "Every Scripture inspired of God *is* also profitable"; at least five uncial MSS. of the Vulgate have *utilis est*. It is regrettable, therefore, that the R.V. margin should suggest, "Or, Every Scripture *is* inspired of God," in this rendering following the Genevan version and A.V., which insert two verbs: "All Scripture *is* given by inspiration of God, and *is* profitable." But St. Paul would not have felt it necessary to state that all divine Scripture is inspired of God, though he would have insisted on its "profitable" character.

[8] See F. C. Cook, *"Deliver Us from Evil": A protest against the change in the last petition of the Lord's Prayer, adopted in the Revised Version of the New Testament,* 1881–82. The resulting controversy between Canon Cook and Dr. Lightfoot in *The Guardian*, 1881–82, was naturally hailed by journalists as "The Devil in the Lord's Prayer."

[9] *A Plain Introduction to the Criticism of the New Testament,* II, 344.

According to the Rhemists, the seven angels were "revested with cleane and white stone" (Apoc. 15:6), a reading based on MSS. of the Vulgate which evidently had for their translator or copyist someone who found λίθον and not λίνον in the Greek text before him. But the Tridentine Revisers replaced *lapide* by *lino,* as Wycliffe had read the passage long before, translating, "clothid with a stole cleene and white." Challoner of course followed suit. The Revisers in 1881, however, on the authority of the margin of B, of Lachmann, Tregelles, and Westcott and Hort, follow the reading λίθον, or stone. Feeling, presumably, that angels could hardly have been clad in stone, they inserted the adjective "precious": "arrayed with *precious* stone." How these revisers persuaded themselves that a patent misprint, λίθον for λίνον, ever stood in St. John's original copy, passes comprehension.

THE RHEMISTS AND THE REVISERS

In numerous places of lesser importance the Revised Version follows the Rhemists rather than the Authorized Version. Wycliffe, Rheims, R.V., "The Spirit of Jesus suffered them not"; Tyndale, Cranmer, Geneva, and A.V. omit "of Jesus" (Acts 16:7); Wycliffe, Rheims, and R.V., "the liberty of the glory of the sons of God"; but Tyndale, Cranmer, Geneva, and A.V., "the glorious liberty" (Rom. 8:21); similarly, Wycliffe, Rheims, and R.V. have, "holiness of truth"; while Tyndale, Cranmer, Geneva, and A.V. read, "true holiness" (Ephes. 4:24); Wycliffe, Rheims, and R.V., "the Lord Christ"; Tyndale, Cranmer, Geneva, and A.V., "the Lord God" (I Pet. 3 15). Wycliffe, Rheims, and R.V., "By their fruits you shall know them"; but Tyndale, Cranmer, Geneva, and A.V. destroy the rhythm by changing the order, "Ye shall know them by their fruits." In Matt. 25:8 the imperfect tense is correctly rendered by Wycliffe, "oure lampis ben quenchid," by Tyndale and Geneva, "go out," and by Rheims, "are going out," followed by R.V ; but Cranmer and A.V have, "are gone out." [10]

In the following five instances the punctilious rendering of the Greek article by the Rhemists is adopted by the Revisers: "the outer darkness" (Matt. 25:30); "the mountain" (Matt. 28·16); "an angel" (Luke 2:9); "the lamp" instead of "a burning . . . light" (John 5:35); "signs" (John 6:26), omitting the superfluous definite article in A.V.

[10] Lupton, in Hastings' *Dictionary of the Bible* (extra vol., pp. 263 f.), gives lists of changes generally accepted as improvements, and the reverse.

Tyndale, followed by Cranmer, substituted "temple" for "altar" in I Cor. 9:13, and Cranmer did the same in 10:18, though Tyndale had not here ventured on this malicious change. In the same insidious spirit Cranmer and the Genevan editions of 1577 and 1579 changed "table" in the temple of Bel (Dan. 14:13, 18, 21) to "altar"; but none of these perversions were endorsed either in A.V. or R.V.

SERIOUS OMISSIONS IN THE TEXT

Few readers are aware of the numberless occasions on which R.V. omits passages familiar to us in the traditional text, by which we do not mean, of course, the *textus receptus,* which is a more or less corrupt form of it; but we mean that form of text which has come down to us through the ages and is attested to by the vast majority of authorities, whether manuscripts (uncial or cursive), the Greek and Latin Fathers, or the early versions.

Concerning the omission of Mark 16:9–20, Dr. Hort, after a lengthy discussion, says: "The conclusion to be drawn from the documentary evidence alone is that verses 9–20 are a very early interpolation, early and widely diffused and welcomed." While he concedes that "this provisional conclusion is however at once encountered by a strong show of intrinsic evidence" (p. 46), his final verdict is that these twelve verses "manifestly cannot claim any apostolic authority; but they are doubtless founded on some tradition of the apostolic age" (p. 51). On the other hand, Dr. Scrivener says: "So powerfully is it [the section in question] vouched for, that many of those who are reluctant to recognize St. Mark as its author, are content to regard it notwithstanding as an integral portion of the inspired record originally delivered to the Church." And he declares that "Dean Burgon's brilliant monograph, '*The Last Twelve Verses of the Gospel according to St. Mark,*' has thrown a stream of light upon the controversy, nor does the joyous tone of his book misbecome one who is conscious of having triumphantly maintained a cause which is very precious to him. We may fairly say that his conclusions have in no essential point been shaken by the elaborate and very able plea of Dr. Hort (Appendix, pp. 28–51)." [11]

Those perplexed by "the second Sabbath after the first" (Luke 6:1)

[11] *Op. cit.,* II, 344, 337. The section actually stands in the text of R.V., but the note in the margin states that "the two oldest Greek manuscripts, and some other authorities, omit"—another example of the Revisers' dependence on codices ℵ and B. [S.B.]

will feel even more puzzled by its omission in R.V., on the authority of ℵ and B, where the text has "it came to pass on a sabbath," and the margin, "many ancient authorities insert *second first.*" On this Scrivener remarks: "Here again Codd. ℵ B coincide in a reading which cannot be approved, omitting δευτεροπρώτῳ by way of getting rid of a difficulty, as do both of them in Mark xvi. 9–20. . . . The very obscurity of the expression . . . attests strongly to its genuineness, if there be any truth at all in canons of internal evidence."[12]

The much discussed passage, "And there appeared to him an angel from heaven, . . . and his sweat became as drops of blood trickling down upon the ground" (Luke 22:43 f.), is printed between double brackets by Westcott and Hort, but the Revisers, though allowing it to stand in their text, state in the margin that "many ancient authorities omit vers. 43–44." But Scrivener declares: "It is a positive relief to know that any lingering doubt which may have hung over the authenticity of these verses, whose sacred words the devout reader of Scripture could so ill spare, is completely dissipated by their being contained in Codex ℵ."[13] Canon Cook also says: "Supporting the whole passage we have an array of authorities which, whether we regard their antiquity or their character for sound judgement, veracity and accuracy, are scarcely paralleled on any occasion."[14]

The long clause on the troubling of the waters by an angel (John 5:5) is omitted by Westcott and Hort, who in their margin are content to refer us to their Appendix (pp. 76 f.); the Revisers, while relegating the passage to the margin, yet concede that "many ancient authorities insert [it] wholly or in part."

The story of the woman taken in adultery (John 7:53–8:11) is omitted by Westcott and Hort,[15] but retained in R.V. with the marginal *caveat*

[12] *Ibid.*, II, 347; cf. Westcott and Hort, *op. cit.*, pp. 58 f.

[13] *Op. cit.*, p. 353.

[14] *The Revised Version of the First Three Gospels*, p. 103.

[15] After a lengthy discussion, Hort arrives at this conclusion: "When the whole evidence is taken together, it becomes clear that the Section first came into St. John's Gospel as an insertion in a comparatively late Western text, having originally belonged to an extraneous independent source" (Appendix, pp. 82–88). Scrivener speaks very guardedly: "The arguments in its favour, internal even more than external, are so powerful, that we can scarcely be brought to think it an unauthorized appendage to the writings of one, who in another of his inspired books deprecated so solemnly the adding to or taking away from the blessed testimony he was commissioned to bear (Apoc. xxii. 18, 19)." Yet Scrivener himself feels compelled to conclude by saying: "We cannot help

that "most of the ancient authorities omit [it]. Those which contain it vary much from each other."

The text of I John 5:7 f. in A.V. reads: "For there are three that bear record in heaven, the Father, the Word, and the Holy Ghost: and these three are one. And there are three that bear witness in earth, the spirit, and the water, and the blood: and these three agree in one." In R.V. the first sentence is omitted, and its authenticity, says Scrivener, "will, perhaps, no longer be maintained by any one whose judgement ought to have weight." [16]

Besides the foregoing omissions of greater importance, the following are but a few examples of the multitude of omissions of minor importance: "without a cause" (Matt. 5:22); "this kind goeth not out but by prayer and fasting" (Matt. 17:21); "the Son of man is come to save that which was lost" (Matt. 18:11); "Verily I say unto you, It shall be more tolerable for Sodom and Gomorrha in the day of judgment than for that city" (Mark 6:11); "as Elias did," and "Ye know not what manner of spirit ye are of; for the Son of man is not come to destroy men's lives, but to save them" (Luke 9:54–56); "in letters of Greek and Latin and Hebrew" (Luke 23:38).[17] These omissions from the Authorized Version, as well as many verbal changes, are due to the application of principles upon which textual critics are far from being agreed.

JUSTIFIED OMISSIONS

But not all passages omitted by the Revisers are to be regretted. In 1582 the Rhemists omitted from their translation various clauses to be found in the current Greek text. For these omissions they were severely censured by Bulkeley; but later textual criticism has justified the action of the Rhemists, whose critical judgment in omitting the following clauses standing in the *textus receptus* and in the Authorized Version has been borne out by textual criticism and is now endorsed by the Re-

---

admitting that if this section be indeed the composition of St. John, it has been transmitted to us under circumstances widely different from those connected with any other genuine passage of Scripture whatever." (*op. cit.*, pp. 364, 368).

[16] *Ibid.*, pp. 401; cf. Hort, *op. cit.*, Appendix, pp. 103–106. For the arguments in favor of the authenticity of the passage—arguments much more forcible than it is generally known—see Pope, *The Catholic Student's "Aids" to the Bible* (1937), V, 331–36.

[17] The list of such omissions might be extended almost indefinitely. Evidence in favor of these passages is given with overwhelming force in Scrivener's *Plain Introduction* and Burgon's volumes, especially his *Revision Revised*, pp. 75 f., 91 f., 137, 144 f., 410 f.

visers: "Bless them that curse you, do good to them that hate you, [and] despitefully use you" (Matt. 5:44); "I am not come to call the righteous, but sinners (to repentance)" (Matt. 9:13); the two clauses, "to be baptized with the baptism that I am baptized with" (Matt. 20:22 f.); "(or mother), or wife (or children)" (Mark 10:29); "and at him they cast stones" (Mark 12:4); "spoken of by Daniel the prophet" (Mark 13:14); "and thy speech agreeth thereto" (Mark 14:70); "Get thee behind me, Satan" (Luke 4:8); "(Thou art) Christ (the Son of God)" (Luke 4:41); "Be of good comfort" (Luke 8:48); "even as Elias did" (Luke 9:54); "Scribes and Pharisees, hypocrites" (Luke 11:44); "and of the chief priests" (Luke 23:23); "the image of (Baal)" (Rom. 11:4).

In Matt. 12:22 the Authorized Version has, "a devil blind and dumb, and he healed him, insomuch that the blind and dumb both spake and saw"; but the *textus receptus,* followed by Westcott and Hort, and the Revised Version, has: so "that the dumb man spoke and saw." The Vulgate, followed by the Rhemists, has simply *ut loqueretur et videret,* omitting "the blind and dumb." In John 6:51, "the bread that I will give is my flesh," "that I will give" is omitted by the Rhemists and the Revisers, though present in Wycliffe's text.[18] In John 21:1 the words "to the disciples," though omitted by Tyndale, Cranmer, Rheims, and the Vulgate, are retained in Wycliffe, Geneva, A.V., and R.V., and also in the Clementine edition of the Vulgate.

LATER ATTEMPTS AT REVISION

The publication of the Revised Version and the discussions it led to induced many scholars to attempt further revisions. Some of these were independent ventures bearing no explicit relation to the Authorized Version or the Revised Version, while others sprang directly from a dissatisfaction with the Revised Version in the same way as many private versions of the eighteenth and nineteenth centuries had their origin in dissatisfaction with the Authorized Version. The work of the American committees in the direction of further revision is the subject of the next chapter, and the attempts of various translators to present the Bible in modern dress, using current idiom, is the subject of the last chapter of this book. Here we are concerned with several private attempts to revise further the Revised Version.

[18] Very rarely do the Revisers adhere to a reading not endorsed by either Wycliffe, the Rhemists, or the Vulgate: but see Matt. 20:15, where they retain "with mine own."

In 1897 *The New Dispensation, translated from the Greek,* by Robert D. Weekes, was published in New York. This text, although it sets out to be a new translation, adopts the style of the Authorized Version, and is, in fact, an attempt to improve the Revised Version.

In 1905 Dr. Samuel Lloyd published his New Testament, which is a revision of the Authorized Version by the critical Greek text of Nestle, which was just completed.[19] The work sets out to be a deliberate improvement on the Revised Version, and intends "to give to the present day reader a freer access to the meaning . . . of the original" than that version provided (Preface).[20]

In 1914 another text appeared in England which again is a revision of the Authorized Version: *The New Testament, or Covenant, of Our Lord and Saviour Jesus Christ.* This revision is the work of the Rev. E. E. Cunnington, and was directly prompted by his dissatisfaction with the Revised Version. "Of that work," writes the translator in his Introduction, "it is little to say that it has not closed the door upon other attempts"; he adds a footnote to quote a remark of Dr. Rendel Harris describing the Revised Version as "a very bad translation." Cunnington's text is handsomely printed, and a revised edition appeared in 1935.

BIBLIOGRAPHY

Beckett, Edmund (Baron Grimthorpe). *Should the Revised Version of the New Testament be Authorised?* 1882.

Cook, F. C. *The Revised Version of the First Three Gospels, considered in its bearing upon the record of Our Lord's words and of incidents in His life,* 1882.

Curry, D. *The New Testament containing the Old and New Versions. The History of the Committee of Revision,* New York, 1882.

Dawson, Benjamin. *Notes on the Revised Version of the Old Testament,* 1886.

[19] Nestle's first edition appeared in 1906; thus it appears that Dr. Lloyd had access to the text before its final publication. Nestle's text is one of the most widely used even now and has been through many editions with improvements.

[20] A popular American edition is *The Modern Reader's Bible. The Books of the Bible with Three Books of the Apocrypha, Presented in Modern Literary Form. Edited, with Introductions and Notes,* by Richard G. Moulton, New York, 1907. At least parts of this work appeared as early as 1895, and there have been many editions or reimpressions. An editor's note states that "the text of the Modern Reader's Bible is one constructed specially for this work, for which the Editor is solely responsible. It is based upon the English Revised Version, with choice between the readings of the text and margin, and such slight changes of wording as are involved in the adaptation to modern literary structure." Chapter and verse numbers are given in the outside margin, but subject headings rather than chapter headings are employed. The Psalms and other poetic passages are set as poetry. [Ed.]

Field, F. *Notes on the Translation [R.V.] of the New Testament,* 1899.

Gillespie, F. G. K. *Revision Reasons: A Manual of the Revised Version of the Old Testament,* 1906.

Goodwin, D. R. *Notes on the Late Revision of the New Testament,* New York, 1883.

Hemphill, S. *A History of the Revised Version of the New Testament,* 1906.

Humphry, W. G. *Commentary on the Revised Version of the New Testament,* 1882.

Lightfoot, John. *On a Fresh Revision of the English New Testament,* 1871, 1872, 1891.

A List of Changes made in the Text of the Greek Testament by the Company of Revisers of the Authorized Version, 1881 (?).

Malan, S. C. *A Plea for the Received Greek Text and for the Authorized Version of the New Testament,* 1869.

Milligan, G. *The Expository Value of the Revised Version,* 1916.

Moon, G. W. *The Revisers' English. . . . Criticisms showing the Revisers' violations of the laws of the language,* 1882.

Newth, S. *Lectures on Bible Revision,* 1881.

Sampson, G. W. *The English Revisers' Greek Text, shown to be unauthorised,* Cambridge, U.S.A., 1882.

Smith, G. Vance. *Texts and Margins of the Revised New Testament Affecting Theological Doctrine,* 1881.

Vaughan, C. J. *Authorised or Revised?* 1882.

Westcott, B. F. *Some Lessons of the Revised Version of the New Testament,* 1897.

See also J. H. Lupton in Hastings' *Dictionary of the Bible,* extra volume, pp. 259–71; C. J. Cadoux in *The Bible in Its Ancient and English Versions,* pp. 235–74.

CHAPTER XLVII

The American Standard Version and Its Revision

IN 1871, the year following the resolution of Convocation instituting the Commission for Revision and the subsequent formation of the two companies of revision, both houses of Convocation passed a further resolution inviting the cooperation of American scholars. Thus two committees were formed in America, one for the Old Testament and one for the New, who were to act in concert with the two English companies on the basis of the principles and rules drawn up by the Committee of Convocation. The English companies then sent to the corresponding American committees the draft of their first revision as the various parts were completed. The American suggestions were then considered during the drafting of the second revision, likewise with the third and final draft. Those suggestions were accepted for the final draft which received the support of two-thirds of the members of the English company present, just as the suggestions coming from the members of the English company were adopted. It was then agreed that the proposals decided upon by the American committees, but rejected by the English companies, should be printed as an Appendix to the final text of the Revised Version. Thus it came about that when the New Testament appeared in 1881 and the Old Testament in 1885, an Appendix to each was also printed with the following notices: "List of readings and renderings preferred by the American Committee, recorded at their desire" (for the New Testament); "The American Old Testament Revision Company, while recognizing the cordial acceptance given to many of their suggestions, present the following instances in which they differ from the English

Company, as of sufficient importance to be appended to the Revision in accordance with the original agreement."[1]

THE AMERICAN STANDARD VERSION, 1901

The above agreement expired in 1901, and the surviving members of the American committees in that year published the text of the Revised Version embodying their own proposals in the text, placing the preferences of the English companies in an Appendix. This edition was known as the American Standard Version, and was published by Thomas Nelson and Sons, New York, who also held the copyright. It came to be used in America much more widely than the Revised Version was used in England.

The differences between the American Standard Version and the English Revised Version are mainly matters of diction: many archaisms, retained in R.V. from A.V., are modernized in A.S.V., such as "who" for "which," when the reference is to a person, and "know" and "knew" for "wot" and "wist," and other similar instances. More striking, however, is the consistent use of "Jehovah" instead of "the LORD" (R.V.) for the Tetragrammaton, and the uniform replacement of "Holy Ghost" by "Holy Spirit," which last has remained current in American usage. The titles of the Gospels do not include "Saint," and St. Paul's name is removed from the title of the Epistle to the Hebrews. In the Old Testament all the marginal renderings from the Septuagint, the Vulgate, and other ancient versions or "authorities" are omitted. But in general and apart from the particular choice of words considered more suitable for the American reader, the American text differs little in substance from the English.

THE REVISED STANDARD VERSION OF THE NEW TESTAMENT, 1946

In 1928 Thomas Nelson and Sons transferred the copyright of the American Standard Version "to the International Council of Religious Education, a body in which the educational boards of forty of the major Protestant denominations of the United States and Canada are associated. This body appointed a committee of scholars to have charge of the text, and authorized it to undertake further revision if deemed necessary. The charter of the Committee contains the provision that 'all

[1] Cf. the Revisers' Preface to the New Testament.

changes in the text shall be agreed upon by a two-thirds vote of the total membership of the Committee'—a more conservative rule than that which had governed revision hitherto, which required only a two-thirds vote of members present." [2]

In 1937 the Council authorized the committee to begin a complete revision of the American Standard Version. Hopes of cooperation from British scholars were thwarted by the circumstances of war. The committee in its Old Testament and New Testament sections has included thirty-one members, of whom death or retirement has removed ten. The chairman, Luther A. Weigle, of Yale University, who has been on the committee in both sections from its inception, edited the booklet introducing the revision in 1946, and is the author of the most recent book on the history of English versions.[3] He was most ably assisted by Professor James Moffatt, secretary to the committee until his death in 1944. Dr. Moffatt had already earned a worldwide reputation through his own translation of the Bible, and another well-known translator of the Bible, Dr. Goodspeed, was also on the New Testament committee.[4] Six other scholars [5] assisted in the production of the Revised Standard Version of the New Testament, published in 1946.

This version is, in fact, an entirely new translation; it is at the time of this writing (1950) the most recent fresh translation of the whole New Testament that has appeared, and is up to date in every sense. The publishers, again Thomas Nelson and Sons, New York, have printed on the jacket: "The Most Important Publication of 1946." The title page reads: *The New Covenant, commonly called the New Testament of Our Lord and Savior* [6] *Jesus Christ. Revised Standard Version. Translated from the Greek, being the Version set forth A.D. 1611, revised A.D. 1881 and A.D. 1901, compared with the most ancient authorities and revised A.D. 1946.* In the Preface two main reasons are given for the necessity of this revision:

One is that these [the R.V. of 1881 and the A.S.V. of 1901] are mechanically exact, literal word-for-word translations, which follow the order of the Greek

[2] From the Preface to the Revised Standard Version; cf. Luther A. Weigle's essay in *An Introduction to the Revised Standard Version,* 1946.

[3] *The English New Testament from Tyndale to the Revised Standard Version,* 1949.

[4] The translations of Moffatt and Goodspeed are described in the next chapter.

[5] Walter Russell Bowie, Millar Burrows, Henry J. Cadbury, Clarence T. Craig, Frederick C. Grant, and Abdel Ross Wentz.

[6] The correct American spelling has been adopted.

words, so far as this is possible, rather than the order which is natural to English; they are more accurate than the King James Version, but have lost some of its beauty and power as English literature. The second is that the discovery of a few more ancient manuscripts of the New Testament and of a great body of Greek papyri dealing with the everyday affairs of life in the early centuries of the Christian era, has furnished scholars with new resources, both for seeking to recover the original text of the Greek New Testament and for understanding its language.

The importance of this version may be studied under four particular heads. In the first place there have been great advances during the last fifty years in the knowledge of New Testament Greek and the exact meaning of words, as well as their significance in everyday life; papyri and inscriptions have come to light, and contemporary authors have been studied anew. Scholars have gradually begun to realize that the language of the New Testament is the language of everyday speech of the time.

This discovery has put New Testament translation in a new perspective. For if it is written in plain informal style, it should be translated in such a style. Here it differs widely from the Old Testament. The prophets and Job used a high style, often imaginative and rhetorical in the extreme. Their books were for the most part poetry. . . . The New Testament is altogether different in literary quality. It owes almost nothing to literary artistry, and everything to the ideas it had to convey. To convey them with the utmost directness, simplicity and vigour was the chief concern of its writers. And if that was indeed the aim of its writers, it should also be that of its translators. The New Testament then calls for a direct, familiar style in translation; an elaborate, elegant style is unsuited to it, and in proportion as it is rendered in a conscious literary syle, it is misrepresented to the modern reader.[7]

The modern speech used in the Revised Standard Version is a direct result of this discovery. It cannot be said that modern knowledge of New Testament Greek has called for the alteration of many passages, yet there are shades of meaning and elucidations of difficult passages that are determined by the understanding of the popular usage of the time. Many examples are cited in chapter 6 of *An Introduction to the Revised Standard Version;* for example, the "milk without guile" in I Pet. 2:2 is found to be simply "pure milk" as a dairyman might describe it. Let us observe here in passing that this rendering, "pure," is already found in the Confraternity Edition of 1941, and that in a number of passages the Revised Standard Version follows the Confraternity Edition; but there is no suggestion of direct indebtedness.

[7] Goodspeed in *An Introduction to the Revised Standard Version,* pp. 32 f.

The second important point is the deeper understanding of the Semitic background of New Testament diction and the value of Hebrew phrases such as "Amen, amen"—a phrase which "proved to be the most troublesome of all," writes one of the revisers; [8] they were not satisfied with "Truly, truly," which they finally adopted.

The third important point is the central question of the Greek text. Studies in the question have progressed far since the days of Westcott and Hort and the production of the Revised Version, which depended so completely on the theory of those eminent scholars. The Old Syriac Version was discovered in 1892; important biblical papyri have come to light since 1930; and Tatian's Greek text was found in 1933—to mention only the more important discoveries. This new evidence, both of manuscripts and of versions, has affected the course of textual criticism in recent years, and Westcott and Hort's theory of a "neutral text" has gradually been entirely abandoned. In its place the revisers have adopted the theory of the five main types of text, as outlined, for instance, by Sir Frederick Kenyon,[9] as follows:

1. Western, represented by *Codex Bezae* and the Old Latin Version.
2. Caesarean, represented by the Koridethi Gospels and others.
3. Alexandrian, represented by codices ℵ and B and the Coptic Version.
4. Syriac, represented by the Old Syriac Version.
5. Other; that is, a classification for readings that do not fall into any of the preceding groups.[10]

Having accepted this theory, the revisers enunciated these principles:

(1) No one type of text is infallible, or to be preferred by virtue of its generally superior authority.

(2) Each reading must be examined on its merits, and preferance must be given to those readings which are demonstrably in the style of the author under consideration.

(3) Readings which explain other variants, but are not contrariwise themselves to be explained by the others, merit our preference. . . .

Each variant reading must be studied on its merits, and cannot be adopted or rejected by some rule of thumb, or by adherence to such a theory as that of a "Neutral Text." It is this eclectic principle that has guided us in the present Revision. The Greek text of this Revision is not that of Westcott-Hort, Nestle, or

[8] Burrows in *ibid.*, p. 27.

[9] *Our Bible and the Ancient Manuscripts* (1948), pp. 109–18.

[10] Grant in *An Introduction to the Revised Standard Version,* p. 39.

Souter; though the readings we have adopted will, as a rule be found either in the text or the margin of the new (17th) edition of Nestle (Stuttgart, 1941).[11]

If the above method is compared with that of ascertaining the Greek text in 1881, it will be noticed that it is quite different.

The fourth important point is the choice of a modern medium of expression, a choice dictated, as has been explained, by the realization of the everyday character of the original Greek. The style adopted is therefore consciously simple and unadorned, avoiding all archaisms on the one hand, while, on the other, not lowering its dignity by the introduction of any unfortunate neologisms. For example, John 1:43–51:

> The next day Jesus decided to go to Galilee. And he found Philip and said to him, "Follow me." Now Philip was from Bethsaida, the city of Andrew and Peter. Philip found Nathanael, and said to him, "We have found him of whom Moses in the law and also the prophets wrote, Jesus of Nazareth, the son of Joseph." Nathanael said to him, "Can anything good come out of Nazareth?" Philip said to him, "Come and see." Jesus saw Nathanael coming to him, and said of him, "Behold, an Israelite indeed, in whom is no guile!" Nathanael said to him, "How do you know me?" Jesus answered him, "Before Philip called you, when you were under the fig tree, I saw you." Nathanael answered him, "Rabbi, you are the Son of God! You are the King of Israel!" Jesus answered him, "Because I said to you, I saw you under the fig tree, do you believe? You shall see greater things than these." And he said to him, "Truly, truly, I say to you, you will see heaven opened, and the angels of God ascending and descending upon the Son of man."

It will be noticed at once how close this is to the Authorized Version, except for the archaic forms. "Can anything good come out of Nazareth?" follows the Confraternity Edition. Various important doctrinal texts are satisfactorily rendered, and the translations are not in any way biased, although thc "wife" of A.V. in I Cor. 9:5 still appears. The word "emptied" is properly retained in the kenotic passage in Phil. 2:7, and the translation of James 2:22 is interesting: "You see that faith was active along with his works," where the phrase "along with," comes from the Confraternity Edition. I John 5:7 f. is simply omitted, as in the Revised Version, without a note; and Mark 16:9–20 is printed in small type with a note to explain.

The titles of the books for the most part follow the American Standard Version of 1901, but "Letter" is substituted for "Epistle," and "Acts of the Apostles" is written without the definite article, as in the Confraternity Edition. The text is printed in paragraphs without chapter head-

[11] *Ibid.*, p. 41.

ings; the chapter number is merely set in the text. Verse numbers are printed in normal size at the opening of a paragraph, and in small raised figures (as for footnotes) in the course of the paragraph. A device that must prove tiresome to all but the very uninstructed reader is that of printing nearly all proper names (except those of the apostles, of Abraham, Isaac, Jacob, and a few others) with phonetic indications every time they occur; e.g., Nic-o-de′ mus.[12]

[12] Most of the facts in this chapter are taken from the prefaces to the versions. The following works, however, are valuable sources, especially for the history of the Revised Standard Version: *An Introduction to the Revised Standard Version of the New Testament,* a booklet containing nine valuable essays by members of the Revision Committee and issued as a companion to the version itself, published at the same time and by the same publisher, Nelson, 1946; Luther Weigle, *The English New Testament from Tyndale to the Revised Standard Version,* Nashville, 1949 (the later chapters of this book include some of the material which had appeared in the above booklet); Ira M. Price, *The Ancestry of Our English Bible,* 2nd revised ed., New York, 1949, which gives a detailed account of the making of the Revised Standard Version.

CHAPTER XLVIII

The Modern-Speech Versions

Already in the eighteenth century we find a desire to have the Scriptures in the "modern speech" of the time. Particularly among Catholics we find the complaint that the sixteenth-century diction of the Rheims translation had become too remote from the current idiom to be easily intelligible. In 1718 Dr. Nary wrote in the Introduction to his New Testament that the people now "speak, in a manner, another Language" and that he has therefore "endeavoured to make this New Testament speak the English tongue now used." Dr. Witham wrote similarly in 1730: "What chiefly makes that Edition [Rheims, 1582] seem so obscure at present, and scarce intelligible, is, the difference of the English tongue, as it was spoken at that time, and as it is now chang'd, and refin'd." Among the Protestants we read in the "Author's Advertisement" printed in Worsley's New Testament of 1770 that his intention is "to make the form of expression more suitable to our *present* language," and he continues: "For as the English tongue, like other living languages, is continually changing, it were to be wished that the translation of the sacred oracles could be revised by public authority, and reduced to *present* forms of writing and speaking, at lest [*sic*] once in a century: but though this be not allowed for *public* use, it is to be hoped some *private* persons may receive benefit by that which is now offered." Thus it is nothing new in the history of the English Bible that there should be a desire to present the Scriptures in the language of the day. The present chapter considers those versions written in the idiom of the twentieth century.

FERRAR FENTON, 1883–1903

The first person to undertake the translation of the Scriptures into modern English, after the American translations of 1855 and 1858,[1] was a business man in London, Ferrar Fenton. About 1852, while he was yet a student, the idea occurred to him that such a translation was needed; so he tells us in the Introduction to the New Testament and in that to the Psalms. Therefore he applied himself to the study of Greek—later of Hebrew—and to the study of the Bible according to the latest researches and theories of the time. In 1883 his translation of St. Paul's epistles appeared, and thereafter at intervals appeared the Gospels, the whole New Testament, the Book of Job ("rendered into the same metre as the original Hebrew"), the Five Books of Moses, and subsequently the rest, until the whole Bible appeared in 1903 as *The Bible in Modern English*. In this edition each section appears with its original Preface. In the Preface to the first section he writes: "I am now old; but in my youth I pledged a resolve to God to use my talents and acquirements to establish the authenticity of the Sacred Scriptures . . . by making them intelligible, through the use of Modern English . . . ; and although I have been engaged in active commercial affairs for over forty years, I never ceased my studies to that end." By the time that the edition of the whole Bible appeared, the text of St. Paul was a sixth edition.

In this version the books of the New Testament are rearranged in a new order, a practice followed even more radically by later translators. John stands first for two reasons: first, because it is "specially the Doctrinal Record of Our Lord's life"; and secondly, because "there is ample reason for believing that the Gospel of John was written at an earlier date than the other three." The Gospel is followed by John's First Epistle; the other books then follow in the usual order. This arrangement is not found in any other edition.

The style is simple and does not indulge in much paraphrase, though occasionally the text is slightly expanded, as in John 1:11: "He came to His own home; but His own family did not welcome him." Strangely, Gen. 1:1 opens: "By periods God created. . . ." A footnote claims that the Hebrew word is plural. But such unusual translations are not common in this version. The text was republished as recently as 1946; this latter edition is a reprint of the fifth edition, 1910.

[1] See above, p. 546.

ERNEST BILTON'S GOSPELS, 1888

Dissatisfaction with the Revised Version caused Mr. Ernest Bilton to publish in 1888 *The Four Gospels, translated into Modern English from the Authorized and Revised Versions.* The translation does not profess to be a work of scholarship, and in the Preface it is said to be "offered principally as a suggestion" how a modern translation should read. It is simply an attempt to modernize the diction of the Authorized Version, and it is interesting to observe how at that date the author felt it necessary to explain that he had no desire whatever "to bring ridicule on the Gospel by thus translating it into the language of everyday life," an apology which would certainly not be needed at the present day. The printing is in the manner of a modern book, with plain chapter headings and no verse numbers. The absence of any running heads to the pages, however, makes reference difficult.

THE TWENTIETH CENTURY NEW TESTAMENT, 1898–1901, 1904

The Twentieth Century New Testament is a translation into modern English from the Greek text of Westcott and Hort. It is the work of "a company of about twenty persons, members of various sections of the Christian Church,"[2] and was published anonymously. It is generally supposed that the anonymous translators were members of the Free Churches. The work first began to appear in 1898, coming out in three parts; and in 1901 it was published in a single volume under the title, *The Twentieth Century New Testament, a translation into Modern English, made from the Original Greek (Westcott & Hort's Text).*[3] This was issued as a "Tentative Edition," and criticisms and suggestions were welcomed. In 1904 appeared the "permanent edition," so called in a note, though on the title page it is called the "Revised edition." It was the result of a desire to bring the translation "to as high a standard of accuracy and simplicity as may be practicable." There are differences between the two editions in almost every verse, usually in the direction of simpler diction. Thus the permanent edition is really a new text. The changes are interesting and show the difficulty of the task and the care bestowed by the translators. In the following example the italics in the

[2] From the Introduction to the 1901 edition.

[3] The edition of 1901 was published in London by Horace Marshall, and in America by the Fleming H. Revell Company; but in later editions the London publisher is The Sunday School Union.

1901 edition are used for passages referring to the Old Testament and noted in a footnote; these italics were abandoned in 1904.

Mark 1:40–44

1901	1904
One day a leper came to Jesus and went down on his knees to him, begging for pity. "If only you are willing," he said, "you are able to heal me." Jesus' heart was moved, and, stretching out his hand, he touched him and said: "I am willing, be healed." Instantly the leprosy left the man, and he was healed; and then Jesus immediately sent him away with urgent injunctions, saying to him: "Take care not to tell anything to any one; but go and *show* yourself *to the Priest,* and make the offerings in connexion with your healing, as Moses directed, for a proof of your cure to the people.	One day a leper came to Jesus and, falling on his knees, begged him for help. "If only you are willing," he said, "you are able to make me clean." Moved with compassion, Jesus stretched out his hand and touched him, saying as he did so: "I am willing; become clean." Instantly the leprosy left the man, and he became clean; and then Jesus, after sternly warning him, immediately sent him away, and said to him: "Be careful not to say anything to anyone; but go and show yourself to the Priest, and make the offerings for your cleansing directed by Moses as evidence of your cure.

One will observe a more precise accuracy in the text of 1904, and a certain clean quality in the prose is more evident in the permanent edition. One delicate feature of this version is that "Thou" is used when Christ addresses the Father; it is also used in the language of prayer, as in the Our Father and in the songs of praise in the Apocalypse. The same practice is also followed in some of the other modern-speech versions, such as those of Moffatt and Weymouth.

The order of the books sets out to be chronological in each section. Thus Mark is placed first, followed by Matthew, Luke, and John. James stands first among the epistles, followed by St. Paul's: "an early group" (I and II Thess.), "the main group" (Gal., I and II Cor., Rom.), the epistles of the captivity, and finally a "late group of pastoral letters." Then follows "an anonymous letter to the Hebrews" and the letters "attributed to" Peter, Jude, and John. Finally "An Apocalypse," "the Revelation of John." Preceding each book are short notes, most of which, however, are colored by the critical theories of the time. The text is printed like an ordinary modern book, without headings to the chapters, but with subject insets throughout. The attractive quality of the style and the generally orthodox diction are a special merit of this version.

DR. HAYMAN'S EPISTLES, 1900

In 1900 Dr. Henry Hayman published *The Epistles of the New Testament, an Attempt to present them in current and popular idiom,* which was the work of many years and is quite independent in its approach. The new version is printed with the text of the Authorized Version in small type on the verso page for purposes of comparison. Although Dr. Hayman's version has a certain modernity of manner, many archaisms are retained (such as "thou") or replaced by phrases which, after fifty years, no longer are current or popular. The text is printed in paragraphs, while that of the Authorized Version, of course, remains in verses. It is worth observing that "wife" of A.V. is here "helpmate" (I Cor. 9:5); though "eat . . . and drink" (I Cor. 11:27) is here wrongly retained, following A.V. Hayman's work is particularly important in that it is the first of the long series of modern-speech translations of the epistles, a section of the Scriptures which, as Dr. Hayman himself said, needs more than any other the clarification that can be brought out by the use of current idiom.

A. S. WAY'S EPISTLES, 1901, 1906

The Letters of St. Paul to Seven Churches and Three Friends, translated by A. S. Way, appeared in 1901, and a second edition was published in 1906 including the Epistle to the Hebrews. The whole text is printed entirely as a modern book, and the idiom is that of plain modern prose, without much use of paraphrase and with the avoidance of neologisms. An unusual modern word is successfully used in I Cor. 1:10: "Let there be no cliques among you."

The title of the book is something of a departure from the general practice, for previous translators had used the traditional word "Epistles"; but "Letters" reappears in the Revised Standard Version and Dr. Wand's paraphrase, and the title of J. B. Phillips work in 1947, *Letters to Young Churches,* is reminiscent of this one.

THE WORK OF JAMES MOFFATT, 1901, 1913–26

Of all the modern-speech versions, the "Moffatt Bible" has probably had by far the most publicity. It has been frequently republished and reprinted in many different formats; in 1946 appeared the ninety-sixth reprint of the New Testament. There has even appeared a text with commentary running to seventeen volumes, and a "Shorter Moffatt Bible" has been published as a popular edition.

It is frequently not understood that Dr. Moffatt made two quite distinct translations of the New Testament, one in 1901 and the other in 1913. Moreover he had, as we have seen, an important part in the production of the Revised Standard Version until his death in 1944. The translation of 1901 appeared in February with the title, *The Historical New Testament, being the literature of the New Testament arranged in the order of its literary growth and according to the dates of the documents. A New Translation, edited with Prolegomena, Historical Tables, Critical Notes, and an Appendix, by James Moffatt, B.D.* By August of the same year a second and revised edition had already been published. This text is not a modern-speech version at all, being written in biblical English; but it is included here because it is a new translation and not merely a revision of the Authorized Version, and because it is the basis of the much more famous work in modern speech by the same translator, published in 1913.

The Historical New Testament of 1901 broke quite new ground in setting out to present all the documents of the New Testament in the chronological order of their appearance, according to the critical hypotheses which were current at the time, so that the whole process of growth could be observed. (*The Twentieth Century New Testament* had only placed the various Gospels and epistles in their supposed chronological order.) Dr. Moffatt furthermore provides lengthy prolegomena and notes to prove his points, and these are excellent expositions of the theories of the day. The resultant order of the text is as follows: I and II Thess., Gal., I Cor., the "stern letter" (II Cor., chaps. 10–13), II Cor., chaps. 1–9, Col., Philem., Eph., Phil., I Pet., Mark, Matt., Heb., Luke, Acts, Apoc., John, the epistles of St. John, Mark 16:9–20, the pastoral epistles, James, Jude, II Pet. It is all a work of notable scholarship in the traditions of higher criticism.

Dr. Moffatt's edition of 1913, *The New Testament, a New Translation,* was an altogether different work, and it was this text that was eventually incorporated into the "Moffatt Bible." It is a translation from the Greek (von Soden's text) into modern English, made quite independently of any existing versions. The translator thus writes in his Preface: "The only version I have kept before me is the one I prepared thirteen years ago for my *Historical New Testament*. But the present version is not a revision of that. It is an independent work." There are no critical introductions or notes, except an occasional footnote explaining the reading followed, and the traditional order of the books is preserved. There is not even any indication in Second Corinthians of the translator's opinion about its composition, though he refers to this opinion in the Preface.

Although this version is the best known and most highly esteemed among the modern-speech versions, and is clearly the work of an eminent scholar, its colloquialisms are sometimes jarring; as, for instance, John 19:5: "So out came Jesus, wearing the crown of thorns and the purple robe; and Pilate said, 'Here the man is!' " and John 8:11, when our Lord says to the woman taken in adultery: "Neither do I; be off, and never sin again." Sometimes the translator has also become an interpreter, and we feel on distinctly unsafe ground when we find Christ represented as saying at the Last Supper (Matt. 26:26 and parallels; also I Cor. 11:24): "Take and eat this, it means my body." This biased rendering has not, I believe, appeared in any other version before or since; but it must be admitted that, serious though it is, it cannot be said to be typical of Dr. Moffatt's translation. Another typically Protestant reading, however, appears in I Cor. 9:5, where "wife" follows the A.V.

The Old Testament appeared in two volumes in 1924, and the *Complete Moffatt Bible* in one volume in 1926.

DR. WEYMOUTH'S NEW TESTAMENT, 1903

Second only to Dr. Moffatt's version in fame, and forming with this and *The Twentieth Century New Testament* a well-known trio during the years before the first World War, is *The New Testament in Modern Speech* by Richard Francis Weymouth, which appeared in 1903.[4] The subtitle of the work is, *An idiomatic translation into everyday English from the text of the Resultant Greek Testament.*[5] Weymouth had finished the work two years before publication, but sickness prevented him from seeing it through the press, so that this work and the final revision,

[4] The Introduction is dated 1902; but the work was published only after Dr. Weymouth's death in 1903.

[5] Dr. Weymouth is renowned for his edition of the Greek Testament, published in 1886, "exhibiting the text in which the majority of modern editors are agreed," and consequently entitled, *The Resultant Greek Testament*. From this Greek text the translation was made.

as well as the provision of subject insets throughout, was entrusted to the translator's friend, Ernest Hampden-Cook, who assumed the responsibilities of editorship.

An interesting point brought out in the Introduction is Dr. Weymouth's solicitous comparison of Greek and English idiom in the use of conjunctions. An average worked out from numerous representative English authors disclosed that the connecting links between sentences are "about one-third conjunctions, about one-third adverbs or relative and interrogative pronouns, while in the case of the remaining third there is what the grammarians call *asyndeton*—no formal connexion at all. But in the writers of the N.T. nearly *two*-thirds of the connecting links are conjunctions. It follows that in order to make the style of a translation true idiomatic English many of these conjunctions must be omitted and for others adverbs, etc., must be substituted."

The books stand in the traditional order, each introduced by a short note. The notes in this version also are colored by the critical theories then current; for example, Matthew was written A.D. 75.

This New Testament had a second edition in 1903, and a third in 1909, all with several reprints. The fifth (pocket) edition, 1929, has been reprinted eleven times, the last time being in 1948. An American edition, "newly revised by James Alexander Robertson," was published by the Pilgrim Press, Boston, in 1929, with a number of additional notes; it has been reprinted several times.

THE SHORTER BIBLE, 1918

The Shorter Bible is a new modern-English translation of the whole Bible history rearranged as a continuous whole, with section headings independent of the biblical chapters. It is the work of Charles Foster Kent, assisted by C. C. Torrey, H. A. Sherman, F. Harris, and Ethel Cutler.

THE WORK OF PROFESSOR GOODSPEED, 1923–31

Professor Edgar J. Goodspeed, of the University of Chicago, published in 1923 *The New Testament, an American Translation*. We have seen that he had an important part in the production of the Revised Standard Version in 1946, but it cannot be said that that text depends on his rendering of 1923 to any notable extent. Yet the principles that he enunciated in the introductory booklet that appeared with the Revised Standard

Version in 1946,[6] largely governed his work in his own earlier text, where he emphasized the discovery that "the New Testament was written not in classical Greek, nor in the 'biblical' Greek of the Greek version of the Old Testament, nor even in the literary Greek of its own day, but in the common language of everyday life. This fact has been fully established by the Greek papyrus discoveries and the grammatical researches of the last twenty-five years. . . . It follows that the most appropriate English form for the New Testament is the simple, straightforward English of everyday expression." [7] Dr. Goodspeed has long been of the opinion that "there is no book in the New Testament that cannot easily be read at a sitting." [8] In this connection he adds: "For American readers, especially, who have had to depend so long upon versions made in Great Britain, there is room for a New Testament free from expressions which, however familiar in England or Scotland, are strange to American ears."

A comparison between a few verses of Dr. Goodspeed's own version of 1923, in which he was free to choose his own idiom, and the Revised Standard Version of 1946, which sets out to be a revision of 1611, 1881, and 1901, and therefore stays closer to the traditional wording, would be of interest.

Matt. 1:18–20

Goodspeed, 1923

Now these were the circumstances of the birth of Jesus Christ. Mary, his mother, was engaged to Joseph, but before they were married it was found that she was about to become a mother through the influence of the holy Spirit. But her husband, Joseph, was an upright man and did not wish to disgrace her, and he decided to break off the engagement privately. But while he was thinking of doing this, an angel of the Lord appeared to him in a dream, and said. . . .

R.S.V., 1946

Now the birth of Jesus Christ took place in this way. When his mother Mary had been betrothed to Joseph, before they came together she was found to be with child of the Holy Spirit; and her husband Joseph, being a just man and unwilling to put her to shame, resolved to divorce her quietly. But as he considered this, behold, an angel of the Lord appeared to him in a dream, saying. . . .

[6] These principles are given in detail in the preceding chapter.

[7] From the Preface of the 1923 edition. These conclusions were again enunciated in 1946; see above, p. 581.

[8] From the Introduction, 1923; cf. *How to read the Bible* (1948), p. 3, where he reckons that the Gospel of St. Mark "can easily be read aloud in an hour and a half, and to yourself in half that time."

There is no doubt that the literal terseness of the version of 1946 is attractive, even if we might take exception to the word "divorce"; yet the freshness and modernity of Dr. Goodspeed's own version strikes us at once. The books stand in the traditional order, and there are no notes. The titles are the same as in the American Standard Version, except that "Letter" is written for "Epistle."

The Old Testament in *An American Translation* was published in 1927 under the editorship of J. M. Powis Smith of Chicago, with the assistance of three other scholars, Alex. R. Gordon, of Montreal, Theophile J. Meek, of Toronto, and Leroy Waterman, of Michigan. Here again the editor's Introduction emphasizes the progress made in the knowledge of Hebrew usage and in textual criticism, and the consequent need of a new translation. An important feature of this edition was the inclusion of an Appendix of ninety-one closely printed pages indicating the passages where the translators departed from the Hebrew text as it now stands. In the Introduction they assure us that when they have rejected the Masoretic text it is usually when a better reading is provided by the versions, and that they have adopted conjectural readings only "along generally approved lines." This was the first version candidly to adopt conjectural emendations in its translation of the Hebrew text. In this matter it has been followed by the Westminster Version, which explains the emendations in its numerous notes, by the Confraternity Old Testament edition of Genesis, which has an Appendix like the present version, and by the Basic English edition, which has no explanation. It should be said that most of the emendations made here are those which receive general acceptance among exegetes today. There are no notes or introductions in this edition.

In 1931 *The Bible, An American Translation* appeared, including Dr. Goodspeed's New Testament, with a short Preface by Powis Smith and Goodspeed. In 1933 an abridged edition, *The Short Bible,* was published. In 1939 there was a further edition including the Apocrypha, translated by Goodspeed, and entitled, *The Complete Bible, an American Translation.* This includes our deutero-canonical books and also those books regarded as apocrypal by the Church, notably II Esdras (IV Esdras in the Appendix to the Vulgate). Concerning these books Dr. Goodspeed writes, without mentioning his own name: "The American Translation of 1938,[9] the only one based directly on the Greek throughout (except for 2 Esdras, which exists only in Latin), is the only fresh version of the whole group of fourteen books made since Coverdale's Bible translated them in 1535." [10] In fact it seems that none of the revisers, in 1611, 1881, or 1901, made much improvement on that text.

In 1948 a handsome edition of Dr. Goodspeed's New Testament was published to mark the twenty-fifth anniversary of its original publication.

THE RIVERSIDE NEW TESTAMENT, 1923 [11]

The Riverside New Testament is a new translation into modern English from the original Greek (Nestle's text of 1901) by W. G. Ballantine, published at Boston in 1923. The translator states that he has been guided by the Authorized Version and the Revised Version, as well as by the various modern-speech translations then existing. The style of printing is entirely modern, without any verse numbers, references, or notes. A revised edition appeared in 1934.

MRS. MONTGOMERY'S NEW TESTAMENT, 1924

To mark the first hundred years of service of the American Baptist Publication Society, Mrs. Helen Barrett Montgomery, of Rochester, New York, published *The Centenary Translation of the New Testament* in two volumes at Philadelphia in 1924. She is the only woman who has produced a modern-speech New Testament. A brief introduction precedes each book, and unusual features are the titles assigned to each chapter, in the manner of many modern books, and the colloquial subject headings affixed to each paragraph, such as "A 'Close-up' of Sin," "Paul's Swan Song," and "Orchestrate your Virtues."

PROFESSOR TORREY'S GOSPELS, 1933

Professor Charles Cutler Torrey, of Yale University, who had been associated with the production of *The Shorter Bible* in 1918, published *The Four Gospels—A New Translation* in 1933. Torrey was of the opinion that the Gospels as we have them in Greek are themselves trans-

[9] Goodspeed's *Apocrypha* had appeared as a separate volume in 1938.

[10] *How to read the Bible* (1948), p. 225.

[11] The information about this and the following two American translations I owe entirely to I. M. Price, *The Ancestry of Our English Bible* (2nd revised ed., 1949), pp. 298 f.

lations of Semitic documents. He reconstructed these documents, and the present work is a translation of these hypothetical documents. The work undoubtedly throws light on the Semitic background of the New Testament, but the fact that the underlying theory is quite unproven must perforce keep such a work in the realm of pure speculation. Furthermore, the evidence that has been coming to light of Greek usage in New Testament times makes highly unlikely the supposition that the Gospels are all translations of Semitic sources. The book was published in England in 1934, though not printed there.

DR. WADE'S TRANSLATION, 1934

Dr. G. W. Wade's large volume of *Documents of the New Testament,* published in 1934, performs a function similar to Dr. Moffatt's translation of 1901, presenting the various documents of the New Testament in their supposed chronological order; but with these differences: Wade's translation is made into modern English, the text is interspersed with symbols indicating the provenance of the passage, explanatory phrases are inserted in italics, and the chronological order proposed is slightly different. Dr Wade's order is also based on the usual critical theories; for instance, in "Matthew" symbols indicate passages from Mark (Mk), Q, and Matthew himself (M). A notable divergence from Moffatt is the supposition that II Tim. is entirely fragmentary, various passages being scattered throughout the whole chronology. The text of the Synoptic Gospels provides a very exact account of the theory current in the earlier part of this century.

The four Gospels were reprinted as separate pamphlets in 1935–36. The version is too closely tied to the critical theories adopted to make pleasant reading except for the student of those theories. The explanatory phrases, however, sometimes make a useful paraphrase.

BASIC ENGLISH EDITIONS, 1941, 1949

The New Testament in Basic English appeared in 1941, and *The Bible in Basic English* in 1949. A "Note" which appears at the beginning both of the New Testament and of the Bible, itself written in Basic English, explains the nature of the translation:

The form in which the Bible is given here is not simply another example of the Bible story put into present-day English. The language used is Basic English. Basic English, produced by Mr. C. K. Ogden of the Orthological Institute, is a simple form of the English language which, with 850 words, is able to give the sense of anything which may be said in English. Working with the Orthological Institute, a Committee under the direction of Professor S. H. Hooke, Professor Emeritus of Old Testament studies in the University of London, has been responsible for a new English form of the Bible made from the Hebrew and the Greek. In this undertaking, the latest ideas and discoveries in connection with the work of putting the Bible into other languages were taken into account, and when the Basic form was complete it was gone over in detail by a Committee formed by the Syndics of the Cambridge University Press

A footnote adds that "by the addition of 50 special Bible words and the use of 100 words listed as giving most help in the reading of English verse, this number (850) has been increased to 1000 for the purpose of putting the Bible into Basic." A further note at the beginning of the Bible states that "when words are used which are not in the Basic list, they are printed in sloping print the first time they are used in any division of any book." Such words, we find, are equivalent to proper names, and are not numerous. For instance, Amos uses only "cedar, oak, fig, olive, Pleiades, bear"; while Micheas uses "jackals, ostriches, fig."

At first it would seem that the limited vocabulary must cramp the style; yet the translation achieves power by its very simplicity. The book of Job is always difficult to translate, and the following well-known passage will illustrate the nature of this translation: "Do you give strength to the horse? is it by your hand that his neck is clothed with power? Is it through you that he is shaking like a locust, in the pride of his loud-sounding breath? He is stamping with joy in the valley; he makes sport of fear. In his strength he goes out against the arms of war, turning not away from the sword" (Job 39:19–22).

The text is printed in verses, as in the Authorized Version, with no special device to indicate poetical passages. An important feature in the Old Testament is that the conjectural emendations which find general acceptance among scholars are included in the text, as in the *American Translation,* but without any indication that the Hebrew text has been abandoned.

DR. WAND'S EPISTLES, 1943

The New Testament Letters, prefaced and paraphrased, by Dr. J. W. C. Wand, first appeared in Australia in 1943 when the translator was archbishop of Brisbane. In 1946 the volume was published in England, with a few small corrections, after he had become bishop of London. In his Introduction, Dr. Wand says that his work "may be called either a free translation or a close paraphrase"; but in fact it is frequently a very close translation. Yet the title "paraphrase" has enabled the translator sometimes to substitute an English idiom and rearrange the sentences, and even occasionally to insert a phrase as a link in the argument. The result is an argument that is astonishingly faithful to the original; and frequently a colloquial phrase in English corresponds exactly to a colloquial phrase in the Greek, such as "your super-apostles" in II Cor. 12:11. The familiar style is seen in the following example (Philem. 7–10):

> I have been especially encouraged lately, my dear brother, by the thought of your love and generosity, for you have relieved the brothers of many anxieties. Consequently, there is no need for me to urge you to do your bounden duty in the particular matter about which I am writing. . . . I want to enlist your sympathy on behalf of a convert I have made here in prison—a veritable son born to me while in chains. It is none other than Onesimus.

Yet the translation is not entirely colloquial; we can find a lovely passage such as the opening of St. John's First Epistle:

> I am going to write to you about the Word of Life. He existed from the beginning, before time was; yet I have listened to Him; I have seen Him with my own eyes; I have really looked at Him, and have touched Him with my own hands. What that Word revealed to us was Life. I have really seen Eternal Life. And now I am testifying to it and announcing it to you.

The text is printed in paragraphs with subject headings, but without notes. The traditional chapter numbers are retained, but verse numbers are inserted only at the beginning of each paragraph to assist reference. The epistles stand in chronological order.

THE EPISTLES OF J. B. PHILLIPS, 1947

Letters to Young Churches, a translation of the New Testament Epistles, was published in 1947 with an Introduction by C. S. Lewis. Rev. J. B.

Phillips had been at work on the version since 1941. The book has had a remarkable sale, having gone through seven printings by the end of 1950. The letters are presented in the manner indicated in the title, as messages of instruction, consolation, and reproof to the first Christians, and equally applicable to ourselves today. With this special object in view, this translation is the freest of all the modern-speech versions, and although it does not represent Holy Writ word for word, yet it cannot be said that the argument is ever injured. An example will show the style of the translation (I Cor. 1:11–17).

> For I know, from what some of Chloe's people have told me, that you are each making different claims—"I am one of Paul's men," says one; "I am one of Apollos'," says another, or "I am one of Cephas' "; while someone else says, "I owe my faith to Christ alone."
>
> What *are* you saying? Is there more than one Christ? Was it Paul who died on the Cross for you? Were you baptised in the name of Paul? It makes me thankful that I didn't actually baptise any of you (except Crispus and Gaius), or perhaps someone would be saying I did it in my own name. (Oh yes, I did baptise Stephanas' family, but I can't remember anyone else.) For Christ did not send me to see how many I could baptise, but to proclaim the Gospel.

This is probably about as far as the experiment with modern idiom can go; and occasionally Mr. Phillips has gone a little too far, as when "Stachys my beloved" (Rom. 16:9) appears as "dear old Stachys," and "Salute one another with a holy kiss" (Rom. 16:16) appears as "Give each other a hearty handshake all round for my sake."

The text is printed in paragraphs with frequent subject headings, while chapter and verse numbers appear in the margin only at the paragraph headings. The epistles stand in the traditional order.

THE LETCHWORTH NEW TESTAMENT, 1948

The Letchworth New Testament is a translation along more traditional lines. It appeared in 1948 as *The New Testament of Our Lord and Saviour Jesus Christ. The Letchworth Version in Modern English,* by T. F. Ford and R. E. Ford. The text is basically that of the Authorized Version, but all archaic words and phrases have been replaced by modern ones. Frequently whole sections read as in A.V. It is therefore not a revision, but rather an adaptation of A.V. to modern speech. In this respect it stands alone among the modern-speech versions, except for Bilton's Gospels of 1888.[12] The text is printed in verses as in A.V., even including the sign to indicate a new paragraph.

All the modern-speech versions mentioned in this chapter were made by Protestants.[13] The only Catholic version using a completely modern medium is the Confraternity Edition of Genesis, 1948. Msgr. Knox's New Testament, 1945, aims at "a sort of timeless English," and in his Old Testament certain archaisms are deliberately retained.[14]

As an epilogue to this interesting study of the numerous English versions of the Bible, these words of the late James Gairdner, written in reference to the Revised Version but applicable to all other versions of Holy Scripture, are indeed appropriate.

> Any translation of such a book as the Bible can only convey the meaning of the original with the help of comment and traditional interpretation; and when a new translation has been familiarised by sufficient use, it makes the atmosphere in which it lives. Even the positive errors it may contain are no serious bar to the reception of a large amount of valuable and far-reaching truth. But, though much is gained by traditional interpretation, it is a drawback to the study of Holy Scripture to this day, that men too easily satisfy themselves with translations as if they could be perfect substitutes for the original. The Revised Version of the New Testament is almost expressly calculated to encourage this superstition. Of course it is a great deal more accurate than King James's version, especially as regards the niceties of Greek grammar. But it is of really far inferior value for general use, for it only gives half the significance of many words, where by varying translations the older version gives a great deal more.
>
> It would have been much more valuable to have had two or three new translations as different from each other as possible, in parallel columns. For instance, the two different meanings of the same Greek word which are actually found in different passages of King James's version: "Thy faith hath saved thee" and "thy faith hath made thee whole," Luke vii.50 and viii 48, might be placed side by side in each case, for both meanings are contained in the original.[15]

[12] See above, p. 587.

[13] Little has been written about these versions; most of the facts in this chapter have been gathered from the editions themselves. Yet some of these versions are mentioned in the following works: Edgar J. Goodspeed, *How to read the Bible,* 1946 (British ed., 1948); F. Harrison, *The Bible in Britain,* 1949; Ira M. Price, *The Ancestry of Our English Bible,* 2nd revised ed. by William Irwin and Allen Wikgren, New York, 1949; P. H. Vogel, "Englische Bibelübersetzungen," in the *Internationale kirchliche Zeitschrift* (Berne), 1949, pp. 227–42; Luther A. Weigle, *The English New Testament from Tyndale to the Revised Standard Version,* Nashville, Tenn., 1949.

[14] Both of these versions have been noticed in chapter 40.

[15] *Lollardy and the Reformation in England,* I, 369 and note. This epilogue is the conclusion of the last chapter of Father Pope's manuscript.

APPENDIX I

Preface to the Rheims New Testament, 1582 [1]

The Preface to the reader, treating of these three points: of the translation of Holy Scriptures into the vulgar tongues, and namely into English: of the causes why this New Testament is translated according to the auncient vulgar Latin text: and of the maner of translating the same.

The holy Bible long since translated by us into English, and the Old Testament lying by us for lacke of good meanes to publish the whole in such sorte as a worke of so great charge and importance requireth: we have yet through God's goodnes at length fully finished for thee (most Christian reader) all the New Testament, which is the principal most profitable and comfortable peece of holy writte: and aswel for all other institution of life and doctrine, as specially for deciding the doubtes of these daies, more propre and pregnant then the other part not yet printed.

Translation of the Scriptures into the vulgar tongues, not absolutely necessarie or profitable, but according to the time

Which translation we doe not for all that publish, upon erroneous opinion of necessitie, that the holy Scriptures should alwaies be in our mother tonge, or that they ought, or were ordained by God, to be read

[1] The Preface is given in part by Pollard, *Records of the English Bible,* pp. 301 ff.; large excerpts by Mombert, *English Versions of the Bible,* pp. 295 ff. The present text is taken from Cotton, *Rhemes and Doway,* who gives in full the Prefaces to both the New Testament and the Old, pp. 249–97. The footnotes and the citations in brackets have been added by the author. In the *British Museum Guide, Biblical Exhibition,* § 68, it is suggested that this Preface "may have been written by Richard Bristow," but this can be only an hypothesis. For further details, see *Notes on the Preface to the Rhemish Testament,* by Pseudo-Catholicus, Dublin, 1813, 1817.

indifferently of all, or could be easily understood of every one that readeth or heareth them in a knowen language: or that they were not often through mans malice or infirmitie, pernicious and much hurtful to many: or that we generally and absolutely deemed it more convenient in itself, and more agreable to Gods word and honour, or edification of the faithful, to have them turned into vulgar tonges, then to be kept and studied only in the Ecclesiastical learned languages: Not for these nor any such like causes doe we translate this sacred booke, but upon special consideration of the present time, state, and condition of our countrie, unto which, divers thinges are either necessarie, or profitable and medicinable now, that otherwise in the peace of the Church were neither moch requisite, nor perchance wholy tolerable.

The Churches wisedom and moderation concerning vulgar translation

In this matter, to marke only the wisedom and moderation of holy Church and the governours thereof on the one side, and the indiscrete zeale of the popular, and their factious leaders, on the other, is a high point of prudence. These later, partly of simplicitie, partly of curiositie, and specially of pride and disobedience, have made claime in this case for the common people, with plausible pretences many, but good reasons none at all. The other, to whom Christ hath given charge of our soules,[2] the dispensing of God's mysteries and treasures [3] (among which holy Scripture is no small store) and the feeding his familie in season with foode fit for every sort, have neither of old nor of late ever wholy condemned all vulgar versions of Scripture, nor have at any time generally forbidden the faithful to reade the same: yet they have not by publike authoritie prescribed, commaunded, or authentically ever recommended any such interpretation to be indifferently used of all men.

The Scriptures in the vulgar languages of divers nations

The Armenians say they have the Psalter and some other peeces translated by S. Chrysostom into their language, when he was banished among them.[4] And George the Patriarch, in writing his life, signifieth no

[2] Matt. 24:45.

[3] I Cor. 4:1.

[4] So Sixtus of Siena, *Bibliotheca sancta,* VIII; cf. St. Chrysostom, *Homilies on the Pentateuch,* ed. by Gaume, II, ii, 548; *De Lazaro,* Concio III, ed. by Gaume, VI, 903; VII, 216, 361.

lesse. The Slavonians affirme they have the Scriptures in their vulgar tonge, turned by S. Hierom, and some would gather so much by his owne wordes in his epistle to Sophronius, but the place in deede proveth it not.[5] Vulpilas surely gave the Scriptures to the Gothes in their owne tonge, and that before he was an Arrian.[6]

Auncient Catholike translations of the Bible into the Italian, Frenche, and Englishe tongue

It is almost three hundred yeres, since James Archbishop of Genua, is said to have translated the Bible into Italian.[7] More then two hundred yeres agoe, in the daies of Charles the fifth the Frenche king, was it put forth faithfully in Frenche, the sooner to shake out of the deceived peoples handes the false heretical translations of the sect called *Waldenses.*[8]

An auncient provincial constitution in England concerning English translations

In our own countrie, notwithstanding the Latin tonge was ever (to use Venerable Bedes wordes) common to all the provinces of the same for meditation or studie of Scriptures,[9] and no vulgar translation commonly used or occupied of the multitude, yet they were extant in English even before the troubles that Wicleffe and his folowers raised in our

[5] The notion that St. Jerome translated the Bible into the language of Dalmatia seems to have arisen from what is commonly regarded as a misunderstanding by Sixtus of Siena of St. Jerome when he speaks of a translation he had made *meae linguae hominibus* (*Praefatio in Psalterium,* in Migne, *P.L.,* XXCIII, 1126; on Zach., chap. 6 and 10:11 f., in Migne, *P.L.,* XXV, 1454, 1496). Sixtus understood this to mean "the language of Strigonia"; possibly he was right, on the assumption that had St. Jerome meant the Latin language he would have said so. The Slavonic version was made by SS. Cyril and Methodius in the ninth century.

[6] For Ulfilas' translation see Socrates, *Historia,* IV, 33, and Sozomen, *Historia,* VI, 37; J. Bosworth, *The Gothic and Anglo-Saxon Gospels in Parallel Columns with the Versions of Wycliffe and Tyndale,* London, 1865, 1888, 1907; G. W. Friedrichsen, *The Gothic Version of the Gospels; a study of its style and textual history,* Oxford, 1926; *idem, The Gothic Version of the Epistles,* 1936. See A. Wilmart, "Les Évangiles Gothiques," in *Revue Biblique,* January, 1927, pp. 46 ff.

[7] James of Voragine, O.P., author of the once popular *Golden Legend,* is said by Sixtus of Siena to have been the first to translate the Old and New Testaments into Italian (*Bibliotheca sancta,* p. 467). But Richard Simon says it was never printed, nor had he ever come across a copy in manuscript (*Critical History of the Versions of the New Testament* [1689], p. 335).

[8] For the Waldensians see S. R. Maitland, *Facts and Documents Illustrative of the History, Doctrines, and Rites of the Ancient Albigenses and Waldenses,* 1832.

[9] *Historia,* I, 1.

Church, as appeareth as well by the testimonie of Malmesburie recording that V. Bede translated divers partes into the vulgar tonge of his time, and by some peeces yet remaining, as by a provincial Constitution of Thomas Arundel Archbishop of Canturburie in a Councel holden at Oxford.[10] Where straite provision was made that no heretical version set forth by Wicleffe, or his adherentes, should be suffered, nor any other in or after his time be published or permitted to be readde, being not approved and allowed by the Diocesan before: alleaging S. Hierom for the difficultie and danger of interpreting the holy Scripture out of one tonge into an other, though by learned and Catholike men. So also it is there insinuated, that neither the Translations set forth before that Heretike's time, nor other afterward being approved by the lawful Ordinaries, were ever in our countrie wholy forbidden, though they were not (to say the truth) in quiet and better times (much lesse when the people were prone to alteration, heresie, or noveltie) either hastily admitted, or ordinarily readde of the vulgar, but used onely or specially of some devoute religious and contemplatives persons, in reverence, secrecie, and silence, for their spiritual comforte.

The like Catholike and vulgar translations in many countries, since Luther's time

Now since Luther's revolt also, divers learned Catholikes, for the more speedy abolishing of a number of false and impious translations put forth by sundry sectes, and for the better preservation or reclaime of many good soules endangered thereby, have published the Bible in the several languages of almost all the principal provinces of the Latin Church, no other bookes in the world being so pernicious as hereticall translations of the Scriptures, poisoning the people under colour of divine authoritie, and not many other remedies being more soveraine against the same (if it be used in order, discretion, and humilitie) then the true, faithful, and sincere interpretation opposed thereunto.

The Churches order and determination concerning the reading of Catholike translations of the Bible in vulgar tongues

Which causeth the holy Church not to forbid utterly any Catholike translation, though she allow not the publishing or reading of any abso-

[10] See *supra*, pp. 65 f.

lutely and without exception, or limitation; knowing by her divine and most sincere wisedome, how, where, when, and to whom these her Maisters and Spouses giftes are to be bestowed to the most good of the faithful; and therfore neither generally permitteth that which must needes doe hurt to the unworthy, nor absolutely condemneth that which may doe much good to the worthie. Whereupon, the order which many a wise man wished for before, was taken by the Deputies of the late famous Councel of Trent in this behalfe, and confirmed by supreme authoritie, that the holy Scriptures, though truely and Catholikely translated into vulgar tonges, yet may not be indifferently readde of all men, nor of any other then such as have expresse licence therunto of their lawful Ordinaries, with good testimonie from their Curates or Confessors, that they be humble discrete and devout persons, and likely to take much good and no harme thereby.[11] Which prescript, though in these daies of ours it cannot be so precisely observed, as in other times and places where there is more due respecte of the Churches authoritie, rule, and discipline; yet we trust all wise and godly persons will use the matter in the meanewhile, with such moderation, meekenes, and subiection of hart, as the handling of so sacred a booke, the sincere senses of God's truth therein, and the holy Canons, Councels, reason, and religion do require.

The holy Scriptures never read of al persons indifferently, at their pleasure

Wherein, though for due preservation of this divine work from abuse and prophanation, and for the better bridling of the intolerable insolencie of proude, curious, and contentious wittes, the governours of the Church guided by God's spirit, as ever before, so also upon more experience of the maladie of this time then before, have taken more exact order both for the readers and translations in these later ages, then of old: yet we

[11] Among the 101 propositions taken from the writings of Quesnel, nos. 79–85 deal with his views on vernacular versions of the Scriptures, which were, he maintained, for the use of all people indiscriminately; cf. Denzinger, *Enchiridion* (1911), §§1429–35. In 1794 Pius VI condemned similar views as "false, rash, and calculated to disturb men's minds" (*ibid.*, §1567). See the Encyclical of Gregory XVI, May, 1844, on the work of the Bible Societies (*ibid.*, §§1630–33), and a similar condemnation by Leo XII, May, 1824 (*ibid.*, §1607). See also the Encyclical of Pius XII, *Divino afflante Spiritu*, September 30, 1943; Innocent III, *Epis.*, II, 141, in Migne, *P.L.*, CCXIV, 695; St. Gregory the Great, *Epis.*, 4 and 40, *ad Theodosium*.

must not imagin that in the primitive Church, either every one that understoode the learned tonges wherein the Scriptures were written, or other languages into which they were translated, might without reprehension reade, reason, dispute, turne and tosse the Scriptures: or that our forefathers suffered every scholemaister, scholer, or Grammarian that had a little Greeke or Latin, straight to take in hand the holy Testament: or that the translated Bibles into the vulgar tonges, were in the handes of every husbandman, artificer, prentice, boies, girles, mistresse, maid, man: that they were sung, plaied, alleaged, of every tinker, taverner, rimer, minstrel: that they were for table talk, for alebenches, for boates and barges, and for every prophane person and companie. No, in those better times men were neither so ill, nor so curious of themselves, so to abuse the blessed booke of Christ: neither was there any such easy meanes before printing was invented, to disperse the copies into the handes of every man, as now there is.

Where and in whose handes the Scriptures were in the primitive Church

They were then in Libraries, Monasteries, Colleges, Churches, in Bishops, Priests, and some other devout principal Laymens houses and handes: who used them with feare and reverence, and specially such partes as perteined to good life and maners, not medling, but in pulpit and schooles (and that moderately to) with the hard and high mysteries and places of greater difficultie.

How the laitie of those daies did read them, with what humilitie and religion, and enformation of life and maners

The poor ploughman, could then in labouring the ground, sing the hymnes and psalmes either in knowen or unknowen languages, as they heard them in the holy Church, though they could neither reade nor know the sense, meaning, and mysteries of the same. Such holy persons of both sexes to whom S. Hierom in divers Epistles to them commendeth the reading and meditation of holy Scriptures, were diligent to searche all the godly histories and imitable examples of chastitie, humilitie, obedience, clemencie, povertie, penance, renouncing the world: they noted specially the places that did breed the hatred of sinne, feare of God's judgement, delight in spiritual cogitations: they referred them selves in all hard places to the judgement of the auncient fathers and their maisters in religion, never presuming to contend, controule, teach or talke of their own sense and phantasie, in deepe questions of divinitie. Then the virgins did meditate upon the places and examples of chastitie, modestie, and demurenesse: the maried, on conjugal faith and continencie: the parents, how to bring up their children in faith and feare of God: the Prince, how to rule: the subject, how to obey: the Priest, how to teach: the people, how to learne.

The fathers sharply reprehend as an abuse, that al indifferently should reade, expound, and talk of the Scriptures

Then the scholer taught not his maister, the sheepe controuled not the Pastor, the yong student set not the Doctor to schoole, not reproved their fathers of error and ignorance. Or if any were in those better daies (as in al times of heresie such must nedes be) that had itching eares, tikling tonges and wittes, curious and contentious disputers, hearers, and talkers rather than doers of God's word: such the Fathers did ever sharply reprehend, counting them unworthy and unprofitable readers of the holy Scriptures. S. Hierom in his epistle to Paulinus,[12] after declaration that no handicrafte is so base, nor liberall science so easy that can be had without a Maister (which S. Augustine also affirmeth, *de utilitate cred.,* cap. 7) nor that men presume in any occupation to teach that [which] they never learned, "Only" (saith he) "the art of Scripture is that which every man chalengeth: this the chatting old wife, this the doting old man, this the brabling sophister, this on every hand, men presume to teach before they learne it." Againe, "Some with poise of lofty wordes devise of Scripture matters among women: othersome (phy upon it) learn of women what to teach men: and lest that be not ynough, by facilitie of tonge or rather audacitie, teach that to others which they understand never a whit themselves. To say nothing of such as be of my facultie: who stepping from secular learning to holy Scriptures, and able to tickle the eares of the multitude with smothe tale, thinke all they speake, to be the law of God." [13] This he wrote then, when this maladie of arrogancie and presumption in divine matters was nothing so outragious as now it is.

[12] *Epis.,* 53, §7.
[13] *Ibid.*

The Scriptures must be delivered in measure and discretion, according to eche man's nede and capacitie

S. Gregorie Nazianzene made an oration of the moderation that was to be used in these matters: where he saith, that some in his time thought themselves to have all the wisedom in the world, when they could once repeat two or three wordes, and them ill couched together, out of Scriptures: but he there divinely discourseth of the orders and differences of degrees: how in Christes mysticall body some are ordeined to learne, some to teach: that all are not Apostles, all Doctors, all interpreters, all of tonges and knowledge, not all learned in Scriptures and divinitie: that the people went not up to talke with God in the mountaine, but Moyses, Aaron, and Eleazar: nor they neither, but by the difference of their callings: that they that rebel against this ordinance, are guilty of the conspiracie of Core and his complices: that in Scripture there is both milke for babes, and meate for men, to be dispensed, not according to every ones greedines of appetit or wilfulnes, but as is most meete for eche ones necessitie and capacitie: that as it is a shame for a Bishop or Priest to be unlearned in Gods mysteries, so for the common people it is often times profitable to salvation, not to be curious, but to folow their Pastors in sinceritie and simplicitie:[14] whereof excellently saith S. Augustine, "Fidei simplicitate et sinceritate lactati nutriamur in Christo: et cum parvi sumus, maiorum cibos non appetamus," that is, "Being fed with the simplicitie and sinceritie of faith, as it were with milke, so let us be nourished in Christ: and when we are litle ones, let us not covet the meates of the elder sort."[15] Who in another place testifieth that the word of God cannot be preached, nor certaine mysteries uttered to all men alike, but are to be delivered according to the capacitie of the hearers: as he proveth both by S. Paules example, who gave not to every sort strong meate, but milke to many, as being not spiritual, but carnal and not capable: and by our lordes also, who spake to some plainely and to others in parables, and affirmed that he had many things to utter which the hearers were not able to beare.[16]

How much more may we gather, that all things that be written, are

[14] *De moderatione in disputationibus servanda,* ed. by Billius, p. 227.

[15] *De agone Christiano,* XXXIII, 35.

[16] *De dono perseverantiae,* XVI, 40; *De Genesi ad litteram,* VII, 9; *Homilies on the Gospel of St. John,* XVIII, 5.

not for the capacitie and diet of every of the simple readers, but that very many mysteries of holy writte be very far above their reach, and may and ought to be (by as great reason) delivered them in measure and meane most meete for them? which in deede can hardly be done, when the whole booke of the Bible lieth before every man in his mother tonge, to make choise of what he list.

The Jewes law for not reading certaine bookes of holy Scripture until a time

For which cause the said Gregorie Nazianzen wisheth the Christians had as good a law as the Hebrues of old had: [17] who (as S. Hierom also witnesseth) tooke order among them selves that none should read the *Cantica Canticorum* nor certaine other pieces of hardest Scriptures till they were thirtie yeres of age.[18]

And truely there is no cause why men should be more loth to be ordered and moderated in this point by God's Church and their Pastors, then they are in the use of holy Sacraments: for which as Christ hath appointed Priestes and ministers, at whose handes we must receive them, and not be our owne carvers: so hath he given us doctors, prophetes, expounders, interpreters, teachers and preachers, to take the law and our faith at their mouthes: because our faith and religion commeth not to us properly or principally by reading of Scriptures, but (as the Apostle saith [Rom. 10:17]) by hearing of the preachers lawfully sent: though reading in order and humilitie, much confirmeth and advanceth the same. Therefore this holy booke of the Scriptures is called of S. Ambrose

[17] His words on this subject are so apt that we give them in full: "There ought to be observed amongst us the same rule as was laid down by the prudent Hebrews, namely, that young people were not to be allowed to read certain portions of the Bible since such reading was likely to harm souls as yet unformed and weak. Similarly the right to discuss matters of faith should not be conceded to all indiscriminately, but only to certain people and on stated occasions, to people, that is, of some understanding and of careful mind. It should not be granted to men who are never satisfied, are full of ambition and an unprofitable and unholy zeal. Such folk should be set down in some place where they can do no harm either to themselves or others. But full freedom to discuss matters of faith should be accorded to such as show themselves modest and self-restrained in discussion" (*De moderatione in disputationibus servanda,* ed. by Billius, pp. 233 f.).

[18] "Nam nisi quis apud eos (scil. Hebraeos) aetatem sacerdotalis ministerii, id est, trigesimum annum impleverit, nec principia Geneseos, nec Canticum canticorum, nec hujus voluminis [scil. Ezechiel] exordium et finem legere permittitur, ut ad perfectam scientiam, et mysticos intellectus, plenum humanae naturae tempus accedat" (St. Jerome in the Prologue to his *Commentary on Ezechiel,* in Migne, *P.L.,* XXV, 17).

Liber sacerdotalis, "the book of priestes," at whose handes and disposition we must take and use it. (L. i. 2. *ad Grat.*) [19]

The popular objections of withholding the Scriptures from the people, answered

The wise will not here regard what some wilful people do mutter, that the Scriptures are made for all men, and that it is of envie that the Priestes do keepe the holy booke from them. Which suggestion commeth of the same serpent that seduced our first parents, who persuaded them, that God had forbidden them that tree of knowledge, lest they should be as cunning as himself, and like unto the Highest [Gen. 3:5].

Why the Church permitteth not every one at their pleasure to reade the Scripture

No, no, the church doth it, to keepe them from blind ignorant presumption, and from that which the Apostle calleth *falsi nominis scientiam, knowledge falsely so called* [I Tim. 6:20]: and not to embarre them from the true knowledge, of Christ. She would have all wise, but *usque ad sobrietatem, unto sobrietie,* as the Apostle speaketh [Rom. 12:3]: she knoweth the Scriptures be ordained for every state, as meates, elements, fire, water, candle, knives, sword, and the like: which are as needful (most of them) for children as old folks, for the simple as the wise: but yet would marre all, if they were at the guiding of other then wise men, or were in the handes of every one, for whose preservation they be profitable.

The holy Scriptures to carnal men and heretikes, are as pearles to swine

She forbiddeth not the reading of them in any language, envieth no man's commoditie, but giveth order how to doe it to edification and not destruction: how to doe it without casting *the holy to dogges,* or *pearles to hogges* [Matt. 7:6]: (see S. Chrysost. *hom.* 24 *in Matth.* declaring these hogges and dogges to be carnal men and Heretikes, that take no good of the holy mysteries, but thereby do both hurt themselves and others:) how to doe it agreably to the soverain sinceritie, maiestie, and depth of Mysterie conteined in the same. She would have the presumptious Here-

[19] *De fide ad Gratianum,* III, xv, 128.

tike, notwithstanding he alleage them never so fast, flying as it were through the whole Bible, and coting the Psalmes, Prophets, Gospels, Epistles, never so readily for his purpose, as Vincentius Lirinensis saith such mens fashion is: yet she would, according to Tertullian's rule, have such mere usurpers quite discharged of all occupying and possession of the holy Testament, which is her old and onely right and inheritance, and belongeth not to Heretikes at all,[20] whom Origen calleth *Scripturarum fures, theeves of the Scriptures.*[21] She would have the unworthy repelled, the curious repressed, the simple measured, the learned humbled, and all sortes so to use them or absteine from them, as is most convenient for every ones salvation: with this general admonition, that none can understand the meaning of God in the Scriptures except Christ open their sense,[22] and make them partakers of his holy spirit in the unitie of his mystical bodie: and for the rest, she committeth it to the Pastor of every province and people, according to the difference of time, place, and persons, how and in what sort the reading of the Scriptures is more or less to be procured or permitted.

S. Chrysostom's exhortations to the reading of holy Scriptures, and when the people is so to be exhorted

Wherein, the varietie of circumstances causeth them to deale diversely: as we see by S. Chrysostom's people of Constantinople, who were so delicate, dull, worldly, and so much given to dice, cardes, specially stage-plaies or theaters (as S. Gregorie Nazianzene witnesseth) [23] that the Scriptures and all holy lections of divine things were lothsome unto them: wherby their holy Bishop was forced in many of his sermons to crie out against their extreme negligence and contempt of God's word, declaring that not only Eremites and Religious (as they alleaged for their excuse) but secular men of all sortes might reade the Scriptures, and often have more neede thereof in respect of them selves, then the other that live in more puritie and contemplation: further insinuating, that though divers thinges be high and hard therein, yet many godly histories,

[20] *De praescriptionibus haereticorum,* chaps. 15–19. "If Heretics wish to base themselves on Scripture, it should be made quite clear before they do so whether they have any right to use the Scripture, . . . for the controversy based on Scripture can lead to nothing save an upset to brain or stomach" (*ibid.,* chap. 15).

[21] On Rom., chap. 2.

[22] Luke 24:27, 45.

[23] *De laudibus Athanasii,* ed. by Billius, p. 183, col. 2.

lives, examples, and precepts of life and doctrine be plaine: and finally, that when the Gentiles were so cunning and diligent to impugne their faith, it were not good for Christians to be to simple or negligent in the defense thereof, as (in truth) it is more requisite for a Catholike man in these daies when our Adversaries be industrious to empeache our beleefe, to be skilful in Scriptures, then at other times when the Church had no such enemies.[24]

S. Chrysostom maketh nothing for the popular and licentious reading of Scriptures used among the Protestants now a daies

To this sense said S. Chrysostom divers thinges, not as a teacher in schole, making exact and general rules to be observed in all places & times, but as a pulpit man, agreably to that audience and his peoples default.

Every simple artificer among them readeth much more the deepest and hardest questions of holy Scripture, then the moral partes

Nor making it therefore (as some perversely gather of his wordes) a thing absolutely needful for every poore artificer to reade or studie Scriptures, nor anywhit favouring the presumptuous, curious, and contentious iangling and searching of God's secretes reproved by the foresaid fathers, much lesse approving the excessive pride and madnes of these daies, when every man and woman is become not only a reader, but a teacher, controuler; and iudge of Doctors, Church, Scriptures and all: such as either contemne or easily passe over all the moral partes, good examples, and precepts of life (by which as well the simple as learned might be much edified) and only in a maner, occupie them selves in dogmatical, mystical, high and hidden secretes of Gods counsels, as of Predestination, reprobation, election, prescience, forsaking of the Jewes, vocation of the gentiles, & other incomprehensible mysteries, "Languishing about questions" [I Tim. 6:4] of onely faith, fiduce, new phrases and figures, "ever learning" but "never coming to knowledge" [II Tim. 3:7], reading and tossing in pride of witte, conceit of their owne cunning, and upon presumption of I can tell what spirit, such books specially and Epistles, as S.

[24] St. Chrysostom, *Hom. in Matt.*, II, 5, ed. by Guame, I, ii, 34 f.; *Hom. de Lazaro,* III, 1 f., ed. by Gaume, I, ii, 903 ff.; *Hom. in II Thess.*, III.

Peter foretold that the unlearned and instable would deprave to their owne damnation [II Pet. 3:16].

They presuppose no difficulties, which al the learned fathers felt to be in the Scriptures

They delight in none more then in the Epistle to the Romans, the *Cantica Canticorum,* the Apocalypse, which have in them as many mysteries as wordes. They find no difficultie in the Sacred booke clasped with seven seales [Apoc. 5:1]: they aske for no expositor with the holy Eunuch [Acts 8:27 ff.], they feel no such depth of Gods science in the Scriptures, as S. Augustine did, when he cried out, "Mira profunditas eloquiorum tuorum, mira profunditas (Deus meus) mira profunditas: horror est intendere in eam, horror honoris, et tremor amoris:" that is, "O wonderful profoundnes of thy wordes: wonderful profoundnes, my God, wonderful profoundnes: it maketh a man quake to looke on it: to quake for reverence, and to tremble for the love thereof." [25] They regard not that which the same Doctor affirmeth, that the depth and profunditie of wisedom, not only in the wordes of holy Scripture, but also in the matter and sense, is so wonderful, that, live a man never so long, be he of never so high a witte, never so studious, never so fervent to attaine the knowledge thereof, yet when he endeth, he shall confess he doth but begin.[26] They feele not with S. Hierom, that the text hath a hard shel to be broken before we come to the kirnel.[27] They will not stay themselves in only reading the sacred Scriptures thirtene yeres together, with S. Basil, & S. Gregorie Nazianzene, before they expound them, nor take the care (as they did) never otherwise to interpret them, then by the uniforme consent of their forefathers and tradition Apostolike.[28]

Maners and life nothing amended: but much worse, since this licentious tossing of holy Scriptures

If our new Ministers had had this cogitation and care that these and all other wise men have, and ever had, our countrie had never fallen to this miserable state in religion, & that under pretence, colour, and countenance of God's word: neither should vertue and good life have bene so

[25] *Confessions,* XII, xiv, 17.
[26] *Epis.,* 137, §§3, 18.
[27] *Epis.,* 58, §9.
[28] Rufinus, *Hist. Eccles.,* II, 9.

pitifully corrupted in time of such reading, toiling, trembling and translating the booke of our life and salvation: whereof the more pretious the right and reverent use is, the more pernicious is the abuse and prophanation of the same; which every man of experience by these few yeres proofe, and by comparing the former daies and maners to these of ours, may easily trie.

Looke whether your men be more vertuous, your women more chast, your children more obedient, your servants more trustie, your maides more modest, your frendes more faithful, your laitie more iust in dealing, your Cleargy more devout in praying: whether there be more religion, feare of God, faith and conscience in al states now, then of old, when there was not so much reading, chatting, and iangling of Gods word, but much more sincere dealing, doing and keeping the same. Looke whether through this disorder, women teach not their husbands, children their parents, yong fooles their old and wise fathers, the scholers their maisters, the sheepe their pastor, and the People the Priest.

Scriptures as profanely cited as heathen poetes

Looke whether the most chast and sacred sentences of Gods holy word, be not turned of many, into mirth, mockerie, amorous ballets & detestable letters of love and leudnes: their delicate times, tunes, and translations much encreasing the same.

Scriptures erroneously expounded according to every wicked mans private fantasie

This fall of good life, & prophaning the divine mysteries, every body seeth: but the great corruption & decay of faith hereby none see but wise men, who onely know, that, were the Scriptures never so truely translated, yet Heretikes and ill men that follow their owne spirit, and know nothing, but their private fantasie, and not the sense of the holy Church and Doctors, must needes abuse them to their damnation: and that the curious simple and sensual men which have no tast of the things that be of the spirit of God, may of infinite places take occasion of pernicious errors. For though the letter or text [in Mark 10:18] have no error, yet (saith St. Ambrose) the Arrian, or (as we may now speake) the Calvinian interpretation hath errors. *lib.* 2 *ad Gratianum, cap.* 1, and Tertullian saith, "The sense adulterated is as perilous as the style corrupted." *De praescript.* [*haereticorum,* 17]. S. Hilarie also speaketh thus: "Heresie riseth about the understanding, not about the writing: the fault is in the sense, not in the word." *lib.* 2. *de Trinitate, in principio.* And S. Augustine saith that many hold the Scriptures as they doe the Sacraments, "ad speciem et non ad salutem: to the outward shew, and not to salvation." *de baptis. cont. Donat. lib.* 3. *cap.* 19. [27].

Al Heretikes pretend Scriptures

Finally, all Sect-Maisters and ravening wolves, yea the divels them selves pretend Scriptures, alleage Scriptures, and wholy shroud them selves in Scriptures, as in the wool and fleese of the simple sheepe, whereby the vulgar, in these daies of generall disputes, can not but be in extreme danger of error, though their bookes were truely translated, and were truely in them selves Gods owne word in deede.

The Scriptures have been falsely and heretically translated into the vulgar tongues, and sundrie other waies sacrilegiously abused, and so given to the people to reade

But the case now is more lamentable: for the Protestants such as S. Paul calleth *"ambulantes in astutia, walking in deceitfulness"* [II Cor. 4:2], have so abused the people and many other in the world, not unwise, that by their false translations they have in steede of Gods Law and Testament, and for Christes written will and word, given them their owne wicked writing and phantasies, most shamefully in all their versions, Latin, English, and other tonges, corrupting both the letter and sense by false translation, adding, detracting, altering, transposing, pointing, and all other guileful meanes: specially where it serveth for the advantage of their private opinions, for which, they are bold also, partly to disauthorise quiet, partly to make doubtful, divers whole bookes allowed for Canonical Scripture by the universal Church of God this thousand yeres and upward: to alter al the authentical and Ecclesiastical wordes used sithence our Christianitie, into new prophane novelties of speaches agreable to their doctrine: to change the titles of workes, to put out the names of the authors, to charge the very Evangelist with following untrue translation,[29] to adde whole sentences proper to their sect, into their Psalmes in meter, even into the very Crede in rime.[30] Al which the poore

[29] Beza, on Luke 1:78.

[30] The margin has: "See the tenth Article of their creede in meter."

deceived people say and sing as though they were Gods owne word, being in deede through such sacrilegious treacherie, made the Divels word.

> Al this their dealing is noted (as occasion serveth) in the Annotations upon this Testament: and more at large in a booke lately made purposely of that matter, called A DISCOVERIE, etc.

To say nothing of their intolerable liberty and licence to change the accustomed callings of God, Angels, men, places and things used by the Apostles and all antiquitie, in Greeke, Latin, and all other languages of Christian Nations, into new names, sometimes falsely, and alwaies ridiculously and for ostentation taken from the Hebrews: to frame and fine the phrases of holy Scriptures after the forme of prophane [writers], sticking not, for the same to supply, adde, alter or diminish as freely as if they translated Livie, Virgil, or Terence.

Calvin complaineth of the new delicat translators, namely, Castalion: him self and Beza being as bad or worse

Having no religious respect to keepe either the maiestie or sincere simplicity of that venerable style of Christes spirit, as S. Augustine speaketh, which kind the holy Ghost did choose of infinite wisedom to have the divine mysteries rather uttered in, then any other more delicate, much lesse in that meretricious maner of writing that sundrie of these new tranlators doe use: of which sort Calvin him selfe and his pue-fellowes so much complaine, that they professe Satan to have gained more by these new interpreters (their number, levitie of spirit, and audacitie encreasing daily) then he did before by keeping the word from the people.[31] And for a paterne of this mischeefe, they give Castalion, adiuring all their churches and scholars to beware of his translation, as one that hath made a very sport and mockery of Gods holy word. So they charge him them selves (and the Zuinglians of Zuricke,[32] whose translations Luther therfore abhorred) handling the matter with no more fidelity, gravitie, or sinceritie, then the others: but rather with much more falsification, or (to use the Apostle's words) *cauponation* and *adulteration* of Gods word [II Cor. 2:17],[33] then they, besides many

[31] Calvin, *Praef. in Novum Testamentum,* 1567.

[32] Cf. Simler, *Vita H. Bullineri.*

[33] *Caupo* means huckster, and here instead of "adulterating," Tyndale and Cranmer

wicked gloses, prayers, confessions of faith, conteining both blasphemous errors and plaine contradictions to them selves and among them selves,[34] all privileged and authorised to be ioyned to the Bible, and to be said and sung of the poore people, and to be beleeved as articles of faith and wholy consonant to Gods word.

The purpose and commoditie of setting forth this Catholike edition

We therefore having compassion to see our beloved countrie men, with extreme danger of their soules, to use onely such prophane translations and erroneous mens mere phantasies, for the pure and blessed word of truth, much also moved thereunto by the desires of many devout persons: have set forth, for you (benigne readers) the new Testament to begin withal, trusting that it may give occasion to you, after diligent perusal thereof, to lay away at lest such their impure versions as hitherto you have ben forced to occupie. How well we have done it, we must not be iudges, but referre all to Gods Church and our superiors in the same. To them we submit our selves, and this, and all other our labours, to be in part or in the whole, reformed, corrected, altered, or quite abolished: most humbly desiring pardon if through our ignorance, temeritie, or other humane infirmitie, we have anywhere mistaken the sense of the holy Ghost. Further promising, that if hereafter we espie any of our owne errors, or if any other, either frende of good wil, or adversarie for desire of reprehension, shal open unto us the same: we wil not (as Protestants doe) for defense of our estimation, or of pride and contention, by wrangling wordes wilfully persist in them, but be most glad to hear of them, and in the next edition or otherwise to correct them: [35] for it is truth that we seeke for, and Gods honour, which being had either by good intention, or by occaseion, al is wel.[36]

---

have "chop and change," Geneva, "disguise and counterfait"; A.V. and R.V., "corrupt," but "make merchandise of" in the margin.

[34] A marginal heading at this point reads: "See the 4 article of their Creede in meter, where they professe that Christ descended to deliver the fathers, and afterward in their confession of their faith, they deny *Limbus patrum*."

[35] In accord with this statement, the marginal note at this place in the second edition reads: "We have accordingly in this second edition amended al such oversights as have hitherto been found, still submitting ourselves and promising as before."

[36] Cf. St. Augustine, *Confessions,* III, 5.

The religious care and sinceritie observed in this translation

This we professe onely, that we have done our endevour with prayer much feare and trembling, lest we should dangerously erre in so sacred, high, and divine a worke: that we have done it with all faith, diligence, and sinceritie: that we have used no partialitie for the disadvantage of our adversaries, nor no more licence then is sufferable in translating of holy Scriptures: continually keeping ourselves as neere as is possible, to our text and to the very wordes and phrases which by long use are made venerable, though to some prophane or delicate eares they may seem more hard and barbarous, as the whole style of Scripture doth lightly to such at the beginning: acknowledging with S. Hierom, that in other writings it is ynough to give in translation, sense for sense, but that in Scriptures, lesse we misse the sense, we must keepe the very wordes. *Ad Pammach. Epistola* 101. *ca.* 2. *in princip.*[37] We must, saith S. Augustine, speake according to a set rule, lest licence of wordes breede some wicked opinion concerning the thinges conteined under the wordes. *De civitate, lib.* 10. *cap.* 12.[38]

The auncient fathers kept religiously the very barbarismes of the vulgar Latin text

Whereof our holy fathers and auncient Doctors had such a religious care, that they would not change the very barbarismes or incongruities of speach which by long use had prevailed in the old readings or recitings of scriptures, *as neque nubent, neque nubentur* [Matt. 22:30], in Tertullian, lib. 4. in Marcion [§38], in S. Hilarie in c. 22. Matt. [chap. 23, §4], and in al the fathers. *Qui me confusus fuerit, confundar et ego sum,* in S. Cyprian. ep. 63. nu. 7.[39] *Talis enim nobis decebat sacerdos* (which was an elder translation then the vulgar Latin that now is) in S. Ambrose, c. 3. *de fuga seculi.* and S. Hierom him self, who otherwise

[37] "Ego enim non solum fateor, sed libera voce profiteor, me in interpretatione Graecorum, absque Scripturis sanctis, ubi et verborum ordo mysterium est, non verbum e verbo, sed exprimere de sensu" (St. Jerome, *Epis.* 57, §5). St. Jerome gives examples from Cicero, who claimed the same freedom for a translator, also from Terence and Plautus, adding from Horace's *De arte poetica:* "Nec verbum verbo curabis reddere, fidus interpres" (Migne, *P.L.,* XXII, 571); cf. *Epis.,* 106, §3.

[38] This reference must be a mistake; see *Contra faustum,* XXII, chap. 25, and *De doctrina Christiana,* II, xii–xiv, 17–20.

[39] In *Epis.,* 58, §15, St. Cyprian has: "Qui me confusus fuerit, confundetur eum filius hominis"; in *De lapsis,* chap. 20, he has: "Qui confessus me fuerit coram hominibus, et ego confitebor. . . ."

corrected the Latin translation that was used before his time, yet keepeth religiously (as himself professeth *Praefat. in* 4 *Evang. ad Damasum*) [40] these and the like speeches. *Nonne vos magis pluris estis illis?* [Matt. 6:26] and, *filius hominis non venit ministrari, sed ministrare* [Matt. 20:28; cf. Mark 10:45]: and, *neque nubent neque nubentur* [Luke 10:33]: in his commentaries upon these places: and, *Non capit Prophetam perire extra Hierusalem,* in his commentaries in c. 2. *Joel. sub finem.* And S. Augustine, who is most religious in al these phrases, counteth it a special pride and infirmitie in those that have a litle learning in tonges, and none in thinges, that they easily take offense of the simple speaches or solecismes in the Scriptures, *de doctrina Christ. li.* 2. *cap.* 13. [20]. See also the same holy father *li.* 3. *de doct. Christ.* c. 3. and *tract.* 2. *in Evang. Ioan.* But of the maner of our translation more anon.

Now, though the text thus truely translated, might sufficiently in the sight of the learned and al indifferent men, both controule the adversaries corruptions, and prove that the holy Scripture, whereof they have made so great vauntes, make nothing for their new opinions, but wholy for the Catholike Churches beleefe and doctrine, in all the pointes of difference betwixt us: yet knowing that the good and simple may easily be seduced by some few obstinate persons of perdition (whom we see given over into a reprobat sense, to whom the Gospel, which in it selfe is the odour of life to salvation, is made the odour of death to damnation, over whose eies for sinne and disobedience God suffereth a veile or cover to lie, whiles they reade the new Testament, even as the Apostle saith the Iewes have til this day, in reading of the old [II Cor. 3:13–16], that as the one sort cannot finde Christ in the Scriptures, reade they never so much, so the other can not finde the Catholike Churche nor her doctrine there neither) and finding by experience this saying of S. Augustine to be most true, "If the prejudice of any erroneous persuasion preoccupate the mind, whatsoever the Scripture hath contrarie, men take it for a figurative speach." [41]

Of the Annotations, why they were made, and what matter they conteine

For these causes, and somewhat to help the faithful reader in the difficulties of divers places, we have also set forth reasonable Annotations,

[40] "Si enim Latinis exemplaribus fides est adhibenda, respondeant, quibus: tot enim sunt exemplaria pene quot codices" (in Migne, *P.L.*, XXIX, 526).

[41] *De doctrina Christiana,* III, x, 15.

thereby to shew the studious reader in most places perteining to the controversies of this time, both the heretical corruptions and false deductions, and also the Apostolike tradition, the expositions of the holy fathers, the decrees of the Catholike Church and most auncient Councels: which meanes whosoever trusteth not, for the sense of holy Scriptures, but had rather folow his private iudgement or the arrogant spirit of these Sectaries, he shal worthily through his owne wilfulnes be deceived: beseeching all men to looke with diligence, sinceritie, and indifferencie, into the case that concerneth no lesse then every ones eternal salvation or damnation.

Heresies make Catholikes more diligent to search and finde the senses of holy Scripture for refelling of the same

Which if he doe, we doubt not but he shal to his great contentment, find the holy Scriptures most clerely and invincibly to prove the articles of Catholike doctrine against our adversaries, which perhaps he had thought before this diligent search, either not to be consonant to Gods word, or at least not conteined in the same, and finally he shal prove this saying of S. Augustine to be most true. "Multi sensus, etc. Many senses of holy Scriptures lie hidden, and are knowen to some few of greater understanding: neither are they at any time avouched more commodiously and acceptably then at such times, when the care to answer heretikes doth force men thereunto. For then, even they that be negligent in matters of studie and learning, shaking of sluggishnes, are stirred up to diligent hearing, that the Adversaries may be refelled. Againe, how many senses of holy Scriptures, concerning Christes Godhead, have been avouched against Photinus: how many, of his Manhood, against Manichaeus: how many, of the Trinitie, against Sabellius: how many, of the unitie in Trinitie, against the Arrians, Eunomians, Macedonians: how many, of the Catholike Church dispersed throughout the whole world, and of the mixture of good and bad in the same until the end of the world, against the Donatistes and Luciferians and others of the like errour: how many against al other heretikes, which it were to long to rehearse? of which senses and expositions of holy Scripture the approved authors and avouchers, should otherwise either not be knowen at al, or not so wel knowen as the contradictions of proud heretikes have made them." [42]

[42] *Enarr. in Ps.* 67, I, 39 (*P.L.*, XXXVI, 837).

Thus he saith of such thinges as not seeming to be in holy Scriptures to the ignorant or heretikes, yet in deede be there. But in other pointes doubted of, that in deede are not decided by Scripture, he giveth us this goodly rule to be folowed in all, as he exemplifieth in one. "Then do we hold (saith he) the veritie of the Scriptures, when we doe that which now hath seemed good to the Universal Church, which the authoritie of the Scriptures themselves doth commend: so that, forasmuch as the holy Scripture cannot deceive, whosoever is afraid to be deceived with the obscuritie of questions, let him therein aske counsel of the same CHURCH, which the holy scripture most certainely and evidently sheweth and pointeth unto." Aug. li. 1. Cont. Crescon. c. 13. [33.]

Many causes why this new Testament is translated according to the auncient vulgar Latin text

NOW TO GIVE thee also intelligence in particular, most gentle Reader, of such thinges as it behoveth thee specially to know concerning our Translation:—We translate the old vulgar Latin text, not the common Greeke text, for these causes: [43]

It is most auncient

1. It is so auncient, that it was used in the Church of God above 1,300 yeres agoe, as appeareth by the fathers of those times.

Corrected by S. Hierom

2. It is that (by the common received opinion, and by al probabilitie) which S. Hierom afterward corrected according to the Greeke, by the appointment of Damasus then Pope, as he maketh mention in his preface before the foure Evangelistes, unto the said Damasus: and *in Catalogo, in fine:* and *ep.* 102.[44]

[43] These are the famous "ten reasons" for preferring the Vulgate text of the New Testament to the Greek text current in the sixteenth century. They were bitterly assailed by E. Bulkeley, *An Answere to ten frivolous and foolish reasons set doun by the Rhemish Jesuits and Papists in their Preface before the New Testament by them lately translated into English, which have mooved them to forsake the originall fountaine of the Greeke, wherein the Spirit of God did indite the Gospell, and the holy Apostles did write it, to follow the streame of the Latin translation translated we know not when nor by whom. With a Discoverie of many great Corruptions and Faultes in the said English Translation set out at Rhemes,* London, 1588; see pp. 289 ff.

[44] *De viris illustribus,* chap. 135; cf. *Praef. in Evangelia, ad Damasum;* also *Epis.,* 27.

Commended by S. Augustine

3. Consequently it is the same which S. Augustine so commendeth and alloweth in an Epistle to S. Hierom.[45]

Used and expounded by the fathers

4. It is that, which for the most part ever since hath been used in the Churches service, expounded in sermons, alleaged and interpreted in the Commentaries and writings of the auncient fathers of the Latin Church.

Only authentical, by the holy Councel of Trent

5. The holy Councel of Trent, for these and many other important considerations, hath declared and defined this onely of al other Latin translations to be authentical, and so onely to be used and taken in publike lessons, disputations, preachings, and expositions, and that no man presume upon any pretence to reiect or refuse the same.[46]

Most grave, least partial

6. It is the gravest, sincerest, of greatest maiestie, least partialiety, as being without al respect of controversies and contentions, specially these of our time, as appeareth by those places which Erasmus and others at this day translate much more to the advantage of the Catholike cause.

Precise in following the Greeke

7. It is so exact and precise according to the Greeke, both the phrase and the word, that delicate Heretikes therfore reprehend it of rudenes. And that it foloweth the Greeke far more exactly than the Protestants translations, beside infinite other places, we appeale to these. *Tit.* 3. 14.

[45] The marginal reference is to *Epis.*, 10 (now 71), but a better reference would have been, *De doctrina Christiana,* II, xv, 22: "Itala ceteris praeteratur, nam est verborum tenacior cum perspicuitate sententiae."

[46] "This holy council, considering that not a little advantage will accrue to the Church of God if it be made known which of all the Latin editions of the sacred books now in circulation is to be regarded as authentic, ordains and declares that the old Latin Vulgate Edition, which, in use for so many hundred years, has been approved by the Church, be in public lectures, disputations, sermons and expositions held as authentic, and that no one dare or presume under any pretext whatsoever to reject it" (Sess. IV, April 8, 1546; in Denzinger, *Enchiridion* [1911], §785, and Schroeder, *Canons and Decrees of the Council of Trent,* pp. 18, 297); cf. Vatican Council, Sess. III, chap. 2, *Constitutio dogmatica de fide Catholica,* in Denzinger, §1787; Leo XIII, Encyclical *Providentissimus Deus,* in Denzinger, §1941.

"Curent bonis operibus praeesse, προίστασθαι. English Bib. 1577. "to mainteine good works."[47] And *Hebr.* 10. 20. "Viam nobis initiavit, ἐνεκαίνισεν. English Bib. "he prepared." So in these wordes, "Justificationes, Traditiones, Idola," etc. In al which they come not neere the Greeke, but avoid it of purpose.

Preferred by Beza himself

8. The Adversaries themselves, namely Beza, preferre it before al the rest. *In praefat. no. Test. an.* 1556. And againe he saith, that the old Interpreter translated very religiously. *Annot. in* 1 *Luc. v.* 1.

Al the rest misliked of the Sectaries themselves, eche reprehending an other

9. In the rest, there is such diversitie and dissension, and no end of reprehending one an other, and translating every man according to his fantasie, that Luther said, If the world should stand any long time, we must receive againe (which he thought absurd) the Decrees of the Councels, for preserving the unitie of faith, because of so divers interpretations of the Scripture.[48] And Beza (in the place above-mentioned) noteth the itching ambition of his fellow translators, that had much rather disagree and dissent from the best, then seeme them selves to have said or written nothing. And Bezas translation it self being so esteemed in our countrie, that the Geneva English Testaments be translated according to the same,[49] yet sometime goeth so wide from the Greek, and from the meaning of the holy Ghost, that them selves which protest to translate it, dare not folow it. For example, *Luc.* 3. 36. they have put the wordes, "The sonne of Cainan," which he wittingly and wilfully left

[47] Wycliffe, "they that be of ouris: lerne to be gouvernouris in good werkis, to necessarie usis"; Tyndale, Cranmer, Geneva, "learn to excell in good works as farforth as nede requyreth"; A.V. and R.V., "to maintain good works for necessary uses."

[48] Cochlaeus, *De canonis Scripturarum auctoritate,* chap. 11. John Dobneck, known as Cochlaeus (1472–1552), at one time dean of the church of the Blessed Virgin at Frankfort and later canon of Warsaw, was instrumental in hindering the printing of Tyndale's New Testament when in exile at Cologne. Needless to say, he was anathema to the Reformers, and even modern writers can find no words strong enough in condemnation of him. He wrote much; among other things, *An expediat laicis legere Novi Testamenti libros lingua vernacula? Ad serenissimum Scotiae regem Jacobum V. Disputatio inter Alexandrum Alesium ct Johannem Cochlaeum Germanum,* 1533; and *De canonis Scripturarum auctoritate.* See Pollard, *Records of the English Bible,* pp. 4, 99 ff.; Anderson, *Annals of the English Bible,* pp. 35, 517 ff.

[49] The edition of 1580.

out: [50] and *Act.* 1. 14. they say "With the women," agreably to the vulgar Latin, where he saith "cum uxoribus," "with their wives." [51]

It is truer then the vulgar Greeke text it self

10. It is not onely better then al other Latin translations, but then the Greeke text itselfe, in those places where they disagree.

The auncient fathers for proofe therof, and the Adversaries them selves

The proofe hereof is evident, because most of the ancient Heretikes were Grecians, & therefore the Scriptures in Greeke were corrupted by them, as the auncient fathers often complaine. Tertullian noteth the Greeke text which is at this day (1 *Cor.* 15. 47.) to be an old corruption of Marcion the Heretike, and the truth to be as in our vulgar Latin, "Secundus homo de coelo coelestis, The second man from heaven heavenly." [52] So reade other auncient fathers, and Erasmus thinketh it must needes be so, and Calvin him self foloweth it. *Instit. li.* 2. *c.* 13. *parag.* 2. Againe, S. Hierom noteth that the Greeke text, (1 *Cor.* 7. 33.) which is at this day, is not the Apostolical veritie or the true text of the Apostle: but that which is in the vulgar Latin, "Qui cum uxore est, solicitus est quae sunt mundi, quomodo placeat uxori, et divisus est. He that is with a wife, is careful of worldly things, how he may please his wife, and is devided or distracted." [53] The Ecclesiastical historie called the Tripartite, noteth the Greeke text that now is (1 *Jo.* 4. 3.) to be an old corruption of the auncient Greeke copies, by the Nestorian Heretikes, and the true reading to be as in our vulgar Latin, "omnis spiritus qui solvit IESUM, ex Deo non est. Every spirit that dissolveth IESUS, is not of

[50] In Bagster's *Hexapla,* "Cainan" is omitted in the Genevan column, but it stands in the edition of 1608 and is retained by Wycliffe, Tyndale, Cranmer, and the rest.

[51] None of the above-mentioned versions follow Beza in this; all read "and with the women."

[52] *Adv. Marcion,* V, chap. 5.

[53] "In the Latin manuscripts we read, *divisa est virgo et mulier.* But though this does bear a definite meaning and I myself have commented on the passage according to that reading, yet it is not 'Apostolic truth.' For the Apostle wrote precisely as I have translated it above: *sollicitus est quae sunt mundi, quomodo placeat uxori, et divisus est;* and when he has said that, he passes on to the question of virgins and those who live continently, and then he says: *mulier innupta, et virgo cogitat quae sunt Domini, ut sit sancta corpore et spiritu*" (St. Jerome, *Adv. Jovinianum,* I, chap. 13, in Migne, *P.L.,* XXIII, 226).

God": [54] and Beza confesseth that Socrates in his Ecclesiastical historie readeth so in the Greeke, πᾶν πνεῦμα ὃ λύει τὸν Ἰησοῦν Χριστὸν, etc.

The Calvinistes them selves often forsake the Greeke as corrupt, and translate according to the auncient vulgar Latin text

But the proofe is more pregnant out of the Adversaries themselves. They forsake the Greeke text as corrupted, and translate according to the vulgar Latin, namely Beza and his scholers the English translatours of the Bible, in these places. *Hebr.* chap. 9. verse 1. saying *The first covenant,* for that which is in the Greeke *the first tabernacle.* Where they put *covenant,* not as of the text, but in an other letter, as to be understood, according to the vulgar Latin, which most sincerely leaveth it out altogether, saying "Habuit quidem et prius justificationes etc. The former also in deede had justifications," etc.[55] Againe, *Rom.* 11. *vers.* 21. they translate not according to the Greeke text, *Tempori servientes, serving the time,* which Beza saith must needes be a corruption: but according to the vulgar Latin, *Domino servientes, serving our Lord.*[56] Againe, *Apoc.* 11. *vers* 2. they translate not the Greeke text, *Atrium quod intra templum est, the court which is within the temple:* but cleane contrarie, according to the vulgar Latin, which Beza saith is the true reading,

[54] Vulgate, *qui solvit Jesum;* hence Wycliffe, "for doith Jesu"; Rheims, "that dissolveth Jesus." In his *Historia Eccles.* (VII, chap. 32), Socrates says that Nestorius "was evidently unacquainted with the fact that this was the reading of the ancient copies" and that in his anxiety to repudiate the use of the term "theotokos" of the Blessed Virgin,—a term which emphasized the union of the two natures in Christ, as opposed to "dissolving" them—he mutilated the text of this passage, "aiming at separating the human nature of Christ from his divinity." Modern criticism, basing itself on manuscripts which were young or even non-existent when the Vulgate version was made, insists on rejecting "dissolveth" in favor of "who confesseth not," though Westcott and Hort admit the reading "dissolveth," and in their margin "annulleth." Tyndale, Cranmer, Geneva, and A.V. read, "who confesseth not."

[55] Heb. 9:1: Wycliffe, "And the former testament hadde justifiyngis of worschip and holi duringe for a tyme"; Tyndale and Cranmer, "ordinaunces and servynges of god, and worldly holynes"; Geneva, "then that first *Covenant* verely, had rites of religion ordeyned, and worldly Sanctuarie"; Rheims, "the former also in deede had justifications of service, and a secular sanctuarie"; A.V., "Then verily the first *Covenant* had also ordinances of divine service and a worldly sanctuary"; R.V., "Now even the first *covenant* had ordinances of divine service, and its sanctuary, *a sanctuary* of this world."

[56] Tyndale and Cranmer, "applying youre selves to the tyme," where they substitute Stephens' τῷ καιρῷ for τῷ κυρίῳ, which even now stands in the R.V. margin: "some ancient authorities read 'the opportunity.' "

Atrium quod est foris templum, the court which is without the temple.[57] Onely in this last place, one English Bible, of the yere 1562,[58] foloweth the errour of the Greeke. Againe, 2 *Tim.* 2. *vers.* 14. they adde, *but,* more then is in the Greeke, to make the sense more commodious and easie, according as it is in the vulgar Latin.[59] Againe, *Ja.* 5. 12. they leave the Greeke, and folow the vulgar Latin, saying, *lest you fall into condemnation.*[60] "I doubt not (saith Beza) but this is the true and sincere reading, and I suspect the corruption in the Greeke came thus," etc. It were infinite to set downe al such places, where the Adversaries (specially Beza) folow the old vulgar Latin and the Greeke copie agreable thereunto, condemning the Greeke text that now is, of corruption.

Superfluities in the Greeke, which Erasmus calleth trifling and rash additions

Againe, Erasmus the best translatour of al the later, by Bezas iudgement, saith, that the Greeke sometime hath superfluities corruptly added to the text of holy Scripture: as *Mat.* 6. to the end of the *Pater Noster,* these wordes, *Because thine is the kingdom, the power, and the glorie, for ever-more.* Which he calleth *nugas,* trifles rashly added to our Lordes praier, and reprehendeth Valla for blaming the old vulgar Latin because it hath it not.[61] Likewise *Ro.* 11. 6. these wordes in the Greeke, and not in the vulgar Latin: "but if of workes, it is not now grace: otherwise the

[57] Wycliffe, "but cast thou out the foryerd that is without the temple"; so also Geneva, Rheims, A.V., and R.V. have "without"; but Tyndale and Cranmer, "the queer [choir] which is within the temple."

[58] An edition of the Great Bible; the first edition, 1539, has "within."

[59] All the versions save R.V. have "profitable for nothing *but* for the subversion . . . ," though "but" finds no place in the Greek and is therefore omitted in R.V., which has, "to no profit, to the subverting. . . ." This may seem a trifling point, but the argument in the Preface is that the revisers, despite their insistence on the pre-eminence of the Greek text, are quite ready to reject it when it suits them.

[60] All the versions retain this clause.

[61] This doxology, based on the so-called *textus receptus,* is given by Tyndale, Cranmer, Geneva, and A.V. In Bagster's *Hexapla* a series of dots would seem to indicate that Wycliffe left a space for it. But as he translated from the Vulgate, no manuscript of which has the clause, it seems most improbable that Wycliffe had ever heard of it. R.V. omits it, but in the margin has: "Many authorities, some ancient, but with variations, add 'For thine is the kingdom, and the power, and the glory, for ever. Amen.' " According to the Rhemists' marginal note, Stephens' folio edition and Crispin's omit this. Jean Crispin (or Crespin) of Arras was a disciple of Pierre de Molin (Molinaeus) and a friend of Theodore Beza. After he became a Huguenot, he went to Geneva in 1547, where he set up as a printer. Amongst other things he published a history of the Huguenots who suffered for their tenets.

worke is no more a worke."[62] and *Mar.* 10. 29. these wordes, *or wife,*[63] and such like. Yea the Greeke text in these superfluities condemneth it self, and iustifieth the vulgar Latin excedingly: as being marked through out in a number of places, that such and such wordes or sentences are superfluous, in al which places our vulgar Latin hath no such thing, but is agreable to the Greeke which remaineth after the superfluities be taken away. For example, that before mentioned in the end of the *Pater Noster,* hath a marke of superfluitie in the Greeke text thus, " and *Marc.* 6. 11. these wordes, "Amen I say to you, it shal be more tolerable for the land of Sodom and Gomorrhe in the day of iudgement, then for that citie";[64] and *Mat.* 20. 22. these wordes, "and be baptized with the baptisme that I am baptized with?" which is also superfluously repeated againe vers. 23,[65] and such like places exceeding many: which being noted superfluous in the Greeke, and being not in the vulgar Latin, prove the Latin in those places to be better, truer and more sincere then the Greeke.

The vulgar Latin translation agreeth with the best Greeke copies, by Bezas owne iudgement

Whereupon we conclude of these premisses, that it is no derogation to the vulgar Latin text, which we translate, to disagree from the Greeke text, wheras it may notwithstanding be not onely as good, but also better. And this the Adversarie him self, their greatest and latest translatour of the Greeke, doth avouch against Erasmus in behalfe of the old vulgar Latin translation, in these notorious wordes. "How unworthely and without cause (saith he) doth Erasmus blame the old Interpreter as dissenting from the Greeke? he dissented I graunt, from those Greeke copies which he had gotten: but we have found, not in one place, that the same interpretation which he blameth, is grounded upon the au-

[62] Tyndale, Cranmer, Geneva, and A.V. have, "If it be of grace, then it is not of workes. For then were grace no more grace. If it be of workes, then is it no more grace. For then were deservyng no more deservynge"; the last clause in Geneva and A.V. runs, "or else were work no longer work." But Wycliffe, Rheims, and R.V., "And if by grace, not now of works, otherwise grace now is not grace."

[63] The words "or wife" are given by Tyndale, Cranmer, Geneva, and A.V.; but Wycliffe, Rheims, and R.V. omit them.

[64] This clause stands in Tyndale, Cranmer, Geneva, and A.V., but not in Wycliffe, Rheims, or R.V.

[65] Tyndale, Cranmer, Geneva, and A.V. add, "and be baptized with the baptism that I am baptized with"; but Wycliffe, Rheims, and R.V. omit the clause in both verses.

thoritie of other Greeke copies, & those most auncient. Yea in some number of places we have observed that the reading of the Latin text of the old Interpreter, though it agree not sometime with our Greeke copies, yet it is much more convenient, for that it seemed he folowed some better and truer copie." [66]

Thus for Beza. In which wordes he unwittingly, but most truely, iustifieth and defendeth the old vulgar Translation against him self and al other cavillers that accuse the same, because it is not alwaies agreable to the Greeke text.

When the Fathers say, that the Latin text must yeld to the Greeke, and be corrected by it, they meane the true and uncorrupted Greeke text

Whereas it was translated out of other Greeke copies (partly extant, partly not extant at this day) either as good and as auncient, such as S. Augustine speaketh of, calling them "doctiores & diligentiores, the more learned and diligent Greeke copies," whereunto the latin translations that faile in any place, must needes yeld. *Li.* 2. *de doct. Christ.* c. 15.

And if it were not to long to exemplifie and prove this, which would require a treatise by it self, we could shew by many and most close examples through out the new Testament, these sundrie meanes of iustifying the old translation.

The vulgar Latin Translation is many waies justified by most auncient Greeke copies, and the Fathers

First, if it agree with the Greeke text (as commonly it doth, and in the greatest places concerning the controversies of our time, it doth most certainely) so far the Adversaries have not to complaine: unles they wil complaine of the Greeke also, as they do *Ja.* 4. *v.* 2. and 1 *Pet.* 3. *v.* 21.[67] where the vulgar Latin foloweth exactly the Greeke text, saying, *occiditis:* and, *Quod vos similis formae,* etc. But Beza in both places correcteth the Greeke text also as false.

[66] *Praefatio in Novum Testamentum,* 1556; see also his Annotations on Acts 13:10.

[67] Jas. 4:2: Vulgate, *occiditis et zelatis;* for *occiditis* Beza, misled by the then accepted Greek text, had *invidetis,* which is now universally rejected in favor of the Greek text underlying the Vulgate; R.V., "ye kill and covet." I Pet. 3:21: Vulgate, *Quod et nunc similis formae salvos facit baptisma";* R.V., "which also after a true likeness doth now save you, *even* baptism," and in the margin, "in the antitype." Beza, *Cui rei nunc respondens exemplar baptismi nos quoque servat;* the Greek text justifies *nos.*

2. If it disagree here and there from the Greeke text, it agreeth with an other Greeke copie set in the margent, whereof see examples in the foresaid Greek Testaments of Robert Stevens and Crispin through out, namely 2 *Pet.* 1. 10. "Satagite ut per bona opera certam vestram vocationem faciatis. διὰ τῶν ἀγαθῶν ἔργων."[68] and *Marc.* 8. *v.* 7. "Et ipsos benedixit, εὐλογήσας αὐτά."[69]

3. If these marginal Greeke copies be thought less authentical than the Greeke text, the Adversaries them selves tel us the contrarie, who in their translations often folow the marginal copies, and forsake the Greeke text: as in the examples above mentioned, *Rom.* 11., *Apoc.* 11., 2 *Tim.* 2., *Jac.* 5., etc. it is evident.

4. If al Erasmus Greeke copies have not that which is in the vulgar Latin, Beza had copies which have it, and those most auncient (as he saith) & better. And if al Beza's copies faile in this point and wil not help us, Gagneie[70] the French King's preacher, and he that might commaund in al the kings libraries, he founde Greeke copies that have just according to the vulgar Latin: & that in such place as would seeme otherwise lesse probable, as *Jac.* 3. *vers.* 5. "Ecce quantus ignis quam magnam silvam incendit. Behold how much fire what a great wood it kindleth."[71]

[68] Rheims, "Labour the more that by good works you may make sure your vocation"; Wycliffe, "be more bisie that by good werkis . . ."; Cranmer retains "good works," but puts the words in brackets; Tyndale, Geneva, A.V., and R.V. omit the words; yet the phrase has very good MSS. authority and stands in all MSS. of the Vulgate.

[69] This reading is endorsed in Weymouth's *Resultant Greek Testament.* But Cranmer omits "them" and has simply "and when he had blessed"; Geneva cuts the knot by rendering "when he had given thanks"; Wycliffe, Tyndale, and R.V. read, "when he had blessed them."

[70] Joannes Gagnaeus, Doctor of Paris University and Almoner to the King of France, published *Scholia* from the Greek and Latin Fathers on the New Testament, *Brevissima et facillima in omnes D. Pauli Epistolas, item in septem canonicas epistolas et D. Joannis Apocalypsim,* Paris, 1543; reprinted, 1629, 1660.

[71] Two variations are possible here: (a) Many Greek MSS. as well as the Vulgate *quantus ignis quam magnam ignem incendit* would justify the Rhemists in rendering, "Behold how much fire, what a great wood it enkindleth," though in the margin they read, "how little a fire, how great a wood . . . ," and the marginal note says that the "Codex veronensis has ἡλίκον πῦρ" (see E. S. Buchanan, *The Four Gospels from the Codex Veronensis,* Oxford, 1911). But Wycliffe, though he translated from the Vulgate, has "Lo, hou litil fier, brenneth a ful greet wood," where "litil" is supported by some Greek MSS. This certainly makes far better sense and is accepted by all the other English versions as well as by Challoner and all his revisers. (b) The Greek ὕλη means primarily a wood or forest, secondarily "material"; the Vulgate reads *silvam,* and Beza seems to have been the first to change this into *materiam: Ecce, exiguus ignis quantam materiam incendit;* he is followed by Tyndale, Cranmer, Geneva, and A.V., though the latter has "wood" in the margin; R.V. seems to try to avoid the difficulty by rendering it, "how much wood."

A man would thinke it must be as in the Greeke text, "A litle fire what a great wood it kindleth!" But an approved auncient Greeke copie alleaged by Gagneie, hath as it is in the vulgar Latin. And if Gagneis copies also faile sometime, there Beza and Crispin supply Greeke copies fully agreable to the vulgar Latin, as *Ep. Judae, vers.* 5. "Scientes semel *omnia,* quoniam JESUS" etc.[72] and *vers.* 19. "Segregant *semetipsos."*[73] Likewise 2 *Ephes.* 2. [*sic*] "Quod elegerit vos primitias";[74] *ἀπαρχὰς* in some Greeke copies. Gagn.; & 2 *Cor.* 9. [2.] "Vestra aemulatio,[75] *ὁ ὑμῶν ζῆλος.*" So hath one Greeke copy. Beza.

The Greeke fathers

5. If al their copies be not sufficient, the auncient Greeke fathers had copies and expounded them agreable to our vulgar Latin: as 1 *Tim.* vi. 20. *"Prophanas vocum novitates":*[76] So readeth S. Chrysostom and expoundeth it against Heretical & erroneous novelties. Yet now we know no Greeke copie that readeth so. Likewise *Jo.* 10. 29. *Pater Meus quod mihi dedit majus omnibus est.*[77] So readeth S. Cyril [of Alexandria] and expoundeth it, *li.* 7. *in Jo.* c. 10. *Likewise* 1 *Jo.* 4. 3. *omnis spiritus qui solvit* JESUM, *ex Deo non est.*[78] So readeth S. Irenaeus [*Adv. Haereses*] *li.* 3. c. 18., S. Augustine *tract.* 6. [14.] *in Jo.,* S. Leo *Epist.* 10. c. 5. besides Socrates in his Ecclesiastical historie, *li.* 7. c. 22., and the Tripartite *li.* 12. c. 4.,[79] who say plainely, that this was the old and the true reading

[72] Rheims, "that once know all things"; so too Wycliffe and R.V.; but Tyndale, Cranmer, Geneva, and A.V., "though ye once knew *this.*"

[73] The versions are all practically the same: Wycliffe, "departen hem silf"; Tyndale, Cranmer, and Geneva, "makers of sects"; Rheims, "segregate themselves"; R.V., "make separations."

[74] II Thess. 2:13. The Vulgate reads, *quod elegerit nos Deus primitias;* but this *nos* in the Sixtine and Clementine editions rests on the authority of only minor MSS. Wycliffe, Tyndale, Cranmer, Geneva, A.V., and R.V. all have "you" (*vos*). This misprint (2. Ephes. for 2. Thess.) is one of the few that escaped the Rhemists' proof reader.

[75] Vulgate, *et vestra aemulatio provocavit plurimos.* On the authority of the Greek text known to him, Beza translated this, *et ex vobis ortus ardor.* Critical investigation, however, has justified the Vulgate reading; R.V. has, "your zeal hath stirred up very many," though the marginal reading has "emulation of you."

[76] Wycliffe, "kepe the thing bitakun to thee"; Tyndale, Cranmer, and Geneva, "save that which is given thee to kepe"; A.V., "keepe that which is committed to thy trust"; see II Tim. 1:12, 14, where the Rhemists have again *depositum;* Challoner follows A.V.

[77] Here is an example of a reading vouched for by the Vulgate despite its improbable character: "The Father is a greater thing than I." Beza decided that the neuter must be a mistake for the masculine; yet the Greek MSS. support the Vulgate.

[78] Instead of *qui solvit Jesum,* all Greek MSS. have "who confesseth not," and Beza, *qui non profitetur;* yet R.V. margin allows that "annuleth" has good authority.

[79] This work was collected by Cassiodorus out of Theodoret, Sozomen, and Socrates,

of this place in the Greeke. And in what Greeke copie extant at this daye is there this text *Jo.* 5. 2. *Est autem Hierosolymis probatica piscina?* [80] And yet S. Chrysostom, S. Cyril, and Theophylacte reade so in the Greeke, and Beza saith it is the better reading. And so is the Latin text of the Romane Masse Booke iustified, and eight other Latin copies that reade so. For our vulgar Latin here, is according to the Greeke text, "*super probatica.*" & *Ro.* 5. *v.* 17. *Donationis et iustitiae.*[81] So readeth Theodorete in Greeke. And *Luc.* 2. *v.* 14. Origen & S. Chrysostom reade *Hominibus bonae voluntatis,*[82] and Beza liketh it better then the Greeke text that now is.

6. Where there is no such signe or token of any auncient Greeke copie in the fathers, yet these later Interpreters tel us that the old Interpreter did folow some other Greeke copie, as *Marc.* 7. 3. *Nisi crebro laverint.*[83] Erasmus thinketh that he did reade in the Greeke πυκνῇ, *often:* and Beza and others commend his coniecture, yea and the English Bibles are so translated. Whereas now it is πυγμῇ, which signifieth the length of the arm up to the elbow. And who would not think that the Evangelist should say "The Pharisees wash often, because otherwise they eate not," rather then thus, *Unless they wash up to the elbow, they eate not?*

The Latin fathers

7. If al such coniectures, and al the Greeke fathers help us not, yet the Latin fathers with great consent wil easily iustifie the old vulgar translation, which for the most part they folow and expound, as *Jo.* 7. 39. *Nondum erat spiritus datus.*[84] So readeth S. Augustin *li.* 4. *de Trinit.* c. 20. [29.] and *li.* 83. *quaest.* q. 62. and *tract.* 52. [8.] in *Joan.,* Leo *ser.* 2. *de Pentecoste.* Whose authoritie were sufficient, but in deede Didymus

whence the title, *Tripartite.* Cassiodorus made unfortunate and inaccurate additions; see *The Catholic Encyclopedia,* "Cassiodorus."

[80] The reading here given, *Jerosolymis probatica piscina,* is that of the Sixtine and Clementine editions only; the Greek and the MSS. of the Vulgate read *super probatica.*

[81] This reading is endorsed by R.V., though the marginal note agrees that some MSS. omit "of the gift."

[82] Wycliffe and Rheims, "men of good will"; R.V., "men in whom he is well pleased," though the margin has, "good pleasure among men."

[83] All MSS. of the Vulgate read *lavent; laverint* is the reading of the Sixtine and Clementine editions only. *Crebro,* "frequently," comes from the reading πυκνῇ; but the accepted reading is πυγμῇ, meaning literally "up to the elbow," therefore "diligently," as in R.V.

[84] The Greek does not express the word "given," hence Tyndale, Cranmer, and Geneva have "was not yet there"; A.V., and R.V., "not yet *given.*"

also a Greeke Doctor readeth so *li.* 2. [33.] *de Sp. sancto,*[85] translated by S. Hierom, and a Greeke copie in the Vaticane, and the Syriake new Testament. Likewise *Jo.* 21. 22. *Sic eum volo manere,* so readeth S. Ambrose, in *Psal.* 45 & *Psal.* 118. *octonario Resh.,* S. Augustine and Ven. Bede upon S. John's Gospel.[86]

8. And lastly, if some other Latin fathers of auncient time, reade otherwise, either here or in other places, not al agreing with the text of our vulgar Latin, the cause is, the great diversitie and multitude that was then of Latin copies, (whereof S. Hierom complaineth) til this one vulgar Latin grew onely into use. Neither doth their divers reading make more for the Greeke, then for the vulgar Latin, differing oftentimes from both, as when S. Hierom in this last place readeth, *Si sic eum volo manere, li.* i. [26] *adv. Iovin,*[87] it is according to no Greeke copie now extant. And if yet there be some doubt, that the readings of some Greeke or Latin fathers, differing from the vulgar Latin, be a checke or condemnation to the same: let Beza, that is, let the Adversarie himself, tell us his opinion in this case also. "Whosoever," saith he, "shal take upon him to correct these things" (speaking of the vulgar Latin translation) "out of the auncient fathers writings, either Greeke or Latin, unles he doe it very circumspectly and advisedly, he shal surely corrupt al rather then amend it, because it is not to be thought that as often as they cited any place, they did alwais looke into the booke or number every word." As if he should say, We may not by and by thinke that the vulgar Latin is faultie and to be corrected, when we read otherwise in the fathers either Greeke or Latin, because they did not alwaies exactly cite the wordes, but folowed some commodious and godly sense thereof.

The few and smal faultes negligently crept into the vulgar Latin translation

Thus then we see that by al meanes the old vulgar Latin translation is approved good, and better then the Greeke text itself, and that there is no cause why it should give place to any other text, copies, or readings. Marie if there be any faultes evidently crept in by those that heretofore wrote or copied out the Scriptures (as there be some) them we graunt

[85] In Migne, *P.L.,* XXII, 132.

[86] St. Augustine, *Homilies on the Gospel of St. John,* CXXIV, 1. St. Bede, *On John,* chap. 21.

[87] The text printed by Valesius has, *Quid ad te si eum volo sic esse;* see Jerome's notes on the passage, also Migne, *P.L.,* XXIX, 686.

no lesse, then we would graunt faultes now a daies committed by the Printer, and they are exactly noted of Catholike writers, namely in al Plantin's Bibles set forth by the Divines of Lovan: and the holy Councel of Trent willeth that the vulgar Latin text be in such pointes throughly mended, & so to be most authentical. Such faultes as these, *in fide* for *in fine; Praescientiam,* for *praesentiam;* [88] *Suscipiens,* for *suspiciens;* [89] and such like very rare, which are evident corruptions made by the copistes, or growen by the similitude of wordes. These being taken away, which are no part of those corruptions and differences before talked of, we translate that text which is most sincere, and in our opinion and as we have proved, incorrupt.

The Adversaries contrarie, translate that text, which them selves confesse both by their writings and doings, to be corrupt in a number of places, & more corrupt then our vulgar Latin, as is before declared.

The Calvinists confessing the Greeke to be most corrupt, yet translate that only, and hold that only for authentical Scripture

And if we would here stand to recite the places in the Greeke which Beza pronounceth to be corrupted, we should make the reader to wonder, how they can either so plead otherwise for the Greeke text, as though there were no other truth of the new Testament but that: or how they translate onely that (to deface, as they think, the old vulgar Latin) which them selves so shamefully disgrace, more then the vulgar Latin, inventing corruptions where none are, nor can be, in such universal consent of al both Greeke and Latin copies. For example, *Matt.* 10. [2.] *The first Simon, who is called Peter.* I thinke (saith Beza) this word πρῶτος, first, hath been added to the text of some that would establish Peter's Primacie.[90] Againe, *Luc.* 22. [20.] The Chalice, *that is shed for you.* It is most

[88] II Pet. 1:16. The majority of Latin MSS. have *praesentiam,* in accord with the Greek, but some have *praescientiam,* whence Wycliffe, "the bifore knowynge"; Tyndale, Cranmer, Geneva, and A.V., "the coming"; R.V., "coming," but in the margin, "presence."

[89] Luke 10:20. The majority of Vulgate MSS. have *suspiciens,* but it is rightly rejected in favor of *suscipiens* (cf. White, *Novum Testamentum Latine . . . . Editio minor*). Wycliffe, however, had "bihelde and seide"; Tyndale, Cranmer, A.V., and R.V., "answered," or "made answer"; Geneva and Rheims, "taking it, said"; Challoner, "answering." The Clementine edition of the Vulgate here corrects the Sixtine edition, which had *suspiciens.*

[90] For all these assertions by Beza, see his Annotations in his *Novum Testamentum* of 1556.

likely (saith he) that these wordes, being sometime but a marginal note, came by corruption out of the margent into the text. Againe, *Act.* 7. [43.] Figures which they made, *to adore them.* It may be suspected (saith he) that these wordes, as many other, have crept by corruption into the text out of the margent. And 1 *Cor.* 15. [57.] He thinketh the Apostle said not νῖκος, *victorie,* as it is in al Greeke copies, but νεῖκος, contention. And *Act.* 13. [20.] he calleth it a manifest errour, that in the Greeke it is 400 *yeres,* for 300. And *Act.* 7. *v.* 16. he reckeneth up a whole catalogue of corruptions, namely *Marc.* 12. *v.* 42 ὅ ἐστι κοδράντης, *Which is a farthing:* and *Act.* 8. *v.* 26. αὕτη ἐστὶν ἔρημος, *This is desert.* And *Act.* 7. *v.* 16. the name of Abraham, & such like. Al which he thinketh to have been added or altered into the Greeke text by corruption.

They standing precisely upon the Hebrue of the old, and Greeke text of the new Testament, must of force denie the one of them

But among other places, he laboureth excedingly to prove a great corruption *Act.* 7. *v.* 14. where it is said (according to the *Septuagint,* that is, the Greeke text of the old Testament) that Jacob went downe into Egypt with 75 soules. And *Luc.* 3. *v.* 36. he thinketh these wordes τοῦ καινὰν, *which was of Cainan,* to be so false that he leaveth them cleane out in both his editions of the new Testament [1556 and 1565]; saying, that he is bold so to doe, by the authoritie of Moyses. Whereby he wil signifie that it is not in the Hebrue text of Moyses or of the old Testament, and therfore it is false in the Greeke of the new Testament. Which consequence of theirs (for it is common among them and concerneth al Scriptures) if it were true, al places of the Greeke text of the new Testament, cited out of the old according to the Septuaginta, and not according to the Hebrue (which they know are very many) should be false; and so by tying them selves onely to the Hebrue in the old Testament, they are forced to forsake the Greeke of the new: or if they wil mainteine the Greek of the new, they must forsake sometime the Hebrue in the old: but this argument shal be forced against them elsewhere.

They say the Greeke is more corrupt then we wil graunt them

By this litle, the Reader may see what gay patrones they are of the Greeke text, and how litle cause they have in their owne iudgements to translate it, or vaunt of it as in derogation of the vulgar Latin translation, and how easily we might answer them in a word why we translate not the Greeke: forsooth because it is so infinitely corrupted. But the truth is, we do by no meanes graunt it so corrupted as they say, though in comparison we know it lesse sincere and incorrupt then the vulgar Latin, and for that cause and others before alleaged we preferre the said Latin, and have translated it.

We preferre not the vulgar Latin text, as making more for us
The Greeke text maketh for us more then the vulgar Latin

If yet there remain one thing which perhaps they wil say, when they can not answer our reasons aforesaid: to wit, that we preferre the vulgar Latin before the Greeke text, because the Greeke maketh more against us: we protest that as for other causes we preferre the Latin, so in this respect of making for us or against us, we allow the Greeke as much as the Latin, yea in sundrie places more then the Latin, being assured that they have not one, and that we have many advantages in the Greeke more then in the Latin, as by the Annotations of this new Testament shal evidently appeare: namely in al such places where they dare not translate the Greeke, because it is for us and against them, as when they translate δικαιώματα, *ordinances,* and not *iustifications,* and that of purpose as Beza confesseth *Luc.* 1. 6. παραδόσεις *ordinances* or *instructions,* and not *traditions,* in the better part. 2 *Thess.* 2. 15 [91]; πρεσβυτέρους, *Elders,* and not *Priests;* εἴδωλα, *images* rather than *idols.*

For the real presence

And especially when S. Luke in the Greeke so maketh for us (the vulgar Latin being indifferent for them and us) [92] that Beza saith it is a corruption crept out of the margent into the text. What neede these absurd divises and false dealings with the Greeke text, if it made for them more then for us, yea if it made not for us against them?

For fasting

But that the Greeke maketh more for us, see 1 *Cor.* 7. [5]. In the Latin, *Defraude not one an other, but for a time, that you give your selves to*

[91] For "traditions" (Wycliffe, Rheims, A.V., and R.V.), Tyndale and Cranmer have "ordinances"; Geneva, "instructions."

[92] The marginal reference is to Luke 22:20, on which see note on p. 636.

prayer; in the Greeke, *to fasting and prayer.*[93] *Act.* 10. 30. in the Latin Cornelius saith, *from the fourth day past until this houre I was praying in my house, and behold a man,* etc.; in the Greeke, *I was fasting and praying.*[94]

For free wil

1 *Io.* 5. 18. in the Latin, *We know that every one which is borne of God, sinneth not, but the generation of God preserveth him,* etc.; [95] in the Greeke, *but he that is borne of God preserveth him self.*

Against only faith

Apoc. 22. 14. in the Latin, *Blessed are they that wash their garments in the bloude of the lambe,* etc.; in the Greeke, *Blessed are they that doe his commandments.*[96]

Against special assurance of salvation

Rom. 8. 38. *Certus sum.* etc. I am sure that neither *death nor life, nor other creature is able to separate us from the charitie of God.*[97] As though he were assured, or we might and should assure our selves of our predestination; in the Greeke, πέπεισμαι, *I am probably persuaded that neither death nor life,* etc.

For the sacrifice of Christs body and bloud

In the Evangelists about the Sacrifice and B. Sacrament, in the Latin thus: *This is my bloud that shal be shed for you* [Luke 22:20]: and in S. Paul, *This is my body which shal be betraied or delivered for you* [I Cor. 11:24]: both being referred to the time to come and to the sacrifice on the crosse; in the Greeke, *This is my bloud which is shed for you:* and, *my body which is broken for you:* both being referred to that present time

[93] Thus have Tyndale, Cranmer, Geneva, and A.V.; but R.V. omits "fasting."

[94] Wycliffe, "I was preiynge and fastynge"; Tyndale, Cranmer, Geneva, and A.V. omit "praying" and retain only "fasting"; R.V., "I was keeping the ninth hour of prayer"; Rheims, "I was praying in my house."

[95] Thus Rheims and Wycliffe; but Tyndale, Cranmer, Geneva, A.V., and R.V. read thus: "but he that is begotten of God keepeth himself."

[96] Tyndale, Cranmer, Geneva, and A.V., "that do his commandments"; Wycliffe, "that waischem her stoolis in the blood of the lamb"; Rheims and R.V. omit "in the blood of the lamb," one of the few instances in which Rheims and Wycliffe differ.

[97] Rheims, "nor Angels, nor Principalities nor Powers"; Tyndale, Cranmer, Geneva, and A.V., "nether angels, nor rule, nether power."

when Christ gave his body and bloud at his supper, then sheading the one and breaking the other, that is sacrificing it sacramentally and mystically. Loe these and the like our advantages in the Greeke, more then in the Latin.

The Protestants condemning the old vulgar translation as making for us condemne them selves

But is the vulgar translation for al this Papistical & therfore do we folow it? (for so some of them call it, and say it is the worst of al other.) If it be, the Greeke (as you see) is more, and so both Greeke and Latin and consequently the holy Scripture of the new Testament is Papistical. Againe, if the vulgar Latin be Papistical, Papistrie is very auncient, and the Church of God for so many hundred yeres wherein it hath used and allowed this translation, hath been Papistical. But wherein is it Papistical? forsooth in these phrases and speaches, *Poenitentiam agite* [Matt. 3:2, etc.], *Sacramentum hoc magnum est* [Ephes. 5:32], AVE GRATIA PLENA [Luke 1:28], *Talibus hostiis promeretur Deus* [Heb. 13:16],[98] and such like. First, doth not the Greeke say the same? See the Annotations upon these places. Secondly, could he translate these things Papistically or partially, or rather prophetically so long before they were in controversie? Thirdly, doth he not say for *poenitentiam agite,* in an other place *poenitemini:* and doth he not translate other mysteries, by the word *Sacramentum,* as *Apoc.* 17. [5.] *Sacramentum mulieris:* and as he translateth one word *Gratia plena,* so doth he not translate the very like word *plenus ulceribus,* which them selves do folow also? is this also Papistrie?

It is voide of al partialitie

When he said *Heb.* 10. 29. *Quanto deteriora merebitur supplicia,* etc. and they like it wel ynough: might he not have said according to the same Greeke word, *Vigilate ut mereamini fugere ista omnia & stare ante filium hominis. Luc.* 21. 36. and *Qui merebuntur saeculum illud & resurrectionem ex mortuis,* etc. *Luc.* 20. 35. and, *Tribulationes quas sustinetis ut mereamini regnum Dei, pro quo et patimini.* 2 *Thess.* 1. 5. Might he not (we say) if he had partially affectated the word merite, have used

[98] Here occurs one of the worst Latinisms in the Rheims version: "for with such hostes God is promerited"; Wycliffe, "bi suche sacrificis God is dissevered"; Tyndale, Cranmer, and Geneva, "pleased"; A.V. and R.V., "well pleased"; Challoner, "God's favour is obtained."

it in al these places, according to his [99] and your owne translation of the same Greeke word *Heb.* 10. 29? Which he doth not, but in al these places saith simply, *Ut digni habeamini,* and, *Qui digni habebuntur.* And how can it be judged Papistical or partial, when he saith *Talibus hostiis promeretur Deus, Heb.* 13. [16.]? Was Primasius also S. Augustine's scholer, a Papist, for using this text, and al the rest that have done the like? Was S. Cyprian a Papist, for using so often this speach, *promereri Dominum iustis operibus, poenitentia, etc.?* [*Epis.* XIV, 18.] Or is there any difference, but that S. Cyprian useth it as a deponent, more Latinly, the other as a passive less finely? Was it Papistrie, to say *Senior* for *Presbyter, Ministrantibus* for *Sacrificantibus,* or *liturgiam celebrantibus* [Acts 13:2], *simulachris* for *idolis* [I Thess. 1:9; I John 5:21], *fides tua te salvum fecit* sometime for *sanum fecit?* [100] Or shal we thinke he was a Calvinist for translating thus, as they thinke he was a Papist, when any word soundeth for us?

The Papistrie thereof (as they terme it) is in the very sentences of the Holy Ghost, more then in the translation

Againe, was he a Papist in these kinde of wordes onely, and was he not in whole sentences? as *Tibi dabo claves,* etc. *Quidquid solveris in terra, erit solutum et in coelis;* and, *Quorum remiseritis peccata, remittuntur eis* [Matt. 16:19]; and, *Tunc reddet unicuique secundum opera sua* [Rom. 2:6]; and, *Nunquid poterit fides salvare eum? Ex operibus justificatur homo & non ex fide tantum* [Jas. 2:24]; and *Nubere volunt, damnationem habentes quia primam fidem irritam fecerunt* [I Tim. 5:11 f.]; and, *Mandata ejus gravia non sunt;* and, *Aspexit in remunerationem* [Heb. 11:26]. Are al these and such like, Papistical translations, because they are most plain for the Catholike faith which they call Papistrie? Are they not word for word as in the Greeke, and the very wordes of the holy Ghost? And if in these there be no accusation of Papistical partiality, why in the other? Lastly, are the auncient fathers, General Councels, the Churches of al the west part, that use al these speaches & phrases now so many hundred yeres, are they al Papistical? Be it so, and let us in the name of God folow them, speake as they speake, translate as they translated, interprete as they interpreted, because we be-

[99] The edition of 1580.
[100] Matt. 9:22; Mark 5:34; 10:52; Luke 7:50; 8:48; 17:19; 18:42.

leeve as they beleeved. And thus far for defense of the old vulgar Latin translation, and why we translated it before al others.

Now of the maner of translating the same.

The maner of this translation, and what hath been observed therein

In this our translation, because we wish it to be most sincere, as becometh a Catholike translation, and have endevoured so to make it: we are very precise & religious in folowing our copie, the old vulgar approved Latin: not onely in sense, which we hope we alwaies doe, but sometime in the very wordes also and phrases, which may seeme to the vulgar Reader & to common English eares not yet acquainted therewith, rudenesse or ignorance: but to the discrete Reader that deepely weigheth and considereth the importance of sacred wordes and speaches, and how easily the voluntarie Translatour may misse the true sense of the holy Ghost, we doubt not but our consideration and doing therein shal seeme reasonable and necessarie: yea and that al sortes of Catholike Readers wil in short time think that familiar, which at the first may seeme strange, & wil esteeme it more when they shal otherwise be taught to understand it, then if it were the common knowen English.[101]

Certain wordes not English nor as yet familiar in the English tongue

Amen

For example, we translate often thus, *Amen Amen, I say unto you.* Which as yet seemeth strange, but after a while it wil be as familiar as *Amen* in the end of al praiers and Psalmes, and even as when we end with *Amen,* it soundeth far better then *So be it:* so in the beginning *Amen Amen* must needes by use and custom sound far better than *Verily Verily.* Which in deede doth not expresse the asseveration and assurance signified in this Hebrue word; besides that is the solemne and usual word of our Saviour to expresse a vehement asseveration, and therfore is not changed, neither in the Syriake nor Greeke nor vulgar Latin Testament, but is preserved and used of the Evangelistes and Apostles them selves, even as Christ spake it, *propter sanctiorem authori-*

[101] A marginal heading at this point directs the reader to "see the last Table, at the end of the booke."

tatem, as S. Augustine saith of this and of *Alleluia, for the more holy and sacred authoritie thereof.* li. 2. doct. Christ. c. 11. [16.]

Alleluia

And therefore do we keepe the word *Alleluia* Apoc. 19. [4.] as it is both in Greeke and Latin, yea and in al the English translations,[102] though in their bookes of common praier they translate it, *Praise ye the Lord.*

Parasceue

Againe, if Hosanna, Raca, Belial, and such like be yet untranslated in the English Bibles, why may not we say *Corbana,* and *Parasceue:* Specially when they Englishing this later thus, *the preparation of the Sabboth,* put three wordes more into the text, then the Greeke word doth signifie. Mat. 27. 62.[103] And others saying thus, after the day *of preparing,* make a cold translation and short of the sense: as if they should translate the Sabboth, *the resting,* for *Parasceue* is as solemne a word for the Sabboth eve, as *Sabboth* is for the Jewes seventh day; and now among Christians much more solemner, taken for Good-friday onely. These wordes then we thought it far better to keep in the text and to tel their signification in the margent or in a table for that purpose, then to disgrace both the text & them with translating them.

Pasche. Azymes

Such are also these wordes, *The Pasche,*[104] *The feast of Azymes, The bread of Proposition.*[105] Which they translate *The Passeover, The feast*

[102] Beza's New Testament, with notes, translated by L. Tomson, 1580; also in the Geneva Bible of 1577. The Protestant versions indeed were not consistent on this point, for they often retain both *Amen* and *Alleluia* without attempting to translate them; see the lengthy note by the Rhemists on Apoc. 19:4.

[103] Wycliffe, 'aftir pask evene"; Tyndale, "the nexte daye that foloweth good frydaye"; Cranmer, "that folowed the day of preparynge"; Geneva, "that folowed the day of the Preparation *of the Sabbath";* A.V., "the day of Preparation"; R.V., "the morrow, which is *the day* after the Preparation."

[104] "Pasch" is, of course, the Anglicized form of the Greek and Latin word, and though it is perhaps not so familiar to us now as "Passover," yet everyone is accustomed to the expression "paschal time."

[105] Matt. 12:4; Mark 2:26; Luke 6:4. Wycliffe, "loves of propocisioun"; Tyndale, "halowed loves"; Cranmer, "shew breades"; Geneva, "shewe loves"; A.V., "Shewbread"; R.V., "shewbread." In Heb. 9:2, Wycliffe has "the setting forth of looves"; Rheims, very awkwardly, "the proposition of loaves," changed by Challoner into Wycliffe's "setting forth of loaves"; the other versions evade the difficulty by simply writing, "shewbread."

of swete bread,[106] *The shew bread.* But if *Pentecost,* Act. 2. [1.] be yet untranslated in their bibles, and seemeth not strange: why should not *Pasche* and *Azymes,* so remaine also, being solemne feastes, as Pentecost was? or why should they English one rather then the other? specially whereas *Passeover* at the first was as strange, as Pasche may seeme now, and perhaps as many now understand *Pasche,* as *Passeover.* And as for *Azymes,* when they English it *The feast of sweete bread,* it is a false interpretation of the word, & nothing expresseth that which belongeth to the feast, concerning unleavened bread. And as for their terme of *shew bread,* it is very strange and ridiculous.

Neophyte

Againe, if *Proselyte* be a received word in the English bibles, Mat. 23. [15.], Act. 2. [11.]: why may not we be bold to say *Neophyte,* 1 Tim. 3. [6.]? specially when they translating it into English, do falsely expresse the signification of the word thus, *a yong scholer.*[107] Whereas it is a peculiar word to signifie them that were lately baptized, as *Catachumenus* signifieth the newely instructed in faith not yet baptized, who is also a yong scholer rather then the other: and many that have been old scholers, may be *Neophytes,* by differring baptisme. And if *Phylacteries*[108] be allowed for English, Mat. 23. [5.] we hope that *Didragmes*[109] also, *Prepuce,*[110] *Paraclete,*[111] and such like, wil easily grow to be currant and familiar. And in good sooth there is in al these suche necessitie, that they can not conveniently be translated, as when S. Paul saith, *concisio, non circumcisio,*[112] how can we but folow his very wordes and allusion? And how is it possible to expresse *Evangelizo,* but as we do, *Evange-*

[106] The Reformers are not consistent: Tyndale and Cranmer have "swete bread" in Matt. 26:17; Mark 14:1; Luke 22:1; but Geneva, A.V., and R.V., "unleavened bread"; yet in Acts 12:3; 20:6; I Cor. 5:7 f., Geneva follows suit and has "swete bread"; while in Acts 20:6 Tyndale has "Ester."

[107] Wycliffe, "new converted"; Tyndale, Cranmer, and Geneva, "yonge skoler"; A.V. and R.V., "novice."

[108] Tyndale and Cranmer, "filateries"; Geneva, A.V., and R.V., "phylacteries."

[109] Wycliffe, "tribute"; Tyndale and Geneva, "poll money"; Cranmer and A.V., "tribute money"; R.V., "the half-shekel."

[110] E.g., Rom. 3:9: Wycliffe, "prepucie"; the rest have "uncircumcision."

[111] Wycliffe, Tyndale, Cranmer, Geneva, A.V., and R.V. all have "Comforter" in John 14:16, 26; 15:26; 16:7; just as all have "Advocate" in I John 2:1. It is remarkable that the Rhemists should here differ from Wycliffe.

[112] Phil. 3:2. Wycliffe, "division"; Tyndale and Cranmer, "dissension"; Geneva, A.V., and R.V., "beware of the concision." "Concision" aptly expresses the play on words; Liddell and Scott have "excision," "abscission," as opposed to true circumcision.

lize? [113] For *Evangelium* being the Gospel, what is *Evangelizo,* or *to Evangelize,* but to shew the glad tydings of the Gospel, of the time of grace of al Christ's benefits? Al which signification is lost, by translating as the English bibles do, *I bring you good tydings,* Luc. 2. 10. Therefore we say *Depositum,* 1 Tim. 6. [20.] and He *exinanited* him self, Philip. 2. [7.] [114] and, You have *reflorished,* Philip. 4. [10.] [115] and to *exhaust,* Heb. 9. 28.[116] because we can not possibly attaine to expresse these wordes fully in English, and we think muche better, that the reader staying at the difficultie of them, should take an occasion to looke in the table folowing, or otherwise to aske the ful meaning of them, then by putting some usual English wordes that expresse them not, so to deceive the reader.

Catholike termes proceding from the very text of Scripture

Sometime also we doe it for an other cause, as when we say, *The advent of our Lord,*[117] and, *Imposing of handes,* because one is a solemne time,

---

An interesting commentary on all the above renderings is furnished by Stephen Gardiner's action in 1542, advocating the transliteration, as opposed to the translation, of technical biblical terms, a "theory partly justified by many of these words being adopted from the Rheims Version by the revisers of 1611 and passing into the English language" (British Museum, *Guide to the Manuscripts and Printed Books exhibited in Celebration of the Tercentenary of the Authorized Version* [1911], §68).

[113] The Rhemists consistently wrote "evangelize," though Wycliffe always has "preche," except in Luke 16:16, "the rewme [realm, kingdom] of God is evangelized." The Rhemists' use of the word "evangelize" is certainly unfortunate, for we have such expressions as "evangelizing the word," "Philippe evangelizing of the kingdom of God," "evangelized unto him [the eunuch] Jesus," "he evangelized to all the citie" (Acts 8:4, 12, 35, 40).

[114] Wycliffe, "he lowide him silf"; Tyndale, Cranmer, Geneva, and A.V., "made himself of no reputation"; R.V., "emptied himself." No one would wish to defend "exinanited him self," which persisted throughout the first five editions, 1582, 1600, 1621 (1630), 1633, and 1738. Challoner first wrote, "emptied himself," 1749 and 1750; but in his third revision, "debased himself," a rendering which prevailed down to 1815, when the edition brought out by the Catholic Bible Society, though ostensibly reproducing Challoner's first revision, 1749, here followed the third revision, 1752. Witham, 1730, followed suit, while Nary, 1719, had "demeaned himself." But Dr. Murray, 1825, apparently following the lead of Coyne, who had in 1820 reproduced Challoner's second revision, 1750, reverted to "emptied himself," a rendering which has ever since held the field.

[115] Wycliffe, "ye flouriden agen"; Tyndale and Geneva, "ye are revived agayne to care for me"; Cranmer, "your care is revived again for me"; A.V., "your care for me hath flourished again"; R.V., "ye have revived your thought for me."

[116] Wycliffe, "to avoide the synnes of many"; Tyndale, Cranmer, Geneva, "to take awaye the synnes of many"; A.V. and R.V., "to bear the sins of many."

[117] In the margin appears this notation: "Why we say, *our Lord,* not, *the Lord* (but in certaine cases) see the Annotations. I Tim. 6. p. 585." The Annotation referred to

the other a solemne action in the Catholike Church: to signifie to the people, that these and such like names come out of the very Latin text of the Scripture. So did *Penance, doing penance, Chalice, Priest, Deacon, Traditions, altar, host,* and the like (which we exactly keepe as Catholike termes) procede even from the very wordes of Scripture.

Certaine hard speaches and phrases

Moreover, we presume not in hard places to mollifie the speaches or phrases, but religiously keepe them word for word, and point for point, for feare of missing, or restraining the sense of the holy Ghost to our phantasie, as Eph. 6. [12.] *against the spiritual of wickednes in the celestials.*[118] And, *What to me and thee woman?* [John 2:4] [119] whereof see the Annotation upon this place. And 1 Pet. 2. [2.] *As infants even now borne, reasonable, milke without guile desire ye.*[120] We do so place *rea-*

reads: "We Catholikes must not say, *The Lord,* but, *Our Lord:* as we say *Our Lady,* for his mother, not, *The Lady.* Let us keepe our forefathers wordes, and we shal easily keepe our old & true faith that we had of the first Christians. Let them say *Amendment, Abstinence, the Lordes Supper, the Communion Table, Elders, Ministers, Superintendant, Congregation, so be it, praise the Lord, Morning-praier, Evening-praier,* and the rest, as they will: Let us avoid those Novelties of wordes, according to the Apostles prescript, and keepe the old termes, *Penance, Fasting, Priest, Church, Bishop, Masse, Mattins, Evensong, the B. Sacrament, Altar, Oblations, Host, Sacrifice, Alleluia, Amen, Lent, Palme Sunday, Christmas,* and the very wordes wil bring us to the faith of our first Apostles, and condemne these new apostates new faith and phrases." Wiseman defended the phrase "Our Lord" against "the Lord" in the *Dublin Review,* April, 1837 (II, 475–92: "Catholic Versions of Scripture").

118 Wycliffe, "spiritual thingis of wickidnesse, in hevenli thingis"; Tyndale, "agaynst spretuall wickednes for hevenly thinges"; Geneva, "against spiritual wickednesses *which are* above"; A.V., "against spirituall wickednesse in high places"; R.V., "against the spiritual *hosts* of wickedness in the heavenly *places.*"

119 Wycliffe, "What to me and to thee Womman?" Tyndale, Cranmer, Geneva, A.V., and R.V., "Woman, what have I to do with thee?" Rheims, 1582–1633 and 1738, "What is to me and to thee, woman?" Challoner inverted the phrasing, "Woman, what is to me and to thee?" in all his five revisions, 1749, 1750, 1752, 1764, 1772, and most subsequent editors or publishers adhered to this reading. But in MacMahon's editions, 1783, 1791, 1794, 1803, 1810, 1847, appeared the reading: "What is *that* to me and to thee?" a rendering which reappeared in an edition published in 1919, in New York, with the approbation of Archbishop Hayes, though the Preface described that edition as "an accurate copy of the Rheims and Douay edition with the Annotations by the learned Dr. Challoner." In an edition published anonymously in 1792, in that published by Moir in Edinburgh, 1797, and that by Worswick in 1812, the word "it" was inserted: "What is it to me and to thee?" This reading stood in the editions of 1804, 1812, 1814, 1825, and in many modern editions. Nary, (1719), Witham (1730), Lingard (1836), and Kenrick (1849) boldly translated, "What has thou to do with me?" thus avoiding the objectionable rendering of the Reformers and their modern followers.

120 It is not easy to justify this punctuation, though several Latin MSS. have *infantes rationabiles* (*rationales*); but others have *rationabile et sine dolo lac,* as in the Greek.

sonable of purpose, that it may be indifferent both to infants going before, as in our Latin text; or to milke that foloweth after, as in other Latin copies and in the Greeke.

The Protestants presumptuous boldnes and libertie in translating

Jo. 3. [8.] we translate, *The spirit breatheth where he wil,* etc.,[121] leaving it indifferent to signifie either the holy Ghost, or winde: which the Protestants translating winde, take away the other sense more common and usual in the auncient fathers. We translate Luc. 8. 23. *they were filled,* not adding of our owne, *with water,* to mollifie the sentence, as the Protestants doe,[122] and c. 22. [20.] *This is the chalice, the new Testament,* etc., not *This chalice is the new Testament.* Likewise Mar. 13. [19.] *Those daies shal be such tribulation,* etc. not as the Adversaries *In those daies,*[123] both our text and theirs being otherwise. Likewise Iac. 4. 6. *And giveth greater grace,* leaving it indifferent to the *Scripture,* or to the *holy Ghost,* both going before. Whereas the Adversaries do to boldly & presumptuously adde, saying *The Scripture* giveth, taking away the other sense, which is far more probable.[124] Likewise *Hebr.* 12. 21. we translate, *So terrible was it which was seen, Moyses said,* etc., neither doth Greeke or Latin permit us to adde *that* Moyses said, as the Protestants presume to doe.[125] So we say, *Men brethren* [Acts 1:16; 2:29], *a widow woman*

Wycliffe, "reasonale without gile," agreeing with "infants"; Tyndale, "reasonable mylke." Rheims agrees with Wycliffe, but Challoner has "the rational milk without guile"; R.V., "spiritual milk"; Geneva and A.V., "the sincere milk of the word"; Cranmer paraphrases: "the mylke (not of the body but of the soul) which is without disceate."

121 Wycliffe and Rheims alone among the English versions here refer to the Holy Spirit. The Vulgate, by spelling the word with a capital "S" here and in the following *qui natus est ex Spiritu,* does the same; but Tyndale, Cranmer, Geneva, A.V., and R.V. all read, "the wind bloweth where he [it] listeth."

122 Wycliffe, "were in peril"; Tyndale, Cranmer, Geneva, "were filled with water"; A.V., the same, but "with water" is italicised; R.V., "were filling *with water.*"

123 Wycliffe, "But thilke daies"; Tyndale, Cranmer, Geneva, and A.V., "in those days"; but Rheims, followed by R.V., omits "in."

124 Wycliffe, "but he geveth the more grace, for whiche thing he seith, god withstondith proude men: but to meke men he geveth grace"; Tyndale omits the verse altogether; Cranmer has it in italics; Geneva, "but *the Scripture* offereth more grace and therfore sayeth, God resisteth the proude, geveth grace to the afflicted"; Rheims (verse 5), "to envie doth the spirit covet which dwelleth in you? And giveth greater grace. For the which cause it saith, God resisteth the proud, and giveth grace to the humble"; A.V. is to all intents the same, reading however, "wherefore he saith," for which R.V. substitutes, "wherefore *the Scripture* saith."

125 Wycliffe, Geneva, and A.V. have, "that Moses said"; R.V. italicises "that."

[Luke 4:26],[126] *A woman a sinner* [Luke 7:37],[127] *James of Alphaeus,*[128] and the like. Sometime also we folow of purpose the Scriptures phrase, as, *The hel of fire,*[129] according to Greeke and Latin, which we might say perhaps, *the fiery hel,* by the Hebrue phrase in such speaches, but not *hel fire,* as commonly it is translated. Likewise *Luc.* 4. 36. What *word* is this, that in power and authoritie he commaundeth the uncleane spirits? as also *Luc.* 2. [15.] Let us passe over, and see the *word* that is done, where we might say, *thing,* by the Hebrue phrase, but there is a certaine maiestie and more signification in these speaches, and therfore both Greeke and Latin keepe them, although it is no more the Greeke or Latin phrase, then it is the English. And why should we be squamish at new wordes or phrases in the Scripture, which are necessarie: when we do easily admit and folow new wordes coyned in court and in courtly or other secular writings?

The Greeke added often in the margent for many causes

We adde the Greeke in the margent for divers causes. Sometime when the sense is hard, that the learned reader may consider of it and see if he can helpe him self better then by our translation, as *Luc.* 11. [sic; Luke 12:29?] *Nolite extolli,*[130] μὴ μετεωρίζεσθε; and again, *Quod superest date eleemosynam,* τὰ ἔνοντα [Luke 11:40 f.].[131] Sometime to take away the ambiguitie of the Latin or English, as *Luc.* 11. [17.] *et domus supra domum cadet,* which we must needes English, *and house upon house, shal fall.*[132] By the Greeke the sense is not, one house shal fal upon an

126 Tyndale, Cranmer, A.V., and R.V., "a woman that was a widow"; Wycliffe and Geneva write simply, "a widowe."

127 Wycliffe, "a sinful woman"; Tyndale, "a woman in that citie, which was a sinner," and so Cranmer, Geneva and A.V.; but R.V., "a woman which was in the city, a sinner."

128 Thus Rheims in Acts 1:13 and in the lists of the apostles: Matt. 10:3; Mark 3:18; Luke 6:15. Wycliffe always, "James alfeye"; the other versions, "the son of Alphaeus," though in Mark 3:18 A.V. italicises "son of"; both Geneva and A.V. do so in Acts 1:14; R.V. always italicises "son of."

129 Matt. 5:22; 18:9; Mark 9:44, 46. Wycliffe, "helle of fier," but in Matt. 5:22, "fier of helle"; Tyndale, Cranmer, Geneva, and A.V., "hell fire"; R.V. has "hell of fire" in Matt. 18:9, but excises Mark 9:44, 46 as being "omitted by the best ancient authorities."

130 The reading here given, *nolite extolli,* has good MSS. authority; see White, *Novum Testamentum Latine. . . . Editio minor.*

131 Wycliffe, "that that is over plus, geve ye almes"; Tyndale, and Cranmer, "neverthelesse geve almose of that ye have"; Geneva, "therefore, geve almos of those thinges which are within"; A.V., "But rather give alms of such things as you have," but in the margin, "as you are able"; Rheims, "But yet that remaineth, give alms"; R.V., "Howbeit, give for alms those things which are within."

132 Wycliffe, "and an hous schal fal on an hous"; Tyndale and Cranmer, "and one

other, but, if one house rise upon it self, that is, against it self, it shal perish, according as he speaketh of a kingdom devided against it self, in the wordes before. And *Act.* 14. [12.] *Sacerdos Jovis qui erat,* in the Greeke, *qui* is referred to Jupiter.[133] Sometime to satisfie the reader, that might otherwise conceive the translation to be false, as *Philip.* 4. v. 6. *But in every thing by praier,* etc., *ἐν πάντι προσευχῇ*, not *in al praier,* as in the Latin it may seeme.[134] Sometime when the Latin neither doth, nor can, reache to the signification of the Greeke word, we adde the Greeke also as more significant. *Illi soli servies, him only shalt thou serve, λατρεύσεις.* And *Act.* 6. [5.] Nicolas a *stranger* of Antioche, *προσήλυτος.*[135] And *Ro.* 9. [4.] *The service ἡ λατρεία.*[136] And *Eph.* 1. [10.] to *perfite, instaurare omnia in Christo, ἀνακεφαλαιώσασθαι.*[137] And, *Wherein he hath gratified us ἐχαρίτωσεν* [Eph. 1:6].[138] & *Eph.* 6. [11.] *Put on the armour, πανοπλίαν,*[139] and a number the like. Sometime, when the Greeke hath two senses, and the Latin but one, we adde the Greeke. 2 *Cor.* 1. [4.] *By the exhortation wherewith we also are exhorted,* the Greeke signifieth also *consolation* etc.; [140] and 2 *Cor.* 10. [15.] *But having hope of your faith increasing, to be* etc., where the Greeke may also signifie, *as* or *when* your faith increaseth.[141] Sometime for ad-

housse shall fall upon another"; Geneva and A.V., "and a house devided against itself falleth"; Rheims, "and house upon house shall fall"; R.V., "and a house divided against a house falleth."

[133] Wycliffe, "the preest of jubiter that was bifor the citee"; so too Rheims and A.V.; Tyndale, "Then Jupiter's Preste, which dwelleth before their cite," followed by Cranmer and Geneva; R.V., "the priest of Jupiter whose *temple* was before the city."

[134] Wycliffe, "in al preier and bisechynge"; Cranmer, "supplication"; Tyndale and Geneva, "in al thinges . . . in prayer and supplication"; Rheims, A.V., and R.V., "in every thing by prayer and supplication."

[135] Wycliffe, "a comelynge"; Tyndale, Cranmer, and Geneva, "a convert"; Rheims, "a stranger"; A.V. and R.V., "a proselyte."

[136] Wycliffe and Rheims, "and the service"; Tyndale and Cranmer add "of God"; so too A.V. and R.V., but they italicise "of God."

[137] Wycliffe, "enstore"; Tyndale, Geneva, and A.V., "gather together"; Cranmer, "set up all things perfectly"; Rheims, "to perfit"; R.V., "to sum up."

[138] Wycliffe, "glorified us"; Tyndale, Cranmer, Geneva, and A.V., "made us accepted"; Rheims, "gratified," an unfortunate Latinism.

[139] Wycliffe, Tyndale, Cranmer, and Rheims, "the armour of God"; Geneva, A.V., and R.V., "the whole armour"; but the Greek means simply "armour."

[140] Wycliffe, "which [God] confortith us in al ure tribulacioun, that also we moun conforte hem, that ben in al disese, bi the monestynge bi whiche also we ben monestid of god"; Tyndale, Cranmer, Geneva, A.V., and R.V., "who comforteth us in all our tribulation, that we may be able to comfort them which are in any trouble, by the comfort, wherewith we ourselves are comforted of God."

[141] Wycliffe, "We han hope of youre feith that wexith in you to be . . ."; Tyndale,

vantage of the Catholike cause, when the Greeke maketh for us more then the Latin, as, Seniores, πρεσβυτέρους;[142] *Ut digni habeamini, ἵνα ἀξιωθῆτε* [II Thess. 1:5];[143] *Qui effundetur, το ἐκχυνόμενον* [Luke 22:20];[144] *Praecepta, παραδόσεις* [II Thess. 2:14];[145] & *Jo.* 21. [15.] *ποίμαινε, Pasce et rege.*[146] And sometime to shew the false translation of the Heretike, as when Beza saith, *Hoc poculum in meo sanguine qui, τὸ ποτήριον ἐν τῷ ἐμῷ αἵματι τὸ ἐκχυνόμενον, Luc.* 22. [20.] & *Quem oportet coelo contineri, ὅν δεῖ οὐρανὸν δέχεσθαι, Act.* 3. [21.][147] Thus we use the Greeke divers waies, & esteeme of it as it is worthie, & take al commodities thereof for the better understanding of the Latin, which being a translation, can not alwaies attaine to the ful sense of the principal tonge, as we see in all translations.

The Latin text sometime noted in the margent

Item we adde the Latin worde sometime in the margent, when either we can not fully expresse it, (as *Act.* 8. [2.] They tooke order for Steven's funeral, *curaverunt Stephanum,*[148] and, Al take not this word, *Non omnes capiunt* [Matt. 19:11])[149] or when the reader might thinke, it

"we hope when youre fayth is increased amonge you, to be . . ."; Cranmer, "We hope it will come to passe, that when youre fayth is increased among you, we shall be . . ."; Geneva, "We hope, when your fayeth shal increase, to be . . ."; A.V., "when your faith is increased . . ."; R.V., "that as your faith increaseth, we shall be . . ."

142 Apart from the expression, "Elders of the people," in the Gospels, Tyndale, Cranmer, Geneva, A.V., and R.V. always render πρεσβυτέρους by "Elders"; in Acts 15:4, 6, 22, 23, and I Tim. 5:2, Rheims renders it by "ancients" or "seniors"; in I Tim 5:17, 19; Tit. 1:5; and Jas. 5:14, Wycliffe writes "priests"; so does Rheims in these places and in Acts 14:22 and 15:2.

143 Wycliffe, Rheims, A.V., and R.V. read in the subjunctive, "that ye may be counted worthy"; Tyndale, Cranmer, and Geneva, in the indicative, "that ye are counted worthy."

144 Wycliffe, Tyndale, and Rheims, "which shall be shed for you"; Cranmer, Geneva, A.V., and R.V., "which is shed." Mark 14:24 joins with the rest as above in reading "is shed."

145 Wycliffe, Rheims, A.V., and R.V., "traditions"; Tyndale and Cranmer, "ordinances"; Geneva, "instructions."

146 Wycliffe and Rheims, "feed thou my lambs, . . . lambs, . . . sheep"; Tyndale, Cranmer, Geneva, and A.V., "feed thou my lambs, . . . sheep, . . . sheep"; R.V., "Feed thou my lambs, . . . tend my sheep, . . . feed my sheep."

147 Wycliffe, Tyndale, Cranmer, Rheims, A.V., and R.V., "must receive"; Geneva, "whom heaven must conteyne."

148 Wycliffe, "biride stevene"; Tyndale and Cranmer, "dressed Stephen"; Geneva and A.V., "carried Stephen among them *to be buried*"; Rheims, "took order for"; R.V., as Wycliffe, "buried Stephen."

149 Wycliffe and Rheims, "Not all men take this word"; Tyndale, "all men cannot awaye with this word"; Cranmer, "cannot comprehend this word"; Geneva, A.V., and R.V., "cannot receive this word."

can not be as we translate, as *Luc.* 8. [23.] A storme of winde descended into the lake, and *they were filled, & complebantur;* [150] and *Jo.* 5. [6.] when Jesus knew that he had now a long time, *quia iam multum tempus haberet,* meaning, in his infirmitie.[151]

In the beginning of bookes, Matthew, Paul, etc., not S. Matthew, S. Paul, etc.[152]

This precise folowing of our Latin text, in neither adding nor diminishing, is the cause why we say not in the title of books, in the first page, S. Matthew, S. Paul: because it is so neither in Greeke nor Latin, though in the toppes of the leaves following, where we may be bolder, we adde S. Matthew, etc. to satisfie the reader.[153] Much unlike to the Protestants

[150] Better, "and they were filling," i.e., "beginning to fill." Wycliffe has the strange rendering, "were driven hither and thither with waves"; Tyndale, Cranmer, Geneva, and A.V., "were filled with water," but A.V. italicises "with water"; R.V., "were filling *with water";* cf. Matt. 8:24; Jo. 5:6.

[151] Wycliffe, "hadde mych tyme"; Tyndale, Cranmer, and Geneva, "had now a long time been diseased"; A.V. and R.V., "had been now a long time in that case."

[152] The paragraph, "This precise . . . *Catholicae Epistolae"* is omitted in the edition of 1738.

[153] The Geneva Bible has, "The Gospel according to Matthew," and so forth, but the pages are headed, "S. Matthewe," and so forth. The Epistles are simply entitled, "The Epistle of the Apostle Paul to the Romanes," and the page headings have merely, "To the Romanes," and so forth. That to the Hebrews is "The Epistle to the Hebrews," with an introductory note on the authorship. The Catholic Epistles are labeled, "The Generall Epistle of James," and so on, while the page heading is simply "James"; the Apocalypse is "The Revelation of John the Divine."

The Authorized and Revised Versions are peculiarly inconsistent: we have "The Gospel according to S. Matthew," but "The Epistle of Paul the Apostle to the Romans," and even "The Epistle of Paul the Apostle to the Hebrews"; but "The Revelation of S. John the Divine."

The earlier editions of the Rheims New Testament betray a curious inconsistency: The first edition, 1582, has "The Gospel according to Matthew," and so forth, but the page headings, "according to S. Matthew"; "The Epistle of Paul the Apostle to the Romans," and ". . . to the Hebrews," also "The Apocalypse of John the Apostle"; but the page headings always insert "S. Paul," or "S. John." In the second edition, 1600, we have "The Gospel according to S. Matthew," but the "S." is omitted in the title of the other Gospels, though they now write, "The Epistle of S. Paul the Apostle to the Hebrews" and "The Apocalypse of S. John." The confusion is even more marked in the editions of 1621 and 1630, which, while having "S. Matthew" both in the title and page headings, yet omit the prefix in the titles of the other three Gospels; they also omit it in the titles and page headings of Romans and Second Corinthians.

According to the reprints by Offer (1836) and Bosworth (1865), Tyndale wrote, "The Gospell of S. Mathewe," and so forth, "The Pistle of Paul the Apostle to the Romaynes," "The fyrst Pistle of S. Peter the Apostle," "The Pistle of Sanct Judas," "The Pistle of S. James," "The Revelation of Sanct Jhon the devine."

our Adversaries, which make no scruple to leave out the name of Paul in the title of the Epistle to the Hebrues, though it be in every Greeke booke which they translate.[154] And their most authorised English Bibles [155] leave out (Catholike) in the title of S. James Epistle and the rest, which were famously knowen in the primitive Church by the name of *Catholicæ Epistolae.* Euseb. hist. Eccles. li. 2. c. 22.

An other reading in the margent

Item we give the Reader in places of some importance, an other reading in the margent, specially when the Greeke is agreeable to the same, as Jo. 4. [sic; 5:24] *transiet de morte ad vitam.* Other Latin copies have, *transiit,* and so it is in the Greeke.[156]

The pointing sometime altered

We binde not our selves to the pointes of any one copie, printe, or edition of the vulgar Latin, in places of no controversie, but folow the pointing most agreable to the Greeke and to the fathers commentaries. As Col. 1. 10. *Ambulantes digni Deo, per omnia placentes. Walking worthy of God, in al thinges pleasing.*[157] ἀξίως τοῦ Κυρίου εἰς πᾶσαν ἀρέσκειαν. Eph. 1. 17. We point thus, *Deus Domini nostri Jesu Christi, pater gloriae,*[158] as in the Greeke and S. Chrysostom, and S. Hierom both in text and commentaries. Which the Catholike reader specially must marke, lest he finde fault, when he seeth our translation disagree in such places from the pointing of his Latin Testament.

[154] This omission of the name of St. Paul in the title of the Epistle to the Hebrews is peculiar to the Anglo-Genevan editions of the Bible, e.g., those of 1557, 1560, 1578, 1579, and 1582. The Apostle's name is not omitted in Coverdale's version, 1537, nor in those of Mathew, 1537, and Taverner, 1539, nor in the Bible published by Day, 1558, nor in the Great Bible, 1562, nor in the Bishops' Bible, 1568. Cf. the Introduction to Fulke's *Defense,* as edited for the Parker Society, p. 29.

[155] The Bibles published in 1562, 1577, 1579, and 1580.

[156] Wycliffe, "passith"; Tyndale, Cranmer, Geneva, "is scaped [escaped]"; A.V., "is passed"; R.V., "hath passed"; Rheims, "shall passe."

[157] Wycliffe, "walke worthili to god plesynge in alle thingis"; Tyndale, "worthy of the Lorde in all thinges that please"; Cranmer and Geneva, "that in al things ye may please"; A.V., "worthy of the Lord unto all pleasing"; Rheims, "worthy of God, in all things pleasing"; R.V., "worthily of the Lord unto all pleasing," and in the margin, "unto all pleasing, in every good work, bearing fruit and increasing."

[158] Wycliffe, Cranmer, Geneva, Rheims, A.V., and R.V., "that the God of our Lord Jesus Christ, the Father of glory"; Tyndale, ". . . Christ and the father of glory."

The Margent reading sometime preferred before the text

We translate sometime the word that is in the Latin margent, and not that in the text, when by the Greeke or the fathers we see it is a manifest fault of the writers heretofore, that mistooke one word for an other. As, *in fine,* not *in fide,* 1 Pet. 3. v. 8.;[159] *praesentiam,* not *praescientiam,* 2 Pet. 1. v. 16.; Heb. 13. [2.] *latuerunt,* not *placuerunt.*[160]

Thus we have endevoured by al meanes, to satisfie the indifferent reader, and to helpe his understanding every way, both in the text, and by Annotations: and withal to deale most sincerely before God and man, in translating and expounding the most sacred text of the holy Testament. Fare wel good Reader, and if we profit the any whit by our poor paines, let us for Gods sake be partakers of thy devout praiers, & together with humble and contrite hart call upon our Saviour Christ to cease these troubles and stormes of his derest spouse: in the meane time comforting our selves with this saying of S. Augustine: *That Heretikes, when they receive power corporally to afflict the Church, doe exercise her patience: but when they oppugne her onely by their evil doctrine or opinion, then they exercise her wisedom.* De Civit. Dei. li. 18. c. 51.[161]

[159] Wycliffe, "and in feith," reading *in fide* for *in fine;* the other versions have "in fine" or "finally."

[160] So Wycliffe, "summen pleseden to aungelis," reading *placuerunt* for *latuerunt* in his Latin text.

[161] Cotton (*Rhemes and Doway,* p. 285) appends the following note to his text of the above Preface: "N.B. The same Preface, with slight differences of spelling, and a few variations in the marginal notes, is given in the editions of 1600, 1621, and 1633. And, with some alterations of the peculiar phraseology, in those of 1738, and 1788: except that in the latter edition three clauses near the end are omitted. In this last form it appears again, prefixed to Dr. Troy's *Bible,* 4°. *Dublin,* 1816." [Ed.]

APPENDIX II

Preface to the Douay Old Testament, 1609[1]

TO THE RIGHT WELL BELOVED ENGLISH READER GRACE AND GLORIE IN JESUS CHRIST EVERLASTING

The cause of delay in setting forth this English Bible

At last through Gods goodnes (most dearly beloved) we send you here the greater part of the Old Testament: as long since you received the New; faithfully translated into English. The residue is in hand to be finished: and your desire therof shal not now (God prospering our intention) be long frustrate.[2] As for the impediments, which hitherto have hindered this worke, they al proceded (as manie do know) of one general cause, our poore estate in banishment. Wherein expecting better meanes; greater difficulties rather ensued. Nevertheles you wil hereby the more perceive our fervent good wil, ever to serve you, in that we have brought forth this Tome, in these hardest times, of above fourtie yeares, since this College was most happely begune.[3] Wherfore we nothing doubt, but you our dearest, for whom we have dedicated our lives, wil both pardon the long delay, which we could not wel prevent, and accept now this fruict of our laboures, with like good affection, as we acknowledge them due, and offer the same unto you.

[1] This Preface, written long after the Preface to the New Testament and presupposing much that was said there, is consequently not so impressive a document as the former. Dr. Worthington is probably its author. The present text is taken from Cotton, *Rhemes and Doway,* pp. 287–97.

[2] "The holy Bible long since translated by us into English, and the Old Testament lying by us for lacke of good meanes to publish the whole": thus begins the Preface to the New Testament of 1582. The translation of the Old Testament had, then, been "lying by" for over thirty years before it was published, 1609–10.

[3] The college at Rheims was founded in 1568; see Gasquet, *A History of the Venerable English College, Rome,* 1920.

Why & how it is allowed to have holie Scriptures in Vulgar tongues

If anie demand, why it is now allowed to have the holie Scriptures in vulgar tongues, which generally is not permitted, but in the three sacred only: for further declaration of this & other like pointes we remite you to the Preface, before the New Testament. Only here, as by an Epitome, we shal repete the summe of al, that is there more largely discussed.

Scriptures being hard are not to be read of al

To this first question therfore we answer, that both just reason, & highest authoritie of the Church judge it not absolutely necessarie, nor alwayes convenient, that holie Scriptures should be in vulgar tongues.[4] For being as they are, hard to be understood, even by the lerned, reason doth dictate to reasonable men, that they were not written, nor ordayned to be read indifferently of al men.

Manie take harme by reading holie Scriptures

Experience also teacheth, that through ignorance, ioyned often with pride and presumption, manie reading Scriptures have erred grosly, by misunderstanding God's word. Which, though it be most pure in itself, *yet the sense being adulterated is as perillous* (saith Tertullian) *as the stile corrupted.*[5] S. Ambrose observeth: that *where the text is true, the Arians interpretation hath errors.*[6] S. Augustin also teacheth that *heresies and perverse doctrines entangling soules, and throwing them downe headlong into the depth, do not otherwise spring up, but when good* (*or true*) *Scriptures are not well* (*and truly*) *understood, and when that which in them is not wel understood, is also rashly and boldly avouched.*[7] For the same cause, S. Jerom utterly disallowed, that al sortes of men & wemen, old & yong, presumed to read and talke of the Scrip-

[4] Buckingham (*The Bible in the Middle Ages,* p. 58) remarks that: "Such restrictions had no existence under the dominion of the Church; even Luther pays this just tribute to her fame, in that remarkable passage in which he declares that 'it was an effect of God's power, that in the Papacy should have remained, in the first place, sacred baptism; secondly, the text of the Holy Gospel, which it was the custom to read from the pulpit in the vernacular tongue of every nation; thirdly, the sacred forgiveness and absolution of sin, as well privately as in public; fourthly, the most holy Sacrament of the Altar' (*De missa privata,* etc.)."

[5] *The Prescription against Heretics,* chap. 17.

[6] *De fide, ad Gratianum,* II, i, 16.

[7] *Homilies on the Gospel of St. John,* XVIII, 1.

tures: whereas *no articene no tradsman dare presume to teach anie facultie, which he hath not first lerned.*[8]

Reading of Scriptures moderated

Seeing therfore that dangers, & hurtes happen in manie, the careful chief Pastores in God's Church have alwaies moderated the reading of holie Scriptures, according to persons, times, and other circumstances; prohibiting some, and permitting some, to have and read them in their mother tongue.

Scriptures translated into divers tongues

So S. Chrysostom translated the Psalmes & some other partes of holie Scriptures for the Armenians, when he was there in banishment.[9] The Slavonians and Gothes say they have the Bible in their languages.[10] It was translated into Italian by an Archbishop of Genua.[11] Into French in the time of king Charles the fifth:[12] especially because the Walden-

[8] *Epis.*, 53, §7.

[9] There does not seem to be any historical proof of this. But the whole Bible was translated into Armenian in Chrysostom's time (between 406 and 411) by Isaac the Great and Mesrob; they made use of a Syriac version and revised their work by the Septuagint and the Hexapla, and the New Testament by the Greek; see Vigouroux, *Dictionnaire de la Bible,* I, 1010. Richard Simon says that the Armenians of his day repudiate the idea that St. Chrysostom was the author of their translation (*Critical Enquiries into the Various Editions of the Bible,* p. 208); but the very denial suggests that there is some foundation for the statement of the Rhemists.

[10] The Slavonic version was made by SS. Cyril and Methodius, who were born in 827 and 826 respectively. St. Cyril died in 869, and St. Methodius in 885, after completing the translation of the Old Testament except the Books of Machabees; see Leger, *Cyrille et Méthode: Etude historique sur la conversion des Slaves au Christianisme,* 1868. The Gothic version referred to is the famous one by Ulfilas, a native of Dacia (c. 311–80). Taken as a hostage to Constantinople, he was educated there, became lector in the Cathedral, and was consecrated bishop for Dacia in 348. He translated the Old Testament from the Septuagint Version, omitting however the Books of Kings on the grounds that the Goths whom he was evangelizing were already too fond of war and military exploits. Little remains of this version; cf. Migne. *P.L.*, vol. 18. Ulfilas translated the New Testament from the Greek; see J. Bosworth, *The Gothic and Anglo-Saxon Gospels in Parallel Columns with the Versions of Wycliffe and Tyndale.* For some account of his life and work, see Scott, *Ulfilas, Apostle of the Goths,* 1885; also Villari, *Barbarian Invasions of Italy* (1902), I, 43 f.

[11] This was James of Voragine, O.P., of whom Sixtus of Siena says: "Utriusque instrumenti volumina divina, primus omnium, in Italicam linguam, summa fide ac diligentia, transfudit" (*Bibliotheca sancta,* p. 397). He is better known as the author of the *Golden Legend.*

[12] This version went only as far as the Psalms; its author was Raoul de Presles in the fourteenth century. There is a MS. copy in the British Museum.

sian heretikes had corruptly translated it, to maintaine their errors.[13] We had some partes in English translated by Venerable Bede: as Malmesburie witnesseth.[14] And Thomas Arundel Archbishop of Canterburie in a Councel holden at Oxford, straictly ordayned, that no heretical translation set forth by Wicliffe, and his complices, nor anie other vulgar Edition should be suffered, til it were approved by the Ordinarie of the Diocese; alleaging S. Jerom's judgement of the difficultie & danger in translating holie Scriptures out of one tongue into an other.[15] And therfore it must nedes be much more dangerous, when ignorant people read also corrupted translations.

A calumnious suggestion of Lutherans

Now since Luther and his folowers have pretended, that the Catholique Romane faith and doctrine should be contrarie to Gods written word, & that the Scriptures were not suffered in vulgar languages, lest the people could see the truth, & withal these new maisters corruptly turning the Scriptures into divers tongues, as might best serve their owne opinions: against this false suggestion and practise, Catholique Pastores have, for one special remedie, set forth true and sincere translations in most languages of the Latin Church. But so, that people must read them with license of their spiritual superior, as in former times they were in like sort limited. Such also of the Laitie, yea and of the meaner lerned Clergie, as were permitted to reade holie Scriptures, did not presume to interprete hard places, nor high Mysteries, much lesse to dispute and contend; but leaving the discussion therof to the more lerned, searched rather, and noted the godlie and imitable examples of good life, and so lerned more humilitie, obedience, hatred of sinne, feare of God, zele of Religion, and other vertues. And thus holie Scriptures may be rightly used in anie tongue, *to teach, to argue, to correcte, to instruct in justice, that the man of God may be perfect, and* (as S. Paul addeth) *instructed to everie good worke* [II Tim. 3:16 f.], when men labour rather to be

[13] Waldo, the founder of the Waldensian sect towards the close of the twelfth century, seems to have had translations made of portions of the Scriptures, though none of these now exist. The Waldensian version, made by the Vaudois or Waldensians, dates from the fourteenth century; see James Todd, *The Books of the Vaudois,* London, 1865; S. Berger, *Les Bibles provençales et vaudois,* 1889; Vigouroux, *Dictionnaire de la Bible,* "Versions Waldensiennes."

[14] *Historia,* I, chap. 47.

[15] On this Constitution see above, pp. 65 ff.

doers of God's wil & *word, then readers* or *hearers only, deceiving themselves* [Jas. 1:22].

Why we translate the old Latin text

But here an other question may be proposed: Why we translate the Latin text, rather then the Hebrew, or Greke, which Protestants preferre, as the fountaine tongues wherin holie Scriptures were first written?

More pure then the Hebrew or Greke now extant

To this we answer, that if in dede those first pure Editions were now extant, or if such as be extant were more pure then the Latin, we would also preferre such fountaines before the rivers, in whatsoever they should be found to disagree. But the ancient best lerned Fathers & Doctors of the Church do much complaine, and testifie to us that both the Hebrew and Greke Editions are fouly corrupted by Jewes and Heretikes, since the Latin was truly translated out of them whiles they were more pure.[16] And that the same Latin hath bene farre better conserved from corruptions. So that the old Vulgate Latin Edition hath bene preferred, and used for most authentical above a thousand and three hundred yeares. For by this verie terme S. Jerom calleth that Version *the vulgate or common,* which he conferred with the Hebrew of the Old Testament and with the Greke of the New: which he also purged from faultes committed by writers, rather amending then translating it. Though in regard of this amending, S. Gregorie calleth it *the new version of S. Jerom:* [17] who nevertheles in an other place calleth the self same *the old*

[16] That the Jews did corrupt the text of the Bible in order to destroy the arguments of the Christians was certainly a common assertion of the Fathers; see St. Justin, *Dialogue,* chap. 71; Lactantius, *Instituta,* IV, chap. 30; and Origen, *Ad Africanum,* where he instances such passages as Heb. 11:38; Matt. 23:29–36; Acts 7:52. Marcion and Tatian also corrupted the text of the New Testament, according to the testimony of Eusebius (*Ecclesiastical History,* IV, xviii, 8; xxiii, 12; xxix, 2 f.). Tertullian thus puts the case in his usual forceful way: "There, then, must the corruption both of the Scriptures and the expositions thereof be regarded as existing where diversity of doctrine is found. On those whose purpose it was to teach differently, lay the necessity of differently arranging the instruments of doctrine. They could not possibly have effected their diversity of teaching in any other way than by having a difference in the means whereby they taught. As in their case, corruption in doctrine could not possibly have succeeded without a corruption also of its instruments, so to ourselves also integrity of doctrine could not have accrued, without integrity in those means by which doctrine is managed" (*The Prescription against Heretics,* chap. 46).

[17] "Haec nova translatio ex Hebraeo cuncta verius transfudisse perhibetur" (*Book of Morals on Job,* XX, chap. 24).

Latin Edition, judging it most worthy to be folowed.[18] St. Augustin calleth it the *Italian.*[19] S. Isidorus witnesseth that *S. Jerom's version* was received and *approved by al Christian Churches.*[20] Sophronius also a most lerned man, seing S. Jerom's Edition so much estemed, not only of the Latines, but also of the Grecians, turned the Psalter and Prophetes, out of the same Latin into Greke. Of latter times what shal we nede to recite other most lerned men? S. Bede, S. Anselme, S. Bernard, S. Thomas, S. Bonaventure, & the rest? who al uniformly allege this only text as authentical. In so much that al other Latin Editions, which S. Jerom saith were in his time almost innumerable,[21] are as it were fallen out of al Divines handes, and growne out of credite and use. If moreover we consider S. Jerom's lerning, pietie, diligence, and sinceritie, together with the commodities he had of best copies, in al languages then extant, and of other lerned men, with whom he conferred: and if we so compare the same with the best meanes that hath bene since, surely no man of indifferent judgement wil match anie other Edition with S. Jerom's: but easely acknowledge with the whole Church God's particular providence in this great Doctor, as wel for expounding, as most especialy for the true text and Edition of Holie Scriptures.

His Edition free from partialitie

Neither do we flee unto this old Latin text, for more advantage. For besides that it is free from partialitie, as being most ancient of al Latin copies, and long before the particular Controversies of these dayes beganne; the Hebrew also, & the Greke when they are truly translated, yea and Erasmus his Latin, in sundrie places, prove more plainly the Catholique Romaine doctrine, then this which we relie upon. So that Beza

[18] In dedicating his *Book of Morals* to Bishop Leander, he says: "I base my comments on the new translation; but according as the exigencies of illustration require, I use testimonies derived now from the old, now from the new; so that since the Apostolic See, over which I by God's authority preside, makes use of either, so my toil may derive support from both."

[19] See Pope, *The Catholic Student's "Aids" to the Study of the Bible,* I, 216–18.

[20] "Presbyter quoque Hieronumus trium linguarum peritus ex Hebraeo in Latinum eloquium easdem Scripturas convertit eloquenterque transfudit; cujus interpretatio merito caeteris antefertur. Nam est in verborum tenacior, et perspicuitate sententiae clarior" (St. Isidore, *De officiis,* I, chap. 12, *de scriptoribus*). Cf. St. Augustine, *Doctrina Christiana,* II, chap. 21).

[21] "Apud Latinos tot sunt exemplaria, quot codices, et unusquisque pro arbitrio suo vel addiderit vel subtraxerit quod ei visum est" (*Praef. in librum Josue; Praef. in Evangelia, ad Damasum*).

and his folowers take also exception against the Greke, when Catholiques allege it against them.

Preferred before all other Editions by Beza

Yea the same Beza preferreth the old Latin version before al others, & freely testifieth, that the old Interpreter translated religiously.

None yet in England allowed for sufficient

What then do our countriemen, that refuse this Latin, but deprive themselves of the best, and yet al this while, have set forth none, that is allowed by al Protestantes, for good or sufficient.

What is done in this Edition

How wel this is donne the lerned may judge, when by mature conference, they shal have made trial therof. And if anie thing be mistaken, we wil (as stil we promise) gladly correct it. Those that translated it about thirtie yeares since, were wel knowen to the world, to have bene excellent in the tongues, sincere men, and great Divines.

Divers readinges resolved upon, & none leift in the margent

Only one thing we have done touching the text, wherof we are especially to geve notice. That whereas heretofore in the best Latin Editions, there remained manie places differing in wordes, some also in sense, as in long processe of time, the writers erred in their copies; now lately by the care & diligence of the Church, those divers readings were maturely and juditiously examined and conferred with sundrie the best written and printed bookes, & so resolved upon, that al which before were leift in the margent, are either restored into the text, or els omitted; so that now none such remaine in the margent. For which cause, we have again conferred this English translation, and conformed it to the most perfect Latin Edition.

They touched not present controversies

Where yet by the way we must geve the vulgar reader to understand, that very few or none of the former varieties touched Controversies of this time; so that this Recognition is no way suspicious of partialitie, but is merely donne for the more secure conservation of the true text; and more ease, and satisfaction of such, as otherwise should have remained more doubtful.

Why some wordes are not translated into vulgar English

Now for the strictnes observed in translating some wordes, or rather the not translating of some, which is in more danger to be disliked, we doubt not but the discrete lerned reader deepely weighing and considering the importance of sacred wordes, and how easely the translatour may misse the sense of the Holie Ghost, wil hold that which is here donne for reasonable and necessarie.

Some Hebrew wordes not translated into Latin nor Greke

We have also the example of the Latin, and Greke, where some wordes are not translated, but left in Hebrew, as they were first spoken & written; which seeing they could not or were not convenient to be translated into Latin or Greke, how much lesse could they, or was it reason to turn them into English?

More authoritie in sacred tongues

S. Augustin also yeldeth a reason, exemplifying in the words *Amen* and *Alleluia, for the more sacred* authoritie therof: which doubtles is the cause why some *names of solemne Feastes,* Sacrifices, & other holie thinges are *reserved in sacred tongues,* Hebrew, Greke, or Latin.[22]

Some wordes can not be turned into English

Againe for necessitie, English not having a name, or sufficient terme, we either kepe the word as we find it, or only turne it to our English termination, because it would otherwise require manie wordes in English, to signifie one word of an other tongue. In which cases, we commonly put the explication in the margent.

Protestantes leave some wordes untranslated

Briefly, our Apologie is easie against English Protestantes; because they also reserve some wordes in the original tongues, not translated into

[22] Fully aware of the difficulty attaching to such expressions, the translators have appended "An Explication of certaine wordes in this Translation, not familiar to the vulgar reader, which might not conveniently be uttered otherwise: agnition, commessations, contristate, Dominical Day, exinanited, prefinition, repropitiate, resuscitate the grace, Sabbatisme, etc.," words certainly strange to English ears.

English: as *Sabbath, Ephod, Pentecost, Proselyte,* and some others. The sense wherof is in dede as soone lerned, as if they were turned so nere as is possible into English. And why then may we not say *Prepuce, Phase* or *Pasch, Azimes, Breades of Proposition, Holocaust,* and the like? rather than as Protestantes translate them, *Foreskinne, Passeover, The feast of sweete breades, Shewbreades, Burnt offerings,* etc. By which termes, whether they be truly translated into English or no, we wil passe over. Sure it is an English man is stil to seke, what they meane, as if they remained in Hebrew or Greke.

Corruptions in Protestantes translations of Holie Scriptures

It more importeth, that nothing be wittingly and falsly translated, for advantage of doctrine in matter of faith. Wherein as we dare boldly avouch the sinceritie of this Translation, and that nothing is here either untruly, or obscurely donne of purpose, in favour of Catholique Romane Religion, so we can not but complaine, and chalenge English Protestantes, for corrupting the text, contrarie to the Hebrew, & Greke, which they professe to translate, for the more shew, and mainteyning of their peculiar opinions against Catholiques, as is proved in the *Discoverie of manifold corruptions.*

Of purpose against Catholique doctrine

For example we shal put the reader in memorie of one or two, Gen. 4. v. 7. whereas (God speaking to Cain) the Hebrew wordes in Grammatical construction may be translated either thus; *Unto thee also perteyneth the lust* THEROF, *& thou shalt have dominion over* IT*:* or thus; *Also unto thee* HIS *desire shal be subject, & thou shalt rule over* HIM*:* [23]

[23] The Rhemists, adhering of course to the Vulgate, wrote: "If thou doe wel, shalt thou not receive againe: but if thou doest il, shal not thy sinne forthwith be present at the dore? but the lust therof shal be under thee, & thou shalt have dominion over it." Coverdale, 1535: "Is it not so? that yf thou do well, thou shalt receave it: but and yf thou do evell, thy sin lyeth open in the dore? Shall he then be subdued unto thee? And wilt thou rule him?" The Rhemists complain of an edition of the Geneva Bible published in 1579 because it reads: "If thou doe well, shalt thou not be accepted? and if thou doest not well, sinne lieth at the doore: also unto thee his desire shall be subject, & thou shalt rule over him." Tremellius and Junius (1585) thus render the passage: "Nonne si bene egeris remissio: si vero non bene egeris prae foribus *est* peccatum excubans? At erga te *est* appetitus illius et tu praees illi." Geddes: "Doth not one, if he have done well, look up, but look down, if he have not done well? Hast thou sinned? Be quiet! He (thy brother) is still subordinate to thee, and thou hast dominion over him." Le Clerc (quoted by Geddes): "If thou behave well shalt thou not retain thy dignity? But if thou behave

though the coherence of the text requireth the former, & in the Bibles printed 1552 and 1577, Protestantes did so translate it: yet in the yeare 1579 and 1603 [24] they translate it the other way, rather saying, that Abel was subject to Cain, and that Cain by Gods ordinance had dominion over his brother Abel, than that concupiscence or lust of sinne is subject to man's wil, or that man hath powre of free wil, to resist (by God's grace) tentation of sinne. But as we heare in a new Edition (which we have not yet sene) [25] they translate it almost as in the first.

Against Melchisedech's Sacrifice

In like sorte Gen. 14. v. 18. The Hebrew particle VAU, which S. Jerom, and al Antiquitie translated ENIM (FOR), Protestantes wil by no meanes admitte it, because (besides other argumentes) we prove therby Melchisedech's Sacrifice.[26] And yet themselves translate the same, as

ill, is not sin at the door? Be quiet, and he (thy brother) will be submissive to thee, thou shalt have dominion over him." The Authorized and Revised versions have: "If thou doest well, shalt thou not be accepted? And if thou doest not well, sin coucheth at the door: and unto thee shall be his desire, and thou shalt rule over him."

All these versions, then, agree in repudiating the rendering insisted on by both St. Augustine and St. Jerome. In the case of the earlier among them, the position is intelligible. For they were determined to get rid of the doctrine of free will. Whitaker declared: "Neither will I believe free will, although the Book of Ecclesiasticus confirms it an hundred times" (*Contra Campion,* p. 17); cf. Ward, *Errata of the Protestant Bible* (1807), p. 29. Luther, with his usual arrogance, entitled his treatise *De servo arbitrio* in opposition to St. Augustine's *De libero arbitrio;* and, as the Rhemists somewhat quaintly express it in their notes on this passage of Genesis, he "denieth that man is in aniewise free to choose, to resolve or determine, but in al things servil, tyed, constrained, and compelled to whatsoever he doth, saith, or thinketh. Further, that man in al his actions is like to a hackney, that is, forced to goe whither the rider wil have him. And knowing the whole world against him shameth not to confesse that he setteth them al at naught in respect of himselfe, concluding thus: 'I have not conferred with anie in this booke, but I have affirmed, and I do affirme. Neither wil I that anie man judge hereof, but I counsail al to obey, or yeelde to mye opinion.'" Calvin exhibits more caution: "I neither myself would use this word [free will], and would wish others, if they ask me counsaile, to abstaine from it."

[24] The Bibles of 1577 and 1579 are editions of the Geneva Bible; that of 1552 may be either a Geneva Bible or a Bishops' Bible, editions of both being published that year. It is not clear what edition of 1603 is referred to; Cotton enumerates five as appearing that year: three of the Geneva Bible and two of the Geneva New Testament, one of which had Tomson's notes.

[25] Presumably the allusion is to the contemplated King James's Version, preparations for which were initiated at the Hampton Court Conference in 1604. Pollard makes the gratuitous suggestion that "it was doubtless the news of the forthcoming new Anglican version which at last brought it [the Douay Version of the Old Testament] to light" (*Records of the English Bible,* p. 37).

[26] Thus Coverdale: "Brought forth bred and wyne. And he beynge the prest of the

S. Jerom doth, *Gen.* 20. *v.* 3 saying, FOR *she is a man's wife, etc.*[27]

And against holie Images

Againe, *Gen.* 31. *v.* 19. the English Bibles 1552 and 1577 translate *Theraphim* IMAGES. Which the edition of 1603 correcting, translateth IDOLES.[28] And the marginal Annotation wel proveth, that it ought to be so translated.

This edition dedicated to al that understand English

With this then we wil conclude most deare (we speake to you al, that understand our tongue, whether you be of contrarie opinions in faith, or of mundane feare participate with an other Congregation, or professe with us the same Catholique Religion) to you al we present this worke: dayly beseching God Almightie, the Divine Wisedom, Eternal Goodnes, to create, illuminate, and replenish your spirites, with his Grace, that you may attaine eternal glorie, everie one in his measure, in those manie Mansions, prepared and promised by our Saviour in his Father's house. Not only to those which first received, & folowed his Divine doctrine, but to al that should afterwardes beleve in him, & kepe the same preceptes.

Christ redeemed al, but al are not saved

For there is one God, one also Mediatour of God and men; Man Christ Jesus. Who gave himself a Redemption for al. Wherby appeareth his wil, that al should be saved. Why then are al not saved? The Apostle addeth, that they must first come to the knowlege of the truth. Because without faith it is impossible to please God.

True faith first necessarie

This groundworke therfore of our creation in Christ by true faith, S. Paul labored most seriously by word and writing, to establish in the hartes of al men. In this he confirmed the Romanes by his Epistle, com-

most hye God, blessed him." The full stop and the unjustifiable "and" instead of "for" can be described only as a subtle evasion of the Catholic doctrine which Coverdale himself must have taught during the years of his own sacrificing priesthood. In their Annotations on this passage of Genesis, the Rhemists afford us a sample of their learning and skill in controversy which, did space permit, we would gladly give in full.

27 Here we have precisely the same construction in Hebrew, and Coverdale rightly renders "for she is a man's wife."

28 Coverdale and A.V., "ymages"; R.V., "teraphim"; Rheims, "idols."

mending their faith, as already received, and renowned in the whole world. He preached the same faith to manie nations. Amongst others, to the lerned Athenians. Where it seemed to some, as absurde as strange; in so much that they scornfully called him a *worde-sower,* and a Preacher of new gods [Acts 17:18].

The twelve Apostles were first Reapers, before they were Sowers. S. Paul at first a Sower, or Seminarie Apostle

But S. Augustin alloweth the terme for good, which was reprochfully spoken of the ignorant. And so distinguishing between *reapers* and *sowers* in God's Church, he teacheth, that wheras the other Apostles reaped in the Jewes, that which their Patriarches and Prophetes had sowne; S. Paul sowed the seede of Christian Religion in the Gentiles. And so in respect of the Israelites, to whom they were first sent, calleth the other Apostles *Messores, reapers,* and S. Paul being specially sent to the Gentiles, *Seminatorem,* a *Sower,* or *Seminarie Apostle.*[29]

Pastoral cures and Apostolical missions

Which two sortes of Gods workmen are stil in the Church, with distinct offices of Pastoral cures and Apostolical missions; the one for the perpetual government of Catholique countries; the other for conversion of such, as either have not received Christian Religion, or are relapsed. As at this time in our country, for the divers sortes of pretended religions, these divers spiritual workes are necessary to teache and feede al Britan people.

New doctrine is falsly called the Gospel

Because some in error of opinions preache an other Gospel, wheras in veritie there is no other Gospel. They preach in dede new doctrines, which can not save.

The seduced and externally conformable are punished with the authors of iniquitie

Others folow them beleving falshood. But *when the blinde leade the blinde* (not the one only, but) *both fal into the ditch* [Matt. 15:14]. Others conforme themselves, in external shew, fearing them that can punish, and kil the bodie. But our Lord *wil bring such as decline unto*

[29] *Sermons,* CI, chaps. 1–3; cf. *Homilies on the Gospel of St. John,* XV, 32.

(unjust) *obligations, and them that worke iniquitie* [Ps. 124:5]. The Reliques and final flock of Catholiques in our country, have great sadnes and sorow of hart; not so much for our own affliction, for that is comfortable, but for you our brethren and kinsemen in flesh and bloud. Wishing with our own temporal damage whatsoever, your salvation.

Grace in the New Testament more abundant then in the old

Now is the acceptable time, now are the dayes of salvation [II Cor. 6:2], the time of Grace by Christ, whose daies manie Kinges and Prophetes desired to see [Luke 10:24]: they saw them (*in spirite*) and rejoyced. But we are made partakers of Christ, and his Mysteries, so that our selves neglect not his heavenly riches: if we receive and kepe the beginning of his substance, firme unto the end; that is, the true Catholique faith; building theron good workes by his grace, without which we can not thinke a good thought, by which we can do al thinges necessarie to salvation. But if we hold not fast this ground, al the building fayleth.

Both wicked workes and omission of good workes are damnable

Or if, confessing to know God in wordes, we denie him in deedes; committing workes of darknes [Tit. 1:16]; or omitting workes of mercie, when we may do them to our distressed neighbours [Matt. 25:31 ff.]; brifly if we have not charitie, the forme and perfection of al vertues, al is lost, and nothing worth [I Cor., chap. 13]. But if we builde upon firme grounde, gold, silver, and precious stones, such building shal abide, and make our vocation sure by good workes, as S. Peter speaketh [II Pet. 1:10]. These (saith S. Paul) are the heyres of God, coheyres of Christ [Rom. 8:17].

Innumerable saved by Christ

Neither is the number of Christ's blessed children counted, as of the Jewes, an hundred fourtie four thousand; of everie tribe of Israel twelve thousand signed [Apoc. 7:4]: but a most great multitude of Catholique Christians which no man can number, of al nations, and tribes, and peoples, and tongues, standing before the throne of the lambe, clothed in white robes, and palmes (*of triumph*) in their handes: having overcome tentations in the vertuous race of good life.

They are more happie that suffer persecution for the truth

Much more those which also indure persecution for the truthes sake, shal receive most copious great rewardes in heaven. For albeit the passions of this time (*in themselves*) are not condigne to the glorie to come that shal be reveled in us: yet our tribulation, which presently is momentarie, and light, worketh (*through grace*) above measure excedingly an eternal weight of glorie. [Rom. 8:18; cf. II Cor. 4:8 ff.]

English Catholiques most happie in this age

What shal we therfore meditate of the especial prerogative of English Catholiques at this time? For to you it is geven for Christ, not only that you beleve in him, but also that you suffer for him. A litle now, if you must be made pensive in divers tentations, that the probation of your faith, much more precious than gold, which is proved by the fire [I Pet. 1:6 f.], may be found unto praise, and glorie, and honour, in the revelation of Jesus Christ. Manie of you have susteyned the spoile of your goodes with joy, knowing that you have a better and a permanent substance. Others have benne deprived of your children, fathers, mothers, brothers, sisters, and nerest frendes, in readie resolution also, some with sentence of death, to lose your own lives. Others have had trial of reproches, mockeries, and stripes. Others of bandes, prisons, and banishments.

The due praise of Martyres, and other glorious Sainctes, excedeth mortal tongues

The innumerable renowned late English Martyres & Confessors, whose happie soules for confessing true faith before men, are now most glorious in heaven, we passe here with silence; because their due praise, requiring longer discourse, yea rather Angels, then English tongues, farre surpasseth the reach of our conceiptes. And so we leave it to your devout meditation. They now secure for themselves and solicitous for us their dearest clientes, incessantly (we are wel assured) intercede before Christs Divine Maiestie, for our happie consummation, with the conversion of our whole countrie.

Patience necessarie to the end of man's life

To you therfore (dearest frendes mortal) we direct this speach; admonishing ourselves & you, in the Apostles wordes, that for so much as we have not yet resisted tentations to (last) bloud (and death itself) patience is stil necessarie for us, that doing the wil of God, we may receive the promise. So we repine not in tribulation, but ever love them that hate us, pittying their case, and rejoicing in our owne.

Persecution profitable

For neither can we see during this life, how much good they do us; nor know how manie of them shal be (as we hartely desire they al may be) saved: our Lord and Saviour having paide the same price by his death, for them and for us. Love al therefore, pray for al. Do not lose your confidence, which hath a greate remuneration. For yet a litle, and very litle while, he that is to come, wil come, and he wil not slacke.

Confession of faith before men necessarie to salvation

Now the just liveth by faith, beleeving with hart to justice, and confessing with mouth to salvation. But he that withdraweth himself shal not please Christ's soule. Attend to your salvation, dearest countriemen. You that are farre of, draw nere, put on Christ. And you that are within Christ's fold, kepe your standing, persevere in him to the end. His grace dwel and remaine in you, that glorious crownes may be geven you. AMEN.

From the English College at Doway, the Octaves of AL SAINCTES. 1609.

The God of patience and comfort geve you to be of one mind, one towards an other in JESUS Christ; that of one mind, with one mouth you may glorifie God.

APPENDIX III

Catholic Editions of the Bible, 1505-1950[1]

The sizes assigned to books, 8vo, 12mo, and so forth, present a problem. In the case of Catholic editions of the Bible or New Testament, I have adhered to the figures given in the catalogue of the British Museum, though these differ noticeably from those given by Dr. Cotton and other authorities. On this point Lea Wilson remarked so long ago as 1845: "In affixing the sizes to the different volumes I found considerable difficulty. Much confusion has hitherto existed; one author considering a book as an octavo, which another styles as a duodecimo; and in many catalogues every size below quarto is rated as octavo." [2] And Cotton, who quotes the above passage, himself says: "There is little doubt that several editions cited by me as well as by my predecessors in these inquiries, owe their supposed existence to misdescriptions; being called folios by one, and quartos by another; or octavos by *this* writer, and duodecimos by *his fellow*." He adds that in the Bodleian catalogue no size below an octavo is specified; "but all the smaller fry of twelves, eighteens, twenty-fours, thirty-twos, forty-eights, etc., are made to take brevet rank and appear as *octavos*." [3]

The accompanying lists are as complete as I can make them. But it is extraordinarily difficult to get accurate information. Publishers them-

[1] Though this list is complete for the sixteenth, seventeenth, and eighteenth centuries, there probably are gaps when we come to the nineteenth century; possibly, too, some duplications. For details concerning each edition see the fuller accounts given in the text; here the versions are given in chronological order and for the sake of completeness.

[2] Wilson, *Catalogue of Bibles, Testaments, Psalms . . . in the collection of L. W., Esq.*, Preface.

[3] *Lists of Editions of the Bible and Parts Thereof in English, MDV to MDCCCL*, p. xv.

selves do not seem always to have kept records of the editions they brought out; in more than one case, too, fires and the war have wrought havoc. I have found it impossible to give lists of editions published in America by Devereux, Carey, Cumminskey, Fielding, Lucas, and others at the beginning of the nineteenth century. The editions published by Moir in Edinburgh in 1805, and by Coyne in 1811 and in 1816, seem to have been reproduced there at one time. See E. B. O'Callaghan, *A List of the Editions of the Holy Scriptures and Parts Thereof Printed in America Previous to 1860,* 1861; also J. Wright, *Early Bibles of America,* 1893. A separate list of American editions is given below, pp. 719 ff.

Editions marked with an * I have personally examined. The figures in parentheses, e.g., (1008.c.9), denote the press mark in the British Museum catalogue.

1505 *The Fruytful Saynges of Davide, in the seven penitential Psalmes; devyded in seven sermons, by John Fysher, bishop of Rochester,* London, R. Pynson, 4to.[4]

1508 The same, London, Wynken de Worde, 4to.

1509 The same, London, Wynken de Worde, 4to.

1510 The same, London, R. Pynson, 4to.

1525 The same, London, Wynken de Worde, 4to.

1529 The same, London, Wynken de Worde, 4to.

1555 *The seven Penitential Psalms,* by Bishop Fisher, London, Thomas Marshe, 16mo.

1555 *An uniforme and Catholike Prymer in Latin and Englishe, set forth by certayne of the cleargye with the assente of the moste reverende father in god, the Lorde Cardinall Pole hys grace,* London, 4to.

1582 * *New Testament,* Rheims, J. Fogny, 4to (1008.c.9).

1589 * *New Testament,* Rheims and Bishops' versions in parallel columns with very acrimonious notes, by W. Fulke, London, fol. (1413.k.9).

1600 * *New Testament* (Rheims), 2nd ed., Antwerp, Vervliet, 4to (1109.f.22).

[4] St. John Fisher's translation of the penitential psalms is the first biblical text ever to be printed in English. The edition of 1505 is inserted on the sole authority of Dr. Cotton (*op. cit.,* p. 133). Cambridge University Library possesses a copy of 1508, and this and the subsequent editions are listed by Gillow (*Bibliographical Dictionary of English Catholics,* II, 267). [S.B.]

1601 * *New Testament,* Fulke (as above, 1589), 2nd ed., fol. (3037. ee.7).

1609–10 * *Old Testament,* Douay, Kellam, 4to (1008.c.7–8).

1617 * *New Testament,* Fulke (as above, 1589), 3rd ed., fol. (466. g.9.I.).

1617 *The Seven Penitential Psalms in the Douay Version,* printed in a *Primer,* 12mo.

1618 * *New Testament* (Rheims), printed by Cartwright with his *Confutation,* fol.

1621 * *New Testament* (Rheims), 3rd ed., Antwerp, Seldenslach, 16mo (1006.a.17).

1630 * *New Testament* (Rheims), 4th ed. (?), Antwerp, Seldenslach, 16mo.

1631 *The Penitential Psalms,* printed in a *Primer,* St. Omer's, 18mo.

1633 * *New Testament* (Rheims), called "fourth edition," Rouen, Cousturier, 4to (1008.d.8).

1633 * *New Testament,* Fulke (as above), 4th ed., fol. (466.g.12. I).

1635 * *Old Testament* (Douay), 2nd ed., Rouen, Cousturier, 4to (1008. c.10–11).

1635 *The Seven Penitential Psalms, a Paraphrase, translated out of the Italian by John Hawkins,* Douay or (?) Paris, 8vo.

1650 *The Seven Penitential Psalms* (altered from the Douay Version), in a *Manual of Prayers,* Antwerp, J. Cnobbart, 16mo.

1658 *The Seven Penitential Psalms in the Douay Version,* in a *Primer,* Antwerp, 12mo.

1675 *The Seven Penitential Psalms* (altered from the Douay version), in *The Key of Paradise,* St. Omer's, 18mo.

1681 *The Ascents of the Soul; paraphrases or descants in verse on the XV. Psalms of Degrees,* by Henry Hare, Lord Coleraine, from the Italian of Francesco Loredano, fol.

1700 * *The Psalmes of David; translated from the Vulgat,* 12mo. Published anonymously by Thomas Caryll, created Lord Dartford by the Pretender.

1704 * The same: *second edition, review'd and corrected, St. Germain en laye, by W. Weston, printer and stationer to the King's most excellent Majesty of Great Britain* [that is, to the Pretender] *for his household and chapel,* 12mo.

1714 * *The Seven Penitential Psalms,* by Bishop Fisher, 12mo.
1718 * *New Testament,* Dr. Nary's version, Dublin (?), 8vo.
1719 * *New Testament,* Dr. Nary's version, 2nd. ed., 8vo (1004.c.6).
1730 * *New Testament,* Dr. Witham's version, Douay (?), 8vo, 2 vols. (3225.b.2).
1733 * *New Testament,* Dr. Witham's version, 2nd ed., Douay (?), 8vo.
1738 * *New Testament,* (Rheims), "fifth edition," fol. (3053.i.11).
1740 * *New Testament,* Dr. Witham's version, 3rd ed., Dublin, 8vo.
1749 * *New Testament,* Dr. Challoner's first revision, 12mo (3049.b.5).
1750 * *Old Testament,* Dr. Challoner's first revision, 12mo, 4 vols. (1411. c.9–12).
1750 * *New Testament,* Dr. Challoner's second revision, 12mo (1411. c.13).
1752 * *New Testament,* Dr. Challoner's third revision, 12mo (3050. b.28).
1763–64 * *Old Testament,* Dr. Challoner's second revision, 12mo, 4 vols. (3006.s.1).
1764 * *New Testament,* Dr. Challoner's fourth revision, 12mo.
1772 * *New Testament,* Dr. Challoner's fifth revision, 12mo, London, Coghlan.
1783 *New Testament,* MacMahon's first revision, 12mo, Dublin, Wogan.
1788 *New Testament, The Sixth edition of the Rhemists' New Testament,* Liverpool, Ferguson, fol.
1789 *New Testament,* the foregoing with reprinted title page, Liverpool, Wogan, fol.
1789–90 * *Holy Bible,* published in parts by M. Carey, Philadelphia, 4to.
1791 * *Holy Bible,* MacMahon's first revision of the Old Testament, second revision of the New Testament, called "the fifth edition," Dublin, Cross, 4to.
1792 * *New Testament,* anonymous edition, Edinburgh (?), 12mo (3051.aaa.3).
1792–97 * *Genesis to Ruth,* new translation by Dr. A. Geddes, London, Faulder, 4to.
1794 * *Holy Bible,* MacMahon's second revision of the Old Testament, third revision of the New Testament, called "the sixth edition," Dublin, Reilly, fol. (3053.k.6).

1796–97 * *Holy Bible,* Challoner's edition, Edinburgh, Moir, 12mo, 5 vols.

1803 *New Testament,* MacMahon's fourth revision of the New Testament, called "the seventh edition," Dublin, Wogan, 12mo.

1804–5 * *Holy Bible,* reprint of the 1796–97 edition, Edinburgh, Moir, 12mo (8vo ?), 5 vols. (3053.cc.1).

1805 *Holy Bible,* "the first American edition," from the fifth Dublin edition (1791), Philadelphia, Carey, 4to.

1807 * *The Psalms,* translation by Dr. Geddes, London, Johnson, 8vo.

1808 *Holy Bible,* the edition of 1804–5 (Moir), with reprinted title page, Dublin, Coyne, 12mo, 5 vols.

1810 * *New Testament,* MacMahon's fifth revision, called "the eighth edition," Dublin, Fitzpatrick, 12mo (3051.aaa.5).

1810 *New Testament* (same as the foregoing), Dublin, Wogan, 12mo.

1811 * *Holy Bible,* reprint of the 1804–5 edition, Dublin, Coyne, 12mo, 5 vols. (3006.s.2).

1811 * *New Testament,* Challoner's edition, Dublin, Coyne, 12mo (3050.aaa.5).

1811–14 * *Holy Bible,* Haydock's edition, Manchester, fol., 2 vols. (3053.k.5).

1812–13 * *Holy Bible,* Haydock's edition, second impression, 2 vols.

1812 * *New Testament,* ed. Dr. Worswick, Newcastle, Preston and Heaton, 12mo (3053.aaa.5).

1813 * *Holy Bible,* Challoner's edition with Dr. Witham's notes in the New Testament, Manchester, Syers, fol. (3053.i.9).

1813 * *Holy Bible,* Haydock's edition, Dublin and Manchester; the New Testament portion is dated 1813 (3049.k.4).

1813–14 *Holy Bible,* to Romans, with the Rhemists' original notes on the New Testament, ed. P. Walsh, Cork, MacNamara, 4to.

1814 * *New Testament,* Challoner's edition, Wogan, Dublin, 12mo (3050.aaa.6).

1815 * *New Testament,* the Catholic Board edition, London, Wilson, 8vo (1411.g.8).

1815 *New Testament* (same as the foregoing), 12mo.

1816 * *Holy Bible,* "Dr. Troy's," reprint and completion of MacNamara's edition, 1813–14, with the Rhemists' original notes in the New Testament, ed. P. Walsh, Dublin, Coyne, 4to (3023. c.1).

1816 * *New Testament,* Challoner's text with selected notes, Manchester, Beegan, 4to.

1816 * *New Testament,* begun in numbers, never completed, London, W. E. Andrews, 4to.

1816–17 * *Holy Bible,* Dr. Gibson, London and Liverpool, Fisher, fol.

1817 * *New Testament,* text of Wogan's edition of 1814, Belfast, Smith, 12mo.

1818 * *Holy Bible,* with the Rhemists' original notes on the New Testament, Cork, MacNamara, 4to.

1818 * *New Testament,* Dr. Poynter's edition, with approbations by Doctors Poynter, Gibson, and Milner, London, Keating & Brown, 12mo (3053.b.18).

1818 * *New Testament,* same as the foregoing, but with the Approbations to the editions of 1582, 1600, and 1749 (3050.bb.7).

1818 * *New Testament,* reprint of the Catholic Board edition (1815), ed. Sidney and Horrabin, London, Hack, 12mo (3051.b.23).

1820 * *Holy Bible,* the New Testament has no notes and is published separately, Dublin, Coyne, 12mo.

1820 * *New Testament,* without notes, often reprinted (last edition 1930), Dublin, Coyne, 12mo (3051.aaa.6).

1821 * *New Testament,* Liverpool, Smith, 12mo.

1822–24 * *Holy Bible,* Haydock's edition with abridged notes, ed. Hamil, Dublin, Pickering, 8vo, 2 vols.

1822–24 * *Holy Bible,* Dr. Gibson, 2nd ed., London, Fisher, fol.

1823 * *New Testament,* reprint of the Catholic Board edition (1815), Bagster, 12mo and 8vo (3051.ee.4).

1823–24 *Holy Bible,* Genesis to Isaias, chap. 13, Christie, Dublin, 4to.

1824 *Holy Bible,* "from the Fifth Dublin Edition" (1791), New York, Cummiskey.

1824 *New Testament,* from the 1822–24 edition of Haydock's Bible, ed. Dr. Hamil, 8vo.

1825 * *Holy Bible,* Dr. Murray, Dublin, Coyne, 8vo.

1825 * *Holy Bible,* Dr. Murray, London, Keating & Brown, 8vo (1003. g.1).

1825 * *New Testament,* Dr. Poynter's edition, reprint of the Catholic Board edition (1815), London, Cudden, 8vo (1109.h.9).

1825 *New Testament,* London, Keating & Brown, 12mo.

1825 * *New Testament,* Dublin, Coyne, with the notes omitted in 1820 inserted at the end, 12mo.[5]

1825 *New Testament,* "reprint of the edition of 1817," Belfast, Smith, 12mo.

1825 *The Epistle of St. Jude, with a Paraphrase and Notes,* H. Rutter (?), London, Keating & Brown, 12mo.

1826 * *New Testament,* reprint of the Catholic Board edition (1815), Dublin, Coyne, 12mo.

1828 *St. Paul's Epistles to Timothy and Titus,* translated from the Latin Vulgate by W. Curray, Dublin, 12mo.

1829 * *Holy Bible,* stereotype, reprint of Dr. Murray's edition of 1825, Dublin, Coyne, 8vo.

1829 * *Holy Bible,* Dr. Bramston, 3rd ed. of Dr. Gibson's edition (1816–17), London, Fisher, fol.

1829 *New Testament,* approbation of Dr. Dubois, bishop of New York, published at Utica.

1831 *Holy Bible,* reprint of Dr. Murray's edition of 1825, Coyne, 12mo.

1832 * *Holy Bible,* Baltimore, F. Lucas, 4to (3049.f.3).

1832 * *Holy Bible,* Dr. Bramston, reprint of the 1829 edition, fol.

1832 * *New Testament,* Keating & Brown, 12mo (3049.bb.10).

1833 *Holy Bible,* reprint of Dr. Murray's edition of 1825, Coyne, 12mo (8vo ?).

1833 * *New Testament,* Coyne, 4to.

1834 * *Holy Bible,* Dr. Crolly, Belfast, Mairs, 8vo.

1834 * *New Testament,* reprint of the 1826 edition (Catholic Board edition), Coyne, 12mo.

1834 * *New Testament,* reprint of the Rheims edition (1582), with the original notes (for controversial anti-Catholic purposes), New York, Leavitt (1003.h.7).

1835 (?) * *Holy Bible,* approbations of the Scottish episcopate, Glasgow, Kennedy (3052.eee.1).

[5] According to Cotton, *Lists of Editions of the Bible and Parts Thereof,* p. 118 note, this absence of the requisite notes led to the production of *A Supplement to the Douay Testament without Note or Comment.* Whether this is identical with the notes inserted at the end of the edition of 1825, the author cannot ascertain.

1835 * *Holy Bible,* reprint of Dr. Murray's edition of 1825, Coyne, 12mo (8vo ?) (3051.c.7).

1835 *New Testament,* reprint of the 1826 edition (Catholic Board edition), Coyne, 12mo.

1835 * *New Testament,* Belfast, Simms & Reves.

1836 * *Holy Bible,* Belfast, Mairs, 8vo (3051.cc.5).

1836 * *New Testament,* Dr. Denvir, Belfast, Simms & Reeves, 16mo.

1836 * *The Four Gospels,* Dr. Lingard's version, London, J. Booker, 8vo.

1837 * *New Testament,* reprint of the 1835 edition (Dr. Murray's edition), Coyne, 12mo.

1837 * *New Testament,* reprint of the 1826 edition (Catholic Board edition), Coyne, 12mo.

1837 * *New Testament,* Dr. Denvir, Belfast, Simms & Co., 24mo.

1838 * *New Testament,* Dr. Denvir, 16mo.

1838 * *New Testament,* Dr. Blake, Newry, Greer, 12mo.

1839 * *Holy Bible,* Dr. Denvir, Belfast, Simms & McIntyre, 18mo (12mo ?) (3052.aaa.11).

1839 * *Holy Bible,* London, Dolman, 12mo (690.a.1).

1839 * *New Testament,* Dr. Denvir, Preface by Curoe, Belfast, Simms & McIntyre, 16mo (3051.a.14).

1840 *Holy Bible,* Dr. Denvir, reprint of the Belfast edition of 1839, London, Dolman, 18mo.

1840 *Holy Bible,* reprint of Dr. Murray's edition of 1825, Coyne, 8vo.

1840 *New Testament,* Coyne, 4to.

1840 *New Testament,* reprint of the 1826 edition (Catholic Board edition), Coyne, 12mo.

1840 * *New Testament,* Dr. Hughes and Dr. Kenrick, Philadelphia, Cummiskey, 8vo (12mo?).

1840 *New Testament,* Dr. Blake, reprint of the 1838 edition, 8vo.

1841 *Holy Bible,* reprint of Dr. Murray's edition of 1825, 8vo.

1841 * *New Testament,* Dr. Denvir, reimpression of the 1839 edition, Belfast, Simms & Co., 16mo (3051.aa.8).

1842 *New Testament,* reprint of Dr. Poynter's edition (1825).

1842 *New Testament,* Newry, Read & Co.

1843 * *New Testament,* reprint of the Catholic Board edition (1815), London, Little & Co. (3052.d.3).[6]

[6] Cotton assigns this edition to 1842 (*Rhemes and Doway*). [Ed.]

1843 *New Testament,* reprint of the 1826 edition (Catholic Board edition), Coyne, 12mo.

1844 *Holy Bible,* reprint of Dr. Murray's edition of 1825, Coyne, 8vo.

1844 *New Testament,* New York.

1845 * *Holy Bible,* Dr. Crolly, copied from Coyne's edition, 1840, Belfast, Simms & McIntyre.

1845–48 *Holy Bible,* Haydock's edition, Glasgow, Fullarton, 4to (3053.i.4).

1845 * *New Testament,* Belfast, 18mo.

1846 *Holy Bible,* Dr. Denvir and Dr. Crolly, Belfast, Simms & McIntyre, 8vo.

1846 * *Holy Bible,* reprint of Dr. Murray's edition of 1825, approbation of Dr. Denvir and Dr. Crolly, Coyne, 8vo (3052.bb.13).

1846 * *Holy Bible,* Dr. Denvir, Belfast, Read & Co., 24mo.

1846 * *New Testament,* Dr. MacHale's edition, Tuam, Brennan, 12mo (3053.bb.16).

1846 * *New Testament,* Dr. Denvir, Belfast, Simms & Co., 24mo.

1846 *New Testament,* reprint of Dr. Blake's edition of 1838, Belfast, 12mo; perhaps the same as the foregoing.

1847 * *Holy Bible,* reprint of Dr. Murray's edition of 1825, Coyne, 8vo (3051.c.8).

1847 * *Holy Bible,* reprint of Dr. Murray's edition of 1825, J. Duffy, 12mo.[7]

1847 *Holy Bible,* Dr. Hughes.

1847 * *Holy Bible,* approbations by Dr. Walsh and Dr. Wiseman, Derby, Richardson, 8vo (3052.cc.6).

1847 * *Holy Bible,* Dr. Denvir, London and Belfast, Simms & Co., 24mo.

1847 * *New Testament,* approbations by Dr. Walsh and Dr. Wiseman, Derby, Richardson, 8vo (3052.dd.3).

1847 * *New Testament,* reprint of the 1826 edition (Catholic Board edition), Coyne, 12mo (3053.bb.14).

1847 *New Testament,* Dr. Blake, reprint of his edition of 1838, Belfast and London, Simms & Co., 12mo.

1848 * *Holy Bible,* Dr. Denvir, Belfast, Simms & Co., 12mo.

[7] This is one of the few editions that avoid the misprint dating from Challoner's 1750 revision, "Jacob," in place of "heaven," in Ps. 90:1.

1849 *Holy Bible,* Dr. Denvir, Belfast, Simms & Co., 16mo.

1849 * *The Four Gospels,* Dr. Kenrick's version, New York, Dunigan, 8vo (3050.d.15).

1850 *Holy Bible,* Dr. Denvir, Belfast, Simms, 24mo.

1850 *New Testament,* Dr. Denvir, the edition of 1846 with new title, Belfast, Simms, 24mo.

1850 * *New Testament,* New York, Sadlier, 12mo (3053.c.10).

1850 *New Testament,* Pictorial Edition, Hewett & Spooner, New York, 8vo (3053.f.5).

1850 *New Testament,* reprint of the 1826 edition (Catholic Board edition), Coyne, 12mo.

1850 *New Testament,* published by Reed & Co.

1851 * *Holy Bible,* Dr. Denvir and Dr. Crolly, London, Dolman, 8vo; identical with Coyne's edition of 1835 (3051.c.7).

1851 * *Holy Bible,* reprint of Dr. Murray's edition of 1825, 8vo (3053.aa.22); perhaps the same as the foregoing.

1851 * *Holy Bible,* Haydock's version, New York, Dunigan, folio (3051. f.4).

1851 * *New Testament,* reprint of Dr. Murray's edition of 1825, Dublin, Duffy, 12 mo.

1851 *New Testament,* reprint of the edition of 1847, with the approbation of Dr. Walsh and Dr. Wiseman, Derby, Richardson, 8vo.

1851 * *New Testament, "permissu superiorum,"* approbation of Dr. Denvir (1836), Derby, Richardson.

1851 * *New Testament,* Challoner's edition (1749), London, Brown, 8vo (12mo ?) (3053.bb.17).

1851 * *New Testament,* Dr. Denvir, Simms & McIntyre, 12mo (3053.aa.22).

1851 *New Testament,* Dr. Denvir, reprint of Dr. Murray's edition, 16mo (8vo ?).

1851 * *The Four Gospels,* Dr. Lingard's version, 2nd ed., London, Dolman, 8vo.

1851 * *The Acts of the Apostles, the Epistles, and the Apocalypse,* Dr. Kenrick's version, New York, Dunigan, 8vo.

1852 * *Holy Bible,* Dr. Crolly, Belfast, Read & Co., 8vo.

1852 * *Holy Bible,* Dr. Denvir, Belfast, Read & Co., 12mo.

1852 *Holy Bible,* Dr. Denvir, Belfast, Read & Co., 8vo.

1852 * *Holy Bible,* Dr. Denvir, Belfast, Simms & Co., 24mo.

1852 * *Holy Bible,* Haydock's edition, reimpression of the 1845–48 edition, Edinburgh, Fullarton, 4to.

1852 * *Holy Bible,* Haydock's edition, New York, Dunigan, fol. (3051.f.4).

1852 * *Holy Bible,* Dr. Hughes, New York, Sadlier, 4to, 2 vols.

1852 *Holy Bible,* Dr. Cullen, Dublin, Duffy.

1852 *New Testament,* Dr. Denvir, 24mo.

1852 *New Testament,* reprint of the 1826 edition (Catholic Board edition), 12mo.

1853 * *Holy Bible,* Haydock's edition with abbreviated notes, ed. Dr. Husenbeth, London, Henry & Co., 4to (2009.g).

1853 * *Holy Bible,* Dr. Denvir, Dolman, 12mo (3051.aa.13).

1853 * *Holy Bible,* Dr. Hughes, New York, Sadlier.

1853 * *Holy Bible,* Drs. Hughes, Kenrick, etc., New York.

1853 *Holy Bible,* reprint of Dr Murray's edition of 1825.

1853 *Holy Bible,* Dr. Denvir, Burns & Lambert.

1853 * *New Testament,* Dr. Murray's edition, Duffy, 16mo (12mo ?) (3053.aa.14).

1853 * *New Testament,* Dr. Murray's edition of 1851 with new title page, Dublin, Duffy, 18mo; perhaps the same as the foregoing.

1854 *New Testament,* Dr. Denvir, Belfast, Read & Co., 18mo.

1855 *New Testament,* Belfast, Read & Co.

1856 * *Holy Bible,* Dr. Cullen, New York, O'Shea.

1856–58 * *Holy Bible,* Haydock's version, Dublin.

1857 * *Holy Bible,* called the "ninth edition," Dr. Crolly, Read & Co., cr. 8vo.

1857 * *Holy Bible,* called the "ninth edition," Dr. Cullen, Dublin, Duffy, 12mo (3050.b.35).

1857 (?) * *Bible,* approbation of Dr. Crolly and twenty-six Irish bishops, no date given.

1857 (?) *New Testament,* Dr. Cullen, no date, Dublin, Duffy, 12mo.

1857 * *New Testament,* published with the approbation of the Irish bishops; perhaps the same as the foregoing.

1857 * *The Psalms and the Sapiential Books,* Dr. Kenrick's version, Baltimore, Lucas, cr. 8vo.

1858 * *New Testament,* approbation of Cardinal Wiseman, Burns & Lambert, 12mo.

1858 *New Testament,* without any approbation, Duffy.

1858 *New Testament,* approbation by Dr. Denvir.

1859 * *New Testament,* reprint of Dr. Murray's edition, 1851, Duffy.

1859 * *Job and the Prophets,* Dr. Kenrick's version, cr. 8vo.

1860 (?) * *Holy Bible,* Dr. Hughes, "The Catholic Family Bible," New York, Sadlier.

1860 * *The Pentateuch,* Dr. Kenrick's version, cr. 8vo.

1860 * *The Historical Books of the Old Testament,* Dr. Kenrick's version, cr. 8vo.

1861 * *Holy Bible,* Duffy.

1862 * *New Testament,* Dr. Kenrick's version, 2nd. ed., cr. 8vo.

1865 * *Holy Bible,* Dr. Cullen, Pictorial Edition, Duffy, 4to (3052.f.8).

1866 * *New Testament,* Dr. Cullen, reprint of Dr. Murray's edition of 1825, 24mo.

1867 * *Holy Bible,* the approbation given by Dr. Cullen in 1857 is prefixed, Duffy, 8vo.

1867 * *New Testament,* with the same approbation as above, but different text, Duffy.

1869 * *Holy Bible,* Dr. Denvir, Booker, Catholic Booksellers' & Publishers' Co.

1870 * *Holy Bible,* New York, O'Shea, 12mo (3053.bb.26).

1872 * *New Testament,* the Vulgate and the Rheims version in parallel columns, Bagster.

1874 * *New Testament,* approbation by the archbishops and bishops of Ireland, Duffy, 16mo (3053.bb.1).

1874 *New Testament,* Dr. Cullen, 8vo.

1874–78 * *Holy Bible,* Haydock's edition, ed. Oakeley & Law, 4to (3015.g.13).

1875 *Holy Bible,* approbation by fifty-one American archbishops and bishops, Philadelphia, Potter, 4to.

1875 *New Testament,* Dr. Cullen, 8vo.

1876 * *Holy Bible,* Dr. Crolly's edition (1857), republished with the approbation of Cardinal Manning, Burns & Oates (3050.cc.5).

1876 * *New Testament,* illustrated edition, McGlashen & Gill, 4to (3052.ee.2).

1876 * *New Testament,* Gill, 12mo.

1876 *New Testament,* reprint of Dr. Crolly's edition, Burns & Oates.

1882 * *New Testament,* Gill, 8vo (3053.c.23).

1882 * *Holy Bible,* Dr. Denvir, Gill, 8vo (3053.e.13).

1885 * *Holy Bible,* reprinted from Dr. Denvir's edition of 1846, Gill.

1886 * *Holy Bible,* Belfast, Mairs, 8vo.

1888 * *Holy Bible,* approbation of the Irish episcopate, Duffy.

1896 *New Testament,* pocket ed., 448 pp., approbation of Cardinal Vaughan, Burns & Oates, 16mo.[8]

1898 * *New Testament,* "pulpit edition," 495 pp., approbation of Cardinal Vaughan (1897), Burns & Oates, cr. 8vo (03051.c.3).

1898 *New Testament,* same as the above, 495 pp., approbation of Dr. Corrigan (1897), New York, cr. 8vo.

1898 (?) *New Testament,* pocket ed., 574 pp., approbation of Cardinal Vaughan, Burns & Oates, 16mo.

1898 * *The Four Gospels,* translated from the Latin Vulgate by Father A. Spencer, O.P., New York.

1897–1901 *Scripture Manuals for Catholic Schools* (with text), the Gospels and Acts, ed. by Rev. Sydney F. Smith, Burns & Oates (03218.g.107).

1897–1907 *St. Edmund's College Scripture Handbooks* (with text), only Mark, Luke, John, and Second Corinthians, Catholic Truth Society (03127.ee.5).

1899 * *Holy Bible,* approbation of Cardinal Gibbons, Baltimore, 16mo (8vo ?).[9]

1899 * *New Testament,* Dublin, Gill.

1900 * *Holy Bible,* reprint of the 1899 edition, Washbourne, 8vo.

1900–1901 *Four Gospels* (separately), with notes by Rev. M'Intyre, Catholic Truth Society. (Some epistles were published later.)

[8] This edition and all the following ones, except those examined by Father Pope (marked *) and those noticed by the editor (marked [Ed.]), have been added to this list of Catholic Editions of the Bible by Rev. Sebastian Bullough, O.P. [Ed.]

[9] This edition is the basis of almost all subsequent American editions, some of which, however, adopted a few more readings from Challoner's revision of 1752; this edition, through Washbourne's reprint of 1900, is likewise the basis of most current British editions.

1901 *The Four Gospels, a new translation from the Greek text direct,* by Father Aloysius Spencer, O.P., New York.

1906 * *Holy Bible,* approbation of Cardinal Farley, New York, Herder.

1909 *New Testament,* pocket ed., 707 pp., Washbourne, 16mo.

1912 * *Holy Bible,* approbation of Cardinal Farley, with Preface by Rt. Rev. H. A. Brann and new introductions, printed in Belgium.

1912 *Holy Bible,* same as the above, but with additional approbations, illustrated, printed in Belgium.

1913–35 * *New Testament,* Westminster Version, ed. by Fathers Cuthbert Lattey and Joseph Keating, S.J. (in separate fascicles), large 8vo.

1914 * *Holy Bible,* Preface by Cardinal Bourne, re-edition of the 1900 edition, Washbourne, 8vo (03051.ff.5).

1914 *Holy Bible,* with approbations by Cardinals Gibbons, Farley, and O'Connell, Murphy, cr. 8vo. [Ed.]

1914 *Holy Bible,* same as the foregoing, "Red Letter Edition." [Ed.]

1914 * *New Testament,* reprint of the "pulpit edition" of 1898 (495 pp.), Burns & Oates, 8vo (03051.e.38).

1919 * *New Testament,* Dr. Hayes, New York, 16mo.

1920 *Four Gospels,* reprint of the edition of 1900–1901, Catholic Truth Society.

1920 *The Psalms,* new translation and commentary by Msgr. Patrick Boylan, 2 vols., Dublin, Gill, large 8vo.

1921–36 *New Testament,* Westminster Version, Longmans, large 8vo, 4 vols.

1922 (?) *New Testament,* approbation of Cardinal Vaughan, reprint of the 1896 edition (448 pp.) with several alterations, Burns, Oates & Washbourne.[10]

1922 (?) *New Testament,* approbation of Cardinal Vaughan, reprint of the 574-page edition (1898?), Burns, Oates & Washbourne.

1922 (?) *New Testament,* reprint of the 1909 edition (707 pp.), Burns, Oates & Washbourne.

1926 * *New Testament,* the version of 1582, the text (not the notes) ed. by G. R. Hudleston, O.S.B., Burns, Oates & Washbourne (W.P. 7458/9).

[10] In 1922 Burns & Oates consolidated with Washbourne, and in this same year or soon after the new firm reprinted existing editions with at least a new title page.

1927 *The Psalms,* new translation and commentary by Rev. T. E. Bird, Burns, Oates & Washbourne, large 8vo, 2 vols.

1928 * *New Testament, The Layman's,* Sheed & Ward, cr. 8vo (03051. e.22).[11]

1928 *New Testament,* Burns, Oates & Washbourne, 12mo.

1929 * *Holy Bible,* approbation of Dr. Hayes, New York, Herder, 8vo.

1931 *Holy Bible,* pocket edition of Cardinal Bourne's edition of 1914 with the same approbation, Burns, Oates & Washbourne, 16mo.

1931 *New Testament,* reprint of Dr. Corrigan's edition of 1898 (495 pp.), with additional approbation of Cardinal Hayes, New York, Benziger.

1934 * *New Testament, The Layman's,* Sheed & Ward, cr. 8vo (03051. a.49).

1934 *New Testament,* reprint of the "pulpit edition" of 1898 and 1914, Burns, Oates & Washbourne, 8vo.

1934 *Malachy,* in the Westminster Version, by Father Cuthbert Lattey, S.J., Longmans, large 8vo.

1935 *Ruth,* in the Westminster Version, by Father Cuthbert Lattey, S.J., Longmans, large 8vo.

1935 *New Testament,* Father Carey's revision of the Challoner version, New York, Wildermann-Brepols, printed in Belgium, 16mo. [Ed.]

1936 * *Holy Bible,* Dr. Hayes, Herder, cr. 8vo.

1936 *New Testament,* Father Carey's revision, republication of the 1935 edition, Dublin, Bassi.

1936 * *New Testament,* Dr. Hayes, 16mo.

1937 *New Testament, . . . translated into English from the Original Greek* by Father Aloysius Spencer, O.P., New York, Macmillan.

1937 *New Testament,* Father Carey's revision, republication of the 1935 edition with new approbation, Wildermann-Brepols.

1937 *Nahum and Habakkuk,* in the Westminster Version, by Dom Hugh Bévenot, O.S.B., Longmans, large 8vo.

1938 *Holy Bible,* containing Carey's revised New Testament, New York, Wildermann, cr. 8vo. [Ed.]

1938 *New Testament,* Father Carey's revision, same as the 1937 edition, but with another new approbation.

[11] Father Pope himself was the editor of this popular edition with new notes. [S.B.]

1938 *Jona,* in the Westminster Version, by Rev. T. E. Bird, Longmans, large 8vo.

1939 *The First Book of Psalms,* in the Westminster Version, by Father Cuthbert Lattey, S.J., Longmans, large 8vo.

1939 *Job,* new translation and commentary by Rev. E. J. Kissane, Dublin, Browne & Nolan, large 8vo.

1940 *New Testament,* reprint of Father Spencer's version (1937).

1941 *Holy Bible,* Challoner's version, New York, The Douay Bible House, cr. 8vo. [Ed.]

1941 * *New Testament,* The Confraternity Edition, Paterson, St. Anthony Guild Press, cr. 8vo.

1941 *New Testament,* reprint of Father Spencer's version (1937).

1941–43 *Isaiah,* new translation and commentary by Rev. E. J. Kissane, Dublin, Browne & Nolan, large 8vo, 2 vols.

1942 *New Testament,* Challoner's version, The Douay Bible House, 16mo.

1943 *New Testament,* reprint of Father Spencer's version (1937).

1944 *Holy Bible,* "Red Letter Edition," approbation of Cardinal Spellman, Preface by Father Charles Callan, O.P., New York, Benziger, cr. 8vo.

1944 * *New Testament . . . Translated from the Vulgate Latin at the Request of Their Lordships, the Archbishops and Bishops of England and Wales,* by Msgr. R. Knox (trial edition), Burns, Oates & Washbourne, cr. 8vo.

1944 *The Psalms,* new translation and notes by Father Charles Callan, O.P., New York, Wagner, large 8vo.

1945 *New Testament . . . Translated from the Vulgate Latin,* by Msgr. R. Knox (definitive edition), Burns, Oates & Washbourne, cr. 8vo.

1945 *New Testament,* reprint of Father Spencer's version (1937).

1945 *The Psalms,* in the Westminster Version, by Father Cuthbert Lattey, S.J., Sands, one-volume edition.

1945 *The Psalms,* reprint of Father Callan's version (1944).

1946 *Holy Bible,* reprint of the 1931 edition with the Preface by Cardinal Bourne, 1914; actually printed in 1939, 16mo.

1946 *New Testament,* reprint of Father Spencer's version (1937).

1947 *Holy Bible,* reprint of the 1946 edition.

1947 *New Testament,* Dr. Arendzen's edition of Challoner's text, Sheed & Ward, cr. 8vo.

1947 *The Psalms,* translated by Msgr. Ronald Knox, Burns, Oates & Washbourne, 16mo.

1948 *New Testament,* Westminster Version, in one volume, Sands.

1948 *New Testament,* Msgr. Knox's version, "Library Edition," Burns, Oates & Washbourne, large 8vo.

1948 *Genesis,* The Confraternity Edition, Paterson, St. Anthony Guild Press, cr. 8vo.

1949 *Old Testament,* translated by Msgr. Ronald Knox, "Library Edition," Burns, Oates & Washbourne, large 8vo, 2 vols.

1949 *Daniel,* in the Westminster Version, by Father Cuthbert Lattey, S.J., Dublin, Browne & Nolan, large 8vo.

1949 *The New Psalter,* Father Callan's work of 1944 adapted to the new Latin text.

1949 *New Catholic Edition of the Holy Bible. The Old Testament, Douay Version (Challoner); a New Translation of the Book of Psalms from the New Latin Version approved by Pope Pius XII; and the New Testament, Confraternity Edition,* New York, Catholic Book Publishing Co. [Ed.]

1950 *New Testament,* reprint of the 574-page edition (1898 ?) with Cardinal Vaughan's approbation, Burns, Oates & Washbourne, 16mo.

APPENDIX IV

Private Versions between the Authorized and the Revised Versions

The sixty-seven versions described in chapters 41, 42, and 43 were private versions produced by Protestants between the publication of the Authorized Version and the completion of the Revised Version. In those chapters the versions were grouped either according to their authors' associations or according to the nature of the translation, so that they were studied according to a rational plan. However, a chronological catalogue has its obvious uses, and this list provides such a catalogue.

A version is entered under the date of its first appearance; subsequent editions, when known, are indicated after the entry. In the case of Dissenters, the denomination is added after the author's name. If the version sets out to be a revision of the Authorized Version, this fact is also noted (rev. A.V.); par. = paraphrase. Exact titles are not given here.

1616–27 Henry Ainsworth (*Ind.*), Pentateuch, Canticle of Canticles, and the Psalms.

1647 John Canne (*Ind.*), Reference Bibles; many editions.

1653 Henry Hammond, New Test., par.; 1659; 17th ed., 1702; 1845.

1675 Woodhead, Allestry, and Walker, epistles, par.; 1684, 1702, 1708, 1852.

1685 Richard Baxter (*Diss.*), New Test.; 1695.

1701–1702 Samuel Clarke, Gospels, par.

1703 Daniel Whitby, New Test., par.; 1706, 1709–10, 1759–60.

1717–25 Thomas Pyle, historical books (Old Test.), par.

1718–24 Edward Wells, Bible, rev. A.V.

1725–35 Thomas Pyle, Acts, epistles, Revelation, par.; 5th ed., 1765.

1726 New Test. from the French of de Beausobre and Lenfant.

1729 W. Mace (*Presb.*), New Test.
1739 Philip Doddridge (*Presb.*), New Test.; 1761.
1739–52 John Guyse (*Ind.*), New Test., par.; 6th ed., 1818.
1745 William Whiston, New Test.
1749–61 John Heylyn, New Test.
1755 John Wesley, New Test., rev. A.V.; 1790.
1764 Richard Wynne, New Test.
1764 Anthony Purver (*Quaker*), Bible.
1768 Edward Harwood (*Presb.*), New Test.
1770 John Worsley, New Test.; 1795, 1820.
1789 George Campbell (*Presb.*), Gospels; 1812, 1813, 1834, 1838.
1791 Gilbert Wakefield, New Test.; 1795, 1820.
1791 W. H. Roberts, Old Test., rev. A.V.
1795 James Macknight (*Presb.*), epistles; 1806, 1816, 1834.
1795 Thomas Haweis, New Test.
1796 William Newcome, New Test., rev. A.V.
1798 Nathaniel Scarlett, New Test.
1799 J. M. Ray, Bible; 1815.
1808 "Improved Version" (*Unit.*), New Test.; 5th ed., 1819.
1808 Charles Thomson (U.S.A.), Old Test. (LXX).
1812 W. Williams, New Test.
1816 William Thomson, New Test.
1817 Benjamin Boothroyd, Bible; 1824.
1818 Presbyterian Version, New Test. of Campbell, Doddridge, and Macknight, re-edited; 1828, 1830, 1898, 1912.
1822 Thomas Belsham (*Unit.*), epistles of Paul.
1822 A. Alexander, Bible.
1823 William Alexander, Bible (vol. 1), rev. A.V.
1828 (Anonymous), New Test.
1832 Charles Eyre (*Unit.*), epistles of Paul.
1832 George Pilkington, New Test., Part I.
1833 Rodolphus Dickinson (U.S.A.), New Test.
1833 Noah Webster (U.S.A.), Bible, rev. A.V.; 1841; New Test., 1839, 1840.
1834 J. G. Tolley, Gospels, rev. A.V.
1836–37 Granville Penn, New Test., rev. A.V.
1837 Edward Barlee, epistles.

1839 William Heberden, epistles and Revelation.
1840 Samuel Sharpe (*Unit.*), New Test., rev. A.V.; 8th ed., 1881.
1840 Edgar Taylor (*Diss.*), New Test., rev. A.V.
1841 Dr. Conquest, Bible, rev. A.V.
1844 Lancelot Brenton, Old Test. (LXX).
1844–45 T. J. Hussey, Bible, rev. A.V.
1854 Joseph Turnbull, epistles of Paul; with Revelation, 1858.
1854 Herman Heinfetter, catholic epistles; New Test., 6th ed., 1864.
1855 Andrew Norton (U.S.A.), Gospels (modern speech).
1858 Leicester Sawyer (U.S.A.), New Test. (modern speech).
1862 Robert Young, Bible; many editions.
1862 H. Highton, New Test., rev. A.V.
1863 G. W. Brameld, Gospels.
1865 Samuel Sharpe (*Unit.*), Old Test., rev. A.V.; 4th ed., 1881.
1869 Robert Ainslie, New Test., rev. A.V.
1869 Henry Alford, New Test., rev. A.V.
1870 John Bowes (*Meth.*), New Test.
1871–81 F. C. Cook (ed.), Bible, rev. A.V.
1872 J. B. Rotherham, New Test.; 1878; Bible, 1897–1902.
1875 Samuel Davidson (*Presb.*), New Test.
1875 J. B. McClellan, New Test., rev. A.V.
1881 W. B. Crickmer, New Test.

Bibliography

Where more than one edition of the same work is listed, the date in boldface numbers indicates the edition usually referred to in the text unless otherwise noted.

Abbott, T. K. (ed.). *Evangeliorum versio antehieronymiana ex Codice Usseriano,* Dublin, 1884, 2 vols.

Abel, F. *Grammaire du Grec biblique,* 1927.

Adye, W. L. *The History of the Printed Greek Text of the New Testament,* 1865.

Aelfric. *Homilies on the Gospels for Sundays and Feasts,* in *The Homilies of the Anglo-Saxon Church, . . . with an English Version,* ed. by B. Thorpe, 1844–46.

———. *The Old English Version of the Heptateuch, Aelfric's Treatise on the Old and New Testament and His Preface to Genesis, together with a reprint of a Saxon treatise concerning the Old and New Testament, with the Vulgate text of the Heptateuch, now first published in print with English of our times by William L'Isle of Wilburgham, 1623,* ed. by S. J. Crawford, London, 1922.

———. *A Saxon Treatise Concerning the Old and New Testament,* ed. by William Lisle and Francis Junius, 1623.

———. *De Vetere et Novo Testamento,* ed. by C. W. Grein (vol. 1 of *Bibliothek der angelsächsischen Prosa*), Cassel and Göttingen, 1872.

Aldhelm. *Opera Sti Aldhelmi quae extant,* ed. by Giles, Oxford, 1844; ed. by Ehwald, 1913–19.

Alesius, Alexander. *Disputatio inter Alexandrum Alesium et Johannem Cochlaeum Germanum: An expediat laicis legere Novi Testamenti libros lingua vernaculari,* 1533.

Alexander, W. L. "Theodore Beza," in Kitto, *Biblical Encyclopaedia.*

Alfred. *The Whole Works of Alfred the Great,* 1852–53.

Allen, William. *An Apologie and True Declaration of the Institution and Endeavors of the Two English Colleges; the one in Rome, the other now resident in Rhemes,* 1581.

———. *Letters and Memorials,* with Introduction by T. F. Knox, London, 1882.

Amann, F. *Die Vulgata Sixtina von 1590,* 1912.

Ambrosius Catharinus (Lancelot Politi). *Annotationes in excerpta quaedam de commentariis Cardinalis Caietani dogmata,* Paris, 1535; Lyons, 1542.

———. *Apologia pro veritate catholicae fidei ac doctrinae adversus impia Martini Lutheri dogmata,* Florence, 1520.

———. *De erroribus annotatis in Caietani commentariis,* 1561.

Ames, Joseph. *Typographical Antiquities, or an Historical Account of the Origin and Progress of Printing in Great Britain and Ireland, Containing Memoirs of Our Ancient Printers,* 1749; "augmented" by William Herbert, 1785–90, 3 vols.; "enlarged" by Thomas Dibdin, 1810–19, 4 vols.

Anderson, Christopher (Baptist minister in Glasgow). *Annals of the English Bible,* London, 1845, 2 vols.; revised editions in one volume, 1849, 1862.

———. *The English Scriptures, their first reception and effects, including Memorials of Tyndale, Frith, Coverdale, and Rogers,* 1836.

———. *The Singular Introduction of the English Bible,* 1849, 1861. *The Answere to the Preface of the Rhemish Testament,* Edinburgh, 1602.

Arber, E. (ed.). *The First Printed English New Testament, Photolithographed from the Unique Fragment in the British Museum,* 1871, 1895.

Archbishop Murray's Douay and Rhemish Bible and the Bordeaux New Testament Examined in Four Letters, by "Phoenix," 1850.

Arias Montanus. *Biblia Hebraica, cum interlineari interpretatione Latina Xantis Pagnini Lucensis.*

Asser. *Annales rerum gestarum Alfredi Magni,* ed. by F. Wise, Oxford, 1722.

———. *Life of King Alfred,* ed. by W. H. Stevenson, Oxford, 1904; tr. by L. C. Jane, London, 1908.

Astle, Thomas. *Origin and Progress of Writing,* 2nd ed., 1802.

Atkinson, John C. *Memorials of Old Whitby,* 1894.

Ayres, S. C., and C. F. Sitterly. *The History of the English Bible Studied by the Library Method,* New York, 1898.

Baber, Henry H. *The New Testament Translated from the Latin in 1380 by John Wiclif, to which are prefixed memoirs of Dr. Wiclif and an historical account of the Saxon and English versions of the Scriptures previous to the opening of the fifteenth century,* 1810.

Babington, Churchill (ed.). Higden's *Polychronicon,* 1865.

Bagster, Samuel (ed.). *The Holy Scriptures faithfully and truly translated in to English by Myles Coverdale, 1535,* a reprint, 1838.

——— (ed.). *The English Hexapla, Exhibiting the Six Important English Translations of the New Testament Scriptures: Wiclif, Tyndale, Cranmer, Genevan, Anglo-Rhemish, Authorised,* 1841, 1845, 1846; Introduction by S. P. Tregelles.

Baikie, James. *The English Bible, Its Story, Its Growth, Its Translators and Their Adventures,* 1928, 1932, 1935.

Baille, R. *Letters and Journals,* ed. by S. Laing, 1842.

Baird, H. M. *Theodore Beza, Counsellor of the French Reformation,* New York, 1899.

Bale, John. *Index Britanniae scriptorum quos . . . collegit Ioannes Baleus,* ed. by R. L. Poole and Mary Bateson, Oxford, 1902.

Barlow, William. "The Summe and Substance . . . of the Conference . . . at Hampton Court, January 14, 1604," in Cardwell's *History of Conferences,* pp. 187 f.

Barnard, James. *The Life of the Venerable and Right Rev. Richard Challoner, D.D.,* London, 1784; Dublin, 1793.

Barry, William. "Our Latin Bible," *Dublin Review,* CXXXIX (1906), 1–23.

Bateson, Mary. *Catalogue of the Library of Syon Monastery, Isleworth,* Cambridge, 1898.

Baum, J. W. *Theodor Beza,* Leipzig, 1843, 2 vols.

Baumgarten, P. M. *Die Vulgata Sixtina von 1590,* 1911.

Baye, J. Baron de. *Industrial Arts of the Anglo-Saxons,* tr. by T. B. Harbottle, 1893.

Beard, Chas. *Martin Luther and the Reformation in Germany,* 1889.

Bebb, Ll. J. M. "The Evidence of the Early Versions and Patristic Quotations on the Text of the Books of the New Testament," in *Studia biblica* (*et ecclesiastica*), (Oxford, 1885–91, 3 vols.), II, 195–240.

Beckett, Edmund (Baron Grimthorpe). *Should the Revised Version of the New Testament be Authorised?* 1882.

Bede the Venerable. *Complete Works,* tr. by J. A. Giles, 1843–44, 12 vols.

———. *The Ecclesiastical History of the English Nation,* tr. by V. D. Scudder, 1910.

———. *Historical Works,* ed. by John Smith, 1722.

———. *Historical Works,* tr. by J. A. Giles, London, 1843, 2 vols. (in *Patres ecclesiae anglicanae,* vols. 1–4).

———. *Historical Works,* tr. by Joseph Stevenson, London, 1853.

———. *The Life and Miracles of St. Cuthbert,* tr. by V. D. Scudder, 1910.

———. *Lives of the First Five Abbots of Wearmouth and Jarrow,* tr. by Peter Wilcock, 1910.

———. *The Lives of the Holy Abbots of Wearmouth and Jarrow,* tr. by V. D. Scudder, 1910.

———. *Opera historica,* ed. by Plummer, Oxford, 1896, 2 vols.; also in Migne, *P.L.,* vols. 94 f.

———. *Vita ss. abbatum monasterii in Wiramutha et Girvum,* in Migne, *P.L.,* vol. 94.

———. *Vita prosaica Sti Cuthberti,* in Migne, *P.L.,* vol. 94.

Bedell, William (tr.). *Leabhuir na Seintiomna, or The Books of the Old Testament translated into Irish by the care and diligence of Dr. William Bedel, late Bishop of Kilmore,* 1685, 1690, 1852.

Berger, Samuel. *La Bible au seizième siècle: études sur les origines de la critique biblique,* 1879.

———. *La Bible française au moyen âge,* 1884.

———. *La Bible italienne au moyen âge,* 1894.

———. *Les Bibles provençales et vaudois,* in *Romania,* 1889.

———. *De l'histoire de la Vulgate en France,* 1887.

———. *Histoire de la Vulgate pendant les premier siècles du moyen âge,* Paris, 1893.

———. *Quam notitiam linguae Hebraicae habuerint Christiani medii aevi temporibus in Gallia,* 1893.

Bernard, Richard. *Rhimes against Rome: or the Removing of the Gagg of the New Gospell,* London, 1626.

Bernous, A. *Notice bibliographique sur Richard Simon,* 1882.

———. *Richard Simon et son Nouveau Testament,* 1869.

———. *Richard Simon et son Histoire critique du Vieux Testament: La critique biblique au siècle de Louis XIV,* 1869.

Bevan, J. O. *Our English Bible, the history of its development, 1611–1911,* 1911.

Beza, Theodore. *Praefatio in Novum Testamentum,* 1556.

Bilson, Thomas. *True Difference between Christian subjection and Unchristian Rebellion,* Oxford, 1585.

Bingham, Joseph. *Origines ecclesiasticae,* 1708–22, 10 vols.; English editions: *Antiquities of the Christian Church,* 1855, 10 vols.; 1878, 2 vols.

Binns, Leonard Elliott. *Erasmus the Reformer. A study in restatement,* Hulsean Lectures for 1921–23, 1928.

———. *The Reformers and the Bible,* 1923.

Birch, Walter de Gray (ed.). *Memorials of St. Guthlac,* 1881.

Bishop, Edmund, and F. A. Gasquet. *The Bosworth Psalter,* 1908.

Blackburn, Francis A. (ed.). *Caedmon: Exodus and Daniel,* Boston, 1907.

Blunt, John H. *A Plain Account of the English Bible from the earliest times of its translation to the present day,* 1870.

———. *The Reformation of the Church of England,* 1868, 2 vols.

——— (ed.). *The Myroure of oure Ladye, edited from the original black-letter text.* Early English Text Society, London, 1873.

Bois, John. *Veteris interpretis cum Beza aliisque recentioribus collatio in quatuor Evangeliis et Apostolorum Actis. In qua annon saepius absque justa satis causa hi ab illo discesserint disquiritur,* London, 1655.

Bonner, C. *The Romance of the English Bible,* 1927.

Bosworth, J., and G. Waring (eds.). *The Gothic and Anglo-Saxon Gospels in Parallel Columns with the Versions of Wycliffe and Tyndale,* London, 1865; 3rd ed., 1888; 4th ed., 1907.

Boutflower, Douglas S. (tr.). *The Life of Ceolfrid, the Abbot of the Monastery at Wearmouth and Jarrow, by an unknown author of the eighth century,* London, 1887, 1912.

Bradley, H. "The Caedmonian Genesis," in *Essays and Studies,* VI (1920), 7–29.

———. "Caedmon," in *Dictionary of National Biography,* and in *The Encyclopedia Britannica,* 11th ed.

Brady, William Maziere. *Episcopal Succession in England, Scotland, and Ireland, 1400–1875,* Rome, 1876–77, 3 vols.

Bramley, H. R. (ed.). *The Psalter or Psalms of David and Certain Canticles, with a translation and exposition in English, by Richard Rolle of Hampole,* Oxford, 1884.

Brewer, John S. *The Reign of Henry VIII,* 1884.

——— and James Gairdner (eds.). *Calendar of Letters and Papers of the Reign of Henry VIII,* 21 vols.

A Brief History of the Versions of the Bible of the English and Roman Churches, Dublin, 1830.

Bright, James W. (ed.). *Evangelium secundum Iohannem; the Gospel of St. John in West-Saxon,* 1904.

——— (ed.). *Evangelium secundum Lucam; the Gospel of St. Luke in West-Saxon,* 1906.

——— (ed.). *Evangelium secundum Mattheum: the Gospel of St. Matthew in West-Saxon,* 1904.

——— (ed.). *The Gospel of St. Luke in Anglo-Saxon,* Oxford, 1893.

Bristow, Richard. *A briefe Treatise of diverse plaine and sure wayes to finde out the truthe in this doubtful and dangerous time of Heresie, conteyning sundry worthy motives unto the Catholike faith, or Considerations to move a man to beleve the Catholikes and not the Heretikes,* Antwerp, 1574, 1599; 3rd ed. by Thomas Worthington (*Motives inducing to the Catholicke Faith*), 1641.

———. *Demaundes to bee proposed of Catholickes to the Heretickes,* 1576.

———. *Motiva omnibus Catholicae doctrinae orthodoxis cultoribus pernecessaria,* ed. by Worthington, Arras and Douay, 1608, 4to; tr. by Worthington (*Motives inducing to the Catholic Faith*), 1641.

———. *A Reply to William Fulke in Defence of M. D. Allen's Scrole of Articles and Booke of Purgatorie,* Louvaine, 1580.

———. *Tabula in Summam Theologicam S. Thomae Aquinatis,* 1579.

———. *Veritates aureae S. R. ecclesiae auctoritatibus veterum patrum* (posthumous), 1616, 4to.

British Museum. *Catalogue of the Western Manuscripts in the Old Royal and King's Collections in the British Museum,* by George Warner and Julius Gilson, 1921, 4 vols. fol.

———. *Facsimiles of Biblical Manuscripts in the British Museum,* ed. by Frederic Kenyon, Oxford, 1900.

———. *Guide to the Manuscripts and Printed Books Exhibited in Celebration of the Tercentenary of the Authorized Version,* British Museum Bible Exhibition, 1911; reprint, 1927.

———. *Queen Mary's Psalter; miniatures and drawings by an English artist of the fourteenth century,* Oxford, 1912.

Broughton, Hugh. *A Censure of the late translation for our churches: sent unto a Right Worshipfull Knight, Attendant upon the King,* 1612.

———. *A Concent of Scripture,* 1588.

———. *An Epistle to the learned Nobilitie of England, Touching Translating the Bible from the original, with ancient warrant for evrie worde, unto the full satisfaction of any that have hart,* Middlesburgh, 1597.

———. *The Works of the Great Albionean Divine, renowned in many Nations for Rare Skill in Salems and Athens Tongues and Familiar Acquaintance with all Rabbinical Learning. Mr. Hugh Broughton,* ed. by John Lightfoot, 1662, 13 vols.; 1825.

Brown, Gerard Baldwin. *The Arts in Early England,* vols. 1 and 2, London, 1903 (vols. 4 and 5 of *The Arts and Crafts of Our Teotonic Forefathers*); vols. 3 and 4, 1915; revised ed., 1926–30, 6 vols.

Brown, John. *The History of the English Bible,* 1911.

Browne, J. *Ten Lectures on Ward's "Errata of the Protestant Bible,"* 1859.

Buchanan, E. S. (ed.). *The Four Gospels from the Codex Veronensis,* Oxford, 1911.

Buckingham, L. S. *The Bible in the Middle Ages,* London, 1853.

Bülbring, K. D. *The Earliest Complete English Prose Psalter. Together with the Eleven Canticles and a Translation of the Athanasian Crede, edited from the only two MSS. in the libraries of the British Museum and Trinity College, Dublin,* Early English Text Society, No. 97, London, 1891 (Part I only).

Buisson, F. *Sébastien Castellion,* Paris, 1892.

Bulkeley, E. *An Answere to ten frivolous and foolish reasons set doun by the Rhemish Jesuits . . . which have mooved them to forsake the originall fountaine of the Greeke,* 1588.

Bullock, C. *Who gave us "the Book"? Or England's Debt to William Tyndale,* London, 1884.

Burgon, J. W. *The Causes of the Corruption of the Traditional Text,* ed. posthumously by E. Miller, 1896.

———. *The Last Twelve Verses of the Gospel according to St. Mark,* Oxford and London, 1871.

———. *The Revision Revised,* London, 1883 (reprinted from the *Quarterly Review,* October, 1881, to April, 1882).

———. *The Traditional Text of the Holy Gospels Vindicated,* ed. posthumously by E. Miller, 1896.

———. *An Unitarian Reviser of Our Authorized Version, Intolerable,* 1872.

Burkitt, Francis Crawford. *The Book of Rules of Tichonius* (vol. 9 of *Text and Studies*), 1894.

———. *The Gospel History and Its Transmission,* 1906, 1907.

———. *The Old Latin and the Itala* (vol. 4 of *Texts and Studies*), Cambridge, 1896.

Burnet, Gilbert. *History of the Reformation,* 1679–1714, 3 vols.; ed. by Pocock, 1865.

———. *The Life of William Bedell, D.D., Bishop of Kilmore in Ireland,* 1685; 2nd ed., Dublin, 1736.

Burton, Edwin H. *Life and Times of Bishop Challoner,* London, 1909, 2 vols.

Butler, Charles. *Historical Memoirs of the English, Irish, and Scottish Catholics,* London, 1819–21, 4 vols.; 3rd ed., 1822, 4 vols.

———. *Horae biblicae,* 1797–99; 1817, 2 vols.

Butterworth, C. C. *The Literary Lineage of the King James Bible, 1340–1611,* Philadelphia, 1941.

Cadoux, C. J. "The Revised Version" in *The Bible in Its Ancient and English Versions,* 1940.

Caedmon, *Exodus and Daniel,* ed. by Francis A. Blackburn, Boston, 1907.

———. *Exodus und Daniel,* ed. by C. W. Grein (in *Bibliothek der angelsächsischen Poesie*), 1857.

The Caedmon Manuscript of Anglo-Saxon Biblical Poetry, Introduction by Israel Gollancz, Oxford, 1927.

The Caedmon Poems, translated into English Prose, by Charles W. Kennedy, New York, 1916.

Caedmonis monachi paraphrasis Geneseos ac praecipuarum sacrae paginae historiarum, abhinc annos MLXX Anglo-Saxonice conscripta, ed. by F. Junius, Amsterdam, 1655.

Caedmon's Metrical Paraphrase of Parts of the Holy Scriptures, in Anglo-Saxon; with an English translation, notes, and a verbal index, by B. Thorpe, 1832.

Cajetan, Thomas de Vio. *Jentacula in selecta Novi Testamenti,* 1525, 1526, 1565, 1623.

———. *Praefatio in Evangelia cum commentariis Caietani,* Venice, 1530.

———. *Psalmi Davidici ad Hebraicam veritatem castigati et juxta sensum quem literalem dicunt enarrati,* 1530, 1532.
———. *Epistolae Pauli et aliorum apostolorum ad Graecam veritatem castigatae,* 1532, 1537, 1540.
Callaway, M. *Studies in the Syntax of the Lindisfarne Gospels,* 1918.
Calvin, John. *Praefatio in Novum Testamentum,* 1567.
Cambridge History of English Literature, 1907–16.
Cambridge Modern History, 1902–11.
Camden, William. *Annales rerum Anglicarum et Hibernicarum, regnante Elizabetha,* 1615–27, 2 vols.; 1625, 1639, 1677; English tr. by A. Darcy (Part I), 1625; by T. Browne (Part II), 1629; by R. Norton (whole), 1635; also 1675, 1688.
———. *Britannia,* 1586, 1587, 1590, 1594, 1600, 1607, 1616.
Cano, Melchior. *Summa apologetica.*
Canton, William. *The Bible and the Anglo-Saxon People,* 1914.
Capelle, Paul (ed.). *Le texte du Psautier latin en Afrique,* Rome, 1913 (vol. 4 of *Collectanea biblica Latina*).
Cardwell, Edward. *A History of the Conferences and other Proceedings connected with the Revision of the Book of Common Prayer from 1558 to 1690,* 1840.
———. *Synodalia; a Collection of Articles of Religion, Canons, and Proceedings of Convocations in the Province of Canterbury from 1547 to 1717,* 1842, 2 vols.
——— (ed.). Gibson's *Synodus Anglicana,* 1854.
Carleton, James. *The Part of Rheims in the Making of the English Bible,* Oxford, 1902.
——— (ed.). *The Psalter of the Church. The Prayer Book Version of the Psalms with Introduction and notes,* Cambridge, 1909.
Carpenter, J. Estlin. *The Bible in the Nineteenth Century,* London, 1903.
Carter, Edward H., and R. A. F. Mears. *A History of Great Britain,* 1937.
Cartwright, Thos. *The Answere to the Preface of the Rhemish Testament,* Edinburgh, 1602.
———. *A Confutation of the Rhemish Translation, Glosses, and Annotations on the New Testament,* 1618.
Catalogue of Bibles, Testaments, Psalms and the Books of the Holy Scriptures in English in the Collection of Lea Wilson, London, 1845, 4to.
Catharinus, Ambrosius (Lancelot Politi); *see* Ambrosius.
Chadwick, H. J. *The Origin of the English Nation,* Cambridge, 1907.
———. *Studies in Anglo-Saxon Institutions,* Cambridge, 1905.
———. *The Study of Anglo-Saxon,* 1941.
Chapman, John. *Notes on the Early History of the Vulgate Gospels,* Oxford, 1908.
———. "The Latin Bible," in the *Dublin Review,* CLXXX (1927), 1–18, 161–72.
Chavasse, C. M. *The English Bible in English History,* 1938.
Chester, J. L. *John Rogers, the Compiler of the First Authorised English Bible, the pioneer of the English Reformation, and its first martyr,* 1861.
Chronicle of Queen Jane and Two years of Queen Mary, Camden Society.
Clapton, Ernest (ed.). *Our Prayer Book Psalter, containing Coverdale's version from his 1535 Bible and the Prayer Book Version by Coverdale from the Great Bible, 1539–1541, printed side by side,* London, 1934.

Clark, Adam. *A Succinct Account of the Principal Editions of the Greek Testament,* 1804.

Clark, Albert C. (ed.). *The Acts of the Apostles. A critical edition,* 1933.

———. *The Descent of Manuscripts,* Oxford, 1918.

Clarke, F. L. *The Life of William Tyndale,* 1883.

Cleaveland, Elizabeth W. *A Study of Tindale's Genesis Compared with the Genesis of Coverdale and of the Authorized Version,* Yale University Press, 1911.

Cochlaeus (Johannes Dobneck). *Commentaria de actis et scriptis Martini Lutheri,* 1549.

———. *De canonis Scripturarum auctoritate.*

———. *Disputatio inter Alexandrum Alesium et Johannem Cochlaeum Germanum: An expediat laicis legere Novi Testamenti libros lingua vernaculari,* 1533.

Colgrave, Bertram. *Two Lives of St. Cuthbert,* Cambridge, 1940.

Collectanea biblica Latina, Rome, 1912–22, 6 vols.

Collette, C. H. *The Authorised Version of the Bible as Compared with the Douay and Rhemish Versions vindicated from the charge of corruption,* 1891.

Collier, Jeremiah. *An Ecclesiastical History of Great Britain,* 1708–14, 2 vols. fol.; ed. by Barham, 1840–41, 9 vols.; ed. by Lathbury, 1852, 9 vols.

Comper, Frances M. *A Life of Richard Rolle,* 1928.

Conant, Hannah. *The English Bible; a Popular History of the Translation of the Holy Scriptures into the English Tongue,* 1856; with an Introduction by C. H. Spurgeon, 1859; new and revised edition by Dr. Conant, 1881.

Condit, Blackford. *History of the English Bible,* New York, 1882.

Constant. *La Réforme en Angleterre,* 1930; English translation, *The Reformation in England,* 1934.

Cook, A. S. *The Authorized Version of the Bible and Its Influence,* 1909, 1910.

———. *A Glossary of the Old Northumbrian Gospels,* 1894.

Cook, F. C. *"Deliver Us from Evil": A protest against the change in the last petition in the Lord's Prayer, adopted in the Revised Version of the New Testament,* 1881.

———. *The Revised Version of the First Three Gospels, considered in its bearing upon the record of Our Lord's words and of incidents in his life,* 1882.

Cook, Stanley. *The Old Testament. A Reinterpretation,* 1936.

Cooke, George A. (ed.). *The Prayer Book Psalter Revised,* Oxford, 1939.

Cooper, Charles H. and F. S. A. *Athenae Cantabrigienses,* Cambridge, 1858–61, 2 vols.

———. *Memorials of Cambridge,* 1858–66, 3 vols.

Cooper, W. B. *The Life and Work of William Tyndale,* 1924.

Copinger, W. A. *Incunabula biblica, or the first half century of the Latin Bible, being a bibliographical account of the various editions of the Latin Bible between 1450 and 1500,* 1892.

Cotton, Henry (Archdeacon of Cashel). *Lists of Editions of the Bible and Parts Thereof in English, from the year MDV to MDCCCXX,* Oxford, 1821; second edition (*MDV to MDCCCL*), 1852. (Most valuable despite many inaccuracies.)

———. *Rhemes and Doway. An attempt to shew what has been done by Roman Catholics for the diffusion of the Holy Scriptures in English,* Oxford, 1855.

———. *The Five Books of Maccabees,* Oxford, 1832.

Coverdale, Myles. *Memorials of Myles Coverdale* (anonymous), London, 1838.

———. *Works,*—including *Writings and Translations* (1844) and *Remains* (1846) —ed. by G. Pearson, Parker Society, Cambridge, 1844–48.

Cranmer, Thomas. *Miscellaneous Writings and Letters of Thomas Cranmer,* Parker Society, 1846.

Crawford, Samuel John. *Anglo-Saxon Influence on Western Christendom,* Oxford, 1933.

———. *Exameron Anglice, or the Old English Hexameron,* 1921.

——— (ed.). *The Old English Version of the Heptateuch, Aelfric's Treatise on the Old and New Testament and His Preface to Genesis, together with a reprint of a Saxon treatise concerning the Old and New Testament, with the Vulgate text of the Heptateuch, now first published in print with English of our times by William L'Isle of Wilburgham, 1623,* Early English Text Society, London, 1922.

Curry, D. *The New Testament Containing the Old and New Versions. The history of the committee of revision,* New York, 1882.

Dabney, J. P. (ed.). *The New Testament Translated by William Tyndale the Martyr, with a memoir of his life and works. To which are annexed the essential variations of Coverdale's, Thos. Matthew's, Cranmer's, the Genevan, and the Bishops' Bible, as marginal readings,* 1837.

Daiches, David. *The King James Version of the English Bible,* 1936; Chicago, 1941.

Darlow, J. H., and H. F. Moule. *Historical Catalogue of the Printed Editions of Holy Scripture in the Library of the British and Foreign Bible Society,* vol. 1 (English versions), 1903.

D'Astros. *La Bible mutilée par les Protestants, ou démonstration de la divinité des Ecritures rejetées par la Reforme,* 2nd ed., 1817; 3rd ed., 1847.

Davies, J. *Ancient Rites and Monuments of the Monastical Church of Durham,* 1672.

Dawson, Benjamin. *Notes on the Revised Version of the Old Testament,* 1886.

Deanesly, Margaret. *The Lollard Bible and Other Medieval Biblical Versions,* Cambridge University Press, 1920.

Delisle, L., and P. Meyer, *L'Apocalypse en français au XIII*[e] *siècle,* Paris, 1901.

Demaus, R. *William Tyndale,* 1871; revised ed. by R. Lovett, 1886; abridged and ed. by N. Watts, 1935.

———. *Hugh Latimer,* 1869, 1882, 1923; abridged and ed. by N. Watts, 1936.

Dictionary of National Biography, London and New York, 1908–9, 22 vols.

Dirksen, Aloys H. *The New Testament Concept of Metanoia,* Washington, 1932.

Disraeli, Isaac. *Curiosities of Literature,* 1859.

Dixon, R. W. *History of the Church of England,* London, 1878–85, 3 vols.

Dobneck, J.; *see* Cochlaeus.

Dobschütz, E. von. *Studien zur Textkritik der Vulgata,* 1894.

Dodd, C. *The Church History of England, from 1500 to 1688,* Brussels, 1737, 3 vols.; ed. by Tierney, 1839–43, 5 vols.

———. *The History of the English College at Douay, . . . by a Roman Catholic, Chaplain to an English Regiment,* London, 1713.

Dore, J. H. *Old Bibles,* 1876; 2nd ed., 1888.[1]

The Douay Bible. Being remarks on what is said by authority in regard to it, 1931.

Douay Diaries, I–II (1568–93), ed. by Knox as *Records of the English Catholics,* London, 1878.

Douay Diaries, III–V (1598–1654), ed. by Burton and Williams, Catholic Record Society, Nos. 10 f., London, 1911.

Drake, Allison. *The Authorship of the West-Saxon Gospels,* New York, 1894.

Driver, S. R., and W. A. Wright. *On the Marginal Notes of the Revised Versions,* 1912.

Ducarel, A. C. *A List of Various Editions of the Bible and Parts Thereof in English, from the year 1526 to 1776,* 1777.

Duff, E. G. *A Short Account of Tindale's Pentateuch,* 1910.

Eadie, John. *The English Bible: an External and Critical History of the Various English Translations of Scripture,* London, 1876, 2 vols.

Eadwine's Canterbury Psalter, ed. with Introduction and notes from the MS. in Trinity College, Cambridge, by F. Harsley, Early English Text Society, No. 92, London, 1892.

Earle, John. *The Psalter of 1539, a Landmark in English Literature,* 1894.

Earle, John. *Remarks on the Prefaces prefixed to the First and Second Volumes of a work entitled "The Holy Bible; . . . translated by the Rev. Alexander Geddes,"* 1799, 12mo.

Eason, Charles. *The Circulation of the Douay Bible in Ireland,* London, 1931.

———. *The Geneva Bible. Notes on Its Production and Distribution,* 1937.

Echard, and J. Quétif. *Scriptores Ordinis Praedicatorum,* Paris, 1719.

Edgar, Andrew. *The Bibles of England. A plain account for plain people of the principal versions of the Bible in English,* London, 1889.

Ellicott, C. J. *Considerations on the Revision of the English Version of the New Testament,* London, 1870.

——— and E. Palmer(?). *The Revisers and the Greek Text of the New Testament* (published anonymously), 1882.

Ellis, Henry J. *Original Letters of Eminent Literary Men,* Camden Society, No. 23, 1843.

———. *An Account of Caedmon's Metrical Paraphrases of Scripture History,* 1833.

Emser, Jerome, *Annotationes in Novum Testamentum Luteri,* 1523.

Encyclopaedia Britannica, 9th edition.

The English Hexapla, ed. by S. Bagster, 1841, 1845, 1846; Introduction by S. P. Tregelles; *see* Bagster.

Faber, F. W. *St. Francis of Assisi,* Oratorian Lives of the Saints, 1847–56.

Faber (Fabri, *or* Lefèvre), J. (Stapulensis). *Biblia Sacra juxta Vulgatam ab aliquot theologis Parisiensibus accurate recognita et emendata . . . accesserunt III Maccabaeorum Liber, etc. cum scholiis Joan. Benedicti,* Paris, 1573.

———. *Epistolae divi Pauli apostoli, cum commentariis,* Paris, 1551.

Felix of Croyland. *Vita et miracula Scti Guthlaci anachoretae, primum Latine scripta, et deinde ab incerto scriptore Saxonice versa,* tr. by Charles Goodwin, London, 1848.

[1] This is a most useful volume and betrays no unworthy religious bias; the author, like Mr. Lea Wilson, must have formed a priceless collection of editions of the Bible.

Firth, F. J. (ed.). *The Acts of the Apostles, the Epistles, and the Revelation of St. John the Divine. A comparison of the text as it is given in the Protestant and Roman Catholic Bible versions in the English language in use in America* (the Authorized, Revised, and Douay versions), New York, 1912.

——— (ed.). *The Holy Gospel. A comparison of the Gospel text as it is given . . . ,* New York, 1911, 1912.

Fish, Simon. *A Supplication for the Beggars, written about 1529,* ed. by F. J. Furnival, Early English Tract Society, 1871.

Forshall, J. M., and Frederick Madden (eds.). *The Holy Bible, with the Apocryphal Books, in the earliest English versions, made from the Latin Vulgate by John Wycliffe and his followers,* Oxford, 1850, 4 vols.

Foulis, H. *History of the Popish Treasons and Usurpations, together with a particular account of many gross corruptions and impostures in the Church of Rome highly dishonourable and injurious to Christian religion. To which is prefixt a large Preface to the Romanists,* London, 1671, 1681.

Foxe, John. (ed.). *The Gospels of the Fower Evangelistes translated in the olde Saxons tyme out of Latin into the vulgare toung of the Saxons, and now published for testimonie of the same,* with Introductions, 1571.

———. *Actes and Monumentes,* 1563; ed. by Townsend, 1844–49, 8 vols.

Freeman, James M. *A Short History of the English Bible,* 1879.

Friedrichsen, G. W. S. *The Gothic Version of the Epistles,* 1936.

———. *The Gothic Version of the Gospels; a study of its style and textual history,* Oxford, 1926.

Frigel, L. *Dissertatio de Cardinale Cajetano.*

Froude, James Anthony. *History of England from the Fall of Wolsey to the Defeat of the Spanish Armada,* 1856–70, 12 vols.

Fry, Francis (ed.). *The Bible by Coverdale MDXXXV,* London, 1867.

———. *A bibliographical description of the Editions of the New Testament: Tyndale's version in English with numerous readings,* London, 1878.

———. *A Description of the Great Bible, 1539, and the six editions of Cranmer's Bible, 1540 and 1541, printed by Grafton and Whitchurch; also of the editions in large folio of the Authorised Version, 1611, 1613, 1617, 1634, and 1640,* London, 1865, fol.

———. *The First New Testament Printed in the English Language (1525 or 1526), translated from the Greek by William Tyndale, reproduced in facsimile, with an Introduction,* Bristol, 1862.

———. "On the Bishops' Bible," in *Notes and Queries,* July 28, 1871.

——— (ed.). *The Prophete Jonas, with an Introduction by Wm. Tyndale, reproduced in facsimile, to which is added Coverdales version of Jonah, with an Introduction,* London, 1863.

——— (ed.). *The Standard Edition of the English New Testament the Geneva Version,* London, 1864; reprinted from the *Journal of Sacred Literature,* July, 1864.

Fulke, W. *A Defense of the Sincere and True Translations of the Holie Scriptures into the English Tong, against the manifolde cavils, frivolous quarels, and impudent slaunders of Gregorie Martin,* London, 1583; edited for the Parker Society by C. H. Hartshorne, Cambridge, 1843.

———. *A Discoverie of the daungerous Rocke of the Popish Churche,* 1580.
———. *The Text of the New Testament of Jesus Christ, translated out of the vulgar Latine by the Papists of the traiterous Seminarie at Rhemes. . . . Whereunto is Added the Translation out of the Original Greeke, commonly used in the Church of England,* London, 1589, 1601, 1617, 1633.
Fuller, Thos. *The Church-History of Britain from the Birth of Jesus Christ untill the year 1648,* London, 1655; ed. by J. Nichols, 1837, 3 vols.; ed. by J. S. Brewer, 1845.
Gairdner, James. *The English Church in the Sixteenth Century,* in Stephens and Hunt's *History of the English Church,* 1902, 1903, 1904, 1912.
———. *Lollardy and the Reformation in England,* 1908–13, 4 vols.
——— and J. S. Brewer (eds.). *Calendar of Letters and Papers of the Reign of Henry VIII,* 21 vols.
Gardiner, Stephen. *A Detection of the Devil's Sophistrie, wherewith he robbeth the unlearned people of the true belief in the Most Blessed Sacrament of the Aulter,* London, 1546.
Gasquet, Francis Aidan (ed.). *Codex Vercellensis jamdudum ab Irico et Bianchino bis editus, denuo cum manuscripto collatus,* Rome, 1914 (vol. 3 of *Collectanea biblica Latina*).
——— (ed.). *Biblia sacra juxta Latinam Vulgatam versionem* (Genesis to Ruth), 1926–39, 4 vols.
———. "English Biblical Criticism in the Thirteenth Century," in the *Dublin Review, CXXII* (1898), 1–21.
———. *A History of the Venerable English College, Rome,* 1920.
———. *The Life of St. Gregory the Great.*
———. "The Pre-Reformation Bible," in the *Dublin Review,* CXV (1894), 122–52.
———. *The Old English Bible, and other essays,* London, 1897.
———. "Revising the Vulgate," in the *Dublin Review,* CXLIII (1908), 264–73.
——— and E. Bishop. *The Bosworth Psalter,* 1908.
Geddes, Alexander. *Address to the Public, on the publication of the first volume of his New Translation of the Bible,* London, 1793, 4to.
———. *Critical Remarks on the Hebrew Scriptures,* London, 1800, 4to.
———. *A General Answer to the Queries, Counsels, and Criticisms . . . since the publication of his Proposals for printing a New Translation of the Bible,* London, 1790.
——— (tr.). *The Holy Bible . . . faithfully translated from the corrected text of the Original: Genesis to Josue,* 1792; *Judges to Chronicles,* London, 1797.
———. *A Letter to the R. R. Bishop of London . . . relative to a vernacular version of the Holy Scriptures,* London, 1787, 4to.
——— (tr.). *A New Translation of the Book of Psalms* (to psalm 117), London, 1807 (posthumous).
———. *Proposals for printing, by subscription, a New Translation of the Holy Bible,* London, 1788.
———. *Prospectus of a New Translation of the Holy Bible, from corrected Texts of the Originals,* London, 1786, 4to.
Gibson, Edmund. *Synodus Anglicana,* ed. by Edward Cardwell, 1854.

Gillespie, F. G. K. *Revision Reasons: A Manual of the Revised Version of the Old Testament,* 1906.

Gillow, Joseph. *Bibliographical Dictionary of the English Catholics,* London, 5 vols.

Gilson, Julius P., and G. F. Warner. *Catalogue of the Western Manuscripts in the Old Royal and King's Collections in the British Museum,* Oxford, 1921, 4 vols. fol.

Giraldus Cambrensis. *Topographia Hiberniae.*

Glass, H. A. *The Story of the Psalters; a history of the metrical versions of Great Britain and America, 1549–1885,* London, 1888.

Glunz, H. *The History of the Vulgate in England from Alcuin to Roger Bacon,* 1933.

Goguel, M. *Le texte et les éditions du Nouveau Testament Grec,* 1920.

Gollancz, Israel (ed.). *The Caedmon Manuscript of Anglo-Saxon Biblical Poetry,* Oxford, 1927.

Goodman, Christopher. *How Superior Powers Ought to be Obeyed,* Geneva, 1558; reproduced with a bibliographical note by Charles McIlwain, Columbia University Press, 1931.

Goodspeed, Edgar J. *How to Read the Bible,* 1946; British ed., Oxford, 1948.

———. *The Making of the English New Testament,* Chicago, 1925.

———. *The Translators to the Reader. Preface to King James' Version,* 1911, 1935.

Goodwin, D. R. *Notes on the Late Revision of the New Testament,* New York, 1883.

Goodwin, J. *Evangelia Augustini Gregoriana. An historical and illustrative description of the MSS. cclxxxvi and cxcvii in the Parker Library of Corpus Christi College, Cambridge, being the Gospels sent by Pope Gregory the Great to Augustine, A.D. DCI,* 1847.

Gordon, Robert K. *Anglo-Saxon Poetry,* 1927.

Graf, K. H. *Essai sur la vie et les écrits de J. Lefèvre d'Etaples,* Strasbourg, 1842.

Graham, Rose. "The Intellectual Influence of English Monasteries between the Tenth and Twelfth Centuries," in *Transactions of the R. Hist. Soc.,* London, 1903.

Gratet-Duplessis, P. A. *Notice sur une traduction de l'Écriture sainte designée ordinairement sous le titre de Bible de Douai et Nouveau Testament de Rheims,* 1841.

Gray, Crete. *William Tyndale and the English Bible,* 1938.

Green, Mary Ann Everett (ed.). *The Life and Death of Mr. William Whittingham, Dean of Durham, who departed this life, A.D. 1579,* Camden Society, No. 187, Miscellany VI, 1871.

Greenslade, S. L. *The Work of William Tindale, with an essay on Tindale and the English Language* by G. D. Bone, 1938.

Grein, C. W. M. (ed.). *Aelfric, de Vetere et Novo Testamento* (vol. 1 of *Bibliothek der angelsächsischen Prosa,* Cassel and Göttingen), 1872.

——— (ed.). *Caedmon, Exodus und Daniel* (in *Bibliothek der angelsächsischen Poesie*), 1857.

Greswell, W. P. *A View of the Early Parisian Greek Press, including the Lives of the Stephani,* 2nd ed., Oxford, 1840, 2 vols.

Grier, Richard. *An Answer to Ward's Errata of the Protestant Bible,* London, 1812.

———. *A Reply to the "End of Religious Controversy,"* London, 1821.
Grimthorpe, Baron: *see* E. Beckett.
Grindal, Edmund. *The Remains of Archbishop Grindal,* Parker Society.
Grisar, H. *Martin Luther, His Life and Work* (adapted from the second German edition by Frank J. Elbe), St. Louis, 1930; 2nd ed., 1939.
———. *Martin Luther* (authorized translation by E. J. Lamond), 1913–17, 6 vols.
Gruber, L. Franklin. *The First English New Testament and Luther; the real extent to which Tyndale was dependent upon Luther,* 1928.
———. *The Truth of the So-called Luther's Testament in English, Tyndale's New Testament,* 1917 (reprinted from *The Lutheran Church Review,* 1916–17).
———. *The Version of 1611: propriety of calling it "Authorized Version"* or *"King James's Version,"* 1914.
Guppy, Henry. *A Brief Sketch of the History of the Transmission of the Bible Down to the Revised Version of 1881–1885,* 1926; new edition, 1936.
———. *Catalogue of an Exhibition Illustrating the History of the Transmission of the Bible,* John Rylands Library, 1935.
———. *Miles Coverdale and the English Bible, 1488–1568,* 1935.
———. "The Royal Injunctions of 1536 and 1538 and the Great Bible," in *Bulletin of the Rylands Library,* April, 1938.
———. *William Tindale and the Earlier Translators of the Bible into English,* 1925.
Gwynn, John. *Liber Armachanus. The Book of Armagh,* 1913.
Hague, Dyson. *Life and Work of John Wycliffe,* London, 1935.
Hales, J. D. *The Bible or the Bible Society? The corruption of God's word in the Italian version of Martini,* London, 1861.
——— and C. E. Stuart. *A Protest against the Circulation of the Papal Latin Vulgate and Its Versions,* London, 1857.
——— and Stuart. *Romish Versions of the Bible: facts and arguments,* 1856.
Da Halgon Godspel on Englisc. The Anglo-Saxon Versions of the Holy Gospels, ed. by Benjamin Thorpe, London, 1842.
Hall, Edward. *Abridgement of the Chronicles of England,* 1542, 1548, 1550, 1809.
Hallam, Henry. *The Introduction to the Literature of Europe in the Fifteenth, Sixteenth, and Seventeenth Centuries,* 5th ed., 1855.
Hamilton, G. *Observations on the present state of the Roman Catholic English Bibles,* 1825.
Harden, J. M. *Dictionary of the Vulgate New Testament,* 1921.
——— (ed.). *Psalterium juxta Hebraeos Hieronymi with Introduction and apparatus criticus,* 1922.
Harris, James Rendel. *Four Lectures on the Western Text of the New Testament,* Cambridge, 1894.
Harris, L. M. *Studies in the Anglo-Saxon Version of the Gospels,* 1901.
Harris, Mattie A. *A Glossary of the West-Saxon Gospels,* Yale University Press, 1899.
Harrison, F. *The Bible in Britain,* 1949.
Harsley, F. (ed.). *Eadwine's Canterbury Psalter,* Early English Text Society, No. 92, London, 1892.

Hart, Richard. *Ecclesiastical Records,* 2nd ed., 1846.

Hastings, James (ed.). *Dictionary of the Bible,* 1902–04, 5 vols.

Hatch, W. *The Principal Uncial MSS. of the New Testament,* Chicago, 1939.

Heaton, W. J. *Our Own English Bible, its translators and their work,* 1905–13, 3 vols.

———. *The Puritan and Other Contemporaneous Protestant Versions,* 1913 (vol. 3 of *Our Own English Bible*).

Hemphill, S. *The Gospels of MacRegol of Birr. A Study in Celtic illumination,* 1911.

———. *A History of the Revised Version of the New Testament,* 1906.

Henderson, E. F. *Select Historical Documents and Charters of the Middle Ages,* 1892.

Henderson, M. H. *The Canon of Holy Scripture, with remarks upon King James' Version, the Latin Vulgate, and the Douay Bible,* 1868.

Henshall, Samuel (ed.). *The Gothic Gospel of St. Matthew from the Codex Argenteus of the Fourth Century,* London, 1807, 1887.

Henslow, G. *The Vulgate the Source of False Doctrines,* 1909.

Hentenius, J. *Biblia ad vetustissima exemplaria nunc reens castigata, Hebraea, Chaldaea, Graeca et Latina nomina restituta cum Latina interpretatione,* 1547, 1563, 1565, 1570.

Heppe, H. *Theodore Beza,* 1861.

Hetzenauer, M. *De recognitione principiorum criticae textus Novi Testamenti,* 1921.

Heylyn, Peter. *Ecclesia restaurata: or the History of the Reformation of the Church of England,* London, 1661, 1670, 1674; ed. by J. C. Robertson, 1849.

———. *Ecclesia vindicata, or the Church of England justified,* 1657.

———. *Examen historicum, or a Discovery and Examination of the Mistakes, Falsities, and Defects in some Modern Histories,* 1658–59.

Hickes, G. *Linguarum veterum septentrionalium thesaurus grammatico-criticus et archaeologicus* 1703–1705.

Higden. *Polychronicon,* ed. by Churchill Babington, 1865.

Historical Catalogue of the Printed Editions of Holy Scripture in the Library of the British and Foreign Bible Society, 1903–11, 2 vols.

The History of the English College at Douay, by a Roman Catholic, Chaplain to an English Regiment That Marched in upon It, London, 1713.

Hoare, H. W. *The Evolution of the English Bible, 1382–1885,* London, 1901; 2nd ed., 1902; 3rd ed., 1911; revised ed. with new title: *Our English Bible; the story of its origin and growth,* 1925.

Hodgkin, R. H. *History of the Anglo-Saxons,* Oxford, 1935, 2 vols.

Hody, Humphrey. *De Bibliorum textibus originalibus,* Oxford, 1705.

Hoepfl, H. *Beiträge zur Geschichte der Sixto-Klementinischen Vulgata,* 1913.

Holland, A. *Histoire du texte du Nouveau Testament,* 1936.

Holland, John. *The Psalmists of Britain. Records . . . of upwards of one hundred and fifty authors who have rendered the whole or parts of the Book of Psalms into English verse,* London, 1843, 2 vols.

Hopkins-James, L. J. *The Celtic Gospels; Their Story and Their Text,* Oxford, 1934.

Horne, T. H. *A Compendious Introduction to the Study of the Bible,* 1827; 10th ed., London, 1862.

———. *An Introduction to the Critical Study and Knowledge of the Scriptures,* 1818, 1823, 4 vols.; 8th ed., 1839.

———. *A Manual of Biblical Bibliography,* 1839.

Horstmann, Carl. *Richard Rolle of Hampole and His Followers,* London, 1895, 2 vols.

Hort, Fenton J., and B. Westcott (eds.). *The New Testament in the Original Greek,* with the Introduction (vol. 2) by Hort, 1881.

Hoskier, Herman C. *Concerning the Genesis of the Versions of the New Testament,* 1910.

Hospinianus, Rodolphus. *Concordia discors: . . . de origine et progressu Formulae Concordiae Bergensis,* Zurich, 1607.

Howlett, J. A. "Textual Criticism of the Hebrew Text," in the *Dublin Review,* CXXV (1899), 121–43.

———. "Textual Criticism of the New Testament," in the *Dublin Review,* CXXII (1898), 320–44.

Hügel, F. von. "The Church and the Bible," in the *Dublin Review,* CXV (1894), 313–41; CXVI (1895), 306–37; CXVII (1895), 275–304.

Humphry, W. G. *Commentary on the Revised Version of the New Testament,* 1882.

Hunt, W. *The English Church to the Norman Conquest,* 1899.

Hurter, H. *Nomenclator literarius theologiae catholicae,* 1871–86, 3 vols.; 3rd enlarged ed., 1906–13, 6 vols.

Husenbeth, Frederick C. *The Life of R. R. John Milner, Bishop of Castabala,* Dublin, 1862.

Hutton, Edward A. *Atlas of Textual Criticism, being an attempt to show the mutual relationship of the authorities for the text of the New Testament up to about 1000 A.D.,* 1911.

Hutton, H. H. "The Ignored Taverner Bible of 1539," in *The Crozier,* July, 1939, pp. 161–76.

Irwin, William A.; *see* Ira M. Price.

Isaacs, J. Contributions to *The Bible in Its Ancient and English Versions,* ed. by H. W. Robinson, Oxford, 1940.

Jackson, John E. "Catholic Tradition and Scripture," in the *Dublin Review,* XXII (1847), 457–86.

Jacquier, E. *Le Nouveau Testament dans l'Église chrétienne,* 1911–13, 2 vols.

James, M. R. Contributions to *Cambridge Modern History.*

———. *Sources of Archbishop Parker's Collection of Manuscripts,* Cambridge Antiquarian Society, 1899.

———. *Two Ancient English Scholars, St. Aldhelm and William of Malmesbury,* 1931.

James, Thos. *Bellum papale sive Concordia discors Sixti Quinti et Clementis Octavi circa Hieronymianam editionem,* London, 1600, 1606, 1678.

———. *A Treatise of the Corruption of Scripture, Councels and Fathers by the Prelats, Pastors, and Pillars of the Church of Rome for maintenance of popery and irreligion,* 1611.

Jenkins, R. C. *Pre-Tridentine Doctrine. A Review of the Commentaries on the Scriptures by Thomas de Vio, Cardinal Cajetan,* 1891.
John, H. *The History of the English Bible,* 1903.
John the Deacon. *Sancti Gregorii Magni vita,* in Migne, *P.L.,* vol. 75.
Johnson, A. *An Historical Account of the Several English Translations of the Bible,* 1730.
Jones, Maurice. *The Four Gospels: their literary history and their special characteristics,* 1921, 1927.
———. *The New Testament in the Twentieth Century,* 1914, 1924, 1934.
Junius, F. (ed.). *Caedmonis monachi paraphrasis Geneseos ac praecipuarum sacrae paginae historiarum, abhinc annos MLXX Anglo-Saxonice conscripta et nunc demum edita a Francisco Junio,* Amsterdam, 1655.
——— and W. Lisle (eds.). *A Saxon Treatise Concerning the Old and New Testament,* 1623.
——— and T. Marshall (eds.). *Quatuor Domini Nostri Jesu Christi . . . Evangeliorum versiones perantiquae duae, Gothica scilicet* [ed. by F. Junius], *et Anglo-Saxonice* [ed. by T. Marshall], Dort, 1665.
Kaulen, Franz. *Geschichte der Vulgata,* Mainz, 1868.
———. *Handbuch zur Vulgata,* 1870.
———. *Sprachliches Handbuch zur biblischen Vulgata,* 1904.
Kennedy, Benjamin H. *The Ely Lectures on the Revised Version of the New Testament,* London, 1882.
Kennedy, C. W. *The Caedmon Poems, Translated into English Prose,* New York, 1916.
Kennedy, Henry A. A. *The Sources of New Testament Greek, or the influence of the Septuagint on the vocabulary of the New Testament,* 1895.
———. "Latin Versions," in Hastings' *Dictionary of the Bible,* vol. III.
Kennedy, William P. M. *Archbishop Matthew Parker,* 1908.
———. *Studies in Tudor History,* 1916.
Kenyon, Frederic. *The Bible and Archaeology,* 1940.
———. *Chester Beatty Biblical Papyri, descriptions and texts of twelve MSS. on papyrus of the Greek Bible,* 1933–36, 10 vols. 4to.
———. "English Versions" in Hastings' *Dictionary of the Bible,* 1909.
——— (ed.). *Facsimiles of Biblical Manuscripts in the* [*British*] *Museum,* Oxford, 1900.
———. *Handbook to the Textual Criticism of the New Testament,* London, 1901; 2nd ed., New York, 1912; 1926.
———. *Our Bible and the Ancient Manuscripts,* 1895; 4th ed., 1939.
———. *Recent Developments in the Textual Criticism of the Greek Bible,* 1933, 1937.
———. *The Story of the Bible,* 1936.
———. *The Text of the Greek Bible,* 1937.
Kilburne, W. *Dangerous Errors in Several Late Printed Bibles to the great scandal and corruption of sound and true religion,* 1659.
King, E. G. (tr.). *The Psalms in Three Collections, translated with notes,* 1898.
Kingdon, J. A. *Incidents in the Lives of Thomas Poyntz and Richard Grafton,* 1895.

Knox, Thomas Francis. Historical Introduction to *Letters and Memorials of William Cardinal Allen,* London, 1882.

Knighton, H. de. *Compilatio de eventibus Angliae,* 1366.

Konrath, M. (ed.). *The Poems of William of Shoreham,* Early English Text Society, 1902.

Kropatschek. *Die deutsche Bibelübersetzung des Mittelalters,* 1889.

La Faye, Antoine. *De vita et obitu Theodori Bezae,* 1606.

Lagrange, M. J. *Critique textuelle, critique rationelle,* 1935.

———. *Histoire ancienne du canon du Nouveau Testament,* 1933.

Lake, Kirsopp. *Codex I of the Gospels and Its Allies,* Cambridge, 1902 (vol. 7 of *Texts and Studies*).

———. *Codex Sinaiticus petropolitanus,* Oxford, 1911, 4to.

———. *Text of the New Testament,* 2nd ed., 1904.

Lappenberg, John Martin. *A History of England under the Anglo-Saxon Kings,* tr. by B. Thorpe, 1881, 2 vols.

Lawlor, H. J. *Chapters on the Book of Mulling,* Edinburgh, 1897.

Leabhuir na Seintiomna, or The Books of the Old Testament translated into Irish by the care and diligence of Dr. William Bedel, late Bishop of Kilmore, 1685, 1690; new edition, 1852.

Le Bachelet, X. M. *Bellarmine et la Bible Sixto-Clementine: Étude des documents inédits,* 1911.

Lechler, G. V. *John Wycliffe and His English Precursors,* tr. and ed. with notes by P. Lorimer, London, 1878; new editions, 1881, 1884.

Lefèvre, Jacques: *see* Faber.

Leger. *Cyrille et Méthode: Étude historique sur la conversion des Slaves au Christianisme,* Poitiers-Paris, 1868.

Le Long, J. *Biblia Sacra seu Syllabus omnium ferme S. Scripturae editionum ac versionum secundum seriem linguarum quibus Vulgatae sunt notis historicis et criticis illustratus,* Antwerp, 1709, 2 vols.

———. *Bibliotheca sacra post Cl.Cl.V.V. Jacobi Le Long et C. F. Boerneri iteratas curas ordine disposita, emendata suppleta, continuata ab Andrea Gottlieb Masch,* 1783, 3 vols.

Lenox, James. *Early Editions of King James' Bible in Folio,* New York, 1861, 4to.

Leo XIII. Encyclical *Providentissimus Deus,* November 18, 1893.

Leonard, G. H. *The Authorized Version of the English Bible,* 1911.

Leonard, H. C. (tr.). *A Translation of the Anglo-Saxon Version of St. Mark's Gospel,* 1881.

The Life of Ceolfrid, the Abbot of the Monastery at Wearmouth and Jarrow, by an unknown author of the eighth century, tr. by Douglas S. Boutflower, London, 1887, 1912.

Le Roux de Lincy. *Les Quatre Livres des Rois traduits en français au XIIe siècle,* 1841.

Lewis, John. *A Complete History of the Several Translations of the Holy Bible and New Testament, etc., into English,* 1731, 1738, 1818.[2]

[2] The first edition of this work (London: 1731) was prefixed to an edition of Wycliffe's translation of the New Testament.

Lightfoot, J. B. *On a Fresh Revision of the English New Testament,* London, 1871, 1872, 1891.

The Lindisfarne Gospels, from the Northumbrian Interlinear Gloss to the Gospels contained in the MS. collated with the Rushworth MS., Surtees Society, 1854.

Lingard, John. *The Antiquities of the Anglo-Saxon Church,* 2nd ed., Newcastle, 1810.

———. *The History and Antiquities of the Anglo-Saxon Church,* appearing in parts, 1820 and after; the whole, 1845, 2 vols.; 2nd ed., 1858.

———. *History of England,* 5th ed.

Lisle, William (tr.). *Saxon-English Remains of the Pentateuch, Josua, Judges, Ruth, etc., out of Sir Robert Cotton's MSS. of most reverend antiquity, now first englished and set out by W. L.*

——— and F. Junius. *A Saxon Treatise Concerning the Old and New Testament,* 1623.

Llewellyn, F. G. *The Bible and the Reformation,* 1938.

Llewellyn, Thomas. *An Historical Account of the British or Welsh Versions and Editions of the Bible,* London, 1768.

Lloyd, R. *Formularies of Faith under Henry VIII,* 1825.

Loftie, William J. *A Century of Bibles, or the Authorised Version from 1611 to 1711,* 1872.

Lopez, Didacus (Stunica). *Annotationes contra Erasmum in defensionem translationis Novi Testamenti,* 1520.

Lovett, Richard. *The English Bibles in the John Rylands Library, 1525–1640,* 1899.

———. *The Printed English Bible, 1525–1885,* London, 1894.

Lowe, E. A. (ed.). *Codices Latini antiquiores, a palaeographical guide to Latin MSS. prior to the ninth century,* 1934–36.

Lupton, J. H. "Versions (English)," in Hastings' *Dictionary of the Bible,* extra vol.

Lupton, Donald. *The History of the Moderne Protestant Divines, faithfully translated out of Latine* [of J. Verheiden and H. Holland], London, 1637.

Lyell, J. P. *Cardinal Ximenes . . . , with an account of the Complutensian Polyglot Bible,* 1917.

Macaulay, G. C. "The English Bible," in the *Quarterly Review,* October, 1911.

McComb, S. *The Making of the English Bible,* 1900, 1909.

McGhee, R. J. *Complete notes of the Douay Bible and the Rhemish New Testament,* 1837.

———. *The Nullity of the Government of Queen Victoria in Ireland; or, the Pope the virtual ruler of the land,* 1839.

———. *Truth and Error Contrasted; being an inquiry into the necessity of promoting the reformation of the Roman Catholics of Ireland,* 1830; enlarged ed., 1841.

——— and O'Sullivan. *Romanism as It Rules in Ireland,* 1840.

Madden, Frederic, and J. M. Forshall; *see* Forshall, J. M.

Maitland, Samuel R. *Notes on the Contributions of the Rev. George Townsend to the new edit. of Fox's "Martyrology,"* 1841–42.

———. *The Dark Ages,* 1844; 2nd ed. with notes, 1845; Catholic Standard Library ed., 1888; 1890.

———. *Essays on Subjects Connected with the Reformation in England,* 1849.
———. *Facts and Documents Illustrative of the History, Doctrine, and Rites of the Ancient Albigenses and Waldenses,* 1832.
———. *Six Letters on Fox's Acts and Monuments,* 1837.
Malan, Solomon C. *The Gospel of St. John Translated from the Eleven Oldest Versions.*
———. *A Plea for the Received Greek Text and for the Authorised Version of the New Testament,* 1869.
———. A *Vindication of the Authorised Version,* 1856.
Mandonnet, P. F. "Cajétan (Thomas de Vio)," in *Dictionnaire de théologie catholique,* 1905; reprinted separately, 1931.
Mangonet, Eugène. *Les travaux des Bénédictins de St. Maur, de St. Vannes et St. Hydulphe sur les anciens versions de la Bible,* 1888.
Margival, H. *Essai sur R. Simon et la critique biblique du XVIIe siècle,* 1900.
Marsh, G. P. *The Origin and History of the English Language,* London, 1862.
Marsh, Herbert. *A History of the Translations of the Scriptures from the Earliest Times to the Present Age,* London, 1812.
Marshall, Thomas, and F. Junius; *see* Junius.
Martin, David. *Histoire du Vieux et du Nouveau Testament,* Amsterdam, 1700, 2 vols.; tr. by Richard Gough: *The History of the Bible,* 1747.
Martin, Gregory. *A Discoverie of the Manifold Corruptions of the Holie Scriptures by the Heretikes of our Daies, Specially the English Sectaries,* Rheims, 1582.
———. *Of the Love of the Soule, with Questions to the Protestants* (posthumous), St. Omer, 1603.
———. *Roma Sancta, The Holy Citie of Rome* (posthumous), 1838; Preface by Martin dated April 9, 1581.
———. *A Treatyse of Christian Peregrination* (posthumous), Rheims, 1583.
———. *A Treatise of Schisme. Shewing that al Catholikes ought in any wise to abstaine altogether from heretical Conventicles,* Douai, 1578.
Martin, P. *La Vulgate Latine au XIIIe siècle d'après Roger Bacon,* Paris, 1888.
———. "Le texte parisien de la Vulgate Latine," in *Le Museon,* 1888–90.
Matthew, F. D. (ed.). *The English Works of Wyclif,* Early English Text Society, 1880.
Merriman, R. B. *Life and Letters of Thomas Cromwell,* Oxford, 1902, 2 vols.
Meyer, P., and L. Delisle. *L'Apocalypse en français au XIIIe siècle,* Paris, 1901.
Michel, F. X. *Bibliothèque Anglo-Saxone,* Paris, 1837.
——— (ed.). *Le Livre des Psaumes, ancienne traduction française, publiée d'après les MSS. de Cambridge et de Paris,* Paris, 1876.
———. *Libri Psalmorum versio antiqua Gallica, e codice manuscripto in Bibliotheca Bodleiana asservato,* Oxford, 1860.
Middendorff, H. *Studien über Richard Rolle von Hampole,* Magdeburg, 1888.
Middleton, T. F. *The Doctrine of the Greek Article Applied to the Criticism and Illustration of the New Testament,* London, 1808, 1828, 1833, 1841.
Migne, Jacques Paul (ed.). *Patrologia Latina,* 1844, 221 vols.
Miles, G. *The Bishops of Lindisfarne, Hexham, Chester-le-Street, and Durham,* 1898.

Millar, E. G. (ed.). *The Lindisfarne Gospels: three plates in colour and thirty-six in monochrome from the Cotton MS. Nero D.IV in the British Museum,* Oxford, 1923.

Miller, E. *The Causes of the Corruption of the Traditional Text,* 1896.

———. *A Guide to the Textual Criticism of the New Testament,* 1886.

———. *The Oxford Debate on the Textual Criticism of the New Testament,* 1897.

———. *The Traditional Text of the Holy Gospels Vindicated,* 1896.

Milligan, George. *The Autographs of the New Testament in the Light of Recent Discovery,* 1910.

———. *The English Bible: a Sketch of Its History,* 1895.

———. *The Expository Value of the Revised Version,* 1916.

———. *The New Testament and Its Transmission,* 1932.

———. *The New Testament Documents, Their Origin and Early History,* 1913.

———. "Versions," in Hastings' *Dictionary of the Bible,* vol. 4.

——— and James Moulton; *see* Moulton, James H.

Milne, J., and J. C. Skeat. *Scribes and Correctors of the Codex Sinaiticus,* 1938.

Milner, John. *A Brief Account of the Life of the Late R. R. Richard Challoner, D.D.,* prefixed to the fifth edition of Challoner's *Grounds of the Old Religion,* 1797; London, 1898.

———. *The End of Religious Controversy,* London, 1818, 3 vols.

———. *Letters to a Prebendary,* Winchester, 1800.

———. *Supplementary Memoirs of English Catholics,* 1820.

———. *A Vindication of Ward's "Errata," in reply to Grier,* published in the 1841 edition of Ward's *Errata.*

Mombert, J. *English Versions of the Bible,* 1883, 1890; new and enlarged ed., 1907.[3]

——— (ed.). *William Tyndale's Five Books of Moses Called the Pentateuch, a verbatim reprint of the edition of 1530,* 1884.

Moon, G. W. *The Revisers' English,* London, 1882.

Morris, R. (ed.). *The Story of Genesis and Exodus, an early English song,* London, 1865; revised ed., 1895.

Morris, W. *The Revised and Arianized Version of the English New Testament,* 1882.

Moulin, P. de (Molinoeus). *Translatio Novi Testamenti.*

Moulton, James H., and G. Milligan. *The Vocabulary of the Greek Testament, illustrated from the papyri and other non-literary sources,* 1914–29, 1930.

——— and W. F. Moulton, *A Grammar of New Testament Greek,* 1906–20, 2 vols.

Moulton, W. F. *The History of the English Bible,* 2nd ed., 1878; 3rd ed., 1884; 1887, 1911; abridged ed., 1937.[4]

Mozley, J. F. *John Foxe and His Book,* 1941.

———. *William Tyndale,* 1937.

——— and J. R. Coates. "The Life of Tyndale" in *Tyndale Commemoration Volume,* ed. by R. M. Wilson, 1939.

Muller, J. A. *Stephen Gardiner and the Tudor Reaction,* 1926.

[3] Though not free from prejudice, this work is of value for the copious specimens it gives of various translations.

[4] Dr. Moulton writes dispassionately and provides specimens of the earlier versions.

The Myroure of oure Ladye, edited from the original black-letter text, by John H. Blunt, Early English Text Society, London, 1873.

Nestle, E. *Introduction to the Textual Criticism of the Greek New Testament,* tr. by W. Edie, ed. by A. Menzies, 1901.

———. *Novum Testamentum Graece cum apparatu critico,* 1898; 14th ed., 1930.

Netter, Thos. (Waldensis). *Fasciculi zizaniorum,* ed. by W. W. Shirley, Rolls Series V, 1858.

Newcome, William. *An attempt towards revising our English Translation of the Greek Scriptures, and toward illustrating the sense by philological and explanatory notes,* Dublin, 1796, 2 vols.

———. *An Historical View of the English Biblical Translations. . . . To which is added, a list of various editions of the Bible, and parts thereof, in English from the year 1526 to 1776,* by A. C. Ducarel, Dublin, 1792.

———. *A List of Various Editions of the English Versions of the Bible,* 1818.

Newglass, E. *The English Bible in Retrospect,* 1943.

Newman, John H. *Grammar of Assent,* 1892.

———. "History of the Text of the Rheims and Douay Version of the Holy Scripture," in the *Rambler,* July, 1859; reprinted in *Tracts Theological and Ecclesiastical* (1891), pp. 405–45.

Newth, S. *Lectures on Bible Revision,* 1881.

Nichols, J. *Narratives of the days of the Reformation, chiefly from the MSS. of John Foxe,* London, 1859.

Nicholas of Lyra. *Postillae super Bibliam,* Cologne, 1478.

Norlie, Olaf M. *The Translated Bible, 1534–1934; commemorating the four hundredth anniversary of the translation by Martin Luther,* 1934.

O'Callaghan, Edmund B. *A List of Editions of the Holy Scriptures and Parts Thereof Printed in America Previous to 1860,* 1861.

Offor, George (ed.). *The New Testament . . . by that eminent scholar and martyr William Tyndale, reprinted verbatim with a Memoir of his life and writings, together with the proceedings and correspondence of Henry VIII, Sir Thomas More and Lord Cromwell,* 1836.

Original Letters Relative to the English Reformation, written during the reigns of King Henry VIII, King Edward II and Queen Mary, ed. by Hastings Robinson, Parker Society, 1846, 2 vols.

Pagninus, Santes (tr.). *Biblia Sacra Latina, Vetus et Novum Testamentum, nova translatio,* 1528.

Palgrave, Francis (Cohen). *A History of the Anglo-Saxons,* London, 1876.

———. *History of England (Anglo-Saxon Period),* London, 1831.

Pallavicino. *Istoria del Concilio de Trento,* Venice, 1802–03, 14 vols.; Rome, 1845–46, 3 vols.

Palmer, E. *The Greek Testament, with the readings adopted by the revisers of the Authorized Version,* Oxford, 1881.

Palmer, Thos. *De versione Bibliorum,* 1405.

Parker, Matthew. *De antiquitate Britannicae Ecclesiae et privilegiis Ecclesiae Cantuariensis cum archiepiscopis ejusdem 70,* Lambeth, 1572; Hanover, 1605; London, 1729.

———. *Correspondence,* Parker Society, 1853.

——— (ed.). *The Gospels of the Fower Evangelistes translated in the olde Saxons tyme out of Latin into the vulgare toung of the Saxons, and now published for testimonie of the same,* 1571.

———. *History of the Archbishops of Canterbury.*

Parsons, Robert. *A Treatise of Three Conversions of England from Paganisme to Christian Religion,* St. Omer, 1603–4, 2 vols.; London, 1688.

Pattison, Mark. "Erasmus," in the *Encyclopaedia Britannica,* 9th ed.

Pattison, T. H. *The History of the English Bible,* 1894.

Paues, A. C. *A Fourteenth Century English Biblical Version,* Cambridge University Press, 1902, 1904.

Payne, J. D. *The English Bible. An Historical Survey,* 1911.

Pearson, G. (ed.). *Writings and Translations* (1844) and *Remains* (1846) *of Bishop Coverdale,* Parker Society, Cambridge.

Pells, S. F. *The Church's Ancient Bible: the Septuagint, the Old Latin, the Latin Vulgate,* 1929.

Penniman, Josiah H. *A Book about the English Bible,* Oxford, 1919, 1931.

Petit, Jean. *Question du tyrannicide au commencement du XVe siècle,* ed. by A. Covelle, 1932.

Petre, E. A. Rumball-. *Rare Bibles,* 1938.

Phillimore, J. S. "Scripture Versions and Variants," in the *Dublin Review,* CLXX (1922), 20–46.

Pick, B. *Translations of the Bible,* American Bible Society, 1913.

Pits, John. *De illustribus Angliae scriptoribus,* Paris, 1619.

Pius VII. *Rescript addressed to the Vicars Apostolic of Great Britain,* 1820.

Pius XII. Encyclical *Divino afflante Spiritu,* September 30, 1943.

Plater, William E., and H. J. White. *A Grammar of the Vulgate,* Oxford, 1926.

Plomer, Henry R. "Antony Marler and the Great Bible," in *The Library,* Series III, I, pp. 200 ff.

Plummer, Charles. *The Life and Times of Alfred the Great,* Oxford, 1902.

Plumptre, Edward H. "Version, Authorized," in Smith's *Dictionary of the Bible,* vol. 3.

Politi, Lancelot; *see* Ambrosius Catharinus.

Pollard, Alfred W. *Records of the English Bible. The documents relating to the translation and publication of the Bible in English, 1525–1611,* Oxford University Press, 1911.

——— (ed.). *Beginning of the New Testament Translated by William Tyndale, 1525; facsimiles of the unique fragment of the uncompleted Cologne edition,* Introduction by Alfred Pollard, Oxford, 1926.

———. *Last Words on the History of the Title Page,* London, 1891.

Pope, Hugh. *The Catholic Student's "Aids" to the Study of the Bible,* vol. 1, revised ed., 1926.

———. "The Lollard Bible," in the *Dublin Review,* CLXVIII (1921), 60–72.

———. "The Origin of the Douay Bible," in the *Dublin Review,* CXLVII (1910), 97–118.

———. "The Rheims Version of the New Testament," in the *Dublin Review,* CLII (1913), 276–300; and in *The Library,* March to June, 1940; and in the *Downside Review,* October, 1944.

———. "The Rheims Version of the New Testament: the hostile reception accorded to it," in the *Clergy Review*, XVII (1939), 311–25.

———. "Some Omissions in the Rheims-Douay Version," in the *Clergy Review*, XIX (1940), 112–21.

———. "An Unhappy Biblical Scholar," in *The Irish Ecclesiastical Record*, LVI (1940), 321–42.

———. "An Unusual Edition of the Rheims New Testament," in *The Irish Ecclesiastical Record*, LV (1940), 468–84.

Powell, M. J. *The Pauline Epistles Contained in MS. Parker 32, Corpus Christi College Cambridge*, Early English Text Society, Oxford, 1916.

Powicke, F. M. *Aelred of Rivaulx and His Biographer, Walter Daniel*, 1922.

Price, Ira M. *The Ancestry of Our English Bible*, 9th ed., New York, 1934; 2nd revised ed. by William A. Irwin and Allen P. Wikgren, New York, 1949.

Pseudo-Catholicus. *Notes on the Preface to the Rhemish Testament, Dublin*, 1813, 1817.

Purdue, W., and N. H. J. Westlake; *see* Westlake.

Purvey, John. *The Dore of Holy Scripture* (attributed to Wycliffe), 1536.

Quentin, Henri. *Essai du critique textuelle*, 1926.

———. *Mémoire sur l'établissement du texte de la Vulgate*, 1922 (vol. 6 of *Collectanea biblica Latina*).

———. *La Vulgate à travers les siècles et la revision actuelle*, 1926.

Quétif, Jacques, and Echard. *Scriptores Ordinis Praedicatorum*, Paris, 1719.

Queen Mary's Psalter; miniatures and drawings by an English artist of the fourteenth century, British Museum, Oxford, 1912.

Radley, J. A. *A Defence of the Proceedings of the British and Foreign Bible Society in reference to the so-called Roman Catholic Versions*, 1842.

Raine, James. *St. Cuthbert, with an account of the state in which his remains were found upon the opening of his tomb in Durham Cathedral in the year 1827*, Durham, 1828.

Rashdall, Hastings. *The Universities of Europe in the Middle Ages*, 1895; ed. by Powicke and Emden, Oxford, 1936, 3 vols.

Reiske, J. R. *De versionibus Germanicis ante Lutherum*, 1697.

"The Revision of the New Testament," in the *Dublin Review*, Third Series, VI (1881), 127–44.

Reynolds, William. *A Refutation of sundry Reprehensions, Cavils, and false Sleightes by which M. Whitaker laboureth to deface the late English translation and Catholick Annotations of the New Testament*, Paris, 1583.

Richards, George. *A Concise Dictionary to the Vulgate New Testament*, 1934.

Roberts, Alexander. *Companion to the Revised Version of the English New Testament*, London, 1881.

Robinson, Hastings (ed.). *Original Letters Relative to the English Reformation, written during the reigns of King Henry VIII, King Edward II and Queen Mary*, Parker Society, 1846, 2 vols.

Robinson, Henry Wheeler (ed.). *The Bible in Its Ancient and English Versions*, Oxford, 1940.

Robinson, Joseph Armitage. *The Times of St. Dunstan*, Oxford, 1923.

Roche, James. "The Complutensian Bible," in *Critical and Miscellaneous Essays*, vol. 1, 1850–51.

Roensch, H. *Itala und Vulgata*, Marburg, 1869.

Rogers, C. *Collation of the Old Testament from the Translations of J. Rogers, the Bishops', the Genevan and the Authorised Version; the New Testament from Wyclif, Rogers, the Rhemes, 1582, the Genevan, the Authorised and G. Wakefield*, 1795; Dundee, 1847.

Rolle, Richard. *English Prose Treatises*, ed. by G. G. Parry, Early English Text Society, 1866.

———. *The Pricke of Conscience, written in English for such as do not understand Latin*, ed. by R. Morris, 1863.

———. *The Psalter or Psalms of David, and Certain Canticles, with a Translation and Exposition in English*, ed. by H. R. Bramley, Oxford, 1884.

Rossi, Giovanni Battista de. *La Bibbia offerta da Ceolfrido Abbate al sepolcro di S. Pietro*, 1888.

Routh, Martin J. *Reliquiae sacrae*, Oxford, 1814–18, 4 vols.; 1846–48, 5 vols.

Rumball-Petre, E. A. *Rare Bibles*, 1938.

Russell, C. "The Bible and the Reformation," in the *Dublin Review*, III (1837), 428–52.

Ryan, E. *An Analysis of Ward's "Errata of the English Bible,"* Dublin, 1808.

Rylands, G. (ed.). *The Psalms of David, Coverdale's Version, edited with Introduction*, London, 1926.

Rymer, Thomas, and R. Sanderson. *Foedera*, 1704–35, 20 vols.; 1737–45, 10 vols.; 1816–30 (incomplete).

Sabatier, P. *Bibliorum sacrorum Latinae versiones antiquae*, Rheims, 1743–49, 3 vols.

Salmon, P. *La revision de la Vulgate, état des travaux*, 1937.

Sampson, G. W. *The English Revisers' Greek Text, shown to be unauthorised*, Cambridge, U.S.A., 1882.

Sanday, William, John Wordsworth, and H. J. White; *see* White, H. J.

Sanders, Nicholas. *De origine et progressu schismatis Anglicani*, Cologne, 1585; Rome, 1586, 1628; English tr. by David Lewis, 1877.

Schlosser, F. *Leben des Theodore Beza und des Peter Martyr Vermili*, Heidelberg, 1809.

Scott. *Ulfilas, Apostle of the Goths*, 1885.

Scrivener, F. H. A. *The Authorized Edition of the English Bible (1611); its subsequent reprints and modern representatives*, Cambridge, 1884; reprinted from the Introduction to *The Cambridge Paragraph Bible, of the Authorised English Version*, 1870–73, 3 vols.

——— (ed.). *Codex Augiensis, an exact transcription of a Graeco-Latin MS. of St. Paul's Epistles*, 1859.

——— (ed.). *Codex S. Ceadae Latinus . . . cum codice versionis Vulgatae Amiatino, contulit, prolegomena conscripsit F. A. A. Scrivener*, 1887.

———. *Contributions to the Criticism of the Greek Testament*, 1859.

———. *A Plain Introduction to the Criticism of the New Testament*, 1861, 1874, 1884; 4th ed. by E. Miller, 1894, 2 vols.

——— (ed.). *The Greek New Testament*, 1860, 1872, 1877, 1887, 1906.

——— (ed.). *The Parallel New Testament, Greek and English, being the Au-*

thorised Version, arranged in parallel columns with the Revised Version of 1881 and with the original Greek, Oxford, 1882.
——— (ed.). *The New Testament in the Original Greek, according to the text followed in the Authorized Version, together with the variations adopted in the Revised Version*, Cambridge, 1881, 1883, 1884, 1886, 1890, 1908.
———. *Six Lectures on the Text of the New Testament*, 1875.
———. *A Supplement to the Authorised English Version of the New Testament*, 1845.
Searle, W. S. *Anglo-Saxon Bishops, Kings and Nobles*, Cambridge, 1899.
Seebohm, Frederic. *Oxford Reformers: John Colet, Erasmus, and Thomas More*, 3rd ed., **1911**: 1913, 1914.
Selden, John. *Table-Talk*, London, 1689; ed. by Arber, **1868**.
Selwyn, W. *Notes on the Proposed Amendment of the Authorized Version*, 1856.
Shea, John D. G. *A Bibliographical Account of Catholic Bibles, Testaments . . . translated from the Latin Vulgate and printed in the United States*, 1859.
Sheahan, J. F. *The English in English Bibles*, Poughkeepsie, N.Y., no date.
Sheppard, L. A. "The Printers of the Coverdale Bible, 1535," in *The Library*, 1935, pp. 280–89.
Shirley, Walter W. *Catalogue of the Extant Latin Works of John Wyclif*, revised by J. Loserth, 1925.
——— (ed.). *Fasciculi zizaniorum* (by Thos. Netter), 1858.
Simeon of Durham. *Epistola ad Hugonem Decanum Eboracensem de archiepiscopis Eboraci*.
Simon, Richard. *Bibliothèque critique*, 1708–10.[5]
———. *A Critical History of the Old Testament*, tr. by "a Person of Quality" (R. Hampden), 1682.
———. *A Critical History of the Text of the New Testament*, tr. by R. Taylor, 1689.
———. *Critical Enquiries into the Various Editions of the Bible*, tr. by N. S., 1684.
———. *The Critical History of the Versions of the New Testament, together with a refutation of such passages as seem contrary to the doctrine and practise of the Church of England*, 1692.
———. *Histoire critique des principaux commentateurs du Nouveau Testament*, 1693.
———. *Histoire critique du Vieux Testament*, 1685.
———. *Lettre à un amy où l'on rend compte d'un livre, qui a pour titre, Histoire critique du Vieux Testament*, 1679.
———. *Nouvelles observations sur le texte et les versions du Nouveau Testament*, 1695.
Sisam, Kenneth. "Aelfric's Catholic Homilies," in *Review of English Studies*, VII (1931), 7–22; VIII, 51–68.
Sitterly, C. F., and S. C. Ayers. *The History of the English Bible Studied by the Library Method*, 1898.
Sixtus of Siena, *Bibliotheca sancta*, Venice, 1566, **1575**, 1591, 1626, 1742.

[5] Simon's views met with such opposition from both Catholics and Protestants that he published the *Bibliothèque critique* to defend the various positions he had taken up. See A. Bernous, *Richard Simon et son Histoire critique du Vieux Testament: La critique biblique au siècle de Louis XIV*, 1869.

Skeat, J. C., and J. Milne. *Scribes and Correctors of the Codex Sinaiticus,* 1938.

Skeat, Walter W. (ed.). *The Gospel of St. Mark in Gothic according to the Translation Made by Wulfila in the Fourth Century,* 1882.

——— (ed.). *The Holy Gospels in Anglo-Saxon, Northumbrian and Old Mercian Versions,* Cambridge, 1871–87.

——— (ed.). *The New Testament in English according to the Version of John Wycliffe, about A.D. 1380, and revised by John Purvey, about A.D. 1388,* with Introduction, 1879.

Slater, J. R. *The Sources of Tyndale's Version of the Pentateuch,* University of Chicago Press, 1906.

Smalley, Beryl. "Gilbertus Porretanus and the Problem of the Glossa Ordinaria," in *Recherches de théologie ancienne et médiévale,* 1936, pp. 51–60.

———. *The Study of the Bible in the Middle Ages,* 1941.

Smith, G. B. *William Tyndale and His Translation of the English Bible,* 1896.

Smith, G. Vance. *The Bible and Popular Theology,* 2nd ed., 1871.

———. *Texts and Margins of the Revised New Testament Affecting Theological Doctrine,* 1881.

Smith, H. P. "The Value of the Vulgate Old Testament for Textual Criticism," in the *Presbyterian Review,* April, 1891.

Smith, Thos. *Memoirs of the Translators of the Authorised Version,* 1827.

Smith, William. *Dictionary of the Bible,* London, 1863, 1893.

Smith, W. E. *A Study of the Great "SHE" Bible,* 1890.

Soames, H. *The Anglo-Saxon Church: its history, revenues, and general character,* London, 1835.

Soden, H. von. *Das lateinischen Neue Testament in Afrika zur Zeit Cyprians,* 1909.

Souter, A. (ed.). *Novum Testamentum Graece. Textui a retractoribus Anglis adhibito brevem adnotationem criticam subjecit,* Oxford, 1910.

———. *The Text and Canon of the New Testament,* 1912; 3rd impression, 1930.

Sparkes, H. F. D. "On the Latin Versions," in *The Bible in Its Ancient and English Versions,* Oxford, 1940.

Spelman, John. *Psalterium Davidis Latino-Saxonicum vetus,* London, 1640.

Standish, John. *A Discourse wherein is debated, whether it be expedient that the Scriptures should be in English for al men to read that will,* London, 1554.

Stapulensis; *see* Faber.

Stenton, F. M. *Anglo-Saxon England* (vol. 2 of *Oxford History of England*), Oxford, 1943.

Stevens, H. *The Bibles in the Caxton Exhibition of 1877,* 1878.

Stevenson, J. *The Truth about John Wyclif,* London, 1885.

——— (ed.). *An Anglo-Saxon and Early English Psalter, now first printed from MSS. in the British Museum,* Surtees Society, 1843–47, 2 vols.

——— and G. Waring (eds.). *The Lindisfarne and Rushworth Gospels,* Surtees Society, No. 48, 1854–65, 4 vols.

Stoughton, J. *Our English Bible: its translations and translators,* London, 1878.

Strype, John. *Annals of the Reformation in England,* 1709, 2nd ed., 1725–31, 4 vols.; 3rd enlarged ed., 1735, 4 vols.

———. *Ecclesiastical Memorials,* 1721, 3 vols.; 1816.

———. *The Life and Acts of John Whitgift, Archbishop of Canterbury,* 1718, 2 vols.; Parker Society, Oxford, 3 vols.

———. *The Life and Acts of Matthew Parker, Archbishop of Canterbury,* London, 1711, 2 vols.; Oxford, 1821, 3 vols.

———. *Memorials of Archbishop Cranmer, Archbishop of Canterbury,* 1694, 2 vols.; Oxford, 1848–54, 3 vols.; London, 1853, 2 vols.

Stuart, C. E. *The Bible and the Versions of the Bible, or, the Vulgate compared with the original Scriptures,* London, 1856.

——— and J. D. Hales; *see* Hales.

Stuart, John. *The Book of Deer,* 1869.

Studer, P. *The Study of Anglo-Norman,* Oxford, 1920.

Sturge, Charles. *Cuthbert Tunstall, Churchman, Scholar, Statesman, Administrator,* 1938.

Sweet, Henry. *Alfred's Anglo-Saxon Version of Gregory's "Pastoral Care," with an English Translation, Latin Text; Notes and Introduction,* London, 1871.

———. *The Oldest English Texts,* Early English Tract Society, No. 83, 1885.

Swift, Dean. *A Proposal for correcting, improving and ascertaining the English Tongue; a Letter to Robert, Earl of Oxford, and Mortimer, Lord High Treasurer of Great Britain,* ed. by John Nichols, 1712.

Taylor, J. *What is the Power of the Greek Article, and how it may be expressed in the English version of the New Testament?* 1842.

Taillepied, N. *Vie de Théodore de Bèze,* 1577.

Thompson, A. Hamilton. *Bede: His Life, Times and Writings,* Oxford, 1935.

Thompson, E. Maunde. *The Wycliffe Exhibition in the British Museum.*

Thomson, W. B. *The History of the English Bible and How It Has Come Down to Us,* 1900.

Thorpe, Benjamin. *Analecta Anglo-Saxonica,* 1834.

——— (ed.). *Caedmon's Metrical Paraphrase of Parts of the Holy Scriptures in Anglo-Saxon, with an English Translation, Notes, and a Verbal Index,* London, 1832.

——— (ed.). *Da Halgan Godspel on Englisc. The Anglo-Saxon Version of the Holy Gospels,* London, 1842.

——— (tr.). *The Homilies of the Anglo Saxon Church, . . . with an English Version,* Aelfric Society, London, 1843–46.

——— (ed.). *Libri Psalmorum versio antiqua Latina cum paraphrasi Anglo-Saxonica,* Oxford, 1835.

Thwaites, Edward (ed.). *Heptateuchus, Liber Job et Evangelium Nicodemi Anglo-Saxonice,* Oxford, 1698.

Tischendorf, C. *An Account of the Printed Text of the New Testament,* 1854.

Todd, H. J. *An Authentic Account of Our Authorised Translation of the Holy Bible,* 1834, 1842.

———. *Memoirs of the Life and Writings of the Rt. Rev. Brian Walton,* 1821, 2 vols.

———. *Vindication of our Authorised Translation and Translators of the Bible,* 1819.

Todd, James H. *The Books of the Vaudois,* London, 1865.

——— (ed.). *The Last Age of the Church, by John Wycliffe,* Dublin, 1840.

Trappes-Lomax, M. *Bishop Challoner,* 1936.

Tregelles, Samuel P. *An Account of the Printed Text of the Greek Testament,* 1854.

———. *Historical Account of the English Versions of the Scriptures* (Introduction to the *English Hexapla,* ed. by S. Bagster), 1841, 1845, 1846.

Trench, Richard C. *On the Authorized Version of the New Testament, in connection with some recent proposals for its revision,* 1858, 1859.

Trevelyan, George M. *England in the Age of Wycliffe,* 1899, 1904, 1909.

Turner, C. H. *Early Printed Editions of the Greek New Testament,* 1904; Oxford, 1924.

———. "Historical Introduction to the Textual Criticism of the New Testament," in the *Journal of Theological Studies,* X (1908–09), 13–28, 161–82, 354–74.

———. *The Oldest Manuscripts of the Vulgate Gospels,* Oxford, 1931.

———. *The Study of the New Testament, 1883 and 1920,* Oxford, 1920, 1924, 1926 (with additional notes).

Turton, Thomas. *The Text of the English Bible . . . Considered,* 2nd ed., 1833.

Ungarelli, L. M. *Praelectiones de Novo Testamento et historia Vulgatae Bibliorum editionis a Concilio Tridentino,* Rome, 1847.

Ussher, James (Archbishop of Armagh). *Annales Veteris et Novi Testamenti,* 1650–54.

———. *Historia dogmatica controversiae inter orthodoxos et pontificios de Scripturis et sacris vernaculis,* ed. by Wharton (who added: *Auctarium historiae dogmaticae Jacobi Usserii*), 1689; Dublin, 1863.

Valentine-Richards, A. V. *History of the New Testament Textual Criticism.*

Variorum Bible, ed. by Cheyne, Driver, and others, 1876.

Vaughan, C. J. *Authorised or Revised?* 1882.

Vaughan, Robert. *The Life and Opinions of Wycliffe, illustrated principally from his unpublished Manuscripts,* 1828, 1831, 2 vols.

Vercellone, C. *Variae lectiones Vulgatae Latinae Bibliorum editionis,* Rome, 1860–64, 2 vols.

Verres, J. *Luther, an Historical Portrait,* London, 1884.

Vigouroux, *Dictionnaire de la Bible.*

Vinogradoff, Paul. *English Society in the Eleventh Century,* Oxford, 1908.

Vising, Johan. *Anglo-Norman Language and Literature,* Oxford, 1923.

Vogel, P. H. "Englische Bibelübersetzungen," in *Internationale kirchliche Zeitschrift,* Berne, 1949, pp. 227–42.

Vogels, H. J. *Handbuch des Neutestamentlichen Textkritik,* 1923.

———. *Vulgatastudien: Die Evangelien der Vulgata,* 1928.

Walden, T. *The Great Meaning of the Word "Metanoia," lost in the old version, recovered in the new,* 1881.

———. *Our English Bible and Its Ancestors,* 1871.

Wall, J. C. *Alfred the Great, His Abbeys of Hyde, Athelney and Shaftesbury,* 1900.

Wallis, Norbert Hardy (ed.). *The New Testament Translated by William Tyndale, 1534. A reprint of the edition of 1534 with the translator's prefaces and notes and the variants of the edition of 1525,* Cambridge University Press, 1938.

Walther, W. *Die deutsche Bibelübersetzung im Mittelalter,* Brunswick, 1889–92.

Walton, Brian. *Biblia sacra polyglotta,* with *Prolegomena,* London, 1657, 6 vols.

Wanley, Humphrey. *Librorum veterum septentrionalium qui in Angliae bibliothecis extant catalogus historico-criticus,* 1705 (vol. 2 of G. Hickes's *Linguarum veterum septentrionalium thesaurus grammatico-criticus et archaeologicus*).

Ward, B. *The Dawn of the Catholic Revival,* London, 1909.

———. *The Eve of Catholic Emancipation,* 1911–12, 3 vols.

Ward, Thomas. *Errata of the Protestant Bible,* 1688; 1841, 1899.

Ward, Wilfrid. *Life of Cardinal Newman,* 1912.

Waring, G., and J. Bosworth; *see* Bosworth.

——— and J. Stevenson (eds.). *The Lindisfarne and Rushworth Gospels,* Surtees Society, No. 48, 1854–65, 4 vols.

Warner, George F. *Illuminated MSS. in the British Museum: miniatures, borders and initials in gold and colours,* Series I–IV, London, 1903.

——— and Julius P. Gilson. *Catalogue of the Western Manuscripts in the Old Royal and King's Collections in the British Museum,* Oxford, 1921, 4 vols. fol.

Waterland, D. *Works,* Oxford, 1823, 1831, 6 vols.

Watson, R. S. *Caedmon, the First English Poet,* 1875.

Weigle, Luther A. *The English New Testament from Tyndale to the Revised Standard Version,* Nashville, Tenn., 1949; British ed., 1950.

——— (ed.). *An Introduction to the Revised Standard Version of the New Testament,* New York, 1946.

Wells, John E. *A Manual of the Writings in Middle English, 1050–1400,* London, 1915, 1916.

Wendell, Prime. *Fifteenth Century Bibles,* 1888.

Westcott, Brooke F. *The Bible in the Church,* 1862, 1864, 1879.

———. *General Survey of the History of the Canon of the New Testament during the First Four Centuries,* 1855, 1866, 1875, 1881, 1896.

———. *General View of the History of the English Bible,* 1868, 1872; 3rd ed. by W. Aldis Wright, London, 1905; 1916.

———. *Some Lessons of the Revised Version of the New Testament,* London, 1897.

———. "The Vulgate," in Smith's *Dictionary of the Bible,* vol. 3.

——— and F. J. Hort (eds.). *The New Testament in the Original Greek,* with the Introduction (vol. 2) by Hort, 1881.

Westlake, N. H. J., and W. Purdue (eds.). *Illustrations of Old Testament History in Queen Mary's Psalter by an Artist of the Fourteenth Century,* 1865.

The West-Saxon Psalms: the first fifty from the so-called Paris Psalter, Boston, 1907.

Westwood, J. O. *Palaeographia sacra pictoria: being a series of illustrations of the ancient versions of the Bible, copied from illuminated manuscripts executed between the fourth and sixteenth centuries,* London, 1843–45.

Wharton, Henry. *Anglia sacra: sive collectio historiarum de archiepiscopis et episcopis Angliae, a prima fidei Christianae susceptione ad annum 1540,* London, 1691, 2 vols.

———. *Auctarium historiae dogmaticae Jacobi Usserii,* in J. Ussher, *Historia dogmatica controversiae inter orthodoxos et pontificios de scripturis et sacris vernaculis,* 1689.

Whitaker, William. *Ad decem rationes Edmundi Campiani . . . Christiana responsio,* London, 1581.

———. *Adversus Tho. Stapletoni Anglopapistae . . . defensionem ecclesiasticae authoritatis . . . duplicatio pro authoritate atque αὐτοπιστίᾳ S. Scripturae,* Cambridge, 1594.

———. *Disputatio de sacra Scriptura contra hujus temporis papistas, imprimis Robertum Bellarminum Iesuitam,* 1588, 1590, 1610.

———. *Praelectiones in quibus tractatur controversia de ecclesia contra pontificios, imprimis Robertum Bellarminum Iesuitam,* Cambridge, 1599.

———. *Works,* Parker Society, 1849.

———. *Dispute with Campion: De auctoritate scripturae,* 1594.

White, C. L. *Aelfric: A New Study of His Life and Writings,* 1898.

White, Henry Julian. "The Codex Amiatinus and Its Birthplace," in *Studia biblica (et ecclesiastica),* (Oxford, 1885–91, 3 vols.), II, 273–308.

———. *The Four Gospels from the Munich MS. Lat. 6224, with a fragment of St. John,* Oxford, 1888.

——— and William Plater. *A Grammar of the Vulgate,* Oxford, 1926.

——— and John Wordsworth (eds.). *Novum Testamentum Domini Nostri Jesu Christi Latine secundum editionem Sancti Hieronymi; ad codicum manuscriptorum fidem recensuit Ioannes Wordsworth, in operis societatem assumpto H. I. White,* Oxford, 1889–1941.

——— and John Wordsworth (eds.). *Novum Testamentum Latine secundum editionem Sancti Hieronymi; recensuerunt Wordsworth et White. Editio minor curante White,* Oxford, 1911, 1912.

——— and John Wordsworth. *On the Question of What Greek Manuscripts or Class of Greek Manuscripts St. Jerome Used in Revising the Latin Gospels,* 1893.

———, John Wordsworth, and W. Sanday (eds.). *Portions of the Gospels according to St. Matthew and St. Mark, from the Bobbio MS. (k),* 1886.

White, Robert Meadows (ed.). *The Ormulum, with Notes and Glossary,* Oxford, 1852; re-edited by Robert Holt, Oxford, 1878, 2 vols.

Whitehead, D. In Whittingham, *A Brieff Discours off the Troubles begonne at Franckford in Germany, anno Domini 1554,* 1575.

Whitley, N. T. *The English Bible under Tudor Sovereigns,* London, 1937.

———. *Roman Catholic and Protestant Bibles* (no date).

Whitley, W. T. "Thomas Matthew of Colchester and Matthew's Bible of 1537," in *The Essex Review,* January, 1934.

Whitney, J. P. "Tyndale" in the *Cambridge History of English Literature,* pp. 58 ff.; ed. of 1907–11, III, 44 ff.

Whitney, S. W. *The Revisers' Greek Testament. A critical examination of certain readings,* 1892, 2 vols.

Whittaker, John W. *An Historical and Critical Enquiry into the Interpretation of the Hebrew Scriptures,* Cambridge, 1819.

Whittingham, William. *A Brieff Discours off the Troubles begonne at Franckford in Germany, anno Domini 1554,* 1575, **1846.**

Wikgren, Allen P.; *see* Ira M. Price.

Wilkins, David. *Concilia Magnae Britanniae et Hiberniae,* 1731.

Wilkins, Henry John. *Was John Wycliffe a Negligent Pluralist? Also John de Trevisa; His Life and Work*, 1915.

William of Malmesbury. (Various works tr. by John Sharp, 1854.)

———. *Gesta pontificum Anglorum*, ed. by N. Hamilton, London, 1870.

———. *Gesta regum Anglorum*, ed. by William Stubbe, London, 1887–89.

———. *Historia novella*, ed. of 1815.

William of Shoreham. *Poems*, ed. by M. Konrath, London, 1902.

———. *Religious Poems*, ed. by Thomas Wright, Percy Society, 1849.

Willoughby, Harold R. *The Coverdale Psalter and the Quatrocentenary of the Printed English Bible*, Chicago, 1935.

———. *The First Authorized English Bible, and the Cranmer Preface*, Chicago, 1942.

Wilmart, A. "Les Évangiles Gothiques," in *Revue Biblique*, January, 1927.

Wilson, Lea. *Catalogue of Bibles, Testaments, Psalms, and Other Books of the Holy Scripture in English in the Collection of L.W., Esq.*, London, 1845, 4to.

Winn, H. E. (ed.). *Select English Writings of John Wycliffe*, Preface by H. B. Workman, Oxford, 1929.

Wise, Francis (ed.). *Annales rerum gestarum Aelfredi Magni, auctore Asserio Menevensi* (Sherborne), Oxford, 1722.

Wiseman, Nicholas. "Catholic Versions of Scripture," in the *Dublin Review*, II (1837), 475–92, and in *Essays on Various Subjects*, vol. 1.

———. "Two Letters . . . on I John 5:7," in *Essays on Various Subjects*, vol. 1.

Wither, George. *A View of the Marginal Notes of the Popish Testament translated into English by the English Fugitive Papists resiant at Rhemes*, London, 1588.

à Wood, Antony. *Athenae Oxonienses*, London, 1691–92, 2 vols.

———. *Fasti Oxonienses*, 1691.

———. *History and Antiquities of the University of Oxford*, 1674, 2 vols.; ed. by Gutch, 1791–96, 2 vols.

Wordsworth, Christopher. *John Wiclif: His Doctrine and Work*, 1884.

Wordsworth, John, and H. J. White; *see* White, H. J.

Workman, H. B. *John Wyclif, a Study of the English Mediaeval Church*, Oxford, 1926, 1936, 2 vols.

Wormald, F. (ed.). *The Book of Psalms from the Version of Miles Coverdale, as published in the "Great Bible" of 1539, with an Introduction*, 1930.

Worthington, Thomas. *An Anker of Christian Doctrine*, Douay, 1622.[6]

Wrangham, Francis. *Briani Waltoni in biblia polyglotta prolegomena specialia*, Cambridge, 1827–28, 2 vols.

Wright, John. *Early Bibles of America*, 1893.

Wright, Thomas. *Biographia Britannica literaria*, or *Biography of Literary Characters of Great Britain and Ireland*, 1842–46, 2 vols.

———. *The Celt, the Roman, and the Saxon*, 1852; 4th ed., 1885.

——— (ed.). *The Religious Poems of William of Shoreham*, Percy Society, 1849.

Wright, William Aldis. *Hexaplar Psalter. The Book of Psalms in Six English Versions*, 1911.

——— and S. R. Driver. *On the Marginal Notes of the Revised Version*, 1912.

[6] Worthington is the author of the annotations in the Douay Version of the Old Testament, 1609–10.

Wycliffe, John (tr.). *The Books of Job, Psalms, Proverbs, Ecclesiastes, and the Song of Solomon,* formerly ed. by Josiah Forshall and Frederic Madden; reprinted, Oxford, 1881.

———. *The Last Age of the Church,* ed. by Todd, Dublin, 1840.

——— (tr.). *The New Testament in English, translated by John Wycliffe circa Mccclxxx. Now first printed from a contemporary manuscript formerly in the Monastery of Sion, Middlesex, late in the collection of Lea Wilson, F.S.A.,* London, 1858.

———(tr). *New Testament,* ed. by Lea Wilson, 1848; *see also* H. Baber, S. Bagster, J. Bosworth, J. Forshall, and W. Skeat.

——— (tr.). *The New Testament of Our Lord and Saviour Jesus Christ, Translated out of the Latin Vulgate by John Wiclif, S.T.P.,* London, 1731.[7]

———. *Select English Writings,* ed. by H. E. Winn, 1929; *see also* F. D. Matthew and E. M. Thompson.

Ziegler, L. *Die lateinischen Bibelübersetzungen vor Hieronymus und die Itala des Augustinus,* Munich, 1879.

Zimmermann, Benedict. *Carmel in England,* 1899.

[7] To this edition was prefixed John Lewis' *Complete History of the Several Translations of the Holy Bible and New Testament, etc., into English,* which was afterwards published separately.

SUPPLEMENT

American Editions of the Catholic Bible

We cannot expect that Fathers Hugh Pope or Sebastian Bullough had an opportunity to examine many American editions of the Bible or New Testament, for earlier American editions are by no means common in England; in fact, they are not too common even in America. Realizing, then, that the list of Catholic versions of the Bible provided by the authors was deficient in American editions, the American editor of this work has undertaken the compilation of a list of American editions of the Catholic Bible and New Testament. He is aware that even this list is not complete, especially for the last half of the nineteenth century; for, since records are scanty and even contemporary publishers cannot give an accurate account of Bibles and Testaments published as recently as twenty years ago, no complete list could be drawn up until every Bible in every library and home in the land were examined.

The difficulty is increased by the fact that during the last half of the nineteenth century many editions were published without date and were frequently re-issued with slight variations in the preliminary matter and illustrations; in fact, such variations are found in the same dated edition. The practice, too, of publishing the same text with different imprints is most confusing. The most extreme example of this practice is seen in the Bible of 1912 printed in Belgium, which not only was printed with various imprints, but also was issued without any imprint at all, so that the individual booksellers could stamp in their own imprints.

For the editions published before 1860 the compiler of this list has been dependent almost entirely on O'Callaghan, *A List of Editions of the Holy Scriptures and Parts Thereof, Printed in America Previous to 1860*

(1861), supplemented by Parsons, *Early Catholic Americana: A List of Books and Other Works by Catholic Authors in the United States: 1729–1830* (1939). The editions between 1860 and 1900 listed here were examined by the compiler himself.[1] The publishers themselves were able to supply some information concerning more recent editions; yet even here the records are incomplete.

This is, as far as we know, the first attempt to compile a list of Catholic editions of the Bible since O'Callaghan published his monumental work nearly a century ago. And although this list is not complete, it shows the efforts made by the bishops and Catholic publishers of this country to present the word of God to the people. The number of editions is all the more remarkable when we consider that until the middle of the nineteenth century the number of English-speaking Catholics in this country was not great, and that during this time the Middle West was frontier country and the Far West was hardly settled at all.

It is our hope that this initial effort will be an incentive to further scholarly study on this interesting subject. We would appreciate, too, information concerning editions not here listed.

The Editor

1790 *Holy Bible. . . . With Annotations for elucidating the principal difficulties of Holy Writ,* Philadelphia: Carey, Stewart, and Co., 4to.[2]

1805 *Holy Bible. . . . First American, from the Fifth Dublin Edition,* Philadelphia: Mathew Carey, 4to.[3]

[1] The compiler is grateful for the assistance of Very Rev. David Kinish, O.S.B., a monk of St. Benedict's Abbey, Atchison, Kansas.

[2] This first Catholic Bible published in the United States first began to appear in weekly numbers in December, 1789, published by Mathew Carey. "In the beginning of 1790, the name of the firm was changed to Carey, Stewart, and Co. The issue in numbers was abandoned about that time, after (as we are disposed to think) between 80 and 90 pages had been printed, when it was determined to publish the work in two volumes" (O'Callaghan, *A List of Editions of the Holy Scriptures and Parts Thereof, Printed in America Previous to 1860,* pp. xxvi f.). Parsons is not exactly correct when he says that this is the "first quarto Bible published in the United States" (*Early Catholic Americana: A List of Books and Other Works by Catholic Authors in the United States: 1729–1830,* p. 23); for in 1663 and again in 1685 Samuel Green printed in quarto John Eliot's Indian translation of the Bible, and in 1743, 1763, and 1776 Christopher Saur published at Germantown a quarto Bible in German. Carey's quarto edition of 1790 is, however, the first quarto Bible in English published in the United States.

[3] O'Callaghan describes two Carey editions of the Bible published this year. Actually

1805 *New Testament. . . . First American, from the fifth Dublin Edition,* Philadelphia: Mathew Carey, 4to.

1811 *New Testament,* reprint of the 1805 edition, Philadelphia: Carey, 4to.

1816 *New Testament,* reprint of the 1805 edition, Philadelphia: Carey, 4to.

1817 *New Testament,* Approbation by Archbishop Neale (February 20, 1817), Georgetown, D.C.: W. Duffy, 12mo.

1824 *Holy Bible. . . . First Stereotype, from the Fifth Dublin Edition,* without the Approbation of Bishop Conwell, Philadelphia: Eugene Cummiskey, 8vo.[4]

1824 *Holy Bible,* same as the preceding, with the Approbation of Bishop Conwell, Philadelphia: Eugene Cummiskey, 8vo.

1824 *New Testament. . . . From the Fifth Dublin Edition,* Approbations of Dr. Troy and Bishop Conwell, Philadelphia: Eugene Cummiskey, 8vo.[5]

1825 *Holy Bible. . . . With Useful Notes, . . . by the Rev. Geo. Leo Haydock,* Philadelphia: Eugene Cummiskey, fol.[6]

1825 *Holy Bible. . . . First Stereotype, from the fifth Dublin Edition,*

---

the texts are the same, but the preliminary matter is differently arranged and the illustrations are different. The New Testament was issued previously to the Bible. "The expression, 'First American from the Fifth Dublin Edition,' meaning only the first American edition of Dr. Troy's Bible (1791), has led many to suppose this the first American Catholic Bible. *Bibliog. Account of Catholic Bibles, &c., printed in the United States.* By J. G. Shea, p. 11. This, however, is an erroneous supposition" (O'Callaghan, *op. cit.*, p. 76).

[4] Both O'Callaghan and Parsons list two octavo editions published by Cummiskey in 1824, one with the Approbation of Conwell, the other without his Approbation. However, in the edition with the Approbation described by O'Callaghan the engraved frontispiece of the Old Testament is dated 1827 and the title page of the New Testament is dated 1831. We may conclude, therefore, that this edition was actually published in 1831 or later despite the date on the title page of the Old Testament. The edition without Conwell's Approbation was reprinted in 1827, 1828, 1831, 1832, and 1835. The New Testament was also published separately.

[5] This is the New Testament to Cummiskey's octavo Bible published separately. Parsons does not list this edition.

[6] "This Cummiskey Bible is a reprint of Haydock's folio, 1811–1814 (J. G. S[hea]). It was published originally in 120 weekly numbers of 16 pages each. . . . The publication was commenced in 1823, . . . and was completed in 1825. The date on the back of the volume is: Philadelphia, 1826. The work, bound, was $35, and the edition consisted of one thousand copies. It was not stereotyped. Other copies are without plates, or date on back" (O'Callaghan, *op. cit.*, p. 171).

Approbations of Dr. Troy and Bishop Conwell (December 13, 1824) before the New Testament, Philadelphia: Eugene Cummiskey, 4to.

1826 *Holy Bible,* reprint of the 1825 edition, Philadelphia: Eugene Cummiskey, 4to.

1827 *Holy Bible,* reprint of the 1824 edition, Philadelphia: Eugene Cummiskey, 8vo.

1828 *Holy Bible,* reprint of the 1824 edition, Philadelphia: Eugene Cummiskey, 8vo.

1828 *New Testament. . . . From the Fifth Dublin Edition,* Philadelphia: Eugene Cummiskey, 32mo.[7]

1829 *New Testament. . . . As approved by the Right Reverend John Dubois, Catholic Bishop of New-York,* Utica, 12mo.[8]

1829 *New Testament,* Philadelphia: Eugene Cummiskey, 12mo.[9]

1829 *New Testament. . . . From the Fifth Dublin Edition,* Philadelphia: Eugene Cummiskey, 32mo.

1831 *Holy Bible. . . . First American, from the Fifth Dublin Edition,* reprint of the 1824 edition, Philadelphia: Cummiskey, 8vo.[10]

1831 *New Testament,* reprint of the 1824 edition, Philadelphia: Cummiskey, 8vo.

[7] Parsons does not list this edition, and O'Callaghan seems not to have seen a copy himself. It is possible that Cummiskey, in his correspondence with O'Callaghan, referred to the 1829 edition but gave the date 1828, when its publication probably was undertaken. O'Callaghan calls this and the 1829 edition 16mo, giving the size of the latter as 4¼ x 2¾ inches (p. 199), whereas Parsons calls the 1829 edition 32mo (p. 234). But on p. 213, in reference to Lucas' 32mo Testament, O'Callaghan refers to a 32mo Testament published by Cummiskey: "Mr. Cummiskey has informed me that he sold the plates of his 32mo Testament to Mr. Lucas in 1830 or 1831."

[8] This is the first edition of what is called the Devereux Testament from the fact that the plates were owned by Nicholas Devereux, of Utica, who had the Testaments printed at his expense for distribution among school children. The text follows Coyne's 1820 Dublin edition, and a misprint in James 5:17, "possible" instead of "passible," was continued in all subsequent reprints. This edition was reprinted at Utica in 1831, 1833, 1835, 1840; and at New York (by Sadlier) in 1842, 1845, and 1847. Cf. O'Callaghan, *op. cit.,* pp. 198 f.; Parsons, *op. cit.,* p. 234. An identical text was published by Lucas in 1831; see below, footnote 12.

[9] Parsons does not list this edition, and O'Callaghan himself did not see a copy. It seems highly probable, however, that Cummiskey would have printed an edition of this 12mo text before selling the plates to Lucas; see below, footnote 12.

[10] O'Callaghan indicates that Cummiskey published an 8vo Bible dated 1831. But he also must have published about this time another impression of his 8vo Bible dated 1824, for O'Callaghan describes such an edition with 1831 on the title page of the New Testament; see above, footnote 4.

1831 *New Testament,* Approbation of Bishop Dubois, reprint of the 1829 edition, Utica, 12mo.[11]

1831 *New Testament,* Approbation of Bishop Whitfield, reprint of Cummiskey's edition of 1829, Baltimore: Fielding Lucas, Jr. (no date), 12mo.[12]

1831 *New Testament,* Approbation of Bishop Whitfield, reprint of Cummiskey's edition of 1829, Baltimore: Fielding Lucas, Jr. (n.d.), 32mo.

1832 *Holy Bible. . . . With Annotations, by the Rev. Dr. Challoner,* reprint of Cummiskey's 4to edition of 1825, Baltimore: Fielding Lucas, Jr. (n.d.), 4to.[13]

1832 *Holy Bible,* reprint of the 1824 edition, Philadelphia: Cummiskey, 8vo.

1833 *Holy Bible. . . . From the last London and Dublin editions. . . . Published with the approbation of the Right Rev. John Dubois,* New York: John Doyle, 8vo.[14]

1833 *New Testament,* reprint of the 1829 edition, Utica, 12mo.

[11] Parsons says that the New Testament printed in Utica in 1829 was reprinted there in 1831 (*op. cit.,* p. 234); but O'Callaghan does not list such an edition. It is to be noted, too, that O'Callaghan calls this edition 12mo, whereas Parsons designates it as 16mo.

[12] "Mr. Cummiskey informs me that he sold the plates of his 12mo Testament [1829] to Mr. Lucas in 1830 or 1831. I have not been able to find a copy of the Cummiskey 12mo, and am therefore unable to say how far that volume agrees with this; but on comparing it with the Devereux Testament of 1829, the text of both appears to be identical; even the error in James, 5:17 is common to one and the other. The preliminary matter of the Devereux Testament, included on pp. ii–xi, is, in the Lucas edition, transferred to the end of the volume, where the 'Table of Controversies' is entitled 'Table of References.' In consequence of this transfer, pp. iii–xii are not enumerated in the Lucas Testament before the text, which begins immediately after the Title leaf and abruptly with p. 13. If, as is represented, this volume is printed from the plates of Cummiskey's 12mo Testament, then it and the Devereux Testament are from duplicate plates manufactured by James Conner, N.Y." (O'Callaghan, *op. cit.,* p. 211.) Unfortunately Lucas did not date his editions of the Bible.

[13] "This edition is from the plates of Cummiskey's 4to, which Mr. Lucas purchased in 1830 or 1831. It omits the Approbation of the Bishop of Philadelphia, but agrees in other respects" (*ibid.,* p. 214).

[14] "This is the first edition of Doyle's Catholic Bible. The Parallel References are printed at the foot, instead of at the side of the Text. . . . A transposition of lines occurs on p. 43, the latter part of v. 29 and the entire of v. 30 of chap. xlix being inserted between the first line of v. 17 and the 18th verse. Approbations of the Rt. Rev. Dr. Dubois and of the Rt. Rev. the Bishop of Charleston are printed on the reverse of the title" (*ibid.,* p. 220). The illustrations vary in different copies, and at the foot of the last page (968) we read: *"Printed by* Wm. Pearson, 60 *Cliff St."*

1834 *New Testament,* Philadelphia: Cummiskey.

1834 *New Testament. . . . First published by the English College of Rheims, Anno 1582. With the Original Preface, Arguments and Tables, Marginal Notes, and Annotations. To which are now added, an Introductory Essay; and a complete Topical and Textual Index,* New York: Jonathan Leavitt; Boston: Crocker and Brewster, 8vo.[15]

1835 *Holy Bible,* reprint of the 1824 edition, Philadelphia: Cummiskey, 8vo.

1835 *New Testament,* reprint of the 1824 edition, Philadelphia: Cummiskey, 8vo.

1835 *New Testament,* reprint of the 1829 edition, Utica, 12mo.

1836 *Holy Bible,* with the Approbation of Bishop Conwell (December 12, 1824), Philadelphia: Cummiskey, 8vo.[16]

1836 *Holy Bible. . . . Published with the approbation of the Right Rev. John Dubois,* reprint of the 1833 edition, New York: John Doyle, 8vo.[17]

1837 *Holy Bible. . . . With the Approbation of the Provincial Council* (April 22, 1837), Baltimore: Fielding Lucas, Jr. (n.d.), 12mo.[18]

1839 *Holy Bible. . . . First Stereotype, from the fifth Dublin Edition,* reprint of the 1836 edition, Philadelphia: Cummiskey, 8vo.[19]

1840 *Holy Bible. . . . First Stereotype, from the fifth Dublin Edition,* reprint of the 1836 edition (as in 1839), Philadelphia: Cummiskey, 8vo.[20]

[15] This edition of the original Rheims New Testament was published by a group of Protestant ministers for controversial purposes; see above, pp. 435–37. *O'Callaghan* gives more than a page of passages where the Protestant edition varies from its examplar, and adds that more examples could be cited (*ibid.*, pp. 234–36).

[16] This edition differs somewhat from the edition of 1824. Here the text of the Old Testament is paged continuously from Genesis to Machabees, whereas in the first edition it was divided into two parts both in paging and in signatures (cf. *ibid.*, pp. 165, 245). Parsons says that new type was used in this edition (*op. cit.*, p. 195).

[17] In this reprint of Doyle's 1833 edition the transposition at page 43 is corrected and Pearson's name is suppressed at the end.

[18] In Gen. 4:14 the words "and from thy face I shall be hid, and I shall be a vagabond and a fugitive on the earth" are omitted.

[19] "This edition agrees with that of 1836. It has, in addition, however, before the printed Title page, Approbations of Archbishop Eccleston of Baltimore; of Bishops Conwell and Kenrick of Philadelphia, and Dr. Hughes, coadjutor Bishop of New York. And an Engraved Title with Vignette, The Finding of Moses" (O'Callaghan, *op. cit.*, p. 260).

[20] O'Callaghan lists also the following publication for 1840: *An Abstract of the*

1840 *New Testament. . . . From the last London and Dublin editions, Published with the approbation of the Right Rev. Francis Patrick Kenrick, and the Right Rev. J. Hughes* (October 1, 1829), Philadelphia: Eugene Cummiskey, 12mo.

1840 *New Testament. . . . As approved by the Right Reverend John Dubois,* reprint of the 1829 edition, Utica, 12mo.

1841 *New Testament,* Philadelphia: Cummiskey, 8vo.

1842 *New Testament. . . . As approved by the Right Reverend John Dubois, Catholic Bishop of New-York,* reprint of the 1829 edition, New York: D. & J. Sadlier, 12mo.[21]

1844 *Holy Bible. . . . From the last London and Dublin Editions. . . . Published with the Approbation of the Right Reverend John Hughes, D.D., Bishop of New York* (January 27, 1844), New York: Edward Dunigan, 8vo.[22]

1844 *New Testament,* reprint of the 1831 edition, Baltimore: Fielding Lucas, Jr. (n.d.), 32mo.

1844 *New Testament,* Philadelphia: Cummiskey.

1845 *Holy Bible. . . . With the approbation of the Right Rev. Bishop Hughes. With a number of Steel Engravings,* New York: D. & J. Sadlier (n.d.); this has Ward's *Errata of the Protestant Bible,* 1844, 4to.

1845 *Holy Bible,* same as the above, but with Ward's *Errata* dated 1845, 4to.[23]

History of the Old and New Testaments, divided into Three parts. Part I. From the Creation to the Birth of Christ. Part II. The Life of our Lord Jesus Christ. Part III. The Acts of the Apostles and the Establishment of the Church throughout the World. By the Ven. and Right Rev. Richard Challoner, D.D., Bishop of Tebra, and V.A. Third American Edition. Revised by the Very Rev. John Power, V.G. with the Approbation of the most rev. Archbishop Ecclison, of Baltimore, and the Rt. Rev. J. Dubois, B-p N.Y. New York: Published by John McSweeny. Stereotyped by Smith & Wright, 1840.

"A considerable part of the New Testament History consists of portions of the Sacred Text, printed, however, in paragraphs. The dedication is dated 15 February 1834" (p. 266).

21 "This is the first edition of Sadlier's Testament, from the plates of the 'Devereux Testament' [1829], which were purchased by the firm. On the verso of the title page is the original approbation of Bishop Dubois, dated 7th Sept. 1828. The error in James 5:17 is continued" (*ibid.,* p. 272).

22 "The Text of this edition is from the Stererotype plates of Doyle's Douay Bible [1833], and has been issued in different styles," with various engravings and illuminated title pages (*ibid.,* p. 276).

23 O'Callaghan does not list such an edition; but I have seen one.

1845 *Holy Bible,* reprint of the 1836 edition, Philadelphia: Cummiskey, 8vo.

1845 *New Testament. . . . As Approved by the Right Rev. John Hughes, Catholic Bishop of New York,* reprint of the 1842 edition with new title page, New York: Sadlier, 12mo.

1845 *New Testament. . . . Approved by the Right Rev. John Hughes, D.D., Bishop of New York,* New York: Edward Dunigan, 18mo.[24]

1845 *The Acts of the Apostles, in four books: With copious notes. . . . By the Rev. Charles Constantine Pise, D.D.,* New York: Johnson, Fry and Company (n.d.), 12mo printed as 4to, 224 pages.

1845 *The Acts of the Apostles,* same as the above, 4to, 77 pages.[25]

1846 *Holy Bible,* reprint of the 1836 edition, Philadelphia: Cummiskey, 8vo.

1847 *Holy Bible,* reprint of the 1836 edition, Philadelphia: Cummiskey, 8vo.

1847 *New Testament,* reprint of the 1842 edition, New York: Sadlier, 12mo.

1848 *Holy Bible. . . . Published with the Approbation of the Right Reverend John Hughes, D.D., Bishop of New York,* reprint of the 1844 edition, New York: Dunigan, 8vo.[26]

1849 *The Four Gospels, translated from the Latin Vulgate, . . . by the Right Rev. Francis Patrick Kenrick,* New York: Edward Dunigan & Brother, 8vo.[27]

1850 *Holy Bible,* New York: Tallis, Willoughby & Co. (n.d.), fol.[28]

[24] O'Callaghan (p. 286) attributes to Mr. Shea the statement that "the text of this Testament is from the plates of a Belfast edition."

[25] In both these editions of the Acts the notice of copyright, dated 1845, appears on the verso of the title page, followed by a "Dedication to Right Rev. J. McCloskey, D.D., Coadjutor of New York." "These editions of the Acts are usually met bound up with Rutter's Life of Christ" (*ibid.,* p. 287).

[26] O'Callaghan does not list this edition.

[27] The Dedication, "To the Hierarchy of the United States, assembled in the Seventh Provincial Council of Baltimore," is dated May 1, 1849. For a further description of Kenrick's translation, see above, pp. 458 ff., and below, footnote 40.

[28] In 1850 Tallis, Willoughby & Co. proposed to publish in thirty parts, with thirty-one beautiful engravings, an edition of Haydock's Bible as revised by Dr. Hamil. But after six numbers were issued, the house dissolved and the plates were bought by D. & J. Sadlier and suppressed. The edition, however, bore the approbations of the Archbishop of New York and the bishops of Albany, Philadelphia, and many other Catholic divines in the United States. Cf. O'Callaghan, *op. cit.,* p. 306.

1850 *Holy Bible. . . . Published with the approbation of the Most Rev. John Hughes, D.D., Archbishop of New York, Most Rev. Samuel Eccleston, D.D., Archbishop of Baltimore, and the Right Rev. Bishop of Boston. With parallel references,* reprint of the 1844 edition, New York: Edward Dunigan & Brother (n.d.), 8vo.[29]

1850 *Holy Bible,* with Approbations of Archbishop Eccleston of Baltimore, Bishops Conwell and Kenrick of Philadelphia, and Bishop Hughes of New York, reprint of the 1836 edition, Philadelphia: Cummiskey, 8vo.

1850 *New Testament. . . . Illuminated after Original Drawings. By W. H. Hewett, Esq.,* New York: Hewett & Spooner, 8vo.[30]

1850 *New Testament,* reprint of the 1845 edition with new title page, New York: Edward Dunigan & Brother, 18mo.

1851 *Holy Bible. . . . With the Approbation of the Most Rev. John Hughes, D.D., Archbishop of New York,* reprint of the 1845 edition, New York: D. & J. Sadlier & Co.; this has Ward's *Errata* without any date on the title page, 4to.[31]

1851 *New Testament,* reprint of the 1842 edition, New York: D. & J. Sadlier (n.d.), 12mo.

1851 *New Testament,* reprint of the 1845 edition, New York: Edward Dunigan & Brother, 18mo.

1851 *The Acts of the Apostles, the Epistles of St. Paul, the Catholic*

[29] "This is called The Illustrated Family Edition. It has an illuminated title and 15 plates. It is the edition of 1844 with new titles" (*ibid.,* p. 308).

[30] This edition bears the Approbations of one archbishop and six bishops, dated 1847 and 1848. It is called "The Pictorial Catholic New Testament," and was originally published in numbers, the first in 1848. It is embellished with nearly 150 fine woodcuts by Mr. Hewett, who is stated to be "one of the best wood engravers that this country has produced." There are also marginal arabesque ornaments adapted to each page, and several hundred ornamental initial letters, one at the head of each chapter. "Mr. Shea says, this Testament was edited by the Rev. James McMahon of New York, who revised it by the Vulgate, and not only made it conform to the division of the verses in the Clementin edition, but in translating availed himself of the Greek, and in the Epistles of St. Paul, of the light which Hebrew throws on the Hebraisms of that Apostle. The edition was purchased in 1854 by John Murphy & Co., Baltimore, by whom the work has since been issued, and the copy before us, though retaining the imprint of Hewett & Spooner, has 'Baltimore, Murphy & Co.,' on the back of the cover" (*ibid.,* p. 310).

[31] One of the plates in the 1845 edition entitled "The Ascent of Elijah, 2nd Kings," now reads: "The Ascent of Elias, 4th Kings"; and "London: George Virtue," is erased from the plates which bore that inscription in the edition of 1845. Cf. *ibid.,* p. 314.

Epistles, and the Apocalypse. Translated from the Latin Vulgate, . . . with Notes, critical and explanatory, by Francis Patrick Kenrick, New York: Edward Dunigan and Brother, 8vo.[32]

1852 *Holy Bible. . . . With Useful Notes, . . . by the Rev. George Leo Haydock,* New York: Edward Dunigan and Brother, 4to.[33]

1852 *Holy Bible. . . . With Annotations by Dr. Challoner,* reprint of the 1845 edition, New York: Sadlier (n.d.); without Ward's *Errata,* 4to.

1852 *Holy Bible. . . . From the Last London and Dublin Editions,* reprint of the 1844 edition, New York: Edward Dunigan & Brother, 8vo.

1852 *Holy Bible,* reprint of the 1836 edition, Philadelphia: Cummiskey, 8vo.

1852 *Holy Bible,* reprint of Cummiskey's 8vo edition (1836, etc.), Boston: Patrick Donahoe, 8vo.[34]

1852 *New Testament,* Boston: Patrick Donahoe, 8vo.

1852 *New Testament,* reprint of the 1845 edition, New York: Edward Dunigan & Brother, 18mo.

1853 *Holy Bible. . . . With Useful Notes, . . . by the late Rev. Geo. Leo Haydock. . . . Abridged by the Very Rev. F. C. Husenbeth,* New York: George Virtue (n.d.), 4to.[35]

[32] In 1851 Patrick Donahoe, Boston, published *The Epistles and Gospels for the Sundays and Principal Festivals throughout the Year.* Cf. *ibid.,* p. 314.

[33] "This is called a New Edition of Haydock's Catholic Bible to distinguish it from that published by Mr. Cummiskey in 1824. It was issued in 38 parts." Rev. J. R. Bayley, later bishop of Newark, edited a few sheets; Rev. J. McMahon, the remainder. The latter is supposed to have made many corrections in the text and notes; but many errors in the Old Testament have been overlooked, including the curious mistake in Gen. 1:16, where light is said to "be nearly 3000 years in coming to us from the remotest star in our stratum" (*ibid.,* p. 321). O'Callaghan (p. 345) noted the following omissions in this edition: "wherein my people is" (Exod. 8:22), "fine linen and goats hair, rams' skins dyed" (Exod. 35:23), "casting for them sockets of silver" (Exod. 36:34), "Zare. Bringing that also by the houses, he found it to be" (Jos. 7:17). See above, p. 466 and note.

[34] This edition by Donahoe is a reprint of Cummiskey's 8vo edition, "the plates of which had been purchased by Mr. Lucas of Baltimore, who sold them to Mr. Donahoe." This edition had the Approbations of the archbishop of Baltimore, of the bishops of Philadelphia and New York, of the bishop of Boston (August 10, 1852), and Bishop Conwell's Approbation of Cummiskey's 4to and 8vo stereotype editions (September 13, 1824). The work was advertised as "The Unrivalled dollar edition of the Douay Bible" (*ibid.,* p. 324). The New Testament was published separately this same year.

[35] "This work was printed originally at Bungay in Suffolk, England, and published in London in 1853, in two volumes with 51 engravings. The plates were afterwards

1853 *Holy Bible. . . . With Useful Notes, . . . by the Rev. Geo. Leo Haydock,* revised edition of the 1852 edition, New York: Edward Dunigan and Brother, 4to.

1853? *Holy Bible. . . . With Annotations by Dr. Challoner,* reprint of the 1845 edition, New Testament dated 1857, New York: Sadlier; with Ward's *Errata,* 4to.[36]

1853 *New Testament,* New York: Sadlier, 4to.

1854 *Holy Bible,* reprint of the 1844 edition, New York: Edward Dunigan & Brother, 8vo.

1854 *New Testament,* reprint of the 1845 edition, New York: Edward Dunigan & Brother, 18mo.

1855 *Holy Bible. . . . With Useful Notes, . . . by the Rev. George Leo Haydock,* reprint of the 1853 edition, with Approbation of Archbishop Hughes and commendatory letter from the Pope (July 6, 1853), New York: Edward Dunigan and Brother, 4to.

1855 *Holy Bible, . . . Published with the Approbation of the Most Reverend John Hughes, D.D.* (January 27, 1844), reprint of the 1844 edition, New York: Edward Dunigan & Brother, 8vo.

1855 *New Testament* (with the Bible of 1856), New York: Edward Dunigan & Brother, 4to.

1855 *New Testament* (with the Bible of 1856), New York: Edward Dunigan & Brother, 8vo.

1855 *New Testament,* reprint of the 1845 edition, New York: Edward Dunigan & Brother, 18mo.

1855 *The Gospels, with Moral Reflections on each Verse. By Pasquier Quesnel. With an Introductory Essay by the Rev. Daniel Wilson, D.D., Bishop of Calcutta. Revised by the Rev. Henry A. Board-Man, D.D.,* Philadelphia: Parry & McMillan, 2 vols., 8vo.

1856 *Holy Bible. . . . With Useful Notes, . . . by the Rev. George Leo Haydock,* reprint of the 1853 edition, with Approbations of six archbishops and twenty-eight bishops, and commendatory letter from the Pope, New York: Edward Dunigan & Brother, 4to.

---

imported into this country and the work is issued in New York in 36 numbers" (*ibid.,* p. 330). Both the text and notes abound in errors. See above, p. 466.

[36] It is strange that these various editions should appear with different dates on the title pages of the Old and the New Testament. The New Testament was also published separately.

1856 *Holy Bible,* same as the above, but with the New Testament dated 1855, 4to.

1856 *Holy Bible. . . . With the approbation of the Most Rev. John Hughes, Archbishop of New York,* reprint of the 1845 edition, New York: D. & J. Sadlier, 4to.

1856 *Holy Bible,* reprint of the 1844 edition, New Testament dated 1855, New York: Edward Dunigan & Brother, 8vo.

1857? *Holy Bible. . . . With Annotations by Dr. Challoner,* reprint of the 1845 edition, New York: Sadlier; with Ward's *Errata,* 4to.[37]

1857 *Holy Bible. . . . With Useful Notes, . by the Rev. George Leo Haydock,* reprint of the 1853 edition with further corrections, New York: Edward Dunigan & Brother, 4to.

1857 *Holy Bible,* reprint of the 1844 edition, New York: Edward Dunigan and Brother (James B. Kirker), 8vo.

1857 *The Psalms, Books of Wisdom, and Canticle of Canticles. Translated from the Latin Vulgate, . . . with Notes critical and explanatory, by Francis Patrick Kenrick,* Baltimore: Lucas Brothers (n.d.), 8vo.

1857? *New Testament,* with Bibles of 1853 and 1858, New York: D. & J. Sadlier & Co., 4to.

1857 *New Testament,* reprint of the 1845 edition, New York: Edward Dunigan & Brother (James B. Kirker), 18mo.

1858 *Holy Bible. . . . With Annotations by the Rev. Dr. Challoner,* reprint of the 1845 edition, New Testament dated 1857, New Yord: Sadlier; with Ward's *Errata,* 4to.[38]

1858 *Holy Bible. . . . With Useful Notes, . . . by the Rev. George Leo Haydock,* reprint of the 1853 edition with corrections, New York: Edward Dunigan & Brother (James B. Kirker), 4to.[39]

[37] The date on the title page to the Old Testament is 1853; but the New Testament is dated 1857.

[38] The engraved title page shows St. John in the wilderness. The Approbations of three archbishops and three bishops precede the Old Testament.

[39] "This is the third edition of Dunigan's Haydock. Several errors in the preceding editions are now corrected. In this copy the Approbation page is replaced by an inserted sheet of eight pages of facsimiles of the Approbation of Archbishop Hughes, a letter of Pope Pius IX, and facsimiles of letters of commendation from Cardinal Wiseman, Archbishops Bedini, Purcell, Romilli, Turgeon, Blanc, Allemany, P. R. Kenrick, F. P. Kenrick, Bishops Charbonnel, Martin, O'Connor, Demers, O'Regan, Rappe, Bayley, Blanchet, Lefevere, Whelan, Spalding, Vandevelde, de St. Palais, Odin, Reynolds, Bacon, Baraga, McCloskey, Henni, Fitzpatrick, Portier, de Goesbriand, Carrell, Cretin,

1858 *Holy Bible,* reprint of the 1844 edition, New York: Edward Dunigan & Brother (James B. Kirker), 8vo.

1858 *Holy Bible,* reprint of the 1852 edition, Boston: P. Donahoe, 8vo.

1858 *New Testament,* Philadelphia: Cummiskey, 8vo.

1858 *New Testament,* New York: Edward Dunigan & Brother (James B. Kirker), 12mo (18mo?).

1859 *New Testament,* from the edition of Haydock's Bible, New York: Dunigan, 4to.

1859 *The Book of Job, and the Prophets. Translated from the Vulgate, . . . with Notes, critical and explanatory, by Francis Patrick Kenrick,* Baltimore: Kelly, Hedian & Piet, 8vo.

1860 *The Pentateuch. Translated from the Vulgate, . . . with Notes, critical and explanatory, by Francis Patrick Kenrick,* Baltimore: Kelly, Hedian & Piet, 8vo.

1860 *The Historical Books of the Old Testament. Translated from the Latin Vulgate, . . . with Notes, critical and explanatory, by Francis Patrick Kenrick,* Baltimore: Kelly, Hedian & Piet, 8vo.[40]

1861? *Holy Bible,* reprint of the 1845 edition, with the Approbation of three archbishops and three bishops, New York: Sadlier (n.d.); without Ward's *Errata,* 4to.[41]

1861? *Holy Bible,* same as the above with added Approbation of Bishop Wood of Philadelphia and different imprint, Philadelphia: P. Gallagher (n.d.); without Ward's *Errata,* 4to.

1863 *Holy Bible,* reprint of the 1845 edition, without the Approbation of three archbishops and three bishops, New York: Sadlier; without Ward's *Errata,* 4to.

Loras, Miles, Loughlin, Timon and Young" (Shea, *A Bibliographical Account of Catholic Bibles,* quoted by O'Callaghan, *op, cit.,* pp. 365 f.).

40 "Archbishop Kenrick's revision of the Douay Version is an immense labor, and one which has as yet been hardly appreciated according to its merits. It is a work on which has been bestowed a vast amount of rare and valuable learning, every text, every word seems to have been the object of diligent study, and of careful comparison with the original text. Few persons, till they compare the two, will suspect its very great superiority over our common Douay Bibles, either in accuracy or elegance" (*Brownson's Review,* quoted by O'Callaghan, *op. cit.,* p. 375).

41 It is impossible to give exactly the dates of this and some of the following editions. According to O'Callaghan (*ibid.,* p. 330), this edition with the Approbation of six bishops and archbishops first appeared in 1853; but that edition was dated, whereas this one is not. Unless otherwise noted, practically all of the following editions have been personally examined.

18—? *Holy Bible,* reprint of the 1845 edition, without the Approbation of three archbishops and three bishops, New York, D. & J. Sadlier, 31 Barclay Street; Montreal: 275 Notre Dame Street (n.d.); with Ward's *Errata,* 4to.

18—? *Holy Bible,* Husenbeth edition of Haydock's Bible, reprint of the 1853 edition, New York: Virtue and Yorston (n.d.), 4to.

18—? *Holy Bible,* with the Approbation of eight archbishops and forty-two bishops of America and seven Vicars Apostolic of Great Britain, and Admonition of Pope Leo XIII, Philadelphia: H. L. Kilner & Co. (n.d.), 8vo.

18—? *Holy Bible,* with the Approbation of Rev. D. Denvir (March, 1846), New York, etc.: Benziger Brothers; Dublin: M. H. Gill & Son, 16mo.

18—? *Holy Bible,* same as the above with new title page, 16mo.

1863–65 *Holy Bible. . . . From the last London and Dublin Editions. . . . Carefully Printed from the edition of 1844, which was published with the approbation of the Most Rev. John Hughes, D.D., Archbishop of New York,* New York: Johnson, Fry & Co. (n.d.), 42 parts, royal 4to.

186–? *New Testament,* reprint of the 1831 edition, Baltimore: Fielding Lucas, Jr. (n.d.), 32mo. [L.C.] [42]

1867 *New Testament,* Boston: P. Donahoe, 18mo. [A.C.B.]

1868 *Holy Bible,* New York: P. O'Shea, fol. [A.C.B.]

1868 *Holy Bible. . . . With the Approbation of the most Rev. John McCloskey, D.D., archbishop of New York,* New York: P. O'Shea, 4to.

1868 *Holy Bible,* New York: P. O'Shea, 12 mo. [A.C.B.]

1869 *Holy Bible. . . . With the Approbation of the Most Rev. John McCloskey, D.D.,* reprint of the 1868 edition, New York: P. O'Shea, 4to.[43]

1869 *Holy Bible,* New York: Catholic Publication Society, 12mo (same as the following?). [A.C.B.]

[42] Editions marked [L.C.] have for their sole source the *Library of Congress Catalogue of Printed Cards;* editions marked [A.C.B.] have for their sole source *The American Catalogue of Books, 1866–1871,* compiled and arranged by James Kelly, 1938 (reprint).

[43] But the only Approbation given is that of Bishop Cullen, given at Dublin on June 10, 1865: "This New edition of the English Version of the Bible, printed with our permission by James Duffy, Dublin, . . . WE by our authority approve."

18—? *Holy Bible. . . . Published with the Approbation of the Right Rev. D. Denvir, R.C. Bishop Down and Connor* (July 7, 1853), New York: The Catholic Publication Society (n.d.), 32mo.

1870 *Holy Bible,* New York: D. & J. Sadlier. [L.C.]

1871 *Holy Bible,* with the Approbation of Archbishop McCloskey (January, 1871), New York: D. & J. Sadlier (not seen), 18mo.

1875? *Holy Bible,* with a "History of the Holy Catholic Bible" by Rev. Ignatius Horstmann (copyright, 1875, by John E. Potter Co.), Chicago: William M. Farrar (n.d.), 4to.

1875 *Holy Bible,* same as the foregoing with different imprint and a few different illustrations, Philadelphia: John E. Potter and Co. (no date), 4to.[44]

1875 *Holy Bible,* with the Approbations of archbishops John McCloskey (February 27, 1872) and James F. Wood (June 23, 1871), New York: Thomas Kelly, 4to.

1875? *Holy Bible,* text reprinted from the 1845 edition with Preface by Rev. James O'Leary and other new introductory matter, New York: D. & J. Sadlier (n.d.), 4to.[45]

1878 *Holy Bible,* reprint of the 1875 edition, New York: Thomas Kelly, 4to.

1879? *Holy Bible. . . . With Annotations by the Rev. Dr. Challoner; to which is added The History of the Holy Catholic Bible, and Calmet's Illustrated and Explanatory Catholic Dictionary of the Bible* [copyright, 1879, by John E. Potter & Co.], *each edited by the Rev. Ignatius F. Horstmann, D.D., . . . and prepared under the special sanction of His Grace, The Most Rev. James F. Wood, D.D., Archbishop of Philadelphia,* Philadelphia: John E. Potter and Company (n.d.), 4to.

1879? *Holy Bible,* same as the above with different imprint, Philadelphia: Moore Brothers & Co. (n.d.), 4to.

1880 *Holy Bible,* reprint of the 1871 edition, New York: D. & J. Sadlier, 12mo (18mo?).[46]

[44] This edition is described above, pp. 475 f.

[45] This has the Approbation of Rt. Rev. Dr. Hughes on an engraved title page and also the Approbations of Cardinal McCloskey (created cardinal March 15, 1875), John Hughes, Martin Spalding, Francis P. Kenrick, and eight bishops and archbishops.

[46] These Bibles have on the reverse of the title page the following notice: "I hereby approve a pocket Bible to be published by Messrs. D. & J. Sadlier & Co. under the di-

1881 *Holy Bible,* reprint of the 1871 edition with new copyright date, New York: D. & J. Sadlier, 18mo.

1880–81 *Holy Bible,* Husenbeth edition of Haydock's Bible, "To which is added a Comprehensive History of the Books of the Holy Catholic Bible," by Rev. Bernard O'Reilly, Boston, Mass.: M. R. Gately, etc. (n.d.), 4to.[47]

1881–82 *Holy Bible,* Husenbeth edition of Haydock's Bible, reprint of the 1880–81 edition with different imprint, New York: Baird & Dillon (n.d.), 4to.

1883–84 *Holy Bible,* Husenbeth edition of Haydock's Bible, reprint of the 1880–81 edition with different imprint, Philadelphia: National Publishing Co. (n.d.), 4to.

1883–84 *Holy Bible,* same as the above with different imprint, New York: Benziger Brothers (n.d.), 4to.

1883–84 *Holy Bible,* same as the above with different imprint, New Orleans, La.: McDonald & Co. (n.d.), 4to.

1885 *Holy Bible. . . . With Useful notes, . . . by the Rev. Geo. Leo Haydock. Only correct and unabridged edition now issued,* New York: T. Kelly (n.d.), 4to.

1885 *Holy Bible,* reprint of the 1871 edition with new copyright (1885), New York: D. & J. Sadlier & Co., 33 Barclay Street and 38 Park Place (n.d.), 18mo.

18—? *Holy Bible,* reprint of the 1845 edition, without the Approbation of three archbishops and three bishops, New York: D. & J. Sadlier & Co., 33 Barclay Street & 38 Park Place. Montreal: 1669 Notre Dame Street (n.d.); with Ward's *Errata,* 4to.

---

rection of Mr. John Gilmary Shea, the text of Bishop Challoner's own edition of 1750 to be followed exactly, correcting merely the typographical errors, and conforming in punctuation and the orthography of proper names to the standard edition of the Vulgate of 1592. New York, January, 1869." Then the Approbation: "I hereby approve the publication by Messrs. D. & J. Sadlier & Co. of the 'Pocket Catholic Bible,' unusual care having been taken to make this edition extremely accurate and faithful. ✠ John, Archbp. of New York. New York, January, 1871." This Bible was reprinted at least in 1881 and 1885 with new copyright dates.

[47] The dates given for this edition and for the six following ones are taken from the respective copyrights. It is strange that two copyright dates should be given in all these Husenbeth editions of Haydock's Bible. These huge Bibles were popular in American homes during the last quarter of the nineteenth century, and the children of those times were attracted by the numerous illustrations, which we would now consider quite old-fashioned.

1890 *New Testament. . . . Published with the Approbation of His Eminence, James Cardinal Gibbons, Archbishop of Baltimore,* Baltimore: The Baltimore Publishing Company, 8vo.

1891 *Holy Bible. . . . Published with the Approbation of the Most Reverend John Hughes, D.D., archbishop of New York,* Baltimore: John Murphy & Co. 8vo.

1897 *Holy Bible. . . . From the last London and Dublin editions. The whole revised and diligently compared with the Latin Vulgate. Published with the Approbation of the Most Reverend John Hughes, D.D., Archbishop of New York,* New York: P. J. Kenedy, Publishers to the Holy See, Excelsior Catholic Publishing House, 5 Barclay Street, 8vo.[48]

189–? *Holy Bible,* reprint of the above but imprint simply: New York: P. J. Kenedy, Excelsior Catholic Publishing House, 5 Barclay Street (n.d.), 8vo.

1898 *New Testament,* with the Imprimatur of Archbishop Corrigan (November 10, 1897), New York: Benziger Brothers, 12mo.[49]

1898 *The Four Gospels,* translated from the Latin Vulgate by Rev. Francis Aloysius Spencer (not seen).

1899 *Holy Bible. . . . The Whole Revised and diligently compared with the Latin Vulgate. Published with the Approbation of His Eminence James Cardinal Gibbons, Archbishop of Baltimore* (September 1, 1899), Baltimore–New York: John Murphy Co. (n.d.), 8vo.[50]

1899 *Holy Bible,* same as the above with illustrations, Baltimore–New York: John Murphy Co. (n.d.), 8vo.

1899 *Holy Bible,* same as the above except that "The Whole Revised and diligently compared with the Latin Vulgate" is replaced by a shield, Baltimore–New York: John Murphy Co. (n.d.), not illustrated, 8vo.

[48] In this edition the reverse of the title page is blank and the Approbation (dated January 27, 1844) is on a second leaf which is page 2, the reverse also being blank. The Approbation is also on an engraving which serves as frontispiece. In the following edition the Approbation is on the reverse of the title page, and the frontispiece is a picture of Aaron in his priestly robes.

[49] For a description of this New Testament see above, p. 481.

[50] This important edition was often reprinted with the imprints of various publishers; it was the most common Bible in America during the first quarter of the twentieth century, and like most 8vo Bibles published since that time, it appeared with and without illustrations. This edition is described above, pp. 482 f.

1899? *Holy Bible,* same as the preceding with new illustrations (as in later Kenedy Bibles), John Murphy Company (n.d.), 8vo.

1899? *Holy Bible,* the Murphy Bible with different imprint, Catholic Bible House (n.d.), 8vo.

1899? *Holy Bible,* the Murphy Bible with different imprint, New York: Benziger Brothers (n.d.), 8vo. [L.C. and Rom.] [51]

1899? *Holy Bible,* the Murphy Bible with different imprint, New York: P. J. Kenedy (not seen), 8vo.

1899? *New Testament. . . . Published with the Approbation of His Eminence James Cardinal Gibbons, Archbishop of Baltimore,* Baltimore–New York: John Murphy Company (n.d.), 8vo.[52]

1900? *Holy Bible. . . . Published with the Approbation of His Eminence James Cardinal Gibbons, Archbishop of Baltimore* (undated), Baltimore, Maryland: John Murphy Company (n.d.), 16mo.[53]

1901 *The Four Gospels. A New Translation from the Greek Text Direct, with Reference to the Vulgate and the Ancient Syriac Version, by the Very Rev. Francis Aloysius Spencer, O.P. Preface by His Eminence James Cardinal Gibbons,* New York: Wm. H. Young & Co. (not seen).

1903 *The Psalms and Canticles in English Verse,* trans. by Edward G. Bagshawe, St. Louis: Herder, 1903. [Rom.]

1912? *Holy Bible,* reprint of the 1899 edition with shield on title page; to the usual approbation of Card. Gibbons (without date) is added the Approbation of John Cardinal Farley (also undated), New York: John Murphy Co. (n.d.), 8vo.[54]

1912 *Holy Bible. . . Published with the Imprimatur and Approbation of His Eminence John Cardinal Farley* (December 4, 1911), also the Imprimatur of Archbishop Prendergast (Philadelphia,

[51] Editions marked [Rom.] have for their source *The Guide to Catholic Literature,* compiled by Walter Romig.

[52] This New Testament seems to be simply the New Testament part of the John Murphy Bible. Cardinal Gibbons' Approbation is not given, for in the complete Bible it appeared only before the Old Testament; and the tables at the end include also the Old Testament, as at the end of the Murphy Bible.

[53] The early history of this edition is obscure; the date given here is conjectural. The edition seems never to have been copyrighted, although it has been reprinted by P. J. Kenedy and Sons as late as 1944.

[54] The date is conjectural. Archbishop John Farley was created Cardinal on November 27, 1911.

September 27, 1911) and of the archbishop of Montreal (December 3, 1912), printed in Belgium by Brepols' Press, illustrated edition, seventeen maps, New York: The C. Wildermann Co. (n.d.), 8vo.[55]

1912 *Holy Bible,* same as the above with the added Imprimatur of Bishop Chatard of Indianapolis (September 5, 1906) before both the Old and New Testaments, illustrated edition with seventeen maps, Chicago, Ill.: Extension Magazine (n.d.), 8vo.

1912 *Holy Bible,* same as the above with the added Imprimatur of Bishop Chatard before the Old Testament only, no illustrations, seventeen maps, St. Louis, Mo.: B. Herder Book Co. (n.d.), 8vo.

1912 *Holy Bible,* same as the above with the added Imprimatur of Bishop Chatard before the Old Testament only, no illustrations, seventeen maps, Omaha, Nebr.: Mid-West Church Goods Co. (n.d.), 8vo.[56]

1912 *Holy Bible,* same as the above with the added Imprimatur of Bishop Chatard before the Old Testament only, no illustrations, only four maps, Brepols' Catholic Press, Turnhout, Belgium; New York: C. Wildermann Co., 33 Barclay Street (n.d.), 8vo.

1912 *Holy Bible,* printed in Belgium by Brepols' Press; New York: P. J. Kenedy (n.d.), 8vo.

1913 *The Psalms. Translated from the Latin Vulgate with Critical and Explanatory Notes, by Francis P. Kenrick,* Baltimore: John Murphy Co. [Rom.]

1914 *Holy Bible. . . . Published with the Approbation of His Eminence James Cardinal Gibbons, Archbishop of Baltimore, reprint* of the 1899 edition, with new maps and illustrations, Baltimore–New York: John Murphy Company (n.d.), 8vo.

1914 *Holy Bible,* same as the above with different imprint, New York: P. J. Kenedy (not seen), 8vo.

1914 *Holy Bible,* same as the above, "Red Letter Edition," Baltimore–New York: John Murphy Company (n.d.), 8vo.

1918? *The New Testament and Catholic prayer-book combined,* New York, etc.: Benziger Brothers (n.d.). [L.C.]

[55] For a further account of these Bibles printed in Belgium see above, pp. 484 f.

[56] The imprint in the copy examined is out of alignment and appears to have been stamped in. Probably all these publishers and booksellers had their imprint in the illustrated as well as the non-illustrated edition.

1918 *New Testament. . . . Special Edition for the Army and Navy,* Washington, D.C.: National Catholic War Council (n.d.), 32mo.

1921 *The Psalms,* by Patrick Boylan, printed in Ireland; St. Louis: B. Herder (not seen), 8vo.

1921 *Gospel according to St. Mark,* Introduction, text, and notes, ed. by Robert O. Eaton, New York: Benziger Brothers, 1921. [Rom.]

1923 *Gospel according to St. John;* with Introduction and annotations (Catholic Scripture Manuals), Benziger, 1923. [Rom.]

1924? *New Testament. . . . With the Imprimatur and Approbation of His Eminence John Cardinal Farley, Archbishop of New York* (August 8, 1924), also that of Cardinal Mercier (Belgium, May 4, 1924), printed in Belgium; New York: P. J. Kenedy & Sons (n.d.), 32mo.

1927 *Book of Exodus, . . . with translation and concise Commentary,* by Henry J. Grimmelsman, Norwood, Ohio. [Rom.]

1929 *Holy Bible. . . . Published with the Imprimatur and Approbation of His Eminence Patrick Cardinal Hayes* (December 16, 1929), with Pope Leo XIII's encyclical and Introduction by Father Lattey, S.J., New York: The C. Wildermann Co. (n.d.), 16mo.

1929 *The Psalms Explained for Priests and Students. . . . By the Rev. Charles J. Callan, O.P., and the Rev. John A. McHugh O.P.,* New York: Joseph F. Wagner (not seen), 8vo.

1930 *The Bible Beautiful; an edition, for general use, of the Douay version of the Old Testament,* by Mother Mary Eaton. With maps and notes, London, New York, etc.: Longmans, Green and Co., 12mo. [L.C.] [57]

1930 *Holy Bible,* with introduction by Cuthbert Lattey, probably same as the 1929 edition, New York: The C. Wildermann Co. [Rom.]

1930 *Apocalypse of St. John,* with expositions of each chapter, Preface by T. E. Bird, St. Louis: B. Herder Book Co. (not seen).

1931 *Book of Ruth,* by Henry J. Grimmelsman, Chicago: Scott, Foresman & Co. [Rom.]

1931 *New Testament,* reprint of the 1898 edition with added Imprimatur of Patrick Cardinal Hayes (New York, November 16, 1931), New York: Benziger Brothers (n.d.), 12mo.

[57] Yet a recent communication from Longmans, Green and Co. informs me that they "do not publish any Bibles."

1934 *The Layman's New Testament; being the Rheims text as first revised by Bishop Challoner, edited with introduction and notes by Father Hugh Pope,* New York: Sheed & Ward, 1934. [L.C.]

1935 *New Testament. . . . With Annotations and References by Dr. Challoner, Canon Haydock and Dr. H. J. Ganss, and . . . a Preface of Rev. James A. Carey, M.A. . . . A Wildermann-Brepols Publication,* Carey's revision of Challoner, printed in Belgium by Brepols' Catholic Press; New York: C. Wildermann Co. (n.d.), 16mo.

1936 *New Testament,* same as the above, C. Wildermann Co. (n.d.), 16mo.

1936 *New Testament,* Westminster Version, vol. 2, Longmans. [Rom.]

1937 *The Holy Bible, an abridgement and rearrangement, by Ronald A. Knox,* New York: Sheed & Ward, 8vo.

1937 *The Psalms and the Canticles of the Divine Office. A New English Translation by George O'Neill, S.J.,* Milwaukee: The Bruce Publishing Company (not seen).

1937 *The New Testament. . . . Translated into English from the Original Greek by the Very Rev. Francis Aloysius Spencer, O.P.,* New York: The Macmillan Company, 8vo.

1938 *Holy Bible. . . . The re-edited edition* [of the New Testament] *by Rev. James A. Carey, M.A., was first published* A.D. *1935. . . . Published with the Imprimatur and Approbation of His Eminence, Patrick Cardinal Hayes* (New York, January 7, 1938), printed in Belgium by Brepols' Catholic Press, with sepia illustrations and seventeen maps, New York: C. Wildermann Co. (n.d.), 8vo.[58]

1938 *Holy Bible,* same as the preceding but without illustrations, seventeen maps, New York: P. J. Kenedy & Sons (n.d.), 8vo.

1938 *Holy Bible,* same as the preceding, without illustrations, seventeen maps, St. Louis, Mo.: B. Herder Book Co. (n.d.), 8vo.

1938 *Holy Bible,* same as the preceding, without illustrations, but only four maps, New York: C. Wildermann Co. (n.d.), 8vo.

1938 *New Testament,* Westminster Version, vol. 1, 2nd edition, Longmans. [Rom.]

[58] Neither the C. Wildermann Co. (the American agents) nor Brepols' Press has been able to give a satisfactory account of Wildermann-Brepols Bibles and New Testaments. The dates of publication and the various imprints are thus difficult to ascertain.

1938 *The World's Classic, Job, Translation from Original Texts . . . by George O'Neill, S.J.,* Milwaukee: The Bruce Publishing Company (not seen).

1938 *The Layman's New Testament,* reprint of the 1934 edition, printed in Belgium, New York: Sheed & Ward, 1938. [L.C.]

1939? *New Testament. . . . With the Imprimatur and Approbation of His Eminence John Cardinal Farley* (August 8, 1924), also that of the Vicar General of Malines, Belgium (April 3, 1939), similar to the 1924 edition but entirely new type, New York: The Regina Press (n.d.), 32mo.

1940 *The Layman's New Testament.* [Rom.]

1940 *New Testament,* reprint of Spencer's version (1937), New York: The Macmillan Company, 8vo.

1941 *Holy Bible. . . . With Notes by Bishop Challoner and also the Encyclical Letter "On the Study of the Holy Scriptures," by Pope Leo XIII, and a Preface by Rev. William H. McClellan, S.J.,* New York: The Douay Bible House, 8vo.

1941 *Holy Bible,* same as the preceding, with illustrations, New York: The Douay Bible House, 8vo.

1941 *Holy Bible,* same as the preceding with different imprint, published with and without illustrations, New York: Benziger Brothers (n.d.—not seen), 8vo.[59]

1941 *New Testament,* same as the following, deluxe edition, 8vo printed as 4to.

1941 *New Testament of Our Lord and Savior Jesus Christ. . . . A Revision of the Challoner-Rheims Version Edited by Catholic Scholars under the Patronage of the Episcopal Committee of the Confraternity of Christian Doctrine,* Paterson, New Jersey: St. Anthony Guild Press, 8vo.

1941 *New Testament,* reprint of Spencer's version (1937), New York: The Macmillan Company, 8vo.

[59] This edition seems to agree with the Douay Bible House edition word for word and line for line, the same kind of type being used for both; but it is not printed from the same plates. For the Douay Bible House edition has a rule between the columns of the text, whereas this one does not. But apparently the two sets of plates were made from the same type. Both editions were printed by Benziger Brothers, and the one with their imprint is still in print. The plates of this edition, except for the psalms and the New Testament, have been used for their *New American Catholic Edition* (1950) with the Confraternity Edition of the New Testament.

1941 *The Layman's New Testament,* reprint of the 1934 edition (?), New York: Sheed & Ward, 8vo.

1942 *Holy Bible,* reprint of the 1941 edition, New York: The Douay Bible House, 8vo.

1942 *The Psalter of the Roman Breviary, with Succinct Notes, by the Rev. L. C. Fillion, S.S.,* St. Louis: B. Herder Book Co., 8vo.

1942 *The Psalms Explained for Priests and Students,* reprint of the 1929 edition, New York: Joseph F. Wagner (n.d.), 8vo.

1942 *My Daily Reading from the Four Gospels and the New Testament. Gospels Unified. Epistles Unified. Prepared for the Use of Catholic Personnel of the Army of the United States. Published under the Direction of Chief of Chaplains,* Washington: United States Government Printing Office, 32mo.

1943 *Holy Bible,* reprint of the 1941 edition, New York: The Douay Bible House, 8vo.

1943 *Holy Bible,* same as the foregoing, with excerpt of Pope Pius XII's encyclical inserted before the Preface, New York: The Douay Bible House, 8vo.

1943 *New Testament,* reprint of Spencer's version (1937), New York: The Macmillan Company, 8vo.

1943 *New Testament,* student's edition of the Confraternity Edition, Paterson, New Jersey: St. Anthony Guild Press, 18mo.

1944 *Holy Bible,* reprint of the 1941 edition, with excerpt of Pope Pius XII's encyclical inserted before the Preface, New York: The Douay Bible House, 8vo.

1944 *Holy Bible,* exact duplicate of the John Murphy Bible (1914) with slight corrections in punctuation, etc., New York: P. J. Kenedy & Sons (n.d.), 8vo.[60]

1944 *Holy Bible,* same as the above with different type on the title page, New York: P. J. Kenedy & Sons (n.d.), 8vo.

1944 *Holy Bible,* reprint of the Murphy 12mo edition (1900?) with new imprint, New York: P. J. Kenedy & Sons (n.d.), 12mo.

1944 *Red Letter Edition. The Holy Bible (Douay Version). . . . An Introduction by Vy. Rev. Charles J. Callan, O.P.,* New York: The Douay Bible House, 18mo.

[60] The date of this edition, as well as that of the 12mo edition published this same year by P. J. Kenedy and Sons, has been supplied by Mr. A. R. Kenedy of that firm. The 12mo edition is still printed from the original Murphy plates. See above, note 53.

1944 *Red Letter Edition. The Holy Bible,* same as the above with different imprint, New York: Benziger Brothers (n.d.), 18mo.

1944 *The Psalms. Translated from the Latin Psalter, . . . with Introductions, Critical Notes and Spiritual Reflections by the Very Rev. Charles J. Callan,* New York: F. Wagner (n.d.), 8vo.

1944 *New Testament of Our Lord and Saviour Jesus Christ. Newly Translated from the Vulgate Latin at the Request of their Lordships, the Archbishops and Bishops of England and Wales,* by Msgr. Ronald Knox, New York: Sheed & Ward, 8vo.

1944 *New Testament,* same as the above, second printing, Sheed & Ward, 8vo.

1945 *Holy Bible,* reprint of the 1941 edition, with excerpt of Pope Pius XII's encyclical inserted before the Preface, New York: The Douay Bible House, 8vo.

1945 *Red Letter Edition. The Holy Bible,* reprint of the 1944 edition (perhaps the same), New York: Benziger Brothers (not seen), 18mo.[61]

1945 *The Psalms,* reprint of Callan's version and commentary (1944), New York: F. Wagner (n.d.), 8vo.

1945 *New Testament,* reprint of Spencer's version (1937), New York: The Macmillan Company, 8vo.

1945 *New Testament of Our Lord and Saviour Jesus Christ. A New Translation,* reprint of the 1944 edition with new title page, third fourth, and fifth printings, New York: Sheed & Ward, 8vo.

1946? *Holy Bible,* reprint of the 1941 edition, with excerpt of Pope Pius XII's encyclical inserted before the Preface, New York: The Douay Bible House (n.d.), 8vo.

1946 *The Psalms,* reprint of Callan's version and commentary (1944), New York: F. Wagner (n.d.), 8vo.

1946 *New Testament of Our Lord and Saviour Jesus Christ. A New Translation,* illustrated edition of Knox's version, "Fifth Printing of the general edition. First Printing of illustrated edition," New York: Sheed & Ward, 8vo.[62]

[61] The publishers maintain that this edition was published in August, 1945; but the copyright is dated 1944.

[62] One can hardly imagine what is meant by "Fifth Printing of the general edition. First Printing of the illustrated edition," especially when a "Fifth Printing" of the general edition appeared in 1945. A more detailed account of Knox's version is given above, pp. 502–504.

1946 *New Testament,* reprint of Spencer's Version (1937), New York: The Macmillan Company, 8vo.

1947 *The Psalms. A New Translation with the Canticles of the Roman Breviary, by Ronald Knox,* New York: Sheed & Ward, 16mo.

1947 *My Daily Psalm Book. The Book of Psalms Arranged for Each Day of the Week. New English Translation from the New Latin Version,* by Rev. Joseph Frey and Rev. John E. Steinmueller, Brooklyn: Confraternity of the Precious Blood (n.d.), 32mo.

1947 *New Testament,* reprint of Knox's version (1945), sixth printing, New York: Sheed & Ward, 8vo.

1947 *New Testament,* Introduction and notes by J. P. Arendzen, New York: Sheed & Ward (not seen).

1947 *New Testament,* Confraternity Edition, reprint of the 1941 edition, a Foreword by Most Rev. Amleto Giovanni Cicognani replaces the letter of Cardinal Tisserant; Paterson, New Jersey: St. Anthony Guild Press, 8vo.

1947 *New Testament,* student's edition of the Confraternity Edition, reprint of the 1943 edition, Paterson, New Jersey: St. Anthony Guild Press, 18mo.

1947 *New Testament,* New York: Benziger Brothers (not seen), 32mo.

1948 *The Old Testament. Newly translated from the Vulgate Latin by Msgr. Ronald Knox at the Request of His Eminence The Cardinal Archbishop of Westminster. Volume I, Genesis to Esther,* New York: Sheed & Ward, 8vo.

1948 *The Holy Bible. . . . The Book of Genesis,* Confraternity Edition, Paterson, New Jersey: St. Anthony Guild Press (not seen), 8vo.

1948 *The Book of Psalms in Latin and English. With the Canticles Used in the Divine Office,* Knox's version, printed in Great Britain, New York: Sheed & Ward, 24mo.

1948 *New Testament,* reprint of Spencer's version (1937), New York: The Macmillan Company, 8vo.

1948 *New Testament,* reprint of Knox's version (1945), eighth printing, New York: Sheed & Ward, 8vo.

1949 *New Catholic Edition of the Holy Bible. . . . The Old Testament, Douay Version, with Newly Edited Annotations of Bishop Challoner and a New Translation of the Book of Psalms from the New Latin Version, . . . and the New Testament, Confraternity*

Edition, copyright 1949, New York: Catholic Book Publishing Company (n.d.), 8vo.

1949 *The Holy Bible. . . . The Book of Genesis,* Confraternity Edition, second printing, Paterson, New Jersey: St. Anthony Guild Press (n.d.), 8vo.

1949 *The New Psalter of Pius XII in Latin and English: with Introductions, Notes and Spiritual Reflections,* by the Very Rev. Charles J. Callan, O.P., New York: Joseph F. Wagner, 8vo.

1949 *New Testament,* reprint of Knox's version (1945), eighth printing, New York: Sheed & Ward, 8vo.[63]

1950 *Holy Bible. Old Testament in the Douay-Challoner Text. New Testament and Psalms in the Confraternity Text. Edited by Reverend John P. O'Connell, with Illustrations by James Joseph Jacques Tissot. Published with the Approbation of His Eminence Samuel Cardinal Stritch* (August 5, 1950), Chicago, Illinois: The Catholic Press, Inc. (n.d.), royal 8vo or small 4to.[64]

1950 *Holy Bible,* reprint of the 1949 edition, copyright 1949–50, New York: Catholic Book Publishing Company (n.d.), 8vo.

1950 *New American Catholic Edition. The Holy Bible. Old Testament, Douay Version, with Psalms from the New Latin Version Authorized by Pope Pius XII. New Testament Confraternity Edition.*

[63] It is indeed strange that the same "Eighth Printing" should appear with two different dates on the title page. These vagaries make it extremely difficult to give an account of American editions, especially since the publishers themselves cannot explain them.

[64] This magnificent volume, measuring seven by ten inches, is the most elaborate Catholic Bible now published. The presentation plate, engraved title page, and numerous illustrations are colorful and most pleasing, and the volume is thumb-indexed. Before the Old Testament we find the encyclical letters on the Sacred Scriptures by Leo XIII, Benedict XV, and Pius XII, and other papal documents. At the end of the New Testament are an explanation of the Mass, "A Practical Dictionary" (256 pages), "A Collation of Texts from the New Testament," and a "Family Register" exquisitely decorated. The beautiful binding has on the back, "Holy Family Edition of the Catholic Bible."

Although it is outside the intended scope of this list, I cannot refrain from mentioning another sumptuous Bible published by the same firm in 1951: *The Holy Bible. Holy Trinity Edition, edited by Reverend John P. O'Connell. Published with the approbation of Samuel Cardinal Stritch, Archbishop of Chicago* (March 29, 1951), The Catholic Press, Inc., Chicago, Illinois (8vo). This edition likewise is thumb-indexed and has an elaborate cover and many beautiful illustrations, which differ, however, from those in the "Holy Family Edition." This edition has 29 pages of introductory matter, including "Facts Catholics Should Know About the Bible." At the end of the New Testament is an explanation of the Mass (different from the preceding one), an extensive Family Register, and "A Practical Dictionary" (256 pages).

. . . *Preface by Rev. William H. McClellan, S.J.*, the Old Testament plates taken from the 1941 edition except for the Psalms, New York: Benziger Brothers, 8vo.

1950 *Holy Bible,* same as the foregoing with different imprint, New York: C. Wildermann Co., 8vo.[65]

1950 *Holy Bible,* same as the 1938 Brepols edition with Pope Pius XII's encyclical inserted after Pope Leo XIII's encyclical, seventeen maps (as in the 1938 edition), no illustrations, St. Paul 1, Minn.: The E. M. Lohmann Co. (n.d.), 8vo.

1950 *Holy Bible,* same as the preceding, but with new maps, no illustrations, New York: The Douay Bible House (n.d.), 8vo.[66]

1950 *Holy Bible,* same as the preceding, but with illustrations, New York: The Douay Bible House (n.d.), 8vo.

1950 *Holy Bible. . . . The Douay Version of the Old Testament. . . . The Confraternity Edition of the New Testament,* Old Testament from the plates of the 1944 edition, New York: P. J. Kenedy & Sons (n.d.), 8vo.

1950 *Holy Bible,* same as the foregoing with beautiful colored illustrations, New York: P. J. Kenedy & Sons (n.d.), 8vo.

1950 *The Old Testament. Newly Translated from the Vulgate Latin by Msgr. Ronald Knox. . . . Volume I,* second printing, New York: Sheed & Ward, 8vo.

1950 *The Old Testament. Newly Translated from the Vulgate Latin by Msgr. Ronald Knox. . . . Volume II, Job to Machabees. With Appendix* (*Alternative Version of the Psalms*), New York: Sheed & Ward, 8vo.

1950 *The Holy Bible. . . . The Book of Psalms and the Canticles of the Roman Breviary,* Confraternity Edition, Paterson, New Jersey, 8vo.

1950 *New Testament,* Confraternity Edition, "Special Student Edition

65 The publishers (Benziger Brothers) inform me that this *New American Catholic Edition* has been published also with the following imprints: Donnelly Co., Kansas City, Mo.; Nebraska Church Goods, Lincoln, Nebraska; Catholic Action Book Shop, Wichita, Kansas; The Cosgrave Co., Omaha, Nebraska; J. B. Reilly, Newark, N.J.; Jay Kay (Catholic Book Shop of New York), New York; Engel & Sharkey, New York; Templegate, Springfield, Ill.

66 Thus it comes about that the Wildermann-Brepols Bible of 1938 now appears with the imprint of the Douay Bible House, while the Old Testament in the Benziger and Douay Bible House editions of 1941, except for the psalms, now appears with the Wildermann imprint.

with Blank Pages and Wide Margins for Notes," New York: Catholic Book Publishing Company (n.d.), 4to.

1950 *New Testament,* Confraternity Edition, reprint of the 1941 edition, Paterson, New Jersey: St. Anthony Guild Press, 8vo.

1950 *New Testament,* reprint of Knox's version (1945), eleventh printing, New York: Sheed & Ward, 8vo.

1950 *New Testament,* student's edition of the Confraternity Edition, reprint of the 1943 edition, Paterson, New Jersey: St. Anthony Guild Press, 18mo.

Index

Aalix de Cunde, 10
Abrek, 208 note
Ad imprimendum solum, 188 and note
Adonis, "mourning for," 105
Adrian, St., 5, 21, 46
Adrian VI (pope), 110
Aelfric, 10, 23-25, 37
Aethelred (king), 35
Aethelstan, 6, 54
Aethelward, 10
Agatho (pope), 20
Aidan, St., 18, 44
Ainslie, Robert: revision of the Authorized Version, 548
Ainsworth, Henry: and the Brownists, 511; version of the Bible, 511 f.
Ainsworth, John, 511
Alcuin, 409
Aldhelm, St., 18-20, 35, 52
Aldred, 7, 42 f. and notes, 50
Alen, E., 128
Alexander II (pope), 33
Alexander, A.: version of the Bible, 542
Alexander, William, 309 note: version of the Bible, 542 f.
Alexandrian Greek text, 556 f., 582
Alford, Henry: editions of the Greek N.T., 545, 548; Revised Version and, 548, 552 f.; revision of the Authorized Version, 548
Alfred (king), 6, 22 f., 37 f.: *Code of Saxon Laws*, 22; Psalter translated by, 9, 22, 54, 59; translation of Bede's *Historia*, 17, 18 note, 22, 38
Alleluia: Geneva Bible's omission of, 285 note; the Rhemists' use of, 258
Allen, William (cardinal), 250 f. and note
  Douay Old Testament and, 294 note
  Fulke's condemnation of, 286
  on the fury of the Reformers, 274
  on the necessity for a Catholic version, 250
  the revision of the Vulgate and, 296 note
  Reynolds' translation of his works, 253
  Rheims New Testament and, 250-52, 254, 302 note
Allestry, Richard, 514, 516 f.: and Hammond, 517; *Paraphrase* by 514 f., 517-19
Ambrose, St.: on Peter's primacy, 125 note
Ambrosius Catharinus, 107
Amen
  Kenrick's translation of, 461
  Lingard's translation of, 444
  Nary's translation of, 345 note
  the Revised Standard Version translation of, 582
  the Rhemists' use of, 258
  Spencer's translation of, 499
  Tyndale's translation of, 136
American Baptist Publication Society, 595
American editions, 369 f., 386, 458-63, 484-96, 667, 719 ff.: *see also* Benziger, Cummiskey, Douay Bible House, Dunigan, Kenrick, Sadlier, Sheed and Ward
American Standard Version, 578 f.: revision of, 579 f., 584
Amsterdam, the Independents at, 511 f.
Anderson, Christopher
  burning of Tyndale's New Testament, 147 note
  editions of the Bible, 92
  on Cochlaeus, 130 note
  on Taverner, 205
  on Thomas More, 146 note
  on Tunstall, 148
  Rheims version disregarded by, 267
Andrews, bishop of Winchester, 123
Andrews, Lancelot, 312, 328
Andrews, W. E.: edition of the New Testament, 412
Anglican versions, 513-21, 528, 530 f., 533
Anglo-Norman, meaning of the term, 15 note
Anglo-Norman literature, 9
Anglo-Norman versions, 8 f.: of the Psalter, 9; of the Apocalypse, 8, 10 and note, 64
Anglo-Saxon, meaning of the term, 15 note
Anglo-Saxons, the
  arts of, 5 f., 41-44
  conversion of, 3 and note
  culture of, 3-6, 41-44
  extent of vernacular versions among, 6-10, 64 f.
  glosses of the Gospels, 31 f., 40-51
  history of, 3

Anglo-Saxons, the (*continued*)
literature of, 3 ff.
love for the Bible, 4
version of the Bible in verse, 58
versions of the Gospels, 7, 9, 31 ff., 64 f.: Aelfric on, 23 and note; by St. Bede, 21; the Ormulum, 25 f.
versions of the Proverbs, 10, 64
versions of the Psalter, 19, 37, 52-61: by King Alfred, 9, 22, 54, 59
Anne (queen), Lenfant and, 521
Anne (of Bohemia), 69, 87 note
Anne (of Cleves), 205
Anne Boleyn, 160
Anselm of Laon, 11, 57, 78 note
Anstruther, Godfrey, 98 note
Anti-Catholic prejudice, 293, 440
Antiochian Greek text, 557
Antiochian revision of the Greek text, 557, 559, 561 f., 564 note
Anti-Trinitarianism: in the Church of England, 524; publication of the doctrine prohibited, 540 note; see also *Unitarianism*
Apocalypse, the
Anglo-Norman versions of, 8, 10 and note, 64
Anglo-Saxon versions of, 10
Authorized Version, 123 note, 312
Bois' translation of, 123 note
Geneva Bible, 224, 228 f.
Junius' annotations on, 123 note
Norman version of, 8, 10 and note, 64
popularity of, 98
Pyle's paraphrase on, 527
Walmesley's version of, 98
Wycliffe's commentary on, 68
Apocrypha, the, 110
Aelfric's translation, 23, 37
Arias Montanus' version, 110
Authorized Version, 129, 312
Baduellus' version, 111 note
Bishops' Bible, 237, 240, 243 and note
Cajetan on, 106
Castalio's version, 120
Cholin's version, 112 and note
Coverdale's version, 157, 163 and note, 166 f., 208, 595
Geddes on, 120
Geneva Bible, 167 note, 223
Goodspeed's translation, 594 f.
Great Bible, 200, 208
in edition of Pagninus' version, 110
Junius' version, 117 note, 127 and note
Matthew's Bible, 158 note, 167 note, 175, 182, 184 f., 208
Pelican's edition, 112 note
Rogers' translation, 158 note
St. Jerome and, 185
Apocrypha, the (*continued*)
Taverner's version, 208
Tigurine Bible, 112
Whitaker on, 291
Wycliffite versions, 76 note
Apostolic Constitutions, 525 note; Whiston on, 525 f. and note
Approbations
by Bernard, 504 note
by Bourne, 468
by Bramston, 414, 433 note
by Carpenter, 372-74
by Chatard, 485
by Corrigan, 481
by Crolly; *see* Crolly
by Cullen; *see* Cullen
by Curtis, 431, 433, 454
by Denvir; *see* Denvir
by Everard, 431
by Farley, 485, 491
by Gibson, 422, 434
by Green, 356, 423
by Griffin, 504 and note
by Hayes: in Bible of 1938, 490 and note; in New Testament of 1919, 487; in New Testament of 1935, 489 f.
by Hughes: in Bibles of 1852, 466 and note; in Bibles of 1853, 467; in Cummiskey's New Test. of 1840, 449 and note; in the "Catholic Family Bible," 469
by Irish bishops; *see* Ireland
by Kelley, 431, 433, 454
by Kenrick, 449 and note, 467
by Laffan, 433, 454
by McCloskey, 467
by MacHale, 451
by Manning, 476
by Milner, 422, 434
by Murray, 393, 429 f., 433 note: in New Testament of 1826, 433; in New Testament of 1847, 454; in New Testament of 1853, 467
by O'Hara, 506
by O'Reilly, 375
by Poynter, 422, 434
by Prendergast, 485
by Purcell, 467
by Scottish bishops, 437
by Spellman, 494, 496 note
by Surmont, 483
by Timon, 467
by Troy, 373 and note, 376 f.: in Coyne's New Testament of 1825, 431; in Gibson's edition, 413
by Vaughan, 480 f.
by Walsh: in Bible of 1847, 378, 453; in Bible of 1888, 478; in New Testament of 1851, 464 f.

Approbations (*continued*)
by Walton, 356, 423
by Wiseman: in Bible of 1847, 378, 453; in New Testament of 1851, 464 f.; in New Testament of 1858, 469
by Wood, 476
Cotton's criticism of, 93-95, 373
for Christie's edition (1823), 429
in Brepols Bibles, 485, 490
in Brown's New Testament (1851), 465
in Carey's edition, 386
in Catholic Board Edition, 405
in Challoner's revisions, 356, 359, 361, 423
in Coyne's New Testaments, 431, 433, 454
in Cummiskey's New Testament (1840), 449 and note
in Douay Old Testament, 294 f.
in Duffy's Bible (1857), 471
in Duffy's New Testament (1874), 475
in Fullarton's edition (1845), 450
in Gibson's editions, 412-14
in Hewett's Pictorial New Testament, 463
in Keating and Brown's New Testaments, 363, 422 f., 434
in Kennedy edition (1830), 437
in Knox's version, 503 f. and note
in Lucas edition of the Bible (1832), 434
in MacMahon's revisions, 372 f. and note, 375-77, 418, 420
in MacNamara's editions, 415 and note
in Nary's version, 339 f.
in New Testaments of 1851, 464 f.
in New York edition of 1850, 463
in Newcastle New Testament (1812), 398
in Rheims New Testaments, 255, 269 f.
in Richardson's Bible of 1847, 453
in Smith's New Testament (1821), 427
in the Confraternity Edition, 506
in Witham's version, 346 note, 347, 353
Kenrick on, 94
lacking in Syers' Bible, 399 f.
nature of, 419
purpose of, 94
Archer and Sons, New Testament by, 440 f.
Arendzen, J. P.: edition of the New Testament, 427, 482, 495 f.
Arianism
Clarke and, 526 f., 539
Guyse's opposition to, 524
Harwood and, 529
in the Church of England, 525 f.
of Eusebius, 561
the Revised Version and, 562
Unitarianism and, 528, 539
Whiston and, 524-26
Whitby's opposition to, 521
Arias Montanus: edition of Pagninus' Bible, 110; version of the Bible, 315
Ariminum, Council of, 290
Armagh, Book of, 4
Arundel (archbishop)
Constitution of, 6 note, 64 note, 65, 85 f.: and Coverdale's Dedications, 161 note; Parker's condemnation of, 236; and the Synod of Canterbury, 146 f.
on the piety of Queen Anne, 69 note
Purvey condemned by, 75
Wycliffe condemned by, 86 f.
Ashburnham, Lord, 157 note
Astruc, 383
Augsburg Confession, 205
Augustine, St. (of Canterbury): books brought by, 4 and note; conversion of England, 3; monastery of, 19, 38, 41; Psalter of, 4 note, 19, 52 f.
Augustine, St. (of Hippo), 108, 239, 269
Canonicity of Second Machabees, 287 and note
Erasmus on, 102
on kissing, 303
on miracles, 569 note
on the reading of Scripture, 254 f.
Soliloquia translated by King Alfred, 22
Austin, St., 188 note
Authorization for the vernacular Scriptures; *see* Arundel, Constitution of
Authorized Version, 308-30
Address to King James, 314
Address to the Reader, 309 f. note, 311-14: and the Rheims Preface, 311 note, 314
Ainslie's revision of, 548
Alford's revision of, 548
antiquity of the language: Scarlett on, 535; Worsley on, 531
Apocalypse in, 123 note
the Apocrypha, 312
authorization of, 313
Barlee's version and, 543
beauty of, 321-24
Beza's influence on, 123 f., 315, 316 note, 317 ff.
Bilton's modernization of, 587
Bishops' Bible and, 310, 313, 315-17
Bois and, 123 note
Broughton's denunciation of, 329 f.
Canne's edition of, 512
Challoner's revisions and, 129, 365 f. and note
Clarke's paraphrase on, 526 f.
companies of revision, 312, 328
Conquest's revision of, 548
Cook's revision of, 548 f.
Cruttwell's edition of, 92
culmination of biblical translations, 129, 337, 509
defects of, 318-21

Authorized Version (*continued*)
demands for the revision of, 551 f.
Douay Old Testament and, 264 and note
editions of, 313 note, 326 f. and notes
Fulke's edition of, 264
Gaelic translation of, 452
Gairdner on, 600
Geneva Bible and, 311, 315 f. and notes, 323
Great Bible and, 238, 244 note, 245 and note, 311 and note, 317
the Greek text, 318-20, 554 f.
Harwood's version and, 530
Hayman's version and, 589
Highton's revision of, 548
Hussey's revision of, 548
italics used in, 166, 324 f. and note, 566
James I and, 308-10
Letchworth New Testament and, 599 f.
McClellan's revision of, 549
Martin's influence on, 332
Matthew's Bible and, 178, 311, 317
misprints in, 325 f.
need for the version, 308 f.
Newcome's revision of, 534 and note
notes in, 275 note, 325 and note
omission of notes, 309 f.
origin of, 308-12, 314
Oxford Movement and, 538
peculiarities of, 324-26
Penn's revision of, 547
predominance of, 337, 509, 538
Preface to, 264 and note: on John of Trevisa, 30
the Psalter, 199 note, 299, 311 f.
Pyle's *Paraphrase* on, 527
Revised Standard Version and, 583
Revised Version and, 322 f., 566-68: Gairdner on, 600
revisions of, 539, 547-49, 575
Rheims New Testament and, 63 f., 261 and note, 263-65, 315-17
Rheims-Douay Version and: Phillimore on, 259 f.
Roberts' revision of, 533
rules for revision, 275 note, 310 f., 315
Sharpe's revision of, 541, 547, 549
size of, 324
sources used, 310 f., 315-18
spelling of the names in, 310 f.
style of, 321-24
subsequent versions and, 509
Taylor's revision of, 547 f.
title page, 313
Tolley's revision of, 547
Tyndale's version and, 135, 178, 311, 317
the Unitarian Version and, 540
Wakefield's revision of, 532 f.
Webster's revision of, 547

Authorized Version (*continued*)
Wells' revision of, 521, 528
Wesley's revision of, 528
Whiston's version and, 526
Whitby's *Paraphrase* on, 520 f.
Woodhead's *Paraphrase* on, 518 f.
Worsley's criticism of, 531
Worsley's version and, 531
Axon, W. E.: on Ainsworth's version, 511 f.
"Azymes," Rhemists' use of, 258, 268

Baber, Henry: edition of Wycliffite N.T., 72 f.; on John of Trevisa, 30; on Wycliffe's translation, 71 note, 72 f.
Babington, Churchill; on John of Trevisa, 29
Bacon, on Rheims New Testament, 259, 260 n.
Baduellus, C., 111 note
Bagster, Samuel
Catholic Board Edition reprinted by, 369, 394, 406 note, 408 and note, 428 note
Coverdale's Bible reprinted by, 157 note, 158 note, 162 f. notes, 171
English Hexapla, 73 and note, 80, 163 note, 202 note
Great Bible reprinted by, 199 note
Rheims New Testament criticized by, 267 f.
Rheims New Testament reprinted by, 267 and note, 474
Vulgate New Testament published by, 474
Whittingham's New Testament reprinted by, 219 note
Baird editions of Challoner's revision, 421
Balbus, William, 255
Bale, bishop of Ossory: the "foul-mouthed," 144; Martin calumniated by, 274; notes on the New Testament, 141; on King Alfred, 22 note; on St. Aldhelm, 19 note
Ball, John: and Baxter, 512
Ballantine, W. G.: and the Riverside New Testament, 595
Baltimore, Councils of, 490: and Kenrick's version, 458 f.
Baltimore editions of the Bible, 434, 479, 482 f., 494
Bancroft (bishop): funds for the Authorized Version, 312 note; Rainolds and, 309 note
Baptists: and the Revised Version, 553; and Scarlett, 536; and Whiston, 526
Barker, Christopher: edition of the Bishops' Bible, 238
Barker, Robert (printer): and the cost of the Authorized Version, 312 note; editions of the Authorized Version, 326 note; editions of the Bishops' Bible, 285 note; editions of the Geneva Bible, 229 note, 285 note; editions of the Genevan New Testament, 232 f.
Barlee, Edward: version of the epistles, 543 f.

Barlow, William: and the Authorized Version, 309 note, 312, 328: and the Bishops' Bible, 237
Barnard, T.: and Challoner, 353, 355 note
Barnes, Dr., 153 f. and note, 156 note
Barrow, and the Revised Version, 552
Baruch, Book of: in Coverdale's version, 167
Basic English version, 594, 596 f.
Basil, St.: Prologue on the Psalms, 239
Bassi, A.: edition of Challoner's New Testament, 490
Bath, monastery at, 33
Baxter, Richard, 512 f., 516, 522: paraphrase of the New Testament, 513; the "Reformed Liturgy," 513
Beausobre, Isaac de: version of the Bible, 521
Becan, Gedde's criticism of, 383
Becke (publisher): Dedication to Edward VI, 181 f.; editions of Matthew's Bible, 178, 180 note, 181 f.; edition of Taverner's version, 207, 208 note, 211, 213 f.
Becon, Thomas, 237 note
Bede, St., 3, 20 f.
  books sent by St. Gregory, 4 note
  death of, 21
  his study of Scripture, 4 note
  monastic life of, 4 note
  on Caedmon, 16 and note, 17 f.
  on St. Benet Biscop, 4 f.
  on SS. Theodore and Adrian, 5
  translation of the Bible, 7, 21, 38: Parker on, 236
Bedell, William: Gaelic version of the Bible, 451 f. and notes
Bedford, earl of, 112
Beegan edition of Challoner's New Testament, 392 f., 412
"Bel and the Dragon," in the Bishops' Bible, 240
Belfast editions of Challoner's revision, 421 ff.; *see also* Simms and McIntyre, Mairs, Read, Denvir
Belgian editions: Bible of 1912, 484 f., 491; Bible of 1931–46, 488; Bible of 1938, 490 f. and note; New Testament of 1935, 489 f.
Bellarmine: Geddes' criticism of, 383; Junius' controversy with, 127; Whitaker and, 280, 291
Belsham, Thomas, 539: and the Unitarian Version, 539 f.; version of the epistles, 540
Benedict XIV (pope), 107
Benedict XV (pope) on the Society of St. Jerome, 486
Benedicti, Joannes, 116 note, 128
Benedictus, the: in Anglo-Saxon Psalters, 55, 57
Benet Biscop, St., 4 f., 20
Bensley, R. L.: and the Revised Version, 553
Benziger Brothers editions of Challoner's revision: Bible of 1941, 360 note, 369, 479, 491 note, 493-95; Bible of 1945, 494 f.; Bible of 1950, 360 note, 496 note; New Testament of 1898, 481
Berger, Samuel: Anglo-Saxon arts, 5, 44; the Bible in the British Isles, 4; Celtic art, 44
Berkeley, chapel at, 29 f.
Bernard, Morrogh: *Imprimatur* for Knox's Old Testament, 504 note
Bernard, Richard, 292 f.
Berthelet (printer), editions of the Bible (1540), 162 note, 203
Bévenot, Hugh, 501 note
Beyerlink, Laurence, 270 note
Beza, Theodore, 121-26
  Authorized Version influenced by, 123, 315, 316 note, 317 ff.
  Calvinism of, 318 note
  Cartwright's *Confutation* and, 276
  Castalio condemned by, 120 f.
  Castalio's version condemned by, 274
  criticism of, 123-26
  English versions influenced by, 121, 123-26
  Fulke's repudiation of, 287
  the Geneva Bible influenced by, 216 note, 229 f., 309, 317
  Greek New Testament, 122: and the Authorized Version, 318, 555; editions of, 318; Tomson's translation of, 123 and note, 129
  heretical tenets of, 121, 124-26
  Latin New Testament, 117 notes, 121 ff.: editions of, 117 notes, 121 f. and notes, 125-27 notes; Scrivener on, 317 f.; Tomson's translation of, 123 and note, 129, 233; variations in editions of, 125 note, 126 note; with Pagninus's Old Testament, 110, 111 note
  Laurence's criticism of, 244 f.
  likened to Marcion, 125 note
  mistranslations of, 123-25
  Molinoeus' condemnation of, 274
  notes by, 125-27
  on the multiplicity of translators, 347
  opponents of, 123 f.
  the Rhemists' condemnation of, 123-25
  Scrivener on, 318 note
  the Vulgate praised by, 290
Bible, the
  Authority of: Geddes on, 383; Kenrick on, 459
  Bohemian editions, 64, 69
  burning of, 137 note, 144 f., 147
  the Catholic Church's concern for, 405, 408 ff.
  Catholic use of, 410

Bible, the (*continued*)
concern for its accuracy, 551
French editions, 64, 69
German editions, 64, 69
in the churches, 238
inspiration of: Geddes' contempt for, 380, 382 and note
interpretation of; *see* Interpretation
Italian editions, 64
lists of editions of, 91 ff.
love for: Aelfric on, 24 f.; in Saxon times, 7
only rule of faith, 85, 249, 293
parts rejected by the Reformers, 282, 287; *see also* Apocrypha
petitions for revising, 551 and note
printed editions of, 91 ff.
reading of; *see* Reading
supposed ignorance of, 62
Bible societies, 401 f. and note, 407 and note
Biblia Eadwini, 57
Biblia Gregoriana, 4 note, 38
Bibliander, 112 and note
Biblical English: in Spencer's version, 499; in Westminster Bible, 500
Bickley, Thomas: and the Bishops' Bible, 237
Bilfrith (Bilfrid), 42 f. and note, 50
Bilson, Thomas: and the Rhemists, 292 and note
Bilton, Ernest: version of the Gospels, 549 f., 587, 599 f.
Bingham, 268 note
Bird, T. E.: 501 note
"Bishop," Fulke concerning the use of, 280
Bishops' Bible, 234-46
Apocrypha in, 237, 240, 243 and note
authorization of, 237
Authorized Version based on, 238, 244 note, 245 and note, 310, 313, 315-17
criticism of, 243-45
defects of, 308 f. and note
edition attacked by Martin, 245, 282 note, 285 and note, 332
editions of, 238, 240-42, 244-46, 281 note
Fulke's edition of, 264, 286
Geneva Bible and, 242 f. and note
Great Bible and, 204, 235 f. and note, 238, 242 f.
Jugge's notes in, 151
Martin's criticism of, 245, 332
Muenster's version and, 114
New Testament, 241 ff.
the notes, 235, 243 note, 245 f., 275
numbering of the verses, 235, 244 and note
Old Testament, 238-41
origin of the name, 236 f.
Parker and, 234 ff., 275
Prefaces by Parker, 236 ff., 241
the Psalter, 237, 239-41, 244 and note
Bishops' Bible (*continued*)
a revision, 242 f.
rules for revision, 235 f.
Tyndale's New Testament and, 243
with edition of Anglo-Saxon versions, 31 note, 34
the work of revision, 234-37
Blair, D. H.: and Charles Butler, 402 f., 410 note; edition of the Authorized Version, 327
Blake (bishop of Dromore): edition of Challoner's New Testament, 439, 449; Preface by, 439, 452
Bliss, Geoffrey, 76 and note
Bloomfield and Kenrick, 462
Blunt, J. H.: early English versions, 8; Tyndale's learning, 134; Tyndale's version, 139; Wycliffe's heretical tenets, 84 f.; Wycliffe's translation, 71 f.
Blyth, Francis, 97, 352 f. and note
Bodley and the Great Bible, 221 and note
Bodley, Thomas: founder of the Bodleian Library, 221
Boethius, translated by King Alfred, 22
Bohemian editions, 64, 69
Bois, John, 104, 123 and note, 312, 328: and the Authorized Version, 123 note; and Beza, 123, 125
Boniface, St., 3
Bonner: and Coverdale's Bible, 191 and note; Cranmer burned by, 191 note; defamed by Foxe, 191 note; and the Great Bible, 190 f. and notes, 195 f.; Matthew's Prologues condemned by, 180 note
Book of Common Prayer: Barker's editions of, 232 f.; the Latin Psalter in, 114 note; revision of, 164 f., 199 note, 216-18; *see also* Prayer Book Psalter
"Book of St. Cuthbert"; *see* Lindisfarne Gospels
Booker, Joseph: and Coyne's New Testament of 1825, 431
Boothroyd, Benjamin: edition of the Hebrew Bible, 542, 549; version of the Bible, 542
Bosch, Herman, 134
Boston of Bury, 22 and note
Bosworth, J.: edition of Anglo-Saxon Gospels, 31, 33, 34 note, 73 and note
Bosworth Psalter, 35, 54
Bourne, 175
Bourne, Francis (cardinal): and Washbourne's Bible, 468, 483, 485, 488
Bowes, John: version of the New Testament, 545
Boylan, P., 500 note
Boyle, Robert, 451 note
Boyse and Walker, 518

Bradshaw, M.: editor of Worsley's New Testament, 531
Brady, Maziere: and Poynter, 407 note
Brameld, G. W.: version of the Gospels, 545
Bramston (bishop), 93, 414 note: Approbation by, 414, 433 note; edition of the Bible, 414 f., 433 note
Brann, H. A., 484 f.
"Breeches Bible," 222, 238
Brennan, Thomas: edition of Challoner's revision, 451 f. and notes
Brenton, Lancelot: version of the Old Testament, 543
Brepols' Press; editions of the Bible, 484 f., 490 f. and note; edition of the New Testament, 489-91
Breviary, the: cost of (1518), 62; prayer before the recitation of, 58 note; recitation of, 6
Brewer, J. S.: Foxe denounced by, 144, 192
Bridfrith, 42 note
Bristow, Richard, 252 f., 396: death of, 252, 254; and Douay Old Testament, 294 note; and Fulke, 253, 286; learning of, 355; and Rheims New Testament, 250, 252 f., 302 note; works of, 253 and note
Brithwald, 33
"British and Foreign Bible Society," 92
British Museum: Bible Exhibition (1911), 64; catalogue of, 509 and note; foreign Bibles in, 64
Broughton, Hugh, 329 f.: Bishops' Bible criticized by, 243, 245
Brown, J.: edition of the New Testament (1851), 465 and note; the text carefully selected by, 472
Browne, J.: on Martin and Fulke's controversy, 281; and Ward's *Errata*, 281, 332 and note
Brownists, the: at Amsterdam, 511 f.; and Ainsworth, 511
Bruce, J.: edition of the Authorized Version, 327
Brut, Walter, 70 note
Bryers, Coyne's noteless New Testament reprinted by, 427
Bucer, 138, 216: and Gairdner, 283
Buckingham, extent of Anglo-Saxon versions, 64 f.
Buelbring, K. D.: edition of the Anglo-Saxon Psalter, 56 n., 59
"Bugge Bible," 177
Bulkeley, Edward: and Erasmus, 290 note; Pighius reproached by, 291; the Rhemists attacked by, 289-91, 332, 574
Bullinger, H., 112 and note
Bullough, Sebastian, 479 note, 511 note
Bunemann, J., 119 note
Burgis, Ambrose, 347
Burgon, J. W.: biblical work of, 565 note; on the last chapter of St. Mark, 572; on the Revised Version, 567 note; on Westcott and Hort's theory, 560 f., 563-65
Burnet, Gilbert: on the Gaelic version, 452 note; on Tunstall, 147
Burns and Lambert editions of Challoner's revision, 453, 467, 469
Burns and Oates, 479: editions of the Bible, 360, 369, 376, 468, 476 f.; editions of the New Testament, 479-84, 486
Burns, Oates and Washbourne, 478, 488 note: editions of the Bible, 479, 488; editions of the New Testament, 479 f., 482, 486 f.; edition of the Rheims N.T., 352 note; Knox's version, 496, 502-504
Burton, Edwin: on Richardson's Bible of 1847, 453 f.; on Witham's character, 346 note
Butler, Alban, 402 note
Butler, Charles: and Blair, 402 f., 410 note; and the Catholic Board Edition, 402 and note, 404 note, 406 f.; on Challoner's last revision, 371; on the need for a Catholic version, 460

Cabbalists, the, 115
Caedmon, 16-18
Caesar, 382 note
Caesarean Greek text, 582
Cajetan, 105-109
Callan, Charles J.: on Challoner's revisions, 494 f.; and Spencer's version, 498
Calligraphy of the Anglo-Saxons, 6, 42-44
Calmet, 396 and note
Calvin, John: and the Edwardine Prayer Book, 217; "Epistle" in Whittingham's New Testament, 219 and note; and the Geneva Bible, 216 note, 229; Molinoeus' condemnation of, 274; and Osiander, 115
Calvinism: at Geneva, 216; in Beza's notes, 124-26; in the Geneva Bible, 234
Cambridge Psalter, the, 55-57
Cambridge University and Erasmus, 102
Cambridge University Library, 509 and note
Camden: Martin slandered by, 274; on Tunstall, 148 note
Camerarius, 127
Campbell, George: version of the Gospels, 523
Campion: Fulke's disputations with, 278 f. and note; Martin's praise for, 279
Canne, John: edition of the Authorized Version, 512; on Presbyterianism, 512
Canterbury, Synod of, 146 f.
Canterbury Psalter, the, 56 f.
Canticle of Canticles
Castalio's doubts concerning its authenticity, 121

Canticle of Canticles (*continued*)
  Martin on, 164 note
  Muenster's version of, 114 note
  title of: in Bishops' Bible, 240; in Coverdale's Bible, 164; in Geneva Bible, 223; in Matthew's Bible, 177; Martin on, 164 note
Canticles of the Church: Anglo-Norman version, 9; in Anglo-Saxon Psalters, 55, 59; in *Psalterium Triplex,* 56 note, 57; Rolle's version of, 27 note
Capellus, Ludovicus, 119 note
Carey, James A.: history of Rheims-Douay version, 489 note, 491; revision of Challoner's New Testament, 479, 489-91
Carey, Mathew: edition of Challoner's revision, 369, 386
Carisbrooke, Charles I at, 514
Carleton, J. G.: on the Rheims and Authorized versions, 316 and note
Carnwaille, John, 29 note, 69
Carpenter, James: and MacMahon's editions, 372-74
Carter, printer of Catholic books, 274 note
Cartwright, Thomas: the *Confutation* by, 276-78, 286, 437; Geddes' criticism of, 380; heretical propositions of, 276 f. note
Cassiodorus, 409
Castalio, Sebastian: version of the Bible, 119-21, 125: Beza's condemnation of, 274; Bishops' Bible and, 235 note
Castillion, 188
Catena aurea, 64, 68
Catherine (queen), 161
Catharinus, Ambrosius, 107
Catholic Board Edition, 358, 363 f., 401-11
  Bagster's reprint of, 369, 394, 406 note, 408 and note, 428 and note
  editions of, 408
  Little's reprint of, 449
  Milner's denunciation of, 256 note, 363 f., 403 f. and note, 422
  the notes in, 402-404, 407, 431
  Poynter and, 402, 407 f., 422
  Poynter's "Address," 405, 408-11
  Poynter's New Testament and, 430
  purpose of, 401, 411
  the text, 404-407
Catholic Book Publishing Co., 360 note, 496
Catholic Booksellers' and Publishers' Co., 471, 474
Catholic Emancipation Act, 433 note, 442, 464
Catholic Evidence Guild, 847
Catholic Family Bible, 469
Catholic Fund, the, 401 f. and note: edition published by, 393 f., 407, 423, 425-27, 430, 432; called "Douay Version," 495
Catholic Truth Society editions of the Gospels, 483 f.
Catholic versions, 93 f., 97 f., 249 ff.
  differences in, 391-94, 455-57, 470-72, 476 f., 486 f.
  in Saxon times, 6 ff.
  lists of, 666 ff., 719 ff.
  necessity for, 250, 252
  omissions in, 359 f., 368-70, 391
  pre-Wycliffite, 62-66
  vicissitudes of, 509
Catullus, 120
Caxton, on John of Trevisa, 29 f.
Ceadwalla, 44
Cecil: and the Bishops' Bible, 234 and note; Catholics tortured by, 275; printing of the Geneva Bible, 221 note
Celibacy, clerical
  attacked in Matthew's Bible, 183, 211
  Cox's remark concerning, 245 note
  Erasmus' doubts concerning, 105
  Jugge's notes deriding, 245
  Rhemists' notes on, 267
  teaching of the Geneva Bible regarding, 228
Centenary Translation of the New Test., 595
Challoner, Richard, 93, 355 and note
  death of, 372 f.
  Douay College and, 346, 353, 355 note
  fifth edition of Rheims N.T., 97 f., 352-55, 358
  Nary's version and, 345
  revisions of Rheims-Douay; *see* Challoner's revisions
  Witham's version censored by, 345, 347, 353
Challoner's revisions, 95, 250, 355-72, 391 ff.
  Authorized Version and, 129, 365 f. and note
  collation of, 95-97
  Cotton on; *see* Cotton
  Kenrick's revision and, 460 f. and note
  Nary's version and, 342-44
  New Testament (1749), 356-58, 367 ff.: and the Catholic Board Edition, 392-94, 405-407; principal reprints of, 369, 424
  New Testament (1750), 361-64, 367 ff.: and Keating and Brown Edition (1818), 422 f.: predilection for, 358, 362 f., 391, 393, 408 and note, 430, 438, 464 ff.
  New Testament (1752), 364 ff., 372, 391-93: and edition of 1792, 390; and MacMahon's revisions, 374
  New Testament (1764), 364, 370, 391
  New Testament (1772), 364, 370 f., 391
  New Testament (1777), 371
  notes in, 357, 361, 364, 371, 389 f. and notes, 403 f. and notes
  Old Testament, 358-60, 370
  omissions in, 359-61, 368 f., 391, 406
  Rheims New Testament compared with, 355, 357 f., 366 f.
  Wiseman on, 442 note

Chapuys, 161: Cromwell and, 188 note
Charlemagne (emperor), 409
Charles I (of England): death of, 514; Dedication to, 288; and Hammond, 514; and the Psalter of James I, 309 note
Charles II (of England): and Allestry, 516; and Baxter, 513
Chastising of Goddis Children, The, 13
Chatard (bishop), *Imprimatur* by, 485
Chaucer and the practice of glossing, 11 note
Cheyne, T. K.: and the Revised Version, 553
Cholin, R., 112 and note
Christ: bloody sweat of, 573; descent into hell denied, 121, 125, 276 note; His life in the Catholic Board Edition, 405
Christ Church, Canterbury, 57
Christ the King, feast of, 488
Christie, James, 428 f.; 472: edition of the Bible, 429
Chronicles, Books of: in Bishops' Bible, 237
Civil War (English): Allestry and, 516; Baxter and, 513; Hammond and, 514
Clario, Isidore, 115 f. and notes
Clarke, Samuel, 526 f.: Arianism of, 526 f., 539
Clement VII (pope), 106, 109 f.
Clement VIII (pope), edition of the Vulgate, 295 f., 409: and the Confraternity Edition, 491; Nary on, 340; Preface to, 396
Clifford and Poynter, 407 note
Cochlaeus, 130 note: and Luther, 130 note; on Tyndale, 134; and Tyndale, 130
Code of Saxon Laws, 22
Codex ℵ, 557 ff., 570, 573, 582
Codex Alexandrinus, 560 note: and Harwood, 529; and Westcott and Hort's theory, 557; and Whiston, 525 f.
Codex Amiatinus, 325 note
Codex argenteus, 128
Codex Arundel, 60, pp. 54 f.
Codex B, 557 ff., 570, 573, 582: Tischendorf on, 560; Scrivener on, 573
Codex Bezae, 32 note, 103 note, 122, 124, 260 note, 582
  age of, 525 and note
  Authorized Version and, 319 note
  Beza and, 122, 124
  corruptions in, 560 note
  Harwood and, 529
  Westcott and Hort's theory, 556
  Whiston and, 525 f.
Codex Cantabrigiensis, 122
Codex Claromontanus, 122 and note: age of, 525 and note; and Harwood, 529; and Whiston, 529
Codex Ephraemi rescriptus, 560 note
Codex Junianus XI, 16 note
Codex Junianus 113, 16 note
Codex Montfortianus, 103 note
Codex Stowensis, 54
Codex Vaticanus, 103 note
Codex Vitellius E.18.6, pp. 54 f.
Codex Vossius, 54
Codrington, Antony, 347
Coghlan (printer), and Challoner's third revision, 364 note
Colet and Erasmus, 100 f.
Collier: on Cromwell, 154 note, 188 and note; on Foxe, 191 note
Cologne (Germany) edition of Tyndale's N.T., 130, 150
Colonna (cardinal), 251
Colvenerius, George, 294
Complutensian Polyglot, 100, 104, 113: and the Authorized Version, 315, 318 and note; and the Great Bible, 189
Confraternity Edition of the New Testament, 479, 491, 496 and note 505: Preface to, 491 f.; and the Revised Standard Version, 581, 583; and the Westminster Version, 492 note, 500 f.
Confraternity Edition of the Old Testament, 505 f., 594
"Congregation"
  in Coverdale's version, 154, 169
  in Protestant versions, 124, 284
  in Tyndale's version, 139, 148, 152, 220, 284
  Martin and Fulke concerning the use of, 280 f.
  not used in A.V. and R.V., 284, 310 and note, 332
  not used in Whittingham's version, 220
Congregationalist, a: and the Revised Version, 553
Congregationalists; *see* Independents
Conjunctions in Greek and English, 592
Conquest, Dr.: revision of the Authorized Version, 548
Constant, on Cromwell, 188
Constantine I (emperor), 118: and the revision of the Greek text, 561
Constitution of Arundel; *see* Arundel
Conventicle Act, 513
Convocation
  the Bishops' Bible and, 237 f.
  Clarke's submission to, 527
  Coverdale's version and, 157 f., 229
  the Great Bible condemned by, 229, 234
  "Our Lord" or "the Lord," 356 note
  the Revised Version and, 541, 552 f., 578
Cook, F. C.
  Lightfoot and, 570 note
  on Christ's bloody sweat, 573
  on Eusebius, 561
  Pope and, 565

Cook, F. C. (*continued*)
  Revised Version criticized by, 549, 559, 568
  revision of the Authorized Version, 548 f.
  The Speaker's Commentary, 548 f.
Cooper, on the Gaelic version of the Bible, 451 note
Coppinger (bishop), 416
Coptic version, 582
"Corbona," the Rhemists' use of, 258
Cornwall, John, 29 note, 69
Corrigan, Michael: *Imprimatur* by, 481
Cost of manuscript Bibles, 62 and note
Cotton, Henry, 92 ff.
  anti-Catholic animus of, 93-95
  Bagster's reprint of the Catholic Board edition, 428
  Catholic Board Edition described by, 406, 408
  Challoner's revisions, 366
  Clario's version, 116 note
  collation of Challoner's revisions, 95-97
  Coyne's New Testament of 1825, 431 f.
  Curoe's Preface, 440 note
  edition of 1792, 388 f.
  editions of Matthew's Bible, 181 note
  editions of the Bishops' Bible, 244
  episcopal approbations, 93-95, 373
  fifth edition of Rheims N.T., 351 f. and note
  Geddes' biblical work, 385 note
  later editions of Challoner's revisions (1796–1850), 391 f. note, 394 ff.
  Lingard's version, 442 note
  Lists of Editions of the Bible, 92, 509, 542
  Mace's New Testament, 521 note
  MacHale's Approbation criticized by, 451 note
  MacMahon's revision, 375 ff.
  Milner criticized by, 403
  Nary's version, 339 note
  Newcastle New Testament, 388 f. and note, 399
  on John Fisher, 97 note
  on John Lewis, 91
  Protestant reprint of Rheims New Testament, 435
  Protestant versions of the nineteenth century, 542 f.
  Ray's Bible, 537
  Rhemes and Doway, 92 ff.
  sixth edition of Rheims N.T., 354 note
  size of Bibles, 449 note, 455 note
  Troy's condemnation of Coyne's edition, 419
  Ward's *Errata* criticized by, 332
  White's proposed revision, 497 note
  Witham's version, 350
Cotton manuscripts: names of, 33 note; *see also* Manuscripts
Cotton Psalter, 51
Couley, Robert, 76
Courtney (archbishop), 86 note
Courtney, W. P.: on Hammond, 514
Cousturier, John: edition of Rheims New Test., 271 f.; second edition of Douay Old Test., 306
"Cove and key," 389 note
Coverdale, Myles, 153 ff.
  apostasy of, 153 note, 154 f.
  Bible translated by; *see* Coverdale's Bible
  compulsion in translating, 154 note, 159, 168
  Cranmer and, 156 note
  Cromwell and, 153, 155 and note, 156 notes, 163, 189
  Erasmus' New Testament translated by, 128
  foul language of, 155
  Geneva Bible influenced by, 230
  Grafton and, 163, 170 note
  Great Bible and, 163, 189 f. and note, 192, 199-201, 203
  Grindal and, 156 note
  heretical tenets of, 155 f., 168
  love for the Bible, 153
  Mass derided by, 155 f.
  Matthew's Bible and, 175 f.
  modesty of, 155, 159, 161 note, 163, 168
  New Testament translated by, 168-71: Bonner's assistance on, 191 and note; editions of, 168-71; Rheims New Testament and, 260 note
  on the Vulgate Bible, 169
  retiring character of, 155, 156 note
  Thomas More and, 153 note, 154 and note
Coverdale's Bible, 156-72
  the Apocrypha, 157, 163 and note, 166 f., 208
  Authorized Version and, 311, 317
  the Dedications in, 155, 157, 159-61, 168-70: compared with Taverner's Dedications, 206 note
  editions of, 156-59, 163 note
  illustrations in, 162 and notes
  Matthew's Bible and, 176-78
  the New Testament, 168-71: Bonner's assistance on, 191 and note; editions of, 168-71; Rheims New Testament and, 260 note
  notes in, 168
  Prologues, 155 and note, 157-59, 166-68, 170
  Prayer Book Psalter, 164-66
  renderings in, 164-66
  sources of, 156 f., 158 note, 159, 163 f.
  title page, 162 and note
  translated under compulsion, 154 note, 159, 168
  unsatisfactory character of, 187 f., 234

Cowgle, John, 76
Cox, bishop of Ely: and the Bishops' Bible, 234 note, 237; and the Geneva Bible, 218; on translating the Psalter, 234 note
Coyne's editions of Challoner's revision
Bible of 1811, 392 and note, 394 f.
Bible of 1816, 392, 410 note, 415 and note, 417-20: Troy's condemnation of, 393 f., 417-19
Bible of 1825, 429 f. and notes: and Duffy's New Testament, 464
Bible of 1829, 430, 433 note
Bible of 1833, 430, 435
Bible of 1835, 437: and Brown's New Testament, 465; and Dolman's edition, 464
Bible of 1840, 430, 448
Bible of 1841, 449
Bible of 1844, 430
Bible of 1846, 450, 455
Bible of 1847, 430, 453, 456
Hamil's edition of Haydock's Bible, 427
New Testament of 1811, 363, 392 and note, 395
New Testament of 1820 (noteless), 94, 97, 363, 393 f., 407, 423-27, 430, 432; late reprint of, 427
New Testament of 1825, 431 f.
New Testament of 1826, 433: reimpressions of, 433, 437, 448, 454, 456 and note
New Testament of 1833, 435 note, 448
New Testament of 1834, 433
New Testament of 1835, 433, 437
New Testament of 1837, 433
New Testaments of 1840, 433, 448
New Testament of 1843, 433
New Testament of 1847, 433, 454, 456
the text carefully selected, 472
Cranmer, Thomas
burning of, 191 note
Coverdale and, 156 note
Cromwell and, 179 f. and notes
frontispiece to the Great Bible, 197
Grafton and, 179 f. and notes
Great Bible and, 193
Matthew's Bible and, 179 f. and notes
on pre-Wycliffite versions, 63
on reading the Bible, 63, 187 note
on vernacular versions, 63
Osiander related to, 115 note
Preface to the Great Bible, 63, 73 note, 188, 202 and note: in the Bishops' Bible, 238 and note
project for new "authorized" revision, 189 note, 218
Tremellius and, 117
triumph of Protestantism and, 216
Cranmer's Bible, 187 f., 202, 205; *see also*, Great Bible
Creation, story of: Geddes' disregard for, 380, 382
Creighton, James: and Scarlett's New Testament, 536
Creighton, W., 78
Crickmer, W. B.: version of the New Testament, 546
Criticism, textual: Archbishop Lee on, 101 f.; in Beza's time, 126, 319; in Erasmus' time, 101-103; Kenyon on, 319
Crolly, Approbations by, 93, 430, 438, 470 f.
in Bible of 1845, 450
in Bible of 1851, 464
in Bible of 1852, 465
in Bibles of 1857, 373 note, 414 note, 430, 468, 471, 476
in Bible of 1876, 476 f.
in Bible of 1886, 478
in New Testament of 1851, 464
in New Testament of 1865, 471
Cromwell, Thomas
character of, 188 and note
Collier on, 154 note
Coverdale and, 153-55, 156 notes, 189
Coverdale's Dedication to, 169 f.
Cranmer and, 179 f. and notes
fall of, 197, 202 note, 205
Foxe on, 154 note
and the frontispiece to the Great Bible, 197
Grafton and, 163, 170 note, 179 f. and notes, 189
the Great Bible and, 163, 187 ff., 204
Hoare on, 154 note
knowledge of the New Testament, 154 note, 188 note
Matthew's Bible and, 179 f. and notes
Cromwell's Bible, 73 note, 187, 202 note; *see also* Great Bible
Cross, Richard, 472: edition of MacMahon's revision, 94, 96, 373, 377, 397 note, 417-19: and Coyne's noteless edition, 425 f.; and Hamil's edition of Haydock's Bible, 428
Cross, sign of the: attacked by Cartwright, 277 note
Cross references in the Catholic Board Edition, 406
Cruttwell, Clement, 92
Cucchi, Thaddeus, 115 f. and notes
Cudden, Ambrose: edition of Challoner's New Test., 431
Cue, John: and Scarlett's New Testament, 536 f. and note
Cullen, Approbations by, 470 f.
in Bible of 1856, 471
in Bible of 1857, 468, 471, 473
in Bible of 1864, 473
in Bible of 1873, 474, 477
in New Testament of 1857, 469-71

Cullen, Approbations by (*continued*)
in New Testament of 1866, 470, 473
in New Testament of 1874, 475, 477
in New Testament of 1875, 475, 477
in New Testament of 1876, 476
in New Testament of 1899, 483
Cumming, James: printer of MacNamara's edition, 415-17, 418 note
Cummiskey, Eugene (printer): editions of Challoner's revision, 369, 449 and note
Cunnington, E. E.: revision of the Revised Version, 576
Curetonian Syriac text, 557
Curoe, Daniel: on the reading of the Bible, 440; Preface to the New Testament of 1839, 440
Curtis, Patrick: Approbations by, 431, 433, 454
Cuthbert, St., 42, 44 f.: destruction of statue of, 217; on St. Bede's death, 21
Cutler, Ethel: and The Shorter Bible, 592
Cyril, St.: on the Eucharist, 288

Daily Readings from the New Testament, 493
Damasus (pope): Erasmus on, 418 note; revision of the Bible, 409
Daniel, Book of: Caedmon's paraphrase on, 17, 18 note; Purvey's notes on, 77 note; St. Jerome's Prologue to, 78
Dano-Saxon, meaning of the term, 15 note
Dano-Saxon versions, 43, 47
Danvers, Anne, 74
Danvers, Thomas and William, 74
Davidson, A. B.: and the Revised Version, 553
Davidson, Samuel: version of the New Testament, 546
Davies (bishop) and the Bishops' Bible, 237
Daye, John (printer): edition of Matthew's Bible, 181; edition of Taverner's version, 213 f. and note
Daye and Seres (printers): edition of Taverner's version, 213 note; edition of Tyndale's New Testament, 101 note, 141, 151 note
"Deacon," Fulke on the use of, 280 f.
Dean, Joseph, 500 note
Deissmann, 342
Deluge, the: Geddes on, 382
Denvir, Approbations by
in Bibles of 1839 and 1841, 439 and note, 449
in Bibles of 1846, 450 f., 455, 471, 474
in Bible of 1849, 455
in Bible of 1851, 464
in Bibles of 1852, 465 f.
in Bible of 1853, 467
in Bible of 1869, 471, 474
Denvir, Approbations by (*continued*)
in New Testament of 1836, 438
in New Testament of 1839, 440
in New Testament of 1846, 452, 455
in New Testaments of 1851, 465
Denvir, editions of the Bible and New Testament, 93, 421, 439 note: called Douay Version, 495
Deuteronomy: Purvey's notes on, 77 note; Tyndale's translation of, 133
"Devil in the Lord's Prayer," 570 and note
Dialogue, The (More), 63, 65, 137, 146, 150, 154
Dibdin, Thomas, 91 note
Dickinson, Rodolphus: version of the New Testament, 543
Dictionary of National Biography, 509 and note
Diodati, Italian version by, 452
Disraeli, Isaac: Geddes criticized by, 380 note
Dissectionists, the: Geddes' contempt for, 383
Dissenters, 513
Divergences in Catholic Bibles, 391-94, 455-57, 470-72, 476 f., 486 f.
Divine right of kings, Douay note on the, 303
Dixon, on Tyndale's New Testament, 148 f.
Dobneck, Johannes; *see* Cochlaeus
Dodd, C.: on Worthington, 300; translator of Rheims-Douay version, 252 f. and note
Doddridge, Philip, 522 f., 529: paraphrase on the New Test., 522 f.
Dolefull Dove, The, 97
Dolman editions of Challoner's revision, 464, 466 f.
Dominicans, the: and Spencer, 498
Dore, J. H.
the Bishop's Bible, 238
burning of Tyndale's New Testament, 145
Coverdale's Dedications, 161 note
Coverdale's translation, 154 note
Douay version of the Psalms, 299
editions of Coverdale's Bibles and New Testaments, 171 note
Foxe's unreliability, 193
the Geneva Bible, 225
inconsistency of heretics, 246
on Tyndale, 134
Rheims New Testament, 275: accuracy of, 262
Tyndale's New Testament, 145, 149
unreliability of title pages, 151, 213 f.
Wycliffe's heretical tenets, 84
Dore of Holy Scripture, The, 76
Dornwillium, William: Gaelic translation of the Bible by, 451 note
Dorpius, Martin, 100
Dort, Synod of, 223

Douay, English college at, 251 f.: and Challoner, 346, 353, 355 note; and Witham, 346 and note, 353, 355 note
"Douay Bible," 249
Douay Bible House, 491 note: edition of Challoner's revision, 360 note, 369, 491 note, 493 f.
Douay Diaries: and Martin's *Discoverie,* 273 note; on Robert Witham, 346 note; and the translation of the Rheims N.T., 251-53
"Douay New Testament," 249 note, 427, 495
Douay Old Testament, 294-306, 504
- appearance of, 305 f. and note
- Approbation in, 294 f., 306
- Authorized Version and, 264 and note
- defects of, 297 f.
- delay of publication, 294 f.
- edition of the Vulgate used for, 295 f. and note
- final revision of, 295 f. and notes
- history of the translation, 249, 294
- Nary's criticism of, 340
- notes and annotations, 253, 300-304
- omissions in, 296 f., 359 f.
- Preface to, 295 f., 651 ff.
- preliminary matter, 295 f.
- the Psalter in, 297-99
- title page, 294
- translators of; *see* Rhemists, the
- second edition of, 306
- supplementary pieces, 304 f.

Douglass (bishop) and Geddes, 384 f.
Doyle edition of Challoner's revision, 369
Driver, S. R.: and the Revised Version, 553
Drusius, 118, 136
Ducarel, A. C., 91
Duff, on the identity of John Hollybusche, 170
Duffey editions
- Bible of 1847, 359, 453, 456
- Bible of 1857, 468
- Bible of 1861, 472
- Bible of 1865, 471, 473
- Bible of 1867, 471, 473 f.
- Bible of 1888, 478
- New Testaments of 1851, 464
- New Testament of 1853, 464, 467 f.
- New Testament of 1857, 468 f.
- New Testament of 1858, 469
- New Testaments of 1859 and 1865, 471
- New Testaments of 1874, 475

Dugdale, *Monasticon,* 64
Du Hamel, 396 note
Dunigan, Edward: edition of Haydock's Bible, 370, 466 and note; and Kenrick's version, 459
Dunstan, St., 61
Durham Book; *see* Lindisfarne Gospels
Durham Ritual, the, 50
"Durham's unworthy Dean," 217
Durrow, Book of, 4

Eadfrid, 18
Eadfrith, 7, 42, 44, 50
Eadgar, King, 54
Eadie, John: the Bishops' Bible, 243 note; Coverdale's Bible, 164 note; the practice of glossing, 11; Rheims New Testament, 260 note; versions of Jonas, 178
Eadmer, 46
Eadwine, 56 note, 57: prayer for the recitation of the breviary, 58 note
Earle, John: Geddes criticized by, 381 note
Ecclesiae regimen, 76 and note
Ecclesiastes, Book of: Purvey's notes on, 78 note; title in the Bishops' Bible, 239 f.
Ecclesiasticus, Book of: Purvey's notes on, 78 note; Purvey's rejection of, 76 note; Whitaker's rejection of, 282
Edgar, Andrew: on the Douay version of the Psalms, 299
Edinburgh edition of 1792, 387-91, 393, 399
Edward VI (of England)
- Becke's Dedication to, 181 f.
- books owned by, 112 note
- Castalio's Dedication to, 119
- childhood drawings of, 171
- coronation of, 198
- Coverdale and, 155
- Coverdale's Dedication to, 159-61
- Taverner's licence to preach, 205

Edwardine Prayer Book, controversy over, 216-18
Egbert, 44
Egyptology, Sharpe's interest in, 541
Eichhorn, 383
"Elders"; *see* Presbyter
Eleazar, deed of, 223
Elizabeth (queen)
- accession of, 219
- Beza's Dedication to, 121 note
- Bodley's licence to print the Geneva Bible, 221
- books owned by, 117 note, 171
- coronation of, 219
- Coverdale and, 155
- death of, 314
- Dedications to, 121 note, 221
- demand for large Bibles, 187
- Foxe's Dedication to, 63 and note, 287
- Geneva Bible dedicated to, 221
- need for a new translation, 308
- refutation of the Rhemists and, 276
- the revision of the Bible and, 551

Elizabeth (*continued*)
Sixtus V and, 302 note
supposed plot against, 274, 302 and note
Tremellius and, 117
Ellicott, C. J.: and Newman, 553 f. note; on the Greek Text of the Revised Version, 554-56, 563 note, 564 and note; on the Rheims and Authorized versions, 315 f.; on Tyndale's version, 135; and the Revised Version, 552 ff.
Ely, Synod of, 146 and note
Emphatic Bible, The, 546
Endhover, Christophell, 131 note, 150
England: bombing of, 488; Saxon invasion of, 3
English (language), development of, 29 note, 69
English Hexapla, The, 73 and note
Ephesus, Second Council of, 290
Episcopacy, Cartwright's attack on, 276 note
Epistles, the: Cajetan's commentary on, 106 note, 107; difficulty of, 589; for Sundays, 98 f., 410
Erasmus, Desiderius, 100-105
Authorized Version influenced by, 318 and note
Bulkeley and, 290 note
English versions influenced by, 309
Greek New Testament by, 100-103, 104 note
heretical tendencies of, 105
Latin New Testament by, 100 f., 103-105, 112 f. and note: English translation of, 128, 203; and the Great Bible, 189, 203; Gualter's revision of, 112 and note; and the Tigurine Bible, 112 f. and note; and Tyndale's version, 133; with Tyndale's version, 141
Laurence's criticism of, 244 f.
on Pope Damasus' approval of St. Jerome, 418 note
Tunstall and, 147
Errata of the Protestant Bible, 331-34: Brown's attack on, 281; in Sadlier Bibles, 466
Escalente, 113
Esdras, Fourth Book of: Goodspeed's translation of, 594 f.; in Castalio's version, 120
Esdras, Third and Fourth Books of
Challoner's note on, 359
Coverdale's version of, 157
in Bishop's Bible, 240
in Douay Old Testament, 299 and note
in Junius' edition, 127
in Matthew's Bible, 184 f.
Taverner's version of, 208
Wycliffite versions and, 76 note, 79 note
Esther, Book of: Aelfric's translation of, 23; in Bishops' Bible, 237
Estius, William, 294, 396 and note
Ethelreda, St., 61
Ethelstan (king), translation attributed to, 23
Ethilwold, 42, 50
Eucharist, the
Beza's opinion concerning, 125
Fulke's denial of, 288
Luther on, 348
Purvey's heretical teaching, 77
Rhemists' note on, 287 f.
teaching of Matthew's Bible regarding, 183 f.
teaching of the Geneva Bible regarding, 227 f.
Woodhead and Walker on, 518 f.
Eunuchus: Coverdale's translation of, 164, 169; Tyndale's translation of, 211
Eusebian (semi-Arian), 525
Eusebian Canons, 41
Eusebius: *Historia ecclesiastica,* 185; and the revision of the Greek text, 561
Everard, Patrick: Approbation by, 431
Exodus, Book of: Alfred's translation of, 22; Caedmon's paraphrase of, 17, 18 note; Douay Version notes on, 301; Parker's revision of, 237
Eyre, Charles, 540 f.: version of the epistles, 540
Ezechiel, Book of: in the Polychrome Bible, 550 note; Purvey's notes on, 77 note

Faber, F. W.: the beauty of the Authorized Version, 322
Faber, Jacques, 99
Faerman, 47 f. and note, 51
Fagan, P.: and Horrabin's edition, 423
Fagius, 216
Fairbairn, 103
Fall, the: Geddes on, 382
Farely, John, 339
Farley, John: *Imprimatur* by, 485, 491
"Father of English biblical criticism," 514
Fathers of the Church: and the Reformers, 284; Vulgate text used by, 290
Feckenham (abbot) and Fulke, 278
Fell, John: and Woodhead's *Paraphrase,* 514, 516-19
"Fell's Paraphrase," 519
Fenton, Ferrar: version of the New Testament, 546, 549, 586
Ferguson, R. (printer): sixth edition of Rheims N.T., 354 note
Field, F.: and the Revised Version, 553
Fielde, John, 278 note
Fisher, Henry: and Gibson's edition, 412-14
Fisher, John: and Erasmus, 100-102; on the reading of Scripture, 236 and note; Penitential Psalms by, 97 f. and note; and Sebastian Muenster, 114

Fitzhenry, Robert, 225 and note
Fitzpatrick, H. (printer): edition of MacMahon's revision, 377
Five-mile Act, 513
Fogarty, M., 340
Fogny, John: printer of Martin's *Discoverie,* 273; printer of Rheims New Testament, 254, 487
Foot, Isaac, 132 note
Ford, R. E. and T. F.: and the Letchworth New Test., 599
Forshall and Madden
  Anglo-Norman versions, 9
  Anglo-Saxon Psalters, 58
  Anglo-Saxon versions of the Gospels, 39
  the "Paris Psalter," 19 note
  Psalter of St. Augustine, 53
  Wycliffe's translation, 67 f., 71, 74 and note
  Wycliffite versions, 78: effect of, 68 f.
Fothergill, John: and the Quakers' Bible, 529
Foulis, Martin accused by, 274
Foxe, John, 39
  Brewer's denunciation of, 144, 192
  Dedication to Queen Elizabeth, 63 and note
  dishonesty of, 144, 192 f.
  edition of Anglo-Saxon Gospels, 21, 31, 34 and note, 39, 63 and note
  Erasmus and, 101
  Grafton's imprisonment, 189 note
  the Great Bible, 190-93, 199 note
  Littledale's denunciation of, 144
  the Lollards, 86
  Matthew's "Table of Pryncypal Matters," 183
  on John Purvey, 75 and note
  on Taverner, 205 note
  on Tunstall, 147
  pre-Wycliffite versions, 63
  "Thomas Matthew," 158 note, 175 f.
  Tyndale's translation of the Old Test., 133 f. note, 158 note, 175
  vernacular versions, 63
  Wycliffite version, 87 note
Francis I (of France) and the printing of the Great Bible, 190 f. and notes
Frankfort, controversy at, 216 and note, 218
Frederic IV (Count Palatine), 127
French, taught in schools, 29 note, 69
French versions of the Bible, 64, 69: by de Beausobre and Lenfant, 521
Frith, John, 134
Froben (printer) and Erasmus, 100
Froschover, Christopher: editions of Coverdale's Bible, 156-58 and note
Froude, James, 62: on Tyndale's version, 135
Fry, Francis: edition of Tyndale's version, 130 note, 150 note
Fryer, William: and Geddes, 384 f.
Fulke, William, 278 ff.
  Bristow and, 253
  Campion's disputations with, 278 f. and note
  Cartwright's *Confutation* and, 277 note, 278, 286
  dishonesty of, 287
  edition of the Bishops' Bible and Rheims New Testament, 242 note, 244, 264, 286-89: and Protestant edition of 1834, 435, 437
  epitaph for, 278 note
  Geddes' criticism of, 380
  the Great Bible, 201
  his *Defense,* 99, 280 ff.
  Isidore Clario misinterpreted by, 116
  Luther's rejection of St. James's Epistle, 282, 287
  Martin's controversy with, 275 and note, 278 ff.
  Martin's *Discoverie* reprinted by, 280
  on the divine right of kings, 283 f.
  on the Eucharist, 288
  the Protestant editions attacked by Martin, 285 note
  St. Ignatius misquoted by, 284
  St. Jerome condemned by, 287
  Sander and, 287
  virulent language of, 278 f., 286
  the Vulgate condemned by, 99
  works of, 279 note
Fullarton editions of Haydock's Bible, 397, 450, 466
Fuller, Thomas
  Geddes' criticism of, 380
  on Cartwright's *Confutation,* 278 note
  on Richard Bristow, 253
  on the demand for revision, 551 f. note
  on Tunstall, 147
  Rheims New Testament criticized by, 268

Gaelic versions of the Bible, 541 f. and notes
Gagg of the New Gospell, The, 292
Gairdner, James
  Bale denounced by, 144
  burning of Tyndale's New Testament, 145 note
  disorders caused by the Great Bible, 195
  effects of the Reformation, 148 note
  on Cromwell, 188
  on Lollardy, 85, 136 f.
  on versions of the Bible, 600
  Tyndale's heretical spirit, 141 f., 149 note
  Tyndale's translation, 135, 137
  Wycliffe's translation, 67 note
  Wycliffite version, 85, 136 f.
Gandolphy, Peter, 398
Ganss, H. J.: notes in Brepols' Bibles, 484, 493

Gardiner, Stephen: Bucer's controversy with, 138, 283; and the burning of Cranmer, 191 note; defamed by Foxe, 191 note; on private interpretation, 140; and the printing of the Great Bible, 192
Garvais, Henry, 191 note
Gasquet (cardinal) on pre-Wycliffite Bibles, 65 f.
Geddes, Alexander
- the Apocrypha, 120
- authority of Scripture, 383
- Authorized Version criticized by, 323
- Bellarmine and Becan criticized by, 383
- biblical work of, 379-85, 497
- Castalio's version praised by, 120
- contempt for Old Testament narratives, 381-83
- Cotton's praise of, 385 note
- death of, 384 f.
- difficulties with ecclesiastical authorities, 379 f., 384 f.
- "dissectionists" criticized by, 383
- Earle's criticism of, 381 note
- epitaph for, 384
- infallibility of the Church, 383
- inspiration of Scripture denied by, 380-82
- Pagninus and, 111, 114
- rational faith of, 383 f. and note
- Rheims New Testament criticized by, 380
- Sebastian Muenster's version praised by, 114
- Tigurine Bible praised by, 112 f.
- tribute to, 385
- Tyndale's version, 135
- works of, 379-81

"Gelded"; *see Eunuchus*
Genebrard, 110: on Castalio's version, 120 note; on translating the Bible, 340
Genesis, Book of
- Ainsworth's version of, 511
- Caedmon's paraphrase of, 16-18
- Confraternity Edition of, 505 f.
- Douay notes on, 301
- Heinfetter's version of, 544
- Junius' commentary on, 127
- Parker's revision of, 237
- Tremellius' heading for, 118
- Tyndale's Preface to, 130 note

Geneva: Calvinism and, 216 f.; English Reformers at, 216
Geneva Bible, 73 note, 216-33
- Alleluia omitted in, 285 note
- the Apocrypha, 223
- apologia for the version, 221 f.
- Authorized Version and, 311, 315 f. and notes, 323
- Beza's influence on, 309, 317
- Bishops' Bible and, 242 f. and note

Geneva Bible (*continued*)
- Calvinistic notes in, 234
- dedication to Elizabeth, 221
- editions of, 222 note, 223, 225, 229 note, 232 f. and note, 281 note: attacked by Martin, 245, 282, 285 and note
- Great Bible and, 230
- heretical teaching in, 223, 224 note, 225-29
- influence of, 229 f.
- italics used in, 324, 350 note
- James I's condemnation of, 309
- Martin's criticism of, 332
- notes in, 222 f., 227-31, 309
- the Old Testament, 220-23, 232 f.
- popularity of, 229 ff., 238
- printing of, 221
- the Psalter, 223, 233
- replaced by Luther's version, 274
- revised New Testament, 224-29: editions of, 230-33; foreign translations of, 232; Tomson's editions of, 123 and note, 129, 230-32
- revisers for, 216-19: Castalio condemned by, 120; plot against the rulers, 302
- Rheims New Testament influenced by, 260 note
- the text, 222 f., 226 f.
- type used in, 222 and note, 233 and note
- unsatisfactory character of, 234
- Whittingham's New Testament, 219 f., 226 and note, 228 note
- with Tomson's New Testament, 129

George, William, 278 note
German editions, 64, 69
Gibbons, James (cardinal): edition of the Bible (1899), 479, 482 f., 494; on the divine inspiration of the Bible, 482
Gibson, William (bishop), 93: Approbations by, 422, 434; editions of the Bible, 393, 412-15; and Syers' Bible, 399 f.
Giffard, William: metrical version of the Apocalypse, 10
Gifford, list of English versions, 91
Gigot, Francis, 500 note
Gilby and the Geneva Bible, 219 note
Gildas, 54
Gill editions of Challoner's revision
- Bible of 1882, 477
- Bible of 1885, 478
- New Testaments of 1876, 476 f.
- New Testament of 1881, 477 f.
- New Testament of 1885, 453 note
- New Testament of 1899, 483
- New Testament of 1912, 453 note, 455

Gillet, T.: printer of Scarlett's New Testament, 535

Gillow, Joseph: on William Reynolds, 253
Glanrikerd, lord of, 278 note
Glas, John, 537 note
Glasgow edition of the Bible (1830), 437
Glassites, 537 note
Glossa interlinearis, 11, 57, 78 note
Glossa ordinaria, 11 and note, 57, 78 note
Glossing: practice of, 11-13; purpose of, 12 f.
Glover, V.: corrector of Gibson's edition, 413
Goade: and Cartwright's *Confutation,* 277 note; disputations with Campion, 278 note
Godemann, 6 and note
Godfried van der Hagen, 132
Golden Legend, the, 222 note
Goodier, 500 note
Goodman, Christopher: and the Geneva Bible, 217 f.
Goodspeed, Edgar J.: on the literary style of the New Test., 581, 593; on the private versions, 509; and the Revised Standard Version, 580 f., 592 f.; time for reading the New Test., 593 and note; version of the Bible, 592-95
Gordon, Alexander: and Goodspeed's work, 594; on Newcome's New Test., 534
Gordon, W.: Fullarton's edition revised by, 450
Gospel of Nicodemus, 10, 33
Gospels, the
  Anglo-Saxon versions of, 7, 9, 31 ff., 64 f.: Aelfric on, 23 and note
  Bilton's version of, 549 f., 587, 599 f.
  Brameld's version of, 545
  Cajetan's commentary on, 106 f.
  Campbell's version of, 523
  Clarke's *Paraphrase* on, 526
  composition of, 445 f., 458 f.
  glossing of, 12 f.
  Kenrick's version of, 458-60, 462
  Lingard's version of, 442-47
  Norton's version of, 546
  Semitic origin of, 596
  Spencer's version of, 498
  Torrey's version of, 595 f.
  Whittingham's titles for, 220
Gospels for Sunday, 410: Anglo-Saxon version of, 10; Lefèvre's Latin version, 99; list of; *see* Tables of Epistles and Gospels; versions of, 98 note
Gospels of St. Chad, 47 note
Gowgle, John, 76
Grafton
  Bibles printed by, 189 note
  Coverdale and, 163, 170 note
  Cranmer and, 179 f.
  Cromwell and, 163, 170 note, 179 f. and notes, 189
Grafton (*continued*)
  edition of Coverdale's New Test., 169 f. and note
  edition of Erasmus' New Test. in English, 128
  Great Bible and, 163, 189
  imprisonment of, 189 note
  Matthew's Bible and, 179 f., 189 note
  on royal licences, 188 note
  on the printing of the Great Bible, 192 note
  printer of Matthew's Bible, 189 note
  printer of the Great Bible, 189 note, 202
  translation of the Psalms by, 97
Granville, 161
Great Bible, 187-204
  the Apocrypha, 200, 208
  "authorized," 202 and note, 313
  Authorized Version and, 311 and note, 313, 317
  Bishops' Bible and, 204, 235 f. and note, 238, 242 f.
  Bonner and, 190 f. and note
  condemnation of, 234
  and condemnation of Tyndale's version, 204
  contents of, 198 f.
  Coverdale and, 163, 177, 189 f. and note, 192, 199-203
  Coverdale's intended notes, 199 f.
  Cranmer and, 193
  Cranmer's Preface to, 63, 188, 202 and note: in Bishops' Bible, 238 and note
  Cromwell and, 163, 187 ff., 204
  editions of, 199, 202-204, 281 note: attacked by Martin, 245, 284 and note
  Erasmus' version and, 189, 203
  frontispiece to, 162 and note, 196-200
  Geneva Bible based on, 230
  Grafton and, 163, 189
  Henry VIII and, 194-98, 201, 204
  in the Churches, 191 and note, 194-96, 202 and note
  Marler and, 204
  Martin's condemnation of, 282, 332
  Matthew's Bible and, 189, 203
  Muenster version and, 189, 203
  New Testament, 200 f.
  notes in, 203 f. and note
  Parker's revision of, 384 and note
  price of, 193, 204
  printed by Grafton, 189 note, 202
  printed by Marler, 189 note, 193
  printed by Regnault, 191
  printing of, 190-92
  reception of, 192 ff.
  sources of, 189 f. and note, 203
  Taverner's version and, 205, 213
  title page of, 196-200

Great Bible (*continued*)
Tyndale's version and, 180 and note, 189, 201
Vulgate Bible and, 189 f. and note, 203
Whitchurch's editions of, 311 note
Greek, knowledge of, 340 f.
Greek article: and the Authorized Version, 321 and note; the Rhemists' attention to, 260-63; Taverner's rendering of, 210
Greek idiom and English, 535 f.
Greek manuscripts, diversity of readings, 405
Greek text: Antiochian revision of, 557, 559, 561 f., 564 note; by Westcott and Hort, 556-65, 570-73; for the Revised Version, 554-65, 570-73
Green, J. R.: on St. Bede, 20
Green, William: Approbation by, 356, 423
Greer, Robert: edition of Challoner's New Test., 439, 449
Gregory I, St. (pope): books sent by, 4 and note, 38, 53; *De cura pastorali,* 22 and note
Gregory VII (pope), 231
Gregory VIII (pope), 51
Gregory XI (pope), 86
Gregory XIII (pope): Allen and, 251 note; Junius' attack on, 127
Grier, Richard: "the Rhemish Jesuits," 277 note; Rheims New Test. misrepresented by, 418 and note; and Ward's *Errata,* 332 and note
Griesbach edition of the Greek text, 545: and Brameld's version, 545; and Kenrick, 462; and Newcome's New Testament, 534; and Sharpe's revision, 541, 547; and Taylor's revision, 547 f.
Griffin (cardinal): *Imprimatur* for Knox's version, 504 and note; Preface to Knox's version, 503
Grimbald, St., 61
Grindal: Bodley's printing of the Geneva Bible, 221 note; Coverdale and, 156 note
Grosart, on Bilson's lack of judgment, 292
Grotius, Hugo: on the accuracy of the Vulgate, 262, 410 note
Gruber, 137
Gualter, R., 112 and note
Guest (bishop) and the Bishops' Bible, 237
Guppy, H.: on Coverdale's character, 156 note
Guthlac, St., 52
Guyse, John, 423 f.: paraphrase on the New Test., 524

Hack, P. and F.: printers of Horrabin's edition, 423
Hackney, academy at, 532, 539
Hagiographa, in the Great Bible, 200
Hales, on Hereford's translation, 71 note
Hall, on Tyndale's translations, 134
Hall, Rowland, printer of the Geneva Bible, 221
Hallam, Authorized Version criticized by, 323
Hamil, edition of Haydock's Bible, 397 and note, 427 f.
Hammond, Henry: and Allestry, 517; paraphrase of the New Test., 514 f. and note
Hampden-Cook, Ernest: and Weymouth's version, 592
Hampton Court Conference, 308 f. and notes, 312, 314
Harding, John, 312, 328
Harewood, 47 and note
Harison, William, 295
Harmony of the Gospels: by Wycliffe, 68; in Catholic Board Edition, 405
Harris, F.: and The Shorter Bible, 592
Harris, Rendel: criticism of the Revised Version, 576
Harrison, Robert, 225 and note
Harrowing of Hell, The, 33
Harsley, editor of the *Psalterium Triplex,* 56
Hart, heresy of the Lollards, 85
Harwood, Edward: version of the New Testament, 528 f., 532, 543
Hastings, Selina: and the Methodist movement, 533
Haudecoeur, on Witham's character, 346 note
Haupt, Paul: the Polychrome Bible of, 550 and note
Haweis, Thomas: version of the New Testament, 533
Hawkins, John, 97
Hay (bishop): Bible of, 392 notes; and Geddes, 379
Haydock, Leo, 395
Haydock, Thomas (printer), 395, 427
Haydock's Bible, 95, 363, 394-98
Dunigan's edition of, 466 and note
editions of, 360, 368-70, 397 and notes
Fullarton's editions of, 397, 450, 466
Hamil's edition of, 397 and notes, 427 f.
Husenbeth's edition of, 397, 466 and note
MacMahon's revisions and, 378, 392 f., 397, 457, 470
misprint in, 450
notes in, 396 and note
omissions in, 360, 368 f., 398, 450
and Richardson's Bible, 454, 470
Hayes, *Imprimatur* of: in Bible of 1938, 490 and note; in New Testament of 1919, 487; in New Testament of 1935, 489 f.
Hayman, Henry: version of the epistles, 589
Heath, Nicholas: revision of the Great Bible, 202 f. and note
Heath and Preston, printers of Newcastle New Test., 398

Heberden, William, 544: version of the epistles, 544
Hebrew: necessity of knowing, 340 f.; tenses in, 545 and note; Young's notions about, 545 f.
Hebrew Bible, numbering of the psalms in, 165 note, 166; *see also* Masoretic
Hebrews, Epistle to the
  authorship of: Cajetan on, 106; Great Bible on, 201; Tyndale on, 138; Whittingham on, 220
  in the American Standard Version, 579
  title of: in the Great Bible, 201; in Whittingham's New Test., 220
  Tyndale's Prologue to, 138
Heinfetter, Herman: version of Genesis and the New Test., 544
Helvidius, St. Jerome's letter to, 320 note
Henry IV (emperor), excommunication of, 231
Henry II (of England), 51
Henry VIII (of England)
  books owned by, 112 notes
  Coverdale's Dedications to, 155, 157, 159 f. and note, 161 note, 168 f.
  Coverdale's title page and, 126
  death of, 216
  "Defender of the Faith," 142, 146, 155
  divorce opposed by Tyndale, 137 note, 168, 180 note
  Erasmus and, 100 and note
  the frontispiece to the Great Bible, 162, 197 f.
  the Great Bible and, 194-98, 201, 204
  Lee's correspondence with, 142
  Luther and, 142 f.
  Matthew's Bible dedicated to, 179
  on private interpretation, 140
  progress toward totalitarianism, 202 and note
  "staying of the Bible," 189 note
  Taverner's Dedication to, 206 f.
  totalitarianism of, 206
  Tyndale's New Test. condemned by, 137 and note
  Tyndale's opposition to, 137 and note, 168, 180 note
Henry III (of France), Genebrard and, 340
Hentine, John de: edition of the Vulgate, 251, 296 note
Heptateuch, 10, 23, 64 f.: Tyndale's version of, 163
Herbert, William, 91 note
Herder Book Co., edition of the Bible, 491 note
Herders (Freiburg) edition of the Greek N.T., 565 note
Hereford, on Tunstall, 147
Heretics: inconsistency of, 266, 273 f., 281 f., 285 f. and note; Ward's denunciation of, 333; *see also* Reformers
Hermit of Hampole, 8, 26-28
Herod, Macrobius' quip about, 210
Herodotus, 382 note
Herry, Robert F., 225 and note
Hester, edition of Coverdale's Bible, 158-60
Hewett, W. H.: illustrated edition of Challoner's N.T., 463
Hewlett, John: Bible published by, 92
Heylyn, John: version of the New Testament, 528
Hickes, George, 16 note
Hierarchy, Catholic: restoration of, 464
Higden, *Polychronicon* by, 29, 69
Highton, H.: revision of the Authorized Version, 548
Hilda, St., 16
Hinnage, Thomas, 278 note
Historia Eliensis, 22 note, 37
Hitchyns, William, 146; *see* Tyndale
Hoadly and Pyle, 527
Hoare, H. W.
  Coverdale's Dedications, 160
  Cromwell's intrigue, 154 note
  the Edwardine councilors, 218 f.
  exploitation of the Church, 218 f.
  frontispiece to the Great Bible, 197
  the Geneva Bible, 228 note
  the Great Bible and disorders in the churches, 195
  Wycliffe's heretical tenets, 85
Holbein, frontispiece to the Great Bible, 162, 196 f., 200
Hollybushe, John, 170 and note
"Holocaust," Rhemists' use of, 268
Homer, 380
Hooke, S. H.: and the Basic English version, 597
Hooper, bishop of Gloucester, 175 f.
Hopkins, John: metrical version of the Psalms, 233, 241
Hopton, Owen, 278 note
Horne, Hartwell: on John of Trevisa, 30; the Rheims New Test. criticized by, 268
Horrabin, Richard, 423 note: edition of Challoner's revision, 363, 394, 403, 407
Hort, A. J.
  edition of the Greek New Testament, 556 ff.
  the Greek text for the Revised Version, 556-65, 570-73, 582
  Introduction to the Greek New Test., 556-58, 563-65, 572
  on John 7:53–8:11, 573 note
  on the last chapter of St. Mark, 572
  the Revised Version and, 552-54, 556 ff.
Hotchyn, William; *see* Tyndale

Hoxton, Woodhead and Walker at, 515 f.
Hudleston, Roger: edition of Rheims N.T., 352 note, 487
Huetius, 110, 114
Hugh of Lincoln, St., 58
Hughes, Approbations by: in Bible of 1847, 453; in Bibles of 1852, 466 and note; in Bibles of 1853, 467; in Cummiskey's New Testament (1840), 449 and note; in the "Catholic Family Bible," 469
Hugo à S. Charo, 220 note
Huguenots, the, 122
Humphry, W. G.: on the Revised Version, 564 notes; and the Revised Version, 552
Hunt, on St. Aldhelm, 20
Huntingdon, countess of: and the Methodist movement, 533
Hurter, on Pagninus, 109
Husenbeth editions of Haydock's Bible, 397, 466 and note
Huss, John: and Wycliffe's translation, 67
Hussey, T. J.: revision of the Authorized Version, 548
Hyll, William (printer): edition of Matthew's Bible, 162 note, 181-83; edition of Taverner's version, 213
Hytchins, William; *see* Tyndale

Ignatius, St.: Martin and Fulke on, 283 f. and note
Illustrations in
  Anglo-Saxon manuscripts, 5 f., 10, 12
  Anglo-Saxon Psalters, 53, 55 and note
  Authorized Version, 313
  Bishops' Bible, 23-40 and note
  Brepols' Bibles, 485
  Coverdale's Bible, 162 and notes
  Coyne's 1811 editions of the Bible, 394 f., 418 note
  Cromwell's Bible, 162 and note
  edition of Fulke's New Testament, 289
  fifth edition of Rheims New Test., 351 f.
  fourth edition of Rheims New Test., 271
  Geneva Bible, 221, 224
  Great Bible, 162 and note, 196-200, 204
  Jugge's edition of Tyndale's New Test., 151
  Lewis' edition of Wycliffe's version, 72 f. note
  Lindisfarne Gospels, 41-44
  MacMahon's revisions, 375
  Matthew's Bible, 177, 182
  New York edition of 1850, 463
  Newcastle New Testament (1812), 398
  Psalterium Triplex, 56 f. and notes
  Queen Mary's Psalter, 61 and note
  Sadlier Bible of 1853, 467
  sixth edition of Rheims N.T., 354
  Whittingham's New Testament, 219
"Immaculate Bible," the, 327
Imposition of hands, Woodhead and Walker on, 519 and note
Imprimatur; see Approbations
Ina (king), 35
Independents
  at Amsterdam, 512
  Belsham and, 539
  Canne and, 512
  Doddridge and, 522
  Guyse and, 523
  Presbyterianism and, 522
Infallibility of the Church, Geddes on, 383
Inquisition and the Great Bible, 191 and notes
Inspiration of the Bible, Geddes' contempt for, 380, 382 and note
International Council of Religious Education, 579 f.
Interpretation of the Bible: Cajetan on, 108; the Geneva Bible on, 228; Pighius on, 291; Purvey on, 77; Surius on, 249
Ireland, Approbations by Bishops of, 378
  Bible of 1857, 471
  Bible of 1888, 478
  New Testament of 1825, 431
  New Testament of 1826, 433
  New Testament of 1847, 454
  New Testament of 1874, 475
Irish versions of the Bible, 451 f. and notes
Isaacs, J.
  the Douay Bible, 304
  Douay version of the Psalms, 298
  introduction of "Jehovah," 136
  Rheims New Testament, 260-63 notes
  Tyndale's heretical spirit, 142
  Wycliffe's translation, 72
Isagoge, 111
Isaias, Book of: in the Polychrome Bible, 550 note; Purvey's notes on, 77 note, 80 note
Itala version, Kenrick on, 461
Italian editions, 64
"Italic" version of the Bible, 409
Italics, use of, 324 f. and notes, 350 note
  by Challoner, 367, 370
  by Witham, 349 f.
  in the Authorized Version, 166, 324 f., 566
  in the fifth edition of Rheims N.T., 367
  in the Geneva Bible, 324, 350 note
  in the Revised Version, 566, 568

Jackson, printer of Bramston's edition, 414
Jacobson (bishop) and "Fell's Paraphrase," 519
James, Epistle of: Luther's rejection of, 282, 287
James I (of England): and the Authorized Version, 308-10; Dedication to, 314; Geneva Bible denounced by, 222 f., 229, 309; Psalter translated by, 309 note

James II (of England): and Baxter, 513; and Walker, 514-17
James, Montague, 10: on Wycliffe's translation, 71
James, Thomas, 314
Jane Grey, 61
Jane Seymour (queen), 160
Januarius, St., 45
Jeffreys and Baxter, 513
"Jehovah": Geddes on, 381; in Spurrell's version, 549; in the American Standard Version, 579; Isaacs on, 136; Tyndale's introduction of the word, 136
Jenkins, R. C., 108 f.
Jennings, David, 529
Jennings, John: academy of, 522, 529
Jeremias, Book of: Rolle's paraphrase of, 27
Jerome, St.
- the Apocrypha and, 185
- asterisks and obeli inserted by, 54
- Bois's defense of, 104, 123
- Cajetan and, 105 f.
- Erasmus and, 102 f.
- Erasmus' edition of, 100 note
- Fulke's condemnation of, 287
- Greek text translated by, 320 and note
- on the purity of the Vulgate, 320 note
- Prefaces of, 41
- revision of the Bible, 409: approved by Pope Damasus, 418 note
- revisions of the Psalter, 56 note, 58; *see also* Psalter
- Society of, 486

Jesuits, Rheims New Test. attributed to, 277 note
Job, Book of
- Aelfric's version of, 23 f.
- Beza's translation of, 122 and note
- Cajetan's commentary on, 107
- Fenton's version of, 586
- in Basic English, 597
- in the Authorized Version, 312
- Kenrick's version of, 459
- Muenster's version of, 114 note
- Purvey's gloss on, 76
- Rolle's version of, 27
- St. Jerome's Prologue to, 78

John XXIII (pope), 86
John Chrysostom, St., 194, 557: on reading the Bible, 194 f.; works of, 104, 312
John the Deacon, 4 note
John of Trevisa, 29 f., 69, 72
Johnson, Francis, 511
Johnson, Samuel: and Hammond's *Paraphrase*, 515
Jonas, Book of: in Coverdale's version, 177 f.; in Matthew's Bible, 176, 178; in the Great Bible, 177 f.; Tyndale's Prologue to, 181 f.; Tyndale's version of, 133 f., 163: rejected in Matthew's Bible, 176, 178
Jonghe, François; *see* Junius
Jonson, Ben: Rheims-Douay Version compared with, 259
Josephus, 185: Whiston's translation of, 525
Josue, Book of: Aelfric's translation of, 10, 23 and note, 64 f.; in the Bishops' Bible, 237; in the Polychrome Bible, 550 note; Tyndale's version of, 134, 163, 176
Joye, editions of Tyndale's version, 131 f., 137 note, 150
Jud, Leo, 112 f. and note, 128: Authorized Version influenced by, 315; and the Bishops' Bible, 235 note
Judges, Book of: Aelfric's translation of, 23 and note, 65; in the Bishops' Bible, 237; in the Polychrome Bible, 550 note; Purvey's notes on, 77 note; Tyndale's version of, 134, 163, 176
Judith, Book of: Aelfric's translation of, 23 and note; Taverner's version of, 208
Jugge (printer): edition of Coverdale's Bible, 159 f.; editions of Tyndale's New Test., 141, 151; notes to the New Testament, 141, 151, 245 f.
Junius, Francis, 10 and note, 126-28
- Anglo-Saxon publications of, 127 f.
- Authorized Version influenced by, 315
- edition of Caedmon's work, 16 note
- edition of the Bible, 117 f., 126 f.
- and Marshall: edition of Anglo Saxon Gospels, 21, 25, 31, 34 note
- notes by, 231
- Tremellius and, 117 and note, 126 f.

Kearney, John: Gaelic version of the Bible by, 451 and note
Keating, George, 422 note
Keating, Joseph, 500 and note
Keating, Patrick, 422 note, 472
Keating and Brown editions, 422 note
- Bible of 1811, 392 and notes
- Bible of 1825, 429 note
- Coyne's edition of 1816, 417 f.
- New Testament of 1818, 96 f., 307 f. and note, 363, 393 f., 422 f. and notes, 430, 434
- New Testament of 1832, 363, 423, 434
- New Testament of 1851, 465 and note

Kelley, Oliver; Approbations by, 431, 433, 454
Kellison, 295
Kells, Book of, 4, 44
Kenedy, J. P.: edition of Challoner's revision, 360 note, 496 note
Kennedy edition of Challoner's revision, 437
Kennedy, B. B.: and the Revised Version, 553

Kennicott and Geddes, 379
Kenrick, Francis Patrick
ancient versions of the Bible, 461
Approbations by, 449 and note, 467
authority of Scripture, 459
composition of the Gospels, 458 f.
Councils of Baltimore and, 458 f.
editions of Challoner criticized by, 460
infallibility of the Church, 459
Newman and, 459 and note
on Lingard's version, 462
on the Book of Proverbs, 461
peculiarities of the Vulgate, 461
purpose of approbations, 94
vernacular translations, 460
version of the Bible by, 458-62, 497: and Knox's version, 504; the notes in, 461 f.
Kent, Charles F.: and The Shorter Bible, 592
Kent, W. H., 500 note
Kent, earl of: disdain for the Rheims New Test., 275
Kenyon, Edward, 400
Kenyon, Frederic
Anglo-Saxon versions of the Gospels, 35 note
Greek basis of the Authorized Version, 319
on John Purvey and the Wycliffite versions, 78
on St. Aldhelm, 19
on the classes of Greek texts, 582 f.
Psalter of St. Augustine, 53
Rheims Version contemned by, 267 note
Keogh, A., 500 note
Key, Thomas, 128
Key of Paradise, The, 97
Kibworth, academy at, 522, 529, 539
Kidderminster, Baxter at, 513
Kilburne and "The Wicked Bible," 326 note
Kimchi, Rabbi David, 301
King, Gaelic version of the Bible by, 451 f. and notes
Kings, Books of
Aelfric's translation of, 23-25
Anglo-Norman version of, 9
Anglo-Saxon version of, 10
in Coverdale's version, 164
in Taverner's Bible, 208
in the Bishops' Bible, 237
Tyndale's version of, 134, 163, 176
Kirkham Psalter, 58
Kissing, St. Augustine on, 303
Knighton and Wycliffe's translation, 67, 72 note
Knox, John: at Frankfort, 217 f.; at Geneva, 216 f.; the Geneva Bible and, 229
Knox, Ronald A., version of the New Testament, 497, 502-504: American editions of, 504 note; and Arendzen's New Testament, 495
Koridethi Gospels, 582
Kyle, and Fullarton's edition of 1845, 450

Lachmann, edition of the Greek text, 545
Laffan (bishop), Approbation of, 433, 454
Lambert (publisher); *see* Burns and Lambert
Lambeth Library, 91
Lamentations, Book of: in Coverdale's version, 167
Lanfranc, 409
Language, changes in the, 535
Laodiceans, Epistle to: Aelfrics version of, 25; in Lefèvre's edition, 99 f. note; in Richard Rolle's version, 27 note; and the Wycliffite versions, 76 note
Last Age of the Church, 68 and note
Latimer, 218
Latin versions of the Bible, 99-129, 408 f.: English translations of, 123 and note, 128 f.; result of, 129; Vulgate Bible and, 250, 258
Latinisms in the Rheims New Testament, 257 f., 263
Lattey, Cuthbert: and Confraternity Edition, 492 note; and Pope Leo XIII's encyclical, 491; and Westminster Version, 492 note, 500 note, 501 note
Laud (archbishop) and "The Wicked Bible," 326 note
Laurence, Giles: and the Bishop's Bible, 244 and note
Laurence, Thomas, 244 note
Lavenham, Richard, 75 note
Law, T. G.; *see* Oakeley and Law
Layman's New Testament, 487 f.
Leavitt, Jonathan: Rheims New Testament published by, 435
Le Besgue, John, 255
Lee, Edward (archbishop of York), 101 f.: exclusion of vernacular versions, 142
Lefèvre, Jacques, 99
Legh, Thomas, 147
Leicester, earl of, 217: and Cartwright's *Confutation*, 276
Le Long, J.: on Andreas and Luke Osiander, 115 note; on the Gaelic version of the Bible, 451 note; on the Latin versions, 116 note; on the translators of Rheims N.T., 253 and note
Lenfant, Jacques: version of the Bible, 521
Leo X (pope), 100, 109, 142: bull of, 145
Leo XIII (pope), encyclical by: in Benziger Bible, 494; in Brepols Bible, 490 f.; in Washbourne Bible (1914), 485
Leofric, 33
Letchworth New Testament, 599 f.
Leviticus, Book of: in the Polychrome Bible, 550 note

Lewis, C. S.: and Phillips' epistles, 598
Lewis, John
  Anglo-Saxon versions, 9, 39
  edition of Wycliffite New Test., 72 and note, 91
  editions of the Bible, 91 f.
  John Purvey's Prologue, 76
  Martin and Fulke's controversy, 281, 283
  Martin's *Discoverie,* 275
  Ward's *Errata,* 332
  Wycliffe's translation, 72 f.
Liber Eadwini Anglici, 57
Liber vitae, 43 note
Lightfoot, John B.: and Cook, 570 note; edition of Broughton's work, 330; on the style of the Authorized Version, 322; and the Revised Version, 552 f.
Linacre and Erasmus, 100
Lindanus, 278
Lindisfarne, 44
Lindisfarne Gospels, 41-51
  and Anglo-Saxon versions, 32, 40
  date of, 50 f.
  description of, 41-44
  history of, 44 f.
  Naples and, 45 f.
  omissions in, 32
  purpose of, 12
  Rushworth Gospels and, 32, 47 ff.
Lindsey, Theophilus: and the Unitarian movement, 539 and note
Lingard, John: on Anglo-Saxon culture, 3 note, 4 note, 5 note; on St. Aldhelm, 20; version of the Gospels by, 442-47, 497
Lingard's version of the Gospels, 442-47, 497
  Challoner's version compared with, 444 f.
  Cotton on, 442 note
  the Introduction, 445 f.
  Kenrick's approval of, 462
  Knox's version and, 504
  the notes in, 445-47
  the text, 443-45
  Wiseman on, 442 f. and note, 446
Lisle, William, 10 and note, 23 note, 61
Lists of editions, 91 ff., 666 ff., 719 ff.
Little, F. A.: reprint of Catholic Board Edition, 449
Littledale, Foxe denounced by, 144
Lively, Edward, 312, 328
Liverpool edition of Rheims New Testament, 353 f., 392
Livy, 382 note
Lloyd (bishop), 325
Lloyd, Samuel: revision of the Revised Version, 576
Lohmann edition of the Bible, 491 note
Lollards, the: heresy of, 85 f. and note
Lollardy: Gairdner's description of, 136 f.; and Tyndale's New Test., 137; and Wycliffe's version, 136 f.
London Polyglot Bible, 551
Long Parliament, the, 551
Lopez, Didacus, 104
Louvain Bible, 295, 296 note
Lowth and Geddes, 379
Lozell, Fulke's condemnation of, 286
Lucas, Fielding: American publisher, 476; edition of Challoner's Bible (1832), 434
Luke of Bruges, edition of the Vulgate, 251
Lumby, J. R.: and the Revised Version, 553
Lupton, Donald: on Bellarmine and Whitaker, 291
Lupton, J. H.: on Wycliffe's translation, 71
Luther, Martin
  Cochlaeus and, 130 note
  condemnation of, 142
  contempt for Zwingli, 274
  Curoe on, 440
  disciple of Wycliffe, 146
  Fulke's repudiation of, 287
  Henry VIII and, 142 f.
  on the preservation of the Bible by the Catholic Church, 64 note, 440
  on the preservation of the sacraments, 64 note
  on the words of consecration, 348
  opponents of, 107
  Osiander and, 115
  St. James's Epistle rejected by, 282, 287
  Tyndale influenced by, 135, 137 f., 143 f., 146
  Warham's condemnation of, 143
  works of, 112
Lutheranism and Wittenberg, 216
Luther's version, 163: burning of, 137 note; Preface to, 137 f.; and Tyndale's Prologue, 178; and Tyndale's version, 135, 137 f., 148; Zwingli's condemnation of, 274
Lynch, John: and Denvir's New Testament, 438
Lyndwood, 142 note
Lyons, sack of, 122

Macauly, G. C.: accuracy of Rheims New Test., 262 f.; Douay Old Testament and Authorized Version, 264 note
McClellan, John B.: revision of the Authorized Version, 549
McCloskey (cardinal), Approbation by, 467
Mace, William: version of the New Testament, 521 f.
McGhee, on Gibson's edition (1822), 414
McGiffert, edition of Eusebius, 561 note
McGlashen and Gill, New Testament of 1876, 476 f.

Machabees, Books of: Aelfric's translation of, 23; in Junius' edition, 127; Whitaker's rejection of, 282; Wycliffite versions and, 76 note, 78 note

Machabees, Fourth Book of, Challoner's note on, 359

Machabees, Second Book of: canonicity of, 184; St. Augustine on, 287 and note

Machabees, Third Book of, 213 note; Challoner's note on, 359; Council of Trent on, 213 note; in Becke's edition of Matthew's Bible, 182; in edition of Taverner's Bible, 213 note

MacHale, John: Approbation of, 451; edition of Challoner's revision, 451 f. and notes; Gaelic version of the Bible, 452 and note

McHugh, John A.: and Spencer's version, 498

M'Intyre (canon), and Catholic Truth Society edition of the Gospels, 483

McIntyre (publisher); *see* Simms and McIntyre

Macknight, James: version of the epistles, 522 f.

MacMahon, Bernard, 337, 372 note

MacMahon's revisions, 337, 372-78, 391-93
- Approbations in, 418, 420
- Bible of 1791, 373-75, 405, 417-19; *see also* Cross, Richard
- Christie's correction of, 429
- criticism of, 378
- edition of 1792 and, 390
- Gibson's editions and, 413
- Haydock's Bible and, 378, 392 f., 397, 457: and Richardson's edition, 470
- Kenrick's condemnation of, 460 note
- New Testament of 1783, 372 f.
- New Testaments of 1803 and 1810, 376-78
- numbering of the editions, 373 note
- and Richardson's edition, 378, 454, 470
- Troy's Approbation and, 417-19

MacNamara's editions: Bible of 1818, 363, 393 f., 419-21; edition of 1813–14, 415-17

McRay, D.: version of the Bible, 537

Macregol, 46 f.

Macrobius, on Herod's cruelty, 210

Madden, Frederic: on the Lindisfarne Gospels, 43

Magnificat, the: in Anglo-Saxon Psalters, 55, 57

Mairs editions of Challoner's revision, 421: Bible of 1836, 438; Bible of 1886, 478

Maitland, Samuel: on the ribaldry of the Rhemists' opponents, 279

Malan, S. C.: and the Revised Version, 522 and note

Manasses, Prayer of: Challoner's note on, 359; in Bishops' Bible, 240; in Douay Old Testament, 299; in Matthew's Bible, 176, 181, 184; in the Geneva Bible, 223

Manning (cardinal), Approbation of, 476

Manuscripts
- age of, 19, 36, 51
- Bodleian 959, pp. 70 and note, 74 note
- Bodleian, Auct. D.ii.19, pp. 46-51
- Bodleian, *Codex Junianus XI*, p. 16 note
- Bodleian, *Codex Junianus 113*, p. 16 note
- Bodleian, Douce 320, p. 55
- Bodleian, Douce 369, pp. 70 and note, 74 note
- Bodleian, Douce 370, p. 74 note
- Bodleian, Hatton 38, pp. 31, 35, 38-40
- Bodleian, Junius I, pp. 25 f.
- Bodleian, Junius 27, p. 54
- Bodleian, Laud. D.85.i, pp. 60 f.
- Bodleian, Laud. E.19, p. 23 note
- Bodleian, Laud. E.33.1, p. 23 note
- Bodleian, N.E.D. 2.19, p. 5
- Bodley 117, p. 70 note
- Bodley 441, pp. 31 and note, 34 and note, 37-40
- Bodley 779, p. 58
- British Museum 1.A.14, p. 9 note
- British Museum, Addit. 15580, p. 75 note
- British Museum, Addit. 17376, pp. 28, 59
- British Museum, Addit. 37517, p. 54
- British Museum, Arundel 57, p. 51
- British Museum, Arundel 60, pp. 54 f.
- British Museum, Arundel 155, p. 55
- British Museum, Royal I.A.xiv, pp. 31, 35-40
- British Museum, Royal I.B.vi, p. 74 note
- British Museum, Royal 2.B.vii, p. 61
- British Museum, Royal 18.D.1, p. 27 note
- Cambridge, Corpus clx, pp. 31 ff., 37-40
- Cambridge, Corpus L.15, p. 4 note
- Cambridge, Corpus O.6, p. 58
- Cambridge University Library F.f.i.23, pp. 55 f.
- Cambridge University Library Ii.2.11, pp. 31 and note, 33 f., 38-40
- Cambridge University Library Ii.6.26, p. 69 note
- Cotton, Caligula A.7, p. 57
- Cotton, Caligula XV, p. 3 note
- Cotton, Claudius B.4, p. 10
- Cotton, Cleop. F.2, p. 147 note
- Cotton, Domitian A.7, pp. 6 note, 45 note
- Cotton, Faustina A.5, p. 45 note
- Cotton, Faustina B.13, p. 5
- Cotton, Nero C.4, pp. 9, 58
- Cotton, Nero D.iv, pp. 41 ff.
- Cotton, Otho C.i, pp. 31 and note, 34 f., 38-40
- Cotton, Tiberius C.6, p. 54
- Cotton, Vespasian A.I(xv), pp. 19, 52 f., 56 note
- Cotton, Vespasian D.6, p. 10
- Cotton, Vespasian D.xxi, p. 52 note
- Cotton, Vitellius E.18.6, pp. 54 f.

Manuscripts (*continued*)
Egerton 617 f., pp. 71 note, 74 note
Foxe 1396, p. 75 note
Harleian 603, p. 57 note
Harleian 606, p. 56 note
Harleian 1170, p. 58
Harleian 3449, pp. 64 f.
Hatten 65, p. 9 note
Lambeth 1140, p. 91
Mareschal 72, p. 10 note
Oxford, Corpus 4, p. 75 note
Oxford, Corpus 94, p. 71 note
Oxford, Rawlinson 258, p. 75 note
Oxford, St. John's College 94, p. 13 note
Parker 32, pp. 13 note, 68 note
Sir Thomas Phillipps 9302, p. 74 note
Royal Library, Paris, 4.A.xiv, pp. 58 f.
Salisbury Cathedral 141, p. 9 note
Trinity College, Cambridge, R.17.1, p. 9 and note
Trinity College, Cambridge, B.14, 19, p. 13 note
Trinity College, Dublin, A.i.10, p. 75
Trinity College, Dublin, A.4.4 (H.32), p. 59
Maps: in Bishops' Bible, 241; in Brepols' edition of the Bible, 485; in Geneva Bible, 224, 233; in Spencer's version, 499; in Washbourne's edition of the Bible, 486
Marcion, 125 note
Mardochai, portrait of, 198
Margaret van Emerson, 133
Market Harborough, Doddridge at, 522
Marler, Great Bible printed by, 189 note, 193, 204
Marot, 122 note
Marsche, Thomas (printer), 97
Marsh (bishop), 398
Marshall, Horace (publisher), 587 note
Marshall, Thomas: edition of Anglo-Saxon Gospels, 21, 25, 31, 34 note; on the Anglo-Saxon versions, 25, 33 f., 37
Marten Le Emperour (de Keyser), editions of Tyndale's version, 131, 150
Martin, Gregory, 251 f.
Bale's accusation against, 274
Beza criticized by, 125 note
Campion praised by, 279
death of, 252, 254
the *Discoverie,* 273 ff.: Fulke's reprint of, 280 note; and Ward's *Errata,* 332
divine right of kings, 283
Douay Old Testament and, 294 note
editions of the Bible attacked by, 245, 282 and note, 284 f. and notes, 332
Foulis' accusation of, 274
Fulke's controversy with, 275 and note, 278 ff.
Martin, Gregory (*continued*)
Great Bible condemned by, 202 note, 282
learning of, 355
mistranslations in Protestant versions, 273, 281-86
on "Salomons ballettes," 164 note
translator of Rheims New Test., 250-52
works of, 252 note
Martin, Raymund, 136
Mary, virginity of: Newcome on, 534
Mary (princess), 128
Mary (Queen of Scots), regard for Rheims New Testament, 275
Mary Tudor, 61: accession of, 216; conspiracy against, 217 f.; Coverdale's imprisonment by, 155; Tremellius and, 117
Masoretes, numbering of verses, 220 note
Masoretic Hebrew Text, 112 f.: emendations of, 505, 594, 597; and the Revised Version, 566
Mass: Coverdale's derision of, 155 f.; derided in edition of Matthew's Bible, 183, 195, 212; Erasmus' doubts concerning, 105; not in the Bible, 183, 195; Woodhead and Walker on, 518 f.
Mathew, Theobald: apostle of Temperance, 450, 453
Matthew, St.: Cajetan on the Gospel by, 106
Matthew, Thomas:
edition of Coverdale's Bible attributed to, 158
edition of Taverner's version attributed to, 213
edition of Tyndale's New Test. attributed to, 150
fictitious name, 158 note, 175 f.
fined by Tunstall, 176
his notes in edition of Tyndale's New Test., 141
Matthew, Tobie: criticism of the Rheims New Test., 257
Matthew's Bible, 175-86, 198 note
the Apocrypha, 158 note, 167 note, 175, 182, 184 f., 208
authorized for public reading, 160, 176, 178-80
Authorized Version and, 178, 311, 317
condemnation of, 143, 185
Coverdale and, 175 f.
Coverdale's Bible and, 176-78
Cromwell and, 188
Dedications in, 179, 181 f.
editions of, 176 f., 180 ff.
fictitious attribution, 158 note, 175 f.
Foxe on, 158 note, 175 f.
Great Bible and, 189, 203
heretical character of, 183-185
Hyll's editions of, 162 note

Matthew's Bible (*continued*)
illustrations in, 177, 182
importance of, 186
influence of, 470-72, 477
initials in, 177 and note
the New Testament: in edition of Taverner's Bible, 213; and Tyndale's New Testament, 130, 158 note, 175 ff., 234
the notes, 175 f., 182-84, 195, 210-12: in Taverner's version, 211 f.
Preface and Prologues, 177 f., 180 note, 181 f.
printed by Grafton, 189
reception of, 178-80
the royal licence, 178-80, 188, 206 and note
"Table of principall maters": in Taverner's version, 207, 212
Taverner's version and, 207-13
the text, 177 f.
the title page, 177
Tyndale's version and, 130, 158 note, 175 ff., 234
Meahan, Patrick: reviser of Duffy's New Test., 467 f.
Meek, T. J.: and Goodspeed's work, 594
Melancthon, 104, 115
Melchisedech's sacrifice, Geddes on, 382
Methodism, 527: and Whitefield and Haweis, 533
Metrical paraphrase of the Bible, 58
Michel (editor) and the *Psalterium Triplex*, 56
Middle-English versions, 25-30
Mill, Vulgate esteemed by, 409
Miller, E., 565
Milner, John
Approbations by, 422, 434
Catholic Board Edition denounced by, 256 note, 363 f., 403 f. and note, 422
Challoner and, 355
Challoner's last revision, 371
Cotton's criticism of, 403
Geddes condemned by, 380
Horrabin's edition denounced by, 424
on Worthington, 300
Roman Catholic Bible Society denounced by, 401 f. and note
Ward's *Errata* and, 332 note
Milton, 380
Miracles: Campbell's dissertation on, 523; St. Augustine on, 569 note
Miraculous, suppression of the, 569
Moberly and the Revised Version, 552
Modern Reader's Bible, 576 note
Modern-speech versions, 505 f., 530, 546 f., 585-600
An American Translation, 592-94
Bilton's version, 549 f., 587, 599 f.
by Catholics, 504-506, 600
Modern-speech versions (*continued*)
the Confraternity Old Testament, 505 f., 600
Fenton's version, 546, 549, 586
Goodspeed's version, 592-95: and the Revised Standard Version, 592-94
Hayman's epistles, 589
in Basic English, 596 f.
Letchworth New Testament, 599
Moffatt's version, 546, 588-91
Montgomery's New Testament, 595
Norton's version, 546
Phillips' epistles, 589, 598 f.
Revised Standard Version, 579-84
Riverside New Testament, 595
Sawyer's version, 546
The Shorter Bible, 592
Torrey's Gospels, 595 f.
Twentieth Century New Testament, 546, 549, 587 f., 590 f.
Wade's New Testament, 596
Wand's epistles, 589, 598
Way's epistles, 589
Weymouth's New Testament, 588, 591 f.
Worsley's New Testament, 530
see also Nary's version, Witham's version
Moeso-Gothic version, 128
Moffat, James: *Historical New Testament*, 550, 590, 596; modern-speech version by, 546, 588-91; and the Revised Standard Version, 580 and note, 590
Moffat Bible, 589 f.
Moir editions of Challoner's revision: Bible of 1796, 391 f. and note, 395, 400, 405; Bible of 1804, 391 f. and note, 395, 400, 404 f.
Molinoeus: Beza's version condemned by, 274; Calvin condemned by, 274
Mombert, J.
Aelfric, 24 note
Bishops' Bible, 243 and note, 244 note
Coverdale's letter to Cromwell, 153 note
Douay version of the Psalms, 298
Great Bible, 203
Hereford's translation, 71 note
identity of John Hollybushe, 170
Martin and Fulke's controversy, 275, note, 281
Rheims New Testament, 260 note: Preface to, 255
sources of the Authorized Version, 315, 319
Taverner's version, 211
Tyndale's translation of the Pentateuch, 134 note
Tyndale's version, 147 note
Ward's *Errata* criticized by, 332 and note
Monachius, 396 note
Monasticon, 64
Montagu, William, 8

Montanus, Arias: edition of Pagninus' Bible, 110; version of the Bible, 315
Montgomery, Helen B.: version of the New Testament, 595
Moore and Coverdale, 153 f.
Moore (bishop of Norwich): and Pyle, 527; and Whiston, 525-27
More, Hubert, 255
More, Thomas (St.)
  Coverdale and, 153 note, 154 and note
  the *Dialogue* by, 63, 65, 137, 146, 150, 154
  Erasmus and, 100 f.
  his knowledge of manuscripts, 63 note
  "licence" to read heretical books, 145 f.
  on Arundel's Constitution, 65
  on pre-Wycliffite versions, 63, 66
  on the burning of Bibles, 66
  on Tunstall's learning, 147
  on Tyndale, 134, 136 f.
  Tyndale and, 145 f., 154
Morerius, 127
Morin, Dom, 45
Morton (bishop of Durham), 329
Moulton, James H.
  Anglo-Saxon versions, 7 f.
  Authorized Version and the Rheims New Test., 265
  the Bishops' Bible, 243 note, 245 note
  Douay version of the Psalms, 297
  the Great Bible, 203
  Preface to Rheims New Testament, 255
  Taverner's notes, 211
  Taverner's version, 215
  Wycliffe's translation, 71 note
Moulton, Richard: *Modern Reader's Bible,* 576 note
Muenster, Sebastian, 114 f. and notes
  Authorized Version influenced by, 315
  Bishops' Bible and, 235, 237
  Coverdale's version and, 163-65
  English versions influenced by, 114 and note, 309
  Geneva Bible influenced by, 230
  Great Bible and, 189, 203
  Isidore Clario and, 116
  use of italics, 324
"Murderers Bible," p. 327
Murray, Daniel, 93, 332
  Approbations by, 393, 429 f., 433 and note, 454, 467
  edition of Challoner's Bible (1825), 358-60, 393, 429 f. and notes: and Blake's edition (1838), 439; and Christie's edition, 429; and Duffy editions, 453, 456, 464; and Mairs edition of 1836, 438; reprints of, 430, 433 note, 435, 437, 448-50, 453, 456, 464 f., 467; and Richardson's New Test. of 1851, 465
Murray, Daniel (*continued*)
  edition of Challoner's Bible (1829), 430, 433 note
  edition of Challoner's Bible (1833), 430, 435
  edition of Challoner's Bible (1835), 437: and Dolman's Bible of 1851, 464
My Sunday Missal (Stedman), 493 and note
Myroure of our Ladye, The, 6 note, 8, 27, 57
"Mystic Doctor," the, 528

Names, table of: in the Geneva Bible, 224
Naples and the Lindisfarne Gospels, 45 f.
Nary, Cornelius, 339 f. and note, 349 and note: Douay Bible criticized by, 340; Preface to his New Testament, 257, 340-42; Rheims New Testament criticized by, 257, 340, 585
Nary's version of the New Testament, 339-45, 497
  Challoner and, 345
  the notes, 345
  Preface to, 257, 340-42
  second edition of, 339 note
  the text, 342-44
  Witham and, 349 and note
Nehemias, Book of: in Matthew's Bible, 178; Tyndale's version of, 134
Nelson, Thomas (publisher): and the American Standard Version, 579; and the Revised Standard Version, 580
"Neophyte," the Rhemists' use of, 258
Nestle, E.: edition of the Greek New Test., 565 note, 576 and note, 582 f.: and Lloyd's revision, 576 and note
Netter, Thomas: on John Purvey, 75; on John Wycliffe and Nicholas of Hereford, 70 note
Neutral Greek text, 556-62, 582
New Testament, the: literary style of, 581, 593; order of books; *see* Order of books; semitic background of, 582, 596; titles of the books of the Wycliffite version, 74
New Theory of the Earth, 525
New York editions of Challoner's revision, 450, 453, 462 f.
Newcastle New Testament, 387 note, 388 note, 393, 398 f., 410 note
Newcome, William, 92
  biblical work of, 533 f. and note
  Historical View, 92, 532, 534
  on the translators of Rheims New Testament, 253 note
  the Revised Version and, 534
  Rheims version disregarded by, 267
  the Unitarian Version and, 540
  Wakefield and, 532 f.
Newman, John Henry: on Henry Cotton, 93; on the beauty of the Authorized Version, 322 and note; on the differences in Catho-

Newman, John Henry (*continued*)
lic Bibles, 394; proposed translation of the Bible by, 459 and note, 497; and the Revised Version, 553 f. note
Newry New Testament (1838), 439
Newth, S.: on the Revised Version, 554; and the Revised Version, 552
Newton, Isaac: and Whiston, 524 f.
Nicholas, St., 280
Nicholas of Hereford, 70 note: condemnation of, 86; translation of the New Testament by, 70 f., 78
Nicholas of Lyra, 11, 77 f.
Nicodemus, Gospel of, 23 note
Nicolson, James: editions of Coverdale's version, 157 f., 168-70
Nonconformists, 513: at the Savoy Conference, 551 note
Norman-French Psalters, 52 note, 55-57
Northampton, academy at, 522
Norton, Andrew: version of the Gospels, 546
Notes in Catholic Bibles, 410: necessity for, 402
Nuns: recitation of the Divine Office by, 6; and vernacular versions, 6 and note, 8
Nycolson (glazier), 188 note

Oakeley and Law, edition of Haydock's Bible, 368, 397 f.
Oates (publisher); *see* Burns and Oates
O'Cassaide, Seamus, 372 note
O'Connell, Daniel, 302 note
O'Donellan and the Gaelic version of the Bible, 451 note
Offor, George, 93 note: edition of Tyndale's version, 130 note, 137 note, 141 note
Ogden, C. K.: and Basic English, 597
Ogden, Hester, 288
O'Hara, Edwin V.: and the Confraternity Edition, 506
Old Latin Version, 582
Old Syriac Version, 582
Olde, J., 128
Olivetan and Matthew's Apocrypha, 184 f.
Ora (coin), 42 and note
Order of books (New Testament) in
Aelfric's version, 25
Coverdale's version, 157
Fenton's version, 586
the *Historical New Testament,* 590
Luther's version, 137
Matthew's Bible, 178 note, 209
Moffatt's version, 590
Taverner's version, 209
the *Twentieth Century New Testament,* 588, 590
Tyndale's version, 137
Wade's version, 596
Wand's version, 598

Order of books (*continued*)
The Westminster Version, 501
Whiston's version, 526
William's version, 542
Wycliffite version, 74
O'Reilly, Richard: Approbation to MacMahon's revision, 375; and MacNamara's edition, 415, 419
Origen, 556 f.
Orm, 25 f.
Ormulum, the, 25 f.
Ornamentation of the Lindisfarne Gospels, 41-44
Orosius, the *Historia* by, 22
Osiander, Andreas, 114
Osiander, Luke, 115
"Our Lord," 355 f. and note
Owun, 47 f. and note, 51
Oxford Movement, the, 538
Oxford Psalter, 55
Oxford University: condemnation of, 86; version of the New Testament, 513 ff.

Packington, Augustine, 145
Pagninus, Santes, 109-11
Authorized Version influenced by, 315 and note, 323
Bishops' Bible and, 235 and note
Coverdale's Bible and, 163
English versions influenced by, 110, 235 and note
numbering of verses, 220 note
translation of the Bible, 109-11, 116 f.
Tyndale's New Testament and, 133, 134 note
Pallavicino, 105 note, 108 note
Palmer, E.: edition of the Greek New Testament, 556 note
Papyri (Greek), discovery of, 581, 593
"Paraclete," the Rhemists' use of, 258
Paralipomenon, Books of: Tyndale's version of, 134, 163, 176
"Parasceve," the Rhemists' use of, 258
Paris, University of: Cajetan's work condemned by, 107; Lefèvre's work condemned by, 99; Stephens' Bible condemned by, 117
Paris Psalter, 19, 22, 59 and note
Parker, F.: version of Genesis and the N.T., 544
Parker, Matthew
Anglo-Saxon versions and, 34 and note
Bishops' Bible and, 234, 275
Bodley's printing of the Geneva Bible, 221 and note
Coverdale and, 155
on Bede's translation of St. John, 236
on John Fisher, 236
on the study of Anglo-Saxon, 6 note

Parker, Matthew (*continued*)
  on vernacular versions, 34 note, 236
  Preface to Bishops' Bible, 236 ff., 241
  revised edition of the Great Bible, 284 and note
  Thomas Sampson and, 218
  Tremellius and, 117 note
Parkhurst (bishop): and the Bishops' Bible, 237; epitaph for Goodman, 217
Parr, Katherine, 156
Participial construction: in Challoner and the Rheims N.T., 368, 444; in Lingard's version, 444
Pascha (or Passover), 211, 345 note, 380 note, 388 f.
Pastorini, 98, 396 note
Pattison, Mark, 103 note
Paul, St.: portrait of, 198
Paulinus, St., 194
Paulist Fathers and Spencer, 498
Pearson, on Coverdale's Dedications, 161 note
Pellican, Conrad, 111 f. and notes
Pencriche, Richard, 29 note
Penda, 44
Penitential Psalms, the, 97
Penn, Granville: revision of the Authorized Version, 547
Pentateuch, the
  Aelfric's version of, 10, 23 and notes, 64 f.
  Ainsworth's version of, 511
  Alexander's version of, 542
  Authorized Version, 312
  Cajetan's commentary on, 106-108
  in Anglo-Saxon, 10, 23 and notes, 64 f.
  Kenrick's version of, 459
  Muenster's version of, 114 note
  Tyndale's Prologue to, 181 f.
  Tyndale's version of, 133 f. and note, 142, 163 and note, 176
Perowne, J. S.: and the Revised Version, 553
Peshitta Syriac version, 557
Peter Lombard, 27 and note
Peter Martyr, 117, 216
Petre, and Geddes biblical work, 377
Petrus, Bartholomew, 294
Philadelphia edition of the Bible (1875), 475 f. and note
Philip II (of Spain), 302 note
Phillimore, J. S.: on the merits of the Rheims-Douay version, 259; on the use of italics, 325
Phillips, J. B.: version of the epistles, 589, 598 f.
Phonetic indications of the R.S.V., 584
"Phylacteries," use of the word, 258
Pickering, William: edition of Wycliffite New Test., 73 note; and Hamil's edition of Haydock's Bible, 427
Pico de la Mirandola, 110
Pictorial editions: Bible of 1865, 471, 473; New Testament of 1850, 463; New Testament of 1865, 471; New Testament of 1876, 476
Pighius, on private interpretation, 291
Pilgrim Press and Weymouth's version, 592
Pilkington, George: version of the New Testament, 543
Pitts, on Bede's learning, 20
Pius VI (pope), letter to Martini: in Horrabin's edition, 423 f.; in MacMahon's revision, 373, 375
Pius VII (pope), rescript to British bishops on reading the Bible, 426
Pius XII (pope), encyclical by, 494: and the Confraternity Old Testament, 505 note
Plumptre, E. H.: and the Revised Version, 552
Pocock, on Junius' anti-Catholic notes, 231
Poissy Debate, 121
Pole (cardinal), 98: and Tremellius, 117
Polen, John: on Thomas More, 63 note
Politi, Lancelot, 107
Pollard, Alfred
  Bishops' Bible criticized by, 244 note
  the Great Bible, 203
  importance of Matthew's Bible, 186
  importance of Taverner's version, 214 f.
  on royal licences, 188 note, 206 note
  printing of the Great Bible, 191 notes, 192
  Rheims New Testament, 264 f., 277 note, 296 note: and the Authorized Version, 264 f.
  Rheims-Douay version, 259
  Tyndale's influence on English versions, 186
  Wycliffe's translation, 71
Polychrome Bible, the, 550 and note
Polychronicon, by Higden, 29, 69
Polydore Vergil, 22
Pope, Hugh: death of, 62 note; and Knox's version, 503 and note; Layman's New Testament edited by, 487 f.; and Vogels' edition of the Greek New Testament, 565 note
Porter, John, 195
Postillae, the, 11, 77 note
Potter, John E.: edition of Challoner's revision, 475 f. and note
Powell (publisher), edition of Erasmus' New Testament in English, 128
Poynes, Nicholas, 278 note
Poynter, William
  Approbations by, 422, 434
  Brady's criticism of, 407 note
  Catholic Board edition and, 363, 402, 407 f., 422: the Address, 405, 408-11; the purpose of, 411
  edition of the New Testament (1825), 394, 431

Poynter, William (*continued*)
Horrabin's edition and, 424
on the antiquity of the Vulgate, 409
on the Church's concern for the Scriptures, 405, 408-11
on the notes in Catholic Bibles, 402, 410
on the pre-eminence of the Vulgate, 405, 409 f.
on the reading of Scripture by Catholics, 410
on the Rheims-Douay version, 410
on the variations in Greek and Hebrew manuscripts, 405, 408
Roman Catholic Bible Society and, 402, 407 note
Poynts, A., 171
Prayer before Communion, 60
Prayer before reciting the breviary, 58 note
Prayer Book Psalter, 114 note, 164-66, 199 note: in editions of the Bishops' Bible, 240 f.; Parker's concession for the use of, 244 note; used in choir, 244 note
Predestination: Beza's teaching concerning, 126; Castalio's rejection of, 119; in the Geneva Bible, 225
Preface to Douay Old Testament, 295 f., 651 ff.
Preface to Rheims New Testament, 255 f., 601 ff.
antiquity of the Vulgate, 319
Arundel's Constitution, 64 note
Bede's translation, 63 note
Bulkeley's attack on, 289-91
the English used in, 258
in MacNamara's edition, 416
in the sixth edition, 354 and note
"ingenius," 255
mistranslations of the Reformers, 123 f., 255
Preface to the Authorized Version and, 264 and note, 311 note, 314
pre-Wycliffite versions, 63 note
the "ten reasons," 256: Bulkeley's attack on, 289-91
use of Hebrew and Greek words, 258
Vulgate defended by, 256, 276
Prendergast (bishop), *Imprimatur* by, 485
"Prepuce," the Rhemists' use of, 258
Presbyter, translation of
Bishops' Bible, 242, 285 note
Coverdale's version, 154
edition of 1792, 388
Matthew's Bible, 178
Nary's revision, 349
Protestant versions, 124, 284
Taverner's note on, 212
Tyndale's version, 132, 139, 148, 154
Presbyterian versions, 522 f.
Presbyterianism: Canne on, 512; and Congregationalism, 522; and Doddridge, 522; and Harwood, 529
Presbyterians and the Revised Version, 553
Preston and Heath, printers of the Newcastle New Test., 398
Pre-Syrian Greek text, 557 f.
Pre-Wycliffite versions, 62-66
Price, Ira M., 584 note, 595 note
Pricke of Conscience, The, 27
Primitive Christianity Revived, 525
Principles of translating
Aelfric, 24
Authorized Version, 310 f.
Bishops' Bible, 235 f.
Carey's revision, 489
Geddes, 380 note, 381
Goodspeed, 581, 592 f.
Knox, 502 f.
Nary, 340-42
Purvey, 77 f.
the Revised Standard Version, 581 f., 592 f.
Richard Rolle, 27
Scarlett's New Testament, 535 f. and note
Wakefield, 532
Wynne, 528
"Proselyte," use of the word, 258
Protectorate, the, 216
Protestant versions, 509 ff.
divergences in, 273, 281 f., 285 f., and note
editions attacked by Martin, 245, 282 and note, 284 f. and notes, 332
MacHale's condemnation of, 451
mistranslations in, 123 ff., 250, 252, 255, 270, 272, 281-85: attacked by Martin, 273, 281-86
multiplicity of revisions, 281 f., 285 f. and note
variety of: Bulkeley on, 290
Protestantism: exploitation of the Church, 218 f.; triumph of, 216
Proverbs, Book of: Anglo-Saxon versions of, 10, 64; Kenrick on, 461; Muenster's version of, 114 note; Purvey's notes on, 78 note
Psalms, the; *see* Psalter
Psalter, the
Ainsworth's version of, 511
Anglo-Norman versions of, 9
Anglo-Saxon versions of, 7, 19, 25, 37, 52-61, 64 f.: by King Alfred, 9, 22, 54, 59
attributed to William of Shoreham, 28, 59 and note
Authorized Version of, 199 note, 299, 311 f.
Barker's editions of, 232 f.
Beza's translation of, 122 and note
the Bishops' Bible version of, 237, 239-41, 244 and note
Book of Common Prayer; *see* Prayer Book Psalter
Cajetan's commentary on, 105, 106 note, 107

Psalter, the (*continued*)
Coverdale's Bible, 164-66
Cox on the uniform translation of, 234 note
Douay Version of, 297-99
the Gallican recension, 52, 54 ff., 297 note: in the Douay Old Test., 297 f. and note
Geneva Bible version of, 223, 233
glossing of, 12 f.
Great Bible version, 164-66, 199 and note: in editions of the Bishops' Bible, 240 f.; *see also* Prayer Book Psalter
Matthew's Bible version, 177: numbering of the psalms, 176
Moulton's *Modern Reader's Bible*, 576 note
James I's translation of, 309 note
Junius' commentary on, 127
Kenrick's version of, 459 f.
Knox's version of, 504
metrical version by Sternhold and Hopkins, 233, 241
Norman-French versions, 9, 52 note, 55-57
numbering of the psalms, 165 note, 166, 199: in Coverdale's version, 166; in Matthew's Bible, 176: in Prayer Book Psalter, 166; in Taverner's Bible, 208; in the Great Bible, 199
Parker's Preface to, 237, 239 f.
Pellican's version of, 111
Prayer Book version; *see* Prayer Book Psalter
Richard Rolle's version of, 26-28
the Roman recension, 19, 52, 54 ff.
St. Aldhelm's version of, 18 and notes
St. Jerome's three revisions of, 56 note, 58
St. Jerome's translation of, 52, 56, 58, 105 f.
Taverner's version of, 208
versions of, 97
the Westminster Version of, 501
Psalter of St. Augustine, 4 note, 19, 52 f.
Psalterium Triplex, 56 f.
Publishers: Dore on the dishonesty of, 213 f., 232 note; freedom of, 150, 158, 170 and note, 181; knowledge of the text, 472; liberty with the text, 232 note, 455, 472, 476 f.; unreliability of title pages, 150 f., 158, 170, 213 f., 232
Purcell (bishop), Approbation by, 467
Puritans; *see* Hampton Court Conference
Purver, Anthony: style of the Authorized Version criticized by, 323; version of the Bible, 528 f.
Purvey, John, 72, 73 note, 75-79
Alfred's translation, 9
Bede's translation, 7 f., 21
condemnation of, 75
heretical tenets of, 76 f.
Prologue to the Old Testament, 76-78
translation of the Bible, 72, 73 note, 75 f., 78 f., 81
Pusey: the *Minor Prophets*, 538; and the Revised Version, 553 note
Pyle, Thomas, 527: *Paraphrase* on the epistles, 527
Pynson, R. (printer), 97 note

Quakers, the, 543
Quakers' Bible, the, 528 f.
Queen Mary's Psalter, 61
Quotation marks, use of: in Newcome's New Testament, 534; in Spencer's New Testament, 499

"Rainbow Bible," 550 note
Rainolds, John, 308 note: and the Authorized Version, 308 and note, 312, 328
Ray, J. M.: version of the Bible, 537
Raynalde, Thomas (printer), 181: edition of Taverner's version, 213
Razias, deed of, 223
Read editions of Challoner's revision, 421: Bible of 1846, 450 f., 455; Bible of 1857, 468, 471
Reading of the Bible, 187 note, 195 f.
Aelfric on, 24 f.
Cranmer on, 63
Curoe on, 440
encouraged by the Church, 440
in Catholic schools, 410
Pius VII on, 426
time required for, 535, 593 and note
"Red Letter Edition" of the Bible (1945), 494 f.
Red Sea, passage of the: Geddes on, p. 381
Redman (printer): edition of Taverner's version, 213; edition of Tyndale's New Test., 141, 151
Reeves (publisher); *see* Simms and Reeves
Reform Bill of 1832, 541
Reformed Liturgy, the, 513
Reformers, the
Beza's influence on, 123-26
Cajetan's opposition to, 106 f.
discord among, 305
dishonesty of, 280
inconsistencies in the text, 281 f., 285 and note, 440
infuriated by Martin and the Rheims N.T., 274 ff.
mistranslations of the Bible by, 123 ff., 250, 252, 255, 270, 272, 281-85
private interpretation and, 249
the Rhemists' condemnation of, 123 f., 255
the Vulgate condemned by, 99, 276
Regnault and the Great Bible, 191
Reich, on the Greek text, 559
Reilly (publisher), edition of MacMahon's revision, 375

Reilly, W. S., 492 note, 500 note
Reims; *see* Rheims
Religion and science, 537
Remigius, Peter, 255, 269
Reppington, Philip, 86 and note
Res sacramenti, 109
Resultant Greek Testament by Weymouth, 556 note, 591 note
Revel, Fleming (publisher), 587 note
Revised Standard Version, the, 579-84
  American Standard Version and, 579 f., 583
  arrangement of the text, 583 f.
  the Confraternity Edition and, 581, 583
  Goodspeed's work and, 580 f., 592 f.
  Moffatt and, 580 and note, 590
  a new translation, 580
  principles of translating, 581 f., 592 f.
  procedure of translating, 579 f.
  style of, 581, 583, 593 f.
  titles of the epistles, 589
Revised Version, the, 334, 509, 551-78
  Alford's contribution to, 548, 552 f.
  American Standard Version and, 578 f.
  Appendix to, 578 f.
  Arian influence on, 561 f.
  Authorized Version and, 322 f., 554 f., 566-68: Gairdner on, 600
  Bilton's dissatisfaction with, 587
  Burgon on, 567 note
  companies of revision, 541, 548, 552-54, 563 f. and note, 566, 578: procedure of, 554, 563 f.
  controversy concerning, 552, 560 f., 566-68, 575
  Convocation and, 541, 552 f., 578
  Cook's opposition to, 549, 559
  criticism of, 566-76, 580 f.
  Cunnington's criticism of, 576
  Cunnington's revision of, 576
  demands for the revision, 551 f.
  Gairdner on, 600
  the Greek text, 554 ff., 582: Burgon on, 560 f., 563-65; Ellicott on, 554-56, 563 note, 564 and note; Hort on, 556-58, 572, 573 note; Scrivener on, 557, 560, 563 f.
  Harris' criticism of, 576
  Humphry on, 564 note
  later revisions of, 575 f. and note
  Lloyd's revision of, 576
  Moulton's adaptation of, 576 note
  a new version, 563
  Newcome and, 534
  Newth's account of the procedure of revision, 554
  the notes, 568
  the Old Testament, 566
  opponents of, 552
  Preface to, 265
Revised Version, the (*continued*)
  publication of, 566
  questionable passages, 561 f.
  revisions of the Authorized Version and, 547-49
  Rheims-Douay version and, 129, 261 f., 366 and note, 571 f.
  rules for revision, 553
  Sharpe and, 541 f.
  unwarranted changes, 567 ff.
  Webster's influence on, 547
  Weekes' revision of, 576
  Wordsworth's criticism of, 567 f.
Reynolds, William: and the Rheims New Testament, 253 f., 302 note; and second edition of Rheims N.T., 270 note; and Whitaker, 253 f., 291
Rheims, English College at, 249, 251 f.
Rheims-Douay version: and the Authorized Version, 259 f.; and Latin versions, 129; Poynter on, 410; vicissitudes of, 337
Rheims New Testament, 249-72
  accuracy of, 260 ff.
  Allen and, 250 f., 254
  Approbations in, 255, 269-72
  attribution to the Jesuits, 277 note
  Authorized Version influenced by, 63 f., 261 and note, 263-65, 315-17
  Bagster's condemnation of, 267 f.
  Bagster's edition of, 474
  Bulkeley's attack on, 574
  Cartwright's "confutation" of, 276-78
  cause for torture, 275
  Challoner's revision and, 355, 357 f., 366 f.
  controversy caused by, 274 ff.
  criticism of, 257 f., 263, 267-69, 314
  defects of, 257 f., 263, 268, 314, 352
  division of the text, 256 and note, 270, 272
  editions of, 269-72: numbering of, 271
  excellent qualities of, 258 ff., 269, 355
  "fifth edition" of, 333 f., 351-53, 355, 358
  "fourth edition" of, 271 f.
  Fulke's attack on, 286-89
  Fulke's edition of, 264, 286-89
  Geddes' criticism of, 380
  Geneva Bible's influence on, 226 note, 260 note
  Greek article observed in, 260-63
  honesty of, 259 ff.
  Horne's criticism of, 268
  Hudleston's edition of, 487
  Latin text used in, 256, 260 and notes, 262 f.
  Macaulay's commendation of, 262 f.
  and Milner's criticism of the Catholic Board edition, 403 f.
  Nary's criticism of, 257, 340, 585

Rheims New Testament (*continued*)
the notes, 252 f.: in Coyne's edition of 1816, 417-19; in MacNamara's editions, 415, 419, 421; in the fifth edition, 352; Troy's condemnation of, 418
notes and annotations, 252 f., 256, 265-67, 270 f., 276, 301: attributed to Worthington, 301 note; Cartwright's "confutation" of, 276-78; Fulke's attack on, 287; Wither's attack on, 289
Preface to; *see* Preface
prejudiced condemnations of, 257, 267-69
preliminary and supplementary matter, 256, 269-72
Protestant reprint of (1834), 435-37
Revised Version and, 129, 261 f., 366 and note, 571 f.
Scrivener's criticism of, 268
second edition of, 269 f.
"sixth edition" of, 353 f., 392
third edition of, 270
the title page, 254 f., 260: in later editions, 269-71
titles of the books, 271
translators of; *see* Rhemists, the
Tyndale's New Testament and, 130 note, 142, 275
Ward's criticism of, 257
Westcott's commendation of, 261, 263
Witham's criticism of, 347, 585
Rhemes and Doway, by Henry Cotton, 92 f.
Rhemists, the, 250-54
abuse heaped on, 273 ff.
Beza condemned by, 123-25
Bulkeley's attack on, 289-91
Geddes' criticism of, 380
honesty of, 280
Reformers condemned by, 123 f.
Reformers' controversy with, 273 ff.
suffering endured by, 254, 265 f., 301-303
Wither's attack on, 289
Rhimes against Rome, 292 f.
Richardson editions of Challoner's revision: Bible of 1847, 94 f., 358 and note, 378 and note, 453 f., 457, 470; New Testament of 1847, 378 and note, 406, 454, 464 f., 469 f.; New Testaments of 1851, 464 f.
Rickaby, J., 500 note
Ridadeneira, 300
Ridley, Nicholas, 143: burning of, 191 note; and Thomas Sampson, 218
Ridley, Robert, 143
Rigby, Thomas: and the Catholic Board Edition, 406 note, 407 and note
Riverside New Testament, 595
Rivington, F. and C. (booksellers), 535
Roberts, W. H.: revision of the Authorized Version, 533
Robertson, James A., 592
Robinson, T.: corrector of Gibson's edition, 413
Rogers, John, 158 and note, 175 f.; *see also* Matthew, Thomas
Rolle, Richard, 8, 26-28
Roman Catholic Bible Society, 401 f., 407 and note; *see also* Catholic Board Edition
Roman Catholic Church: concern for the Scriptures, 405, 408 ff.; interpreter of Scripture, 459; reading of the Bible encouraged by; *see* Reading
Romans, Epistle to: Tyndale's Prologue to, 137 f., 143, 178
Rome, English college at, 251
Rosen Bible, the, 299
Rotherham, J. B.: *The Emphatic Bible,* 546; version of the New Testament, 546
Roy, the heretic, 145: condemned by Ridley, 143
Ruremond, Hans von, 170
Rushworth, John, 46
Rushworth Gospels, 46-51
Anglo-Saxon versions and, 32, 40
date of, 50 f.
description of, 46 f.
the Lindisfarne Gospels and, 32, 47 ff.
omissions and other errors in, 32, 48 f.
purpose of, 12
Ruth, Book of: Anglo-Saxon version of, 23 note, 65; in Bishops' Bible, 237; omitted in Coyne's list of books, 450, 453; Tyndale's version of, 134, 163, 176
Rutland, earl of, 61
Ryan, bishop of Ferns, 416: and Ward's *Errata,* 331 and note

Sacraments, the
Beza on, 318 note
Coverdale's attitude toward, 155 f.
Erasmus' doubts concerning, 105
in the Old Testament, 318 note
"Matthew's" teaching regarding, 183 f.
Purvey's heretical teaching regarding, 76 f.
Stokesley on, 138
teaching of the Geneva Bible regarding, 225, 227 f.
Tyndale's attitude towards, 132, 138 note, 139
Woodhead and Walker on, 519
Sadler, Thomas, 400
Sadlier editions of Challoner's revision, 369: Bible of 1852, 466; Bible of 1853, 467; the "Catholic Family Bible," 469; New Testament of 1850, 462, 467
St. Anthony Guild Press and the Confraternity Edition, 491, 505
St. Paul's Church, the Great Bible in, 191 note, 195 f.

Salamanca, theologians of: edition of Stephens' Bible, 117; edition of the Tigurine Bible, 112 note
Salust, 382 note
Samaritan Pentateuch and Spurrell's version, 549
Sampson, Thomas: and the Geneva Bible, 218, 219 note
Samson de Nantuil, 10
Sandeman, Robert, 537 note
Sandemanians, the, 537 and note
Sander: and Fulke, 287; and Whitaker, 291
Sandys: and the Bishops' Bible, 237; on the influence of Muenster's version, 114
Sanger, E. (bookseller), 517
Saturday, religious observance of, 277 note
Saunders, Laurence, 175
Savile, Henry, 104, 312, 328
Savonarola, disciples of, 107, 109
Savoy Conference and Baxter, 513, 551 note
Sawyer, L. A.: version of the New Testament, 546
Sayce, A. H.: and the Revised Version, 553
Scaliger, 329
Scarlett, Nathaniel, 536 f.: principles of translating, 535 f. and note; version of the New Testament, 535-37
Scholz and Kenrick, 462
Science and religion, 537
Scott (bishop) and Fullarton's edition of 1845, 450
Scotus, Duns: and Baxter, 512
Scripture, Holy
  authority of: Geddes on, 383; Kenrick on, 459
  and the Catholic Church, 405, 408 ff., 440
  inspiration of: Geddes' contempt for, 380, 382 and note
  interpretation of; *see* Interpretation
  love for, 10, 24 f.
  only rule of faith, 85, 249, 293
  reading of; *see* Reading
  supposed ignorance of, 62
  see also Bible
Scrivener, F. H.
  Anglo-Saxon versions of the Gospels, 39
  the Authorized Version, 311 f. and note: the psalms in, 299; the sources of, 315 note, 317 f. and note; style of, 322, 324
  Beza's influence on the Authorized Version, 123, 317 f.
  Christ's bloody sweat, 573
  Coverdale's renderings, 164 note
  edition of the Greek New Testament, 555 and note, 556 note
  the Geneva Bible, 229
  Greek basis of the Authorized Version, 317 f., 319 note
Scrivener, F. H. (*continued*)
  on Eusebius, 561
  on John 7:53–8:11, 573 note
  on Luke 6:1, 573
  on I John 5:7 f., 574
  on the last chapter of St. Mark, 572
  on the notes to Rheims New Testament, 293 note
  on the Rheims New Testament, 268: its accuracy 262
  Pope and, 565
  the Revised Version and, 553 f., 563 f.
  Westcott and Hort's theory, 557, 560, 563 f.
  Wycliffite versions, 79
Sealy (publisher), Coyne's noteless New Test. reprinted by, 427
"Selah," 166, 173, 177
Selden, on the style of the Authorized Version, 323
Seldenslach, James: editions of Rheims N.T. printed by, 270 f.
Septuagint, the: Kenrick on, 461; the Sixtine edition of, 251; and Spurrell's version, 549; translations of, 542 f.
Seres, William (printer): edition of Matthew's Bible, 181
Sergius (pope), 35
Servetus, edition of Pagninus' Bible, 110
Seven Sobs of a Sorrowful Soul, 97
Shaftesbury Psalter, 58
Shakespeare: Rheims-Douay version compared with, 259; Rheims version quoted by, 275 note
Sharpe, Samuel: Hebrew grammar, 541; and the Revised Version, 541 f.; revision of the Authorized Version, 541, 547, 549
Sheed and Ward editions: Knox's version, 404 note; Layman's New Testament, 847 f.; New Testament of 1947, 495 f.
Sheppard, L. A.: edition of Coverdale's Bible, 156 f. note
Sherman, H. A.: and The Shorter Bible, 592
Shirley, Walter: date of the *Ecclesiae regimen,* 76 note; on the *The Last Age of the Church,* 68 note
Shorter Bible, The, 592
"Shorter Moffatt Bible," 590
Sidney, Marlow, 423 note: edition of Challoner's revision, 423 f. and note
Sidney and Horrabin editions of Challoner's version, 363, 394, 403, 407
Simeon of Durham, 20 f.
Simms and Co., editions of the Bible, 449, 455, 465
Simms and McIntyre editions of Challoner's revision, 421
  Bible of 1839, 439 f.: reimpression of, 449
  Bible of 1845, 450

Simms and McIntyre (*continued*)
New Testament of 1829, 465 note
New Testament of 1846, 439 note
New Testament of 1847, 455
New Testament of 1851, 465 and note
Simms and Reeves editions of Challoner's revision: New Testament of 1835, 438; New Testament of 1836, 438; New Testament of 1846, 452 f., 455
Simon, archbishop of Canterbury, 28
Simon, Richard
Arias Montanus, 110 note, 111
Beza's version, 123, 126
Cajetan's work, 105 note
Castalio's version, 119 f.
Didacus Lopez, 104
Isidore Clario's version, 116
John Bois, 123
the Latin Vulgate, 102-104
Muenster's version, 114
Pagninus' work, 110 note, 111
Tigurine Bible, 113
Sion House Monastery, 8, 57, 73 f. and note
Sixtus V (pope), revision of the Vulgate by, 251, 295, 296 note, 409: Nary on, 340; Preface to, 396
Sixtus of Siena: on Pagninus, 109; on Richard Rolle, 26 and note
Skeat, Walter: on Anglo-Saxon manuscripts, 5; Anglo-Saxon versions of the Gospels, 33 ff., 37 ff.; the Lindisfarne Gospels, 42, 48; the practice of glossing, 11
"Skipover," used by Geddes, 380 note
Slater, M. T., 488
Smith, C. (bookseller), 517
Smith, E.: edition of Challoner's revision, 427
Smith, G. V.: on the Revised Version, 562 note
Smith, J. M. Powis: and Goodspeed's work, 594
Smith, Miles: and Preface to the Authorized Version, 311, 313 f.; Rheims New Testament criticized by, 314
Smith, W. R.: and the Revised Version, 553
Society for Promoting Christian Knowledge, 540
Society for Promoting Primitive Christianity, 525
Society of Friends, 528 f.
Society of St. Jerome, 486
Socinian controversy, 524
Soden's edition of the Greek New Test., 590
Souter, Alexander: edition of the Greek New Test., 556 note, 582 f.
Sparke, Thomas, 45
Speaker's Commentary, The, 548 f.
Spellman (cardinal), *Imprimaturs* by, 494, 496 note: in Knox's version, 504 note
Spelman, Psalter published by, 25, 37, 53 f.
Spencer, Aloysius: versions of the New Testament, 497-99
Spenser, Edmund: Rheims-Douay version compared with, 259
Spurrell, Helen: version of the Bible, 549
Stamford Priory, 206
Stanley and the Revised Version, 553
Stapelton: Fulke's condemnation of, 286; and Whitaker, 291
Stapulensis, Jacques, 99
Stedman, Joseph, 493 and note
Stenton: on Anglo-Saxon culture, 4, 6; on St. Aldhelm, 20 note
Stephen (king), 56 note, 57
Stephen of Citeaux, St., 409
Stephen, Leslie: on Clarke, 526
Stephens, Henry, 116
Stephens, Robert, 116 f. and notes
Authorized version influenced by, 123, 318 and note
edition of Beza's New Testament, 121 f. notes
edition of Pagninus' Bible, 110, 111 note, 116 f.
edition of the Greek New Testament, 318: numbering of verses in, 220 note
edition of the Vulgate New Test., 121 f. note
edition of the Zurich Bible, 116
Sternhold, Thomas: metrical version of the psalms, 233, 241
Stevenson, on the *Psalter of St. Augustine,* 53
Stinchcombe, Gloucestershire, 130
Stock (bishop) and Belsham, 540
Stokesley, on vernacular versions, 138
Strasburg, the English Reformers at, 216, 218
Strype, John
the Bishops' Bible, 235
the Great Bible, 203 note
on Giles Laurence, 244
on Tyndale, 140
Tunstall's learning, 147
Wycliffe's translation, 67 note
Stunica, 104
Subordinationism, 539
Sudbury (archbishop), 86
Sunday School Union, the, 587 note
Surius, on the religious situation in 1550, 249
Surmont, *Imprimatur* by, 483
Susanna, portrait of, 198
Sweet, Henry: on the *Psalter of St. Augustine,* 53
Swift, on the style of the Authorized Version, 322
Syers, Oswald, 399, 410 note
Syers' Bible (1813), 363, 392 f., 395, 399 f., 410 note, 430, 473
Syriac version, 582
Syrian Greek text, 557

Tables of Epistles and Gospels
  correct in Coyne's New Testament of 1847, 454
  correct in Washbourne Bible of 1914, 486 and note
  incorrect in Challoner's revision, 361
  incorrect in MacMahon's revision, 375
  incorrect in the "fourth" edition of Rheims N.T., 272
  incorrect in the sixth edition of Rheims N.T., 354
Tatian's Greek text, 582
Taverner, Richard, 205 ff.: the Greek article observed by, 210
Taverner's version, 205-15
  the Apocrypha, 208
  contents of, 206 f.
  Dedication to Henry VIII, 206 f.
  editions of, 211, 213-15: with New Test. from Matthew's Bible, 213
  Great Bible and, 205, 213
  importance of, 214 f.
  Matthew's Bible and, 207-13 and note
  the notes in, 211 f.
  the Psalter in, 208
  the text, 207-11
  the Vulgate Bible and, 208
Tavistock, nuns of, 6 note
Taylor, Edgar: revision of the Authorized Version, 547 f.
Taylor, John, 529, 548
Taylor, Rowland, 175
Tertullian, 125 note
Textus receptus, 557, 559 f. note, 572: and the Revised Version, 569, 572, 574 f.
Theodore, St., 5, 21, 45 f.
Thomas Aquinas, St., 64, 68: Baxter's study of, 512
Thomas à Becket, St., 19, 58, 61, 155 and note, 198
Thomas de Vio; *see* Cajetan
Thompson, Charles: version of the Old Testament, 542
Thomson, William: version of the New Testament, 542
Thorpe, Benjamin: edition of Anglo-Saxon Gospels, 31, 34 note; edition of Anglo-Saxon Psalter, 19 and note, 58 f.; edition of Caedmon, 18 note; the Ormulum, 25 f.
Thucydides, 282 note
Tibullus, 120
Tichonius the Donatist, 76
Tigurine Bible, 112 f. and note, 116
Time required to read the Bible, 535, 593 and note
Timon (bishop), Approbation by, 467
Tirinus, 396 and note
Tischendorf, edition of the Greek text, 545, 565 note: and Brameld's version, 545; and Davidson's version, 546
Title pages, unreliability of, 150 f., 158, 170, 213 f., 232
Titles of the chapters in Montgomery's New Test., 595
Tobias, Book of: Muenster's version of, 114 note; Taverner's version of, 208; Whitaker's rejection of, 282
Tolley, J. G.: revision of the Authorized Version, 547
Tomson, Laurence, 230: anti-Catholic notes by, 231 f.; Beza's New Testament translated by, 123 and note, 129, 233; editions of Genevan New Testament, 123 and note, 129, 230-32
Torrey, Charles: and The Shorter Bible, 592, 595; version of the Gospels, 595 f.
Traditional Text of the Greek, 559 and note, 572
Translation, principles of; *see* Principles of translation
Treacle Bible, 299
Treatise Concerning the Old and New Testament, 10 and note, 23
Treatise on the Ten Commandments, 13
Tregelles edition of the Greek text, 545: and Brameld's version, 545; and Rotheram's version, 546
Tremellius, John Immanuel, 117 f., 126 f.: Authorized Version influenced by, 315; English versions influenced by, 118; and Thomas Sampson, 218
Trench, R. C.: on the Geneva Bible, 229; and the Revised Version, 552 f., 555 note
Trent, Council of: authenticity of the Vulgate, 340, 409; Bulkeley's disdain for, 290; Isidore Clario at, 116; on the canon of the Bible, 375; revision of the Vulgate, 129, 296 note; Whitaker's disdain for, 292
Tristram, Henry, 554 note
Troy, J. T. (bishop)
  Approbations by: for MacMahon's revision, 373 and note, 376 f.; in Coyne's New Testament of 1825, 431; in Gibson's edition, 413
  and Christie's edition (1823), 429
  and Coyne's edition of 1816, 393 f., 410 note, 415 and note, 417-19: his disclaimer of, 417 note, 418 f.
  and Coyne's noteless edition (1820), 94, 425 f.
  edition of Challoner's revision (1816), 360, 363
  Hamil's edition of Haydock's Bible, 397 note, 427 f.

Troy, J. T. (*continued*)
MacMahon's edition of 1791, 417-19; *see also* Cross, Richard
MacNamara's edition of 1813, 415 and note, 417
"Troy's Bible," 417 note
Tunstall, Cuthbert
Bibles burned by, 144 f., 147
Erasmus and, 100 f. and note, 147
errors in Tyndale's New Test., 270, 272
justification of, 147-49
Matthew fined by, 176
More and, 146
revision of the Great Bible, 202 f. and note
Tyndale denounced by, 144-48
Turnbull, Joseph: version of the epistles, 544 f.
Tutet, Mark, 91
Twentieth Century New Testament, 546, 549, 587 f., 590 f.
Tyndale, William, 130 ff.
Cochlaeus and, 130
condemnation of, 141 ff.
difficulties with Joye, 131 and note
execution of, 149
Henry VIII's divorce opposed by, 137 note, 168, 180 note
heretical tenets of, 132, 136-44
honesty of translation by, 137, 139
learning of, 134 f.
Lutheranism of, 137 ff., 143 f., 146, 148 f.
More's attack on, 154
subjectivism of, 140 f.
supposed translation of the whole Old Test., 158 note, 175
Tunstall and, 144 f.
Tunstall's denunciation of, 144-48
Tyndale's New Testament, 130-51
Authorized Version and, 311, 317
Bishops' Bible and, 243
burning of, 144 f. and note, 147
condemnation of, 86, 137 and note, 141-49
editions of, 101 note, 130-32, 140 f. and note, 144, 150 f.
Erasmus' influence on, 133
errors in, 270, 272
Great Bible and, 189, 201
honesty of the translation, 137, 139
Luther's influence on, 135, 137 f., 143 f., 146, 148
Luther's Preface in, 178
Matthew's Bible and, 132, 176-79, 234
mistranslations in, 138 f. and note, 145
modern editions of, 130 note, 131 f. note, 141 note
notes in, 132 and note, 139-42, 148, 151
Pagninus' influence on, 133
Prefaces and Prologues in, 130 f., 137-39, 143, 148, 150: in Matthew's Bible, 178, 180 note, 182
Prologues: in edition of Coverdale's New Test., 171; in edition of Matthew's Bible, 178, 180 note; in edition of Taverner's version, 214
Rheims New Testament and, 142, 275
unsatisfactory character of, 234
Whittingham's version and, 220
Wycliffe's version and, 136 f.
Tyndale's version
Authorized Version and, 178
condemnation of, 204
Foxe on, 158 note
Great Bible and, 180
influence on other English versions, 135, 186
Matthew's Bible and, 158 note, 175 ff.
translation of the Old Testament, 133 f., 139, 142, 145 note: and Coverdale's version, 163 and notes; in Matthew's Bible, 176-79; the Prologues in Matthew's Bible, 181 f.; supposed translation of the whole, 158 note, 175
Tyre, Council of, 290

Udall, N., 128
Ulfilas, version by, 128
Ulster, Synod of, 440
Uniformity, Act of, 513
Unitarian, a: and the Revised Version, 553 and note
Unitarian Version, 539 f.: Wakefield and, 532, 540
Unitarianism: and Arianism, 528; doctrine of, 539; of Pyle, 527; prohibition of, 540 note; *see also* Anti-Trinitarianism
Unitarians: history of, 539; versions by, 532, 538-42
Ussher: dates *Anno Mundi,* 325; on St. Aldhelm, 18; on St. Bede, 21

Valla, 100
Van der Gucht, 351 f.
Van Meteren: edition of Coverdale's Bible, 156 and note; editions of Tyndale's New Test., 150
Vatablus, 110, 111 note, 112 note
Vatican Codex (B), 103 note
Vaughan, C. J.: and the Revised Version, 553
Vaughan, Herbert (cardinal), editions of the New Testament, 480-82, 486
Vermigli, 216: and Tremellius, 117
Vernacular versions
Cranmer on, 63
demand for, 69, 193
Foxe on, 34, 63
in French, 6, 8

Vernacular versions (*continued*)
in Saxon times, 6-10, 39, 64 f.
Kenrick on, 460
Lee on, 142
need for, 62, 69 and note, 250, 252, 313 f.: Tunstall on, 138
of the Epistles and Gospels, 98 note
Pius VI on, 423 f.
Stokesley on, 138
Tunstall on, 138
Verses in the Bible, numbering of, 220 note: in Bishops' Bible, 235, 244 and note
Vervliet, Daniel: printer of second edition of Rheims New Test., 269 note
Vidler, William: and Scarlett's New Testament, 536
Vigouroux, on Osiander, 115 note
"Vinegar Bible," 327
Virgil, 380
Vising, on Anglo-Norman literature, 9
Vitalian (pope), 20
Vitus, St., 45
Vogels, edition of the Greek New Test., 565 note
Voltaire, on Clarke, 527
Voysey, bishop of Exeter, 155: Warham's correspondence with, 143
Vulgate Bible
accuracy of, 262 and note
antiquity of, 262 and note, 290, 319, 409
authenticity of, 340
Authorized Version influenced by, 315, 318
Bagster's edition of the New Testament, 474
Benedicti's edition of, 128
Beza and, 122 note, 290
Bishops' Bible and, 239 note, 241
Bois's defense of, 104, 123
Bulkeley's attack on, 290 f.
Cajetan's work and, 106 f.
Clario's editions of, 115 f.
Confraternity Edition and, 491
Coverdale's New Testament and, 168-70
Coverdale's opinion of, 169
Coverdale's version and, 163 f.
Erasmus on, 102 f. and notes
errors in, 116 and note
excellence of, 290
Fulke's condemnation of, 287
Geddes' criticism of, 380
Great Bible and, 189 f. and note, 201
Greek text underlying, 320 and note
Grotius on, 262 note
Hentenius' edition of, 251, 296 note
history of, 405, 408 f.
Latin versions and, 250, 258
Lee on, 101 f.
Lefèvre's edition of, 99
Kenrick on, 461
Vulgate Bible (*continued*)
Nary on, 340
numbering of the psalms in, 165 note, 166, 199
origin of, 409
Osiander's editions of, 115
Poynter on, 405, 409 f.
pre-eminence of, 405, 409 f.
purity of, 319 f. and note, 347, 409 f.
the Reformers' disdain for, 99, 106, 276
Rheims New Testament and, 256, 260 and note, 262 f.
Rheims Preface in defense of, 276
Simon on, 102 f.
Stephens' editions of, 111 note, 116
superiority of, 101 f.
Taverner's version and, 208
translations of, 410
Tyndale's version and, 134 note, 135, 148
Ward on, 319
with edition of Beza's New Testament, 122 note
Witham on, 347
Wordsworth and White on, 320

Wade, G. W.: version of the New Testament, 596
Wakefield, Gilbert, 531 f., 539: and Newcome, 532-34; and the Unitarian Version, 532, 540; version of the New Testament by, 532 f. and note
Wakeman and Walker, 516
Walafrid Strabo, 11, 57, 78 note
Walde-grave, Robert (printer), 277 note
Walker (printer), Coyne's noteless New Testament reprinted by, 427
Walker, Obadiah, 514-18: *Paraphrase* by, 514 f., 517-19
Wallis, N. H., 132 note, 150 note
Walmesley, 98, 396 note
Walsh, David: Approbations by: in Bible of 1847, 94 f., 358 and note, 378, 453, 457; in Bible of 1888, 478; in New Testament of 1851, 464 f.
Walsh, Nicholas: Gaelic version of the Bible by, 451 note
Walsh, P. A.: reviser of MacNamara's edition, 415, 417
Walsh, William (archbishop): and Nary, 339 and note
Walsingham, Francis: and Cartwright's *Confutation,* 276 note
Walton, Brian: on Beza's version, 216 note; the Polyglot Bible, 551; the Vulgate esteemed by, 409
Walton, William: Approbation by, 356, 423
Wand, J. W. C.: and Knox's version, 503 f. note; version of the epistles, 589, 598

Wanley, Humphrey
Anglo-Saxon calligraphy, 6, 42
Anglo-Saxon Gospels, 31 ff.
Anglo-Saxon Psalters, 54 ff.
date of manuscripts, 36
the Lindisfarne Gospels, 42 f. and note
on Caedmon, 16 note
the Pentateuch in Anglo-Saxon, 10
Psalter of St. Augustine, 53
the Rushworth Gospels, 46 and note
Ward (publisher); *see* Sheed and Ward
Ward, Thomas, 331
Cantos on the Reformation, 331 f.
Errata of the Protestant Bible, 331-34: Brown's attack on, 281; in Sadlier Bibles, 466
heretics denounced by, 333
the purity of the Vulgate, 319
Rheims New Testament criticized by, 257
Warham (archbishop): and Erasmus, 100 note, 101; on Tyndale's New Testament, 143
Waring, G.: edition of Anglo-Saxon Gospels, 73 and note; on Anglo-Saxon versions, 48; on the Lindisfarne and Rushworth Gospels, 50; on the history of the Lindisfarne Gospels, 44 f.; the practice of glossing, 12
Warrington, academy at, 529, 532, 539, 548
Washbourne, R. and T., 479: editions of the Bible, 479, 482 f., 485 f. and note, 453; editions of the New Testament, 479; *see also* Burns, Oates and Washbourne
Waterland, Daniel, 526: on John Purvey, 75 note; two Wycliffite versions, 72 and note, 79, 81
Waterman, Leroy: and Goodspeed's work, 594
Watson (bishop) and Fulke, 278
Way, A. S.: version of the epistles, 589
Webster, Noah: *American Dictionary* by, 547; revision of the Authorized Version, 547
Weekes, Robert: revision of the Revised Version, 576
Weigle, Luther: on Dickinson's version, 543; on Mace's New Testament, 521; and the Revised Standard Version, 580, 584 note; Webster's version, 547
Weiss, edition of the Greek New Test., 565 note
Wells, Edward: revision of the Authorized Version, 521, 528
Werung, Bible possessed by, 21
Wesley, John, 527 f.: revision of the Authorized Version by, 528
Westcott, B. F.
the Authorized Version: influenced by Rheims New Test., 263, 316 and notes; merits of, 324
Beza's version, 126
Westcott, B. F. (*continued*)
Bishops' Bible, 236, 243 f.
Castalio's version, 119
Douay Version of the psalms, 297
edition of the Greek New Test. by, 556 ff.: and the *Twentieth Century New Testament,* 587
Geneva Bible, 230
the Great Bible, 201, 203
the Greek text for the Revised Version, 556-65, 570 f., 573, 582
Matthew's Bible, 179 f. note: importance of, 186
and the Revised Version, 553, 555 note, 556 ff.
the Rheims New Testament: accuracy of, 260 note, 261, 263; Authorized Version influenced by, 263, 316 and notes; Preface to, 255
Taverner's version, 215
Tyndale's version, 132 f.
Western Greek text, 556 f., 582
Westminster, Synod of (1855): and Newman's proposed translation of the Bible, 459 note, 497
Westminster Confession, 440
Westminster Version, 498, 500 f.: and the Confraternity Edition, 492 note, 500 f.; emendations of the Hebrew, 594
Westwood, J. O.: date of manuscripts, 36; on Caedmon, 16 note; on the Lindisfarne Gospels, 41, 43 f.; Psalter of St. Augustine, 53
Weymouth, Richard: edition of the Greek New Testament, 556 note, 591 note; the *New Testament in Modern Speech,* 556 note, 588, 591 f.
Wharton, two Wycliffite versions, 72
Whiston, William: Arianism of, 524-26; honesty of, 526; translation of Josephus, 525 note; version of the New Testament, 525-27
Whitaker, William, 291 f.
and Bellarmine, 280, 291
and Cartwright's *Confutation,* 277 note
dishonesty of the Reformers, 280
Luther's rejection of St. James's Epistle, 282
on Andreas Osiander, 115
on the Church Fathers, 284
Reynolds' controversy with, 253 f., 291
the Rhemists opposed by, 291 f.
Sander and, 291
Stapleton and, 291
Tobias and Machabees rejected by, 282
Whitby, Daniel: *Paraphrase* by, 520 f.
Whitchurch, E.: edition of Coverdale's New Test., 169 f.; edition of Erasmus' New Test. in English, 128; edition of the Great

Whitchurch, E. (*continued*)
Bible, 202, 311 and note; edition of the psalms, 97
White, proposed revision of the New Testament by, 497 and note
Whitefield, George: and the Methodist movement, 527, 533
Whitgift, John: and the Bibles in the churches, 238; Cartwright opposed by, 276; editions of the Bishops' Bible, 238; on the need for a new translation, 308
Whitley, W. T.: on Thomas Matthew, 175
Whitney, S. W.: edition of the Greek New Test., 556 note
Whittingham, William: the Geneva Bible and, 73 note, 217, 219 f., 226 and note, 228 note
Whole Duty of Man, The, 515
"Wicked Bible," 326 and note
Wildermann editions of Challoner's revisions, 489-91
Wilfrid, St., 3
William of Malmesbury, on King Alfred, 22
William of Orange, 127
William of Shoreham, 28 f., 59 and note
Williams, W.: version of the New Test., 542
Willoughby, H. R., 197 note
Wilson, bishop of Sodor, 213 note
Wilson, Lea: *Catalogue of Bibles,* 92; on the illustrations in an edition of the Great Bible, 204; on Wycliffe's translation, 71 note, 73 f. and note
Wisdom, Book of: Purvey's notes on, 78 note; Purvey's rejection of, 76 note
Wiseman, Nicholas (cardinal), 93
Approbations by: in Bible of 1847, 94 f., 394, 453, 457, 469; in New Testament of 1858, 464 f., 469
Challoner criticized by, 365, 442 note
criticism of the 1792 edition of the New Test., 387
on Lingard's version, 442 f. and note, 446
"Our Lord," 355 f.
Richardson's edition and, 378 note
Witham, Robert, 346 and note, 353, 355 note, 396 note: Nary's version and, 349 and note; Rheims New Testament criticized by, 347, 585
Witham's version of the New Testament, 346-50
Challoner and, 345, 347, 353
Knox's version and, 504
the notes in, 348 f.: in Syers' Bible, 400
Poynter on, 410
the Preface to, 347
second edition of, 346 note
the text, 349 f.
Wither, George: the Rhemists' notes attacked by, 289
Wittenberg and Lutheranism, 216
Wittingham, Charles (printer): edition of Wycliffite New Test., 73 note
Wodforde, William, 8
Wogan, David (publisher): Bible of 1814, 392 and note, 400; and Hamil's edition of Haydock's Bible, 427
Wolsey, Thomas (cardinal): burning of Luther's New Test. by, 137 note; and Erasmus, 100 note, 101; and Luther, 143; and Taverner, 205
Wogan, P. (printer): edition of MacMahon's revision, 377; selection of texts by, 472; sixth edition of Rheims New Test., 353, 354 note
Wood, Antony à: on Bilson's learning, 292; on Christopher Goodman, 217; on John of Trevisa, 29; on Taverner, 205 f.; on William Whittingham, 217
Wood, James: Approbation by, 476; archbishop of Philadelphia, 475 note
Woodhead, Abraham, 514 f., 517: *Paraphrase* by, 514 f., 517-19
Worcester Bible, 204
Wordsworth, John: on the Revised Version, 567 f.; and the Revised Version, 553, 563
Workman, H. B.: on Hereford's translation, 70 note; on John Purvey's Prologue, 76; on Luther's Prologue to Romans, 137 f.; on Queen Anne's book of the Gospels, 70 note
Worms (Germany): Diet of, 249; edition of the Tyndale's version printed at, 130 f., 150
Worsley, John: on the necessity of new translations, 585; and Scarlett's principles of translating, 535 note; version of the New Testament, 530 f.
Worsley, S.: editor of J. Worsley's New Test., 531
Worswick and the Newcastle New Test., 393, 398 f.
Worthington, Thomas, 300 f., 396 note: notes in Douay Old Testament, 300 f.; notes in Rheims New Testament, 301 note; second edition of Rheims New Testament, 270 note
Wright, John, 295
Wright, Thomas: on Anglo-Saxon versions, 7; on Caedmon, 17; on St. Aldhelm, 20
Wright, W. Aldis: Preface to Revised Version, 566; and the Revised Version, 553
Wulfri (king), 35
Wyatt's rebellion, 175

Wycliffe, John
- commentaries on the New Testament, 68 and note
- condemnation of, 86
- *The Dore of Holy Scripture,* 76
- heretical tenets of, 66, 84-86
- *Last Age of the Church,* 68 and note
- legends concerning, 62, 65-67
- spelling of the name, 67 note
- translation of the Bible by, 67 f., 71 f., 73 note

Wycliffite versions, 8, 67-87
- genesis of, 68, 70 ff., 80
- importance of, 68 f.
- John Purvey and, 72, 73 note, 75-79, 81
- modern editions of, 68 note, 71 note, 72 f. and notes, 718
- never condemned, 86, 87 note
- Nicholas of Hereford and, 70 f., 78
- notes in, 77 f. note, 80 note, 81 note, 84
- order of books in the New Testament, 74
- title of books in the New Testament, 74

Wycliffite versions (*continued*)
- two different versions, 72-83
- Tyndale's version and, 136 f., 146
- Wycliffe's work and, 67 f., 71 f., 73 note

Wycliffites; *see* Lollards

Wynken de Worde (printer), 97 note

Wynn, Richard: and Scarlett's principles of translating, 535 note; version of the Bible, 528

Young, Robert: *Analytical Concordance to the Bible,* 544; version of the Bible, 544 f.

Young, William H. (publisher): and Spencer's version, 498

Zagorola, memorial at, 251

Zurich Bible, 112 f. and note, 116: and Coverdale's version, 163 f.

Zwingli: disciple of, 112; Luther's contempt for, 274; Luther's version condemned by, 274